THE LAW OF CORPORATE INSOLVENCY

THE LAW OF CORPORATE INSOLVENCY

by

IAN SNAITH BA (Keele), MA (Manchester)
Solicitor, Lecturer in Law at Leicester University

with the assistance of
FIONA COWNIE BA (Bristol); LLB (Leicester);
LLM (London); of Lincoln's Inn Barrister,
Lecturer in Law at Leicester University

WATERLOW PUBLISHERS

First edition 1990
© Ian Snaith 1990

Waterlow Publishers
Paulton House
8 Shepherdess Walk
London N1

A division of Pergamon Financial and Professional Services PLC

ISBN 0 08 039205 9

British Library Cataloguing in Publication Data
Snaith, Ian
    The law of corporate insolvency.—(Waterlow
    practitioner's library)
    1. Great Britain. Companies. Insolvency. Law
    I. Title
    344.106′78

Printed in Great Britain by BPCC Wheatons Ltd, Exeter

To the memory of
Roger W Benedictus and Victoria M Fisher,
two colleagues who are sadly missed.

Contents

Preface	xx
Table of cases	xxii
Table of statutes	li
Table of statutory instruments	lxix
Introduction	lxxix

Chapter 1—CORPORATE BORROWING AND SECURITY INTERESTS — 1

1.01	Corporate borrowing	1
1.02	Capacity of the company	1
1.02	The *ultra vires* doctrine before the Companies Act 1989	1
1.10	The Companies Act 1989	4
1.13	The powers of the company's agents	5
1.13	Agency	5
1.22	Companies Act 1989	8
1.28	The development and nature of security interests	10

Chapter 2—SECURITY OVER LAND — 15

2.01	Available securities	15
2.02	Legal mortgages of land	15
2.07	Equitable mortgages of land	17
2.08	Deposit of title deeds	17
2.14	Agreement to create a legal mortgage or express equitable charge	19
2.16	A mortgage of an equitable interest	20

Chapter 3—SECURITY INTERESTS IN CHATTELS — 21

3.01	Forms of security	21
3.10	Pledge	24
3.11	Possession by the pledgee	25
3.17	Security interests in ships	28
3.18	Legal mortgages of ships	28
3.22	Equitable mortgages of ships	29
3.23	Registration and mortgagee's rights	30
3.26	Bottomry bonds and respondentia	31
3.28	Aircraft as security	31

Chapter 4—SECURITY INTERESTS IN CHOSES IN ACTION — 33

4.01	The nature of security rights over choses in action	33
4.05	Statutory (legal) assignment of a chose in action	34
4.10	Equitable assignments of choses in action	36
4.15	Insurance policies	38
4.19	Mortgages of shares	39

4.33	Partnership shares	45
4.35	Book debts	46
4.49	Negotiable instruments	51
4.56	Interests in trust funds	55
4.58	Intellectual property	56
4.59	Patents	56
4.62	Copyright	57
4.65	Registered designs	58
4.67	Trade marks	59

Chapter 5—THE FLOATING CHARGE 61

5.01	The development of the floating charge	61
5.11	The legal nature and creation of a floating charge	65
5.19	The ordinary course of business	67
5.24	The crystallisation of a floating charge	69
5.26	Liquidation	70
5.27	Appointment of a receiver, cessation of business or enforcement by other creditors	71
5.27	Actions of the chargee	71
5.29	Cessation of business	72
5.32	Acts of other creditors	73
5.42	Partial crystallisation and reflotation	77

Chapter 6—SECURITY BY OPERATION OF LAW 79

6.01	Basis of non-consensual security	79
6.03	Liens	79
6.06	Common law liens	80
6.08	Particular liens	81
6.13	General liens	84
6.14	Solicitors	85
6.24	Bankers' and stockbrokers' liens	88
6.28	Insurance brokers' liens	90
6.29	Factors	91
6.31	Liens on the sale of goods	91
6.38	Equitable liens	94
6.39	Vendor's lien	94
6.46	Maritime liens	97
6.50	Execution	99
6.50	Nature of execution	99
6.55	The writ of *fieri facias*	102
6.60	Writ of possession	104
6.62	Writ of delivery	105
6.64	Sequestration	105
6.66	Garnishee proceedings	106
6.74	Charging orders	110
6.83	Stop orders and stop notices	113
6.85	Appointment of a receiver	114
6.90	Mareva injunctions	116
6.91	Payment into court	116
6.92	Distress	117
6.93	Distress for rent	117

6.97	Subject matter of distress for rent	119
6.98	The statutory exemptions for goods not belonging to the tenant	120
6.99	The Law of Distress Amendment Act 1908	121
6.101	Procedure for distress	123
6.106	Intervention by third parties—the procedure	124
6.109	Distress for taxes	125
6.110	Value added tax	126
6.113	Income tax, capital gains tax and corporation tax	126
6.115	Distress for rates	127
6.122	Distress under the Magistrates' Court Act 1980	128

Chapter 7—THE ENFORCEMENT OF A SECURITY INTEREST 130

7.01	Introduction	130
7.05	Possession	132
7.11	Receivership	135
7.17	Sale by the mortgagee	138
7.31	Foreclosure	144

Chapter 8—PRIORITY OF SECURITY INTERESTS 147

8.01	General principles	147
8.04	Legal and equitable mortgages and charges	147
8.05	Conduct resulting in loss of priority	148
8.11	Notice outside registration systems	150
8.13	Actual notice	152
8.14	Constructive notice	152
8.18	Imputed notice	154
8.19	Tacking further advances	154
8.20	Agreement between mortgagees	155
8.21	Absence of notice	155
8.23	Obligation to make further advances	156
8.24	Tacking and registered land	156
8.25	Registration of company charges	157
8.25	Registrable charges	157
8.42	Effects of failure to register	164
8.51	Rectification and registration out of time	167
8.55	Effect of registration	168
8.61	Companies Act 1989	170
8.62	Reform of registrable charges	171
8.69	New effects of failure to register	172
8.70	Registration out of time or of inaccurate particulars	173
8.75	New effects of registration	174
8.76	Overseas companies	174
8.77	Priority rules as to floating charges	175
8.78	Priorities between floating charges	175
8.79	Priority against fixed charges	175
8.88	Floating charges and liens	178
8.89	Floating charges and execution	178
8.95	Floating charges and distraint	180
8.97	Specific rules and registration systems	181
8.97	Land	181
8.98	Mortgages of legal estate or equitable interests	181

8.100	Mortgages protected by deposit of title deeds	181
8.101	Competition between mortgages protected by deposit	182
8.105	Competition between protection by deposit and registration	183
8.106	Competition between two or more registrable mortgages	183
8.108	Registered land	184
8.112	Choses in action and intellectual property	186
8.113	Rule in *Dearle v Hall*	186
8.119	Register of patents	188
8.123	Register of trade marks	189
8.124	Register of designs	189
8.125	Shares	189
8.127	Insurance policies	190
8.128	Chattels	190
8.129	Bills of Sale Acts	191
8.130	Priority of security interests over ships	191
8.135	Register of aircraft mortgages	193
8.136	Pledge and liens	194
8.137	Execution and priorities	194
8.138	*Fieri facias*	194
8.139	Garnishee orders	195
8.140	Charging orders	195
8.141	Receivers appointed by the court	196
8.142	Distraint	196

Chapter 9—SECURITY BY THE USE OF OWNERSHIP RIGHTS   197
9.01	Nature of such methods	197
9.06	Retention of title	198
9.07	Title to unmixed goods before subsale	199
9.11	Security over mixed goods	200
9.22	The effect of a subsale of goods subject to a retention of title clause	205
9.26	Proceeds of sale	206
9.45	Securing the whole account	212
9.49	Trust property	214
9.59	Leasing, hire purchase and factoring	218

Chapter 10—THE QUALIFICATIONS OF INSOLVENCY PRACTITIONERS   222
10.01	The insolvency practitioner	222
10.02	The origins of the system of qualifications	222
10.04	Acting as an insolvency practitioner	223
10.06	Recognised professional bodies	224
10.09	Authorisation by a competent body	224
10.10	Application	225
10.11	Criteria	225
10.20	Procedure and the tribunal	228
10.31	Disqualifications	231
10.34	Surety	232
10.36	Records	233

Chapter 11—ADMINISTRATIVE RECEIVERS 235

11.01	Receivers—their role	235
11.02	The origin of the administrative receiver	235
11.05	Definition of an administrative receiver	236
11.09	Qualifications of an administrative receiver	237
11.15	Disqualifications	239
11.16	Corporate bodies	239
11.17	Undischarged bankrupts	240
11.18	Disqualified person	240
11.19	Grounds of appointment	241
11.24	Validity of appointment	242
11.25	Satisfaction of conditions in the debenture	243
11.26	Validity of the debenture itself	243
11.29	Liability for invalid appointment	244
11.29	Indemnity	244
11.31	Defect in appointment	245
11.32	No protection from s 42(3) Insolvency Act 1986	245
11.33	Appointment	246
11.35	Appointment of joint receivers	246
11.39	Appointment of receiver if company in liquidation	247
11.40	Acceptance of appointment	247
11.40	Time within which acceptance must be made	247
11.41	Time of appointment	248
11.42	Mode of acceptance	248
11.43	Notification that administrative receiver appointed	248
11.44	Appointment to be entered in register of charges	249
11.45	Advertisement of appointment	249
11.46	Notice to company and creditors	249
11.50	Advertisement of appointment	250
11.51	Non-application of s 46	251

Chapter 12—DUTIES AND LIABILITIES OF THE ADMINISTRATIVE RECEIVER 252

12.01	Agency and liability for contracts	252
12.05	Position after liquidation	253
12.07	Personal liability for contracts entered into in the course of receivership	254
12.13	Statement of affairs	256
12.14	Notice to deponents	257
12.15	Content of statement	257
12.18	Limited disclosure of statement of affairs	258
12.19	Concurrence in the statement of affairs	259
12.20	Administrative receiver's discretion to release from obligations	259
12.22	Application to the court	260
12.25	Abstract of receipts and payments	260
12.27	Enforcement of duty to make returns	261
12.28	Other duties to supply information	262
12.31	Duty to publicise appointment	263
12.32	Duty to make a report	263
12.37	Content of the report	265

12.39	Limited disclosure of contents of report	266
12.40	Creditors' meeting—setting up a committee	266
12.45	Creditors' committee—membership	268
12.48	Creditors' committee—actions	269
12.51	Creditors' committee—holding meetings	270
12.53	Procedure at meetings	271
12.54	Postal resolutions	271
12.56	Expenses	271
12.57	Creditors' committee—resignation	272
12.58	Automatic termination of membership	272
12.59	Removal	272
12.60	Vacancies	272
12.61	Duty to issue certificate of insolvency	273
12.63	General duties of receivers	273
12.64	Duty of care	274
12.67	Contractual duties	275
12.68	Fiduciary duties	275
12.69	Powers of the administrative receiver	276
12.69	General	276
12.71	Seeking the guidance of the court	276
12.72	General powers given by schedule 1	277
12.73	Disputes arising over the exercise of the administrative receiver's powers	277
12.74	Protection of persons dealing with the administrative receiver	278
12.75	Getting in the property of the company	278
12.78	Selling the company's property	279
12.81	Sale as a going concern	280
12.84	Hive down	281
12.88	Sale of property subject to a security	282
12.93	Alternatives to sale—schemes	284
12.94	Powers of administrative receiver as officeholder	285
12.96	Confidentiality of records of insolvency	285
12.98	Supplies by utilities	286
12.100	Delivery up of company property to the officeholder	286
12.101	Duty to cooperate with officeholder	287
12.102	Summoning people before the court	287
12.112	Effect of liquidation	292
12.120	Ending the receivership	294
12.120	Distribution	294
12.126	Administrative receivers and distribution	297
12.127	Special priority of preferential creditors	297
12.128	Categories of preferential claims	297
12.129	The relevant date	299
12.130	The Insolvency Act 1986 s 115	299
12.131	The Insolvency Act 1986 s 45(3)	299
12.132	Vacation of office	300
12.135	Removal of administrative receiver	301
12.137	Resignation of administrative receiver	302
12.138	Death of an administrative receiver	303
Chapter 13—ADMINISTRATION ORDERS		304

13.01	Introduction	304
13.08	Application for an order	306
13.13	Hearing and criteria for order	309
13.27	The administration order	314
13.34	The moratorium	317
13.41	Supplies by public utilities	320
13.43	Other effects of administration order	321
13.46	Invoices etc.	322
13.47	Copies and notice of order	322
13.48	Statement of affairs	323
13.54	Variation or discharge of order	325
13.55	The role of the administrator	326
13.55	Appointment	326
13.57	The powers of the administrator	327
13.58	General powers	327
13.63	Powers within the company	329
13.66	Powers to deal with third parties	330
13.69	Power to deal with charged property	331
13.83	The duties of the administrator	336
13.89	Vacation of office by the administrator	338
13.93	Release of the administrator	339
13.94	Remuneration of the administrator	340
13.99	The administrator's proposals	341
13.103	Presenting the proposal	342
13.106	Consideration of the proposals	344
13.118	Creditor protection	349
13.119	Requisitioning meetings	350
13.121	The creditors' committee	350
13.129	Unfair prejudice to creditors or members	354

Chapter 14—WINDING UP: COMMENCEMENT; PROCEDURE;		
MEETINGS AND EFFECTS		356
14.01	Part 1—The nature and scope of the winding up process	356
14.07	Part 2—Commencement and effects of voluntary winding up	358
14.07	Creditors' voluntary winding up	358
14.08	Resolutions for creditors' voluntary winding up	358
14.10	Procedure for passing resolution	358
14.31	The conduct of the creditors' meeting	366
14.32	Members' voluntary winding up	366
14.41	Effects of winding up resolution	370
14.41	Business and status of the company	370
14.43	Share transfers	371
14.44	Directors' powers	371
14.45	Effect on employment contracts	371
14.47	Use of s 112 to restrain proceedings against the company	372
14.51	Part 3—Commencement and effects of winding up by the court	373
14.51	Jurisdiction	373
14.58	Petitioners	376
14.61	The company or its directors as petitioners	377
14.65	Petition by a creditor	379

14.77	Petition by a contributory	384
14.77	Who may petition?	384
14.81	Restrictions on a contributory's petition	385
14.90	Secretary of State's petition	389
14.96	The official receiver	392
14.97	The petition: form, service and advertisement	392
14.106	The grounds for a winding up by the court	396
14.107	Special resolution—s 122(1)(a)	396
14.108	Public companies not complying with share capital requirements—s 122(1)(b)	396
14.110	Old public companies—s 122(1)(c)	397
14.111	Suspension of business—s 122(1)(d)	398
14.114	Number of members below minimum—s 122(1)(e)	399
14.115	Inability to pay debts	399
14.116	Overall financial position	400
14.124	Statutory demand	403
14.130	Execution unsatisfied	405
14.131	Just and equitable ground—s 122(1)(g)	406
14.137	Fraud, illegality and the need for investigation	408
14.139	Disappearance of the company's substratum	408
14.143	Paralysis of the decision-making process	410
14.145	The partnership analogy	411
14.150	Oppression and misconduct	413
14.153	Specialist grounds	415
14.154	Insurance companies	415
14.156	Banks	416
14.157	Companies carrying on investment business	416
14.160	The hearing	417
14.163	The decision and the order	418
14.175	The effect of a winding up order	424
14.176	Rescinding or staying a winding up order	424
14.179	Effect on proceedings against the company	425
14.181	Avoidance of dispositions and share transfers	426
14.189	Effect on execution against the company	429
14.190	Effect on employees and agents of the company	429
14.193	Effect on director's status and powers	431
14.194	Part 4—Meetings of creditors and contributories	431
14.195	When and by whom meetings can be called	432
14.196	Calling meetings in winding up by the court	432
14.199	Calling meetings in a voluntary liquidation	433
14.201	Notice of meetings and information to creditors in any winding up	434
14.207	Venue, chair and adjournment in any liquidation	436
14.210	Attendance voting and proxies at meetings in any liquidation	438
14.222	Resolutions and minutes at meetings in any liquidation	442
14.224	Expenses of meetings	443
Chapter 15—THE LIQUIDATOR		**444**
15.02	Part 1—Appointment of liquidator	444
15.02	General requirements for appointment	444
15.04	Appointment in a compulsory winding up	445

15.04	Provisional liquidator	445
15.18	Termination of the appointment of a provisional liquidator	451
15.19	Special managers	451
15.24	The powers of the special manager	453
15.26	The appointment of a liquidator in a compulsory winding up	454
15.40	The effect of the appointment on the powers of the directors	458
15.41	Appointment in a voluntary winding up	459
15.49	Part 2—Powers, duties and role of the liquidator	462
15.49	Legal status of the liquidator	462
15.50	The liquidator as agent	462
15.58	The liquidator as fiduciary	465
15.76	The liquidator as an officer of the court	472
15.80	The duty of care and skill	474
15.84	The statutory powers of the liquidator	476
15.86	Unfettered powers	477
15.97	Qualified powers in compulsory liquidations	485
15.102	Powers exercisable only with sanction in all liquidations	489
15.106	Part 3—Removal from and vacation of office by a liquidator and release	492
15.106	Resignation	492
15.115	Ceasing to be a qualified insolvency practitioner	495
15.116	Vacation of office on the making of a winding up order	495
15.117	Removal of a liquidator	496
15.118	By the court	496
15.123	By creditors meeting or company meeting	498
15.131	By the Secretary of State	502
15.132	Death of the liquidator	502
15.133	Completion of the winding up	503
15.134	Duties of the liquidator on leaving office	503
15.135	The release of a liquidator	504
15.136	Release in a voluntary liquidation	504
15.138	Release in a compulsory liquidation	506
15.140	Part 4—Remuneration of liquidators	507
Chapter 16—INVESTIGATION, ENFORCEMENT, RECORDS AND THE CREDITORS' COMMITTEE		511
16.01	Inspection of books and public and private examinations	511
16.03	Inspection of the company's books	512
16.10	Private examination	514
16.24	Public examination	520
16.36	Duty of liquidator to report matters to the authorities	524
16.47	Accounts and the handling of monies	528
16.48	The insolvency services account	528
16.53	Administrative and financial records and audits	530
16.59	Unclaimed funds and payments of dividend	533
16.61	Investments	533
16.62	Summary proceedings	534
16.63	Payments by contributories etc.	535
16.65	Enforcing the delivery of books, papers, etc.	536
16.66	Misfeasance summonses	536

16.67   The applicants   536
16.68   The respondents   537
16.72   The rights enforceable   538
16.81   Orders available   543
16.83   Procedure   544
16.85   The liquidation committee   545
16.86   Appointment of committee   545
16.94   Proceedings of liquidation committee   548
16.98   Vacation of membership   550
16.101   Transactions by committee members and their associates   551
16.108   Functions of the liquidation committee   553
16.114 Reports to creditors   556

Chapter 17—CONTRIBUTORIES   558
17.01   Significance of contributories   558
17.03   Definition of a contributory   558
17.04   Every past and present member of the company   559
17.08   Private company purchasing own shares from capital   561
17.10   Directors and managers with unlimited liability   561
17.11   Settlement of list of contributories   562
17.18   Rectifying the register of members   564
17.20   Calls and the liability of contributories   565
17.30   Set off by contributories   568

Chapter 18—THE WINDING UP PROCESS: GATHERING ASSETS   571
18.05   Part 1—The right to disclaim property   572
18.05   The property that may be disclaimed   572
18.07   Procedure   573
18.10   Effect of disclaimer   574
18.14   Vesting orders   575
18.16   Disclaimer of leaseholds   576
18.22   Part 2—Gathering particular assets   579
18.23   Land   579
18.29   Chattels   581
18.30   Effect of liquidation on distress or execution   582
18.35   Effect of liquidation on actions or proceedings   584
18.38   Incomplete execution or attachment   585
18.47   Sale of goods contracts   589
18.48   Choses in action   589
18.49   Third Parties (Rights Against Insurers) Act 1930   589
18.51   Set off   590
18.55   Scope of set off   591
18.61   Mutuality   593
18.67   The account   596
18.68   Exclusion of set off   596
18.70   The statutory recission of contracts   597
18.73   The realisation of assets   598

**Chapter 19—THE DISTRIBUTION OF ASSETS ON WINDING UP
            AND THE DISSOLUTION OF THE COMPANY**   600
19.01   General order of distribution of assets   600
19.06   The expenses of winding up   601

19.06	Priority of expenses	601
19.09	Usual order of priority of expenses inter se	602
19.17	Preferential debts	606
19.18	The priority of preferential debts	606
19.23	The "Relevant Date"	608
19.25	The categories of preferential debts	609
19.26	Category 1: Debts due to the inland revenue	609
19.27	Category 2: Debts due to the customs and excise	609
19.30	Category 3: Social security contributions	610
19.31	Category 4: Contributions to occupational pension scheme	610
19.32	Category 5: Remuneration and other sums due to employees	611
19.33	Amounts paid by the Department of Employment	612
19.38	Levies on coal and steel production	614
19.39	Ordinary debts	614
19.39	What is provable?	614
19.46	Procedure for proving debts	617
19.56	Quantification of debts	619
19.58	Debts of uncertain value	620
19.61	Negotiable instruments	621
19.62	Secured creditors	621
19.71	Discounts	624
19.72	Foreign currency debts	624
19.73	Post liquidation interest	624
19.77	Preliquidation interest	625
19.80	Periodic payments	626
19.83	Set off	627
19.84	Dividend and final distribution	627
19.84	Dividend	627
19.92	The final distribution	629
19.99	Post liquidation interest	631
19.100	Section 215(4) orders and Bathampton orders	631
19.101	Distributions to contributories	632
19.101	Liability arising from purchase or redemption of own shares	632
19.103	Deferred debts to members	632
19.105	Expenses of contributories' meetings	633
19.106	Return of capital	633
19.113	Distribution of surplus after repayment of capital	636
19.118	Distributions to employees	637
19.119	The final meetings	637
19.121	Dissolution	638
19.122	Voluntary liquidation	638
19.123	Compulsory liquidation	638
19.123	Early dissolution	638
19.128	The usual procedure	640
19.130	Striking companies off the register	641
19.134	The effects of dissolution and striking off	642
19.137	Revival of dissolved companies	643
19.138	Use of s 651	643
19.141	Use of s 653	644

Chapter 20—SETTING ASIDE TRANSACTIONS 647

20.03	Transactions at an undervalue	648

20.03	Application and nature of transaction	648
20.07	The statutory defence	649
20.10	The relevant time	650
20.16	Connected persons	652
20.18	"Associates"	653
20.19	Associates of individuals	653
20.22	Associates of corporate bodies	654
20.30	The order	657
20.31	Transactions defrauding creditors	657
20.32	Transaction at an undervalue	658
20.33	The purpose of the transaction	658
20.35	Applicants	659
20.37	Court order	659
20.40	Preferences	660
20.49	Orders of the court on proof of a preference or a transaction at an undervalue	663
20.49	Scope of court orders	663
20.51	Possible orders	665
20.59	Extortionate credit transactions	668
20.66	The avoidance of certain floating charges	671

Chapter 21—PERSONAL LIABILITY OF DIRECTORS AND OTHERS		**674**
21.02	Part 1—Personal liability	674
21.05	Wrongful trading	676
21.06	Definition	676
21.09	Preconditions for an order	678
21.10	Insolvent liquidation	678
21.12	Knowledge or negligence	678
21.21	Commencement	683
21.22	The statutory defence	684
21.24	The application	685
21.25	Fraudulent trading	686
21.26	The meaning of fraudulent trading	686
21.31	The parties to fraudulent trading	689
21.34	The court order under ss 213 and 214	690
21.39	Phoenix companies	693
21.46	Exclusions from the Phoenix rules	697
21.47	Leave of court	697
21.48	Cases where leave not required	698
21.51	Part 2—Disqualification of directors	699
21.51	The nature of a disqualification order	699
21.57	Consequences of breach of an order	701
21.61	Applications for disqualification orders	702
21.65	Disqualification orders on grounds not necessarily involving insolvency	703
21.65	Conviction for an indictable offence	703
21.68	Persistent default in complying with companies legislation	704
21.73	Disqualification after the investigation of a company	706
21.75	Grounds specifically relating to corporate insolvency	706

21.76	Fraud becoming apparent in the course of winding up	706
21.77	Wrongful trading	707
21.78	Unfitness in the context of insolvency	707
21.78	Investigation and report	707
21.84	The order on the basis of unfitness	709
21.88	The criteria for unfitness	710

Chapter 22—VOLUNTARY ARRANGEMENTS **715**

22.01	The liquidator's powers	715
22.02	Sections 110–111 Insolvency Act 1986	715
22.09	Voluntary arrangements under Part 1 of the Insolvency Act 1986	718
22.10	The proposal and the nominee	718
22.13	Proposal by directors	719
22.23	A proposal by a liquidator or administrator	724
22.24	Summoning meetings	724
22.24	Nominee not liquidator or administrator	724
22.27	Liquidator or administrator himself the nominee	725
22.28	All meetings	726
22.29	The decision on a proposal and its effects	726
22.43	Challenges to the arrangement	731
22.49	Implementing the arrangement	734
22.52	Accounts reports and records	735
22.55	Completion of the arrangement	736
22.56	Arrangements and reconstructions under ss 425 to 427	736
22.56	Scope of s 425	736
22.60	Convening class meetings	737
22.65	The meetings	739
22.66	Court sanction and orders	740
22.69	Mergers and divisions of public companies	741
22.74	Agreements with creditors at common law	743
	Index	745

Preface

This book has been long in gestation. In part this was because of the consolidation, in the Insolvency Act 1986, of the reforming Insolvency Act 1985 and the relevant sections of the Companies Act 1985 as well as the delay in producing the final version of the Insolvency Rules 1986. It is to be hoped that the book benefits from the opportunity provided by the delay to take account of developments in the area since the 1986 Act came into force. The purpose of the work is to provide those concerned with corporate insolvency with a comprehensive picture and analysis of the law in that field with some regard to matters of procedure. Responsibility for the book is divided as follows.

Chapters 1 to 7; 9; 10 and 13 to 22 are the responsibility of Ian Snaith who conceived the plan for the project. Chapters 11 and 12 are the work of Fiona Cownie and chapter 8 was prepared by Ian Snaith with the assistance of Fiona Cownie.

During the course of writing the book debts have been incurred to many. Spouses and family have suffered neglect and inconvenience. Tedious and lengthy typing assignments have been undertaken by many of the secretarial staff in the Law Faculty Office at Leicester University.

Ian Snaith wishes to thank Judith, Sarah, John and Kate for the tolerance thay have shown of his frequent absences from home and his preoccupied state while there. Judith did not act as an editorial assistant or typist but is thanked instead "for the agreeable fact of her continuing presence which in twenty years I have never presumed to expect" (see Barbara Trapido, *Brother of the More Famous Jack*, Black Swan, London 1983).

Tony Bradney did act as unpaid typist as well as putting up with inconvenience and neglect. Barbara Goodman, Christine Driver and other members of the secretarial staff of Leicester University Law Faculty worked efficiently and effectively on tedious and lengthy typing assignments. Heather Langman played a crucial role in organising and collating the manuscript as well as typing large sections of it—showing enormous initiative, resourcefulness and good humour while doing so.

A number of colleagues in the Law Faculty at Leicester provided support and assistance during the course of the project. In particular, Tony Arnull and Fiona Patfield were always willing to engage in vigorous discussions of issues as they arose. Mark Thompson discussed some of the real property law matters dealt with in the book.

The experience gained by Ian Snaith in September 1986 in the offices of Coward Chance (shortly before the creation of Clifford Chance) was invaluable. Thanks are due to Michael Mockridge, Mark Dyer and Daniel Kossoff for their hospitality, the stimulating problems they produced and their willingness to spend time discussing the issues raised.

The forbearance of James Lamb, Kim Corker and Jo Bushell of Waterlow Publishers at the inordinate delay in producing a final manuscript was remarkable. They have the gratitude of the authors for their tolerance and understanding. Jane Cairney of Waterlows spent many hours editing and improving the text and we are grateful for her efforts.

It goes without saying that responsibility for the infelicities of style and other faults in the work lie only with the authors who take that responsibility divided along the lines set out above.

The book deals with the law as at 31st March 1989 as it appeared on the basis of materials available to the authors at that time. It has also been possible to include references to the Companies Act 1989 and to some later cases. It does not deal with the law applicable to transactions taking place before the Insolvency Act 1986 and the Insolvency Rules 1986 came into effect.

Ian Snaith
Fiona Cownie
Leicester
1989

Table of Cases

A v B [1984] 1 All ER 265   6.18
AB & C Chewing Gum, Re [1975] 1 WLR 579   14.147, 14.152
ABC Coupler and Engineering Co Ltd, Re (No. 2) [1962] 1 WLR 1236   14.160
ABC Coupler and Engineering Co Ltd, Re (No 3) [1970] 1 WLR 702,
  [1970] 1 All ER 650   15.12, 18.33, 19.82
ACL Metals Ltd, Re (1989) 5 BCC 749   15.96
AE Realisations (1985) Ltd, Re [1987] BCLC 486   18.18
A Line (1839) 1 W Rob 111   8.132, 8.134
ARV Aviation Ltd, Re (1988) 4 BCC 708   13.75, 13.78
Aberdeen Railway v Blaikie (1854) 1 Macq 461   15.61
Aberman Ironworks v Workers (1868) 4 Ch App 101   6.44
Abingdon RDC v O'Gorman [1968] 2 QB 811   6.105
Acraman v Bates (1860) 29 LJQB 78   1.30
Aga Estate Agencies Ltd, Re [1986] BCLC 346   19.142
Agra & Masterman's Bank, Ex p (1871) 6 Ch App 206   15.73, 15.93
Agra & Masterman's Bank, Re (1896) LR 12 Eq 509n   15.93, 22.01, 22.04
Agra Bank Ltd v Barry (1874) LR 7 HL 135   8.06
Aidall Ltd, Re [1933] 1 Ch 323   16.63
Air Ecosse Ltd v CAA (1987) 3 BCC 492   13.34
Alabama, New Orleans, Texas & Pacific Junction Railway Co, Re [1891] 1
  Ch 213   22.67
Albemarle Supply Co Ltd v Hind & Co [1928] 1 KB 307   6.06, 6.11
Allcester (David) Ltd, Re [1922] 2 Ch 211   3.15, 8.31, 8.37
Allied Produce Ltd, Re [1967] 1 WLR 1469   14.92
Altack v Bramwell (1863) 3 B & S 520   6.104
Alton Corporation, Re [1985] BCLC 27   2.09
Aluminium Industries Vaasen BV v Romalpa Aluminium Ltd [1976]
  1 WLR 676, [1976] 2 All ER 552   8.37, 9.06, 9.12, 9.15,
  9.22, 9.28–9.29, 9.31, 9.35, 9.36
Amalgamated Investment and Property Co Ltd, Re (1984) 1 BCC 104   19.73
American Concentrated Must Corporation v Hendry (1893) 65 LJQB 388   6.102
American Express International Banking Corporation v Hurley [1986]
  BCLC 52, [1985] 3 All ER 564   7.22, 7.23, 7.26, 12.05,
  12.64, 12.66, 12.82, 12.113
American Pioneer Leather Co, Re [1918] 1 Ch 556   14.144
Anchor Lines (Henderson Bros) Ltd, Re [1937] Ch 1   15.93
Anderson v Midland Railway Co (1861) 2 E & E 614   6.93
Andrabell Ltd, Re [1984] BCLC 522   9.22, 9.38, 9.45
Andrew, Re [1937] Ch 122   18.39
Anglesea Colliery Co, Re (1866) 1 Ch App 555   17.07
Anglesea Island Coal and Coke Co Ltd, Re, ex p Owen (1861) 4 LT 684   14.128
Anglo-Continental Carpet Manufacturing Co, Re [1903] 1 Ch 914   8.52

xxii

Anglo-Continental Produce Ltd, *Re* [1939] 1 All ER 99   14.61, 14.133
Anglo-French Co-operative Society, *Re, ex p* Pelly (1882) 21 Ch D 492 16.79, 18.66
Anglo-Moravian Hungarian Junction Railway Company, *Re* (1875)
    1 Ch D 130   15.52, 15.53, 15.84
Annangel Glory Compania Naviera SA v Goldetz ME Marketing Corp
    [1988] PCC 37   5.17, 8.37
Ant Jurgens Margarinenfabriken v Lois Dreyfus & Co [1914] 3 KB 40   3.12
Apex Film Distributors Ltd, *Re* [1960] Ch 378   17.04, 17.25
Apex Leisure Hire v Barratt [1984] ICR 452   12.87
Aquila Design (GRP Products) Ltd v Cornhill Insurance plc (1987) 3 BCC
    364   18.03
Arctic Engineering Ltd, *Re* (No 2) [1986] BCLC 253   21.72
Argentum Reductions (UK) Ltd, *Re* [1975] 1 All ER 608   14.183
Armagh Shoes Ltd, *Re* [1982] NI 59   4.45
Armavent Ltd, *Re* [1975] 1 WLR 1679   14.92
Armstrong Whitworth Securities Ltd, *Re* [1947] 1 Ch 673   15.81
Arnold (RM) & Sons Ltd, *Re* [1984] BCLC 535   8.52
Arrow (Leeds) Ltd, *Re* [1986] BCLC 538   14.171
Art Reproduction Co Ltd, *Re* [1952] Ch 89   19.42
Ashbury Railway Carriage Co v Riche (1875) LR 7 HL 653   1.05
Ashford's Case (1880) 16 Ch D 411   4.32
Attika Hope [1988] 1 Lloyd's Rep 439   8.118
Attorney-General v Lindi St-Claire (Personal Services) Ltd *Financial Times*
    18 December 1980   14.137
Audio Systems Ltd, *Re* [1965] 1 WLR 1096   14.55
Auriferous Properties Ltd, *Re* [1898] 1 Ch 691   17.35
Automatic Bottle Makers Ltd, *Re* [1926] 1 Ch 412   5.33, 8.78, 8.84
Aveling Barford Ltd, *Re* [1989] BCLC 122   6.02, 6.17,
                                        12.103, 12.111, 16.09–16.11
Ayerst v C & K (Construction) Ltd [1976] AC 167   15.01, 15.58, 18.04

Badeley v Consolidated Bank (1888) 38 Ch D 238   6.70
Baglan Bay Tin Plate Co Ltd v John (1895) 72 LT 805   6.118
Bailey v Barnes [1894] 1 Ch 25   8.04, 8.87, 8.104
Bailey Hay & Co Ltd, *Re* [1971] 1 WLR 1357   14.12
Baku Consolidated Oilfields Ltd, *Re* [1944] 1 All ER 24   14.142
Ball v Faulkner (1848) 2 De G & Sm 722   6.44
Bamford Publishers Ltd, *Re The Times* 4 June 1977   14.94
Bank of Baroda v Panessar [1986] BCLC 497   11.21
Bank of Cyprus (London) Ltd v Gill [1980] 2 Lloyd's Rep 51   7.23
Bank of Montreal v Woodtown Developments Ltd (1979) 99 DLR (3d) 739 5.41
Bankers' Trust v Galadari [1986] 3 WLR 1099   6.54, 6.56, 8.138
Banner v Berridge (1881) 18 Ch D 254   7.28
Banner v Johnston (1871 LR 5 HL 157   6.24
Barber v Richards (1851) 6 Exch 63   4.53
Barclays Bank Ltd v Bird [1954] Ch 274   7.07
Barclays Bank Ltd v Kiley [1961] 2 All ER 849   6.94
Barclays Bank Ltd v Quistclose Investments Ltd [1970] AC 567   9.51
Barclays Bank Ltd v Taylor [1974] 1 Ch 137   8.111
Barclays Bank Ltd v TOSG Trust Fund Ltd [1984] AC 626   19.44

Barker (George) (Transport) Ltd v Eynon [1974] 1 All ER 900   6.03, 6.04,
           6.08, 8.88
Barleycorn Enterprises Ltd, *Re* [1970] Ch 465   12.130, 19.12
Barnet v Eastman (1898) 67 LJQB 517   6.68
Barnett (Augustus) & Son Ltd, *Re* [1986] BCLC 170   21.30, 21.32
Barnhart v Greenshields (1853) 9 Moo PC 36   8.13
Barrow Borough Transport Ltd, *Re* (1989) 5 BCC 646   8.52, 13.34
Barrows v Chief Land Registrar *The Times* 20 October 1977   14.192
Bastable, *Re* [1901] 2 KB 518   18.06
Bateman v Hunt [1904] 2 KB 530   4.08
Bateman & Co v Ball (1887) 56 LJQB 291   14.41
Bateson (John) & Co Ltd, *Re* [1985] BCLC 259   8.52, 15.79
Bath Glass Ltd, *Re* (1988) 4 BCC 130   21.93, 21.94
Bathampton Properties Ltd, *Re* [1976] 1 WLR 168   14.171, 19.100
Bayswater Trading Co Ltd, *Re* [1970] 1 WLR 343   14.80, 19.142
Beaufort (Jon) (London) Ltd, *Re* [1953] Ch 131   19.42
Bede Steam Shipping Co, *Re* [1917] 1 Ch 123   4.28
Beirnstein, *Re* [1925] Ch 12   6.38
Belfast Ropework Co v Bushell [1918] 1 KB 210   6.08
Bell, *Re* [1896] 1 Ch 1   4.57
Bellaglade Ltd, *Re* [1977] 1 All ER 319   14.179, 18.32, 18.39
Bellamy v Brickenden (1861) 2 J & H 137   4.27
Belmont Finance Corporation Ltd v Williams Furniture Ltd [1979]
    Ch 250   15.65
Benwell Tower (1895) 8 Asp Mar Law Cas 13   8.131
Berkeley Applegate (Investment Consultants) Ltd, *Re* (1988) 4 BCC 274   9.53
Berkeley Applegate (Investment Consultants) Ltd, *Re* (No 2) (1988) 4 BCC
    280   15.144
Berry (Herbert) Associates v IRC [1978] 1 All ER 161   14.49, 18.35
Berwick & Co v Price [1905] 1 Ch 632   8.15
Bibby (James) Ltd v Woods & Howard [1949] 2 KB 449   6.70
Biggs & Rocke, *Re* (1897) 41 Sol Jo 277   6.14
Birch v Cropper (1889) 14 App Cas 525   19.117
Birmingham, *Re* [1959] Ch 523   6.40
Bishop v Bonham (1988) 4 BCC 347   7.25, 12.66
Bishop v Smyrna and Cassaba Railway Co [1895] 2 Ch 265   19.114
Bisset v Caldwell (1791) Peake 50   6.97
Black v Williams [1895] 1 Ch 408   3.22, 8.130
Blackburn Building Society v Cunliffe Brooks (1883) 22 Ch D 61   1.09
Blaina Colliery, *Re* [1926] WN 30   14.183
Blakeley v Dent (1876) 15 WR 663   18.32
Blakeley Ordnance Co, *Re* (1867) LR 4 Eq 135   17.14
Blakeley Ordnance Co, *Re* (1873) 8 Ch App 800   17.04, 17.05
Blanche (1887) 58 LT 592   7.03, 7.09
Bland, *Ex p* (1814) 2 Rose 91   6.46
Blenkinsopp v Blenkinsopp (1852) 1 De GM & G 495   6.64
Bleriot Manufacturing Aircraft Co, *Re* (1916) 32 TLR 253   14.140, 14.152
Bletchley Boat Company Ltd, *Re* [1974] 1 WLR 630   16.13
Bloomenthal v Ford [1887] AC 156   19.56
Blue Jeans Sales Ltd, *Re* [1979] 1 All ER 641   18.27
Blum v OCP Repartition SA (1988) 4 BCC 771   21.04

Boardman v Phipps [1967] 2 AC 46   15.63
Bolton (HL) Engineering Co Ltd, *Re* [1956] 2 WLR 84   14.79
Bolton (HL) Engineering Co Ltd v Graham (TJ) & Sons Ltd [1957]1 QB
    159   6.93
Bond Worth, *Re* [1980] Ch 228, [1979] 3 All ER 919   5.41, 9.09,
                                                                 9.12, 9.22, 9.32
Bondina v Rollaway Shower Blinds Ltd [1986] 1 WLR 517   21.03
Boodle Hatfield & Co v British Films (1986) PCC 176   6.39
Borax Co, *Re* [1901] 1 Ch 326   5.19, 5.21, 5.22, 5.26
Borden (UK) Ltd v Scottish Timber Products [1979] 3 All ER 961   9.12, 9.14,
                                                                 9.17, 9.30, 9.33
Born, *Re* [1900] 2 Ch 433   19.11
Borough of Portsmouth Tramways Co, *Re* [1892] 2 Ch 362   14.65
Bostels, *Re* [1968] 1 Ch 346   19.09
Boston Timber Fabrications Ltd, *Re* [1984] BCLC 328   14.164
Bowes, *Re* (1886) 33 Ch D 586   6.24
Bowes v Directors of Hope Life and Insurance Guarantee Co (1865) 11 HL
    Cas 389   14.75, 14.76
Bowling and Welby's Contract, *Re* [1895] 1 Ch 663   14.114
Boxco Ltd, *Re* [1970] Ch 442   19.147
Bradford Banking Co v Briggs & Co (1886) 12 App Cas 29   8.114
Bradley v Eagle Star Insurance Co *The Times* 3 March 1989   18.49
Bradley v Ricks (1898) 9 Ch D 189   8.104
Braemar Investments Ltd, *Re* [1988] BCLC 556   8.52
Brandao v Barnett (1846) 12 Cl & Fin 747   6.24, 6.26
Brendacot Ltd, *Re* (1986) 2 BCC 164   22.75
Briggs v Jones (1870) LR 10 Eq 92   8.07
Brightlife, *Re* [1987] Ch 200, [1986] BCLC 418, [1986] 3 All ER 673   4.38,
                            5.28, 5.31, 5.38–5.40, 9.46, 19.15
Brightmore, *Re, ex p* May (1884) 14 QBD 37   14.53
Brighton Arcade Company v Dowling (1868) LR 3 CP 175   17.17
Brighton Club and Norfolk Hotel Ltd, *Re* (1865) 32 Beav 204   14.71, 14.127
Brighty v Norton (1862) 3 B & S 302   7.32
Brinds Ltd v Offshore Oil NL (1986) 2 BCC 98, 917   14.71
Brinsmead (Thomas Edward) & Sons Ltd, *Re* (1867) LR 3 Eq 355   14.137,
                                                                            14.139
Bristow, *Re* [1906] 2 IR 215   6.88, 8.141
British and Foreign Generating Apparatus Co Ltd, *Re* (1865) 12 LT 368   14.127
British Eagle International Airlines Ltd v Compagnie Nationale Air France
    [1975] 1 WLR 758   18.68, 19.03, 19.85
British Equitable Bond and Mortgage Corporation Ltd, *Re* [1910] 1 Ch
    574   14.70
British Mutoscope & Biograph Co Ltd v Homer [1901] 1 Ch 671   6.97
Broad's Patent Night Light Co, *Re* [1892] WN 5   14.101
Brocklesby v Temperance Permanent Building Society [1895] AC 173   8.07
Brompton Securities Ltd, *Re* (1988) 4 BCC 189   18.27
Brompton Securities Ltd, *Re* (No 2) (1988) 4 BCC 436   15.95, 18.27
Brooke Marine Ltd, *Re* [1988] BCLC 546   13.07, 13.65, 13.98
Brooks v Greathed (1820) 1 Jac & W 176   6.65
Brown v Cork [1985] BCLC 363   18.59
Brown v Shevill (1834) 2 Ad & El 138   6.97

Brown (Henry) & Sons v Smith [1964] 2 Lloyd's Rep 476   21.02
Brown Shipley & Co v Kough (1885) 29 Ch D 848   4.11
Browne v Savage (1859) 4 Drew 635   8.13
Brunton v Electrical Engineering Corpn [1892] 1 Ch 434   5.40, 6.18, 8.25, 8.88
Brush Aggregates, *Re* [1983] BCLC 320   4.38, 8.35
Bryanston Finance v De Vries (No 2) [1976] 2 WLR 41   14.73
Bryant Investment Co Ltd, *Re* [1974] 1 WLR 826   14.127
Building Societies Trust, *Re* (1890) 44 Ch D 140   14.99
Burn v Carvalho (1839) 4 My & Cr 690   6.44
Burnes v Trade Credits [1981] 1 WLR 805   8.19
Burston Finance Ltd v Godfrey [1976] 1 WLR 719   6.78, 6.79
Burston Finance Ltd v Speirway Ltd [1974] 1 WLR 1648   6.42, 11.28
Burton & Deakin, *Re* [1977] 1 WLR 390   14.184
Business Computers International Ltd v Registrar of Companies and Alex
     Lawrie Factors [1987] 3 WLR 1134, [1987] BCLC 621   14.104, 14.178
Business Properties Ltd, *Re* (1988) 4 BCC 685   13.13, 13.18
Byblos Bank SAL v Khudairy (AL) [1987] BCLC 232   14.120
Byng v London Life Association Ltd (1989) 5 BCC 227   14.208

CU Fittings Ltd, *Re* (1989) 5 BCC   21.96
Calahurst Ltd, *Re* (1989) 5 BCC 318   14.174
Caldwell v Sumpters [1972] Ch 478   6.18
Calgary and Edmonton Land Co Ltd, *Re* [1975] 1 WLR 355   14.178
Callao Bis Co, *Re* (1889) 42 Ch D 169   22.05, 22.08
Calmex Ltd, *Re* (1988) 4 BCC 761   14.177
Cambrian Mining Co Ltd, *Re* (1881) 50 LJCh 536   14.65
Campbell v Holyland (1877) 7 Ch D 166   7.33
Campbell Coverings Ltd, *Re* (No 2) [1954] 1 Ch 225   16.35
Cane v Jones [1981] 1 WLR 1457   14.11, 14.32
Cannon Street Entertainment Ltd v Handmade Films (Distributors) Ltd
     (1989) 5 BCC 207   14.127
Cape Breton Co v Fenn (1881) 17 Ch D 198   15.99
Capel v Buszard (1829) 6 Bing 150   6.95
Capital Annuities Ltd, *Re* [1979] 1 WLR 170   14.118
Capital Finance Co Ltd v Stokes [1969] 1 Ch 261, [1968] 3 All ER 625   6.41,
                                                                 6.42, 8.33
Capital Fire Assurance Association, *Re* (1882) 21 Ch D 209   14.113
Capital Fire Insurance Association, *Re* (1883) 24 Ch D 408   6.15, 16.08
Carden v Albert Palace Association (1886) 56 LJCh 166   15.12
Cardiff Workmen's Cottage Co Ltd, *Re* [1906] 2 Ch 627   8.45
Cargo ex Sulton (1859) Swab 504   3.27
Caribbean Products v Swains Packaging Ltd [1966] 1 Ch 331   18.39, 18.40
Carreras Rothman v Freeman Mathews Treasure Ltd [1985] Ch 207,
     [1984] BCLC 420   9.52, 18.57
Carruth v ICI [1937] AC 707   22.67
Carter v Wake (1877) 4 Ch D 605   2.08, 4.30, 4.53
Carter & Ellis, *Re*, *ex p* Savill Bros [1905] 1 KB 735   18.19
Casey's Patents, *Re* [1892] 1 Ch 104   4.59
Castell and Brown Ltd, *Re* [1898] 1 Ch 315   8.80
Castle, *Re* [1917] 2 KB 725   18.72
Castle (Henry) & Sons Ltd, *Re* (1906) 94 LT 396   18.25

Castle New Homes Ltd, *Re* [1979] 1 WLR 1075   16.14
Catholic Publishing & Bookselling Co Ltd, *Re* (1864) 2 De GJ & S 116   14.124
Cave v Cave (1880) 15 Ch D 639   8.18
Cavendish Bentinck v Fenn (1887) 12 App Cas 652   16.67, 16.74
Cella (1888) 13 PD 82   6.49
Central Newbury Car Auctions Ltd & Unity Finance Ltd [1957] 1 QB 371   3.12
Centrebind Ltd, *Re* [1967] 1 WLR 377   14.13, 14.17
Centrifugal Butter Co Ltd, *Re* [1913] 1 Ch 188   16.81
Chancellor v Webster (1893) 9 TLR 568   6.93
Chapel House Colliery Co, *Re* (1883) 24 Ch D 259   14.166
Charge Card Services Ltd, *Re* (No 2) [1987] Ch 510, [1987] BCLC 17,
    [1988] 3 All ER 702   8.36, 18.58
Charlotte Wylie (1846) 2 Wm Rob 495   6.48
Charnley Davies Ltd, *Re* [1988] BCLC 243   13.102, 13.129
Charterland Goldfields Ltd, *Re* (1909) 26 TLR 130   15.69
Chellaram (K) & Sons (London) Ltd v Butlers Warehousing and
    Distribution Ltd [1978] 2 Lloyd's Rep 412   6.10, 6.12
Chelsea Cloisters Ltd, *Re* (1978) 41 P & CR 98   9.50
Chesham Automobile Supply Ltd v Beresford Hotel (Birchington) Ltd
    (1913) 29 TLR 584   6.09
Chesterfield Catering Co, *Re* [1976] 3 All ER 294   14.86
Choice Investments v Jeromnimon [1981] 1 All ER 225   6.67
Chow Yoong Hong v Choong Fah Rubber Manufactory [1962] AC 209   4.47
Christie v Edwards [1939] 1 DLR 158, [1940] 2 DLR 65   15.63
Christonette International Ltd, *Re* [1982] 1 WLR 1245   12.130, 19.12
Church of England Building Society v Piskor [1954] 1 Ch 553   8.86
Churchill Hotel (Plymouth) Ltd, *Re* (1988) 4 BCC 112   21.64, 21.94, 21.95
Cilfoden Benefit Building Society, *Re* (1868) 3 Ch App 462   15.07
City Bank, *Ex p* (1868) LR 3 Ch 758   1.04
City Equitable Fire Insurance Co Ltd, *Re* [1925] Ch 407   15.57, 21.14, 21.19
City Land & Property (Holdings) Ltd v Dabrah [1968] Ch 166   2.06
City Life Assurance Company Ltd, *Re* [1926] Ch 191   18.66
Clandown Colliery Co, *Re* [1915] 1 Ch 369   14.166
Clark v West Ham Corporation [1909] 2 KB 858   6.08
Clarke, *Re* [1898] 1 Ch 366   8.138
Clarkson (H) (Overseas) Ltd, *Re* (1987) 3 BCC 606   19.141
Clasper Group Services Ltd, *Re* (1988) 4 BCC 673   16.70, 20.45
Clayhope Properties Ltd v Evans [1986] 2 All ER 795   7.15, 8.141
Clayton's Case, Devayner v Noble (1816) 1 Mer 529, 572   8.22, 9.55–9.57,
                                                               19.32, 20.70
Clifton Place Garage Ltd, *Re* [1970] Ch 477   14.188
Clough Mill v Martin [1984] 3 All ER 982   9.09, 9.12, 9.15–9.19,
                                                         9.22, 9.30, 9.39, 9.45
Cloverbay Ltd, *Re* (1989) 5 BCC 732   16.13
Coalport China, *Re* [1895] 2 Ch 404   4.28
Coglan v Lock (SH) (Australia) Ltd (1987) 3 BCC 183   21.02
Cole v Muddle (1852) 10 Hare 186   6.45
Cole v North Western Bank (1875) LR 10 CP 354   4.54, 6.06
Collins, *Re* [1925] Ch 556   9.68
Collins v Collins (No 2) (1862) 31 Beav 346   6.39, 6.42
Collins v Martin (1797) 1 B & P 648   4.53, 4.54

Colonial Bank v Hepworth (1887) 36 Ch D 36   4.26
Colonial Bank v Whinney (1886) 11 App Cas 426   4.24
Colonial Trusts Corporation, *Re* (1879) 15 Ch D 465   5.26
Coltman v Chamberlain (1890) 25 QBD 328   3.19
Columbian Fireproofing Co, *Re* [1910] 2 Ch 120   20.70
Combined Weighing and Advertising Machine Co, *Re* (1889) 43 Ch D 99   14.68
Commercial and Industrial Insulators Ltd, *Re* [1986] BCLC 191   14.86, 14.162
Commissioner of Customs & Excise v TH Knitwear Ltd [1988] BCLC 195   15.76
Compania Colombiana De Seguros v Pacific Steam Navigation Co [1965] 1 QB 101   4.07
Compania de Electricidad de la Provincia de Buenos Aires Ltda, *Re* [1980] 1 Ch 146   19.39, 19.94, 19.110
Company, *Re* [1894] 2 Ch 349   14.82
Company, *Re* [1973] 1 WLR 1567   14.67
Company, *Re* [1974] 1 All ER 256   15.04
Company, *Re* [1980] Ch 138 (reversed on other grounds by [1981] AC 374)   16.69
Company, *Re* [1983] 1 WLR 927   14.88, 14.189
Company, *Re* [1983] BCLC 492   14.165
Company, *Re* (No 0065 of 1983) (Goodwin Squires Securities Ltd) (1983) 1 BCC 927   14.60
Company, *Re* (No 001573 of 1983) [1983] Com LR 202   14.70
Company, *Re* [1984] 1 WLR 1090   14.127
Company, *Re* [1984] BCLC 307   14.59, 14.103
Company, *Re* [1984] BCLC 322   14.71
Company, *Re* [1985] BCLC   14.71
Company, *Re* [1985] BCLC 37   14.127
Company, *Re* [1986] BCLC 127   14.72
Company, *Re* [1986] BCLC 261   14.120
Company, *Re* (No 00477 of 1986) [1986] PCC 372   22.44
Company, *Re* [1987] 3 WLR 339   21.34
Company, *Re* (No 001761 of 1986) [1987] BCLC 141   22.44
Company, *Re* (No 07523 of 1986) [1987] BCLC 200   14.184
Company, *Re* (No 00175 of 1987) [1987] BCLC 467   13.12, 13.23, 13.24, 13.56
Company, *Re* (No 001951 of 1987) [1988] BCLC 182   14.172
Company, *Re* [1988] BCLC 282   14.132
Company, *Re* (No 001992 of 1988) [1989] BCLC 9   13.21, 13.25, 14.98
Company, *Re* (No 005009 of 1987), *ex p* Copp [1989] BCLC 13   4.42, 4.44, 4.45, 5.16, 20.46, 21.07
Company, *Re* (No 005686 of 1988) (1989) 5 BCC 79   14.184
Competitive Insurance Co v Davies Investments [1975] 1 WLR 1240   15.72
Connolly Bros Ltd, *Re* (No 2) [1912] 2 Ch 25   8.85
Consolidated Goldfields of New Zealand Ltd, *Re* [1953] Ch 689   17.07, 19.104
Consolidated South Rand Mines, *Re* [1909] 1 Ch 491   22.06
Consumer and Industrial Press Ltd, *Re* (1988) 4 BCC 68   13.15, 13.17, 13.20
Consumer and Industrial Press Ltd, *Re* (No 2) (1988) 4 BCC 72   13.76, 13.102
Contract Corporation, *Re* (1866) 2 Ch App 95   17.25
Cook v X Chair Patents Co Ltd [1960] 1 WLR 60   14.48
Cooper (a bankrupt), *Re, ex p* Trustee v Peterborough and Huntingdon Registrars and the High Bailiff [1958] Ch 922   6.56, 8.138
Cooper (Gerald) Chemicals Ltd, *Re* [1978] 1 Ch 262   21.27, 21.32, 21.36
Cope (Benjamin) & Sons, *Re* [1914] 1 Ch 800   8.78, 8.84

Corbenstoke Ltd, *Re* (1989) 5 BCC 197   14.105
Corbenstoke Ltd, *Re* (No 2) (1989) 5 BCC 767   15.69, 15.120
Coregrange, *Re* [1984] BCLC 453   18.37
Cornhill Insurance v Improvement Services [1986] 1 WLR 114   14.74
Cornish Manures Ltd, *Re* [1967] 2 All ER 875   19.122
Cotman v Brougham [1918] AC 514   1.03, 14.139
Coulson Sanderson & Ward Ltd v Ward (1986) 2 BCC 29, 207, 992   14.73,
                                                                         14.89
Coulter (Martin) Enterprises Ltd, *Re* [1988] BCLC 121   14.84
Coventry and Dixon's Case (1880) 14 Ch D 660   16.70, 16.73
Cramer & Co Ltd v Mott (1870) LR 5 QB 357   6.102
Craven Insurance Co Ltd, *Re* [1968] 1 WLR 675   14.166
Creative Handbook, *Re* [1985] BCLC 1   14.59, 14.103, 14.162
Cretanor Maritime Co Ltd v Irish Marine Management Ltd, The Cretan
    Harmony [1978] 1 WLR 966   6.90, 8.94
Crichton's Oil Co, *Re* [1902] 2 Ch 86   19.114
Cripps v Wickenden [1973] 1 WLR 955, [1973] 2 All ER 606   11.21,
                                                                  11.33, 11.41
Cripps v Wood (1882) 51 LJCh 584   7.32
Crompton & Co Ltd, *Re* [1914] 1 Ch 954   5.26
Crossley v Lee [1908] 1 KB 86   6.97
Crossmere Electrical and Civil Engineering Ltd, *Re* (1989) 5 BCC 37   14.184
Crown Bank Ltd *Re* (1890) 44 Ch D 634   14.139
Cryne v Barclays Bank plc [1987] BCLC 548   11.24
Crystal Reef Gold Mining Co, *Re* [1892] 1 Ch 408   14.87
Cuckmere Brick Co Ltd v Mutual Finance Ltd [1971] Ch 949, [1971] 2 All
    ER 633   7.22, 7.24, 7.26, 18.73
Cullen (RA) Ltd v Nottingham AHA (1986) 2 BCC 367   18.64
Cunard SS Co Ltd v Hopwood [1908] 2 Ch 564   8.38
Cunningham & Co Ltd, *Re*, Attenborough's Case (1885) 28 Ch D 682   8.29
Currie v Consolidated Kent Collieries Corporation Ltd [1906] 1 KB 134   14.48
Curtis (DH) (Builders) Ltd, *Re* [1978] Ch 162   18.54, 18.58, 18.64
Curtis's Furnishing Stores Ltd v Freedman [1966] 1 WLR 1219   16.70
Cushla, *Re* [1979] 3 All ER 415   18.64
Cyona Distributors Ltd, *Re* [1967] 1 Ch 889   21.36

DPR Futures Ltd, *Re* (1989) 5 BCC 603   15.99
Daintry, *Re* [1900] 1 QB 546   18.57
Dallman v King (1837) 4 Bing NC 105   6.96
Dallow v Garrold (1884) 14 QBD 543   6.72
Danish Mercantile Co Ltd v Beaumont [1951] Ch 680   15.99
Dank Rekylriffel Syndikat Aktieselskab v Snell [1908] 2 Ch 123   6.39
Davie & Co v Williamson & Son Ltd [1898] 2 QB 194   5.41, 8.91
Davis & Collett Ltd, *Re* [1935] Ch 693   14.143
Davis Investments (East Ham) Ltd, *Re* [1961] 1 WLR 1396   14.143, 14.160
Dawson Print Group Ltd, *Re* [1987] BCLC 601   21.97
De Courcy v Clement [1971] 1 Ch 693   14.33
Dearle v Hall (1828) 3 Russ 1   4.56, 8.111, 8.112, 8.125, 9.67
Debtor, *Re* (No 2 of 1977), *ex p* Debtor v Goacher [1979] 1 WLR 956   14.69
Debtor, *Re* (No 1 of 1989) [1988] 1 WLR 419   14.126
Denney Gasquet and Metcalfe v Conklin [1913] 3 KB 177   4.08

Dennison v Ashdown (1897) 13 TLR 226	4.62
Derham and Allen Ltd, *Re* [1946] Ch 31	17.19
Detillon v Gale (1802) 7 Ves 583	4.27
Diamond Fuel Co, *Re* (1879) 13 Ch D 400	14.84, 14.193, 15.40, 15.85
Dibble v Bowater (1853) 3 E & B 564	6.95
Dillow v Garrold, *ex p* Adams (1884) 13 QBD 543	6.23
Dinn v Grant (1852) 5 De G & Sm 45	6.44
Diplock, *Re* [1948] Ch 465	9.56
Discoverer's Finance Corporation Ltd, *Re* [1910] 1 Ch 312	17.19
Distributors and Warehousing Ltd, *Re* [1986] BCLC 129	18.21
Dixon (CW) Ltd, *Re* [1947] Ch 251	19.140
Dorman Long & Co Ltd, *Re* [1934] Ch 635	22.64
Douglas Construction Services, *Re* [1988] BCLC 397	21.96
Downer Enterprises Ltd, *Re* [1974] 1 WLR 1460	19.16
Dry Docks Corporation of London, *Re* (1888) 39 Ch D 306	15.11, 15.12
Dublin City Distillery v Doherty [1914] AC 823	3.10, 3.11, 8.30, 15.99
Duckworth, *Re* (1867) 2 Ch App 578	17.34
Dufaur v Professional Life Assurance Co (1858) 25 Beav 599	1.34
Dunderland Iron Ore Co Ltd, *Re* [1909] 1 Ch 446	14.66
Dunk v Hunter (1822) 5 B & Ald 322	6.93
Dunlop & Ranken Ltd v Hendall Steel Structures Ltd [1957] 3 All ER 344	6.68
Duomatic Ltd, *Re* [1969] 2 WLR 114	14.11
Durham Bros v Robertson [1898] 1 QB 765	4.07, 4.10, 4.14
Durham Fancy Goods Ltd v Jackson (Michael) (Fancy Goods) Ltd [1968] 2 QB 839	21.03
EVTR Ltd, *Re* [1987] BCLC 646	9.51
Eagle Star Insurance Co Ltd v Spratt [1971] 2 Lloyd's Rep 116	8.16
Eastern Capital Futures Co Ltd, *Re* (1989) 5 BCC 223	9.56, 15.144
Eastern Holdings Establishment of Vaduz v Singer & Friedlander Ltd [1967] 2 All ER 1192	14.180
Eastern Telegraph Co, *Re* [1947] 2 All ER 104	14.112, 14.142
Ebeed v Soplex Wholesale Supplies [1985] BCLC 404	1.18
Eberle's Hotels and Restaurant Co Ltd v Jonas (1887) 18 QBD 459	18.65
Ebrahimi v Westbourne Galleries Ltd [1973] AC 360, [1972] 2 WLR 1289	14.131, 14.145, 14.147, 14.151–14.152
Eckman v Midland Bank Ltd [1973] QB 519	8.94
Edge v Worthington (1786) 1 Cox Eq Cas 211	2.08
Edmonds v Blaina Furnaces Co (1887) 36 Ch D 215	8.26
Edwards v Standard Rolling Stock Syndicate [1893] 1 Ch 574	7.03
Ehrmann Bros Ltd, *Re* [1906] 2 Ch 697	8.45, 8.54
Elmore v Stone (1809) 1 Taunt 458	1.29
Elwell v Jackson (1885) 1 TLR 454	6.68
Embassy Art Products Ltd, *Re* [1988] BCLC 1	16.14
Emmadart, *Re* [1979] Ch 540, [1979] 2 WLR 868	14.64, 15.85
Emmerson's Case (1866) 1 Ch App 433	14.183
Empire Mining Co, *Re* (1890) 44 Ch D 402	22.59
Engle v South Metropolitan Brewing and Bottling Company [1892] 1 Ch 442	16.03
English & Scottish Mercantile Investment Co Ltd v Brunton [1892] 2 QB 700	8.16, 8.80–8.82
English Bank of the River Plate, *Re* [1892] 1 Ch 391	17.13

English Joint Stock Bank Corporation, *Re ex p* Harding (1866) LR 3 Eq
341   14.190
English Joint Stock Bank, *Re* (Yelland's Case) (1867) LR 4 Eq 350   14.191
English, Scottish and Australian Chartered Bank, *Re* [1893] 3 Ch 385   22.67
Equiticorp International plc (1989) 5 BCC 599   13.08
Ernest v Nicholls (1857) 6 HL Cas 401   1.16
Esal (Commodities) Ltd, *Re* [1989] BCLC 59   16.10, 16.15
Etic Ltd, *Re* [1928] Ch 861   16.76, 16.81
European Assurance Society, *Re* (1869) LR 9 Eq 122   14.116, 14.119
Evans v Brook [1959] 2 All ER 399   6.118
Evans v Clayhope Properties Ltd [1987] BCLC 418   6.89, 7.15
Evans v Elliott (1838) 9 Ad & El 342   6.94
Evans v Rival Granite Quarries Ltd [1910] 2 KB 979   5.15, 5.30, 5.41, 5.42
Exchange Securities and Commodities Ltd, *Re* [1983] BCLC 186   18.36
Exchange Securities and Commodities Ltd, *Re* (No 2) [1985] BCLC 392 15.144
Exchange Securities and Commodities Ltd, *Re* (No 3) (1987) 3 BCC 48
                                                      18.02, 19.56, 22.65
Expanded Plugs Ltd, *Re* [1966] 1 WLR 69   14.85
Eyton (Adam) Ltd, *Re, ex p* Charlesworth (1887) 36 Ch D 299   15.119

Fahey v Tobin [1901] 1 IR 511   6.88
Fairbairn Engineering Co, *Re* (Ladd's Case) [1893] 3 Ch 450   14.44
Falcon (RJ) Developments Ltd, *Re* [1987] BCLC 437   14.169
Fanchon (1880) 5 PD 173   3.19
Fargo Ltd v Godfroy [1986] 3 All ER 279   15.99, 16.82
Farley v Housing and Commercial Developments Ltd [1984] BCLC 442   18.66
Farnol, Eades, Irvine & Co, *Re* [1915] 1 Ch 22   7.32
Farrar v Farrars Ltd (1888) 40 Ch D 395   7.27
Farrow's Bank Ltd, *Re* [1921] 2 Ch 164   14.193, 15.38, 15.40, 15.85, 15.93
Fearman (WF) Ltd, *Re* (1988) 4 BCC 139   15.07
Fearman (WF) Ltd, *Re* (No 2) (1988) 4 BCC 141   13.08, 13.26, 15.31
Federal Business Development Bank v Red Lion Restaurant Ltd (1979) 101
    DLR (3d) 480   5.41
Fenton, *Re* [1931] 1 Ch 85   18.59
Fenton, *Re* (No 2) [1932] 1 Ch 178   19.44
Feuer Leather Corporation v Johnstone (Frank) & Sons [1981] CLR 251 8.16
Filby Bros (Provender) Ltd, *Re* [1958] 1 WLR 683   14.55
Fildes Bros Ltd, *Re* [1970] 1 WLR 592   14.146, 14.147
Firbank v Humphreys (1886) 18 QBD 54   1.09
Fitzroy v Cave [1905] 2 KB 364   4.02
Flagstaff Silver Mining Co of Utah, *Re* (1875) LR 20 Eq 268 14.123, 14.130
Floors of Bristol (Builders) Ltd, *Re* [1982] Com Lr 55   14.166
Florence Land & Public Works Co, *Re* (1878) 10 Ch D 530   5.21, 5.27
Ford, *Re* [1900] QB 211   6.91
Forster v Baker [1910] 2 KB 636   4.07
Forte (Charles) Investments Ltd v Amanda [1964] Ch 240, [1963] 3 WLR
    662   14.101, 14.144, 14.152
Forth v Simpson (1849) 13 QB 680   6.06
Foss v Harbottle (1843) 2 Hare 461   14.88, 15.59, 15.99, 16.67
Foulds (RA), *Re* (1986) 2 BCC 99, 269   14.71
Four Maids Ltd v Dudley Marshall (Properties) Ltd [1957] Ch 317   7.07

Four Point Garage v Carter [1985] 3 All ER 12   9.22, 9.23
Fowler v Broad's Patent Night Light Company [1893] 1 Ch 724   14.193
Fowler v Commercial Timber Co Ltd [1930] 2 KB 1   14.46
Fox Bros (Clothes) Ltd v Bryant [1979] ICR 64   14.46
Free Vale Ltd v Metro Store (Holdings) [1984] BCLC 72   12.08
Freeman and Lockyer v Buckhurst Park Properties (Mangal) Ltd [1964]
    2 QB 480, [1964] 2 WLR 618   1.18, 15.54, 21.17
French's (Wine Bar) Ltd, *Re* [1987] BCLC 499   14.182
Frith v Forbes (1862) 4 De GF & J 409   6.06

Gale v Laurie (1826) 5 B & C 156   1.30
Gamlen Chemical Co (UK) Ltd v Rochem [1980] 1 All ER 1049   6.19
Gandolfo v Gandolfo [1980] 1 All ER 833   6.67
Gapp v Bond (1887) 19 QBD 300   3.18
Garage Doors Associates Ltd, *Re* [1984] 1 WLR 35   14.78
Gardner v Lachlan (1838) 4 My & Cr 129   8.118
Garfitt v Allen (1887) 37 Ch D 48   7.07
Garton (Western) Ltd, *Re* (1989) 5 BCC 198   14.105
Gartside v Silkstone Co (1882) 21 Ch D 762   8.78
Garwood's Trust, *Re* [1903] 1 Ch 236   4.34
Gaskell v Gosling [1896] 1 QB 669   7.12
Gattopardo Ltd, *Re* [1969] 1 WLR 619   14.82
General Credit & Discount v Glegg (1883) 22 Ch D 549   7.31
General Motor Cab Co, *Re* [1913] 1 Ch 377   22.06
General Radio Co Ltd, *Re* [1929] WN 172   19.32
General Rolling Stock Co, *Re* (Chapman's Case) (1866) LR 1 Eq Cas 346 14.190
General Share & Trust Co v Wetley Brick & Pottery Co (1882) 20 Ch
    D 260   8.95, 18.26
Geoghegan v Greymouth Point Elizabeth Railway & Coal Co Ltd (1898)
    16 NZLR 749   5.41
Gerard v Worth of Paris Ltd (1936] 3 All ER 905   15.95
German Date Coffee Co, *Re* (1882) 20 Ch D 169   14.139
Gertzenstein, *Re* [1937] Ch 115   15.62
Gibbs, *Re, ex p* Price (1844) 3 Mont D & De G 586   8.113
Giles v Grover (1832) 9 Bing 128   6.52
Gill v Downing (1874) LR 17 Eq 316   4.18, 7.03
Gilman v Elton (1821) 3 Brod & Bing 75   6.97
Gisbourn v Hurst (1710) 1 Salk 249   6.97
Gladstone v Padwick (1871) LR 6 Exch 203   6.59
Glascott v Lang (1847) 2 Ph 310   3.27
Glasspoole v Young (1829) 9 B & C 696   6.57
Glegg v Bromley [1912] 3 KB 474   6.70
Globe New Patent Iron and Steel Co, *Re* (1875) Lr 20 Eq 337   14.123
Gluckstein v Barnes [1900] AC 240   16.71
Gold Co, *Re* (1879) 11 Ch D 701   14.152
Gold Company, *Re* (1897) 12 Ch D 77   16.12
Goldberg, *Re* (No 2) [1912] 1 KB 606   11.26
Golden Chemical Products, *Re* [1976] Ch 300   14.90
Goldthorpe & Lacey Ltd, *Re* (1987) 3 BCC 595   14.97, 14.164
Gomba Holdings Ltd v Homan [1986] 1 WLR 1301, [1986] BCLC 331
                                    7.23, 12.26, 12.28–12.30, 12.68

Gomba Holdings Ltd v Minories Finance Ltd (1989) 5 BCC 27
                                    12.02–12.03, 12.30, 12.68
Goodman v Robinson (1886) 18 QBD 332   6.67
Gorringe v Irwell Rubber Company (1886) 34 Ch D 128   4.11, 5.08
Goscott (Groundworks) Ltd, *Re* [1988] BCLC 363   13.08, 19.09
Gosling v Gaskell [1897] AC 575   14.191
Gough's Garages v Pugsley [1930] 1 KB 615   12.112
Goulandris [1927] P 182   6.47
Government of India v Taylor [1955] 1 All ER 292   15.78
Government of Newfoundland v Newfoundland Railway Company (1883)
   13 App Cas 199   18.66
Government Stock and Other Securities Investment Co Ltd v Manila
   Railway Co Ltd [1897] AC 81   5.30
Graham v Allsopp (1848) 3 Exch 186   6.96
Grand Junction Co Ltd v Bates [1954] 2 QB 160   2.05
Gray's Inn Construction Co Ltd, *Re* [1980] 1 WLR 711, [1980] 1 All ER
   814   14.184, 14.188
Great Eastern Electricity Co Ltd, *Re* [1941] 1 Ch 241   15.98, 19.08
Great Northern Railway v Swaffield (1874) LR 9 Exch 132   6.08
Great Western Forest of Dean Coal Consumers Co Ltd, *Re* (1886) 31 Ch 42   16.70
Great Western Railway v Crouch (1858) 3 H & N 183   6.08
Green McAllan & Fielden Ltd, *Re* [1891] WN 127   14.161
Greene, *Re* [1949] Ch 333   4.25
Greer Napper v Farnshaw [1895] 2 Ch 217   6.67
Gregg v National Guardian Assurance Co [1891] 3 Ch 206   7.06
Griffin Hotel Ltd, *Re* [1941] Ch 129   5.44
Griffith v Paget (1877) 6 Ch D 511   19.115
Grissell's Case (1866) 1 Ch App 528   17.30, 17.31, 17.35, 19.104, 19.112
Groome v Cheesewright [1895] 1 Ch 730   6.23
Grosvenor Metal Co, *Re* [1950] Ch 63   18.40
Guardian Assurance Co Ltd, *Re* [1917] 1 Ch 431   22.10, 22.57
Gurnell v Gardner (1863) 4 Giff 626   4.12
Gustaf (1862) Lush 506   8.134

Halcyon Skies [1976] 2 WLR 514   6.48
Hale v Victoria Plumbing Co Ltd [1966] 2 QB 746   6.71
Halesowen Presswork and Assemblies Ltd v Westminster Bank Ltd [1970]
   3 WLR 624   6.24
Hall, *Re, ex p* Close (1884) 14 QBD 386   8.29
Hallett's Estate, *Re* (1880) 13 Ch D 696   9.12, 9.35, 9.41, 9.43, 9.55
Halliday (LB) & Co Ltd, *Re* [1986] BCLC 227   19.104
Halvanon Insurance Co Ltd v Central Reinsurance Corporation [1988]
   3 All ER 857   6.22
Hamilton Young & Co, *Re, ex p* Carter [1905] 2 KB 772   3.15, 8.31
Hamiltons Windsor Ironworks, *Re, ex p* Pitman & Edwards (1879) 12
   Ch D 707   5.21, 5.28
Hammersmith Town Hall Co, *Re* (1877) 6 Ch D 112   15.09
Hardwick, *Re, ex p* Hubbard (1886) 17 QBD 690   3.10
Hari Sankar Paul v Kedar Nath Sahah [1939] 2 WLR 737   2.13
Harley v Harley (1860) 11 I Ch R 451   6.58
Harriet (1868) 18 LT 804   6.46

Harris Simons Construction Ltd, *Re* (1989) 5 BCC 11   13.16
Harrison v Harrison (1888) 13 PD 180   6.23
Harrold v Plenty [1901] 2 Ch 314   4.30, 4.31, 6.26
Harvest Lane Motor Bodies Ltd, *Re* [1969] 1 Ch 457   19.142
Hatton, *Re* (1872) 7 Ch App 723   22.10
Hatton v Car Maintenance Co Ltd [1915] 1 Ch 621   6.06, 6.11
Hawkes, *Re* [1898] 2 Ch 1   6.14
Heaton & Dugard Ltd v Cutting Bros Ltd [1925] 1 KB 655   8.90
Helbert v Banner, *Re* Barned's Bank (1871) LR 5 HL 28   17.04, 17.05, 17.25
Helgoland (1859) Swab 491   3.27
Hellenic & General Trust Ltd, *Re* [1976] 1 WLR 123   22.62
Hely-Hutchinson v Brayhead Ltd [1968] 1 QB 549   1.16, 1.18, 21.17
Hendy Lennox v Puttick (Grahame) Ltd [1984] 2 All ER152   9.13, 9.24, 9.36–9.37
Hercules Insurance Company, *Re* (1870) LR 9 Eq 589   17.19
Herlakenden's Case (1589) 4 Co Rep 62a   1.30
Hewitt v Loosemore (1851) 9 Hare 449   8.06
Hi-Fi Equipment (Cabinets) Ltd, *Re* [1988] BCLC 65   3.02
Higgs v Higgs [1934] P 95   6.23
Higgs v Northern Assam Tea Co (1869) LR 4 Exch 387   4.23
Highfield Commodities Ltd, *Re* [1985] 1 WLR 640, [1984] 3 All ER 884   14.93, 15.10
Highgrade Traders Ltd, *Re* [1984] BCLC 151, [1983] BCLC 137   16.10, 16.16
Hill (William) (Contractors) Ltd, *Re* [1967] 1 WLR 948, [1967] 2 All ER 1150   19.22, 19.32
Hillman v Crystal Bowl Amusements Ltd [1973] 1 WLR 162   15.55, 15.58
Hills v Parker (1866) 14 LT 107   4.51, 4.52
Hill's Waterfall Estate & Gold Mining Co, *Re* [1896] 1 Ch 947   15.76, 16.73
Hilton v Tucker (1888) 39 Ch D 669   3.11, 7.06
Hirachand Punamchand v Temple [1911] 2 KB 330   22.74
Hire Purchase Furnishing Co v Richens (1888) 20 QBD 387   14.41, 15.98
Hoare v British Columbia Development Association [1912] WN 235   8.38
Hockley and Papworth v Goldstein (1920) 90 LJKB 111   4.08
Hockley (William) Ltd, *Re* [1962] 1 WLR 555, [1962] 2 All ER 111   14.67, 14.69, 14.129
Holmes (Eric) Ltd, *Re* [1965] Ch 1052   8.55
Holohan v Friends Provident & Century Life Office [1966] IR 1   7.24
Holroyd v Griffiths (1856) 3 Drew 426   6.45
Holroyd v Marshall (1862) 10 HL Cas 191   1.34, 3.05–3.06, 4.35, 4.37, 4.63, 5.08, 5.11
Holt v Heatherfield Trust Ltd [1942] 2 KB 1   4.08
Holt Southey v Catnic Components Ltd [1978] 1 WLR 630   14.73
Home and Colonial Insurance Co Ltd, *Re* [1930] 1 Ch 102   15.80, 16.82
Hope v Haley (1856) 5 E & B 830   1.30
Hopkinson v Rolt (1861) 9 HL Cas 514   8.22
Horne and Hellard, *Re* (1885) 29 Ch D 736   5.39–5.41
Horsey Estate Ltd v Steiger [1899] 2 QB 79   18.23
Horsley & Wright, *Re* [1982] Ch 442   1.02
Houghton & Co v Northard Lowe & Wills Ltd [1927] 1 KB 246   1.18
Hubbard, *Ex p* (1886) 17 QBD 690   3.11
Hubbard & Co, *Re* (1898) 68 LJCh 54   5.27

Hudson v Viney [1921] 1 Ch 98   8.06
Hudson and Howes' Contract, Re (1887) 35 Ch D 668   7.20
Humber Iron Works Co, Re (1866) LR 2 Eq 15   14.171
Humber Ironworks and Shipbuilding Co Ltd, Re (1869) 4 Ch App 643   19.57
Humberstone Jersey Ltd, Re [1977] 74 LS Gaz 711   14.127
Hunt v Luck [1902] 1 Ch 428   8.14
Hunter v Hunter [1936] AC 222   4.28
Hutchinson v Johnson (1787) 1 Term Rep 729   6.54
Hymas v Ogden [1905] 1 KB 246   6.63

I v K [1884] WN 63   6.85
Ida (1860) Lush 6   6.48
Ijaola [1979] 1 Lloyd's Rep 103   6.11
Ilkley Hotel Company, Re [1893] 1 QB 248   14.52
Illingworth v Holdsworth [1904] AC 355   4.42, 5.14
Imperial Continental Water Corporation, Re (1886) 33 Ch D 314   16.13
Imperial Motors (UK) Ltd, Re (1989) 5 BCC 214   13.13, 13.17
Independent Automatic Sales Ltd v Knowles and Foster [1962] 3 All ER
    27   8.44
Industrial and Commercial Securities plc, Re (1989) 5 BCC 320   14.174
Industrial Development Consultants v Cooley [1972] 1 WLR 443   15.63
Industrial Insurance Association Ltd, Re [1910] WN 245   14.76
Inglis v Robertson & Baxter [1898] AC 616   3.13
Instrumentation Electrical Services Ltd, Re [1988] BCLC 191, (1988)
    4 BCC 301   13.08, 14.63, 14.86
Intermain Properties Ltd, Re [1986] BCLC 265   14.177
International Contract Co Ltd, Spartali & Tabor, Re (1866) 14 LT 726   14.88
International Life Assurance Association, Re (1870) LR 10 Eq 312   17.31
International Sales and Agencies Ltd v Marcus [1982] 3 All ER 551   1.06
International Tin Council, Re [1988] BCLC 44   14.03
Introductions Ltd, Re [1968] 2 All ER 1221   1.02
Irrigation Company of France, Re ex p Fox (1871) 6 Ch App 176   14.151
Irvine v Union Bank of Australia (1877) 2 App Cas 366   1.18

JN2 Ltd, Re [1978] 1 WLR 183   14.78, 14.82
Jacob (Walter L) & Co Ltd, Re (1989) 5 BCC 244   14.91, 14.93–14.94, 14.134
James, Re (1874) 9 Ch App 609   13.84, 15.76, 15.78, 15.93
James W Elwell [1921] P 351   6.57
Jay's Furnishing Co v Brand & Co [1915] 1 KB 458   6.100
Jessel Trust, Re [1985] BCLC 119   22.64
Joachinson v Swiss Bank Corporation [1921] 3 KB 110   6.69
Jobson v Palmer [1893] 1 Ch 71   15.57, 15.83
Johnson v Ribbins (1975) 235 EG 757   7.24
Johnson (B) & Co (Builders) Ltd, Re [1955] 1 Ch 634   15.57, 16.69, 16.74, 16.76
Joint Stock Account Co, Re (No 2) (1870) LR 10 Eq 11   19.69
Joint Stock Discount Co, Re (1867) 3 Ch App 119   17.19
Jones v Consolidated Investment Assurance Co (1858) 26 Beav 256   4.15
Jones v Humphreys [1902] 1 KB 10   4.11
Jones v Jenner (1836) 24 QBD 103   6.67
Jones v Peppercorne (1858) Johns 430   6.27
Jones v Smith (1843) 1 Ph 244   8.15

Joseph v Lyons (1884) 15 QBD 280   8.04
Joule v Jackson (1841) 7 M & W 450   6.97
Juson v Dixon (1813) 1 M & S 601   6.113

K/9 Meat Supplies (Guildford) Ltd, *Re* [1966] 1 WLR 1112   14.79, 14.146
Karnos Property Co Ltd, *Re* (1989) 5 BCC 14   14.66
Kaslo-Slocan Mining & Financial Corporation Ltd, *Re* [1910] WN 13   14.84
Kasofsky v Keegers [1937] 4 All ER 374   11.22
Katherine et Cie, *Re* [1932] 1 Ch 70   18.11
Katingaki [1976] 2 Lloyd's Rep 372   6.11, 6.46
Kayford Ltd, *Re* [1975] 1 All ER 604   9.50, 9.57, 9.58
Keenan Bros Ltd, *Re* (1984) *Irish Law Times* 205   4.43, 4.44
Kekewich v Manning (1851) 1 De GM & G 176   2.16
Kennedy v De Trafford [1867] AC 180   7.23
Kennedy v Green (1834) 3 Myl & K 699   8.18
Kent and Sussex Sawmills Ltd, *Re* [1947] Ch 177   8.36
Keypack Homecare Ltd, *Re* [1987] BCLC 409   15.120
Kinatan (Borneo) Rubber, *Re* [1923] 1 Ch 124   19.112
King's Cross Industrial Dwellings Co, *Re* (1870) LR 11 Eq 149   14.71
Kingston Cotton Mill Co, *Re* (No 2) [1896] 2 Ch 279   16.78
Kitson & Co Ltd, *Re* [1946] 1 All ER 435   14.140, 14.141
Klauber v Weill (1901) 17 TLR 344   6.68
Knowles v Scott [1891] 1 Ch 717   15.58, 15.82
Koscot Interplanetary (UK) Ltd, *Re* [1972] 3 All ER 829   14.100, 14.160
Krasnapolski Restaurant Co, *Re* [1892] 3 Ch 174   14.166
Kruger v Wilcox (1755) Amb 252   6.29

LHF Wools Ltd, *Re* [1969] 3 WLR 100   14.75, 14.76
Ladenbury Co v Goodwin Ferreira & Co [1912] 3 KB 275   8.37
Lakeglen Construction Ltd, *Re* [1980] IR 347   4.45
Lamburn Petroleum Products, *Re* [1979] 3 All ER 297   14.166
Lames v Winram (1987) 3 BCC 156   15.75
Lampet's Case (1613) 10 Co Rep 46b, 48a   4.02
Lanaghan Bros, *Re* [1977] 1 All ER 265   14.171
Lancashire & Yorkshire Reversionary Interest Co Ltd v Crowe (1970) 114
   SJ 435   7.33
Lancashire Cotton Spinning Company, *Re* (1887) 35 Ch D 656   18.30
Lancaster [1980] 2 Lloyd's Rep 497   6.11
Langen and Wind Ltd v Bell [1972] Ch 685   6.39
Langham Skating Rink Co, *Re* (1877) 5 Ch D 669   14.97, 14.111, 14.112, 14.166
Langley Construction (Brixham) Ltd v Wells [1969] 1 WLR 503   18.36
Latex Investments Ltd v Hotel Terrigal Property Ltd (1965) 113 CLR 265   7.26
Lathia v Dronsfield Bros Ltd [1987] BCLC 321   12.66
Lee & Chapman's Case (1885) 30 Ch D 216   18.62
Legard v Hodges (1792) Ives Jun 477   1.32
Leitch (William C) Bros Ltd, *Re* [1932] 2 Ch 71   21.28
Lemon v Austin Friars Investment Trust [1926] 1 Ch 1   8.26
Leon v York-O-Matic [1966] 1 WLR 1450   15.88–15.90
Leslie (J) Engineers Co Ltd, *Re* [1976] 1 WLR 292   14.184
Levy v Abercorris Slate & Slab Co (1887) 37 Ch D 260   5.10, 8.26
Levy v Barnard (1818) 8 Taunt 149   6.28

Levy v Stogdon [1898] 1 Ch 478   6.44
Lewis v Powell [1897] 1 Ch 678   6.15
Lewis and Smart, _Re_ [1954] 1 WLR 755   19.140
Lewis Merthyr Consolidated Collieries, _Re_ [1929] 1 Ch 498   12.121, 19.18
Leyton & Walthamstow Cycle Co Ltd, _Re_ (1901) 50 WR 93   14.76
Liberator Permanent Benefit Building Society, _Re_ (1894) 71 LT 406   16.70
Lilley v Barnsley (1844) 1 Car & Kir 344   6.11
Lind, _Re_ [1915] 2 Ch 345   4.35, 9.68
Linda Marie, _Re_ [1989] BCLC 46   15.81, 15.82, 19.09
Lindsay Bowman, _Re_ [1969] 1 WLR 1443   19.144
Littlehampton, Havre & Honfleur SS Co Ltd, _Re_ (1865) 34 KJ Ch 237   14.77
Liverpool Corporation v Hope [1938] 1 KB 751   6.116
Llandown Colliery Co, _Re_ [1915] 1 Ch 369   14.138
Lloyds and Scottish Finance Ltd v Prentice (1977) 121 SJ 847   8.36
Lloyds and Scottish Trust v Britten (1982) 44 P & CR 249   7.31
Lloyds Bank Ltd v Medway Upper Navigation Co [1905] 2 KB 359   6.87
Lo Line Electric Motors, _Re_ [1988] BCLC 698   21.92
Loch v Blackwood (John) Ltd [1924] AC 783   14.152
Lockiel (1843) 2 W Rob 34   3.26
Loescher v Dean [1950] Ch 491   6.21
London & Birmingham Flint Glass & Alkali Co Ltd, _Re_, _ex p_ Wright
   (1859) 1 De G F &J 257   14.130
London & Cheshire Insurance Co Ltd v Laplagrene Property Co Ltd
   [1971] Ch 499   2.11, 6.38–6.40, 8.33
London & County Coal Co Ltd, _Re_ (1867) LR 3 Eq 355   14.137
London and General Bank, _Re_ [1895] 2 Ch 166   16.69
London & Manchester Industrial Association, _Re_ (1875) 1 Ch D 466   15.10
London & Mediterranean Bank, _Re_, ex p Birmingham Banking Co (1868)
   3 Ch App 651   15.73, 15.93
London & Norwich Investment Services Ltd, _Re_ [1988] BCLC 226   15.07
London Cotton Co, _Re_ (1886) LR 2 Eq 53   18.31
London Fish Market Co, _Re_ (1883) 27 SJ 600   14.160
London Metallurgical Co, _Re_ [1897] 2 Ch 262, [1895] 1 Ch 758   15.99, 19.10
London Pressed Hinge Co Ltd, _Re_ [1905] 1 Ch 576   5.07
London Suburban Bank, _Re_ (1871) 6 Ch App 641   14.87, 14.88
London Wine Co (Shippers) Ltd, _Re_ (1976) 126 NLJ 977   9.50
Lowestoft Traffic Services Ltd, _Re_ [1986] BCLC 81   14.169
Lubin Rosen & Associates Ltd, _Re_ [1975] 1 WLR 122   14.93, 14.134, 14.166
Lucan (Earl), _Re_ (1890) 45 Ch D 470   2.16, 4.07
Lucy's case (1853) 4 De G M & G 356   15.103
Lundie Bros Ltd, _Re_ [1965] 1 WLR 1051   14.152
Lympne Investments Ltd, _Re_ [1972] 1 WLR 523   14.124, 14.127
Lyrma (No 2) [1978] 2 Lloyd's Rep 30   6.48

MB Group Ltd, _Re_ (1989) 5 BCC 684   22.64
MCH Services Ltd, _Re_ [1987] BCLC 535   14.169
MIG Trust Ltd, _Re_ [1937] Ch 542   8.52, 8.54
McCarthy & Co (Builders) Ltd, _Re_ (No 2) [1976] 2 All ER 338   14.162, 14.171
Macdonald v Hollister (1855) 3 WR 522   6.68
Macdonald, Sons and Co, _Re_ [1894] 1 Ch 89   17.18
Mace Builders v Lunn [1985] 3 WLR 465   11.27

Mace Builders (Glasgow) Ltd v Lunn [1987] BCLC 55   20.74
McGuinness Bros (UK) Ltd, *Re* (1987) 3 BCC 571   14.187
Mack v Ward [1884] WN 16   6.68
McKinnon v Armstrong (1877) 2 App Cas 531   18.56
Mackreth v Symmons (1808) 15 Ves 329   6.38, 6.42
Macnicoll v Parnell (1887) 46 WR 773   6.85
McNulty's Interchange Ltd, *Re* (1988) 4 BCC 533   21.94
Madden v Kempster (1807) 1 Camp 2   6.06
Madrid Bank v Bayley (1886) LR 2 QB 37   14.193
Mahony v East Holyford Mining Co (1875) LR 7 HL 869   1.17
Maidstone Building Provisions Ltd, *Re* [1971] 1 WLR 1085   21.33
Majestic Recording Studios, *Re* [1989] BCLC 1   21.92, 21.95, 21.96
Malpas v Ackland (1827) 3 Russ 273   8.15
Manchester Trust v Furness [1895] 2 QB 539   8.16
Manchester Unity Life v Sadler (1974) 232 EG 201   7.07
Manlon Trading Ltd, *Re* (1988) 4 BCC 455   4.101, 13.08, 13.21
Mann v Goldstein [1968] 1 WLR 1091   14.72
Manurewa Transport Ltd, *Re* [1971] NZLR 909   5.41
Marchant v Morton, Down & Co [1901] 2 KB 829   4.07
Margot Bywaters Ltd, *Re* [1942] 1 Ch 121   14.49
Marlborough Club Company, *Re* (1868) LR 5 Eq 365   16.64
Marley Tile Co v Burrows [1978] QB 241   18.43
Marriott v Anchor Reversionary Co (1861) 3 De GFJ 177   7.09
Martin v Reid (1862) 11 CBNS 730   3.11
Masonic & General Life Assurance Co, *Re* (1885) 32 Ch D 373   14.66
Maude, *Ex p* (1870) 6 Ch App 51   19.112
Maugham v Sharpe (1864) 17 CBNS 443   3.03
Mawcon Ltd, *Re* [1969] 1 WLR 78   14.57, 14.193, 15.14, 15.24
Maxwell v Ashe (1752) 7 Ves Jun 184n   4.32
Measures Bros Ltd v Measures [1910] 2 Ch 248   14.190, 14.193, 15.40
Mechanisations (Eaglescliff) Ltd, *Re* [1966] Ch 20   8.55
Medical Battery Co, *Re* [1894] 1 Ch 444   14.96
Medisco Equipment Ltd, *Re* [1983] BCLC 305   14.168, 15.47
Meguerditchian v Lightbound [1917] 2 KB 298   6.21
Memco Engineering Ltd, *Re* [1986] Ch 86, [1985] 3 WLR 875, [1985]
    3 All ER 267   14.180, 18.35, 19.21
Mercantile Bank of India v Chartered Bank of India [1938] AC 278, [1937]
    1 All ER 23   5.28, 8.38
Mercantile Investment & General Trust Co v International Company of
    Mexico [1893] 1 Ch 484n   15.103, 22.56
Mercantile Investment & General Trust v River Plate Trust Loan & Agency
    Co [1892] 2 Ch 303   14.66
Mercantile Trading Co, *Re* (Stringer's Case) (1869) 4 Ch App 475   16.63, 16.74
Mercer & Moore, *Re* (1880) 14 Ch D 287   18.11
Merchant Banking Co of London v London Hanseatic Bank (1886) 55
    LJCh 579   7.32
Merchant Navy Supply Association, *Re* [1947] 1 All ER 894   19.109
Metals and Ropes Co Ltd v Tattersall [1966] 3 All ER 401   6.63
Metropolitan Bank, *Re* (1876) 2 Ch D 366   15.73, 15.75
Metropolitan Bank and Jones, *Re* (1876) 2 Ch D 366   15.93
Metropolitan Railway Co Ltd, *Re* (1867) 36 LJCh 827   14.112, 14.113

Middlesburgh Assembly Rooms Co, *Re* (1880) 14 Ch D 104   14.111, 14.113
Mid-Kent Fruit Factory, *Re* [1896] 1 Ch 567   18.62
Midland Bank PLC v Pike [1988] 2 All ER 434   6.82
Midland Coal, Coke & Iron Co, *Re* [1895] 1 Ch 267   14.65
Midland Counties District Bank Ltd v Attwood [1905] 1 Ch 357   14.45
Midland Land and Investment Corporation, *Re* (1887) 22 WN 58   15.75
Milan Tramways Co, *Re, ex p* Theys (1884) 25 Ch D 587   18.60
Milford Docks Co, *Re* (1883) 23 Ch D 292   14.67
Milford Haven Shipping Co, *Re* [1895] WN 16   14.53
Miller's Case, *Re* (1876) 3 Ch D 661   14.176
Mills v Mills (1938) 60 CLR 150   15.60, 15.71
Mills v Northern Railway of Buenos Ayres & Co (1870) 5 Ch App 621   5.22
Milward v Caffin (1779) 2 Wm BL 1330   6.118
Minster Assets plc, *Re* [1985] BCLC 200   22.64
Misa v Currie (1876) 1 App Cas 554   6.10, 6.24
Molton Finance Ltd, *Re* [1968] Ch 325   8.33, 8.63
Monolithic Building Co, *Re* [1915] 1 Ch 643   8.47
Moor v Anglo-Italian Bank (1879) 10 Ch D 681   14.65
Moore v North Western Bank [1891] 2 Ch 599   8.125
Moore's (Sir John) Goldmining Co, *Re* (1879) 12 Ch D 325   15.69, 15.119
Moorgate Mercantile Co v Twitchings [1977] AC 890   8.08
Morcambe Bowling Ltd, *Re* [1969] 1 WLR 133   16.84
Morris v Harris [1927] AC 252   19.140
Morris v Kanssen [1946] AC 459   1.17, 11.31
Morritt, *Re, ex p* Official Receiver (1886) 18 QBD 222   6.26, 7.17
Moss v Gallimore (1779) 1 Doug 279   6.94
Mountford v Scott (1823) Turn & R 274   2.08
Multi Guarantee Co Ltd, *Re* [1987] BCLC 257   9.52, 15.79
Multinational Gas and Petroleum Co Ltd v Multinational Gas and
    Petroleum Services Ltd [1983] 3 WLR 492   21.04
Municipal Permanent Investment Building Society v Smith (1888) 22 QBD
    70   6.94
Munns v Isle of Wight Railway Co (1870) 5 Ch App 414   6.43
Murray v Legal and General Assurance Society Ltd [1970] 2 QB 495   18.50
Mutual Life Assurance Society v Langley (1886) 32 Ch D 460   8.115

NFU Development Trust Ltd, *Re* [1972] 1 WLR 1548, [1973] 1 All ER 135   22.10,
        22.57, 22.65
NRG Vision Ltd v Churchfield Leasing (1988) 4 BCC 56   11.22
Nadler Enterprises Ltd, *Re* [1981] 1 WLR 23   19.27
Narada [1977] 1 Lloyd's Rep 256   6.11
Nation Life Insurance co, *Re* [1978] 1 WLR 45   19.11
National Commercial Bank of Scotland Ltd v Arcam Demolition and
    Construction Ltd [1966] 2 QB 573   6.59
National Employers Mutual Association v Jones [1988] 2 WLR 952   8.10
National Funds Assurance Co, *Re* (1878) 10 Ch D 118   16.75, 16.76
National Permanent Building Society, *Re* (1869) LR 5 Ch App 309   14.66
National Provincial and Union Bank of England v Charnley [1924] 1 KB
    431   2.15, 8.55, 8.60
National Provincial Bank v United Electric Theatres [1916] 1 Ch 132   5.16
National Savings Bank Association, *Re* (1866) 1 Ch App 547   14.77, 17.07

National Westminster Bank Ltd v Halesowen Presswork Assemblies Ltd
   [1972] AC 785   6.25, 18.68
National Westminister Bank v Stockman [1981] 1 WLR 67   6.75
Nelson (Edward) & Co Ltd v Faber & Co [1903] 2 KB 367   5.30
New City Constitutional Club, *Re* (1886) 34 Ch D 646   8.95
New Finance and Mortgage Co Ltd, *Re* [1975] 2 WLR 443   19.42
New Gas Co, *Re* (1877) 5 Ch D 703   14.139
New Oriental Bank Corporation, *Re* (No 2) [1895] 1 Ch 753   19.82
New Timbiqui Gold Mines Ltd, *Re* [1961] 1 All ER 865   19.142
New Travellers Chambers Ltd v Cheese & Green (1894) 70 LT 271   14.127
New York Taxi Cab Co Ltd, *Re* [1913] 1 Ch 1   7.03
Newman & Howard Ltd, *Re* [1961] 3 WLR 192   14.85
Newport County AFC, *Re* [1987] BCLC 582   13.33
Newstead v Frost [1980] 1 All ER 363   4.33
Noble (RA) & Sons (Clothing) Ltd, *Re* [1983] BCLC 273   14.147
Nokes v Doncaster Amalgamated Collieries Ltd [1940] Ac 1014   15.93
Norcross Ltd v Amos (1980) transcript No 0079 of 1980 Lexis, (1981) 131
   NLJ 1213   21.28, 21.29, 21.31
Norris v Wilkinson (1806) 12 Ves 192   2.08
North Brazilian Sugar Factories Ltd, *Re* (1887) 37 Ch D 83   16.07
North Western Bank Ltd v Poynter (John) & Son and MacDonalds [1894]
   AC 56   3.11, 3.15
Northern Counties of England Fire Insurance v Whipp (1884) 26 Ch
   D 482   8.08
Norton v Yates [1906] 1 KB 112   6.70, 8.92, 8.139
Norton Warburg Holdings Ltd, *Re* [1983] BCLC 235   16.12
Norwegian Titanic Iron Co, *Re* (1866) 35 Beav 223   14.111, 14.139
Norwest Holst v Secretary of State for Trade and Industry [1978] 3 WLR
   73   14.91
Norwich Yarn Co, *Re* (1850) 12 Beav 366   14.86
Nott v Eastern [1900] 1 Ch 29   7.26
Nourse Self Build Association Ltd, *Re* [1985] BCLC 219   14.03
Nuneaton Borough Association Football Club, *Re* (1989) 5 BCC   14.80
Nylstroom Co Ltd, *Re* (1889) 60 LT 477   14.138

Ocean Accident & Guarantee Corporation v Ilford Gas Co [1905] 2 KB
   493   7.07
Oceanic Steam Navigation Co, *Re* [1939] Ch 41   22.58
O'Donovan v Goggin (1892) 30 LR Ir 579   6.85
Offical Assignee of Madras v Mercantile Bank of India Ltd [1935] AC 53   3.12,
    7.06, 8.29
Official Custodian for Charities v Parway Estates Ltd [1984] BCLC 309   18.25,
    18.44
Offshore Ventilation Ltd, *Re* (1989) 5 BCC 160   6.108, 8.96, 8.115
Olds Discount Co Ltd v Playfair (John) Ltd [1938] 3 All ER 275   4.04,
    4.47, 8.36
Oliver v Hinton [1899] 2 Ch 264   8.06, 8.07
Olivier (1862) Lush 484   3.27
Openshaw v Fletcher (1916) 32 TLR 372   16.70
Opera Ltd, *Re* [1891] 2 Ch 154   15.78
Orelia (1833) 3 Hagg 75   3.26

Oriel Ltd, *Re* [1986] 1 WLR 180, [1985] BCLC 343, [1984] BCLC 241   8.42
Oriental Banking Corporation, *Re* (1884) 54 LJCh 481   14.03
Oriental Banking Corporation, *Re* (McDowall's Case) (1886) 32 Ch D 366 14.190
Oriental Commercial Bank, *Re* (1872) 7 Ch App 99, (1868) LR 6 Eq 582 19.44,
                                                                    19.61
Oriental Credit, *Re* [1988] 2 WLR 172   16.11
Oriental Inland Steam Co, *Re* (1874) 9 Ch App 557   15.58
Orthomere Ltd, *Re* (1981) 125 SJ 495   14.176
Oshkosh B'Gosh Inc v Marbel (Dan) Inc Ltd (1988) 4 BCC 795   21.03
Othery Construction Ltd, *Re* [1966] 1 WLR 69   14.84, 14.85
Overend Gurney and Co, *Re* (1867) LR 2 HL 325   17.19
Overmark Smith Warden, *Re* [1982] 1 WLR 1195   19.42
Owen, *Re* (1894) 3 Ch 220   7.31
Oxenham v Esdaile (1829) 3 Y & J 262   6.40

Pain, *Re* [1919] 1 Ch 38   4.06, 4.56
Paine, *Re* [1897] 1 QB 122   19.60
Palmer v Barclays Bank Ltd (1971) 23 P & CR 30   7.24
Palmer Marine Surveys Ltd, *Re* [1986] 1 WLR 573, [1986] BCLC 106   14.169,
                                                        15.47, 15.120, 15.121
Panama, New Zealand and Australian Royal Mail Co, *Re* (1870) 5 Ch App
    318   1.35, 5.12, 5.26
Paragon Holdings Ltd, *Re* [1961] 1 Ch 346   17.12
Park Gate Wagon Works Co Ltd, *Re* (1881) 17 Ch D 239   15.93, 18.73
Parke v The Daily News [1962] Ch 927   15.105
Parker v Housefield (1834) 2 Myl & K 219   2.14, 7.31
Parkes Garage (Swadlincote) Ltd, *Re* [1929] 1 Ch 139   20.74
Patent Elastic Pavement and Kamptulicon Co, *Re* (1850) 3 De G &
    Sm 146   4.27
Patent File Co, *Re* (1870) LR 6 Ch 83   1.04
Patent Steam Engine Co, *Re* (1878) 8 Ch D 464   14.82
Patrick and Lyon Ltd, *Re* [1933] 1 Ch 786   21.28
Paul & Frank Ltd v Discount Bank (Overseas) Ltd [1967] Ch 348   4.16, 8.35
Pawson's Settlement, *Re* [1917] 1 Ch 541   4.57, 7.10
Payne v Cardiff RDC [1932] 1 KB 241   7.13
Payne v Hornby (1858) 25 Beav 250   6.45
Peachdart, *Re* [1983] 3 All ER 204   9.12, 9.16, 9.20, 9.22, 9.30, 9.34, 9.35
Peacock v Pursell (1863) 32 LJCP 266   4.52
Pearson v Gee & Braceborough Spa Ltd [1934] AC 272   18.25
Peat v Clayton [1906] 1 Ch 659   6.27
Pelly v Wathen (1851) 1 De G M & G 16   6.18
Pen y Van Colliery Co, *Re* (1877) 6 Ch D 477   14.67
Pennel v Dawson (1856) 18 CB 355   3.04
Pentalta Exploration Co, *Re* [1898] WN 55   14.66
Performing Rights Society v London Theatre of Varieties Ltd [1924] AC 1   4.63
Permanent Houses (Holdings) Ltd, *Re* (1989) 5 BCC 151   4.38, 9.46, 12.122
Perry v Phoenix Assurance plc [1988] 1 WLR 940   6.75, 6.80, 8.140
Peruvian Amazon Co, *Re* (1913) 29 TLR 384   14.138
Peruvian Guano Co v Dreyfus Bros Co [1892] AC 170   6.45
Peruvian Railway Construction Co, *Re* [1915] 2 Ch 144   17.30
Peter v Russell (1716) 1 Eq Co Abr 321   8.06

Peveril Gold Mines Ltd, *Re* [1898] 1 Ch 122   14.89
Pfeiffer (E) v Arbuthnot Factors [1987] BCLC 522   4.06, 8.37, 8.116, 9.40, 9.46
Phene v Gillan (1845) 5 Hare 1   4.27
Phillips v Highland Railway Co, The Ferret (1883) 8 App Cas 329   6.48
Phillips v Phillips (1862) 4 De G F & J 208   8.102
Phoenix Bessemer Co, *Re* (1875) 44 LJCh 683   1.04
Phoenix Oil & Transport Co Ltd, *Re* (No 2) [1958] Ch 560   15.96,
    17.12, 19.107
Piers, *Re* [1898] 1 QB 627   19.63
Pilcher v Rawlins (1872) LR 7 Ch App 259   15.93
Pioneer Concrete (UK) v National Employer's Mutual Insurance Associ-
    ation [1985] 2 All ER 395   18.50
Pioneers of Mashonaland Syndicate, *Re* [1893] 1 Ch 731   14.138
Pitman (Harold M) & Co v Top Business Systems (Nottingham) Ltd
    [1984] BCLC 593   15.89, 18.74
Platt v Mendel (1884) 27 Ch D 246   7.33
Portman Building Society v Gallwey [1955] 1 All ER 227   10.32, 11.16
Portra Frame Ltd, *Re* [1986] BCLC 533   19.141
Potter's Oils Ltd, *Re* [1985] BCLC 203   18.05
Potter's Oils Ltd, *Re* (No 2) [1986] 1 WLR 201, [1986] BCLC 98, [1986]
    1 All ER 890   7.12, 11.23, 12.115, 12.118
Potts v Hickman [1941] AC 212   6.120
Powell v London & Provincial Bank [1893] 2 Ch 555   4.31
Practice Directions [1971] 1 WLR 4, 757   14.176
Practice Note [1934] WN 142   22.62
Precision Dippings Ltd v Precision Dippings Marketing Ltd [1986] 1 Ch
    447   14.44
Prekookeanska v LNT Lines Srl [1988] 3 All ER 897   6.21
Pretoria Pietersburg Railway Co, *Re* (No 2) [1904] 2 Ch 359   19.54
Priestmen (Alfred) & Co (1929) Ltd, *Re* [1936] 2 All ER 1340   5.17
Prime Metals Trading Ltd, *Re* [1984] BCLC 543, (1984) 1 BCC 265   14.119,
    14.212, 19.60, 19.62
Primlaks (UK) Ltd, *Re* (1989) 5 BCC 710   13.16
Princess of Reuss v Bos (1871) LR 5 HL 176   14.01, 14.137
Priscilla (1859) Lush 1   3.27
Pritchett v English Syndicate Ltd [1899] 2 QB 428   14.68
Probe-Data Systems Ltd, *Re* (1989) 5 BCC 384   21.78
Proctor v Nicholson (1835) 7 C & P 67   8.138
Produce Marketing Consortium Ltd, *Re* (1989) 5 BCC 399, 569   21.18, 21.20,
    21.23, 21.35
Professional, Commercial and Industrial Benefit Society, *Re* (1871)
    6 Ch App 856   14.88
Property and Bloodstock Ltd v Emerton [1968] Ch 94   7.26
Property Discount Corporation v Lyon Group Ltd [1981] 1 WLR 300   8.33
Pryce v Bury (1853) 2 Drew 41   2.12
Puddephatt v Leith [1916] 1 Ch 200   4.26
Pulsford v Devenish [1903] 2 Ch 625   15.57, 15.81, 15.82, 16.80, 22.07

Quartz Hill Mining Co v Eyre (1883) 11 QBD 674   14.74
Quest Cae Ltd, *Re* [1985] BCLC 266   5.18
Quickdome Ltd, *Re* (1988) 4 BCC 296   14.82

R v Andrews Weatherfoil Ltd [1972] 1 WLR 118   20.07
R v Austen (1985) 1 BCC 99, 528   21.66
R v Campbell [1984] BCLC 83   21.41, 21.52
R v Consolidated Churchill Copper Corporation Ltd [1978] 5 WWR 652   5.41,
                                                                5.44
R v Cox & Hodges [1983] BCLC 169   21.29
R v Georgiou (1988) 4 BCC 322   21.67
R v Grantham [1984] 1 QB 675   21.28
R v Inman [1967] 1 QB 140   21.26
R v Kemp [1986] BCLC 217   21.26
R v Lockwood (1986) 2 BCC 99, 333   21.27
R v Registrar of Companies, *ex p* Central Bank of India [1986] QB 1114,
    [1985] BCLC 465   8.56
R v Secretary of State for Transport, *ex p* Factortame Ltd *The Times*
    24 March 1989   3.21
R-R Realisations, *Re* [1980] 1 WLR 805   19.93
Radford & Bright Ltd, *Re* (No 1) [1901] 1 Ch 272   16.92
Rainbow v Moorgate Properties Ltd [1975] 1 WLR 788   6.79, 22.75
Ramel Syndicate Ltd, *Re* [1911] 1 Ch 749   19.106
Ramsey v Hartley [1977] 1 WLR 686   4.07
Rapid Road Transit Co Ltd, *Re* [1909] 1 Ch 96   6.15
Rayland Financiers Association, *Re* (1878) 10 Ch D 269   15.120
Read v Burley (1597) Cro Eliz 549   6.97
Real Estates Co, *Re* [1893] 1 Ch 398   14.54
Redman Builders, *Re* [1964] 1 WLR 541   18.41
Reeves v Capper (1838) 5 Bing NC 136   3.02, 3.11
Regal (Hastings) Ltd v Gulliver [1942] 1 All ER 443   15.63
Regent Finance & Guarantee Corporation, *Re* [1930] WN 84   15.78
Regent's Canal Ironworks Co, *Re, ex p* Grissell (1875) 3 Ch D 411   15.93, 19.11
Reid v Furnival (1833) 1 Cr & M 528   4.52
Reigate v Union Manufacturing (Ramsbottom) Ltd [1918] 1 KB 592   14.45
Reliance (1833) 3 Hagg 66   3.26
Rendell v Roman (1893) 9 TLR 192   6.93
Reprographic Exports (Euromat) Ltd, *Re* (1978) 122 SJ 400 14.171
Republic of Bolivia Exploration Syndicate Ltd, *Re* [1914] 1 Ch 139   16.82
Rhine Film Corporation (UK) Ltd, *Re* (1986) 2 BCC 849   14.170
Rhodes v Allied Dunbar Pension Services [1989] BCLC 186 6.108, 8.115
Rhodes (JT) Ltd, *Re* [1982] BCLC 77   16.14
Riby Grove (1843) 2 W Rob 52   6.48
Rica Gold Washing Co, *Re* (1879) 11 Ch D 36   14.84, 14.97
Rice v Rice (1854) 2 Drew 73   8.104
Richards v Kidderminster Overseas (1886) 2 Ch 212   3.01
Richardson v Richardson [1927] P 228   6.67
Ridout v Fowler [1904] 2 Ch 93   6.85
Rimmer v Webster [1902] 2 Ch 163   8.07
Ripon City [1897] P 226   6.47, 6.48
Roberts v Crowe (1872) LR 7 CP 629   17.04
Roberts v Death (1881) 8 QB 319   6.70
Roberts and Cooper Ltd, *Re* [1929] 2 Ch 383   19.115
Roberts Petroleum Ltd v Kenny (Bernard) Ltd [1983] AC 192, [1983]
    BCLC 28   6.73, 6.78, 6.82, 18.39

Robins & Co v Gray [1895] 2 QB 501	6.09
Robinson v Burnell's Vienna Bakery Co [1904] 2 KB 624	8.90
Rodick v Gandell (1852) 1 De G M & G 763	4.11
Roehampton Swimming Pool Ltd, *Re* [1968] 1 WLR 1693	19.138, 19.139
Rolled Steel Products (Holdings) Ltd v British Steel Corporation [1986] Ch 246, [1984] BCLC 466	1.02, 1.03, 11.26, 11.27, 13.66, 19.42
Rolls Razor Ltd, *Re* (No 2) [1970] 1 Ch 576	16.12
Rolls Razor Ltd v Cox [1967] 1 QB 552	6.29, 18.61, 18.65
Rolus Properties, *Re* (1988) 4 BCC 446	21.92
Romalpa Case, *see* Aluminium Industries Vaasen BV v Romalpa Aluminium Ltd	
Romford Canal Co, *Re* (1883) 24 Ch D 85	4.23
Rose v Sims (1830) 1 B & Ad 521	4.50
Roselmar Properties, *Re* (No 2) (1986) 2 BCC 156	14.105, 14.168
Ross v Buxton (1889) 42 Ch D 190	6.21
Roundwood Colliery Co, *Re* [1897] 1 Ch 373	8.95
Row Dal Constructions Proprietary Ltd [1966] VR 249	8.44
Roxburghe v Cox (1881) 17 Ch D 520	4.09, 4.13, 6.24
Royal Arch (1857) Swab 269	3.27, 8.132
Royal British Bank v Turquand (1856) 6 E & B 327, (1856) 25 LJQB 317	1.17, 15.54
Royal Trust Bank v Buchler [1989] BCLC 130	13.35
Royal Wells, The [1983] 3 WLR 698	6.48
Rubber & Produce Investment Trust, *Re* [1915] 1 Ch 382	15.70
Ruben v Great Fingall Consolidated [1906] AC 439	1.17
Rudow v Great Britain Mutual Life Assurance Society Ltd (1881) 17 Ch D 600	18.31
Rushforth v Hadfield (1805) 6 East 519, 7 East 224	6.12
Russel v Russel (1783) 1 Bro CC 269	1.33, 2.08
Russell (J) Electronics Ltd, *Re* [1968] 1 WLR 1252	14.96
Rutherford (James R) & Sons Ltd, *Re* [1964] 1 WLR 1211	19.32
Ryall v Rolle (1749) 1 Atk 165	3.10
S & A Conversions Ltd, *Re* (1988) 4 BCC 384	16.37
SBA Properties, *Re* [1967] 1 WLR 799	14.70
SCF Finance Co Ltd v Massri (No 3) [1987] 2 WLR 81	6.67
SCL Building Services Ltd, *Re* (1989) 5 BCC 746	13.16
Sabina (1843) 7 Jur 82	8.134
Safety Explosives Ltd, *Re* [1904] 1 Ch 226	6.20, 19.63, 19.64, 19.70
Saffron Walden Second Benefit Building Society v Rayner (1880) 14 Ch D 406	8.117
St Ives Windings Ltd, *Re* (1987) 3 BCC	13.62
St Piran Ltd, *Re* [1981] 1 WLR 1300	14.93, 14.150, 14.160
Salcombe Hotel Development Co Ltd, *Re* (1989) 5 BCC 807	14.24
Sale Continuations Ltd v Austin Taylor & Co Ltd [1968] 2 QB 849	18.70
Sale Hotel and Botanical Gardens Ltd, *Re, ex p* Hesketh (1898) 78 LT 368	16.77
Sanders (GL) Ltd, *Re* [1986] BCLC 40	19.18
Sandwell Copiers Ltd, *Re* [1988] BCLC 209	19.09
Sarflax Ltd, *Re* [1979] 1 Ch 262	21.27, 21.29
Sauter Automation Ltd v Goodman Mechanical Services Ltd [1986] 2 FTLR 239	9.08

Savory (EW) Ltd, *Re* [1951] 2 TLR 1071   19.106
Savoy Hotel Ltd, *Re* [1981] 3 All ER 646   22.57, 22.60
Saxton (EV) & Sons Ltd v Miles (R) (Confectioners) Ltd [1983] 1 WLR
    952   14.13, 14.17
Scad Ltd, *Re* [1941] Ch 386   19.138
Schiffshypotheken Bank v Luebeck, A-G v Compton *The Times* 5 January
    1988   3.25
Scotch Granite Co, *Re* (1868) 17 LT 533   15.73
Scott v Knowles [1891] 1 Ch 717   15.50
Scottish Insurance Corporation v Wilson & Clyde Coal Co [1949] AC 462   19.111
Scottish Workmen's Assurance Co Ltd (Liquidator) v Waddle 1910 SC 670   6.12
Sea Spray [1907] P 133   8.134
Secretary of State for Employment v Spence [1986] 3 WLR 380   12.87
Security Trust Co v Royal Bank of Canada [1976] AC 503   8.85
Selangor United Rubber Estates Ltd v Cradock [1967] 1 WLR 1168   16.77
Selangor United Rubber Estates Ltd v Cradock (No 3) [1968] 1 WLR 1555   15.65
Selwyn v Garfit (1888) 38 Ch D 273   7.26
Senbrook Estate Co Ltd v Ford [1949] 2 All ER 94   6.68
Sewell v Burdick (1885) 10 App Cas 74   3.12, 6.26, 7.03
Shakel v Marlborough (Duke) (1819) 4 Madd 463   7.15
Shamji v Johnson Matthey Bankers [1986] BCLC 278   7.12, 11.23
Sharpe v Fowle (1884) 12 QBD 385   6.106
Shaw v Hudson (1879) 48 LJCh 689   6.83
Shaw & Sons (Salford) Ltd v Shaw [1935] 2 KB 13   14.63
Shaw (Joshua) & Sons Ltd, *Re* (1989) 5 BCC 188   19.42
Sherbro (1883) 52 CJ 28   8.132
Sheridan Securities Ltd, *Re* (1988) 4 BCC 200   13.93, 13.98
Sherratt (WA) Ltd v Bromley (John) (Church Stretton) Ltd [1985] QB
    1038, [1985] BCLC 170, [1985] 1 All ER 216   6.91, 18.32, 19.62
Shillitoe v Hinchcliffe [1922] 2 KB 236   6.118
Shipley v Marshall (1863) 14 CBNS 566   4.04, 4.38, 8.35
Shippey v Grey (1880) 49 LJQB 524   6.70
Shusella Ltd, *Re* [1983] BCLC 505   14.171
Sichel v Mosenthal (1862) 30 Beav 371   2.15
Sidney Cove (1815) 2 Dods 1   8.134
Siebe Gorman & Co Ltd v Barclays Bank Ltd [1979] 2 Lloyd's Rep 142
                                              4.41–4.42, 4.44–4.46, 5.16, 8.81
Siemens Bros & Co Ltd v Burns [1918] 2 Ch 324   4.26
Signland Ltd, *Re* [1982] 2 All ER 609   14.105, 14.162
Silkstone & Haigh Moor Coal Co, *Re* [1900] 1 Ch 167   15.93
Silkstone Coal Co v Edey [1900] 1 Ch 167   15.68
Silver Valley Mines Ltd, *Re* (1882) 21 Ch D 381   15.56, 15.99
Sinclair v Brougham [1914] AC 398   1.09
Singer v SW Railway Co [1894] 1 QB 833   6.10
Singer (A) & Co (Hat Manufacturers) Ltd, *Re* [1943] Ch 121   16.84
Six Arlington Street Investments v Persons Unknown [1987] 1 WLR 188   6.60
Skinner v Upshaw (1702) 2 Ld Raym 757   6.08
Skipper & Tucker v Holloway [1910] 2 KB 630   4.07
Slade v Rigg (1843) 3 Hare 35   4.32
Slavenburg's Bank NV v Intercontinental National Resources Ltd [1980] 1
    WLR 1076, [1980] 1 All ER 955   3.08, 8.26, 8.31, 8.76
Slee, *Re, ex p* North Western Bank (1872) LR 15 Eq 69   3.09

Smallman Construction Ltd, *Re* (1988) 4 BCC 785   13.117
Smart v Sanders (1848) 5 CB 895   6.29
Smart Bros v Holt [1929] 2 KB 303   6.100
Smith v Manchester (Duke) (1883) 24 Ch D 611   14.62
Smith v Smith (1833) 2 C & M 231   8.118
Smith & Fawcett Ltd, *Re* [1942] Ch 304   4.28
Smith (James) and Sons (Norwood) Ltd v Goodman [1936] Ch 216   15.81
Smith (ML) (Plant Hire) Ltd v Mainwaring (D) [1986] BCLC 342   19.134
Smithett v Hesketh (1890) 44 Ch D 161   7.33
Sneath v Valley Gold Ltd [1893] 1 Ch 477   15.103
Snow (John) & Co Ltd v DBG Woodcraft & Co Ltd [1985] BCLC 54   9.06
Société Générale de Paris v Walker (1885) 11 App Cas 20   4.22, 4.26, 8.114, 8.125
Somes v British Empire Shipping Co (1860) 8 HLCas 338   6.46
Sorge (AV) & Co Ltd, *Re* (1986) 2 BCC 99, 306   19.09
South London Fish Market, *Re* (1888) 39 Ch D 324   14.03
South Rhondda Colliery Co, *Re* [1928] WN 126   18.35
South Wales Atlantic Steamship Co, *Re* (1875) 2 Ch D 763   14.66
Southall, *Ex p* (1848) 17 LJ Bcy 21   6.12
Southard & Co Ltd, *Re* [1979] 1 WLR 1198   14.166
Southern Livestock Producers Ltd, *Re* [1964] 1 WLR 24   6.11
Sovereign Life Assurance Co v Dunn [1892] 2 QB 573   22.61
Sowman v Samuel (David) Trust Ltd [1978] 1 WLR 22, [1978] 1 All ER 616   12.114, 14.192
Space Investments Ltd v Canadian Imperial Bank of Commerce Trust Co (Bahamas) [1986] 3 All ER 75   9.54
Specialist Plant Servicing Ltd v Braithwaite Ltd [1987] BCLC 1   9.13
Spence v Clarke (1878) 9 Ch D 137   4.15, 8.127
Spink, *Re, ex p* Slater (1913) 108 LT 811   16.106
Spiraflite Ltd, *Re* [1979] 1 WLR 1096   16.14
Spiral Globe Co, *Re* (No 2) [1902] 2 Ch 209   8.27
Stacey v Hill [1901] 1 KB 660   18.13
Staffordshire Gas Co, *Re* [1893] 3 Ch 523   19.10
Standard Chartered Bank v Walker [1982] 1 WLR 1410, [1982] 3 All ER 938   7.26, 7.30, 12.65, 12.66, 12.80
Standard Manufacturing Co, *Re* [1891] 1 Ch 627   3.01, 7.08, 8.29, 8.89, 8.128
Standard Rotary Machine Co Ltd, *Re* (1906) 95 LT 829   8.81
Stanford Services, *Re* [1987] BCLC 607   21.94
Stanton (F & E) Ltd, *Re* [1928] 1 KB 464   14.52
Stead Hazel & Co v Cooper [1933] 1 KB 840   15.53, 15.77
Steadman v Steadman [1976] AC 536   2.14
Steel Wing Co Ltd, *Re* [1921] 1 Ch 349   4.07, 4.10–4.11, 14.66, 14.128
Stein v Saywell (1969) 121 CLR 529   5.33
Sterling, *Ex p* (1809) 16 Ves 258   6.06
Stetzel Thomson & Co Ltd, *Re* (1988) 4 BCC 74   9.49
Stevens v Hince (1914) 110 LT 935   6.58
Stocks v Dobson (1853) 4 De Gm   4.13
Stonegate Securities v Gregory [1980] 3 WLR 168   14.73
Stoneleigh Finance Ltd v Phillips [1965] 2 QB 537   8.32
Storey v Robinson (1795) 6 Term Rep 138   6.97
Stratford v Twyman (1822) Jac 418   7.27
Stream Fisher [1927] P 73   8.134

Stubbs v Slater [1910] 1 Ch 632   7.17
Suburban Hotel Co, *Re* (1867) 2 Ch App 737   14.140
Sudair International Airways, *Re* [1951] Ch 165   18.40
Sugar Properties (Derisley Wood) Ltd, *Re* [1988] BCLC 146   8.32, 14.186
Sullivan v Henderson (1972) 116 SJ 969   14.183
Sullivan (Walter) Ltd v Murphy (J) & Sons Ltd [1955] 2 QB 584   4.07
Sunlight Incandescent Gas Lamp Co, *Re* (1900) 16 TLR 535   16.82
Surplus Properties (Huddersfield) Ltd, *Re* [1984] BCLC 89   14.168
Sussex Brick Co, *Re* [1940] 1 Ch 598   17.19
Sussman (J & P), *Re* [1958] 1 WLR 519   14.101
Swain (JD) Ltd, *Re* [1965] 1 WLR 909   14.76, 15.47
Swaledale Cleaners Ltd, *Re* [1968] 1 WLR 1710   4.28
Swan [1968] 1 Lloyd's Rep 5   21.02
Swan v Maritime Insurance Co [1907] 1 KB 116   4.15
Swiss Bank Corporation v Lloyds Bank Ltd [1979] 3 WLR 201, [1981]
    2 All ER 449   8.125, 9.51

TCB v Gray [1986] 1 All ER 587   1.07
TH Knitwear (Wholesale) Ltd, *Re* [1988] BCLC 195   19.29
Tahiti Cotton Co, *Re, ex p* Sargent (1874) LR 17 Eq 273   4.31
Tailby v Official Receiver (1888) 13 App Cas 523   1.34, 4.04, 4.35
Taldica Rubber Co Ltd, *Re* [1946] 2 All ER 763   14.140
Tancred v Delgoa Bay & East Africa Railway Co (1889) 23 QBD 239   4.07
Tapling & Co v Weston (1883) Cab & El 99   6.97
Tapp v Jones (1875) LR 10 QB 591   6.68, 6.71
Tasbian Ltd, *Re* (1989) 5 BCC 729   21.87
Tatung (UK) Ltd v Galex Telesure Ltd (1989) 5 BCC 325   8.37, 9.06, 9.19, 9.43
Taunton v Sheriff of Warwickshire [1895] 2 Ch 319   5.27, 8.89
Tavistock Ironwork Co, *Re* (1871) 24 LT 605   15.72
Taylor v H'Keand (1880) 5 CPD 358   5.22
Taylor, Stileman & Underwoood, *Re* [1891] 1 Ch 590   6.19
Tea Corporation, *Re* [1904] 1 Ch 12   22.60
Telescriptor Syndicate Ltd, *Re* [1903] 2 Ch 174   14.178
Television Parlour plc, *Re* (1988) 4 BCC 95   14.170
Temple Fire & Accident Assurance Co, *Re* (1910) 129 LTJo 115   15.78
Tesco Supermarkets Ltd v Nattrass [1970] 2 QB 133   20.07
Test Holdings (Clifton) Ltd, *Re* [1970] Ch 285   19.137, 19.145
Thaper v Singh [1987] FLR 369   6.12
Thompson and Riches, *Re* [1981] 1 WLR 682   19.133
Thomsons Mortgage Trust, *Re* [1920] 1 Ch 508   7.28
Thorne (HE) & Son, *Re* [1914] 2 Ch 438   18.56
Thorpe (William) & Son Ltd, *Re* (1989) 5 BCC 156   14.168
Thurso New Gas Co, *Re* (1889) 42 Ch D 486   14.48
Time Furnishing Co Ltd v Hutchings [1938] 1 KB 775   6.100
Tolhurst v Associated Portland Cement Manufacturers [1903] AC 414   4.07
Tomlin Patent Horse Shoe Co Ltd, *Re* (1886) 55 LT 314   14.111
Topham v Greenside Co (1888) 37 Ch D 281   8.26
Torkington v Magee [1902] 2 KB 427   4.06, 4.07, 4.22, 4.56
Torzillu Pty Co Ltd v Brynac Pty Ltd [1983] 8 ACLR 52   5.22
Townsend, *Re, ex p* Parsons (1886) 18 QBD 532   3.10
Train v McIntyre Ltd 1925 SLT 280   6.12

Tramway Building and Construction Co Ltd, *Re* [1987] BCLC 632   14.185
Transport and General Credit Corporation v Morgan [1939] Ch 331   6.39
Trench Tubeless Tyre Co, *Re* [1900] 1 Ch 408   15.41
Trent v Hunt (1853) 9 Exch 14   6.94
Treuttel v Barandon (1817) 8 Taunt 100   4.54
Trix Ltd, *Re*; Ewart Holdings Ltd, *Re* [1970] 1 WLR 1421   15.104, 22.56
Trueman's Estate, *Re* (1872) LR 14 Eq 278   15.51, 15.53, 19.11
TSE Kwang Lan v Wong Chit Sen [1983] 3 All ER 54   7.27
Tucker v New Brunswick Trading Co (1890) 44 Ch D 249   14.176
Turner (P) (Wilsden) Ltd, *Re* [1987] BCLC 149   15.11
Tweeds Garages Ltd, *Re* [1962] 2 WLR 38   14.71, 14.127
Twentieth Century Banking Corporation Ltd v Wilkinson [1976] 3 WLR
    489   7.13, 7.20, 7.32, 7.33
Twyne's Case (1602) 3 Co Rep 80b   3.04
Tymans Ltd v Craven [1952] 2 QB 100   19.147

Union (1860) 1 Lush 128   8.134
Union Accident Insurance Co, *Re* [1972] 1 WLR 640, [1972] 1 All ER
    1105   14.193, 15.08–15.14
Union Bank of London v Ingram (1882) 20 Ch D 463   7.33
Unit 2 Windows Ltd, *Re* [1985] 1 WLR 1383   18.55
United Provident Assurance Co, *Re* [1910] 2 Ch 477   22.62
Universal Banking Corporation, *Re* (1870) 5 Ch App 492   17.34
Urethane Engineering Products Ltd, *Re* (1989) 5 BCC 614   12.128, 19.36
Uruguay Central & Hygueritas Railway of Monte Video, *Re* (1879) 11
    Ch D 372   14.66

VGM Holdings, *Re* [1942] Ch 235   16.82
Valletort Sanitary Steam Laundry Co Ltd, *Re* [1903] 2 Ch 654   8.80
Van Gelder, Apseman & Co v Sowerby Bridge United District Flower Society
    (1890) 44 Ch D 374   4.61
Vandervell's Trusts, *Re* (No 2) [1974] Ch 269   6.45
Varieties Ltd, *Re* [1893] 2 Ch 235   14.88
Vaughan v Vanderstegen (1854) 2 Drew 408   6.14
Venners Electrical Cooking and Heating Applicances Ltd v Thorpe [1915]
    2 Ch 404   14.179
Veritas [1901] P 304   8.134
Vernon Heating Co Ltd, *Re* [1936] Ch 289   14.54
Victor (1860) Lush 72   6.48
Victoria Housing Estates Ltd v Ashburton Estates [1982] 3 WLR 964   8.52,
                                                                   8.54
Victoria Steamboats Ltd, *Re* [1897] 1 Ch 158   5.26, 5.30, 7.03
Videofusion, *Re* [1974] 1 WLR 1548   14.101
Vivian (HH) & Co Ltd, *Re* [1900] 2 Ch 654   5.21, 5.22
Vron Colliery Co, *Re* (1882) 20 Ch D 442   18.41
Vulcan Ironworks, *Re* [1888] WN 37   6.40
Vyse v Brown (1884) 13 QBD 199   6.68

Waddell v Hutton 1911 SC 575   4.32
Wakefield Rolling Stock Co, *Re* [1892] 3 Ch 165   19.112
Wala Wynaad Indian Gold Mining Co, *Re* (1882) 21 Ch D 849   14.81

Walkden Sheet Metal Co, _Re_ [1960] Ch 170   18.39
Walker v Birch (1795) 6 Term Rep 258   6.06, 6.29
Walker v Linom [1907] 2 Ch 104   8.07
Wallis, _Re_ [1902] 1 KB 719   4.15
Wallis and Simmonds (Builders) Ltd, _Re_ [1974] 1 All ER 561   2.11, 6.42, 8.33
Walsh v Lonsdale (1882) 21 Ch D 9   6.93, 7.07
Wapshore Tube Co Ltd v Hyde Imperial Rubber Co (1900) 18 RPC 374   8.122
Ward v Fielden [1985] CLY 2000   6.06
Ward v Turner (1751) 2 Ves Sen 431   3.11
Ward (Alexander) Co v Samyung Navigation Co [1975] 1 WLR 673   15.55
Ward (RV) Ltd v Bagnall [1967] 1 QB 534   6.36
Wardle v Oakley (1864) 36 Beav 27   2.08
Warnford Investments Ltd v Duckworth [1979] Ch 127   18.13
Wasdale, _Re_ [1899] 1 Ch 163   8.118
Washington Diamond Mining Co, _Re_ [1893] 3 Ch 95   16.75, 16.76
Watson v Duff Morgan Vermont Holdings Ltd [1974] 1 WLR 450, [1974]
   1 All ER 794   8.53, 8.69
Watson v Marston (1853) 4 De GN & G 230   7.33
Watson v Maskell (1834) 1 Bing 366   6.21
Watts v Driscoll [1901] 1 Ch 294   4.34
Wavern Engineering Co Ltd, _Re_ (1987) 3 BCC 3   14.104
Wear Engine Works Co, _Re_ (1875) 10 Ch App 188   14.97
Wearmouth Crown Glass Co, _Re_ (1882) 19 Ch D 640   15.84
Webb v Smith (1885) 30 Ch D 192   6.11, 6.30
Webb v Stenton (1883) 11 QB 518   6.85
Webb v Whiffin (1872) LR 5 HL 711   17.05
Webb Electrical Ltd, _Re_ (1988) 4 BCC 230   14.186
Webb Hale & Co v Alexandria Water Co (1905) 93 LT 339, 21 TLR 572   4.23,
   4.29
Welsh Irish Ferries, _Re_ [1986] Ch 471, [1985] 3 WLR 610, [1985] BCLC
   327   6.04, 8.37, 8.38, 8.65
Wenlock (Baroness) v River Dee (1885) 10 App Cas 354   1.04
West v Pryce (1825) 2 Bing 455   18.62
West v Reid (1843) 2 Hare 249   8.13, 8.15
West Coast Goldfields, _Re_ [1906] 1 Ch 1   19.112
West London Commercial Bank v Reliance Permanent Building Society
   (1885) 29 Ch D 954   7.28
West Mercia Safetywear Ltd (Liquidator) v Dodd [1988] BCLC 250
   16.77, 20.40, 20.47
West of England Bank, _Re, ex p_ Brown (1879) 12 Ch D 823   19.45
West Surrey Tanning Co, _Re_ (1866) LR 2 Eq 737   14.138
Westbury v Twigg & Co [1892] 1 QB 77   14.49, 15.95, 18.26
Western Bank v Schindler [1977] 1 Ch 1, [1976] 3 WLR 341   7.03, 7.07
Western Canada Oil Lands and Works Co, _Re_ (1873) LR 17 Eq 1   14.166
Western Welsh International System Buildings Ltd, _Re_ (1985) 1 BCC 920
   14.162, 14.187
Western Welsh International System Buildings Ltd, _Re_ (1988) 4 BCC 449   21.89
Westerton, _Re_ [1919] 2 Ch 104   4.56
Westminster (1841) 1 Wm Rob 229   6.48
Westminister Corporation v Haste [1950] 1 Ch 442   12.128, 19.22
Wheatley v Silkstone & Haigh Moor Coal Co (1885) 29 Ch D 715   5.21, 8.79

Whistler v Foster (1863) 14 CBNS 248 4.50
Whitbread & Co Ltd v Watt [1902] 1 Ch 835 6.44
White Rose Cottage, *Re* [1965] Ch 940, [1965] 1 All ER 11 2.12, 2.13, 7.20
Whitehouse & Co, *Re* (1878) 9 Ch D 595 16.64, 17.31
Whiteley's Case [1900] 1 Ch 365 17.19
Whitting, *Re, ex p* Hall (1879) 10 Ch D 615 2.14
Whitworth v Smith (1832) 1 Mood & R 193 6.104
Wilcocks v Wilcocks (1706) 2 Vern 558 1.32
Wilkes (John) (Footwear) Ltd v Lee International (Footwear) Ltd [1985] BCLC 444 21.03
Williams v Atlantic Assurance Co Ltd [1933] 1 KB 81 4.07
Williams v Aylesbury & Buckingham Railway Company (1873) 28 LT 547 6.43
Williams v Morgan [1906] 1 Ch 804 7.32
Williams v Quebrada Railway Land & Copper Co [1895] 2 Ch 751 5.22
Williams v Thorp (1828) 2 Sim 257 8.117
Williams v Wellingborough BC [1975] 1 WLR 1327 7.27
Willis v Association of Universities of the British Commonwealth [1965] 1 QB 140 14.42
Willis Winder & Co v Combe (1884) Cab & El 353 6.52
Wills, *Ex p* (1790) 1 Ves Jun 162 1.32
Wilson v Kelland [1910] 2 Ch 306 8.41, 8.47, 8.57, 8.81
Wilson v Wilson (1872) LR 14 Eq 32 3.24
Wilson (D) (Birmingham) Ltd v Metropolitan Property Developments Ltd [1975] 2 All ER 814 6.73, 8.139, 14.179, 22.75
Wilson (EK) & Sons Ltd, *Re* [1972] 1 WLR 791 14.171
Wiltshire Iron Co v Great Western Railway Co (1871) LR 6 QB 776 6.08
Windsor Refrigerator v Branch Nominees [1961] Ch 375 11.36
Windsor Steam Coal Company (1901) Ltd, *Re* [1928] Ch 609, [1929] 1 Ch 151 15.58, 15.81, 16.78
Wing v Tottenham and Hampstead Junction Railway Co (1868) LR 3 Ch App 740 6.43
Winkworth v Baron (Edward) Development Co Ltd [1986] 1 WLR 1512, [1987] BCLC 193 16.77, 21.04
Wise v Landsell [1921] 1 Ch 420 4.32
Wolverhampton Steel & Iron Co Ltd, *Re* [1977] 1 WLR 860 14.79
Wood & Martin (Bricklaying) Contractors Ltd, *Re* [1971] 1 All ER 732 19.138
Woods v Winskill [1913] 2 Ch 303 12.128
Woodworth v Conroy [1976] 1 QB 884 6.12
World Industrial Bank Ltd, *Re* [1909] WN 148 14.76
Wreck Recovery & Salvage Co, *Re* (1880) 15 Ch D 353 15.98
Wright v Redgrave (1879) 11 Ch D 24 6.58
Wyllie v Pollen (1863) 21 LJCh 782 8.18

Yenidje Tobacco Co Ltd, *Re* [1935] Ch 693 14.143
Yeoman v Ellison (1867) LR 2 CP 681 6.93
Yeovil Glove Co, *Re* [1965] Ch 148 20.70, 20.73
Yorkshire Railway Wagon Co v Maclure (1882) 21 Ch D 309 8.32
Yorkshire Woolcombers' Association Ltd, *Re* [1903] 2 Ch 284 4.41, 4.42, 5.13

Zinotty Properties Ltd, *Re* [1984] 1 WLR 1249, [1984] BCLC 375 14.12, 14.89, 14.135, 14.142, 14.146

Table of Statutes

Administration of Justice Act 1970
s 36   7.10
Administration of Justice Act 1973
s 8   7.10
Administration of Justice act 1977
s 26   8.109

Banking Act 1979   14.156
Banking Act 1987   14.98, 14.156, 16.49
s 3   14.156
s 49   19.40
s 92   14.60, 14.156
s 92(1), (6)   14.156
s 106(1)   14.156
Bankruptcy Act 1914
s 25   16.02
s 31   17.34
s 42   20.01
s 80   15.88
Bankruptcy and Deeds of
   Arrangement Act 1913
s 15   6.59
Betting and Gaming Duties Act 1981
s 28(1)   6.112
Bills of Exchange Act 1882   4.49
s 26   21.03
s 31(2)–(4)   4.50
s 34(1)   4.50
s 89   4.50
Bills of Sale Act 1878   3.01–3.03,
     3.07–3.08, 3.10, 3.13–3.14,
     3.28, 5.08, 7.08–7.10, 7.17,
     8.29, 8.135, 9.46
s 4   3.06, 3.09, 3.13–3.15, 3.18,
     4.04, 4.24, 7.09, 8.31
s 10   8.129
s 34   8.29
Bills of Sale Act (1878) Amendment
   Act 1882   3.01–3.03, 3.07–3.08,
     3.10, 3.13–3.14, 3.28, 5.08,
     7.08–7.10, 7.17, 8.29,
     8.135, 9.46

s 3   3.09, 3.13
s 5   5.08
s 7   7.08, 7.10, 7.17
s 9   3.07, 5.08
s 17   5.08, 8.128
Bills of Sale Act 1890
s 1   3.08, 3.13–3.14, 8.31
Bills of Sale Act 1891
s 1   3.08

Charging Orders Act 1979   6.74
s 1(1), (5)   6.76
s 2(1)   6.75
s 2(2)   6.74
s 2(2)(b)   6.84
s 3(4)   6.80, 7.28, 8.93
s 7(2)   8.140
Charities Act 1960
s 30(1)   14.60
new s 30   1.11
Cheques Act 1957   4.49
Companies Act 1862   15.121
s 141   15.119
Companies Act 1948
s 28   4.28
s 95   6.41
s 243(1)   15.12
s 322   20.66
s 366   11.11, 11.16
Table A, Art 79   1.14
Companies Act 1980   4.28
s 8   4.21
s 74   15.105
s 96   21.25
Companies Act 1985   1.14, 8.33,
   13.34, 13.105, 14.95, 14.121, 15.124,
     16.44, 20.50, 21.18, 21.20, 21.66,
     21.89
s 1(3)   4.28
ss 4–5   1.12
s 14   14.89
s 22(2)   14.80, 14.114

Companies Act 1985—*cont.*		s 211	6.15
s 23	4.20	s 221	14.154
s 24	14.81, 14.114	s 222	12.62, 12.133, 14.154
s 35	1.05, 1.09, 1.10, 1.16, 1.20,	s 285	11.31
	1.22, 13.66, 14.66, 15.55, 19.42	s 288	6.15
s 35(1)	1.06, 1.19	s 300	21.92
s 35(2)	1.06	s 306(1)	17.10
s 35A	1.22–24, 1.27	s 322A	1.24
s 35B	1.24, 1.26	s 325	6.15
s 42	15.40, 18.44	s 346	20.27
s 53	14.109	s 346(2)(a)	20.27
s 53(1)–(2)	14.109	s 346(4)–(5)	20.27
s 54	14.109	s 349(2)	21.03
s 54(1)–(3)	14.109	s 349(4)	21.04
s 54(5)–(9)	14.109	s 353	6.15
s 55	14.109	s 359	15.77
s 80	1.14	s 359(3)	17.19
s 80(4)	14.116	s 360	4.26, 8.114
ss 89–96	1.14	s 369(1)(b)(ii)	14.10
s 94(2)–(3)	1.14	s 369(2)(b)	14.10
s 117	14.95, 14.108, 14.109	s 369(3)–(4)	14.10, 14.32
s 118	14.109	s 375	12.45, 12.46, 13.123, 14.221
ss 135–141	22.58	s 378	14.13
s 143(3)(b)	22.58	s 378(2)	14.10
s 146	4.20	s 380	14.14–14.15
s 150	4.21	s 380(4)(j)	14.14
s 150(4)	4.21	s 380(5)	14.34
ss 151–158	4.21	s 386(1)(a)	8.63
s 151	22.58	s 386(2)(a)	8.63
ss 159–181	4.19, 22.58	ss 395–409	8.61
s 160(4)	4.19	s 395	2.11, 3.07, 3.09–3.10,
s 162(2)	4.19		3.14–3.16, 4.04, 4.16, 4.24,
ss 171–181	17.08		6.04, 6.38, 6.41, 6.42, 7.04,
s 173(3)	17.08		8.01, 8.25, 8.41, 8.42, 8.45,
s 178	19.05		8.47, 8.57, 8.84, 8.128–8.130,
s 178(4)	19.05, 19.101–19.102		8.135, 9.04, 9.12–9.14, 9.43,
s 178(5)(a)–(b)	19.101		9.44, 9.46, 9.65, 11.27,
s 178(6)(a)–(b)	19.102		13.40, 15.79, 19.147
s 182	4.23	s 395(1)	8.25, 8.49
s 182(1)(b)	4.25	s 395(2)	8.44, 8.62
s 183(1)	4.25	s 395(2)(c)	3.01–3.02, 3.04
s 183(4)	4.26	s 395(2)(h)	3.23
s 183(5)	4.28	s 396	7.04, 8.62, 11.27
s 184	4.26	s 396(1)	8.25, 8.27, 8.38
s 190	6.15	s 396(1)(a)	4.04, 8.27
s 195	2.15	s 396(1)(b)	4.24, 8.39, 8.64
s 196	5.25, 5.34–5.35, 5.44, 12.122,	s 396(1)(c)	3.07–3.09, 3.13, 4.04,
	12.127, 19.13, 19.19		4.24, 8.65, 9.46
s 196(2)	19.19	s 396(1)(d)	8.66
s 196(3)	12.128	s 396(1)(e)	4.04. 4.38, 8.67, 9.46
s 196(4)	19.19	s 396(1)(f)	4.04, 4.63, 9.46

Companies Act 1985—*cont.*
s 396(1)(g)	4.24
s 396(1)(h)	3.28, 4.16, 9.46
s 396(1)(i)	4.04
s 396(1)(j)	9.46
s 396(2)	8.36
s 396(2)(c)–(e)	8.65
s 396(3)	8.26, 8.62
s 396(3)(a)	8.66
s 396(4)	8.25, 8.62
s 396(5)–(6)	8.62
s 397(1)	8.27
s 397(5)	8.75
s 399	8.43, 8.69
s 399(1)–(2)	8.69
s 400	8.25, 8.42, 8.71
s 401	8.70
s 401(2)	8.55, 8.60, 11.28
s 402	8.74
s 403	8.25
s 404	8.42
s 404(1)	8.51
s 404(2)	8.52
s 405	11.44
s 405(1)	5.33, 11.44
s 405(2)	12.132
s 406	8.58, 8.68
s 407	8.25, 8.42
s 407(1)	8.69
s 408	8.25, 8.58
ss 425–427	15.104, 22.09, 22.56, 22.69, 22.74
s 425	6.79, 13.01, 13.19, 13.61, 13.130, 22.01, 22.10, 22.56–22.59, 22.66, 22.71
s 425(1)	22.56, 22.60, 22.69
s 425(2)	22.65, 22.72
s 425(3)	22.67
s 425(6)(b)	22.56
s 426	22.64
s 426(2)–(7)	22.63
s 427	22.68
s 427(2)	22.68
s 427(3)	22.68
s 427(3)(d)	14.01
s 427(4)–(5)	22.68
s 427A	22.69, 22.71
s 427A(1)	22.69
s 427A(1)(a)	22.69
s 427A(1)(b)	22.70
s 427A(1)(c)	22.69
s 427A(2)	22.70
s 427A(4)–(5), (8)	22.69
ss 433–436	16.44
s 437	14.134, 21.73
s 440	14.91, 14.106, 14.134, 15.10
s 441	14.160
ss 447–448	14.91, 14.134, 21.73
s 458	21.05, 21.25, 21.26, 21.29–21.31, 21.36, 21.76
s 459	13.129, 14.59, 14.78, 14.89, 14.113, 14.148, 14.184, 21.22, 22.44
s 461	14.148, 14.163
s 497(b)	12.28
s 551	16.65
s 561	16.15
s 566	15.20
s 580(1)	15.140
s 582(2)	22.03
s 588	14.10, 14.13
s 593	22.03
s 612	18.54
s 617	20.66
s 631	16.66, 16.72
s 631(1)	16.72
s 651	15.82, 19.122, 19.135, 19.137, 19.138, 19.140, 19.143, 19.147
s 651(1)	19.138
s 652	14.01, 14.113, 19.129, 19.130, 19.137, 19.141
s 652(1)–(2)	19.130, 19.131
s 652(3)	19.131
s 652(4)	15.43, 15.48, 19.129, 19.131
s 652(5)	19.131
s 652(6)	19.133
s 652(7)	19.132
s 653	15.82, 19.135, 19.137, 19.140–19.141, 19.143–19.144
s 653(1)	19.141
s 653(2)	19.141, 19.144
s 653(3)	19.146
s 654	19.135, 19.137
s 655(1)	19.135
s 655(2)	19.140
s 655(2)(a)–(b)	19.135
s 656	19.136
s 657(1)–(2)	19.136
s 658	19.136
s 680	4.21
s 691	8.76

Companies Act 1985—*cont.*	
ss 703A–703N	8.76
s 711(1)(p)	18.44
s 711(2)	18.44
s 711A	1.25–1.27, 8.75
s 719	15.105
s 726	18.03
s 727	21.23
s 735	14.03, 14.05
s 736	20.26
s 736(1)	20.26
s 740	20.22
s 741	20.46
s 741(1)	16.69, 20.16, 21.07
s 741(2)	20.16, 20.29, 21.07
s 743	20.21
s 744	5.10, 16.69
Sch 13 Part I	20.27
para 15	20.27
Sch 15A	22.69, 22.71
para 1	22.72
paras 2–6	22.71
para 8	22.72
para 9(2)–(3)	22.73
para 10	22.71
Companies Act 1989	1.01–1.02,
	1.04–1.05, 1.09–1.10, 1.12,
	1.16, 1.18–1.20, 1.22, 1.27,
	1.36, 3.09, 5.37, 6.04, 8.37,
	8.61, 14.66, 15.55, 18,69, 19.42
s 93	8.62–8.67
s 94	8.75
s 95	8.69, 8.71
s 96	8.70
s 97	8.74
s 99	8.69
s 100	8.68
s 105	8.76
s 108	1.10
s 108(1)	1.16, 1.23, 1.24
s 109(1)	1.24
s 110	1.12
s 111	1.11
s 111(1)	1.12
s 142	1.16, 1.25, 8.75
Part VII	18.69
Sched 15	8.76
Companies Consolidation	
(Consequential Provisions) Act	
1985	
s 1	14.95, 14.110
s 6(3)	4.21

Companies (Winding Up) Act 1890	
s 1(6)	14.52
Company Directors Disqualification	
Act 1986	10.37, 11.13, 11.18,
	15.02, 21.39, 21.41
s 1	21.51
s 1(1)(b)	15.02
s 1(1)(d)	21.53
s 1(2)–(4)	21.54
ss 2–5	21.61
s 2	21.66, 21.75
s 2(1)–(2)	21.65
s 2(3)	21.66
s 3	21.69–21.71, 21.75
s 3(1)	21.68
s 3(2)	21.69
s 3(2)(b)	15.02, 21.69, 21.71
s 3(3)	21.69
s 3(4)–(5)	21.68
s 4	21.75, 21.77
s 4(1)	21.76
s 4(1)(a)–(b)	21.76
s 4(2)	21.76
s 5	21.71, 21.75
s 5(5)	21.71
s 6	21.54, 21.61–21.62,
	21.74–21.75, 21.78, 21.84,
	21.87, 21.91
s 6(1)	21.85
s 6(1)(a)	21.86
s 6(1)(b)	21.87
s 6(2)	21.87
s 6(2)(a)–(b)	21.86
s 6(2)(c)	13.43, 21.86
s 6(3)	21.84, 21.87
s 6(4)	21.85
s 7	21.75, 21.82, 21.83
s 7(1)	21.84
s 7(2)	21.87
s 7(3)	21.78, 21.80–21.81
s 7(4)	21.83
s 7(4)(a)–(b)	21.83
s 8	21.61–21.62, 21.75
s 8(2)–(4)	21.74
s 9	21.87, 21.88
s 9(1)	21.88, 21.90
s 9(3)	21.91
s 9(4)–(5)	21.88
s 10	21.77
s 13	15.02, 21.57
s 14(1)–(2)	21.57
s 15	15.02, 21.58

Company Directors Disqualification
  Act 1986—*cont.*
  s 15(1)(a)   21.58
  s 15(1)(b)   15.02, 21.59
  s 15(2)–(3)   21.60
  s 15(4)   21.58
  s 15(5)   21.59
  s 16(1)–(3)   21.61
  s 17(1)   21.55
  s 17(1)(b)   15.02
  s 17(2)   21.55
  s 18   21.56
  s 22(3)   21.86
  s 31   10.33
  Sch 1   21.87–21.89, 21.91
  Sch 1 Part I   21.88
    paras 1–5   21.89
    paras 6–10   21.90
  Sch 1 Part II   21.88, 21.90
Consumer Credit Act 1974   7.10,
                             13.39
  s 8(1)   3.10, 7.10
  s 76(1)   7.10
  s 87   6.100
  s 87(1)   7.10
  ss 88–89   6.100
  s 126   7.10
  s 138(2)–(4)   20.62
  s 189(1)   3.10, 7.10
Conveyancing Act 1881
  s 21(1)   7.20
Copyright, Designs and Patents Act
  1988
  Chapter IV   4.62
  s 90   4.58
  s 90(2)–(3)   4.62
  s 91   4.63
  s 94   4.62
  s 96(1)   4.63
  ss 213–216   4.64
  s 222   4.64
  s 222(1)   4.58
  s 224   4.64
County Courts Act 1984
  s 40(1)   14.53
  s 41(1)   14.53
  s 42   14.53
  s 75(3)(b)   14.53
Customs and Excise Management Act
  1979
  s 117(5)   6.112

Distress for Rent Act 1689
  s 1   6.92, 6.96
Distress for Rent Act 1737
  ss 1–3   6.97
  ss 8–9   6.103
  s 10   6.92, 6.103
Drug Trafficking Offences Act 1986
  s 1   19.40

Electric Lighting Act 1882
  s 25   6.98
Electric Lighting Act 1909
  s 6   6.98
Electricity Act 1947
  s 57(1)   6.98
Employment Protection
  (Consolidation) Act 1978   12.128,
                    14.46, 19.34
  s 12(1)   19.32
  s 19   19.32
  s 27(3)   19.32
  s 31(3)   19.32
  s 31A(4)   19.32
  s 49   19.34
  s 72   19.34
  s 101   19.32
  s 122   19.35
  s 122(2)   19.35
  s 122(3)(a)–(e)   19.34
  s 122(4)   19.34
  s 122(5)   19.35
  s 123   19.36
  s 124   19.35
  s 125   19.36
  s 125(2)–(3)   19.36
  Part VII   19.33
Energy Act 1983   13.41
European Communities Act 1972
  s 9(1)   1.05
  s 9(4)   18.44

Factors Act 1889   4.47, 9.25, 9.65
  s 1(4)   3.12
  s 2   6.06, 8.10, 9.64
  s 3   3.12, 8.30
  s 7   6.30
  s 9   8.10, 9.64
Finance Act 1984   9.63
Finance (No 2) Act 1975
  s 69   19.26

Financial Services Act 1986
s 6   19.40
s 44   14.158
s 72   14.60, 14.95, 14.157–14.159
s 72(1)   14.159
s 72(2)   14.158
s 72(3)   14.159
s 94   14.91, 21.73
s 105   14.91, 21.73
s 109   14.94
s 177   21.73
s 207(1)   14.158
Fraudulent Conveyances Act 1571
                                       20.01

Gas Act 1986
s 15   6.98
Sch 5 para 19(1)   6.98
General Rate Act 1967
s 1(1)   6.116
ss 16–17A   6.117
s 17B(6)   6.116
s 24   6.117
ss 28–29   6.117
s 36(5)   6.117
ss 55–56   6.117
s 62   6.117
s 96(1)   6.117, 6.118
s 99(2)   6.120
s 99(3)   6.119
Part VI   6.116
Sch 1   6.117
    para 13   6.116

Harbours, Docks and Piers Clauses
    Act 1847
s 44   6.49
Hosiery Act 1843
s 18   6.98

Income and Corporation Taxes Act
    1970
s 204   19.26
Industrial and Provident Societies Act
    1965   14.03
Insolvency Act 1985   4.46, 5.06,
            5.37, 9.48, 9.58, 10.03,
        11.11, 15.123, 18.64, 19.17,
                        19.37, 21.05
s 5   10.16
s 88   14.06
s 235   5.08, 14.10

Sch 6 para 14   5.34
    para 45   19.138
Sch 10 Part II   14.10
    Part III   5.08
    Part IV   3.04
Insolvency Act 1986   9.02, 9.68,
            10.01, 10.03, 11.01, 11.04,
            11.09, 11.12, 11.14–11.15,
            13.19, 13.57, 13.69, 13.130,
        14.13, 14.186, 15.49, 15.123,
            16.02, 16.85, 18.70, 19.02,
                19.73, 20.02, 21.66
Part I   6.79, 10.04, 13.06, 14.164,
            15.06, 15.26, 18.49, 19.23,
                        20.35, 22.75
ss 1 – 7   14.02, 15.104, 22.01,
            22.09, 22.56, 22.59, 22.74
s 1   22.10, 22.12
s 1(1)   22.10
s 1(2)   22.12
s 1(3)   22.11
s 2   22.25
s 2(2)   22.17, 22.18
s 2(3)   22.18
s 2(4)   22.22
s 3   22.45
s 3(1)   22.24
s 3(2)   22.27
s 3(3)   22.24
s 4(1)–(2)   22.29
s 4(3)–(4)   22.09, 22.29
s 4(5)   22.30
s 4(6)   22.33, 22.40
s 5(1)   22.41
s 5(2)   22.41
s 5(2)(b)   22.31, 22.32
s 5(3)–(4)   22.42
s 6   22.27, 22.43, 22.45, 22.47, 22.48
s 6(1)–(3)   22.43
s 6(4)–(5)   22.46
s 6(6)   22.47
s 6(7)   22.45
s 7(2)   22.49
s 7(3)   22.50
s 7(4)   14.58, 22.50
s 7(5)–(6)   22.51
ss 8–27   13.02
s 8(1)   13.16
s 8(1)(a)   13.13, 13.17
s 8(1)(b)   13.14, 13.17
s 8(2)   13.27, 13.58

Insolvency Act 1986—cont.
s 8(3)   13.10–13.11,
               13.14–13.16, 13.20, 13.27
s 8(4)   13.22
s 9(1)   13.08, 13.09
s 9(2)(b)   13.12
s 9(3)   12.134, 13.23
s 9(4)   13.23, 13.56
s 9(5)   13.24
s 10   4.48, 13.26
s 10(1)   9.59, 13.25
s 10(1)(b)   9.05, 13.38–13.40
s 10(3)   13.26
s 10(4)   9.05, 9.59, 13.38, 13.39
s 11   4.48, 12.37
s 11(1)   13.28, 13.65
s 11(1)(b)   12.134
s 11(2)   13.28
s 11(3)   9.68
s 11(3)(a)   13.32, 13.65
s 11(3)(b)   13.32
s 11(3)(c)   9.05, 9.68, 13.30, 13.32,
               13.35, 13.36, 13.38, 13.40
s 11(3)(d)   13.30, 13.32, 13.36
s 11(4)   12.134, 13.28
s 11(5)   13.29
s 12(1)–(2)   13.46
s 13   13.24
s 13(1)–(3)   13.55
s 14   14.58
s 14(1)(a)–(b)   13.58
s 14(2)(a)   13.63
s 14(2)(b)   13.63, 13.105, 13.107
s 14(3)   13.117
s 14(4)   13.59, 13.60
s 14(5)   13.66, 13.84
s 14(6)   12.74, 13.66
s 15   12.88, 13.36, 13.68,
               13.75, 13.80. 13.82, 13.129
s 15(1)   13.70, 13.90
s 15(2)   13.73–13.78, 13.81
s 15(3)   13.70, 13.73
s 15(4)   13.70
s 15(5)   13.75, 13.78
s 15(6)   13.78
s 15(7)   13.79
s 17(1)   13.85
s 17(2)(a)–(b)   13.86
s 17(3)   13.87, 13.107
s 17(3)(a)   13.119
s 18   13.54, 13.103

s 18(1)   13.15, 13.54
s 18(3)–(5)   13.54
s 19(1)   13.89
s 19(2)   13.26, 13.89
s 19(4)   13.90
s 19(5)   13.91, 13.92
s 20(1)–(3)   13.93
s 21   11.45, 12.31
s 21(1)–(3)   13.47
s 22(1)   13.48
s 22(2)   13.51
s 22(3)   13.48, 13.49
s 22(4)   13.50
s 22(5)   13.50, 13.52
s 22(6)   13.53
s 23   13.76, 13.103–13.104,
       13.106–13.108, 13.110, 13.113,
                         13.120, 13.122
s 23(1)   13.103, 13.108
s 23(1)(a)–(b)   13.104
s 23(2)(b)   13.104
s 23(3)   13.104
s 24   13.86, 13.130
s 24(1)–(3)   13.113
s 24(4)   13.110, 13.114
s 24(5)–(6)   13.114
s 25   13.117, 13.130
s 25(1)   13.116
s 25(2)   13.108, 13.115, 13.116
s 25(3)–(4)   13.115
s 25(6)   13.115
s 26   13.55
s 26(1)   13.121
s 26(2)   13.121, 13.124
s 27   13.82, 13.102, 13.130
s 27(1)   13.129
s 27(2)–(3)   13.130
s 27(4)   13.131
s 27(5)   13.82, 13.129
s 29   11.04, 11.07
s 29(2)   5.44, 10.04,
               11.05, 11.09, 11.19
s 29(2)(b)   11.06
s 30   10.32, 11.16
s 31   11.17
s 32   11.39, 12.119
s 33   11.37
s 33(1)   11.40
s 33(1)(b)   11.41
s 34   11.26, 11.29
s 35   12.71, 12.120

Insolvency Act 1986—*cont.*

s 36	12.117
s 36(2)–(3)	12.117
s 39(1)–(2)	11.43
s 40	5.06, 5.25, 5.35, 12.121–12.122, 12.127, 13.29, 19.13, 19.19,. 19.23
s 40(2)	12.127, 19,13, 19.19
s 40(3)	12.128, 19.13, 19.19
s 41	12.27, 12.28
s 41(1)–(2)	12.27
s 42	5.04, 7.11, 11.34, 14.58, 14.192, 18.46
s 42(1)	12.69, 12.72–12.73, 12.75–12.76, 12.78, 12.80–12.83, 12.85, 12.93, 12.115, 14.64
s 42(1)(b)	12.70
s 42(2)(b)	12.75
s 42(3)	11.32, 12.74
s 43	5.04, 12.88, 12.91
s 43(1)	12.89, 12.90
s 43(2)	12.91
s 43(3)–(4)	12.92
s 43(5)–(6)	12.90
s 43(7)	12.89
s 44	5.04, 15.53
s 44(1)(a)	7.26, 12.01, 12.68, 12.112, 14.64, 14.192
s 44(1)(b)	12.07, 12.11, 12.67, 12.116
s 44(1)(c)	12.06, 12.11, 12.113
s 44(2)	12.09, 12.27
s 44(3)	12.11
s 45	5.04, 21.82
s 45(1)	12.135, 12.137
s 45(2)	12.95, 12.134
s 45(3)	12.126, 12.131
s 45(4)	12.120, 12.132
s 45(5)	12.132
s 46	5.04, 11.45, 12.31
s 46(1)(a)	11.46, 11.50
s 46(1)(b)	11.46
s 46(2)	11.51, 12.32
s 46(3)	11.51
s 46(4)	11.50
s 47	12.37
s 47(1)	12.13, 12.21
s 47(2)	12.15, 12.16, 12.21
s 47(3)	12.13, 12.19
s 47(4)	12.14, 12.20, 12.21
s 47(5)	12.14, 12.21, 12.22
s 47(5)(b)	12.21
s 47(6)	12.14
s 48	12.32–12.33, 12.36
s 48(1)	12.35, 12.37
s 48(2)	12.33–12.35, 12.40
s 48(4)	12.35
s 48(5)	12.37
s 48(6)	12.39
s 48(7)	12.32
s 49(1)	12.40, 12.41
s 49(2)	12.42
s 59	13.29
s 62(3)	12.136
s 73	14.03
s 74(1)	14.77, 14.80, 17.04, 17.07
s 74(2)	17.07
s 74(2)(a)–(b)	17.04, 17.14
s 74(2)(c)	17.06, 17.07, 17.14
s 74(2)(d)	14.77, 17.01, 17.07
s 74(2)(f)	19.05, 19.45, 19.94, 19.103, 19.104
s 74(3)	17.07
s 75	17.10
s 76	14.83
s 76(1)–(2)	17.08
s 76(3)	17.08, 17.09
s 76(4)	17.09
s 76(5)	17.08
s 77	17.23
s 78	17.24
s 79(1)	14.77, 17.03, 17.07
s 79(2)	17.03
s 79(3)	17.08
s 80	17.20, 17.21
s 81	17.21, 19.106
s 82	17.21, 19.106
s 82(1)	17.33
s 82(2)	14.79, 17.33
s 82(3)–(4)	17.33
s 84	14.199
s 84(1)	14.08, 14.14, 14.32, 15.92
s 84(3)	14.14, 14.34
s 85	14.15
s 86	5.26, 14.40, 20.10, 20.66
s 87(1)	14.41
s 87(2)	14.42
s 88	14.43, 17.22
s 89	14.199, 15.02
s 89(1)	14.33
s 89(2)	14.36

Insolvency Act 1986—*cont.*
s 89(2)(a) 14.34
s 89(2)(b) 14.33
s 89(3) 14.34
s 89(4) 14.35
s 89(5) 14.36
s 89(6) 14.34
s 90 14.36, 14.199
s 91 15.140
s 91(1) 14.37, 14.199, 18.01
s 91(2) 14.44, 15.40, 15.41, 15.85
s 92(1) 14.37, 14.199, 15.41, 15.42
s 92(2) 14.37, 14.199, 15.42
s 92(3) 14.37, 15.42
s 93(1) 15.92
s 93(2)–(3) 16.116
s 94 15.136, 19.119, 19.122
s 94(1) 14.199, 15.92, 16.116
s 94(2) 19.119
s 94(3) 15.133, 15.136, 16.37, 19.119
s 94(4) 16.116
s 94(5) 19.119
s 94(6) 16.116
s 95 14.25, 14.29, 14.39, 14.40,
14.199, 14.205–14.207,
15.92, 16.114
s 95(1) 14.37, 15.92
s 95(2) 14.27, 14.37
s 95(2)(a) 14.38, 15.92
s 95(2)(b)–(c) 14.38, 14.206
s 95(2)(d) 14.38
s 95(3) 14.27, 14.38
s 95(3)(c) 14.207
s 95(4)–(7) 14.38
s 95(8) 16.116
s 96 14.37, 14.39, 14.199, 15.92
s 96(3) 16.116
s 98 14.21, 14.25, 14.27, 14.29,
14.38–14.39, 14.205–14.207,
14.211, 14.224, 15.43–15.44,
15.92, 16.86, 16.114, 18.60, 18.67,
21.90
s 98(1) 14.17, 15.92
s 98(1)(a) 14.19, 15.44
s 98(1)(b)–(c) 14.20, 14.206
s 98(2)(a) 14.22
s 98(2)(b) 14.23
s 98(3)–(5) 14.20
s 98(6) 14.21, 16.116
s 99 15.43, 15.44
s 99(1) 14.207, 14.211

s 99(1)(a), (c) 14.24
s 99(2)–(3) 14.24
s 100 14.28
s 100(1) 15.44, 18.01
s 100(2) 15.44
s 100(3) 15.46
s 101 15.92, 16.86
s 101(1) 14.28
s 101(2)–(3) 14.28, 16.86
s 102 14.39
s 103 14.15, 14.44, 15.40, 15.85
s 104 14.200, 15.46
s 105 15.92
s 105(1) 14.200, 15.92
s 105(2)–(3) 16.116
s 106 14.200, 15.92, 15.137,
19.119, 19.122
s 106(1) 15.92, 16.116
s 106(2) 19.119
s 106(3) 15.133, 15.137,
16.37, 19.119
s 106(4) 16.116
s 106(5) 19.119
s 106(6) 16.116
s 107 18.68, 19.03, 19.05,
19.85, 19.109
s 108 15.43, 15.118, 15.121, 15.126
s 108(1) 15.46
s 109 15.48, 18.44
s 110 15.104, 22.01–22.02,
22.04–22.08, 22.59, 22.74
s 110(1)–(2) 22.02
s 110(3) 22.03, 22.05
s 110(3)(a)–(b) 22.03
s 110(4) 22.02
s 110(5) 22.04
s 110(6) 22.05
s 111 15.104, 22.01–22.02,
22.04–22.05, 22.07, 22.59, 22.74
s 111(1)–(3) 22.06
s 112 6.51, 9.49, 14.47, 15.59, 15.92,
15.95, 15.99, 16.07, 17.22, 17.29,
18.26, 18.35, 19.07, 19.58, 19.109,
22.08
s 112(1) 14.179, 15.87, 15.89,
16.35, 19.07
s 112(2) 14.179, 15.87, 15.90
s 114 15.43
s 114(1) 14.15
s 114(2) 14.15, 14.16
s 114(3) 14.16

Insolvency Act 1986—*cont.*
s 115   12.130, 15.140, 19.07
s 117(1)–(2)   14.51
s 117(4)   14.51
s 117(5)   14.52
s 118   14.53
s 119   14.57
s 122   13.13, 14.97
s 122(1)   14.106
s 122(1)(a)   14.107, 14.133
s 122(1)(b)   14.95, 14.108
s 122(1)(c)   14.95, 14.110
s 122(1)(d)   14.111
s 122(1)(e)   14.114
s 122(1)(f)   14.115
s 122(1)(g)   14.85, 14.131,
14.133, 14.136
s 122(4)   14.95
s 123   8.71, 13.13, 14.67, 14.115,
14.154, 14.156, 14.159, 20.67
s 123(1)(a)   14.73, 14.76, 14.118,
14.121, 14.124, 14.128–14.129
s 123(1)(b)–(d)   14.118, 14.130
s 123(1)(e)   14.117, 14.118
s 123(2)   14.117, 14.118, 14.120
s 124   14.58
s 124(1)   13.08, 14.58–14.59,
14.62–14.63, 14.70, 14.77,
14.128, 14.138
s 124(2)   14.81, 14.83, 14.114
s 124(2)(b)   14.79, 14.80
s 124(3)   14.83
s 124(4)   14.58, 14.108, 14.110,
14.134, 14.136
s 124(5)   14.58, 14.96, 14.134,
14.138, 14.167, 14.169
s 125   12.115
s 125(1)   12.115, 14.76, 14.84,
14.138, 14.163
s 125(2)   12.128, 14.149,
14.152, 14.163
s 126   6.51, 18.31
s 126(1)   14.179, 18.32
s 127   12.114, 14.162,
14.181–14.183, 14.187–14.188,
17.22, 21.90
s 128   6.51, 14.189, 18.30–18.31,
18.33–18.34, 19.21
s 128(1)   18.30
s 129   5.26, 14.99, 14.174,
20.10, 20.66

s 129(1)   15.116
s 129(2)   15.19
s 130   6.51, 14.47, 18.26
s 130(1)   14.173, 14.177
s 130(2)   14.180, 15.95, 15.98, 18.26,
18.35–18.36
s 131   16.24
s 131(2)   16.25
s 131(3)   16.24
s 131(4)–(5)   16.25
s 131(6)   16.24
s 131(7)   16.26
s 132   16.26, 16.83
s 132(1)   16.39
s 132(2)   16.26, 16.83
s 133   16.39
s 133(1)   12.119, 16.27
s 133(2)   12.119, 16.28
s 133(3)   16.29
s 133(4)   16.30
s 134(1)–(3)   16.32
s 135   15.04, 15.07
s 135(1)–(2)   15.04
s 135(4)–(5)   15.04, 15.13
s 136   14.30
s 136(1)   15.26, 15.32
s 136(2)   14.30, 15.26, 15.32, 15.116
s 136(3)   14.30, 15.26, 15.128–15.129
s 136(4)   14.196, 15.27, 15.30
s 136(5)   14.199, 14.201
s 136(5)(a)   15.27, 15.131
s 136(5)(b)   14.202, 15.27, 19.47
s 136(5)(c)   14.202, 15.27–15.28
s 137(1)–(2)   15.29, 15.131
s 137(3)   15.131
s 137(4)–(5)   15.30
s 139   14.196
s 139(2)   15.30
s 139(3)   14.196, 15.30
s 139(4)   14.196, 15.30, 15.32, 19.48
s 139(4)(a)   15.129
s 140   15.26, 15.32, 19.48
s 140(1)   15.129
s 141   14.196, 15.29, 16.87, 16.90
s 141(1)   16.87
s 141(2)   14.196, 16.87
s 141(3)   16.87
s 141(4)   15.100, 16.88, 16.113
s 141(5)   15.100–15.101, 16.88,
16.113
s 143   15.12, 16.39

Insolvency Act 1986—*cont.*		s 166(5)	15.92
s 143(1)	18.01, 19.107	s 166(5)(a)–(b)	14.21
s 143(2)	16.38	s 166(6)	15.92
s 144	16.03, 16.08	s 166(7)	15.92, 16.116
s 144(1)	13.85, 15.12, 16.09	s 167	15.12, 22.56
s 145	18.04	s 167(1)	15.99, 16.111, 22.01
s 145(1)–(2)	15.99	s 167(1)(a)	15.98
s 145(3)	13.62	s 167(1)(b)	15.93
s 146	14.203, 15.139	s 167(2)	15.101, 16.111
s 146(1)	14.198, 15.92, 19.120	s 167(2)(a)	15.101
s 146(1)(a)	16.116	s 167(2)(b)	15.99
s 146(2)	14.203, 19.120	s 167(3)	15.59, 15.86, 15.88–15.89,
s 146(3)	14.198		15.99
s 147	14.176–14.178	s 168	19.58
s 148(1)	15.91, 17.12, 17.13	s 168(2)	14.197, 14.202, 15.77,
s 148(2)	15.91, 17.12		15.92, 15.128
s 148(3)	17.14	s 168(3)	15.95
s 149(1)	16.63, 17.27	s 168(4)	15.86, 15.88
s 149(2)	16.63, 17.31	s 168(5)	15.59, 15.86,
s 149(3)	17.32		15.88–15.89, 15.99
s 150(1)	17.17, 17.25–17.26, 17.29	s 170	16.116
s 150(2)	17.26	s 170(4)	16.116
s 151(1)	17.27	s 171(2)	15.118
s 152	17.27	s 171(2)(a)	15.124
s 152(1)	17.17	s 171(2)(b)	15.125
s 154	15.96, 17.36, 19.05, 19.107	s 171(3)	15.126
s 155	16.07	s 171(4)	15.02, 15.115
s 156	19.07	s 171(5)	15.106
s 158	17.28	s 171(6)	15.133
s 160(1)	15.77	s 171(6)(a)	15.136
s 160(1)(a)	14.197	s 171(6)(b)	15.137
s 160(1)(b)	15.91, 17.13	s 172(2)	15.18, 15.118, 15.121
s 160(1)(d)	15.100, 17.25	s 172(3)	15.129
s 160(2)	15.91, 15.100, 17.13, 17.29	s 172(4)	15.131
s 164	15.46	s 172(5)	15.02, 15.115
s 165	14.40, 22.04	s 172(6)	15.106, 15.112
s 165(1)	22.01	s 172(8)	15.139, 16.37, 19.120,
s 165(2)	16.111		19.128
s 165(3)	15.73, 15.93	s 173(2)(a)–(b)	15.136
s 165(4)	17.11	s 173(2)(d)	15.136
s 165(4)(a)	15.91, 17.17	s 173(2)(e)	15.137
s 165(4)(b)	15.91, 15.100, 17.25	s 173(2)(e)(i)	15.137
s 165(4)(c)	14.44, 14.199–14.200,	s 173(4)	15.135
	15.92	s 174(2)(a)–(b)	15.138
s 165(5)	17.36, 19.109	s 174(3)	15.138
s 165(6)	15.101, 16.111	s 174(4)(a)–(c)	15.139
s 166	14.10, 14.15, 14.40	s 174(4)(d)(ii)	15.139
s 166(1)–(2)	15.44	s 174(5)	15.138
s 166(3)	14.16, 15.44	s 174(6)	15.135
s 166(3)(a)	18.01	s 175	5.25, 19.19
s 166(4)	16.116	s 175(1)	19.06

Insolvency Act 1986—*cont.*

s 175(2)(a)	19.06, 19.22
s 175(2)(b)	19.19
s 176	19.20–19.21
s 176(3)	19.20
s 176(10)	19.21
s 177	15.19, 15.22, 15.95
s 177(2)	15.21
s 177(3)–(4)	15.24
ss 178–180	19.136
s 178	18.05, 18.14, 18.16, 18.32
s 178(2)	18.05–18.07
s 178(3)(a)–(b)	18.06
s 178(4)	18.10, 18.13, 19.136
s 178(4)(b)	18.12
s 178(5)	18.08
s 178(6)	18.12, 18.14
ss 179–182	19.136
s 179	18.05, 18.16
s 179(1)–(2)	18.16
s 180	18.11
s 181	15.94, 18.16
s 181(2)	18.15
s 181(3)	18.14
s 181(5)	18.14
s 181(6)	18.15
s 182(1)	18.17
s 182(2)–(4)	18.20
s 183	8.46, 14.50, 18.32, 18.38, 18.45
s 183(1)	6.53, 6.56, 6.82, 18.40
s 183(2)	18.40
s 183(2)(a)	6.53, 14.50
s 183(2)(b)	6.53, 18.40, 18.43
s 183(2)(c)	6.53, 18.30, 18.36, 18.40
s 183(3)	6.53, 6.82, 18.38
s 183(4)	18.39
s 184	18.38, 18.42, 18.45–18.46
s 184(1)	6.53, 18.42, 18.46
s 184(2)	6.53, 18.42, 18.43
s 184(3)	6.53
s 184(4)–(5)	6.53, 18.43
s 186(1)–(2)	18.71
s 187	15.105, 19.118
s 188(1)	14.174
s 189	14.37, 19.74, 19.76
s 189(1)	19.74–19.75
s 189(2)	19.59, 19.74–19.75
s 189(3)	19.75, 19.100
s 189(4)	19.76

s 191	16.07
s 192	16.37, 16.58
s 195	14.197, 14.200, 15.92
s 195(1)	14.165
s 195(2)–(3)	14.166
ss 201–205	19.137
s 201	19.128
s 201(1)	19.122, 19.126
s 201(2)–(4)	19.122
s 202	15.31, 19.123, 19.128
s 202(2)	19.123
s 202(3)–(4)	19.125
s 202(5)	19.123
s 203	19.123, 19.128
s 203(2)–(3)	19.126
s 203(4)–(5)	19.127
s 205	19.128
s 205(1)–(4)	19.128
s 205(6)	19.128
s 212	13.44, 13.93, 15.57, 15.59, 15.68, 15.82, 15.93, 15.135, 16.66–16.67, 16.72, 16.76–16.78, 16.81–16.82, 20.40
s 212(1)	13.44, 16.68, 16.72
s 212(1)(b)	16.69
s 212(1)(c)	16.70–16.71
s 212(3)	16.67, 16.81
s 212(3)(a)	15.93, 16.81
s 212(3)(b)	15.93, 16.79, 16.82
s 212(4)	16.71
s 212(5)	16.67
s 213	21.05, 21.14, 21.24–21.26, 21.29–21.30, 21.35–21.38, 21.42, 21.77
s 213(1)	13.44, 21.34
s 213(2)	21.25, 21.31
s 214	21.05, 21.07, 21.09–21.10, 21.14, 21.23, 21.26, 21.30, 21.35, 21.37–21.38, 21.42, 21.77
s 214(1)	13.44, 21.06–21.07, 21.10, 21.24, 21.34
s 214(2)	21.06, 21.09, 21.12
s 214(2)(a)	21.12
s 214(2)(b)	21.12, 21.23
s 214(2)(c)	21.21
s 214(2) proviso	21.21
s 214(3)	13.08, 21.14, 21.22–21.23
s 214(4)	21.13–21.14, 21.16–21.17, 21.22

Insolvency Act 1986—*cont.*

s 214(4)(a)–(b) 21.19
s 214(5) 21.16–21.17
s 214(6) 21.11
s 214(7) 21.07
s 214(8) 21.24
s 215(2) 21.37–21.38
s 215(2)(b) 21.38
s 215(3) 21.37
s 215(3)(b) 21.37
s 215(4) 19.04, 19.100
s 216 21.39–21.46, 21.49–21.50, 21.52
s 216(1)–(2) 21.40
s 216(3) 21.40, 21.46–21.49
s 216(4) 21.42
s 216(6)–(7) 21.40
s 217 21.39, 21.42, 21.44–21.45, 21.58
s 217(1)(a)–(b) 21.42
s 217(2)–(3) 21.44
s 217(4) 21.42
s 217(5) 21.43
s 218 16.45
s 218(1) 16.40
s 218(2) 16.41
s 218(3) 19.35
s 218(4) 16.43–16.44
s 218(5) 16.43–16.44
s 218(5)(a)–(b) 16.44
s 219(1)–(2) 16.44
s 219(3) 16.45
s 219(4) 16.46
ss 220–229 14.03–14.04
s 220 14.03
s 220(1) 14.03
s 221 14.159
s 221(4)–(5) 14.04
ss 222–224 14.154
s 230 12.75, 12.95, 13.55
s 230(2) 12.134
s 230(3) 15.02
s 230(4) 15.04
s 230(5) 15.02
s 231 11.36, 12.94, 15.03, 15.31, 15.75
s 232 11.31, 12.95, 15.14
s 233 12.99
s 233(1) 13.42
s 233(2) 12.99, 13.41–13.42

s 233(3) 12.99, 13.42
s 233(5) 13.41
s 234 15.14, 15.77, 16.03, 16.13, 16.65
s 234(1) 16.03
s 234(1)(c) 16.11
s 234(2) 12.100, 16.03–16.04, 16.08–16.09
s 234(3)–(4) 12.75, 12.100, 16.04
s 235 12.14, 12.101–12.102, 12.111, 13.48, 13.50, 14.210, 16.05, 16.39
s 235(1) 13.50
s 235(2) 12.101, 13.50
s 235(2)(a) 12.14
s 235(2)(b) 12.14, 12.101
s 235(3) 12.14, 12.101, 13.50, 16.05
s 235(4)–(5) 12.101
s 236 6.02, 6.17, 12.102–12.105, 12.109–12.111, 16.10, 16.20–16.23, 16.39, 16.83
s 236(1) 16.11
s 236(1)(c) 16.16
s 236(2) 12.102, 16.10, 16.17
s 236(2)(c) 12.109, 16.10
s 236(3) 12.102, 16.09, 16.17
s 236(4) 12.107, 16.18
s 236(5) 12.107, 16.18–16.19
s 236(6) 12.107, 16.18
s 237 12.104–12.105, 12.109–12.110, 16.22–16.23
s 237(1) 12.110, 16.23
s 237(2) 12.110, 16.23, 16.83
s 237(3) 12.105, 16.21
s 237(4) 16.20
ss 238–240 11.27, 12.116, 14.52, 21.90
s 238 6.70, 13.23, 13.43, 20.08, 20.10, 20.31, 20.49–20.50, 20.63, 20.65, 22.15
s 238(1) 13.43, 20.03
s 238(2) 20.04
s 238(3) 20.30, 20.49, 20.51, 20.54
s 238(4) 20.04, 20.32
s 238(5) 20.07
s 239 6.70, 13.23, 13.43, 20.10, 20.42, 20.49–20.50, 20.63, 22.15
s 239(1) 13.43, 20.03
s 239(3) 20.49, 20.51, 20.54
s 239(4) 20.40
s 239(5) 20.43

Insolvency Act 1986—*cont.*

s 239(6)	20.46
s 239(7)	20.47
s 240	13.12, 20.09–20.10, 20.42
s 240(1)	20.02, 20.10
s 240(1)(a)	20.11–20.12
s 240(1)(b)	20.12, 20.48
s 240(1)(c)	20.10
s 240(2)	20.13, 20.15
s 240(3)	20.10
s 241	11.27, 12.116, 14.52, 20.30, 20.52
s 241(1)	20.37, 20.51, 20.58
s 241(1)(a)	20.38, 20.52
s 241(1)(b)	20.53
s 241(1)(c)	20.54
s 241(1)(d)	20.55
s 241(1)(e)	20.56
s 241(1)(f)	20.57
s 241(1)(g)	20.58
s 241(2)	20.39, 20.49, 20.51–20.52
s 241(2)(a)–(b)	20.49
s 241(3)	20.49
s 241(3)(a)–(b)	20.49
s 241(4)	20.50
s 244	11.27, 11.29, 12.116, 20.59, 20.65, 22.15
s 244(1)	13.43, 20.03, 20.59–20.60
s 244(2)	20.59, 20.61
s 244(3)	20.61
s 244(4)	20.63, 20.65
s 244(4)(a)	20.63
s 244(4)(b)–(e)	20.64
s 244(5)	20.65
s 245	5.08, 11.27, 11.29, 12.116, 13.43, 14.52, 20.66, 22.15
s 245(1)	13.43. 20.03, 20.66
s 245(2)	20.66, 20.68–20.69
s 245(2)(a)	20.70–20.71, 20.73
s 245(2)(b)	20.72–20.73
s 245(3)	20.66
s 245(3)(a)–(b)	20.67
s 245(3)(c)	20.66
s 245(4)	20.67
s 245(6)	20.71
s 246	6.02, 6.16–6.17, 16.08
s 246(1)	13.43
s 246(2)	6.16
s 246(3)	16.09
s 247(2)	14.192, 15.19, 20.59, 21.11, 21.40, 21.86
s 248	19.70
s 248(b)	13.73, 13.111
s 248(b)(i)	20.54
s 248(d)(i)	19.70
s 249	15.101, 16.111, 20.16–20.17, 20.22, 22.15
s 250	17.04
s 251	5.10, 5.25, 13.38–13.39, 19.13, 20.69
ss 278–282	11.18
s 287(3)(a)	13.43
s 323	17.34
s 328(4)	19.59
s 386	5.06, 12.127, 19.17, 19.19
s 387	12.129
s 387(2)	19.23
s 387(3)	19.24
s 387(3)(a)	12.129, 13.92
s 387(3)(b)–(c)	12.129
s 387(4)	12.129, 19.24
ss 388–398	10.12
s 388	12.95
s 388(1)	10.04
s 388(1)(a)	11.12, 15.02
s 389	10.04, 12.134, 13.55
s 389(1)	11.12, 12.95, 15.115
s 390	11.12, 11.18, 12.134
s 390(1)	10.32, 11.13, 11.16, 15.03
s 390(2)	11.13
s 390(2)(b)	10.09, 11.13
s 390(3)	11.13, 15.16
s 390(4)	11.13, 11.17–11.18
s 390(4)(a)	10.33, 15.03
s 390(4)(b)	10.33, 15.02
s 390(4)(c)	10.33, 15.03
s 391	10.05, 11.13
s 391(1)	10.06
s 391(2)	10.06, 10.08
s 391(3)	10.06
s 391(4)–(5)	10.08
s 392	10.10–10.11
s 392(2)	10.09
s 392(3)–(4)	10.10
s 392(6)–(7)	10.10
s 393	10.05, 10.09, 10.16, 10.20, 11.13
s 393(1)–(2)	10.11
s 393(2)(b)	10.17
s 393(3)	10.11
s 393(4)–(5)	10.12
s 394	10.21

Insolvency Act 1986—*cont.*
s 394(1)   10.20
s 394(2)   10.20–10.21
s 394(3)   10.20
s 395   10.20–10.21
s 396   10.20
s 396(2)   10.21, 10.23
s 396(3)   10.21
s 397   10.24
ss 403–409   16.48–16.49
s 410   16.49
s 414   19.09
ss 423–425   21.89
s 423   3.04, 6.70, 12.77, 20.01,
  20.31, 20.33–20.35, 20.37,
  20.39, 20.49
s 423(1)   20.32
s 423(1)(a)–(b)   20.34
s 423(1)(c)   20.32
s 423(2)   20.36–20.37, 20.49
s 423(3)   20.33–20.34
s 423(4)   20.36
s 423(5)   20.34–20.35
s 424   12.77, 20.01, 20.03, 20.31,
  20.34–20.35
s 424(1)(a)–(c)   20.35
s 425   12.77, 20.01, 20.31,
  20.34–20.35, 20.49
s 425(1)   20.37
s 425(1)(a)   20.38
s 425(2)–(3)   20.39
s 430   11.16, 11.43, 12.14, 12.26,
  12.36, 12.90, 12.132, 12.134
s 435   15.65, 15.101, 20.17–20.18,
  20.21–20.23, 20.26–20.27
s 435(1)   20.18
s 435(2)   20.19, 20.22
s 435(3)–(5)   20.21–20.22
s 435(6)   20.25
s 435(7)   20.23
s 435(8)   20.19–20.20
s 435(9)   20.22
s 435(10)   20.25
s 435(10)(a)   20.29
s 435(10)(b)   20.28
s 435(11)   20.22
s 436   13.39, 20.06
Sch 1   5.04, 7.11, 11.34,
  12.69–12.72, 12.80, 12.127, 14.192
  para 1   12.75–12.76, 13.61
  para 2   12.78, 13.67

  para 3   12.83, 13.67
  para 4   12.73, 13.67
  para 5   12.73, 12.76, 13.67
  para 6   12.73, 13.67
  para 7   13.67
  paras 8–9   12.80, 13.67
  para 10   12.83, 13.67
  para 11   12.72, 13.67
  para 12   12.83, 13.61
  para 12   12.83, 13.61
  para 13   12.72
  para 14   12.81, 13.64
  paras 15–16   12.85, 13.64
  para 17   12.78, 13.67
  para 18   12.93, 13.67
  para 19   12.76, 13.64
  para 20   12.76, 13.67
  para 21   12.72, 12.115, 13.65,
  14.58, 14.64
  para 22   12.72, 13.64
  para 23   12.72, 13.58
Sch 4   15.12
  Part I   16.111–16.112, 22.01
  paras 1–2   15.104
  para 3   15.103
  para 4   15.99, 16.62, 16.111
  para 5   15.98, 16.111
  paras 6–7   15.93, 22.04
  para 8   15.91
  paras 9–10   15.93
  para 11   15.91
  para 12   15.73, 15.96, 15.99
  para 13   15.99, 22.01, 22.04
  para 20   16.111
Sch 6   5.06, 12.128–12.129, 19.17,
  19.19, 19.25
  para 13(1)(a)–(b)   19.32
  para 13(2)   19.32
  para 15(1)   19.32
  para 15A   19.38
Sch 7   10.24
  para 1(1)   10.25
  paras 2–3   10.25
  para 4(1)–(3)   10.26
Sch 10   11.16, 11.43, 12.14,
  12.26, 12.36, 12.90, 12.132,
  12.134, 21.42
Sch 13   5.34, 12.122, 19.13
Insurance Companies Act 1982   13.22,
  14.154
s 53   14.154

Insurance Companies Act 1982—*cont.*
s 54(1)   14.60, 14.95, 14.154
s 54(4)   14.154
s 57   14.155
Interpretation Act 1978   15.65
s 5   21.65
Sch 1   21.65, 21.71

Judgments Act 1838
s 12   6.57
s 17   19.76, 19.78–19.79
Judicature Act 1873
s 25(g)   4.03

Land Charges Act 1925
s 2(1), (4)   8.09
s 4(5)   8.12
Land Charges Act 1972   6.80,
          8.13, 8.33
s 2(4)(iii)   8.99
s 3(7), (8)   8.33
s 4(5)   8.105–8.107
s 6   6.52
s 6(1)   8.140
s 6(1)(b)   7.15, 8.33, 8.141
s 17(1)   8.105
Land Registration Act 1925   6.40,
          6.80, 8.34
s 25(2)   2.06
s 26   8.110
s 27(1)   7.07
s 29   8.108
s 30   8.19, 8.24
s 30(1)–(3)   8.24
s 49   8.110
s 49(1)(c)   8.34
s 52   8.109–8.110
s 54   7.15, 8.110
s 54(1)   8.34, 8.141
s 55   8.109–8.110
s 58(1)   8.34
s 59   6.52
s 59(1)   8.140
s 59(2)   8.34
s 106   8.109
s 106(1)   8.110
s 106(2)   2.06, 2.15
s 106(4)   8.110
Land Registration Act 1986
s 5(1), (5)   8.111
Landlord and Tenant Act 1709
ss 6–7   6.93

Landlord and Tenant Act 1954   6.61,
          18.28
Part II   6.93
s 23(1)   18.28
s 24(1)   6.93
Law of Distress (Amendment) Act
1888
s 7   6.101
Law of Distress Amendment Act 1908
          6.98, 8.96
s 1   6.99, 6.108, 8.95
s 2   6.107
s 4   6.100
s 4(1)   6.100
s 6   6.108
s 9   6.99
Law of Property Act 1925   7.31
s 1(1)–(2)   2.02
s 30   6.82
s 40   2.10, 2.12–2.13, 2.16
s 40(1)   2.14
s 40(2)   2.08
s 53(1)(c)   2.15, 4.12, 4.57
s 61(c)   11.35
s 85   2.02
s 85(1)   2.03, 2.05
s 85(2)   2.04
s 86   2.02
s 86(1)   2.04–2.05
s 87(1)   2.03, 2.05, 7.07
s 88(1)   7.20
s 88(2)   7.31
s 89(1)   7.20
s 89(2)   7.31
s 90   7.20
s 90(1)   7.32
s 91   7.32
s 91(2)   7.20
s 94   8.19
s 94(1)   8.19
s 94(1)(b)   8.21
s 94(1)(c)   8.23, 8.131
s 94(2)   8.21–8.22
s 95(4)   7.07
s 97   8.105–8.107
s 99   6.94
s 101   2.15, 4.57, 7.12, 7.20, 11.33
s 101(1)   2.12, 4.32, 7.20, 7.23
s 101(1)(iii)   7.13, 7.15
s 103   4.32, 7.20
s 104(2)   7.21, 7.26
s 104(3)   7.21

Law of Property Act 1925—*cont.*
s 105   7.28
s 107(1)   4.57
s 107(2)   7.28
s 109   5.04, 7.12
s 109(1)   7.13
s 109(2)   7.12
s 109(4)–(5)   7.13
s 109(8)   7.14
s 121   6.95
s 136   4.03, 4.05–4.06, 4.10–4.12,
     4.14–4.15, 4.17, 4.22–4.23, 4.34,
       4.56–4.57, 7.10, 8.116, 9.67
s 136(2)   4.17
s 137   8.99, 9.67
s 137(1)   4.08, 8.111, 8.113
s 137(2)–(3)   8.117
s 137(8)   8.113
s 146   18.24
s 146(2)   18.27
s 146(9)–(10)   18.25
s 172   3.04, 20.01, 20.31
s 198   8.11, 8.13
s 198(1)   8.12
s 199   8.11–8.12
s 199(1)(ii)(a)   8.14
s 199(1)(ii)(b)   8.18
s 205(1)(xvi)   7.15
Law of Property (Miscellaneous
  Provisions) Act 1989
s 2   2.10, 2.12–2.14, 2.16
s 2(5)   2.10
Limitation Act 1980   16.80, 19.147
s 8(1)   17.20
s 19   6.96
s 24(1)   6.51
Limitation of Actions and Costs Act
  1842
s 2   6.105
Local Government (Finance) Act 1988
Sch 4 para 7   6.121
Sch 9 para 3(2)   6.121

Magistrates' Courts Act 1980   6.92,
                   6.124
s 76   6.122
s 78   6.123
s 125(2)   6.123
s 148   6.123
Marine Insurance Act 1906
ss 50–51   4.15
s 53(2)   6.28

Matrimonial Causes Act 1973
s 16   20.19
Mental Health Act 1983   15.03, 16.33
Part VII   10.33, 11.13, 11.18
Merchant Shipping Act 1894   3.23
s 31(1)–(2)   3.18
s 33   8.131
s 34   3.19, 7.09, 8.131
s 35   7.19
ss 56–57   3.22, 8.130
s 544(2)   8.134
Sch 1 Form B   3.18
Merchant Shipping Act 1970
s 18   6.48
Merchant Shipping Act 1988
s 8   3.21
ss 13–23   3.20
Sch 2 para 5   7.19
Sch 3   3.20
  para 2(1)–(2)   3.20
  para 2(3)–(4)   3.21
  para 3   3.21, 8.131
  paras 4–6   3.21
  para 8   3.21

Partnership Act 1890
s 31   4.34
s 33   4.34
Patents Act 1949   4.59
Patents Act 1977   4.59
s 30(1)–(2)   4.59
s 30(4)   4.59
s 30(4)(a)   4.60
s 30(6)   4.59
s 32(3)   4.61, 8.119
s 33   8.119, 8.121
s 33(1)   8.120
s 33(1)(b)–(c)   8.120
s 33(2)–(3)   8.41
s 33(3)(b)–(c)   4.61
s 33(4)   8.120
s 36(3)   4.59
s 67(1)   4.60
s 127(3)   4.59
s 130(1)   4.61
Sch 2 para 1   4.59
Policies of Assurance Act 1867   4.17
ss 1–2   4.17
s 3   4.17, 8.127
ss 4–5   4.17
Sch   4.17

Powers of Criminal Courts Act 1973
s 32(1),(3),(5)   6.122

Railway Rolling Stock Protection Act 1872
s 1–3   6.98
Registered Designs Act 1949   4.66
s 19   4.65
s 19(4)   4.66, 8.124
s 19(5)   4.65
Rent Act 1977
s 147   6.92, 6.101
Rent (Agriculture) Act 1976
s 8   6.92, 6.101
Reserve Forces (Safeguard of Employment) Act 1985   19.32

Sale of Goods Act 1893   9.07
Sale of Goods Act 1979   6.31, 6.37, 6.39, 9.07
s 19(1)   9.07
ss 21–22   9.25
s 24   8.10
s 25(1)   8.10, 9.23–9.24, 9.64
s 25(2)   8.30
s 27   15.93
s 38(1)   6.31
s 39(2)   6.33
s 41(1)–(2)   6.32
ss 42–43   6.32
s 44   6.33
s 45(1), (3)–(4)   6.33
s 46   6.33
s 47(1)–(2)   6.34
s 48(1)   6.34–6.36
s 48(2)   6.35
s 48(3)–(4)   6.35–6.36
s 61(4)   6.32
Social Security Act 1975   19.30
Social Security (Pensions) Act 1975
Sch 3   19.17, 19.31
Solicitors Act 1974
s 73   6.23
Stock Transfer Act 1963   4.25
Sch 1   4.25

Stock Transfer Act 1982   4.25
Supreme Court Act 1981   8.138
s 37   6.85, 7.15, 16.11
s 37(1)   6.85
s 40(1), (3)   6.69
s 40A   6.69
s 61(1)   14.53
s 138   6.56, 8.46, 8.138
Sch 1 para 1   14.53
Sch 7   8.46

Taxes Management Act 1970
s 61   6.113
s 61(2)–(3), (5)   6.114
Theft Act 1968   21.66
Third Parties (Rights Against Insurers) Act 1930   18.49
s 1(1)   18.49
s 2   18.50
Tort (Interference with Goods) Act 1977
s 1(a)–(b)   6.45
s 4   6.12
Trade Marks Act 1938
s 22(1)–(3)   4.67
s 22(4)–(6)   4.68
s 22(7)   4.67
s 24   4.67, 8.123
s 25(1)   4.69
s 64(1)   4.69
s 64(2)   4.67, 4.69, 8.123
Trade Marks (Amendment) Act 1984
s 1(4)   4.68
Trustee Act 1925   15.58

Unfair Contract Terms Act 1977 12.66

Value Added Tax Act 1983   12.133, 19.27
s 38   6.110
Sch 7 para 4   6.110
Sch 17 para 6(4)(a)   6.110

Water Act 1945
s 35   6.98
s 59(1)   6.98

Table of Statutory Instruments

Attachment of Debts (Expenses)
Order 1983, SI 1983 no 1621 6.69

Banks (Administration Proceedings)
Order 1989, SI 1989 no 1276
                                13.22

Civil Courts Amendment Orders 1984,
SI 1984 nos 297, 1075   14.51
Civil Courts Order 1983, SI 1983
no 713   14.51
Companies (Disqualification Orders)
Regulations 1986, SI 1986
no 2067   21.56
Companies (Mergers and Divisions)
Regulations 1977, SI 1987
no 1991   22.69
Companies (Tables A to F)
Regulations 1985, SI 1985 no 805
Table A Art 38   14.10
       Art 53   14.11, 14.21
       Art 70   1.14, 13.08, 15.140
Companies (Winding-Up) Rules 1949
SI 1949 No 330
r 134   14.212

Distress for Rates Order 1979, SI 1979
no 1038   6.119
Distress for Rates Order 1980, SI 1980
no 2013   6.119
Distress for Rent Rules 1953, SI 1953
no 1702
r 22   6.103
App 2 Form 5   6.103
       Form 6   6.105

Financial Services Act 1986
(Delegation) Order 1987, SI 1987
no 942   14.95, 14.157

Insolvency Amendment Regulations
1987, SI 1987 no 1959   16.49
Insolvency Amendment Rules 1987,
SI 1987 no 1919   13.12,
    13.47–13.48, 13.103, 13.108,
    13.112, 13.114, 13.124, 13.128,
    14.19, 14.26–14.27, 14.207,
    14.214, 15.18, 15.32, 15.108,
    15.114, 15.143, 16.97,
    16.114, 19.40, 21.47, 22.37
Insolvency (European Coal and Steel
Community Levy Debts)
Regulations 1987, SI 1987
no 2093   19.38
Insolvency Fees Order 1986, SI 1986
no 2030   19.09
Insolvency of Employer (Excluded
Classes) Regulations 1983,
SI 1983 no 624   19.33
Insolvency Practice Amendment
Regulations 1986, SI 1986
no 2247   10.34
Insolvency Practitioners (Recognised
Professional Bodies) Order 1986,
SI 1986 no 1764   10.07
Insolvency Practitioners Regulations
1986, SI 1986 no 1995
reg 4   15.61
reg 4(1)(a)–(b)   10.14
reg 4(1)(d)–(e)   10.15
reg 4(1)(f)   10.14
reg 4(2)   10.13
reg 5   10.16
reg 6   10.17
reg 6(2)   10.17
reg 6(3)(a)–(b)   10.18
reg 6(4)   10.19
reg 6(6)–(7)   10.17
reg 7   10.10
reg 8   10.11
reg 10(1)(a)–(c)   10.34
reg 10(2)   10.34

Insolvency Practitioners Regulations		reg 32	16.55
1986, SI 1986 no 1925—*cont.*		reg 33	16.59
regs 11–12	10.35	reg 35	16.60
reg 14	10.36	Insolvency Rules 1986, SI 1986	
reg 15	10.37	no 1925	14.31, 14.194,
reg 16(1)–(2)	10.38		18.53–18.54
regs 17–18	10.38	r 1.2	22.13
Sch 1 Part I	10.16	r 1.3(1)	22.13
Sch 2 Part I	10.34	r 1.3(2)	22.15
Sch 3	10.34, 10.37	r 1.3(3)	22.17
Insolvency Practitioners' Tribunal		r 1.4	22.17
(Conduct of Investigations) Rules		r 1.5(1)–(2)	22.19
1986, SI 1986 no 952	10.24	r 1.5(3)	22.20
r 2(1)	10.22	r 1.5(4)	22.18
r 2(2)	10.22, 10.27	r 1.6(1)–(3)	22.21
rr 3–4	10.27	r 1.7(1)–(4)	22.18
rr 5–7	10.28	r 1.8	22.22
r 8	10.29	r 1.9(1)	22.24
r 9	10.27	r 1.9(2)	22.24–22.25
rr 10–11	10.29	r 1.9(3)	22.25
rr 13–14	10.29	r 1.10(1)–(2)	22.23
r 15	10.30	r 1.11	22.27
Insolvency Regulations 1986, SI 1986		r 1.12(1)–(6)	22.23
no 1994	10.36, 19.09	r 1.12(7)	22.23–22.55
reg 2(1)	16.49	r 1.13	22.28
reg 4(1)–(4)	16.49	r 1.14(1)–(2)	22.30
reg 6(1)	16.49	r 1.15	22.30
reg 6(2)–(6)	16.50	r 1.16(1)–(2)	22.31
reg 7	16.50	r 1.17(1)–(3)	22.32
reg 8	16.53	r 1.17(5)–(9)	22.33
reg 9(1)–(2)	16.54	r 1.18(1)–(3)	22.36
reg 10	16.54, 16.57	r 1.19(1)–(3)	22.34
reg 10A	16.54	r 1.19(4)–(7)	22.35
reg 11	16.50, 16.52	r 1.20(1)	22.37
reg 12	16.54	r 1.20(2)–(3)	22.36
reg 12(1)–(7)	16.55	r 1.21(1)–(6)	22.38
reg 13	16.54	r 1.22(1)–(4)	22.39
reg 14	16.55	r 1.23(1)–(6)	22.49
regs 16–17	16.59	r 1.24(1)	22.40
reg 18(1)–(7)	16.61	r 1.24(4)–(5)	22.40
reg 18(8)	16.60–16.61	r 1.25(2)–(5)	22.48
reg 18(9)	16.61	r 1.26(1)	22.52
regs 19–22	15.151	r 1.26(2)–(4)	22.53
reg 24	16.51	r 1.26(5)(a)–(b)	22.53
reg 25	16.52	r 1.27	22.54
reg 26	16.53	r 1.27(1)–(3)	22.54
reg 27	16.56	r 1.28	22.15
reg 28	16.57	r 1.29	22.55
reg 29	16.52	r 2.1	13.09
reg 30	16.56	r 2.1(2)	13.08–13.09
reg 31(1)–(2)	16.58	r 2.1(4)	13.09

Insolvency Rules 1986, SI 1986
  no 1925—*cont.*

r 2.2(1)–(3)	13.10
r 2.3(1)–(6)	13.11
r 2.4(1)	13.12
r 2.4(3)	13.08
r 2.4(4)–(6)	13.12
r 2.5(1)–(4)	13.12
r 2.6(1)–(2)	13.12
r 2.6A	13.12
r 2.7	13.12
r 2.7(1)	13.12
r 2.7(3)–(4)	13.12
r 2.8	13.12
r 2.9(1)–(2)	13.12
r 2.10	13.47
r 2.10(5)	13.47
r 2.11	13.48
r 2.12	13.51
r 2.12(1)–(6)	13.51
r 2.13	13.53
r 2.14(1)–(5)	13.52
r 2.14(7)	13.52
r 2.15(1)–(3)	13.52
r 2.16	13.103–13.104
r 2.17	13.104, 13.115
r 2.18(1)–(3)	13.107
r 2.18(4)	13.108, 13.113
r 2.19	13.115
r 2.19(2)–(6)	13.108
r 2.19(7)	13.108, 13.114
r 2.20	13.108
r 2.21(1)–(6)	13.119
r 2.22(1)–(5)	13.109
r 2.23(1)–(4)	13.110
r 2.23(6)	13.110
rr 2.24–2.26	13.111
r 2.27(2)	13.111
r 2.28(1), (1A)	13.112
r 2.28(2)–(3)	13.112
r 2.29	13.114, 13.115
r 2.30	13.115
r 2.30(1)	13.114
r 2.31	13.105
r 2.32(1)–(3)	13.122
r 2.33(1)–(5)	13.122
r 2.34(1)	13.121
r 2.34(2)–(4)	13.123
rr 2.35–2.36	13.123
r 2.37(1)–(6)	13.123
r 2.38	13.125
r 2.39(1)(a)–(c)	13.125
r 2.40	13.125
r 2.41(2)–(3)	13.126
r 2.42	13.123
r 2.43(1)–(5)	13.123
r 2.44(1)–(3)	13.124
r 2.45	13.127
rr 2.46–2.46A	13.128
r 2.47(1)–(4)	13.94
r 2.47(5)–(6)	13.95
r 2.47(7)	13.95–13.96
r 2.48	13.95
r 2.49(1)–(4)	13.97
r 2.50(1)–(5)	13.98
r 2.51(2)	13.74
r 2.51(3)	13.79
r 2.52(1)–(4)	13.88
r 2.53(1)–(3)	13.89
r 2.54	13.89
r 2.55	13.55, 13.89
r 2.58(4) (7)	14.211
r 3.1	11.42
r 3.1(1)	11.37
r 3.1(2)–(5)	11.38, 11.42
r 3.2	11.47
r 3.2(2)(a)–(c)	11.47
r 3.2(2)(d)–(g)	11.48
r 3.2(3)	11.50, 12.33
r 3.2(4)	11.50
r 3.3(1)–(3)	12.14
r 3.3(4)	12.16
r 3.4(1)	12.16
r 3.4(2)	12.19, 12.36
r 3.4(3)	12.19
r 3.4(4)	12.16
r 3.4(5)–(6)	12.19
r 3.5	12.18, 12.36, 12.39
r 3.5(1)	12.18
r 3.5(2)	12.18, 12.39
r 3.5(3)	12.18, 12.36
r 3.6(1)	12.21
r 3.6(2)	12.22
r 3.6(3)	12.22, 12.23
r 3.6(4)	12.23
r 3.6(5)–(6)	12.24
r 3.7	12.17
r 3.7(1)–(3)	12.17
r 3.8(1)	12.33
r 3.8(2)	12.34
r 3.8(3)–(4)	12.36
r 3.16(1)–(3)	12.45

Insolvency Rules 1986, SI 1986
no 1925—*cont.*

r 3.17(1)	12.48	r 4.10	14.98
r 3.17(2)	12.45	r 4.11(1)–(3)	14.101
r 3.17(3)–(5)	12.48	r 4.11(5)	14.101
r 3.18(1)	12.41	r 4.12	14.100, 14.160
r 3.18(2)–(3)	12.51	r 4.12(3)	14.100
r 3.18(4)	12.51, 12.53	r 4.12(b)	14.100, 14.160
r 3.19	12.51	r 4.13	14.98
r 3.19(1)–(2)	12.52	r 4.14	14.102
r 3.20	12.45, 12.53	rr 4.16–4.17	14.161
r 3.21(1)	12.45–12.46	r 4.18(1)–(2)	14.160
r 3.21(2)–(3)	12.46	r 4.19	14.129, 14.162
r 3.21(4)	12.45, 12.47	r 4.19	14.129, 14.162
r 3.21(5)	12.47	r 4.20(1)	14.173, 15.22
r 3.21(6)	12.46	r 4.20(3)	14.173
r 3.22	12.57	r 4.21(1)–(3)	14.173
r 3.23(1)	12.58	r 4.25(1)	15.04
r 3.24	12.59	r 4.25(2)	15.05
r 3.25(2)–(3)	12.60	r 4.25(3)–(4)	15.06
r 3.26(1)–(3)	12.53	r 4.26(1)	15.06, 15.13
r 3.27(1)–(2)	12.54	r 4.26(2)–(3)	15.06
r 3.27(3)–(5)	12.55	r 4.27	15.15, 15.17
r 3.28(1)–(3)	12.43	rr 4.28–4.29	15.16
r 3.29	12.56	r 4.30(1)–(2)	15.17
r 3.30(1)–(2)	12.50	r 4.30(3)	14.172, 15.18
r 3.30A	12.49	r 4.30(3A)	15.18
r 3.31(2)–(4)	12.90	r 4.31	15.18
r 3.32	12.25	r 4.31(1)	15.18
r 3.32(1)–(2)	12.25, 12.133	r 4.32	16.25
r 3.32(3)–(4)	12.26, 12.133	r 4.33	14.25, 16.25
r 3.33	12.137	r 4.34(2)–(4)	14.27
r 3.33(1)–(3)	12.137	r 4.34A	14.27
r 3.34	12.138	r 4.37	19.09
r 3.35(1)	12.120, 12.132	r 4.41	19.09
r 3.35(2)	12.132	r 4.43	16.115
r 3.36(1)	12.61	rr 4.45–4.47	14.205, 16.115
r 3.37(1)–(2)	12.62	r 4.48	14.205
r 3.37(3)	12.61	rr 4.49–4.49A	16.114
r 3.38(1)	12.62, 12.133	r 4.50(1)–(5)	14.201
r 3.38(2)	12.61, 12.133	r 4.50(6)	14.202
r 4.1(1)	15.140	r 4.51(2)	14.22, 14. 206
r 4.3	14.101	r 4.52(1)	14.29
r 4.4	14.127	r 4.52(1)(e)	14.30
r 4.4(2)–(3)	14.125	r 4.52(2)–(3)	14.30
r 4.5	14.127	r 4.53	14.29
r 4.5(1)–(2)	14.125	r 4.53A	14.19
r 4.6	14.127	r 4.53B	14.26
r 4.6(1)–(2)	14.125	rr 4.54–4.71	15.77
r 4.7(2)–(6)	14.98	r 4.54	14.206, 15.92
rr 4.8–4.9	14.102	r 4.54(1)	14.197, 14.203, 15.128
		r 4.54(2)–(3)	14.203
		r 4.54(4)	14.203, 15.77

Insolvency Rules 1986, SI 1986
  no 1925—*cont.*
r 4.54(6)   14.203
rr 4.55–4.56   14.207
r 4.56(1)   14.207
r 4.57   14.202, 15.129
r 4.57(1)–(3)   14.202, 15.128
r 4.57(4)   14.202
r 4.58(2)–(3)   14.210
r 4.59   14.206
r 4.60(1)–(2)   14.207
r 4.60(3)   14.216
r 4.61(1)–(3)   14.224
r 4.61(4)   14.224, 19.05, 19.105
r 4.62(3)–(4)   14.224
r 4.63   15.130
r 4.63(1) 14.212, 14.222, 15.44–15.45
r 4.63(2)(a)–(c)   14.222, 15.45
r 4.63(2A)   14.222
r 4.63(3)–(4)   14.222
r 4.64   14.214–14.215
r 4.65(2)–(3)   14.208
r 4.65(4)–(7)   14.209
r 4.67(1)   14.212
r 4.67(2)   14.212, 19.46
r 4.67(3)–(4)   14.212
r 4.67(5)   14.213
r 4.68   14.212
r 4.69   14.213
r 4.70(1)–(6)   14.213
r 4.71(1)–(4)   14.223
r 4.73(1)–(5)   19.46
r 4.73(6)   19.49
r 4.73(7)   19.50
r 4.74   19.48
r 4.75(1)   19.48
r 4.75(1)(g)   19.62
r 4.75(2)–(3)   19.48
r 4.76   19.49
r 4.78   19.50–19.51
rr 4.79–4.81   19.52
r 4.82   19.53
r 4.83   19.58
r 4.83(1)   19.53
r 4.83(2)–(4)   19.54
r 4.83(6)   19.54
r 4.84   19.55
r 4.85(1)   19.55
r 4.86   18.58, 19.51, 19.58
r 4.87   19.61
r 4.88(1)   19.62

r 4.88(2)   19.63
r 4.89   19.71
r 4.90   18.54, 18.64
r 4.90(1)   18.54, 18.56, 18.59, 18.61
r 4.90(2)   18.58, 18.67–18.68
r 4.90(3)   18.60, 18.67–18.68
r 4.90(4)   18.67
r 4.91   19.72
r 4.92(1)–(2)   19.80
r 4.93(1)   19.41, 19.77
r 4.93(2)   19.77
r 4.93(3)   19.78
r 4.93(4)–(5)   19.79
r 4.93(6)   19.78–19.79
r 4.94   19.59, 19.82
r 4.95(2)   19.65–19.66
r 4.96   6.20
r 4.96(1)   19.63
r 4.96(2)   19.64
r 4.97(1)–(3)   19.66
r 4.97(4)   19.67
r 4.98   19.68
r 4.99   19.69
r 4.100   15.32
r 4.101A   14.200, 15.41–15.42
r 4.102   15.122
r 4.102(2)   15.32
r 4.102(3)   15.33
r 4.102(4)   15.32
r 4.102(5)–(6)   15.33
r 4.103   15.122
r 4.104   15.34
r 4.106   15.34
r 4.106(1)–(3)   15.48
r 4.107(1)–(5)   15.36
r 4.107(6)–(8)   15.37
r 4.108   15.113
r 4.108(1)–(3)   15.108
r 4.108(4)   15.106 15.113
r 4.108(5)   15.107, 15.113
r 4.108(6)   15.108
r 4.109(2)–(5)   15.110
r 4.109(6)   15.110, 15.139
r 4.110(2)–(3)   15.109
r 4.111   15.113
r 4.111(1)   15.111, 15.113
r 4.111(2)–(4)   15.111
r 4.111(5)   15.112
r 4.112   15.109, 15.130
r 4.112(1)–(5)   15.130
r 4.113   15.127

Insolvency Rules 1986, SI 1986		r 4.144(2)	15.136
no 1925—*cont.*		r 4.144(3)	15.136–15.137
r 4.113(3)	14.208	r 4.144(4)	15.136
r 4.114	15.127	r 4.144(5)	15.137
r 4.114(1)	15.125	r 4.145(1)–(2)	15.132
r 4.114(2)	15.127	r 4.146	15.136
r 4.114(3)	14.208, 15.127	r 4.146(2)	15.115
r 4.115	15.127, 15.130	r 4.146(3)	15.137
r 4.116	15.130	r 4.147	15.116, 15.137
r 4.117	15.127, 15.136	r 4.148	15.134
r 4.118	15.127	r 4.149	15.66–15.67, 18.75
r 4.119	15.121	r 4.149(1)	15.64–15.65
r 4.119(2)	15.118, 15.122	r 4.149(2)–(3)	18.75
r 4.119(4)–(6)	15.122	r 4.150(1)–(2)	15.39
r 4.120	15.121	r 4.151(6)	16.90
r 4.120(2)	15.122	r 4.152(1)	16.90
r 4.120(4)–(6)	15.122	r 4.152(2)	16.86
r 4.121	15.108	r 4.152(3)	16.91
r 4.121(1)–(2)	15.139	r 4.153	16.93
r 4.121(3)	15.137, 15.139	r 4.153(2)–(8)	16.93
r 4.122	15.108, 15.137	r 4.154	16.90, 16.94, 16.96
r 4.122(1)–(3)	15.136	r 4.155(1)	16.108
r 4.122(3)(b)	15.137	r 4.155(2)	16.108, 16.113
r 4.123(1)–(3)	15.131	r 4.155(3)–(5)	16.110
r 4.124(1)–(3)	15.138	r 4.156	16.94
r 4.126	15.116	r 4.156(3)	16.94
r 4.126(3)	15.137	rr 4.157–4.158	16.94
rr 4.127–4.131	15.141, 16.112	r 4.159	16.91
r 4.127(1)–(3)	15.141	r 4.159(1)–(2)	16.91, 16.95
r 4.127(4)	15.142	r 4.159(3)–(5)	16.95
r 4.127(5)–(6)	15.141	r 4.160	16.98
r 4.128(1)	19.68	r 4.161(1)(a)–(b)	16.98
r 4.128(2)	13.95, 15.143	r 4.161(2)–(3)	16.98
r 4.128(3)	13.96, 15.62, 15.143	r 4.162	16.98
r 4.129	15.143	r 4.163(2)–(5)	16.99
r 4.130(1)–(4)	15.143	r 4.164(2)–(6)	16.99
r 4.132(1)–(4)	15.132	rr 4.165–4.166	16.96
r 4.133(1)–(2)	15.132	r 4.167	16.53
r 4.134(2)	15.115	r 4.167(1)–(7)	16.97
r 4.135(2)	15.115	r 4.168(1)–(2)	16.108
r 4.136	15.137	r 4.169	16.100, 19.09
r 4.137(1)–(2)	15.135	r 4.170(1)	16.101
r 4.138(1)–(2)	15.134	r 4.170(2)	16.102
rr 4.139–4.150	15.140	r 4.170(3)(a)	16.105
r 4.142(1)–(2)	15.114	r 4.170(3)(b)	16.104
r 4.142(3)	15.106	r 4.170(3)(c)	16.105
r 4.142(4)	15.107	r 4.170(4)	16.105
r 4.142(4A)	15.114	r 4.170(5)	16.106
r 4.142(5)	15.114	r 4.170(6)–(7)	16.107
r 4.143(2)	15.122	r 4.171	16.96
r 4.143(4)–(5)	15.122	r 4.171(1)–(3)	16.89

Insolvency Rules 1986, SI 1986
  no 1925—*cont.*

r 4.171(5)–(8)	16.89
r 4.172(1)	16.113
r 4.172(2)	15.101, 16.113
r 4.172A	16.97
rr 4.173–4.178	16.113
r 4.179(1)–(2)	15.77
r 4.180(1)–(3)	19.84
r 4.181	19.85
r 4.182(1)	19.86
r 4.182(2)	19.87
r 4.182(3)	19.88
r 4.182A(1)	19.84
r 4.182A(4)	19.87
r 4.182A(5)	19.84
r 4.183	18.73, 19.89
r 4.184	16.112
r 4.184(1)–(2)	15.102, 16.112
r 4.185	15.77, 16.03, 16.65
r 4.186(1)–(2)	19.92
r 4.186(3)–(4)	19.98
r 4.187	18.07
r 4.188	18.07
r 4.188(2)–(5)	18.07
rr 4.189–4.190	18.07
r 4.191	18.08
rr 4.192–4.193	18.09
r 4.194(1)	18.15
r 4.194(3)–(6)	18.15
r 4.194(7)	18.16
r 4.195	15.77, 15.91, 17.13
rr 4.196–4.201	15.77
r 4.196	15.77, 17.15
r 4.196(1)	15.91
r 4.197(1)–(2)	17.15
r 4.198(1)–(2)	17.16
r 4.198(3)–(4)	17.17
rr 4.199–4.201	17.17
r 4.202	15.77, 15.91, 15.100, 17.25
r 4.203	15.91, 17.29
r 4.203(1)–(3)	15.00
r 4.204	15.91, 15.100, 17.29
r 4.205	17.29
r 4.205(2)	16.63, 17.26
r 4.206(3)	15.22
r 4.206(5)	15.24
r 4.206(6)	15.23
r 4.207	15.23
r 4.207(5)–(6)	15.23
rr 4.208–4.209	15.25
r 4.210(1)–(2)	15.22
r 4.211(1)	16.29
r 4.211(2)(a)	16.27
r 4.211(3)	16.29
r 4.211(4)	16.27
r 4.212	16.29
r 4.213(1)–(6)	16.28
r 4.214(1)–(4)	16.33
r 4.215(1)–(4)	16.30
r 4.215(5)	16.30, 16.83
r 4.215(6)	16.31
r 4.216(1)–(3)	16.31
r 4.217(1)	16.28
r 4.217(2)	16.31
r 4.218	19.09
r 4.218(1)	19.07
r 4.218(1)(c)(ii)	15.15
r 4.218(1)(e)	15.23
r 4.218(1)(o)	19.09
r 4.218(1)(p)	19.09
r 4.218(2)	19.09
r 4.219	19.09
r 4.220(1)	19.07
r 4.220(2)	19.10
r 4.221	19.108
r 4.222(1)–(2)	19.108
r 4.223(2)	16.60
rr 4.224–4.225	19.127, 19.128
r 4.227	21.47
r 4.228	21.49
r 4.228(1)–(4)	21.49
r 4.229	21.47
r 4.230	21.50
r 6.5(4)	14.126
r 7	21.24
rr 7.1–7.10	13.74
r 7.4(6)	15.07
r 7.9(3)	16.83
r 7.11	14.54, 14.56
r 7.11(2)	14.56
r 7.12	14.56
r 7.13(1)–(3)	14.56
r 7.20(1)(c)	16.06
r 7.20(2)(d)	16.06
r 7.20(3)	16.06
r 7.21(2)	16.19
rr 7.23–7.24	16.19
r 7.34	19.09
r 7.47	14.177
r 7.55	14.101
r 8	12.47

Insolvency Rules 1986, SI 1986	
no 1925—*cont.*	
rr 8.1–8.7	12.45
r 8.1(1)–(2)	14.214
r 8.1(3)–(5)	14.215
r 8.1(6)	14.214
r 8.2(1)–(3)	14.216
r 8.3(1)–(3)	14.217
r 8.3(4)–(6)	14.218
rr 8.4–8.5	14.219
r 8.6	14.220
r 8.7	14.221
r 9.2(1)–(2)	12.102, 16.12
r 9.2(3)	12.104, 16.12
r 9.2(3)(c)	12.103
r 9.2(4)	12.102, 12.104, 16.12
r 9.3(1)	16.17
r 9.3(2)–(3)	12.104, 16.17
r 9.3(3)(a)	12.103
r 9.3(4)–(5)	12.104, 16.17
r 9.4(1)–(2)	12.106, 16.20
r 9.4(3)	16.20
r 9.4(4)	12.106, 16.20
r 9.4(5)	12.105, 16.20
r 9.4(6)	12.108, 16.21
r 9.4(7)	12.108, 16.83
r 9.5	16.21
r 9.5(1)–(3)	12.108
r 9.6(1)	12.111, 16.22
r 9.6(2)	16.22
r 9.6(2)(a)–(b)	12.111
r 9.6(3)	12.111, 16.22
r 9.6(4)	12.111
rr 11.2–11.3	19.94
r 11.4	19.95
r 11.5(1)–(2)	19.95
r 11.6(1)–(3)	19.96
r 11.6(4)–(5)	19.97
r 11.7	19.97
r 11.8(1)–(3)	19.87
r 11.9(2)–(3)	19.90
r 11.10	19.90
r 11.11	19.91
r 11.12	19.98
r 11.13	19.59
r 11.13(2)–(3)	19.59
r 12.3	19.40
r 12.3(2)	19.40
r 12.3(2A)(a)–(c)	19.40
r 12.3(3)	19.40, 19.44
r 12.4(1)–(2)	11.49
r 12.4A	12.45

r 12.5	14.223
r 12.7	14.97
r 12.8	15.16
r 12.9	13.12
r 12.10	14.204
r 12.13(1)–(3)	12.96
r 12.16	14.204, 22.31
rr 12.17–12.18	14.205
r 12.18(1)–(2)	12.97
r 12.21	11.16, 12.97, 12.133
r 13.3	11.47
r 13.5	11.36
r 13.12(1)–(2)	19.41
r 13.12(3)–(4)	19.43
Sch 5	11.16, 12.97, 12.133
App Form 2.9	13.48, 13.51
Form 2.11	13.108
Form 4.1	14.125
Form 4.2	14.97
Form 4.7	14.102
Form 4.9	14.161
Form 4.17	14.25, 16.25
Forms 4.18–4.19	14.25
Form 4.54	18.08
Form 8.1	14.214
Form 8.2	13.108, 14.214
Forms 8.3–8.5	14.214
Insolvent Companies (Disqualification of Unfit Directors) Proceedings Rules 1986, SI 1986 no 612	21.62
rr 2–3	21.62
rr 4–5	21.63
r 6(1)–(2)	21.63
r 7	21.63
r 8	21.64
r 9	21.63
Insolvent Companies (Reports on Conduct of Directors) No 2 Rules 1986, SI 1986 no 2134	21.79
r 3	21.79, 21.82
r 4	21.82
r 4(1)	21.79
r 4(2)	21.79, 21.81
r 4(4)	21.82
r 4(5)	21.79–21.80, 21.82
r 4(7)	21.81
r 5	21.83
Land Registration (Official Searches) Rules 1981, SI 1981 no 1135	
r 2	8.108

Land Registration Rules 1925,
  SR & O 1925 no 1093
  r 139   2.06
  r 140   8.108
  r 225   8.110
  Sch Form 45   2.06

Magistrates' Courts Amendment
  Rules 1983, SI 1983 no 553   6.123
Magistrates' Courts Rules 1981,
  SI 1981 no 552
  r 53   6.122
  r 54   6.123
  r 95   6.123
Merchant Shipping Regulations 1988,
  SI 1988 no 1926   3.20
Mortgaging of Aircraft Order 1972,
  SI 1972 no 1268   3.28
  Art 2(2)   3.28
  Art 4(4)–(5)   8.135
  Art 14(1)–(2)   8.135
  Art 16(1)   3.28, 7.09
  Art 16(2)   3.28

Rules of the Supreme Court 1965,
  SI 1965 no 1776 as amended
  Ord 1 r 3   6.64
  Ord 3 r 6   6.51
  Ord 14   6.91
  Ord 15 r 6   19.141
  Ord 22   6.91, 18.32
  Ord 23   6.91
  Ord 45 r 3   6.61
    r 3(2)   6.60
    r 5(1)(i)   6.64

  r 7(1)–(3)   6.51
  r 7(4)(a)   6.64
  r 12   6.62
  Ord 46 r 2(1)(a)   6.51
  Ord 48 r 1   6.54
  Ord 49   8.46
    r 1   6.69
    r 1(1)   6.67, 8.139
    r 4(1)   6.72
    r 9(1)   6.67
  Ord 50 r1(2)   6.76
    r 9A   6.81
    r 10   6.83, 8.118
    rr 11–12   6.84, 8.118, 8.126
    rr 13–15   6.84, 8.118
  Ord 51 r 1   6.85
    r 2   6.87
  Ord 77 r 6   18.63
  Ord 113 r 7(1)   6.60

Transfer of Undertakings (Protection
  of Employment) Regulations
  1981, SI 1981 no 1794   12.86
  reg 4   12.87
  reg 8   12.86

Value Added Tax (Bad Debt Relief)
  Regulations 1978, SI 1978
  no 1129   19.29
Value Added Tax (General)
  Regulations 1980, SI 1980
  no 1536
  reg 58   6.110
  reg 58(2)   6.110
  reg 58(3)–(4)   6.111

Introduction

This book provides an account of those legal rules which affect insolvent companies and those concerned with them. It was inspired by the changes introduced by the reform of insolvency law in 1985 but its lengthy gestation period has provided an opportunity to take account of developments up to 31st March 1989 insofar as they were available in the materials to which the authors had access. All aspects of corporate insolvency are addressed to provide a convenient picture of the issues and procedures that arise or are available. The basic rules governing security interests in property belonging to an insolvent company are outlined in addition to the procedures available under the Insolvency Act 1986. Administrative receivership, liquidation, administration and voluntary arrangements are all included in the interest of providing a comprehensive account of the law in this field. The book is organised as follows.

Chapters 1 to 9 deal primarily with the forms of real security available to those lending to a company. By this is meant the assignment by a company of some proprietary interest in its assets to secure its debts. However, in addition to those forms of real security created by contract, those which exist by operation of law are considered. Real security attaches to the debtor's property. Security in this sense has nothing to do with the popular use of the phrase to describe a company's shares or debentures—although debentures (which are documents evidencing a debt due from a company) are frequently secured by a charge on the company's assets. Security in the form of guarantees given by some other person of the payment of a debt by a company is also excluded as such security may be personal although insofar as a mortgage or charge is granted by a guarantor against his own property real security will be involved.

The justification for dealing with real security in a work on corporate insolvency is the fact that although property subject to the rights of a secured creditor is excluded from the winding up process, in reality those who hold security usually scoop the pool of assets owned by an insolvent company. The validity and priority of the claims of the secured creditors will be of vital importance in determining how the company's assets are to be distributed. In a case of administrative receivership the whole procedure applied to the insolvent company is based on the rights of the holder of a floating charge. It is thus difficult to paint any clear picture of the law of corporate insolvency without dealing with such security interests. By way of contrast guarantees and sureties are not treated in detail as they do not, as such, affect the priority of the distribution of company property.

The method chosen is to deal first with the nature and creation of consensual security interests by reference to the assets subject to them (chapters 1 to 4). This will give guidance to the practitioner who has to determine whether a security interest has been properly created and, if so, what is the nature of the interest. Secondly, the floating charge which is a consensual form of security capable of encompassing assets of any kind, is described in chapter 5. Thirdly, those forms of real security such as liens and execution which are created by operation of law are the subject of chapter 6 and, finally, the principles determining the remedies of secured creditors, the priority of security interests, and the use of ownership retention for security purposes, are explored with reference to rules of law and equity and, for priorities, registration procedures applicable to particular classes of asset and under the companies registration system (chapters 7 to 9).

Chapters 10 to 22 deal with insolvency procedures. Chapter 10 considers the new regime of qualifications for insolvency practitioners introduced by the 1985 reforms. Chapters 11 and 12 examine the role of the administrative receiver and the process of receivership. In chapter 13 the new process of administration is considered as a means of corporate rescue.

Chapters 14 to 19 deal with the process of liquidation by examining the role of the liquidator and the procedures involved in winding up a company while chapters 20 and 21 examine the possibility of setting aside colourable transactions and the personal liability of individuals involved in corporate insolvency respectively. Chapter 22 considers the use of voluntary procedures to deal with corporate insolvency.

CHAPTER 1

Corporate Borrowing and Security Interests

CORPORATE BORROWING[1]

1.01 It is necessary to consider a company's powers to borrow before dealing with the forms of security that can be granted as, unlike an individual, a company has been circumscribed by the common law in its activities by the *ultra vires* doctrine which could, under the law as it stood before the Companies Act 1989, avoid those transactions of a company which were outside the objects clause contained in its memorandum of association. The Companies Act 1989 significantly reduces the importance of the *ultra vires* doctrine for those lending to companies or otherwise dealing with them. Consequently this chapter deals with the old *ultra vires* doctrine and then outlines the reforms in the Companies Act 1989. It is also necessary to consider briefly the consequences of borrowing by a company which is *intra vires* but in respect of which there may be doubt about the authority of the human person who agreed to the loan to bind the company as its agent. Once again, the reforms in the Companies Act 1989 are dealt with after a discussion of the law applicable before the Act.

THE CAPACITY OF THE COMPANY TO BORROW

The *ultra vires* doctrine before the Companies Act 1989

1.02 Before the reforms introduced in the Companies Act 1989 the contents of the objects clause of a company's memorandum could affect the validity of the company's transactions with third parties. Lenders were therefore subject to the possibility that their loans would be *ultra vires* transactions. If the company's objects clause stated that borrowing was an object of the company, there was likely to be no difficulty. However, it was held that where such a provision existed in the objects clause of a trading company, the right to borrow was, by definition, a power and had to be exercised in relation to one of the company's other objects. Thus where the company borrowed in order to carry on a business which was outside the

---

1 See generally Palmer's *Company Law*, Stevens & Sons 24th edition, chapters 9, 21 and 43.

range of those specified in the clause, the transaction could not be held to be *intra vires* merely because of the status of borrowing as an object although a transaction amounting to a misuse of an express power to borrow was not outside the company's capacity but only that of its directors.[2] It has always been possible for a company to have as an object some purpose, such as the promotion of charitable ends, which does not involve trading for profit.[3]

1.03   The question of whether a particular provision of a company's objects clause amounted to a substantive object which could be carried out without reference to any other object was one of construction[4] subject to the possibility that certain provisions might, by their very nature, be incapable of having that status. Only those actions which were outside the capacity of the company were *ultra vires*. This term did not extend to transactions which were entered into in breach of the directors' fiduciary duty or for a purpose other than one described in the memorandum, providing the transaction itself was of a type which fell within the substantive objects of the company or which was capable of being carried out for a purpose reasonably incidental to such a substantive object.[5] In such cases the question of the ability of the third party to enforce the transaction would depend on the state of his knowledge of the misuse of the power.

1.04   In the absence of an express provision in the memorandum of the capacity of the company to borrow, such a power would be implied by the courts in the case of a trading company as one which was reasonably incidental to the objects which specified the company's trading activities.[6] In the case of a non-trading company some provision of the memorandum had to give grounds for an inference of a power to borrow.[7] The power to grant security for loans would readily be implied once a power to borrow was established and, unless a contrary intention had to be inferred from the limited wording of an express power to grant security, the power would extend to a mortgage of uncalled capital.[8] The power to borrow could be exercised by the use of any method of borrowing; negotiable instrument, bank overdraft, debenture or promissory note.[9] These rules on objects and powers will still apply after the Companies Act 1989 insofar as the objects clause has to be construed to determine questions of breach of duty by

2   *Re Introductions Ltd* [1968] 2 All ER 1221 and *Rolled Steel Products (Holdings) Ltd v British Steel Corporation* [1984] BCLC 466.
3   *Re Horsley & Weight* [1982] Ch 442.
4   *Cotman v Brougham* [1918] AC 514.
5   *Rolled Steel Products (Holdings) Ltd v British Steel Corporation* [1984] BCLC 466.
6   *Ex p City Bank* (1868) LR 3 Ch 758.
7   *Baroness Wenlock v River Dee* (1885) 10 App Cas 354.
8   *Re Patent File Co* (1870) LR 6 Ch 83; *Re Phoenix Bessemer Co* (1875) 44 LJ Ch 683.
9   See Palmer, *op cit*, paras 43-01 to 43-12.

directors. They will also be relevant to the validity of certain transactions in the case of companies that are charities. Paragraphs 1.10 and 1.22 outline those situations.

1.05   If a company borrowed when it did not have power to do so the loan contract itself would be void according to the traditional *ultra vires* doctrine.[10] However, the lender might still have been able to recover either by virtue of the statutory abrogation of the *ultra vires* rule by s 35 of the Companies Act 1985[11] (as it existed prior to the Companies Act 1989) or in equity. If a power to borrow did exist and was used for an *ultra vires* purpose the transaction would be within the company's capacity but beyond that of those who decided to exercise it improperly.

1.06   The original s 35(1) provided that, in favour of a person dealing with a company in good faith, a transaction decided on by the directors was deemed to be within the capacity of the company. Section 35(2) abrogated the constructive notice rule in favour of such a party and imposed the burden of proof of the absence of good faith, on the part of that party, on the company. It seemed that a lack of good faith would be established by proof either that the person dealing with the company actually knew that the transaction was *ultra vires* or that he could not have been unaware of that fact.[12]

1.07   The interpretation of the phrase 'decided on by the directors' was uncertain. The wording of article 9 of EEC Directive 68/151/EEC on which the provision was based refers to the 'organs' of the company. It is clear that a decision of a sole effective director to whom all actual authority to act on behalf of the company had been delegated came within the section.[12] It is probable that a decision of a director with express, implied, or apparent authority would also have done so. In *TCB v Gray*[13] it was held that the consent of all directors given, other than at a normal board meeting, fell within the section. However, it is unclear whether a decision of some other person (such as a non-managerial employee of the company) acting within the framework of a policy or managerial structure laid down by the board or those to whom the board had devolved its authority could have amounted to a transaction 'decided on by the directors'.

1.08   In the light of the reference in the Directive to the acts of a company's organs and the need, in the interests of commercial convenience, for normal

10   *Ashbury Railway Carriage Co v Riche* (1875) LR 7 HL 653.
11   Formerly s 9(1) European Communities Act 1972.
12   *International Sales and Agencies Ltd v Marcus* [1982] 3 All ER 551 per Lawson J at 559.
13   [1986] 1 All ER 587.

managerial structures to be recognised, it is submitted that this would have been the case. It is likely that an act of a director or other employee without any authority whatsoever would have fallen outside the scope of the section. The section presupposed a 'dealing' by the third party and this was satisfied by a loan, although not by the receipt of a gift or of funds known to have been used wrongfully. A person who, because of such knowledge, was a constructive trustee could not claim the protection of the section.[12]

1.09   It is probable that the usual insertion of express borrowing powers in a company's objects clause; the willingness of the courts to imply them in the case of a trading company and the effect of the original s 35 made most loan agreements enforceable even before the Companies Act 1989. However, if the agreement was void as a result of the *ultra vires* rule and was not saved by the original s 35 or the *Rolled Steel* doctrine a lender could trace his money if it was still in the company's hands—despite his inability to enforce the loan agreement or to sue for money had and received.[14] If the money had been used to pay creditors with *intra vires* debts, the lender would have a right to stand in the shoes of those creditors and to claim to the extent that his money was used in this way.[15] This right did not, however, entitle the lender whose loan was *ultra vires* to any security held by the *intra vires* creditors whose debts were paid with his money. There may also be a right to recover damages from directors or other company officials who, by their acts impliedly represented that they are acting within their powers if this representation causes the lender to enter the transaction.[16]

The Companies Act 1989

1.10   The Act substitutes a new s 35 in the Companies Act 1985. The new section provides that the validity of a company's acts are not to be called into question on the ground of lack of capacity by reason of anything, or the lack of anything, in its memorandum of association. However, this provision does not affect the right of a member of the company to bring proceedings to restrain such an act unless the act is done in fulfilment of a legal obligation arising from a previous act of the company. Nor does it affect the liability of directors for such acts which will remain a breach of their duty unless ratified by special resolution. Relief from liability for directors requires a separate special resolution.[17]

1.11   In the case of a company that is a charity the prohibition on

14   *Sinclair v Brougham* [1914] AC 398.
15   *Blackburn Building Society v Cunliffe Brooks* (1883) 22 Ch D 61; *Sinclair v Brougham* (*supra*).
16   *Firbank v Humphreys* (1886) 18 QB D 54.
17   Companies Act 1989, s 108.

questioning *ultra vires* acts can only operate in favour of a person, giving full consideration in money or money's worth, who is unaware at the time that the act is done that it is beyond the company's objects.[18] That limitation does not apply if the person in question did not know, at the time of the company's act, that the company was a charity; in such a case the person has full protection.

1.12 The Act substitutes new ss 3 and 4 to the Companies Act 1985. The new section specifies that the objects of a company can be stated in any manner and provides that a statement that the object of the company is to carry on business as a general commercial company allows it to carry on any trade or business whatsoever as a general commercial company. Power to do all such things incidental or conducive to the carrying on of any trade or business is expressly conferred in such a case. Companies are given power to alter the objects clause by special resolution without proof of any ground although the procedure for objections to an alteration under s 5 of the 1985 Act is retained.[19] In the case of charitable companies the prior written permission of the Charity Commissioners is required for such an alteration to be effective and the effect of an alteration causing the body to cease to be a charity is strictly limited in its application to certain property of the company.[20] The Act substantially implements the recommendations of the Prentice report on the abolition of the *ultra vires* rule.[21] Its provisions as to the capacity of directors are dealt with in paragraphs 1.22–28.

THE POWERS OF THE COMPANY'S AGENTS

Agency

1.13 A transaction which is within the capacity of the company may nonetheless fail to bind it if it was not entered into by a person with the authority to borrow on the company's behalf. The power conferred by the company's memorandum of association to borrow will usually be exercisable by the company's board of directors although the power may be limited. The articles of association will deal with the allocation of this power between the organs of the company.

1.14 Table A provides that the power to manage the company is in the hands of the directors subject only to the Companies Act 1985, the memorandum and articles and to any directions by special resolution of the

---

18   *Ibid* s 111 inserting a new s 30B in the Charities Act 1960.
19   *Ibid* s 110.
20   *Ibid* s 111(1).
21   D Prentice, "Reform of the Ultra Vires Rule: a Consultation Document" DTI 1986.

company general meetings.[22] Some articles of association may, however, limit the power of the directors to borrow more than a specified amount by requiring the agreement of the company general meeting.[23] The allotment of any debenture convertible into shares must always be carried out in accordance with s 80 of the Companies Act 1985 which requires authorisation by the articles of the company or a general meeting which authorisation can last for only 5 years before renewal. The pre-emption rights of members under ss 89 to 96 of the Act will also apply to such debentures unless they are excluded or replaced by another scheme in accordance with those sections.[24]

1.15 Borrowing on behalf of a company must be the act of an agent with authority to bind the company. This follows from the fact that the company as an abstract entity can only act through human agents. That authority will ultimately derive from the provision of the articles of association which will usually give borrowing powers to the board. An agent may have express, implied or apparent authority. The authority conferred, by the articles, on the board is express authority. They may in turn confer express authority on other officers of the company, or on individual directors.

1.16 Implied authority may result from any behaviour by agents of the company with express authority which suggests that transactions of the type in question may be entered into by the agent on the company's behalf. Past conduct in adopting such transactions may result in the agent having implied authority. The appointment of a director as a managing director which confers on him the usual authority of such an officer or the acquiescence of the board in actions by a person who acts as if he occupied such an office will suffice.[25] However, subject to the original s 35 of the Companies Act 1985 such implied authority could be negated by the constructive notice doctrine (which confers notice of the contents of the memorandum and articles of association on those dealing with the company) before the provisions of the Companies Act 1989 came into effect.[26]

1.17 The rule in *Turquand*'s case preventing those who are outsiders from being put on notice of purely internal matters of 'indoor management' will save the lender from the effects of the constructive notice doctrine where the articles require some step by the company to authorise a loan (for example, an ordinary resolution of a general meeting) which would not become part

---

22   The Companies (Tables A to F) Regulations 1985 SI 1985 No 805 Article 70.
23   See eg the former Article 79 under the Companies Act 1948 Table A.
24   s 94(2)(3).
25   *Hely-Hutchinson v Brayhead* [1968] 1 QB 549.
26   *Ernest v Nicholls* (1857) 6 HL Cas 401 but see Companies Act 1989 s 142 and para 1.25 *infra*.

of the public record by registration (as a special resolution would).[27] This doctrine extends to the validity of the appointment of directors.[28] However, only genuine outsiders (and not, for example, other directors) who have no knowledge of a breach of internal procedures and who have not been put on enquiry are protected.[29] There is no protection in the case of a forgery not represented as genuine by an agent of the company.[30]

1.18 A director or other officer of a company who has no express or implied authority may still bind the company by virtue of apparent or ostensible authority. This will occur when the lender relies on a representation (whether verbal or by conduct) made to him by some person with express or implied authority (commonly the board) that the officer has authority to bind the company by entering a transaction of the kind in question, providing the memorandum and articles of association of the company do not deprive the company of the capacity to enter such a contract or to delegate the authority to do so to that officer.[31] The representation cannot be deduced from the content of the company's memorandum and articles by the operation of the doctrine of constructive notice to confer apparent authority to enter an unusual transaction. The doctrine of constructive notice is purely negative in its effect.[32] If a person who purports to bind the company to a loan agreement has no authority it is possible for the company in general meeting to ratify the decision by ordinary resolution and thus to bind itself—so long as the transaction is within the capacity of the company itself although outside that of the person in question or indeed, the board.[33] There will also be the possibility of action by the lender, against the person without authority who purported to bind the company, for his breach of warranty of authority.[34] Paragraph 1.22 deals with the position after the provisions of the Companies Act 1989 come into effect.

1.19 In many cases where no authority to enter the loan transaction on behalf of the company exists, s 35(1) of the Companies Act 1985 (as it stood before the Companies Act 1989 replaced it) operated to rescue the lender. In addition to its effect in cases where an act is beyond the capacity of the company, the section deemed the power of the directors to bind the company to be free of any limitation under the memorandum or articles providing the transaction in question was decided on by the directors and the third party

27 *Royal British Bank v Turquand* (1856) 6 E&B 327.
28 *Mahony v East Holyford Mining Co* (1875) LR 7 HL 869.
29 *Morris v Kanssen* [1946] AC 459.
30 *Ruben v Great Finall Consolidated* [1906] AC 439.
31 *Freeman and Lockyer v Buckhurst Park Properties (Mangal) Ltd* [1964] 2 QB 480; and *Ebeed v Soplex Wholesale Supplies* [1985] BCLC 404.
32 *Houghton & Co v Northard Lowe & Wills Ltd* [1927] 1 KB 246.
33 *Irvine v Union Bank of Australia* (1877) 2 App Cas 366.
34 *Hely-Hutchinson v Brayhead* [1968] 1 QB 549 at 596.

acted in good faith.[35] The section operated for the protection of the third party only and abrogated the doctrine of constructive notice as it applies to limitations on the powers of directors in the memorandum or articles. Apparently it did not assist a third party who dealt with an officer who is not a director.

1.20   In the case of a transaction entered into before the Companies Act 1989 was in force, the liquidator, administrative receiver or administrator who is concerned with the validity of the claims of creditors must initially investigate the validity of the loan, or other transaction giving rise to the debt, by reference to the company's capacity and s 35 of Companies Act 1985. He must then consider the question of whether the transaction was within the authority of the agent who entered into it; having regard to constructive notice, the indoor management rule and the agency rules as well as to s 35.

1.21   If the transaction was within the express or implied authority of the agent the company will be liable and is unlikely to have a remedy against the agent for exceeding his authority; although there will be an action for breach of fiduciary duty by a director or other agent if the facts amounted to such a breach. However, where there was apparent authority which was used to enter a transaction outside express or implied authority given to the agent there may be liability on the part of the agent to the company for acting in excess of his authority and causing loss to the company. The grounds on which a transaction may be impugned on the onset of liquidation or administration are dealt with below.[36]

Companies Act 1989

1.22   In furtherance of the policy of abrogating the effect of problems of the capacity of the company or its directors on those dealing with the company while protecting members of companies from the abuse of power by directors, the Companies Act 1989 deals with limitations on the capacity of directors. It substitutes a new s 35A in the Companies Act 1985. This provides that, in favour of a person dealing with a company in good faith, the power of the board of directors to bind the company or authorise others to do so is to be deemed free from any limitation under the company's constitution. It will be noted that this overcomes a number of the problems of the former s 35. There is no limitation of the rule to transactions decided on by the directors. The board is recognised as the relevant organ and its authorisation of others to bind the company is expressly within the section. There is no limitation of the section on 'transactions'. A person deals with the company for the purpose of the section if he is a party to any transaction

---

35   See paras 1.02–1.09 above.
36   See chapter 22.

or other act to which the company is party. Bad faith on the part of someone dealing with a company is not established by proving, without more, his knowledge that the act is beyond the directors' powers. The section applies to limitations deriving from resolutions of the company, shareholder agreements or meetings of classes of shareholder as well as those contained in its memorandum or articles of association.

1.23 The new s 35A expressly preserves any existing right of members to seek to restrain acts beyond the capacity of directors and not done in fulfilment of a legal obligation arising from a previous act of the company. The liability of directors for such acts is preserved. Such liability will frequently be for breach of duty owed to the company rather than to members but the section leaves that matter open. It provides for the ratification by the company by special resolution of acts of the directors that exceed limitations on their powers flowing from the company's objects clause and requires a separate special resolution to relieve directors of liability. The issues of directors' authority to bind the company and of liability for breach of duty must thus be addressed separately. This contrasts with the ability of the company under the existing rules to ratify many other excesses of the directors by ordinary resolution but is consistent with the need for a special resolution to alter the objects clause.[37]

1.24 A new s 322A deals with transactions entered into by the company with a director of the company or of its holding company or a person connected with such a director or a company with which such a director is associated. It lays down that such transactions, in relation to which the board exceeded its authority or authorised others to do so, are voidable[37a] at the instance of the company as between the company and the party linked to the company in that way. The effect of the new s 35A in deeming the directors' powers to be free from limitations is preserved for others who act in good faith but who are also parties to such a transaction. The court is given power to sever or set aside on just terms a transaction which is voidable against one person and valid in favour of another.[38] A new s 35B stipulates that no party to a transaction with the company is bound to enquire whether it is within the objects of the company to enter into it or what limitations there are on the power of the board to bind the company or to authorise others to do so.[39]

1.25 The concept that anyone is deemed to have notice of any matter merely because it is disclosed in any document available for inspection at

---

37   s 108(1).
37a   New s 322A(5) lays down that the transaction ceases to be voidable if: restitution is no longer possible; the company has been indemnified for loss or damage; rights acquired *bona fide* for value without notice by a non-party would be affected by avoidance; or the company ratifies the transaction.
38   s 109(1).
39   s 108(1).

the companies registry or from the company is revoked by a new s 711A inserted by s 142 of the Act. This is, however, qualified by the fact that the section is stated not to affect the question of whether someone is affected by notice because of a failure to make inquiries that ought reasonably to be made. This means that the public availability of documents does not in itself give notice of their contents but that if, on the other grounds (such as the fact that a person had possession of the documents), notice arises because of a failure to make inquiries, the fact of public availability does not absolve the person from the consequences of that failure. Mere failure to inspect the register will not fix a person with notice unless such an inspection is an inquiry that ought reasonably to have been made by that person in the situation in issue.

1.26 The new s 711A will not have to be relied upon by a party to a transaction with the company who is given the higher level of protection conferred by the new s 35B. Such a person is not bound to inquire at all about the objects of the company or limitations on the powers of the board on the question of whether the transaction is affected by such matters. Section 711A is of greater concern in relation to the registration of company charges.

1.27 The effect of the 1989 Act's provisions is to improve the security of transactions with companies. It will not be possible for companies to use the formalities of the decision making process or even the actual knowledge of the other party of limitations on the powers of the board to challenge the validity of loans or other transactions. In any case in which express or implied authority has been conferred on another as agent by the board, the third party is protected from the effects of any limitation on the board's powers. This will also apply for the purpose of deciding whether a representation, used as the basis of a claim of apparent authority, was made by a person with express or implied authority. The fact that no party to any transaction (whether in good faith or not) is bound to enquire about the objects clause or any limitations on the board's powers, is likely to avoid the possibility that a representation on which apparent authority is founded is negated by provisions of the memorandum, articles or resolutions of the company.

THE DEVELOPMENT AND NATURE OF SECURITY INTERESTS[40]

1.28 Having ensured that the loan and the security were *intra vires* and that they bind the company the liquidator, administrative receiver or

---

40   See Pennington "Fixed Charges over Future Assets of a Company" (1985) 6 *Company Lawyer* 9 at 9-17, on which this passage is based.

administrator will be concerned to establish that any necessary formalities for the creation of a security interest have been completed and to discover the nature of that interest. Chapters 2 to 5 deal with the creation and nature of particular security interests but in this paragraph some of the broader issues as to such interests are considered.

1.29   At common law security could be granted over assets only by way of a mortgage or a pledge. A mortgage involved a transfer of the borrower's ownership of the asset to the lender. This would be subject to the condition that ownership would be returned to the borrower on repayment of the loan by an agreed date. Equity gave the borrower an equity of redemption which enabled him to reclaim his property on repayment, after that date, of all amounts secured by the mortgage until that right was ended by a foreclosure order. Consequently, a mere contractual agreement, that assets should be used as security, would not create a valid security interest at law and, since a transfer of ownership presupposed the existence of the borrower's right over identified assets, a mortgage of future property, not yet in existence or not yet owned by the borrower, was impossible. In the case of a debt or other chose in action the impossibility of a legal assignment of the asset precluded the creation of a security interest at law. It was possible for future property to be subject to an anticipatory mortgage and for the ownership rights in the assets to pass by virtue of a further deed transferring ownership or by a transfer of the possession of goods to the lender. However, only on the occurrence of such an event were the assets subject to the security interest.[41]

1.30   A licence for the lender to seize goods was implied for this purpose at common law in mortgages of after acquired goods, but no security interest could exist until it was exercised and the lender's interest was subject to the legal rights of others which were acquired before that time.[42] Only accretions or additions to the property subject to the legal mortgage, such as chattels to land or equipment placed on board a ship for its navigation or employment would automatically become subject to the mortgage on the principle that they were additions to the original asset and not new assets.[43]

1.31   A pledge could be created at common law over goods or documents by a transfer of possession to the lender. However, without such a transfer an agreement for a pledge did not create a security interest. Only the extensive development of the common law doctrine of constructive

---

41   *Elmore v Stone* (1809) 1 Taunt 458.
42   *Hope v Haley* (1856) 5 Eard and B 830; *Acraman v Bates* (1860) 29 LJQB 78.
43   *Herlakenden's Case* (1589) 4 Co Rep 62a, and *Gale v Laurie* (1826) 5B and C156, and see Pennington *op cit* p 11.

possession enabled the pledge to be used while actual possession was in the hands of the borrower or a bailee.[44] The inability of a lender to grant a security at common law over future property or property not susceptible to legal assignment, and the need to transfer ownership rights or possession to create a security right at law was remedied by the development of equitable security rights.

1.32   The courts of equity developed the equitable charge as a means of facilitating the payment of a testator's debts, and implementing certain provisions of family settlements.[45] This was later extended to commercial contractual arrangements whereby it was agreed that certain specific items of a debtor's property were to be made available to secure a loan or were charged with its repayment. This could apply to future property and gave the lender an immediate equitable proprietary interest on the creation of the charge (in the case of present property) or at the time of the later acquisition of future property by the borrower.[46] Thus an equitable charge overcame the problems of form and subject matter which applied to legal security interests.

1.33   An equitable mortgage differed from an equitable charge in that it was based on the existence of a contractual arrangement to create a legal mortgage which equity regarded as creating an immediate equitable proprietary interest. Such an agreement could be expressly created and was inferred from a deposit of title deeds to secure a loan.[47] This gave the right to specific performance of the contract but was significant for the immediate proprietary right conferred on the lender. Both an equitable charge and an equitable mortgage gave the lender priority over any successor in title to the borrower such as a purchaser, a trustee in bankruptcy or a later mortgagee unless such a person was the purchaser in good faith of a legal estate without actual or constructive notice of the equitable charge or mortgage.[48]

1.34   The only substantial difference between an equitable charge and an equitable mortgage is the absence of the remedy of foreclosure in the case of a charge as there has been no transfer of ownership subject to an equity of redemption which the court can extinguish. An equitable mortgage is a transfer of ownership rights in equity subject to an equity of redemption

---

44   See paras 3.11–3.16 below.
45   See eg *Wilcocks v Wilcocks* (1706) 2 Vern 558; *Legard v Hodges* (1792) 1 Ves Jun 477 and Pennington, *op cit* at p 13.
46   *Ex p Wills* (1790) 1 Ves Jun 162 and Pennington, *op cit*.
47   *Russel v Russel* (1783) 1 Bro CC269.
48   See Pennington, *op cit* at p 14.

and thus foreclosure is available.[49] The fact that in modern times receivership, possession and sale have replaced foreclosure in practice as remedies for the enforcement of the security makes the distinction between an equitable charge and an equitable mortgage of little significance. The development of these equitable forms of security interest enabled assets to be used for security purposes even if ownership of them could not be transferred at common law. Thus it was possible in equity to use a chose in action such as a debt or an insurance policy as security[50] and to charge or mortgage future property.[51]

1.35   The need for businesses in the nineteenth century to grant security over assets which were bought and sold in the course of the business or which were subject to a production process was met by the development of the equitable security over future property. It developed into the concept of the floating charge which can exist as a present security interest over assets but allows the borrowing company to deal with them in the course of its business without the lender's consent until the charge crystallises and attaches to those assets of the class affected by the charge in existence at that time.[52]

1.36   The confusing array of security interests available over property other than land and the complex rules affecting priorities have been the subject of a report by Professor Aubrey Diamond.[53] Were his recommendations to be implemented a simplified system of a single register of such security interests created by companies, partnerships and sole traders in the course of business would be established. It would replace the present system for the registration of company charges in the Companies Registry and, in the case of certain forms of property, a variety of other registers.[54] Priority would be determined by date of filing and the registration requirement would extend to a purchase money security interest by retention of title or hire purchase. Chattel leases for a term of three years or more would likewise be capable of registration as security interests. The report's proposals would also lay down requirements for the creation of security interests which would distinguish between possessory and non-possessory interests.[55] Although none of the report's recommendations for the radical reform of the whole system applicable to security interests has been implemented, the Companies Bill 1989 adopts a number of its recommen-

---

49 See below, paras 7.31–7.33.
50 *Tailby v Official Receiver* (1888) 13 App Cas 523; *Dufaur v Professional Life Assurance Co* (1858) 25 Beav 599.
51 *Holroyd v Marshall* (1862) 10 HLC 191.
52 *Re Panama New Zealand and Australian Royal Mail Co* (1870) 5 Ch App 318 and see paras 5.01–5.18 below.
53 Prof A L Diamond, "A Review of Security Interests in Property" DTI 1989.
54 *Ibid* paras 1.9 to 1.15 outline the broad thrust of the recommendations.
55 *Ibid* para 9.7 and chapters 10 and 17.

dations for the immediate reform of the system of registration for company charges.[56]

1.37   Having considered the broad perspective within which security interests have developed in English law, it is possible to deal with the nature and creation of security interests which apply to assets of different types.

---

56 *Ibid* Part III and see para 8.61 *infra*.

CHAPTER 2

Security Over Land

AVAILABLE SECURITIES

2.01   Land can be the subject of a legal or an equitable mortgage. The type of mortgage created may affect both priority and the mortgagee's remedies. Since 1925, the distinction between legal and equitable mortgages has been of less importance for priorities than the question of whether a particular mortgage is protected by deposit of title deeds or by registration, and the remedies available are affected by whether the mortgage is by deed or not; a distinction which does not wholly coincide with the legal/equitable distinction. However, the question of whether a mortgage is legal or equitable retains sufficient significance to require some elaboration.

LEGAL MORTGAGES OF LAND

2.02   A legal mortgage can only be granted by the owner of a legal estate in the land. The Law of Property Act 1925 s 1(1) provides that the only legal estates are fee simple absolute in possession and a term of years absolute. Sections 85 and 86 provide for a legal mortgage of each of these. All other estates exist only in equity and s 1(2) exhaustively lists those interests or charges which can exist at law. Before 1925 a mortgage of land would be created by a conveyance of the mortgagor's legal estate to the mortgagee subject to a covenant to reconvey on payment of the debt. This method still applies to legal mortgages of pure personalty. The Law of Property Act 1925 sought to ensure that as far as possible the legal estate in land remained with the beneficial owner.

2.03   In pursuance of this policy, the form of a legal mortgage of a freehold interest in land has become the grant of a lease ('demise') for a term of years absolute subject to a proviso for cesser on redemption, or a charge by deed expressed to be by way of legal mortgage[1] which has the same effect as a mortgage by demise.[2] Thus a legal mortgage is invariably created by deed. The fact that a mortgagor who holds the legal estate retains that estate after granting a legal mortgage means that subsequent mortgages can also be legal.

1   Law of Property Act 1925 s 85(1).
2   Law of Property Act 1925 [hereafter LPA] s 87(1).

This was not possible when the creation of a legal mortgage involved the conveyance of the mortgagor's legal estate to the mortgagee.

2.04 A company which owns a fee simple interest in land can create a legal mortgage by deed by granting a term of years absolute (a lease) for a period (usually 3,000 years) to the mortgagee. A later legal mortgage will be granted by granting a term of years one day longer. Any attempt to create a mortgage by a purported conveyance of the fee simple will be treated as creating such a demise.[3] If a mortgage is to be granted of leasehold property it will be by sub-demise. That is to say that the mortgagor company grants the mortgagee a term of years a few days shorter than the one it holds. The sub-demise is subject to a proviso for 'cesser on redemption' which ensures that the mortgagee's term of years ends when the mortgage is repaid.[4] Later legal mortgages of the leasehold interest can be created by granting sub-demises of terms of years longer than that granted to the first mortgagee.

2.05 The creation of legal mortgages by demise or sub-demise has the disadvantage that the same deed cannot deal with both freehold and leasehold property. This problem can be overcome by the use of a 'charge by deed expressed to be by way of legal mortgage'. This is applicable to either form of property[5] and gives the mortgagee the same protection, powers and remedies as if a demise or sub-demise had been granted.[6] It also has the advantage of greater simplicity and that, in the case of leasehold property, the granting of such a mortgage will probably not amount to a breach of a covenant against sub-letting, although it may violate a covenant not to part with possession.[7]

2.06 The forms of legal mortgage described so far are applicable to unregistered land. The usual form of mortgage for registered land is a registered charge. This can be created by the use of a simple Land Registry form, or by any of the methods available for unregistered land.[8] However, a mortgage created by one of the methods appropriate for unregistered land must describe the registered land subject to the charge by reference to the register or in some other manner which enables it to be identified without reference to any other documents. It must not refer to any other interest or

---

3 LPA s 85(2).
4 LPA s 86(1).
5 LPA s 85(1) and 86(1).
6 LPA s 87(1).
7 See, eg obiter statement in *Grand Junction Co Ltd v Bates* [1954] 2 QB 160 per Upjohn J at 168. A legal mortgagee is entitled to immediate possession on the creation of the mortgage unless the mortgage provides for possession by the mortgagor.
8 Land Registration Rules 1925 Rule 139, Schedule Form 45. This is a legal mortgage by way of legal charge although the deed does not include those words. *City Land & Property (Holdings) Ltd v Dabrah* [1968] Ch 166 at 171–172.

charge affecting the land which would have priority over it and which is not protected or registered on the register and is not an overriding interest.[9] Any such mortgage of registered land not registered as a legal charge or protected by the registration of a notice or caution at the Land Registry takes effect in equity only and may be overriden as a minor interest.[10]

EQUITABLE MORTGAGES OF LAND

2.07 An equitable mortgage of land can be created in three ways:

(a) by a deposit of title deeds;
(b) by an agreement to create a legal mortgage, or the creation of an equitable charge;
(c) by any mortgage of an equitable interest.

Deposit of title deeds

2.08 The act of depositing the title deeds to land with the creditor or his agent for the purpose of giving security creates an equitable mortgage.[11] Not all material deeds need be deposited, and in the case of registered land a deposit of a Land Certificate will suffice. An equitable mortgage will be created providing the deposit was for the purpose of security and was not by mistake or for some other purpose.[12] The essential question is whether there is an immediate intention to give security by the deposit.[13] The deposit is taken to be part performance and evidence of a contract to create a legal mortgage and thus is effective without writing.[14] Further advances are secured by the deposit but amounts provided earlier are not unless there is evidence of an intention that they should be.[15]

2.09 A loan accompanied by the simultaneous deposit of deeds or the Land Certificate raises a strong inference that an equitable mortgage or charge is being created—even in the absence of express agreement to that effect. However it is for the person seeking to establish such an interest to prove it, and evidence of another form of security (eg a cash deposit) may indicate that an equitable mortgage or charge was not intended even if the deposit of deeds was simultaneous with payment of the loan.[16]

9   Land Registration Act 1925 [hereafter LRA] s 25(2).
10   LRA s 106(2).
11   *Russel v Russel* (1783) 1 Bro CC269.
12   See *Wardle v Oakley* (1864) 36 Beav 27 at 30, and *Norris v Wilkinson* (1806) 12 Ves 192 where the purpose of the delivery was to enable a solicitor to draft a legal mortgage.
13   *Edge v Worthington* (1786) 1 Cox Equ Cas 211.
14   *Carter v Wake* (1877) 4 Ch D 605 at 606, and LPA s 40(2).
15   *Mountford v Scott* (1823) Turn & R 274.
16   *Re Alton Corporation* [1985] BCLC 27 Ch D.

2.10 From 27 September 1989 s 2 of the Law of Property (Miscellaneous Provisions) Act 1989 provides that a contract for the sale of other disposition of an interest in land can only be made in writing and only by incorporating all the items expressly agreed by the parties. This repeals s 40 of LPA 1925 for contracts made on or after 27 September 1989. Since the doctrine of part performance is contained in s 40 it seems that the creation of an equitable mortagage by deposit of title deeds without a contract made in writing and signed by both parties is no longer possible. Section 2(5) does not exclude mortages from the operation of the 1989 Act although the creation and operation of resulting implied and constructive trusts is excluded. It is only if the courts hold that the creation of an equitable mortgage by deposit of title deeds is not a contract for the disposition of an interest in land but a disposition of the interest that this form of security will remain available. This presupposes that it is not by virtue of the doctrine of part performance but by a separate rule that equitable mortages may be created that deposit has its effect.

2.11 Where the deposit is by a company the mortgage is registrable under s 395 of the Companies Act 1985 as the right of the mortgagee to retain the deeds does not represent a lien separate from the mortgage itself. The retention of the document is possible only on the basis of the mortgage created by the company and the effectiveness of the security against other creditors and the liquidator is therefore dependent on registration.[17] This is so even if the deposit of the deeds represents security for the debt of someone other than the company which deposited them. This is in contrast to the position when the deeds are held on the basis of a possessory lien which exists by operation of law and was not created by the company. In this case there is no need for registration under s 395.[18]

2.12 In practice, mortgagees will rarely accept a deposit of title deeds without more as security. While it is true that an equitable mortgage by deposit creates a contract for a legal mortgage and gives the mortgagee the right to call for the creation of a legal mortgage, and that the deposit creates an equitable mortgage and not merely an equitable charge, the mortgagee will normally demand the deposit of a memorandum with the title deeds. This was not necessary to allow enforcement under s 40 of the Law of Property Act 1925 but will prevent uncertainty about the intention with which the deeds were deposited and the terms of the loan.[19] The mortgagee can use the remedies of sale and the appointment of a receiver granted by the Law of

---

17   *Re Wallis and Simmonds (Builders) Ltd* [1974] 1 All ER 561.
18   *London & Cheshire Insurance Co Ltd v Laplagrene Property Co Ltd* [1971] Ch 499 at 514.
19   *Pryce v Bury* (1853) 2 Drew 41 at 42 and see LP (Misc Prov) Act 1989 s 2 which repeals s 40, and para 2.10.

Property Act 1925 s 101 if, but only if, the mortgage is made by deed.[20] The question of whether the mortgage is made by deed or by deposit is a question of the construction of the deed. In *Re White Rose Cottage*,[21] the Court of Appeal unanimously held that where a Land Certificate was deposited with a mortgagee by a mortgagor and a deed was executed by the mortgagor containing provisions for the existence and extent of the charge, an agreement to execute a legal mortgage if the mortgagee required this, together with a declaration of trust by the mortgagor in favour of the mortgagee and a grant of a power of attorney to the mortgagee to sell the legal estate free of the mortgagor's equity of redemption, the charge was created by the deed and not by the deposit.[22]

2.13   It would seem that the test of how the mortgage is created is whether the contractual document is itself an operative instrument and not merely evidential.[23] However, a document under seal which provides for the matters dealt with in *Re White Rose Cottage*, including a power of attorney or a declaration of trust allowing the sale of the legal estate by the equitable mortgagee, will create an equitable mortgage. Deposit provides additional security, affects the question of registration for priority and means that a failure of the document to comply with s 40 of the Law of Property Act 1925 will not be fatal to the enforceability of the mortgage since deposit is a form of part performance. From 27 September 1989 s 2 of the Law of Property (Miscellaneous Provisions) Act 1989 may be fatal to the existence of a mortgage based on a contract for the creation of a legal mortgage, or on deposit, if that is taken to be a form of part performance. The issues of registration or notice which determine priorities are dealt with below.[24]

Agreement to create a legal mortgage or express equitable charge

2.14   If there is no deposit of title deeds an equitable mortgage of land will have to be evidenced by a memorandum in writing signed by the party to be charged or some other person authorised by him or her to do so.[25] A contract for valuable consideration to execute a legal mortgage over the property identified in the memorandum or written contract when required to do so will create an equitable mortgage. An imperfect legal mortgage also takes effect as an agreement for a mortgage and thus is an equitable mortgage.[26]

---

20   s 101(1).
21   [1965] 1 All ER 11.
22   *Ibid* see pp 15, 16 and 17.
23   See *Hari Sankar Paul v Kedar Nath Sahar* [1939] 2 WLR 737 at p 742.
24   See paras 8.97–8.111 below.
25   LPA s 40(1). The payment of money lent has been held not to be a sufficient act of part performance under the section—*Re Whitting ex p Hall* (1879) 10 Ch D 615 at 619, but see *Steadman v Steadman* [1976] AC 536. From 27 September 1989 the contract must be in writing and signed by both parties – s 2 LP (MP)A 1989.
26   *Parker v Housefield* (1834) 2 MY & K 219.

2.15 A mortgage of registered land in the form appropriate to a legal mortgage of unregistered land but not registered or protected on the register takes effect in equity by virtue of Land Registration Act 1925, s 106(2). It is necessary that the money should have been advanced before an equitable mortgage will exist as the court will not specifically enforce a contract to lend money but will only award damages for its breach, and it is the possibility of specific performance of the obligation which creates the real security interest.[27] In practice a document creating an equitable mortgage will usually be under seal to take advantage of the power of sale and to appoint a receiver in s 101 of the Law of Property Act 1925. However, the necessary conditions for an enforceable equitable mortgage by agreement to create a legal mortgage are that the agreement shows an intention to create a present security right[28] against property that is sufficiently identified and that the requirement of writing or part performance has been observed.[29] Such a document which does not specifically grant a right to take a legal mortgage may none the less be effective as an equitable charge.

A mortgage of an equitable interest

2.16 The forms of equitable mortgage dealt with above are methods which can be used by the owner of a legal estate to create an equitable mortgage. For that reason they have to be evidenced by a memorandum under s 40 of the Law of Property Act 1925 or by an act of part performance—including a deposit of title deeds. After 27 September 1989 the contract must be in writing and signed by both parties and part performance will not be sufficient.[30] An equitable mortgage will also be created if the owner of an equitable interest mortgages his interest. Such a mortgage, which will usually be a mortgage by a beneficiary under a trust of his interest, must be by will or in (and not merely evidenced by) writing signed by the mortgagor or by his agent authorised in writing. A mortgage of an equitable interest can be made without consideration, but only if it is drafted to operate as a complete assignment of the whole of the mortgagor's interest. Although equity will not give effect to an incomplete assignment or one resting only on an executory contract as an order of specific performance is not available to a volunteer,[31] a completed voluntary assignment of equitable rights will be effective.[32] Written notice to the trustees who own the legal estate in which the mortgagor has a beneficial interest is desirable in order to ensure that priority is retained and that payment is not made to the mortgagor.[33]

---

27 *Sichel v Mosenthal* (1862) 30 Beav 371, but this is not true of a contract to take a debenture in a company—Companies Act 1985 s 195.
28 *National Provincial Bank & Union Bank of England v Charnley* [1924] 1 KB 431 at 440.
30 s 2 LP(MP)A 1989.
31 *Re Earl of Lucan* (1890) 45 Ch D 470.
32 *Kekewich v Manning* (1851) 1 DeGM & G 176.
33 See below, 4.01–4.10 and 8.112.

CHAPTER 3

Security Interests in Chattels

FORMS OF SECURITY

3.01 This section deals with property which can be described as tangible moveables or choses in possession. It differs from real property (land) and chattels real (leasehold interests in land) which were dealt with under the heading of 'land'. It is also distinguishable from choses in action which cannot be reduced to possession and are not tangible. All goods fall into this category but mortgages of ships and aircraft are dealt with separately as they are subject to special rules. The use of chattels as security is dominated by the Bills of Sale Acts of 1878 and 1882. For a company, the main importance of these Acts is that, although documents used by companies to grant security over their chattels are not covered by the Acts,[1] the scope of the Acts as they apply to such documents determines whether it is necessary to register the security under s 395(2)(c) of the Companies Act 1985.[2]

3.02 A security interest in a chattel can take the form of a mortgage (legal or equitable) or a pledge. The essence of a pledge, which operates only at common law, is that the pledgee has possession of the property pledged. A mortgage transfers property in the goods in law or at equity to the creditor but does not necessarily give him possession. There is no need for a mortgage (even a legal mortgage) or a pledge of chattels to be in writing.[3] If a document is used the goods subject to the charge will be defined in it. A fixed charge on 'fixed plant and machinery' only applies to plant or machinery attached to the mortgagor's premises. Any such goods not so attached will not be covered by the fixed charge but may fall within a floating charge created by the same document—which will be subject to the claims of preferential creditors.[4] If writing is used the Bills of Sale Acts 1878–1882 will apply, and a company will be required to register the charge under s 395(2)(c).

3.03 A legal mortgage of a chattel will be created by the assignment of the property in the goods to the mortgagee subject to the mortgagor's right of

---

1 *Re Standard Manufacturing Co* (1891) 1 Ch 627 and *Richards v Kidderminster Overseers* (1886) 2 Ch 212.
2 See para 8 below on the registration system for company charges.
3 *Reeves v Capper* (1838) 5 Bing NC 136.
4 *Re Hi-Fi Equipment (Cabinets) Ltd* [1988] BCLC 65.

21

redemption. Possession by the lender is not necessary.[5] A transfer of title can be by delivery, by sale, or by deed. Delivery of the goods is unlikely to be used to create a mortgage of chattels without a document in practice as giving possession to the lender will be inconvenient to the borrower and, if it is acceptable to him, it can be used to create security by way of pledge rather than by mortgage.[6] Sale is not a method of transferring title by way of security unless it is clear that the transaction is subject to a right of re-transfer on redemption. Hence it is normal for a conditional bill of sale to be used for this purpose. Since, in practice, writing will be desirable to effect a transfer in order to create a legal mortgage of chattels, the Bills of Sale Acts 1878–1882 will apply to such mortgages.

3.04   Possession of the goods by the borrower where property is transferred by a conditional bill of sale was not subject to the rule in *Twyne's Case*[7] that it amounts to a fraudulent alienation under s 172 of the Law of Property Act 1925. However, this rule did apply where an absolute bill of sale was used.[8] Section 172 was repealed by the Insolvency Act 1985 Schedule 10 Part IV, and s 423 of the Insolvency Act 1986 which replaces it only applies to transactions at an undervalue. It will be a question of fact in each case whether a Bill of Sale could be attacked under that section. Chapter 21 deals with s 423. A mortgagor's possession has never been *prima facie* evidence of fraud in the case of a *bona fide* mortgage. However, failure to register under s 395(2)(c) of the Companies Act 1985 makes the security unenforceable against secured creditors and the liquidator.

3.05   An equitable mortgage of chattels can be created by the legal owner of the chattels making a contract which charges them in equity with the repayment of a loan, or by an agreement to grant a legal mortgage which can be the subject of an order for specific performance because the money has been paid. This will apply where no legal mortgage has been effectively created. The most common situation in which it will be impossible to create a legal mortgage will be one which involves future property. Since there is no need for writing to create a legal mortgage of chattels it is unlikely that an ineffective legal mortgage will result in an equitable mortgage. Providing the agreement identifies the property sufficiently and the loan has been paid to the borrower, property not yet owned by the borrower will be subject to an equitable mortgage as soon as he acquires it.[9]

3.06   In *Holroyd v Marshall* an agreement that the security for a loan was

---

5   *Maugham v Sharpe* (1864) 17 CBNS 443.
6   See paras 3.11–3.16 below on pledge and the possibility of constructive possession.
7   (1602) 3 Co Rep 80b.
8   *Pennel v Dawson* (1856) 18 CB 355.
9   *Holroyd v Marshall* (1862) 10 HL Cas 19.

to include a mortgage of machinery later installed in the borrower's mill created an equitable mortgage of such machinery effective as soon as the borrower acquired it. The owner of an equitable interest in a chattel may mortgage his chose in action if he is a beneficiary under a trust or charge his interest by a bill of sale if some other equitable interest is held.[10] This will create an equitable mortgage of the equitable interest held by the borrower.

3.07   In any case in which writing is used to create an equitable mortgage of a chattel it will be necessary for the company borrowing on that security to register the charge under s 396(1)(c) of Companies Act 1985 as such a charge would require registration as a bill of sale if it were executed by an individual. Failure to register a bill of sale granted by a company will render the security void against other secured creditors or the liquidator.[11] Non-registration of a bill of sale granted by an individual under the Bills of Sale Acts 1878–1882 makes the security void even as between the parties, and will frequently render the loan irrecoverable by the lender.[12]

3.08   It is possible to create an equitable charge on chattels whereby no legal or equitable interest is transferred to the chargee and possession remains with the chargor. This appropriates particular chattels to the payment of a debt. If an equitable charge is created by writing, the Bills of Sale Acts 1878–1882 will apply and registration under s 396(1)(c) of the Companies Act 1985 will be necessary. A common example of an equitable charge on goods is the letter of hypothecation (or charge) used by banks. A trading company wishing to buy goods (particularly imports) may borrow the purchase price from its bank on the security of the goods themselves. The security will be given by the company charging either all goods to be imported by it over a period by a general letter of hypothecation, or by a letter dealing only with the goods involved in a specific transaction. A general letter of hypothecation is outside the exception in s 1 of the Bills of Sale Act 1890 as replaced by s 1 of the Bills of Sale Act 1891, which relates only to charges on imported goods although a letter of hypothecation or a trust receipt dealing with identified goods, as opposed to future goods, would be within the exception so long as the goods were imports.[13]

3.09   The question of whether the Bills of Sale Act exemption for imported goods applies will determine whether registration by the company under

---

10   Bills of Sale Act 1878 s 4.
11   See below para 8 for a full discussion of registration under s 395.
12   Bills of Sale Act (1878) Amendment Act 1882 s 9.
13   *MV Slaveburg's Bank v Intercontinental Natural Resources Ltd* [1980] 1 All ER 955 per Lloyd J at p 977.

the Companies Act 1985, s 396(1)(c) is necessary. Any document which could be treated as being used in the ordinary course of business to prove the possession of goods would fall outside the definition in s 4, Bills of Sale Act 1878 of a bill of sale which is applied to securities by the Bills of Sale Act (1878) Amendment Act 1882 s 3. However, it is unlikely that a letter of hypothecation covering future goods by applying generally to any imports by the company could fall within this category.[14] A common form of security in international trade is a combination of the pledge of a bill of lading and a trust receipt—each relating to identifiable goods. This is dealt with below. The changes introduced by the Companies Bill 1989 to s 395 of the Companies Act 1985 which affect the charges that are registrable under that section are dealt with in chapter 8.

PLEDGE

3.10   A pledge of chattels is created by a transfer of possession to the lender, unlike a mortgage which operates by transfer of ownership.[15] Such a security can exist only at common law. 'Possession' has a wide meaning for this purpose as it can be that of the pledgee or of his agent. A pledge only lasts during the pledgee's possession of the goods and does not affect ownership. Registration under the Bills of Sale Acts 1878–1882 is not required—nor is registration under the Companies Act 1985 s 395.[16] This exemption from the need to register will only apply where the lender has taken actual or constructive delivery and does not claim the security by virtue of a document while the borrower remains in possession.[17] This form of security only applies to chattels or documentary intangibles— documents which represent the goods title to which they establish. It is likely that a company will borrow on the strength of a pledge most commonly when a bank finances purchases by reference either to a bill of lading which confers possession of the goods that it represents on endorsement and delivery or to the constructive possession of goods not physically held by the borrower or the lender. The fact that the lender has possession of pledged goods makes other uses of this security inconvenient in commercial transactions—the use of pawnbrokers by individuals being the other common example of the use of the security.[18] For that reason the

14   See *Re Slee ex parte North Western Bank* (1872) LR 15 Eq 69 where the letter of hypothecation applied to specific listed goods.
15   *Ryall v Rolle* (1749) 1 ATK 165.
16   *Re Hardwick ex parte Hubbard* (1886) 17 QBD 690; *Re Townsend ex parte Parsons* (1886) 18 QBD 532.
17   *Dublin City Distillery v Doherty* (1914) AC 823.
18   Such transactions are regulated by the Consumer Credit Act 1974 as personal credit agreements—ss 8(1) and 189(1), but this can never apply to a loan to a company.

meaning of 'possession' and the concept of constructive possession must be considered in some detail.

Possession by the pledgee

3.11 There can be no equitable pledge; a contract to pledge chattels does not confer any property in the chattels on the pledgee even if money is advanced on the strength of it. Delivery must take place before the pledge is completed.[19] This prevents a pledge from being available as a way of using a chose in action as security. The *ipsa corpora* of a document which incorporates a right can be pledged. A bill of lading is a document of title and thus a pledge of the bill is a pledge of the goods it represents without any attornment by the third party with actual custody of them. However, the common law has developed a broad doctrine of constructive delivery which means that the actual transfer of the custody of chattels from one party to the other is not always necessary for there to be delivery and therefore a change of possession.[20] The delivery of a key to a warehouse or other store where goods have been placed amounts to a constructive delivery as the key represents a way of taking possession or making use of the goods.[21] It has been held that there can be constructive delivery even where the goods are left with or returned to the pledgor providing this is done in his capacity as agent for the pledgee for a particular purpose.[22] This special purpose can include the sale of the goods and the pledgee's security will remain valid against the liquidator or other creditors of the pledgor should liquidation intervene.[23] Constructive delivery to the pledgee will prevent any document used to regulate the rights of pledgor and pledgee from being a bill of sale as the document does not create the security interest which arises because of the transfer of possession.[24] The taking of possession by a pledgee, although essential to the existence of a pledge, need not be simultaneous with the debt being incurred—it can take place before or after the debt arises.[25] However, the security only takes effect from the time when the pledgee takes possession.

3.12 A common situation for trading companies will be the use of goods as security for a bank loan at a time when the goods are in the possession of a third party and not of the company. The third party may be a warehouseman or a carrier. In these circumstances English law requires

19 *Dublin City Distillery v Docherty* (1914) AC 823.
20 *Martin v Reid* (1862) 11 CBNS 730.
21 *Ward v Turner* (1751) 2 Ves Sen 431 at 443.
22 *Reeves v Capper* (1838) 5 Bing NC 136.
23 *North Western Bank Ltd v John Poynter & Son and MacDonalds* [1894] AC 56.
24 *Ex parte Hubbard* (1886) 17 QBD 690.
25 *Hilton v Tucker* (1888) 39 Ch D 669.

that there be an instruction from the pledgor to the third party who has custody of the goods to hold them on behalf of the pledgee and an acknowledgement by the third party that he does so hold them. This is known as an attornment.[26] The attornment is necessary to perfect the security, and the delivery to the pledgee of a document (other than a bill of lading)[27] which evidences the pledgor's title to the goods does not amount to delivery of the goods themselves.[26] A bill of lading when endorsed and delivered by way of pledge constitutes a delivery of the goods themselves to the pledgee and therefore creates a pledge without the attornment or even the knowledge of the master of the ship on which the goods are being carried.[27] No other document has this effect at common law, although under s 3 of the Factors Act 1889 a pledge of a document of title by a mercantile agent in possession of it operates in favour of a *bona fide* pledgee without notice of any irregularity as a pledge of the goods so long as the pledge was for money lent at the time of the pledge or later. 'Documents of title' for this purpose include:

"Any bill of lading, dock warrant, warehouse-keeper's certificate, and warrant, or order for the delivery of goods, and any other document used in the ordinary course of business as proof of the possession or control of goods, or authorising or purporting to authorise, either by endorsement or by delivery the possessor of the document to transfer or receive goods thereby represented."[28]

This definition includes a delivery order relating to goods that are not specific (in the Sale of Goods Act sense) and even one created by the owner of the goods,[29] but not the registration documents of motor vehicles.[30]

3.13   It is clear that the delivery of documents within that definition only represents a delivery of the goods where the pledge is by a mercantile agent.[31] He thus has greater power than the true owner—even if he is defrauding the true owner. Documents used in the ordinary course of business as proof of possession, or control of goods or authorising or purporting to authorise either by endorsement or by delivery the possessor of such document to transfer or receive goods thereby represented, and letters of hypothecation made before imported goods are deposited in store, reshipped for export, or delivered to a purchaser are exempted from the definition of a bill of sale within the meaning of the Bills of Sale Acts 1878–1891. This means that a company need not register such documents

26 *Official Assignee of Madras v Mercantile Bank of India Ltd* [1935] AC 53.
27 *Sewell v Burdick* (1885) 10 App Cas 74 at 83.
28 Factors Act 1889 s 1(4).
29 *Ant Jurgens Margarinenfabriken v Lois Dreyfus & Co* [1914] 3 KB 40.
30 *Central Newbury Car Auctions Ltd v Unity Finance Ltd* [1957] 1 QB 371.
31 *Inglis v Robertson & Baxter* [1898] AC 616.

under the Companies Act 1985 s 396(1)(c).[32] The fact that a pledgor is unable to make use of pledged goods causes difficulties with this form of security. It is most frequently used in conjunction with letters of hypothecation and trust receipts.

3.14   If a bill of lading is delivered to a bank, properly endorsed, then this will amount to a pledge of the goods which it represents. This transaction need not be registered under the Bills of Sale Acts 1878–1891 as it is a security based on possession and there is no document of transfer. A bill of lading is exempt as a document used as proof of the possession and control of goods under s 4 of the Bills of Sale Act 1878 and, in any event, s 1 of the Bills of Sale Act 1890 would exempt a charge over imported goods. Consequently there is no charge registrable under s 395 of the Companies Act 1985.

3.15   However, in order to sell the goods the company will require the use of the bill of lading. This is achieved by the release by the bank to the company of the bill of lading and any other necessary documents in return for a trust receipt (or letter of trust) in which the company acknowledges that it has received the documents and will hold them (and the goods and proceeds of sale thereof) as trustees for the bank. This means that redelivery of the pledged goods or documents to the pledgor is for a specific purpose of the pledgee bank (sale) which the pledgor company will carry out as the agent of the bank. Thus the pledge continues even while the documents are in the pledgor's hands.[33] The trust receipt is not registrable as a bill of sale (or under the Companies Act 1985 s 395) as it is not an independent security device but a means of continuing the pledge.[34] It does not create a charge—and even if it did so it would be outside the definition in s 4 of the Bills of Sale Act 1878 as a document used in the ordinary course of business as proof of the possession or control of goods.[35] The bank's claim to the goods or the proceeds of sale therefore takes priority over a claim by the liquidator of the company without registration of any document and despite the release of the bill of lading to the company.[34]

3.16   The liquidator, administrative receiver, or administrator of an insolvent company must therefore take considerable care to ascertain the precise nature of any security granted by the company over chattels. It will be vital to ascertain whether the security is based on any transfer of title and

32   See Bills of Sale Act 1878 s 4; Bills of Sale Act 1878 (Amendment) Act 1882 s 3, and Bills of Sale Act 1890 s 1.
33   *North Western Bank Ltd v John Poynter & Son* [1895] AC 56.
34   In *Re David Allester Ltd* [1922] 2 Ch 211 at 216.
35   In *Re Hamilton Young & Co* [1905] 2 KB 772 at 785 but see para 8.62 re Companies Bill 1989.

is effected by a document in which case registration under the Companies Act 1985 s 395 will be necessary for the validity of the transaction, or whether the security is based on possession, in which case registration may not be necessary.[35]

SECURITY INTEREST IN SHIPS[36]

3.17 Ships are chattels, but the creation of a legal mortgage over a ship is governed by statute, and for that reason this topic requires separate treatment.

Legal mortgages of ships

3.18 A legal mortgage of a British ship or a share or shares in such a ship[37] must be registered by the registrar of the ship's port of registration.[38] The mortgage should take the form set out in Form B of Schedule 1 of the Merchant Shipping Act 1894, or be as near to it as circumstances permit. Separate forms are laid down to secure principal and interest on the one hand or to secure a current account on the other. The mortgage may make the ship, or the share in a ship, security for a loan or other valuable consideration. Mortgages are recorded by the registrar in the order in which he receives notice of them.[39] Transfers or assignments of ships or vessels or shares therein are outside the definition of a bill of sale[40] whether or not the vessel is one the ownership and therefore the mortgaging of which must be registered under the Merchant Shipping Act 1894. Thus certain vessels which operate on non-tidal waters are outside each statute.[41]

3.19 A registered mortgage applies to all articles necessary for the navigation of the ship or the adventure on which it is used and articles substituted for them after the date of the mortgage.[42] When a mortgage is granted all the rights and powers of the owner of a registered ship remain with the mortgagor except those that are necessary for the purpose of making the ship (or share of it) available as a security for the mortgage debt.[43] The mortgagee is normally bound by a charterparty granted by a

---

36 See generally as to this heading and para 3.28 *infra* N Meeson, "Ship and Aircraft Mortgages", Lloyds of London 1988.
37 There are 64 shares in a ship.
38 Merchant Shipping Act 1894 s 31(1).
39 Merchant Shipping Act 1894 s 31(2).
40 Bill of Sale Act 1878 s 4.
41 *Gapp v Bond* (1887) 19 QBD 300.
42 *Coltman v Chamberlain* (1890) 25 QBD 328.
43 Merchant Shipping Act 1894 s 34.

mortgagor in possession even if this means that the ship is taken out of the jurisdiction.[44]

3.20 The Merchant Shipping Act 1988 and regulations made under it introduce a separate system of registration for fishing vessels.[45] An instrument creating a mortgage of such a vessel must be on a form prescribed by the secretary of state.[46] All securities over such a vessel or a share in one which are for the repayment of a loan or the discharge of some other obligation are referred to as 'mortgages'.[47] When executed the document must be produced for the secretary of state for registration and endorsement of the fact of registration.

3.21 The registration of mortgages of fishing vessels takes place in order of production of the form to the secretary of state, and priorities of mortgages of the same vessel are determined by order of registration and not by reference to any other matter.[48] A system of prior notification of proposed mortgages is instituted to give priority for up to thirty days with the possibility of renewal for further thirty day periods. Initial registration of a ship after such a notification is registration subject to the proposed mortgage.[49] A registered mortgagee may transfer his interest by prescribed instrument or operation of law and has a power of sale and to give a receipt subject, in the case of prior mortgages of the same ship or share in the ship, to the consent of the prior mortgagee or a court order.[50] The discharge of a registered mortgage of a fishing vessel has to be registered but the termination of the registration of a vessel under the Act's provisions does not affect entries in the register of undischarged mortgages of fishing vessels or shares in them.[51] At the time of writing the system of registration is subject to challenge in the English courts on the grounds of incompatibility with European Community Law.[52]

Equitable mortgages of ships

3.22 An equitable mortgage of a registered ship can be created by the same methods as are available for other chattels. However, the statutory rules for registration make this an ineffective security against earlier or later legal mortgagees or subsequent registered owners of the vessel. No notice of

---

44 *The Fanchon* (1880) 5 PD 173, and see chapter 7 below on mortgagee's remedies.
45 Merchant Shipping Act 1988 ss 13 to 23 and sch 3 and SI 1988/1926.
46 *Ibid* sch 3 para 2(2).
47 *Ibid* paras 2(1) and 2(2).
48 *Ibid* paras 2(3)(4) and 3.
49 See *Ibid* para 4 and para 8.130 *infra* in this book.
50 *Ibid* paras 5 and 6.
51 *Ibid* para 8 and s 8 of the Act.
52 See *R v Secretary of State for Transport ex parte Factortame Ltd* (1989) The Times 24th March 1989.

any trust can be registered and the registered owner has power absolutely to dispose of his ship or share in accordance with the Merchant Shipping Act 1894, subject only to rights registered under that Act.[53] However, equitable interests can be enforced in relation to ships in the same way as those applicable to any other personal property.[54] There are no formalities laid down by statute for the creation of equitable mortgages of ships and notice of them cannot be registered but the mortgagor will be bound and the competing rights of holders of equitable interests will be governed by the normal rules of equity.[55] A mortgagee whose legal mortgage is registered will take free of any prior equitable mortgage (including a floating charge)[56] whether or not he has notice of it, and the purchaser of the ship who is registered as its owner will also be bound only by registered mortgages. This is in contrast to the position in relation to other property.

Registration and mortgagee's rights

3.23   A corporate mortgagor will have to register any mortgage of a ship under s 395(2)(h) of the Companies Act 1985, but if this is done the liquidator of the mortgagor company will take subject to any valid mortgage of a ship whether it is legal or equitable. An attempt to create a legal mortgage which is unsuccessful because of non-registration under the Merchant Shipping Act 1894 will take effect as an equitable mortgage. There may also be an equitable charge against a ship, for example, for any excess hire paid under an uncompleted charterparty.

3.24   A mortgagee in possession of a ship has the right to freight payable to the mortgagor under a charterparty and a mortgagee not in possession may intercept it when the mortgagor defaults by giving notice to the charterer to pay it to him.[57] However, until this is done, the right to be paid freight is a chose in action which can be used as security separately from the ship by the person entitled to it.[58] However, the right of the mortgagee of a ship to freight will take priority over an earlier assignment of the freight unless he had notice of the assignment when his mortgage was created.[57]

3.25   The use of the cargo of a ship as security is also excluded from the statutory rules that apply to mortgages of ships and is governed by the common law rules that apply to other chattels. However, the special status of the bill of lading which enables delivery of the document to amount to delivery of the goods makes it easier to pledge a cargo than it is to pledge

53   Merchant Shipping Act 1894 s 56.
54   *Ibid*, s 57.
55   See para 8.130 below, Priorities.
56   *Black v Williams* [1895] 1 Ch 408.
57   *Wilson v Wilson* (1872) LR 14 Eq 32.
58   See chapter 4 below on security over choses in action.

other chattels. A mortgagee of a ship who has his own separate insurance policy on the vessel—unconnected with the ship owner—can claim on the policy even if the constructive total loss of the ship has been caused by the deliberate act of the shipowner.[59]

Bottomry bonds and respondentia

3.26 These forms of security are peculiar to ships and are not now commonly used. A bottomry bond charges the ship, and sometimes the freight, with the repayment of a loan after the voyage is completed. A respondentia bond charges the cargo on similar terms and can be granted in similar circumstances. Both forms of security are granted by the master of the ship on the basis of implied authority and are only valid if there is a necessity to raise the money by bottomry or respondentia because of unforeseen necessity or distress and in order to complete a voyage already begun.[60] The lender is obliged to make reasonable inquiries about the necessity for the money he lends.[61] A bottomry bond (unlike a mortgage) will always place the risk of the voyage on the lender so that no repayment of principal or interest will be due if the ship is lost before the end of the voyage as defined by the parties to the bond.

3.27 The master must contact, or attempt to contact, the owner of the ship (or of the cargo in the case of respondentia) before charging the ship or the cargo.[62] Failure to do so will make the bond invalid unless there was urgency which made communication impractical.[63] There is no duty on the holder of a bottomry bond to notify a mortgagee when the ship is in the possession of the mortgagor although it has been said that it is desirable to do so.[64] Bottomry bonds and respondentia bonds rank in priority among themselves in reverse order of creation, the latest ranking first, and a later bond takes priority over an earlier registered mortgage subject to unreasonable delay in enforcement causing prejudice to the mortgagee who may then use the doctrine of laches against the bond holder.[65]

AIRCRAFT AS SECURITY

3.28 Aircraft are chattels. The creation of mortgages over them does not require registration under the Mortgaging of Aircraft Order 1972[66] but

59   *Schiffshypotheken Bank v Luebeck AG v Compton* (1988) The Times 5th January 1988.
60   *The Reliance* (1833) 3 Hagg 66 and *The Lockiel* (1843) 2 WRob 34.
61   *The Orelia* (1833) 3 Hagg 75.
62   *Glascott v Lang* (1847) 2 Ph 310.
63   *Cargo ex Sulton* (1859) Swab 504; *The Olivier* (1862) Lush 484.
64   *The Helgoland* (1859) Swab 491.
65   *The Priscilla* (1859) Lush 1; *The Royal Arch* (1857) Swab 269.
66   SI 1972 No 1268.

such registration is necessary for priority purposes.[67] There is no specified form of mortgage but a registrable mortgage may only extend to a store of spare parts and to the aircraft itself—the definition does not otherwise include a mortgage created as a floating charge.[68] A mortgage by a company of any aircraft (whether the aircraft or mortgage is registered or not) must be registered under s 396(1)(h) of the Companies Act 1985.[69] The Bills of Sale Acts 1878 and 1882 do not apply to any mortgage of an aircraft which is registered in the United Kingdom nationality register. This exemption applies whether the mortgage is registered or not, so long as the aircraft is registered.[70] Subject to these provisions and the effect of registration or non-registration of aircraft mortgages on priorities, the general law as to mortgages of chattels applies to mortgages of aircraft.

---

67 See para 8.135 below, Priorities.
68 Article 2(2) of the Mortgaging of Aircraft Order 1972.
69 As amended by the Mortgaging of Aircraft Order 1972 Article 16(2) which inserts the word 'aircraft' without any qualification as to registration.
70 *Ibid*, Article 16(1).

CHAPTER 4

Security Interests over Choses in Action and Intellectual Property

THE NATURE OF SECURITY RIGHTS OVER CHOSES IN ACTION

4.01 Choses in action are 'all rights and incorporeal things, not being chattels real or choses in possession'.[1] Choses in possession are tangibles which can be reduced to possession and were dealt with in chapter 3 as 'personal chattels'. Both choses in action and personal chattels represent personal property as opposed to real property, which is an interest in land. Leases are strictly chattels real (a form of personal property) but for all practical purposes can be treated as land. Choses in action are rights rather than things, and the classic example is the debt; a right to sue for money. However, this category of intangibles includes shares, copyrights, patents and trademarks as well as rights under executory contracts (for example of insurance). A company which grants fixed security over the benefits of concessions or franchises which it holds, or of agency or distribution agreements (or any agreements for the exploitation of intellectual property rights), is offering choses in action as security. A leasehold is not a chose in action but a corporate landlord's right to rent is such an asset.

4.02 The importance of the distinction between choses in action and personal chattels before 1873 was that, at common law, choses in action could not be assigned, whereas assignment by delivery was always possible for personal chattels which, by definition, can be reduced to possession.[2] As a result of this, specific methods were laid down by statute for the legal assignment of shares in companies, life assurance policies, patents and other particular choses in action. Negotiable instruments and bills of lading are unusual in that the document has always been treated as the chose and thus delivery is possible. This derives from the adoption by English law of the rule of the Law Merchant. The debt is locked up in the document.[3] For this reason such documentary intangibles could be transferred by delivery—and they could be subject to the possessory security of a pledge. Other choses in action could only be subject to an equitable assignment.

---

1 Crossley Vaines, *Personal Property*, 5th edn 1973, p 11.
2 *Lampet's Case* (1613) 10 Co Rep 46b, 48a; *Fitzroy v Cave* [1905] 2 KB 364 at 372.
3 See R Goode, *Commercial Law*, 1982, p 66.

4.03   For the purpose of using choses in action as security, assignment is crucial and s 136 of the Law of Property Act 1925[4] makes this possible at common law as well as in equity. The whole range of legal mortgages, equitable mortgages and equitable charges is available for choses in action. However, it is also necessary to consider the particular methods of creating a security interest which apply to particular forms of chose in action when special statutory rules are laid down.[5]

4.04   For a company there is no general rule on whether charges over choses in action have to be registered under s 395 of the Companies Act 1985. Since such property is specifically excluded from the definition of personal chattels in the Bills of Sale Act 1878[6] a charge of it does not need to be registered under s 396(1)(c). However, a charge on goodwill, patents, copyrights or trademarks will be registrable under s 396(1)(i); a charge over book debts is registrable under s 396(1)(e);[7] a charge over any property to secure an issue of debentures is registrable under s 396(1)(a) and a floating charge needs to be registered under s 396(1)(f). The only major exclusion in respect of a chose in action is a charge over debts which do not come within the definition of book debts if it is not granted either to secure an issue of debentures or in the form of a floating charge.

STATUTORY ASSIGNMENT OF A CHOSE IN ACTION

4.05   As with chattels, a mortgage of a chose in action is created by assignment with a proviso for redemption. To create a legal mortgage the assignment must comply with s 136 of the Law of Property Act 1925 which states:

"(1) Any absolute assignment by writing under the hand of the assignor (not purporting to be by way of charge only) of any debt of other legal thing in action, of which express notice in writing has been given to the debtor, trustee or other person from whom the assignor would have been entitled to claim such debt or thing in action is effectual in law (subject to equities having priority over the right of the assignee) to pass and transfer from the date of such notice—
    (a) the legal right to such debt or thing in action;
    (b) all legal and other remedies for the same; and

---

4   This replaced s 25(g) of the Judicature Act 1873.
5   See below, paras 4.15–4.18, 4.19–4.32, 4.58.
6   Bills of Sale Act 1878 s 4—thus assignments of book debts (present or future) are excluded—*Tailby v Official Receiver* (1888) 13 App Cas 513.
7   This does not include a sale of such receivables—*Olds Discount Co Ltd v John Playfair Ltd* [1938] 3 All ER 275. A book debt is a debt arising in the course of a trade or business or connected with the same and due to the proprietor (in this context the company)—*Shipley v Marshall* (1863) 14 CBNS 566 and see paras 8.25–8.41 and 8.62–8.68.

(c) the power to give a good discharge for the same without the concurrence of the assignor:

provided that if the debtor, trustee or other person liable in respect of such debt or thing in action has notice—

    (a) that the assignment is disputed by the assignor or any person claiming under him;

or

    (b) of any other opposing or conflicting claims to such debt or thing in action;

he may, if he thinks fit, either call upon the persons making claim thereto to interplead concerning the same, or pay the debt or other thing in action into court under the provisions of the Trustee Act 1925.

(2) This section does not affect the provisions of the Policies of Assurance Act 1867."

4.06 The assignment must be absolute, by writing under the hand of the assignor, and must not purport to be by way of charge only. Despite the use of the words "other legal thing in action" equitable choses in action are within this section.[8] Indeed, while s 136 gives the assignee all the procedural advantages of legal title, for priority purposes his position is no better than it was before a statutory provision existed. Priorities are determined on the basis that the assignment was effected in equity and not at law.[9]

4.07 An assignment will be regarded as absolute even if it is subject to a proviso for redemption so that the morgagee may, in future, be subject to a duty to assign the debt back to the mortgagor.[10] On the other hand, a direction to pay an amount out of a sum due may merely be a charge[11] and be valid only in equity.[12] An assignment by deed is effective under the section despite the requirement that the document be 'under the hand of the assignor'.[13] It is uncertain whether there can be an absolute assignment of part of a debt, but it seems that this is not possible.[14] The application of the section to 'any debt or other legal thing in action' has been held to exclude shares in companies from this procedure as they are not 'debts'.[15] Also, it does not enlarge the class of assignable things in action which existed in equity before 1873.[16] The right to sue in tort or contract is assignable only if

---

8   *Re Pain* [1919] 1 Ch 38 and *Torkington v Magee* [1902] 2 KB 427 at 430.

9   *E Pfeiffer v Arbuthnot Factors* [1987] BCLC 522.

10 *Tancred v Delgoa Bay & East Africa Railway Co* (1889) 23 QBD 239.

11 *Durham Brothers v Robertson* [1898] 1 QB 765 where there was automatic reverter to the assignor without retransfer—the assignment itself was conditional.

12 *Re Earl of Lucan* (1890) 45 Ch D 470—The validity of such a charge in equity depends on the presence of valuable consideration.

13 *Marchant v Morton, Down & Co* [1901] 2 KB 829

14 See *Forster v Baker* [1910] 2 KB 636; *Williams v Atlantic Assurance Co Ltd* [1933] 1 KB 81; *Walter Sullivan Ltd v J Murphy & Sons Ltd* [1955] 2 QB 584, and contrast *Skipper & Tucker v Holloway* [1910] 2 KB 630; *Re Steel Wing Co Ltd* [1921] 1 Ch 349, and *Ramsey v Hartley* [1977], 1 WLR 686.

15 *Torkington v Magee* [1902] 2 KB 427 at 430—and see paras 4.19–4.32 below for the special rules applying to shares.

16 *Tolhurst v Associated Portland Cement Manufacturers* [1903] AC 414 at 424.

equity would, at that time, have forced the assignor to sue on the contract or for the damages in tort on behalf of the assignee.[17]

4.08   In addition to these matters, it is necessary that express notice in writing of the legal assignment be given to the debtor, trustee or other person who owes the obligation which is the subject matter of the assignment. The notice, which is essential before an assignee can sue in his own name, can be given at any time before the action is begun[18] although early notice is important for priority purposes under the rule in *Dearle v Hall* as extended by s 137(1) of the Law of Property Act 1925 and so that the debtor knows who to pay. Notice must be given in the statutory form even if the debtor cannot read and became aware of the assignment in some other way.[19] No rigid form of notice is laid down by the Act, but the fact of assignment must be indicated with sufficient certainty and the name of the assignee must be indicated—albeit only by an express and accurate reference in the notice to the assignment document.[20] The notice (and therefore the legal assignment) is effective on the date of receipt of the notice by or on behalf of the debtor.[21]

4.09   The mortgagee takes subject to any prior equities that existed between the mortgagor and the debtor. This includes any right of the debtor—for example a right of set-off—that arose before the assignment took effect. This will be the position regardless of whether the assignee had notice of that right.[22] This rule applies quite apart from the question of the priorities of the different assignees of the same chose in action.[23]

EQUITABLE ASSIGNMENTS OF CHOSES IN ACTION

4.10   An equitable assignment of a chose in action for security purposes can be created in the familiar ways. Any attempt to create a legal mortgage by assignment under s 136 of the Law of Property Act 1925, which fails because of the absence of some of the statutory requirements, will result in an equitable mortgage, providing the intention to create a mortgage is clear and consideration has been provided. This takes effect as an agreement to create a legal mortgage (hence the need for consideration). An assignment which grants a determinable interest, and is not 'absolute' for the purposes

17 *Compania Colombiana De Seguros v Pacific Steam Navigation Co* [1965] 1 QB 101.
18 *Bateman v Hunt* [1904] 2 KB 530 CA.
19 *Hockley and Papworth v Goldstein* (1920) 90 LJ KB 111.
20 *Denney Gasquet and Metcalfe v Conklin* [1913] 3 KB 177.
21 *Holt v Heatherfield Trust Ltd* [1942] 2 KB 1.
22 *Roxburghe v Cox* (1881) 17 Ch D 520.
23 See below, paras 8.11–8.117.

of s 136, will result in an equitable mortgage.[24] If it is the case that an assignment of part of a debt cannot be absolute then an equitable charge may nonetheless be created by an attempt to do this.[25]

4.11 An equitable mortgage of a chose in action may be created by an express agreement to create a legal mortgage (rather than a failure in the attempt to do so). After a debt has been mortgaged by legal assignment under s 136 any later mortgage of it must be an equitable mortgage of the equity of redemption.[26] It is also possible to create an equitable charge so that the chargee is entitled to claim the amount owed by the chargor from the chose in action and not to claim the whole of the chose. Such a security can never be a legal mortgage.[27] The fund against which the chargee can claim must be clear[28] and there must be an intention that property will pass.[29] There must either be a direction to the person who owes the money to pay the chargee or an agreement between the chargor and the chargee that the debt is to be charged.[30]

4.12 An equitable mortgage or charge of a chose in action can be oral or in writing[31] subject to the rule that a disposition of an equitable interest in or trust of land subsisting at the time of the disposition must be in writing, and signed by the mortgagor or his agent authorised in writing or by will.[32] In practice a deed is normally used to mortgage an interest in a trust fund by assignment of the interest with a proviso for re-assignment on redemption. Since an equitable chose in action can be assigned under s 136 Law of Property Act 1925, it may be that such property can be subject to a legal mortgage (contrary to the rule which applies to land).[33] However, it is commonly believed that a mortgage of an equitable interest must be an equitable mortgage.

4.13 An equitable mortgage of a chose in action is effective despite the absence of any notification of the original debtor or the trustee. However, notice is important for priority reasons as between assignees of the chose in action; to prevent the original debtor or trustee from effectively discharging his obligation by paying the assignor and to prevent further equities arising between the debtor and the assignor from binding the assignee.[34] The

24 *Durham Bros v Robertson* [1898] 1 QB 765.
25 See the cases at footnote [14] above—especially *Re Steel Wing Co Ltd* [1921] 1 Ch 349.
26 *Jones v Humphreys* [1902] 1 KB 10.
27 *Re Steel Wing Co Ltd* [1921] 1 Ch 349.
28 *Brown Shipley & Co v Kough* (1885) 29 Ch D 848.
29 *Gorringe v Irwell India Rubber Works* [1886] 34 Ch D 128.
30 *Rodick v Gandell* (1852) 1 De G M & G 763.
31 *Gurnell v Gardner* (1863) 4 Giff 626.
32 LPA 1925 s 53(1)(c).
33 See paras 2.02–2.06 above.
34 *Stocks v Dobson* (1853) 4 De Gm and see paras 8.113–8.118 below on priorities.

assignment is subject to equities such as right of set-off between the debtor and the assignor which arose before the creation of the mortgage or charge, but later equities will only affect the assignee if no notice of the assignment has been given to the debtor.[35]

4.14   In the case of an equitable mortgage of a legal chose in action the mortgagee must join the mortgagor as plaintiff (if he is willing) or defendant (if he is not) in any action against the original debtor.[36] The general rules for the use of choses in action for security allow the creation of a legal mortgage by the use of s 136 of the Law of Property Act 1925 or of an equitable mortgage or charge providing there is a clear intention to create a mortgage or charge and that consideration has been provided. There are, however, specific rules which apply to particular types of chose in action.

INSURANCE POLICIES

4.15   The most common use of insurance policies as security is by individuals who can mortgage life policies. A life policy is a useful asset for security purposes because of the certainty that payment will be made by the insurer. A company, since it cannot enter a contract of life assurance, will never use such a policy as security for its own debts. It may be that it will hold, as mortgagee, insurance policies on the lives of individual mortgagors. It may also use, as part of the security it provides for a loan to the company, a policy which insures some other asset which is given by the company as security. A mortgage of a ship owned by a company will frequently be supported by a mortgage of the insurance policy which covers the ship.[37] Such a mortgage is no different from a mortgage of any other chose in action and can be created either by the use of the procedure laid down in s 136 of the Law of Property Act 1925 or by way of an equitable mortgage of the policy. Such an equitable mortgage can be created by a deposit of the policy;[38] or agreement to create a legal mortgage[39] or an equitable charge can be created expressly.[40]

4.16   Unless the mortgage or charge over an insurance policy is a floating charge or is to secure an issue of debentures, it need not be registered under s 395 of the Companies Act 1985. This seems to be true even if the mortgage is of a policy of marine insurance and is made in connection with a

---

35 *Roxburghe v Cox* (1881) 17 Ch D 520.
36 See eg *Durham Bros v Robertson* [1898] 1 QB 765.
37 *Swan v Maritime Insurance Co* [1907] 1 K B 116, and see Marine Insurance Act 1906 ss 50 and 51 on the assignability of such policies.
38 *Re Wallis* [1902] 1 K B 719.
39 *Spencer v Clarke* (1878) 9 Ch D 137.
40 *Jones v Consolidated Investment Assurance Co* (1858) 26 Beav 256.

mortgage of a ship. Section 396(1)(h) applies to 'a ship', not to an insurance policy on a ship. A charge over an insurance policy is unlikely to be registrable as a charge over a book debt since even a policy issued by the Export Credit Guarantee Board to indemnify a company for the non-payment of debts due on export sales has been held not to be registrable.[41]

4.17 All the available methods of creating legal or equitable mortgages or charges apply to life policies but in addition there is a specific statutory method for creating a legal mortgage of such a policy. This requires the use of an absolute assignment under the Policies of Assurance Act 1867 subject to a right of redemption. This procedure is unaffected by the Law of Property Act 1925 s 136.[42] If the formalities required by the 1867 Act are followed then s 1 of that Act allows the assignee (mortgagee) to sue in his own name. The assignment must be in writing and either indorsed on the policy or made by a separate document which is in the form laid down in the Schedule to the 1867 Act.[43] By s 3 written notice of the assignment and the date of it must be given to the insurance company at one of their principal places of business as specified in the policy.[44] The mortgagee takes subject to any equities between insurer and insured which have arisen, for example, because of the failure of the insured to comply with the high level of disclosure to the insurer demanded by the fact that the contract of insurance is a contract *uberrimae fidei*.[45]

4.18 The mortgage will normally stipulate that the mortgagor must pay premiums on the policy and that if he fails to do so the mortgagee will pay and the amount paid will be a charge on the policy monies. Even if the mortgage does not contain such a provision, a mortgagee who has to pay premiums to keep the policy alive may add that amount to the sum otherwise secured on the policy.[46] Apart from the possibility of a mortgage of a life policy, a creditor can take out a policy of life assurance on the life of his debtor. Subject to the additional method of creating legal mortgages of life policies laid down by the 1867 Act, the general rules as to mortgages of choses in action apply to insurance policies.

MORTGAGES OF SHARES

4.19 Shares, as an asset of a company, may be subject to security rights. Usually, such shares will be those of another company. They may be those

41   *Paul and Frank v Discount Bank (Overseas) Ltd* (1967) Ch 348.
42   Law of Property Act 1925 s 136(2).
43   s 5 1867 Act.
44   *Ibid*, s 4.
45   *Ibid*, s 2.
46   *Gill v Downing* (1874) LR 17 Eq 316.

of a subsidiary company or shares in a completely separate company held as an investment or as a prelude to some form of takeover of that company. The circumstances in which a company can own its own shares beneficially, and mortgage or charge them, are limited. Where a company purchases or redeems its own shares in accordance with ss 159–181 of the Companies Act 1985, the shares are treated as cancelled immediately and the company's issued share capital is reduced by the amount of their nominal value.[47] Such shares could never, therefore, be mortgaged or charged by the company.

4.20 Shares forfeited or surrendered to a public company or those acquired by such a company or its nominee in which it has a beneficial interest must be cancelled within three years of the acquisition unless they are disposed of first. In cases where a public company has a beneficial interest in shares in itself which were acquired by a person with financial assistance from the company the period is one year.[48] It is, however, possible that a public company, during the period before the cancellation of such shares, or a private company at any time, could grant a mortgage or charge over shares in itself which it held beneficially. As a general rule no company is allowed to be a member of its own holding company. This rule applies to holdings through a nominee except that this is permitted where the subsidiary company is concerned as a trustee or is beneficially interested only by way of security for the purposes of a transaction entered into by it in the ordinary course of a business which includes the lending of money.[49] It is possible for a company to hold a beneficial interest in shares in its own holding company by way of security if the subsidiary which holds the shares engages in the business of lending money and if the shares are taken as security in the course of that business.

4.21 A public company is prohibited from taking any charge or lien over its own shares and such charge or lien is void unless it is for an uncalled amount on partly paid shares or is a charge arising in connection with a transaction entered into in the course of the company's ordinary business of lending money, providing credit or hiring goods out on hire purchase.[50] For this purpose a public company does not include an 'old public company' which did not apply to re-register as a public company under s 8 of the Companies Act 1980, insofar as a charge on its shares was in existence on or immediately before the 22nd March 1982.[51] A company which has

47   s 160(4) and s 162(2) Companies Act 1985.
48   s 146 Companies Act 1985.
49   s 23 Companies Act 1985.
50   s 150 Companies Act 1985.
51   Companies Consolidation (Consequential Provisions) Act 1985 s 6(3).

registered or re-registered as a public company under s 680 of the Companies Act 1985 does not have a charge on its shares avoided if the charge was in existence immediately before the company's application for re-registration or registration.[52] There is no prohibition against a private company accepting its own shares as security subject to the general prohibition on the provision by any company of financial assistance for the purchase of its own shares.[53]

4.22 The creation of a mortgage or charge of shares is subject to particular rules as the legislature provided a statutory method of transferring shares in registered companies and thereby creating legal mortgages before 1873. The Law of Property Act 1925 s 136 does not apply to such transactions.[54] The courts have developed particular rules for priorities because the fact that the company is not a trustee for its shareholders makes notice to the company as trustee or debtor under the rule in *Dearle v Hall* inappropriate as a method of ascertaining the priorities of equitable assignment of shares.[55] Instead, an equitable owner may protect himself by the service of a 'stop notice' on the company after obtaining the issue of such a notice from the court. This will force the company to notify the equitable mortgagee or chargee of any application by the owner of the share to transfer it.[56] The general rules applicable to the priority of mortgages and charges apply to such interests in shares subject to appropriate rules to deal with the possibility of delay in the registration of a transfer as a result of provisions of the articles or the existence of stop notices.[57]

4.23 One consequence of the fact that the legal assignment of shares in a company is not carried out in accordance with s 136 of the Law of Property Act 1925 is that such an assignment is free from any equities which existed between the company and the original allottee or the transferor. A person who takes a transfer of shares without notice of any defect in the title of the allottee is protected from a claim of the company by a waiver when the company registers the transfer[58] and by the transferability conferred on shares by s 182 of the Companies Act 1985. This enables the transferee to take the shares free of any equity of which he was unaware.[59] These factors will also prevent a company from being able to enforce against the transferee a set-off to which it is entitled against the transferor. A transfer by

52 s 150(4) Companies Act 1985.
53 ss 151–158 Companies Act 1985.
54 *Torkington v Magee* [1902] 2 KB 427 at 430.
55 *Societe Generale de Paris v Walker* (1885) 11 App Cas 20 at 30.
56 See below, paras 8.125–8.126, priorities.
57 See Pennington, *Company Law*, 4th edn, ch 10.
58 *Higgs v Northern Assam Tea Co* (1869) LR 4 Exch 387.
59 *Re Romford Canal Co* (1883) 24 Ch D 85.

share warrant will protect the transferee who gives value and has no notice of any equities affecting the shares because of the nature of the warrant as a negotiable instrument.[60]

4.24   A mortgage or charge of shares, unless it is a floating charge or secures an issue of debentures, will not usually be registrable under s 395 of the Companies Act 1985. As shares are choses in action[61] charges over them do not fall within s 396(1)(c) because of s 4 of the Bills of Sale Act 1878 which expressly excludes shares from the scope of the Acts. However, a charge over the company's own uncalled share capital or on calls made but not paid is registrable.[62] The absence of any obligation to register a charge on, for example, shares held by a company in its subsidiary is a major omission from the list of charges registrable under s 395 and from the protection given to creditors by the disclosure of the interest.

4.25   A legal mortgage of shares is created by transferring the shares to the mortgagee subject to a proviso for retransfer on repayment of the loan. The transfer will either be by the method specified in the company's articles of association, or by the method laid down in the Stock Transfer Act 1963.[63] All transfers must be made by a proper instrument and must therefore be in writing regardless of any provision to the contrary in the company's articles.[64] The provisions of companies' articles often require a transfer to be executed by both transferor and transferee in the presence of witnesses, so the Stock Transfer Act 1963 was passed to allow a transfer signed by the transferor only without witnesses to be valid regardless of the requirements of the company's articles. The form set out in Schedule 1 of the Act can be used only in respect of fully paid shares or debentures. Certain transfers of shares may be made under procedures allowed by the Stock Transfer Act 1982 which provides for the systems of transfer used on the Stock Exchange.

4.26   It is generally accepted that the legal title to shares passes on registration of the transferee as a member in the company's register of shareholders.[65] Either transferor or transferee can apply for registration of the transfer, although it is usual for the transferee to do this.[66] Where only some of the shares comprised in a share certificate are to be transferred then

60   *Webb Hal & Co v Alexandria Water Co* (1905) 93 LT 339.
61   *Colonial Bank v Whinney* (1886) 11 App Cas 426.
62   s 396(1)(b)(g).
63   s 182(1)(b) Companies Act 1985.
64   s 183(1) Companies Act 1985 and *Re Greene* [1949] Ch 333.
65   *Societe Generale de Paris v Walker* (1885) 11 App Cas 20 and *Colonial Bank v Hepworth* (1887) 36 Ch D 36. However for a different view see Pennington, *op cit*, p 312.
66   s 183(4) Companies Act 1985.

the share certificate may be produced to the company secretary who will certify on the instrument that the share certificate was lodged on the transfer.[67] Where the mortgagee is registered as legal owner of the shares the mortgagor's equity of redemption will not appear on the register of shareholders.[68] The mortgagee will have the right to vote in company meetings but an agreement by him to vote in accordance with the mortgagor's instructions can be enforced by injunction, although in the absence of such a provision in the mortgage agreement the mortgagee may vote in accordance with his own wishes without consulting the mortgagor.[69] This means that a company which mortgages shares in its subsidiary may lose control unless the mortgage permits it to retain its voting rights.

4.27 If shares are not fully paid then the mortgagee will be responsible as against the company for paying any calls and, it seems that in respect of calls made during the existence of a mortgage the mortgagee will be liable as between mortgagor and mortgagee in the absence of agreement to the contrary.[70] However, the mortgagor is responsible for calls made before the creation of the mortgage. This rule appears to be contrary to principle in that when a call must be paid to avoid forfeiture of the shares to the company in accordance with its articles, payment is necessary to preserve the security and such costs incurred by a mortgagee can normally be added to the amount due from the mortgagor on the security.[71]

4.28 If the transfer of shares in a company is restricted by the company's articles of association then the directors may be justified in refusing to register a transfer. As such restrictions were necessary for a private company under the Companies Act 1948 s 28 until the changes introduced by the Companies Act 1980 abolished this requirement,[72] it is still common for the articles of association of private companies to give directors an absolute discretion on whether to register share transfers. This must be exercised properly in what the directors consider to be the interests of the company and not for some collateral purpose.[73] If their approval is won by fraud or concealment then the transaction may be set aside and rectification may be available to a transferor who is not estopped from claiming it.[74] The

---

67   s 184 Companies Act 1985 deals with the meaning and effect of certification by the company.
68   s 360 Companies Act 1985.
69   *Puddephatt v Leith* [1916] 1 Ch 200; *Siemens Bros & Co Ltd v Burns* [1918] 2 Ch 324.
70   *Phene v Gillan* (1845) 5 Hare 1, and *Re Patent Elastic Pavement and Kamptulicon Co* (1850) 3 De G & Sm 1 146.
71   See eg *Bellamy v Brickenden* (1861) 2 J & H 137, and *Detillon v Gale* (1802) 7 Ves 583.
72   See now Companies Act 1985 s 1(3).
73   *Re Smith & Fawcett Ltd* [1942] Ch 304.
74   *Re Bede Steam Shipping Co* [1917] 1 Ch 123, and *Hunter v Hunter* [1936] AC 222.

transferee can claim rectification if he proves that the directors acted improperly in refusing to register a transfer, but the discovery of the reasons or grounds for the directors' decision may be difficult or impossible.[75] Notification of a refusal to register a transfer must be sent to the transferee within two months of the transfer being lodged, and undue delay in dealing with the request for registration will cause a later refusal of registration to be invalid.[76]

4.29   A public company whose shares are quoted on the Stock Exchange will not be allowed to restrict the transferability of its fully paid shares. If share warrants are issued by a company it will be impossible for their transfer to be restricted because of the negotiability of the warrant.[77] This negotiability makes the use of such shares as security dependant on possession of the warrant which amounts to possession of the chose in action which it represents.

4.30   In the light of such potential difficulties and of the mortgagee's possible liability in the case of partly paid shares, it is hardly surprising that an equitable mortgage of shares protected by the deposit with the mortgagee of the share certificate and a blank transfer executed by the mortgagor is a common form of security. It seems that a deposit of a share certificate, without any other evidence of the form of security intended, creates an equitable mortgage in the same way that a deposit of title deeds to land would create such a security interest. This effect is achieved rather than the alternative which would be the creation of a pledge of the *ipsa corpora* of the share certificate.[78]

4.31   This represents an agreement to create a legal mortgage, and if the mortgagor has deposited a signed blank transfer the mortgagee has the right to enter his own name and apply for registration of a transfer to convert the mortgage into a legal one.[79] If a deed is required for a transfer the mortgagee will have to have a power of attorney from the mortgagor to allow him to complete the transfer.[80] However, he could insist on a new transfer because of the agreement to create a legal mortgage and, if the shares are fully paid, the provision on creation of the mortgage of a blank signed transfer in the common form laid down in Schedule 1 of the Stock Transfer Act 1963 will enable the shares to be transferred without any deed, regardless of the provisions of the company's articles.

75   *Re Coalport Chine* [1895] 2 Ch 404.
76   s 183(5) Companies Act 1985, and see *Re Swaledale Cleaners Ltd* [1968] 1 WLR 1710.
77   *Webb Hale & Co v Alexandria Water Co* (1905) 21 TLR 572.
78   *Harrold v Plenty* [1901] 2 Ch 314; contrast *Carter v Wake* (1877) 4 Ch D 605.
79   *Re Tahiti Cotton Co ex parte Sargent* (1874) LR 17 Eq 273 and see *Harrold v Plenty* (above).
80   *Powell v London & Provincial Bank* [1893] 2 Ch 555.

4.32 In practice it is usual for the deposit of the certificate and blank transfer to be supported by a memorandum of deposit under seal setting out the terms of the transaction such as the power of the mortgagee to sell (and his appointment as the mortgagor's attorney). The amount of principal and interest secured and the right of the mortgagee to include any bonus issue in the security will also be included.[81] The use of a document under seal in the creation of the mortgage will give rise to the statutory power of sale under the Law of Property Act 1925, s 101(1) and 103. The position of the mortgagee in relation to rights issues made by the company to its shareholders is unclear, but a Scottish case indicates the need for consultation with the mortgagor on whether such an issue should be taken up before it is declined by the mortgagee unless the mortgagor has already refused to pay for the new shares.[82] As is the case with land, an equitable charge of shares can be created and any agreement (or attempt) to create a legal mortgage will constitute an equitable mortgage.[83] If the interest in shares that is mortgaged is itself equitable then the mortgage of it will also be equitable.[84]

PARTNERSHIP SHARES

4.33 Although it is unlikely that a company would hold such property and therefore be able to use it as security, such a transaction is possible. Providing the activity of the partnership which the company joins is within the company's objects as set out in the memorandum of association and the power to enter a partnership is expressed in, or can be implied into, that clause there is nothing to prevent a limited company from being a partner in a firm.[85] It may be convenient for a company to enter a consortium with others and leave the organisation in the form of a partnership. This may be advantageous for tax or other reasons. In such a case the shares of the company in the partnership could be used by the company as security for a loan, and might well be subject to floating charge which sought to cover all of the company's undertaking and property.

4.34 The use of a partner's share as security by charging it in favour of a mortgagee in respect of the separate debts of the chargor partner gives the

---

81   It would seem that both the security right and the right of redemption applies to such bonus shares in any event by analogy with accretions to mortgaged land—*Maxwell v Ashe* (1752) 7 Ves Jun 184 note and *Ashford's case* (1880) 16 Ch D 411.
82   Although the problem is more likely to arise in the case of a legal mortgage, this principle will presumably apply whether the mortgage is legal or equitable. See *Waddell v Hutton* 1911 SC 575.
83   *Wise v Landsell* [1921] 1 Ch 420.
84   *Slade v Rigg* (1843) 3 Hare 35.
85   *Newstead v Frost* [1980] 1 All ER 363.

other partners the right to dissolve the partnership.[86] On dissolution (whether under s 33 or for any other reason) an assignee from a partner is entitled to an account from the date of the dissolution to ascertain the share of the assets to which he is entitled.[87] However, during the course of the partnership an assignee of a partner's share is not entitled, as against the other partners, to accounts or to the inspection of books or to take part in the management of the partnership business.[88] The assignee is only entitled to the assignor's share of profits. The methods of creating a mortgage of a partnership share are the same as those which apply to other choses in action, and notice to the other partners is important for priority purposes and their agreement to the mortgage may provide some practical assurance that there will not be a dissolution of the firm under s 33 of the Partnership Act 1890 by reason of the charge. Notice to the other partners will create a legal assignment under s 136 of the Law of Property Act 1925 and will be a priority point for the purpose of the rule in *Dearle v Hall*.[89]

BOOK DEBTS

4.35   The creation of a mortgage over debts is governed by the rules on the assignment of choses in action outlined above.[90] A charge over book debts will deal not only with those due to the borrower at the time of the creation of the charge but with those which are to become due in the future. It is well established that future debts can be the subject of an equitable charge.[91] This applies to any property not yet owned by the borrower although books debts are the commonest example in practice. The security over such debts must be granted by an agreement made for consideration which shows an intention that a security interest is to be conferred and makes it possible to determine at the time when particular property is acquired by the borrower whether it falls within the classes of asset described in the charge.[92] The agreement must be within that class of agreements for which an order of specific performance would be available in equity; for example, in the case of a loan agreement the money must have been advanced—but it is probably not necessary for a decree of specific performance to be available in the particular case before an equitable charge exists.[93]

4.36   The effect of this rule is that a borrower can agree to grant a fixed

86   Partnership Act 1890, s 33.
87   *Watts v Driscoll* [1901] 1 Ch 294.
88   Partnership Act 1890, s 31; *Re Garwood's Trust*, [1903] 1 Ch 236.
89   See paras 8.113–8.118 on Priorities.
90   See paras 4.05–4.14.
91   *Holroyd v Marshall* (1862) 10 HL Cas 191.
92   *Tailby v Official Receiver* (1888) 13 App Cas 523.
93   *Tailby v Official Receiver* (1888) 13 App Cas 523, *Re Lind* (1915) 2 Ch 345.

charge over any assets which he has not yet acquired, providing they can be identified as falling within the agreement. This creates a contractual right in the lender which attaches as an equitable charge to any assets falling within the terms of that agreement as soon as they are acquired. This occurs on acquisition of the asset without any further step being taken by the borrower,[91] and amounts to an equitable proprietary interest in the asset rather than a mere contractual right. There is no question of the breadth of the definition of assets covered by a charge making the agreement void for uncertainty *ab initio* providing it can be decided at the time of acquisition whether the asset which was acquired falls within its scope.[92] The question of the priority of such an equitable interest against the claims of other secured creditors depends on the rules on priority which apply to choses in action, but the holder of the equitable interest does have a real security which gives priority over unsecured creditors.[94]

4.37 Before there can be a mortgage at common law of property acquired after the execution of the document granting the security there must be some new act by the borrower passing ownership to the lender. This could be a further mortgage, delivery of the goods, attornment by the borrower to the lender as bailee, or seizure by the lender under express or implied licence. The development after *Holroyd v Marshall*[95] of the possibility of making an agreement which results in the creation of an equitable proprietary interest in favour of the lender on the acquisition by the borrower of an asset within the class described in the agreement avoids the need for such a *novus actus* although it may still be desirable for a mortgagee to establish that he has a legal rather than an equitable mortgage for the purpose of gaining priority.

4.38 Any charge (fixed or floating) on the book debts of a company must be registered under s 396(1)(e) of the Companies Act 1985. However, a charge over a debt which falls outside the definition of 'book debt' will not be registrable unless it falls into one of the other categories in the section because, for example, it is a floating charge or secures an issue of debentures. A book debt is defined as a debt arising in the course of a trade or business or connected with the same and which is due to the proprietor. This means that the courts will tend to interpret the phrase as dealing with a debt which, in the ordinary course of business, would be entered into the books of a well run enterprise.[96] This will include payments under a sale agreement if expert opinion on accounting practice indicates that they would be recorded in the company's books. A credit balance in a bank

94   See paras 8.113–8.118 on Priorities.
95   (1862) 10 HL Cas 191.
96   *Shipley v Marshall* (1863) 14 CBNS 566 *Re Brush Aggregates* [1983] BCLC 320.

account may be excluded because it is not, as a matter of business and accounting practice, usually seen as a debt. The whole question is one of fact and the construction of the document creating the charge on which evidence of accounting practice and the view of the parties on the nature of the asset will be important.[97]

4.39   For insolvent companies the issue of how a bank or other creditor can take a fixed charge rather than a floating charge on book debts is of great importance because of the effect the nature of the charge will have on the priority accorded to preferential creditors and the question of the priority of such a claim as against any later dealing with the book debts by the company.[98]

4.40   It has become common for a company's bankers to seek to take a fixed charge on the company's trade debts (or receivables) despite their nature as 'floating' assets which are constantly and inevitably changing while business carries on. There is some uncertainty about the requirements to be satisfied before such a charge is effective as a fixed charge rather than a floating charge.

4.41   In *Siebe Gorman & Co Ltd v Barclays Bank Ltd* [1979][99] Slade, J looked to the wording of the document creating the charge and the nature of the dealings between the bank and the company to decide the issue. He held that a charge expressed to be a 'first fixed charge' on 'all book debts . . . now and from time to time due and owing to the company' covered all the bills of exchange involved in the case and that there was no reason to deny the contractual intention of the parties since the mortgagor company could not dispose of unencumbered title to the subject matter of the charge without the mortgagee's consent. This was regarded as sufficient to indicate the creation of a fixed charge despite the fact that the charge applied to present and future assets of a class which changed in the ordinary course of business.[100]

4.42   The fact that the company was required by the debenture to pay all the proceeds of its book debts into its account which was subject to a lien by the bank whenever it was in credit was crucial to the decision.[101] This

97   *Re Brightlife* [1987] Ch 200 but see *Re Permanent Houses (Holdings) Ltd* (1989) 5 BCC 151 where the expressions 'book debt' or 'other debt' were construed not to encompass the credit balance on a bank account on the basis that it was unlikely that the company believed that it could only be used with the consent of the debenture holder.
98   See ch 5 on floating charges.
99   2 Lloyds Rep 142.
100   [1979] 2 Lloyds Rep at 142; see *Re Yorkshire Woolcombers' Association Ltd* (1903) 2 Ch 284 at 295.
101   [1979] 2 Lloyds Rep 142 at 159.

meant that the charge was not 'ambulatory' or 'shifting' (the features of a floating charge).[102] The restriction in the debenture on the company assigning (or creating further charges over) the debts subject to the lender's charge and limiting the company's dealings with its equity of redemption was not regarded as a necessary condition for the charge to be fixed.[103] It would therefore seem that the central issue is whether the company is free to dispose of the proceeds without paying them into a designated account. If this is so, the charge will be a floating one.[104] If not, the question is open. The courts tend to use the question of the use the company can make of the assets in the ordinary course of its business as both a quality of a floating charge and a criterion to decide whether a particular charge is fixed or floating. The description given to the charge is only one factor taken into account.

4.43   The application of this test has resulted in a decision in the Republic of Ireland that a charge described as a first fixed charge on present and future book debts was a floating charge despite a requirement that the proceeds of the debts be paid into the company's account with the bank. The latter stipulation was seen as evidence of an intention to allow the company to use the proceeds in the ordinary course of its business until the bank chose to freeze the account. The description given to the charge in this debenture did not displace that intention which was deduced from the court's examination of the document as a whole.[105]

4.44   This approach was forcefully rejected by Knox J at first instance in *Re a Company (005009 of 1987) ex parte Copp*.[106] In that case a debenture which followed the wording of the relevant clause in *Re Siebe Gorman* was held to confer a fixed charge over the company's debts by stipulating for such a security and requiring the proceeds of the debts to be paid into the company's account with the chargee bank. The absence of any express prohibition on the disposal of the proceeds of the book debts did not prevent that outcome as the role of precedent in providing security for commercial transactions and guidance for advisers required that the approach in *Siebe Gorman* be followed when a similar clause was used.[107] The existence of the decision in *Re Keenan Brothers* was not to be regarded as putting advisers on notice that such an express prohibition was required. The fact that a fluctuating overdraft was the advance secured by the charge

102   See *Illingworth v Holdsworth* (1904) AC 355 at 358.
103   Per Slade, J at p 160 and see *Re a Company ex parte Copp* [1989] BCLC 13.
104   *Re Yorkshire Woolcombers' Association Ltd* (1903) 2 Ch 284.
105   *Re Keenan Brothers Ltd* (1984) Irish Law Times 205, and see Pennington, 1985, *op cit* at p 20.
106   [1989] BCLC 13.
107   *Ibid* at p 25.

was regarded as collateral to the issue of the status of the charge and not as the badge of a floating charge.

4.45   Certainly the absence of any requirement for the payment of the proceeds of book debts into a separate account has been held to be fatal to the argument that a fixed charge exists—even where the charge is so described.[108] It is possible that in a later case the Court of Appeal will overrule *Siebe Gorman*[99] on the adequacy of a requirement to pay the proceeds of debts into an account with the lending bank as an indication of the existence of a fixed charge. It is at least possible that a greater emphasis will be placed in future on the need for restrictions on the use made by the company of money in such an account and on its availability to the company. It may be that restrictions on further dispositions by the company of the debts charged or their proceeds should be a significant factor in determining whether the asset subject to the charge can be used by the company in the normal course of business. This, however, is not the position according to *Siebe Gorman* and *Re a Company (005009 of 1987) ex parte Copp.*[106]

4.46   The Cork Report recommended a statutory definition of a floating charge which would have reversed *Siebe Gorman* by preventing restrictions on the creation of further charges; on the assignment of book debts; on the debtors' dealings with the proceeds of such debts or requirements for the prior consent of the lender to any transactions from being taken into account in determining whether the debtor was free to deal with the assets subject to the charge.[109] However, this proposal was not included in the Insolvency Act 1985.

4.47   It must be noted that it is only a charge or mortgage over book debts which represents a security interest. If the book debts are assigned outright by way of sale to a factor (in the usual commercial sense of the term rather than the legal sense used in the Factors Act 1889) there will be no need for any form of registration for priority purposes. The owner of the book debts will not be a creditor (secured or otherwise) on the company's insolvency.[110] The factor will be the owner of the debts even if he has the right of recourse against the company and the fact that the debts are discounted and cash is paid to the company but later repaid, as would be the case if the debts had been mortgaged, is irrelevant.[110] The factor will be

---

108   *Re Armagh Shoes Ltd* [1982] NI 59, and see *Re Lakeglen Construction Ltd* [1980] IR 347.
109   Cork Report 1982 Cmnd 8558, para 1586.
110   *Olds Discount Co Ltd v John Playfair Ltd* [1938] 3 All ER 275; *Chow Yoong Hong v Choong Fah Rubber Manufactory* [1962] AC 209.

a creditor to the extent that the agreement assigning the debts gives him recourse against the company in respect of bad debts. The factor who has purchased the company's book debts is in much the same position as the owner of goods leased or hired to the company, or of goods supplied under a hire purchase agreement, or a sale agreement which includes a retention of title clause.

4.48 Property in the debts having passed to him, the purchaser of the debts does not come within the range of creditors. It must be noted, however, that the assignment of the debts to him will be subject to any equities which the company may be entitled to raise against the original debtor. Under the Insolvency Act 1986 the factor to whom debts have been assigned by way of sale is in a better position than the vendor whose contract contains a retention of title clause or the hirer or lessor of goods to the company in that during the course of an administration order against the company the rights of a purchaser of the company's receivables cannot be suspended as part of the general moratorium.[111] It may be that the fact that a substantial part of the company's income from receivables has been factored and the terms on which this has been done would influence a court's decision whether to make an administration order. Since suppliers of finance who customarily use trade debts as security will usually buy the debts, the most common source of attempts to create a fixed charge over a company's present and future debts will be those debentures used by the clearing banks to secure their lending to companies on overdraft.

NEGOTIABLE INSTRUMENTS

4.49 Such instruments include cheques or other bills of exchange, promissory notes and bearer debentures or shares. It is unusual for negotiable instruments to be the subject of a security interest—particularly a mortgage—since they represent an exception to the general common law rules against the assignment of choses in action and can therefore be 'negotiated' to a holder in due course who will be unaffected by any defects in the title of an earlier holder providing the instrument is taken for value, in good faith, and without notice of any defect in the transferor's title. The instrument, if it is a bill of exchange, must not be overdue or have notice of dishonour endorsed on it.[112]

4.50 A bill of exchange payable to the bearer is negotiable simply by

---

111   Insolvency Act 1986, ss 10 and 11.
112   The provisions of Bills of Exchange Act 1882 and Cheques Act 1957 will apply to that form of negotiable instrument.

delivery. Where a bill is payable to order, both delivery and indorsement are required for negotiation.[113] The indorsement may be in blank, which will effectively convert the bill into a bearer instrument and allow negotiation by delivery only.[114] An indorsement which is special because it specifies in whose favour the instrument is indorsed will allow further negotiation of the instrument only by both delivery and further indorsement by the indorsee. If an order bill is transferred for value but without an indorsement then the transferee acquires such title as the transferor had and also the right to have the bill indorsed by the transferor,[115] and that right is enforceable by action against the transferor.[116] Until the instrument is indorsed the transferee is not a holder in due course and is in the same position as any other equitable assignee of a chose in action. Notice of fraud, to him before indorsement, affects his rights,[117] and he can neither sue on the bill in his own name nor negotiate the bill to another party. For these reasons the delivery of an instrument payable to order gives a mortgagee a poor title. Therefore such a mortgagee would demand that the instrument be indorsed and delivered so that he obtains the benefit of being a holder in due course.

4.51   The negotiability of negotiable instruments means that a company can use them to obtain credit by issuing or discounting bills or promissory notes rather than by mortgaging such documents. A mortgagor cannot easily guard against a mortgagee negotiating the instrument at any time and leaving the borrower with only a personal remedy against the lender. In the case of *Hills v Parker*[118] Lord Cranworth LC expressed his unfamiliarity with mortgages of bills of exchange and stated that when a bill becomes due it is no longer a security as the holder can get payment from the acceptor of the amount due in full or partial discharge of the debt.[119] In principle, it would seem that the appropriate method of creating a mortgage of a negotiable instrument would be to assign it with an agreement for reassignment on payment of the debt for which it is security. Since a valid negotiation of the instrument would be required by a prudent lender to avoid taking a transfer subject to defects in the title of earlier holders, the need for a mortgage would be academic if the instrument were for the full amount due or less as the lender as holder in due course could demand full payment from the acceptor because of the nature of the instrument.

---

113 Bills of Exchange Act 1882, ss 31(2), 31(3) and 89.
114 *Ibid*, ss 34(1) and 31(2).
115 *Ibid*, ss 31(4).
116 *Rose v Sims* (1830) 1 B & Ad 521.
117 *Whistler v Foster* (1863) 14 CBns 248.
118 (1866) 14 LT 107.
119 *Ibid*, at 108–109.

4.52 The decision in *Hills v Parker*[118] that a negotiable instrument for a lower amount than the sum borrowed can also be redeemed by the borrower at face value regardless of other debts due to the lender makes such an instrument unsatisfactory from a lender's point of view. The assignment of an instrument of face value greater than the amount of the debt is hard to distinguish from the issue or discounting of a promissory note or other instrument—a more straightforward means of using a negotiable instrument to obtain or provide finance. A borrower would be unwise to assign as security a negotiable instrument, the face value of which exceeded the debt due and any interest thereon, although if he did so the agreement between him and the lender would result in the lender holding any balance over the amount needed to pay off the debt on trust for the borrower. The lender would be entitled as a holder in due course to enforce payment for the full amount, but would have to hand over the surplus.[120] This results from the fact that the assignment of ownership necessary to create a mortgage would make the lender a holder in due course as it would amount to a negotiation of the bill. Full negotiation by indorsement and delivery (or delivery only depending on the type of instrument) would create a legal mortgage, and agreement to do so would be specifically enforceable in equity. In *Peacock v Pursell*[121] it appears that a bill indorsed to a borrower by the payee was assumed to be enforceable against earlier holders and the acceptor by a lender with possession of it without any indorsement in his favour.

4.53 A company is more likely to assign negotiable instruments absolutely than to transfer title by way of mortgage because the benefits of discounting make mortgaging unnecessary in the case of bills of exchange. A pledge is, however, more likely to be intended where a bearer bond or share warrant is deposited. It is well established at common law that negotiable instruments can be pledged as security for a debt. In *Carter v Wake*[122] the remedy of foreclosure was held not to be available where a bond had been deposited as an order for sale is the appropriate remedy in a case of pledge. However, where a bill of exchange is indorsed in blank and delivered to a holder who provides value and acts in good faith the acceptor will be liable to that holder despite the fact that it was deposited by way of pledge.[123]

4.54 This will not be the case where the negotiable instrument (not being a

---

120   This is certainly the case where the negotiable instrument is used by way of pledge or where the holder has a lien—*Peacock v Pursell* (1863) 32 LJCP 266 per Byles, J at 268, and *Reid v Furnival* (1833) 1 Cr & M 528.
121   (1863) LJCP 266.
122   (1877) 4 Ch D 605.
123   *Collins v Martin* (1797) 1 B & P 648, and *Barber v Richards* (1851) 6 Exch 63.

bearer instrument negotiable by delivery alone) is indorsed in favour of someone other than the borrower or in favour of the borrower in a particular capacity, for example as agent. In such a case the lender has a remedy against the borrower, but the true owner of the instrument can recover it as it is held by the lender by way of deposit and has not been delivered to him by way of discount which would allow him to demand payment from the acceptor because of the negotiability of the instrument.[124] The lender has notice of the limited right of the depositor by virtue of the indorsements. The deposit of an instrument not negotiable by delivery will give the depositee the security of a common law pledge which depends on the right of the pledgor to create a pledge and continues so long as possession is retained.[125] This application of the general rule, that an owner of property is unable to confer a title which he does not himself hold (*nemo dat quod non habet*), is subject to exceptions where, for example, the pledgor has a title defeasible on grounds of fraud or misrepresentation; where the true owner is estopped by his own conduct which gave apparent authority to the pledgor; and where a factor holds goods with the owner's permission. If it can be established that an instrument was properly negotiated—whether by delivery alone or indorsement and delivery—to a holder who took in good faith and gave value he will be a holder in due course. This gives ownership rights and not mere possession. This can be explained on the basis that every holder of a bill takes the property in it, and that the property and possession are inseparable. This is part of the negotiability of a bill and distinguishes it from goods of which the property and possession may be held by different persons.[126] The nature of the instrument and the method used when possession was passed to the lender will determine whether he becomes the owner of the instrument or pledgee.

4.55   Negotiable instruments are therefore, in practice, subject to a form of security more commonly used for chattels than for choses in action owing to the ease with which they have always been assignable and the nature of bills of exchange or promissory notes which can be used to obtain credit by the drawer of the document (or a later holder) directly and not by way of mortgage. A right to foreclose on a negotiable instrument which is worth a larger amount than the sum lent and the interest due on it would be even more obviously inequitable than that remedy is when it is applied to other assets.[127] The availability to a pledgee of the right to sell provides a lender with a sufficient remedy. The disadvantage of this form of security is the need for the lender to retain possession in order to keep the security alive.

---

124   See *Treuttel v Barandon* (1817) 8 Taunt 100.
125   The right of the pledgor to pledge will usually depend on him having authority to do so—*Cole v North Western Bank* (1875) LR 10 CP 354.
126   *Collins v Martin* (1797) 1 B & P 648 per Eyre, CJ at p 651.
127   See below ch 7 on remedies.

INTERESTS IN TRUST FUNDS

4.56   It is possible to use as security an interest owned by the borrower in a trust fund. A company which has such an interest may mortgage it. Such a situation may arise if money is held by a customer on trust for the company. The mortgage of the borrower's interest will be by assignment with a proviso for re-assignment on redemption. It is generally assumed that a mortgage of an interest in a trust fund, necessarily being a mortgage of an equitable interest, must be an equitable mortgage. However, there is authority for the availability of the method of assignment contained in s 136 of the Law of Property Act 1925 for the creation of a mortgage of an interest in a trust fund.[128] This means that if the requirements of s 136 are satisfied an assignment of the whole interest of the borrower is possible under the section. The question of whether this creates a legal or an equitable mortgage will rarely be important in practice as priorities in either case will be determined in accordance with the rule in *Dearle v Hall*.[129] There is no need for consideration if the assignment is made under s 136 and the assignee can sue in his own name without joining the assignor as a party.[130]

4.57   Whether s 136 of the Law of Property Act 1925 is used or not it is necessary for an assignment of an equitable interest which exists at the time of the assignment to be in writing and signed by the assignor or his agent.[131] Even a mortgage created by an assignment not satisfying s 136 must comply with s 53(1)(c). A deed will be necessary if statutory powers of sale are to be incorporated[132] and notice to the trustees is desirable for the purposes of priority and because an instruction to them to pay income to the mortgagee is necessary for the assignment to amount to a taking of possession by the mortgagee of the interest to place the trustees under an obligation to pay any income due from the interest to the mortgagee. Notice which does not contain such an instruction will not have that effect.[133] Where a mortgage is taken of a reversionary interest in a trust fund the trustees may pay the full amount to the mortgagee[134] or, if they choose to do so, they may pay to him only the amount of the principal, interest and costs due under the mortgage and pay the balance to the mortgagor/beneficiary.[135]

---

128   In *Re Pain* [1919] 1 Ch 38 at 44 and *Torkington v Magee* [1902] 2 KB 427 at 430–431.
129   (1828) 3 Rus 1.
130   *Re Westerton* [1919] 2 Ch 104 and s 136 LPA 1925.
131   LPA 1925 s 53(1)(c).
132   *Ibid*, s 101.
133   *Re Pawson's Settlement* [1917] 1 Ch 541.
134   LPA 1925 s 107(1).
135   *Re Bell* [1896] 1 Ch 1.

INTELLECTUAL PROPERTY

4.58   It will commonly be the case that a company will own patents, copyrights, designs or trade marks. Such property[136] can be the subject of security interests but because they are created by statute the method of assignment for the creation of a legal mortgage will be laid down by the relevant legislation.

Patents

4.59   Patents are governed by the Patents Act 1977 although for some purposes those granted under the Patents Act 1949 are still governed by the provisions of that Act. However, the provisions on assignment, registration and its effects apply whenever the patent was granted.[137] Mortgages or assignments of patents, applications for patents and licences and sub-licences of patents are specifically provided for by s 30(2) and (4). Such assignments and mortgages are required to be in writing and signed by or on behalf of the parties to the transaction or to be under the seal of a corporation.[138] A mortgage by one of joint proprietors of a patent without the consent of the other or others is not permitted[139] and any assignment or mortgage which fails to conform to the statutory requirements as to form is said to be void.[138] To create a legal mortgage of a patent it is necessary to use writing (but not a deed) and for all parties (not only the mortgagor) to sign the document. Despite the statement that an assignment failing to comply with these requirements is void it is clear that such an act can amount to an agreement to assign which will be specifically enforceable and will, under the normal rule, provide an effective equitable assignment or mortgage. There emerges the familiar pattern of a requirement for a formally correct assignment with a proviso for re-assignment on redemption to create a legal mortgage and the creation of an equitable mortgage by an ineffective attempt to do this or an agreement for a mortgage.[140]

4.60   In the context of patents it is important to distinguish the assignment of all rights under the patent which places the assignee in the same position as the assignor and enables him to deal with the patent freely, from a licence which permits the licensee to do acts which would otherwise enable the

---

136   By s 30(1) Patent Act 1977, a patent or an application for a patent is not a thing in action but is personal property. Copyrights, designs and trademarks are choses in action, but ss 90 and 222(1) of the Copyright Designs & Patents Act 1988 lay down that a copyright and a design right are transmissible as personal or moveable property.
137   Patent Act 1977 s 127(3) and sch 2 para 1.
138   s 30(6).
139   ss 30(2) and 36(3).
140   *Re Casey's Patents* [1892] 1 Ch 104. It would seem that only an assignment which is not void for want of formalities can be registered and therefore that an equitable interest created by a contract to assign is not registrable under the 1977 Act.

patent holder to sue for a violation of his rights. An exclusive licence may be given which may amount to a property interest rather than a mere contractual right as the Patent Act 1977 s 67(1) gives such a licensee the rights to sue for an infringement in his own name. No formalities are required for the grant of a licence as opposed to an assignment. The assignment of a licence can be used as a form of security.[141]

4.61 The registration of an assignment by way of legal mortgage will show the assignee as mortgagee if the true nature of the transaction is made clear on registration. However, the mortgagor will always have the right to sue any person who infringes the patent because he retains the equity of redemption.[142] Registration is not necessary for the creation of legal or equitable mortgages of patents but it is important for priority purposes for a legal mortgage. Registration is available in the case of a charge for securing money or money's worth, but no notice of any trust (express, implied or constructive) can be entered on the register or affect the comptroller.[143]

Copyright

4.62 A legal mortgage of a copyright will take the form of an assignment of it with a proviso for re-assignment on redemption. Such an assignment must be in writing and signed by or on behalf of the assignor.[144] The 'moral rights' to a copyright conferred by Chapter IV of the 1988 Act are not assignable.[145] However, no special form of words is required and a lost written assignment may be presumed from a course of dealings between the parties.[146] The assignment may be of the whole interest of the assignor or it may be limited as to the acts authorised on behalf of the owner or on the part of the period of the copyright to which it applies.[147].

4.63 Where a legal mortgage is taken by assignment the assignee can sue in his own name for breach of the copyright. An equitable mortgage may be created by agreement for a legal mortgage and gives the mortgagee a right to call for the creation of a legal mortgage. It does not, however, give the mortgagee the right to restrain a breach of copyright without joining the mortgagor as a party to the action.[148] It is possible for a mortgagor to grant

141 s 30(4)(a).
142 *Van Gelder, Apseman & Co v Sowerby Bridge United District Flower Society* (1890) 44 Ch D 374.
143 ss 33(3)(b), (c); 130(1) and 32(3) Patent Act 1977.
144 Copyright Designs and Patents Act 1988 s 90(3).
145 s 94.
146 *Dennison v Ashdown* (1897) 13 TLR 226.
147 Copyright Designs and Patents Act 1988 s 90(2).
148 *Performing Rights Society v London Theatre of Varieties Ltd* [1924] AC 1 and see s 96(1) of the Copyright Designs and Patents Act 1988.

a security interest in a future copyright. If this is done by an agreement signed by, or on behalf of, the prospective copyright owner then as soon as the copyright comes into existence the assignment will be effective without any further assurance by the mortgagor if the mortgagee is entitled as against all other persons to insist that the copyright vests in him.[149] This means that the holder of a mortgage on future copyrights can obtain a legal mortgage as soon as the property comes into existence providing the agreement to grant the mortgage was in writing and signed by the mortgagees. Without this statutory provision such a mortgagee would obtain only an equitable interest unless some further act of assurance were done by the mortgagor.[150] Unlike patents, a copyright is not subject to its own system of registration although s 396(1)(f) of the Companies Act 1985 does apply to charges on patents and copyrights or licences granted under them. Such security interests must be registered under that section in order to be enforceable against other secured creditors or the liquidator or administrator of the company.

4.64 The 'design right' created by ss 213 to 216 of the Copyright Designs and Patents Act 1988 can be assigned in writing under the hand of the assignor by virtue of s 222. Section 224 lays down a presumption that an assignment of the right to a registered design in which design right subsists is also an assignment of the design right if the proprietor of the registered design is also the design right owner.

Registered designs

4.65 Although copyright exists in registered designs, particular statutory provisions cover their registration and provide for them to be dealt with in the same way and by the same registry as patents. By s 19 of the Registered Designs Act 1949 any assignment of a registered design or a share in such a design must be registered. This includes an assignment by way of mortgage. The mortgagee will usually be registered as such—although it would be possible for him to be registered as proprietor. Notice of the mortgagee's interest will be registered on proof of title being provided to the Registrar. A document in respect of which no entry has been made on the register cannot be used in any court as evidence of any person's title to, or interest in, any registered design or share in a registered design unless the court otherwise directs. The only exception to this rule is an application to rectify the register.[151]

4.66 Unlike the law governing patents, the Registered Designs Act 1949

---

149 *Ibid*, s 91.
150 *Holroyd v Marshall* (1862) 10 HL Cas 191.
151 Registered Design Act *1949* s 19(5).

does not lay down any formalities to be observed in the assignment of registered designs. The registered proprietor of the design has power to deal with it subject only to other registered interests but equities in a design may be enforced in like manner as for any other personal property.[152] A legal mortgage can be created by any method which the Registrar will accept as creating a registrable interest and a mortgagee whose mortgage is unregistered may enforce his right to registration of his interest against the mortgagor and would presumably be entitled to an order of specific performance against the mortgagor to ensure that sufficient evidence was provided to convince the Registrar of the mortgagee's title and to obtain registration of the mortgagee's interest. The need to prove the mortgagee's interest for the purpose of registration makes it desirable that the assignment by way of mortgage be in writing.

Trade marks

4.67   The Trade Marks Act 1938[153] gives the registered proprietor of a trade mark the power to assign the trade mark subject to anything recorded in the register but the right to enforce equities which applied to a trade mark are preserved and can be enforced as they would be in the case of any personal property.[154] The assignment can be with or without the goodwill of a business and can be in respect of all or only some of the goods in relation to which the trade mark was registered.[155] An unregistered trade mark is subject to the same rules providing that, at the time of its assignment, it was used in the same business for the same goods as a registered trade mark and is assigned at the same time, to the same person and in respect of the same goods as that registered trade mark.[156] However, where a trade mark is assigned separately from the goodwill of the business the assignee must apply to the Registrar for directions on the advertisement of the assignment and must then advertise as the Registrar directs.[157] This can be done within 6 months after the date of the assignment unless the Registrar allows longer periods.[158]

4.68   A difficulty with a mortgage of a trade mark by a full assignment lies in the restrictions imposed by the Act on an assignment which results in more than one person each holding exclusive rights concerning the use of identical trade marks (or ones sufficiently similar to be likely to deceive or

152   *Ibid*, s 19(4).
153   s 24.
154   s 64(2).
155   s 22(1)(2).
156   s 22(3).
157   s 22(7).
158   *Ibid*.

cause confusion) if those trade marks relate to the same goods, or the same description of goods or, from the 1st October 1987, associated goods and services or descriptions thereof.[159] This restriction also applies to assignments leading to the exclusive right of more than one person to use such trade marks in respect of such goods in different parts of the United Kingdom.[160] It is important that both mortgagor and mortgagee do not have exclusive rights of use at the same time. The assignment must ensure that such rights are in one person only at any given time. It is possible for a proposed assignment to be certified by the Registrar in advance as valid.[161]

4.69   The assignee of a registered trade mark must be registered as such but no formal requirements are laid down by the Act for an effective assignment.[162] Any unregistered mortgage would only give the mortgagee the right to specific performance against the mortgagor so as to ensure registration.[163] Providing care is taken to avoid prohibited simultaneous rights to exclusive use, a mortgage of a registered trade mark may be created by assignment with a proviso for re-assignment on redemption. Equitable mortgages are possible but will be of little value if they are not registered.

---

159   1938 Act s 22(4) as amended by Trade Marks (Amendment) Act 1984 s 1(4).
160   s 22(6) as amended.
161   s 22(5).
162   Trade Marks Act 1938 s 25(1).
163   Equities are preserved by s 64(2) but may not appear on the register—s 64(1).

CHAPTER 5

The Floating Charge

THE DEVELOPMENT OF THE FLOATING CHARGE

5.01 The security interests examined so far have been what are usually called 'fixed charges'. Although they may be mortgages, charges or pledges they attach to particular property and may (in the case of mortgages) be legal or equitable. A mortgage is created by the transfer of the ownership of the asset mortgaged so it was necessary to examine the different types of property which might be mortgaged in order to ascertain how ownership might be transferred and what formalities are required for the creation of a legal mortgage. It emerged that a failure to comply fully with the formalities necessary for a legal mortgage would give rise to an equitable mortgage providing that the requirements necessary for such a security were met.[1]

5.02 It has also been noted that a charge can exist only in equity and gives rise to different remedies from those available to a mortgagee. However, since the remedies of possession and sale of the assets subject to the security are the most commonly used of those available to lenders the distinction between mortgages and charges as regards remedies is of little importance. Foreclosure, which is the remedy peculiar to the mortgagee, has been rendered substantially obsolete for practical purposes because of the need for court proceedings. The widespread use of registration systems to determine priorities either on the basis of registration amounting to notice or by a rule that priority is in order of registration has reduced the importance of the distinction between legal and equitable security interests in respect of many types of asset. It is usual in the context of an insolvent company to refer to fixed and floating 'charges' as encompassing all forms of security interest held over the company's assets.

5.03 It has been noted that those creditors who have some form of security are likely to stand outside the winding up process and to rely entirely on the assets on which their debts were secured for the satisfaction of their claims. It is only to the extent that their security is ineffective or is not of sufficient value to pay the full amount owed that they will prove as

---

1 See para 2.15 for the need for agreement; consideration and clarity as regards the assets mortgaged.

unsecured creditors in the winding up of the company. The development by the courts of equity of the floating charge as a form of security over the assets of the company was responsible for a large scale expansion of the assets which could be subject to security and removed from the winding up process. Broadly, it allowed the use of 'circulating assets' such as stock, work in progress and trade debts to be the subject of a security interest.

5.04   The fact that a floating charge is usually combined with certain fixed charges in the same document and that it is expressed to cover the whole of the company's undertaking has been responsible for a substantial expansion of the role of the receiver and manager. That role has received statutory recognition in the Insolvency Act 1986 which codifies the powers of the administrative receiver of the whole, or substantially the whole, of a company's assets.[2] The powers of a receiver appointed, either in accordance with the terms of a security instrument in respect of a fixed charge or by the court as a remedy available to the mortgagee, will either be defined in the instrument creating the charge or by the Law of Property Act 1925 s 109.

5.05   The entirely new concept in corporate insolvency, of administration, is itself modelled on the role of the receiver and manager under a fixed and floating charge, with greater emphasis on the role of 'manager' than that of 'receiver'. The development of the floating charge has been seen as a powerful engine for the development of the financing of British industry. It can be argued that while the limited liability company allowed the investor in shares to protect his personal wealth while investing in a company, the floating charge allowed the powerful provider of loan finance (classically the banker) to secure his position, in the case of the company's failure and to gain priority over the unsecured creditors (usually trade creditors or customers). Others have seen that device as an imposition on the general class of the creditors of a company and an invitation to fraud on the part of its owners.[3] Cork accepted the impossibility of abolishing the floating charge but suggested a '10% fund' to be provided from the net amount realised by the holder of a floating charge which would assist the unsecured creditors.

5.06   The rest of the report suggests that this was intended to achieve a substantial accretion to the funds available to the unsecured creditors in payment of debts due to them but the function of this fund could be seen as the provision of resources to enable a liquidator, acting on behalf of the

2   Insolvency Act 1986 ss 42–46 and schedule 1 and see chs 11 and 12.
3   See Cork paras 105–109.

unsecured creditors, to pursue directors who might be personally liable and otherwise to add to the funds at his disposal.[4] However neither the view of the fund as a resource for distribution to unsecured creditors nor its role as a fighting fund for the liquidator appealed sufficiently to the government for such a measure to be included in the Insolvency Act 1985. This was despite the fact that in the face of opposition to its original proposals the government did reduce the amount payable to preferential creditors, with priority over a floating chargee, along the lines of the Cork recommendations.[5]

5.07   The net effect of the Act was to increase the amount available after the payment of creditors with fixed charges and the preferential creditors without ensuring any redistribution between those with a floating charge and those without any security at all. This results in even greater benefit to the holders of floating charges than the law before the Act.[6] This is hardly calculated to molify those suppliers of goods or credit referred to by Buckley J in *Re London Pressed Hinge Co Ltd:*[7] "He may have lent his money, or consigned his goods, to the company last week: but if he has the audacity to ask for payment and to enforce his legal remedies to obtain it, the debenture holder obtains a receiver in a proceeding to which the execution creditor is not a party,[8] and thus closes the door against him, taking his money or his goods as part of the security and leaving the creditor who supplied the money or the goods to go unpaid."[9]
    It is hardly surprising that the supply of goods subject to Romalpa clauses and on the basis of leasing or hire purchase has been adopted by those with the economic power to insist upon such arrangements.[10]

5.08   One justification for the development and use of the floating charge was probably the inadequacy of the chattel mortgage in English law. While it has been accepted since *Holroyd v Marshall*[11] that equity will recognise a charge which attaches to future property as soon as it is obtained by the debtor without further action by him, the demands of the Bills of Sale Acts 1878–1882 prevent individuals or partnerships from using the floating charge in respect of chattels. Apart from the clumsiness of the registration system under those Acts and the draconian consequences of non-

4   Cork paras 1538–1549.
5   Insolvency Act 1986 ss 40, 386 and schedule 6.
6   See Cork paras 1488–1489.
7   (1905) 1 Ch 576 at 581—see Cork para 106.
8   In modern times the receiver will normally be appointed without any proceedings. As for the priority between an execution creditor and the holder of a floating charge see paras 8.89–8.94.
9   See ch 8 for priorities. This statement is certainly true unless the enforcement by the creditor reaches its final stage.
10   See ch 9 below.
11   (1862) 10 HLC 191.

registration (which results in the invalidity of the bill against the debtor), the requirement that a mortgage bill should have a schedule listing the property subject to it makes the creation of a charge which will attach to unknown future property impossible.[12] It is only the exemption of companies from the Bills of Sale Act requirements which permits the floating charge to exist.[13] The fact that the provision applies to individual traders and partnerships prevents the use of the floating charge by them.It is also important to note that the doctrine of reputed ownership which used to apply to an individual bankrupt did not apply to a company in liquidation.[14] This meant that the complaint that a company apparently in possession of substantial assets could gain credit from suppliers while the semblance of the strength of those assets was falsified by the existence of a floating charge did not affect the right of the holder of a floating charge to enforce it against the liquidator of a company.[15] It is clear that although a fixed charge may provide greater priority in the case of the insolvency of the debtor company (it is not subject to the payment of preferential debts and may bite on assets before a floating charge does) the floating charge remains a powerful weapon in the armoury of lenders supplying corporate finance.

5.09   While it is possible for any supplier of finance to a company to use the device of the floating charge to secure payment of a loan, there are two types of lender who will normally have the benefit of this security. One is the single creditor (usually a bank) which lends by way of overdraft (or other form of credit), and which insists on the execution and registration of a debenture by the company. The other is the more traditional debenture holder who will supply funds raised by the company in the market place. The latter may hold one of a series of debentures (forming part of one issue) and may have bought a debenture (or loan stock) in the market. In the case of the latter class of creditor, it is convenient and usual for a trust structure to operate so that a trustee acting on behalf of the debenture holders as a class will enforce the security if that becomes necessary. In the case of both the single creditor who holds a document conferring a security interest in the company's assets and the class of debenture holders the security granted will normally provide a fixed charge over certain assets—land, buildings and other fixtures thereon—and a floating charge over the remainder of the company's assets and undertaking.

5.10   The word *debenture* has no significance in the context of security

---

12   Bills of Sale Act 1882 ss 5 and 9.
13   *Ibid* s 17.
14   Insolvency Act 1985 s 235 sch 10 Part III abolished the doctrine for individuals. See *Gorringe v Irwell Rubber Company* (1886) 34 Ch D 128 on companies.
15   Subject to the invalidity of the floating charge under s 245 Insolvency Act 1986. See ch 20.

interests. It is merely a document evidencing a loan and may be supported by no charge or security right whatsoever.[16] There has been a tendency in recent times for those seeking security over a company's assets (particularly when the loan secured is a medium or long term bank loan) to extend the range of assets subject to a fixed charge to include intellectual property, the benefit of contracts and the book debts of the borrower company in addition to real property while obtaining a floating charge over all its other assets.[17] What then, is the legal nature of a floating charge, how can it be created and how does it attach itself to assets which are subject to it?

THE LEGAL NATURE AND CREATION OF A FLOATING CHARGE[18]

5.11 A fixed security over property prevents the borrower from disposing of the property without the lender's permission. While in *Holroyd v Marshall*[11] an equitable mortgage of machinery required that the mortgagor hold for the mortgagee the machinery subject to the charge, any machinery substituted for it (permission for the substitution being given) and any additional machinery brought into the mill, the removal of the machinery otherwise than for the purpose of replacing it would have entitled the mortgagee to an injunction according to Lord Westbury.[19] While that case facilitated the creation of charges over future property in equity without the need for the *novus actus* required at common law,[20] it did not deal with, or recognise, a form of security that could be used over assets which would be freely bought and sold in the course of the borrower's business. Assets such as stocks of unsold finished products or raw materials, work in progress or, arguably, book debts[21] cannot be subject to fixed charges without the inconvenience of requiring the lender's permission on each occasion when the borrower wishes to deal with them. It was such assets which became the classic subject matter of the floating charge.

5.12 The genesis of this form of security was the case of *Re Panama, New Zealand and Australian Royal Mail Company.*[22] In that case a charge of the debtor company's 'undertaking and all sums of money arising therefrom'

---

16 See *Levy v Abercorris Slate & Slab Co* (1887) 37 Ch D 260; and the Companies Act 1985 s 744 defining a 'debenture' for the purpose of that Act and (by virtue of Insolvency Act 1986 s 251) the Insolvency Act 1986.
17 See Pennington (1985) No 6 *Co Lawyer* 9.
18 See W J Gough, *Company Charges*, Butterworths 1978 Part Two.
19 (1862) 10 HLC 191 at 211–212.
20 See above para 1.28.
21 But see above paras 4.35–4.48.
22 (1870) 5 Ch App 318.

was held to include the present and future property of the company so that the debenture holder chargees could realise their security over the company's assets on the winding up of the company and were held to: 'stand in a position superior to that of the general creditors who can touch nothing until they are paid.'[23] However the chargees could not interfere with the running of the company's business before the commencement of its winding up.

5.13 One of the two best known descriptions of a floating charge was given in *Re Yorkshire Woolcombers' Association Ltd* in Romer LJ's judgment in the Court of Appeal:[24]

"If a charge has the three characteristics that I am about to mention it is a floating charge. (1) If it is a charge on a class of assets of a company present and future; (2) if that class is one which in the ordinary course of business of the company would be changing from time to time; and (3) if you find that by the charge it is contemplated that, until some future step is taken by or on behalf of those interested in the charge, the company may carry on its business in the ordinary way as far as concerns the particular class of assets I am dealing with."

5.14 The other is to be found in the contrast of a fixed charge with a floating charge in Lord McNaghton's speech in the same case when it reached the House of Lords:[25]

"A specific charge, I think, is one that without more fastens on ascertained and definite property or property capable of being ascertained and defined; a floating charge, on the other hand, is ambulatory and shifting in its nature, hovering over and, so to speak, floating with the property which it is intended to affect until some event occurs or some act is done which causes it to settle and fasten on the subject of the charge within its reach and grasp."

5.15 A consequence of the nature of the charge is that before crystallisation:

"a floating security is not a specific mortgage of the assets, plus a licence to the mortgagor to dispose of them in the course of his business but it is a floating mortgage applying to every item comprised in the security but not specifically affecting any item . . ."[26]

The floating charge creates an immediate security interest on creation but it is only on crystallisation that it can be said to attach itself to any specific assets. This is the vital point in time so far as its priority against the claims of others with real interests is concerned.[27]

23   *Ibid* at 323.
24   [1903] 2 Ch 284 at 295.
25   *Sub nom Illingworth v Houldsworth* [1904] AC 355 at 358.
26   Per Buckley LJ in *Evans v Rival Granite Quarries Ltd* [1910] 2 KB 979 at 999.
27   See paras 5.24–5.25 and 8.77–8.96.

5.16 The creation of a floating charge is achieved by the use of wording which stipulates the security to be provided and indicates an intention that the assets should be available for the company's use during the existence of the security. The court, in deciding on the type of security created, will be guided by the intention of the parties as ascertained from the document as a whole and will not necessarily be bound by the description of the security used in the documents.[28] A security described as a fixed charge may be held to be a floating charge if the intention appears to be that the company can make use of the assets which it covers without the consent of the chargee.[29] Conversely, it follows that the use of the word 'floating charge' may not establish the nature of the charge conclusively if there is a clear intention to give the chargee control over the assets involved to prevent their use by the company in the ordinary course of its business.

5.17 A charge which is said to extend to the whole undertaking or business of the company is likely to be regarded as a floating charge as is any charge which can be construed as encompasing all present and future property of the borrower.[30] A contractual lien on sub-freights granted to the owner of a ship in a charterparty has been held to be a floating charge if it attaches to the subfreights when they come into existence and remains dormant until the point at which the sums for which it is security become due, at which point it assigns them to the owner.[31]

5.18 The scope of the liabilities secured by a charge is a matter of construction. A debenture issued to cover all monies due from the company to the debenture holder does not cover the company's liability on unsecured loan stock issued to another party and later bought by the debenture holder as the monies are not owed as a result of a transaction between the parties and the liability is not initially recorded in accounts between them.[32]

THE ORDINARY COURSE OF BUSINESS[33]

5.19 The 'hovering' quality of a floating charge continues during the company's use in the ordinary course of business of the assets over which the security floats. Until the charge crystallises it is not a fixed charge. The

---

28   *Siebe Gorman & Co Ltd v Barclays Bank* [1979] 2 Lloyds Rep 142.
29   See eg *National Provincial Bank v United Electric Theatres* [1916] 1 Ch 132 but see *Re a Company (005009 of 1987) ex parte Copp* [1989] BCLC 13.
30   *Re Alfred Priestmen & Co (1929) Ltd* [1936] 2 All ER 1340.
31   *Annangel Glory Compania Naviera SA v Golodetz ME Marketing Corp* [1988] PCC 37.
32   *Re Quest Cae Ltd* [1985] BCLC 266.
33   See generally Picarda *op cit* at pp 9–11 and Gough Ch 7.

use of company assets for a purpose which falls outside the definition of the company's ordinary course of business is a breach of the agreement between the company and the chargee. Apart from other factors giving rise to crystallisation, such behaviour entitles the chargee to apply to a court for the appointment of a receiver on the ground that his security is in jeopardy and gives him a right to restrain the transaction. This is the case despite the absence of any other breach of agreement such as a failure to pay interest on capital.[34] It is uncertain whether such an act by the chargee results in automatic crystallisation on, or immediately before, the use of the assets outside the ordinary course of business.[35] The use of assets outside the ordinary course of business can be distinguished from a cessation of business—which is itself a circumstance that can lead to the crystallisation of the charge.[36]

5.20 Subject to the effectiveness of a negative pledge clause restricting later mortgages or charges with priority over or *pari passu* to the floating charge,[37] any dealing by a company with assets subject to a floating charge before that charge crystallises will take priority over the floating charge so long as such transactions are in the ordinary course of the company's business. Raw materials can be made up into stock or work in progress completed and the finished product sold without the purchaser taking subject to the floating charge. However, can the whole business or undertaking of the company be sold or made subject to some other security interest with similar effect? Can some part of the business or shares in a subsidiary be sold? What of fixed assets?

5.21 The assignment of specific assets subject to the floating charge clearly falls within the power to deal in the ordinary course of business. This may be by way of sale, exchange, or security.[38] This is clearly necessary for the floating charge to be of any value to the borrower and is inherent in the normal description of such a charge. However, it has also been held that unusual transactions which involve a disposal of a large part of the company's undertaking may still be within the ordinary course of business at least where the company, on the facts, has not stopped business or ceased to be a going concern. The sale of part of the company's business can be in the ordinary course of business so that the sale of one of three plants owned by a company has been held not to be a ground for granting an injunction to

---

34 *Re Borax* [1901] 1 Ch 326 per Vaughan Williams LJ at 341–342.
35 As for the doubts about the possibility of automatic crystallisation in any event see paras 5.24–5.42 below.
36 See below paras 5.29–5.31.
37 See para 8.78.
38 *Re H H Vivian & Co Ltd* [1900] 2 Ch 654; *Re Florence Land & Public Works Co* (1878) 10 Ch D 530; *Re Hamiltons Windsor Ironworks ex p Pitman & Edwards* (1879) 12 Ch D 707 and *Wheatley v Silkstone & Haigh Moor Coal Co* (1885) 29 Ch D 715.

prevent the transfer.[39] In *Re Borax Co*,[40] a security over the undertaking of the company was held not to cease being a floating charge on the sale of all of the company's property and assets except certain investments in return for shares and debentures in a purchasing company—one of the classic forms of company takeover and a form of reconstruction expressly authorised by the company's memorandum and articles.

5.22   The courts will examine evidence on the past business activities of the company and its objects as set out in the memorandum of association to establish whether a particular transaction is within the course of business.[41] It seems clear that a transaction outside the objects clause, and therefore *ultra vires* the company, could not be held to be within the ordinary course of business although whether this gives the holder of a floating charge the right to obtain an injunction to restrain such an act is unclear.[42] It may be the case that even an *intra vires* transaction could fall outside the normal course of business because of fraud, the unusual behaviour by, or intention of, the parties or (distinguishing *Re Borax*) the large scale nature of the disposition of assets involved combined with the termination of the company's activities.[43]

5.23   It must be emphasised that the question of the freedom of the company to create other mortgages or charges over the assets subjected to a floating charge will depend on the existence and effectiveness of a negative pledge clause. Such clauses will almost invariably be included in a document creating a floating charge and as between the company and the holder of the charge they are clearly effective. There is however doubt about the effect they have on the priorities as between those holding charges granted by the company in breach of the clause and the proprietor of a floating charge.[44]

THE CRYSTALLISATION OF A FLOATING CHARGE

5.24   The vital time relevant to determining the nature and therefore the priority of the interest held by a person with a floating charge over the assets

39   *Re H H Vivian & Co Ltd* (above).
40   [1901] 1 Ch 326.
41   Regard was had to the latter in both the *Re Borax Co* [1901] 1 Ch 326 at 341–342 and *Re H H Vivian & Co Ltd* [1900] 2 Ch 654.
42   Contrast *Re Borax & Co* [1901] 1 Ch 326 per Vaughan Williams LJ at 341 with *Mills v Northern Railway of Buenos Ayres & Co* (1870) 5 Ch App 621 which is authority against the right of an unsecured creditor to obtain such relief. See Gough *op cit* at p 114.
43   *Williams v Quebrada Railway Land & Copper Co* [1895] 2 Ch 751; *Taylor v H'Keand* (1880) 5 CPD 358 cited by Gough at p 111. See also the Australian case of *Torzillu Pty Co Ltd v Brynac Pty Ltd* [1983] 8 ACLR 52 cited by Picarda *op cit* at p 10–11.
44   See below, para 8.78.

of a company is the moment at which the charge becomes fixed. This process of the conversion of a floating charge into a fixed charge is known as *crystallisation*. The circumstances which can give rise to the metamorphosis of the security interest are not entirely agreed. There are certain events which definitely result in the crystallisation of a floating charge but there are others which are the subject of debate among commentators and about which there is no clear English precedent but only *obiter dicta* in the case law. It is the effect of crystallisation on the priorities of the security of the holder of the erstwhile floating charge and others who claim some interest in the property subject to it that makes the moment of crystallisation so important. Those who use floating charges as their security have an interest in ensuring that crystallisation takes place in the widest possible range of circumstances. Those who have a conflicting claim emphasise the importance of notice to others dealing with the company and the status of existing security to which its property is subject as the central issue.[45]

5.25   As a result of ss 40, 175 and 251 of the Insolvency Act 1986 and s 196 of the Companies Act 1985, any charge that was floating at the time of its creation is treated as a floating charge even after it has crystallised for certain purposes. Consequently the priority accorded to preferential debts is not undermined by the crystallisation of the charge before a receiver is appointed or before the lender takes possession of the assets.[46] This makes the question of the time of crystallisation less important in that context. However, if priorities have to be determined between a floating charge and some other security interest the rules about the date of crystallisation may be relevant.

Liquidation

5.26   It is universally agreed that a floating charge crystallises on the commencement of the winding up of the company. This applies whether the winding up be voluntary[47] (in which case crystallisation occurs on the passing of the resolution for the winding up of the company[48]); or compulsory.[49] The presentation of a winding petition does not in itself amount to a crystallising event unless the winding up order is subsequently

---

45   See eg Cork Report paras 1570–1582; Picarda *op cit* pp 15–25; Gough *op cit* chap 6 and Goode *op cit* 795–803.
46   See chapter 19 on preferential debts.
47   *Re Colonial Trusts Corporation* (1879) 15 Ch D 465 which indicates that crystallisation will occur on the appointment of a provisional liquidator in a compulsory liquidation.
48   Insolvency Act 1986 s 86.
49   *Re Panama, New Zealand & Australian Royal Mail Co* (1870) 5 Ch App 318 (in which case the operative date will be that of the presentation of a successful winding up petition or the earlier date of a resolution passed for the voluntary winding up of the company— Insolvency Act 1986 s 129).

made.[50] However, a winding up in the course of a company reconstruction causes the crystallisation of a floating charge despite a provision in the document creating the charge that the principal does not become payable by virtue of such a winding up.[51] This indicates that the effect of the liquidation of a company on its floating charges is automatic as a matter of law—if contractual intent were of significance the document in that case could have been construed as not giving rise to crystallisation in such circumstances. The case also highlights the importance of the choice of method of reconstruction of a company if the crystallisation of floating charges is to be avoided. The sale of substantially the whole of the undertaking in return for shares in, or debentures of, a different company may be within the course of business of the company and not be a breach of the agreement giving the chargee a right to a remedy which will result in crystallisation.[52] On the other hand the use of a method of restructuring, involving the winding up of the company, will result in the crystallisation of the floating charge regardless of the terms of the document which creates it or, presumably, the intentions of the parties.

Appointment of a receiver, cessation of business or enforcement by other creditors

Actions of the chargee
5.27 The appointment of a receiver by the chargee under the power which he will almost invariably be given in the document creating the charge or the appointment of a receiver by the court will crystallise the floating charge.[53] However, the commencement of a debenture holder's action with a view to having a receiver appointed does not crystallise the charge without an order resulting from it.[54]

5.28 Other actions by the chargee to enforce his security will also cause the crystallisation of the floating charge. They include taking possession of property and the sale of assets.[55] The most usual form of intervention is, of course, the appointment of a receiver but the cases support the proposition that possession has the effect of crystallising the charge and it would seem to follow that sale, even if it is not carried out by the chargee after taking possession, will have the same effect. The service of notice to crystallise the

50 *Re Victoria Steam Boat Co Ltd* [1897] 1 Ch 158.
51 *Re Crompton & Co Ltd* [1914] 1 Ch 954—a case on whether a receiver should be appointed by the court.
52 *Re Borax (supra).*
53 See eg *Re Florence Land & Public Works Co* (1878) 10 Ch D 530 per Jessel MR at 541; *Taunton v Sheriff of Warwickshire* [1895] 2 Ch 319; Gough at p 86 and Picarda at p 16.
54 *Re Hubbard & Co* (1898) 68 LJ Ch 54.
55 See eg *Re Hamiltons Windsor Ironworks* (1879) 12 Ch D 707 at 710; *Mercantile Bank of India v Chartered Bank of India* [1937] 1 All ER 23.

charge is also effective if done in accordance with the provisions of the debenture it secures.[56]

Cessation of business

5.29   The more doubtful causes of crystallisation[57] include the cessation of business (outside the circumstances, such as liquidation, agreed to give rise to crystallisation in themselves); the appointment of a receiver—or possibly some other act of enforcement by another creditor; and automatic crystallisation on the occurrence of any events stipulated in the document creating the charge to have that effect.

5.30   All acts which are generally accepted as giving rise to crystallisation can be argued to be based on either the withdrawal of managerial authority from the normal controllers of the company (usually the directors) or the cessation of the company's business. Professor Goode has argued that despite the retention of theoretical powers of management on the part of the directors the *de facto* cessation of business is a crystallising event. This view is supported by strong *dicta* in a number of cases.[58] Picarda classifies this area as doubtful and raises a possible distinction between 'ceasing to carry on business' and 'ceasing to be a going concern'. He observes that the former is easier to assess objectively than the latter but his primary objection to either as a cause of crystallisation is the possible absence of knowledge on the part of third parties or of the lender that such an event has occurred.[59] This might be answered by the adoption of Professor Goode's approach which distinguishes the position as between the parties to the charge from that in relation to other parties.[60] There is little doubt on the authorities[58] that crystallisation results from a voluntary cessation of business by the company.

5.31   *Dicta* in *Re Brightlife* suggest that the English courts will give effect to a contractual provision for automatic crystallisation despite its effects on third parties.[61] This implies that there is no objection to the cessation of business or the ending of the company's status as a going concern as a basis for automatic crystallisation in accordance with a contractual stipulation

---

56   *Re Brightlife* [1986] BCLC 418.
57   See Picarda pp 16–24 where a typology based on the certainty with which causes can be put forward is adopted.
58   See, for example, *Government Stock and Other Securities Investment Co Ltd v Manila Railway Co Ltd* [1897] AC 81 per Lord MacNaughten at 86; *Evans v Rival Granite Quarries* (1910) 2 KB 979 per Vaughan Williams LJ at 990 and per Fletcher Moulton LJ at 993; *Edward Nelson & Co Ltd v Faber & Co* [1903] 2 KB 367 per Joyce J at 376–7; *Re Victoria Steamboats Ltd* [1897] 1 Ch 158 per Kekewich J at 161 and see Gough *op cit* p 86.
59   *Op cit* pp 17–18.
60   Goode *op cit* at 795–6 and 798–9.
61   [1986] BCLC 418.

to that effect. This will be the case if it is assumed that the floating quality of the charge is intended by the parties to exist only during and for the purpose of the continuation of the company's business. In most debentures the wording and the behaviour of the parties will point to such an intention. It may be that the courts will be rather less reluctant to uphold automatic crystallisation in cases of ambiguity where the ground is the cessation of business than in the case of other events stated to have that effect.

Acts of other creditors
5.32 There is no English authority on the question of whether the appointment of a receiver by the holder of a later floating charge will crystallise an earlier one. If it is assumed that the test of withdrawal of the power to manage a company from its directors is one of the fundamental principles to be applied in determining whether crystallisation occurs then it should follow that any act by another secured creditor having that effect would result in crystallisation.[62] This would certainly be the case if the receiver were appointed over the whole or substantially the whole of the company's undertaking. Picarda assumes that such an event can only give rise to crystallisation if it is analogous to one known to have that effect: winding up; cessation of business as a going concern or inconsistency of the continued flotation of the earlier charge with the crystallisation of the later one. He finds none of these grounds persuasive. This is because, in contrast to winding up, receivership does not necessarily involve the cessation of business. The second ground is treated as a *de facto* question on the continuation of the business and not one of the power of the company to do this and the third is seen as an issue of priorities rather than the control of the company over its undertaking.

5.33 Such authority as exists does seem to point to the crystallisation of an earlier charge on the appointment of a receiver under a later one but it is far from decisive.[63] Given that the priority of the earlier charge is retained as against the later charge regardless of the date of crystallisation—which as between the floating charges will be the case in the absence of express words to the contrary in the earlier charge[64]—the priority of the holder of the first charge will be retained so long as he acts before a receiver, appointed under the later one, hands over assets to preferential creditors or his own appointor.[65] This makes the question of whether a floating charge is crystallised by the appointment of a receiver under a later one of limited

---

62 See Goode *op cit* p 797.
63 It was assumed without argument that an appointment of a receiver under an earlier charge crystallised a later one in the Australian case of *Stein v Saywell* (1969) 121 CLR 529.
64 *Re Automatic Bottle Makers Ltd* [1926] Ch 412.
65 Picarda *op cit* p 23.

practical importance—given the need for public notice of the appointment of any receiver.[66]

5.34 Two difficulties arose under s 196 of the Companies Act 1985 and its predecessors about the priority of preferential creditors over the holder of a floating charge in circumstances where there was automatic crystallisation or in circumstances where there were two floating charges. The problem of automatic crystallisation has been resolved by an amendment to the section introduced by the Insolvency Act 1985.[67] This amendment ensures that providing a charge was a floating charge at the time when it was created, the preferential creditors will have priority over the chargee on the appointment of a receiver or the taking of possession by the chargee despite the fact that an automatic crystallisation which took place before the appointment of the receiver or the chargee's entry into possession has converted the charge into a fixed charge.

5.35 The use of the plural 'debentures' in s 196 as amended and in s 40 of the Insolvency Act 1986 ensures that there is an obligation to pay preferential debts in advance of the claim of the holders of any debentures; not only the one under which the receiver was appointed or possession was taken of the assets. This remedies the problem identified by the Cork Report; the loss of rights by preferential creditors by effluxion of time if there was delay in the appointment of a receiver in a case where more than one debenture existed.[68]

Automatic crystallisation and notice to the company
5.36 Perhaps the most important doubt about the events which can give rise to crystallisation is the uncertainty about the effect of an express agreement in a document creating a charge that certain events will result in the automatic crystallisation of the charge.[69] Such provisions have become common in debentures and the events which are stated to give rise to crystallisation can include an attempt by the company to grant a further mortgage or charge with priority over or *pari passu* with the floating charge itself; the levying of execution against the company's assets by a creditor; the act of the company in exceeding a borrowing limit; or a failure by the company to repay an instalment of the principal or interest. Objection to such clauses can be made on the basis of the undesirability of an

---

66 Companies Act 1985 s 405(1).
67 Insolvency Act 1985 sch 6 para 14 and see now Insolvency Act 1986 sch 13 for the substituted section.
68 Paras 1581–1582.
69 See Boyle "The Invalidity of Automatic Crystallisation" [1979] JBL 231; Farrar "The Crystallisation of a Floating Charge" (1976) 40 Conv 397 and "World Economic Stagnation puts the Floating Charge on Trial" (1980) 1 Co Law 83.

unpublicised event affecting the interests of third parties who are unaware of it; and indeed because of the possibility of crystallisation occurring without the knowledge of the chargor and the chargee themselves. Some of these objections could be overcome by an approach which distinguished the effect of an event as between the parties to the charge from its effects as against third parties. Crystallisation may deprive the company of actual authority but third parties can argue that the company retained apparent authority to deal with its assets in the absence of some act by the chargee publicly depriving it of authority.[70] The difficulties as between the parties to the charge which could arise when a breach by the company which causes automatic crystallisation is treated by the lender as not having that effect could be dealt with by an application of the rules on waiver.[71]

5.37   However, while the policy considerations have been explored by commentators, the law in England is not entirely clear. The proposal of the Cork Report, that it should be clarified by the enactment of an exhaustive list of the circumstances in which a floating charge crystallises and the exclusion of the possibility of automatic crystallisation, was not taken up by the Insolvency Act 1985.[72] Nor had any provision for the registration of notices of the crystallisation of floating charges of the kind suggested in 1973 by the Land Law Committee of the Law Society been introduced before the presentation of the Companies Bill 1989.[73]

5.38   In the case of *Re Brightlife*[74] Hoffman J held that crystallisation by the service of notice by the lender on the company was possible and, in that case, resulted in crystallisation of the charge before the commencement of winding up. Under the law applicable to the case this permitted the chargee to take the assets free from the claims of the preferential creditors—a result that would not now arise as the charge was a floating charge at the time of creation.[67] Hoffman J expressed the view, *obiter*, that while the commercial inconvenience of automatic crystallisation might give rise to a presumption against it, there was no rule of law excluding it. The combination of this *obiter* statement, with the effect given in the case to a clause allowing crystallisation on the service of a notice, appears to resolve the issue on the side of upholding the contract freely entered into by the parties.

5.39   This is subject only to a rule of construction against automatic

---

70   See Goode *op cit* pp 798–799.
71   See Picarda p 19 and Goode *Legal Problems of Credit and Security* (1982) pp 36–40.
72   Cork para 1580.
73   See Cork para 1576. The Companies Bill 1989 does provide for making regulations to introduce such a system and make the effectiveness of the crystallising event dependant on registration.
74   [1986] BCLC 418.

crystallisation which can presumably only operate in cases of ambiguity.[75] In *Re Brightlife* third parties were affected on the basis of a notice served only on one of the parties to the debenture. As a matter of principle this clears the way for automatic crystallisation without such notice in cases where the clause is unambiguous in the context of the debenture and the factual situation in which the parties are involved. The courts may be cautious if the event resulting in automatic crystallisation might not be known to the company and be impossible for third parties to discover on enquiry. This would be the case with a breach of borrowing limits if crystallisation were to occur without the service of notice.[76] According to Pearson J in *Horne and Hellard*,[77] failure to pay principal and interest can readily be ascertained by such an enquiry and should therefore be permissible as an event giving rise to automatic crystallisation.

5.40   *Dicta* in cases before *Re Brightlife* also support the validity of automatic crystallisation clauses. The strongest support is to be found in the case of *Re Horne and Hellard*[77] in which Pearson J held that a purchaser was entitled to reasonable evidence that there had been no default by the debtor. The charge in question contained a provision that the charge should be a floating security until default in the payment of the principal and interest. Pearson J clearly regarded the clause as meaning that the charge would crystallise on default by the debtor and emphasised the desirability of giving effect to the contractual intention of the parties.[78] However, there has been criticism of this first instance case[79] and although, like *Re Brightlife*, on crystallisation by the service of notice, it may well be binding on a first instance court, the Court of Appeal or House of Lords would be free to decide the matter at large.

5.41   In addition to the decision in *Re Horne and Hellard*, there were statements in a number of cases which could be taken to support the effectiveness of automatic crystallisation clauses[80] but, equally, the majority in the Court of Appeal in *Evans v Rival Granite Quarry Ltd*[81] disapproved the view expressed by Lord Russell CJ in *Davie & Co v Williamson & Son Ltd*.[82] The majority in *Evans* emphasised the need for

75   Per Hoffman J at p 426.
76   See Picarda *op cit* at p 21.
77   (1885) 29 Ch D 736 and see Farrar (1976) 40 Conv 397 at 400–403 and Picarda pp 18–19.
78   See especially (1885) 29 Ch D 736 at p 744.
79   By Kekewich J in *Brunton v Electrical Eng Corpn* [1882] 1 Ch 434 at 440.
80   See eg Buckley LJ in *Evans v Rival Granite Quarries Ltd* [1910] 2 KB 979 at 1000; *Davie & Co v Williamson & Sons Ltd* [1898] 2 QB 194 per Lord Russell CJ at 201.
81   [1910] 2 KB 979 per Fletcher Moulton LJ at 997 and implied in the judgment of Vaughan Williams LJ at 989–990.
82   [1898] 2 QB 194 at 201.

active intervention by the lender before crystallisation occurs.[83] More recently the concept of automatic crystallisation on the occurrence of an agreed event was supported in a *dictum* of Slade J in *Re Bond Worth*.[84] Additional support for the existence of automatic crystallisation could be found in a group of Australian and New Zealand decisions upholding the concept.[85] However, it appears that the Canadian courts took the opposite view.[86]

Partial crystallisation and reflotation

5.42   The nature of a floating charge is such that it is clear that the normal interpretation of a document, which simply creates such a charge without more, must be that the charge is either to crystallise over the whole of the assets with which it deals or over none of them.

> "It is inconsistent with the nature of a floating security that the holder should be able to pounce down on particular assets and to interfere with the Company's business while still keeping his security a floating security; he cannot at once give freedom and insist on servitude."[87]

5.43   However, it would seem that, as with the concept of express automatic crystallisation there is no reason to deny the parties to a charge the freedom to agree that there can be partial crystallisation. An express provision having that effect will probably be accepted by the courts. This could be combined with an automatic crystallisation clause to ensure that the charge crystallised only on an asset in jeopardy because of, for example, an attempt by the borrower to charge or mortgage it. This has not been tested in the English courts but there can be no objection in principle to giving effect to this contractual intention of the parties to the charge if the principle of automatic crystallisation is accepted in cases of crystallisation over all the assets of the company.

5.44   If a receiver is appointed over only some of the assets subject to the charge then the charge is likely to be held to float over the remaining assets. The basis of this is that such an appointment by the chargee would only be

83   See Moulton Fletcher LJ at 993 and 997 and Vaughan Williams LJ at 984 and 986/7. See also the discussion of the cases in Farrar *op cit* at 400–4 and Gough *op cit* at pp 97–100.

84   [1980] Ch 228 at 266 and see Picarda *op cit* at p 18.

85   See *Re Manurewa Transport Ltd* [1971] NZLR 909 and *Geoghegan v Greymouth Point Elizabeth Railway & Coal Co Ltd* (1898) 16 NZLR 749 at 768 and 771 and see Picarda pp 19–20 and Gough 99–100.

86   See eg *R v Consolidated Churchill Copper Corporation Ltd* [1978] 5 WWR 652; *Bank of Montreal v Woodtown Developments Ltd* (1979) 99 DLR (3d) 739 at 744 and *Federal Business Development Bank v Red Lion Restaurant Ltd* (1979) 101 DLR (3d) 480 at 484 and see Picarda at pp 20–21.

87   *Evans v Rival Granite Quarries* [1910] 2 KB 975 per Fletcher Moulton LJ at 998 cited at Picarda p 25.

justifiable if it were allowed by the wording of the charge—otherwise there would be a breach of the general rule expressed by Fletcher Moulton LJ and applicable in the absence of express provision to the contrary.[88] If a receiver is appointed by the court then the court order will define the assets over which he is to be appointed and the charge will crystallise with regard to those assets but will continue to float over the others to which it applies.[89] It will be a question of fact whether such a receiver is an administrative receiver on the basis of being appointed over the whole, or substantially the whole, of the company's property in accordance with the definition in s 29(2) of the Insolvency Act 1986.

5.45   It seems that it is at least theoretically possible for the holder of a floating charge to restore to the company the powers removed from it on crystallisation and to 'refloat' the charge. This would presumably only be possible if a provision in the charge permitted it. If a receiver had been appointed then the preferential creditors and the receiver's costs would have to be paid first.[90] The receiver would then be removed and not be replaced (if the chargee had such power under the terms of the charge document) and the management powers restored to the company's directors. Reflotation would not be possible if the company were in liquidation.[91]

5.46   The effects of crystallisation are dealt with below in so far as they concern the priority of different secure creditors over a company's assets.[92] As between the parties to the charge, crystallisation ends the power of the company to deal with the assets which are subject to the crystallised charge without the consent of the chargee. In other words, the charge becomes a fixed charge at that time. The remedies of the holder of the floating charge are similar to those of fixed chargee although the appointment of a receiver and manager and, commonly, the exercise by him of the power of sale are most frequently used. Remedies generally,[93] and the appointment of a receiver in particular,[94] are dealt with below.

88 *R v Consolidated Churchill Copper Corpn Ltd* [1978] 5 WWR 652.
89 *Re Griffin Hotel Ltd* [1941] Ch 129.
90 Companies Act 1985 s 196.
91 See generally Picarda p 24.
92 See below, chapter 8.
93 See chapter 7.
94 See paras 7.11–7.16.

CHAPTER 6

Security by Operation of Law

BASIS OF NON-CONSENSUAL SECURITY

6.01 In addition to those forms of security interest which are created by contractual agreement between borrower and lender, it is possible for property to be subject to a right based on a real security interest by virtue of the operation of a legal rule. This chapter deals with such forms of security. They are dealt with under three headings: liens, distress and execution. Liens and distress are remedies normally available to a private party without recourse to the courts as a condition of the existence of the right. However the forms of distress available to a person other than a landlord or the tax authorities require court sanction. Execution is a process which is available to enforce a judgment or order of the court and which may therefore be used by an unsecured creditor against the debtor's property to secure his right to payment after judgment has been obtained. The stage reached by an execution process will be important for the purpose of determining its priority as against a person claiming by virtue of some other security interest.

6.02 Section 246 of the Insolvency Act 1986 makes any lien or other right to retain possession of a company's books, papers or other records unenforceable to the extent that enforcement of such a right would deny possession of such documents to an administrator, liquidator or provisional liquidator. The section applies to a company in liquidation, subject to an administration order, or in respect of which a provisional liquidator has been appointed. Although s 246 does not apply to an administrative receiver he may still apply under s 236 and obtain an order for the production of documents. A lien does not prevent a court from making such an order.[1]

LIENS

6.03 A lien can take two forms. The word is sometimes used to describe any right to retain property until the payment of a debt. Such a right may be given by contract in which case it will give the person with the right an

---

1 *Re Aveling Barford Ltd* [1989] BCLC 122.

advantage over unsecured creditors if the right arises before the commencement of a liquidation or receivership. It has been held that such a right exists from the time of the contract and gives the person claiming it priority over a receiver acting on behalf of a floating chargee whose charge crystallised after the date of the contract granting the 'contractual lien', but before the goods subject to it came into the hands of the holder of the lien.[2] Such a consensual security can be created by contract and gives a right over the property to which it applies. The basis of the right of the holder of the lien in that case was that the receiver as agent of the company continued to be subject to the contract which contained the lien and since that contract was not terminated before the receivership began he could only take the benefit of it subject to the right to a lien that it gave to the other party.

6.04 A lien granted by contract can only take effect as between the parties to the contract unless it amounts to a charge on particular property and has been subjected to the necessary steps (such as registration) or is created at a time which gives it priority over other securities. In *George Barker (Transport) Ltd v Eynon* the contractual 'lien' had priority only as a contract made by a company in the ordinary course of business before the crystallisation of the floating charge under which the debenture holders claimed. Insofar as it was a right to retain possession of goods as a security for a debt to be paid it is arguable that the provision in that case was a pledge of the goods.[3] In any event, the receiver could only take benefit of the contract subject to the right of retention already granted by the company in that contract. In a case where a contract conferred a lien on cargoes and sub-freights carried by a chartered ship in favour of the owners it has been held that the right created was an equitable charge and registrable under the Companies Act 1985 s 395.[4]

6.05 Since a contractual lien will give rise to a right of retention as between the parties to the contract but not to a security right valid against third parties the rest of this section will deal only with those liens which arise by operation of law. The categories of lien that can exist by operation of law may be said to be common law or (possessory) liens; equitable liens and maritime liens.

Common law liens

6.06 A common law lien is dependent on possession of the property over which it exists. Such a lien may be general or particular. The possession of

---

2 *George Barker (Transport) Ltd v Eynon* [1974] 1 All ER 900.
3 Note the significance attached to constructive possession in argument—[1974] 1 All ER at 906–907.
4 In *Re Welsh Irish Ferries Ltd* [1985] 3 WLR 610 to be reversed by Companies Bill 1989.

the property must not have been wrongfully obtained. Property obtained by a misrepresentation[5] cannot be subject to a lien which would otherwise exist and, subject to the exceptions to the rule *nemo dat quod non habet*,[6] possession obtained because of the wrongful act of another person does not give rise to a lien.[7] Where possession is obtained lawfully it must continue for a lien to be available to the person in possession. If possession of the property is subject to a right of the owner to remove it at his discretion no lien will exist. A garage which maintains a car under a contract which gives the owner the right to remove it when he pleases will have no lien.[8] Similarly the trainer of a race horse who operates under a contract allowing the horse to be removed by the owner for entry into races cannot have a lien.[9] However, where delivery of the property is for a specific limited purpose only, this may not interrupt the possession of the lienee and the lien can remain—as where a garage allowed taxis to be removed only for the purpose of plying for hire with the intention that the lien should continue.[10] A contract may be held to exclude a person's right to a lien if it is clear that possession is obtained by that person for a particular purpose but if the evidence points only to an intention to give that purpose priority over the lien then the lien may remain subject to that purpose being carried out.[11] If property remains in the possession of a person otherwise entitled to a lien after the particular purpose of its deposit with him is carried out, then the lien will exist.[12]

6.07   The common law recognises particular liens and general liens. The former gives the person in possession of the property a right to hold the property until the payment of a specific debt connected with the property over which the lien is available. It does not provide security for any other debt which exists between the parties. A garage proprietor has a lien over a vehicle for the sum due for repair work done on that vehicle but not on other vehicles or the supply of other goods or services. A general lien, on the other hand, allows the lienee to retain property until all debts due from the owner have been paid, whether arising in connection with that property or not. The common law has been reluctant to extend the number of situations where a general lien can be taken.

Particular liens

6.08   The common law grants a particular lien to those persons who are

---

5   *Madden v Kempster* (1807) 1 Camp 2.
6   Eg under Factors Act 1889 s 2.
7   *Cole v North Western Bank* (1875) LR 10 CP 354.
8   *Hatton v Car Maintenance Co Ltd* [1915] 1 Ch 621.
9   *Forth v Simpson* (1849) 13 QB 680 and *Ward v Fielden* [1985] CLY 2000.
10   *Albemarle Supply Co Ltd v Hind & Co* [1928] 1 KB 307.
11   *Walker v Birch* (1795) 6 Term Rep 258; *Frith v Forbes* (1862) 4 De GF & J 409.
12   *Ex parte Sterling* (1809) 16 Ves 258.

obliged by law to receive goods. Such an obligation applies to a limited range of people. Common carriers and innkeepers are the commonest subjects of such a duty and, in the context of corporate insolvency, common carriers are the more significant of those two groups. Common carriers are those who exercise the public profession of carrying goods or passengers and hold themselves out to carry for hire as a business at a reasonable price.[13] Most UK carriers of goods reserve the right to reject goods and are not common carriers, but they will often stipulate for a contractual lien over the goods that they carry.[14] A common carrier's lien is over the goods carried for the freight payable in respect of those goods against the owner of the goods.[15] Only a contractual lien can give the right to hold the goods for payment of any more than the price of carriage. An express or implied agreement that the common carrier will give credit for the cost of carriage destroys the lien and the right to exercise the lien only arises when the carriage of the goods ends although a contractual lien is treated as being granted at the date of the contract.[16] When the lien is exercised the carrier must store the goods at his own expense somewhere reasonably convenient for the owner to collect them on tendering payment.[17]

6.09   An innkeeper obliged to receive and accommodate any person who asks to be his guest has a lien over the goods that such a person brings with him for the cost of the accommodation and food provided. This is a particular lien in that it applies only to debts due as a result of the stay and not other debts, although the lien is applicable to amounts due for food and accommodation and not simply for storage of the goods.[18] The lien extends to property which is brought to the inn by the guest but which belongs to another person. A company's property could be subject to a lien if taken to an hotel by one of its officers or employees.[19]

6.10   A custodian of goods such as a warehouseman has no lien over goods stored with him in the absence of a contract (which may be evinced by usage) or, possibly, a statutory obligation to store the goods.[20] This is because of the absence of the kind of obligation to provide a service which is imposed on an innkeeper or a common carrier and the fact that the

---

13   *Clark v West Ham Corporation* [1909] 2 KB 858; *Belfast Ropework Co v Bushell* [1918] 1 KB 210.
14   See eg *George Barker (Transport) Ltd v Eynon* [1974] 1 All ER 900.
15   *Skinner v Upshaw* (1702) 2 Ld Raym 757.
16   *Wiltshire Iron Co v Great Western Railway Co* (1871) LR 6 QB 776 and see *George Barker (Transport) Ltd v Eynon* (above).
17   *Great Northern Railway v Swaffield* (1874) LR 9 Exch 132 and *Great Western Railway v Crouch* (1858) 3 H & N 183.
18   *Chesham Automobile Supply Ltd v Beresford Hotel (Birchington) Ltd* (1913) 29 TLR 584.
19   See *Robins & Co v Gray* (1895) 2 QB 501.
20   *Chellaram & Sons (London) Ltd v Butlers Warehousing and Distribution* [1978] 2 Lloyds Rep 412 and *Singer v S W Railway Co* [1894] 1 QB 833.

custodian does not work on the goods for their improvement or repair. The use of skill and labour for the improvement or repair of goods or the existence of the relationship of principal and agent are the most common sources of particular, as opposed to general, liens. An agent has a particular lien over the goods and chattels of his principal for any amount due to him from his principal in respect of the goods or chattels in question. A general lien exists for certain specific classes of agent as a result of usage. The agent's claim must be under the same agency as results in the goods being held.[21]

6.11   The commonest liens of agents are those of solicitors, bankers, stockbrokers, and factors who all have general liens. However, an auctioneer has a particular lien over the proceeds of sale of goods as against the vendor. This covers the charges for that particular transaction.[22] As a factor he may also have a general lien to cover the balance over a series of transactions on behalf of a principal. A particular lien based on the exercise of skill and labour to repair or improve (but not merely to maintain) goods exists for any person whose business involves such activities.[23] This will secure payment for the work done. The goods must have been delivered into the possession of the lienee with the owner's express, implied or ostensible authority for the work to be done. In the case of a ship the repairer may have sufficient control despite the continued presence of the master and crew on board.[24] The lien will not extend to insurance monies which neither represent nor constitute the product of the chattel over which the lien existed.[25] The labour expended on the goods must represent completed work unless completion is prevented by the owner, in which case a lien exists for the price of the work that has been done.[26] However, the maintenance of a herd of pigs, which were fed and accommodated and produced progeny while in the custody of the lienee who did not provide boars to service the sows, was held to have been not an improvement but merely the supervision of a natural increase.[27] The lien of a ship repairer does not extend to damages incurred because of the ship's continued occupation of his dock after repairs have finished.[28] However, such a lien does extend to a part of a ship in the repairer's possession to cover the owner's liability for repairs to the whole ship.[29] The range of such artificer's liens extends from those given to vehicle repairers to the lien of the

21   *Misa v Currie* (1876) 1 App Cas 554.
22   *Webb v Smith* (1885) 30 Ch D 192.
23   *Hatton v Car Maintenance Co Ltd* [1915] 1 Ch 621.
24   See *Albemarle Supply Co Ltd v Hind & Co* [1928] 1 KB 307 and *The Narada* [1977] 1 Lloyds Rep 256.
25   *The Lancaster* [1980] 2 Lloyds Rep 497 (a case involving a contractual lien).
26   *Lilley v Barnsley* (1844) 1 Car & Kir 344.
27   *Re Southern Livestock Producers Ltd* [1964] 1 WLR 24.
28   *The Katingaki* [1976] 2 Lloyds Rep 372.
29   *The Ijaola* [1979] 1 Lloyds Rep 103.

accountant or the parliamentary agent—in each case it is based on the improvement, by skill and labour, of the property over which the lien exists for the cost of that work.

6.12   The case law indicates that an accountant's lien is based on his work on the books held, rather than on a position as agent. Presumably the precise nature of the work done by an accountant would determine the basis on which the lien was granted. Without contractual stipulation to the contrary it would seem that there can be no general lien over property held by an accountant. If such stipulation were laid down then the lien would depend on the contractual term. Sufficiently widespread use of such contractual terms might result in a usage in favour of a general lien for accountants. However, the case law suggests that accountants only have a particular lien over books of account in their possession for work done on those books.[30] This provides the possibility that even when books are delivered up to the liquidator of an insolvent company, under the liquidator's statutory powers the accountant may preserve his lien by stipulation to this effect or by virtue of acting in accordance with a Court Order. This can prevent the operation of the usual rule that a lien only lasts while the lienee has possession of the property.[31] It may be that the courts would be willing in the future to recognise a general lien for accountants if it could be established that a usage to this effect had developed. The analogy with the rights of solicitors would point in this direction but the policy of the common law is against the creation of further general liens.[32] This policy is based on the desirability of a *pari passu* distribution among creditors in bankruptcy (or company liquidation) but has not prevented recognition, by the courts, of frequent usage and acceptance of such conduct as part of the common law.[33] An accountant's lien covers files and papers delivered to him by clients and any documents which come into his possesison whilst acting for clients in the ordinary course of business.[34] The lien can be defeated by a claim under s 4 of the Tort (Interference with Goods) Act 1977 if the accountant fails to produce evidence of the work done.[35]

General liens

6.13   A general lien can exist at common law and is based on possession by the lienee. It will only result from the acceptance by the courts of a general

30   *Ex parte Southall* (1848) 17 LJ Bcy 21; *Woodworth v Conroy* [1976] 1 QB 884.
31   Scottish cases suggest this, see *Liquidator of Scottish Workmen's Assurance Co Ltd v Waddle* 1910 SC 670 and *Train v McIntyre Ltd v Forbes* 1925 SLT 280.
32   *Rushforth v Hadfield* (1805) 6 East 519 at 528 and 7 East 224 at 229.
33   *K Chellaram & Sons (London) Ltd v Butlers Warehousing and Distribution Ltd* [1977] 2 Lloyds Rep 192.
34   *Woodworth v Conroy* [1976] 1 QBD 884.
35   *Thaper v Singh* [1987] FLR 369.

usage in a particular trade or business. It gives the lienee a right to hold property in his possession until payment has been made of all claims and debts due to him from the owner. It is not limited to claims relating to work done on, or in, connection with, the goods that are held. Such a lien is often provided for by the terms of a contract but the number which exist purely by operation of law is limited.

Solicitors

6.14 A solicitor has a general lien over documents and any other personal chattels in his possession until he is paid all costs due from his client. The lien covers chattels which came into his possession in the course of his employment as a solicitor.[36] It does not extend to property held as mortgagee or trustee[37] or to property handed over for a particular purpose or to the original of the client's will. The most common documents subjected to a lien are the title deeds to land but negotiable instruments, insurance policies, share certificates, letters of patent or money in the client account can all be subject to the lien.[38] A lien over the title deeds to land does not give any right over the land; only the right to retain the deeds and to deny the client access to them.[39]

6.15 The lien of the solicitor over the documents is only against the client and can be no better than the client's right to retain the documents. If the client is ordered by the court to produce them, the solicitor's lien is no defence.[40] As against the liquidator of a company, the company's solicitor has no right to retain documents such as the register of members required by the Companies Act to be kept at a certain place. This will extend to all documents required by the Companies Act to be kept at the company's registered office.[41] In the case of such documents it is the statutory requirement that they be kept in a particular place to be available for public inspection which is the reason for their non-availability for a solicitor's lien.[42] However, as against the liquidator there is no effective lien over documents that come into the solicitor's hands after the commencement of the liquidation. There is no lien against the liquidator for costs arising before the commencement of the liquidation.[43]

6.16 If a company goes into liquidation, has a provisional liquidator

---

36 *Re Hawkes* [1898] 2 Ch 1.
37 *Vaughan v Vanderstegen* (1854) 2 Drew 408.
38 See Halsbury's Laws 4 Edition Vol 44 p 227.
39 *Re Biggs & Rocke* (1897) 41 Sol Jo 277.
40 *Lewis v Powell* [1897] 1 Ch 678.
41 See eg Companies Act 1985 ss 190, 211, 288, 325 and 353.
42 *Re Capital Fire Insurance Association* (1883) 24 Ch D 408.
43 *Ibid* and *Re Rapid Road Transit Co Ltd* [1909] 1 Ch 96.

appointed, or is subject to an administration order, all liens are unenforceable against its books, papers or other records to the extent that their enforcement would deny such documents to the office holder. The office holder for this purpose is the administrator, liquidator or provisional liquidator. This provision does not apply to a lien on documents which give title to property and which are held as such.[44] It will apply to a consensual security interest as well as to a lien as s 246(2) refers to a lien 'or any other right to retain possession.'

6.17 Although s 246 does not apply to administrative receivers a solicitor's lien will not prevent a successful application by an administrative receiver under s 236 for an order against the solicitor that documents should be produced. The role of the administrative receiver as agent of the company does not prevent the court from making an order, under s 236, in his favour. That section is concerned with the collection of information, not the possession of property, and it is available to an administrative receiver. As inspection of documents is possible without removing them from the solicitor's possession the lien which relates to possession is unaffected. The fact that the lien may in practice be without value once the information in the documents is disclosed is immaterial as the lien is over the document and not the information. For the same reason it has been said, *obiter*, that an order may be made under s 236 for the inspection of documents of title protected from the effect of s 246 on liens. Legal professional privilege will only protect the information if it relates to a client other than the company or group of companies in receivership.[45]

6.18 Even in the absence of notice, the solicitor's lien does not normally have priority over an earlier equity[46] although a lien which arises before a floating charge crystallises will have priority over it.[47] In accordance with the general rule on liens a solicitor who parts with possession of documents will lose his lien unless he gives possession to a later solicitor only to his order or hands the documents to the agent of a third party subject to the lien.[48] The arrest by the solicitor of the client's ship will not amount to a waiver of his lien over the client's documents.[49]

6.19 Solicitors who discharge themselves from acting for a client must usually hand the papers over to the new solicitors on an undertaking that

44 Insolvency Act 1986 s 246.
45 *Re Aveling Barford Ltd* [1989] BCLC 122.
46 *Pelly v Wathen* (1851) 1 De GM & G 16.
47 *Brunton v Electrical Engineering Corpn* [1892] 1 Ch 434.
48 *Caldwell v Sumpters* [1972] Ch 478.
49 *A v B* [1984] 1 All ER 265.

they will be redelivered at the end of the litigation. There is no right for the 'old' solicitors to hold the papers pending the outcome of litigation as to whether they had good cause to withdraw from acting for the client.[50] However, in a case in which the solicitors acted properly throughout and in which the client is simply trying to avoid the payment of money clearly owed, no order will be made to require solicitors who have withdrawn from the case to hand papers over. This judicial discretion is exercised on the basis of the overriding principle that the order made should be that which best serves, or is least likely to frustrate, the interests of justice.[49] The lien secures all costs, charges and expenses due, from the client who owns the document, to the solicitor but not costs due to the solicitor in some other capacity. As a general lien, it extends to all costs due to the solicitor and is not limited to those relating to the documents in question or the matter to which they are relevant.[51]

6.20   Apart from terminating if the solicitor parts with possession of the property subject to it, the lien will be discharged on payment of the costs; on proof by the solicitor in a winding up for the costs it secures without valuing the lien and stating that it exists;[52] and by waiver of the lien by the solicitor. The latter will most commonly occur where a solicitor takes some other form of security for the costs over property to which the documents are relevant without denying abandonment of the lien. It is unclear whether the security merely has to be more advantageous than the lien for waiver to take place or whether it is necessary for the security to be inconsistent with it.[51]

6.21   In addition to the general lien, a solicitor has a particular lien over funds recovered by him for the client in a court action or an arbitration. This does not extend to the proceeds resulting from a process of negotiation which is not the compromise of litigation.[53] This right differs from the general lien which allows retention in that it gives the solicitor a right to ask the court to charge the property in favour of the solicitor and it is only then that he has a right to the money. It extends only to the costs of the proceedings in which the fund was recovered and not to any other costs owed by the client.[53] Where the money is held by the solicitor he may deduct his costs from it and where it is payable under a judgment he can give notice to the person liable to pay it to hand it to the solicitor. If it is handed to the client after receipt of the notice then the party who paid it to the client

---

50   *Gamlen Chemical Co (UK) Ltd v Rochem* [1980] 1 All ER 1049.
51   *Re Taylor, Stileman & Underwood* [1891] 1 Ch 590.
52   *Re Safety Explosives Ltd* [1904] 1 Ch 226; and see Chapter 19 as to proof of debts and Rule 4.96 Insolvency Rules 1986 SI 1986/1925.
53   *Meguerditchian v Lightbound* [1917] 2 KB 298.

will have to make a further payment to the solicitor.[54] This right, effectively to seize money for payment of costs, is in addition to the general lien over any of the client's property which gives a right to retain any money in the client account for any amount due from the client to the solicitor for services as such.[55] The lien on client account funds prevents such funds from being included in a *Mareva* injunction freezing the client's assets.[56]

6.22 Funds paid into a joint account held by the parties' solicitors as a condition of leave to defend the action being given are held by the solicitors as bare trustees. No lien can be asserted over the account as it can only be dealt with in accordance with a court order. However, the solicitors may benefit from the equitable interference of the court which can order payment for their work in recovering or preserving the property to the extent of their own client's interest in the fund.[57]

6.23 A further analogous right is granted to solicitors by the Solicitors Act 1974 s 73 which empowers any civil court in which a solicitor has been employed in a suit to declare that he is entitled to a charge on any property recovered or defended by him. All later dealings in the property will then be subject to the charge. Normally a solicitor will be entitled to a charging order providing he shows that he will not obtain his costs in the absence of one.[58] Only a breach of faith or conduct which would make it unfair to a third party to grant an order or the fact that a solicitor proves in liquidation or takes some other security will prevent an order from being granted where the solicitor is entitled to costs in the action which resulted in the recovery or preservation of the property.[59]

Bankers' and stockbrokers' liens
6.24 A banker has a general lien over all securities deposited with him in his capacity as banker by a customer or on his account.[60] This can include not only cheques paid in for collection but also insurance policies, share certificates and orders for payment.[61] In the case of monies the right is one of set-off rather than lien because normally the money in question is not earmarked and no particular money can be repaid—it can only be used to set off debts due to the banker. The same applies to the customer's account[62] and it has been doubted whether any of the rights granted to

54 *Watson v Maskell* (1834) 1 Bing 366 and *Ross v Buxton* (1889) 42 Ch D 190.
55 *Loescher v Dean* [1950] Ch 491.
56 *Prekookeanska v LNT Lines Srl* [1988] 3 All ER 897.
57 *Halvanon Insurance Co Ltd v Central Reinsurance Corporation* [1988] 3 All ER 857.
58 *Harrison v Harrison* (1888) 13 PD 180.
59 *Dillow v Garrold ex parte Adams* (1884) 13 QBD 543; *Higgs v Higgs* [1934] p 95; *Groome v Cheesewright* [1895] 1 Ch 730.
60 *Brandao v Barnett* (1846) 12 Cl & Fin 747.
61 *Re Bowes* (1886) 33 Ch D 586; *Misa v Currie* (1876) 1 App Cas, 554.
62 *Banner v Johnston* (1871) LR 5 HL 157; *Roxburghe v Cox* (1881) 17 Ch D 520.

bankers by law can rightly be described as 'liens'. Terms suggesting a right to combine accounts or setoff may be more appropriate.[63] There is, however, a well established case law on this right which is usually referred to as a lien.

6.25 The two major limitations on the right which may make it inapplicable in many circumstances are that it does not operate where there is an agreement which expressly or impliedly excludes the lien and that it does not apply to documents held by the banker for safekeeping. Circumstances indicating that documents such as title deeds to land have been deposited by way of equitable mortgage will make the lien irrelevant. If there is an agreement excluding the right of set-off it ends when the banker/customer relationship ends and as soon as this occurs the lien arises and is enforceable.[64] A lien can exist as long as the documents are in the banker's hands in the course of business. It is unclear whether securities deposited for safekeeping are excluded because this function is not regarded as part of the business of banking or because this arrangement indicates a contract excluding the right to a lien. It is, however, clear, that such deposits are excluded from the lien.[65] It has become common for some banks to seek to include securities deposited by way of safekeeping in their charge documents. This may be successful in creating an equitable charge but it does not affect the position as regards a lien which exists by operation of law.[66]

6.26 A lien depends on the banker's possession of securities and on there being debts due from the customer but, of course, being a general lien those debts need bear no relation to the documents held. It is immaterial whether documents come into the banker's possession before the debts arise or afterwards. The banker's lien has been said to be in the nature of an implied pledge[67] and because of this the courts have held that, unlike most lienees, bankers have a right to sell property subject to their lien without statutory authority. The right to sell can be exercised on default if there is a fixed time for payment or after reasonable notice of the intention to do so if no time was fixed. This accords with the rules applicable to a pledge.[68] This remedy will, of course, be irrelevant in the large number of cases where the securities held by a banker are negotiable instruments, such as cheques or bills of exchange, which can be dealt with by the banker as holder when they are

---

63 See *Halesowen Presswork and Assemblies Ltd v Westminster Bank Ltd* [1970] 3 WLR 624 per Buckley LJ at 645.
64 *National Westminster Bank Ltd v Halesowen Presswork Assemblies Ltd* [1973] AC 785.
65 *Brandao v Barnett* (1846) 12 Cl & Fin 787 at 808.
66 See Paget's "Law of Banking" 9th Edition p 414.
67 *Brandao v Barnett* (1846) 12 Cl & Fin 787 at 806.
68 *Sewell v Burdick* (1884) 10 App Cas 74; *Re Morritt* (1886) 18 QBD 222.

due without reference to the lien. Any proceeds received can then become the subject of a set-off or combination of accounts. The lien is most likely to be used where bearer bonds or share certificates are held—although deposit of the latter may amount to an equitable mortgage which will exclude the lien.[69] The banker's lien occupies the narrow range of situations which fall between those circumstances in which securities are negotiable and are held in due course and those where they are held as security by virtue of a mortgage or charge. The right of sale suggests that the 'lien' is an implied pledge and 'set off' is the appropriate remedy where money or customer's accounts are involved. The remedy of the lien did, however, develop by virtue of the common law's recognition of an established usage of the law merchant and it is a right granted by operation of law.[70]

6.27 A stockbroker has a general lien for any amount due to him from a client in respect of dealings with shares. It extends to any securities in his possession (such as share certificates) which relate to shares owned by the client but the lien is displaced by any contrary agreement and does not apply to documents that do not come into the broker's possession in the course of his business as such.[71] The stockbroker's lien extends only to the client's interest in the property hence after an equitable assignment of shares the assignee's interest has priority over the stockbroker's lien when he is given the share certificates for sale.[72] It remains to be seen how the stockbroker's lien will develop after the creation, since 1986, of financial conglomerates operating in the securities markets.

Insurance broker's liens

6.28 A broker who is left in possession of an insurance policy has a particular lien over the policy for the premiums payable under it and for his charges in respect of it. In the case of a marine insurance policy he will also have a general lien for all amounts due on accounts between the broker and the insured which relate to insurance providing he deals with the insured and not with an agent. However, so long as he deals with the person who has deposited the policy as principal he will have the right unless, when the debt was created, he had reason to believe that the person he dealt with was an agent.[73] Loss of possession extinguishes the lien but it revives if possession is regained and the broker's knowledge of the status of the other party for the purpose of his general lien will be decided according to his knowledge at the time of regaining possession.[74]

---

69 *Harrold v Plenty* [1901] 2 Ch 314.
70 *Brandao v Barnett* (1846) 12 Cl & Fin 787.
71 *Jones v Peppercorne* (1858) Johns 430.
72 *Peat v Clayton* [1906] 1 Ch 659.
73 Marine Insurance Act 1906 s 53(2).
74 *Levy v Barnard* (1818) 8 Taunt 149.

Factors

6.29 A factor, in the strict legal sense of the word, has a lien. This does not relate to the purchaser of debts. A factor for this purpose is an agent who is entrusted with the possession of goods by the owner of those goods for the purpose of sale or who buys on behalf of a principal and who is remunerated by commission. He must buy or sell in his own name without disclosing the name of his principal.[75] A factor has a general lien over goods which come into his possession in the ordinary course of his business as against the owner of those goods for all amounts due arising from the course of dealing between the owner and the factor. The ordinary course of business of the factor may be sale by him on behalf of the owner, or the purchase of goods for his principals. The lien extends beyond the goods to the price received by the factor on his sale of them.[76] This is not, however, a right of sale because of the lien but rather a sale under the authority already given by the principal.[77] The lien does not apply if the goods are deposited for a particular purpose or if the factor is claiming for a debt which does not arise from acts done as a factor for the person against whom the lien is claimed.[78]

6.30 Where goods are consigned or shipped in the name of a person other than the owner, any lien that the consignee would have over the goods (as common carrier or by contract) as against the owner is good against the person in whose name they were consigned.[79] An auctioneer, if he comes within the definition of a factor, will have a general lien in addition to his own particular lien over the proceeds of sale for the costs of a particular transaction.[80]

Liens on the sale of goods[81]

6.31 If a contract exists for the sale of goods, property in the goods will usually pass to the buyer before payment by him. A seller may take effective security for the price by stipulating in the contract that the property in the goods will not pass to the buyer until payment has been made—in which case, although there is not a security interest in the real sense, the seller remains the owner and therefore has a right to regain possession of the goods if there is no payment.[82] If this is not done ownership may well have passed to the buyer before he is in possession of the goods. In these

75 *Rolls Razor Ltd v Cox* [1967] 1 QB 552 at 568.
76 *Kruger v Wilcox* (1755) Amb 252.
77 *Smart v Sanders* (1848) 5 CB 895.
78 *Walker v Birch* (1795) 6 Term Rep 258.
79 Factors Act 1889 s 7.
80 *Webb v Smith* (1885) Ch D 192.
81 See generally Goode, "Commercial Law" pp 366–371.
82 See below, paras 9.06–9.15 on such retention of title clauses.

circumstances the Sale of Goods Act 1979 provides certain real remedies for the unpaid seller so long as the conditions laid down in the statute are satisfied. Those rights are a lien over goods in which property has passed to the buyer but which remain in the seller's possession; the right to refuse to deliver the goods if property remains in the seller; a right to stop the goods in transit; and a right of resale. These statutory rights are legal and not equitable. A seller is deemed to be unpaid for this purpose when part of the price remains unpaid or where a cheque or other bill of exchange accepted in payment is dishonoured.[83] A seller is treated as unpaid even if he has agreed to grant credit.

6.32   An unpaid seller has a lien over the goods sold for the price of those goods (not including other expenses unless the contract stipulated this) if he is in possession of the goods and he has sold without granting the buyer any credit or the term of the credit granted has expired or the buyer becomes insolvent.[84] His possession can be as the buyer's bailee or agent[85] but it is lost if the goods are delivered to a carrier for transportation to the buyer without the reservation of a right of disposal, or if the buyer or his agent lawfully obtain possession or if the lien is waived by the seller.[86] An intention to waive the lien may be shown by the delivery of some of the goods to the buyer but if such intention is not shown the lien remains over those goods which were not delivered.[87] The effect of the lien is that delivery by the seller can be made conditional on the payment of the price. If a seller has not been paid before the commencement of a winding up or the appointment of a receiver[88] he is entitled to retain the goods in his possession.

6.33   The right to withhold delivery is similar to and co-extensive with the lien and right of stoppage in transit. It exists only when the seller retains the property in the goods. It is not a lien as the right exists over the seller's own property and not that of another person.[89] The right to stop goods in transit can only be exercised by an unpaid seller if the buyer becomes insolvent. This right applies while the goods are in the hands of the carrier or other bailee for transmission to the buyer, and ends on delivery to the buyer or his agent or acknowledgement by the carrier that the goods are held for the buyer. Attornment by acknowledgement by the carrier that he

---

83   Sale of Goods Act 1979 s 38(1).
84   *Ibid* s 41(1).
85   s 41(2).
86   s 43.
87   s 42.
88   Assuming that at this time the buyer is insolvent within the meaning of the Sale of Goods Act 1979 s 61(4) because it cannot pay its debts as they fall due or has ceased to pay its debts in the ordinary course of business.
89   s 39(2).

holds for the buyer will not end the period of transit if the buyer refuses to take delivery. However, wrongful refusal by the carrier to deliver to the buyer or his agent brings the transit period to an end.[90] The seller's right to stop the goods in transit is exercised by the repossession of the goods or by serving notice on the carrier. On receipt of such notice the carrier must deliver the goods, to the seller's directions, at the latter's expense.[91]

6.34 Dispositions of the goods by the buyer do not affect the seller's right to a lien or to stoppage in transit unless either the seller assents to it or documents of title have been given to the buyer and transferred to a *bona fide* purchaser for value. If the recipient of the documents of title is a buyer the rights of lien and of stoppage in transit are lost altogether. If the transfer of the documents of title was, for example, by way of pledge, then the seller retains those rights but they are subject to the rights of the transferee.[92] The contract of sale is not rescinded by the exercise by the unpaid seller of his lien or right of stoppage in transit.[93]

6.35 Section 48(2) makes it clear that if a seller who has exercised the right to a lien or to stop the goods in transit resells them the new buyer gets good title to the goods by way of exception to the rule *nemo dat quod non habet* despite the fact that the property in the goods had passed to the buyer under the original contract before the seller's lien or right of stoppage was exercised. It is clear that good title will be passed to the new buyer where the seller retained the property in the goods in the original sale contract.[94] Despite the good title conferred on the new buyer by s 48(2), a sale of goods, the property in which had passed to the original buyer, will make the seller liable to that buyer for breach of the contract as, according to s 48(1), the original contract is not rescinded by his exercise of his lien or right of stoppage in transit. This will not be the case if the sale was allowed by a term of that contract or by ss 48(3) or (4).

6.36 Sections 48(3) and (4) lay down the grounds on which the seller is entitled to resell the goods as against the original buyer. These are, in the case of perishable goods, that the buyer has not paid or tendered payment of the price within a reasonable time, in the case of any goods, that notice is given to the buyer of the seller's intention to resell and there is no payment or tender of it. The latter is merely a restatement of the common law position that the time of payment is not of essence but may be made such by

---

90 ss 44; and 45(1), (3) and (4).
91 s 46.
92 s 47(1) and (2).
93 s 48(1).
94 See s 48(2) which refers to the 'right of retention'.

notice.[95] The exercise of either an express right of resale or of the statutory right gives rise to rescission of the original sale contract without prejudice to any damages claim.[96]

6.37   These rights will clearly be of importance in the context of an insolvent company which has entered into contracts to buy or sell goods. A liquidator, receiver or administrator will have no better right in relation to such goods than the company had under the Sale of Goods Act 1979 or the sale contract to which the company was a party.

Equitable liens

6.38   Unlike a common law lien an equitable lien is not based on possession by the lienee of the property over which it operates. On the contrary, it is based on the principle that one who has obtained property under a contract for payment will not be allowed to keep it without payment. It is often a right of a person who does not have possesison of property and, unlike a common law lien which does not give a right of sale unless a statute so provides, gives the holder of the lien a right to obtain a sale of the property by order of the court.[97] The lien is a security created by operation of law rather than by agreement between the parties since it applies because of the relationship between them. Consequently it can be distinguished from a mortgage or charge created by the parties and is not registrable under the Companies Act 1985 s 395.[98] In other circumstances a lien will be held to exist because of the course of conduct or the agreement of the parties in situations where there is no equitable lien on the basis of the relationship itself. The characteristics of an equitable lien resemble those of an equitable charge but are imposed by law in a situation in which justice demands it.

Vendor's lien
6.39   The form of equitable lien most likely to be relevant to the circumstances of an insolvent company is that which arises between vendor and purchaser. It would seem that this lien applies to any property where specific performance of the contract of sale is available other than contracts relating to goods which are subject to the legal lien and other rights created in favour of the unpaid vendor by the Sale of Goods Act 1979.[99] It certainly

---

95   See Goode, "Commercial Law" pp 369–371.
96   s 48(4) and *R V Ward Ltd v Bagnall* [1967] 1 QB 534.
97   *Mackreth v Symmons* (1808) 15 Ves 329 and *Re Beirnstein* [1925] Ch 12.
98   See *London and Cheshire Insurance Co Ltd v Laplagrene Property Company Ltd* [1971] Ch 499.
99   See paras 6.32–6.38 above and *Transport and General Credit Corporation v Morgan* [1939] Ch 331; see *London & Cheshire Insurance Co Ltd v Laplagrene* (above).

applies to the unpaid vendor of land, shares, patents or debts.[100] A third party can be subrogated to the unpaid vendor's lien if he has provided the purchase money at the purchaser's request from his own funds and if subrogation does not lead to an unjust result. There must be no evidence of any arrangement which would be inconsistent with such a claim.[101]

6.40 The vendor's lien exists to secure the purchase price of the property to which the lien attaches until that price is paid in full. It first arises when the contract of sale is entered into but is not enforceable until after the date fixed for completion of the transaction by transfer of the property.[102] It succeeds the legal lien over land which exists in the vendor until execution of the conveyance and to title deeds until they leave the vendor's possession.[103] The lien will apply to chattels affixed to land which is subject to the lien, and continues despite an acknowledgement of receipt of payment in a conveyance of land or in the Register in the case of land governed by the Land Registration Act 1925.[104]

6.41 A difficulty will sometimes arise about whether the unpaid vendor's lien is replaced by a security interest created between the same parties or whether the lien subsists despite such a transaction. This is of particular importance in the corporate context as a mortgage or charge is registrable under the Companies Act 1985 s 395 whereas a lien is not as it is a security created by operation of law.[98] There is a question of whether an unpaid vendor who takes a consensual security can later fall back on his lien if the mortgage or charge he took is not registered. In *Capital Finance Co Ltd v Stokes*[105] an agreement for the sale of land to a company in return for cash for part of the price and the grant of a legal mortgage by the purchaser in favour of the vendor for the balance was held to entitle the vendor to the grant of such a mortgage together with the amount of cash agreed. The consequences of a failure to register the mortgage under the Companies Act 1948 s 95 (now the Companies Act 1985 s 395) could not be avoided by claiming an unpaid vendor's lien when the vendor had been provided with the consensual security that he was promised.

6.42 Similarly, the security granted by a deposit of title deeds is created by an agreement of the parties and results in an equitable mortgage that must

---

100   *Langen and Wind Ltd v Bell* [1972] Ch 685; *Dank Rekylriffel Syndikat Aktieselskab v Snell* [1908] 2 Ch 123 and *Collins v Collins (No 2)* (1862) 31 Beav 346 respectively.
101   *Boodle Hatfield & Co v British Films* (1986) PCC 176.
102   *Re Birmingham* [1959] Ch 523.
103   *Oxenham v Esdaile* (1829) 3 Y & J 262.
104   *Re Vulcan Ironworks* [1888] WN 37 and *London & Cheshire Insurance Co v Laplagrene Property Co Ltd* [1971] Ch 499.
105   [1969] 1 Ch 261.

be registered under s 395. The right to retain the deeds is not to be classified as a lien and registration of the security interest is required.[106] In cases in which consensual security is given it is a matter of construction whether the grant of the security is itself the 'price' as in *Capital Finance & Co Ltd v Stokes*[105] or whether the security is merely intended to secure payment of the price in which case the status of the lien will depend upon the intention of the parties whether it was to be supplanted by the consensual security.[107] If the security is completely unenforceable from the beginning it would seem that the lien can continue in existence.[108]

6.43   The vendor's lien is an equity which binds all successors of the purchaser except *bona fide* purchasers of a legal or equitable estate without notice of it. Registration requirements will affect the question of notice where they apply.[109] The lien is enforceable by any of the remedies available to an equitable chargee. In addition to its power to order a sale of the property (which can be exercised despite the fact that works have been carried out by the purchaser on the property since he took possession of it[110]) the court may appoint a receiver or award possession of the property to the unpaid vendor. As in the case of an equitable charge, however, foreclosure is not available.[111]

6.44   The purchaser of property who pays a deposit or other money on account of the purchase price has a lien on the property which was subject to the sale contract if there is a failure to complete which is not the result of his default.[112] The lien is subject to the same rules as the vendor's lien. It is not defeated by delay or justified rescission by the purchaser unless he abandons the contract[113] and is available to a sub-purchaser from the purchaser to the extent of the purchaser's interest in the property as against his deposit if it is recovered from the vendor.[114] The equitable lien of a purchaser or a vendor may be assigned and the benefit of the lien can be passed with the debt to which it relates.[115]

6.45   Apart from the equitable lien of the purchaser or vendor of property, a lien arises over the partnership property on the dissolution of a

106   *Re Wallis & Simmonds (Builders) Ltd* [1974] 1 All ER 561.
107   See *Mackreth v Symmons* (1808) 15 Ves 329 and *Collins v Collins (No 2)* (1862) 31 Beav 346.
108   *Burston Finance Ltd v Speirway Ltd* [1974] 1 WLR 1648 at 1652.
109   See chapter 8.
110   *Wing v Tottenham and Hampstead Junction Railway Co* (1868) LR 3 Ch App 740.
111   *Munns v Isle of Wight Railway Co* (1870) 5 Ch App 414; *Williams v Aylesbury & Buckingham Railway Company* (1873) 28 LT 547.
112   *Whitbread & Co Ltd v Watt* [1902] 1 Ch 835.
113   *Levy v Stogdon* [1898] 1 Ch 478 and *Dinn v Grant* (1852) 5 De G & Sm 45.
114   *Aberman Ironworkers v Workers* (1868) 4 Ch App 101.
115   *Burn v Carvalho* (1839) 4 My & Cr 690; *Ball v Faulkner* (1848) 2 De G & Sm 772.

partnership in favour of the retiring partner (or his successors) and the continuing partners in respect of amounts due on the dissolution.[116] Such interests may affect a company which has taken part in a consortium with others in the form of a partnership—especially if the consortium has been dissolved on the winding up of one of its corporate members. Such a lien ends if the partnership assets are distributed among the partners and become their property unless distribution is agreed to be subject to the lien.[117] Equitable liens can also exist in the case of a person with a limited interest in property under a trust who commits waste which injures the interests of others. The lien is for the benefit of the remaindermen and applies to the profits due to the limited owner during his term. The same principle applies to waste by a trustee—any beneficial interest that he holds is subject to the lien.[118] In a limited number of cases, an equitable lien will exist in favour of a person who expends resources on the improvement of property belonging to another. This is an exception to the general rule that a lien is not available in such cases.[119] They apply to cases of family relationships, mistake, subrogation or express or implied contract and their scope is uncertain.[120] If an equitable lien exists in such a case its characteristics will be the same as those of an equitable lien arising in favour of a vendor or purchaser.

Maritime liens

6.46   Three types of lien can exist in relation to ships. Firstly, as chattels, they can be subject to the liens already described. The most likely such lien to apply in practice is the particular lien of the repairer. If a ship is in the possession of one who has repaired or improved it then he will have a lien over the ship to the same extent and in the same circumstances as any other repairer of a chattel.[121] The lien secures the amount due for repairs but not the cost of keeping the ship to enforce the lien.[122] The lien ends when possession is lost[123] and, unlike a maritime lien proper, it does not affect ownership rights over the ship once possession is relinquished.[124]

6.47   Maritime liens, *strictu sensu*, were developed by the Court of

---

116   *Payne v Hornby* (1858) 25 Beav 250.
117   *Holroyd v Griffiths* (1856) 3 Drew 426.
118   *Cole v Muddle* (1852) 10 Hare 186.
119   *Peruvian Guano Co v Dreyfus Bros Co* [1892] AC 170 *Re Vandervell's Trusts (No 2)* [1974] Ch 269 and see Torts (Interference with Goods) Act 1977 ss 1(a) and (b).
120   See Goff and Jones "Law of Restitution" pp 237 *et seq* and Halsbury's Laws 4th Edition Vol 28 paras 569 to 573.
121   *Ex parte Bland* (1814) 2 Rose 91.
122   *Somes v British Empire Shipping Co* (1860) 8 HLC 338 and *The Katingaki* [1976] 2 Lloyds Rep 372.
123   *The Harriet* (1868) 18 LT 804.
124   See paras 6.06 *et seq*.

Admiralty but are extended and reinforced by statutory rights conferred on certain persons who would not have had any lien under the case law rules. The claim of a maritime lienee arises by operation of law but otherwise resembles the remedies of the grantee of a bottomry bond.[125] A right is conferred on the lienee which is not based on possession and which is enforceable by a court action *in rem* against the ship or other property that is subject to the lien. Such an action will result in the enforcement of the lien by the sale of the property which is subject to it and the payment of claimants in the appropriate order out of the proceeds of sale. The right however, arises at the time when the lien attaches and a judgment which enforces it relates back to that time. Being a right *in rem*, it applies to later owners of the ship unless there has been a sale by the court in an action *in rem*.[126] This makes the maritime lien an important limitation on the rights of the ship's owner and his successors in title whether mortgagees or purchasers—even if they have no notice of its existence. The lien remains attached to its subject matter and does not transfer to the purchase money.

6.48   A lien is granted in favour of the following:

(1) *The Crew*. The master and seamen of a ship have a lien over the ship and its freight for wages earned under an ordinary contract on board the ship. It does not apply to special contracts such as those under which the pay of the crew takes the form of a share in the proceeds of the voyage[127] although if the wages were earned on board ship the lien will take effect against the ship and the freight earned by it even if the crew were hired by a person who had no authority to do so.[128] As well as wages the lien covers subsistence or travel allowances, compensation for wrongful dismissal and contributions to a pension fund.[129] The master also has a lien in respect of any disbursements made by him or liabilities incurred by him in the ordinary course of his employment by virtue of his authority.[130] The claims of master and crew are *pari passu*. The claim of the crew does not have priority.[131]

(2) *Salvage*. A person who assists in saving a ship, its cargo or, sometimes, the lives of those on the ship is entitled to payment under maritime law in respect of those services.[132] The provision of those services creates a lien over the ship and its cargo. If the freight earnings of the ship

---

125   See paras 3.26–3.27 and 7.19.
126   *The Ripon City* [1897] p 226 and *The Goulandris* [1927] p 182.
127   *The Riby Grove* (1843) 2 W Rob 52.
128   *Phillips v Highland Railway Co, The Ferret* (1883) 8 App Cas 329.
129   *The Halcyon Skies* [1976] 2 WLR 514.
130   Merchant Shipping Act 1970 s 18 and *The Ripon City* [1897] p 226.
131   *The Royal Wells* [1984] 3 WLR.
132   See Halsbury's Laws 4th Edition Vol 43 para 1027.

are saved by the salvage operation then they too are subject to the lien. Each form of property is separately subject to a lien in proportion to its volume but there is not joint liability of each to contribute to the salvage due in respect of the other. If the salvage due in respect of the cargo is satisfied by an amount lower than the cargo's full value, the balance of the cargo's value cannot be used to pay the amount of salvage due in respect of the ship.[133] The salvor preserves property out of which other claims can be met so his claim has priority over those of others—such as the crew—whose lien arose earlier. He has priority over the claim of the crew for wages for the period both before and after salvage services were rendered unless this rule leads to a result that is plainly unjust.[134]

(3) *Damage caused by act of navigation.* A lien attaches to the ship and her freight but not her cargo as soon as damage is done by her.[135] It applies to damage inflicted by a ship on another ship or other property in port or at sea owing to negligence on the part of those responsible for her navigation. The damage may be done by the owners or their servants or those with authorised control of the ship. This includes charterers who have control or anyone else in authorised possession of the ship.[136] There can be no lien when the owners have not given at least implied authority for a person to take possession of the ship nor will it arise when damage is caused wilfully by the ship's master.[137]

6.49 In addition to the liens in respect of the crew's wages, salvage and damage, a range of statutory liens are created in respect of ships. The arrest of a ship in an Admiralty action *in rem* creates a lien[138] as does detention of a vessel by dock or harbour authorities in pursuit of rights granted under their own private statutes[139] for unpaid dues or for damage to harbours or docks.

EXECUTION

Nature of execution

6.50 When a creditor is unpaid and obtains a judgment of the court for the amount of the debt he will be entitled to use the methods of enforcement open to him by law to obtain satisfaction of the judgment. The fact of obtaining judgment does not of itself provide any security for the creditor or

133 *The Westminster* (1841) 1 Wm Rob 229; *The Charlotte Wylie* (1846) 2 Wm Rob 495.
134 *The Lyrma* (No 2) [1978] 2 Lloyds Rep 30.
135 *The Victor* (1860) Lush 72.
136 *The Ripon City* [1897] P 226.
137 *The Ida* (1860) Lush 6.
138 *The Cella* (1888) 13 PD 82.
139 See Harbours, Docks and Piers Clauses Act 1847 s 44.

any priority for him over the claims of other creditors. When enforcement of a judgment is sought a number of devices may be used which will provide the creditor with a real right against the property of the debtor company— at least once a certain stage in the process is reached. The forms of execution available in the High Court[140] which are likely to be used against a corporate debtor are: writs of *fieri facias*, possession and delivery; the attachment of debts or garnishee proceedings charging orders on shares, stock, land or interests in land and stop orders in relation to funds in court or stop notices in relation to funds not in court or shares in a company.

6.51   Before execution can be levied a judgment must have been entered. In the case of a judgment or unconditional order for the payment of money or the transfer of property from one person to another there is no need for a demand to be made or for the order to be served on the debtor before execution is levied but this is necessary in the case of an order granting possession of land or requiring someone to do or to refrain from doing something.[141] Execution must be used within 6 years of the judgment to which it relates but leave may be given for it to be issued after that time so long as it has been kept alive for the purpose of the Limitation Act 1980.[142] Execution can be issued by the judgment creditor or those who succeed to his rights—for example, his trustees in bankruptcy or assignees—against the judgment debtor. The making of a winding up order in relation to a company stays all proceedings by way of execution and the commencement of voluntary liquidation or the service of a winding up petition gives the court power to order a stay on application.[143] The effect of an administration petition and order is dealt with in chapter 13.

6.52   Once issued, the writ of execution is delivered to the undersheriff of the appropriate county for execution although the order will actually be executed by bailiffs acting under a warrant issued by the sheriff or undersheriff. A writ or order issued to enforce a judgment in relation to land must be registered to retain priority against later purchasers or mortgagees.[144] Execution by the bailiffs is under the supervision of the sheriff and the sheriff is responsible to the judgment creditor, and the judgment debtor for the way in which the execution is carried out. His duty to the creditor is to carry out the execution as soon as possible. This will usually involve the seizure of property followed by its sale and the

140   Similar remedies are available in the County Court.
141   RSC ord 45 r 7(1) to (3).
142   RSC Ord 3 r 6, Ord 46 r 2(1)(a) and Limitation Act 1980 s 24(1) which imposes a six year limitation period.
143   Insolvency Act 1986 ss 126, 128, 130 and 112 and see paras 14.47–14.50 and 14.189.
144   Land Charges Act 1972 s 6 and Land Registration Act 1925 s 59 require registration of a writ or order for the enforcement of a judgment.

application of the proceeds to meet the costs of execution and then their transmission to the creditor. The goods will be kept until sale. The sheriff is liable to proceedings by the creditor if he negligently allows the goods to be seized or destroyed before sale.[145] The duty to the debtor is to do only those things authorised by the writ. Goods belonging to the debtor remain his until the sale.[146]

6.53 In the case of an insolvent debtor company, the creditor is not allowed to retain the benefit of any execution against goods or land or of any attachment of debts as against the liquidator unless the process is completed before the commencement of the winding up.[147] If the creditor had notice of a meeting called to pass a resolution for a voluntary winding up then the date on which he received notice is the date before which the execution process must have been completed.[148] However, the title of a person buying in good faith, on a sale by the sheriff, goods on which execution was levied will always be good against the liquidator and the court has power to set aside the liquidator's rights in favour of the creditor.[149] The completion of the execution process for this purpose is the seizure and the sale of goods, the making of a charging order on land or the receipt of an attached debt.[150] When goods are seized in execution the sheriff must deliver the goods and money seized or received in part execution to the liquidator if he is required to do so after being served with notice that a winding up order has been made, a provisional liquidator has been appointed, or a resolution for a voluntary winding up passed. The costs of execution are a first charge on such property and the liquidator may sell it to satisfy the charge.[151] Again the court has power to set aside the liquidator's rights in favour of the creditor.[152] Where the execution is levied in respect of a judgment for more than £500, the sheriff must deduct his costs from the proceeds of sale or any money paid to him to avoid a sale and retain the balance for 14 days. The balance must be handed to the liquidator if notice is given to the sheriff within the 14 day period of the presentation of a winding up petition or the calling of a meeting at which a resolution for voluntary winding up is to be proposed. The petition or meeting must in fact result in a winding up of the company before this provision applies.[153] To succeed against a liquidator the judgment creditor's execution must have been completed by seizure and sale and, in

---

145   *Willis Winder & Co v Combe* (1884) Cab & El 353.
146   *Giles v Grover* (1832) 9 Bing 128.
147   Insolvency Act 1986 s 183(1) and see paras 18.38–18.46.
148   s 183(2)(a).
149   s 183(2)(b) and (c) and see paras 18.38–18.46.
150   s 183(3).
151   s 184(1) and (2).
152   s 184(5).
153   s 184(3) and (4).

the case of the sale of goods in enforcement of a judgment for more than £500, 14 days must have passed after receipt of the sale proceeds by the sheriff without notice having been served on him of the presentation of a petition or the calling of a meeting to consider a winding up resolution.

6.54 When a number of creditors issue writs of execution they will be carried out in the order of their delivery to the sheriff.[154] If a judgment on which the writ was based is overturned and then restored the writ regains its original priority over all similar writs delivered to the sheriff after its original delivery. However in the case of *fieri facias* the sheriff is not liable to the creditors for the actions he takes on other writs after being told that the judgment was set aside. He should seek directions from the court before proceeding beyond possession on the other writs in these circumstances.[155] It is possible for an officer of a debtor company to be ordered to appear before a master or registrar to be examined on the property available to the debtor to satisfy the judgment. He may also be ordered to produce any relevant books or documents. The statement of the officer will be recorded and he will be asked to sign it.[156]

The writ of *fieri facias*

6.55 This is the commonest method of enforcing a judgment. The writ instructs the sheriff to seize the goods of the debtor to an amount sufficient to meet the debt. The goods are sold and the proceeds used to defray the debt and the costs of execution. Any balance is returned to the debtor. Where several writs are issued the goods are seized and sold under the first one and the proceeds are applied to satisfy the debts in the order in which the writs were delivered to the sheriff. The seizure takes place by the entry of the sheriff's officers on to the premises (whether of the debtor or of another person) where the debtor's goods are stored. Entry cannot be made by breaking down an external door although there may be entry through an open door or window and internal doors (of rooms or cupboards) may be broken if this is the only way to gain access to the goods. The fact that an external door is broken does not invalidate the seizure and sale but does give the owner of the premises the right to sue in trespass.

6.56 Any property subject to the writ is bound by it from the date of the delivery of the writ to the sheriff but this is subject to exceptions in favour of a purchaser in market overt, the Crown, a purchaser of goods within the Sale of Goods Act definition who is in good faith and without notice of the

154 *Hutchinson v Johnston* (1787) 1 Term Rep 729.
155 *Bankers' Trust v Galadari* [1986] 3 WLR 1099.
156 RSC Order 48 r 1.

delivery of the writ[157] and the liquidator of the corporate debtor.[158] Subject to these exceptions the binding force of the writ of *fieri facias* means that any transfer or assignment of goods subject to the writ after its delivery to the sheriff is subject to the sheriff's rights to levy an execution against them.[159]

6.57 The property subject to a writ of *fieri facias* must belong to the debtor. There is no power to seize property belonging to someone else.[160] However, jointly owned property may be seized although the co-owner can intervene to ensure that the proceeds of sale are divided.[161] It includes all goods and chattels but not land. The common law test was whether the property could be sold but, by statute, money or other securities for money such as cheques, promissory notes, bonds etc can be seized if they are in the possession or control of the debtor.[162] Money will be applied to discharge the debt and securities can be enforced by the sheriff so that the monies due can be applied for the debt. Any balance after payment of the costs of execution and the debt is handed over to the debtor. The debtor's leasehold interest in land can be sold under *fieri facias* but the sheriff is not entitled to possession and so cannot seize the land.

6.58 Land owned by the debtor, and fixtures which have become part of the land to which they are attached, are not subject to a writ of *fieri facias* but will be subject to a charging order.[163] Choses in action—other than securities for money in the debtor's possession or control—cannot be subject to *fieri facias* but may be subject to a charging order on securities or to garnishee proceedings.[164] Execution against any property other than land owned (rather than leased) by the debtor or choses in action not being securities for money in his possession or control takes the form of the writ of *fieri facias*. Ships are subject to it[165] as are equitable interests where the debtor holds the whole beneficial interest. Other forms of beneficial interest which can be recognised as representing a debt can be subject to a garnishee order.[166] Property held by a debtor as trustee cannot be seized.[167]

6.59 Seizure of the goods is achieved by the expression of an intention to

---

157 Supreme Court Act 1981 s 138 and see *Banker's Trust v Galadari* [1986] 3 WLR 1099.
158 Insolvency Act 1986 s 183(1).
159 *Re Cooper (a bankrupt) ex parte the Trustee v Peterborough and Huntingdon Registrars and the High Bailiff* [1958] Ch 922.
160 *Glasspoole v Young* (1829) 9 B & C 696.
161 *The James W Elwell* [1921] P 351.
162 Judgments Act 1838 s 12.
163 See paras 6.74–6.82.
164 See paras 6.67–6.82.
165 Seizure is by attaching a warrant to the mast but the writ binds British ships without seizure. *Harley v Harley* (1860) 11 I Ch R 451.
166 *Stevens v Hince* (1914) 110 LT 935.
167 *Wright v Redgrave* (1879) 11 Ch D 24.

seize after an entry on to the premises where the goods are kept.[168] Its significance is that after seizure the sheriff can bring an action in respect of any tort against the goods. Normally goods are subject to 'walking possession' by the sheriff after seizure by agreement with the debtor—this is usually regarded by debtors as preferable to the physical removal of the goods or the continuing presence of an officer of the sheriff which are the practical alternatives.[169] After seizure the goods must be sold within a reasonable time and at a reasonable price. The goods never become the property of the judgment creditor. The sheriff has certain special property rights to which the debtor's ownership rights are subject and the sheriff can pass good title to a purchaser who buys in good faith so long as no claim has been made to the goods.[170] The writ is normally returned by the sheriff to the court after it has been enforced with a statement on how it has been executed.

Writ of possession

6.60   This form of enforcement applies to a judgment or order giving possession of land. It is normally issued only with the leave of the court, although this is not necessary where an order is made against trespassers or in a mortgage action.[171] It must be distinguished from a charging order which uses the debtor's interest in land to enforce the judgment for a debt. The essence of a writ of possession is that the sheriff assists the plaintiff to obtain possession and that this can be done by the forcible eviction of other persons who are on the land without permission. The sheriff has a discretion on the timing of the execution of the writ. So long as he does this as soon as is reasonably practicable the court will not interfere.[172]

6.61   Before leave is obtained from the court for a writ of possession to issue, notice will have to be given to any person in actual possession of the land to allow him to apply to the court for any relief to which he may be entitled. The rights of tenants under the Landlord and Tenant Act 1954 are also protected by the suspension of the writ or order entitling the plaintiff to possession and a refusal of leave for a writ of possession to issue unless the court is satisfied that no notice has been served by the tenant to gain relief under the Act.[173] A writ of possession against the land of a debtor company will deprive the company, or its liquidator, administrator or administrative

---

168   *Gladstone v Padwick* (1871) LR 6 Exch 203.
169   See *National Commercial Bank of Scotland Ltd v Arcam Demolition and Construction Ltd* [1966] 2 QB 593.
170   See Bankruptcy & Deeds of Arrangement Act 1913 s 15.
171   RSC Ord 45 r 3(2) and Ord 113 r 7(1).
172   *Six Arlington Street Investments v Persons Unknown* [1987] 1 WLR 188.
173   RSC Ord 45 r 3.

receiver of the use of the land which is subject to the writ. It is, however, the final stage of possession proceedings in relation to the land and if the company was entitled to possession it would presumably have defended the proceedings successfully. It is unlikely that a liquidator, receiver or administrator will frequently encounter a writ of possession.

Writ of delivery

6.62 This form of execution enforces a judgment which requires the defendant to deliver goods to the plaintiff. This may give the defendant the option of paying the assessed value of the goods instead. If it does so, leave is needed before a writ of specific delivery can be issued requiring the sheriff to obtain the goods and hand them over to the plaintiff. However, a writ of delivery which requires the defendant either to hand over the goods or to pay their assessed value can be issued without leave. This is the usual form of the writ.[174] In cases where the original order which is to be enforced required that the goods be handed over without the option of payment of the assessed value a writ of specific delivery may be issued without the leave of the court.

6.63 The detailed rules applicable to these writs are much the same as those applying to *fieri facias* except that the sheriff will seize the goods to hand them to the plaintiff and not to sell them or (in the case of a writ of delivery allowing the defendant the option) will obtain the assessed value from him. Where the defendant is given the option either to deliver or to pay, the plaintiff may obtain *fieri facias* against any of the defendant's goods (and not only the ones subject to the writ of delivery) to obtain the assessed value unless the defendant informs the plaintiff that the goods subject to the writ of delivery are at the plaintiff's disposal.[175] Where an order for specific delivery directs that the goods be delivered by the defendant, remedies available for contempt, such as the sequestration of his assets or, in the case of an individual, committal to prison will be available for non-compliance.[176]

Sequestration

6.64 This remedy is only available in cases of contempt where the person against whom a court order was made was required to do certain things (or to refrain from doing them) within in a specified period of time. The writ of sequestration binds property from the time it is issued and can apply to the

---

174 Ord 45 r 12.
175 *Metals and Ropes Co Ltd v Tattersall* [1966] 3 All ER 401.
176 *Hymas v Ogden* [1905] 1 KB 246.

property of corporate bodies.[177] Notice of the judgment or order to be enforced by sequestration must have been served on the company and must have been endorsed with a warning that disobedience would result in a process of execution.[178] The writ is carried out by officers of the court, called sequestrators, who are nominated by the plaintiff and their duty is to sequestrate all the property of the contemnor. Property purchased for value without notice of the writ of sequestration is exempt but all other property of the contemnor is affected. However, it is only the interest of the contemnor which is subject to the writ. Secured creditors with a fixed charge over particular property will retain priority as will those with a crystallised floating charge. However, any transfer or creation of an interest in the contemnor's property, executed for the purpose of evading the sequestration, will be ineffective against the sequestrators and any voluntary transfer or transfer to someone aware of the writ's existence will be ineffective against the sequestrators who will be entitled to the delivery of such property.[179]

6.65 The sequestrators have the same power to take possession of property without entering with force as the sheriff but cannot use the sheriff to assist them. They have to seek the assistance of the court which may provide assistance by issuing injunctions or other orders giving the sequestrators rights over the contemnor's property and, for example, requiring others to pay debts due to the contemnor directly to the sequestrators. The court's powers to imprison for contempt can be used against those resisting or interfering with sequestrators.[180] Unlike a sheriff acting under the writ of *fieri facias*, the sequestrators have no power to sell the property in their possession. They simply hold it until the contempt is cleared up and act in accordance with the orders of the court, which may include an order for sale or orders to permit the sequestrators to manage the property in their hands, to enter contracts or to act on behalf of the contemnor in relation to the estates. The sequestration ends as it begins; by an order of the court terminating it and not, as in the case of *fieri facias*, by the return of the writ.

Garnishee proceedings

6.66 Since *fieri facias* only enables execution to be levied against a limited range of property, other remedies have been developed to extend the enforcement of judgment to forms of property such as choses in action or

---

177 RSC Ord 1 r 3 and Ord 45 r 5(1)(i).
178 RSC Ord 45 r 7(4)(a).
179 *Blenkinsopp v Blenkinsopp* (1852) 1 De GM & G 495.
180 *Brooks v Greathed* (1820) 1 Jac & W 176.

land owned by the debtor. Garnishee proceedings apply to debts due to the debtor against whom enforcement is sought. They are a method of attaching such debts for the benefit of the judgment creditor and, apart from applying to trade debts can, for example, be used to obtain for the creditor money held on behalf of the debtor in a bank account.

6.67 The third party who owes money to the debtor (the garnishee) is ordered to pay directly to the creditor either the whole amount due to the debtor from the third party or the amount necessary to discharge the judgment and the costs of the garnishee proceedings. Subject to the judgment or order requiring at least £50 to be paid, any judgment creditor who is entitled to issue a writ of *fieri facias* can use garnishee proceedings. This includes an assignee of the debt from the original creditor with the leave of the court.[181] The proceedings cannot be used against a garnishee who is located or indebted outside the jurisdiction or in respect of money held in court for the debtor or to enforce an order that money be paid into court.[182] An order may be obtained to enforce an undertaking given by a party and embodied in a court order[183] and is available against a bank account denominated in a foreign currency to satisfy a judgment given in sterling.[184] The temporary presence of a garnishee in England is sufficient for the court to make the order if he has submitted to the court's jurisdiction by instructing solicitors to accept service.[185]

6.68 Only debts can be attached. The tests of whether a debt is due are that the debtor can maintain an action for a liquidated amount and that the debt is not contingent. A legacy, money held by a receiver for a debenture holder and preferential creditors, and an insurance company's liability under a motor policy, are not attachable as they have not yet become debts.[186] The dividend due from a liquidation is not a debt.[187] On the other hand, an amount to be paid under an enforceable agreement made in settlement of an insurance claim, arrears of rent due from the debtor's tenant (but not future rent under the lease) or the amount due to a subcontractor from the main contractor after an architect's certificate has been issued under a RIBA building contract, are all attachable as an action

181 RSC Ord 49 r 1(1) *Jones v Jenner* (1836) 24 QBD 103 and *Goodman v Robinson* (1886) 18 QBD 332.
182 *Richardson v Richardson* [1927] P 228; RSC Ord 49 r 9(1) and *Re Greer Napper v Farnshawe* [1895] 2 Ch 217 respectively.
183 *Gandolfe v Gandolfo* [1980] 1 All ER 833.
184 *Choice Investments v Jeromnimon* [1981] 1 All ER 225.
185 *SCF Finance Co Ltd v Massri (No 3)* [1987] 2 WLR 81.
186 See *Macdonald v Hollister* (1855) 3 WR 522; *Senbrook Estate Co Ltd v Ford* [1949] 2 All ER 94; *Vyse v Brown* (1884) 13 QBD 199.
187 *Mack v Ward* [1884] WN 16 but there may be attachment if the liquidator consents: *Klauber v Weill* (1901) 17 TLR 344.

for the amount due could be brought by the debtor against the garnishee.[188] A debt which was formerly contingent can be attached after the contingency has occurred. A debt payable in future instalments can be attached by a garnishee order which has effect as and when each instalment is due. While future rental payments are not attachable the instalments of an existing debt are.[189] If a cheque or promissory note has been given to the judgment debtor by the garnishee no attachment order can be made until it is dishonoured or, in the case of a cheque, stopped until that time no debt exists which can be the subject of attachment.[190]

6.69   Amounts in the debtor's current account with a bank are attachable despite the need for a demand by the debtor before he could bring an action, as the order *nisi* of garnishee served on the bank is treated as the demand.[191] A garnishee order can be made in respect of money held in the debtor's deposit account with any bank or deposit taking institution or in any withdrawable share account with any deposit taking institution subject to the specific inclusion or exclusion of particular accounts by order.[192] Such a garnishee is entitled to deduct up to £30 from the sum attached for the administrative and clerical expenses involved in giving effect to the order.[193]

6.70   Only debts which are enforceable by the judgment debtor for his own benefit can be attached. A debt which has been assigned before the garnishee proceedings cannot be attached unless the assignment can be attacked on the basis of being a transaction at an undervalue or under some other provision of the insolvency legislation.[194] A debt due to the judgment debtor as trustee should not be made the subject of a garnishee order absolute.[195] The judgment creditor takes no better interest in the garnisheed debt than that of the judgment debtor. It is taken subject to all equities and rights which have attached to it in the garnishee's hands.[196] Any charge created over the debt before the service of the garnishee order *nisi* has priority over the garnishee order. This applies to any charge legal or equitable and even when no notice had been given of the creation of the charge.[197] A floating charge takes priority even if a receiver is appointed

188   *Barnet v Eastman* (1898) 67 LJ QB 517; *Dunlop & Ranken Ltd v Hendall Steel Structures Ltd* [1957] 3 All ER 344.
189   *Tapp v Jones* (1875) LR 10 QB 591.
190   *Elwell v Jackson* (1885) 1 TLR 454.
191   *Joachinson v Swiss Bank Corporation* [1921] 3 KB 110.
192   RSC Ord 49 r 1 and Supreme Court Act 1981 ss 40(1) and (3).
193   *Ibid* s 40A and The Attachment of Debts (Expenses) Order 1983.
194   *Glegg v Bromley* [1912] 3 KB 474 and Insolvency Act 1986 ss 238, 239 or 423.
195   *Roberts v Death* (1881) 8 QB 319.
196   *Norton v Yates* [1906] 1 KB 112.
197   *Badeley v Consolidated Bank* (1888) 38 Ch D 238.

after the date of service of the order *nisi*.[196] The order is also subject to any existing liens.[198]

6.71   A garnishee is entitled to set off debts due to him from the judgment creditor up to the date of the garnishee order *nisi* (but not those arising after that date) and to rely on any counter claim he may have in relation to the same transaction as that which involved the debt subject to the garnishee order.[199]

6.72   The procedure for obtaining a garnishee order falls into two parts. An application for an order *nisi* is made *ex parte* and it is the service of this order on the garnishee which binds the debt and marks the point after which later dispositions are subject to the order.[200] The next stage is a hearing which takes place at least 15 days after service on the garnishee (service on the judgment debtor has to be at least 7 days before the hearing). Unless some reason is found for refusing to do so (such as the fact that the garnishee is not indebted to the judgment debtor or that the debt is due to some person other than the judgment debtor or is subject to a charge or lien) the court may make a garnishee order absolute requiring the garnishee to pay the amount of the debt or such lesser amount as is necessary to satisfy the judgment and the costs of the garnishee proceedings.[201] That order may then be enforced against the garnishee as an order to pay money, by the use of *fieri facias* other garnishee proceedings or any other appropriate execution procedure.

6.73   The garnishee order absolute is an equitable remedy and thus is discretionary and may be refused on the grounds of its inequitable effects. The interests of judgment creditor, judgment debtor and garnishee must be taken into account but so must those of other creditors of the judgment debtor. Where the order is sought to enforce a debt due from an insolvent company the principle of *pari passu* treatment of its creditors may prevent the making of a garnishee order absolute against a debtor of the company.[202] A similar tenderness towards the interests of beneficiaries lies behind the refusal of the court to grant a garnishee order where the money is due from the garnishee to the judgment debtor as trustee for others.

198   *Shippey v Grey* (1880) 49 LJ QB 524. But a solicitor's right to a charging order only gains priority if that order is made absolute: *James Bibby Ltd v Woods & Howard* [1949] 2 KB 449.
199   *Tapp v Jones* (1875) LR 10 QB 591; *Hale v Victoria Plumbing Co Ltd* [1966] 2 QB 746.
200   *Dallow v Garrold* (1884) 14 QBD 543.
201   RSC Ord 49 r 4(1).
202   *D Wilson (Birmingham) Ltd v Metropolitan Property Developments Ltd* [1975] 2 All ER 814 and *Roberts Petroleum Ltd v Kenny Ltd* [1983] AC 192 and see paras 6.74–6.82 below where similar considerations are dealt with in relation to charging orders.

Charging orders

6.74 In order to enforce a judgment against property which cannot be classified as a debt to which garnishee proceedings will apply or as goods which can be subject to *fieri facias* a charging order may be used. Such orders are governed by the Charging Orders Act 1979 and may be obtained against:

(a) land;
(b) government stock;
(c) the stock of any corporate body, except a building society, incorporated in England or Wales, or of one incorporated outside England and Wales if the stock is registered in a register within that area; or
(d) units of any unit trust of which a register of unit holders is held in England and Wales; or
(e) funds in court.[203]

6.75 The charging order can deal with any beneficial interest of the debtor in such property or under any trust.[203a] An interest held by the debtor as trustee can be attached if the judgment is against him in that capacity. If he holds the property unencumbered as trustee for himself as the sole beneficiary or if he and any other debtors liable for the same debt together hold the whole beneficial interest unencumbered and for their own benefit his beneficial interest can be attached.[204]

6.76 The order is available where a judgment or order of either the high court or the county court requires the debtor to pay a sum of money.[205] The procedure for obtaining a charging order falls into two stages which resemble the procedure for a garnishee order. To obtain payment of the debt, however, it is necessary to go through the third stage of obtaining an order for the sale of the property charged by the charging order. The initial stage in obtaining an order is an application which may be *ex parte*—and the first order requires the debtor to show cause why an order should not be made absolute at a time and place specified in the order but it does not impose a charge until that time.[206] Thus, as with a garnishee order, the charging order binds the property which it is stated to cover from the time

---

203   Charging Orders Act 1979 s 2(2).
203a   *Perry v Phoenix Assurance plc* [1988] 1 WLR 940.
204   *Ibid* s 2(1). The list may be amended by statutory instrument. An order can be made over a beneficial interest in the proceeds of sale of land held on a trust for sale: *National Westminster Bank v Stockman* [1981] 1 WLR 67.
205   s 1(1).
206   RSC Ord 50 r 1(2).

of the initial order. The practical difficulty for the creditor at this stage is in obtaining adequate information about the property owned by the debtor which may be susceptible to an order. In deciding whether to make a charging order the court must consider the circumstances of the debtor and whether any other creditor or debtor would be likely to be prejudiced by the making of the order.[207]

6.77 When an initial order is made notice of its creation must be served on the judgment debtor and the keeper of the register of any stock subject to the order. This will be the Bank of England in the case of much government stock, the corporate body whose stock is subject to the order in the case of the shares of a company incorporated in England and Wales, or the keeper of the register in the case of any other corporate body or of a unit trust. An order over money held in court must be served on the Accountant General at the Court Funds Office and in any case where the judgment debtor's interest in a trust fund is charged the trustees should be served. The court may, in addition, order service on any other interested party—including the other creditors of the judgment debtor.

6.78 At the second stage of the proceedings, when cause has to be shown against the making of a charging order absolute, the court will proceed to make the order unless reasons to the contrary are shown by the judgment debtor or some other interested party. In a case where a corporate debtor appears to be insolvent the fact of the commencement of liquidation before the date fixed for making a charging order absolute is sufficient, in itself without any other factor, to justify a refusal by the court to make the order absolute.[208] This is so despite the fact that the charging order *nisi* provides for the appointment of a receiver and despite the absence of the possibility of any scheme of arrangement before the liquidation. In a case where the debtor company is insolvent but liquidation has not yet commenced the court retains a discretion but the presence of imminent liquidation or an imminent scheme of arrangement between the company and its creditors may not result in a refusal to make the charging order absolute. In *Roberts Petroleum Ltd* the House of Lords disapproved *Burston Finance Ltd v Godfrey*[209] in which the Court of Appeal upheld a charging order absolute made after the prior making of a receiving order and adjudication of bankruptcy.[210] However, the disapproval related to the circumstances of *Roberts* where a liquidation commenced before the charging order was made absolute.

---

207 Charging Order Act 1979 s 1(5).
208 *Roberts Petroleum Ltd v Kenny Ltd* [1983] AC 192.
209 [1976] 1 WLR 719.
210 Per Lord Brandon [1983] AC 192 at 211–212.

6.79   In a case where liquidation is only imminent and has not commenced before the charging order is made absolute the possibility of a scheme under s 425 of the Companies Act 1985 or Part I of the Insolvency Act 1986 will be a relevant consideration in deciding whether or not the charging order should be made absolute. This accords with the importance attached by the courts to treating all creditors *pari passu* once liquidation begins and to exercising its discretion equitably in their favour if; 'a scheme of arrangement formal or informal agreed or being negotiated amongst creditors'[211] exists. In the absence of the actual commencement of liquidation and of a scheme of arrangement—existing or discussed and with a chance of being agreed—insolvency will not be a ground for refusing an order absolute. The diligent creditor is entitled to his advantage if others are unable to begin the winding up process. Inequitable conduct on the part of the creditor seeking the order absolute will justify a refusal of the order as, for example, where he purports to take part in good faith in discussions merely to delay liquidation by attempting to make a scheme of arrangement while secretly seeking to secure his own position by means of a charging order.

6.80   The nature of the charging order is dealt with by the Charging Orders Act 1979. It is laid down that it 'shall have the like effect and shall be enforceable in the same courts and in the same manner as an equitable charge created by the debtor by writing under his hand'.[212] For priority purposes a charging order made over land must be registered under the Land Charges Act 1972 or the Land Registration Act 1925 as an order or writ for the enforcement of a judgment. This provision only applies to orders over an interest in land and thus a charging order over the undivided share of a co-owner is not registrable in that way as it is a charging order on an interest under a trust.[212a]

6.81   Registration only provides protection against later charges or transactions. If it is satisfied that it is necessary to protect the judgment creditor's interest or that the debtor is likely to dispose of property, the court can grant an injunction restraining dealings in the property subject to the order on, or after, granting an order *nisi* or absolute.[213] The remedy for an equitable chargee is sale and this can be sought in the same way as it would be if the security were consensual. Similarly a receiver may be appointed to enforce the order. The appointment of a receiver is not

---

211   Per Scarman LJ at p 734 in *Burston Finance v Godfrey* and see *Rainbow v Moorgate Properties* [1975] 1 WLR 788.
212   s 3(4).
212a   *Perry v Phoenix Assurance plc* [1988] 1 WLR 940.
213   RSC Ord 50 r 9A.

necessary to complete the execution against land and therefore can only be obtained on enforcement of the order after it has been granted.

6.82 Sale will usually be the desired remedy so receivers are unlikely to be appointed in this context. Section 183(3) of the Insolvency Act 1986 lays down that execution is complete by the making of a charging order against goods or land; by seizure or appointment of a receiver against land or by receipt of the debt where a debt is attached. A charging order *nisi* creates a charge but refusal to make the order absolute has the effect of preventing any priority from accruing to the creditor as a result of that charge. Once the charging order is made absolute the execution is complete against the liquidator but if winding up intervenes the court may refuse to make the order absolute and the judgment creditor loses any priority gained as a result of the charging order. For the purpose of s 183(1) a charging order is not completed by a charging order *nisi* and the creditor does not retain the benefit of the execution against the liquidator under that section.[214] The holder of a charging order over the share of a co-owner is entitled to use s 30 of the Law of Property Act 1925 to apply for an order of sale as a 'person interested' in the land.[214a]

Stop orders and stop notices

6.83 Where any funds are held in court and a debtor has an interest in them the judgment creditor of the debtor or the mortgagee, chargee or assignee of that interest may apply by summons for a stop order which will prohibit a transfer, sale, or other dealing with those funds, by the person with an interest in them without notice being given to the person who applied for the stop order.[215] A stop order can be obtained without a charging order first being granted and despite the fact that funds ordered to be paid into court have not yet been paid in.[216]

6.84 Anyone who claims to be beneficially entitled to an interest in any securities not in court which come within s 2(2)(b) of the Charging Orders Act 1979 (ie government stock or the stock of corporate bodies incorporated in England or Wales other than building societies, or of those incorporated elsewhere or of unit trusts if the register of stock or of unit holders is kept in England or Wales), can apply for a stop order (replacing the former writ of *distringas*) which requires the person on whom it is served to notify the applicant of any proposed transfer of the securities and to

---

214 See *Roberts Petroleum Ltd v Kenny Ltd* (above).
214a *Midland Bank PLC v Pike* [1988] 2 All ER 434.
215 RSC Ord 50 r 10.
216 *Shaw v Hudson* (1879) 48 LJ Ch 689.

refrain from transferring them until 14 days after the notice was sent. This enables a judgment creditor who has obtained a charging order to prevent the transfer of the securities that are subject to it or any other dealing specified in the stop notice. Such a creditor has a beneficial interest only after the charging order has been made.[217] It is also possible for the court to make an order prohibiting outright the registration of any transfer of such securities if application is made by a person with a beneficial interest.[218] Such an order may later be discharged on application by the person who obtained it. This procedure applies to judgment creditors and can be used by equitable mortgagees of securities. It provides a useful protection for such mortgagees.

Appointment of a receiver

6.85   As well as being a remedy open to mortgagees this remedy is available in limited circumstances to judgment creditors to enforce their judgments. As an additional means of enforcing judgments relating to interests in land, it is possible for a receiver of the debtor's interest to be appointed by the court. This will only be done if it appears to be a more effective means of enforcement of a judgment debt than a charging order. This power is additional to the power to appoint a receiver to enforce a charging order.[219] In the case of other forms of property a receiver will only be appointed if there is no remedy of execution at law—by *fieri facias* or garnishee or charging order—or if such remedy is ineffective for some reason. The court may, for example, appoint a receiver of the debtor's interest under the contract where he is bound by contract to sell land[220] or where a debt is payable to two or more people jointly but the beneficial interest is in the hands of the debtor.[221] Similarly, the appointment may relate to a legacy or an interest under a settlement.[222] In all these cases the appointment of a receiver can be justified either because other forms of execution are not available or because of the complexity of the circumstances which makes the appointment of a receiver desirable on the grounds of justice and convenience. As with all equitable remedies the court has a discretion which is exercised on the basis of consistent principles but not rigid precedent.[223] Before making an order the court will consider the sum claimed by the creditor and the costs of receivership as against the amount likely to be recovered.[224]

217 RSC Ord 50 rr 11–15.
218 RSC Ord 50 r 15.
219 Supreme Court Act 1981 s 37.
220 *Ridout v Fowler* [1904] 2 Ch 93 CA.
221 *O'Donovan v Goggin* (1892) 30 LR Ir 579.
222 *Macnicoll v Parnell* (1887) 35 WR 773; *Webb v Stenton* (1883) 11 QB 518.
223 Supreme Court Act 1981 s 37(1).
224 *I v K* (1884) WN 63; RSC Ord 51 r 1.

6.86   A receiver will not be appointed where one is already in place. In such circumstances the court will extend the authority of an existing receiver appointed by the courts. If an administrative receiver has been appointed by debenture holders, a receiver on behalf of a judgment creditor will not usually be appointed. If there was evidence that there would be assets left over after the receivership for the debenture holders terminated then it is possible that the judgment creditor could obtain an order that the receiver appointed by the court should take over at that time. Presumably a court would be disposed to appoint the same individual as receiver on behalf of the judgment creditors. Given that in most cases it is unlikely that any assets will remain after debenture holders' claims and the claims of preferential creditors have been satisfied this is likely to be a rare occurrence. A receiver would only be appointed on behalf of judgment creditors if this was necessary on the grounds of justice and convenience. It would have to offer some benefit which was not available by a straightforward liquidation of the company on the termination of receivership instigated by the debenture holders.

6.87   An application by way of summons or motion for the appointment of a receiver is made in the proceedings in which the judgment to be enforced was made. An injunction may be sought *ex parte*, ancillary to the application for a receiver to be appointed. This can be granted before the application is heard in order to prevent any dealings with the property in question before the application for a receiver is heard.[225] Such an injunction will only be granted if the judgment creditor establishes by affidavit that there is a risk that the property in issue may be disposed of before the hearing.[226]

6.88   The appointment of a receiver does not create a charge on the property but entitles the receiver to receive the money or property due to the debtor. The receiver can apply to the court for any assistance by way of injunction that may be needed to prevent the interests of the judgment creditors being defeated. Assignments or dealings in the debtor's interest in the property before the date of the order appointing the receiver are unaffected and take priority.[227] Later incumbrances will be subject to the interest of the judgment creditor. The court will order the receiver to pay the money which comes into his possession to the judgment creditor in priority to the claims of those holding incumbrances of a date later than that of the order appointing the receiver. This will be the case where the later incumbrancers are aware of the appointment of the receiver. If it could

225   RSC Ord 51 r 2.
226   *Lloyds Bank Ltd v Medway Upper Navigation Co* [1905] 2 KB 359.
227   *Re Bristow* [1906] 2 IR 215.

be shown that such a person did not have notice of the appointment and acted in good faith and for value then the 'interest' of the judgment creditor would presumably be subordinated to that of the incumbrancer on the basis of the usual principles which apply to priorities. It may well be however that the public nature of a court order appointing a receiver would be regarded as notice to all parties. It seems that a creditor who obtains a charging order on a fund in court gains priority over a receiver.[228]

6.89 A receiver appointed in litigation is an officer of the court and will be paid his remuneration and expenses from the amount he collects. If that is insufficient the court cannot order one of the parties to pay him. It is incumbent on the receiver either to ensure that he will collect sufficient assets to cover his expenses or to obtain an indemnity from one of the parties to the litigation.[229]

Mareva injunctions

6.90 An injunction which restrains a person from removing assets from the jurisdiction (a Mareva injunction) is a purely personal form of relief and does not give the plaintiff security over the frozen assets. As against other creditors the existence of such an injunction provides no security.[230]

Payment into court

6.91 Where money is paid into court, either as a condition of leave being granted to defend the suit or in satisfaction of a claim or an order for security of costs, insolvency after the date of the payment will not affect the right of the other party in the proceedings to claim the money paid into court. That party will prove in the liquidation of the insolvent company for any balance due which the amount paid into court did not satisfy.[231] These orders, like other forms of execution attached to specific property, create a real interest which is unaffected by later insolvency on the part of the property owners. By contrast, a Mareva injunction merely restrains a person from dealing with property in certain ways. Orders of this kind do not create any real interest on the part of the other party in the proceedings.[232]

---

228   *Fahey v Tobin* [1901] 1 IR 511 CA.
229   *Evans v Clayhope Properties Ltd* [1987] BCLC 418.
230   *Cretanor Maritime Co Ltd v Irish Marine Management Ltd*, *The Cretan Harmony* [1978] 1 WLR 966.
231   See RSC Orders 14, 22 and 23; *Re Ford* [1900] QB 211; *W A Sherratt Ltd v John Bromley (Church Stretton) Ltd* [1985] BCLC 170.
232   See R M Goode "Commercial Law" at pp 732–733.

DISTRESS

6.92 Distress is analogous to execution in that it is a procedure whereby goods become subject to the claim of a creditor which will take priority over the claims of unsecured creditors or of secured creditors whose security attached later in time than the distraint. At common law distress is the right to take goods without legal process as a pledge to compel the satisfaction of a debt or the performance of a duty or the redress of an injury.[233] There was no right at common law to sell the goods distrained to pay the debt but such rights are provided to landlords by statute[234] and are part of the powers granted by statute for distress for unpaid taxes, rates and under the summary jurisdiction of magistrates.[235] The right to levy distress for rates and under the magistrates' summary jurisdiction does not arise without an application to a court and in the case of protected or statutory tenancies, protected occupancies, or agricultural statutory tenancies of dwelling houses leave of the court is required before a landlord can distrain for rent.[236] However in the case of other types of tenancy (including business tenancies) a landlord does not require any form of sanction from the court to levy distress. It is this which distinguishes distress for rent and for taxes from execution. In the case of distress for rates an application to a court is required but there is no need for an earlier judgment which is to be enforced as is the case with *fieri facias*. Distress is levied against goods. It exists in respect of rent, rates, taxes and under the Magistrates' Courts Act 1980. Each form of distress is considered in turn.

Distress for rent

6.93 The right to distrain for rent is an incident of the relationship of landlord and tenant. There must be a demise of the property or an agreement for a lease which can be enforced by an order of specific performance or later executed by the grant of a lease.[237] There must be more than a mere licence although a weekly tenancy or a tenancy at will gives the landlord the right to distrain.[238] At common law the right to distrain ends with the tenancy. By statute distress can be levied for rent arrears due on a lease after the determination of the lease as it might have been levied but for the determination of the lease. This is providing it is done within six months of the end of the lease and during the continuance of

---

233 See Halsbury's Laws Vol 13 paras 201–500.
234 Distress for Rent Act 1689 s 1; Distress for Rent Act 1737 s 10.
235 See paras 6.109–6.122 below.
236 Rent Act 1977 s 147. Rent (Agriculture) Act 1976 s 8.
237 *Dunk v Hunter* (1822) 5 B & Ald 322; *Walsh v Lonsdale* (1882) 21 Ch D 9.
238 *Rendell v Roman* (1893) 9 TLR 192; *Yeoman v Ellison* (1867) LR 2 CP 681 and *Anderson v Midland Railway Co* (1861) 3 E & E 614.

the landlord's interest. Possession by the tenant of the demised premises is also necessary.[239] Business tenancies within Part II of the Landlord and Tenant Act 1954 do not end unless they are terminated in accordance with the Act. The landlord probably retains the right to levy distress while the tenant is still in possession.[240] If the landlord obtains judgment for the rent due he is unable to distrain even if the judgment is unsatisfied.[241]

6.94 The right to distrain is lost if the landlord assigns his reversion but if the landlord's right in the property is mortgaged the mortgagee may distrain after giving the tenant notice of the mortgage. The distraint may be for rent due before or after the service of the notice.[242] If the tenancy is created by estoppel after the landlord mortgaged his interest in the property the mortgagee will not be able to distrain unless he has the relationship of landlord and tenant with the tenant by agreement or conduct.[243] If the mortgagor makes a lease under the Law of Property Act 1925 s 99 the mortgagee will be able to distrain after giving notice to the tenant that he intends to act as lessor.[244] A mortgagor can distrain while he is in possession before that time.[245]

6.95 The owner of a rent charge will have a right of distress by virtue of the deed creating it without having a right to the reversion as this is the definition of a rent charge.[246] Distress cannot be levied for rent reserved out of an incorporeal hereditament.[247] The payment in respect of which it is levied must be due.[248]

6.96 The amount will depend on the terms of the lease. Only a limited range of payments by a tenant can be set off against rent due to the landlord. These include sums which it was the landlord's duty to pay and which were charged on the land[249] and sums which the lease authorises the tenant to deduct from the rent.[250] No distress can be levied for rent more than six years after it fell due.[251] In addition to the rent due chattels may be distrained to cover the costs of the distraint.[252]

239 Landlord and Tenant Act 1709 ss 6 and 7.
240 Landlord and Tenant Act 1954 s 24(1) and *H L Bolton Engineering Co Ltd v T J Graham & Sons Ltd* [1957] 1 QB 159.
241 *Chancellor v Webster* (1893) 9 TLR 568.
242 *Moss v Gallimore* (1779) 1 Doug 279.
243 *Evans v Elliott* (1838) 9 Ad & El 342; *Barclays Bank Ltd v Kiley* [1961] 2 All ER 849.
244 *Municipal Permanent Investment Building Society v Smith* (1888) 22 QBD 70.
245 *Trent v Hunt* (1853) 9 Exch 14 at 23.
246 LPA 1925 s 121.
247 *Capel v Buszard* (1829) 6 Bing 150 and ?????.
248 *Dibble v Bowater* (1853) 3 E & B 564.
249 *Graham v Allsopp* (1848) 3 Exch 186.
250 *Dallman v King* (1837) 4 Bing NC 105.
251 Limitation Act 1980 s 19.
252 Distress for Rent Act 1689 s 1.

Subject matter of distress for rent

6.97 The general rule on the goods which can be seized is that the landlord has the right to seize all goods and chattels on the demised premises, whether or not they belong to the tenant. Any goods belonging to the tenant and fraudulently or clandestinely moved from the premises can also be the subject of distress off the premises unless they have been sold in good faith for valuable consideration to someone ignorant of the fraud. The offence of fraudulent removal results in a penalty of twice the value of the goods.[253] The right to distrain against goods on the premises subject to the lease includes goods not belonging to the tenant on the ground that the right arises because of the place where the goods are found and not because of their ownership. However statutory protection is now available for goods belonging to persons other than the tenant.[254] Property which cannot be physically seized such as choses in action or patent rights cannot, however, be subject to distraint.[255] A list of exceptions to the general rule has developed and this gives certain property a privilege against seizure on distraint. Some of the exceptions have developed at common law and others by statute. Those which are most likely to apply to a corporate tenant are as follows:

(a) *Things which cannot be returned.* Anything which cannot be returned undamaged and in the condition in which it was seized cannot be the subject of distress. Thus loose money cannot be taken as there can be no proof that the same coins and notes will be returned whereas money in a sealed bag can be seized as it is identifiable. Fixtures which cannot be restored in the same condition as they were in when taken also fall within this exemption.[256]

(b) *Goods seized in execution.*[257]

(c) *Things in actual use.* Such goods are exempt at common law as otherwise there would be a constant danger of a breach of the peace.[258] The exemption extends to clothes worn at the time of distraint[259] in the case of an individual tenant or to any other item which is in use. Presumably the exemption could extend to valuable machinery or equipment on the premises of a debtor company so long as it was in use.

(d) *Goods delivered for the purpose of a trade.* In addition to the rules

---

253 Distress for Rent Act 1737 ss 1–3.
254 See below, paras 6.98–6.100.
255 *British Mutoscope & Biograph Co Ltd v Homer* [1901] 1 Ch 671.
256 *Crossley v Lee* [1908] 1 KB 86.
257 See paras 6.51–6.91 and 8.142.
258 *Storey v Robinson* (1795) 6 Term Rep 138.
259 *Bisset v Caldwell* (1791) Peake 50 in which seizure of clothes not being worn was allowed.

applying to goods not owned by the tenant, there is an exemption from distress for goods delivered, to a person exercising a public trade, to be dealt with by way of the trade. This is analogous to the class of goods which give rise to a repairer's lien. This may be a trade which involves the carriage of goods, repairs to them or work on them. The exemption extends to a car left at a garage for repair; to cloth left with a tailor to be made up; or to goods in the hands of a carrier.[260] The trade must be public in the sense of being carried on for the benefit of anyone who chooses to make us of it.[261] Goods held by an agent acting for only two principals are not privileged whereas those in the hands of a factor who operates as an agent selling on behalf of anyone who hires him will be within the exemption.[262] The trade must be carried on in the trader's premises and the goods must be there for the purpose of the exercise of the trade—which may be storage or sale. Goods stored for some purpose other than the trade are not exempt. Brewer's casks sent to a publican to contain beer until it was sold were not privileged. The beer would have been.[263]

(e) *The tools of a tenant's trade.* This exemption is unlikely to apply to a corporate debtor. It is subject to a very low financial limit and it is hard to see how a company may have tools of its trade as opposed to items which are currently in use.

The statutory exemptions for goods not belonging to the tenant
6.98   (a) *Specific exemptions.* At common law goods present on the demised premises are subject to distress even if they do not belong to the tenant. By statute a number of specific exceptions are laid down to this rule. In these cases no particular procedure needs to be followed by the owner of the goods. This is in contrast to the general exception laid down by the Law of Distress Amendment Act 1908.

(b) *Gas, water and electricity fittings.* Gas and water pipes, meters, fittings and apparatus cannot be subject to distress providing that they bear a mark or brand indicating that they are owned by a gas supplier or the statutory water undertaker.[264] This applies in each case to fittings let out by the supplier. Electricity fittings (lines, meters, accumulators, works or apparatus) placed on premises by an electricity board for the purpose of supplying electricity enjoy a similar immunity.[265]

---

260   *Read v Burley* (1597) Cro Eliz 549 and *Gisbourn v Hurst* (1710) 1 Salk 249.
261   *Brown v Shevill* (1834) 2 Ad & El 138.
262   *Gilman v Elton* (1821) 3 Brod & Bing 75; *Tapling & Co v Weston* (1883) Cab & El 99.
263   *Joule v Jackson* (1841) 7 M & W 450.
264   Gas Act 1986 s 15, sch 5 para 19(1) and Water Act 1945 ss 35 and 59(1).
265   Electricity Act 1947 s 57(1); Electric Lighting Act 1882 s 25 and Electric Lighting Act 1909 s 6.

(c) *Railway rolling stock and hosiery equipment*. If the ownership of railway rolling stock such as carriages, trucks, waggons or engines is sufficiently indicated by a mark or metal plate affixed to it, it cannot be distrained for rent due from a tenant of a 'work' where it is situated unless the rolling stock belongs to him. A 'work' includes any railway siding, pier jetty, wharf, quarry, mine, colliery, factory or warehouse.[266] By virtue of the Hosiery Act 1843 s 18 specific protection is given to frames, looms and other equipment used in the manufacture of silk, cotton, flax, linen, woollen or mohair materials unless the rent is due from the owner of the equipment. It would seem that equipment used to manufacture man-made fibres is not included in this protection.

(d) *Agricultural holdings*. Certain goods belonging to someone other than the tenant of an agricultural holding are exempt from distress. However this is unlikely to apply to a corporate debtor.

The Law of Distress Amendment Act 1908
6.99 Other goods not belonging to the tenant may be covered by this legislation. It provides protection for goods belonging to a person other than the tenant providing the procedure laid down in the Act is followed. The person claiming benefit of the Act as the owner of goods must either be a sub-tenant paying a full rent for all or part of the premises or some other person with no beneficial interest in any part of the premises occupied by the tenant.[267] This is intended to prevent abuse.

6.100 However, the Act excludes certain categories of goods. The major exclusions which are likely to be relevant to a corporate tenant are as follows:

(a) The goods of a partner of the tenant (a company may be a member of a partnership). Goods belonging to another company which has formed a consortium in the form of a partnership with the company which is the tenant will be liable for seizure and the procedure contemplated by the 1908 Act cannot apply.

(b) The goods of a company or other corporation which are present in its offices or on premises the tenant of which is an officer, director or other employee of the corporation. This is unlikely to apply unless company property is on the premises of a person falling into the category described.

(c) The goods of a sub-tenant which are on premises where a trade or business is carried on in which both the tenant and the sub-tenant have an

266 Railway Rolling Stock Protection Act 1872 ss 1–3.
267 Law of Distress Amendment Act 1908 ss 1 and 9.

interest. This will only apply if a company has a relationship with a sub-tenant or sub-landlord which involves some factor other than that relationship. This could be the case if a group of companies is involved and a number of companies share the same business and are also sub-landlord and sub-tenant.

(d) Goods which are left at an office or warehouse for more than one month after notice has been served on their owner to remove them and to vacate the premises. The notice must give one calendar month for the removal of the goods and must be given in the same way as notice to quit.

(e) Goods possessed by a tenant with the consent of their true owner in such circumstances that the tenant is reputed owner of them. This exception reflects the doctrine of reputed ownership which formerly applied to individuals on bankruptcy. It has never applied in cases of company liquidation or receivership and no longer applies on individual bankrupt-cies. For these reasons it is unlikely that a court would use this exception to prevent the true owner of goods from using the protection of the 1908 Act. The exception could cause difficulties for a receiver who sought to use the 1908 Act to protect goods which were subject to a crystallised floating charge from later distress on behalf of the landlord. However the appointment of a receiver who goes into possession must surely avoid any implication of reputed ownership by the tenant of goods subject to a crystallised floating charge. Greater difficulties may be experienced by the owner of goods which are leased to the company or which are subject to hire purchase. A separate provision of the 1908 Act seeks to exclude goods subject to hire purchase agreements from its terms. As will be seen this is frequently avoided by the termination of the hire purchase agreement on the signing of a distress warrant by a landlord. A similar provision in the case of a lease of chattels—which is normal—will presumably terminate the possession of the tenant lessee for the purpose of this provision. The provision does however indicate the importance of ensuring that the possession of a tenant company of goods which are owned by another terminates before those goods are seized for the purpose of distress. Should the provision apply it might be argued that the abolition of the doctrine of reputed ownership in individual bankruptcy and the fact that it has never applied to corporate liquidation should cause the courts to be cautious in their interpretation of s 4 of the 1908 Act.

(f) As a general rule goods comprised in any hire purchase agreement or conditional sale agreement are excluded from protection under the 1908 Act.[268] However the Consumer Credit Act 1974 amends the 1908 Act so

---

268 Law of Distress Amendment Act 1908 s 4(1).

that during the period between the service of a default notice under ss 87–89 of that Act and the date on which the notice expires or is complied with goods do receive protection under the 1908 Act. Hire purchase agreements involving a company as hirer and conditional sale agreements under which a company is the buyer are not however subject to such a procedure. The general rule excluding goods on hire purchase from the 1908 Act applies. In practice a termination clause will prevent this. Goods will remain within a hire purchase agreement and therefore outside the protection of the 1908 Act if any contractual right or obligation still subsists after the time at which the agreement purported to effect an automatic termination. The right of the owner to enter and retake goods can be such a right and may prevent termination of the agreement.[269] A clause providing for automatic termination of both the agreement and the owner's consent to the hirer's possession of the goods if a landlord distrains or threatens to do so will remove the goods from the category of those comprised in a hire purchase agreement as soon as the landlord signs the distress warrants.[270] However, such a clause does not automatically end the hirer's reputed ownership of such goods with the owner's consent for the purpose of s 4(1) without some notice or other act by the owner to terminate his consent[271] and on this ground the goods may still be outside the protection afforded by the 1908 Act. Goods leased to a company will be subject to similar difficulties and the rule laid down in the *Times Furnishing Company Ltd* case will apply. It is important in the case of either form of agreement that an appropriate clause be present.[272]

Procedure for distress
6.101 The right to levy distress for rent does not depend on a court order except in the case of a company in compulsory liquidation and in the case of a dwelling house let on a protected or statutory tenancy or a protected occupancy or agricultural statutory tenancy.[273] A landlord may levy distress himself (or more usually) by employing a bailiff certificated under the hand of a county court judge as authorised to act as a bailiff.[274] A distress warrant is normally given by the landlord to the bailiff as authority. This impliedly indemnifies the bailiff against acts properly done and warrants the landlord's right to distrain.

6.102 A person levying distraint has a right to enter peaceably between

---

269 *Jay's Furnishing Co v Brand & Co* [1915] 1 KB 458, c/f *Smart Brothers v Holt* [1929] 2 KB 303.
270 *Times Furnishing Co Ltd v Hutchings* [1938] 1 KB 775.
271 *Ibid.*
272 The exemptions listed above are contained in s 4 of the 1908 Act.
273 Rent Act 1977 s 147 and Rent (Agriculture) Act 1976 s 8.
274 Law of Distress (Amendment) Act 1888 s 7.

sunrise and sunset on a day other than a Sunday and has power to break down internal (but not outer) doors.[275] The goods are seized either by taking hold of one chattel and declaring that it is taken in the name of them all or by intervening to prevent the removal of goods—even if the intervention is unsuccessful.[276]

6.103   A notice of distress stating when the goods will be sold and listing them and stating the amount for which distress is levied and the fees and charges due must be served before goods can be sold. This can take place not less than 6 days after the seizure but that period is extended to 15 days if the tenant or the owner of the goods gives security for any extra costs and demands an extension in writing. The sale must be at the best price and can be at the demised premises or elsewhere.[277] It is usually by auction.

6.104   If distress is illegal as being wrongful from its beginning, because for example it was levied by forcible entry or in circumstances where there was no rent due, then the sale passes no title to the purchaser. If it was merely irregular because some of the proceedings after the levy were conducted unlawfully, or excessive because more goods than were reasonably necessary to satisfy the rent and costs were received then the purchaser does get a good title.[278]

6.105   Between seizure and sale the goods are 'impounded' on or off the premises on which they were seized. Removal of the goods by anyone aware of the distress is a criminal offence and allows the landlord to reclaim the goods and to seek an indemnity.[279] The tenant can require an appraisal (or valuation) of the goods before sale. In practice goods are usually impounded on the demised premises and the tenant is asked to sign a form agreeing to 'walking possession' to avoid the allegation that the landlord has abandoned the distraint. The goods may also be labelled.[280] If a distraint is unlawful, a tenant can seek an injunction to prevent the distraint; reclaim the goods before sale (replevy); or sue for damages for his loss.

Intervention by third parties—the procedure
6.106   Any person who claims protection under the Law of Distress

---

275   *American Concentrated Must Corporation v Hendry* (1893) 65 LJ QB 388.
276   *Cramer & Co Ltd v Mott* (1870) LR 5 QB 357.
277   Distress for Rent Act 1737 ss 8, 9 and 10. See also Distress for Rent Rules 1953 (SI 1702) r 22 and Appendix 2 Form 5.
278   *Altack v Bramwell* (1863) 3 B & S 520; *Whitworth v Smith* (1832) 1 Mood & R 193.
279   *Abingdon RDC v O'Gorman* [1968] 2 QB 811 and Limitation of Actions and Costs Act 1842 s 2.
280   See Distress for Rent Rules 1953 (SI 1702) Appendix 2 Form 6.

Amendment Act 1908 against distress being levied on his goods must serve a written declaration on the landlord or the bailiff after the seizure or threat of seizure of his goods. The declaration must state that the tenant has no property, right or beneficial interest in the goods which are the property of, or in the lawful possession of, the person serving the declaration. It must also state that the chattels in question are not ones to which the 1908 Act is expressed not to apply. A sub-tenant serving such a declaration must state in it the amount of the rent (if any) due from him to his immediate landlord (ie the tenant) and the amount of future instalments of rent and when they are due. He must undertake to pay all such rent to the superior landlord (ie the landlord levying distress). The declaration must have attached to it an inventory of all chattels for which protection is claimed signed by the person claiming protection.[281] It is an offence to make a statement known to be false in such a declaration or inventory. The 1908 Act does not lay down a time limit within which a declaration must be made and served and sale by the landlord does not protect him. Indeed after sale a claim may be made under the 1908 Act by the owner of goods even if no declaration has been served.[282]

6.107 A person protected by the 1908 Act can apply to the magistrates for an order that the goods be returned if distress is levied after a declaration has been served. Such an action amounts to an illegal distress. In addition to obtaining a magistrates' order for the recovery of the goods the owner may sue the landlord or the bailiff at common law.[283]

6.108 By s 6 of the Act it is possible for a superior landlord to serve an under tenant with notice that rent is in future to be paid direct to him and not to the tenant until arrears specified in the notice have been paid off. This transfers to the superior landlord the right to give a good discharge for such rent. A floating charge which has, to the landlord's knowledge, crystallised before he serves notice under s 6 has priority over his claim when it has attached to the rent due from subtenants as book debts of the insolvent tenant.[284]

Distress for taxes

6.109 A statutory power to levy distress for unpaid taxes is conferred on various revenue authorities in respect of different taxes. Like distress for

---

281 Law of Distress (Amendment) Act 1908 s 1.
282 *Sharpe v Fowle* (1884) 12 QBD 385.
283 s 2.
284 *Rhodes v Allied Dunbar Pension Services* [1989] BCLC 186, but see appeal *Re Offshore Ventilation Ltd* (1989) 5 BCC 160 in which the charge in this case was held to be a first fixed charge entitling the company to rent as a mortgagor in possession.

rent this remedy does not depend upon the existence of a court order. A warrant may be issued by the revenue authorities themselves.

Value Added Tax

6.110 Distress can be levied against the goods and chattels of any person refusing or neglecting to pay any Value Added Tax due.[285] After a demand for the tax due distress may be levied by a collector of the Customs and Excise or by a person authorised by him by warrant. Distress cannot be levied until 30 days after an amount of tax becomes due by being assessed and notified to the tax payer under the VAT Act 1983 s 38 sch 7 Para 4. A warrant authorising the person levying distress to break a house or premises open during daytime may be issued by the collector of the Customs and Excise.[286]

6.111 The goods taken in distress must be kept for 5 days and may then be sold by public auction after appraisal and the proceeds must be used to meet the sum due and the costs of the distress. Any balance is returned to the owner of the goods.[287]

6.112 The power to levy distress under VAT regulations is limited to the goods and chattels of the person who owes the tax. There is no right to distrain on other goods present on the taxpayer's premises. Similar powers to distrain the taxpayer's goods exist for the non-payment of excise duty by a revenue trader and non-payment of general betting duty, gaming licence duty, pool betting duty or bingo duty.[288]

Income Tax, Capital Gains Tax and Corporation Tax

6.113 The power to levy distress for these taxes will normally be available only against the goods and chattels of the taxpayer.[289] However, in the case of taxes assessed in respect of land—such as tax under sch A on income from the receipts of rents or rentcharges, or under sch B on income from the occupation of woodlands managed on a commercial basis, the power to distrain extends to any goods found on the premises.[290]

6.114 A reasonable time after the tax due is demanded the collector of taxes may distrain. He requires no warrant to do this but with a warrant

---

285 VAT Act 1983 s 38 sch 17 para 6(4)(a) and VAT Regulations 1980 (SI 1980 no 1536) reg 58.
286 Reg 58(2).
287 Reg 58(3) and (4).
288 Customs & Excise Management Act 1979 s 117(5) and Betting and Gaming Duties Act 1981 s 28(1).
289 Taxes Management Act 1970 s 61.
290 *Juson v Dixon* (1813) 1 M & S 601.

signed by the general commissioners he may break open in the daytime any house or premises.[291] This must be done by, or under the direction of, and in the presence of the collector who has power to require a constable to assist him.[292] The goods must be kept for 5 days and may then be sold by public auction after appraisal.[293] The cost of the distraint and the tax due are retained and any balance returned to the owner of the goods.

Distress for rates

6.115 Unlike distress for rent or taxes, distress for unpaid rates can only be levied after a hearing in the magistrates' court. It is perhaps analogous to execution rather than to distress for rent or taxes. However, this remedy, like the remedy of distress as a means of enforcing certain summary judgments, is known as distress and, for that reason, is dealt with here.

6.116 Rates are a local tax payable to rating authorities. These are London Borough Councils and, elsewhere in the country, district councils.[294] Distress and committal are the primary methods of enforcing the payment of rates except in the case of empty property when the rate is recoverable as a contract debt.[295]

6.117 By the General Rate Act 1967 s 96(1) distress is levied against a person who fails to pay a sum legally due from him in respect of rates. This is usually the occupier of the premises.[296] The goods subject to distress are those of the ratepayer. However where the owner is rated under s 55 of the Act or has agreed to pay the rates under s 56 the occupier's goods can be distrained for rates which accrued during his occupation up to the limit of the amount due from the occupier for rent on the premises if those rates have not been paid by the owner providing the rate has been demanded from the occupier in writing and more than 14 days has elapsed.[297]

6.118 Proceedings can be begun 7 days or more after a demand for rates has been made if the ratepayer has neglected or refused to pay.[298] The rating authority makes a complaint to the magistrates' court which issues a summons requiring the ratepayer to appear and show why the rate has not been paid. The only objections that will prevent the court from issuing a

---

291 Taxes Management Act 1970 s 61(2).
292 *Ibid* and s 61(3).
293 s 61(5).
294 General Rate Act 1967 s 1(1).
295 *Liverpool Corporation v Hope* [1938] 1 KB 751 and General Rate Act 1967 Part VI; ss 17B(6) and sch 1 para 13.
296 *Ibid* s 16 but see the exceptions in ss 17, 17A, 24, 28, 29, 36(5), 55, 56 and sch 1.
297 General Rates Act 1967 s 62.
298 *Ibid* s 96(1).

distress warrant are that the property is not occupied by the person summoned or is not in the area subject to the rate; that a relief from rates applies; that a demand was not properly made or that the rate has been paid. Matters relating to the rateable value of the property cannot usually be raised as an objection to the enforcement of the rate by distress.[299]

6.119   Once the warrant is issued distress may be levied in execution of it by the person authorised or by a constable.[300] The goods can be left on the premises subject to an agreement with the ratepayer and a copy of the Distress for Rates Order should be left with the ratepayer as should a memo setting out the sum due and a copy of any possession agreement.[301]

6.120   Any goods of the ratepayer are subject to distress whether or not they are in the property rated or even the area of the rating authority.[300] The common law exemptions applicable to goods which might otherwise be subject to distress do not apply to distress for rates but the statutory protection of railway rolling stock, hosiery machinery and water, gas and electricity fittings do apply.[302] This reflects the similarities between distress for rates and execution and the statutory basis of the former.

6.121   The Local Government (Finance) Act 1988 Sch 4 para 7 retains a similar system for the collection of the community charge (or Poll Tax) and for non-domestic rates. Sch 9 para 3(2) allows regulations to be made to provide for distress to be levied to recover sums that are due.

Distress under the Magistrates' Court Act 1980

6.122   Distress can be levied under a warrant issued by a magistrates' court against the goods of any person who defaults in paying a sum payable under a conviction or order of a magistrates' court.[303] This includes costs, damages, compensation or a fine imposed as a punishment and can also include amounts due as a result of certain orders of the crown court and other courts.[304] A sum enforceable as a civil debt in a magistrates' court may be the subject of a distress warrant providing the defendant has been previously served with a copy of the minute of the order or providing the order was made in his presence and the warrant issued at that time.[305] A

---

299   See *Milward v Caffin* (1779) 2 Wm Bl 1330; *Baglan Bay Tin Plate Co Ltd v John* (1895) 72 LT 805; *Evans v Brook* [1959] 2 All ER 399 and *Shillitoe v Hinchcliffe* [1922] 2 KB 236.
300   General Rate Act 1967 s 99(3).
301   See Distress for Rates Orders 1979 (SI 1038) and 1980 (SI 2013).
302   *Potts v Hickman* [1941] AC 212 at 219 and 248 and General Rate Act 1967 s 99(2).
303   Magistrates' Court Act 1980 s 76.
304   Powers of Criminal Courts Act 1973 s 32(1), (3) and (5).
305   Magistrates' Court Rules 1981 (SI 552) r 53.

company may thus be subject to this form of distress as it is possible that it would have been convicted of an offence and fined or that it would have been ordered to pay compensation.

6.123   A warrant is issued by a magistrates' court in the same petty sessions area as the one which made the order and is signed by a justice or clerk of the court.[306] It is normally directed to and enforced by the police. Magistrates are protected from liability for irregularities in the warrant. The warrant can be executed anywhere in England and Wales by a constable acting within his police area.[307] Goods seized must be sold no earlier than the 6th day after seizure and no later than the time stated in the warrant or, if no time is stated, the 14th day after the distress was levied.[308] Earlier sale is possible with the written consent of the person against whom distress was levied. On sale the costs and the amount due are deducted from the proceeds and the balance is handed over to the owner of the goods which were sold. Money can be seized on a warrant to levy a sum payable on summary conviction or order. Such money is dealt with in the same way as the proceeds of sale of the distress.[309]

6.124   Water, gas and electricity fittings are protected from distress under the Magistrates' Courts Act 1980 but none of the common law exemptions to the right to levy distress for rent applies.

---

306 Magistrates' Court Act 1980 s 148 and Magistrates' Court Rules 1981 r 95.
307 Magistrates' Court Act 1980 ss 78 and 125(2).
308 Magistrates' Court Rules 1981 r 54.
309 *Ibid* r 54 as amended by SI 1983/553.

CHAPTER 7

The Enforcement of a Security Interest

INTRODUCTION

7.01 The holder of a security interest in property is entitled to use that property to recoup the amount lent to the borrower together with interest on that amount and the costs of realisation of the security. To do this he will make use of a remedy which operates against the property itself. The property on which the remedy operates will be that which is subject to the charge—but in the case of a floating charge that will often be the whole of the company's assets at the time of crystallisation. It will usually be the case that the company borrower is personally liable for the debt due to the security holder apart from the question of security and this means that one remedy open to the creditor is a proceeding for that debt on the basis of the borrower's covenant to repay. That, however, puts the lender in no better position than any other unsecured creditor so those who have security will seek to enforce it against the assets subject to it. This gives them priority over unsecured creditors. If those assets are not of sufficient value to meet the whole amount of the debt then the secured creditor can prove in a liquidation of the company for the balance due.[1] If there is an excess, after the debt is paid out of the proceeds of sale of the assets which were subject to security, then that will be returned to the company (or the liquidator if winding-up has commenced) in the absence of later secured or preferential creditors with a claim on the proceeds of sale of the assets.

7.02 The remedies available to the secured creditor will determine the steps that can be taken to obtain payment by the use of the assets on which the debt is secured. The availability of remedies under the general law depends on the type of security and, often, on the form in which it was taken; whether by deed or under hand. However, as will be noted, it is normally the case that powers and remedies given by the document creating the security will be upheld and applied by the courts—detailed provisions about the right of the lender to sell the asset, the powers of a receiver appointed by the lender or the position as regards possession of the property subject to the security right are normally contained in agreements

---

1 For the options available to a secured creditor in the winding up of a company see paras 19.62–19.70.

stipulating for such rights. Foreclosure alone is exercisable only by court order and is not amenable to contractual agreement between the parties. It is also available only in respect of a limited range of security interests. This is a result of the importance that Equity attaches to the preservation of the mortgagee's equity of redemption.[2]

7.03 The security holder has a right to preserve the assets from deterioration or jeopardy. Debenture holders who hold a floating charge can apply to the court for the appointment of a receiver even if the amount secured is not due and the situation is not one which allows an appointment under the terms of the debenture if the company's assets are endangered, for example, by execution being levied on behalf of an unsecured creditor[3] or by the insolvency of the company combined with the presentation of a winding up petition.[4] This principle applies to situations where the security is threatened by the use to which the assets subject to the security are put. For example, a mortgagee has a right even against third parties to bring action to prevent deterioration of the property[5] and he may have rights because of his status as one who has a demise of property (in the case of a legal mortgage of land) or possession of it; either because of the nature of the security or because of the provisions of the document creating the security.[6] The use of a mortgaged ship for a purpose likely to injure the security can result in an order for an arrest on the application of the mortgagee.[7] The right of a mortgagee to keep up the premiums on a mortgaged insurance policy and to add the amount to the sum secured is based on the same principle.[8]

7.04 The holder of an equitable mortgage is entitled to complete the security by obtaining specific performance of an agreement to create a legal mortgage and the transfer of any property necessary to do this. However, given that the equitable mortgage is binding on later mortgagees or owners who have notice of it this process will be of less importance than ensuring that proper registration of the mortgage occurs in order that later mortgagees or purchasers will be deemed to have notice of it. If title deeds to land, a share certificate or a bill of lading are deposited with the equitable mortgagee this, together with any necessary registration, will provide

---

2 See paras 7.31–7.33.
3 *Edwards v Standard Rolling Stock Syndicate* [1893] 1 Ch 574.
4 *Re Victoria Steamboats Ltd* [1897] 1 Ch 158. It would seem that the mere insufficiency of assets does not amount to jeopardy but that there must be a threat of seizure of assets by execution—*Re New York Taxi Cab Co Ltd* [1913] 1 Ch 1. See Gough *op cit* at pp 95 and 114.
5 *Western Bank v Schindler* [1977] 1 Ch 1 at 9 and 10.
6 Eg see *Sewell v Burdick* (1884) 10 App Cas 74 at 92 (a case of pledge).
7 *The Blanche* (1887) 508 LT 592.
8 *Gill v Downing* (1874) LR 17 Eq 316.

considerable protection of the security without the need for the creation of a legal mortgage.[9] In the case of an equitable charge there is no right to a transfer of a proprietary interest in the property. The primary remedy is the sale of the property charged; there can be no creation of a legal mortgage followed by foreclosure. Such a course is theoretically available to the equitable mortgagee although, in practice, the rights to possession, sale and the appointment of a receiver normally granted in the document creating the charge will be preferred if enforcement is necessary. Even a legal mortgagee will not use foreclosure.[10]

POSSESSION

7.05   The possession of the assets which are subject to a security right is only likely to be used by a mortgagee either to prevent further disposal of assets (in the case of goods or documents of title) or as a preliminary to the exercise of the right of sale.[11] This is because the mortgagee in possession is subject to stringent duties and liabilities to account strictly for the use made of the property. On the other hand, the appointment of a receiver[12] can result in the recovery of income generated by the property without exposing the mortgagee to the risks involved in taking possession. Possession by the lender before default is inconvenient if the borrower wishes to make use of the property during the subsistence of the security interest.

7.06   The underlying position in relation to the possession of the assets subject to the security interest will vary according to the nature of that interest and of the assets themselves. In the case of a pledge of chattels it has already been noted that possession by the pledgee is fundamental to the existence of the security interest—although the meaning of 'possession' extends beyond the physical custody of the assets to allow possession by the pledgee's agent who may be the pledgor.[13] However, in cases where the pledgee does not have the chattels in his custody he must have access to them[14] or control over them.[15] There can therefore be no question of the pledgee taking possession but he may take custody of goods using the existence of the pledge if his possession up to that time has been

9   See chapter 8 on priorities between different interests in the same property. The registration required will depend on the nature of the mortgaged assets and the requirements of Companies Act 1985 ss 395 and 396.
10 See below paras 7.31–7.33.
11 See below paras 7.17–7.30.
12 See below paras 7.11–7.16.
13 See above paras 3.10–3.16.
14 *Hilton v Tucker* (1888) 39 Ch D 669.
15 Eg by the attornment of a third party or because of instructions by the pledgee to the third party *Gregg v National Guardian Assurance Co* [1891] 3 Ch 206.

'constructive'. The possession of a document of title (eg a bill of lading) by way of pledge gives the pledgee *de jure* possession of the goods that it represents.[16]

7.07 In other forms of security, possession by the lender is not essential to the existence of the security. A mortgage involves a transfer of ownership and a charge a transfer of no proprietary interests. In the case of a mortgage there is usually a provision, in the document creating the security, giving the borrower a right to retain possession until default. This is necessary in the case of a legal mortgage of land as the mortgagee is entitled to possession as soon as the mortgage is granted because of the estate that is granted to him.[17] While the mortgagee's power of sale is exercisable only on default by the mortgagor, a possession order is available to protect the mortgagee's security unless he has bound himself not to exercise his right to possession.[18] This is so whether the mortgage is of registered or unregistered land and, in the latter case, whether it is created by demise or by legal charge.[19] In the case of an equitable mortgage of land the mortgagee is generally considered to have no right to possession in the absence of a provision in the document creating the security, a court order, or the permission of the mortgagor.[20] This would seem to be contrary to the principle that equity looks on that as done which ought to be done and that an equitable interest is a proprietary interest.[21] Clearly, an equitable mortgagee who, as opposed to a chargee, has a right to call for the execution of a legal mortgage will have the rights to possession of a legal mortgagee if he goes through that formality. An equitable chargee who has no right to the transfer of ownership of assets subject to the charge will only have the right to possession if such a right is granted by the contract creating the charge or if a court order is obtained.[22] In the case of loans to companies, the mortgage or charge agreement will normally contain a provision dealing with possession.

7.08 Where security is taken over chattels the method of creating a mortgage will, in principle, pass the right to possession to the mortgagee as it involves an assignment with a proviso for reassignment on redemption.

---

16   *Official Assignee of Madras v Mercantile Bank of India Ltd* [1935] AC 53.
17   *Four Maids Ltd v Dudley Marshall (Properties) Ltd* [1957] Ch 317. Thus a possession action is not strictly a mortgagee's remedy but an action for the recovery of land available against the person actually in possession—whether that is the mortgagor or not, *Manchester Unity Life v Sadler* (1974) 232 EG.
18   *Western Bank v Schindler* [1976] 3 WLR 341.
19   Land Registration Act 1925 s 27(1) and LPA 1925 ss 87(1) and 95(4).
20   *Ocean Accident & Guarantee Corporation v Ilford Gas Co* [1905] 2 KB 493 and *Barclays Bank Ltd v Bird* [1954] Ch 274.
21   *Walsh v Lonsdale* (1882) 21 Ch D 9.
22   *Garfitt v Allen* (1887) 37 Ch D 48.

The assignment may, however, allow possession to the mortgagor until default. These rules are abrogated in bills of sale to which the Bills of Sale Acts 1878 to 1882 apply and are replaced by a provision limiting the right of the assignee to seize the assets covered by a bill to five situations and allowing the borrower five days to pay or challenge the seizure.[23] However, since securities granted by a company are not subject to those Acts[24] the underlying position would seem to apply in any case of the assignment of chattels by way of security. In practice, a floating charge is the most likely security to affect a company's chattels and in that case there can be no right to possession until crystallisation, and at that stage the appointment of a receiver is the normal remedy.

7.09   In the case of mortgages and charges of ships or mortgages of registered aircraft, the Bills of Sale Acts 1878–1882 can never apply.[25] In the absence of a contractual provision to the contrary, possession of a mortgaged ship remains with the mortgagor who is entitled to the use of it so long as he does not impair the security.[26] He has the right to retain the character of owner except to the extent that this is inconsistent with making the ship (or a share of it) available for the mortgage debt.[27] If a mortgagee takes possession in default his primary obligation is to sell but he is entitled to use the ship as a prudent owner would before selling.[28] The possession of a mortgaged aircraft is not the subject of specific legislative provision and will, therefore, be dealt with on the basis of the contract creating the mortgage which will usually give the mortgagor possession until default. If this is not done, mortgage by assignment of ownership will pass the right to possession to the mortgagee.

7.10   In the case of mortgages of things in action, possession means the right to any income due on the debt or other right. This will most commonly apply where a share in a trust fund is mortgaged. The notice given to a trustee or debtor to effect a statutory assignment under s 136 of the Law of Property Act 1925 does not, in itself, give possession of the assignor's interest to the assignee or mortgagee. In this context (as in the context of land which is subject to a lease) 'possession' means the right to payment due and in the case of a trust fund this is any payment of income made by the trustees in respect of the mortgaged interest in the fund. Before the trustee is obliged to pay the mortgagee the trustee must be given notice

---

23 Ie default in payment; bankruptcy or distress; fraudulent removal; failure to produce receipts; execution against goods—s 7 Bills of Sale Act (1878) Amendment Act 1882.
24 *Re Standard Manufacturing Co* [1891] 1 Ch 627.
25 Bills of Sale Act 1878 s 4 and Mortgaging of Aircraft Order 1972 SI 1268 Article 16(1).
26 *The Blanche* (1887) 58 LT 592.
27 Merchant Shipping Act 1894 s 34.
28 *Marriott v Anchor Reversionary Co* (1861) 3 De GFJ 177.

specifically requiring him to do this. This gives the mortgagee possession.[29] In certain cases, the exercise by the mortgagee of his right to possession under the agreement or because of the assignment of ownership rights is restricted by statute.[30] This will not usually apply where the mortgagor is a company even if it has mortgaged dwelling houses.[31] Its borrowings are subject to neither the Consumer Credit Act 1974 nor the Bills of Sale Acts 1878–1882.[32]

RECEIVERSHIP

7.11 The detailed rules governing the appointment, removal, powers and liabilities of an administrative receiver appointed over substantially the whole of a company's assets are dealt with in chapters 11 and 12. It is this type of receivership which is normally involved in cases of corporate insolvency. However, the practice of appointing such receivers to enforce a debenture secured by a fixed and floating charge grew out of the remedy developed in the courts of equity on behalf of mortgagees of land. It is possible for the holder of a legal or equitable mortgage or of an equitable charge to appoint a receiver over those assets which are subject to his security interest. The wide powers of the administrative receiver developed because a floating charge usually extends to the whole of a company's undertaking and the powers given by the Insolvency Act 1986 s 42 and Schedule 1 reflect those normally conferred by documents creating fixed and floating charges.

7.12 The conditions for the appointment of receivers to act for those with a fixed charge only and the powers and functions of such receivers are governed by the document creating the security or by the provisions of the Law of Property Act 1925 ss 101 and 109 if they apply and are not modified by the provisions of the mortgage document. Although a receiver is appointed by the mortgagee he is the agent of the mortgagor[33] and the mortgagee is not liable for default in relation to the property as he would be if he took possession. The mortgagor is responsible for all acts and defaults of the receiver. A receiver appointed by the court is responsible to the court

---

29   *Re Pawson's Settlement* [1917] 1 Ch 541.
30   Eg Consumer Credit Act 1974 s 76(1); 87(1) and 126; Administration of Justice Act 1970 s 36; Bills of Sale Act (1878) Amendment Act 1882 s 7.
31   It is improbable that a court would use its powers of adjournment under the Administration of Justice Act 1970 s 36 and Administration of Justice Act 1973 s 8 in favour of a corporate mortgagor even if they were applicable.
32   Consumer Credit Act 1974 ss 8(1) and 189(1).
33   LPA 1925 s 109(2) where the agent is appointed under the statutory power or *Gaskell v Gosling* [1896] 1 QB 669 where the appointment is under an express power.

as its officer. The decision of a mortgagee to appoint a receiver cannot be challenged except on grounds of bad faith. There is no duty of care to the mortgagor or guarantors of the debt in making that decision as distinct from the manner in which the receiver's powers are exercised after appointment, at which point meddling by the mortgagee may result in liability.[34] The mortgagee is entitled to make the decision to appoint with regard to his own interests and need not subordinate them to the interests of the company or of other creditors.[35]

7.13   The statutory power only applies to mortgages or charges made by deed. The power arises when the mortgage money becomes due. This is the legal date of redemption if one is specified in the deed. Otherwise it is the date when each instalment becomes due.[36] The power can be excluded for a longer period by a provision of a deed.[37] However the power is not exercisable until notice is served requiring repayment of the mortgage money and default in payment by the mortgagor for three months after the service of the notice; or until interest is two months in arrears; or there is a breach by the mortgagor of some other provision of the deed or of the Act.[38] Once the power arises its use is valid as against third parties but until it is exercisable there can be no valid appointment as between mortgagor and mortgagee. This ensures that a person dealing with a receiver appointed under the statutory power need only check that the mortgage or charge was by deed and that the legal date for repayment in that document has arrived. Questions on whether there has been default, arrears of interest or other breaches of the provisions of the Act or deed need not be investigated by a person dealing with the receiver.[39] The appointment or removal of a receiver must be in writing under the mortgagee's hand.[40]

7.14   A receiver appointed under the statutory provision is not a manager and has powers only to recover income from the property to apply it to the payment of his own expenses and remuneration, any outgoings affecting the property, payments having priority over the mortgage under which he was appointed, and the interest and, if the mortgagee so directs him in writing, the principal due under that mortgage.[41] Powers to manage the property are not granted and for this reason it is normal for mortgage deeds to confer wider powers on a receiver and to enable him to operate as a

---

34   *Shamji v Johnson Matthey Bankers* [1986] BCLC 278.
35   *Re Potter's Oils (No 2)* [1986] BCLC 98.
36   *Payne v Cardiff RDC* [1932] 1 KB 241.
37   *Twentieth Century Banking Corporation Ltd v Wilkinson* [1976] 3 WLR 489.
38   LPA 1925 ss 101(1)(iii) and 109(1).
39   LPA 1925 s 109(4).
40   ss 109(1) and (5).
41   s 109(8).

manager as well as simply a receiver. Any residue of monies collected by the receiver after he has made the payments provided for under s 109(8) are to be passed to the person who would have been entitled to the income had he not been appointed—normally this will be the mortgagor but it may sometimes be the holder of a later mortgage. The statutory power is applicable to any form of property but is most suitable to land subject to a lease when rent can be collected and used to discharge interest on the lessor-mortgagor's debt. The power is so limited that it will not often be used for property other than land and, even in the case of mortgages of land, more extensive powers will usually be granted by the mortgage deed to a receiver appointed under it. Apart from the particular case of a charge securing a debenture granted by a company, it is more common for mortgagees or chargees to use the power of sale and to take possession (if this is necessary) as a preliminary to sale.[42]

7.15 An equitable mortgage or charge[43] granted by deed will confer the statutory power to appoint a receiver. In the case of such a mortgage or charge not granted by deed, the mortgagee or chargee may use the right to apply to the court for the appointment of a receiver should the mortgagor default.[44] This right is available to legal and equitable mortgagees and to chargees.[45] The duty of such a receiver will be to collect the income of the mortgaged property and to apply it as the court directs although the court may appoint a receiver and manager with more extensive powers than those available to a receiver appointed under the Law of Property Act 1925 s 101(1)(iii). If the amount collected by a court appointed receiver is insufficient to meet his own remuneration and expenses he cannot claim them from a party to the litigation in which he was appointed as he is an officer of the court and not an agent of either party.[46] A court order appointing a receiver of land must be registered under s 6(1)(b) of the Land Charges Act 1925 or s 54 of the Land Registration Act 1925 as a land charge or caution for priority purposes whether or not the receivership is of a kind that could bind a purchaser.[47]

7.16 The availability of the statutory power in the case of mortgages or charges by deed and of an express power to appoint a receiver in most documents creating mortgages or charges (whether or not they are deeds) has made this jurisdiction one that is little used. Where property does not generate income or where, as will usually be the case, the mortgagee or

---

42   See paras 7.17–7.30 below.
43   LPA 1925 s 205(1)(xvi).
44   *Shakel v Duke of Marlborough* (1819) 4 Madd 463.
45   Supreme Court Act 1981 s 37.
46   *Evans v Clayhope Properties Ltd* [1987] BCLC 238.
47   *Clayhope Properties Ltd v Evans* [1986] 2 All ER 795.

chargee is concerned to realise the capital value of the security, the appointment of a receiver is not likely to occur. Even in the case of an appointment by debenture holders the realisation of the security will often be the object of the receivership; it is the nature of the property charged which makes receivership a more appropriate method of achieving this as the sale of a company as a going concern may realise a larger amount than the sale of its assets at a break-up value.

SALE BY THE MORTGAGEE

7.17   The power of sale is normally expressly provided for in a document creating a consensual security interest. However, it exists in the case of certain securities as an incident of the security held by the mortgagee. This is the case where a legal mortgage is given over things in action such as shares or insurance policies or over chattels where posession is delivered to the mortgagee.[48] A pledgee has an implied right of sale if the pledgor defaults after being given a reasonable time to pay.[49] An equitable mortgagee probably requires the assistance of the court to sell and there is uncertainty over the ability of such a mortgagee to pass title to the legal estate on a sale under the statutory power whatever form of property is involved.[50] The power of sale of a mortgagee of chattels subject to the Bills of Sale Acts 1878–1882 is restricted by those Acts, whether it be incidental to the security, express or statutory. By s 7 of the Bills of Sale Act (1878) Amendment Act 1882 the goods may only be taken into the lender's possession on the grounds specified in that section[51] and they must then be held for five days during which time the borrower may apply to a court for the release of the goods or for an order restraining the lender from removing or selling them.

7.18   An equitable chargee may only sell if the statutory power of sale applies because the charge was created by deed or if there is an express power to sell in the document creating the charge. Otherwise, sale by a chargee is only possible by a court order. This is the result of the nature of a charge which, unlike a mortgage, does not operate by virtue of a transfer of ownership but merely indicates that certain property is charged with the debt.[52]

---

48 *Stubbs v Slater* [1910] 1 Ch 632 and *Re Morritt ex parte Official Receiver* (1886) 18 QBD 222.
49 *Re Morritt* (1886) 18 QBD 222.
50 See below text to footnotes 56–60.
51 See below paras 7.05–7.10.
62 See above paras 1.13–1.27.

7.19 The registered mortgagee of a ship or fishing vessel is statutorily empowered to sell a mortgaged ship or a mortgaged share of it but, if there are prior mortgages, he must have the concurrence of any prior registered mortgagee or a court order authorising sale.[53] In cases where the court's order is necessary, the ship will be arrested and sale and appraisement will be ordered.

7.20 Where a mortgage or charge is made by deed then a statutory power of sale exists under the Law of Property Act 1925 s 101. This arises and becomes exercisable in the same circumstances as the statutory right to appoint a receiver. The legal repayment date must be past and the mortgage or charge must be by deed[54] before the power can arise and it only becomes exercisable if notice is served requiring repayment of the mortgage money and the mortgagor defaults for three months; or interest is two months in arrears; or the mortgagor breaches some other provision of the deed or of the Act.[55] It is common for an express power to be included in a mortgage or charge even if it is made by deed and for the circumstances in which the power is exercisable to be more widely drawn than they are in the statute. It is also common in the case of an equitable mortgage for the deed to give the mortgagee a power of attorney to convey the legal estate on behalf of the mortgagor or to declare that the legal estate is held by the mortgagor on trust for the mortgagee. This is necessary because of the uncertainty of whether an equitable mortgagee can pass title to the legal estate under the statutory power.[56] A ruling that this was not possible was made by the Court of Appeal in a decision dealing with the power of sale under the Conveyancing Act 1881 s 21(1)[57] where it was held that an equitable mortgagee merely transferred his equitable interest on a sale under the statutory power given in that Act. In *Re White Rose Cottage*[58] *obiter* statements in the Court of Appeal indicated that an equitable mortgagee could sell the legal estate, but it is nonetheless usual to draft a document creating an equitable mortgage to include a device ensuring that there can be a transfer of the legal estate. The grant of a power of attorney to the mortgagee operates to enable the legal estate to be transferred without the need for a legal mortgage to be called for first.[59] If such a device is not used an equitable mortgagee may have to apply to the court for an order for sale

---

53 Merchant Shipping Act 1894 s 35 and Merchant Shipping Act 1988 sch 2 para 5.
54 LPA 1925 s 101(i). Where there is no principal sum to become due before the end of the loan period the statutory power will not arise but foreclosure and sale may be ordered by the court: *Twentieth Century Banking Corporation v Wilkinson* [1976] 3 WLR 489.
55 Law of Property Act 1925 s 103.
56 *White Rose Cottage* [1965] Ch 940.
57 *Re Hodson and Howes' contract* (1887) 35 Ch D 668.
58 [1965] Ch 940.
59 *Re White Rose Cottage* [1965] Ch 940 at 955–956.

in which case the court has power to vest a legal term of years in the mortgagee so that he can sell as legal mortgagee.[60] The legal mortgagee has statutory power to sell the fee simple if the mortgage is of freehold property or the whole leasehold interest of the mortgagor if a leasehold is mortgaged.[61]

7.21 A purchaser from a mortgagee under the statutory power of sale is protected from the impeachment of his title on the grounds that the power of sale was not exercisable—so long as it had arisen[62] and any conveyance on a sale by a mortgagee is deemed to have been made in exercise of the statutory power unless a contrary intention appears.[63] This provision will thus usually protect the purchaser under an express power of sale.

7.22 Whatever the source of the power of sale—statutory, express or an incident of the security—the duty of the mortgagee who exercises the power of sale is the same.[64] The mortgagee is not the trustee of the power for the mortgagor and is apparently entitled to choose the time of sale once the power is exercisable. He is not required to wait for a time when the price is at a high level.

> "It matters not that the moment may be unpropitious and that by waiting a higher price could be obtained. He has the right to realise his security by turning it into money when he likes."[65]

7.23 There is no power in the court to require a receiver appointed under a debenture or any other agent of a mortgagee to give advance notice of an intention to exercise the power of sale.[66] The older authorities suggest that the duty of the mortgagee on sale is only one of good faith.[67] However, it is now clear that he also has a duty to the mortgagor, to other mortgagees and to guarantors of the debt to take reasonable care to obtain the best price that the circumstances permit at the moment of sale.[68] Sale by auction[69] is permissible and will not represent a breach of duty even if the auction is poorly attended through no fault of the mortgagee. However, a failure

---

60 LPA 1925 ss 90 and 91(2). This may amount to no more than specific performance of the equitable mortgagee's right to have a legal mortgage.
61 LPA 1925 ss 88(1) and 89(1).
62 LPA 1925 s 104(2).
63 *Ibid* s 104(3).
64 See Fisher & Lightwood 9th ed Ch 20 pp 367–370.
65 *Cuckmere Brick Co Ltd v Mutual Finance Ltd* [1971] Ch 949 per Salmon LJ at 965–966 and *American Express International Banking Corporation v Hurley* [1986] BCLC 52.
66 *Gomba Holdings Ltd v Homan* [1986] BCLC 331.
67 *Kennedy v De Trafford* [1867] AC 180.
68 There is no duty to delay a sale in the hope of an upturn in the property market—*Bank of Cyprus (London) v Gill* [1980] 2 Lloyds Rep 51.
69 LPA 1925 s 101(i) allows sale by public auction or private treaty and subject to any conditions that the mortgagee thinks fit in the case of a sale under the statutory power.

sufficiently to advertise the auction or the negligent omission of information about the property which results in a sale at a price below the market value will make the mortgagee liable to the mortgagor for the amount of the deficiency. A failure by a mortgagee who is not a valuer to take any professional advice about valuation and method of sale or to advertise property in an appropriate specialist journal can amount to a breach of duty.[70]

7.24 In *Cuckmere Brick v Mutual Finance Ltd*[71] a failure to publicise the existence of planning permission for the building of a hundred flats on land made the mortgagee liable to the mortgagor for the loss caused by the lower sale price resulting from the mortgagee's negligence. The negligence of an agent of the mortgagee is his responsibility. A number of authorities provide specific examples of breaches of duty. A sale of commercial property without goodwill may be a breach if this affects the price because the sale of property and goodwill together would fetch a higher price than the sale of each separately[72] although in *Palmer*'s case a sale of the freehold was held to include a sale of such goodwill as could be disposed of by the mortgagee. In a case where it is clear that a sale with vacant possession will fetch an amount greater than the price of the property subject to a tenancy added to the cost of buying out the tenants, then a sale by a mortgagee without any attempt to obtain vacant possession may be a breach of duty.[73] However, the actions of the mortgagee must, it is submitted, always be tested against what steps are reasonable in the light of the interests of the mortgagors. The mortgagee must balance a firm lower offer against a higher one that is not firm and will not be held to be in breach of duty simply because of disagreements between different valuers on the market value.[74]

7.25 The Court of Appeal has held that since the general law imposes a duty to act with reasonable care in exercising the power of sale a term authorising a person to carry out the transaction on such terms and in such manner and for such consideration as he thinks fit is construed as giving such authority within the limits of the duty to take reasonable care. Similarly an exemption from liability contained in a document conferring authority to sell in that way for losses arising in connection with 'any such sale' means such a sale that is not in breach of the chargee's duty under the general law. An allegation of a breach of that duty can be used as a defence to a mortgagee's action for specific performance of an agreement to grant a

---

70 *American Express Corporation v Hurley* [1986] BCLC 52 and *Tse Kwang Lam v Wong Chit Sen* [1983] 3 All ER 54.
71 [1971] ch 949.
72 See *Palmer v Barclays Bank Ltd* (1971) 23 P & CR 30.
73 *Holohan v Friends Provident & Century Life Office* [1966] IRI (Ireland).
74 See eg *Johnson v Ribbins* (1975) 235 Estates Gazette 757.

legal mortgage of shares where an executed transfer is required to enable the mortgagee to carry out a sale that he has agreed. It is, however, possible to limit or exclude that mortgagee's duty by an appropriately worded provision.[75]

7.26 A breach of duty may be restrained prior to sale or may result in damages for breach being awarded to the mortgagor or other mortgagees.[76] A purchaser who has knowledge of the facts constituting the mortgagee's breach of duty may be subject to an injunction restraining completion of the sale and will not take a right superior to that of the mortgagor. However after contracts are exchanged a sale will not be restrained because the mortgagee tenders payment of the mortgage debt if there has been no breach of duty by the mortgagee in his conduct of the sale.[77] The sale can be set aside if the purchaser had actual or constructive knowledge of the impropriety of the sale.[78] The right of a mortgagor to have the sale set aside is a mere equity. It is defeated by the mortgagor's delay in seeking a remedy in which case the equitable doctrine of laches will apply and it will not affect any purchaser for value of a legal or equitable interest who has no notice of the impropriety involved in the sale.[79] Alternatively, the conveyance of the property to the purchaser from the mortgagee may be treated as a transfer of the mortgage and the debts secured by it and not of the mortgagor's interest.[80] Both of these remedies against a purchaser are only available if he had actual or constructive knowledge of the mortgagee's impropriety. In the absence of this the statutory protection will ensure that he gets good title even if the power of sale was not exercisable.[81]

7.27 Unless a sale is by court order and the court gives leave, a mortgagee is not allowed to purchase the mortgaged property himself—whether as sole or joint purchaser or by a nominee—even if such a sale is at full value.[82]

75   *Bishop v Bonham* (1988) 4 BCC 347.
76   *Cuckmere Brick v Mutual Finance Ltd* [1971] ch 949; *Standard Chartered Bank v Walker* [1982] 1 WLR 1410—on sale by a receiver a duty to obtain the best price the circumstances permit is owed to a guarantor of the debt as well as to the mortgagor. The mortgagee may be liable for a receiver's fault if the mortgagee interferes with the conduct of the receivership despite the fact that the receiver is the agent of the mortgagor. Once liquidation begins a debenture holder's receiver may become the mortgagee's agent without interference by the mortgagee but the mortgagee has a right of indemnity against the receiver for breaches of duty under a term that will be implied into the contract unless expressly excluded. *American Express International Banking Corporation v Hurley* (*supra*) and see s 44(1)(a) of Insolvency Act 1986 as to administrative receivers.
77   *Property and Bloodstock Ltd v Emerton* [1968] Ch 94.
78   *Nott v Eastern* [1900] 1 ch 29. This is so providing relief is sought promptly.
79   This is supported by Australian authority. See *Latex Investments Ltd v Hotel Terrigal Property Ltd* (1965) 113 CLR 265.
80   *Selwyn v Garfit* (1888) 38 Ch D 273.
81   Law of Property Act 1925 s 104(2).
82   *Williams v Wellingborough BC* [1975] 1 WLR 1327; *Farrar v Farrars Ltd* (1888) 40 Ch D 395.

However, a sale to a company in which the mortgagee has an interest may be upheld after close scrutiny if it is in good faith and for the best price reasonably obtainable.[83] It seems that an execution creditor is allowed to purchase property sold as part of the process of execution.[84] This rule can be justified on the grounds that such a sale, unlike a sale by a mortgagee under an express or statutory power, is conducted by the sheriff and not by the creditor himself.

7.28 The purchase money received by a mortgagee after the sale of the mortgaged property must be used to pay off the holders of any prior incumbrances attaching to the mortgaged property unless the property was sold subject to those incumbrances. The balance is held on trust by the mortgagee to be applied to pay the costs, charges and expenses that he incurred in the sale or any attempted sale and the amount due on the mortgage. The latter includes interest, costs and other money due as well as the principal sum.[85] Any surplus must then be paid to the next incumbrancer. This includes a mortgagee whose mortgage ranks after the one in respect of which the power of sale was exercised but also, for example, a bank with a lien or an execution creditor with a charging order.[86] A mortgagee with notice of a later incumbrance will be liable to its holder for handing the surplus over to the mortgagor.[87] Registration of a later mortgage or charge will constitute notice of that incumbrance but actual knowledge of an unregistered incumbrance may make the mortgagee liable.[88] If there is any dispute about who should receive the surplus then it should be paid into court. In the absence of later incumbrances the surplus must be paid to the mortgagor or other person entitled to the equity of redemption. Where that is subject to a trust for sale payment should be to the trustee.

7.29 In the case of a sale by any mortgagee these rules ensure that the proceeds of the sale are dealt with in accordance with the priorities of any security interests attached to the property that was sold. In the unlikely event of the purchaser agreeing to take the property subject to them, prior incumbrances remain attached to the property after sale. Otherwise property is sold free of them but they are paid off by the selling mortgagee out of the proceeds of sale before payment of even the expenses of sale. Later

---

83   *Tse Kwang Lan v Wong Chit Sen* [1983] 3 All ER 54 PC.
84   *Stratford v Twyman* (1822) JAC 418.
85   LPA 1925 s 105 lays down this rule for the statutory power. In other cases there will be a constructive trust to the same effect—*Banner v Berridge* (1881) 18 Ch D 254 and see LPA s 107(2) which imposes the same directions on sale under an express power.
86   *Re Thomsons Mortgage Trust* [1920] 1 Ch 508. Charging Orders Act 1979 s 3(4).
87   *West London Commercial Bank v Reliance Permanent Building Society* (1885) 29 Ch D 954.
88   See Fisher and Lightwood 9th edn p 374.

incumbrances are paid in the appropriate order of priority after the payment of the amount due and the expenses of earlier incumbrances.

7.30   As a preliminary to sale the mortgagee will usually seek to obtain possession of the property if he does not already hold it because of the nature of his security or as a result of agreement.[89] The use of these two enforcement methods in tandem is the commonest technique for the enforcement of fixed security interests against the debtor's assets. In the case of a floating charge, or, more commonly, a debenture secured by a fixed and a floating charge over different assets of a corporate debtor, the appointment of a receiver is the usual preliminary as this keeps open the possibility of a sale of the whole enterprise or some part of it as a going concern rather than of separate assets. It is also a method that can be used speedily and without court order under the terms usually found in such debentures. It does not impose on the chargee the liabilities and responsibilities of a mortgagee in possession.[90]

FORECLOSURE

7.31   This method of enforcing a security interest is available only to a mortgagee. It applies to legal and equitable mortgages but not to equitable charges as in that case there is no express or implied agreement to grant a legal mortgage.[91] The very concept can only be applied to a mortgage. Since, in the case of mortgages of property other than land, legal ownership is usually assigned to the mortgagee, the interest of the mortgagor is limited to the equity of redemption. That is the right to pay all sums due under the mortgage and to have the ownership of the property transferred back to the borrower. This was formerly the case with land but since the Law of Property Act 1925 the mortgagor retains legal title but the mortgagee has a term of years.[92] The remedy of foreclosure involves an application by the mortgagee to the court for the mortgagor's equity of redemption to be extinguished. In the case of a mortgage of property other than land (such as chattels or things in action[93]) where there has been an assignment to the mortgagee such an order, in itself, will vest full ownership rights in the mortgagee without leaving the mortgagor any right to redeem the property.

---

89   See para 7.05–7.10.
90   *Standard Chartered Bank v Walker* [1982] 1 WLR 1410 suggests that the mortgagee may incur duties during a receivership where he interferes in the conduct of the receivership.
91   An equitable mortgage by deposit of title deeds gives a right to foreclosure as it is taken to represent an agreement to grant a legal mortgage: *Parker v Housefield* (1834) 2 Myl & K 419. An equitable charge does not imply such an agreement: *Re Owen* (1894) 3 Ch 220.
92   See para 2.02 above.
93   *General Credit & Discount v Glegg* (1883) 22 Ch D 549.

In the case of mortgages of land, statute specifically provides for the transfer of the legal estate of the mortgagor to the mortgagee on foreclosure so that the mortgagee becomes the legal and equitable owner of the property.[94] The mortgagee's interest after foreclosure will be subject to earlier incumbrances but will be free of all claims of later incumbrancers of the property as well as those of the mortgagor. After foreclosure and sale a mortgagee cannot sue the mortgagor on any covenant of the mortgage and guarantors of the mortgagor's obligations under those covenants are also relieved of liability.[95] The injustice that would flow from a frequent resort to this remedy in such cases means that it is seldom used.

7.32 Foreclosure can only be achieved by court order.[96] It is expensive when compared to a sale out of court or the appointment of a receiver. More significantly, in any case where the value of the property subject to the mortgage is greater than the amount of the debt secured by that mortgage, foreclosure is potentially unjust to the mortgagor who loses his whole interest in the property if the court allows the foreclosure. If there are other mortgagees ranking lower in order of priority than the one who seeks foreclosure, they will be subject to total loss if foreclosure is allowed as their interests, like that of the mortgagor, will be extinguished. For those reasons a court will almost invariably order a sale rather than foreclosure if either of those factors exist although the mortgagee seeking foreclosure may be entitled to the payment into court, by those seeking a sale order, of a sum sufficient to secure him against loss—especially if the assumption that there will be a surplus after payment of the mortgaged debt is based on speculative gain.[97] The power to order sale by judicial process instead of foreclosure is now governed by statute.[98] Foreclosure is available after the payment of the debt has become due at law (that is the time fixed in the deed for redemption whether a specific date or an event such as a failure to pay interest or principal or some other breach of the terms of the mortgage) as it is not until then that an equitable right to redeem exists.[99] If no legal redemption date is fixed then a demand for payment followed by the passage of a reasonable time will give rise to a right of foreclosure.[100]

7.33 The mortgagee (or a successor in title[101]) begins proceedings for a

---

94 LPA 1925 ss 88(2) and 89(2).
95 *Lloyds and Scottish Trust v Britten* (1982) 44 P & CR 249.
96 *Re Farnol, Eades, Irvine & Co* [1915] 1 Ch 22, 24.
97 *Cripps v Wood* (1882) 51 LJ Ch 5840 *Merchant Banking Co of London v London Hanseatic Bank* (1886) 55 LJ Ch 579.
98 LPA ss 90(1) and 91.
99 *Williams v Morgan* [1906] 1 Ch 804. In *Twentieth Century Banking Corporation v Wilkinson* [1976] 3 WLR 489 arrears of interest sufficed.
100 *Brighty v Norton* (1862) 3 B & S 305.
101 *Platt v Mendel* (1884) 27 Ch D 246 at 247.

foreclosure order. Initially, a foreclosure order *nisi* will be made and an account of the amount due on the mortgage taken. The mortgagor will be given a fixed period (often six months) to redeem the mortgage; failing which the order will be made absolute. Each subsequent mortgagee also has the right to redeem earlier mortgages and, in effect, to purchase them. Further periods may be given for this process.[102] At any stage before a foreclosure order absolute is made any party may apply for a judicial sale[103] with considerable hope of success if the value of the property exceeds the debt or if there are later mortgages of the property. Even after a foreclosure order absolute is made, it is possible for it to be reopened if this appears to be necessary in the interests of justice. This will only be so if an application is made reasonably promptly by a mortgagor who is able to redeem and who can show good reasons for the matter to be reopened. This includes an explanation of the failure to redeem before the order was made and may also include the special value of the particular property to the mortgagor.[104] A combination of the mortgagor's failure to understand the effect of the orders made with a large discrepancy between the amount of the debt and the value of the property has been held to be sufficient to warrant the reopening of a foreclosure order absolute.[105] It is even possible for an order to be reopened against a purchaser from the mortgagee who was aware of the facts which affected the mortgagee's right to the foreclosure order absolute—at least where the purchase took place shortly after the order was made.[104] If a sale by the mortgagee was carried out in circumstances that would allow sale under the statutory power then the purchaser's title will be unimpeachable as the statutory power is still available after foreclosure.[106] However, the foreclosure can be reopened between mortgagor and mortgagee in relation to the purchase money paid to the mortgagee. These rules make it clear why foreclosure is not usually considered to be a desirable remedy if others are available. In the absence of a statutory or express power of sale, it may be an appropriate remedy for an equitable mortgagee although a judicial sale is likely to be the most satisfactory outcome of any such application.[107]

---

102 *Smithett v Hesketh* (1890) 44 Ch D 161 but see *Platt v Mendel* (1884) 27 Ch D 246.
103 *Union Bank of London v Ingram* (1882) 20 Ch D 463.
104 *Campbell v Holyland* (1877) 7 Ch D 166.
105 *Lancashire & Yorkshire Reversionary Interest Co Ltd v Crowe* (1970) 114 Sol Jo 435.
106 *Watson v Marston* (1853) 4 De G N and G 230.
107 See, for example, *Twentieth Century Banking Corporation v Wilkinson* [1976] 3 WLR 489 where foreclosure and sale were possible on the basis of interest arrears but there was no power of sale out of court until the principal sum became due at the end of the loan period.

CHAPTER 8

The Priority of Security Interests

GENERAL PRINCIPLES

8.01   The complexity of this topic derives from the fact that the rules which govern priorities represent the accumulation of layers of rules which interact with each other. The distinction between mortgages of legal and equitable interests is significant as is the difference between legal and equitable mortgages. The question of the notice of the existence of one mortgage or charge given to the holder of a later one forms an important element in the rules and this, in turn, is often replaced by the operation of a system of registration of charges over particular types of asset. In the case of companies there is, for most consensual security interests, the additional requirement of registration under the Companies Act 1985 s 395.

8.02   In the case of personal property certain security interests operate and attach to property by virtue of possession. This is the case with a pledge of goods or documents of title. In such cases the question of when possession was granted and whether it was retained actually or constructively will be relevant to the question of priority. In the case of certain registration systems priority is simply accorded by date of registration. In the case of others registration operates as notice and therefore complements, but does not wholly replace, the underlying system based on common law and equity.

8.03   In this chapter the matter is dealt with by looking first at the broad principles which can apply to a security interest over any kind of asset. Secondly, the detailed rules applicable to particular categories of asset are dealt with, with special reference to the registration systems which operate for different types of property. The effect that the very existence of an administration order or a liquidation has on the priority of the security interests that exist over the property of a company is dealt with in chapters 13, 14 and 20.

Legal and equitable mortgages and charges

8.04   Before the reform of property law in 1925, the question of whether a mortgage was legal or equitable was a major factor in determining priority.

While the basic rule as between competing mortgages in the same category was that they would rank in order of creation (*Qui prior est tempore potior est jure*), a legal mortgage would prevail over an equitable mortgage of earlier date providing 'the equities are equal'. This 'equality' of the equities meant 'the non-existence of any circumstance which affects the conduct of one of the rival claimants and makes it less meritorious than that of the other.'[1] Subject to the importance of registration in the case of mortgages of land, this remains a fundamental rule of priorities after 1925.[2] The legislation does not amend these rules of priorities in relation to a mortgage of a legal estate but where the interest mortgaged is an equitable interest (whether in land or pure personalty) the rule in *Dearle v Hall*,[3] which determines priority on the basis of the order in which notice is served on the person holding the legal estate, applies. Rules governing mortgages of chattels and choses in action are dealt with below.

Conduct resulting in loss of priority

8.05   The rule that priority depends on the date of creation of an incumbrance may be ousted where it is established that the holder of the earlier security interest behaved in such a way that it would be unjust to allow him to retain priority as against a later mortgagee or chargee. Similarly, where priorities are affected by the status of a mortgage as legal or equitable, the legal mortgagee may lose such priority as he gains over the holder of an earlier equitable mortgage because of his conduct, although it is notice of the existence of the earlier equitable mortgage which will most commonly have this effect. The doctrine of constructive notice imposes liability on the later mortgagee for behaviour which amounts to a failure to take reasonable precautions by making inquiries about earlier incumbrances.[4]

8.06   Fraud, gross negligence and conduct clothing the mortgagor with apparent authority will all cause a loss of priority. The fraud must cause the creation of the later incumbrance and result in absence of notice of the earlier legal title on the part of the later mortgagee.[5] It must be attributable to the earlier mortgagee or his solicitor. The presence of such behaviour is a clear and uncontroversial ground for deferring the claim of a mortgagee. Gross negligence by the legal mortgagee normally relates to the deeds of the property subject to the mortgage. The degree of negligence required is that which makes it unjust to enforce the usual order of priority. It must be

1 *Bailey v Barnes* [1894] 1 Ch 25 per Lindley LJ at 36.
2 *Joseph v Lyons* (1884) 15 QBD 280.
3 (1828) 3 Russ 1.
4 See paras 8.11–8.18.
5 *Peter v Russell* (1716) 1 Eq Co Abr 321.

'aggravated' carelessness and involve a failure to take precautions which a reasonable man would have observed, indicating an attitude of indifference to obvious risks.[6] A failure to make any inquiry about the whereabouts of deeds or to investigate title will postpone a legal mortgagee, as will the acceptance of an inadequate explanation for a failure to produce them.[7] As regards later incumbrances a failure to take custody of the deeds will postpone the mortgagee to a later incumbrancer who assumes that their presence in the hands of the mortgagor indicates an absence of existing charges.[8] This is subject to the application of the registration system to puisne mortgages and general equitable charges.

8.07 It is probable that the same rule would apply if the deeds are released to the mortgagor while the mortgage continues. There is no doubt that where they are released to allow the mortgagor to raise further loans and the mortgagor fails to declare the existence of the first mortgage to later mortgagees, or borrows in excess of the amount agreed with the first mortgagee, the first mortgagee loses priority because of his action in clothing the mortgagor with apparent authority on the basis of which the later mortgagee lends and takes security.[9] The representation of the first mortgagee, which results in the deception of the later incumbrancer, estops him from asserting his priority against the later mortgagee. Apart from parting with the deeds, the representation can take the form of the grant of a receipt or a statement in a deed which appears to show that the mortgage is discharged when that is not the case.[10] It would seem that there is a duty in equity on the part of the holder of a legal interest to take sufficient care to protect his interest by, for example, retaining the deeds after the creation of the interest to prevent the mortgagor from granting further mortgages or insisting on the production of deeds when the legal interest is purchased or created.[11]

8.08 In *Northern Counties of England Fire Insurance v Whipp*[12] the Court of Appeal appeared to recognize a distinction between the obligation on a legal mortgagee to obtain deeds in the first place, which exists and is breached by carelessness or imprudence, and the obligation to retain them, which will not be breached by negligent conduct but only by assistance or connivance in deliberate fraud or behaviour making the mortgagee his agent. However, omission to use ordinary care in inquiring about title

---

6   *Hudson v Viney* [1921] 1 Ch 98 at 104 and *Oliver v Hinton* [1899] 2 Ch 264
7   *Hewitt v Loosemore* (1851) 9 Hare 449 and *Oliver v Hinton (supra)*
8   *Agra Bank Ltd v Barry* (1874) LR 7 HL 135.
9   *Briggs v Jones* (1870) LR 10 Eq 92; *Brocklesby v Temperance Permanent Building Society* [1895] AC 173.
10 *Rimmer v Webster* [1902] 2 Ch 163.
11 *Walker v Linom* [1907] 2 Ch 104 and *Oliver v Hinton* [1899] 2 Ch 264.
12 (1884) 26 Ch D 482.

deeds or retaining them may be evidence of fraud.[13] It seems that at law, as opposed to equity, there is no obligation on the owner of a legal interest actively to safeguard his rights over the property in order to be able to assert those rights against another.[14]

8.09 This may indicate that there is a distinction between inaction by the mortgagee, which will not affect his rights, such as a failure to take adequate precautions to prevent theft of the deeds, and an act, such as handing the deeds to the mortgagor, which will result in deferral to the rights of the first later incumbrancer (because of the representation to him implicit in the action) and also to subsequent incumbrancers because of his breach of his obligation in relation to his custodianship of the deeds. If a mortgage of a legal estate in land is not protected by deposit of the title deeds from the beginning it is registrable and obtains priority under the rules applicable to that system. If deeds are retained but later given up it is unclear whether the mortgage then becomes registrable (and can be rescued from vulnerability to later dispositions by registration after creation) or remains outside the system and subject to later incumbrances created by the mortgagor on the basis of either the grant of apparent authority by the mortgagee or some other culpable failure of the mortgagee to retain custody of the deeds.[15]

8.10 The importance of the act of a person with a prior claim on goods in entrusting the goods or documents representing them to another before he loses priority is underlined by the House of Lords decision in *National Employers Mutual Association v Jones*.[16] In that case the issue was the interpretation of ss 2 and 9 of the Factors Act 1889 and ss 24 and 25(1) of the Sale of Goods Act 1979. Those provisions were held to operate as exceptions to the *nemo dat* rule conferring title on a *bona fide* purchaser only when the true owner entrusts the goods or documents to a factor or buyer. If the goods were stolen from the true owner his title is not defeated by the claim of a later purchaser in good faith from another party. The statutory exceptions to the maxim *nemo dat quod non habet* depend on an act of the person with the original title and can only divest him of his title on that basis.

Notice outside registration systems

8.11 The relationship between legal and equitable interests under the pre-1925 real property law was governed by notice because an equitable interest

13 *Ibid* per Fry LJ at 491–492 and 494.
14 *Moorgate Mercantile Co v Twitchings* [1977] AC 890 per Lord Fraser of Tullybelton at 925–926.
15 See Land Charges Act 1925 s 2(1) and (4).
16 [1988] 2 WLR 952.

was good against anyone other than a *bona fide* purchaser of the legal estate for value without notice of the equitable interest. For this purpose the courts had to develop the concept of notice in order to define the degree of security enjoyed by equitable interests. It is this doctrine which determines the priorities between a legal mortgage and a later equitable mortgage of the same legal estate. However, in relation to land the reforms of 1925 substituted the fact of registration or non-registration for the concept of notice in relation to interests which are registrable.[17] As against subsequent encumbrances (legal or equitable) an equitable mortgage not protected by deposit of title deeds is secure so long as it is registered. As between mortgages of a legal estate in land which are not protected by deposit of title deeds, the ranking is in order of registration—legal and equitable mortgages all have their priorities determined on that basis and questions of notice are irrelevant.

8.12   However, mortgages of land protected by deposit of title deeds (not being registrable) are not subject to the rule that priorities are determined by order of registration and their priorities depend on date of creation and other pre-1926 rules. If a first legal mortgage and a second equitable mortgage compete, loss of priority for the legal mortgage can only come about because of the behaviour of the legal mortgagee since, subject to that, the priority of his mortgage is secured by being first in time and by taking a legal mortgage.[18] However, where the first mortgage is equitable and the second is legal, the priority of the legal mortgage depends on the second mortgagee having no notice of the earlier equitable mortgage. If the earlier equitable mortgage were registrable and unregistered no later purchaser could be prejudicially affected by notice of it.[19] If it were registrable and registered, the registration of it would constitute actual notice to all persons for all purposes connected with the land from the date of registration.[20] Where the earlier mortgage is not registrable, recourse must be had to the definitions of actual, constructive and imputed notice developed by the courts. In the case of mortgages of property other than land which are not covered by a registration system affecting notice, those concepts will be of more widespread importance in making decisions about the priority ranking of legal and equitable mortgages than they are in the case of land. However, the extensive scope of the doctrine of constructive notice will not apply in cases where commercial practice prevents a thorough investigation of title.[21]

17   LPA 1925 ss 198 and 199.
18   For fraud, gross negligence and the grant of apparent authority to the mortgagor see para 8.06 *supra.*
19   LPA 1925 s 199 and s 4(5) of Land Charges Act 1923 make it void against a purchaser.
20   LPA 1925 s 198(1).
21   See paras 8.14–8.17 *infra.*

Actual notice

8.13   Actual notice is knowledge. The question of whether a later mortgagee has actual notice of an earlier incumbrance is one of fact. Although the source of the knowledge which constitutes actual notice can be oral or written,[22] it would seem that it must be given by a person interested in the property[23] and for the purpose of actual notice, as opposed to constructive notice, suspicious circumstances are not enough. There must be evidence of notice as such.[24] Registration of a document or matter under the Land Charges Act 1972 is deemed to constitute actual notice.[25] Although there may be practical or evidential problems about ascertaining a person's state of knowledge, there are few difficulties with the concept of actual notice itself.

Constructive notice

8.14   The courts of equity extended the concept of notice beyond the state of knowledge of the purchaser for value of the legal estate, as a failure to do so would have undermined the security of equitable interests by encouraging such purchasers to avoid actual notice by refraining from inquiry. It seems, however, that the doctrine will not be applied with the same rigour to transactions of a commercial nature dealing with property other than land. Constructive notice is that knowledge which a person is irrebuttably presumed to have because he would have had it had he made such inquiries and inspections as he ought reasonably to have made.[26] It may arise from his actual knowledge of something which should have caused him to make further inquiries or from his wilful abstention from inquiry to avoid notice. Negligence is sufficient to cause the doctrine to apply and the standard applied is that of the inference to be drawn by an impartial person from the facts available to the person concerned.

8.15   The usual inquiries which a purchaser would make into the mortgagor's title and each link in it are demanded and failure to make them will not prevent constructive notice of anything which they would have revealed to a professional person who made them; irrespective of whether the mortgagee was such a person or not.[27] This establishes that the test is based on the usual practice of conveyancers. Actual notice of the existence of a deed which necessarily affects title, is notice of its contents although where the deed does not necessarily have that effect only fraud or gross negligence in failing to ascertain its import will result in constructive notice

---

22   *Browne v Savage* (1859) 4 Drew 635.
23   *Barnhart v Greenshields* (1853) 9 Moo PC at 36.
24   *West v Reid* (1843) 2 Hare 249.
25   LPA s 198.
26   LPA 1925 s 199(1)(ii)(a) and *Hunt v Luck* [1902] 1 Ch 428.
27   *Berwick & Co v Price* [1905] 1 Ch 632.

of its contents.[28] The recitals of or references to important transactions contained in a deed of which a mortgagee has notice may lead to the imputation of notice of details of those transactions if normal inquiries would have revealed them.[29] These rules are peculiarly applicable to land where the practice of an extensive investigation of title is well established. In the case of other forms of property there will be less scope for the doctrine of constructive notice.[30] Observations to the effect that the doctrine will be used less extensively in commercial cases involving assets other than land are to be found in a number of cases.

8.16　In *English & Scottish Mercantile Investment Co v Brunton*[31] both Lord Esher MR and Bowen LJ emphasised the distinction between deeds relating to land and the debenture giving securities over a company's debt which concerned them in that case. They also emphasised the limits which the courts of equity had begun to impose on the extent of the doctrine, in the mid-nineteenth century, even in relation to land.[32] It was an exchange between the parties to the transaction which was decisive in that case—not a finding as to constructive notice. The reason for this approach of the courts was put well by Lindley LJ in *Manchester Trust v Furness:*[33]

> "In dealing with estates in land title is everything, and it can be leisurely investigated; in commercial transactions possession is everything, and there is no time to investigate title; and if we were to extend the doctrine of constructive notice to commercial transactions we should be doing infinite mischief and paralysing the trade of the country."

8.17　Since the case law on constructive notice is based on conveyancing practice—real or ideal—it is submitted that the approach of the courts to these issues in other contexts should depend on the process of investigation that might be expected in the situation in question. This should be decided on the basis of the nature of the transaction, the parties to it and the usual practice. A financier or banker lending to a company might be expected to inspect the companies register but a purchaser of goods in the ordinary course of business would not be subject to the same assumption.[34] In practice the registration systems applicable to some forms of property have drastically reduced the importance of the doctrine of notice by providing

---

28　*Jones v Smith* (1843) 1 Ph 244, and see *West v Reid* (1843) 2 Hare 249.
29　See *Malpas v Ackland* (1827) 3 Russ 273.
30　See R M Goode, *Legal Problems of Credit and Security*, pp 774–776.
31　[1892] 2 QB 700.
32　*Ibid* at pp 708 and 711, and 713 respectively.
33　[1895] 2 QB 539 at 545, and see Rigby LJ at 549 and Lopes LJ at 547. See also *Eagle Star Insurance Co Ltd v Spratt* [1971] 2 Lloyds Rep 116 and *Feuer Leather Corporation v Frank Johnstone & Sons* [1981] CLR 251.
34　See R M Goode, *op cit* p 775.

that registration amounts to notice and non-registration to its absence. Other forms of notice thus become irrelevant.[35]

Imputed notice

8.18   In addition to the actual or constructive notice which the mortgagee himself possesses, he is treated as having notice which his agent acquired in the course of the same transaction.[36] This notice is imputed to him. Either actual or constructive notice to the mortgagee's agent will provide notice to the mortgagee. However, matters known to the agent but which the agent has no duty to communicate to the mortgagee, or which it is not relevant for him to know, will not affect the mortgagee with notice,[37] and where the agent is involved in a fraud in a transaction which he effects and this makes it certain that he would conceal certain information, notice will not be imputed to the principal.[38] In practice, these rules give the client the constructive and actual notice available to the solicitor who acts for him, providing the notice is obtained by the solicitor in the same transaction. In relation to property other than land it is unlikely that a solicitor will be employed to investigate title but, in principle, notice to an agent will affect the principal.

Tacking further advances

8.19   The concept of 'tacking' enables a mortgagee to obtain a higher level of priority than he would otherwise have. Before 1925 the doctrine of *tabula in naufragio* allowed an equitable mortgagee who, at the time of making his advance had no notice of an earlier equitable mortgage to obtain priority over it by getting in the legal estate. If property was subject to a legal mortgage and two later equitable mortgages, a purchase of the interest of the legal mortgagee by the second of the two equitable mortgagees would enable him to gain priority over the earlier equitable mortgage so long as he had no notice of it at the time of making his advance. This application of the superiority of the legal estate was abolished by s 94 of the Law of Property Act 1925. However, the ability to tack further advances, made by a mortgagee with priority so that they achieve the same priority as the original advance and defeat the priority otherwise obtained by an intervening mortgage, remains. The rule, which now applies to all property operates regardless of whether the mortgages in question are legal or equitable.[39] A mortgagee may tack a further advance to gain priority over

---

35   See paras 8.97 *et seq infra*.
36   LPA 1925 s 199(1)(ii)(b).
37   *Wyllie v Pollen* (1863) 32 LJ Ch 782.
38   *Kennedy v Green* (1834) 3 Myl & K 699; *Cave v Cave* (1880) 15 Ch D 639.
39   LPA 1925 s 94(1). Section 30 of the Land Registration Act 1925 provides a similar system in the case of registered land.

subsequent mortgages (but not other interests) in three cases. In the context of determining the liability of a guarantor the expression 'further advances' has been construed as excluding the extension of the term allowed for the repayment of an amount due.[40] The same interpretation may apply for the purpose of tacking. The three cases are as follows.

Agreement between mortgagees

8.20   If agreement is reached between the earlier mortgagee and the holder of the subsequent mortgage to permit tacking then the priorities will be affected in accordance with it. This might occur if the later mortgagee is unwilling to lend more to the mortgagor despite the fact that the use to which the money advanced will be put will increase the value of the security. It will then be in the interest of the later mortgagee to agree to subordinate his security to that of the first mortgagee who makes the advance.[41]

Absence of notice

8.21   If the further advance by the earlier mortgagee is made without notice of the existence of a mortgage created after the first advance was made then that advance is 'tacked' to give the earlier mortgagee priority in respect of it.[42] The question of what will amount to notice depends on the registration system which applies to the mortgaged property and on whether the earlier mortgage was expressed to secure further advances. If the mortgage does expressly secure such advances (even if it does not oblige the mortgagee to make them) the registration (in the case of land) of the second mortgage as a land charge will not in itself amount to notice unless it was so registered before the last search made by the earlier mortgagee.[43]

8.22   Actual, constructive or imputed notice is required before tacking is prevented. Such doctrines will also apply in any case in which the later mortgage of land was not registrable because it was protected by deposit of title deeds. However, in a case in which the later mortgage is registered and the first one does not expressly secure further advances, registration will have its usual effect of constituting actual notice to the first mortgagee of the existence of the later mortgage. If an earlier mortgage secures further advances it is important that a later mortgagee gives actual notice of his interest to the person holding the earlier mortgage. The rationale for the exception to the usual rules about notice is that it is unreasonable to expect a lender whose security covers further advances (for example, a bank which has secured a loan by way of overdraft) to search the register before making

40   *Burnes v Trade Credits* [1981] 1 WLR 805.
41   See Megarry and Wade, *The Law of Real Property* 4th ed p 982.
42   LPA 1925 s 94(1)(b).
43   *Ibid* s 94(2).

the agreed further advances. However, it is important to note that tacking can only apply as between existing mortgages and in relation to further advances. A search before the initial advance is necessary as mortgages registered before the creation of the one on which an advance is to be made are protected.[44] Notice of a later mortgage to an earlier mortgagee gives the former priority in relation to all later advances—even if the earlier mortgagee has made no advance at the time when notice was served.[45] Bank lenders may also be affected by the rule in *Clayton's case*[46] in this context. This has the effect that any money paid into an account by the debtor is taken to clear the earliest outstanding advance. Unless the old account is closed and a new account is opened, as soon as notice of a later mortgage is received payments into the account reduce the indebtedness as to which there is priority over the later mortgage while further advances are subordinated to it.

Obligation to make further advances
8.23   Where a mortgage obliges a mortgagee to make further advances to the mortgagor, then such advances can be tacked regardless of whether notice of a later mortgage (whether actual, constructive, imputed or by virtue of registration) is received by the earlier mortgagee.[47] Where there is a clear enforceable duty to lend further amounts the mortgagee subject to it is secure against later mortgages regardless of his state of knowledge about them.

Tacking and registered land
8.24   The rules on tacking further advances described above will apply in the case of a series of registered charges and protection is conferred on the earlier mortgagee by s 30 of the Land Registration Act 1925. This lays down that the land registry must serve notice by registered post on the proprietor of a registered charge which secures further advances of any intended entry on the register which would prejudice the priority of further advances to be made. The priority of the charge which secures further advances will not be affected by the entry in respect of such advances which were made before the date on which the notice ought to have been received in the due course of post.[48] Any loss to the earlier chargor in relation to the advance because of a failure of the Post Office or the registry can be indemnified from registry funds as if an error had been made on the register unless the loss was caused by the chargor's failure to register a change of address or to register the

---

44   *Ibid.*
45   *Hopkinson v Rolt* (1861) 9 HL Cas 514, and see Goode, *op cit* pp 766–767 and Megarry and Wade, *op cit* p 984.
46   *Devaynes v Noble* (1816) 1 Mer 572.
47   LPA 1925 s 94(1)(c).
48   Land Registration Act 1925 s 30(1).

correct address in the first place.[49] In cases in which a charge obliges its proprietor to make further advances this fact will be noted on the register and all later charges take effect subject to such further advances.[50]

REGISTRATION OF COMPANY CHARGES[51]

The Companies Act 1989 substitutes new provisions for the registration of company charges into the Companies Act 1985. Paras 8.61–8.76 deal with the major changes introduced by the Act. In other respects the new provisions do not change the previous law which is considered first.

Registrable charges

8.25 Section 395(1) of the Companies Act 1985 requires that the charges listed in s 396(1) be registered with the Registrar of Companies. A charge for this purpose includes a mortgage[52] but a security obtained by operation of law is not a 'charge' for this purpose. Liens are excluded.[53] The requirement in s 395 is additional to the need to register a charge or mortgage under any other registration system which applies to a particular type of asset. If a company acquires property that is already subject to a charge which would have been registrable under s 395 had it been granted by the company, particulars of it must be notified to the Registrar of Companies. However, failure to do so does not affect the priority or validity of the charge although the company can be fined for failing to submit particulars.[54] A company must also keep a register of charges at its registered office. This applies to all fixed and floating charges over its property but failure to register a charge in this register results in a fine and does not affect priority.[55] A copy of the instrument creating a registrable charge must also be kept there and the instruments and register are open to inspection, free of charge, by members and creditors and, for a small fee, by others.[56] A memorandum of satisfaction indicating that a registrable charge has been discharged is also registrable.[57] The charges to which s 395 applies are dealt with in order.

49 *Ibid* s 30(2).
50 *Ibid* s 30(3).
51 See generally W J Gough, "Company Charges", Butterworth 1978 for an authoritative treatment of this area.
52 Companies Act 1985 s 396(4).
53 *Brunton v Electrical Engineering Co* [1892] 1 Ch 434.
54 Companies Act 1985 s 400.
55 *Ibid* s 407.
56 *Ibid* s 408.
57 *Ibid* s 403.

Debentures

8.26   "(a) A charge for securing any issue of debentures." This category will frequently overlap in practice with the category of floating charges or of fixed charges over particular categories of company assets, although the holding of debentures entitling the creditor to a charge on land is not deemed to be an interest in land for the purpose of the section.[58] The word debenture does not have any precise technical legal meaning. It has been said to be a document which creates a debt or acknowledges it, although not all documents with such characteristics will necessarily be debentures.[59] A document called by some other name which in fact acknowledges a debt may be a debenture, even if it is not secured by a charge[60] and a failure to stipulate the exact amount of the debt at the date of the creation of the document will not prevent a document from being a debenture.[61] Debentures can be issued singly or as part of a series.[62]

8.27   This gives rise to the question whether s 396(1) applies to a single debenture. The use of the wording 'for the purpose of securing any issue of debentures' would seem to imply a series of more than one debenture. However, since single debentures are in practice likely to be issued to bank lenders, who will ensure that the debenture is secured by a floating charge and, usually, a fixed charge over assets subject to the requirement of registration, there will be few circumstances in which a debenture will not be registrable. A series of debentures will also usually be secured by charges over assets which are dealt with in s 396(1) or by a floating charge. Section 396(1)(a) is only likely to apply to the rare case of a series of debentures secured only by a fixed charge over assets not referred to elsewhere in the subsection. Where a series of debentures is secured by a charge to which the debenture holders are entitled *pari passu*, the requirements to be submitted to the registrar are limited to the total amount secured by all the debentures in the series, the dates of resolutions authorising the issue and of a document creating the charge, a general description of the property charged and the names of the trustees for the debenture holders. The document creating the charge or, if there is no separate deed, a sample of the debenture from the series secured, must be filed within 21 days of the execution of the deed or of the execution of the debentures in the series. A failure to meet the requirement to send the registrar details of the date and the amount of each debenture issued in the series will not affect the validity of the debentures.[63]

---

58   *Ibid* s 396(3).
59   *Levy v Abercorris Slate & Slab Co* (1887) 37 Ch D 26; but contrast *Topham v Greenside Co* (1888) 37 Ch D 281.
60   *Lemon v Austin Friars Investment Trust* [1926] 1 Ch 1.
61   *NV Slavenberg's Bank v Intercontinental Resources* [1980] 1 All ER 955.
62   *Edmonds v Blaina Furnaces Co* (1887) 36 Ch D 215.
63   Companies Act 1985 s 397(1) and *Re Spiral Globe Co (No 2)* [1902] 2 Ch 209.

Uncalled share capital
8.28 "(b) a charge on the uncalled share capital of the company." This category of charge is limited to those over the company's own uncalled share capital. One of the omissions from the registration requirement is a fixed charge granted by the company over shares which it holds in another company. This results from the drafting of the section which lists registrable charges by reference to specific assets over which they operate or, in the case of debentures and floating charges the nature of the debt secured or the charge. A floating charge over shares in another company held by the debtor, or a charge over shares in another company which secures a debenture are registrable. The decline in the number of companies issuing shares partly paid makes charges over a company's uncalled share capital rare.

Bills of sale
8.29 "(c) a charge created or evidenced by an instrument which, if executed by an individual would require registration as a bill of sale." The Bills of Sale Acts 1878 and 1882 do not apply to mortgage bills of sale created by companies,[64] although the 1878 Act does apply to absolute bills issued by companies.[65] The requirement to register, like the Bills of Sale Acts 1878 to 1882, applies only to documents and not to transactions. A bill of sale is a mortgage or charge on personal chattels. This includes goods and other articles capable of transfer by delivery but not shares in companies or choses in action.[66] Any document creating a charge over goods or other tangible personal property will be registrable subject to certain exceptions. A pledge is not registrable and a creditor whose debt is secured by possession of the goods and not solely by a charge created by the document need not register the document as it is not a bill of sale.[67] However, possession of the goods must be delivered to the pledgee, or a bailee must attorn to him—it is not enough that a document is delivered to the pledgee unless that document is a document of title, possession of which is regarded as amounting to possession of the goods.[68]

8.30 There are exceptions which allow the transmission of a document letting the holder obtain possession of goods, such as a warehouse warrant, to transfer possession for the purposes of a pledge in the case of a pledge by a mercantile agent or by a buyer in possession under the Sale of Goods Act 1979.[69] If a document does create a charge on goods, it will be registrable as

---

64 *Re Standard Manufacturing Co* [1891] 1 Ch 627.
65 *Re Cunningham & Co Ltd, Attenborough's Case* (1885) 28 Ch D 682.
66 Bills of Sale Act 1878 s 34.
67 *Re Hall ex parte Close* (1884) 14 QBD 386.
68 *Official Assignee of Madras v Mercantile Bank of India Ltd* [1935] AC 53 at 58–60—a bill of lading falls into this class, and see paras 3.10–3.15.
69 Factors Act 1889 s 3 and Sale of Goods Act 1979 s 25(2).

a bill of sale despite being handed to the creditor simultaneously with a document which enables him to obtain possession if the latter does not actually transfer possession of the goods.[70] The test is whether the document creates a charge, or merely represents the goods for the purpose of giving possession of them to the creditor.

8.31 In addition to the exception for a pledge of goods, the Bills of Sale Act 1878 s 4 lays down a statutory rule excluding from the definition of a bill of sale documents used in the ordinary course of business to prove the possession or control of goods. Similarly, a document charging imported goods or creating trusts of them executed before their deposit in a warehouse, factory or store or their being reshipped for export or delivered to a purchaser, is exempt.[71] A trust receipt which continues a previous pledge while the debtor has possession of the goods for a defined purpose such as sale is not registrable.[72] The s 4 exception will extend to a letter of lien or a hypothecation on the basis of its status as a document which is used in the ordinary course of business as proof of the possession or control of goods.[73]

8.32 A transaction whereby goods are sold by a company and repurchased on hire purchase may be regarded as a grant of a security interest, over the goods, by the company if that is seen by the courts as the substance of the transaction.[74] However, so long as one party to the transaction regarded it as a genuine sale and rehiring, the fact that the total payable under the hire-purchase agreement is equal to the sale price with interest will not make the document containing the agreement registrable under this heading.[75] A charge on a share in a racehorse has been held to be a charge on a chose in action rather than a chattel and not to be registrable under this or any other category.[76]

Land
8.33 "(d) A charge on land (wherever situated) or any interest in it but not including a charge for any rent or other periodical sum issuing out of the land." This category includes a charge or mortgage of a legal or equitable interest in land and it includes a charge by way of equitable mortgage created by deposit of title deeds—even if no document exists and the charge

70 *Dublin City Distillery Ltd v Doherty* [1914] AC 823.
71 Bills of Sale Act 1890 s 1 so long as the goods are identified—*Slavenburg's Bank NV v Intercontinental National Resources Ltd* [1980] 1 All ER 955.
72 *Re David Allcester Ltd* [1922] 2 Ch 211.
73 *Re Hamilton Young & Co ex parte Carter* [1905] 2 KB 772.
74 *Yorkshire Railway Wagon Co v Maclure* (1882) 21 Ch D 309.
75 *Stoneleigh Finance Ltd v Phillips* [1965] 2 QB 537.
76 *Re Sugar Properties (Derisley Wood) Ltd* [1988] BCLC 146.

arises by presumption from the deposit. Such a transaction is categorised as a consensual security and not merely a lien on the documents deposited.[77] If a company's land is subject to an unpaid vendor's lien, that claim will not be registrable, as it is a security arising by operation of law. However, if a mortgage is granted by the company as security for payment and the lien is extinguished, the mortgage must be registered and, if it is not, the vendor is unable to rely on the extinguished lien.[78] A sub-mortgage by a company of a charge secured on land must be registered under this paragraph.[79] In addition to registration under this provision, a mortgage or charge of the company's land will need to be registered under the Land Charges Act 1972 if the land is unregistered and the mortgage is not protected by a deposit of the title deeds. In the case of registered land the mortgage will require registration as a registered charge or protection by caution or notice if it is not in that form. A floating charge is exempt from registration under the Land Charges Act 1972,[80] protection being available if it is registered under the Companies Act 1985. This protection continues to suffice after crystallisation, as the security is the same. However, the appointment of a receiver by court order should be registered under the Land Charges Act 1972 as a writ or order affecting the land.[81]

8.34   In the case of registered land, registration of fixed charges is required under Land Registration Act 1925 as a registered charge or by way of caution or notice if the mortgage is created by the methods applicable to unregistered land.[82] A floating charge can be protected by a notice or caution which will show that it is a floating charge.[83] If later fixed mortgages are prohibited by the document granting the floating charge, this may be specified on the notice or a restriction may be entered to that effect on the land register.[84] However, the fact that the system of land registration operates against land and not owners makes it difficult to ensure that entries are made to protect a floating charge every time land is bought by the company. The best that can be done is to use a covenant in the charge document to oblige the company to notify the chargee of all dealings in land and to facilitate the registration of the charge. This will not in itself give priority to the chargee over later mortgagees or chargees although it could be made an event giving rise to automatic crystallisation.

77   *Re Wallis and Simmonds (Builders) Ltd* [1974] 1 All ER 561.
78   *Capital Finance Co v Stokes* [1968] 3 All ER 625; *London & Cheshire Insurance Co Ltd v Laplagrene Property Co Ltd* [1971] Ch 499.
79   *Re Molton Finance Ltd* [1968] Ch 325.
80   s 3(7) and (8), and see *Property Discount Corporation v Lyon Group Ltd* [1981] 1 WLR 300 CA.
81   Land Charges Act 1972 s 6(1)(b), and see Pennington, "Company Law" 4th ed p 345.
82   See para 8.108 *infra*.
83   Land Registration Act 1925 ss 49(1)(c), 54(1) and 59(2).
84   *Ibid* s 58(1).

That, however, may not assist the chargee against a later mortgagee unaware of the facts.[85]

Book debts

8.35 "(e) A charge on the book debts of the company." This is one form of a charge on a chose in action. A book debt is one owed to the company and arising out of carrying-out its business.[86] A charge will only require registration under this head if its subject matter is a book debt at the time of the charge being granted. A charge over an insurance policy covering export credit is not registrable even if a claim later arises because at the date of the charge the company's right under the policy was contingent.[87] However, payments due to a company under a sale agreement that were contingent on the size of the reserves in a gravel mine sold by the company have been held to be book debts on the basis of expert evidence of the treatment of entries relating to them.[88]

8.36 Where a company receives a negotiable instrument in payment of its book debts the deposit of the instrument to secure an advance will not amount to a charge on the book debts.[89] On the other hand, where a company's receivables are used as security for a loan the transaction will require registration.[90] However, a sale of receivables to a factor or other person will not be registrable as the receivables are not used as security in law and this is true whether or not the purchaser has recourse against the vendor in respect of unpaid debts.[91] A right of retention given to a purchaser of receivables as a form of security for the payment by the vendor of the book debts of amounts due under the agreement is not a 'charge' if the amount retained is taken into account in calculating the balance due. It is not possible conceptually for a right given in favour of a debtor over his own indebtedness to be a charge.[92]

8.37 If a trust receipt is used to allow a pledgor company to sell pledged goods so that the proceeds of sale are to be paid to the pledgee, this does not amount to a charge on the proceeds of sale but merely a continuation of the pledge and so the transaction is not registrable as a charge on book debts.[93] If, however, a charge on goods or proceeds of sale is created after the goods

85   See Pennington, *op cit* pp 436–437 on which this section is based.
86   *Shipley v Marshall* (1863) 14 CB NS 566 and see para 4.38 *supra*.
87   *Paul & Frank Ltd v Discount Bank (Overseas) Ltd* [1967] Ch 348.
88   *Re Brush Aggregates Ltd* [1983] BCLC 320.
89   Companies Act 1985 s 396(2).
90   *Re Kent and Sussex Sawmills Ltd* [1947] Ch 177.
91   *Olds Discount Co Ltd v John Playfair Ltd* [1938] 3 All ER 275 and *Lloyds and Scottish Finance Ltd v Prentice* (1977) 121 Sol Jo 847.
92   *Re Charge Card Service Ltd (No 2)* [1987] BCLC 17—a point that did not arise on appeal at [1988] 3 All ER 702.
93   *Re David Allcester Ltd* [1922] 2 Ch 211.

have in fact been sold by the chargor then the transaction is a charge of a book debt and is registrable as such, *if* the lender was aware of the sale.[94] In the case of a successful attempt by a vendor to retain title to goods and to have a right to the proceeds of sale received by the purchaser, no asset belonging to the company is ever charged as both goods and book debt belong to the vendor.[95] The failure of such an attempt is likely to result in a charge registrable as a floating charge. However, a charge on book debts may be created in such a case.[96] In the controversial case of *Re Welsh Irish Ferries*[97] it was held that a lien on subfreights created by a company under a time charter of a ship in favour of the ship owner was registrable as an equitable charge on a book debt and that a charge over such assets created at a time when they did not exist was registrable as a floating charge. This decision is explicitly reversed by the Companies Act 1989 as it flew in the face of longstanding commercial practice and created considerable uncertainty and difficulty.

Floating charges

8.38   "(f) A floating charge on the company's undertaking or property." The concept, and priority of a floating charge are dealt with in detail elsewhere.[98] The wording of this paragraph of s 396(1) shows that a floating charge over the whole of the company's undertaking or any part of its property must be registered. Floating charges limited to particular classes of asset are registrable.[99] If the company is given power in the charge document to substitute other property as security with the chargor's consent, then a charge on the new property need not be registered as it is subject to the charge already registered.[100] In any other case, the charge over additional or substituted property must be registered.[101]

Calls made

8.39   "(g) A charge on calls made but not paid." This provision complements s 396(1)(b) by requiring the registration of a charge on a company's own share capital which is not uncalled but not yet paid. This presumably includes the instalments due as part of the issue price of shares which are not strictly subject to a call. If it did not do so an unfortunate gap in the registration requirements would be revealed.[102]

---

94   *Ladenbury Co v Goodwin Ferreira & Co* [1912] 3 KB 275.
95   *Aluminium Industrie Vaasen BV v Romalpa Aluminium Ltd* [1976] 1 WLR 676.
96   See paras 9.26ff and see *Pfeiffer v Arbuthnot Factors* [1987] BCLC 522 and *Tatung (UK) Ltd v Galex Telesure Ltd* (1989) 5 BCC 325.
97   [1986] Ch 471 and see *Annangel Glory Compania SA v Goldetz* (1988) PCC 37.
98   See Ch 5 and paras 8.77–8.96, and see *Re Welsh Irish Ferries, supra.*
99   *Mercantile Bank of India v Chartered Bank of India, Australia and China* [1938] AC 278.
100 *Cunard SS Co Ltd v Hopwood* [1908] 2 Ch 564.
101 *Hoare v British Columbia Development Association* [1912] WN 235.
102 See Pennington, *op cit* p 421 n 1.

Ships and aircraft

8.40 "(h) A charge on a ship, aircraft or any share in a ship." The registration requirements for these assets have been dealt with above.[103] It is, however, essential that mortgages or charges of such property should be registered in the Companies Registry as failure to do so will have the effects described below despite the fact of registration in the register at a ship's port of registry or the register of aircraft mortgages.

Goodwill and intellectual property

8.41 "(j) A charge on goodwill; on a patent or a licence under a patent, on a trademark or on a copyright or a licence under a copyright." Mortgages and charges of patents, trademarks or registered designs have already been dealt with.[104] As for a patent, the requirement of actual knowledge of an earlier mortgage not registered in the Patent Register means that registration of such a mortgage in the Companies Registry will only provide protection against a later mortgagee or other holder of property in the patent if the latter has in fact searched the Companies Register and discovered the earlier mortgage.[105] A floating charge which was secured on a patent, trademark or design would have to be registered against each asset of that kind owned by the company or later acquired by it.[106] As with other types of property the requirement of registration in the Companies Registry is additional to the registration requirement applicable to the assets under the general law and failure to register under s 395 will have its detrimental effect on the mortgagee's priority.

Effect of failure to register

8.42 Section 395 provides that a failure to register a charge at the Companies Registry results in any security which it confers over the company's property or undertaking being avoided against the liquidator and any creditor of the company. This invalidity applies even in a solvent liquidation.[107] This applies if there is no registration within the 21 days from the date of creation of the charge laid down by the section. The court does, however, have power to extend the period.[108] It is only a failure to register under s 395 has this effect on the charge's priority. Failure to register under s 407 in the company's own register of charges and a failure to send particulars to the registrar of an existing charge over property acquired by a company under s 400 do not have this effect.

---

103 Paras 3.17–3.28.
104 See paras 4.58–4.67.
105 Patents Act 1977 s 33(2) and (3) and *Wilson v Kelland* [1910] 2 Ch 306.
106 Pennington, *op cit* p 437.
107 *Re Oriel Ltd* [1984] BCLC 241—a point not raised on appeal at [1985] BCLC 343; [1986] 1 WLR 180.
108 s 404 and paras 8.55ff *infra*.

8.43   It is possible for either the company or the chargee to register the charge and, as it is the chargee who is most likely to lose as a result of failure to do so, it is common for him to ensure that the charge is registered although the statutory duty to do so is imposed on the company.[109]

8.44   The effect of non-registration is limited. The obligation to pay the money secured by the charge remains as between company and chargee and is accelerated so that the whole of the money immediately falls due when the charge becomes void.[110] The charge itself remains valid as security against the company and enforcement by sale or foreclosure by the chargee against the property charged before the company goes into liquidation or administration confers good title on the purchaser or mortgagee as against the liquidator or administrator as they are owners of the property and not the holders of an unregistered charge.[111]

8.45   Despite the wording of the Act, it is not against all creditors that an unregistered charge is void. While a company is not in liquidation or subject to an administration order only those holding a security interest that enables them to prevent the company from disposing of its assets are able to prevent the payment by the company of the amount secured by the charge or enforcement of the security by the chargee against the company's property. This reflects the absence of any right over the company's property in an unsecured creditor before liquidation or administration commences.[112]

8.46   However, those against whom the charge is void include both consensual security holders and lienees or other whose security is conferred by law. An execution creditor whose execution is completed can contend that an unregistered charge is void. For this purpose a charge is imposed on property when a writ of *fieri facias* in the High Court is delivered to the sheriff, or a warrant of execution in the County Court is applied for, or a charging order or garnishee order is made.[113] It seems that, at this point, such a creditor obtains priority over an unregistered charge although as against a liquidator the execution by *fieri facias* or garnishee must have been fully completed by seizure and sale or payment of the debt respectively before the execution creditor can retain property.[114] Similarly, the holder

109   s 399.
110   s 395(2).
111   *Independent Automatic Sales Ltd v Knowles and Foster* [1962] 3 All ER 27 and *Row Dal Constructions Proprietary Ltd* [1966] VR 249; and see Pennington *op cit* p 425.
112   *Re Ehrman Bros Ltd* [1906] 2 Ch 697; *Re Cardiff Workmen's Cottage Co Ltd* [1906] 2 Ch 627. As to administration, s 395 as amended makes the charge void against the administrator.
113   Supreme Court Act 1981 s 138 and Sch 7, and RSC O 49.
114   Insolvency Act 1986 s 183.

of a possessory lien over property, or a vendor taking advantage of the lien available because he was unpaid, will take free of an unregistered charge.

8.47   Where a later registered mortgage or charge is created it will take priority over the earlier unregistered charge by virtue of s 395, despite actual knowledge on the part of the later mortgagee of the existence of the earlier charge.[115] If an earlier charge is registered and the later one unregistered then, *a fortiori*, the former will have priority. If two charges are registered, then the main significance of the registration procedure under the Companies Act 1985 will be that registration constitutes constructive notice of the existence of a mortgage[116] and consequently, when that determines priority, the earlier mortgage or charge will gain priority. A later legal mortgagee will have notice of an earlier equitable mortgage registered under s 395. However, this registration system does not lay down that priority is determined by date of registration and its effect will vary according to the priority rules applicable to the particular asset involved and the rules derived from any other registration system under which the security also needs to be registered.

8.48   Where a second mortgage is created before the first mortgage is registered but both are properly registered within 21 days of creation then there will be no constructive notice and the company registration system can have no positive effect on priorities which will be wholly governed by the rules governing the asset in question.

8.49   As between two unregistered charges, the priority position is uncertain. It can be argued that each is void as against the other as s 395(1) specifies that a charge is void against 'any creditor' and since an unregistered charge retains its owner's security right over the property charged as against the company, each chargee is a 'creditor' within the meaning of that section as neither is an unsecured creditor.[117] However, it has also been suggested that since the first charge is void for want of registration, the order of ranking is reversed and the later charge has priority as between the two. A further possible solution is that the general law will apply to determine priorities in this situation and that the company registration system has no effect. If the interpretation of the Act is to resolve the difficulty, it would seem that Professor Pennington's solution is more satisfactory as each chargee is undeniably a creditor within the meaning given to the section by the courts.

8.50   This emphasis on the status of a person as a 'creditor' at the time of

---

115   *Re Monolithic Building Co* [1915] 1 Ch 643.
116   *Wilson v Kelland* [1910] 2 Ch 306.
117   Pennington *op cit* p 430.

the priority dispute is surely the answer to Professor Goode's concern that this solution implies an inappropriate effect of registration on prior parties.[118] The suggestion implicit in this solution that 'creditor' means 'in the context . . . secured creditor other than a registered secured creditor'[119] is surely reasonable, since such a creditor does retain his status of security as against the company. Those whose interests arise by operation of law and do not require registration fall within the class of 'creditor' and this would seem to imply that the actual notice provided by registration is not regarded as vital for this purpose.

Rectification and registration out of time

8.51   An omission or misstatement of any particular can be rectified on application to the court if the defect was inadvertent, accidental or the result of some other sufficient cause. A failure to register a charge within the 21 day time limit may also be corrected by order of the court. This relief can be granted so long as the error or omission is not of a nature to prejudice the position of creditors or shareholders of the company or on the grounds that it is just and equitable to grant relief.[120]

8.52   Rectification or an extension of the time available for registration can be granted by the court on such terms as it considers just and expedient.[121] This will normally be granted before a winding up commences but not when it is imminent or has begun, as rights will crystallise at that point.[122] However, in a case in which the failure to register was the result of a breach of duty by the chargee's solicitor and the application to register late was made promptly after discovery of the omission, an extension was granted on the basis that it was just and equitable despite the imminence of liquidation.[123] Similarly the fact that unsecured creditors will be unpaid in the liquidation in any event and that the dispute is purely between two secured creditors may justify an extension despite a liquidation but this is done strictly on the basis that the unsecured creditors cannot be prejudiced.[124] In the case of an extension of the time for registration the order does not amount to registration. Only actual registration in accordance with the order protects the chargee against a liquidator or other secured creditors.[125]

118   Goode, *op cit* p 777.
119   *Ibid* p 336.
120   Companies Act 1985 s 404(1).
121   *Ibid* s 404(2).
122   *Re MIG Trust Ltd* [1937] Ch 542; *Victoria Housing Estates Ltd v Ashburton Estates* [1982] 3 WLR 964. *Re Barrow Transport Ltd* (1989) 5 BCC 646.
123   *Re Braemar Investments Ltd* [1988] BCLC 556.
124   *Re R M Arnold & Sons Ltd* [1984] BCLC 535 and *Re John Bateson & Co Ltd* [1985] BCLC 259.
125   *Re Anglo-Continental Carpet Manufacturing Co* [1903] 1 Ch 914.

8.53 The standard term imposed by the court in cases of registration out of time specifies the date to which the time is extended and states that this is to be without prejudice to the rights of parties acquired between the date of creation of the charge and the date of its actual registration. The effect of this is to protect other duly registered charges created during the 21 day period originally available for the registration of the charge, in respect of which the extension is granted, as well as those created outside that period but before registration in accordance with the extension. It avoids the implication that registration within the extended time validates the charge *ab initio.* If another charge, created during the period originally available for registration of the one in respect of which the order was made, is expressed to be subject to it then this order of priority will take effect.[126]

8.54 In the absence of the commencement of a winding up before registration, the terms on which an order extending the time for registration is made will not protect an unsecured creditor.[127] A failure by the company to oppose an application for an extension of time may amount to the granting of a fraudulent preference and thus jeopardise the security of the applicant even if he succeeds in registering pursuant to the extension.[128]

The effect of registration

8.55 Section 401(2) lays down that the certificate issued by the Companies Registrar of the registration of a charge 'is conclusive evidence that the requirements of this chapter as to registration have been satisfied.' The courts have accepted that this means that even if the particulars registered omitted assets covered by the security[129] or the date of the creation of the charge or if the amount secured by the loan is incorrectly stated[130] the registration remains valid.

8.56 However, the decision of the Registrar whether to register a charge is open to judicial review on the application of the Attorney-General.[131]

8.57 Registration under s 395 has the effect of giving constructive notice of the existence of the registered charge and of any particulars required to be registered.[132] It is uncertain what effect, if any, the registration of matters

---

126 *Watson v Duff Morgan & Vermont Holdings Ltd* [1974] 1 All ER 794.
127 *Re Ehrman Brothers Ltd* [1906] 2 Ch 697.
128 *Re MIG Trust Ltd* [1937] Ch 542; *Victoria Housing Estates Ltd v Ashburton Estates* [1982] 3 WLR 964.
129 *National Provincial and Union Bank of England v Charnley* [1924] 1 KB 431.
130 *Re Eric Holmes Ltd* [1965] Ch 1052; *Re Mechanisations (Eaglescliff) Ltd* [1966] Ch 20.
131 *R v Registrar of Companies ex p Central Bank of India* [1985] BCLC 465; [1986] QB 1114 CA.
132 *Wilson v Kelland* [1910] 2 Ch 306.

not required to be registered has and whether any notice of the contents of a registered document is given by registration. The significance of this issue is that notice of a term of a floating charge which prohibits the chargor from granting further charges will prevent a later fixed chargee from gaining priority. It may also be relevant to the effects of an event stipulated as giving rise to automatic crystallisation to know whether notice of the term to this effect was held by a person seeking to claim priority for a dealing with the company after he knew that such an event had happened. If such a person had knowledge, both of the events specified in the charge as giving rise to automatic crystallisation and the fact that such an event had occurred, it would be difficult for him to contend that the company had the apparent authority of the chargee to deal with assets subject to the floating charge.

8.58 It is often assumed that the registration of particulars of a restrictive clause will give constructive notice of that information and it is usual for such details to be registered. Where a search of the file is in fact carried out the searcher will doubtless have actual notice of the registration. This will also be the case if the document creating the charge is inspected.[133] However, there must be doubt whether a person who fails to search or to read the charge can be held to have constructive notice of a matter which the statute does not require to be present on the register. This argument is persuasively put forward by Professors Goode and Farrar.[134] It is argued by Professor Farrar that notice of the existence of a document which will arise from its registration may give rise to inferred knowledge of its contents at common law. This is based on the assumption that a further search would have revealed the information and is reinforced by the argument that the existence of terms restricting a chargor's power to grant further charges or mortgages is now so common as to be a reasonable inference of fact from the existence of a floating charge. Such an argument is certainly persuasive if it is to be applied to those persons who might usually be expected to search the Companies Register. This would include bankers or financiers granting loans, but would not include trade suppliers or customers. The former groups might be argued to be deliberately turning a blind eye to the information on restrictions which would be discovered were a search to be made and this is the common law requirement before knowledge can be inferred. This is essentially the solution propounded by Professor Goode,[135] who argues that the doctrine of constructive notice developed in the context of equitable rights to real property is inappropriate to commercial law situations. The argument is that the courts should treat the

---

133   ss 406 and 408 give creditors that right.
134   See Farrar, "Floating Charges and Priorities" (1974) 38 Conv 315 and Goode, *op cit* pp 772–776.
135   *op cit* pp 775–776.

question of notice on the basis of whether a particular party might reasonably be expected to search the register in the light of the dealing and the asset involved. This would protect purchasers in the ordinary course of business and bankers making further advances on a current account secured by an earlier charge. It would also protect those claiming on the basis of dealings after an event which caused automatic crystallisation unless they were in the class of persons who could reasonably be expected to search the register and were also aware of the existence of the crystallising event.

8.59 It might be argued that such a doctrine puts a premium on the development of practices of failing to search and penalises the unusually diligent customer or supplier who chooses to do so. However, the more closely the doctrine of the courts reflects the commercial practice of particular groups, the greater will be the ability of the law to give effect to the contractual intention of the parties in matters such as restrictions on later charges and automatic crystallisation without excessive hardship to third parties affected by the contractual stipulations agreed.

8.60 While a failure to file certain information among the particulars required to be registered, or the filing of inaccurate information, will not vitiate the registration of the charge,[136] it is uncertain whether the omission of certain assets from the list of those on which the charge is secured will prevent the chargee from claiming priority over a later chargee of those assets who was deprived of notice by the inaccuracy of the registered information. If it is correct that neither constructive nor inferred notice of the contents of the documents creating the charge arises from registration, it would seem to follow that such an error would prevent a later chargee from being, on notice of the earlier charge affecting assets not stated in the registered particulars, subject to it.[137] This is more likely to arise in the case of a fixed charge because of the general nature of the description usually filed of property affected by a floating charge.

Effects of the Companies Act 1989

8.61 The Companies Act 1989[138] substantially reforms the system for the registration of company charges. It does not implement the full recommendations of the Diamond Report on security interests for radical reform of the whole system governing security interests in property other

136 s 401(2) and *National Provincial & Union Bank of England v Charnley* [1924] 1 KB 431.
137 Goode p 773.
138 See R Pennington, "An Introduction to the Companies Bill" (1989) 133 SJ 236.

than land. However, it tackles a number of the problems associated with the workings of the system of registration for company charges. Its provisions are dealt with here under the headings used above to deal with the previous system of company charges. The Act repeals and replaces ss 395 to 409 of the Companies Act 1985.

Reforms to registrable charges

8.62 The new s 396[139] specifies the charges that are registrable. By the new s 396(4) to (6) the Secretary of State for Trade and Industry is given power to add charges to the list and to remove them from it by regulations. The charges on a company's property[140] that are registrable are as follows.

8.63 (a) *Land.* Charges on land and on any interest in land are registrable but a rentcharge or other charge for a periodical sum issuing out of the land is excluded and the holding of debentures entitling the holder to a charge on land is not treated as an interest in land.[141] The latter exclusion reverses *Re Molton Finance Ltd.*[142]

8.64 (b) *Goods.* A charge on goods or any interest in goods other than a charge under which the chargee is entitled to possession of either the goods or a document of title to them is included. Goods are defined as any tangible movable property.[143] Charges over ships and aircraft will now fall within this category. This formulation simplifies the category which formerly dealt with instruments needing registration as bills of sale. There is no longer a reference to an instrument but a pledge is still excluded as that security operates by possession of goods or documents of title. The phrase 'document of title' is not defined in the 1989 Act.

8.65 (c) *Intangible movable property.* An exhaustive list of the forms of property of this kind, which render charges over them registrable, is provided. They are goodwill, intellectual property, book debts, uncalled share capital of the company and calls made but not paid.[144] Intellectual property is defined as including only patents, trade marks, service marks, registered designs, copyright or design right or any licence under or in respect of any of them.[145] Book debts are not defined but the deposit of a

---

139 Companies Act 1989 s 93.
140 A 'charge' includes a 'mortgage' but not a charge arising by operation of law (new section 396(3)) and 'property' in the context of that which is subject to a charge includes future property and the whole or part of the company's undertaking (new section 395(2)).
141 Companies Act 1989 s 93 substituting new section 386(1)(a) and (2)(a).
142 [1968] Ch 325.
143 *Ibid* s 93 substituting new section 396(2)(b),(c).
144 New s 396(1)(c).
145 New s 396(2)(d).

negotiable instrument to secure the payment of a book debt is excluded from that category. A shipowner's lien on subfreights is excluded from both this category and the 'floating charge' category.[146] It will be noted that the exhaustive definition of intangible movable property excludes from the list of categories of property in respect of which a charge is registrable the shares in other companies held by a company.

8.66   (d) *Debentures.* Charges for securing an issue of debentures are included. A charge other than a floating charge securing a single debenture is still excluded from the need for registration.[147] A debenture which is part of an issue or series is not to be treated as a book debt.[148]

8.67   (e) *Floating charges.* A floating charge on the whole or any part of the company's property, wherever that property is situated, is included.[149]

8.68   A new s 410 inserted by the Act gives the Secretary of State power to require, by regulation, the registration of notice of the occurrence of events causing the crystallisation of a registered floating charge, as well as prescribed actions affecting the nature of the security under the powers conferred by any registered charge (fixed or floating) or by court order. The regulations can provide that failure to file notice will cause the act in question to be treated as ineffective until notice is filed subject to a power of the court to waive such consequences.[150]

New effects of failure to register
8.69   The new s 399[151] lays down the consequences of failure to register the charge within 21 days of its creation or of the acquisition of the property it covers. As a general rule, the charge is void against the administrator or liquidator of the company and any person who for value acquires an interest or right over the property subject to the charge. This applies whether the 'relevant event' occurs during or after the 21 day period allowed for registration.[152] For the purpose of invalidity against a liquidator or administrator, a 'relevant event' is the beginning of insolvency proceedings; either the presentation of an administration petition or winding up petition leading (in each case) to an order or the passing of a resolution for voluntary liquidation. For the purpose of invalidity against someone acquiring an interest in, or right over, the property it is the

---

146   New s 396(2)(f) and (g), reversing *Re Welsh Irish Ferries* [1985] BCLC 327.
147   New s 396(1)(d).
148   New s 396(2)(e).
149   New s 396(1)(e).
150   *Ibid* s 100.
151   *Ibid* s 95.
152   New s 399(1) reversing *Watson v Duff Morgan Vermont Holdings Ltd* [1974] 1 WLR 450.

acquisition of the right or interest.[153] When a 'relevant event' happens and causes the charge to become void to any extent the whole of the money secured on it is repayable with interest on demand.[154]

Registration out of time or of inaccurate particulars
8.70 There is no longer any need to obtain a court order to permit registration out of time or the delivery of further particulars to correct omissions or misstatements in the particulars delivered or to record changes which render the original particulars no longer accurate. The date of delivery of such further particulars will be recorded by the Registrar and further particulars must be signed on behalf of both company and chargee, although a procedure is laid down to allow the court to waive the latter requirement in cases of refusal or inability to sign.[155]

8.71 If particulars are delivered for registration more than 21 days after the creation of the charge, 'relevant events' occurring after the delivery do not have the above consequences. The charge is not avoided as a result of such events. However, if, at the date of delivery, the company is unable to pay its debts or if it subsequently becomes unable to pay them as a result of the transaction under which the charge was created and, in either case, insolvency proceedings begin against the company within the relevant period after the date of delivery, the charge is void against the liquidator or administrator and the whole amount secured by it is repayable with interest on demand. The test of the company's inability to pay its debts is the one laid down in s 123 of the Insolvency Act 1986. The 'relevant period' referred to is, two years in the case of a floating charge created in favour of a person connected with the company, one year in the case of any other floating charge and six months in the case of any other charge.[156]

8.72 The effect of these provisions is to ensure that later mortgagees or chargees are protected from the priority of earlier unregistered charges since the later mortgagee acquires an interest in the property for value. Later registration of the earlier charge will not affect that. However, even if the first charge is registered outside the 21 day period, it will have priority over later mortgages created after its registration although not necessarily over the rights of the liquidator or administrator in later insolvency proceedings.

8.73 If the particulars registered are inaccurate or incomplete the charge is void against a liquidator, an administrator or a person who acquires an

153   1989 Act ss 95 and 104; new ss 399(2) and 419(5).
154   *Ibid* s 99; new s 407.
155   *Ibid* s 96; new s 401.
156   *Ibid* s 95; new s 400.

interest for value. It is void to the extent that it confers rights that would have been disclosed had the particulars been accurate and complete but which are not disclosed providing a 'relevant event' occurs when the particulars are inaccurate in a relevant respect. The omission or misstatement of the name of the chargee is not a ground for regarding the particulars of a charge as inaccurate or incomplete. The accuracy of the particulars is assessed by reference to the terms of the charge and is judged at a particular date by reference to the original particulars and any amendments or additions filed at that date.

8.74 The court has power to order, on the application of the chargee, that the charge should not be void as a result of an inaccuracy or omission. In the case of invalidity against a liquidator or administrator the court must be satisfied about one of two factors. First, that the omission or inaccuracy is not likely to have misled, materially to his prejudice, any unsecured creditor of the company or, second, that no person became an unsecured creditor of the company at the time when the particulars of the charge were incomplete or inaccurate. In the case of a person acquiring an interest in the property the court can only waive the invalidity of the charge if it is satisfied that that person did not rely on the particulars that were incomplete or inaccurate in connection with the acquisition.[157]

Changes to the effects of registration
8.75 The new provisions for the registration of charges stipulate that a person is not to be taken to have notice of any matter because of its being disclosed in the register or a document kept by the registrar and open to inspection. There is no doctrine of 'deemed notice' of matters which can be ascertained from the registry. However, that rule is expressly stated not to have any bearing on the question of whether a person is affected by notice of a matter by reason of a failure to make such inquiries as ought reasonably to be made.[158] A certificate of registration is conclusive only as to its date. Details of the particulars to be registered may be prescribed by the Secretary of State and may include a negative pledge clause in a charge document.

Overseas companies
8.76 New ss 703A to 703N extend similar rules to those set out above to charges over the property of overseas companies registered under s 691 of the 1985 Act. This reverses the decision in *Slavenberg's Bank NV v Intercontinental Natural Resources Ltd*.[159] The system applied is to require registration of charges over property situated in Great Britain 21 days after

---

157 *Ibid* s 97; new s 402.
158 *Ibid* ss 94 and 142; new ss 397(5) and 711A.
159 [1980] 1 WLR 1076.

the charge is created or the property acquired. A charge over future property need not be registered if that property cannot be situated in Great Britain after being acquired or coming into existence. A charge that is not registrable because property is outside Great Britain becomes registrable at the end of a four month period during which the property was continuously situated in Great Britain.[160]

PRIORITY RULES ON FLOATING CHARGES

8.77   A floating charge is a form of equitable charge. It has been noted that it does not attach to particular assets until an event occurs which gives rise to crystallisation.[161] The process of crystallisation is thus important in determining the order of priority as between fixed charges or other security interests (such as execution against goods or the attachment of debts) on the one hand and a floating charge on the other hand.

Priorities between floating charges

8.78   A floating charge which secures a debenture will normally rank, in relation to other floating charges, in order of creation. Where a series of debentures is issued then equal ranking is usually stipulated by the terms of the series for the charges supporting all the debentures in the series; otherwise the charges would have priority *inter se* on the basis of the order in which the debentures containing them were issued.[162] Subject to this, the general rule is that a floating charge ranks behind earlier floating charges and ahead of later ones. This will be the case even if the later floating charge purports to rank *pari passu* with the earlier one.[163] However, it is possible for an earlier debenture to specify that later floating charges can be granted with priority over it, or *pari passu* with it, and if this is how the wording of the earlier charge is construed then the later charge will have priority or rank *pari passu*.[164] This rule reflects the normal priority system applicable to equitable charges and the implication that once a floating charge has been granted any later floating charge will rank behind it.

Priority against fixed charges

8.79   The position of other fixed mortgages or charges of specific property is different because of the nature of a floating charge which allows the

---

160   Companies Act 1989 s 105 and Sch 15.
161   See paras 5.24–5.42.
162   *Gartside v Silkstone Co* (1882) 21 Ch D 762.
163   *Re Benjamin Cope & Sons* [1914] 1 Ch 800.
164   *Re Automatic Bottle Makers* [1926] 1 Ch 412.

chargor company to deal with the assets subject to the floating charge in the normal course of business.[165] This means that a mortgage or charge of those assets granted in the ordinary course of business before the crystallisation of the floating charge will have priority unless a contrary intention appears in the document creating the floating charge.[166] If such a contrary intention does appear, then the question of whether the later chargee had notice of it arises.[167]

8.80   A later legal mortgagee who has no notice of the restriction in the earlier charge takes free of it, because he is a *bona fide* purchaser for value of the legal estate without notice of the restriction.[168] A later equitable mortgagee has a stronger equity. The usual priority rule depending on the order of creation is defeated by the inequality of the equities where the later chargee has no notice of the restriction and the floating chargee left title deeds in the possession of the company, giving apparent authority for the creation of later mortgages.[169]

8.81   Registration in the Companies Register of a charge gives constructive notice of its existence, but not of its contents.[170] Knowledge of registration without more may not affect the priority of a later mortgagee in a case where the earlier charge contains a restriction.[167] Knowledge of the existence of the charge does not, in itself, give constructive notice of its contents.[171]

8.82   If the later chargee has notice of the restriction he will take subject to the floating charge as, although the floating charge has not attached to the assets, it is regarded as a personal equity to which his charge is subject on the grounds of the unconscionability of permitting the holder of a fixed charge priority in such circumstances.[172] Where the grant of a particular fixed charge is outside the ordinary course of a company's business, it would seem that it will not have priority over the floating charge unless the company had the apparent authority of the holder of the floating charge to create it. This follows from the limitation, of the use allowed to a company

165   See paras 5.19–5.23.
166   *Wheatley v Silkstone & Haigh Moor Coal Co* (1885) 29 Ch D 715 at 724.
167   See para 8.58 as to the question of whether the registration of details of the restriction in the register of company charges fixes later chargees with notice of it.
168   *English and Scottish Mercantile Investment Co Ltd v Brunton* [1892] 2 QB 700.
169   *Re Castell and Brown Ltd* [1898] 1 Ch 315; *Re Valletort Sanitary Steam Laundry Co Ltd* [1903] 2 Ch 654.
170   *Wilson v Kelland* [1910] 2 Ch 306, and *Siebe Gorman & Co Ltd v Barclays Bank Ltd* [1979] 2 Lloyd's Rep 142.
171   *English and Scottish Mercantile Investment Co v Brunton* [1892] 2 QB 700 and *Re Standard Rotary Machine Co Ltd* (1906) 95 LT 829. See paras 8.58 and 8.75 *supra*.
172   See *English and Scottish Mercantile Investment Co* per Lord Esher MR at 707 and Gough, *op cit* pp 156–157.

of assets subject to a floating charge, to disposals in the ordinary course of business and assumes that whatever the position between a chargor and chargee, the effect of a stipulation on a third party must be subject to the rules as to apparent authority.[173]

8.83 The latter doctrine may, however, be more readily applied in cases in which particular definitions of the ordinary course of business are contained in individual charges. A transaction evidently outside the ordinary course of business of the chargor company in the light of its objects clause and its usual business practice may lose priority to the floating charge unless some conduct of the chargee clearly conferred apparent authority. It is hard to see why a charge granted in circumstances outside the broad definition given by the courts to 'the ordinary course of business'[174] should gain priority over the floating charge without a very clear representation by the holder of the floating charge to the other chargee that the company had authority to dispose of the assets by charging them.

8.84 After crystallisation, a floating charge will have priority on the basis of its existence as a fixed charge from that date. Earlier fixed charges whether legal or equitable will have priority over it assuming that they have been registered under the Companies Act 1985 s 395 and under any system of registration applying to particular assets. Fixed charges created after crystallisation of the floating charge will be subject to it. In the case of competing floating charges the rule of priority in order of creation,[175] regardless of the date of crystallisation, will apply unless the earlier floating charge specifically permitted the creation of later floating charges which would rank *pari passu* or in priority to it.[176]

8.85 Where a mortgage or a charge over an asset is granted to a person who supplies the purchase money for that asset, that charge will have priority over any earlier charge applicable to the chargor's future property if there is a binding agreement by the purchase money financier entitling him to security before the property is owned by the borrower. If this is the case, his security interest attaches to the asset from the very moment at which it becomes the property of the borrower and any other security interest can only attach to it at a later time. Priorities relating to the security interests in that asset work in favour of the person who supplied the finance for its purchase.[177]

---

173 See para 5.19—5.23 *supra* and Goode, *op cit* p 801.
174 See para 5.19–5.23.
175 *Re Benjamin Cope & Sons* [1914] 1 Ch 800.
176 *Re Automatic Bottle Makers* [1926] 1 Ch 412.
177 See *Re Connolly Bros Ltd (No 2)* [1912] 2 Ch 25 and *Security Trust Co v The Royal Bank of Canada* [1976] AC 503.

8.86 Any floating charge can only apply to the asset as it stands when it becomes the property of the chargor, so the priority of the purchase price financier will prevail regardless of notice of the existence of the floating charge or its terms. In the absence of a binding agreement between the chargor and the supplier of the purchase money finance before the completion of the purchase, a *scintilla temporis* will arise between the acquisition of the property by the chargor and the grant of security, during which the asset can become subject to the floating charge.[178] If this happens, the priority of the purchase money financier will depend on the normal rules applicable to a fixed charge granted later than a floating charge, and notice to him of any restriction on the company's power to grant such charges will cause him to lose priority.

8.87 It would seem that an agreement to advance purchase money to a chargor made after a contractual obligation to purchase exists would lose priority over the equitable interest of the purchaser arising from the agreement to buy which would have become subject to the floating charge on its creation and before the agreement to grant security to the purchase money financier. However, if the purchase money financier then made his advance without notice of the floating charge (or without notice of the restriction contained in it which would affect his interest) and then got in the legal estate (in the form of a legal mortgage of the property) he would gain priority under the doctrine of *tabulo in naufragio*.[179] However, there is no decided case directly on this point.

Floating charges and liens

8.88 A lien against a company's property will take priority over an uncrystallised floating charge[180] and, indeed, if the lien arises before crystallisation it will have priority even if it is exercised later—even if the common law right of retention is complemented by a contractual right of sale.[181]

Floating charges and execution

8.89 The priority of execution as against a floating charge will be governed by crystallisation. A writ of *fieri facias* will only give priority to execution creditors if the goods have been seized and sold and the proceeds

---

178 See *Church of England Building Society v Piskor* [1954] 1 Ch 553, which concerned subtenancies by estoppel which was fed during such a *scintilla temporis*.
179 See Goode p 781 and *Bailey v Barnes* [1894] 1 Ch 25.
180 *Brunton v Electrical Engineering Corporation* [1892] 1 Ch 434.
181 *George Barker (Transport) Ltd v Eynon* [1974] 1 All ER 900.

handed, by the sheriff, to the execution creditor before crystallisation.[182] At any earlier stage the holder of a crystallised floating charge takes the goods or the proceeds of sale.[183]

8.90 If the company, on the seizure of its goods, pays the whole or part of the amount due to avoid the sale of its goods, it would seem that the judgment creditors are entitled to keep the money paid.[184] This is logical as it places the judgment creditor in the same position as an unsecured creditor whom the company pays off voluntarily.

8.91 It is unlikely that a modern court would take the view that the act of seizure under an execution is outside the company's ordinary course of business.[185] For this reason the competition between execution creditors and those holding a floating charge is determined by the stage reached by a process of execution before the floating charge crystallises. Seizure of goods in execution will often be a ground for automatic crystallisation under the terms of the charge. The effect of this is uncertain.[186]

8.92 Where a garnishee order is made attaching debts due to a company, the rules are analogous to those applicable where a writ of *fieri facias* is issued against goods. The execution creditor is only able to retain the debt against the holder of a crystallised floating charge if, before execution, a garnishee order absolute has been made and the garnishee has paid him the debt attached by it.[187] For this purpose the debts are not attached by a garnishee order *nisi* to give priority to the execution creditor over a floating charge which crystallises later.

8.93 Where a charging order is made against land, shares or other securities owned by a company, the charging order takes effect as if a specific charge had been created at the date of the charging order *nisi*.[188] Crystallisation of a floating charge after that date will not affect the execution creditor unless the court refuses to make the charging order absolute.

8.94 A Mareva injunction, which prohibits a company from removing its assets from the jurisdiction, will not affect the claim of a holder of a floating charge against the assets—even if the crystallisation of the charge occurs

---

182 *Taunton v Sheriff of Warwickshire* [1895] 2 Ch 319.
183 *Re Standard Manufacturing Co* [1891] 1 Ch 627.
184 *Heaton & Dugard Ltd v Cutting Bros Ltd* [1925] 1 KB 655; *Robinson's v Burnell's Vienna Bakery Co* [1904] 2 KB 624.
185 *Davey v Wilkinson & Sons Ltd* [1898] 2 QB 194 per Russell CJ at 200.
186 See para 5.36–5.41.
187 *Norton v Yates* [1906] 1 KB 112.
188 Charging Orders Act 1979 s 3(4).

after the injunction was granted.[189] This is because the injunction imposes a personal obligation on the company and, while sanctions can be imposed against others who knowingly assist the company to defy the order, the injunction does not amount to a real security interest against the assets to which it applies. For the same reason, a sequestration order is not regarded as a form of execution and does not create a real interest in assets which are subject to it.[190]

Floating charges and distraint

8.95   A landlord who levies distress for rent against property on the demised premises is unaffected by any charge as he is able to levy distress against property regardless of who owns it.[191] If he has distrained before crystallisation he can sell afterwards and retain the proceeds.[192] Distress can also be levied after crystallisation[193] subject to a possible right of a chargee to apply under s 1 of the Law of Distress Amendment Act 1908. If goods are in the possession of a receiver appointed by the court the landlord must apply for leave to distrain which will seldom be refused.[194] However, in practice most receivers of insolvent companies are appointed by a floating chargee. A levy of distress by a company's landlord will often be specified as a ground for automatic crystallisation.

8.96   If a landlord serves notice on the subtenants of the company under the Law of Distress (Amendment) Act 1908 for the payment of rent on a sublease to him he becomes entitled to rent from that time. If the charge over the lease given by the company is a first fixed charge the receiver is entitled to the rent up to that time as the agent of the lessee company which remains in possession.[195] In the case of a floating charge over the rents due from the subtenants, the priorities between the landlord's assignment by notice, under the Act, of the rents from the subtenants and the interest of the holder of the floating charge would depend on the rule in *Dearle v Hall* and the landlord's knowledge of the existence of the floating charge at the time of effecting the assignment.[196] All enforcement rights of execution creditors and the rights of all those entitled to distrain on the company's goods will be subject to the statutory *moratorium* if an administration order is made in relation to the company.[197]

---

189   *Cretanor Maritime Co Ltd v Irish Marine Management Ltd* [1978] 1 WLR 966.
190   *Eckman v Midland Bank Ltd* [1973] QB 519.
191   See para 8.142 *infra*.
192   *Re Roundwood Colliery Co* [1897] 1 Ch 373.
193   *Re New City Constitutional Club* (1886) 34 Ch D 646.
194   *General Share & Trust Co v Wetley Brick & Pottery Co* (1882) 20 Ch D 260.
195   *Re Offshore Ventilation Ltd* (1989) 5 BCC 160.
196   See paras 8.113ff *infra*.
197   See paras 13.34ff *infra*.

SPECIFIC RULES AND REGISTRATION SYSTEMS

Priority of mortgages and charges of land

8.97 The priority of mortgages of land is predominantly governed by registration rules. However, some types of mortgage are not registrable.

Mortgages of a legal estate or equitable interests
8.98 A mortgage of land which affects the legal estate can itself be either legal or equitable.[198] The legal estate which is mortgaged must either be the fee simple or a term of years absolute. Any other interest is equitable. The legislation which governs the priority of such mortgages makes a fundamental distinction between those which are protected by the deposit of the deeds with the mortgagee and those which are not so protected. As has been noted in chapter 2, such protection can be granted to either a legal or an equitable mortgagee. When considering the priority of mortgages of land the fundamental question is not the nature of the mortgage, but the nature of the interest which has been mortgaged (legal or equitable) and whether or not that mortgage is protected by a deposit of the deeds.

8.99 In the case of a mortgage of an equitable interest in land to which the registration system does not apply, priority is determined by the rule in *Dearle v Hall* and s 137 of the Law of Property Act 1925. That system is dealt with in para 8.113. A general equitable charge is registrable under the Land Charges Act 1972. By s 2(4)(iii) of that Act such a charge is an equitable charge which is not secured by the deposit of documents relating to the legal estate affected does not arise or affect an interest arising under a trust for sale or settlement and is not a charge given by way of indemnity against equitably apportioned rents or certain other obligations. Effectively this maintains the position that it is only mortgages or charges of the legal estate not protected by deposit of title deeds which are registrable.

Mortgages protected by deposit of title deeds
8.100 Since such mortgages are excluded from registration requirements,[199] registration cannot affect priority. The rules governing their priority depend on the pre-1926 rules when they compete *inter se*. Consequently, registration rules will only affect priority in this context when a mortgage of the legal interest, protected by a deposit of the title deeds is in competition with a mortgage which is not so protected.

---

198 See chapter 2 *supra*.
199 Subject to the Land Registration Act 1925 in the case of registered land—see paras 8.108ff *infra*.

Competition between two mortgages protected by deposit

8.101   This situation will rarely occur, as a first mortgagee will normally ensure that he holds all the deeds and no later mortgage protected by deposit will be possible. However, in the case of unregistered land, there is always the possibility that some deeds will be provided to each of the mortgagees.[200] If the mortgagor deposits all the deeds with the first mortgagee and later conveys the property subject to the mortgage to a purchaser, the purchaser could create a mortgage of the legal estate by deposit of the conveyance to him. In such a case, the former rules on priority will apply. Legal mortgages rank *inter se* in order of creation. Equitable mortgages also rank in time order, providing 'the equities are equal'. However, as between a legal and an equitable mortgage, the legal mortgage will prevail unless the legal mortgagee had notice of an earlier equitable incumbrance or behaves in a way which causes him to lose priority to a later equitable incumbrance.

8.102   The fundamental principle *nemo dat quod non habet* lays down that no person can pass a title which they do not possess; once an interest in specified property has been granted to a mortgagee, the mortgagor has no power to grant a further mortgage or other disposition with priority over the first mortgagee. However, the principle is subject to exceptions where the first mortgagee behaves in such a way as to make the application of the rule unjust, or where the rule is overridden by Parliament, as where a mortgagee is authorised to sell property free of the mortgagor's equity of redemption. This concept also supports the ordering of equitable interests with priority according to time of creation, providing the equities are equal, in circumstances where the registration system does not oust the rule.[201]

8.103   If a later mortgage by deposit is possible because of the failure of the first mortgagee to ensure all existing deeds were deposited, then the first mortgagee may lose his priority. The most likely cause of this will be the fraud or gross negligence of an earlier legal mortgagee, (usually in relation to the title deeds) which defers him to the later equitable mortgagee.[202] If an earlier equitable mortgagee establishes that a later legal mortgagee had actual, constructive or imputed notice of the equitable mortgage, then the equitable mortgage will retain its priority despite the normal rule that a legal mortgage will prevail.[203]

8.104   Two legal mortgages protected by deposit would rank in order of creation, unless the holder of the first in time had been fraudulent or grossly

---

200   A court may decide that only one (or neither) are protected by deposit of title deeds.
201   See *Phillips v Phillips* [1862] 4 De G F & J 208 per Lord Westbury at 215.
202   See para 8.11 *supra*.
203   See paras 8.19ff *supra*.

negligent. A first legal mortgagee by deposit would prevail over a later equitable mortgagee by deposit, because legal mortgages prevail and his was first in time, unless fraud or gross negligence was shown to exist. A first equitable mortgagee could prevail over a second legal mortgagee only if the legal mortgagee were shown to have notice of the first mortgage. Two equitable mortgagees would rank in order of the creation of the mortgages, unless the equities were unequal in that circumstances existed which affected the conduct of one of the claimants and made it less meritorious than that of the other.[204] This might be founded on the negligence of the first mortgagee or the better claim of the second.[205] A vendor who endorses a receipt on a conveyance and hands over the deeds without receiving payment gives a better equity to a later mortgagee.[206]

Competition between protection by deposit and registration
8.105 If a first mortgage is protected by deposit of title deeds it takes its priority from the date of its creation. It would have priority over a later registrable mortgage, unless the mortgagee had behaved fraudulently or negligently and lost priority. A first mortgage which is not protected by deposit, and which is therefore registrable will prevail if it is registered before a second mortgage protected by deposit of title deeds is created. This is because by s 97 of the Law of Property Act 1925, every mortgage ranks according to its date of registration and by registering the earlier mortgage priority is gained over a later mortgage which is not subject to the registration system because it is protected by deposit of title deeds. If, on the other hand, the first (registrable) mortgage has not been registered by the date of the creation of the second mortgage (which is protected by deposit of the title deeds) the first will be void as against the second by virtue of s 4(5) of the Land Charges Act 1972 which provides that a puisne mortgage or general equitable charge is void as against a purchaser[207] of the land or any interest in it unless the mortgage is registered before completion of the 'purchase'. Failure to register by the date of creation of the second mortgage results in a loss of priority and later registration will not restore the position, as the registered mortgage will only rank according to the date of registration.[208]

Competition between two registrable mortgages
8.106 In this case the registration system determines the priority of successive mortgages. If both mortgages are in fact registered,[209] then the

---

204 *Bailey v Barnes* [1894] 1 Ch 25.
205 *Bradley v Ricks* (1878) 9 Ch D 189.
206 *Rice v Rice* (1854) 2 Drew 73.
207 By Land Charges Act 1972 s 17(1). This includes a mortgage for valuable consideration.
208 LPA 1925 s 97.
209 See paras 8.108ff *infra* as to registered land.

priority will be in order of registration, regardless of whether one or both mortgages are legal or equitable. This is the result of s 97 Law of Property Act 1925. If neither mortgage is registered, then the last in time will prevail. This is because s 4(5) Land Charges Act 1972 lays down that an unregistered (but registrable) mortgage is void as against a later mortgagee (or other 'purchaser') so long as the transaction is completed before registration of the earlier mortgage. If the second mortgage is registered before the first one, then it will prevail by virtue of s 97 (priority from date of registration).

8.107   If the first mortgage is registered after the creation of the second one (but before the second is registered), then the notorious conflict between the effects of s 97 of the Law of Property Act 1925 and s 4(5) Land Charges Act 1972 operates. If both have been registered then s 97 lays down that they should rank in order of registration, but s 4(5) lays down that as against the second mortgagee, the first mortgage is void. The most attractive approach to solving this difficulty is to suggest that if by s 4(5) the first mortgage is void as against the second mortgagee, it cannot gain priority over the second mortgage by registration after the event, ie completion of the second transaction which made it void. This seems to be the prevailing view on the resolution of this conflict, but the matter awaits decision by the courts.[210]

Mortgages of registered land
8.108   (a) *Mortgages by registered charge.* Registered charges, which affect the same land, rank in order of entry on the register, rather than in order of creation.[211] The system of official searches of the register with a priority period enables a mortgagee to ensure priority over mortgagees seeking to register charges during the period of protection, which is 30 working days from the date of the search providing the charge is registered within the priority period.[212] The priority rule laid down by s 29 of the Land Registration Act 1925 can be varied as it is stated to be subject to the expression of a contrary rule in the register. This can be achieved by the registration of an instrument or charge which in fact varies the normal rule[213] but in practice an entry is made in the register itself in all cases where a priority different from that laid down in s 29 is intended to apply.

8.109   (b) *Unregistered mortgages of registered land.* Subject to any entry to the contrary on the register, the proprietor of registered land can mortgage by deed or otherwise the land or any part of it by any method

---

210   See Goode, "Commercial Law" p 768 and Megarry & Wade, "Law of Real Property" 4th ed pp 972 *et seq.*
211   Land Registration Act 1925 s 29.
212   Land Registration (Official Searches) Rules 1981 r 2 (SI 1981/1135).
213   Land Registration Rules 1925 r 140.

allowed if the land was unregistered and with the same effect. However, such a mortgage takes effect in equity only and is capable of being overridden as a minor interest unless it is protected by a notice or caution.[214] If such a mortgage is so protected it ranks for priority purposes at the date of registration of the notice, as all dispositions by the registered proprietor take effect subject to valid interests protected in that way.[215] A caution gives the person who lodged it a right to notice of applications for registration of an interest that affects his right and to challenge the registration of that interest.[216] Consequently these forms of protection preserve the existing right of the mortgagee against the rights of later mortgagees or owners from the date of the caution or notice.

8.110   Once such a mortgage becomes a registered charge it no longer requires protection by notice or caution and mortgages protected by the special mortgage caution which was available before 29th August 1977 can be converted into registered charges by the registrar.[217] After that date a mortgage which is in a form applicable to unregistered land can only be protected by a notice or the standard form of caution against dealing. There is no longer a separate, specially prescribed, form of caution applicable to mortgages. However, a caution against dealing which protects an unregistered mortgage cannot be warned off.[218] Subject to these provisions, a mortgage of this kind has effect and may be transferred, discharged, and otherwise dealt with and will devolve as it would if the land were unregistered.[219]

8.111   If such a mortgage remains unregistered and is not protected by a notice or caution it is effective in equity only and its priority is determined accordingly. The ordinary rules of equity as regards the priority of equitable interests in land will apply. Among a number of such unregistered mortgages the first in time will prevail.[220] Subject to the fact that they are all subject to mortgages appearing on the register or protected on it, the normal rules applicable to a series of equitable mortgages conferring priority in order of creation if the equities are equal, will apply to mortgages of registered land by deposit of the Land Certificate, or submortgages by deposit of the Charge Certificate. Since the abolition of the minor interests index, priorities among minor interests will be determined on the basis of

---

214   Land Registration Act 1925 s 106 as substituted by Administration of Justice Act 1977 s 26.
215   *Ibid* s 52.
216   *Ibid* s 55.
217   *Ibid* s 26 (as substituted) and ss 49, 52, 54 and 55.
218   Land Registration Rules 1925 r 225.
219   Land Registration Act 1925 s 106(1) and (4) as substituted.
220   *Barclays Bank v Taylor* [1974] 1 Ch 137.

s 137(1) of the Law of Property Act 1925 and the rule in *Dearle v Hall*.[221] This rule will apply to a mortgage of an equitable interest in registered land.

Choses in action and intellectual property

8.112 Priorities between choses in action are governed by the rule in *Dearle v Hall*.[221a] In this section that rule is analysed and specific matters affecting particular forms of property are briefly considered.

The rule in Dearle v Hall
8.113 (a) *The property covered.* In the case of an equitable interest, whether in land or personalty, the priority of incumbrances is determined by the order in which notice is given to the trustee or holder of the legal estate. This applies to choses in action (except negotiable instruments[222]) and to all equitable interests in land, in capital money, and in securities representing capital money.[223] This rule supplants the public registration system and can be said to be a private system of registration with the holder of the legal estate or, in the case of debts, the debtor, administering the register.[224] It also represents a recognition that for a chose in action or an equitable interest, notice to the debtor or the holder of the legal estate is the closest possible analogy to reducing a chattel to possession.

8.114 The system is clearly at its weakest when the property subject to the incumbrances is a trade debt. The need for a creditor taking as security the receivables of a corporate borrower to inquire of the debtor about earlier dealings with the debts, makes the factoring of debts by way of security interest rather than assignment by way of sale unnecessarily difficult.[225] The system developed as one applicable to trusts where the stability of the constitution of the body of trustees meant that the maintenance of a private 'register' of security interests was practical. Its application to the trade debts of a body corporate is less satisfactory. When the property subject to the security is company shares, the statutory prohibition on notices of trusts in the company share register[226] suggests that the rule is inapplicable, although notice to the directors of an incumbrance may prevent the company from exercising a lien on those shares with priority over the

---

221 (1828) 3 Russ 1. See Land Registration Act 1986 s 5(1) and (5) and para 8.113 *infra*.
221a (1828) 3 Russ 1.
222 *Re Gibbs ex parte Price* (1844) 3 Mont D & De G 586.
223 LPA 1925 s 137(1).
224 Note *ibid* s 137(8) which governs the custody of notices given to trustees.
225 See Goode *op cit* pp 762–763 and A L Diamond, *A Review of Security Interests in Property*, DTI, 1989.
226 Companies Act 1985 s 360 and see *Société Générale de Paris v Walker* (1885) 11 App Cas 20 per Lord Selbourn at p 30.

incumbrance if the lien is for a debt to the company of a later date than the company's receipt of the notice.[227]

8.115   The rule does not apply if the person who takes an assignment of a chose in action is already aware of the existence of a prior equitable interest at that time. This qualification to the rule applies because the second assignee knows of the earlier assignment when he takes his security. If he is not aware of it at that point but is aware of it when he later gives notice of the assignment to the debtor the order of giving notice will determine priorities. Where this second branch of the rule in *Dearle v Hall* applies, the priority of the interests will be determined by their order of creation.[228]

8.116   (b) *Nature of notice.* When a chose in action is assigned under s 136 of the Law of Property Act 1925 the written notice of the assignment will also serve as notice for the purpose of the rule in *Dearle v Hall*. Since that section gives the assignee all the procedural advantages of legal title but does not make the priorities position of an assignment any better than it was before the existence of the statutory procedure for assignment, notice to the debtor will determine priorities regardless of order of creation or notice as between assignees even if assignment is carried out under the section.[229]

8.117   In other cases the notice must also be in writing.[230] The notice must be given to the trustee[231] or debtor personally or by means of an agent authorised to accept it. The authorisation may be express or implied. A solicitor must have such authorisation for notice to him to be effectively served on the trustee.[232] The trustee or debtor is obliged to accept the notice and will be liable to the incumbrancer for disregarding it and parting with the funds or paying the debt to someone not entitled to it.[233] If it is impossible to serve a valid notice on trustees the result of securing priority may be achieved by indorsement of the notice on the trust instrument, but this will not be available where the property subject to the security interest is a debt or some other security not subject to a trust instrument.

227   *Bradford Banking Co v Briggs & Co* (1886) 12 App Cas 29.
228   *Mutual Life Assurance Society v Langley* (1886) 32 Ch D 460 and *Rhodes v Allied Dunbar Pension Services Ltd* [1988] BCLC 186, a case of a landlord's notice under the Law of Distress (Amendment) Act 1908 which only effects assignment on notice being given to subtenants for the payment of rent on the sublease to the landlord. On appeal the continuing possession of the company despite a first fixed charge over its interest under the lease entitled a receiver to rent as its agent until the landlord served the notice. See *sub nom. Re Offshore Ventilation Ltd* (1989) 5 BCC 160 CA.
229   *Pfeiffer Weinkellerei v Arbuthnot Factors Ltd* [1987] BCLC 522.
230   LPA 1925 s 137(3).
231   In the case of settled land notice must be given to the trustees of the settlement and not the tenant for life who holds the legal estate—LPA 1925 s 137(2).
232   *Saffron Walden Second Benefit Building Society v Ragner* (1880) 14 Ch D 406.
233   *Williams v Thorp* (1828) 2 Sim 257.

8.118   In the case of company shares or government stocks, application may be made to the court for a 'stop notice' which will ensure that before any transfer of the assets the mortgagee or chargee will be notified and will have sufficient time to obtain a court order preventing the transfer.[234] The notice must be given to a properly constituted trustee or to the debtor.[235] In a case where there are two or more trustees or joint debtors then notice to one will preserve priority as an intending mortgagee or chargee has an obligation to inquire of all of them, but it is prudent to give notice to all of them,[236] as this preserves the mortgagee from the need to give further notice to new trustees if the only one retires or dies without passing on the notice to his fellow trustees. Notice to all trustees or debtors absolves the mortgagee from any duty to watch for changes in the trusteeship.[237] In the case of competing equitable assignments of the same subfreights notice must be given to the person from whom they are due.[238]

Register of patents
8.119   A legal mortgage of a patent can, but need not, be registered in the Register of Patents[239] but it is not possible to register an equitable mortgage of a patent and the rules applicable to notice in respect of equitable interests in personal property apply to such mortgages.[240]

8.120   Where a legal mortgage of a patent is not registered and a later transaction takes place in relation to the patent, a person claiming property in the patent by virtue of the later transaction will prevail unless he knew of the earlier mortgage.[241] Actual knowledge is required before the earlier mortgage retains priority.[242] For this purpose, an application for registration is treated as registration.[243] In the case of an unpublished application for a patent, notice to the Controller of Patents of the mortgage is treated as registration.[244]

8.121   The Act does not specifically provide that legal mortgages of patents rank in order of registration but, since only legal mortgages are governed by s 33, its provision (that if the first mortgage is unregistered at the time of the later transaction the latter has priority in the absence of actual knowledge, of the earlier mortgage, on the part of the person

---

234   See RSC O 50 rr 10–15 and para 8.125 *infra*.
235   *Gardner v Lachlan* (1838) 4 Myl & Cr 129.
236   *Smith v Smith* (1833) 2 C & M 231.
237   *Re Wasdale* [1899] 1 Ch 163.
238   *The Attika Hope* [1988] 1 Lloyd's Rep 439.
239   Patents Act 1977 s 33.
240   *Ibid* s 32(3).
241   *Ibid* s 33(1).
242   *Ibid* s 33(1)(c).
243   *Ibid* s 33(4).
244   *Ibid* s 33(1)(b).

claiming by virtue of the later transaction), effectively means that such mortgages will rank in order of registration unless the later claimant has actual knowledge of the existence of the earlier unregistered legal mortgage. The system ensures that a person who checks the Register of Patents before entering into a transaction and registers his own transaction will have full protection.

8.122   A person taking a legal mortgage after an unregistrable equitable mortgage or agreement for a mortgage will take priority over it in the absence of notice of the equitable interest.[245] As between competing equitable mortgages, the ordinary rule that they rank in order of creation if the equities are equal will apply. It is, however, unlikely that the mortgagee of a patent would willingly rely on an equitable mortgage because of the danger of losing the security if a legal mortgage is created and registered in favour of a mortgagee without notice of the equitable interest.

Register of trade marks
8.123   The registered proprietor of a trade mark has, subject to anything appearing on the register, power to assign it and to give receipts for any consideration, but equities in respect of a trade mark may be enforced as in the case of other personal property.[246] Consequently, the rules for trade marks are similar to those for patents but registration of title is mandatory for an assignee of a trade mark. In practice it is unwise to rely on a security interest in a trade mark without registering its transmission. However, the general rules governing equitable interests will apply for security interests which are not created by assignment.

Register of designs
8.124   Registered designs are assignable by the registered proprietor subject to rights, notice of which is entered on the register, and equities in respect of which can be enforced as they can in respect of other personal property.[247] Consequently mortgages in the form of registered assignments will prevail and equitable mortgages, although enforceable, are vulnerable. The general rules on the priority of equitable interests will apply.

Shares
8.125   Although shares in a company are choses in action, they are not subject to the rule in *Dearle v Hall*,[248] as the company does not fulfill the role of the debtor or trustee for the purpose of accepting notice of interests

---

245   *Wapshore Tube Co Ltd v Hyde Imperial Rubber Co* (1900) 18 RPC 374.
246   Trade Marks Act 1938 s 24 and 64(2).
247   Registered Designs Act 1949 s 19(4).
248   (1828) 3 Russ 1; see paras 8.112ff *supra*.

in its shares.[249] Consequently while the usual rules on priority can apply as between legal and equitable mortgagees, as between a number of claimants to shares registered in the name of another, priorities are determined by the order of creation of the equitable interests,[250] unless a claimant under a later title has acquired the status of shareholder or an unconditional right to be registered as such before the company has notice of the claim of the other person.[251]

8.126   The stop notice procedure is the method which has to be used to preserve the position of a person with an equitable interest in shares. It does not, of itself, confer priority but prevents the registration of any transfer of the shares until the person who has obtained the order has had a chance to obtain an order restraining transfer. This is done by filing the stop notice and an affidavit in Chancery Chambers or the District Registry of the High Court. A copy is then served on the company. Notice of any application to transfer the shares is then served by the company on the person who filed the notice and the transfer is delayed for 14 days to give that person a chance to obtain a court order preventing it.[252]

Insurance policies
8.127   Mortgages and charges of insurance policies are subject to the rule in *Dearle v Hall*.[253] Notice is given to the insurer and priorities are in the order of such notices, whether they are given under that rule or s 3 of the Policies of Assurance Act 1867. However, it has been held that failure to produce the policy can affect a second mortgagee with notice of the first mortgage.[254]

Chattels

8.128   In the case of a company there is no need to register an instrument granting security over chattels under the Bills of Sale Acts.[255] However, registration under s 395 of the Companies Act 1985 is necessary. Subject to that requirement, which is dealt with in paras 3.01–3.09 and 8.25–8.41, the priority of security interests over goods depends on the general rules as to priority between and among legal and equitable interests described in para 8.04. The importance of possession as a source of security rights over

---

249   *Société Générale de Paris v Walker* (1885) 11 App Cas 20 at 30.
250   *Swiss Bank Corporation v Lloyds Bank Ltd* [1979] 3 WLR 201.
251   *Moore v North Western Bank* [1891] 2 Ch 599.
252   RSC O 50 rr 11 and 12.
253   See paras 8.112ff *supra*.
254   *Spence v Clarke* (1878) 9 Ch D 137.
255   Bills of Sale Act (1878) Amendment Act 1882 s 17 and *Re Standard Manufacturing Co* [1891] 1 Ch 627.

these tangible movables has been noted. In the case of pledge and liens it is the point at which possession is taken at which priority arises.

Bills of Sale Acts

8.129 Securities which have to be registered under these Acts have priority in order of registration[256] but in the case of securities granted by a company the rules discussed in para 8.01–8.18 will apply with the effect of registration or failure to register under s 395 of the Companies Act 1985 operating in that context.[257]

Priority of security interests over ships

8.130 (a) *The Register of Shipping.* Mortgages of ships are registrable in the register in which the ship, over which the mortgage is taken, is registered. Chapter 3 dealt with the workings of that register and the separate register of fishing vessels. Only legal mortgages of ships are registrable and equitable mortgages, although they can be granted,[258] lose priority to later legal mortgages which are registered.[259] An unregistered mortgage or an equitable mortgage will lose priority to a later registered mortgage, even if the later mortgagee had notice of the earlier mortgage. It will also be postponed to those with priority under the usual rules, such as earlier equitable mortgagees who have not lost priority by their conduct. For example, a later legal mortgage of a ship which is registered prevails over an earlier floating charge which is necessarily equitable.[260] However, as against the mortgagor, an equitable mortgage of a ship is enforceable and this position applies to the liquidator of a mortgagor company. So long as the mortgage is registered under the Companies Act 1985, an equitable mortgagee of a ship retains security in the winding-up, subject to the priority obtained by registered mortgagees.

8.131 As between registered mortgagees, priority is determined by the order of registration and not by the date of creation of the mortgages. This applies, regardless of express, implied or constructive notice, to later mortgagees of the earlier unregistered mortgage.[261] However, when further advances are made by a mortgagee whose mortgage secures such advances and he, although registered first, has notice of a later mortgage, he cannot claim priority in respect of them.[262] This maintains the general rule in relation to tacking in such circumstances, and it seems that the registration of the second mortgage does not constitute notice for the purpose. It would

---

256 Bills of Sale Act 1878 s 10 and see paras 8.29ff.
257 See paras 8.42ff and 8.55ff.
258 Merchant Shipping Act 1894 s 57.
259 *Ibid* s 56.
260 *Black v Williams* [1895] 1 Ch 408.
261 Merchant Shipping Act 1894 s 33 and Merchant Shipping Act 1988 Sch 3 para 3.
262 *The Benwell Tower* (1895) 8 Asp Mar Law Cas 13.

seem to follow that a first mortgage which obliges the mortgagee to make further advances will enable him to retain priority regardless of the creation or registration of later mortgages, whether he has notice of them or not.[263] A registered mortgagee of a ship is protected against a sale of the ship by an execution creditor.[264]

8.132 (b) *Security interests over ships created by operation of law.* A mortgagee (whether the mortgage is registered or not) does not have priority over the claims of lienees. The holder of a possessory lien who has repaired or maintained the ship and supplied equipment has priority over the mortgagee regardless of the date of creation or registration of the mortgage.[265] Similarly, the holder of a maritime lien has priority over a mortgagee whenever the mortgage was created or registered.[266] These rules reflect the nature of a lien as a security created by law and are based on the principle that the mortgagee's security is subject to incumbrances imposed on the ship by law for the benefit of third parties. The doctrine extends to the holder of a bottomry bond to the extent of the bond—providing it is enforced within a reasonable time after the end of the voyage in respect of which it was granted.[267] The principle is that the holder of a lien granted by law prevails over any contractual claim. The holder of a maritime lien will prevail over a bottomry bond holder whose bond was earlier, but a bottomry bond is given priority over a mortgage which was granted earlier than the bond on the basis of the necessity giving rise to the bond— although it is a contractual security.[268]

8.133 Among themselves, liens are subject to priority rules which differ markedly from those applicable to other forms of property. The principle applicable[269] is that the preserver of the property ranks ahead of others. This gives priority to salvage liens over, for example, those available to unpaid seamen. Similarly, it is accepted that since the action of a later salvor preserves the property for the benefit of an earlier one, such claims rank in reverse order of attachment to the ship; a later salvor has priority over an earlier one. This principle applies with like effect as between holders of bottomry bonds. It is also a principle that those whose claim results from voluntary actions lose priority to those whose claims do not. A lienee whose claim results from damage caused by the ship will have priority over the claim of the crew for wages earned after the collision. In the absence of such distinctions, liens of the same class and quality rank *pari passu*, subject to

---

263   LPA 1925 s 94(1)(c).
264   Merchant Shipping Act 1894 s 34.
265   *The Sherbro* (1883) 52 CJ 28.
266   *The A Line* (1839) 1 W Rob 111.
267   *The Royal Arch* (1857) Swab 269.
268   *The A Line, supra.*
269   See L A Sheridan, "Rights in Security" pp 199–200.

the right of the holder of a security interest who sells the property, to his costs of sale which will have priority over other claims against the fund created.

8.134 A lien for damage done by the ship has priority over prior liens and securities.[270] This is based on the principle that the other claims are based on voluntary acts whereas the person who suffered the damage had no choice. However, where a bottomry bond is granted, after a collision, to pay for repairs to the ship after damage giving rise to the lien was done, the bondholder will have priority since the party who suffered the damage has benefited from the repairs to the ship over which he has a lien.[271] Similarly, a salvage lien ranks before a damage lien if the salvors rescued the ship after the damage had been done. This will not be the case where the salvage operation preceded the damage.[272] Among themselves damage liens rank *pari passu* in the absence of laches.[273] Among themselves, salvage liens rank in reverse order of attachment subject to the rule that the lien for the rescue of human life has priority over other salvage liens.[274] While bottomry bonds rank in reverse order of creation between themselves, they are subject to a lien for seamen's wages and master's disbursements.[275] A possessory lien has priority over later maritime liens, but is subject to those attached to the ship when she comes into possession. Seamen's wages due before a ship is docked for repairs or the claims of salvors who bring her in for repairs have priority over the shipwright's possessory lien, but such claims attaching after she is in his hands do not have priority.[276] A lien for seamen's wages has priority over earlier and later bottomry bonds but is subject to salvor's liens.[277]

Register of aircraft mortgages
8.135 Mortgages of aircraft are registrable separately from the aircraft itself. This contrasts with the position with ships since the mortgage of the ship is registrable in the same register as the vessel itself. Chapter 3 dealt with those issues. Registered mortgages of aircraft have priority over any other mortgage or charge over that aircraft except another registered mortgage.[278] As between registered mortgages, priority is according to time of registration. A priority notice system operates which allows a mortgage priority from the date of registration of the notice, providing the

---

270 *The Veritas* [1901] P 304.
271 *The A Line, supra.*
272 *The Sea Spray* [1907] P 133.
273 *The Stream Fisher* [1927] P 73.
274 Merchant Shipping Act 1894 s 544(2).
275 *The Sidney Cove* (1815) 2 Dods 1.
276 *The Gustaf* (1862) Lush 506.
277 *The Union* (1860) 1 Lush 128; *The Sabina* (1843) 7 Jur 82.
278 The Mortgaging of Aircraft Order 1972 (SI 1972/1268) reg 14(1).

mortgage itself is registered within 14 working days of the registration of the priority notice.[279] These provisions have effect regardless of any express, implied or constructive notice that a mortgagee may have of an earlier mortgage, but registered mortgages have no priority over a possessory lien in respect of work done on the aircraft (whenever it was done) on the authority of someone lawfully entitled to possession of it, or over any statutory right to detain the aircraft.[280] The Bills of Sale Acts 1878 and 1882, as they relate to bills given for security, do not apply to registered mortgages of aircraft, but registration, under s 395 of the Companies Act 1985, is necessary.[281] The register constitutes express notice of all facts appearing on it, but the registration of a mortgage is not evidence of its validity. This provision will rarely affect priorities between mortgages, as they are governed by the order of registration of registered mortgages and the priority accorded to registered mortgages over unregistered ones. However, this provision will result in any purchaser of an aircraft subject to a registered mortgage having actual notice of the existence of the mortgage.

Pledge and liens
8.136   The basis of pledges and liens in the possession or (in the case of pledge) the constructive possession of goods by the pledgee was discussed in paras 3.10–3.16 and 6.03–6.50. The priority of these interests over other security interests is determined by that factor. The lien or pledge begins when possession is taken and ends when it is relinquished. The possessory security is subject to subsisting security interests, attached before possession is taken, and defeats those that only attach during possession.

EXECUTION AND PRIORITIES

8.137   The priority of levies of execution or of distress against other security interests depends on the point at which the execution or distress attaches to its subject matter. As a general rule, other interests arising before that time take priority over the execution process and those that arise later are subject to it.

Fieri Facias
8.138   A writ of *fieri facias* binds the goods of the debtor at the time of delivery to the sheriff for execution.[282] However, it only binds the property subject to the existing rights of others which are already attached to

279   *Ibid* reg 14(2).
280   *Ibid* reg 4(4) and (5).
281   See paras 8.25ff and 8.64 *supra*.
282   Supreme Court Act 1981 s 138.

them.[283] Once the writ binds the goods of the debtor any later dealings with them are subject to the right of the sheriff to seize the goods under the writ.[284] However, a purchaser in good faith for value without notice of the writ takes free of the sheriff's right.[285] It is only on seizure that the judgment creditor becomes a secured creditor.[286] Among themselves different orders have priority in the order in which they reach the sheriff, but if the judgment on which a writ is based is erroneously overturned, then when it is restored it regains priority over writs that reached the sheriff between the date on which the judgment was overturned and the date of its restoration.[287]

Garnishee orders

8.139 Since the decision of the court to make a garnishee order (whether *nisi* or absolute) is discretionary, it will not be made if it will prefer one creditor in a case of corporate insolvency.[288] Once the order is made absolute there is an obligation on the garnishee to pay the garnishor but it is subject to pre-existing rights and equities attached to the garnisheed debt in priority over the rights of the debtor.[289]

Charging orders

8.140 A charging order on land is enforceable as an equitable charge created by the debtor over the land or the interest in land.[290] However, like other writs of execution or orders of a like nature, it is subject to registration as a writ or order affecting land under the Land Charges Act 1972 or the Land Registration Act 1925.[291] However, in the case of unregistered land, a charging order over the undivided share of one joint tenant is not so registrable as it affects an interest under a trust and not an interest in land. For that reason the registration of a charging order *nisi* against the name of only one of two joint tenants in error failed to protect the execution creditor from the priority accorded to a later mortgage.[292] Priority is determined by the operation of the appropriate registration system—together with rules on notice in the case of unregistered land.

283   See eg *Proctor v Nicholson* (1835) 7 C & P 67 as to a lien.
284   See *Re Cooper* [1958] Ch 922.
285   Supreme Court Act 1981 and see paras 8.89ff and 14.89ff as to floating charges and liquidations respectively.
286   *Re Clarke* [1898] 1 Ch 366; but note the effect of winding up—see paras 14.189ff.
287   *Bankers Trust v Galadari* [1986] 3 WLR 1099.
288   See *D Wilson (Birmingham) Ltd v Metropolitan Property Developments Ltd* [1975] 2 All ER 814 and para 6.67–6.73.
289   RSC O 49 r 1(1) and *Norton v Yates* [1906] 1 KB 112.
290   Charging Orders Act 1979 s 7(2).
291   Land Charges Act 1972 s 6(1) and Land Registration Act 1925 s 59(1).
292   *Perry v Phaenix Assurance plc* [1988] 1 WLR 940.

Receiver appointed by way of execution

8.141   Such an order only affects the debtor's interest in property. Consequently it is subject to all earlier incumbrances whether legal or equitable.[293] Any receivership order over land is registrable under s 54(1) of the Land Registration Act 1925 or s 6(1)(b) of the Land Charges Act 1925 so as to retain priority.[294]

Distraint

8.142   Distress as a remedy applicable to the goods of the debtor gains priority on the basis of possession. Seizure is the point at which it attaches. This rule applies between competing levies of distress and as against execution levied on the same goods so that goods seized by way of execution cannot be subject to distraint. For priorities as between a floating charge and a levy of distress (the most likely conflict) see paras 8.75–8.96.

---

293   *Re Bristow* [1906] 2 IR 215.
294   *Clayhope Properties v Evans* [1986] 2 All ER 795.

CHAPTER 9

Security by the Use of Ownership Rights

NATURE OF SUCH METHODS

9.01 In commercial practice security will sometimes be sought against assets by methods which the law does not regard as forms of security but as means of retaining or transferring ownership. It is possible for a company to assign its receivables by way of sale rather than mortgage. Companies, like individuals, may purchase property by way of hire purchase so that until a final instalment is paid and an option exercised the asset subject to the contract remains in the ownership of the seller. Some equipment will be leased by a company so that ownership never passes and the lessor retains title throughout the course of the transaction. These methods all represent ways of raising finance for the business of the company or of obtaining resources on credit without actually entering into what is legally classified as an arrangement creating contractual security.

9.02 The Diamond Report has recommended that retention of title clauses, hire purchase agreements and leases for a period of 3 years or more should be treated as security interests. Pending a reform of the law along those lines and the development of a reformed registration system for security interests over property other than land, the mismatch between the commercial and the legal classification of such transactions is mitigated only by the provisions of the Insolvency Act 1986 on the moratorium that arises under an administration order.[1]

9.03 On the insolvency of the company those assets which do not belong to the company cannot be claimed by the receiver or liquidator, and are not available for distribution among creditors. This is because the doctrine of reputed ownership which formerly applied in the case of individual bankruptcy does not apply on the winding up or, *a fortiori* the receivership of a company. It is thus impossible for the creditors of an insolvent company to make any claim against goods owned by others which are in the possession, custody or control of the company even if the company was made to appear to have a wealth and substance which it in fact lacked.

---

1 Professor A L Diamond, *A Review of Security Interests in Property*, DTI 1989, and see note 2 and text below.

9.04   Since s 395 of the Companies Act 1985 only applies to charges created by the company and since the registration systems which apply to various forms of asset frequently do not require the registration of equitable interests, a transaction involving assignment, leasing, hire purchase, or retention of title may in fact mislead creditors. The assignment of a company's debts by way of sale does not require registration in any register although it may be that the debtor will be notified to give priority to the assignee under the rule in *Dearle v Hall* and to ensure payment of the debt to the factor. Retention of title on the sale of goods to a company by a supplier does not require registration in any form. The establishment by the company itself of a trust fund, so that the assets in it are excluded from distribution to its general creditors as the property of the fund's beneficiaries, does not require registration or notice to creditors. In the case of assets such as registered land, ships, and patents the ownership of the asset is registered. However, this may not be publicly available information and the registration systems affecting particular forms of property are inconsistent in this respect.

9.05   This chapter deals with assets which are unavailable to creditors on company insolvency because ownership of them does not vest in the company rather than on the basis of priority of a security interest (in the strictly legal sense). The Insolvency Act 1986 recognises the use of some of these methods as a *de facto* form of security by including them in the scope of the moratorium provisions applicable on the administration of a company.[2]

RETENTION OF TITLE

9.06   This form of *de facto* security is often called a '*Romalpa* clause'. It is normally used by those supplying goods to a business in an attempt to provide some security for the supplier in the case of the customer's insolvency.[3] This reflects the fact that suppliers are often the group with the greatest economic bargaining power among those who are likely to be unsecured creditors in the event of the company's liquidation or receivership and who are thus likely to have no priority over the claims of those (usually banks) with fixed and floating charges or over preferential

---

2   ss 10(1)(b) and 11(3)(c) Insolvency Act 1986 apply to hire purchase agreements, conditional sale agreements, chattel leasing agreements (capable of subsisting for more than 3 months) and retention of title agreements (whereby no charge is created but whereby the seller gains priority over all other creditors of the company as respects the goods or property representing them if the company is wound up before the seller is paid—s 10(4)).

3   The fact that this is the motive does not make such a clause a charge—*John Snow & Co Ltd v DBG Woodcraft & Co Ltd* [1985] BCLC 54.

creditors. Such attempts to gain security have been the subject of much debate[4] as the case law has developed after the leading case of *Aluminium Industries Vaassen v Romalpa Aluminium.*[5] Since the clauses named after this case may seek to achieve a number of related but distinct objectives they are dealt with here by considering:[6]

(a) The retention of ownership in goods by the seller before such goods are processed, mixed with others or sold by the purchasing company.

(b) Attempts to use as security goods created by the mixing of the goods supplied with other goods or labour.

(c) The effect of a subsale of the original goods or their product.

(d) Attempts to secure the proceeds of a subsale of the goods or the sale of their product by the purchasing company; either as debts or as money once the debts are paid.

(e) Which debts as between the seller and the company may be secured by any of these methods.

Title to unmixed goods before subsale

9.07 It has long been accepted that under the Sale of Goods Act 1979, and its predecessor the 1893 Act, goods can be sold on the basis of a 'conditional sale'. It is not necessary that the ownership of the goods should pass from one party to another at the time of delivery or of entering the contract for their sale. The passing of property is a matter left to the agreement of the parties to the sale, subject to the rule that the property in unascertained goods cannot pass until they have been ascertained. It is always possible for a contract for the sale of goods to stipulate that the ownership ('property') in the goods shall remain with the seller until the goods have been paid for.[7]

9.08 Such a clause will be effective providing it has been incorporated into the contract between the parties and will enable the seller to prevent the sale by the receiver or liquidator for the benefit of other creditors of goods delivered to the insolvent company as the goods remain the property of the seller.[8] If a provision is added to the clause allowing the seller to enter the premises of the company to repossess the goods then clearly their recovery will be possible. It may be possible even in the absence of such a clause if the

---

4 See Generally J Parris, "Effective Retention of Title Clauses", Collins 1986.
5 [1976] 2 All ER 552.
6 For a useful summary of the state of the case law see *Tatung (UK) Ltd v Galex Telesure Ltd* (1989) 5 BCC 325 at 332.
7 Sale of Goods Act 1979 s 19(1) expressly provides that this is the case for 'specific goods'. Goods are not likely to be unascertained by the time payment is made. If they were, then that would merely delay the passing of property to the advantage of the seller.
8 As to incorporation see eg *Sauter Automation Ltd v Goodman Mechanical Services Ltd* [1986] 2 FTLR 239.

courts are willing to imply a term giving a licence to enter and recover goods in the particular agreement between the parties. If the company's receiver or liquidator in fact sells the goods which were subject to the clause this will give rise to personal liability on his part in conversion.[9] The seller's claim is not simply as an unsecured creditor of the company.

9.09   The clarity of the position where title is simply retained and goods have not been mixed with others or sold by the company was accepted by the court of appeal in the *Romalpa* case and in *Clough Mill v Martin,*[10] where the presence of the provisions dealing with mixed goods in the same clause was held not to result in the simple retention of title clause being regarded as a charge on the goods. This will be so providing the clause does retain the legal title to property in the goods. An attempt to 'retain' equitable or beneficial title will be construed as a transfer of legal title and a grant back in the form of either a charge or a trust.[11]

9.10   In many cases the use of a provision simply reserving the title to the goods to the seller will be inadequate. If goods are being bought in the course of business they are not likely to remain in the possession of the buyer in unaltered form for very long. The purpose of the purchase of the goods is likely to be either their resale at a profit without any processing by the buyer, or their inclusion together with other goods in a process resulting in an end product to be sold by the company which bought the goods from the supplier. Only the supplier of capital equipment can rely on a simple reservation of title as only such goods are likely to remain in the possession of the buyer unaltered. Such suppliers are more likely to use leasing or hire-purchase arrangements than reservation of title. The supplier of raw materials or stock has to face the likelihood of processing or resale and the fact that the use to which goods required by him are likely to be put make a floating charge a more appropriate form of security. However, attempts have frequently been made to retain title to such goods.

Security over mixed goods

9.11   The difficulties referred to above mean that some suppliers have sought to include in a retention of title clause a provision to deal with the use of the goods supplied in the manufacture of some other product. Attempts to extend the effective security to the proceeds of sale of the product or of the original goods are dealt with below.

---

9   See H. Picarda, "The Law of Receivers and Managers", Butterworths 1984 p 88 as to receivers.
10   [1984] 3 All ER 982.
11   *Re Bond Worth* [1979] 3 All ER 919, where it was held that the creation of a floating charge by the company buyer was the true intention of the parties.

9.12 In the *Romalpa* case[12] the second part of the clause in question sought to ensure that the product made from aluminium foil supplied by the seller would be the property of the seller. The effect of this clause did not however need to be decided by the court as the claim in the case related only to unmixed foils. It is arguable that even in the absence of a term of an agreement expressly dealing with the matter, the product of any processing or mixing of the original goods can be subject to tracing by the seller as the owner of the goods processed or mixed.[13] However, it would seem that where the mixed goods have lost their identity in new goods and the mixture is of heterogeneous goods, mere ownership of the original goods which are ingredients of the final product is not of itself sufficient to give rise to a tracing remedy.[14] It is necessary that an express stipulation of the contract should allow the seller property rights in goods produced by the use of those he has supplied. Not all such stipulations will be effective in retaining title as opposed to creating a charge which will be invalid unless it has been registered under s 395 of the Companies Act 1985.[15] It would seem that even where the identity of goods is not lost, the absence of any requirement that new goods be set aside or recorded as being produced from the supplier's input of material may be fatal to the effectiveness of a clause seeking to preserve his property. It may also prevent tracing in the absence of such a clause.[16]

9.13 If there is no express provision dealing with mixed goods, it would seem that goods, such as an engine fitted to a generator, which can be detached from other goods with which they are assembled and which retain their identity may remain the property of the seller. In *Hendy Lennox*[17] it was the effect of the attachment of engines to generators in putting the generators in a deliverable state and thus passing property to a sub-buyer which prevented ownership of the engine from remaining with the seller. Had sub-buyers not existed for assembled generators, the property of the seller in the engines would not have disappeared merely because of their incorporation into generators given that disconnection would take only a few hours and would not involve any change to the engines. The engines retained their character despite being attached to generators and could be distinguished from leather used in the manufacture of handbags, Acrilan

12   [1976] 2 All ER 552, para 9.06 *supra*.
13   *Re Hallett's Estate* (1880) 13 Ch D 696.
14   *Borden (UK) Ltd v Scottish Timber Products* [1979] 3 All ER 961 per Bridge LJ at 969–971, Templeman LJ at 973 and Buckley LJ at 974.
15   *Ibid* at 971 and *Re Bond Worth* (n 11 *supra*)
16   *Re Peachdart* [1983] 3 All ER 204; *Borden (UK) Ltd (supra)* per Bridge LJ at 971, who presumed that the clause in *Romalpa* would be effective. That clause did provide for the separation of goods produced from aluminium supplied under the contract if the seller required this. See also *Clough Mill v Marten* (n 10 *supra*) per Robert Goff LJ at p 986.
17   *Hendy Lennox v Grahame Puttick Ltd* [1984] 2 All ER 152.

which becomes yarn, or resin which is lost in chipboard.[18] In the absence of any provision dealing with 'mixed goods', a simple retention of title clause may succeed in giving effective security to a seller whose goods, although attached to other property, may still be detached. It will not, without more, protect him from the consumption or loss of identity of his goods. A term in an agreement for the repair of machinery which gives ownership of the repaired machines with the spare parts inserted by the repairer to him as surety for payment creates a charge which is registrable under s 395.[19]

9.14   If it is accepted that the law on tracing does not, in itself, allow the seller who has retained title to trace his goods into others if their identity has been lost in a manufacturing or other process, the question arises of whether an express stipulation in the agreement can have such an effect. In *Borden*,[20] where there was no clause dealing with mixed property, it was suggested by Templeman LJ that the existence of such a clause might cause the product resulting from the processing of goods to be used as security by the seller of those goods. This, however, would suggest a charge rather than an ownership interest in the product. It was accepted by Templeman LJ that the title of the owner of resin disappeared when it became incorporated in chipboard. However, Bridge LJ suggested that a properly drafted clause could give a seller title to the product into which his goods disappeared when he recognised the possibility of the *Romalpa* clause to this effect being valid, although he referred to this as the reservation of effective security.[21] Buckley LJ suggested the possibility in a different case of 'common' ownership of the product or a transfer of ownership by an express term of the contract.[22] While the majority of the Court of Appeal may leave open the possibility of drafting an effective clause to provide a seller with property in the product of his goods, the tenor of their judgments indicates that the creation of a charge is the more likely outcome. Registration of the clause under s 395 is therefore prudent.

9.15   In the *Romalpa* case itself the clause dealing with mixed goods was not in issue but some *dicta* seem to support its effectiveness in retaining the property in such goods in the hands of seller.[23] That clause allowed the seller to require the separate storage of mixed goods produced by the use of his goods. The effectiveness of an appropriately worded clause seeking to allow a seller to retain title in mixed goods by a method other than the grant of a charge on the goods by the buyer is supported by *dicta* in the Court of

---

18   *Ibid* per Staugton J.
19   *Specialist Plant Servicing Ltd v Braithwaite Ltd* [1987] BCLC 1.
20   [1979] 3 All ER 961 at 973.
21   *Ibid* at 971.
22   *Ibid* at 974.
23   [1976] 2 All ER 552 per Roskill LJ at 562.

Appeal in *Clough Mill v Martin*.[24] That case, like *Romalpa*, was concerned with the effect of a retention of title clause on unmixed goods but considered the clause dealing with mixed goods only because of its relevance in indicating the intention of the parties as to the whole contractual arrangement. There was unanimous agreement that, although on the facts of the particular case the clause seeking to 'reserve' title in mixed goods to the seller was an unregistered charge granted by the buyer, the separate part of the clause reserving title in unmixed goods was effective as a reservation of title. The whole clause was not to be treated as an unregistered charge merely because that was the nature of one part of it. In the words of Robert Goff LJ:

> "The fact that I feel driven to do violence to the language of the fourth sentence of the condition is not of itself enough to persuade me that further violence must be done to the language of the first."[25]

9.16   The reason for the decision that the clause in *Clough Mill* dealing with mixed goods would amount to a charge was that it sought to give the supplier the ownership of the whole of the product into which his goods were converted. No allowance would be made for labour or other materials supplied by the buyer; for payment by the buyer of part of the price of the seller's goods used in production; or for the ownership of some goods used in production by other sellers using reservation of title clauses. Such practical difficulties and the injustice resulting from this failure to make allowance for the claims of others were significant factors in leading the court to infer that a trust or a charge was intended by the clause. Of the two a charge was more likely.[26]

9.17   However, it was recognised by Robert Goff and Oliver LJJ that, while the matter was unsettled, there was no reason in principle or in law why the parties could not agree that the ownership of mixed goods should vest in the seller. This suggests that a clause which laid down that such goods must be subject to common ownership by the seller, the buyer and any other owners of material incorporated in the mixed goods in suitable proportions could be effective in preserving that element of the seller's ownership rights without the creation of a charge by the buyer. The co-owners could hold the legal or beneficial interest as either joint tenants or tenants in common. A clause which stated the proportional ownership right—or a method for determining such a right—and that the property was held as tenants in common could overcome the difficulties, referred to

---

24   [1984] 3 All ER 982.
25   *Ibid* at 990.
26   See Robert Goff LJ in *ibid* at 989–990 and Oliver LJ at 993, and *Re Peachdart* [1983] 3 All ER 204 as to the inappropriate nature of a trust.

in the context of tracing by Templeman LJ in *Borden*,[27] of discovering with precision the proportion of the value of the mixed goods attributable to the seller's materials.

9.18   Such a clause may, for example, stipulate a formula to be used to ascertain the share in the mixed goods to be retained by the seller by reference to the relative value of his input and that of other parties (including the buyer). In none of the decided cases has a clause on the ownership of mixed goods reached such a level of sophistication. There is no reason why the common ownership of mixed goods stipulated in such a clause should not survive repudiation of the contract by the seller and leave the seller with limited ownership rights but not a charge.[28] The constraints preventing the seller from receiving a windfall would be inherent in his ownership right and not merely terms of a contract.

9.19   It has to be accepted that even such a clause may be susceptible to interpretation as a charge since it cannot answer the difficulties which arise if another supplier of material incorporated in the mixed goods has claimed a higher proportion of ownership rights than is possible under the first supplier's clause. These factors suggest that there is a risk that even a clause seeking to overcome the difficulties raised in *Clough Mill* would fail in its purpose. The question, as Oliver LJ put it, is whether a clause seeking to create or retain title on the part of the seller to mixed goods can be given 'sensible operation' other than as a charge in any particular case. However, it seems that a seller's interest in mixed goods need not necessarily derive from the grant by the buyer and thus amount to a registrable charge.[29]

9.20   If a suitably refined clause on the ownership of mixed goods is to be upheld by the courts, it may be necessary that the agreement provide a suitable mechanism for the separate storage and identification of such goods. A failure to provide for this may give rise to insuperable problems of identification as to which goods are subject to the clause and this, in turn, may cause the court to infer that the intention of the parties as regards ownership was not that expressed in the clause but rather that the whole ownership of the mixed goods was to vest in the buyer; subject, perhaps, to a floating charge granted by him. An effective clause to reserve title in mixed goods may require a stipulation on identification by storage, marking of goods, or otherwise.[30] Such a provision was contained in the clause in the

27   [1979] 3 All ER 961 at 972.
28   This difficulty was expressed by Robert Goff LJ in *Clough Mill* (n 23 *supra*) at 990.
29   [1984] 3 All ER 982 per Oliver LJ at 993. Contrast *Tatung (UK) Ltd v Galex Telesure Ltd* (1989) 5 BCC 325 as to proceeds of the sale or other disposal of the goods.
30   See eg *Re Peachdart* [1983] 3 All ER 204 at 210, and *Hendy Lennox* [1984] 2 All ER 152 at 154, where the engines were identifiable by serial numbers.

Romalpa case. The content of such a provision will differ according to the nature of the goods concerned. A clear obligation has to be imposed on the buyer to enable goods to be accurately identified.

9.21 In any circumstances in which ownership has passed to the buyer and any rights of the seller arise by grant of the buyer after that event, a charge is likely to be created and require registration. Any effective right over mixed goods must amount to property retained by the seller if he is to keep priority on the basis of ownership rights. Where goods supplied to a buyer become annexed to real property the title of those goods will vest in its owner, as they will be fixtures.[31]

The effects of a subsale of goods subject to a retention of title clause

9.22 When, as is usual, goods subject to a retention of title clause are supplied for resale (whether or not this is after they have been mixed with other goods or subjected to some other process), the clause will either expressly stipulate that title is retained only until such resale or will have such a provision implied into it by the court in order to give the contract business efficacy.[32]

9.23 Even in the absence of such a contractual term, s 25(1) of the Sale of Goods Act 1979 enables a sub-purchaser receiving the goods in good faith and without notice of the buyer's lack of title to obtain a good title to goods if the buyer is in possession of the goods or documents of title to the goods with the seller's consent. This occurs when the goods are delivered or transferred by the buyer to his sub-purchaser. The rule will apply even where the delivery of the goods to the sub-purchaser is made by the seller (and not the buyer); despite the seller's belief that the delivery is by way of some transaction (such as hire) other than sale of the goods.[33]

9.24 Where s 25(1) is relied upon delivery or transfer of the goods (or documents of title to them) to the sub-purchaser is necessary. However, where the retention of title clause in the contract between the seller and the buyer expressly or impliedly gives the buyer the right to sell, the transfer of property in the goods to a sub-purchaser will suffice to extinguish the seller's title. In *Hendy Lennox*[34] the fact that the attachment of engines supplied under the retention of title clause put the generators of which they

31   See Picarda, *op cit* at p 128.
32   For express provisions see *Clough Mill* (n 23 *supra*); *Re Peachdart* (n 25 *supra*); and *Re Bond Worth* (n 17 *supra*). For implied provisions see *Four Point Garage v Carter* [1985] 3 All ER 12; *Re Andrabell Ltd* [1984] BCLC 522; and *Romalpa* (n 5 *supra*).
33   *Four Point Garage v Carter* [1985] 3 All ER 12.
34   [1984] 2 All ER 152.

were part into a deliverable state so that property passed from buyer to sub-purchaser, extinguished the seller's title to the engines. Delivery of the generators to the sub-purchaser was unnecessary.

9.25   A sale by a buyer of goods subject to a retention of title clause in any other circumstances which operate to confer a good title on a sub-purchaser will also end the seller's title. This may be by estoppel under s 21 of the Sale of Goods Act 1979; sale in market overt under s 22; or sale by a mercantile agent under the Factors Act 1889. In practice, the extinction of the seller's title on a sub-sale will usually be a result of the express or implied terms of the contract containing the *Romalpa* clause. It is possible that the behaviour of the seller will give the buyer apparent or ostensible authority to sell on his behalf. This will result in a transfer of title to the sub-purchaser.

Proceeds of sale

9.26   Since the sub-sale of goods by a buyer is likely to terminate the seller's title in the goods, the seller will seek to establish a claim against the proceeds realised by the sub-sale. This may be attempted either by the use of the doctrine of legal or equitable tracing or by the insertion of a provision in the sale contract giving the seller a claim to such proceeds.

9.27   If it can be established that a fiduciary relationship exists between the buyer and the seller in relation to the proceeds of sale, the claim of the seller to such money will have priority over those of other creditors on the grounds that money held by an insolvent company on trust for another is not subject either to receivership or to winding up.[35] It has been the issue of whether a relationship resulting in a claim to proceeds of sale exists which has been the most difficult question to determine in the *Romalpa* line of cases.

9.28   In the *Romalpa* case, it was accepted on all sides that under the agreement the buyer had the right to sell unmixed aluminium foils. The second part of the clause clearly contemplated the sale of mixed goods. However, the right of the seller to trace the proceeds of a sale of unmixed goods (which were in fact kept separate from other monies by the receiver for that purpose) was held to depend on whether, on the facts, and on the true construction of the bargain there was a fiduciary relationship between the parties[36] or whether the buyers were entitled to sell the goods on their

---

35   See paras 9.49 ff below.
36   [1976] 2 All ER 552 per Roskill LJ at 561, and see Goff LJ at 566 and Megaw LJ at 568. It was conceded by the buyers that they were bailees—Mocatta J at 555.

own account rather than as bailees of the seller's goods and as agents for the sellers.

9.29 In construing the clause in that case the court insisted that the implied right to sell must be consistent with the intent of the whole clause. The fact that a fiduciary relationship was referred to in relation to the proceeds of sale of mixed goods dealt with in the second part of the clause was regarded as an important factor pointing to the need to treat the implied right of sale of unmixed goods as a sale by the buyer as a fiduciary on behalf of the seller.[37] Although this would not promote the business efficacy of the buyer it did serve that purpose from the seller's point of view and thus could be part of the implied term.[31] The fact that this finding might negate the advantage of the period of credit given to the buyers by another term of the contract was not regarded as an obstacle to the implication of such a term. This was despite the fact that the clause tied the passing of property to the payment of all debts due to the seller from the buyer. Such considerations were outweighed by the need to fulfil the intentions of the parties as gleaned from the clause as a whole. The essence of the decision was in Roskill LJ's words:[38]

"I see no difficulty in the contractual concept that, as between the defendants and their sub-purchasers, the defendants sold as principals, but that, as between themselves and the plaintiffs those goods which they were selling as principals within their implied authority from the plaintiffs were the plaintiffs goods which they were selling as agents for the plaintiffs to whom they remained fully accountable. If an agent lawfully sells his principal's goods, he stands in a fiduciary relationship to his principal and remains accountable to his principal for those goods and their proceeds. A bailee is in like position in relation to his bailor's goods. What, then, is there here to relieve the defendants from their obligation to account to the plaintiffs for those goods of the plaintiffs which they lawfully sell to subpurchasers!"

9.30 This suggests that if it is accepted that goods which are sold by a buyer to a sub-purchaser remain the property of the seller at the time of the subsale the buyer will necessarily be selling as an agent or as bailee and will have a fiduciary duty to account to the seller for the proceeds of sale. In principle this will apply whether the goods subject to subsale are unmixed and unprocessed by the buyer or are 'mixed goods'. In the latter case, however, there is no possibility of any ownership rights in the mixed or processed goods remaining with the seller unless the clause dealing with this satisfies the conditions of the identification of goods and the specification of a clear proportional ownership mentioned above.[39] It would seem that

---

37   *Ibid* per Roskill LJ at 563 and Goff LJ at 565–566.
38   *Ibid* at 563–564.
39   See above para 9.17; *Re Peachdart* (n 29 *supra*); and *Clough Mill* (n 23 *supra*).

without an express provision specifying the title to be obtained in mixed goods, tracing will not operate where the identity of the original good is lost in a process of production.[40]

9.31   Since the *Romalpa* case the courts have displayed a considerable reluctance to allow title to the proceeds of sub-sale to sellers. The tendency has been to construe provisions attempting to achieve this as charges in need of registration. Even in the *Romalpa* case[41] the difficulties inherent in a finding that the buyer was entitled to resell the goods only on account of the seller were recognised and the reality that until difficulties arose those proceeds would be used by the buyer to finance his own business was accepted.[37]

9.32   In *Re Bond Worth*[42] the issue of the proceeds of sale was dealt with on the basis that property passed on delivery since only equitable and beneficial title was reserved until payment. This resulted in there being no bailor-bailee relationship as a bailor retains general property and only special property passes to a bailee. Only a trust or charge was possible. The factors pointing to a charge were the presumed right of redemption of the buyer and the fact that a surplus on a forced sale would go to the buyer. This last point was taken to be the intention of the parties and if this is the intention clearly it does distinguish the relationship from that of bailor and bailee or principal and agent where the fiduciary is accountable for the whole proceeds of sale and not merely the price due to the seller. In this case a clause expressly seeking to give the sellers an interest in the proceeds of sale of both unmixed fibre and other products of which it was a constituent or into which it was converted failed to affect the proceeds of sale because the reservation of only equitable and beneficial title was held, on the facts, to create a floating charge which was void for non-registration.

9.33   In *Borden (UK) Ltd v Scottish Timber Products Ltd*[43] the clause did not deal with proceeds of sale of mixed goods and it was found that the resin supplied was received by the buyers to the seller's knowledge for use in the manufacture of chipboard. The court found that this meant that the receipt of the resin did not produce a fiduciary relationship. There was no intention that the sellers should be able to call for the return of the resin in its original or altered form. Bridge J doubted whether tracing could ever apply to goods which lost their identity in new goods. In this case it is clear that only a right of ownership (as opposed to a security interest) by sellers in the

---

40 *Borden (UK) Ltd v Scottish Timber Products* (n 14 *supra*), and see para 9.12 above.
41 [1976] 2 All ER 552 at 561, 566, 568.
42 [1979] 3 All ER 919.
43 [1979] 3 All ER 961.

mixed property could result in a right to trace to the proceeds of sale of those mixed goods. Such a right was clearly not going to be implied from a simple reservation of title to the unmixed goods.

9.34 In *Re Peachdart*[44] a clause which sought expressly to confer tracing rights against processed or mixed goods and the proceeds of their sale was held not to compel an assumption of bailment throughout the process. It was held that on the facts (despite the wording of the clause) property in the leather supplied to the buyer passed to him on its application to the manufacture of a particular handbag. Consequently a charge on handbags and later proceeds of sale was granted by the buyer after this stage. The absence of any system of recording which of the handbags sold by the buyer were made from the seller's leather, or of any obligation on the buyer to hold the proceeds of a sale of handbags separately in an interest bearing account and to refrain from using them in his business, was important.[45] This was stated to be so despite the possibility canvassed by counsel for the seller that an expert could identify the leather used to manufacture a particular handbag as being from a particular parcel of skin.

9.35 The detailed nature of the clause in this case and its precise reference to a right to trace under *Re Hallett* makes it a strong precedent against the efficacy of clauses applying to the proceeds of sale in the absence of an obligation to hold such proceeds in a separate account. It must be noted, however, that in *Romalpa* there was a willingness in the Court of Appeal to accept that a practice of permitting the use of proceeds in a buyer's business was not necessarily fatal to the seller's claim against the proceeds.[46] However, in *Romalpa* the funds in question were in fact separately held and had been since their receipt by the receivers. This was not the case in *Re Peachdart*.

9.36 In *Hendy Lennox v Grahame Puttick Ltd*[47] the question of a claim against proceeds of sale primarily arose only on the issue of whether such a term could be implied into a clause which only dealt expressly with the retention of title to unmixed goods. It was held that there was no fiduciary relationship on the facts of the case whether or not the buyers were bailees. The absence from the clause of any treatment of mixed or processed goods; of a requirement for separate storage of any of the goods; and of any reference to a fiduciary relationship and the fact that in this case the proceeds of sale would be those of generators and not simply of 'unmixed'

44 [1983] 3 All ER 204.
45 per Vinelott LJ at 210.
46 [1976] 2 All ER 552 at 563 and 565–566.
47 [1984] 2 All ER 152.

engines supplied by the seller was held to distinguish the case from *Romalpa*. The fact that the contract allowed 1 to 2 months credit and the business inconvenience of an implied requirement to hold proceeds of sale separately both gravitated against such an implication.

9.37   *Hendy Lennox* therefore reinforces the difficulty of showing a fiduciary relationship to enable the tracing of the title to goods into the proceeds of sale and the courts' reluctance to imply a term to this effect because of lack of business efficacy. Insofar as arguments against a clause relate to business efficacy they are irrelevant to a clear express term. The problem of a requirement that proceeds of sale be held separately remains as does the contradictory effect of granting a credit period which implies a right of the buyer to use the proceeds of a sub-sale in his business.

9.38   *Re Andrabell*[48] was another case which involved the question of whether a clause concerning proceeds of sale should be implied. In this case there was no express clause relating to mixed goods or the proceeds of sale. The case does not decide whether the buyer was a bailee because this was regarded as unnecessary. The only question regarded as relevant was whether he was a fiduciary and it was found that he was not. The reasons for this finding included the fact that the price of each item sold was secured by reservation of title but not the whole indebtedness and that it was only contended that the buyer was a fiduciary for the debt and not the whole proceeds of sale as would be the case with a bailee. There was no obligation to keep the goods or the proceeds of sale separate and a 45-day credit period was allowed which resulted in an assumption that the proceeds might be used in respect of the buyer's own business. In this case it was sufficient that the business efficacy of the contract was adequate without an implied clause which related to the proceeds of sale.

9.39   In *Clough Mills v Martin*[49] however the statements about the proceeds of sale suggest that the buyer may be a bailee of goods without having a fiduciary relationship with the seller with regard to the proceeds of sale if this intention is shown in the agreement. It would seem to be possible for a relationship of bailment to exist without a fiduciary relationship resulting in a claim by the seller against the proceeds of sale.

9.40   In *Pfeiffer v Arbuthnot*[50] it was held that if a seller allows sub-sale by the buyer the normal implication will be that sale is allowed on the buyer's own account and not as bailee or agent of the seller unless express wording

---

48   [1984] BCLC 522.
49   [1984] 3 All ER 982 at 987 and 993.
50   [1987] BCLC 522.

rebuts that presumption. If the wording of a clause suggests the proceeds of sub-sales belong to the buyer and that he is only to pass money on to the extent of his liability to the seller that will suggest that proceeds are not held as a fiduciary for the seller. Such a conclusion is reinforced by the commercial improbability of an intention that all proceeds of sale are held as fiduciary for the seller.

9.41 The case law considered above leads to the conclusion that a right of a seller against the proceeds of a sub-sale is unlikely to arise by the insertion of an implied term by the court or by the application of the doctrine of tracing in *Re Hallett*.[51] It would seem that buyers may be held to be bailees of goods sold subject to simple retention of title clause applicable to unmixed goods but that this will not be sufficient of itself to impose a fiduciary relationship as regards the proceeds of a sub-sale. Only a clear intention of the parties that a fiduciary relationship should exist will suffice. This must appear in an express stipulation of the contract which must not be contradicted by a stipulation elsewhere, or possibly, by an established practice of granting credit to allow the use of the proceeds of sale in the buyer's business. The express clause must require proceeds of sale to be kept separate from other monies in the buyer's ownership.

9.42 Even with such provisions a clause which holds the buyer accountable only for any sum owed to the seller as opposed to the whole proceeds of sale may be classified as a charge due to the surplus allowed to be retained by the buyer and the apparent dissimilarity between that provision and the more usual fiduciary obligation of an agent or bailee. However, it is hard to see why an agreement which clearly expresses the intention of the parties, that a proportion of the proceeds of sale of goods supplied by the seller (or those manufactured in part from such goods) the equivalent to the value of the input represented by the seller's good is to remain the property of the seller, should not take effect as a fiduciary obligation on the buyer.

9.43 The case of *Tatung UK Ltd v Galex Telesure Ltd*[52] provides further evidence of the difficulty of creating an effective trust over the proceeds of sale or other dealings with goods by express agreement. In that case a clause, which laid down that the proceeds of hiring out and selling the goods supplied to the defendant were to be kept in a separate account on trust for the seller, was held to create a charge registrable under s 395 of the Companies Act 1985. The right to sell or otherwise deal with the goods was

51   (1880) 13 Ch D 696.
52   (1989) 5 BCC 325.

conferred by the agreement which sought to create a trust in respect of the proceeds of such transactions. The clause was held to create a registrable charge because the interest of the supplier in the hire debts due to the company was defeasible on payment by the company of sums due from it which is an indication of a security interest. This view was held to be consistent with the *Romalpa* case because the nature of the equitable interest of the seller in the foil in that case was not explored. Since, in *Tatung (UK) Ltd v Galex Telesure Ltd*, the right over the monies in the account arose by agreement of the parties and not by the right conferred by law to trace under the *Re Hallett* doctrine it was a charge by way of security created by the defendant company. Even if the security arose at the same time as the debt to which it attached it conferred security on the company's future property by encumbering such property when it vested in the company. This case further reinforces the view that registration is necessary if any interest claimed in the proceeds of a sub-sale or other disposal of goods is to be enforceable against a receiver or liquidator.

9.44   It seems from the case law that only unmixed goods are ever likely to be subject to a successful reservation of title clause. The requirements of physical separation or identification apparently required for such a clause to succeed in the case of mixed goods or proceeds of sale combined with sophisticated 'proportional clauses' required in the case of mixed goods or their proceeds of sale[53] are impractical. Even if that obstacle is overcome the defeasibility of the interest of the seller by the payment of the amounts due is likely to be evidence of a security interest which, if created by the buyer's agreement over its property will be registrable under s 395. The case law since the *Romalpa* case itself certainly indicates that there is substantial doubt about the possibility of drafting an agreement to avoid this outcome.

Securing the whole account

9.45   A *Romalpa* clause may seek either to secure merely the price of the goods title to which is retained by the seller or the whole amount due under a particular contract (or generally) from buyer to seller. Where the former applies, it has been suggested that this creates a difficulty in arguing for the existence of a fiduciary relationship as the duty to account will be argued to apply to only part of the proceeds of sale.[54] If the retention of title secures the whole account the claim of the seller is more likely to be for the whole

---

53   Even if goods are unmixed and unprocessed, the proceeds of their subsale are likely to include a mark up for the buyer. If they are sold at less than the cost of purchase by the buyer, then presumably the seller can only claim the actual proceeds of sale if his claim to reserve title and trace succeeds.

54   per Peter Gibson J in *Re Andrabell* [1984] BCLC 522.

proceeds of sale of sufficient goods to meet that amount. This may be seen by a court as being more compatible with the existence of an agreement that the buyer owes a fiduciary duty to the seller. However, it has to be accepted that logically even the amount due for the whole account may leave certain particular goods whose proceeds of sale will only be claimed in part. Where a seller has retained title to goods and exercises his right to resell them because of the buyer's non-payment before the goods have become mixed or processed or have been resold, and where the seller retains title to all goods until all debts due to him under the contract with the buyer have been paid then there is a question who is entitled to any surplus monies. It would seem that if the contract still subsists and has not been terminated for example by repudiation and acceptance of it, then the seller may only resell sufficient goods to recoup the debts due from the buyer and if he in fact realises any surplus he will be required to account to the buyer for it. However, if the contract has terminated the seller may resell the goods and retain the whole proceeds subject to returning any amount actually paid by the buyer. This results from the extinction of contractual restraints on the seller by the termination of the contract.[55]

9.46 If the court in any particular case decides that on the true construction of the clause in the context of the dealings between the parties to the transaction and their whole agreement, a charge on the buyer's property is created; it will be void against the liquidator, administrator, or secured creditors (and thus a receiver) if it was not registered under s 395 of the Companies Act 1985. A charge over uncollected proceeds of sale will require registration as a charge over a book debt.[56] A charge over assets which can be sold and otherwise dealt with by the debtor company in the ordinary course of its business will be registrable as a floating charge.[57] A document creating a charge over chattels may be registrable because, had it been granted by an individual, the Bills of Sale Acts 1878–1882 would have applied to it.[58] A charge over proceeds of sale held by a buyer in a separate account might also require registration as a charge over book debts,[59] although this is more doubtful as monies held in a bank account (despite being a debt due to a company from the bank) may not be regarded as a book debt. In the case of certain assets registration of a charge may be required because of the nature of the property charged.[60].

---

55   *Clough Mill v Martin* [1984] 3 All ER 982 per Robert Goff LJ at 987–988.
56   s 396(1)(e), and see *Pfeiffer v Arbuthnot* [1987] BCLC 522; *Re Brightlife* [1987] Ch 200; and *Re Permanent Houses (Holdings) Ltd* (1989) 5 BCC 151.
57   s 396(1)(f).
58   s 396(1)(c).
59   s 396(1)(e).
60   s 396(1)(h) & (j). Ships, aircraft and intellectual property are the most likely categories.

9.47   If a *Romalpa* clause is interpreted as creating a charge; whether floating or fixed over chattels or receivables; non-registration will cause it to be void. However, registration will not, in most cases, give priority over a charge granted to a financier as that is likely to precede the registered charge granted to the supplier. In a case where a supplier has registered a fixed charge priority over preferential creditors and uncrystallised floating charges will be obtained but in the case of a floating charge earlier floating charges and preferential creditors will have priority.

9.48   The Cork Report recommended that a form of registration should be introduced for reservation of title clauses other than those in consumer sales[61] and that such clauses should only be effective in cases of the insolvency of buyers if registered as such. Only a clause which secured the amount due in respect of goods supplied under the contract containing it would be regarded as a reservation of title clause. A clause seeking to reserve title for the purpose of securing amounts due on any account between the seller and the buyer would require registration as a charge.[62] These recommendations have not been implemented. It is unfortunate that this recommendation was not enacted in the Insolvency Act 1985 because a requirement of notice would recognise the true nature of such clauses as a form of security. The justification for treating reservation of title clauses in this way while not requiring the registration of hire purchase agreements or leasing arrangements used as a form of security is the prospect of the resale of goods subject to reservation of title which is contemplated by the agreement itself. This does not apply to the capital goods which are usually the subject of hire purchase or leasing agreements. The recommendation that reservation of title clauses should be subject to a moratorium during an administration has been enacted but does not extend to cases of receivership as the Cork Committee suggested.[63]

TRUST PROPERTY

9.49   The rule that a liquidator or a receiver and manager under a fixed or floating charge can deal only with property beneficially owned by an insolvent company is well established. Any property subject to an express, implied or constructive trust will not be available to the company's creditors. A liquidator can use a summons in a voluntary liquidation under s 112 of Insolvency Act 1986 to determine whether property is subject to a

---

61   Paras 1639–1641.
62   Paras 1644–1645.
63   Para 1650 and see below.

trust but the court may refuse to allow this if the beneficiaries can litigate to protect their own position.[64]

9.50 In order to establish such an arrangement it is necessary that a trust be declared or that the circumstances are such that a court can imply a trust or that a constructive trust arises and that the property which is subject to the trust be clearly identified. If a company declares an express trust in favour of its customers as regards monies received by it as advance payment by those customers for its goods and services and if it retains such monies in separate trust accounts the monies will not fall into its assets and cannot be used in a liquidation to pay the company's creditors. Those who made the advance payments will be entitled to their money with priority over all other claimants.[65] Such an arrangement will also preserve the assets concerned against a receiver acting under a fixed or floating charge. However, if there is uncertainty about the property subject to a trust from its inception the mechanism will not succeed.[66]

9.51 Where the terms of a contract under which a company borrows money specify the use to which the advance is to be put this can give rise to a trust in favour of those to whom the money is to be paid. An agreement that a loan will be used to pay off certain particular creditors will amount to a trust in their favour. If the money is not used by the company for this purpose a resulting trust in favour of the lender arises and the money does not become part of the company's general assets. Similarly, a loan for the purpose of a specific purchase will result in the money advanced being held on a resulting trust for the lender if the purchase fails.[67] If the money advanced on loan is paid to the company's bank, knowledge or notice of the trust is necessary to bind it but notice given after the receipt of the money may suffice.[68] The *Barclay's Bank case* did, however, involve money paid into a clearly identifiable separate account. This will assist in establishing knowledge on the part of the bank of the trust with which the money is impressed.

9.52 A trust will be completely constituted if it is the parties' intention that money paid into a separate account be used for a specific purpose and an identified beneficiary can compel the trustee which holds legal title to carry it out. In *Carreras Rothman v Freeman Mathews Treasure Ltd*[69] an

64 *Re Stetzel Thomson & Co Ltd* (1988) 4 BCC 74.
65 *Re Kayford Ltd* [1975] 1 All ER 604, and *Re Chelsea Cloisters Ltd* (1978) 41 P & CR 98.
66 See *Re London Wine Co (Shippers) Ltd* (1976) 126 NLJ 977 and Picarda, *op cit* at pp 130–131.
67 *Re EVTR Ltd* [1987] BCLC 646.
68 *Barclays Bank Ltd v Quistclose Investments Ltd* [1970] AC 567; *Swiss Bank Corporation v Lloyds Bank Ltd* [1981] 2 All ER 449.
69 [1984] BCLC 420.

agreement that money be paid into a specially opened account to be used only for an agreed purpose was held to satisfy that requirement. However, the existence of a separate account to hold monies is not sufficient in itself to establish a trust. There must be certainty of words about the intention and, while the words 'trust' or 'confidence' need not be used, a certainty about the intention of both parties is required. Its absence on the part of one of them will be fatal.[70] It is also necessary that there be certainty about the beneficiaries of the trust.[71] The existence of a separate account may create certainty of subject-matter but that is not sufficient to create a trust if the other two certainties are absent.

9.53   The system of accounting in relation to holdings of monies can be crucial. If an accounting system makes it clear that monies held in designated client accounts are held for particular persons and the three certainties are present, interest on capital sums on such accounts is also held on trust. An appropriate system of recording investments made on behalf of such clients can result in such investments also being held on trust.[72] In the *Berkeley Applegate* case a trust was established of the benefit of mortgages securing advances which were recorded as being of the money of particular clients. This was the case despite a change in beneficiary when one client withdrew money and another was substituted for him as holding the mortgage. The clarity of the system of records was essential to that decision.

9.54   A bank holding funds as the trustee of various settlements with authority from the settlors to deposit some of the money with itself as banker and power to treat itself as beneficially entitled to such funds (as it does with other deposits that it holds) does not hold such deposits subject to a trust impressed upon them. The settlor is regarded as having taken the risk of the bank's insolvency by authorising such dealings and does not have a beneficial interest in such a fund but claims as an unsecured creditor.[73]

9.55   If a trust is established but the money or other property to which it applies is no longer held in its original form the beneficiary/creditor may be able to use the equitable doctrine of tracing to establish a claim over property with which the trust property has been mixed or into which it has been converted. A sale of property subject to a trust (whether or not the sale

---

70   *Re Multi Guarantee Co Ltd* [1987] BCLC 257.
71   *Ibid* at 268–269.
72   *Re Berkeley Applegate (Investment Consultants) Ltd* (1988) 4 BCC 274.
73   *Space Investments Ltd v Canadian Imperial Bank of Commerce Trust Co (Bahamas)* [1986] 3 All ER 75.

is a breach of trust) gives the beneficiary a right to the proceeds of sale if he can identify them. If the proceeds have been used to acquire property without being mixed with other monies, the beneficiary can claim that property as of right or charge it with the amount of the trust money. Where, as will usually be the case on insolvency, the money representing the subject matter of the trust has been mixed with other monies in a bank account they can be traced into that account or property purchased from it. However, if some time has elapsed since the transfer of the trust monies into the bank account this will be a difficult process. Trust monies will be regarded as the last to be used up as the trustee is taken to use his own monies first.[74] This is a modification of the general rule in *Clayton's case*[75] that payments out of a bank account are taken to use up the earliest amounts paid in.

9.56 The rule in *Clayton's case* can also be displaced if it is impossible to ascertain the ownership of assets purchased with payments out of an account. In *Re Eastern Capital Futures Co Ltd*,[76] in which clearly identified client accounts existed, both money in the hands of brokers paid to them from the accounts to be used to buy futures contracts and contracts purchased by the brokers were held to be the authorised form of investment for the trust fund and thus trust assets not available to the creditors. In this context, when payments into the accounts were intended to discharge the contractual obligation of the brokers to the company and the fiduciary obligation of the company to the account holders while payments out were to pay for the clients' contracts, the rule in *Clayton's case* was displaced. Not only was it impossible to ascertain which future contracts were held for particular clients but payments in and out of each account were intended to benefit only the client in question and not other clients. In that situation the fact that all clients were equally innocent led to a *pari passu* distribution of the benefit of contracts and of monies not identified as the property of any particular client by being in a specific client account or otherwise. They all shared deficiencies on contracts equally.

9.57 Equitable tracing is not available against a person who takes a legal interest in the property claimed without notice of the rights of the beneficiary and, to the extent that amounts which represent trust money because of the rule in *Clayton's case* are paid to such persons after the trustee's own monies in the account are exhausted, the right to trace will be lost. The complexity of ascertaining which property in the hands of the debtor company can be subject to tracing will be enormous if the trust monies have been placed in the company's current bank accounts and used

---

74   *Re Hallett's Estate* (1880) 13 Ch D 696.
75   (1816) 1 Mer 529.
76   (1989) 5 BCC 223, following *Re Diplock* [1948] Ch 465.

in the ordinary course of business to pay debts and expenses. For this reason the absence of a separate and distinct account into which trust money is paid is likely to defeat a claim by a beneficiary even where a trust can be established in the first place.[77]

9.58   Despite some pressure in favour of such a measure during the passage of the Insolvency Act 1985 through the legislature, no preference is given to the claims of the customers of an insolvent company who have made advance payments or deposits for goods. In the absence of a clear trust of the kind found in *Re Kayford*[78] such claimants will be unsecured creditors.

LEASING, HIRE PURCHASE AND FACTORING[79]

9.59   On the basis of the principle that property which is not owned by the company is not subject to winding up or receivership procedures, any property leased to the company will be available in full to the lessor. In the case of an administration order in relation to a company this is subject to the effect of the statutory moratorium on the enforcement of the right of the owner in the case of assets subject to certain leasing agreements, retention of title clauses, and hire purchase or conditional sale agreements.[80]

9.60   The forms of agreement commonly found in relation to assets include leasing, hire purchase and conditional sale. A lease will not contemplate a transfer of ownership of assets to the lessee. There is a bailment of the property by the lessor to the lessee and there is no automatic transfer of property on the completion of payment of the price of the goods as is the case with a conditional sale agreement. Nor is there any option to purchase the goods for a nominal sum at the end of the period of hire as is the case with hire purchase agreements. A lease will not always be a form of financing for the use of assets by the lessee.

9.61   An 'operating lease' will normally involve the provision of equipment for a relatively short period (a shorter period than its useful life) at a rental reflecting its use value. During its lifetime the equipment is likely to

---

77   The absence of effective banking arrangements is not necessarily fatal to the existence of a trust—*Re Kayford* [1975] 1 All ER 604 per Megarry J at 607. However, in the case of trade creditors it may establish unanswerably an intention that funds be used on the company's own account and therefore the absence of a fiduciary relationship.
78   [1975] 1 All ER 604.
79   See generally T M Clark, "Leasing" (1978) and R Goode, "Commercial Law" (1985) Chs 29 to 31.
80   Insolvency Act 1986 s 10(1) & (4).

be subject to a number of leases at different times in favour of different lessees. The equipment will usually have been acquired by the lessor without consultation with lessees or reference to their individual needs.

9.62 A 'financial lease', on other hand, represents a means of financing the *de facto* acquisition of equipment by the lessee. Equipment may be chosen by the lessee for purchase by the lessor. The period of the lease will normally be the whole period of the useful life of the asset and the rental payments during that period will be sufficient to cover the cost of the asset to the lessor together with interest and profits. It is assumed that at the end of the period covered by the lease the equipment will have little or no secondhand value and, often, that the lessee may set such value against a future transaction. The equipment may be purchased and, at the end of the lease period, sold by the lessee as agent of the lessor. This may be done in some cases by the lessee without disclosing the existence of the lessor as principal.

9.63 The use of this form of financing developed because of the advantages to a lessee of not disclosing the financing of the acquisition of the equipment on its balance sheet as a capitalised liability or, for example, by registration of any charge granted to secure finance. The tax advantage to a company which would not have sufficient profits to make use of capital allowances for corporation tax purposes was that the hire payments were expenses deducted in calculating profits while the lessor obtained any capital allowance and would reflect this, to some degree, in the amount of the rental payable under the lease. This advantage was greatly reduced by the provisions of the Finance Act 1984 in relation to capital allowances for corporation tax purposes.

9.64 In a case of insolvency, leasing, hire purchase and conditional sale agreements all share the advantage, from the point of view of the supplier, that the assets provided are not subject to claims by other creditors and that, as the interest of the supplier is that of an owner and not a security interest, no registration is necessary to achieve this result. It is only possible for a charge granted by the lessee or hirer and attached to the assets to be valid against the true owner if an exception to the *nemo dat* rule applies.[81] A lessee or hirer is not a buyer in possession[82] and is unlikely to be a mercantile agent.[83] Only annexation of the asset to land presents a danger to the claim of the owner for its return. A leasing, hire purchase or conditional sale agreement will usually provide that insolvency of any kind

---

81   *See* Goode, *op cit* p 847.
82   Sale of Goods Act 1979 s 25(1) and Factors Act 1889 s 9. This contrasts with the position in the case of a conditional sale agreement.
83   Factors Act 1889 s 2.

on the part of the lessee, hirer or buyer will give the right to the owner to terminate the agreement or will result in automatic termination.

9.65 Similar considerations apply to an outright sale, by a company of its receivables, to a factor.[84] This may be done on the basis that the purchaser of the receivables has the right of recourse against the vendor in respect of debts not paid by the debtor to the purchaser. It may or may not involve the notification of the debtor of the factoring of his debt. Where receivables are sold the purpose of the transaction is to provide finance but as with financial leasing the legal form represents a sale of the assets involved. The sale of receivables is not treated in law as a security interest and registration is not necessary. Subject to the possible effects of notice held by the assignee of a clause in a prior floating charge restricting the company's power to dispose of assets subject to the charge,[85] the right granted to a company to dispose of assets subject to a floating charge prior to the crystallisation of the charge will result in priority over receivables going to the purchaser of them (or indeed to an assignee by way of fixed charge) if title to the debts is obtained before the crystallisation of the floating charge.

9.66 Where the floating charge is created after the assignment of receivables then if the assignment vests the company's debts automatically in the factor and he has advanced money to the company his equitable interest will attach as soon as the debt exists and the floating charge will not affect his interest. If the factor is only entitled under his contract to be offered an assigment then the charge will apply to receivables but assignment of them before the floating charge crystallises will give the factor priority unless he has notice of a prohibition in the floating charge document against factoring.

9.67 Any other assignment of receivables (whether a fixed or floating charge or a sale) will have priority over a later assignee's claim unless, under the rule in *Dearle v Hall*[86] the later assignee, having had no notice of a fixed charge when he took the assignment, gives notice of his interest to the debtor before the prior assignee. It is uncertain whether the provision of s 137 of the Law of Property Act 1925 that a statutory assignment is subject to equities having priority over the right of the assignee regardless of notice,

---

84 'Factor' is here used in the commercial sense of one who provides finance to a business in return for security over debts owed to the business. That 'security' may amount to a purchase of the debts or a charge over them. This contrasts with the use of the word 'factor' in the context of Factors Act 1889 to describe a commercial agent with usual authority to buy and sell the goods of others in his own name. See Goode *op cit* chapter 32.

85 See para 8.55–8.60 for the effect of registration under s 395 Companies Act 1985 for this purpose.

86 (1823) 3 Russ 1.

will enable a person with an equitable claim against the receivables at the date of the assignment to prevail regardless of the order of notification of the debtor. It would seem, however, that the section will result in the application of the rule in *Dearle v Hall*; at least when the equity in question has its origins in a contractual provision as in the case of an equitable right to trace which derives from a *Romalpa* clause.[87] An assignee who notifies the debtor in accordance with s 136 of the Law of Property Act 1925 will probably gain priority over a person who has an equity against the debt which has not been so notified.

9.68   The protection afforded by the ownership rights of an assignee of future debts will prevail as to the debts due to the company before the making of a winding up order or the passing of a winding up resolution. Debts incurred by the liquidator in continuing trading will not be subject to such a claim. For the purpose of the Insolvency Act 1986 the date of the disposition of the company's future debts will be the date of the assignment and not the date of the creation of the debts and if this precedes the commencement of the winding up the disposition will not be prohibited. The same rule will apply to a registered charge over the company's future book debts.[88] In the case of a receivership or administration the position of the receiver or the administrator as agent of the company results in debts due to the company after their appointment being subject to the priorities determined by the rules described above with the qualification that any floating charge will have crystallised on the appointment of a receiver.[89] This will not affect the right of an assignee of receivables whose claim to future debts arises as soon as the debts are created. It may, however, postpone him to the fixed charge created on crystallisation in relation to debts then due or future debts if they are subject to the charge, if the assignment does not give him a right which operates on the creation of the debt. Liquidation, receivership and administration will usually give the assignee of book debts the right to terminate the factoring agreement under which assignments take place. The statutory moratorium in the case of an administration order will apply to a charge on debts but not to an assignment by way of sale of future debts, but proceedings to enforce a contract to assign will require the consent of the administrator or the leave of the court.[90]

---

87   See Goode, *op cit* pp 872–873 and the literature cited there.
88   *Re Lind* [1915] 2 Ch 345; *Re Collins* [1925] Ch 556.
89   Administration will have the same effect if the document creating the charge so provides.
90   Insolvency Act 1986 s 11(3) The statement in the text assumes that an assignment by way of sale would not be regarded as a 'security' under s 11(3)(c).

CHAPTER 10

The Qualifications of Insolvency Practitioners

THE INSOLVENCY PRACTITIONER

10.01 Many of the issues involving the role of insolvency practitioners are dealt with elsewhere in this book. The functions and powers of the administrative receiver, the liquidator, the administrator or the supervisor of a voluntary arrangement are dealt with in the chapters dealing with each of those procedures. This includes those powers and rights common to more than one such officeholder such as calling for the co-operation of company officers, seizing documents and demanding supplies from public utilities as well as rules about the remuneration of the practitioner, the records he is required to keep, and the procedures he must follow when handling money.[1] This chapter is concerned with the system of qualification and disqualification set up by the Insolvency Act 1986 for those who act as insolvency practitioners.

THE ORIGINS OF THE SYSTEM OF QUALIFICATIONS

10.02 The Cork Committee concluded that the system which existed before the time of its report was open to abuse and did not command public confidence.[2] It recommended that there should be a requirement of membership of a professional body approved by the DTI and of experience of general practice for at least five years before acting as an insolvency practitioner. Conditions were to be laid down for the bodies to be approved as regards their insistence on an ethical code to be observed by members, (including an obligation to account strictly for funds passing through their hands), effective disciplinary sanctions, an annual practising certificate requirement and a competitive examination to ensure competence.[3]

10.03 The rules which now govern the qualifications of insolvency practitioners come close to meeting these requirements. Great reliance is

---

1 See the following chapters: 11 (administrative receivers); 13 (administrators); 15 and 16 (liquidators); 21 Part 2 (as to disqualification orders) and 22 (supervisors of voluntary arrangements).
2 Cmnd 8558, para 756.
3 *Ibid*, para 758.

placed on the effectiveness of this system of regulation by professional bodies to eliminate the 'cowboy' practitioners who, in the past, have prevented a proper investigation of the affairs of insolvent companies or have colluded with those responsible for their insolvency to defeat the claims of creditors. The disciplinary procedures available for this purpose and the willingness of the professional bodies to use them will be of crucial importance in this respect as the mere fact of professional qualification is not, in itself, a guarantee of probity and competence. The whole scheme introduced by the Insolvency Acts 1985 and 1986 depends on the competence and honesty of those acting as receivers, liquidators, administrators or supervisors to ensure that malpractice in the running of the company in the past is reported to the appropriate authorities and that all assets which can be made available to the creditors are gathered in by setting aside transactions and making any claims which are available against former directors or others involved with the company. In addition, of course, the assets held by the insolvency practitioner must be secure against depletion as a result of his own incompetence or dishonesty.

ACTING AS AN INSOLVENCY PRACTITIONER

10.04   It is an offence for a person other than the official receiver to act as an insolvency practitioner in relation to a company if he is not qualified to do so at the time.[4] The concept of acting as an insolvency practitioner in relation to a company applies to anyone acting as its liquidator, provisional liquidator, administrator, or administrative receiver or as the supervisor of a voluntary arrangement approved by it under Part I of the Act.[5] This excludes a receiver who is not an administrative receiver within the definition laid down in s 29(2) of the Act. The qualification requirement only extends to a person appointed as receiver or manager of the whole or substantially the whole of a company's property by or on behalf of the holders of a debenture secured by a floating charge. Receivers appointed by the court or by the holders of fixed charges are not subject to the requirements of the Act as regards qualifications.

10.05   At the time of acting as an insolvency practitioner a person must satisfy one of two conditions. He must either be authorised so to act by virtue of his membership of a professional body recognised under s 391, the rules of which permit him to act in such a capacity, or he must hold an authorisation granted by a competent body under s 393.

---

4   Insolvency Act 1986 s 389.
5   s 388(1).

RECOGNISED PROFESSIONAL BODIES

10.06   Section 391(1) allows the Secretary of State, by order, to grant recognition to professional bodies for this purpose. He may recognise only bodies which regulate the practice of a profession and maintain and enforce rules to secure that such of their members as are permitted by those rules to act as insolvency practitioners are fit and proper persons so to act and meet acceptable requirements as regards education, practical training and experience.[6] The reference to members in that subsection and, indeed generally under the section is to persons subject to the rules of the professional body in the practice of the profession whether or not they are members.[7] The concept of a 'fit and proper person' implies the need for disciplinary procedures to ensure that a person whose conduct falls below the standard of such a paragon can be prevented under the rules of the body from acting as an insolvency practitioner.

10.07   The Secretary of State has, with effect from 10th November 1986, recognised the following bodies in the Insolvency Practitioners (Recognised Professional Bodies) Order 1986:[8]

The Chartered Association of Certified Accountants;
The Insolvency Practitioners' Association;
The Institute of Chartered Accountants in England and Wales;
The Institute of Chartered Accountants in Ireland;
The Institute of Chartered Acountants of Scotland;
The Law Society;
The Law Society of Scotland.

10.08   A further order can be made by the Secretary of State revoking the recognition of a body if it appears to him that the body no longer satisfies the conditions in s 391(2).[9] Such an order may, however, authorise the members of such a body to continue to act as insolvency practitioners for a specified period after the revocation takes effect.[10]

AUTHORISATION BY A COMPETENT BODY

10.09   A person who is not a member of a recognised professional body may operate as an insolvency practitioner if he is authorised to do so by a

6   s 391(2).
7   s 391(3).
8   SI 1986 No 1764.
9   s 391(4).
10   s 391(5).

'competent authority' under s 393.[11] The competent authorities are those specified by the Secretary of State in relation to particular circumstances and in all other cases, the Secretary of State himself.[12] At the time of writing the only competent authority is the Secretary of State. The Department of Trade and Industry publishes an Annual Directory of Authorised Insolvency Practitioners. The first edition was published by HMSO in 1987. It was accurate up to 1st August 1987.

Application

10.10 An application to the competent authority may be made under s 392 of the Act. It is for the competent authority to lay down directions as to the form which the application takes. It must be accompanied by such information as the authority reasonably requires to reach a decision on the application, and by the prescribed fee of £200. The authority is empowered to direct that notice of the application be published.[13] Additional information can be required after the receipt of the application by the competent authority and the form in which any information is provided and the way in which it is to be verified (for example by affidavit) can be laid down by the competent authority.[14] An application can always be withdrawn before it is granted or refused.[15]

Criteria

10.11 An application made under s 392 may be either granted or refused by the competent authority and in determining which course of action to take the authority will consider whether the applicant is a fit and proper person to act as an insolvency practitioner and whether he meets the requirements laid down in the regulations as regards education, practical training and experience. If it appears to the authority from the information available to it that these conditions are satisfied it must grant the application.[16] The authorisation granted will, unless it is withdrawn, continue in force for the period specified in it but that period may not be more than three years from the date on which it was granted.[17]

10.12 Withdrawal may be on the grounds that the holder of the authorisation is no longer a fit and proper person to act as an insolvency

11 s 390(2)(b).
12 s 392(2). From 1 April 1990 a person seeking authorisation will be required to have passed an exam set by the Joint Insolvency Examining Board.
13 s 392(3) and reg 7 of the Insolvency Practitioners Regulations 1986, SI 1986 No 1995.
14 s 392(4) and (6).
15 s 392(7).
16 s 393(1) and (2).
17 s 393(3) and reg 8.

practitioner or that he has failed to comply with the requirements of s 388 to 398 of the Act or with regulations made under the Act. This will include a failure to provide security or to keep or produce proper records to the authority.[18] Any purported compliance with those provisions by providing false, inaccurate or misleading information to the authority will, in itself, be a ground for the withdrawal of authorisation.[19] Authorisation may also be withdrawn at the request or with the consent of the person who holds it.[20]

10.13   The regulations elaborate on the matters which the competent authority must take into account in deciding whether an applicant is a fit and proper person to act as an insolvency practitioner or to continue so to act. These specific matters do not limit the generality of the 'fit and proper person' test. They apply both when an application for authorisation is being considered and when the competent authority is deciding whether to withdraw an authorisation on the ground that its holder is not a 'fit and proper person'.[21]

10.14   Those matters include (in respect of the applicant) convictions for offences involving fraud, dishonesty or violence, or the contravention of insolvency legislation in the UK or elsewhere.[22] In addition, business practices on his part which appear to be deceitful, oppressive, unfair or improper or which otherwise cast doubt on his probity or competence for discharging the duties of an insolvency practitioner will be taken into account whether they are unlawful or not.[23] The ethics of a person's behaviour in a business context (whether while operating as an insolvency practitioner or in some other business) can be considered in addition to his criminal record.

10.15   His record as an insolvency practitioner in the past will be examined for any failure fully to disclose a conflict of interest to persons who might reasonably be expected to be affected by an actual or apparent conflict between his personal, financial or other interests and his duty as an insolvency practitioner. Such non-disclosure will not be taken into account if the persons in question gave appropriate consent to the applicant to act or continue to act in spite of the existence of those circumstances.[24] His conduct or likely conduct of any past, present or future insolvency practice will be checked for the independence, integrity and professional skills

---

18   See paras 10.36–10.38 below.
19   s 393(4).
20   s 393(5).
21   Insolvency Practitioners Regulations 1986 reg 4(2).
22   reg 4(1)(a) and (b).
23   reg 4(1)(f).
24   *Ibid.*

appropriate to its range and scale and the proper performance of the duties of an insolvency practitioner.[25] The adequacy of the control systems, records (including accounts) and of their maintenance will be considered in respect of any past or current insolvency practice carried on by the applicant.[26]

10.16 Regulation 5 and Part I of the schedule of the Insolvency Practitioner Regulations 1986[27] lay down the educational qualifications required of anyone who had not attained the age of 35 on or before 15th December 1986 and who had not held an authorisation either under s 393 of the Insolvency Act 1986 or its predecessor section.[28] The required standard is either a degree or a combination of ordinary and advanced level GCE passes at the appropriate level or their equivalents.

10.17 The level of practical training and experience required under s 393(2)(b) is laid down in reg 6. For those already holding an authorisation under either the 1985 or the 1986 Insolvency Acts, the requirement is only that the applicant has been appointed officeholder in at least one case under either English or Scottish law during the currency of his authorisation.[29] For others the requirements hinge on proof of appointment as an officeholder on a minimum number of occasions over the previous ten years or of employment by a person, firm or partnership which carried on an insolvency practice or was an officeholder during that period combined with a specified amount of experience at the level stipulated in the regulation.[30]

10.18 Provision is made to leave out of account the appointment of a person as a receiver or as the liquidator in a members' voluntary winding up in cases where the appointment was effected by his associates.[31] Similarly, appointment as an officeholder to two or more associated companies or two or more individuals in partnership with each other at the time count as only one appointment.[32]

10.19 No separate stipulation is made as regards experience in corporate or personal insolvency. It would therefore be possible for a person whose experience was limited to one field to practice in the other without

25   reg 4(1)(e).
26   reg 4(1)(d).
27   SI 1986 No 1995.
28   s 5 of the Insolvency Act 1985.
29   reg 6(7).
30   reg 6(2) and (6).
31   reg 6(3)(a).
32   reg 6(3)(b).

constraint. However, a minimum amount of experience within the English and Scottish jurisdictions is required where experience elsewhere is relied on. A good command of English will also be demanded in such cases.[33]

Procedure and the tribunal

10.20   Notice of the fact that an authorisation has been granted under s 393 must be given to the applicant by the competent authority and the date on which the authorisation commences must be specified.[34] If the authority proposes to refuse the application or to withdraw an authorisation already held then it must give the applicant or the holder of the authorisation written notice of its intention; of the grounds on which it proposes to act; of his rights to make representations or to have the matter referred to the Insolvency Practitioners' Tribunal under ss 395 and 396; and, in the case of the withdrawal of an authorisation, the date from which that decision will take effect.[35] This procedure is designed to enable the person to whom the notice is given to make representations to the competent authority (to which it is bound to have regard in making its decision to refuse or withdraw authorisation) within 14 days of the date of service.[36]

10.21   The person on whom the notice under s 394 has been served can choose to have the matter referred to the Insolvency Practitioners' Tribunal either within 28 days after the service of that notice on him or, if he has made a representation under s 395, within 28 days after the date on which notice is served on him that the authority 'does not propose to alter its decision'.[37] The wording of this provision is odd since s 394(2) refers to a situation in which the authority proposes to refuse an application or to withdraw an authorisation and does not assume that a decision has been made at that stage; although one is proposed. It is submitted that it is clear that the intention is to allow a person to insist on the case being referred to the tribunal if the decision goes against him after he has made representations. Written notice must be given by a person who seeks a reference to the tribunal to require this to be done. The case must then be referred unless the competent authority gives notice of a decision in favour of the person who required a reference within 7 days of the making of that requirement.[38]

10.22   On referring a case to the tribunal the authority must send the

---

33   reg 6(4).
34   s 394(1).
35   s 394(2) and (3).
36   s 395.
37   s 396(2).
38   s 396(3).

tribunal a copy of the written notice it served on the applicant and a copy of the applicant's notification that he wishes the case to be referred to the tribunal. It must give notice to the applicant of the fact that it has referred the case to the tribunal and of the tribunal's address.[39] Within 21 days of referring the case the authority must send to the tribunal such further information and documents that the authority considers would be useful to it and copies of the same to the applicant.[40]

10.23   The competent authority has power to give written notice of the refusal or withdrawal of authorisation if it has not been required to refer the case to the tribunal within the time limit laid down in s 396(2). That time limit is 28 days from the original notice of the proposal to withdraw or refuse authorisation in cases where no representation was made or, in cases in which representations were made, 28 days from the service of notice that the authority does not intend to alter its decision as a result of the representations made to it.

10.24   The composition and procedure of the tribunal is laid down in sch 7 of the Act and in the Insolvency Practitioners' Tribunal (Conduct of Investigations) Rules 1986.[41] Section 397 requires the tribunal to investigate cases referred to it and to report to the competent authority its opinion on the appropriate decision and its reasons for that opinion. The competent authority is obliged to decide the matter in accordance with the tribunal's report; a copy of which is sent to the applicant or the holder of the authorisation who referred the matter to the tribunal. The competent authority has power to publish the report of the tribunal and must serve a copy of its own decision on the person to whom it relates.

10.25   The tribunal consists of members chosen from a panel drawn up by the Secretary of State for Trade and Industry consisting of persons experienced in insolvency matters and barristers and solicitors of at least 7 years' standing.[42] The remuneration of members if fixed by the Secretary of State with Treasury approval.[43] The tribunal can sit as a single tribunal or in two or more divisions but its functions must be exercised by three members chosen from the panel; two persons experienced in insolvency matters and a chairman who is legally qualified.[44]

10.26   The tribunal is required to conduct all its investigations to give a

39   Rule 2(1) of Insolvency Practitioners Tribunal (Conduct of Investigations) Rules 1986, SI 1986 No 952.
40   Rule 2(2).
41   SI 1986 No 952.
42   sch 7 para 1(1).
43   *Ibid* para 2.
44   *Ibid* para 3.

reasonable opportunity to the applicant to make representations to it.[45] It has power to require people to attend and give evidence or produce books, papers or other documents in their possession and may take sworn evidence.[46] Refusal to attend or to give evidence or the deliberate alteration, suppression, destruction or refusal to produce a required document result in a fine.[47]

10.27 The initial stage of the tribunal's investigation of a case is the service on the applicant by the competent authority of all relevant documents under r 2(2) of the Rules. Within 21 days of that material being sent, the applicant is required to send the tribunal a statement of his grounds for requiring the tribunal to investigate the case. A copy of that statement is sent to the authority. It must specify which matters the applicant disputes in the notice from the authority of its refusal or withdrawal of authorisation in addition to any other matters that he considers should be drawn to the attention of the tribunal and a list of the names and addresses of witnesses whose evidence he wishes the tribunal to hear.[48] The applicant may be represented before the tribunal and the Treasury solicitor and counsel may be appointed to assist the tribunal in its task and to represent the public interest.[49]

10.28 After the time limit for the statement of the applicant is up the tribunal will investigate the case by carrying out inquiries.[50] It will decide on the method that it is to use as soon as possible and inform the two sides of its decision and in particular whether it intends to take oral evidence. It must then give the parties the opportunity to make oral or written representations (as they choose) about the manner in which its inquiries are to be carried out. It will then notify the two sides of its decision on that matter. Every time the tribunal proposes to change its *modus operandi* it must follow that procedure.[51] Whenever witnesses are examined orally during the inquiry both parties must be given notice of the time and place so that they can attend or be represented and put questions to the witness. Similarly, both sides must be allowed an opportunity to inspect and take copies of documentary or other recorded evidence considered by the tribunal.[52]

10.29 After the tribunal has finished the stage of its investigation which

45 *Ibid* para 4(1).
46 *Ibid* para 4(2).
47 *Ibid* para 4(3).
48 Rule 3.
49 Rules 9 and 4.
50 Rule 5.
51 Rule 6.
52 Rule 7.

involves collecting evidence, it must give both sides the opportunity of making final representations on the evidence and on the subject matter of the investigation. Those representations may be oral or in writing at the option of each part.[53] Copies of any representations made by one side must be sent to the other.[54] Hearings will be in private unless the applicant requests that sessions for the taking of oral evidence or making oral representations shall be in public in which case those parts of the procedure can be in public.[55] Apart from taking evidence, deciding how the investigation will proceed and considering representations, the chairman of the tribunal has all the powers of the tribunal.[56] The tribunal has a general power to extend the time limit laid down in the rules for any act or sending any document.[57]

10.30   There is an obligation on the tribunal to report to the authority within 4 months of the date of the reference unless the authority extends the time limit on the ground that there appear to be exceptional circumstances which prevent the tribunal from reporting within the 4 month period.[58]

DISQUALIFICATIONS

10.31   Apart from the requirement that insolvency practitioners have an appropriate standard of education, practical experience and competence and the availability of either the competent authority or a recognised professional body to discipline them, the Act lays down certain factors that prevent a person from acting as an insolvency practitioner.

10.32   The first stipulation is the requirement that only an individual can act as insolvency practitioner. No corporate body can act in that capacity.[59] In addition corporations are prevented from acting as receivers of the property of a company by s 30 of the Act; although only administrative receivers are required to be qualified insolvency practitioners. The effect of s 30 is that any purported appointment is a nullity and the appointee fails to become the agent of the company in respect of which he is appointed.[60] The effect of s 390(1) is likely to be the same in respect of all the acts of a corporate body seeking to carry out the function of an

---

53 Rule 8.
54 Rule 10.
55 Rule 11.
56 Rule 14.
57 Rule 13.
58 Rule 15.
59 s 390(1).
60 *Portman Building Society v Gallwey* [1955] 1 Ch D 227.

insolvency practitioner as the section provides that such persons are not qualified to act in that capacity but it may be that the reference to acting in that capacity rather than to the appointment of the body indicates that the appointment itself is not a nullity.

10.33   A person adjudged bankrupt and not yet discharged cannot act as an insolvency practitioner and someone subject to a disqualification order under the Company Directors' Disqualification Act 1986[61] is also disqualified.[62] Section 31 of the Act prevents an undischarged bankrupt from acting as the receiver or manager of the property of a company on the appointment of debenture holders. A mental patient within the definition of Part VII of the Mental Health Act 1983 is similarly prohibited from acting as an insolvency practitioner.[63]

SURETY

10.34   At the time at which a person acts as an insolvency practitioner in relation to a company it is necessary that he have in force a security for the proper performance of his functions which meets the requirements laid down in Part III of the Insolvency Practitioners Regulations 1986.[64] Those requirements are that a bond making the surety liable jointly and severally with the practitioner for the proper performance of the latter's duties has been issued and is held by the recognised professional body or the competent authority which covers the practitioner.[65] The bond must cover both a general penalty sum of at least £250,000 and a specific penalty sum of the value of the assets of the company in respect of which he is acting within a band from £5000 to £5,000,000. Claims under the latter provision are to be made first. The valuation of the company assets for this purpose is carried out in accordance with sch 3 of the Regulations. Liability is for the amount equivalent to the losses caused by the fraud or dishonesty of the practitioner. A certificate of the specific penalty must be issued under the bond as soon as possible after the appointment of the practitioner to act in relation to a particular company and the bond must make provision for this.[66] If, before the practitioner obtains his release, it appears that the assets of the company have a higher value than was estimated for the purpose of the specific penalty then a new certificate for the higher amount must be issued forthwith.[67]

61   See chapter 21 part 2.
62   Insolvency Act 1986 s 390(4)(a) and (b).
63   s 390(4)(c).
64   SI 1986 No 1995 as amended by SI 1986 No 2247.
65   reg 10(1)(a) and (b) and (2) and sch 2 Part I.
66   reg 10(1)(b) and sch 2 Part I.
67   reg 10(1)(c).

10.35 Where an administrator, a voluntary liquidator or a provisional liquidator is appointed liquidator by the court, and a certificate of specific penalty has already been issued no new certificate need be issued.[68] The certificate must be delivered to the registrar of companies within 14 days of receipt by an administrative receiver or the liquidator in a voluntary liquidation. In the case of any other insolvency proceedings it must be filed with the court within the same time limit.[69]

RECORDS

10.36 As part of the regulation of insolvency practitioners to protect the public from dishonest or incompetent operators, obligations for the maintenance and inspection of records are imposed. These rules apply to all persons appointed to act as insolvency practitioners on or after the commencement date of the legislation.[70] They supplement the obligations specifically imposed on liquidators by the Insolvency Regulations 1986.[71]

10.37 The regulations require that a full up to date record in the form laid down in sch 3 of the Regulations should be kept in respect of each insolvency case in which a practitioner acts.[72] The information to be recorded includes the name, number and business address of the practitioner and the competent authority or recognised professional body authorising him to practice. Details of the security held by the practitioner, the date of his appointment, vacation of office and release are demanded. In addition, the date of the commencement of the insolvency proceeding involved together with information on all significant steps in its progress such as the holding of members' and creditors' meetings, the submission of reports on directors under the Company Directors' Disqualification Act 1986, and the distribution of assets and the filing of necessary statutory returns must be included.[73]

10.38 These records must be preserved by the practitioner for a period of ten years from the date of his discharge or release in respect of a particular estate or, if later, the date on which his security in relation to that estate ceases to have effect.[74] The records must be produced by the practitioner to the 'authorising body' or its representative. The authorising body is the

---

68 reg 11.
69 reg 12.
70 Insolvency Practitioners Regulations 1986, SI 1986 No 1995 reg 14.
71 SI 1986 No 1994; see chapter 16 paras 16.47–16.61.
72 SI 1986 No 1995 reg 15.
73 See the form in sch 3 of the Regulations for full details.
74 *Ibid* reg 18.

competent authority or the recognised professional body, membership of which is necessary to enable the practitioner to act.[75] In addition the Secretary of State has a right to inspect the records if the practitioner is authorised to act by a recognised professional body.[76] A duty is imposed on the practitioner to notify the authorising body of where the records are kept and (if different) where they can be inspected.[77]

---

75 *Ibid* reg 16(1).
76 *Ibid* reg 16(2).
77 reg 17.

CHAPTER 11

Administrative Receivers

RECEIVERS—THEIR ROLE

11.01 Generally speaking, a receiver is a person, appointed by a creditor of a company, who has a charge over the company's assets. When the company gets into difficulties and the security is therefore threatened, the charge will usually contain a power enabling the charge holder to appoint a receiver. The receiver's job is to receive the income and preserve the assets of the company, pending their realisation, to satisfy the debt which is owed to the creditor. A receiver will, in the end, deal with the assets of the company in very much the same way as a liquidator, satisfying the claims of any preferential creditors first, then the claims of the charge holder. The advantage of appointing a receiver is that he is given the power to continue to manage the company and to allow it to continue trading, so that it can be sold more profitably as a going concern, rather than breaking it up and selling it for 'scrap value'. It is in deciding whether or not to trade on, and in pursuing the appropriate course with skill and enterprise, that the expertise of the receiver comes into play. The success or otherwise of the receiver in performing his function will affect not only the charge holder who appoints him, but also all the unsecured creditors and members of the company, who will benefit from any surplus which remains after the prior claims have been satisfied. This chapter is concerned with a particular kind of receiver—the administrative receiver; a role created by the Insolvency Act 1986.

THE ORIGIN OF THE ADMINISTRATIVE RECEIVER

11.02 For many years, the law relating to receivers developed as part of the common law. It grew up alongside the law relating to floating charges, with which it is intimately connected, since many receivers are appointed under powers contained in floating charges. This piecemeal development of the law gave rise to a great deal of uncertainty; the nature and extent of important aspects of the law relating to receivers was contained in a large number of reported cases.

11.03 When the Cork Committee came to examine this area of the law of insolvency, it found that central aspects of the receiver's position were far from clear.[1] Particular concern was expressed, for instance, about the uncertainty regarding the receiver's liability for his acts as receiver.[2] In certain circumstances a receiver acts as agent of the debtor company, at other times he is personally liable for his actions, yet the true position could only be deduced after a close study of the reported cases.

11.04 The Cork Committee's examination of the process of receivership gave rise to many recommendations which sought to ensure that the major uncertainties running through this area were overcome. Many of these recommendations were enshrined in statutory form in the Insolvency Act 1986. The Insolvency Act 1986 not only made changes regarding the process of receivership. It also implemented changes designed to ensure that receivers themselves fitted into the general scheme of insolvency law. The Cork Committee had been concerned that anyone could be appointed as a receiver,[3] regardless of the fact that it was a highly specialised job requiring considerable expertise. The statute acknowledged this concern and created a new type of receiver; the administrative receiver.[4] The effect of the statute is that since it came into force,[5] receivers appointed as receiver or manager of the whole, or substantially the whole, of a company's property, who are appointed by, or on behalf of, the debenture holders of a company which is secured by a floating charge are administrative receivers. Administrative receivers are subject to the requirements laid down by the Act which include requirements as regards their qualifications and conduct.[6] In practice, most creditors of companies who can appoint a receiver will have a fixed and floating charge over the whole of the company's assets and the receiver they appoint will fall within the statute. It is with this type of receiver, the administrative receiver, with which this chapter is concerned.

DEFINITION OF AN ADMINISTRATIVE RECEIVER

11.05 An administrative receiver is defined by s 29(2) of the Insolvency Act 1986 as follows:

(2) In this chapter 'administrative receiver' means—
(a) a receiver or manager of the whole (or substantially the whole) of a company's property appointed by or on behalf of the holders of any

1 *Insolvency Law and Practice*, Report of the Review Committee, Cmnd 8558, ch 8.
2 Cork, paras 455–459.
3 Cork, paras 440–441.
4 Insolvency Act 1986 s 29.
5 On 15 December 1986.
6 See ch 10 on qualifications required by insolvency practitioners. See ch 7 on the appointment of a receiver by the holder of a fixed charge.

debentures of the company secured by a charge which, as created, was a floating charge, or by such a charge and one or more other securities; or

(b) a person who would be such a receiver or manager but for the appointment of some other person as the receiver of part of the company's property.

11.06 An administrative receiver must firstly be the receiver or manager of the whole or substantially the whole of a company's property; or if he is not, the only reason for his failure to fulfil that requirement is that some other person has been appointed as receiver of part of the company's property. It is only s 29(2)(b) which permits a receiver to be regarded as an administrative receiver even if he is not receiver of 'substantially' the whole of the company's property and then only for the specified reason, that another person has been appointed as the receiver of part of the company's property. To be an administrative receiver it is only necessary that the instrument under which a person is appointed should provide for their appointment as either a receiver or a manager. In practice most floating charges will provide for the appointment of a receiver and manager, to provide the widest possible ranges of powers to the appointee.

11.07 Secondly, an administrative receiver must be appointed by or on behalf of the holders of any debentures of the company. It is possible for receivers to be appointed in a variety of other ways, eg by the court, but if that is the case, such a receiver will not fall within the definition in s 29.

11.08 Thirdly, the debentures in question must be secured by a charge which, as created was either a floating charge alone or consisted of a floating charge and one or more other securities. It can be seen that it is vital for the potential administrative receiver to know under what type of charge he will be appointed. If, for instance, the charge turns out to be a fixed charge alone, he will not fall within the statutory definition.[6a]

QUALIFICATIONS OF AN ADMINISTRATIVE RECEIVER

11.09 Whilst an administrative receiver must fall within the definition in s 29(2) of the Insolvency Act 1986 in order to be an administrative receiver, fulfilment of the statutory definition alone is not sufficient to enable a receiver to act as an administrative receiver. It is a very important feature of the scheme of insolvency law established by the Insolvency Act 1986 that administrative receivers should be subject to a common regime, along with

---

6a   See ch 7 on the appointment of a receiver by the holder of a fixed charge.

other insolvency practitioners.[7] This follows recommendations made by the Cork Committee,[8] which was concerned with improving public confidence in the insolvency system. In order to achieve this, the Committee felt that it was necessary to ensure not only a high standard of competence in practitioners, but also, insofar as that were possible, that practitioners would act with integrity. Consequently the Committee recommended that all those involved in the administration of the insolvency system, whom it termed 'insolvency practitioners' should be properly qualified and should also be subject to a professional code of practice.[9] The Insolvency Act 1986 embodies these and other similar recommendations in statutory form.

11.10 As far as an administrative receiver is concerned the statutory scheme has the effect both of acknowledging the skill and expertise which is required to undertake the job of receivership, reflected in the need to gain the requisite qualifications, and of introducing an amount of statutory control over the practice of administrative receivership, reflected in the requirement that administrative receivers will henceforth be subject to a relevant professional code.

11.11 Before the introduction of the Insolvency Act 1985, very little attention was paid to the formal qualifications of any potential appointee to carry out the task of receivership. There were certain disqualifications; eg a body corporate could not act as a receiver[10] but there was no positive requirement that a receiver should hold any particular professional qualification. The choice of a receiver appeared to be made on purely pragmatic grounds, so that if a complex receivership involving a very large company was to be undertaken, a firm specialising in receivership work might be chosen, whereas a simpler situation might be judged not to require that level of expertise.

11.12 The situation under the Insolvency Act 1986 is very different; an administrative receiver acts as an insolvency practitioner in relation to a company[11] and this means that he must be qualified so to act, since s 389(1) of the Act creates a criminal offence, whereby a person may be criminally liable if he acts as an insolvency practitioner when he is not qualified to do so. Section 390, sets out a series of requirements which a person must meet if they are to act lawfully as an insolvency practitioner in relation to a company.

---

7   For more detailed information on insolvency practitioners, see ch 10.
8   Cork, chs 15, 16 and 17.
9   Cork, para 758.
10   This was enshrined in statutory form in Companies Act 1948 s 366.
11   Insolvency Act 1986 s 388(1)(a).

11.13   The administrative receiver must, as an insolvency practitioner, be an individual (as opposed to a company)[12] and must be authorised to act as an administrative receiver by virtue of his membership of a professional body which is recognised by the secretary of state in accordance with s 391, or by virtue of an authorisation granted by a competent authority[13] in accordance with s 393.[14] As an insolvency practitioner, the administrative receiver must also have furnished the necessary security for the proper performance of his function[15] and he must not be an undischarged bankrupt, or subject to a disqualification order made under the Company Directors Disqualification Act 1986, or a patient within the meaning of Part VII of the Mental Health Act 1983.[16]

11.14   The need for the administrative receiver to meet these requirements, in common with all other insolvency practitioners, is part of the underlying purpose of the Insolvency Act 1986. However, it is interesting to note that the administrative receiver is not an officer of the court, whereas a liquidator in a winding up by the court is an officer of the court. The position of the administrative receiver, as a receiver appointed out of court, appears to be analogous to the position of a liquidator in a voluntary winding up.

DISQUALIFICATIONS

11.15   The Insolvency Act 1986 contains a number of sections which have the effect of disqualifying certain bodies or persons from acting as an administrative receiver.

Corporate bodies

11.16   Under s 30 a body corporate is not qualified for appointment as an administrative receiver. This rule has already been noted in relation to insolvency practitioners who are required to be individuals by s 390(1),[17] but s 30 establishes the rule specifically in relation to the administrative receiver. Corporations have been disqualified from acting as receivers for some time under English law[18] and the Cork Committee recommended that the *status quo* should be maintained in this respect.[19] However, it is a rule which has been the subject of some criticism, as embodying an irrational distinction between individuals and companies in this particular

---

12   s 390(1).
13   s 390(2)(b).
14   s 390(2).
15   s 390(3).
16   s 390(4).
17   See ch 10.
18   See eg Companies Act 1948 s 366.
19   Cork, para 744.

instance.[20] Under the general law, if a body corporate does act as a receiver, the appointment is void.[21] S 30 provides that a body corporate which acts as an administrative receiver will be liable to a fine.[22]

Undischarged bankrupts

11.17 S 31 of the Act provides that an undischarged bankrupt may not act as an administrative receiver. If such a person does so act, he is liable to imprisonment, or a fine, or both. Again, it has already been noted that an undischarged bankrupt may not act as an insolvency practitioner;[23] s 31 is concerned specifically with the administrative receiver. This particular disqualification has also existed for some time; it can first be found in a recommendation made by the Cohen Committee.[24] Section 31 specifically provides that this particular disqualification does not apply to receivers appointed by the court, although it would seem unlikely that a court would wish to appoint an undischarged bankrupt as a receiver, other than in exceptional circumstances.

Disqualified as insolvency practitioner

11.18 Since he must be qualified as an insolvency practitioner,[25] an administrative receiver will be disqualified from acting if he is subject to one or more of the disqualifications listed in s 390(4) in relation to insolvency practitioners ie:

(a) If he is an undischarged bankrupt; ss 278 to 282 of the Insolvency Act 1986 provide a clear statutory framework governing the bankruptcy of individuals. The bankruptcy begins on the day on which the bankruptcy order is made and continues until either the debtor is discharged or the bankruptcy order is annulled.[26]

(b) If he is subject to a disqualification order made under the Company Directors' Disqualification Act 1986.[26a]

(c) If he is a patient within the meaning of Part VII of the Mental Health Act 1983. A 'patient' under this statute is a person who has been found to be incapable, by reason of mental disorder, of managing or administering his own affairs.

---

20   For criticism of this rule see eg Gower, "Principles of Modern Company Law" 4th edn 1979 p 488.
21   *Portman Building Society v Gallwey* [1955] 1 All ER 227.
22   For punishments under the Act, see s 430 and Sch 10; punishments under the Rules are governed by Rule 12.21 and sch 5 to the Rules.
23   s 390(4) and see relevant part of ch 10.
24   Cmnd 6659, para 69.
25   See paras 11.10ff *supra* and s 390.
26   Insolvency Act 1986 s 278.
26a   See ch 21 part 2.

(d) If he is no longer allowed to act as a qualified insolvency practitioner.[27]

Grounds of appointment

11.19 An administrative receiver is, by definition, a receiver appointed by or on behalf of the debenture holders.[28] The grounds on which the debenture holders may appoint a receiver are generally set out, in very broad terms in the debenture itself. The debenture holders will usually have tried to ensure that the debenture is drafted to cover all the potential circumstances in which they may wish to appoint a receiver, since this is a very important way of safeguarding their security.

11.20 Often the right to appoint a receiver arises on the occurrence of certain events which are specified on the debenture. It will be a question of construing the debenture in any particular case to see whether a relevant event has occurred, thus giving rise to a right to appoint a receiver. Typical events which appear in many debentures as giving rise to this right include failure by the company to fulfil any of its obligations under the debenture, if the assets are in jeopardy, the inability of the company to pay its debts or a cessation by the company of its business.[29] It is very common for debentures to include a right to appoint a receiver if there is a failure by the company to repay principal monies or interests when it is demanded. It is a question of construing the debenture to see if it requires that the demand should be made in any particular form. There has been a great deal of debate on what payment 'on demand' means. Clearly, the company may wish to have a reasonable time to raise the sum required from other financial sources, but the debenture holders will not be in favour of allowing too much time to elapse, in case assets are seized by other creditors or their security is otherwise threatened.

11.21 The traditional view is that if the debenture requires payment on demand, then the borrower must have the money ready and is not entitled to have time to try and raise it.[30] However, it has been held in both Canada and Australia that the borrower is entitled to a reasonable time to raise the money; it remains to be seen whether the English courts will relax their rule. In *Bank of Baroda v Panessar*,[31] Walton J held that if money due under a

---

27 For a discussion of insolvency practitioners, see ch 10.
28 Insolvency Act 1986 s 29(2).
29 For more detailed discussion of events giving rise to a right to appoint a receiver see one of the standard works on receivership, eg Kerr, "Law and Practice as to Receivers"; and see ch 5 on events leading to the crystallisation of a floating charge.
30 *Cripps v Wickenden* [1973] 2 All ER 606.
31 [1986] BCLC 497.

debenture was payable on demand, it was repayable immediately, but the debtor would not be in default in making the payment unless and until he had had a reasonable opportunity of implementing 'whatever reasonable mechanics of payment' he needed to operate in order to discharge the debt. The reasonable opportunity which the debtor is given is, however, limited to the operation of the mechanics of payment; it does not mean the debtor is to be given time to raise the money.

11.22 It is clear that the burden of proof is placed on the debenture holder to show that an event has occurred which gives rise to the right to appoint a receiver.[32] In *NRG Vision Ltd v Churchfield Leasing*[33] the question was whether there had been a demand sufficient for the purposes of clause 6 of the debenture, which gave the debenture holder the right to appoint a receiver after he had 'demanded payment'. The court held that it was sufficient for the purposes of such a clause if a demand is sent to the relevant party which makes it clear to him that the creditor requires to be paid a sum which is, in fact, due. The fact that in this particular case there was an offer to accept instalments and not to appoint a receiver if those instalments were paid did not detract from the efficacy of the demand. However the judge did not go on to decide the difficult question of whether an excessive demand would be valid for the same purpose.

11.23 If the power to appoint a receiver has become exercisable, then the debenture holder owes no duty of care to the company in deciding whether to exercise it, provided that he acts in good faith.[34] The attitude of the court is that provided the debenture holder acts in good faith he is entitled to act to protect his security by appointing a receiver and he does not have to take anyone else's interests into account. In *Re Potter's Oils (No. 2)*[35] it was held that a debenture holder who was contractually entitled to appoint a receiver was entitled to do so in order to protect his own interests. Although the debenture holder owes a duty of care to the company, this duty is qualified, in that it is subordinated to the debenture holders' own interests; he is under no duty to refrain from appointing a receiver merely because that may cause loss to the company or its creditors.

VALIDITY OF APPOINTMENT

11.24 Provided the receiver is qualified to act as an administrative receiver,[36] the validity of his appointment will depend on various other

32 *Kasofsky v Keegers* [1937] 4 All ER 374.
33 (1988) 4 BCC 56.
34 *Shamji v Johnson Matthey Bankers Ltd* [1986] BCLC 278.
35 [1986] 1 All ER 890.
36 See paras 11.10 to 11.21 above on qualification and disqualification.

factors, including whether on its true construction, in the light of the events which have happened, the debenture has given rise to a right to appoint. In *Cryne v Barclays Bank plc*[37] the court would not readily imply a term into the debenture entitling the debenture holder to appoint a receiver when he considered, on reasonable grounds, that his security was in jeopardy. Such a term could only be implied where it was necessary to give business efficacy to the contract. Since this particular debenture contained a number of express provisions designed to protect the debenture holder's security, there was no justification for implying such a term. Other factors which may affect validity of the appointment include whether any relevant conditions laid down by the debenture have been satisfied and whether the debenture itself is valid.

Satisfaction of conditions in the debenture

11.25　The potential administrative receiver will wish to check that any conditions which the debenture requires to be satisfied before an appointment can be made are satisfied. Usually the directors of the company will have the power to ask the debenture holder to appoint a receiver; the directors may also have the power to waive any condition for the making of an appointment which has not yet been satisfied; this can be a particularly useful power from the administrative receiver's point of view.

Validity of the debenture itself

11.26　It is very important that the administrative receiver should check the validity of the charge under which he is going to be appointed, since if it is invalid, his appointment will be invalid. This means that if the administrative receiver nevertheless goes on and acts, he may be liable as a trespasser in respect of his acts as receiver.[38] It is also possible that he may be treated as a constructive trustee of the assets belonging to the company which are in his hands.[39] In practice, the receiver may have a contractual right to an indemnity from his appointor,[40] should this situation occur, but it is preferable to establish the validity of the charge as soon as possible.

11.27　The charge under which the administrative receiver is appointed may be invalid for a number of reasons, the following are some of the most likely sources of invalidity;

37　[1987] BCLC 548.
38　*Re Goldberg (No 2)* [1912] 1 KB 606.
39　*Rolled Steel Products (Holdings) Ltd v British Steel Corporation* [1986] Ch 246.
40　See also paras 11.29 *et seq* on s 34 Insolvency Act 1986.

(a) The grant of the charge may have been *ultra vires* the company; eg the company may lack capacity under its memorandum of association to enter into the relevant transaction or the agents purporting to enter into an *intra vires* transaction may have lacked authority.[41]

(b) The charge may be liable to be set aside as a voidable preference or a transaction at an undervalue under the Insolvency Act 1986 ss 238–241.

(c) If the charge was granted as part of an extortionate credit transaction and it was entered into in the period of 3 years ending with the day on which the company went into liquidation or an administration order was made, then the liquidator or administrator may apply for relief in respect of that transaction under the Insolvency Act 1986 s 244.[41a]

(d) If the floating charge was granted less than one year before the appointment of the administrative receiver and the company goes into liquidation or an administrator is appointed before that period expires, then the floating charge may be found to be void under the Insolvency Act 1986 s 245. If s 245 applies, the invalidation of the floating charge only takes effect as at the date of commencement of the winding-up or presentation of petition for the administration order. The invalidation has no retrospective effect so the receiver can properly act until the invalidation takes effect.[42]

(e) The charge may not have been duly registered under the Companies Act 1985 ss 395 and 396. These sections require that all the most common types of charge must be registered with the Registrar of Companies.

11.28 If the charge is void for non-registration, it seems that the receiver may act safely unless and until challenged by a liquidator or other party able to invoke lack of registration.[43] However, if the charge has been registered, then under s 401(2) of the Companies Act 1985, the registrar's certificate of registration is conclusive evidence that all the requirements of the statute with regard to registration have been complied with, as between the company and all persons other than the Attorney-General.

Liability for invalid appointment

Indemnity

11.29 If the administrative receiver becomes liable owing to the fact that he was invalidly appointed, he may be able to rely on s 34 of the Insolvency Act 1986. This gives the court a discretionary power to order the appointor to indemnify the person appointed against any liability which arises solely

41 *Rolled Steel Products (Holdings) Ltd v British Steel Corporation* [1986] Ch 246.
41a See ch 20.
42 *Mace Builders v Lunn* [1985] 3 WLR 465; and see ch 20.
43 *Burston Finance Ltd v Speirway* [1974] 1 WLR 1648 at 1657C; and see ch 8.

as a result of the invalidity of the appointment. The section covers liability in all cases of invalidity; it specifically provides that it includes invalidity not only as a result of the invalidity of the instrument of appointment, but also 'otherwise'. This could include a situation where the charge which contained the appointor's right to make the appointment was itself found to be invalid, perhaps under ss 244 or 245 of the Insolvency Act 1986.

11.30 The court's discretion allows it to order the appointor to indemnify the person appointed against liability which arises solely by reason of the invalidity of the appointment. Thus the indemnity would not extend to damages incurred by the administrative receiver in carrying out the abortive receivership incompetently. It is, of course, always open to the potential administrative receiver to require the appointor to accept the risk of any invalidity as a condition of accepting the appointment and if this is the case, a deed of indemnity will generally be required.

Defect in appointment

11.31 If there is a slight defect in the appointment, as opposed to an invalid appointment (and the two must be clearly distinguished) then recourse may be had to s 232 of the Insolvency Act 1986. This section provides, *inter alia*, that the acts of an administrative receiver will be valid, notwithstanding a defect in his appointment, nomination or qualifications. The language of s 232 is very similar to that found in s 285 of the Companies Act 1985. From the case law on that section it would seem that s 232 is confined to minor defects in appointment, so that it would not apply, for instance, to validate acts where the appointor had no right to make the appointment at all.[44] However, a minor mistake in the appointment would be covered by this section.

No protection from s 42(3) Insolvency Act 1986

11.32 This section provides that a person dealing with an administrative receiver, in good faith and for value, need not be concerned to inquire whether or not the receiver is acting within his powers. However, it would appear that this section will not assist a person dealing with an invalidly appointed administrative receiver, since it assumes that the receiver has been validly appointed. It also limits its protection to persons dealing with the administrative receiver, which excludes the receiver himself and possibly the person who appointed him.

---

44 See *Morris v Kanssen* [1946] AC 459.

APPOINTMENT

11.33   The appointment of the administrative receiver must be made in accordance with any requirements laid down in the debenture and these will be strictly construed, so that if the requirement is to appoint in writing, it need not be made by deed.[45] However, it is usual for the debenture to be under seal and this may be preferable, since a mortgagee may exercise certain statutory powers only if the mortgage is by deed.[46]

11.34   The statute itself is silent on whether there is any particular method which should be used to appoint a receiver. It is common for the appointment to be made in writing, but this is not a requirement of the statute. When appointing a receiver who is not an administrative receiver it may be important to make the appointment by deed, since if he is to execute a deed as agent for the company he must be appointed by deed, but when appointing an administrative receiver, it is not necessary to make the appointment by deed, since an administrative receiver will have power, (subject to any contrary provision in the debentures) to use the company's seal and to execute deeds and other documents, in the name of, and on behalf of, the company.[47]

Appointment of joint receivers

11.35   It is necessary to construe the debenture to find whether it is possible to appoint more than one person to act as joint administrative receivers. The usual rule under the Law of Property Act 1925 s 61(c) is that if no contrary intention is apparent, then the singular in the debenture would be construed as including the plural, so that a power to appoint one administrative receiver should be construed as a power to appoint joint administrative receivers.

11.36   Joint receivers are not able to act severally as well as jointly unless there is an express provision in the debenture.[48] In addition, s 231 of the Insolvency Act 1986 provides that if more than one person is appointed as an administrative receiver, then the appointment must specify whether any act required or authorised under any enactment is to be done by all those appointed or can be done by any one of them. Clearly, if joint receivers can act only jointly, this may increase the practical difficulties if some particularly urgent action is required on their part. However, where joint administrative receivers are acting as the responsible insolvency practi-

---

45   *Cripps v Wickenden* [1973] 1 WLR 955.
46   Eg power of sale, cf s 101 LPA 1925.
47   s 42 and Sch 1 Insolvency Act 1986.
48   *Windsor Refrigerator v Branch Nominees* [1961] ch 375.

tioner in any proceedings, delivery of a document to one of them is to be treated as delivery to them all.[49]

11.37 Section 33 of the Insolvency Act 1986, which governs the time from which the appointment of a person as an administrative receiver is effective, applies to joint receivers as well, in accordance with the modifications made by the Insolvency Rules 1986.[50] The Rules provide[51] that where joint receivers are appointed, acceptance of the appointment must be made by each of them, in accordance with s 33, just as if they were both sole appointees. However, the joint appointment will only take effect when all the joint appointees have accepted and it will be deemed to have been made at the time when the instrument of appointment was received by or on behalf of all the joint appointees.

11.38 Similarly, both joint appointees must confirm their acceptance of the appointment in writing to the appointor, within 7 days of acceptance,[52] unless they accepted the appointment in writing in the first place[53] The statement of confirmation of acceptance should state the time and date on which the instrument of appointment was received and the time and date of acceptance.[54] Just as with sole appointees, the acceptance and the confirmation of acceptance can be given by any person duly authorised for the purpose on behalf of the joint receiver.[55] Joint administrative receivers must, of course, comply with all the other requirements of the statute.

Appointment of receiver if company in liquidation

11.39 It is still possible to appoint a receiver if the company is in liquidation; under s 32 of the Insolvency Act 1986, the court can appoint the official receiver where an application is made on behalf of the debenture holders or other creditors of a company which is being wound up.

ACCEPTANCE OF APPOINTMENT

Time within which acceptance must be made

11.40 The Insolvency Act 1986 s 33(1) lays down statutory rules relating to the acceptance of an appointment as a receiver. The section follows the recommendations of the Cork Committee[56] in that it provides that the appointment must be accepted before the end of the business day next

---

49 Rule 13.5.
50 See paras 11.45ff on acceptance of appointment.
51 Rule 3.1(1).
52 Rule 3.1(2).
53 Rule 3.1(3).
54 Rule 3.1(5).
55 Rule 3.1(4).
56 Cork, paras 470–474.

following that on which the instrument of appointment is received by or on behalf of the appointee. In setting down a brief timetable for this to occur, the Cork Committee hoped to overcome the difficulties caused previously, when a receiver could be validly appointed some time before the appointment was published.

Time of appointment

11.41 The Committee also recommended that the law should be expressly enacted as it had been stated in the case of *Cripps v Wickenden*;[57] that the appointment should run from the time of receipt of the instrument of appointment by or on behalf of the appointee, provided that the appointment is accepted and that if the appointment is not so accepted, it should lapse. This is the effect of the statute, which provides[58] that if the appointment is accepted it will be deemed to have been made at the time at which the instrument of appointment is received by the appointee.

Mode of acceptance

11.42 The section is silent as to the mode of acceptance, but it is clear from a reading of Rule 3.1 of the Insolvency Rules 1986 that the initial acceptance may be oral or in writing. However, if the initial acceptance is made orally, a written confirmation of acceptance must be sent to the appointor within 7 days.[59] The statement of confirmation, if sent, must include a statement of the time and date when the instrument of appointment was received and a statement of the time and date of acceptance,[60] but it is expressly stated that if an appointment is initially accepted in writing, it does not later have to be confirmed in writing.[61] Although the rules do not expressly state that a written acceptance should be in the same form as a written confirmation, it would seem to be wise to follow the same form, for the avoidance of doubt. In the case of both acceptance and confirmation of acceptance of appointment, the act may be carried out on behalf of the appointee by any person who is duly authorised for the purpose.[62]

NOTIFICATION THAT AN ADMINISTRATIVE RECEIVER APPOINTED—BUSINESS COMMUNICATIONS

11.43 When an administrative receiver has been appointed, s 39(1) of the Insolvency Act 1986 provides that all invoices, business letters and orders

---

57 [1973] 1 WLR 944.
58 Insolvency Act 1986 s 33(1)(b).
59 Rule 3.1(2).
60 Rule 3.1(5).
61 Rule 3.1(3).
62 Rule 3.1(4).

for goods which are issued by or on behalf of both the company and the administrative receiver, must contain a statement that a receiver has been appointed, insofar as they are documents on or in which the company's name appears. Clearly it is important for those dealing with the company to know that it is in receivership as they may wish to adjust their position accordingly. The section goes on to provide a sanction for non-compliance with the notification requirements;[63] any receiver, liquidator or officer of the company who knowingly and wilfully authorises or permits the default will be liable to a fine.[64]

Appointment to be entered in register of charges

11.44   Under s 405(1) of the Companies Act 1985, the appointment of the administrative receiver must be entered in the register of charges. S 405 provides that the appointor must give notice that an administrative receiver has been appointed within 7 days of the appointment and then this fact will be registered accordingly.

Advertisement of appointment

11.45   When an administrative receiver is appointed, he must comply with various requirements of the statute which try to ensure that all those who deal with the company, together with the company's creditors, are aware of the appointment. These requirements, imposed by s 46 of the Insolvency Act 1986 are similar to those imposed on the liquidator by s 21 of the Act.[65]

Notice to company and creditors

11.46   As soon as an administrative receiver is appointed, he must immediately send a notice of his appointment to the company.[66] Unless the court directs otherwise, he must also send a notice to all the creditors of the company insofar as he is aware of their addresses, but he has 28 days from the date of his appointment to comply with this requirement.[67]

11.47   The contents of these notices are prescribed by the Rules,[68] which impose requirements relating to the company's name so that it can be easily identified by any interested party.[69] The notices must contain a statement

---

63   Insolvency Act 1986 s 39(2).
64   For penalties under the Act see s 430 and sch 10.
65   See ch 15.
66   s 46(1)(a).
67   s 46(1)(b).
68   Rule 3.2.
69   Any reference in the Rules to the giving of a notice means that the document can be sent by post, unless a particular Rule specifically requires that service should be effected personally (Rule 13.3).

not only of the registered name and number of the company as at the date of the administrative receiver's appointment, but also of any other name under which the company has been registered in the twelve months preceding the date of his appointment, together with details of any name under which the company has traded at any time during that year, if its trading name was substantially different from the name under which it was then registered.[70]

11.48   The notices must contain the name and address of the administrative receiver and the date on which he was appointed. They must also give a brief description of the instrument which confirmed the power of appointment, its date and the name of the person who made the appointment.[71] Finally, the notices must contain a brief description of any of the company's assets in respect of which the administrative receiver is not made receiver.[72]

11.49   As with all notices required by the Rules, notice must be given in writing unless the court permits notice to be given in some other way (or an alternative method is expressly provided).[73] The sending of any notice by an insolvency practitioner, such as the administrative receiver, may be proved by means of a certificate that the notice was duly posted. This can be given by the insolvency practitioner, his solicitor, or an employee or partner of either of them.[74]

Advertisement of appointment

11.50   S 46(1)(a) also obliges the administrative receiver to publish a notice of his appointment in the manner prescribed by the Rules,[75] as soon as he is appointed. The advertisement of the appointment must appear once in the *London Gazette* and once in any newspaper thought by the administrative receiver to be the most appropriate for ensuring that the advertisement comes to the notice of the company's creditors.[76] The advertisement must contain a statement of the registered name and number of the company as at the date of the administrative receiver's appointment, together with any other name under which the company has been registered in the twelve months preceding the date of his appointment, together with details of any name under which the company has traded at any time during

---

70   Rule 3.2(2)(a)–(c).
71   Rule 3.2(2)(d)–(f).
72   Rule 3.2(2)(g).
73   Rule 12.4(1).
74   Rule 12.4(2).
75   See Rules 3.2(3) and (4).
76   Rule 3.2(3).

that year, if its trading name was substantially different from the name under which it was registered. The advertisement must also contain the name and address of the administrative receiver, the date of his appointment and the name of the person who made the appointment.[77] This section implements a recommendation made by the Cork Committee[78] who wished to ensure, insofar as it was possible, that creditors would have notice of the administrative receiver's appointment. However, the Committee felt that shareholders would have to rely on the general advertisement since the cost of notifying them individually was unjustifiable. The sanction for failure to comply with the requirements of the section without reasonable excuse is a fine; if the default continues, the fine will be levied on a daily default basis.[79]

Non-application of s 46

11.51   If any administrative receiver is merely appointed to act together with an already existing administrative receiver, or to replace an administrative receiver who is ceasing to act, or who has died, then it is not necessary for him to repeat the notification procedures laid down by s 46, provided they have already been fully complied with by the existing administrative receiver or the one being replaced. If the requirements of s 46 have not already been fully complied with then the new administrative receiver and any continuing administrative receiver will have to go through the whole notification process himself.[80] If the company is being wound up, the notification section will still apply, notwithstanding that the administrative receiver and the liquidator are the same person, although the statute allows for any necessary modifications which arise from the fact.[81]

---

77   Rule 3.2(4).
78   Cork, para 476.
79   s 46(4). For penalties, see s 430 and Sch 10.
80   s 46(2).
81   s 46(3).

CHAPTER 12

Duties and Liabilities of the Administrative Receiver

AGENCY AND LIABILITY FOR CONTRACTS

12.01 It has been a common feature of debentures to provide, in relation to a receiver, that when he is appointed he will act as the agent of the insolvent company. However, such a provision was not required by law and the uncertainty surrounding the exact status of the receiver was a source of considerable concern to the Cork Committee.[1] The Committee recommended[2] that until liquidation a receiver appointed out of court should be deemed to be the agent of the company (except so far as the charge provided otherwise). The Insolvency Act 1986 provides in s 44(1)(a) that the administrative receiver of a company is deemed to be the company's agent, unless and until the company goes into liquidation. This means that it is the company which will be the contracting party in all its new business arrangements. The position of the administrative receiver is a very complicated one in conceptual terms, since he is appointed by the debenture holders and will be concerned to protect their interests, but as an agent, he will also owe certain duties to the company which is his principal. However, it is not correct to treat the agency of a receiver as an ordinary example of the law of agency.

12.02 The special position of the receiver was discussed by the Court of Appeal in the case of *Gomba Holdings Ltd v Minories Finance Ltd*[3]. Fox LJ gave the judgment of the court, and made it quite clear that the agency of a receiver is not an ordinary agency. The Court of Appeal agreed with the analysis of Hoffmann J at first instance, when he explained that the particular situation of the receiver arose from the fact that although he is the agent of the company, his primary duty is to realise the assets in the interests of the debenture holder, so that his powers of management are really ancillary to that duty. As the Court of Appeal pointed out,[4] the receiver also owes fiduciary duties to the debenture holder, who has a right, *inter alia*, to be put in possession of all the information concerning the receivership which is available to the receiver. The receiver is in the position of

1 Cork Report para 457.
2 Cork Report para 469b.
3 (1989) 5 BCC 27.
4 (1989) 5 BCC 27 at 29F.

performing duties on behalf of the debenture holder as well as the mortgagor, which puts him in a different position from that of an ordinary agent, who is generally concerned only with his relationship with his principal.

12.03   The Court of Appeal summarised the particular position of the receiver as follows:[5]

> "The agency of a receiver is not an ordinary agency. It is primarily a chance to protect the mortgagee or debenture holder. Thus the receiver acts as agent for the mortgagor in that he has power to affect the mortgagor's position by acts which, though done for the benefit of the debenture holder, are treated as if they were the acts of the mortgagor. The relationship set up by the debenture, and the appointment of the receiver, however, is not simply between the mortgagor and receiver. It is tripartite and involves the mortgagor, the receiver and the debenture holder. The receiver is appointed by the debenture holder upon the happening of specified events, and becomes the mortgagor's agent whether the mortgagor likes it or not. And as a matter of contract between the mortgagor and the debenture holder, the mortgagor will have to pay the receiver's fees. Further, the mortgagor cannot dismiss the receiver since that power is reserved to the debenture holder as another of the contractual terms of the loan. It is to be noted also that the mortgagor cannot instruct the receiver how to act in the conduct of the receivership."

12.04   In the context of the receiver's agency, it is also interesting to note that while the receiver is acting as agent of the company, the debenture holder or mortgagee is not responsible for what the receiver does, unless he interferes with the receiver's activities, or directs the receiver to act in some particular way. However, clearly the debenture holder is responsible for what the receiver does whilst he is the debenture holder's agent, although unless there is an express exclusion clause in the agency contract between the debenture holder and the receiver the debenture holder will be entitled, under an implied term of that contract, to an indemnity from the receiver in respect of any negligence on his part.[6]

Position after liquidation

12.05   The administrative receiver will generally act as agent for the company until it goes into liquidation, at which point his agency is terminated, although not necessarily his role as administrative receiver. The administrative receiver can still exercise his power to manage the undertaking and the assets of the company, but that power cannot be exercised to create any new liabilities.

5   (1989) 5 BCC 27 at 29C–E.
6   *American Express International Banking Corp v Hurley* [1985] 3 All ER 564.

12.06 If the receivership is to carry on after liquidation (or if it is to commence after liquidation) the administrative receiver will be concerned to establish that the instrument of appointment clearly indicates his status in these circumstances. After liquidation he cannot be the agent of the company, but he can act as agent for his appointor or he can simply act as principal in his own right. Clearly it is important for the administrative receiver to clarify his status, since if he acts as agent for the appointor the appointor as principal will be responsible for the administrative receiver's acts and unless there is a provision to the contrary in the instrument of appointment, the administrative receiver will be entitled to an indemnity from the appointor. If the administrative receiver acts as principal he will be personally liable for his actions of the administrative receiver, but with a right to an indemnity out of the assets of the company,[7] subject always to the terms of his appointment.

Personal liability for contracts entered into in the course of receivership

12.07 The Cork Committee was particularly keen to clarify the administrative receiver's position in relation to contracts entered into by him in the carrying out of his functions. The committee found that in practice it was often very difficult to decide whether or not a receiver had assumed personal liability under a particular contract and a great deal of evidence was submitted on this point.[8] The position was particularly complex in relation to contracts made between the company and third parties and entered into before the receiver's appointment. The Committee found that various factors had to be taken into account:

(a) Receivers commonly notified creditors on their appointment, making it clear that post-receivership debts would be met in full.

(b) Receivers felt morally responsible for post-receivership debts and wished to pay them in full to avoid damage to their own reputation, regardless of the strict legal position.

(c) Contracts which appeared to be pre-receivership contracts had often become fresh post-receivership contracts because of new terms being agreed.

In these circumstances, there was often a great deal of uncertainty whether or not a receiver had undertaken personal liability on contracts and the Cork Committee recommended[9] that legislation should be enacted to clarify the situation. Section 44(1)(b) of the Insolvency Act 1986 provides

7 Insolvency Act 1986 s 44(1)(c).
8 See Cork Report paras 455–470.
9 Cork Report para 469.

that the administrative receiver is personally liable on any contract entered into by him in the carrying out of his functions except insofar as the contract provides otherwise.

12.08   As far as contracts made by the company prior to his appointment are concerned, the administrative receiver will have to make a commercial judgment whether the company should give effect to them or not. If it is decided that the company will repudiate the contract, the other contracting party will have a claim in damages against the company, but generally no claim against the administrative receiver. In this context, it is interesting to note that if a company has entered into a contract for the sale of land, which is a specifically enforceable contract, then if the debenture holder of the company subsequently appoints a receiver, it seems that that does not deprive the purchaser of the land of his equitable interest in it, nor does it prevent the court from making an order of specific performance.[10]

12.09   Clearly contracts of employment may play an important role in this area, and the statute makes specific provision for them. Section 44(1)(b) goes on to state expressly that the administrative receiver will be personally liable on any contract of employment adopted by him in the carrying out of his functions. In this context, it is important to note that there is no definition of what the receiver must do in order to adopt a contract of employment within the meaning of the section. The administrative receiver is given a period of 14 days' grace, however, starting from the date of his appointment, during which time he is not to be taken to have adopted a contract of employment by reason of anything he does or omits to do.[11] This implies that the most likely means of 'adopting' a contract will be its continuation after the appointment of the administrative receiver.

12.10   Set off can prove another complex area when the administrative receiver is considering whether to cause the company to repudiate its contracts or not, since in some cases a debtor of the company will be permitted to set off. The administrative receiver will generally want to cause the company to repudiate any particularly onerous set off arrangements. However, the more liberal set off provisions dealt with in chapter 18 do not apply in a receivership; only those acknowledged under the general law of contract will be applicable.

12.11   Although the administrative receiver's personal liability is clearly spelt out in the legislation, he is not left without remedy, should he become

10   *Free Vale Ltd v Metro Store (Holdings)* [1984] BCLC 72.
11   Insolvency Act 1986 s 44(2).

liable on any relevant contracts, since s 44(1)(c) provides that he is entitled to an indemnity out of the assets of the company in respect of the personal liability for contracts which he assumes as a result of s 44(1)(b). For the avoidance of doubt the statute also provides[12] that this section is not to be taken as limiting the liability of the administrative receiver in respect of contracts which he enters into or adopts without authority, nor is it to be read as conferring any right to an indemnity in respect of that liability. Equally, the statute makes it clear[13] that this section does not limit any right to indemnity which the administrative receiver may otherwise possess; thus, he may have an express indemnity granted by the instrument of appointment which would be unaffected by the existence of the statutory indemnity.

12.12   The administrative receiver may wish to protect himself by excluding or limiting his liability in some way. If he does so, it will be a matter of construing the relevant instrument to see whether the exclusion clause covers any breach of duty which has occurred. Under the general law of contract, the *contra proferentem* rule will be applied and in the event of ambiguity the clause will be construed against the interest of the administrative receiver who seeks to rely on it.

STATEMENT OF AFFAIRS

12.13   As soon as the administrative receiver is appointed he must gather together the information which he needs in order to allow him to make an evaluation of the state of the company's affairs. Section 47(1) of the Insolvency Act 1986 places an immediate duty on the administrative receiver to require information to be supplied by some or all of the people who are regarded by the statute as most likely to be able to supply relevant information. The administrative receiver can thus require some or all of the following to submit information to him about the company's affairs:[14]

(a) those who are or have been officers of the company;

(b) those who have taken part in the formation of the company at any time within one year before the date of the appointment of the administrative receiver;

(c) those who are in the company's employment, or have been in its employment within that year, and are in the administrative receiver's opinion capable of giving the information required;

(d) those who are or have been within that year officers of or in the

---

12   Insolvency Act 1986 s 44(3).
13   Insolvency Act 1986 s 44(3).
14   Insolvency Act 1986 s 47(3).

employment of a company which is, or within that year was, an officer of the company.

Notice to deponents

12.14 When the administrative receiver decides to require a statement of the company's affairs to be made out by one of the relevant persons (who are known as 'deponents' because they also have to supply relevant affidavits),[15] he must send them a notice requiring them to prepare and submit a statement.[16] The notice which is sent to each deponent must inform them[17] of the names and addresses of all other persons to whom a similar notice has been sent. They must also be told the amount of time which is available for them to supply the statement. The period of time laid down by the statute is 21 days[18] but the administrative receiver has power to extend the amount of time allowed and if he refuses to exercise this power the deponent may apply to the court for an extension of time.[19] The deponents must also be reminded, in the notice which is sent to them, of the effect of s 235 of the Insolvency Act 1986, which imposes on them a duty to give to an office holder (including an administrative receiver), such information concerning the company and its affairs as he may reasonably require. That section also imposes a duty on the deponents to attend on the receiver if required to do so.[20] Finally, the notice which is sent to the deponents must remind them that under s 47(b) of the Insolvency Act 1986, it is a criminal offence to fail, without reasonable excuse, to comply with the obligations imposed by the section; contravention of this requirement will result in liability to a fine, which will be levied on a daily default basis for continued contravention.[21]

Content of statement

12.15 The statement of affairs which is submitted by each deponent must contain the information specified in s 47(2) of the Insolvency Act 1986, namely:

(a) particulars of the company's assets, debts and liabilities;
(b) the names and addresses of its creditors;
(c) the securities held by them respectively

---

15 r 3.3(2).
16 r 3.3(1).
17 r 3.3(3).
18 s 47(4).
19 s 47(5).
20 See s 235(2)(a) and (b) and s 235(3).
21 For punishments under the Act, see s 430 and sch 10.

(d) the dates when the securities were respectively given, and
(e) such further or other information as may be prescribed.

The information which is required by this subsection follows the same pattern as the information which is obtained under the administration order procedure[22] and also where a company is wound up by the court.[23]

12.16   When the relevant information has been gathered together, it must be set out on Form 3.2.[24] If requested by the deponents concerned, the administrative receiver is under a duty to supply them with the forms which are required for the preparation of the statement of affairs.[25] Each of the deponents must verify by affidavit the statement of affairs which he has been required to submit[26] and the statement itself, together with a copy of the verified statement, must then be delivered to the receiver by the deponent.[27]

12.17   The administrative receiver must pay any expenses which are in his opinion reasonably incurred by a deponent in making the statement of affairs and affidavit of verification;[28] any decision made by the receiver in relation to these matters is subject to an appeal to the court.[29] However, Rule 3.7 expressly provides that its contents are not to be taken as relieving any deponent from any of their obligations with respect to the preparation, verification or submission of the statement of affairs.[30]

Limited disclosure of the statement of affairs

12.18   Rule 3.5 allows the administrative receiver to use his discretion to prevent disclosure of any part of the statement of affairs which he feels would prejudice the conduct of the receivership. He may apply to the court for an order of limited disclosure which may apply to the whole or part of the statement of affairs.[31] If the court grants the application, it has power to order that the statement, or the relevant part of it, is only open to inspection with the leave of the court.[32] The procedure is quite flexible, since the court may also give directions on the delivery of documents to the registrar of companies and the disclosure of relevant information to other persons.[33]

---

22 See ch 13.
23 See ch 15.
24 r 3.4(1).
25 r 3.3(4).
26 s 47(2) and r 3.4(1).
27 r 3.4(4).
28 r 3.7(1).
29 r 3.7(2).
30 r 3.7(3).
31 r 3.5(1).
32 r 3.5(2).
33 r 3.5(3).

Concurrence in the statement of affairs

12.19 The administrative receiver may require any of the persons specified in s 47(3) of the Insolvency Act 1986 to submit an affidavit of concurrence, stating that the individual concerned concurs in the statement of affairs under consideration.[34] However, it is possible for the affidavit of concurrence to be qualified if the person making it is without the direct knowledge necessary for concurrence, or where the statement is considered to be erroneous or misleading, or where the maker disagrees with the deponent.[35] All the affidavits of concurrence, together with a copy of each one, must be delivered to the receiver by the person making the affidavit.[36] The administrative receiver must retain the verified copy of the statement of affairs, together with any affidavits of concurrence, as part of the records of the receivership.[37]

Administrative receiver's discretion to release from obligations

12.20 As a general rule, the deponents have 21 days in which to submit their statement of affairs to the administrative receiver, beginning with the day after that on which the notice requiring them to submit a statement of affairs is given to them.[38] The basic time limit is very short; the Cork Committee commented that a more realistic time limit for the production of a statement of affairs made in relation to a major company would be 3 months, and recommended that the time limit should be extended accordingly. The Committee also acknowledged the need for speedy information by recommending that an approximate and summary form of the statement should be supplied within 21 days.[39]

12.21 However, the statute does not closely resemble the pattern which the Cork Committee recommended. Instead, s 47(4) lays down a basic time limit of 21 days for the submission of the statement of affairs and s 47(5) makes provision for an extension of time at the discretion of the administrative receiver, with the possibility of an application to the court if he refuses to exercise his discretion. The administrative receiver may extend the time available for submission of the statement either when he gives the deponents notice of their obligations in the first place, or at a subsequent stage of the procedure.[40] He also has a discretion to release a person from any obligation imposed by s 47(1) or (2) and the Rules[41] make it clear that

---

34   r 3.4(2).
35   r 3.4(3).
36   r 3.4(5).
37   r 3.4(6).
38   Insolvency Act 1986 s 47(4).
39   Cork Report paras 482–485.
40   Insolvency Act 1986 s 47(5)(b).
41   r 3.6(1).

these powers may be exercised by the receiver either of his own motion or at the request of any deponent.

Application to the court by deponents

12.22 If the administrative receiver refuses to exercise the powers conferred on him when he is requested to do so by a deponent, the deponent may apply to the court for an extension of time or release from the obligations in question,[42] since s 47(5) gives the court the necessary powers. The deponent must satisfy the court that there is sufficient cause for his application, since if it thinks that insufficient cause is shown, it can dismiss the application. However, the application cannot be dismissed unless the applicant has had an opportunity to attend an *ex parte* hearing of the matter, of which he has been given at least 7 days' notice.[43]

12.23 If the application is not dismissed, the court must fix a hearing and give notice of it to the deponent,[44] who must then give the administrative receiver at least 14 days' notice of the hearing. The notice which is sent to the administrative receiver must state the venue of the hearing and it must be accompanied by a copy of the application and of any evidence in support which the deponent intends to adduce.[45]

12.24 When the hearing takes place the administrative receiver may appear and be heard; whether or not he does so he may file a written report of any matters which he considers ought to be drawn to the court's attention. If he decides to file such a report, he must send a copy to the deponents not later than 5 days before the hearing.[46] If the court makes an order as a result of hearing the application, sealed copies of the order must be sent to the deponent and the administrative receiver.[47] As far as costs are concerned the applicant must generally pay his own costs in any event; in addition, the Rules provide that unless the court orders otherwise, no allowance towards them shall be made out of the assets under the control of the administrative receiver.[48]

ABSTRACT OF RECEIPTS AND PAYMENTS

12.25 Under Rule 3.32 the administrative receiver must send an account of his receipts and payments as receiver to the registrar of companies, to the

---

42 r 3.6(2).
43 r 3.6(3).
44 r 3.6(3).
45 r 3.6(4).
46 r 3.6(5).
47 r 3.6(6).
48 r 3.6(7).

company itself, to his appointor and to each member of the creditors' committee (if one has been formed). These accounts must be sent within 2 months after the end of 12 months from the date of his appointment and within 2 months after the end of every subsequent 12 months. In addition, they must be sent within 2 months after he ceases to act as administrative receiver. It is possible for the administrative receiver to apply to the court for an extension of the 2 months' period, should he need more time in which to comply with these requirements.[49]

12.26   The accounts which are sent must be in the form of an abstract which shows all the receipts and payments during the relevant period. Where the administrative receiver has ceased to act, the accounts must show all receipts and payments made during the period from the end of the last 12 month period to the time when he ceased to act. If there has been no previous abstract, then the accounts should show all the receipts and payments made in the period since his appointment as administrative receiver.[50] It is a criminal offence for the administrative receiver to fail to comply with this Rule; contravention brings with it liability to a fine which will be levied on a daily default basis for continued contravention.[51]

Rule 3.32(4) expressly states that this Rule is without prejudice to the receiver's duty to render proper accounts required otherwise than by this Rule. This means that such duties imposed on the receiver by equity or the law of contract must also be fulfilled.[52]

ENFORCEMENT OF DUTY TO MAKE RETURNS

12.27   In addition to the criminal penalties imposed on the administrative receiver, should he fail to file, deliver or make any return, account or other similar document or fail to give any notice required by the Act or by the Rules, s 41 of the Insolvency Act 1986 provides for the enforcement of these duties by means of a court order, which can be made on the application of any member or creditor of the insolvent company or by the registrar of companies.[53] Similarly, if the company is in liquidation, the liquidator can apply for an order to compel the administrative receiver to render proper accounts of his receipts and payments, and to vouch for them and pay over to the liquidator the amount properly payable to him.[54] In either case, the

---

49   rr 3.32(1) and (2).
50   r 3.32(3).
51   r 3.32(4); and see s 430 and sch 10 for punishments imposed by the Act.
52   See Hoffman J in *Gomba Holdings UK Ltd v Homan* [1986] 1 WLR 1301.
53   Insolvency Act 1986 s 41(1) and (2).
54   Insolvency Act 1986 s 41(1) and (2).

court's order may provide that all costs of and incidental to the application shall be borne by the receiver.[55]

OTHER DUTIES TO SUPPLY INFORMATION

12.28   Although it has been suggested that the statutory provisions above embody the sole obligation on the administrative receiver to provide information, that does not seem to be the correct view. In *Gomba Holdings UK Ltd v Homan*,[56] Hoffmann J held that s 497(b) of the Companies Act 1985 (from which s 41 of the Insolvency Act 1986 is derived) left unaffected any obligation on a receiver to provide information which may exist in equity or contract. Since the receiver's primary duty was to realise and manage the assets of the company in the interests of the debenture holder, he could refuse to disclose information which was contrary to the interests of the debenture holder. However, he must of course supply information to the company in accordance with the statute, and since his duty of disclosure was not limited to that imposed by the statute alone, he might have to disclose further information where the company could show that it needed the information.

12.29   In *Gomba*, the receivers were ordered to deliver up to the plaintiffs or their solicitors, within 2 months, all documents belonging to the plaintiff company and other companies in the group. The receivers delivered up a great many documents, but declined to deliver up various other documents which they said were not the property of the plaintiff. Hoffmann J dismissed the motion and the plaintiffs appealed. On appeal, the appellants argued that the receivers were agents of the companies and that all documents concerning the principal's affairs prepared or received by the agent belonged to the principal and must therefore be delivered up on termination of the agency. However, the Court of Appeal dismissed the appeal. The agency of a receiver was not an ordinary agency, since it operated within a tripartite relationship operated by the debenture, involving the mortgagor, the receiver and the debenture holder.

12.30   The Court of Appeal agreed with Hoffmann J that the ownership of documents in this tripartite situation depends on whether the documents were brought into being as a result of the receiver's duties to the mortgagor or debenture holder or neither. The Court of Appeal identified three separate categories of document.[57]

---

55   Insolvency Act 1986 s 41(2).
56   [1986] 1 WLR 1301.
57   (1989) 5 BCC 27 at 30B–D.

(a) All documents created or received in pursuance of the receivers' duty to manage the affairs of the company are the property of the company.

(b) Documents created for the purpose of advising the debenture holders regarding the conduct of the receivership are not the property of the company.

(c) Documents prepared by or on behalf of the receivers to enable them to prepare such documents or perform such duties as they are required to do for the purpose of their professional duties to the debenture holder or the companies are the property of the receivers.

It is quite clear that the statutory duties to supply information are not exhaustive, and that the administrative receiver also has duties arising from the tripartite relationship in which he is involved.

DUTY TO PUBLICISE APPOINTMENT

12.31   As stated previously, s 46[58] of the Insolvency Act 1986 provides that the administrative receiver has a duty to advertise the fact that he has been appointed. He must also notify the company and all its creditors, insofar as he is aware of their addresses. These notification requirements are very similar to those imposed on an administrator which are found in s 21 of the Act, and chapter 13 of this work.

DUTY TO MAKE A REPORT

12.32   The administrative receiver has a period of 3 months (or such longer period as the court may allow) from the date of his appointment in which to send a report on the financial state of the insolvent company to those people specified by the Insolvency Act 1986.[59] The relevant people are: the registrar of companies, any trustees for secured creditors of the company and all secured creditors of the company themselves, insofar as the administrative receiver is aware of their addresses. These people constitute a much broader range of interested parties than those who might have expected to have been kept informed before the passing of the Insolvency Act and their inclusion is as a result of recommendations made by the Cork Committee.[60] The wider dissemination of information about insolvent companies when in receivership was one of the main concerns of that committee; and the requirements of s 48 form one of the major planks

---

58   For more detailed discussion of s 46, see ch 11.
59   Insolvency Act 1986 s 48.
60   Cork Report para 480.

of its attempt to change the existing situation. Since s 46(2) of the Insolvency Act 1986 applies for the purposes of s 48 as well,[61] once the requirements of s 48 have been complied with, there is no need to repeat the exercise when an additional administrative receiver is appointed, nor if a replacement is appointed, for an administrative receiver who dies or ceases to act.

12.33 Section 48 is of particular interest to unsecured creditors, since it also enables them to gain access to a much more extensive range of information than they could have obtained previously. Under s 48(2) the administrative receiver has the same period of 3 months (or such longer period as the court may allow) in which either to send a copy of the report to all the unsecured creditors of the company (insofar as he is aware of their addresses) or to publish a notice stating an address to which those creditors may write for a free copy of the report. Any notice which is published for this purpose must be published in the same newspaper in which the administrative receiver's appointment was advertised.[62] This is logical, because Rule 3.2(3) specifies that the newspaper chosen for that purpose must be the one which the administrative receiver thinks is most appropriate for ensuring that the notice comes to the attention of the company's creditors. Within the same time, unless the court directs otherwise, the administrative receiver must lay a copy of the report before a meeting of the company's unsecured creditors which is summoned, on not less than 14 days' notice, for that purpose.

12.34 The court may not make such a direction, however, unless the administrative receiver has stated his intention to apply for the direction in the report which he has submitted and he has not less than 14 days before the hearing of the application sent a copy of the report to all the unsecured creditors of the company insofar as he is aware of their addresses, or published a notice stating an address to which unsecured creditors can write for a free copy of the report. In addition, if the administrative receiver proposes to apply to the court to dispense with the holding of a meeting of unsecured creditors which would otherwise be required by s 48(2), he must state the venue which is fixed by the court for the hearing of the application, either in his report to the creditors or in the notice which is published in the relevant newspaper.[63]

12.35 Where the company goes into liquidation, the administrative receiver has either an additional 7 days after his compliance with s 48(1)

---

61 Insolvency Act 1986 s 48(7).
62 r 3.8(1).
63 r 3.8(2).

(duty to supply financial information to specified persons) or 7 days from the appointment of the liquidator if that occurs later to send a copy of the report to the liquidator.[64] If the administrative receiver carries out his obligation to send a copy of the report to the liquidator within the time allowed for notifying the unsecured creditors, he does not have to comply with the obligations towards those creditors imposed by s 48(2).[65]

12.36 The copy of the receiver's report which is to be sent to the registrar of companies must have attached to it a copy of the statement of affairs, together with copies of any affidavits in concurrence.[66] However, this requirement is subject to any order of the court made under Rule 3.5,[67] which may limit disclosure of information contained in the statement. The court also has the power to give directions for the delivery of documents to the registrar of companies.[68] If the statement of affairs or affidavits of concurrence have not been submitted to the administrative receiver by the time he sends a copy of his report to the registrar of companies, copies must be sent on as soon as the relevant documents are received.[69] Failure to comply with the requirements of s 48 is a criminal offence, punishable by a fine, which will be levied on a daily default basis for continued contravention.[70]

Content of the report

12.37 The administrative receiver is required to include in his report all the matters listed in s 48(1), namely:

(a) the events leading up to his appointment, so far as he is aware of them;

(b) the disposal or proposed disposal by him of any property of the company and the carrying on or proposed carrying on by him of any business of the company;

(c) the amounts of principal and interest payable to the debenture holders by whom or on whose behalf he was appointed and the amounts payable to preferential creditors; and

(d) the amount (if any) likely to be available for the payment of other creditors.

The report must also contain a summary of the statement of affairs made in

---

64 Insolvency Act 1986 s 48(4).
65 Insolvency Act 1986 s 48(4).
66 r 3.4(2) and r 3.8(3).
67 r 3.8(3).
68 r 3.5(3).
69 r 3.8(4).
70 s 48; and see s 430 and sch 10 for punishments imposed by the Act.

accordance with s 47, together with the administrative receiver's comments upon it.[71]

12.38   The wide range of information contained in the report is largely as a result of recommendations made by the Cork Committee.[72] The Committee expressed their dissatisfaction with the information contained in the receiver's returns, which consisted solely of abstracts of receipts and payments and the receiver's comments on the statement of affairs. The Committee felt that this was not sufficient to give creditors any real guidance on the length of the receivership and its likely outcome, which were vital issues, particularly for unsecured creditors. Consequently, the Committee made detailed recommendations about the receiver's report and these have largely been incorporated into the statute.

Limited disclosure of content of report

12.39   Although the Act enables the administrative receiver to provide creditors with a great deal more information than was previously available, it is also clear that the administrative receiver may use his discretion to exclude from the report any information which, if disclosed, would seriously prejudice his ability to carry out his functions.[73] This is a very widely-worded provision and is clearly open to abuse. Strictly, it only allows information to be withheld if it would 'seriously prejudice' the conduct of the receivership, so the intention of the statute appears to be that information should not be withheld as a matter of course, but only if the consequences of disclosure would be serious. If the administrative receiver is of the opinion that it would prejudice the conduct of the receivership for the whole or part of the statement of affairs to be disclosed, he may make an application to the court under Rule 3.5, in which case the court may have ordered that the statement, or the relevant part of it, is only open to inspection with the leave of the court.[74]

Creditors' meeting—setting up a committee

12.40   Unless the court directs otherwise, the administrative receiver must lay his report before a meeting of the company's unsecured creditors.[75] At this meeting, the unsecured creditors may decide to exercise the right given to the meeting by s 49(1) to establish a creditor's committee. The Cork

---

71   s 48(5); and see s 11 on the s 47 statement of affairs.
72   Cork Report para 480.
73   s 48(6).
74   r 3.5(2).
75   s 48(2).

Committee was particularly concerned that creditors' committees should be established, as a way of increasing the ability of unsecured creditors to obtain information about the position of the insolvent company. It was also seen as a method of enabling the unsecured creditors to make representations if they felt that the receiver was not acting in accordance with his powers and duties.

12.41 The Act itself is unhelpful about the precise functions of the creditors' committee in the context of receivership, the only reference being to the committee's ability to 'exercise the functions conferred on it by or under this Act'.[76] The Rules do not give much help in this context either; Rule 3.18(1), which is solely concerned with the functions of the creditors' committee merely provides that it 'shall assist the administrative receiver in discharging his functions, and act in relation to him in such manner as may be agreed from time to time'.

12.42 The only specific function of the committee expressly referred to in the Act appears to be that in s 49(2), which provides that if a committee is established, it may require the administrative receiver to appear before it at any reasonable time, upon giving 7 days' notice. It may then require him to supply such information relating to the carrying out by him of his functions as it may reasonably require. Clearly the Cork Committee intended that the creditors' committee should constitute a method by which the administrative receiver would be accountable to the unsecured creditors, but s 49(2) relates solely to the provision of information, which does not go very far, in terms of accountability, when compared with the Cork Committee's recommendation that there should be a specific right for the creditors' committee to refer any grievances to the court.

12.43 When the committee decides to exercise its right to require the administrative receiver to attend before it, it must send out a notice to him to that effect, and the notice must be signed by the majority of the members of the committee for the time being.[77] When the meeting takes place, the administrative receiver must stand down from his usual position as chairman of the meeting, and the committee may elect one of their number to be the chairman of that particular meeting.[78] The meeting must be held on a business day, and at the convenience of the administrative receiver; at such time and place as he may decide.[79]

12.44 Under these provisions, it is clearly up to the committee to summon

---

76 s 49(1).
77 r 3.28(1).
78 r 3.28(3).
79 r 3.28(2).

the administrative receiver to appear before it, for example if it wishes to receive a report on the progress of the receivership, whereas the Cork Committee recommended[80] that the administrative receiver should be under a duty to make regular reports, as well as to notify the committee of any specific action which he proposed to take.

Creditors' committee—membership

12.45 If it is decided to set up a creditors' committee, it must consist of at least three and not more than five creditors of the company who are elected at the creditors' meeting.[81] Two members of the committee will constitute a quorum.[82] Any creditor of the company is eligible to be a member of the creditor's committee, provided that his claim has not been rejected for the purpose of his entitlement to vote at the creditor's meeting.[83] However, nobody may act as a member of the committee unless and until they have agreed to do so. It is possible to agree by using a proxy or by authorising some other person to agree on one's behalf, but such agreement may only be given by a proxy-holder or a representative within s 375 of the Companies Act 1985 who is present at the meeting when the creditors' committee is established.[84] It is possible for a body corporate to be a member of the creditors' committee, but it can only act by a representative duly authorised for the purpose[85] and that representative may not be a company[86] or a member of any of the other excluded categories under Rule 3.21(4)

12.46 Any member of the creditors' committee may be represented by a duly authorised representative.[87] That representative must hold a letter of authority, signed by or on behalf of the committee member, and he can be authorised to act generally or specially.[88] Where a representative signs any document on behalf of the committee member whom he is representing, a statement which he signs as a representative must be made below his signature.[89] Unless a statement to the contrary is included, a proxy or authorisation under s 375 of the Companies Act 1985 given in relation to a creditors' meeting will be treated as a letter authorising the holder to act generally on behalf of a committee member.[90] Anyone claiming to act as a

80 Cork Report para 935.
81 r 3.16(1).
82 r 3.20—for general rules as to quorum, see r 12.4A.
83 r 3.16(2).
84 r 3.17(2)—for general rules as to proxies, see rr 8.1–8.7 and ch 14.
85 rr 3.16(3) and 3.21(1).
86 r 3.21(4).
87 r 3.21(1).
88 r 3.21(1) and (2).
89 r 3.21(6).
90 r 3.21(2).

representative of a member of the creditors' committee can be required to produce his letter of authority by the chairman of the committee and any deficiency in the authority may result in exclusion from the committee meeting.[91]

12.47 The Rules exclude certain categories of persons from acting as representatives in this way, namely undischarged bankrupts, bodies corporate or anyone who is subject to a composition or arrangement with his creditors.[92] Equally, no one person may act as the representative of more than one member of the committee. Nor may a person act both as a committee member in their own right and as the representative of another member.[93]

Rule 8 covers the operation both of proxies and the representation of companies. This rule is dealt with in chapter 14 of this work.

The creditors' committee—actions

12.48 The creditors' committee can only act after the administrative receiver has issued a certificate of its due constitution,[94] which must be sent to the registrar of companies.[95] The administrative receiver's certificate cannot be issued until at least three of the persons who are to be members of the committee have agreed to act.[96] If additional members of the committee agree to act at a later date, the administrative receiver must issue an amended certificate[97] and this too must be sent to the registrar of companies,[98] together with notification of any change in the membership of the committee which occurs after it has first been established.[99]

12.49 The Rules provide[100] that defects in the formalities surrounding the appointment of members of the creditors' committee, or defects in the formalities of the establishment of the committee itself will not cause the acts of the committee to be invalid. Similarly, defects in the election or qualifications of members of the committee or their representatives will not invalidate the committee's acts. However, it is submitted that this Rule may be confined to 'defects' and may not therefore be applicable to fundamental flaws, just as a slight defect in the appointment of a receiver must be distinguished from an invalid appointment.[101]

---

91   r 3.21(3).
92   r 3.21(4).
93   r 3.21(5).
94   r 3.17(1).
95   r 3.17(4).
96   r 3.17(3).
97   r 3.17(3).
98   r 3.17(4).
99   r 3.17(5).
100   r 3.30A.
101   See ch 11.

12.50   Whilst the receiver is acting, it is still permissible for a member of the creditors' committee to enter into dealings with the company, provided that any such transactions are entered into *bona fide* and for value.[102] However, any interested person may apply to the court to set aside a transaction which appears to the court to be contrary to the requirements of this rule.[103] The court also has power to give such consequential directions as it thinks fit to compensate the company for any loss which it may have incurred as a result of the transaction.[104]

The creditors' committee—holding meetings

12.51   The Rules make it quite clear that the primary responsibility for organising meetings of the creditors' committee rests with the administrative receiver[105] and it is the administrative receiver or his representative who is given responsibility for chairing the meetings.[106] Once the committee has been established, responsibility lies with the administrative receiver to call the first meeting within 3 months of the date of its establishment. After that time, he must also call a meeting if the committee passes a resolution which states the date of the next meeting. In addition, a meeting must be called within 21 days of the administrative receiver receiving a request from an individual member of the committee that a meeting should be held.[107] The administrative receiver must give each member of the committee or their representative 7 days' written notice of meetings of the committee, although it is permissible for committee members to waive the notice requirement either at or before the meeting.[108]

12.52   It is expected that the administrative receiver will act as chairman of the creditors' committee when it meets, although it is possible for him to make a written nomination of another person to act for him.[109] Any such person must either be one who is qualified to act as an insolvency practitioner in relation to the company, or an employee of the receiver or his firm who is experienced in these matters. By laying down these qualifications, the Rules are acknowledging the importance of the creditors' committee and ensuring that it is given direct access to expert advice, even if the administrative receiver is unable to be present at the meeting.[110]

102   r 3.30(1).
103   r 3.30(2).
104   r 3.30(2).
105   r 3.18(2).
106   r 3.19.
107   r 3.18(3).
108   r 3.18(4).
109   r 3.19(1).
110   r 3.19(2).

Creditors' committee-procedure at meetings

12.53 Meetings of the creditors' committee will be duly constituted, provided that there is a quorum (at least 2 members) and that due notice has been given to all the members[111] though it seems that the notice requirement can be waived in accordance with Rule 3.18(4). Each member of the committee is entitled to one vote and resolutions are passed a simple majority of those present.[112] All resolutions must be recorded in writing, and the record of each resolution has to be signed by the chairman and kept as part of the records of the receivership.[113]

Creditors' committee—postal resolutions

12.54 It is possible for the administrative receiver to try and obtain the agreement of the committee members to a proposed resolution without having to call a full meeting of the committee, by using the postal resolution system provided for in the Rules. In order to do this, the administrative receiver must post to each member a copy of the relevant proposal, set out in such a way that each recipient can indicate his agreement or dissent to each separate proposed resolution on the copy which he is sent.[114]

12.55 If they wish to discuss the proposals further, committee members have 7 days from the date of the administrative receiver sending out a resolution to require him to summon a meeting of the creditors' committee to consider matters raised by the relevant resolution.[115] If no such action is taken, the resolution is deemed to have been passed by the committee if and when the receiver is notified in writing of the agreement of the majority of committee members.[116] A record of resolutions passed under this procedure, together with a note that the committee's concurrence was obtained, must be kept with the records of the receivership.[117]

Creditor's committee—expenses

12.56 Members of the creditors' committee are entitled to recoup any reasonable travelling expenses directly incurred by them or their representatives in relation to committee business or attendance at committee meetings. The administrative receiver must pay these out of the assets of the company. However, this rule does not apply to any meeting of the creditors' committee which is held within 3 months of a previous meeting, unless the

111   r 3.20.
112   r 3.26(1).
113   r 3.26(2) and (3).
114   r 3.27(1) and (2).
115   r 3.27(3).
116   r 3.27(4).
117   r 3.27(5).

meeting in question is summoned by the administrative receiver, rather than by a member of the creditors' committee or as a result of a resolution passed by the committee.[118]

Creditors' committee—resignation

12.57 It is possible for any member of the creditors' committee to give written notice of his resignation from the committee.[119] The notice must be delivered to the administrative receiver. The Rules do not give precise directions about the contents of the notice, but it would seem sensible to include clear details of the name of the relevant committee member and the date on which resignation is to be effective, together with any other information which the administrative receiver may reasonably require.

Creditors' committee—automatic termination of membership

12.58 Membership of the creditors' committee will cease automatically if the relevant person ceases to be a creditor or if it is discovered that he never was a creditor.[120] Similarly, any member entering into a composition or arrangement with his creditors, or becoming bankrupt, will automatically cease to be a member of the committee, although in the case of bankruptcy, the trustee in bankruptcy automatically replaces the relevant member of the committee. In general, membership will end automatically if a committee member is neither present nor represented at three consecutive meetings of the committee, unless on the third occasion a resolution is passed to the effect that this rule is not to apply in a particular case.[121]

Creditors' committee—removal

12.59 If it is wished to remove a member of the creditors' committee, this is possible if a suitable resolution is passed at a meeting of creditors, provided that at least 14 days' notice has been given of the intention to move the resolution.[122]

Creditors' committee—vacancies

12.60 If a vacancy occurs in the membership of the creditors' committee, it is possible for the administrative receiver to appoint any creditor who is suitably qualified under the Rules to be a member of the committee and fill the vacancy, provided that the creditor concerned agrees to act and that a

---

118   r 3.29.
119   r 3.22.
120   r 3.23(1).
121   r 3.23(1).
122   r 3.24.

majority of the remaining members of the committee agree to the appointment.[123] However, it is also possible to leave the vacancy unfilled if the administrative receiver and a majority of the remaining members of the committee so agree, as long as the total number of committee members does not fall below three.[124]

Duty to issue certificate of insolvency

12.61 As soon as the administrative receiver is of the opinion that, if the insolvent company went into liquidation, its assets would be insufficient to cover the payment of any dividend in respect of debts which are neither secured nor preferential, he is under a duty to issue a certificate to that effect so that such creditors can claim bad debt relief for value added tax purposes.[125] If the administrative receiver vacates his office, he is also under a duty to bring this rule to the attention of anyone who succeeds him as receiver, or to the directors of the company, whichever is applicable.[126] However, although the certificate is issued for the convenience of unsecured creditors, the administrative receiver is not under any obligation to provide a copy of the certificate to any creditor,[127] but only to give them notice of the issue of the certificate.

12.62 Notice of the issue of the certificate must be given by the administrative receiver to all those unsecured creditors of the company of whose address he is aware at the relevant time who have, to his knowledge, made supplies to the company with a charge to value added tax at any time before his appointment. This notice must be issued within 3 months of his appointment or within 2 months of issuing the certificate, whichever is the later.[128] If he later becomes aware of any other such creditor, the administrative receiver must also give them a copy of the notice.[129]

The certificate of insolvency which is issued for these purposes must be kept, in accordance with s 222 of the Companies Act 1985, together with the company's accounting records.[130]

GENERAL DUTIES OF RECEIVERS

12.63 The administrative receiver has various duties in his capacity as receiver. A more detailed treatment of these duties can be found in one of

---

123 r 3.25(3).
124 r 3.25(2).
125 r 3.36(1).
126 r 3.38(2).
127 r 3.37(3).
128 r 3.37(1).
129 r 3.37(2).
130 r 3.38(1).

the standard works on receivers.[131] The following is an indication of some of the general duties imposed on administrative receivers at common law.

Duty of care

12.64 A receiver is under a common law duty of care in tort, at least in relation to his powers of realising the company's assets. He has a duty to the company as explained in the case of *American Express International Banking Corporation v Hurley*,[132] to take reasonable care to obtain the true market value of the property which he is selling in his capacity as receiver. Consequently, if he is dealing with specialised equipment, for which there is a very specialised market, he should take expert advice on how to go about selling the equipment and a failure to do so will be negligent.

12.65 The duty of care owed by a receiver in disposing of the company's assets is owed not only to the company, but also to the guarantor of the company's liability under the debenture. In the case of *Standard Chartered Bank Ltd v Walker*[133] it was held that this must follow, since the liability of the guarantor was dependent on the amount which was realised by the company's assets by the receiver. The receiver thus owed the guarantor a duty to obtain the best possible price in the circumstances.

12.66 In general, the debenture holder is not responsible for what the receiver does in this respect but if the debenture holder interferes in the conduct of the receivership, for example by giving the receiver instructions about the sale of the company's assets, then that operates to make the receiver the agent of the debenture holder. If the receiver becomes the agent of the debenture older, then the debenture holder will be liable, on the basis of principal and agent, for the negligence of the receiver.[134] However, in the absence of an express exclusion in the agency contract between debenture holder and the receiver, the debenture holder will generally be entitled, under an implied term of the contract, to an indemnity from the receiver in respect of any negligence on the part of the receiver.[135] It may, in principle, be possible to exclude the duties of care outlined above, but any exclusion clause would have to be very clear and the application of the Unfair Contract Terms Act 1977 carefully considered.[136] It is interesting to note that in the case of *Lathia v Dronsfield Bros Ltd*[137] it was held that since the

---

131 eg *Kerr on Receivers*.
132 [1985] 3 All ER 564.
133 [1982] 3 All ER 938.
134 *Standard Chartered Bank v Walker* (n 133 *supra*).
135 *American Express v Hurley* (n 132 *supra*).
136 See *Bishop v Bonham* (1988) 4 BCC 347 and ch 7 on this.
137 [1987] BCLC 321.

receivers were agents of the company, they were immune from a claim for inducing a breach of contract by their principal unless they had not acted *bona fide* or had acted outside the scope of their authority.

Contractual duties

12.67 As has already been discussed,[138] s 44(1)(b) of the Insolvency Act 1986 provides that an administrative receiver will be:

> "personally liable on any contract entered into by him in the carrying out of his function (except insofar as the contract otherwise provides) and on any contracts of employment adopted by him in the carrying out of those functions".

In addition, the offer and acceptance of the position of administrative receiver gives rise to a contract between the receiver and his appointor, and it is likely that even if there is no express term covering the point, a term will readily be implied that the administrative receiver should use reasonable care in relation to the performance of his function as administrative receiver.

Fiduciary duties

12.68 An administrative receiver is the agent of the insolvent company unless and until the company goes into liquidation.[139] However, as the Gomba Holdings cases made clear,[140] the fiduciary duties owed by a receiver in his capacity as agent are not the same as the duties owed by any other kind of agent. The relationship set up by the debenture is a complicated, tripartite one involving the company, the receiver and the debenture holder. Consequently, the receiver has to perform his duties not only on behalf of his principal, the company, but also on behalf of the debenture holder. Clearly the administrative receiver does owe fiduciary duties to the company but those duties have to be adapted to the particular circumstances. The fiduciary duties owed by the administrative receiver to the company arise within the scope of his agency relationship. They will apply to his conduct in managing the affairs of the company. He must avoid even the possibility of a conflict of interests in his dealings on the company's behalf and he will be accountable for any secret profits or misuse of company property. In this respect he must maintain independence from the debenture holder who appointed him.

---

138 See ch 12.
139 Insolvency Act 1986 s 44(1)(a).
140 [1986] 1 WLR 1301 and (1989) 5 BCC 27 and see ch 12. Ch 15 deals with the analogous rules applicable to a liquidator.

POWERS OF ADMINISTRATIVE RECEIVER

General

12.69 The Cork Committee recommended[141] that the powers of a receiver should be listed in statutory form, so that it would not be necessary to refer to the particular debenture in every instance in order to determine what powers the receiver could exercise in a specific case.

However, the Insolvency Act 1986 does not adopt this recommendation in its entirety. Section 42(1) of the Act, whilst referring to the statutory powers, given to administrative receivers (and administrators),[142] makes it quite clear that although in general every administrative receiver is to be able to exercise the powers contained in sch 1, this is only the case insofar as those powers are consistent with the provisions in the debenture. This means that if there are any terms in the debenture which are inconsistent with the statutory powers in sch 1, the debenture will prevail. Consequently, it is very important for the administrative receiver to be quite clear whether the particular debenture under which he is appointed contains any relevant provisions.

12.70 Section 42(1)(b) of the Insolvency Act 1986 clarifies the position in relation to references in sch 1 of the Act to 'the property of the company'. Such references are to be regarded as references to the property covered by the charge under which the administrative receiver was appointed, since that will be the property falling within the definition provided by s 42(1)(b); 'the property over which [the administrative receiver] is or, but for the appointment of some other person as receiver of part of the company's property, would be the receiver or manager'.

Seeking the guidance of the court

12.71 It is when he is faced with the decision as to whether or not to exercise the powers granted to him, either under sch 1 to the Insolvency Act 1986 or by the debenture, as appropriate, that the administrative receiver may, in particular, find it necessary to seek the guidance of the court.

Under s 35 of the Insolvency Act 1986, the administrative receiver can apply to the court for directions in relation to any particular matter which arises in connection with the performance of his functions as receiver. This provision gives the court a real discretion over the way in which it can provide help or guidance when such an application is made. The provision originally arose out of a recommendation made by the Cohen Committee

---

141 Cork Report para 494.
142 See ch 13.

on the Reform of Company Law,[143] which noted that doubts often arise about the powers which an be exercised by receivers and the precise way in which they should be used; consequently the Committee thought it advisable that receivers should be able to obtain the court's directions concerning such matters.

General powers given by sch 1

12.72 The administrative receiver is given a number of generally applicable powers by sch 1 of the Insolvency Act 1986, but these are all subject to any contrary provision in the debenture.[144] They include the following:

(a) The administrative receiver has power to appoint an agent to do any business which he is unable to do himself or which could more conveniently be done by an agent.[145] Given the demanding nature of receivership, this is clearly an important power.

(b) The schedule also gives a broad general power to the administrative receiver, which allows him to make any payment which is necessary or incidental to his function.[146]

(c) The administrative receiver has a statutory power to defend or present a petition for the winding up of the company.[147] The power to present such a petition may be useful in order to complete the receivership.

(d) The schedule also gives power to change the situation of the company's office.[148] This arose out of a recommendation made by the Cork Committee,[149] who had in mind situations when the old address had become manifestly unsuitable, or had to be vacated by the company.

The schedule also contains the useful catch-all: '. . . power to do all other things incidental to the foregoing powers'.[150]

Disputes arising over the exercise of administrative receiver's powers

12.73 If any dispute arises in matters concerning the exercise of his powers, the administrative receiver has the statutory powers[151] which are necessary to take appropriate professional advice, whether from lawyers or

---

143   Cmnd 6659, para 67 and page 36 III.
144   Insolvency Act 1986 s 42(1).
145   Insolvency Act 1986 sch 1 para 11.
146   Insolvency Act 1986 sch 1 para 13.
147   Insolvency Act 1986 sch 1 para 21.
148   Insolvency Act 1986 sch 1 para 22.
149   Cork Report para 825.
150   Insolvency Act 1986 sch 1 para 23.
151   Subject to any contrary provision in the debenture (s 42(1)).

accountants or other professionals.[152] Should litigation ensue, the schedule also gives a statutory power[153] to bring or defend legal proceedings on behalf of the company[154] or to refer questions to arbitration.[155]

Protection of persons dealing with the administrative receiver

12.74   When the administrative receiver exercises the powers which are given to him, it is possible that he may do something which is beyond his powers. If challenged by third parties there would normally be the possibility in such circumstances that the administrative receiver would plead *ultra vires*. However, the Insolvency Act 1986 provides[156] that persons who deal with the administrative receiver acting as such will not be concerned to inquire whether he is acting within those powers, provided that they deal with him in good faith and for value. This provision is designed to protect third parties dealing with the administrative receiver and it reflects the protection similarly given to those dealing with an administrator.[157]

Getting in the property of the company

12.75   The power given in the first paragraph of sch 1[158] is a very wide one, to: 'take possession of, collect and get in the property of the company and, for that purpose, to take such proceedings as may seem to him expedient'.

Since the property which is referred to is limited by s 42(2)(b) to; 'property of which he is or, but for the appointment of some other person as the receiver of part of the company's property, would be the receiver or manager', care must be taken not to seize property which is not the property of the company. However, s 234(3) and (4) of the Insolvency Act 1986 has the effect of providing that where the administrative receiver seizes or disposes of property which does not belong to the company, he will not be liable, provided that the liability does not arise out of his own negligence and that at the time of the seizure or disposal he believed, on reasonable grounds, that he was entitled to do so. This is one of the privileges which attaches to the administrative receiver in his capacity as 'officeholder' under the Insolvency Act 1986.[159]

---

152   Insolvency Act 1986 sch 1 para 4.
153   Subject to any contrary provision in the debenture (s 42(1)).
154   Insolvency Act 1986 sch 1 para 5.
155   Insolvency Act 1986 sch 1 para 6.
156   s 42(3).
157   s 14(6) and see ch 13.
158   Subject to any contrary provisions in the debenture (s 42(1)).
159   ss 230 *et seq.*

As far as the expenses incurred by the administrative receiver in connection with the seizure and disposal of the company's property are concerned, he is also given a lien on the property or the proceeds of sale so that such expenses can be paid.[160]

12.76 If it is necessary to institute legal proceedings in order to establish the true ownership of the relevant property the administrative receiver is given a statutory power[161] to employ solicitors and counsel,[162] in addition to the power in para 1 of sch 1 to take such proceedings as may seem to him expedient in connection with getting in the company's property.

Provided there is no contrary provision in the debenture,[163] the statute also gives the administrative receiver power to claim in the bankruptcy, insolvency, liquidation etc of the company's debtors. Equally, he has the power to accede to trust deeds for the creditors of any such persons.[164] Clearly these are useful powers when getting in the company's property, as is the statutory power to call up any uncalled capital of the company.[165]

12.77 Another potentially useful power can be found in s 423 of the Insolvency Act 1986, which relates to transactions entered into at an undervalue. This section enables the court to make a variety of orders[166] to protect the position of a person prejudiced by such a transaction, basically by restoring the position to what it would have been if the transaction had not been entered into. Since the administrative receiver does not come within the definition of 'persons prejudiced' in s 424 of the Act, he will have to arrange for the appointor (who does fall within the definition) to get leave to make the application. If the company is in liquidation, the application can also be made by the liquidator.

Selling the company's property

12.78 When it comes to selling the company's property, the administrative receiver is given a statutory power[167] by para 2 of sch 1 to the Insolvency Act 1986, to; 'sell or otherwise dispose of the property of the company by public auction of private contract'. Paragraph 17 of the schedule gives him the power[168] to grant or accept the surrender of a lease or tenancy of any of the property of the company, and to take a lease or

---

160 Insolvency Act 1986 s 234(4).
161 Subject to any contrary provision in the debenture (s 42(1)).
162 Insolvency Act 1986 sch 1 para 5.
163 See s 42(1).
164 Sch 1 para 20.
165 Sch 1 para 19.
166 Detailed in s 425; and see ch 20.
167 Subject to any contrary provision in the debenture (s 42(1)).
168 *Ibid.*

tenancy of any property required or convenient for the business of the company.

12.79   If the administrative receiver decides to grant a lease of the company's property as part of his functions as receiver it is important that he remembers that before a good title can be passed to the lessee, there must be no further charges over the property precluding the exercise of such a power. If the company is a lessee the lease may contain a provision for forfeiture on the appointment of a receiver. It may also contain a provision against assignment. This may preclude the disposal of the company's interest under the lease.

12.80   Subject to any contrary provisions in the debenture[169] sch 1 of the Insolvency Act 1986 provides the administrative receiver with many powers which may be useful when engaging in a sale of the company's assets. The administrative receiver can use the company seal[170] and do all acts and execute in the name or on behalf of the company any deed, receipt or other document.[171] He has a duty to the company, and to any guarantor of the company's liability under the debenture, to take reasonable care to obtain the true market value of the property when selling the company's property.[172]

Sale as a going concern

12.81   One of the basic ideas behind the concept of a receiver is that it affords the debenture holder the possibility that he might get a better return from the insolvent company because a receiver can decide that the company should continue trading and then be sold as a going concern. This may enable the receiver to sell the company for a much better price than if it is sold on a 'break-up' basis. Consequently, the power contained in para 14 of sch 1 to the Insolvency Act 1986, which enables the administrative receiver[173] to carry on the business of the company, is particularly important.

12.82   It is in the context of trading on that the administrative receiver may find the power[174] to appoint an agent to do any work he is unable to do himself most useful. He can also use this power to appoint an agent to do work which can more conveniently be carried out by an agent.

---

169   s 42(1).
170   Sch 1 para 8.
171   Sch 1 para 9.
172   *Standard Chartered Bank v Walker* [1982] 3 All ER 938.
173   Subject to any contrary provisions in the debenture (s 42(1)).
174   *Ibid.*

In deciding whether or not to trade on, the administrative receiver must remember that his primary duty is to realise the security in the interests of the debenture holder. He may wish to consult the debenture holder about his decision, but the debenture holder must not give directions to the administrative receiver on how he should exercise his powers of sale, otherwise the debenture holder may find himself liable for the acts of the receiver.[175]

12.83   The administrative receiver[176] has all the necessary incidental powers to carry on the business of the company; for example, he has the power to raise or borrow money and to grant security over the property of the company in order to do so[177] and also has the power to draw, accept, make and endorse any bill of exchange or promissory note in the name and on behalf of the company.[178] He has the broad power to do all things, including repair works, which may be necessary in order to realise the property of the company.[179]

Hive-down

12.84   The administrative receiver may decide that the best method of realising the assets of the insolvent company would be to undertake a hive-down. This manoeuvre basically involves transferring the business of the insolvent company to a wholly owned subsidiary, which is usually newly formed for the purpose. A hive-down may enable the administrative receiver to make a much more advantageous sale in the interests of the debenture holder because, for example, it enables him to transfer only the most profitable assets, or because the new subsidiary company will not have the debt problems of the old company nor the credit problems associated with such debts.

12.85   Schedule 1 of the Insolvency Act 1986 includes the powers which are necessary for the administrative receiver to undertake a hive-down. Provided there is no contrary provision in the debenture,[180] the administrative receiver can establish subsidiaries of the company[181] and transfer to those subsidiaries the whole or any part of the business and property of the company.[182]

---

175   *American Express v Hurley* [1985] 3 All ER 564.
176   In all cases subject to any contrary provisions in the debenture (s 42(1)).
177   Sch 1 para 3.
178   Sch 1 para 10.
179   Sch 1 para 12.
180   Insolvency Act 1986 s 42(1).
181   Sch 1 para 15.
182   Sch 1 para 16.

12.86   If the administrative receiver does decide to hive-down, he should be aware of the Transfer of Undertakings (Protection of Employment) Regulations 1981[183] which purport to implement EEC Council Directive 187 of 14 February 1977. These regulations provide, *inter alia*, for the automatic transfer of contracts of employment when a transfer of business is undertaken. The administrative receiver will wish to ensure that any transfer of contracts of employment which takes place is limited to the contracts of those workers whom the new company wishes to be transferred to it, otherwise it could be very expensive for the new company and defeat the objective of the hive-down. In general, the Regulations have the effect of automatically transferring contracts of employment in the case of certain transfers of commercial undertakings to another person. If an employee is dismissed in connection with the transfer, the dismissal will be unfair, unless it takes place for an economic, technical or organisational reason.[184]

12.87   The principle of automatic transfer of contracts of employment would normally create a problem for receivers if they were contemplating a hive-down, but the Regulations create an exception for a hive-down operation by a receiver. They provide[185] that the transfer shall be deemed not to have been effective for the purposes of the Regulations until immediately before; (i), the transferee company ceases to be a wholly owned subsidiary of the transferor company (otherwise than by reason of its being wound up) or (ii), the relevant undertaking is transferred by the transferee company or to another person, whichever event occurs first. This means that the parent company can dismiss any surplus employees up until the time 'immediately before' the transfer and liability will remain with it. Much difficulty was caused in this respect by the decision in *Apex Leisure Hire v Barratt*[186] that the question of what period of time amounted to 'immediately before' the transfer was a question of fact in each case. However, that decision has now been overturned by the case of *Secretary of State for Employment v Spence*[187] and it is clear that a receiver can avoid the statutory automatic transfer by dismissing employees at any time prior to the moment of transfer.

Sale of property subject to a security

12.88   The Cork Committee was concerned that a secured creditor could refuse to allow the charged assets to be disposed of without his consent, unless his security was redeemed by full repayment, since this could

183   SI 1981 No 1794; hereafter TU(PE).
184   TU(PE) reg 8.
185   TU(PE) reg 4.
186   [1984] ICR 452.
187   [1986] 3 WLR 380.

effectively inhibit a rescue scheme or an advantageous sale.[188] Consequently, the Committee recommended[189] that both the administrative receiver and the administrator who find themselves in the position of wishing to sell the charged property, yet cannot obtain the consent of the creditor, should be able to apply to the court for leave to sell the asset free from the charge. The provisions in the Insolvency Act which relate to administrators (s 15)[190] and administrative receivers (s 43, below) are quite different in detail, though both have the same basic aim.

12.89 If the administrative receiver makes an application to dispose of charged property, the statute makes it quite clear that the property in question must be 'relevant property' within s 43(1). It must be the property of which the administrative receiver is or, but for the appointment of some other person as the receiver of part of the company's property, would be receiver or manager.[191]

12.90 If the administrative receiver makes such an application, he must give notice of the venue for the hearing to the holder of the security.[192] He must then satisfy the court that the disposal of the property in this way would be likely to result in a more advantageous realisation of the company's assets than would otherwise be effected.[193] If he is successful in so doing, then the court can make an order, authorising the administrative receiver to dispose of the property as if it were not subject to the security.[194] If an order is made under s 43(1), the administrative receiver must immediately give notice of that fact to the security holder.[195] The court will send two sealed copies of the order to the administrative receiver, who must send one on to the security holder.[196] The administrative receiver must also send an office copy of any order under s 43(1) to the Registrar of Companies within 14 days of the making of the order.[197] It is a criminal offence to fail to comply with that requirement without reasonable excuse and contravention will result in liability to a fine, which will be levied on a daily default basis for continued contravention.[198]

12.91 However, the administrative receiver's power to apply to sell charged property is not a general one, since it does not apply; 'in the case of

188   Cork Report para 1511.
189   *Ibid* para 1512.
190   See ch 13.
191   Insolvency Act 1986 s 43(7).
192   r 3.31(2).
193   s 43(1).
194   *Ibid.*
195   r 3.31(3).
196   r 3.31(4).
197   s 43(5).
198   s 43(6). For punishments under the Act, see s 430 and sch 10.

any security held by the person by or on whose behalf the administrative receiver was appointed, or of any security to which a security so held has priority'.[199] It cannot be applied by the administrative receiver to a fixed charge contained in the same deed on the floating charge under which he was appointed. Nor can any fixed or floating charge ranking in priority behind a charge held by the appointor be subject to the administrative receiver's power to apply for the sale of charged property. Charges held by the appointor will not inhibit the activities of a receiver in most cases as he is likely to have control over the property subject to them. Those security interests over which such charges have priority can be paid off from the proceeds of realising that property. Although this is the usual situation the section is also inapplicable to all securities held by the appointor of the receiver so that one in relation to which the insolvency practitioner has not been appointed will also be outside its scope. This is reasonable since the appointor can consent to a sale and presumably will do so when it is in his own interests. It would be inappropriate for the court to have to adjudicate a dispute between the receiver and the debenture holder under s 43.

12.92 If an order allowing an administrative receiver to sell charged property is made, then the net profit accruing from the sale (ie the net amount remaining after deduction of the costs and expenses incurred in making the sale) must be applied towards discharging the sums secured by the security.[200] In addition, there is a statutory formula to ensure that the sum applied towards discharging the security will not fall below a certain level. If the net profit referred to above is less than the amount which the court decides is the net amount which would be realised on an open market sale by a willing vendor, then the deficiency must be made good from other funds and that sum applied towards discharging the amount secured by the security.[201] Clearly this formula could be open to abuse, if the person whose charge is to be overreached artificially raises the market value of the charged property in some way, eg by making an inflated offer to buy in the property. If two or more securities are involved, the sums applied towards discharging the amount secured by those securities must be applied in the order of their priorities.[202]

Alternatives to sale—schemes

12.93 The administrative receiver is given a power to mount a scheme of reconstruction[203] by para 18 of sch 1 of the Insolvency Act 1986.

---

199 s 43(2).
200 s 43(3).
201 s 43(3) and see ch 13.
202 s 43(4).
203 Subject to any contrary provisions in the debenture (s 42(1)). See ch 21.

Powers of administrative receiver as officeholder

12.94 The concept of an 'officeholder' has a special meaning in the Insolvency Act 1986, where it refers to the persons who play a major role in insolvency proceedings as administrators, administrative receivers, liquidators and provisional liquidators. All of these persons are regarded as officeholders within the meaning of the statute.[204] They are given a special status in the conduct of insolvencies, which brings with it both responsibilities and privileges.

12.95 The most basic requirement which an officeholder must fulfil is that he must be a person who is qualified to act as an insolvency practitioner in relation to the insolvent company.[205] A large part of the Cork Report concerned the introduction of a legal regime applicable to insolvency practitioners.[206] It is a result of recommendations made by the Cork Committee that insolvency practitioners not only have to demonstrate a high level of competence; they are also subject to the disciplinary code of a recognised professional organisation.[207] If an officeholder is not qualified to act as an insolvency practitioner, but purports to do so, he commits a criminal offence[208] and will be required to vacate his office.[209] However, the statute provides a measure of protection for those dealing with officeholders, since s 232 provides that the acts of an officeholder will be valid, notwithstanding any defect in appointment, nomination or qualification.

Confidentiality of records of insolvency

12.96 Whenever, in insolvency proceedings, an insolvency practitioner considers that a document which forms part of the records of the insolvency should be treated as confidential, or that its nature is such that its disclosure would be injurious to the interests of the insolvent's creditors, members, or the contributories in its winding up, he may decline to allow it to be inspected by a person who would otherwise be entitled to inspect it,[210] and that includes members of the creditors' committee.[211] If inspection of a document is refused in this way, the person wishing to inspect it may apply to the court for a determination that the insolvency practitioner's decision be overruled; the court may either overrule it or sustain it, subject to such conditions as it thinks fit.[212]

---

204   See s 231.
205   ss 230 and 388 and see ch 10.
206   Cork Report chs 15–17.
207   See ch 10.
208   Insolvency Act 1986 s 389(1).
209   See Insolvency Act 1986 s 45(2).
210   r 12.13(1).
211   r 12.13(2).
212   r 12.13(3).

12.97 Confidentiality is also protected in that where the Rules provide for creditors or members etc of a company to inspect any documents, whether on the court's file or in the hands of a responsible insolvency practitioner, it is an offence for a person falsely to claim a status which would entitle him to carry out such an inspection, with the intention of obtaining a sight of documents which he has not under the Rules any right to inspect.[213] This offence is punishable by imprisonment or a fine or both.[214]

Supplies by utilities

12.98 The Cork Committee noted the particular problems which could arise concerning the supply of public utilities (gas, water, electricity etc) to insolvent companies.[215] These monopoly suppliers commonly threatened to cut off supplies to premises of the insolvent company unless their accounts were paid in full. They could use their monopoly position to ensure payment, even though they were not secured creditors. To overcome this problem, the Cork Committee recommended[216] that once an officeholder was in place, statutory undertakings should be required to treat them as a new customer, who would have the usual statutory right to receive supplies. The officeholder was to be regarded as distinct from the old entity which was in arrears and was not to be held responsible for its debt. This recommendation is largely taken up by the statute.

12.99 Section 233 of the Insolvency Act 1986 provides that where an officeholder, for example an administrative receiver, is appointed, if he makes a request, after his appointment, for the supply of gas, electricity, water or telecommunication services,[217] the utility may not make it a condition (nor do anything which has the effect of imposing such a condition) that any outstanding charges in respect of supplies given to the company before the officeholder's appointment are paid.[218] However, the supplier may make it a condition of the giving of supply that the officeholder personally guarantees the payment of any charges in respect of the supply.[219]

Delivery up of company property to the officeholder

12.100 In his capacity as officeholder, the administrative receiver is entitled, after he is appointed, to apply to the court for an order for delivery

---

213 r 12.18(1).
214 r 12.18(2). For punishments under the Rules see r 12.21 and sch 5 to the Rules.
215 Cork Report ch 33.
216 Cork Report para 1462.
217 s 233(3).
218 s 233(2).
219 s 233(2).

up of books, papers, records or other property to which the company appears to be entitled.[220] This is a very wide provision, which provides for the delivery up of property by 'any person'. Clearly, the officeholder is only entitled to take such action in relation to property which actually belongs to the company, but he is protected from liability, should he make a *bona fide* mistake. Section 234(3) and (4) provides that if the officeholder seizes or disposes of any property which does not belong to the company, but that at the relevant time he believes, and has reasonable grounds for believing that he is entitled to act as he did, then he will not be liable to any person in respect of any loss or damage arising from the seizure or disposal, except insofar as he was negligent. In addition, he will have a lien on the property or the proceeds of sale, as the case may be, for the expenses which he incurred in the seizure or disposal.

Duty to cooperate with officeholder

12.101   Another useful power which accrues to the administrative receiver in his capacity as officeholder is that of requiring cooperation from a variety of persons who may be able to provide information which will help him carry out his function.[221] At any time after his appointment,[222] the officeholder can require information to be provided by a wide range of persons,[223] including those who have at any time been officers of the company and those who are in the employment of the company. The information which is required can cover a wide spectrum, including such information concerning the company and its promotion, formation, business dealings, affairs or property as the officeholder may reasonably require.[224] Failure to comply with such a request without reasonable excuse is a criminal offence, bringing with it liability to a fine, levied on a daily default basis for continued contravention.[225] In addition, the officeholder may require the relevant persons to attend before him at such times as he may reasonably require.[226]

Summoning people before the court

12.102   Under s 236 of the Insolvency Act 1986, the administrative receiver may make an application to the court in his capacity as officeholder to summon various people to appear before it.[227] This power will be of

220   Insolvency Act 1986 s 234(2).
221   Insolvency Act 1986 s 235.
222   s 235(4).
223   s 235(3).
224   s 235(2).
225   s 235(5).
226   s 235(2)(b).
227   s 236(2).

particular use where the person who is the subject of the order has failed to cooperate under s 235. The correct procedure would seem to be for the officeholder to use his powers under s 235 first, before proceeding to the more Draconian powers in this section. The persons covered by the section include any officer of the company, any person known to possess or suspected of possessing any of the company's property, the company's debtors and any person whom the court thinks is capable of giving information about the promotion, formation, business dealings, affairs or property of the company. This application can be made *ex parte*[228] and it must be made in writing, stating briefly the grounds on which it is made[229] and identifying the particular person in respect of whom it is made.[230] The court can require any of the relevant people to submit to the court an affidavit containing an account of their dealings with the company.[231] Such persons can also be required to produce any papers, books or other records which they have in their possession or control and which relate to any other matters about which the officeholder may require information under the section.[232]

12.103 In *Re Aveling Barford*[233] the receivers sought an order under s 236 of the Insolvency Act 1986 to compel the solicitors of the insolvent company to make disclosure and to supply an affidavit giving an account of their dealings with the company. The solicitors appealed against the order which was made, on the grounds that they had a solicitor's lien over the documents for unpaid costs, some of the documents were subject to legal professional privilege and in addition the terms on which they had to make their affidavit were too wide. As far as the solicitors' lien was concerned, the court held that despite its existence, the administrative receivers were entitled to inspect any documents in the solicitors' possession relating to the company. A proper claim of professional privilege by a client other than the company in receivership would be a sufficient reason for withholding a document, but the claim must be made in sufficient particularity to enable the receivers to form a view on whether or not the claim is valid; those making the claim must specify the nature of the document, the client who claims privilege and the grounds on which the claim is made. As for the affidavit, the order required the solicitors to submit an affidavit containing 'an account of the full particulars of all dealings by [the solicitors] with the companies'. Taking into account the requirements of specificity in Rules 9.2(3)(c) and 9.3(3)(a), and since the solicitors had acted for the

228   r 9.2(4).
229   r 9.2(1).
230   r 9.2(2).
231   s 236(3).
232   s 236(3).
233   [1989] BCLC 122.

company in numerous transactions of varying complexity over several years, this order was too wide. What the receivers wanted in the first instance was a list of matters in which the solicitors have dealt on behalf of the company in receivership, giving enough detail to enable the receivers to decide whether to pursue their inquiries any further; the order was amended accordingly.

12.104   The Rules make it clear that a wide variety of applications can be made under s 236, and all applications can be made *ex parte*.[234] Applications can be made for the court to order persons to appear before it, to answer interrogatories, to submit affidavits or to produce books, papers or other records.[235] In each case reasonable particulars should be given by the officeholder.[236] If anyone is ordered to appear before the court as a result of such an application, the court must specify a time and place for his appearance, which must not be less than 14 days from the date of the order.[237] If a person is ordered to submit affidavits, the order must specify the matters which are to be dealt with and the time within which the affidavits are to be submitted to the court.[238] Similarly, if the order is to produce books or papers etc, the time and manner of compliance must be specified in the order.[239] In all cases, the order must be served immediately on the respondent, and it must be served personally, unless the court orders otherwise.[240]

12.105   If a person is ordered to submit to an examination, he may employ a solicitor and counsel at his own expense.[241] They may put to him such questions as the court permits in order to enable him to explain or qualify any answers he may give. They may also make representations on his behalf. The court has a discretion to order the examination of persons abroad, provided that they are persons who, if within the jurisdiction of the court, would be liable to appear before the court under ss 236 or 237 of the Insolvency Act 1986. Such persons may also be examined in any part of the United Kingdom where they may be at the time.[242]

12.106   When an examination is conducted, the officeholder may attend in person or be represented by a solicitor. He may have a barrister as well if he chooses. The officeholder or his representative can put such questions to

---

234   r 9.2(4). See also s 237.
235   r 9.2(3).
236   r 9.2(3).
237   r 9.3(2).
238   r 9.3(3).
239   r 9.3(4).
240   r 9.3(5).
241   r 9.4(5).
242   s 237(3).

the respondent as the court may allow.[243] The Rules also make provision for any other person who could have applied for a similar order to attend the examination; he may put questions to the respondent through the applicant officeholder. However, this particular procedure can only take place with the leave of the court and provided that the applicant officeholder does not object.[244] A similar procedure applies if the original application was made on information provided by a creditor of the insolvent company; the creditor may attend the examination and put questions to the respondent, but only through the applicant officeholder and again, with the leave of the court and provided that the applicant officeholder does not object.[245]

12.107   Section 236(4) of the Insolvency Act 1986 applies if a person fails, without reasonable excuse, to appear before the court when he is summoned to do so under this section. It also applies where there are reasonable grounds for believing that a person has absconded, or is about to abscond, with a view to avoiding an appearance before the court under the section. In such cases, s 236(5) provides that, in order to bring that person and anything in his possession before the court, a warrant may be issued, authorising a police officer or other prescribed person to arrest such a person or to seize any books, papers, records, money or goods in his possession. If someone is arrested under this section, the court may authorise him to be kept in custody and anything seized under the warrant to be held until the person is brought before the court, or until such other time as the court may order.[246]

12.108   A written record of the examination will be made to the extent that the court thinks proper.[247] This must be read over to or by the respondent and signed by him at a time and place fixed by the court.[248] That written record may then be used in any proceedings, whether they take place under the Insolvency Act or not, as evidence against the respondent of any statement made by him in the course of the examination.[249] The written record of the respondent's examination, together with any answer given by him to interrogatories and any affidavits which he submitted to the court in compliance with the Act, will not be filed in court unless the court directs otherwise.[250] In addition, those items will not be open to inspection

---

243   r 9.4(1).
244   r 9.4(2).
245   r 9.4(4).
246   s 236(6).
247   r 9.4(6).
248   r 9.4(6).
249   r 9.4(7).
250   r 9.5(1).

without an order of the court, by persons other than the applicant officeholder and other persons who could have applied for such an order in respect of the affairs of the same insolvent company.[251] The same restriction as regards inspection is put on so much of the court file as shows the grounds of the application and to any copy of the proposed interrogatories.[252]

12.109 When the court has before it the information which has been gained as a result of the officeholder's exercising the powers given to him by s 236 of the Insolvency Act 1986, the court may decide to use the enforcement powers given to it by s 237 of the Act. The section gives the court a wide variety of powers, including the power to examine on oath any person brought before it, either under s 236 or under the instant section, orally or by interrogatories, concerning the company or any other matters specified in s 236(2)(c).

12.110 In addition, the officeholder can apply to the court for an order that a relevant person should deliver up any property of the company which he has in his possession, at such time and place and on such terms as the court thinks fit. The court has a discretion to grant an order if it appears to be the case that such a person is in possession of property belonging to the company on consideration of evidence obtained under s 236 or 237.[253] Similarly the court has a discretion to order payment, by any debtor of the company, of the whole or part of the debt due.[254]

12.111 As far as the costs of such proceedings are concerned, if the court orders an examination of any person and it appears to the court that the examination was made necessary because information had been unjustifiably refused by the person in question, then the court has a discretion to order that the respondent pays the costs of the examination.[255] The sort of unjustifiable refusal referred to here may take place if someone does not comply with their duty to cooperate with the officeholder under s 235 of the Insolvency Act 1986. The court has a similar discretion to order the respondent to pay the costs of the relevant application, if it makes an order to deliver up property which is in the possession of the respondent but belongs to the insolvent company,[256] or to pay any amount in discharge of a debt due to the company.[257] However, apart from those instances, the applicant's costs will be paid by the insolvent company unless the court

251 r 9.5(2).
252 r 9.5(3).
253 s 237(1).
254 s 237(2).
255 r 9.6(1).
256 r 9.6(2)(a).
257 r 9.6(2)(b).

orders otherwise.[258] If any person is summoned to attend for examination, they may claim a reasonable sum for travelling expenses incurred in connection with that attendance; other similar costs which he incurs may be paid at the court's discretion.[259] In *Re Aveling Barford*[260] Hoffmann J said that he saw no reason to distinguish between those persons and persons not summoned to attend but required to comply with an order to produce books etc. A person summoned to attend for examination in this context would therefore seem to include a person required to give information by the alternative methods permitted under s 236.

Effect of liquidation

12.112 It is clear from the Insolvency Act 1986 s 44(1)(a) that liquidation will terminate the administrative receiver's role as agent for the company. However, this does not mean that his role as receiver also comes to an end. Liquidation does not destroy the receiver's powers of realisation, and he may continue to exercise those powers, provided that he does not exercise them to create debts or liabilities which bind the company.[261]

12.113 The administrative receiver should be careful to establish what his precise status is once his agency for the company has ended. He can either carry on as principal, in which case he is personally liable for his acts, with recourse only to the statutory indemnity under s 44(1)(c) of the Insolvency Act 1986 (subject to any relevant provision in his appointment) or he can become the agent of the debenture holder, in which case the debenture holder, as principal, is responsible for the acts of the administrative receiver and the receiver is entitled (subject to any contrary provision in the terms of his appointment) to an indemnity from the debenture holder.[262] The debenture holder must be careful not to constitute the administrative receiver as his agent without meaning to do so; as Mann J said in *American Express International Banking Corp v Hurley*;[263] 'If the receiver continues to act, he does not automatically become agent of the mortgagee, but he may become so if the mortgagee treats him as such'.

12.114 In *Sowman v David Samuel Trust Ltd*,[264] Goulding J considered the effect of a statutory provision equivalent to s 127 of the Insolvency Act 1986, which provides for the invalidation of dispositions of company property after the commencement of the winding up. He held that the

---

258 r 9.6(3).
259 r 9.6(4).
260 [1989] BCLC 122.
261 *Gough's Garages v Pugsley* [1930] 1 KB 615.
262 *American Express International Banking Co v Hurley* [1985] 3 All ER 564.
263 At 568ff.
264 [1978] 1 WLR 22.

section does not prejudice realisation of charged company property by a receiver appointed under the terms of the charge, because such realisations are not 'dispositions' of company property within the meaning of the section.

12.115   A debenture holder can appoint an administrative receiver after liquidation, if the debenture holder's interests would best be served by such appointment.[265] If the receiver is appointed after a winding up he will require leave of the court to take possession from the liquidator, but leave will be given as a matter of course. Subject to contrary provision in the debenture,[266] para 21 of sch 1 to the Insolvency Act 1986 expressly empowers the administrative receiver to defend a petition to wind up, but under s 125 of the Act, a winding up order will not be refused '. . . on the ground only that the company's assets have been mortgaged to an amount equal to or in excess of those assets . . .'.[267]

12.116   Administrative receivers may also be affected by the provisions in ss 238 to 241 of the Insolvency Act 1986 which enables various kinds of transactions to be set aside when a company goes into liquidation.[268] A liquidator may also apply for relief in respect of any extortionate credit transaction entered into by the company within the period of 3 years before the company went into liquidation.[269] In addition, the provisions of s 245 of the Insolvency Act 1986 mean that certain floating charges created prior to the liquidation may be avoided.[270]

Under s 44(1)(b) of the Insolvency Act 1986, a liquidator can require an administrative receiver to render accounts of receipts and payments and to pay over any sums properly payable to the liquidator.

12.117   A liquidator also has the statutory power under s 36 of the Act, to apply to the court to fix the remuneration of a receiver, but, given that the world of the insolvency practitioner is a relatively small one, it seems unlikely that this provision will be much used. However, s 36(2) provides that the court's power, where no previous order has been made in this respect,

'(a) extends to fixing the remuneration for any period before the making of the order or the application for it,

(b) is exercisable notwithstanding that the receiver or manager has died or ceased to act before the making of the order or the application, and

---

265   *Re Potters Oils Ltd* [1986] 1 WLR 201.
266   Insolvency Act 1986 s 42(1).
267   s 125(1).
268   See ch 20 on this.
269   s 244 and see ch 20.
270   See chs 11 and 20.

(c) where the receiver or manager has been paid or has retained for his remuneration for any period before the making of the order any amount in excess of that so fixed for the period, extends to requiring him or his personal representatives to account for the excess or such part of it as may be specified in the order.'

Unless the court decides that there are special circumstances which lead it to act otherwise, this power will not be exercised in respect of any period before the application is made.[271] It is also possible for either the liquidator or the administrative receiver to apply to vary or amend an order which has been made under this section.[272]

12.118   In *Re Potter's Oils*[273] it was held that the court's jurisdiction under the equivalent previous provision was restricted to interfering with the remuneration of the receiver and that the jusidiction would not be exercised lightly. The court said that when it exercised its jurisdiction under the statute, it would be intefering with existing contractual rights in order to protect the interests of unsecured creditors. Since it was interfering with existing contractual rights, it would only do so when the remuneration was excessive.

12.119   Where a company is being wound up by the court, the official receiver may at any time before the dissolution of the company apply for the public examination of any person who acted as receiver or manager of the company.[274] Unless the court orders otherwise, the official receiver must make such an application if he is requested to do so by one half, in value, of the company's creditors, or three-quarters, in value, of the company's contributories.[275]

Under s 32 of the Insolvency Act 1986, where a company is being wound up and the debenture holders or other creditors apply to the court to appoint a receiver, the official receiver may be appointed. This power has long existed in companies legislation.

ENDING THE RECEIVERSHIP

Distribution

12.120   The receivership will come to an end when the administrative receiver has realised all the available assets which are covered by the charge

271   Insolvency Act 1986 s 36(2).
272   s 36(3).
273   [1986] 1 All ER 890.
274   Insolvency Act 1986 s 133(1) and see ch 16.
275   s 133(2).

and has made all relevant distribution to the correct parties in the order determined by law. Distribution of the available assets may raise some particularly complex problems for the administrative receiver. Consequently, this is one of the situations where he may wish to seek the guidance of the court under s 35 of the Insolvency Act 1986.

When he vacates his office at the end of the receivership, the administrative receiver must give immediate notice of the fact to the company (or, if it is liquidation, to the liquidator) and to members of the creditors' committee (if there is such a committee).[276] In addition, notice must be given to the Registrar of Companies within 14 days after the receiver has vacated his office.[277]

Where there is a series of charges, any prior incumbrances also have to be dealth with in the correct order.[278] This means that he will have already paid off the holders of prior charges before he turns to the floating charge held by his appointor.

12.121 Commonly, the administrative receiver will be responsible for a fixed charge also held by his appointor; the order of payments under a fixed charge is very similar to that under a floating charge, except that s 40 of the Insolvency Act 1986 does not apply to fixed charges. In *Lewis Merthyr Consolidated Collieries*[279] the Court of Appeal held that the priority given to preferential creditors in respect of realisation of assets subject to a floating charge applied only to assets caught by the floating charge, even where the receiver was also appointed under a fixed charge.

12.122 In *Re Permanent Houses (Holdings) Ltd*[280] the receiver was appointed under a debenture; there were some preferential debts, including some money owed to the Customs and Excise. The debenture contained a fixed charge over the company's 'book debts and other debts' and provided that on the occurrence of certain events, including a demand for payment, the floating charge would crystallise. The receiver held a large sum, including money in a bank account. The receiver sought guidance from the court on whether the money in the bank account was subject to the fixed or floating charge, whether, if it was subject to the floating charge, that charge had crystallised before the appointment of the receiver, ie on the making of the unsatisfied demand for payment and whether, if the charge had crystallised, the Customs and Excise were entitled to priority under s 196 of the Companies Act 1985. It was held that the credit in the bank was not a

276   r 3.35(1).
277   Insolvency Act 1986 s 45(4); and see ch 12 on vacation of office.
278   See ch 8 as to priorities and ch 7 as to the application of proceeds of sale.
279   [1929] 1 Ch 498 and see ch 19.
280   (1989) 5 BCC 151 and see ch 19.

'book or other debt' within the meaning of the debenture, so that the balance on the account was subject to the floating charge. However the making of the demand for repayment was an event of default as defined in the debentue which caused the floating charge to crystallise. Since s 196 as it then stood, required that the charge over the assets should be floating when the receiver was appointed, and the assets in question were secured by a charge which at the date of the receiver's appointment was a fixed charge, s 196 did not apply. Section 40 of the Insolvency Act 1986 and the s 196 substituted in the Companies Act 1985 by sch 13 of the 1986 Act ensure that for appointments after 15th December 1986 preferential debts will have priority over any charge which was created as a floating charge regardless of whether it has crystallised before the appointment of a receiver or possession has been taken of the assets.

12.123 It is during this stage of the receivership that the administrative receiver may encounter difficulties with retention of title clause. An unpaid supplier of goods faced with a receivership will find that he is a mere unsecured creditor. Consequently, he may try to gain priority by means of a retention of title clause inserted in his contract with the insolvent company.[281] Chapter 9 covers this area in more detail.

12.124 Difficulties may also be faced by an administrative receiver who deals with property subject to a lease. Unless there is a contrary provision in the lease, a lessee is free to charge his interest under the lease and the granting of such a charge will not generally have any effect on the rights and obligations of lessor and lessee; similarly with the crystallisation of a floating charge over the lessee's assets. However, most leases contain provisions prohibiting the granting of charges over the lessee's interest. Such a prohibition may be absolute, or operate unless the prior consent of the lessor is obtained. There is often a clause in the lease providing for forfeiture upon crystallisation of any floating charge or on the appointment of a receiver, and even if this is not the case the receiver can have no better interest in the leased property than the company had.[282]

12.125 The order of distribution[283] of the proceeds of realisation which an administrative receiver makes will usually involve paying the costs of realising the company's property first, followed by the costs and outgoings incurred by the receiver in collecting and recovering that property and in carrying on the business. The payment of the receiver's remuneration and of

---

281 See ch 9.
282 See ch 9 on leases, hire purchase and the sale of receivables.
283 See below para 12.126.

the preferential creditors will be followed by the interest to the debenture holder, together with the capital sum secured by the debenture. Any residue which is left must either be returned to the company or passed to the liquidator if there is one although if there is a series of incumbrancers, surplus proceeds should be paid to the incumbrancers next in order. Again, it may be necessary to seek the directions of the court if the administrative receiver is faced with a particularly complex situation.[284]

Administrative receivers and distribution

12.126   The administrative receiver should note, in particular, the provisions relating to the special priority of preferential creditors and, if there is a winding up, of the costs and expenses of winding up, together with the statutory provisions about his own remuneration.[285]

Special priority of preferential creditors
12.127   Section 40 of the Insolvency Act 1986 provides that where a receiver is appointed on behalf of the holders of any debentures of the company secured by a charge which, as created, was a floating charge, then, if the company is not at the time being wound up, its preferential debts are to be paid out of the assets coming to the hands of the receiver in priority to any claims for principal or interests in respect of the debentures. Section 196 of the Companies Act 1985 applies the same rule at the point at which possession is taken of the company property subject to the charge on behalf of the debenture holder. The object of the sections is to ensure that crystallisation of a floating charge at any time between its creation and the appointment of a receiver does not defeat the rights of the preferential creditors. The section expressly provides[286] that the meaning of 'preferential debts' is that given by s 386 of the Insolvency Act 1986, so that the preferential debts which are referred to are those in sch 1 of the Act (debts due to the Inland Revenue for income tax deducted at source, debts due to the Customs and Excise for VAT, car tax and betting and gaming duties, social security contributions, contributions to pension schemes and the remuneration of employees).[287]

12.128   Section 40(3) of the Insolvency Act 1986 and s 196(3) of the Companies Act 1985 expressly provide that payments made under the sections will be recouped, as far as possible, out of the assets of the company

---

284   See, for example, (1988) 4 BCC 192.
285   Insolvency Act 1986 s 45(3).
286   s 40(2).
287   Rates are no longer preferential debts. Liability for rates will have to be looked at in the light of the Community Charge legislation.

available for the payment of general creditors. This means that although the debenture holder will be disadvantaged by the fact that preferential creditors take priority, it will ultimately be the unsecured creditors who bear the payments.

If the administrative receiver ignores the right of the preferential creditors to be paid out of the assets in his hands, he will be personally liable for breach of statutory duty and for payment of damages in the sums that he should have paid over.[288]

Categories of preferential claims[289]
(a) *Income Tax deducted at source (PAYE)*. Category 1 includes PAYE deductions which have been made or should have been made in the 12 months before the relevant date and deductions in the same period in respect of subcontractors in the construction industry.

(b) *Debts due to Customs and Excise*. Category 2 includes any VAT which is referable to the 6 months preceding the relevant date and this category contains provisions for apportionment if necessary. Also included are; car tax which became due within the 12 months preceding the relevant date; general betting duty; gaming licence duty and bingo duty which was payable during the same period.

(c) *Social security contributions*. Category 3 covers both Class 1 and Class 2 contributions payable during the period of 12 months before the relevant date.

(d) *Pension contributions*. Category 4 covers sums payable as pension contributions both to occupational pension schemes and as state scheme premiums.

(e) *Remuneration of employees*. Category 5 includes sums owed to employees or former employees by way of remuneration in respect of whole or part of a 4 month period before the relevant date, up to a limit set by the Secretary of State. It also includes sums owed by way of accrued holiday remuneration in respect of any period prior to the relevant date and due to a person dismissed on or before that date. In *Re Urethane Engineering Products Ltd*[290] the Court of Appeal held that in a receivership the Secretary of State for Employment could only claim the amount which the employee would have received had the Secretary of State not paid the

---

288 *Woods v Winskill* [1913] 2 Ch 303; *Westminster Corporation v Haste* [1950] Ch 442.
289 Insolvency Act 1986 sch 6 and see ch 19 for a more detailed treatment of preferential debts.
290 The Times 7 April 1989.

employee's claim under the Employment Protection (consolidation) Act 1978. He is not entitled to be paid in priority over any other unsatisfied claim of the employee as is the case with a liquidation. Section 125(2) only gives rights to the Secretary of State in a liquidation, not in a receivership. The court drew attention to the fact that there are two regimes, imposing different priorities, one in relation to winding up and the other in relation to receivership.

The relevant date

12.129 Section 387 of the Insolvency Act 1986 defines the phrase 'the relevant date' for the purposes of sch 6 to the Act. This is the date which operates to determine the existence and amount of a preferential debt. Provided that the company is not being wound up, the relevant date is the date of the appointment of the receiver by the debenture holder.[291] Where the company is being wound up, if the winding up order followed immediately upon the discharge of an administrative order, the relevant date is that of the making of the administrative order.[292] Otherwise, where there is a resolution to wind up the company, that is the relevant date;[293] if there is no such resolution, the relevant date is the date of the winding up order or the date of the appointment of a provisional liquidator, if that is earlier.[294]

Insolvency Act 1986 s 115

12.130 This section provides that all expenses properly incurred in the winding up, including the liquidator's remuneration, are payable out of the company's assets in priority to all other claims. Since 'assets' have been construed by the courts as including assets subject to a floating charge at the commencement of the winding up,[295] this means that the costs and expenses of the liquidation will be payable out of assets subject to the floating charge in priority to the debenture holder's claims. However, it has been held that where a receiver was appointed before the winding up commenced, ie the floating charge crystallised prior to liquidation, the expenses of the liquidation should not take priority.[296]

Insolvency Act 1986 s 45(3)

12.131 This section provides protection for the receiver after his receivership is ended, since his entitlement to remuneration and any expenses properly incurred by him, together with any indemnity to which

---

291   s 387(4).
292   s 387(3)(a).
293   s 387(3)(c).
294   Insolvency Act 1986 s 387(3)(b).
295   *Re Barleycorn Enterprises Ltd* [1970] Ch 465.
296   *Re Christonette International Ltd* [1982] 1 WLR 1245.

he is entitled, are given priority over any securiy held by the debenture holder.

Vacation of office

12.132   When the administrative receiver vacates his office (which may occur on completion of the receivership, or otherwise) s 45(5) of the Insolvency Act 1986 creates a criminal offence if he fails without reasonable excuse to notify the Registrar of Companies of the vacation which is taking place. The administrative receiver has 14 days after he has vacated office in which to carry out the notification[297] and failure to do so results in a fine, levied on a daily default basis for continued contravention.[298] The notice to the Registrar of Companies may be given by means of an indorsement on the notice which is required by s 405(2) of the Companies Act 1985, for the purposes of the register of charges.[299] On vacating office, the administrative receiver must also notify the members of the creditors' committee (if one has been established) and send a notice to the company itself, or if it is in liquidation, to the liquidator.[300] This notification procedure must be carried out 'forthwith' when vacation of office takes place.

12.133   Within 2 months of the date on which he ceases to act as receiver (or such longer time as the court may allow)[301] the administrative receiver must send accounts to the Registrar of Companies, the company, to his appointor and to each member of the creditors' committee (provided one has been established).[302] The accounts must be in the form of an abstract which shows receipts and payments during the period from the end of the last 12 month period[303] to the time when he ceased to act as administrative receiver. Alternatively, if there has been no previous abstract, the document should show the receipts and payments in the period since his appointment as administrative receiver.[304] It is a criminal offence to fail to comply with this rule, bringing liability to a fine, which will be levied on a daily default basis for continued contravention.[305] It is also the duty of the administrative receiver, on vacating his office, to bring to the attention of the directors, or any successor of his as receiver (as the case may be), Rule 3.38(1), which povides that the certificate of insolvency for the purposes of the Value Added Tax Act 1983 must be retained with the company's accounting

---

297   s 45(4).
298   For punishments under the Act, see s 430 and sch 10.
299   r 3.35(2).
300   r 3.35(1).
301   r 3.32(2).
302   r 3.32(1).
303   As defined by r 3.32(1).
304   r 3.32(3).
305   r 3.32(4) and see r 12.21 and sch 5 to the Rules for punishments.

records. He should also inform the relevant person that s 222 of the Companies Act, which makes provision for where and for how long records are to be kept, applies to the certificate as it applies to the company's accounting records.[306]

12.134 If the administrative receiver is no longer qualified to act as an insolvency practitioner in relation to the insolvent company, then the statute requires him to vacate office.[307] He will cease to be so qualified if for some reason he ceased to satisfy the criteria laid down in s 390 of the Insolvency Act 1986. Section 45(2) of the Act, which refers in particular to the duty of an unqualified insolvency practitioner to vacate his office as administrative receiver, is reinforced by s 230(2), which provides that when the administrative receiver is appointed, he must be a qualified insolvency practitioner. In addition, a sanction is provided by s 389, which creates a criminal offence if any person acts as an insolvency practitioner in relation to a company when he is not qualified to do so.[308]

The statute also compels an administrative receiver to vacate his office on the making of an administration order.[309] The debenture holder must give his consent to the making of an administration order[310] if he has previously chosen to appoint an administrative receiver, so that his position is safeguarded. Section 11(4) of the Insolvency Act 1986 provides for the payment of the administrative receiver's remuneration and expenses if an administrator is appointed by the courts.

Removal of administrative receiver

12.135 Section 45(1) of the Insolvency Act 1986 lays down the only method of removing an administrative receiver from office. Anyone wishing to remove an administrative receiver from his office as such must obtain a court order to that effect. To emphasise the point that this is the only way in which an administrative receiver can be removed from office, the statute expressly provides that he cannot be removed otherwise than by court order. This subsection implements a recommendation made by the Cork Committee,[311] who were of the opinion that the existing law, which allowed an appointor to remove a receiver at will, should be changed. The statute embodies their recommendations, since under s 45(1), even an appointor must obtain a court order if he wishes to remove an administrative receiver from office. The effect of this provision is to

306　r 3.38(2).
307　Insolvency Act 1986 s 45(2).
308　For punishments under the Act see s 430 and sch 10.
309　Insolvency Act 1986 s 11(1)(b).
310　s 9(3).
311　Cork Report para 492.

emphasise the independence of the administrative receiver, so that he is not so easily regarded as the puppet of his appointor. It is also in keeping with the policy behind the creation of the office of administrative receiver that a qualified insolvency practitioner should not be subject to removal at the whim of the appointor.

12.136　The section does not specify by whom an application for an order to remove an administrative receiver can be made, nor on what grounds the order may be granted. The Rules appear to give no further guidance on these matters. In Scotland the position is clarified by s 62 of the Insolvency Act 1986, which provides[312] that the holder of the floating charge by virtue of which the administrative receiver was appointed may apply to the court for the removal of an administrative receiver for cause. This would be a very straightforward system to apply by analogy, although it provides for a narrower range of applicants than those who may make an application to remove a non-administrative receiver under the inherent jurisdiction of the court. Under the inherent jurisdiction of the court such an application may be made by the appointor, the receiver himself, the company or another debenture holder. Those applicants all have to show cause for the removal, and the court is generally cautious in intervening. If this analogy was followed, it would have the advantage of enabling a wide range of persons to make an application and would have the additional advantage that it would reflect the position in relation to the removal of a liquidator.[313]

Resignation of administrative receiver

12.137　An administrative receiver may resign his office, provided that he does so by giving notice in accordance with the Rules.[314] Rule 3.33 provides that the administrative receiver must give at least 7 days' notice of his intention to resign. He must give notice to his appointor, the company (or the liquidator, if it is in liquidation) and to the members of the creditors' committee (provided that this has been established).[315] The Rules do not specify the contents of the notice, other than to require that the notice specifies the date on which the administrative receiver intends that his resignation should take effect.[316] There is an exception to the requirement that an administrative receiver must give notice of his resignation and that is if he resigns in consequence of the making of an administration order, when no notice is required.[317]

312　s 62(3).
313　See ch 15 on this.
314　Insolvency Act 1986 s 45(1).
315　r 3.33(1).
316　r 3.33(2).
317　r 3.33(3).

Death of administrative receiver

12.138   If the administrative receiver dies whilst in office, then it is up to his appointor to comply with notice requirements equivalent to those which normally have to be complied with by the administrative receiver himself on vacation of office. As soon as he becomes aware of the administrative receiver's death, the appointor must immediately give notice to the Registrar of Companies, the company itself (or, if it is in liquidation, the liquidator) and to the members of the creditors' committee (provided that one has been established).[318]

---

[318] r 3.34.

CHAPTER 13

Administration Orders

INTRODUCTION

13.01 The Cork Report recognised the value of the procedure of appointing a receiver under a floating charge. Sometimes it is possible to rescue a company by returning it to profitability during the course of a receivership. The whole or part of the company's business might be sold as a going concern to the benefit of employees, the public and the commercial world at large. However, in cases where no floating charge had been granted there was no possibility of using receivership or any similar procedure for the purpose of corporate rescue. Any informal moratorium was dependent on the agreement of all creditors and so could be prevented by the resistance of a tiny minority. The procedure now found in s 425 of the Companies Act 1985 is time consuming and expensive—with a large element of court involvement. The Cork Committee argued that this resulted in certain companies ceasing to trade and being forced into liquidation with the consequence that potentially viable businesses were closed down.

13.02 The report therefore recommended the establishment of a procedure for the appointment of an administrator by the court with a view to carrying on the company's business and borrowing for that purpose. Although this procedure would bear some resemblance to the United States Chapter 11 bankruptcy procedure it would differ in that the company would be run by an outside and independent person appointed by the court and not by the company's existing management. Sections 8 to 27 of the Insolvency Act 1986 implement that proposal in substantially the way that Cork envisaged.

13.03 The procedure is effectively made subject to the veto of the holder of a floating charge as his consent is required if a receiver is in office and sufficient notice of the application for an administration order is given for him to decide whether to appoint one before the order is made. This accords with the view expressed by Cork which recognised the importance of the preservation of the legal rights of the holders of floating charges to the continued availability of corporate finance. The legislation ensures that in any case in which a floating charge exists over the company's assets the administration procedure will only be used in circumstances where the holder of the charge considers the procedure to be to his advantage.

13.04 The fact that preferential debts do not need to be paid at the stage of appointing the administrator will be a factor to take into account, although it is balanced by the priority accorded to the costs of the administration and the debts incurred during it. If the period of moratorium will improve the chances of corporate rescue and thus increase the value of the assets to be realised then an order may indeed be beneficial to the holder of a floating charge. The practice of most secured creditors of taking a fixed and floating charge means a major creditor such as a bank will have regard to the powers of the administrator to use assets subject to a fixed charge in making its decision.

13.05 It is unfortunate that the legislation does not provide for an application to be made by an individual director or by the Secretary of State. The former was recommended by Cork with the leave of the court which provides a sufficient safeguard against frivolous applications and the latter would have enabled the procedure to be used in the public interest.

13.06 The procedure appears to have been remarkably successful in the first year of its operation. A survey published in 1989, of the 166 administration orders made in 1987, showed that in 55% of the 129 cases in which a response was received the whole or part of the business was continued as a going concern. This was achieved by the sale of the business as a going concern and the liquidation of the company in 36% of cases, the use of a voluntary arrangement under Part 1 of the Act in 11%, and a return to solvency of the company itself in 8%. This indicates that the procedure is more useful than the gloomiest commentators might have expected, but it does presumably reflect the careful process of selection by the advisers of insolvent companies of those cases in which the use of the procedure is advised. The 45% of cases in which the assets of the company were disposed of on a break up basis in a liquidation or by a voluntary arrangement may have resulted in a more beneficial realisation, but this is difficult to confirm in the absence of information about the dividend paid in insolvent liquidations.[1]

13.07 In *Re Brooke Marine Ltd* Harman J observed[2] that the achievements in that case in selling off viable parts of the business as going concerns

---

1 See M Homan, *A Survey of Administrations under the Insolvency Act 1986: The Result of Administration Orders made in* 1987, Institute of Chartered Accountants 1989. Reported in *The Independent* 4 April 1989.
2 [1989] BCLC 546 at 547.

for more than the price which would have been realised on a forced sale, as well as avoiding the liability for redundancy payments and breach of contract which would have arisen had the business ceased:

> "showed that the administration procedures invented by the Insolvency Act 1986 as a result of the Cork Committee recommendations are proving useful and of advantage to the public and this country at large."

APPLICATION FOR AN ORDER

13.08   An application for an administration order may be made by the company, or the directors, or by a creditor, or creditors of the company. Contingent and prospective creditors are included and joint petitions by several parties are possible.[3] The possibility of an application by directors overlaps considerably with the right of the company to apply. It is clear that the decision is expected to be one of the whole board and the articles of association of most companies will provide for the board to exercise all the powers of the company.[4] Thus in most cases the application of a company could be decided on by the board, so the power of the directors to apply adds little. However, the right conferred on directors is the corollary of their potential liability for wrongful trading, because an application for an administration order will be one of the actions which amount to a step taken to minimise the losses of the company's creditors. Such steps are required by the Insolvency Act 1986 as a means of avoiding wrongful trading.[5] One might expect that the right to petition for an order would be available to each individual director for this reason and it is unfortunate that the Cork recommendation that an individual director be allowed to apply with leave was not followed. Rule 2.1(2) lays down that the accompanying affidavit must be signed by the secretary or a director 'stating himself to make it on behalf of . . . the directors', and r 2.4(3) states that from and after presentation of the petition it is to be treated for all purposes as that of the company. In *Re Instrumentation Electrical Services Ltd*[6] it was held that the word 'directors', used in s 124(1) in relation to the right to petition for the winding up of a company, required unanimity among all board members. It is submitted that a majority in a properly constituted board meeting should suffice. The directors will normally be ordered to bear the costs of an unsuccessful administration petition, even if they presented it in good faith, as an order that it be met out of the estate of

3   Insolvency Act 1986 s 9(1).
4   For example see Table A art 70 in SI 1985 No 805.
5   s 214(3).
6   (1988) 4 BCC 301 and see *Re Equiticorp International plc* (1989) 5 BCC 599.

the insolvent company would penalise all claimants.[7] However, where a director behaved responsibly in seeking an administration order in good faith and on professional advice, and the proceedings were withdrawn after a winding up order was made at the first hearing, the costs were ordered to be regarded as costs of the liquidation rather than being awarded against the director or being made irrecoverable.[8]

13.09 An application for an order will be by petition and supported by an affidavit.[9] The affidavit must be made by the company secretary or a director, if the application is by the company or the directors, and must be stated to be sworn on behalf of the company or the directors, as the case may be.[10] Where the creditors petition for an order, the affidavit must be made by a person acting on their authority who need not be a creditor himself. The affidavit must state the nature of his authority and the means of his knowledge of the matters to which the affidavit relates. A petition presented by the supervisor of a voluntary arrangement is treated as a petition by the company for this purpose.[11]

13.10 In addition to the affidavit, which must be provided in all cases, provision is made in the rules for the submission of a report recommending the appointment of an administrator. The report will be exhibited to the affidavit which supports the petition and it is desirable that one be prepared in all cases.[12] In practice the report will often be compiled by the person who is to become administrator. The rules require that the author of the report be either the proposed administrator or a person with adequate knowledge of the company's affairs who is not a director, secretary, manager, member, or employee of the company. There is no requirement that he be a qualified insolvency practitioner.[13] The report (if one is prepared) must specify which of the purposes in s 8(3) the making of the order is expected to achieve.[14]

13.11 The affidavit must state the deponent's view that the company is or is likely to become unable to pay its debts and his reasons for that view.[15] It must also state the purpose in s 8(3) that the order is expected to serve. Details of the company's financial position—including assets and liabilities

---

7 *Re W F Fearman (No 2)* (1988) 4 BCC 141; and see *Re Manlon Trading Ltd* (1988) 4 BCC 455.
8 *Re Gosscott Groundworks Ltd* [1988] BCLC 363.
9 s 9(1) and r 2.1.
10 r 2.1(2).
11 r 2.1(4).
12 r 2.2(1).
13 r 2.2(2).
14 r 2.2(3).
15 r 2.3(1).

(contingent and prospective) and of the security held by creditors (with particular reference to the power to appoint an administrative receiver or the fact that one has been appointed) and of any winding up petitions presented against the company—must appear in the affidavit.[16] Other matters likely in the view of the petitioners to assist the court must also be included, together with either the fact that a report is exhibited or an explanation for the failure to provide one.[17]

13.12 The petition must state the name of the petitioner and his address for service. If it is presented by the company or the directors that will be the company's registered office in the absence of special reasons to the contrary.[18] In the case of a petition by a number of creditors the address of a single representative must be used, although the fact that there are several petitioners should be stated.[19] The name of the proposed administrator and his status as a qualified insolvency practitioner must be stated in the petition, and his consent to act must be exhibited to the affidavit together with a copy of the petition and of any independent report recommending that an order be made.[20] The petition must be filed in court with sufficient copies to serve all those entitled to service.[21] All copies are then sealed and endorsed with the date and time of filing and the venue fixed for the hearing.[22] Once the petition has been filed, the petitioner must notify the court of any winding up petition presented against the company as soon as he becomes aware of it.[23] Sealed copies of the petition together with the affidavit in support of it and all exhibited documents except the copy petition must be served on the company (if creditors are petitioning) and:

(a) any person who has appointed or is or may be entitled to appoint an administrative receiver;
(b) the administrative receiver if one has been appointed;
(c) anyone who has presented a pending winding up petition and the provisional liquidator (if one has been appointed); and
(d) the person proposed as administrator.[24]

In addition, the petitioner must give notice to the sheriff or other officer whom he knows to be charged with an execution or other legal process

16 r 2.3(2) and (3) and (4).
17 r 2.3(5) and (6).
18 r 2.4(1).
19 r 2.4(4).
20 r 2.4(5) and (6).
21 r 2.5(1).
22 r 2.5(2) and (3).
23 r 2.5(4).
24 r 2.6(1) and (2).

against the company or its property and anyone whom he knows has levied distress.[25] Once the petition has been filed it may not be withdrawn without the leave of the court.[26] Service is the responsibility of the petitioner and must be achieved not less than 5 days before the date fixed for the hearing.[27] The company is served at its registered office or, if that is not practicable, at its last known principal place of business in England and Wales. Individuals are to be served at their usual or last known address unless an address for service has been notified previously.[28] Proof of service is by affidavit.[29] Banks are to be served; at the address where the company's account is held if they are entitled to appoint an administrative receiver; or their registered office; or usual or last known place of business.[30] The period of notice to a person entitled to appoint an administrative receiver may be reduced under rule 12.9 if the company's state is perilous and the person in question knows that an application is to be heard.[31] As the Cork Report (para 502) recommended, there is no provision for the advertisement of a petition. This may protect the company from some of the commercial problems likely to arise if its position becomes widely known before an order is made. At the hearing of the petition the petitioner, the company, and all those entitled to service may appear or be represented, as may any other person who appears to have an interest justifying an appearance and who obtains the leave of the court.[32] The costs of the petitioner, and of others whose costs are allowed by the court, are payable as an expense of the administration if the order is made.[33]

HEARING AND CRITERIA FOR ORDER

13.13 The court may make an administration order if it is satisfied that the company is or is likely to become unable to pay its debts. This expression has the same meaning in this context as it does in s 122 of the Act where it appears as a ground for a winding up petition. It encompasses all of the circumstances set out in s 123: statutory notice for a debt of £750 or more;[34] unsatisfied execution; and proof by other means that the company is unable to pay its debts as they fall due. If the value of the company's assets is shown to be less than that of its liabilities (including contingent and

25   r 2.6A, inserted by SI 1987 No 1919.
26   s 9(2)(b).
27   r 2.7(1), but under r 12.9 the court may shorten that period.
28   r 2.7(3) and (4).
29   r 2.8.
30   r 2.7 (inserted by SI 1987 No 1919).
31   *Re A Company (No 00175 of 1987)* [1987] BCLC 467.
32   r 2.9(1).
33   r 2.9(2).
34   See eg *Re Imperial Motors (UK) Ltd* (1989) 5 BCC 214.

prospective liabilities) this will also suffice.[35] The order is only available to an insolvent company.

13.14 In addition to proof of the company's inability to pay its debts, the court must be persuaded that the making of an administration order would be likely to achieve one of the statutory purposes.[36] The purposes are:

> "(a) the survival of the company and the whole or any part of its undertaking as a going concern;
> (b) the approval of a voluntary arrangement under Part I;
> (c) the sanctioning under s 425 of the Companies Act 1985 of a compromise or arrangement between the company and any such persons as are mentioned in that section; and
> (d) a more advantageous realisation of the company's assets than would be effected on a winding up."[37]

It would appear that it is not necessary for the petitioner to establish the purpose referred to in the affidavit in support of the petition so long as one of the statutory purposes is established. The order must specify the purpose or purposes for which it was made. This provides guidance to the administrator in formulating his proposal. This requirement reflects the function of the administration order procedure. It can be the rescue of viable businesses or parts of businesses from an insolvent company. The first of the statutory purposes involves the survival of both the company and the whole or part of its undertaking as a going concern. This might be achieved by a plan involving the disposal of certain assets or parts of the business so that others will survive. A change of management is likely to be involved. Conceivably, a renewal of the company's capital base would be another possible method. At the stage of making the order there need not be a detailed plan of how to achieve this. The court simply has to be satisfied that the purpose would be likely to be achieved. The independent report will be important evidence on this issue.

13.15 It has been said that the court must be satisfied that it is more likely than not that one of the purposes laid down in s 8(3) will be achieved and the order will specify those purposes about which the court takes that view. Any change in the purposes to be pursued by the administrator must be the subject of an application under s 18(1) to vary the order.[38] This approach reflects the view that there must be a probability of more than 50% that one of the purposes set out in s 8(3) will be satisfied before the court has jurisdiction to exercise the discretion whether to make an order.

---

35 s 8(1)(a) and s 123, and see *Re Business Properties Ltd* (1988) 4 BCC 685, where the company was asset – solvent but cash – insolvent.
36 s 8(1)(b).
37 s 8(3).
38 *Re Consumer and Industrial Press Ltd* (1988) 4 BCC 68.

13.16 However, in a convincing and closely reasoned analysis of the wording of the statute Hoffmann J in *Re Harris Simons Construction Ltd*[39] held that there need only be a real prospect that one or more of the purposes in s 8(3) of the Act might be achieved. He argued that it was not necessary for the court to be able to say that it was more probable than not that this would be the case for one of the specified purposes. The fact that the court must 'consider' that the making of the order would be 'likely' to achieve one of the statutory purposes to comply with s 8(1), in contrast to the need for it to be 'satisfied' of the company's insolvency, was an important factor supporting this view. In addition, Hoffmann J suggested that a cumulative likelihood of less than a 50% chance of achieving each of a number of the statutory purposes should be sufficient to permit the court to exercise its discretion whether to make an order. It is submitted that this liberal approach to overcoming the statutory obstacles to the court's jurisdiction in this area is to be preferred as allowing greater flexibility to save businesses. Once the discretion arises the court can balance the interests of those involved in deciding whether to make an order.

13.17 Once the court is satisfied that the conditions in s 8(1)(a) and (b) exist it has a discretion to make an order which it will exercise to further and not to frustrate the purpose of the Act in the circumstances of the particular case. While the benefit of an order to secured creditors can be taken into account, their interests are to be given less weight than those of the unsecured and preferential creditors as they are likely to lose less in any event.[40] In *Re Imperial Motors (UK) Ltd*[41] the interests of a petitioning secured creditor in a more advantageous realisation of assets were outweighed by those of the company's proprietors in not having the business taken from them and sold despite the fact that an administration order would lead to a speedier realisation of assets by sale as a going concern. In that case the offer, by a director of the company to pay a supporting creditor personally and to subordinate his own loan account to make the company solvent on a balance sheet basis, made such an outcome possible.

13.18 No order will be made in cases of deadlock and total breakdown of confidence and trust as winding up or receivership are the more appropriate solutions in those circumstances. The intensive care provided by this remedy is inappropriate and a more beneficial realisation of assets by means of an administration order is unlikely in such cases.[42]

39 (1989) 5 BCC 11, followed in *Re Primlaks (UK) Ltd* (1989) 5 BCC 710 and by Peter Gibson J in *Re SCL Building Services Ltd* (1989) 5 BCC 746. The test is the 'real prospect' of achieving one or more of the stated purposes.
40 *Re Consumer and Industrial Press*, n 38 *supra*.
41 (1989) 5 BCC 214.
42 *Re Business Properties Ltd* (1988) 4 BCC 685.

13.19 If the purpose of the administration is the approval of a voluntary arrangement under the Insolvency Act 1986 or a scheme or compromise under s 425 of the Companies Act 1985, the administrator will negotiate with the company's creditors to try to achieve a workable scheme which can be agreed through the statutory procedures involved in finalising the arrangement scheme or compromise. The statutory moratorium will assist in the achievement of this goal. Chapter 22 considers these possibilities in more detail.

13.20 The final purpose laid down in s 8(3) envisages a process of realising the assets of the company rather than a rescue of its business. It will be necessary to establish that the use of an administration order will result in a more advantageous realisation than a winding up. This is likely in a situation where the passing of time during which there is a statutory moratorium will result in a better price being obtained on the disposal of assets. This could be the disposal of part of the company's business or of individual assets. It enables the business of the company to be continued under the protection of the moratorium; any continuation of the business by a receiver would not have this advantage. This purpose will be the appropriate one to use where it is not envisaged that the company itself will survive and where no scheme, compromise or arrangement with creditors is to be negotiated. An order of short duration may be made for this purpose on the basis that a deficiency after sale can result in a winding up order with the resulting investigation by an independent liquidator with appropriate powers to deal with any fraudulent or wrongful trading.[43]

13.21 If there is no evidence to show that an administration order is more likely to provide more money for distribution to the creditors than would be available on a winding up, the petition based on the better realisation of assets will be dismissed. There should be no order to restrain the advertisement of a winding up petition just because an administration petition may be presented unless the company undertakes to take that step. However, such an order will be made in the case of a winding up petition presented after an administration petition has been presented but before it is heard.[44]

13.22 The special regulatory system which applies to them means that insurance companies covered by the Insurance Companies Act 1982 cannot be the subject of an administration order. The Banks (Administration Proceedings) Order 1989[44a] allows the Bank of England to petition for an administration order in respect of a bank and applies the scheme of the Act

---

43 *Re Consumer and Industrial Press*, n 38 *supra*.
44 *Re Manlon Trading Ltd* (1988) 4 BCC 455 and *Re a Company (No 001992 of 1988)* [1989] BCLC 9.
44a SI 1989 no 1276 (in force on 23/8/89).

to banks with some modifications. No company which has already gone into liquidation can have an administration order made against it.[45]

13.23 If an administrative receiver has been appointed before the petition is heard, then the petition will be dismissed unless the court is satisfied that the person by whom or on whose behalf the receiver was appointed consents to the making of an administration order, or the security by virtue of which the appointment was made would be set aside as a preference, a transaction at an undervalue or a recent floating charge under ss 238 to 240 of the Insolvency Act 1986.[46] Unless the court decides on hearing the petition that the security under which a receiver was appointed would definitely be set aside should an administrator take office, the holder of a security (normally a floating charge) which entitles him to appoint an administrative receiver has a complete right of veto over the making of an administration order. The courts may interpret this provision as requiring only *prima facie* proof that the charge would be set aside were an administrator appointed. However, the wording of s 9(3) (to the effect that the courts must be satisfied that the security 'would' be set aside) suggests more than *prima facie* proof. Anyone with the power to appoint an administrative receiver must be given notice of the application for an administration order. This enables them to appoint a receiver in the period between the filing of the petition and the making of the order, to prevent an order from being made. The mandatory nature of s 9(3) of the Insolvency Act 1986 prevents an adjournment of the hearing or any decision other than the dismissal of the petition in these circumstances.[47] Subject to that right of veto, the court may, on hearing the petition, dismiss it, adjourn the hearing conditionally or unconditionally, or make any other order it thinks fit including an *interim* order.[48]

13.24 An *interim* order may restrict the exercise of the directors' powers or those of the company. This may be done by requiring the consent of the court or of a qualified insolvency practitioner or otherwise.[49] In *Re a Company (No 00175 of 1987)*,[50] Vinelott J suggested *obiter* that this power could be used to appoint the proposed administrator or some other person to take control of the property of the company and to manage its affairs pending the hearing of the petition where the time for service was abridged and an *ex parte* order made. Such an appointment would be analogous to the appointment of a receiver by the court to protect the property which

---

45 s 8(4).
46 s 9(3).
47 *Re a Company (No 00175 of 1987)* [1987] BCLC 467.
48 s 9(4).
49 s 9(5).
50 [1987] BCLC 467.

was in jeopardy. The appointment would be for a very brief period during which the person with a right to appoint an administrative receiver was deciding whether to do so. The duration of the appointment could be until the hearing, with liberty for any party to apply to terminate it earlier or until an administrative receiver was appointed if that occurred before the hearing. It is clear from s 13 of the Act that such a person could not be appointed as an administrator as the appointment of an administrator is only possible on the making of an administration order or to fill a vacancy which arises later.

13.25 As soon as a petition for an administration order is presented, a form of moratorium applies to the company. Under s 10 it is not possible for any form of winding up of the company to begin; whether by order or resolution. However, a winding up petition may be presented because of the significance of the date of that event if an order is later made, but advertisement of the petition will be restrained and no further steps will be taken on it until the administration petition is heard.[51] Similarly no steps may be taken to enforce any security over the company's property or to repossess goods possessed by the company under a hire purchase agreement, conditional sale agreement, chattel leasing agreement or a retention of title agreement (see paras 13.36–13.40 below for a full discussion of the meaning of these terms). No other proceedings, execution or other legal process may be begun nor continued or may distress be levied against the company or its property without leave of the court.[52]

13.26 If the petition is presented at a time when an administrative receiver of the company has already been appointed the s 10 moratorium will not begin until and unless the appointer of the receiver gives his consent to the making of an administration order, but once that consent is given no revocation of it will prevent s 10 from operating.[53] It will be noted that the presentation of a winding up petition, as opposed to the making of an order, and the appointment and functioning of an administrative receiver are not subject to the leave of the court or in any other way inhibited by the presentation of a petition for an administration order.[54]

THE ADMINISTRATION ORDER

13.27 The nature of an administration order and its primary effect are set out in s 8(2) of the Act. The order is one directing that the affairs, business

---

51 *Re a Company (No 001992 of 1988)* [1989] BCLC 9.
52 s 10(1).
53 s 10(3).
54 s 19(2); and see *Re W F Fearman (No 2)* (1988) 4 BCC 141.

and property of the company shall be managed during the period for which it is in force by the administrator who is appointed for that purpose by the court. During the currency of the order the control of the company is vested in the administrator. The order will specify the purpose or purposes for which it was made.[55]

13.28 The other major effect of the order is the moratorium imposed by s 11. This requires the dismissal of any winding up petition and the vacation of office by any administrative receiver on the making of the order.[56] The latter requirement can only arise where the appointor of the administrative receiver consented to the administration order or the court decided that the security under which the appointment had been made could be avoided or set aside. In some cases the appointor of the administrative receiver may have consented to the administration order on condition that the former administrative receiver be appointed administrator. The question of whether a receiver of part only of the company's property has to vacate office is left to the administrator; there is no automatic requirement that he vacate office on the order being made but he must leave office if the administrator requires him to do so.[57] Where a receiver leaves office under s 11(1) or (2), his remuneration, expenses and any indemnity to which he is entitled out of the assets of the company, are charged on and must be paid out of any company property which was in his custody or under his control at the time of his vacation of office. Such amounts have priority over any security held by the person on whose behalf he was appointed but the payment of the amounts is subject to the general moratorium while the administration order is in force.[58]

13.29 It is worth noting that the property subject to the charge is that possessed or controlled by the receiver at the time at which he vacates office and not any property which was previously held by him but ceased to be so held before the end of his period in office. In addition to the provisions securing the remuneration, expenses and indemnity of the receiver, he is absolved from any duty under ss 40 or 59 of the Act to pay preferential creditors on or after vacating office.[59] It is interesting that this provision, like the one giving security and priority, applies to receivers of only part of the company's property as well as administrative receivers.

13.30 The position of the non-administrative receiver is distinguished

55 s 8(3).
56 s 11(1).
57 s 11(2).
58 s 11(4).
59 s 11(5).

from that of the administrative receiver, whose function would necessarily conflict with that of the administrator. The receiver of part of the company's assets will commonly have been appointed by the holder of a fixed charge, as any floating charge is likely to have been granted over the whole of the company's assets. His function is likely to be the collection of income from a particular asset for transmission to the mortgagee rather than the management role which an administrative receiver will often fulfil. The administrator may not wish to remove a non-administrative receiver if the purpose of the administration is to reach some arrangement or compromise with creditors and this may be jeopardised by a non-consensual removal of the nominee of a particular creditor. However, where the continuation of all or part of the company's business as a going concern is the purpose of the administration, the administrator may regard the diversion of income to the receiver as undesirable. No sale of the assets held by the receiver will be possible during the currency of the order, as that would be a step to enforce a security or the continuation of an execution or legal process.[60]

13.31 The priority given to a displaced receiver for his expenses and renumeration over the property which was in his possession or under his control amounts to a fixed charge. It will have priority over any security of the person who appointed him—including a fixed charge—which existed at the time at which the receiver vacated office.

13.32 Apart from the effect of an order on an existing receiver, the appointment of an administrative receiver is prohibited during the currency of the administration order.[61] There is no express restriction on the appointment of a non-administrative receiver after an administration order has been made but this would also amount to a step to enforce a security and therefore falls within the prohibition on such acts without leave of the court or consent of the administrator.[62] In addition to the Act's requirement that any winding up petition be dismissed on the making of the administration order, no such order can be made or winding up resolution passed while the administration order is in force.[63] This ensures that administration and liquidation are mutually exclusive alternatives and that the administration order should have either come to the end of its fixed duration or have been terminated by the court before any winding up of the company can begin. This feature of the administration order is fundamental to the whole concept of providing an opportunity for the feasible parts of the business to be saved or sold off. The administrator is able to carry on the

---

60   s 11(3)(c) and (d).
61   s 11(3)(b).
62   s 11(3)(c) and (d).
63   s 11(3)(a).

business without the threat of winding up proceedings being set in motion by creditors. This protection is not available to an administrative receiver.

13.33   The normal duration of an administration order is three months and although the company does have standing to apply for an extension an application by the administrator is preferable as he is in a position to offer the court an independent and detached view of the company's affairs.[64]

The moratorium

13.34   When an administration order is made, the inability of creditors to enforce charges or securities, to bring or continue any proceedings or execution, to levy any distress or to use other legal process against the company or its property continues. However, the requirement to obtain leave to proceed against the company only extends to actions by creditors and not to other litigation such as proceedings for the revocation of a licence under a statutory provision unconnected with insolvency.[65] It does not extend to an application for an extension of time to register a charge under the Companies Act 1985.[65a]

13.35   On an application by a secured creditor under s 11(3)(c) for leave to enforce its security while an administration order is in force it is not necessary to prove any matter amounting to a criticism of the administrator's behaviour to obtain leave. The court examines all the circumstances and considers the interests of all concerned. The fact that the costs of a sale by the administrator in accordance with the scheme approved for the administration will be less than those of the later sale by a receiver appointed by the creditor, may cause leave to be refused if sale by the administrator will not prejudice the secured creditor. A substantial delay in achieving the sale of the asset, which was the purpose of the administration order, does not of itself justify leave to a creditor to enforce its security if the administrator has acted properly and on professional advice.[66] In that case the original intention to sell a building repaired and fully let had proved unattainable and the administrator was proposing to sell it with vacant possession and without repairs.

13.36   The moratorium extends not only to creditors with charges or securities but also to the owners of goods in the company's possession under hire purchase agreements, conditional sale agreements, chattel leasing agreements and retention of title agreements who may not repossess their goods.

64   *Re Newport County AFC* [1987] BCLC 582.
65   *Air Ecosse Ltd v CAA* (1987) 3 BCC 492.
65a   *Re Barrow Borough Transport Ltd* (1989) 5 BCC 646.
66   *Royal Trust Bank v Buchler* [1989] BCLC 130.

However, such steps can be taken with the consent of the administrator or the leave of the court. The latter may be subject to terms.[67] This wide ranging protection against action by those with security interests or, indeed, in the case of goods, ownership rights, is complemented by the power of the administrator to deal with such property (in some cases with the leave of the court).[68]

13.37   The prohibition on the enforcement of securities or charges extends to the holders of fixed or floating charges or of mortgages of any kind over the company's property. Security, in the sense of a guarantee provided by the company of a debt of another company or of an individual, will be subject to the restrictions on the commencement or continuation of proceedings or other legal process against the company. The secured creditor cannot enforce his real security against the company's property and the unsecured creditor cannot bring proceedings to enforce any judgment already obtained by any method of execution or any other legal process. The landlord, the rating authority and the tax authorities are unable to levy distress. These provisions are similar to those which apply when a company is in compulsory liquidation.

13.38   However, in the case of an administration order the prohibition extends to the repossession by the owner of goods not owned by the company but in its possession under certain types of contract.[69] Firstly, any 'chattel leasing agreement' falls within this category. This is defined as an agreement for the bailment of goods which is capable of subsisting for more than three months.[70] Repossession will be prevented in the case of any lease of goods which lasts for more than three months or contemplates a renewal or extension of the period of bailment beyond that length of time. Repossession will not be possible at any time from the presentation of a petition for an administration order until the dismissal of the petition, or the termination of the order in respect of the lessee company.[71] A provision in a lease granting an option to renew the bailment would make the goods subject to the prohibition. Any agreement which clearly ended after a period of less than three months might escape the effects of the administration order but if the goods were in fact retained by the lessee company for a longer period this might well indicate the existence of an agreement capable of lasting for a longer period. Such conduct could show an intention to continue the written agreement; if a hire charge were paid and accepted after the expiration of the original agreement and the evidence

---

67   s 11(3)(c) and (d).
68   See paras 13.57 *et seq* below and s 15.
69   ss 10(1)(b) and 11(3)(c).
70   ss 10(4) and 251.
71   s 10(4).

indicated an acceptance by the parties that the same terms were to apply. If a series of separate agreements were made in respect of the same goods, each agreement lasting less than three months, it would be a matter of construction whether they amounted to one agreement. The fact that the terms of all of the agreements were the same and the absence of time gaps between them might result in a finding that there was only one agreement.

13.39 Secondly, goods in the company's possession under any conditional sale or hire purchase agreement are subject to the prohibition on repossession.[72] The definition of such agreements in the Consumer Credit Act 1974 is adopted by the Act.[73] Goods subject to a retention of title agreement will be caught by the prohibition on repossession.[74] Such an agreement is defined as:

> "an agreement for the sale of goods to the company, being an agreement
> (a) which does not constitute a charge on the goods, but
> (b) under which, if the seller is not paid and the company is wound up, the seller will have priority over all other creditors as respects the goods or any property representing the goods'.[75]

This definition seeks to ensure that clauses which are not held to grant a charge over goods but to succeed in preserving the ownership in the seller until payment either of the price of those goods or of all outstanding amounts due to the seller from the company, either under a particular contract or over the whole account between them. In such circumstances the court will either find that the goods belong to the seller or that they belong to the company and the seller has a charge against some part of the company's property.[76]

13.40 'Property representing the goods' may be new goods manufactured by the use of the goods sold to the company or the proceeds of sale of the goods or goods made by the use of them. It is submitted that since ss 10(1)(b) and 11(3)(c) prohibit steps taken to repossess goods in the company's possession under a retention of title agreement, they do not have the effect of preventing the seller (as principal) from claiming proceeds of sale held on trust for the seller by the company under the terms of such a clause. Since nothing in these sections gives the administrator power to deal with property other than goods which are now owned by the company (as opposed to property owned by the company and subject to a charge) it would seem that a finding that the proceeds of sale of goods subject to a

---

72   s 10(1)(b) and (4).
73   s 436.
74   s 10(4).
75   s 251.
76   See ch 9 paras 9.06–9.48.

retention of title clause were held by the company as a fiduciary would prevent their use by the administrator. It is hard to see how proceeds of sale can be called goods and although the definition of a retention of title agreement refers to 'property representing the goods', the sections concerned with the effects of an administration order or petition refer only to the repossession by the owner of 'goods' possessed by the company under such an agreement. It is, however, clear that the greater the propensity of a clause to extend the ownership of the seller to goods made out of those he originally sold or to proceeds of sale, the greater the likelihood that the agreement will be held to create a charge; enforcement of which is likely to fall foul of s 395 of the Companies Act 1985. If it were effective under that section its enforcement would be restrained during the period after the administration petition.

Supplies by public utilities

13.41 In common with a liquidator or an administrative receiver, the administrator is protected from the imposition, by certain public utilities, of a condition on the supply of their services that outstanding charges due in respect of a supply given before the date of the administration order should be paid. The prohibition extends to anything which has the effect of imposing such a condition and extends from a demand for a deposit before any supply is provided where the deposit relates to earlier unpaid debts, to the utility in respect of supplies. It is possible for the public utility to require a personal guarantee from the administrator of the payment of charges in respect of the supplies provided after the date of the administration order.[77] The public utility supplies covered by this provision are a public supply of gas by British Gas or another public gas supplier; a supply of electricity by an electricity board within the meaning of the Energy Act 1983; a supply of water by a statutory water undertaker; or a supply of telecommunication services by a public telecommunications operator. Telecommunication services do not include services consisting in the conveyance of programmes included in cable broadcasting services.[78]

13.42 It is only payments of earlier charges for 'supplies' of the kind referred to in s 233(3) in connection with each utility which cannot be made a condition of such supplies in the future. The provision of other goods and services by a utility (for example, electrical equipment by an electricity board) can be denied until payment is made for a supply of the kind covered by the provision and made before the administration order was made.

77   s 233(2).
78   s 233(5).

Similarly, a supply, for example, of electricity can be denied until other goods or services have been paid for as the connection of a supply after the date of the administration order would not then be made conditional on earlier supplies of the kind specified in the section. The inability of the supplier to make supplies conditional depends on a request being made by or with the concurrence of the administrator during the existence of the administration order.[79]

Other effects of administration order

13.43 The making of an administration order brings into effect a number of provisions common to the administration of a company and other forms of insolvency proceedings; particularly liquidation. Transactions at an under-value and preferences granted by the company can be challenged under ss 238 and 239 of the Act[80] on an application to the court by the administrator: extortionate credit bargains can be reopened by the court on his application;[81] any lien over the company's books, papers or other records which would deny possession of them to the administrator is unenforceable against him and he can seek the avoidance of floating charges under s 245 of the Act.[82] Where the discharge of an administration order is followed immediately by a winding up order made by the court the date fixed for determining the period in respect of which preferential debts can be claimed in the winding up is the date on which the administration order was made.[83] For the purpose of seeking an order disqualifying a person from acting as a director under s 6 of the Company Directors Disqualification Act 1986, a company is 'insolvent' if an administration order is made.[84]

13.44 An administration order does not allow a director to be made liable for wrongful or fraudulent trading[85] and does not enable the administrator to make use of s 212; the misfeasance summons procedure.[86] The Cork Committee recommended that a remedy against directors for wrongful trading should be available to the administrator and, while it did not contemplate a continuing civil remedy for fraudulent trading, its report suggested that there was no reason for the limitation of that remedy to companies in liquidation.[87] It is hard to see why these devices for making

79 s 233(1) and (2).
80 ss 238(1) and 239(1) and see ch 20.
81 s 244(1).
82 ss 246(1) and 245(1).
83 s 287(3)(a).
84 s 6(2)(c) Company Directors Disqualification Act 1986.
85 ss 213(1) and 214(1).
86 s 212(1).
87 Cork Report, Cmnd 8558, paras 1791 and 1792.

assets available to creditors on the grounds of the misconduct of those in control of the company should not be available when an administration order is made. It would be unfortunate if the inability of an administrator to use these remedies were to encourage creditors to seek the liquidation of a company capable of rescue or reconstruction if an administration order were made.

13.45 Certain of the remedies available to the administrator are not available to an administrative receiver of a company although a liquidator may use them. This category includes an application to set aside preferences; transactions at an under value and extortionate credit transactions. A receiver does not have statutory priority over a lien on the company's documents and his appointment does not affect the time limit for the avoidance of a floating charge. This is a recognition of the fact that even after the reforms of 1986 the receiver's primary duty is to the creditor who appointed him,[88] whereas the administrator is answerable to the court and acts in accordance with its directions or with proposals which it has approved.

Invoices etc
13.46 While an administration order is in force any invoice, order for goods or business letter on or in which the company's name appears and which is issued by or on behalf of the company or the administrator must contain a statement that the company is being managed by an administrator and name him.[89] The penalty for failure to do this can be imposed on the administrator or any officer of the company if they authorise or permit the default without reasonable excuse.[90]

Copies and notice of order
13.47 The administrator is required to send a copy of the administration order to the company and to publish it in the Gazette and in such other newspaper as he thinks most appropriate for ensuring that it comes to the attention of the company's creditors. In addition he must give notice of the making of the order to:

(a) all the creditors (so far as he is aware of their addresses) within 28 days after the making of the order;
(b) any person who has appointed an administrative receiver or who is or may be entitled to do so;

88 See ch 12.
89 s 12(1).
90 s 12(2).

(c) any administrative receiver who has been appointed;
(d) any person who has petitioned for a winding up order and
(e) any provisional liquidator;

and notice together with an office copy of the order to the registrar of companies. The order must be sent within 14 days of it being made and the notice 'forthwith'.[91] Failure by the administrator to comply with these requirements without reasonable excuse is an offence punishable by a fine and a daily default fine.[92] Any order other than the making of an administration order must be the subject of notice to such persons and in such form as the court directs.[93]

Statement of affairs

13.48   Once an administration order has been made the administrator is obliged to require one or more of the persons listed in s 22(3) to make out and submit to him a statement of affairs for the company in the form of Form 2.9 of the Insolvency Rules 1986.[94] He does this by sending notice to each of the persons whom he wishes to make responsible for a statement of affairs. The notice must give each such person details of all the others to whom the same notice has been sent; a time limit within which the statement must be delivered; and information about the penalty for non-compliance and about the duties imposed by s 235 of the Act. On request he must also provide forms required for the preparation of the statement.[95]

13.49   The administrator has a choice of who is to be required to submit the statement of affairs. It will be usual to impose this obligation on the directors of the company but the full list of those from whom the administrator may choose is:

(a) those who are or have been officers of the company;
(b) those who have taken part in the company's formation at any time within a year before the date of the order;
(c) those who are in the company's employment or have been within that one year period and who are, in the administrator's opinion capable of giving the information required; and
(d) those who are or have been within that year officers of or in the employment of another company that is, or was within that year, an officer of the company.

---

91 r 2.10 as amended by SI 1987 No 1919, and s 21(1) and (2).
92 s 21(3).
93 r 2.10(5).
94 s 22(1).
95 r 2.11 as amended by SI 1987 No 1919.

For this purpose 'employment' includes employment under a contract for services.[96]

13.50 The persons required by the administrator to co-operate in this way are required to submit a statement within 21 days unless a longer period is stipulated by the administrator. The period runs from the day after that on which the notice of the requirement is given to them and the period can later be extended by the administrator who also has power to release a person from this obligation.[97] Section 235 imposes a general obligation on such persons to co-operate with the administrator by providing any information about the company which he may reasonably require and by attending on him at such times as he may reasonably require.[98]

13.51 The Act and the Rules specify the content and form of the statement of affairs and the affidavits which are required to be provided in verification of it.[99] The statement of affairs itself must include all the information required by Form 2.9. This includes details of the company's assets, debts and liabilities; and the names and addresses of creditors as well as details of any security that they hold. The same form is used to provide the affidavit of verification.[100] Separate affidavits of concurrence; suitably qualified where the deponent does not agree with those who have verified the statement of affairs or is without direct knowledge, are necessary for concurrence. All affidavits of concurrence are to be delivered to the administrator as are the affidavit of verification and the statement of affairs. In each case the person who swore the affidavit is responsible for this. All the documents are filed in the court by the administrator.[101]

13.52 The administrator's power to give an extension of time or to release someone from their obligations may either be exercised at his own discretion or at the request of the person on whom he has served notice requiring a statement of affairs to be provided.[102] If a release or extension of time is requested but is refused by the administrator, the person who made the request may apply to the court for it to exercise the power to grant an extension or a release.[103] The court must then give at least 7 days' notice to the applicant to attend an *ex parte* hearing after which it may dismiss the application if no sufficient cause is shown for a release or an extension. If

---

96 s 22(3).
97 s 22(4) and (5).
98 s 235(1)(2) and (3).
99 s 22(2) and r 2.12.
100 r 2.12(1).
101 r 2.12(2) to (6).
102 r 2.14(1).
103 s 22(5) and r 2.14(2).

the application is not dismissed at that stage a venue is fixed of which notice is served on the administrator by the applicant together with any evidence to be called by the applicant.[104] The administrator may appear and be heard at the hearing and (whether or not he is heard) may submit a report to the court of matters which he considers should be brought to its attention. A copy of the report must be sent to the applicant at least 5 days before the hearing.[105] The costs of the applicant are to be paid by him in any event and no allowance may be made towards them out of the company's assets unless the court so orders.[106] In contrast to this the reasonable expenses incurred by any person in making the statement of affairs and the affidavit of verification are to be allowed and paid by the administrator out of his receipts.[107] An appeal lies to the court against the administrator's decision on this matter but a dispute over the payment of expenses can never relieve a person of his obligation to prepare, verify and submit a statement of affairs and to provide information to the administrator.[108]

13.53　If the court so orders, on the application of the administrator all or part of the statement of affairs may be excluded from the requirement of filing or filed separately and not open to inspection without the leave of the court. Such an order may include directions to prevent the delivery of all or part of the statement to the registrar of companies and the disclosure of certain information to other persons. The administrator may apply to the court for such orders if he thinks that it would prejudice the conduct of the administration for the whole or part of the statement of affairs to be disclosed.[109] A person who fails without reasonable excuse to comply with his obligations under these provisions is liable to a fine and a daily default fine for continued contravention.[110]

Variation or discharge of order

13.54　Section 18 of the Act empowers an administrator to apply to the court for the discharge or variation of an administration order at any time during its currency. The variation will be to specify an additional purpose.[111] Such an application must be made if it appears to the administrator that the purpose or each of the purposes for which the order was made either have been achieved or are incapable of achievement. He is

---

104　r 2.14(3) and (4).
105　r 2.14(5).
106　r 2.14(7).
107　r 2.15(1).
108　r 2.15(2) and (3).
109　r 2.13.
110　s 22(6).
111　s 18(1).

also obliged to apply if required to do so by a meeting of creditors called for the purpose.[112] On hearing such an application the court may vary or discharge the administration order and make such consequential provisions as it thinks fit. An office copy of an order of variation or discharge must be sent to the registrar of companies by the administrator within 14 days of it being made on penalty of a fine and daily default fine if there is a failure to comply without reasonable excuse.[113]

THE ROLE OF THE ADMINISTRATOR

Appointment

13.55 The appointment of the administrator will always be by court order. An appointment will be made by the administration order itself.[114] In this case the requirements for publicising the order will ensure the dissemination of the identity of the appointee. The court also has power to make an order appointing an administrator if a vacancy in the office occurs by death, resignation or otherwise.[115] An application for an order to fill such a vacancy must be made by the continuing administrator of the company, if one exists. If there is no continuing administrator the application is to be made by the creditors' committee established under s 26 and if no such committee exists the company, the directors or any creditor can apply.[116] An order made on such an application must be advertised and notice must be given of it in the same way as occurs on the making of an administration order.[117] The person appointed as administrator must be a qualified insolvency practitioner.[118] It is an offence for a person to act as the administrator of a company at a time when he is not a qualified insolvency practitioner.[119]

13.56 The Insolvency Act 1986 does not provide for the appointment of an administrator before an administration order is made but it does allow the court to make an *interim* administration order or any other order that it thinks fit[120] on hearing the petition. An *interim* appointment of an administrator could be one of the provisions of an *interim* administration order. It has been held that on an *ex parte* application by a prospective

112 s 18(1).
113 s 18(3) to (5).
114 s 13(1).
115 s 13(2).
116 s 13(3).
117 r 2.55.
118 s 230.
119 s 389.
120 s 9(4).

petitioner before the petition has been filed or served for an order abridging the period for service of the petition there is no power to appoint an *interim* administrator. However, it seems that in such a case the court can appoint a suitable person to manage the affairs, business and property of the company pending the hearing of the administration petition.[121]

The powers of the administrator

13.57 The powers of the administrator reflect his function. They are stipulated in the Insolvency Act 1986, as are his duties. It is proposed to deal with the administrator's statutory powers by looking first of all at those broad and general provisions which illustrate the relationship between the powers of the administrator and his functions. The specific powers which focus on the internal workings of the company and the administration itself and those which allow the creation of relationships between the company and others will then be considered. The paragraphs dealing with the process of administration will illustrate the way in which the powers are likely to be exercised and the genesis of the proposal according to which the whole process will continue.

General powers
13.58 The nature of an administration order is that it directs that the affairs, business and property of the company shall be managed by the administrator while the order is in force.[122] The Act therefore gives the administrator power to:

> "do all such things as may be necessary for the management of the affairs, business and property of the company". (s 14(1)(a))

This broad power is supplemented by a list of specific powers set out in the First Schedule to the Act. However, s 14(1)(b) stipulates that those powers are without prejudice to the generality of the basic power. It would be possible for the court to add to the list of specific powers in the schedule (which apply to both administrators and administrative receivers) on the basis of the power in para 23 of the schedule to do all other things incidental to the listed powers or by use of the wider general power in s 14(1)(a). This provides ample scope for the administrator to carry out his functions.

13.59 His control of the company to which the administration order applies is secured by s 14(4) which provides that any power of the company or its officers conferred by the memorandum or articles of association of the company which could be exercised in such a way as to interfere with the

---

121 *Re a Company (No 00175 of 1987)* [1987] BCLC 467.
122 s 8(2).

exercise of the administrator's powers is exercisable only with the administrator's consent. No managerial powers of the board may be exercised without the consent of the administrator. Nor may any power of the general meeting which is likely to affect the management of the affairs, business or property of the company. It is possible that a residual category of powers, involving the adjustment of the rights of shareholders would be exercisable without consent. However, in any particular case such decisions might well affect matters within the administrator's remit such as the company's capital structure or the chances of reaching agreement with creditors or shareholders. In such cases the administrator's consent would be required.

13.60 The consent of the administrator to the exercise of the powers of others may either be given generally or in relation to particular cases.[123] The way in which an administrator will deal with this will depend on the purpose and nature of the administration. In some cases of corporate rescue and reconstruction the continuation of the company's business may be left in the hands of the board; at least after a new management has been put in place by the administrator. In other cases the administrator or his own employees and agents may take full control of all aspects of the company's operations. Apart from the purpose of the administration and the information available about the company's financial position and history, the size of the company will be an important factor in the decision on this issue.

13.61 The administrator has power to gather in all of the company's property and to take proceedings to that end.[124] He may do all things necessary for the realisation of that property.[125] These powers will not always be exercised if the purpose of the administration is the survival of the company or the approval of a voluntary arrangement or a compromise or arrangement under s 425 of the Companies Act 1985. It will be crucial if the purpose is a more advantageous realisation of assets and may be useful as a means of achieving other purposes if some rationalisation is necessary.

13.62 The powers of the administrator are, however, limited by reference to the purposes for which the order was made. If the order specifies the survival of the company and the advantageous realisation of its assets as the objective, there will be no power for the administrator to distribute the proceeds of sale by means of a binding distribution among creditors or

123 s 14(4).
124 sch 1 para 1.
125 sch 1 para 12.

members without the amendment of the order to allow for the approval of a voluntary arrangement as a purpose.[126] It is always open to the administrator to seek the directions of the court in relation to any matter arising in connection with the carrying out of his functions.[127]

Powers within the company

13.63 In addition to his general control of the company and his ability to limit the exercise by others of powers conferred by the memorandum and articles, the administrator has full control of the composition of the board of the company. He may remove any director and appoint any person to the board whether to fill a vacancy or otherwise.[128] The dismissal of a director may result in a contractual claim against the company, although such a claim will be subject to the moratorium during the course of the administration procedure. In contrast with the United States' Chapter 11 Bankruptcy procedure the control of the company is not left in the hands of its existing management. Equally, the administrator may call meetings of the members and creditors as he thinks fit (see paras 13.118–13.120 below on protection of creditors and paras 13.106–13.117 on the procedure involved in dealing with the administrator's proposal).[129]

13.64 The specific powers which may be used by administrator include the power to carry on the company's business and to set up subsidiaries to which the whole or part of the company's business may be transferred.[130] This facilitates the use of a hivedown to sell the whole or part of the company's business. It also permits the continuation of the whole undertaking while recapitalisation is arranged. Uncalled capital may be called by the administrator, whether or not as part of this process,[131] and he may change the location of the company's registered office.[132]

13.65 Ultimately he is given power to present or defend a winding up petition. The power to defend such a petition is of limited significance since no such petition may remain on the file and no winding up order may be made while the administration order is in existence. After the purpose of the administration order has been carried out the administrator may apply for a winding up order. Any such application must be made by petition; a power exercised by the administrator as agent of the company. Discharge and release of the administrator may be granted on presentation of the

---

126 *Re St Ives Windings Ltd* (1987) 3 BCC.
127 s 145(3).
128 s 14(2)(a).
129 s 14(2)(b).
130 sch 1 paras 14, 15 and 16.
131 sch 1 para 19.
132 sch 1 para 22.

winding up petition and it is possible for the administrator to be appointed as provisional liquidator at that stage.[133]

Powers to deal with third parties

13.66 The control exercised by the administrator over the affairs of the company extends to its dealings with others as well as internal matters. The administrator acts as the agent of the company in exercising his power.[134] He binds it to contracts and creates a relationship between the company and outsiders. However, even if he acts outside his powers there is no need for the other party to rely on concepts of apparent or ostensible authority;

> "a person dealing with the administrator in good faith and for value is not concerned to inquire whether the administrator is acting within his powers."[135]

This will protect contracting parties from any difficulties resulting from the administrator exceeding his own powers. Section 35 of the Companies Act 1985 and the doctrine in *Rolled Steel Products v BSC*[136] may protect them from the consequences of acts which exceed the company's powers, providing in the former case that the transaction decided on by the administrator can be regarded as one decided on by the directors of the company.[137]

13.67 The specific powers of the administrator include those which enable him to deal with others on the company's behalf. He has power to sell or otherwise dispose of company property by public auction or private contract and power to use the company seal, to do any act and execute any document in the company's name.[138] He may draw, endorse, accept and make bills of exchange and promissory notes; borrow and raise money on security; make payments necessary for the performance of his function; insure company property; and grant, accept the surrender of, or take leases of real property.[139] He has full power to litigate on behalf of the company; to refer matters to arbitration; to make arrangements or compromises on its behalf; and to claim in the insolvency of any company or individual indebted to the company.[140] He can employ and dismiss employees and to appoint agents to do things more conveniently done by them or which he is unable to do himself.[141] Solicitors, accountants and other professionally

---

133   sch 1 para 21; but see s 11(1) and (3)(a) and *Re Brooke Marine Ltd* [1988] BCLC 546.
134   s 14(5).
135   s 14(6).
136   [1986] ch 246.
137   s 35 Companies Act 1985 and see ch 1 on the effect of the Companies Bill 1989.
138   sch 1 paras 2, 8 and 9.
139   sch 1 paras 10, 3, 7 and 17 respectively.
140   sch 1 paras 5, 6, 18 and 20.
141   sch 1 para 11.

qualified people may be appointed to assist him in the performance of his functions.[142] This separate power may imply that such professionals may be given greater autonomy than other agents or employees used by the administrator. These specific powers are identical to those conferred on the administrative receiver.

13.68 The particular role of the administrator and the existence of the moratorium during the period of the administration make it necessary for special powers to be conferred on him to deal with charged property or property otherwise encumbered. Section 15 of the Insolvency Act 1986 deals with this matter.

Power to deal with charged property
13.69 In order to assist in carrying out his function it is important that the administrator should be able to dispose of the assets of the company. This implies the need for him to be able to deal with company property subject to some form of security. However, if the order of priority of the security granted by the company over its property could be altered in the course of the administration this would weaken the ability of companies to borrow readily; a matter of great concern to the Cork Committee. Consequently the power given to the administrator by the Insolvency Act 1986 preserves the priority of the holder of the security but makes it attach to different assets. In the case of the holder of a floating charge the administrator is given power to deal with the charged assets without the need to obtain a court order but holders of other forms of security have the additional protection of the requirement that a court order be obtained. This is consistent with the effective veto held by the holder of a floating charge over the making of an administration order in the first place.

13.70 In the case of property subject to security which, as created, was a floating charge, the administrator may exercise any of his powers (including the power of disposal) in relation to the property as if it were not subject to the security.[143] This allows sale, consumption in a manufacturing process, borrowing on the security of the property or any other step in relation to it. However, the holder of the floating charge has the same priority in relation to any property of the company directly or indirectly representing the original property as he would have had in relation to the original property.[144]

13.71 This retention of priority will survive numerous transactions. The

142 sch 1 para 4.
143 s 15(1) and (3).
144 s 15(4).

classic forms of property subject to a floating charge—raw materials, work in progress, stock and receivables—may turn over frequently during the course of administration. On each occasion the property (of whatever kind) which represents the original subject matter of the floating charge will have a security interest attached to it in favour of the holder of the original security. This interest will, presumably, usually be a crystallised floating charge as most such charges will have a clause providing for automatic crystallisation on the making of an administration order.

13.72 Difficult questions will arise where the property originally subject to the floating charge merges with other property not subject to such a charge to create wholly new property. Such difficulties are less likely to arise in this area than in the context of wide retention of title clauses as the breadth of most floating charges will mean that all raw materials, work in progress or other categories of goods owned by the company will be subject to the charge. However, competition between the holder of a floating charge and a supplier who has retained title will be possible although the use of goods subject a retention of title clause will only be possible if the administrator has a court order authorising it.

13.73 The right of the administrator to deal with the property will remain after the floating charge has crystallised as it applies to any charge which was created as a floating charge even if it is now fixed because of crystallisation.[145] The right of the administrator to deal with company property which is subject to other forms of security is limited to a disposal of the property. This is dependent on his success in applying for a court order.[146] Such an order may be obtained in relation to property subject to any form of security other than a floating charge. The security may be over any type of property. Security means 'any mortgage, charge, lien or other security'.[147] It is clear that the expression includes securities granted by agreement of the parties and those, such as liens, created by operation of law. In addition to property owned by the company and subject to a security interest, the possibility of an order authorising the administrator to dispose of property exists for goods owned by another person but in the possession of the company under a hire purchase agreement, a chattel leasing agreement, a conditional sale agreement or a retention of title agreement.[148]

13.74 On application to the court for an order under s 15(2), the court will

---

145 s 15(3).
146 s 15(2) and (3).
147 s 248(b).
148 See paras 13.36–13.40 above on the scope of these expressions.

fix a venue and the administrator must give notice of this forthwith to the holder of the security or the owner of the goods.[149] The application must be made in the form of an originating application under Rules 7.1 to 7.10. On such an application the court must be satisfied that the disposal of the property or the goods whether with or without other assets would be likely to promote the purpose, or one or more of the purposes, set out in the administration order.[150] For example, an order might be obtained to authorise the sale of buildings and land subject to a mortgage as part of a disposal of the business which uses them. The purpose of corporate rescue, the agreement of a compromise or voluntary arrangement or the better realisation of the company's assets may justify the application for an order and only those purposes set out in the administration order can be used.

13.75   The court's discretion whether to authorise a sale under s 15(2) will be exercised by balancing any prejudice to the secured creditor against the interests of those favouring the administration scheme. During this process it will be borne in mind that the purpose of s 15(5) is to protect the rights of the secured creditor to the maximum extent practicable. The balancing process will include consideration of whether the amount likely to be available from the sale of the company's other assets or otherwise by carrying out the purpose of the administration order will be sufficient to prevent prejudice to the secured creditor when applied in accordance with s 15. Any dispute between the valuations placed on the property in question by those advising the parties will be relevant although that is not the only ground on which an order can be made.[151]

13.76   An order under s 15(2) will rarely be made where it will deprive a creditors' meeting, under s 23, of any useful purpose by pre-empting the consideration of the administrator's proposal to sell assets of the company since the aim of the legislation is to give the creditors influence before the decision is made.[152]

13.77   Where an order is made it will authorise the administrator to dispose of the property as if it were not subject to the security or the goods as if the rights of the owner were all vested in the administrator.[153] The sale, mortgage or other disposal of the goods can go ahead and the purchaser, lender or other third party need not be concerned with any claim of the creditor who holds the security interest or, in the case of goods not owned

149   r 2.51(2).
150   s 15(2).
151   *Re ARV Aviation Ltd* (1988) 4 BCC 708.
152   *Re Consumer and Industrial Press Ltd (No 2)* (1988) 4 BCC 72.
153   s 15(2).

by the company, the rights of the owner. However, all orders made under s 15(2) must be subject to a condition which is clearly intended to preserve the position of the person with the security interest or ownership rights. The condition is that the net proceeds of sale be applied towards the discharge of the amount secured by the security or due under the agreement between the owner of the goods and the company.

13.78 On making the order the court will determine a sum which it regards as the net amount which would be realised by the sale of the assets in question on the open market by a willing vendor. While it is desirable for a proper valuation of the asset to be in evidence when the court is deciding how to exercise its discretion, it is possible for the court to engage in a two stage process by making the order under s 15(2) and then ordering an inquiry to fix the sum necessary to make up the deficiency between the net proceeds of sale and the open market value of the property.[154] An amount equal to that deficiency must be provided by the administrator towards discharging the amount secured or due under the agreement with the owner of the goods.[155] It is clear that the amount handed over to the creditor who held the security interest or the ownership rights in the property disposed of will be the market value of the property after the deduction of the expenses of the sale. The order will ensure that if a lower price is fetched by the administrator's disposal, the balance will be handed over from company assets. These amounts will be applied to different securities over the same property in the order of priority applicable under the general law.[156] In s 15(5) 'the sums secured by the security' include capital, interest and all the costs of the secured creditor added either under the general law or by virtue of a provision of the instrument.[157]

13.79 The administrator is required to send an office copy of an order made under this section to the registrar of companies within 14 days of it being made on penalty of a fine if he fails to do so without reasonable excuse.[158] A copy notice of the order must also be given forthwith to the owner of the goods or the holder of the security.[159]

13.80 The power conferred on the administrator by s 15 will be of limited use where company property is subject to a security other than a floating charge or is owned by another person but is in the company's possession

154   *Re ARV Aviation* (n 151 *supra*).
155   s 15(5).
156   s 15(6) and see ch 8 above on priorities.
157   *Re ARV Aviation* (n 151*supra*).
158   s 15(7).
159   r 2.51(3).

under one of the agreements covered by the section. He is required to dispose of the asset for its full market value and use that amount to pay off the creditor in question. Alternatively, he may sell the asset for less and find the balance out of other assets of the company. In each case the freedom to dispose of assets is not likely to be useful as a source of cash unless the amount secured on property is less than the amount of its market value. This position is an inevitable consequence of the policy of fully protecting the security of those with a fixed charge or ownership rights. In the case of property subject to a floating charge, the power to deal with the property is more extensive and the result of the section is that the security interest effectively continues to float for the duration of the administration; although in law the floating charge may well have crystallised. This is a rather more useful power.

13.81 In the case of the disposal of assets subject to a floating charge, there is a possibility that the value of the property which is subject to the security will decline as the assets are transmuted in the course of the administration. The principles which would determine the possible liability of the administrator to the creditor for such a loss would be those developed under the common law in the field of negligence. A duty of care is likely to exist but the standard of care should be such that an administrator acting competently in pursuit of the purposes set out in the administration order could not be held liable. In the case of assets dealt with under s 15(2) the fallback figure determined by the court as the market value of the assets will protect an administrator who sells for at least that amount. If the sale is at a lower figure the loss will fall on the company unless it has insufficient assets to comply with the condition laid down by the court for the full payment of the creditor whose rights were abrogated by the order. No claim by the company against the administrator would be likely to succeed if he could show that the decision to sell at the lower price was made competently in pursuit of the purposes of the administration. Since the Act clearly contemplates sale at less than market value that fact in itself could hardly amount to a breach of the duty of care and skill. It could amount to a breach of fiduciary duty if there were a conflict of interest and duty on the part of the administrator. A claim by a creditor on the basis that the company had insufficient assets to make up the proceeds of sale to the market value of the asset sold would appear to have a much stronger chance of success on the basis of a breach of duty by the administrator. The amount and the accuracy of the information provided to the court before the order was made would be relevant in determining whether there had been such a breach of duty as an administrator who had been frank with the court before the order was made and who sold within a reasonable time after the date of the order could hardly be held to be in breach of duty.

13.82 An application by a creditor or a member under s 27 on the basis of unfair prejudice is possible despite the fact that a court order was made under s 15.[160] A disposal in accordance with a s 15 order may be held to give rise to unfair prejudice to the interests of members or creditors.[161]

The duties of the administrator

13.83 The functions to be performed by the administrator are such that the duties of a fiduciary will be imposed on him. He will be under an obligation to avoid any conflict between his interest and his duty and in this respect is in a similar position to the liquidator and the administrative receiver. There must be no question of financial or other self interest affecting his behaviour or decision making. Such duties arise because they apply to the directors of the company whom he supersedes; or if they remain in office, controls. He shares a role which combines the function of trustee with that of agent. The consequence of this is that he owes the duty of a fiduciary. The detailed obligations stemming from this are dealt with in paras 15.58–15.75 (on liquidators). Like the liquidator, the administrator will owe his duty to the company as he has no direct relationship with creditors or members. He will be liable for breaches of his statutory duty if he performs those duties dishonestly, in bad faith, or, possibly, negligently. If the purpose of the administration is corporate rescue the administrator will be running the business of the company and should therefore be in the position of a company director for the purpose of protection against liability for losses caused by taking legitimate commercial risks. In this sense his position can be distinguished from that of a trustee.

13.84 On the other hand, in carrying out the function of calling the necessary meetings to receive his proposals, of ensuring that the priority of the holders of charges over property with which he deals is protected in accordance with the statute, and in the exercise of his other specific statutory functions he should be regarded as being in the same position as a liquidator. Like the liquidator he is an officer of the court to whom the rule in *Re James*[162] should apply. His role as agent is clear from s 14(5). He will owe the duties of an agent to the company as his principal when he exercises his powers.

13.85 Many of the specific statutory duties of the administrator will be dealt with in the section on the process of administration. However, certain of those matters call for attention here. Section 17(1) lays down that on his

---

160 s 27(5).
161 See paras 13.129–13.131 below.
162 (1874) 9 Ch App 609.

appointment the administrator shall take into his custody or under his control all the property to which the company is or appears to be entitled. This reflects the obligation imposed on the liquidator by s 144(1). This of course gives him full power to take control but it is also a duty. If loss results from a failure of the administrator to comply with his duty in this respect then he will be liable at the suit of the company.

13.86   The other major general duty of the administrator is to use his power to manage the affairs, business and property of the company in accordance with the court's directions during the period between the making of the order and the approval of his proposals for the administration under s 24.[163] After proposals have been approved he must act in accordance with the proposals as revised from time to time.[164] The duty imposed on him, like many of his powers, is designed to ensure that he works towards the objective set for the administration by the purposes laid down in the order and, more specifically, in approved proposals. Unless an act of the administrator could be shown to be directly contrary to a specific stipulation of the proposal or of the court in its directions, the requirement is that the administrator can justify his activities and decisions by reference to those criteria. This is unlikely to prove to be a major constraint as the proposals drawn up and approved by the use of the statutory procedure are likely to be broad and strategic in their content and the directions of the court will usually add little to the purposes set out in the order unless the administrator has gone to the court to seek more detailed guidance.

13.87   In order to ensure a degree of control by creditors over the process of administration, the administrator is required by s 17(3) to call meetings of creditors when requested to do so by one tenth in value of the creditors, or directed to do so by the court. The rules governing such meetings are dealt with in paras 13.107–13.117 below.

13.88   The administrator is required by the Insolvency Rules 1986 to submit to each member of the creditor's committee and to the registrar of companies, accounts in the form of an abstract of receipts and payments covering each 6 month period of the administration and any remaining period before he ceases to act.[165] The accounts must be submitted within 2 months of the end of each 6 month period or of the date he ceases to act unless the court grants an extension on the application of the administrator.[166] Default gives rise to a fine.[167]

---

163   s 17(2)(a).
164   s 17(2)(b).
165   r 2.52(1) and (3).
166   r 2.52(2).
167   r 2.52(4).

Vacation of office by the administrator

13.89 The court has power to remove the administrator at any time.[168] He must also vacate office if he ceases to be qualified to act as an insolvency practitioner in relation to the company or if the administration order is discharged.[169] Resignation is permitted on the same conditions as apply to administrative receivers. Notice must be given on the grounds of ill health or because he intends to cease being in practice as an insolvency practitioner. If neither of these grounds applies the resignation must be based on the existence of some conflict of interest or change of personal circumstances which makes the further discharge by him of the duties of an administrator impractical or precludes it altogether.[170] However, it is possible for the administrator to obtain the leave of the court to resign on other grounds.[171] At least 7 days' notice must be given of the administrator's intention to resign or to apply to the court for leave to do so. Such notice must be given to any continuing administrator, or if there is none, the creditor's committee. If there is no such administrator and no creditor's committee, notice must be given to the company and to its creditors.[172] Notice of the death of an administrator may be given to the court by a partner in his firm or any other person who produces a death certificate. Failing this it must be given by his personal representatives.[173] A court order filling a vacancy in the office of administrator is subject to the same rules as regards giving notice and advertising as apply in the case of the original appointment on the making of the administration order.[174]

13.90 At any time when a person ceases to be an administrator—regardless of the reason for him vacating office—his remuneration and expenses are charged on and paid out of any property of the company in his custody or under his control at that time, in priority to any security which, as created, was a floating charge and to which s 15(1) then applies.[175] The priority accorded to the remuneration and expenses of the administrator will make the whole process unattractive to the holders of floating charges. It also follows the pattern of maintaining the priority accorded to the holders of fixed charges.

13.91 Amounts payable in respect of debts or liabilities incurred during the course of the administration process under contracts entered into by the administrator or contracts of employment adopted by him in carrying out

168 s 19(1).
169 s 19(2).
170 s 19(1) and r 2.53(1).
171 r 2.53(2).
172 r 2.53(3).
173 r 2.54.
174 r 2.55.
175 s 19(4).

the function of administrator are charged on and payable out of the property in the custody or under the control of the administrator at the time at which he vacated office, in priority to the administrator's remuneration and expenses.[176] This applies to contracts entered into or adopted by the administrator or his predecessor providing the creation or adoption of the contract occurred in the carrying out of the functions of the administrator. This gives the administrator power to create charges or other liabilities (including those which are unsecured) in priority to pre-existing floating charges over company property as s 19(5) gives the debts and liabilities which he creates priority over his remuneration and expenses which in turn have priority over any floating charge which affected the property in his hands at the end of the administration.

13.92   In common with the administrative receiver, the administrator may 'adopt' contracts of employment which originally exist between an employee and the company. The Act specifies that nothing done or omitted to be done by the administrator in the first 14 days after his appointment is to be regarded as causing him to adopt a contract of employment.[177] It is possible for the administrator to terminate employment contracts as agent for the company during the first 14 days of the administration without giving the remuneration of those employees priority as a liability of the administration process. If he continues the contract after the 14 days, amounts due to the employees for the period of the administration gain priority over claims whcih existed before the order was made and over floating charges as against the property under the control of the administrator at the end of the administration. This justifies the fact that in the event of a later liquidation of the company the 'relevant date' for the purpose of preferential debts is the date of the making of the administration order.[178] Wages and other claims under employment contracts which accrue during the administration are given priority as claims on property held by the administrator at the end of that process. The concept of adopting a contract means that the administrator is given some time to decide whether to act (or omit to act) in a way which indicates an intention to continue the contractual relationship between employee and company during the administration.

Release of the administrator

13.93   The effect of the release of the former administrator is that from the time of being given his release he is discharged from all liability for his acts

176   s 19(5).
177   *Ibid.*
178   s 387(3)(a).

and omissions in the administration and otherwise in relation to his conduct as an administrator.[179] Liability under s 212 should a misfeasance summons be issued will, however, remain.[180] If an administrator dies release is obtained from the time at which notice of the death is given to the court. In any other case (including resignation) the court will determine the time of release and may postpone it if, for example, it is necessary to consider allegations that the administrator may have spent time and money pursuing purposes not specified in the order.[181]

Remuneration of the administrator

13.94   Like a liquidator, an administrator can be remunerated on the basis of a percentage of the value of the property with which he has to deal or of the time properly given by him and his staff in attending to matters arising out of the administration.[182] The rules set out his entitlement to receive remuneration[183] and give the creditors' committee power to decide the basis on which he will be remunerated and the percentage to be fixed if that basis is chosen.[184] In making that decision they are to have regard to the complexity of the case; any exceptional degree or kind of responsibility; his effectiveness in carrying out his duties and the value and nature of the property with which he has to deal.[185]

13.95   If no creditors' committee exists or one which does exist fails to make a decision, the meeting of creditors may fix the remuneration by resolution having regard to the same factors.[186] Failing this the court will fix the remuneration on application by the administrator.[187] If an administrator is dissatisfied with the remuneration fixed by the creditors' committee, he may request the creditors' meeting to increase the amount by resolution.[188] Joint administrators are to decide the apportionment of remuneration between them by agreement. If they fail to do so the creditors' committee or creditors' meeting may resolve their dispute by resolution or the court may resolve it by order if they refer it to one of those bodies.[189]

13.96   Profit costs for acting in the administration can only be paid to the

179   s 20(2).
180   s 20(3).
181   s 20(1) and *Re Sheridan Securities Ltd* (1988) 4 BCC 200.
182   r 2.47(2).
183   r 2.47(1).
184   r 2.47(3).
185   r 2.47(4).
186   r 2.47(5).
187   r 2.47(6).
188   r 2.48.
189   rr 2.47(7) and 4.128(2).

firm or partner of a solicitor administrator with the authorisation of the creditors' committee, the creditors' meeting or the court.[190]

13.97 If the administrator is dissatisfied with the amount of remuneration fixed by the creditors' committee or the creditors' meeting, he may apply to the court for an increase.[191] He must give 14 days' notice to the members of the creditors' committee or, if none exists, to such creditors as the court may direct. The creditors or the committee as the case may be may then nominate one or more of their number to appear or be represented and be heard at the hearing.[192] The costs of the application may be paid as expenses of the administration if the court so directs.[193]

13.98 Creditors representing at least 25% in value of the creditors may apply to the court for a reduction in the administrator's remuneration if they regard it as excessive.[194] Such an application may be dismissed at an *ex parte* hearing of which 7 days' notice was given to the applicants. If it is not dismissed in this way, a venue will be fixed of which the applicant must give notice to the administrator together with the application and any evidence in support of it.[195] The court may then reduce the administrator's remuneration but the costs of the applicant will not be paid as an expense of the administration unless the court so orders.[196] The administrator's remuneration and expenses are a charge on the assets of the company after he leaves office and those assets remain so charged in the hands of the official receiver.[197] They constitute a pre-preferential debt.[198]

THE ADMINISTRATOR'S PROPOSALS

13.99 It has already been noted that the administrator is under a duty to deal with the affairs of the company in accordance with court directions pending the approval of his proposals for achieving the purposes set out in the order. Those proposals represent a crucial part of the administration process. They amount to a business plan for the realisation of the objectives set for the whole administration process when the order was made. They are likely to build on the independent report drawn up before the order was made, if one exists. In the period after the making of the order the administrator's control over the company's management and the access he

---

190   rr 2.47(7) and 4.128(3).
191   r 2.49(1).
192   r 2.49(2) and (3).
193   r 2.49(4).
194   r 2.50(1).
195   r 2.50(2) and (3).
196   r 2.50(4) and (5).
197   *Re Sheridan Securities Ltd* (1988) 4 BCC 200.
198   *Re Brooke Marine Ltd* [1988] BCLC 546.

has had to information about its past performance present position and future prospects will have enabled him to prepare a strategy for the achievement of the purpose which the order is intended to promote. He may also have been able to raise additional finance to assist in this process on the basis of his plans. The first 3 months after the order was made may be used to develop proposals but the urgency of the situation of the insolvent company is likely to require speedy action.

13.100   Although the moratorium protects the company from litigation or the enforcement of debts, the continuation of the business will require continuing finance and the company's public difficulties may affect cash flow and business with suppliers or customers. The willingness of the company's bankers to provide overdraft facilities may be crucial; although as the bank will frequently hold a floating charge it may have agreed to the administration process in the first place.

13.101   The Act lays down substantial guidance on the procedures to be followed for the approval or modification of the proposals once they are produced. This role is conferred on the creditors as a body who may approve, modify or reject the proposals brought forward by the administrator. Consultation with the major creditors by value will presumably ensure that the proposals to be put to the creditors are acceptable to them but the Act and the Rules lay down a system for dealing with the proposals which can result in their acceptance as drawn, their modification or their rejection. The results of this process are reported to the court but it will only intervene if the proposals have been rejected by the creditors or if a minority of creditors object to the proposals or the way in which the administration has been carried out. The scheme of the Act is to put the creditors in control of the strategic planning of the administration process while leaving the administrator with day to day control.

13.102   The court will seek to avoid any action which reduces the role of the creditors' meeting in the decision making process under the administration order.[199] Behaviour by the administrator which denies the creditors their right to consider his proposal may be grounds for an action by creditors under s 27 on the basis that they have been unfairly prejudiced by the actions of the administrator.[200]

Presenting the proposal

13.103   The administrator is required to produce a statement of his proposals for achieving the purpose or purposes set out in the administra-

---

199   *Re Commercial and Industrial Press Ltd (No 2)* (1988) 4 BCC 72.
200   *Re Charnley Davies* [1988] BCLC 243.

tion order within 3 months of the order being made, or such longer time as the court may allow.[201] The proposals must have annexed to them a statement by the administrator showing:

(a) details of the appointment of the administrator and of the purposes for which the administration order was made and any subsequent variation of those purposes;

(b) details of the directors and secretary of the company;

(c) an account of the circumstances leading to the application for an administration order;

(d) Either

    (i) a copy or summary of the statement of affairs submitted to the administrator with his comments on it or

    (ii) if none has been submitted details of the financial position of the company at the most recent practicable date, which must be no later than the date of the administration order unless the court orders that a later date be taken

(e) the way the company's affairs have been managed so far during the administration and the way they will be managed and the means of finance to be used for the business if the proposals are approved;

(f) any other information that the administrator considers necessary to assist the creditors in voting on whether to adopt the proposals.

If the administrator decides to apply to the court for the discharge of the administration order under s 18 before the s 23 meeting he must send full details of his proposals at least 10 days before making the application.[202]

13.104 Section 23(1)(a) lays down that the administrator must send copies of the statement of his proposals to the registrar of companies and (insofar as he knows their addresses) to all the company's creditors. He is also required to lay the document before a meeting of creditors summoned for the purpose with at least 14 days notice.[203] Rule 2.16 only provides that the full statement of information set out above must be sent to the registrar and laid before the meeting but it is desirable to send it to individual creditors together with the proposals themselves. There is also a requirement that the members of the company be notified of the proposals; again the rules do not insist that they are sent the annexed statement. That notification may either be by sending a copy of the proposals to all the members insofar as the administrator is aware of their addresses or by publication of a notice in the Gazette and in the newspaper in which the administration order was advertised. The notice must inform the members of an address from which they can obtain copies of the statement of the proposals free of charge.[204] Failure by the administrator to comply with the notification requirement of s 23 without reasonable excuse will result in a fine.[205]

13.105 There is no obligation on an administrator to call a meeting of the members of the company to receive his proposals but he has power to call members' meetings at any time under s 14(2)(b). Such meetings are to be called and conducted in accordance with Rule 2.31. The venue must be fixed with regard to the convenience of the members and the meeting will be chaired by the administrator or someone nominated by him in writing. Such a nominee must either be a qualified insolvency practitioner or an employee of the administrator or his firm who is experienced in insolvency matters. If no-one is present to chair the meeting it is adjourned to the same time and place one week later, or on the first business day after that if that is not a business day. Subject to these provisions the meeting is summoned and conducted as if it were a company general meeting and the company articles of association and the Companies Act 1985 apply accordingly.

CONSIDERATION OF THE PROPOSALS

13.106 The decision whether to adopt, reject or modify the proposals of the administrator is taken by the creditors meeting called under s 23. The rules on the conduct of creditors' meetings generally are dealt with here—in addition to those applicable only to meetings called under s 23. The rules governing the creditors' committee and the right of groups of creditors to requisition meetings or to go to the court for relief are dealt with in paras 13.118–13.131 below.

13.107 A creditors' meeting called under s 23 must be convened by notice being given to all the creditors of the company who are identified in the statement of affairs or are known to the administrator. They must have had claims against the company at the date of the administration order.[206] Notice must also be given to past or present officers of the company whom the administrator requires to be present at the meeting.[207] In addition, the notice of the meeting must be advertised in the newspaper in which the administration order was advertised.[208] The general rules governing the

204 s 23(2)(b) and r 2.17.
205 s 23(3).
206 r 2.18(1).
207 r 2.18(3).
208 r 2.18(2).

calling and conduct of creditors' meetings apply to the s 23 meeting as well as those called by the administrator by the use of his general power under s 14(2)(b) to approve revisions to the proposals already adopted and meetings requisitioned by creditors under s 17(3).

13.108 In fixing the venue of the meeting the administrator must have regard to the convenience of the creditors and the time of the beginning of the meeting must be between 10 am and 4 pm on a business day unless the court directs otherwise.[209] Twenty one days' notice must be given of any meeting other than one called under s 23(1) or 25(2) (in those cases only 14 days' notice is required by the Act) to all creditors known to the administrator with claims against the company at the date of the order. The notice must set out the purpose of the meeting and the rules for giving notice of claims for voting purposes and for lodging proxies.[210] Form 2.11 should be used for the notice of the meeting and proxy forms (Form 8.2) should be sent out with it.[211] Where the administrator has called the meeting he should act as chairman. However, he may nominate an employee of his or of his firm who is experienced in insolvency matters or another qualified insolvency practitioner to act in his place. The nomination must be in writing.[212] If no-one is present who can act as chaiman within 30 minutes of the time fixed for the meeting to start, the meeting stands adjourned until the same time and place the following week or the first business day thereafter if that is not a business day.[213] The chairman has power to adjourn a creditors' meeting for not more than 14 days from the date for which it was fixed and, in the case of a meeting called under s 23 at which there is not a sufficient majority to approve the administrator's proposals, he must do so if a resolution is passed to that effect.[214]

13.109 Rule 2.22(1) lays down the conditions to be satisfied by a creditor to be able to vote at a creditors' meeting. He must have given the administrator details in writing of the debt, which he claims is due to him from the company, not later than 12 pm on the last business day before that day of the meeting. If a proxy is to be used it must have been lodged with the administrator. The chairman of the meeting may allow a creditor to vote despite a failure to give written details of the debt in time if he is satisfied that the failure was the result of circumstances beyond the creditor's control.[215] The administrator or the chairman may call for documentary or

---

209   r 2.19(2) and (3).
210   r 2.19(4) as amended by SI 1987 No 1919.
211   r 2.19(5).
212   r 2.20.
213   r 2.19(6).
214   rr 2.19(7) and 2.18(4).
215   r 2.22(2).

other evidence to substantiate the creditor's claim. Voting rights are calculated on the basis of the amount outstanding at the date of the meeting. This is ascertained by taking the amount due at the date of the administration order and deducting any sums paid in respect of that debt after that date.[216] Creditors are not generally entitled to vote in respect of unliquidated or unascertained debts but the chairman may agree an estimated minimum value for the purpose of voting and admit the claim for that purpose.[217]

13.110   The chairman has a general power to admit or reject the claims of creditors at the meeting for the purpose of determining voting rights. The power may be exercised with respect to the whole or any part of a claim.[218] A creditor is entitled to appeal to the court against such a decision and the court may reverse or vary the chairman's decision; calling another meeting or making such other order as it thinks just.[219] The threat of the result of a meeting being invalidated on an application to the court can be avoided if the chairman uses the power conferred on him by Rule 2.23(3) to allow the creditor to vote, to mark the claim as objected and to make the vote subject to being declared invalid if the objection is subsequently sustained. Where an appeal to the court is made in respect of a chairman's decision in a s 23 meeting it must be made not later than 28 days after the delivery of the administrator's report on the meeting under s 24(4). In no case can the administrator or other person nominated to chair the creditors' meeting be made personally liable for the costs of an appeal unless the court makes an order to that effect.[220]

13.111   Creditors with some form of security are required by the rules to deduct the value of that security from the amount of the claim in order to determine the value to be attached to their votes. Rule 2.24 applies this requirement to those with security in the usual sense of the word; 'a mortgage charge, lien or other security' in the words of s 248(b) of the Insolvency Act 1986. Rule 2.25 applies the same rule to the holders of bills of exchange and promissory notes where the debt of the company is either on the bill or note or secured by it. The creditor in this position must treat the liability of every person who is liable on it antecedently to the company, and who is not bankrupt or (in the case of the company) in liquidation, as security; the value of which is deducted from the amount of the claim for voting purposes. The unpaid seller of goods to the company under a

216   r 2.22(3) and (4).
217   r 2.22(5).
218   r 2.23(1).
219   r 2.23(2) and (4).
220   r 2.23(6).

retention of title agreement must similarly value his rights under the agreement in respect of goods in the custody of the company and deduct that amount from the amount of his claim for voting purposes.[221] The owner of goods hired to the company under a hire purchase agreement or a chattel leasing agreement or the seller of goods to the company under a conditional sale agreement can claim the amount due on the agreement but must exclude in the calculation of that amount any sums due because of the exercise by the owner or the seller of a right which became exercisable solely as a result of the presentation of the administration petition or the making of the order or any matter arising in consequence of the petition.[222] This prevents the debt claimed from including amounts due because of the termination of the agreement under a clause allowing the owner or seller to terminate it on the presentation of an administration petition or the making of an order on it. A right which arose because instalments or rental had not been paid by the company in the period before the presentation of the petition would not be covered by the rule as it would not have become exercisable solely because of the petition or the order.

13.112 A resolution will be passed if a majority, by value of those present and voting in person or by proxy, votes in favour of it, unless more than half in value of the creditors to whom notice was sent and who are not persons connected with the company vote against it, in which case it is invalid.[223] The chairman is responsible for ensuring that minutes are kept of the meeting in the company's minute book. The minutes must include a list of creditors attending by proxy or in person and the names and addresses of those elected to any creditors' committee established at the meeting.[224]

13.113 The meeting convened under s 23 to consider the administrator's proposal may approve it or reject it.[225] If it is proposed that the proposal be modified the administrator's consent is required to each modification.[226] This ensures that the administrator, who will have to carry out the proposal, has a veto on its contents. It would clearly be unsatisfactory for him to have thrust upon him a plan which he regarded as impracticable. Thus the control of the creditors over the administration process is limited by the requirement that the administrator consents to modifications to his proposals. It is possible for the administrator as chairman to adjourn the creditors' meeting for up to 14 days to give himself time to consider the modifications before deciding whether to accept them. He is also obliged to

221   r 2.26.
222   r 2.27(2).
223   r 2.28(1) and (1A) as amended by SI 1987 No 1919.
224   r 2.28(2) and (3).
225   s 24(1).
226   s 24(2).

grant an adjournment of the meeting if the creditors resolve in favour of that course of action and there is no majority in favour of the proposal with any modifications agreed by the administrator.[227]

13.114 The outcome of the meeting must be reported to the court by the administrator and reports must also be sent to the registrar of companies and to all the creditors who received notice of the meeting; and any others of whom the administrator has since become aware.[228] Further progress reports must be sent to all creditors by the administrator every 6 months after the approval of his proposals. A report must be sent when the administrator vacates office unless he leaves office because of removal by the court or on ceasing to be qualified to act as an insolvency practitioner. No report is necessary if the administration is immediately followed by the company going into liquidation. The first report must contain details of the proposals considered by the meeting and of any modifications proposed.[229] If the meeting rejected the administrator's proposals, the court may order either that the administration order be discharged and make consequential provisions, or make any order it thinks fit; including a conditional or unconditional adjournment or an interim order.[230] If the order is discharged the administrator must send an office copy of the order to the registrar of companies within 14 days.[231] If the administrator's proposal is approved with or without modifications he must continue the administration in accordance with it and the court will take no action on the basis of the report of the meeting unless it receives an application and gives directions.

13.115 If the administrator wishes substantially to revise the proposals agreed at a later date he must call a creditors' meeting by serving the notice required by Rule 2.19 together with a statement of the proposed revisions in form.[232] The members of the company are entitled to a copy of the statement either directly or by advertisement in the same way as they are entitled to notice of the original proposal.[233] As with the original proposal, revisions may be approved or rejected by the creditors' meeting but modifications can only be accepted with the consent of the administrator.[234] Notice of the result of the meeting is sent to the registrar of companies and to creditors by the administrator in the same way as

---

227   rr 2.19(7) and 2.18(4).
228   s 24(4) and r 2.30(1).
229   r 2.29 as amended by SI 1987 No 1919.
230   s 24(5).
231   s 24(6).
232   s 25(2).
233   s 25(3) and r 2.17.
234   s 25(4).

notice of the result of the meeting which considered the original proposals.[235] Voting and other aspects of the conduct of the meeting are governed by the same rules as the original meeting.

13.116 Some leeway is left to the administrator as to which revisions of the agreed proposal need to be referred to a further creditors' meeting. Revisions must not be made without the agreement of the meeting once they have been proposed by the administrator but he is only obliged to follow the procedure where he proposes to make revisions which appear to him to be substantial.[236] That statutory wording will prevent the courts from readily intervening to challenge his view as to what is substantial. They are likely to adopt a test of whether a reasonable administrator in the position of the present administrator could have considered the revisions to be substantial. There will be a duty to consider the matter in good faith but providing that is done the court will not wish to interfere readily in the discretion conferred on the administrator.

13.117 Once the original proposal has been aproved the courts will be reluctant to allow any variation without the use of the s 25 procedure. In particular a provision in the proposal allowing an orderly realisation of assets not required for the continuation of the business will not be construed as analogous to a residual legacy in a will to permit a substantial deviation from the scheme agreed, even if the realisation of that scheme has become impractical. However, if it is not commercially realistic to wait for the period necessary to call a s 25 meeting the court can use its power under s 14(3) to give directions to permit the substitution of a new scheme approved by the creditors' committee.[237]

CREDITOR PROTECTION

13.118 The control exercised by creditors over the process of administration has already been noted. The creditors' meeting has a hand in determining the strategy of the administrator by approving, rejecting or modifying the proposals of the administrator. However, three forms of continuing control or influence are available to creditors in an administration in addition to the initial creditors' meeting. The obligation of the administrator to provide regular reports on his conduct of the administration to the creditors has already been noted. Such information may form the basis of action by creditors in calling special creditors' meetings. or

---

235   s 25(6) and rr 2.29 and 2.30.
236   s 25(1) and (2).
237   *Re Smallman Construction Ltd* (1988) 4 BCC 785.

applying to the court under the provisions outlined here. It is also possible for creditors to decide at an early stage to appoint a creditors' committee to oversee the process of administration.

Requisitioning meetings

13.119 An administrator is obliged to summon a creditors' meeting if he is requested to do so by one tenth in value of the company's creditors.[238] The request must be made in accordance with the rules. It must be accompanied by a list of the creditors concurring in the request, written confirmation of each creditor's concurrence and a statement of the purpose of the proposed meeting, unless a single requisitioning creditor alone has a debt of one tenth in value of the total of the company's debts, in which case none of these requirements applies.[239] On receiving a request which he considers to be properly made out, the administrator must summon a meeting of all creditors by at least 21 days' notice to take place not more than 35 days after he received the request.[240] A deposit sufficient to secure the expenses of summoning and holding the meeting must be provided by the requisitionists before the administrator is allowed to act.[241] However, the meeting may resolve that those expenses are to be payable out of the assets of the company as an expense of the administration.[242] If this is not done the expenses must be met by those who requisitioned the meeting and will be taken out of the amount deposited, with any surplus being returned to the depositor.[243]

13.120 The meeting does not have the power to reject or modify the proposal which was agreed at the s 23 meeting. However, it provides an opportunity for the views of the creditors to be brought to the attention of the administrator and for the creditors to seek information and explanations from him. Any action to control the behaviour of the administrator against his wishes or to remove him will require a court order. However, the threat of such action will lie in the background and may cause the administrator to give some weight to the views of the majority of creditors as expressed in a resolution of a requisitioned creditors' meeting.

The creditors' committee

13.121 Such a committee can only be set up at the meeting called under s 23 to consider the administrator's proposals. The meeting may establish a

---

238 s 17(3)(a).
239 r 2.21(1).
240 r 2.21(2).
241 r 2.21(4).
242 r 2.21(5).
243 r 2.21(3) and (6).

creditors' committee only after it has approved the proposal (either with or without modifications).[244] The function of the committee is:

'to assist the administrator in carrying out his functions and act in relation to him in such manner as may be agreed from time to time".[245]

However, the committee may, on giving at least 7 days notice, require the administrator to attend before it at some reasonable time and provide it with such information relating to the carrying out of his functions as it may reasonably require.[246] The committee has the function of assisting in the process of administration and may, at the end of the day, only make recommendations or reach agreement with the administrator about the progress of the administration process. However, it represents a forum for discussion between creditors and administrators and, with its statutory power to demand the attendance of the administrator and the provision of facts, a major source of information for creditors about the administration. The largest creditors of the company are likely to be the ones represented on the committee and in practice it will be important for the administrator to retain their confidence during the administration process. The committee has no role in the compilation or approval of the administrator's proposal. It oversees the execution of the strategy contained in that document and endorsed by the s 23 creditors' meeting which sets up the committee.

13.122   The committee must consist of not less than 3 or more than 5 creditors of the company. Its members are elected at the s 23 meeting from those whose claims have not been rejected for the purpose of entitlement to vote at that meeting.[247] A body corporate may be a member but will always act through a representative.[248] The committee cannot act and does not come into existence until the administrator issues a certificate of its due constitution. This will be done when at least 3 of the eligible creditors elected at the s 23 meeting have agreed to act.[249] The certificate and any amended certificate or report showing changes in the committee's membership must be filed with the court.[250]

13.123   The first meeting of the committee must be called within 3 months of its establishment and thereafter within 21 days of a request by a member of the committee or on dates fixed by resolutions or earlier committee meetings.[251] Subject to those rules, the administrator has power to decide where and when the committee meets.[252] Seven days' notice of a meeting

244   s 26(1).
245   r 2.34(1).
246   s 26(2).
247   r 2.32(1) and (2).
248   r 2.32(3).
249   r 2.33(1) and (2).
250   r 2.33(3), (4) and (5).
251   r 2.34(3).
252   r 2.34(2).

must be given by the administrator to each committee member or his designated representative unless a member has waived that requirement either at or before the meeting.[253] Meetings are chaired by the administrator or a person nominated by him who must be either a qualified insolvency practitioner or an employee of the administrator or his firm who is experienced in insolvency matters.[254] A meeting is only duly constituted if notice has been given to all members and at least 2 are present or represented.[255] A committee member may be represented by an individual who is not an undischarged bankrupt or subject to a composition or arrangement with his creditors if that person is provided with a letter of authority signed by the committee member entitling him to act generally or specifically on that occasion or holds authorisation, under s 375 of the Companies Act 1985, from a corporate committee member.[256] The chairman of the meeting may demand to see the letter and may exclude the representative if it appears that his authority is deficient.[257] No corporate body may act as a representative and no-one may represent more than one member at a time or act both as a member and a representative.[258] The fact that a representative signs a document on behalf of a member must be stated below his signature.[259] Each member present or represented at the meeting of the committee is entitled to one vote and resolutions are passed by a majority, signed by the chairman and minuted.[260] It is possible for a resolution to be dealt with by post. If the administrator wishes to follow this procedure he must send a copy of the resolution to every member or representative incorporated in a statement and with each resolution (if there is more than one) set out in a separate document so that agreement with or dissent from each resolution can be indicated.[261] Any member may demand that a meeting be called by requiring this within 7 business days of the date on which the resolution was sent out.[262] If no such request is made, the resolution is deemed to be passed by the committee when a majority of members notify the administrator that they concur in it. A copy of the resolution and a note of the concurrence of the committee must be placed in the company's minute book.[263]

13.124 If the committee resolves to use the power conferred on it by

---

253 r 2.34(4).
254 r 2.35.
255 r 2.36.
256 r 2.37(1), and (2) and (4) as amended by SI 1987 No 1919.
257 r 2.37(3).
258 r 2.37(4) and (5).
259 r 2.37(6).
260 r 2.42.
261 r 2.43(1) and (2) as amended by SI 1987 No 1919.
262 r 2.43(3).
263 r 2.43(4) and (5).

s 26(2), to require the attendance of the administrator at a meeting, the written notice to him must be signed by a majority of current committee members or their representatives.[264] The meeting must be fixed for a business day; the committee decides the day and the administrator decides the time and place according to Rule 2.44(2). It may be chaired by an elected committee member rather than the administrator or his nominee if the meeting so decides.[265]

13.125 Members of the committee can resign by delivering written notice to the administrator and can be removed by a resolution of a creditors' meeting providing at least 14 days' notice has been given of the intention to move that resolution.[266] Membership of the committee will also terminate if the member becomes bankrupt (but he is replaced by his trustee in bankruptcy) or compounds or arranges with his creditors.[267] If a member ceases to be a creditor or is found never to have been one or if he misses 3 consecutive committee meetings and is not represented at them and no resolution is passed at the third meeting to prevent it, he ceases to be a member.[268]

13.126 A vacancy on the committee caused by whatever means may be filled by any qualified creditor appointed by the administrator and agreed by a majority of the remaining committee members providing the nominee consents.[269] However, the administrator and the majority of the committee may agree to leave the vacancy unfilled if at least 3 committee members will remain.[270]

13.127 The reasonable travelling expenses of committee members or their representatives in relation to attending meetings or dealing with other committee business may be met by the administrator out of company assets as an expense of the administration. However this does not apply to a meeting called other than by the administrator within 3 months of the previous meeting.[271]

13.128 Members of the committee may deal with the company for value and in good faith during the currency of the administration order but any transaction not satisfying those conditions may be set aside by the court on

264   r 2.44(1).
265   r 2.44(3).
266   rr 2.38 and 2.40.
267   r 2.39(1)(a).
268   r 2.39(1)(b) and (c).
269   r 2.41(3).
270   r 2.41(2).
271   r 2.45.

the application of any interested person and directions to compensate the company for losses caused by the transaction may be given.[272] Defects in the appointment, election or qualifications of committee members or their representatives do not affect the validity of the committee's acts.[273]

Unfair prejudice to creditors or members

13.129   Section 27 of the Act allows any creditor or member of the company to apply to the court at any time when the administration order is in force on the ground that:

"(a) that the company's affairs business and property are being or have been managed by the administrator in a manner which is unfairly prejudicial to the interests of its creditors or members generally, or of some part of its creditors or members (including at least himself) or,
(b) that any actual or proposed act or omission of the administrator is or would be so prejudicial."[274]

This provision is modelled on s 459 of the Companies Act 1985 which permits the members of a company to apply on the same basis. It is notable that while the concept of unfair prejudice to a member has been developed under that section, the idea will more often apply to creditors in the context of an administration order. The most obvious source of prejudice will be a reduction in the value of the assets available to a particular class of creditors as a result of the conduct of the administrator. It will be necessary for those who consider that they have been prejudiced in this way to prove an element of unfairness in the conduct which led to that result. This is most likely to result from an allegation that the administrator dissipated the assets of the company by using them for a purpose other than those specified in the administration order.[275] Presumably, the fraudulent or negligent exercise of powers that the administrator does have could also form the basis of an application. Applications from creditors who hold security over assets with which the administrator deals under s 15 are possible as the Act specifically provides that nothing in that section or its Scottish equivalent is to be taken as prejudicing applications under s 27.[276]

13.130   The court may make such order as it thinks fit on the application but providing it does not make an order that would prejudice or prevent the implementation of a voluntary arrangement under the Insolvency Act 1986 or s 425 of the Companies Act 1985. If the application for an order under

---

272 r 2.46.
273 r 2.46A, inserted by SI 1987 No 1919.
274 s 27(1).
275 See eg *Re Charnley Davies Ltd* [1988] BCLC 243.
276 s 27(5).

s 27 was made more than 28 days after the approval of any proposals or revised proposals under s 24 or 25 the order made cannot prejudice or prevent the implementation of those proposals.[277]

13.131 The orders which may be made include those which regulate the future management of the company and its affairs by the administrator, require the administrator to rectify acts or omissions of which the applicant has complained or insist that a meeting be convened to consider designated matters. Alternatively, the court may discharge the administration order.[278]

---

277   s 27(2) and (3).
278   s 27(4).

CHAPTER 14

Winding Up: Commencement, Procedure, Meetings and Effects

PART 1: THE NATURE AND SCOPE OF THE WINDING UP PROCESS

14.01   The terms *liquidation* and *winding up* are used interchangeably to describe the process whereby the existence of a company is brought to an end by the realisation of its assets and the payment of its debts. Any surplus is applied in a distribution among members according to their entitlement under the company's articles to a return of capital or to participation beyond that in any remaining assets. This will be followed by the formal dissolution of the company (see paras 19.121–19.147). Apart from the power of the Registrar under s 652 of the Companies Act 1985 which applies to defunct companies, or a court order under s 427(3)(d) of that Act, if a reconstruction or amalgamation takes place, winding up is the only method whereby a company's existence can be brought to an end.[1]

14.02   A decision to wind up an insolvent company may be taken by the directors—perhaps under pressure from creditors—or may be directly precipitated by a petition brought by a creditor. Directors should seek advice on the comparative merits of winding up, an administration order, or, if a creditor holds a floating charge, the appointment of an administrative receiver. Such a receiver can only be appointed by the holder of the floating charge but this may be done with the agreement of the directors or at their request. In any of these events, control of the company will be transferred from the directors to an insolvency practitioner. In some cases it may be possible for the company and its creditors to enter a voluntary arangement under ss 1–7 of the Insolvency Act 1986.

14.03   Section 73 of the Insolvency Act 1986 lays down that the procedure for the winding up of a company voluntarily, or by the court, applies to a company as defined by s 735 of the Companies Act 1985. That provision essentially provides for the inclusion of registered companies in the process. In addition, ss 220 to 229 of the Insolvency Act 1986 apply to the winding up of an 'unregistered company'. Section 220(1) defines this term as meaning any association and any company except a railway company

---

1   *Princess of Reuss v Bos* (1871) LR 5 HL 176 at 193, where it was held that the former writ of *scire facias* was not available to end the existence of a company.

incorporated by Act of Parliament or a company registered in any part of the United Kingdom under the legislation (past or present) relating to companies in Great Britain. While this provision includes, for example, companies incorporated by special Act of Parliament or Royal Charter, it does not include industrial and provident societies. These are to be wound up, under the Act, as registered companies since the Act applies to them by virtue of a provision of the Industrial and Provident Societies Act 1965, under which they are registered.[2] Section 220 is also to be interpreted to exclude jurisdiction to wind up an international organisation established by treaty between sovereign states. To hold otherwise would be to assume a parliamentary intention to confer a jurisdiction incompatible with established constitutional practice and with international law and which could only be exercised by putting the United Kingdom in breach of its treaty obligations.[3]

14.04   The provisions of s 220 to 229 do not allow for the voluntary winding up of an unregistered company. Only compulsory liquidation is available to unregistered companies. The grounds on which the court may wind up such a company are limited to its inability to pay its debts, the just and equitable ground, and the fact that the unregistered company has already been dissolved, has ceased to carry on business, or is carrying on business only for the purpose of winding up its affairs.[4]

14.05   Section 735 includes, within the general definition of a company for the purposes of the winding up provisions of the Insolvency Act 1986, companies formed and registered under the Companies Act 1985 as well as companies subject to the Act by virtue of their registration either under previous Companies Acts or under the 1985 Act. This does not include companies registered in Ireland before 1922.

14.06   If a registered company is to be wound up this may be done compulsorily or voluntarily. In the latter case the winding up may take the form of a creditors' voluntary winding up or a members' voluntary winding up. An insolvent company will be unable to begin a members' voluntary winding up. However, that procedure will be dealt with briefly as such a winding up may be started in the belief that the company is solvent and may later be continued on the basis of its actual insolvency. The obsolete procedure known as winding up under the supervision of the court was abolished by the Insolvency Act 1985 s 88.

2   *Re South London Fish Market* (1888) 39 Ch D 324; *Re Oriental Bank Corporation* (1884) 54 LJ Ch 481; and *Re Nourse Self Build Association Ltd* [1985] BCLC 219.
3   *Re International Tin Council* [1988] BCLC 44.
4   s 221(4) and (5).

PART 2: COMMENCEMENT AND EFFECTS OF VOLUNTARY
WINDING UP

CREDITORS' VOLUNTARY WINDING UP

14.07 This is the commonest procedure used for winding up insolvent
companies as it is cheaper and speedier than a winding up by the court. The
process is initiated by a resolution of a company general meeting despite the
fact that the process will be for the benefit of its creditors and that control of
the winding up process is shared by creditors and members.

Resolutions for creditors' voluntary winding up

14.08 Section 84(1) of the Insolvency Act 1986 provides that such a
resolution may be:

(a) An extraordinary resolution to the effect that the company cannot by
reason of its liabilities continue its business and that it is advisable to wind it
up.
(b) A special resolution that the company be voluntarily wound up.
(c) An ordinary resolution requiring that the company be wound up
voluntarily if the duration of the company was fixed by its articles by
reference to either a period of time or the occurrence of an event. The
ordinary resolution will be effective if passed after the passage of the
specified length of time or the occurrence of the event which is to precipitate
dissolution.

14.09 In the case of a creditors' voluntary winding up an extraordinary
resolution is almost invariably used owing to the shorter period of notice
usually required for such a resolution in comparison with that needed for a
special resolution. Winding up will rarely be commenced by an ordinary
resolution as it is unusual for articles of association to specify either a period
for the company's existence or an event on the occurrence of which it is to be
dissolved. Where such a provision does exist a resolution is necessary for
winding up to commence since there can be no automatic dissolution of the
company by virtue of the provision in its articles.

Procedure for passing resolution

14.10 The period of notice required to call a meeting to pass an
extraordinary resolution will be 14 days[5] or such longer period as the

5 Companies Act 1985 s 369(1)(b)(ii).

articles specify.[6] This contrasts with the period of 21 days' notice required for a meeting which is to consider a special resolution.[7] If the holders of 95%, in nominal value of the shares giving a right to attend and vote agree, the notice requirement in the case of either a special or extraordinary resolution can be waived.[8] The Insolvency Act 1985 repealed the former provision[9] requiring a minimum of 7 days' notice for the members' meeting at which a resolution to put the company into voluntary liquidation was proposed. Instead, the consequences of a members' appointee acting as liquidator during the period of up to 14 days before it is necessary to call a creditors' meeting are dealt with by s 166 of the Insolvency Act 1986. The notice given for a meeting must be in writing in respect of either an extraordinary resolution or a special resolution. However, it would seem that the consent of a 95% majority to shorter notice need not be in writing although it would be imprudent not to obtain written agreement.

14.11 It is possible for even a special or extraordinary resolution to be passed without a meeting being called if all the members of the company unanimously agree to it.[10] This had long been acknowledged to be the case where ordinary resolutions were concerned.[11] Table A specifically provides that a resolution in writing executed by or on behalf of each member who would have been entitled to vote on it in a general meeting is as effectual as if it had been passed at a general meeting duly convened.[12] Where there is unanimity among members a written agreement to an extraordinary resolution is adequate. Where such agreement cannot be obtained a meeting must be called but those with 95% of the voting power may waive the notice requirement.

14.12 If a meeting is called irregularly and purports to pass a resolution for voluntary winding up then members of the company will be bound by the resolutions initiating the liquidation and appointing a liquidator if they allow the resolutions to be passed while knowing of their power to stop them or if they behave in such a way as to indicate their assent to the resolutions. This includes cooperating with the liquidator and proving debts in the liquidation. If no assent to the passing of the resolution can be deduced from the behaviour of the objecting members at the meeting or subsequently, the equitable doctrine of laches may apply to prevent an

6 Art 38 of Table A in SI 1985 no 805 specifies 14 days. In the absence of any provision at all s 369(2)(b) provides for 14 days' notice.
7 Companies Act 1985 s 378(2).
8 *Ibid* s 369(3) and (4).
9 s 588 of the Companies Act 1985 was repealed by s 235 and sch 10 Part II of the 1985 Insolvency Act.
10 *Cane v Jones* [1981] 1 WLR 1457.
11 *Re Duomatic Ltd* [1969] 2 WLR 114.
12 Art 53; SI 1985 no 805.

action by the dissenters if they delay in making an application to the courts.[13] This makes the liquidation process binding as against those members but not necessarily against others such as creditors unless they have also assented by attending and voting at a creditors' meeting, proving in the liquidation, or otherwise participating in the winding up whilst knowing of the irregularity. In the absence of conduct indicating assent to it, an irregularly passed resolution will be void and the winding up will not have commenced.[14]

14.13 The case law on s 588 of the Companies Act 1985 and its predecessor sections indicated that a meeting called with inadequate notice could pass a valid resolution to commence a winding up and effectively to appoint a liquidator.[15] Under the Insolvency Act 1986 that remains the position where assent by all shareholder exists or where the statutory provision for the waiver of notice requirements applies. In other circumstances the validity of the resolutions may be challenged by those who have not indicated their assent. A majority of 75% of the votes of those present and voting is required to pass either a special resolution or an extraordinary resolution.[16]

14.14 A copy of a resolution passed under s 84(1) must be forwarded to the Registrar of Companies under s 380 of the Companies Act 1985 within 15 days of being passed.[17] It must also be embodied in, or annexed to, every copy of the company's articles issued after it was passed. A failure to do so will make the company and every officer in default liable to a fine. For this purpose a liquidator is an officer of the company. The need to notify the registrar and to insert the resolution in the company's articles applies whether a meeting was held or the resolution was signed by all shareholders entitled to vote.

14.15 In addition to the requirements of s 380 as to notification of the Registrar of Companies, a winding up resolution must be advertised in the *Gazette* within 14 days of the date on which it was passed. The penalty for default in this requirement is a fine on the company and any defaulting officer (including a liquidator).[18] It is usual for the members' meeting to pass a resolution appointing a liquidator at the same time as passing the winding up resolution. If it does so, the directors of the company will lose

---

13 *Re Bailey Hay & Co Ltd* [1971] 1 WLR 1357.
14 *Re Zinotty Properties Ltd* [1984] 1 WLR 1249 (where there was no quorum).
15 *Re Centrebind Ltd* [1967] 1 WLR 377 and *E V Saxton & Sons Ltd v R Miles (Confectioners) Ltd* [1983] 1 WLR 952.
16 Companies Act 1985 s 378.
17 Insolvency Act 1986 s 84(3) and Companies Act 1985 s 380(4)(j).
18 Insolvency Act 1986 s 85.

their powers.[19] However, until the creditors' meeting is called, the liquidator appointed by the company will have limited powers in a creditors' voluntary liquidation.[20] If no liquidator is appointed by the company when a winding up resolution is passed then the directors' powers may not be exercised without the sanction of the court. The latter position applies to both a members' and a creditors' voluntary winding up.[21]

14.16 There are two exceptions to this prohibition on the use of the directors' powers. One is their right, in the case of a creditors' voluntary winding up, to call the creditors' meeting and their duty to prepare and verify the statement of affairs to be presented to that meeting.[22] The other is the right to dispose of perishable goods or other goods the value of which is likely to diminish if they are not immediately disposed of and to do all other things as may be necessary for the protection of the company's assets.[23] These restrictions reflect those which apply to the powers of a liquidator, appointed by the company at its general meeting during the period before a creditors' meeting is called, except that the liquidator has power to gather in property to which the company is, or appears to be, entitled.[24]

14.17 These rules are designed to protect the position of creditors in advance of the meeting at which they take control of the winding up by appointing their own liquidator. This is necessary under the scheme introduced by the Insolvency Act 1985 whereby the creditors' meeting can be called up to 14 days after the commencement of the winding up at the company meeting which passed the winding up resolution.[25] Formerly, there was a statutory requirement that the creditors' meeting be held on the same day as the members' meeting or the day after. This was, however, undermined by the validity conferred on the resolutions appointing a liquidator and commencing the winding up even if inadequate notice were given of the meeting and the full powers available to a liquidator appointed by the company before confirmation of the appointment by the creditors' meeting.[26] The possibility of abuse by a liquidator acting in the interests of the company's members and directors before the creditors' meeting is reduced by the limitations now imposed on his powers. The fact that only qualified insolvency practitioners can now act as liquidators will also assist in the prevention of abuse.[27]

19   *Ibid* s 103.
20   s 166 and see below para 14.16.
21   s 114(1) and (2).
22   s 114(2).
23   s 114(3).
24   s 166(3).
25   s 98(1).
26   *E V Saxton & Sons Ltd v R Miles (Confectioners) Ltd* [1983] 1 WLR 952 and *Re Centrebind Ltd* [1967] 1 WLR 377; see para 14.13 above.
27   See ch 10.

14.18   The restriction in the case of both directors and liquidator is on the exercise of their powers. They retain their powers and the validity of actions in breach of the statutory restriction will remain unless the other party to the transaction was aware of the circumstances giving rise to the restriction. The penalty for a breach of the statutory provisions is a fine on the directors or the liquidator, as the case may be.

14.19   After the members' meeting has passed a winding up resolution it is necessary that a creditors' meeting be called in the case of a creditors' voluntary winding up. The statutory provision requiring the creditors' meeting clearly contemplates that notices calling the creditors' meeting will be sent before the members' meeting[28] is held, but providing the creditors' meeting is held not later than the fourteenth day after the company meeting and providing at least 7 days' notice of the creditors' meeting is sent, the statutory requirement will be satisfied. If the company meeting is adjourned and the creditors' meeting is held before the adjourned meeting, resolutions of the creditors' meeting have effect on and from the passing of the winding up resolution by the company.[29]

14.20   The notice to creditors must be sent by post not less than 7 days before the date fixed for the creditors' meeting.[30] Notice must also be advertised once in the *London Gazette* and at least once in two newspapers circulating in the area in which the company's principal place of business was situated.[31] The local newspapers in which advertisements are to appear will be determined by the situation of the company's principal place of business in Great Britain during the 6 months before the notices were sent out summoning the company meeting at which the winding up resolution was passed.[32] If the principal place of business was situated in different localities in Great Britain during that 6 month period, then the creditors' meeting must be advertised in a newspaper in each such locality.[33] If the company had no principal place of business in Great Britain at any time during the 6 month period before the members' meeting, then the registered office is substituted for the principal place of business.[34] The latter provision will apply where there was a principal place of business situated outside Great Britain or where the company had no principal place of

---

28 Insolvency Act 1986 s 98(1)(a) refers to 'the fourteenth day after the day on which there *is to be held* the company meeting at which the resolution for voluntary winding up *is to be proposed*' (emphasis added).
29 r 4.53A, inserted by SI 1987 no 1919.
30 Insolvency Act 1986 s 98(1)(b).
31 s 98(1)(c).
32 s 98(5).
33 s 98(3).
34 s 98(4).

business at all because it did not conduct any business during the relevant six month period.

14.21   The obligation to call the creditors' meeting is placed on the company which is liable to a fine if the meeting is not called.[35] If a liquidator appointed by the company meeting is in post he has a duty to apply to the court for directions if the company fails to fulfil its obligation to call a creditors' meeting under s 98.[36] The liquidator must take this step within 7 days of the appointment or of his later discovery of the company's default. Failure to make such an application without reasonable excuse will make the liquidator liable to a fine.

14.22   The notice of the creditors' meeting must, in addition to stating the time, place and nature of the meeting and the time by which, and place at which, proofs or proxies are to be lodged,[37] indicate the source from which creditors can obtain certain information in advance of the meeting. It may state the name and address of a qualified insolvency practitioner able to act in relation to the company who will furnish creditors free of charge with such information as they may reasonably require concerning the company's affairs during the period before the day of the creditors' meeting.[38] The information to be provided will usually be available from the practitioner who is to be appointed as liquidator or who has already been nominated by the earlier company meeting as such.

14.23   Alternatively, the notice of the creditors' meeting must specify a place in the locality in which the company had its principal place of business in Great Britain during the 6 months before the company meeting where a list of name and addresses of the company's creditors can be inspected free of charge.[39] Creditors will at least be able to contact each other although the list of names and addresses need only be available on the last two business days before the day of the creditors' meeting and the information available from an insolvency practitioner has to be made available only for an unspecified 'period' before the day of the meeting.

14.24   In addition to the provision of notice of the creditors' meeting and of advance information to those creditors who require it, the Insolvency Act 1986 imposes a duty on the directors of the company to prepare a statement of affairs and to lay it before the creditors' meeting.[40] Some or all of the

35   s 98(6).
36   s 166(5)(a) and (b).
37   r 4.51(2) Insolvency Rules 1986 (SI 1986 no 1925). The deadline for lodging proofs or proxies must be no earlier than 12 noon on the day before the meeting.
38   Insolvency Act 1986 s 98(2)(a).
39   s 98(2)(b).
40   s 99(1)(a).

directors must verify the contents of the statement of affairs by affidavit[41] and one of their number must be prepared to attend and preside over the creditors' meeting.[42] The person given this task commits an offence if he or she fails to attend or preside without reasonable excuse and all directors are liable for a failure to supply a statement of affairs containing the full information required by the Insolvency Act.[43] The statement of the affairs must contain:[44]

(a) particulars of the company's assets, debts and liabilities;
(b) the names and addresses of the company's creditors;
(c) the securities held by each secured creditor;
(d) the dates when those securities were given.

14.25 The format of a statement of affairs is laid down in forms 4.18 (for a s 95 meeting) and form 4.19 (for a s 98 meeeting). Those forms (like form 4.17 which applies to a compulsory liquidation by virtue of Rule 4.33) require that estimated deficiencies or surplusses be provided in respect of the different classes of creditor and the claims of members.

14.26 The preparation of the company's statement of affairs is likely to be carried out by an accountant or other qualified insolvency practitioner but responsibility for its presentation and for its accuracy lies with the directors. The statement will reflect the company's financial position on being wound up. The effect of the commencement of the winding up on assets and liabilities will be taken into account. Floating charges will crystallise and become fixed, leasing or hire purchase contracts are likely to terminate and give the owner of the goods a right to reclaim them. All such factors must be taken into account in drafting the statement. If the statement of affairs does not state the position of the company at the time of the meeting, the directors are required to ensure that a written or oral report is made to the meeting on any material transactions relating to the company between the date of the statement and the date of the meeting. The report will be made by either the director presiding at the meeting or some other person with knowledge of the matters with which it deals. The report will be minuted.[45]

14.27 The statement of affairs made by the directors in a creditors' voluntary liquidation must be made up to a date not more than 14 days before the passing of the winding up resolution.[46] It must be delivered by

---

41 s 99(2).
42 s 99(1)(c).
43 s 99(3). The absence of the director nominated to attend and preside does not make the proceedings invalid; _Re Salcombe Hotel (Development) Co Ltd_ (1989) 5 BCC 807.
44 ss 99(2).
45 r 4.53B of Insolvency Rules 1986, inserted by SI 1987 no 1919.
46 r 4.34(4), substituted by SI 1987 no 1919.

them to the liquidator in office after the s 98 meeting forthwith after that meeting and he must then deliver it to registrar to companies within 7 days of receiving it.[47] However, if the company general meeting nominated a liquidator on a day before the s 98 creditors' meeting was held, the directors must deliver a copy of the statement of affairs to him immediately after his nomination or the preparation of the statement—whichever is later.[48] In a members' voluntary liquidation which is being converted into a creditors' voluntary liquidation the statement of affairs is made by the liquidator under s 95(3). In that case it must be delivered by him to the registrar of companies within 7 days after the creditors' meeting held under s 95(2).[49]

14.28   Apart from receiving the statement of affairs the main function of the creditors' meeting will be the appointment of a liquidator. Matters will usually be arranged so that the company meeting and the creditors' meeting appoint the same qualified insolvency practitioner, but in the event of different persons being appointed, the person appointed by the creditors' meeting will act as sole liquidator unless the court, on the application of a director, member, or creditor of the company, makes an order to different effect.[50] A liquidation committee may also be appointed by the creditors' meeting. It must consist of not more than five persons who are usually appointed by the creditors' meeting.[51] The company meeting may nominate members but, if the creditors' meeting resolves that the company nominees should not serve, a court order is required for them to do so and the court may appoint to act in place of those to whom the creditors object.[52] The creditors' meeting cannot alter the fact that a winding up has commenced as a result of the winding up resolution passed at the company meeting but it will usually take control of the process by appointing its own liquidator and liquidation committee. It is this creditor control which distinguishes a creditors' voluntary winding up from a members' voluntary liquidation.

14.29   The rules limit the resolutions that may be taken at the first creditors' meeting. Rules 4.52(1) and 4.53 list exhaustively the resolutions permitted at a creditors' meeting under s 98 (in a creditors' voluntary liquidation) or under s 95 (in a members' voluntary liquidation which has been continued on the basis that the company is insolvent). Those matters are:

   (a) A resolution to appoint a named insolvency practitioner to be liquidator or two or more insolvency practitioners to be joint liquidators;

---

47   r 4.34(3), substituted by SI 1987 no 1919.
48   r 4.34A, inserted by SI 1987 no 1919.
49   r 4.34(2).
50   Insolvency Act 1986 s 100, and see paras 14.58 *et seq* below.
51   s 101(1).
52   s 101(2) and (3).

(b) A resolution to establish a liquidation committee;

(c) In cases where it has not been resolved that a liquidation committee be appointed, a resolution specifying the terms on which the liquidator is to be remunerated or to defer consideration of that matter;

(d) In cases in which two or more joint liquidators have been appointed, a resolution specifying whether acts are to be done by both or all of them or only by one;

(e) A resolution to adjourn the meeting for not more than 3 weeks;

(f) Any other resolutions which the chairman thinks it right to allow for special reasons.[53]

14.30 In the case of a first creditors' meeting in a compulsory liquidation the same list of possible resolutions applies. However, if that meeting was requisitioned under s 136 by one quarter in value of the company's creditors it may pass a resolution authorising the payment out of the assets of the cost of summoning and holding the meeting and of any contributories' meeting so requisitioned and held.[54] A meeting of contributories in a compulsory liquidation may pass the same list of resolutions except that it is not permitted to deal with the liquidator's remuneration or the costs of summoning and holding the meeting if it was requisitioned.[55] Neither a creditors' nor a contributories' meeting in a compulsory liquidation is permitted to consider any resolution to appoint the official receiver as liquidator although under s 136(2) and (3) he will hold that office at any time when no other liquidator is in office.[56]

The conduct of the creditors' meeting

14.31 The Insolvency Rules 1986 lay down provisions for meetings of contributories and creditors. Many of those rules apply to the creditors' meeting in a creditors' voluntary winding up. All of the rules on the conduct of meetings of creditors and contributories are dealt with in Part 4 of this chapter. Where a rule applies only to a winding up by the court or a members' voluntary liquidation that fact is noted in the text.

MEMBERS' VOLUNTARY WINDING UP

14.32 Where a company is solvent it may be voluntarily wound up by the use of this procedure. The control of the winding up will then remain in the

53   r 4.52(1) as applied by r 4.53.
54   r 4.52(1)(e).
55   r 4.52(2).
56   r 4.52(3), and see ch 15.

hands of the members. A members' voluntary winding up is usually commenced by a special resolution that the company be wound up. It is not possible to use an extraordinary resolution as, in the case of a solvent company, it is not accurate to state that the company is unable to continue its business by reason of its liabilities. If the company is solvent and a period is laid down in the articles for the duration of the company's existence or an event is specified on the occurrence of which the company is to be dissolved, an ordinary resolution may be used.[57] Unless the holders of 95% of the nominal value of the shares giving the right to attend and vote at the general meeting agree to waive the notice required, 21 days' notice is required of the meeting at which the special resolution is to be put.[58] Unanimous agreement by all members enables the resolution to be passed without a meeting if it is in writing and signed by or on behalf of all members.[59]

14.33   Before the resolution to place the company in members' voluntary winding up is passed, a majority of the directors if there are more than two, or all of the directors if there are only two, must make a statutory declaration at a directors' meeting on the solvency of the company. The declaration must state that the directors have made a full inquiry into the affairs of the company and have formed the opinion that the company will be able to pay its debts in full within a specified period of time not more than 12 months from the passing of the resolution to wind up the company.[60] The declaration must contain a statement of the company's assets and liabilities at the latest practicable date before the declaration is made.[61] Providing the statement does contain a list of assets and liabilities it will be valid even if it contains some inaccuracies or some liabilities are omitted and the winding up will not be set aside.[62]

14.34   The declaration may be made on the date of the passing of the resolution so long as it precedes the decision to pass the resolution and is made at a directors' meeting. Alternatively it may be made at any time in the 5 weeks preceding the date on which the resolution is passed.[63] A copy of the statement and of the resolution must be delivered to the registrar of companies within 15 days of the date on which the resolution was passed. Failure to deliver the statement or the resolution is an offence by the company and every officer in default.[64]

57   Insolvency Act 1986 s 84(1).
58   Companies Act 1985 s 369(3) and (4).
59   Table A Art 53 (SI 1985 no 805) and *Cane v Jones* [1981] 1 WLR 1451.
60   Insolvency Act 1986 s 89(1).
61   *Ibid* s 89(2)(b).
62   *De Courcy v Clement* [1971] 1 Ch 693.
63   s 89(2)(a).
64   Companies Act 1985 s 380(5) and Insolvency Act 1986 ss 84(3) and 89(3) and (6).

14.35 A director who makes a declaration of solvency without having reasonable grounds for the opinion that the company will be able to pay its debts in full within the period specified commits an offence punishable by imprisonment or a fine or both. The offence will be committed even if there were reasonable grounds to believe that the debts would be paid within 12 months of the commencement of the winding up if a shorter period was specified and there were no reasonable grounds to believe that full payment of debts would be achieved within that shorter period.[65]

14.36 If a winding up resolution is passed within 5 weeks of the declaration of solvency and the company's debts are not paid or provided for in full within the period specified in the declaration, there is a statutory presumption that the directors who made the declaration did not have reasonable grounds for their opinion.[66] If the resolution is passed more than 5 weeks after the declaration was made or if the declaration contains no statement of the company's assets and liabilities then the winding up must be conducted as a creditors' voluntary winding up from the beginning.[67]

14.37 In a members' voluntary winding up it is the company general meeting which is required to appoint the liquidator and which fills any vacancy in that office.[68] A general meeting to fill the vacancy may be called by any contributory or by the liquidator and must be held in the manner laid down by the Companies Act 1985 or by the company's articles unless the court, on application by a member or the liquidator, lays down a different procedure.[69] There is no obligation to call any creditors' meetings in the course of a members' voluntary winding up so long as the liquidator is of the opinion that the company will be able to pay its debts in full with interest at the rate laid down in s 189 of the Insolvency Act 1986 within the period specified in the directors' declaration of solvency. If it becomes clear to the liquidator during a members' voluntary winding up that the company is insolvent, in that it will be unable to pay its debts in full within the specified period, he is required to call a creditors' meeting and from the date of that meeting the winding up becomes a creditors' voluntary winding up.[70]

14.38 The creditors' meeting must take place within 28 days of the date on which the liquidator formed the opinion that the company would be unable

---

65 s 89(4).
66 s 89(5).
67 ss 89(2) and 90.
68 ss 91(1) and 92(1).
69 s 92(2) and (3)—the phrase 'this Act' is used in error in s 92(3).
70 Insolvency Act 1986 ss 95(1)(2) and 96.

to pay its debts in the period specified in the declaration of solvency.[71] Notices must be posted to creditors at least 7 days before the date of the meeting which must be advertised once in the *Gazette* and at least once in two newspapers circulating in the locality of the company's principal place of business in Great Britain.[72] The rules for ascertaining the principal place of business are similar to those applicable to the creditors' meeting required under s 98 in a creditors' voluntary winding up.[73] The liquidator is responsible for supplying the creditors with such information concerning the affairs of the company as they may reasonably require in advance of the day of the meeting and this obligation must be stated in the notice calling the meeting[74] which will otherwise contain the same information as a notice issued under s 98. In addition to supplying in advance such information as creditors require the liquidator must lay before the meeting and verify by affidavit a statement of affairs showing the same details as are required in such a statement in a creditors' voluntary liquidation. The liquidator presides at such a meeting.[75]

14.39   The creditors' meeting called under s 95, when a liquidator takes the view that a company in a members' voluntary winding up is insolvent, has all the powers of a creditors' meeting in a creditors' voluntary winding up.[76] It may appoint a liquidator who will replace the liquidator who was appointed by the company general meeting to conduct the members' voluntary winding up and it may appoint a liquidation committee. Such decisions will be deemed to have been made by a s 98 meeting and the resolution passed at the company general meeting has effect from the date of the creditors' meeting as if it had been passed under s 98.

14.40   Since the conversion of the winding up into a creditors' voluntary winding up only takes effect from the date of the creditors' meeting, the restrictions in s 166 of the Insolvency Act 1986 on the exercise of the powers of a liquidator appointed by the company in the period before the creditors' meeting do not apply. He is able to deal with the company's assets in accordance with s 165 of the Insolvency Act 1986. Presumably the rule that only qualified insolvency practitioners can be appointed as liquidators; the penalties imposed on directors who swear declarations of insolvency without having reasonable grounds for their opinion and the obligation of the liquidator to call a creditors' meeting within 28 days of forming the view that the company will not be able to meet its debts within the specified

---

71   *Ibid* s 95(2)(a).
72   s 95(2)(b) and (c).
73   s 95(5), (6) and (7) and see paras 14.20–21 *supra*.
74   s 95(2)(d).
75   s 95(3) and (4).
76   ss 96 and 102.

period, make it unlikely that a liquidator's powers will be abused to the detriment of creditors in the period before a creditors' meeting takes place. It may also be unwise to impose a restriction on a liquidator's powers by reference to the time at which he forms a particular opinion—particularly since the formation of the opinion may occur some considerable time after the commencement of the winding up. From the date of the creditors' meeting called by a liquidator under s 95 of the Insolvency Act 1986 the winding up will take identical course to that followed by a creditors' voluntary winding up. Both creditors' and members' liquidations commence at the time of the passing of the resolution by the company general meeting.[77] This contrasts with the doctrine of 'relation back' which applies to a compulsory winding up.[78]

EFFECTS OF WINDING UP RESOLUTION

Business and status of the company

14.41 Section 87(1) of the Insolvency Act 1986 lays down that the company must cease to carry on its business from the commencement of the liquidation except so far as may be required for a beneficial winding up. The section's similarly worded predecessor was held at first instance not to render contracts, not required for a beneficial windig up, void for illegality as between the company and the other party.[79] However, should it be the case that this is incorrect the onus is on the person alleging that a contract is void for illegality to establish that it was not required for a beneficial winding up.[80]

14.42 The requirement that business be continued so far as required for a beneficial winding up can be interpreted widely. The purpose of the winding up may be the reconstruction of the company by the transfer of its undertaking as a going concern and the continuation of the business may be intended to facilitate that end. This, rather than a short term financial objective, can justify the continuation of the business in the case of either a commercial or a non-profit making company.[81] Whether or not the company continues its business its corporate status and powers continue until dissolution, regardless of any contrary provision in its articles of association.[82]

---

77 s 86.
78 See paras 14.179 *et seq*, *infra*.
79 *Bateman & Co v Ball* (1887) 56 LJ QB 291.
80 *Hire Purchase Furnishing Co v Riches* (1888) 20 QBD 387.
81 *Willis v Association of Universities of the British Commonwealth* [1965] 1 QB 140 at 149 and 151, and see para 15.98.
82 Insolvency Act 1986 s 87(2).

Share transfers

14.43 Any transfer of shares made after the commencement of a voluntary winding up is void unless it is made to, or with, the sanction of the liquidator. Similarly, any alteration of the status of members of the company made after that time is void.[83]

Directors' powers

14.44 The powers of the directors are not affected by the commencement of the voluntary liquidation as such. However, on the appointment of the liquidator they cease.[84] Since that appointment will usually be virtually simultaneous with the resolution to wind the company up, the directors' powers are normally affected immediately. It is possible for the continuance of the directors' powers to be sanctioned. In a creditors' voluntary winding up that must be done by the liquidation committee or, if there is none, the creditors. In a members' voluntary liquidation either the company general meeting or the liquidator take that step.[85] A general meeting called by the liquidator under s 165(4)(c) may still elect directors in either a members' or a creditors' voluntary liquidation.[86] However, it is only in a members' voluntary liquidation that it can sanction a continuation of the powers of the directors. The general meeting does not have power to ratify earlier decisions or to authorise transactions which are contrary to the statutory scheme of distribution after the commencement of the liquidation.[87]

Effect on employment contracts

14.45 Unlike the making of a winding up order by the court, a resolution for voluntary liquidation does not of itself terminate the employment of company employees.[88] This rule follows the pattern applicable to receivers whereby the appointment of a receiver out of court does not terminate employment whereas the appointment of a receiver by the court in a debenture holders' action does. However, a resolution for the voluntary liquidation of the company can amount to a notice of dismissal if

---

83 *Ibid* s 88.
84 ss 91(2) and 103.
85 *Ibid*.
86 *Re Fairbairn Engineering Co (Ladd's Case)* [1893] 3 Ch 450.
87 This is the case in a creditors' voluntary winding up according to the Court of Appeal in *Precision Dippings Ltd v Precision Dippings Marketing Ltd* [1986] 1 Ch 447 per Dillon LJ at 456. Since this view was based on the potential breach of the statutory scheme of distribution involved in such a decision and on the rights of the liquidator, it is submitted that the same rule applies in a members' voluntary winding up, despite the reference in this case to the ratification of earlier acts of the directors to the detriment of the creditors.
88 *Midland Counties District Bank Ltd v Attwood* [1905] 1 Ch 357.

it amounts to an intimation that the company no longer intends to carry out its contract with the employee.[89] If the commencement of a particular voluntary liquidation involves the immediate cessation of the company's business then it is likely that the resolution will operate to discharge the employees.

14.46 Such a dismissal will be a breach of a fixed term contract and without the necessary notice will be a wrongful dismissal in breach of a periodic employment contract. The fact that the employee was a director and a shareholder of the company and supported the voluntary liquidation resolution will not prevent a claim in the liquidation for damages unless an express term of the contract lays down such a rule.[90] However, without some further element the dismissal will not, in itself, be an unfair dismissal under the Employment Protection (Consolidation) Act 1978.[91]

Use of s 112 to restrain proceedings against the company

14.47 In contrast to the position in a winding up by the court, there is no automatic prohibition on the commencement or continuation of proceedings against the company without the leave of the court.[92] However, s 112 of the Insolvency Act 1986 can be used to seek an order of the court restraining proceedings against the company.

14.48 The principle of the *pari passu* distribution of assets in the liquidation of an insolvent company should cause the court to look favourably on such applications to prevent an unseemly scramble for priority in the liquidation. However, a distinction is made between the resolution of a dispute which will, *prima facie*, be settled by the appropriate court or tribunal, and the priority accorded to any amount awarded as a result of the proceedings. An action will be allowed to continue to settle issues of liability and quantum of damages.[93] It will only be in cases in which expenses may be saved and good done by granting the liquidator's application that the discretion will be exercised. If the effect of the suspension of the proceedings will be that the plaintiff enters a proof almost certain to be rejected and subjected to a dispute procedure whereby it returns to court, then no restraining order will be made as regards the original action.[94] However once the issues in the proceedings have been

---

89 *Reigate v Union Manufacturing (Ramsbottom) Ltd* [1918] 1 KB 592 at 601 and 606.
90 *Fowler v Commercial Timber Co Ltd* [1930] 2 KB 1.
91 *Fox Brothers (Clothes) Ltd v Bryant* [1979] ICR 64.
92 s 130 of the Insolvency Act 1986 has this effect in a compulsory liquidation.
93 *Currie v Consolidated Kent Collieries Corporation Ltd* [1906] 1 KB 134.
94 *Cook v X Chair Patents Co Ltd* [1960] 1 WLR 60.

resolved, the amount awarded will be subject to proof in the liquidation and will be dealt with on the same basis as the claims of other creditors.[95]

14.49   If execution or distress is levied after a resolution for voluntary liquidation is passed, the court will take a similar view and will restrain the execution process in order to uphold the principle of *pari passu* distribution.[96] Indeed, it seems that some exceptional circumstance must be established before the court's discretion is exercised in a different way.[97] However, in a case in which distress or execution is levied before the resolution is passed, the onus is on the liquidator, who seeks to prevent the creditor from proceeding to sale, to show that it would be inequitable to allow him to do so.[98]

14.50   Section 183 of the Insolvency Act 1986, which prevents a creditor whose execution or attachment is not completed before the commencement of the winding up from retaining the benefit of it against the liquidator, applies to a voluntary liquidation. For the purpose of the section the commencement of the voluntary liquidation is the date on which notice of the meeting at which the winding up resolution was proposed was received by the creditor. If he had no notice of the resolution, the usual rule applies and the commencement date is the date on which the resolution was passed.[99]

PART 3: COMMENCEMENT AND EFFECTS OF WINDING UP BY THE COURT

JURISDICTION

14.51   The High Court has jurisdiction to wind up any company registered in England or Wales[100] and in practice it is usual for winding up petitions to be presented in the High Court despite the concurrent jurisdiction of the county court of the district in which the company's registered office is situated in cases where the company's paid up capital is £120,000 or less.[101] Those county courts listed in the Civil Courts Order 1983[102] do not have jurisdiction and other county courts can hear petitions relating to a company with its registered office in the area of such a court.[103]

---

95   *Re Thurso New Gas Co* (1889) 42 Ch D 486 at 491.
96   *Westbury v Twigg & Co* [1892] 1 QB 77.
97   *Re Margot Bywaters Ltd* [1942] 1 Ch 121.
98   *Herbert Berry Associates v IRC* [1978] 1 All ER 161 at 168–169 and 171–172.
99   Insolvency Act 1986 s 183(2)(a) and see para 18.
100   Insolvency Act 1986 s 117(1).
101   *Ibid* s 117(2).
102   SI 1983 no 713 as amended by SIs 1984 nos 297 and 1075.
103   Insolvency Act 1986 s 117(2) and (4).

14.52   All courts which have a winding up jurisdiction in England and Wales have all the powers of the High Court for that purpose and their officers may perform the duties which might be discharged by an officer of the High Court.[104] In matters which arise in, and in consequence of, the winding up the county court has jurisdiction even over matters which involve sums well beyond the normal limits of its jurisdiction.[105] This will include dealing with transactions at an undervalue or preferences under s 238 to 241 of the Insolvency Act 1986 and the avoidance of floating charges under s 245. However, a matter which arose before the winding up, owing for example to a defect in the title conferred on a third party to property transferred by the company, cannot be dealt with by the county court if it would fall outside its jurisdiction were it not for the existence of the winding up. Such a matter is not within the scope of s 117(5) as the power to be exercised could have been used had no winding up order been in existence.[106]

14.53   If proceedings are brought in the wrong court they nonetheless remain valid and may be continued in the court in which they were commenced although proceedings wilfully brought in the wrong court will be dismissed.[107] This provision is clearly necessary since the doctrine of relation back means that the winding up will commence at the date of the filing of the petition if an order is made and to make proceedings invalid if they are brought in the wrong court could cause great confusion and detriment to creditors and others. There is power for the Companies Court (the collective description of the judges of the Chancery Division to whom winding up cases are assigned[108]) to transfer any case at any stage to a county court or to itself from a county court and for a county court to transfer a case to the Companies Court or to a different county court.[109]

14.54   Rule 7.11 of the Insolvency Rules 1986 permits a High Court judge to order that the proceedings in any court other than the High Court be transferred to the High Court or that proceedings in the High Court be transferred to any other court. Such an order may be made by the court of its own motion or on the application of either the official receiver or some other person appearing to the court to have an interest in the proceedings. The criterion for such an order is that good cause has been shown and the

104   s 117(5).
105   *Re F & E Stanton Ltd* [1928] 1 KB 464.
106   See *Re Ilkley Hotel Company* [1893] 1 QB 248, where such a matter was held at first instance to be outside the jurisdiction of a county court judge despite the provisions of s 1(6) of the Companies (Winding Up) Act 1890 which were identical to those of s 117(5).
107   Insolvency Act 1986 s 118 and see *Re Milford Haven Shipping Co* [1895] WN 16 and *Re Brightmore ex p May* (1884) 14 QBD 37.
108   Supreme Court Act 1981 s 61(1) and sch 1 para 1.
109   County Courts Act 1984 s 40(1), 41(1), 42 and 75(3)(b).

transfer from the High Court may be to any court with winding up jurisdiction—even if the jurisdiction is limited as is the case in the county court.[110]

14.55 If petitions are presented in the High Court and a county court by different creditors then the way in which they will be dealt with will depend on how close are the dates for the hearing of the two petitions and the order of their presentation. In *Re Filby Bros (Provender) Ltd*,[111] where the county court petition was presented earlier, and was due to be heard a few days after the High Court hearing, the county court proceedings were transferred to the High Court and a winding up order was made on both petitions. An order was made that any objection to the petition received by the county court should result in an immediate High Court application so that any opposing creditor might be heard before the winding up order was drawn up. The effect of this order is that the commencement of the winding up relates back to the date of the earlier county court petition. However, in *Re Audio Systems Ltd*[112] a winding up order was made on the High Court petition which was heard a month before a hearing of the county court petition was due and the county court proceedings were transferred to the High Court and then stayed. The *Filbey Bros* case was distinguished on the grounds that the High Court petition had been presented first; that a full month remained before it was due to be heard and that the county court petitioner supported the High Court petition. In both cases the costs of both petitions were allowed from the company's assets as no one was at fault.

14.56 Rule 7.11(2) provides for the transfer of proceedings from one county court to another. Notice of applications for a transfer by persons other than the official receiver under Rules 7.11 and 7.12 must be served by the applicant on the official receivers attached to the courts to and from which proceedings are sought to be transferred.[113] An application by the official receiver for proceedings to be transferred is made in a report by him which sets out why it is more convenient for the case to be heard in a different court and that the petitioner either consents to the transfer or has been given at last 14 days' notice of the application.[114] If winding up proceedings are commenced in the wrong court the court may strike them out, transfer them to the correct court or order them to be continued in the court in which they were commenced.[115]

---

110 *Re Real Estates Co* [1893] 1 Ch 398 and *Re Vernon Heating Co Ltd* [1936] Ch 289.
111 [1958] 1 WLR 683.
112 [1965] 1 WLR 1096.
113 Insolvency Rules 1986 r 7.13(3).
114 r 7.13(1) and (2).
115 r 7.12.

14.57 A county court dealing with a winding up case may refer a question to the High Court by way of case stated. Section 119 of the Insolvency Act 1986 allows all the parties to the proceedings, or any one of them together with the county court judge, to decide to state the facts in the form of a special case for the opinion of the High Court. The special case and such of the proceedings as are required are then transmitted to the High Court for its decision. Facts will usually be agreed for the purpose of the reference of the special case to the High Court and a set of questions may also be agreed for answer by the High Court which will make an order answering the questions put to it.[116] The procedure is rarely used as cases likely to involve complex legal issues will either be brought in the High Court or transferred there.

PETITIONERS

14.58 Section 124 of the Insolvency Act 1986 lays down who can present a petition for the winding up of a company. Possible petitioners for any company are:

(a) the company itself or its administrator, administrative receiver or the supervisor of a voluntary arrangement in respect of it;[117]
(b) the directors;
(c) a creditor;
(d) a contributory;[118]
(e) the Secretary of State for Trade and Industry;[119]
(f) the official receiver.[120]

14.59 Joint petitions are permitted by s 124(1) to be presented by any number of contributories or creditors with or without the company as a party. Only one company may normally be the subject of a petition although it may be possible for more than one member of a group of companies to be wound up on the basis of a single petition. Common shareholders between companies will not justify winding up on one petition.[121] Where more than one person wishes to petition for the winding up of a company it is the almost invariable practice of the Companies Court to ensure that only one petition is presented. Even where a contributory

116   See *Re Mawcon Ltd* [1969] 1 WLR 78.
117   Insolvency Act 1986 ss 7(4), 14, 42 and sch 1 para 21.
118   *Ibid* s 124(1).
119   s 124(4).
120   s 124(5).
121   *Re a Company* [1984] BCLC 307.

petitions and applies under s 459 of the Companies Act 1985, a creditor may be substituted as petitioner to prevent multiple petitions. This is justified on the basis of convenience and savings of costs. In a case where a different category of petitioner and a different ground for the petition are involved, readvertisement, amendment and reservice of the petition may be ordered.[122]

14.60 In certain special circumstances persons other than those listed above may petition for the winding up of a company:

(a) the Attorney General may petition for the winding up of a company registered as a charity;[123]
(b) the Bank of England may present a petition to wind up a company which is or was an authorised institution under the Banking Act 1987;[124]
(c) the Secretary of State for Trade and Industry has additional powers to present a petition in case of a company which carries on the business of insurance in Great Britain[125] or which carries on an investment business and is subject to the Financial Services Act 1986.[126]

The company or its directors as petitioners

14.61 It is rare for the company to present a petition for its own winding up. This is because a members' or creditors' voluntary winding up is cheaper and less cumbersome and can be used if a sufficient majority of company's members wish the company to be wound up. The company will merely have to pass an ordinary resolution to present a winding up petition, but some ground apart from the wish of a simple majority of members of the company that it be wound up will be necessary if the petition is to succeed.[127]

14.62 If grounds for a winding up order exist then the company or its directors will be able to present a petition. An article conferring power on the directors to commence or prosecute legal proceedings on behalf of the company has been held not to give them power to present a petition on the company's behalf[128] but under the Insolvency Act 1986 the directors may

---

122   *Re Creative Handbook* [1985] BCLC 1.
123   Charities Act 1960 s 30(1).
124   Banking Act 1987 s 92 and see eg *Re a Company (0065 of 1983) (Goodwin Squires Securities Ltd)* (1983) 1 BCC 98927.
125   Insurance Companies Act 1982 s 54(1).
126   Financial Services Act 1986 s 72.
127   *Re Anglo-Continental Produce Co Ltd* [1939] 1 All ER 99, and see paras 14.106 *et seq infra* as to the grounds for a winding up order.
128   *Smith v Duke of Manchester* (1883) 24 Ch D 611.

present a petition in their own right.[129] This will be useful for directors who fear liability for wrongful trading if the company continues to trade and who are unable or unwilling to apply for an administration order. It avoids the need for a simple majority of members to present a company's petition or a 75% majority to begin a voluntary winding up as the ground of the company's inability to pay its debts can be used.

14.63 It has been held that 'the directors' in s 124(1) means all the directors and not one or more directors. This was taken to exclude action by the majority of directors or even by a majority in a properly constituted board meeting.[130] Since the powers of the directors under the Companies Act are normally exercised by the board, it is submitted that this provision should be construed to give that organ the right to decide by a majority to petition for a winding up order. The doctrine that the general meeting and the board are separate organs, each competent to act within their own sphere, will make the directors' statutory power to petition exercisable even if a majority at a general meeting opposes the move. However the court, in deciding whether to make an order on the petition, will have some regard to the wishes of contributories and creditors.[131]

14.64 A receiver appointed by the holder of a fixed and floating charge also has power to present a petition on the just and equitable ground to protect the company's assets. Where the company was about to be subjected to a levy of rates which could be avoided if a winding up order was made, the receiver succeeded in a petition brought on the just and equitable ground. Such a step to preserve the company's assets was incidental and conducive to his power under the debenture to take possesion of the company's assets.[132] This power formerly only existed if a receiver was an agent of the company. However every administrator and administrative receiver is given power under the Insolvency Act 1986 to present or defend a winding up petition unless, in the case of an administrative receiver, any provision of the debenture under which he was appointed is inconsistent with that power.[133] A failure to provide that the administrative receiver should act as the company's agent will now be immaterial as, once it is established that a person has been appointed as an administrative receiver, he is deemed to be the company's agent until the company goes into liquidation.[134] A specific provision in the debenture denying his power to petition is required to deprive him of that right.

---

129 Insolvency Act 1986 s 124(1).
130 *Re Instrumentation Electrical Services Ltd* (1988) 4 BCC 301.
131 *Shaw & Sons (Salford) Ltd v Shaw* [1935] 2 KB 13 and see paras 14.163 *et seq, infra.*
132 *Re Emmadart* [1979] 2 WLR 868.
133 Insolvency Act 1986 s 42(1) and sch 1 para 21.
134 *Ibid* s 44(1)(a), and see paras 15.50 *et seq, infra.*

Petition by a creditor

14.65 A creditor is able to petition for the winding up of a company. The term is stated by statute to include those whose claims are contingent or prospective and has generally been broadly construed by the courts. It includes all who have pecuniary claims against the company.[135] Secured creditors are included[136] and need not, at the stage of presenting the petition, value their security. Even if a secured creditor has appointed a receiver he may petition for a winding up order although a mortgagee petitioning as contributory has been restrained from exercising his power of sale pending the hearing of his petition.[137]

14.66 A legal or equitable assignee of a debt may petition without the need to join the assignor as a party to the petition but a person who has assigned his whole beneficial interest in a debt will not succeed on a petition without joining the assignee.[138] A beneficiary for whom a debt from the company is held on trust, such as the holder of debentures secured by a trust deed, may not petition, since there is no direct covenant between the company and the beneficiary.[139] However, it is possible for the stock-holders of debentures secured by a trust to compel the trustees to take action in respect of a breach of covenant by the company.[140] A creditor whose claim is based on subrogation, as for example where money borrowed _ultra vires_ is applied to pay debts which are _intra vires_, is entitled to petition as a debt may be legal or equitable and yet give a person the status of creditor. However, any loan to a company or other transaction which is _ultra vires_ the company and which is not saved as regards the other party, by s 35 of the Companies Act 1985 or Companies Act 1989, will not ground a winding up petition.[141] Similarly, a transaction rendered illegal on any other grounds or time barred at the date of the petition will not enable a creditor to present a petition.[142] An executor of a deceased creditor is able to petition providing probate has been granted.[143]

14.67 Since a claim in debt is necessary before a person can be regarded as

---

135 _Re Midland Coal, Coke & Iron Co._ [1895] 1 Ch 267 at 277.
136 _Moor v Anglo-Italian Bank_ (1879) 10 Ch D 681.
137 _Re Borough of Portsmouth Tramways Co_ [1892] 2 Ch 362 and _Re Cambrian Mining Co Ltd_ (1881) 50 LJ Ch 536.
138 _Re Steel Wing Co._ [1921] 1 Ch 349; _Re Pentalta Exploration Co._ [1898] WN 55.
139 _Re Uruguay Central & Hygueritas Railway of Monte Video_ (1879) 11 Ch D 372; _Re Dunderland Iron Ore Co Ltd_ [1909] 1 Ch 446.
140 See eg _Mercantile Investment and General Trust v River Plate Trust Loan & Agency Co_ [1892] 2 Ch 303.
141 _Re National Permanent Building Society_ (1869) 5 LR Ch App 309 at 312–313.
142 _Re South Wales Atlantic Steamship Co_ (1875) 2 Ch D 763 and _Re Karnos Property Co Ltd_ (1989) 5 BCC 14.
143 _Re Masonic & General Life Assurance Co_ (1885) 32 Ch D 373.

a creditor a person with an unliquidated claim against the company in contract or tort is not able to petition for its winding up until judgment has been entered on his behalf.[144] It has been suggested that this rule may not now apply as it was decided before the legalisation specifically provided for petitions by contingent or prospective creditors.[145] However, this does not take account of the argument that a claim in tort or contract may prove to be unfounded and that, should the claim succeed, it is impossible to establish the amount of the claim and therefore whether it falls within the financial limits applicable for a successful petition.[146] These factors take unliquidated claims outside of the definition of a contingent creditor given by Pennycuick J in *Re William Hockley Ltd*,[147] which requires an existing obligation of the company to the petitioner which will, or may, at a future date, or on the happening of a future event, make the company subject to a present liability. In cases where no judgment has been entered on a contract or tort claim there is arguably no existing obligation. Whether such a claim might qualify a person as a 'prospective' creditor is unclear. If the word 'creditor' is taken to require a debt on the part of the company this again points to the need for judgment on an unliquidated claim. The word 'prospective' is apparently rendered superfluous.

14.68 A person who obtains a garnishee order against a company in respect of money held by the company on behalf of his debtor is unable to petition unless he obtains judgment against the company itself and petitions as a creditor. The garnishee order does not operate as an assignment to the garnishor of the debt due from the company to its creditor but merely as a lien. Consequently, until judgment is obtained by the garnishor against the company he is not a creditor.[148]

14.69 The debt must exist at the date of the petition and if it has been recovered without the creditors' knowledge on an execution levied by him before his petition was lodged he is no longer a creditor and will have the petition dismissed.[149] This rule has been criticised on the grounds that an action by the judgment creditor against the sheriff to recover monies paid to him as monies had and received would not succeed until the end of the period of 14 days for which the sheriff must hold money lest a winding up commences during that time, in which case the monies will be paid to the liquidator. It was argued that the monies do not vest in the creditor until the

---

144 *Re Milford Docks Co* (1883) 23 Ch D 292; *Re Pen y Van Colliery Co* (1877) 6 Ch D 477.
145 *Re a Company* [1973] 1 WLR 1567 per Megarry J at 1571.
146 Insolvency Act 1986 s 123 and see para 14.76 *infra*.
147 [1962] 2 All ER 111 at 113.
148 *Re Combined Weighing and Advertising Machine Co* (1889) 43 Ch D 99 and *Pritchett v English Syndicate Ltd* [1899] 2 QB 428.
149 *Re William Hockley Ltd* [1962] 2 All ER 111.

14 days are up.[150] However, since the *William Hockley* case was distinguished in *Re a Debtor ex parte Debtor v Goacher* the rule stands and applies whereever money is recovered before a petition is filed. Recovery between the date of filing and the date of the hearing will not have this effect and the creditors' petition will be heard subject to the outstanding debt being of a sufficient amount.

14.70 A person will qualify as a contingent creditor if there is an existing obligation which will or may give rise to a present liability on its part.[151] A holder of a bill of exchange which is not yet payable, a guarantor of a debt of the company who has not yet paid it or a landlord who wishes to claim for future rent will all qualify as petitioners as they are contingent creditors. A person, whose claim is for an amount for which the company will only be liable if certain actions taken on its behalf are later ratified, is not a contingent creditor as the company has done nothing and some action by the person bound is a necessary precondition for a contingent debt. If these conditions are satisfied there is no need to establish that the creditor could succeed in an action in debt at the date of the petition providing the claim will be so enforceable on the date at which liability arises or on the occurrence of the contingency on which liability depends. Both future debts and contingent debts are within s 124(1) of the Insolvency Act 1986 and a petition can be presented on the strength of the petitioner's actual or possible ability to bring an action in debt at a later date.[152] The costs of an action are a disputed debt until they are taxed or agreed and it is not proper to use a winding up petition to enforce such an unascertained debt if it has never been demanded.[153.]

14.71 A creditor's petition will fail if the company establishes a dispute about the debt which is supported by *prima facia* evidence and is put forward in good faith. If this occurs the court will usually dismiss the petition and require the dispute to be decided in favour of the petitioner before granting a further petition.[154] However, where it is clear that the company is indebted to the petitioner for an amount which would enable a winding up order to be made, a dispute on the precise amount will not prevent the court from making an order.[155] Once it is clear that the petitioning creditor has an undisputed claim for part of the total amount

150 *Re a Debtor (No 2 of 1977) ex p Debtor v Goacher* [1979] 1 WLR 956.
151 *Re SBA Properties* [1967] 1 WLR 799 at 802–83.
152 *Re British Equitable Bond and Mortgage Corporation Ltd* [1910] 1 Ch 574.
153 *Re a Company (No 001573 of 1983)* [1983] Com LR 202.
154 See *Re Brighton Club and Norfolk Hotel Ltd* (1865) 35 Beav 204; *Re Kings Cross Industrial Dwellings Co* (1870) LR 11 Eq 149; *Re a Company* [1984] BCLC 322 and *Re a Company* [1985] BCLC 000 (a striking out application).
155 *Re Tweeds Garages Ltd* [1962] 2 WLR 38.

the petition is not struck out automatically as an abuse of the process of the court because it would be extinguished by cross claims. In such a case the court exercises a judicial discretion and can take account of the class nature of a winding up petition to consider whether the company is in fact solvent. If it has negative current assets the petition will go to a hearing. This contrasts with the situation in which the whole debt is disputed and the petition is based on the statutory notice procedure. In such a case the insolvency of the company will not of itself justify a refusal to strike the petition out.[156] The process of deciding whether to make an order on the petition may involve the court in deciding the substantive dispute about the debt. Such a course of action is within the discretion of the court.[157]

14.72　If the company applies at an earlier stage for injunctive relief the court may restrain a creditor from petitioning until he has obtained judgment on his debt. The prosecution or advertisement of a petition already lodged will be restrained as an abuse of the process of the court where the petitioner lacks *locus standi* as a result of the substantial grounds on which the existence of the debt is disputed. For example, a director claiming for arrears of fees, when unauthorised drawings have been made without deduction of tax, may be so restrained.[158] Such applications to restrain petitions should be made by originating summons in the Companies Court. An order to restrain the advertisement of a petition based on a disputed debt is intended both to protect the company's reputation and to stop that particular step in the winding up proceedings. Consequently the court has jurisdiction to restrain other forms of publication of the fact that a petition was presented.[159]

14.73　An injunction to restrain a winding up petition should only be granted in cases where the petition would be found to be an abuse of the process of the court; or if irreparable damage to the company is possible as a result of such proceedings and there is insufficient time for an adequate consideration of the issues.[160] The presentation of a petition may be restrained where the statutory demand served under s 123(1)(a) of the Insolvency Act 1986 relates to a disputed debt. Once the *bona fides* of a dispute are established the company is entitled to an injunction as of right and no undertaking to file a declaration of solvency should be imposed on the directors. Winding up proceedings are not usually the appropriate method for deciding, either whether a debt exists or whether it is present or

156　*Re R A Foulds* (1986) 2 BCC 99, 269.
157　*Brinds Ltd v Offshore Oil NL* (1986) 2 BCC 98, 917 (PC).
158　*Mann v Goldstein* [1968] 1 WLR 1091.
159　*Re a Company* [1986] BCLC 127.
160　*Coulson Sanderson & Ward Ltd v Ward* (1986) 2 BCC 99, 207 and *Bryanston Finance v De Vries (No 2)* [1976] 2 WLR 41.

contingent, and a court considering an application to restrain the presentation of a petition is not obliged to leave the Companies Court to resolve all the issues between the parties.[161] The fact that the debt is prospective and that the company alleges that it is not payable at the time of the presentation of the petition is not sufficient to justify restraining a petition. The Act permits petitions by prospective creditors and the question of whether a winding up order should be made in such case should be decided at the eharing of the petition.[162]

14.74 If it is established that a petition was presented maliciously, damages are payable in tort without proof of special damage and there is no need for the company to prove that it sought relief before the hearing at which it successfully defended the petition.[163] However, where a company fails to pay an undisputed debt and fails to reply to correspondence about it, the fact that it is a reputable and well known enterprise does not make the presentation of a petition, on the ground that it is unable to pay its debts, an abuse of the process of the court. The company will be refused relief as it could pay the debt rather than seeking to have the petition restrained.[164]

14.75 Where a judgment has been obtained against the company the creditor will normally succeed in obtaining a winding up order as the company will be estopped from disputing the claim unless it can be established that the judgment was obtained fraudulently or collusively.[165] A pending appeal will not prevent the court from making a winding up order on the basis of the judgment debt but a cross claim equal to, or in excess of, the amount of the judgment debt, or the fact that a claim against a petitioning creditor by the company can be pursued more readily by the directors than by a liquidator (for example because of their easier access to resources to finance litigation), may cause the court to stay proceedings on the petition pending the outcome of the counterclaim.[166]

14.76 The opposition of other creditors, or of shareholders, to the making of a winding up order may be taken into account by the court in exercising its discretion whether to make an order, but a creditor whose debt is due for payment immediately and is not either a contingent or a future debt has a right, as against the company, to an order.[167] A winding up order cannot be

161 *Stonegate Securities v Gregory* [1980] 3 WLR 168.
162 *Holt Southey v Catnic Components Ltd* [1978] 1 WLR 630.
163 *Quartz Hill Mining Co v Eyre* (1883) 11 QBD 674.
164 *Cornhill Insurance v Improvement Services* [1986] 1 WLR 114.
165 *Bowes v Directors of Hope Life and Insurance Guarantee Co* (1865) 11 HL Cas 389.
166 *Re LHF Wools Ltd* [1969] 3 WLR 100.
167 *Bowes v Directors of Hope Life* (note 165 supra); *Re J D Swain Ltd* [1965] 1 WLR 909; and *Re LHF Wools* (n 166 supra).

refused by the court on the grounds only that a company's assets have been mortgaged to an amount equal to or exceeding their value or because the company has no assets.[168] The court will, as a general rule, refuse an order if the amount of the debt on which the petition is based is less than the amount for which a creditor may serve a demand to establish the company's inability to pay its debts. However several creditors whose debts together reach that total may join together in a single petition which will not be dismissed on the grounds of the value of their individual claims.[169] If there is a deliberate refusal to pay a debt for a smaller amount and winding up represents the only effective method of enforcement then a petition may be allowed.[170]

Petition by a contributory

Who may petition?

14.77   A winding up petition may be presented by any 'contributory' or 'contributories'.[171] This expression includes not only those who can be required to contribute money to the company in the course of the winding up, but also the holders of fully paid shares in a company limited by shares who will not be required to make payment to the company during the winding up by virtue of their shareholding.[172] A person holding scrip certificates for shares in a company may petition, despite not being a member, if he agrees to do all acts necessary to become a shareholder and admits his liability as a contributory.[173] The holder is required to admit his liability to contribute as scrip—unlike a letter of allotment—does not place a contractual obligation to take shares on the holder but merely gives him the option to do so.[174] It is clear, however, that membership past or present of the company is not a necessary qualification for a contributory. The question is whether the person is liable to contribute.

14.78   An allottee whose name has never been entered in the register of members is allowed to petition in principle although the existence of a *bona fide* dispute whether there has been an allotment of shares to the petitioner and whether he is a contributory will result in the dismissal of the petition.[175] However, where a contributory's petition also includes an

---

168 Insolvency Act 1986 s 125(1).
169 *Re Industrial Insurance Association Ltd* [1910] WN 245 and *Re Leyton & Walthamstow Cycle Co Ltd* (1901) 50 WR 93; and see Insolvency Act 1986 s 123(1)(a). The current sum is £750.
170 *Re World Industrial Bank Ltd* [1909] WN 148.
171 Insolvency Act 1986 s 124(1).
172 *Ibid* ss 74(1) and (2)(d) and 79(1); *Re National Savings Bank Association* (1866) 1 Ch App 547; and see ch 17.
173 *Re Littlehampton, Havre & Honfleur SS Co Ltd* (1865) 34 LJ Ch 237.
174 See R R Pennington, *Company Law* 5th ed p 849.
175 *Re JN2 Ltd* [1978] 1 WLR 183.

alternative claim that the petitioner's shares be purchased by the company or other members, under s 459 of the Companies Act 1985, on the grounds that the company's affairs have been conducted in a manner unfairly prejudicial to the petitioner, it is proper for the question of the beneficial ownership of the petitioner's shares to be considered under s 45 and then for the petition to be dealt with if necessary.[176]

14.79 The trustee in bankruptcy of a contributory represents him for all purposes of the winding up[177] but his right to petition for a winding up is subject to a requirement that the trustee has been registered as a shareholder for the necessary statutory 6 month period.[178] Section 82(2), which treats him as a contributory, only begins to operate after the winding up period has begun.[179] This means that during the whole period of subsistence of the original contributory's bankruptcy after the shares have been registered in the trustee's name the bankrupt is not regarded as a contributory and only the trustee can present a petition. This applies even to shares which were held by the bankrupt as a trustee.[180] However, while the bankrupt is still registered as a member and the trustee is not, the bankrupt can petition at the instance of the trustee.[181]

14.80 Any person on whom shares have devolved on the death of a former holder is contemplated as a possible petitioner.[182] A personal representative of the deceased shareholder can petition even if he has not been registered as a shareholder.[183] However it is not yet settled whether an unregistered beneficiary in whom the shares have been vested by the personal representative can petition. Since the shares would seem to have 'devolved on him through the death of a former holder'[184] it is submitted that such a person should be entitled to present a petition. A person who assents to take shares allotted to him and to registration as a member is a member of the company within s 22(2) of the Companies Act 1985 even if there was no binding contract to take the shares.[185] Such a person would consequently be a contributory under s 74(1) of the Insolvency Act 1986.

Restrictions on a contributory's petition

14.81 The Insolvency Act 1986 limits the right of a contributory to

---

176   *Re Garage Doors Associates Ltd* [1984] 1 WLR 35.
177   Insolvency Act 1986 s 82(2).
178   *Ibid* s 124(2)(b) and see paras 14.81 *et seq, infra.*
179   *Re HL Bolton Engineering Co Ltd* [1956] 2 WLR 84.
180   *Re Wolverhampton Steel & Iron Co Ltd* [1977] 1 WLR 860.
181   *Re K/9 Meat Supplies (Guildford) Ltd* [1966] 1 WLR 1112.
182   Insolvency Act 1986 s 124(2)(b).
183   *Re Bayswater Trading Co Ltd* [1970] 1 WLR 343.
184   s 124(2)(b).
185   *Re Nuneaton Borough Association Football Club* (1989) 5 BCC 000.

petition by reference to the length of time during which shares have been held by him and registered in his name. Unless the number of members of the company has been reduced below two; or some or all of the shares have been devolved on the petitioner on the death of a former holder, or were originally allotted to him, the shares must have been held by him and registered in his name for at least 6 months during the 18 months before the petition is presented.[186] The purpose of this provision is to prevent persons from buying shares in a company with the intention of immediately having it wound up. The exception relating to the reduction in the number of members below two recognizes the potential personal liability of members in such cases if the situation continues for 6 months.[187] The special rights of allottees and those on whom shares devolve on the death of a shareholder recognise that in such cases there is no danger of a purchase of shares solely to enable a petition to be presented. The requirement of registration prevents a holder of a bearer share warrant from presenting the petition unless he is the original allottee as although shares are held by him they are not registered in his name.[188] The renouncee of a letter of allotment is not the original allottee and has not been registered as holding shares; therefore he can only petition if the number of members has fallen below two.

14.82 It seems that where a contributory has applied to be registered as a member and the company has defaulted in registering his name as a shareholder, the date of registration may be taken from the date on which the transfer was presented for registration for the purpose of deciding whether the 6 month period has been completed. Where a court order requiring the company to allot shares to the petitioner and to register him as a member was made more than 6 months before the date of the presentation of the petition it has been held at first instance that the statutory period should be treated as completed and the petition allowed if the company's default is the only reason for the failure to register.[189] However, the Court of Appeal has distinguished this case in circumstances in which an order was made against a shareholder and the company was not a party to it.[190] It therefore seems unlikely that a court would treat the requirement that shares be held and registered for at least 6 months as satisfied in any case where registration has not lasted for that period, in the absence of a court order binding on the company and requiring registration of the petitioner as a shareholder. The general rule is that if there is a genuine dispute whether shares were allotted to the petitioner the petition

186 Insolvency Act 1986 s 124(2).
187 Companies Act 1985 s 24.
188 *Re Wala Wynaad Indian Gold Mining Co* (1882) 21 Ch D 849.
189 *Re Patent Steam Engine Co* (1878) 8 Ch D 464.
190 *Re Gattopardo Ltd* [1969] 1 WLR 619; and see *obiter* statement of Vaughan Williams J in *Re a Company* [1894] 2 Ch 349 at 351.

will be dismissed if the petitioner does not satisfy the requirement of registration.[191] The existence of a blank transfer giving the petitioner an equitable right to shares is not sufficient to make him a contributory in the absence of registration.[192]

14.83 A person liable to contribute in a winding up under s 76 of the Insolvency Act 1986, because of his part in the company's purchase or redemption of its own shares within 1 year before a winding up commences may petition on the ground of the company's insolvency. Alternatively he may do so on the just and equitable ground without reference to the conditions of s 124(2) regarding holding shares for 6 months or the number of members being less than two. However, to petition on any other ground such a person must satisfy one of those requirements.[193]

14.84 In addition to the statutory restrictions on petitions brought by contributories, the courts will not, as a general rule, uphold a petition unless the petitioner stands to gain from the winding up process. In the absence of exceptional circumstances, a petition by a holder of fully paid shares in a limited company will not succeed if there will not be any surplus for distribution to shareholders after the claims of the creditors and the costs of the winding up have been met.[194] This rule is unaffected by s 125(1) of the Insolvency Act 1986, which lays down that a winding up order should not be refused on the grounds that the company has no assets or has mortgaged its assets for an amount in excess of their value.[195] The petition must allege there are sufficient assets to provide a tangible surplus and this must be proved *prima facie* at the hearing of the petition.[196] It is, however, sufficient to show that the affairs of the company require investigation in respects likely to produce a surplus, for example, because of preferences or transactions at an undervalue which may be set aside, allegations of misfeasance by directors or other reasons.[197] The question of whether the petitioning contributory has a tangible interest is *prima facie* one for the hearing of the petition and consequently an application to strike the petition out on that ground will fail unless it is plain and obvious at that stage that there is no surplus. That will not be the case if, for example, the surrender value of a lease held by the company is not known at the time of the application to strike the petition out.[198]

---

191   *Re JN2 Ltd* [1978] 1 WLR 183.
192   *Re Quickdome Ltd* (1988) 4 BCC 296.
193   Insolvency Act 1986 s 124(3).
194   *Re Rica Gold Washing Co* (1879) 11 Ch D 36.
195   See *Re Kaslo-Slocan Mining & Financial Corporation Ltd* [1910] WN 13.
196   *Re Rica Gold Washing Co* (note 194 *supra*).
197   *Re Diamond Fuel Co* (1879) 13 Ch D 400; *Re Othery Construction Ltd* [1966] 1 WLR 69.
198   *Re Martin Coulter Enterprises Ltd* [1988] BCLC 121.

14.85 A petition on the basis of s 122(1)(g) (the just and equitable ground) may succeed if it is established that it is not possible to tell whether the company is solvent as the result of a failure to provide members with accounts and information about the company to which they are entitled.[199] It is, however, no justification for a contributory's petition that he is concerned to protect creditors or to bring to light the conduct of the company's affairs which has affected them.[200] The fact that a petition is brought in respect of a 'quasi partnership' in the form of a company does not exempt the contributory petitioner from the need to show the likelihood of a surplus.[201]

14.86 A contributory may succeed in showing that he has an interest in a winding up order being made, even if no surplus will exist for distribution to shareholders, where he is likely to have to contribute funds in a winding up since the amount required of him may increase if an order is not made on his petition. A member of an unlimited company is not required to establish the existence of a surplus.[202] A fully paid up member of a company in which the membership has fallen below two is liable to contribute if the state of affairs continues for more than 6 months. Consequently he may petition when the company is insolvent to minimise his loss. However, some private advantage in a capacity other than that of member will not justify a contributory's petition.[203] The petition must allege some advantage or the avoidance of some disadvantage to the contributory if an order is made.[204] If a contributory petitioner has no tangible interest in that capacity but does have such an interest as, for example, a guarantor of the company's debts and is a contingent creditor he may be substituted as a creditor petitioner and no readvertisement is necessary if there is no actual or potential opposition from other creditors.[205]

14.87 A holder of partly paid shares will have a possible loss which may increase if the company is not wound up on his petition but the court retains a discretion to refuse a petition where the liability of the petitioner is small and a large majority of members oppose a winding up.[206] A petitioner in arrears with calls on his shares will be required to pay the arrears to the company or into court before his petition is considered.[207]

199 *Re Newman & Howard Ltd* [1961] 3 WLR 192—a case allowing the costs of a petition on those grounds.
200 *Re Othery Construction* (note 197 *supra*).
201 *Re Expanded Plugs Ltd* [1966] 1 WLR 69.
202 *Re Norwich Yarn Co* (1850) 12 Beav 366.
203 *Re Chesterfield Catering Co* [1976] 3 All ER 294.
204 *Re Instrumentation Electrical Services* [1988] BCLC 550.
205 *Re Commercial and Industrial Insulators Ltd* [1986] BCLC 191.
206 *Re London Suburban Bank* (1871) 6 Ch App 641.
207 *Re Crystal Reef Gold Mining Co* [1892] 1 Ch 408.

14.88 In exercising its discretion whether to make a winding up order the court will have regard to the wishes of the majority of members by value and will refuse an order if they oppose it.[208] However, where a fraud on the minority is suspected on the part of the majority an order may be made.[209] This is a reflection of the rule in *Foss v Harbottle*[210] and the principle of majority rule. It applies to the petitions of contributories but not those of creditors even where the majority argues that the company will be able to pay its debts by virtue of the proceeds of a call already made.[211] Where the other members had expressed a willingness to comply with the petitioner's request to buy his shares and would pay a price fixed by the valuation of a competent valuer, the petition was dismissed as a result of his unreasonable rejection of the method of valuation.[212]

14.89 The power of the court to grant an injunction restraining the presentation of a winding up petition should normally only be used if such a step would be an abuse of the process of the court or if the company would suffer irreparable damage and there is not sufficient time to permit an adequate consideration of the issues. If a contributory petitions on the just and equitable ground and it is clear that he was excluded from the company on the breakdown of a quasi partnership relationship, suspicion of his motives for using the winding up remedy rather than seeking an order under s 459 of the Companies Act 1985 will not justify a finding of an abuse of the process of the court.[213] The memorandum and articles of association of a company cannot exclude or limit the statutory right of a contributory to petition for a winding up order despite the contractual effect conferred on them by s 14 of the Companies Act 1985.[214] Where a voluntary winding up has already begun this is a *prima facie* reason against upholding a contributory's petition but such an order will be made if the petitioner shows that he will be prejudiced if his petition is refused.[215] This discretion, like that which governs the attitude of the court to the views of the majority on any contributory's petition is a reflection of the company law principle of majority rule and the exceptions to it.

Secretary of State's petition

14.90 As part of his role in policing and investigating the activities of companies, the Secretary of State for Trade and Industry has certain

208 *Re London Suburban Bank* (note 206 above).
209 *Re Varieties Ltd* [1893] 2 Ch 235.
210 (1843) 2 Hare 461; and see *Re Professional, Commercial and Industrial Benefit Society* (1871) 6 Ch App 856.
211 *Re International Contract Co Ltd, Spartali & Tabor* (1866) 14 LT 726.
212 *Re a Company* [1983] 1 WLR 927.
213 *Coulon Sanderson & Ward v Ward* (1986) 2 BCC 992.
214 *Re Peveril Gold Mines Ltd* [1898] 1 Ch 122.
215 *Re Zinotty Properties* [1984] BCLC 375.

powers to apply to the court for the winding up of a company. These powers may be exercised by a senior official of the Department of Trade and Industry who may decide to exercise them and swear, in his own name, the necessary affidavit supporting the petition.[216]

14.91 Under s 440 of the Companies Act 1985 the Secretary of State may present a petition on the just and equitable ground. He may do so only if it appears to him from the report of an inspector who has investigated the company, or from information or documents obtained under the powers granted under s 447 or 448 of the Companies Act 1985, or s 94 or 105 of the Financial Services Act 1986, that it is expedient in the public interest that the company should be wound up. A Secretary of State's petition under this provision can only be presented after the result of an investigation by an inspector or an inspection of documents has persuaded the Secretary of State that winding up is in the public interest. The decision of the Secretary of State to appoint inspectors is not subject to the rules of natural justice and the court cannot interfere with it so long as the decision was made in good faith and is within the powers conferred by the legislation used.[217] The Court of Appeal has held that the view of the Secretary of State as regards the public interest is a precondition for his petition. Any challenge on the issue of whether that precondition is satisfied must be made by judicial review proceedings and not on the hearing of the winding up petition.[218]

14.92 An inspector's report is admissible as *prima facie* evidence of matters to which it relates and can result in the success of a petition in the absence of any other evidence but the court will hear any evidence to a different effect and decide the case by weighing all the evidence.[219] In cases where serious misconduct is alleged the court may require further evidence in addition to the inspector's report.[220]

14.93 A petition may be presented by the Secretary of State even if the company is already in voluntary liquidation. This is because the courts recognise the special status of the Secretary of State as petitioner since he decides to petition on the basis of the public interest and not, as a creditor or other petitioner would, on the basis of personal interest. Consequently the court, while retaining its proper judicial function and its discretion, will consider the views of the Secretary of State on the public interest and they

---

216 *Re Golden Chemical Products* [1976] Ch 300.
217 *Norwest Holst v Secretary of State for Trade and Industry* [1978] 3 WLR 73.
218 *Re Walter L Jacob & Co Ltd* (1989) 5 BCC 244.
219 *Re Armavent Ltd* [1975] 1 WLR 1679.
220 *Re Allied Produce Ltd* [1967] 1 WLR 1469.

may well outweigh the views of the contributories.[221] However, the Court of Appeal has laid down that the views of the Secretary of State are not entitled to any special weight.[222] An inspector's report may be used by a contributory to support his petition so long as the relevant matters and passages in it are identified.[223] The 'public interest' element in a petition by the Secretary of State makes it inappropriate for an undertaking on damages to be required as a condition of continuing the appointment of a provisional liquidator and a special manager on the petition being heard.[224]

14.94 If, as is often the case, the petition by the Secretary of State is brought because of concern about trading practices of the company, it will not be appropriate for the court to accept an undertaking from the company to change its trading methods in the future in return for refusing to make a winding up order. It is not the court's function to police the trading practices of companies accused of practices of doubtful commercial morality.[225] If the petition is based on evidence gathered under s 109 of the Financial Services Act 1986 the same principle should apply as a regulatory system which can perform that function exists under that Act. Poor accounting records, commercial dishonesty and unacceptable methods of selling securities can all be taken into account in such cases.[226]

14.95 Apart from the power of the Secretary of State to petition in the public interest as part of his supervisory role, he has specific powers in the case of companies which fail to comply with the requirements imposed on public companies under Companies Act 1985. A company which was a public company immediately before 22nd December 1980 and which has failed to re-register as a public or a private company can be subject to a Secretary of State's petition, as can a company incorporated as a public company after that date which has not, within a year of its incorporation, obtained a registrar's certificate under s 117 of the Companies Act 1985 that it may do business and borrow.[227] A company which engages in the investment business may be wound up on the petition of the Secretary of State under s 72 of the Financial Services Act 1986. His power to petition has been devolved to the Securities and Investment Board which is the most likely petitioner but the Secretary of State does retain a concurrent power to

221 *Re Lubin Rosen & Associates Ltd* [1975] 1 WLR 122.
222 *Re Walter L Jacob* (note 218 *supra*).
223 *Re St Piran Ltd* [1981] 1 WLR 1300.
224 *Re Highfield Commodities Ltd* [1984] 3 All ER 884.
225 *Re Bamford Publishers Ltd The Times* 4 June 1977.
226 *Re Walter L Jacob* (note 218 *supra*).
227 See Insolvency Act 1986 s 122(1)(b), (c) and (4) and Companies Consolidation (Consequential Provisions) Act 1985 s 1.

petition.[228] An insurance company may be subject to a Secretary of State's petition under s 54(1) of the Insurance Companies Act 1982 as amended.

The official receiver

14.96 Where a company is being wound up voluntarily, the official receiver (in common with other categories of petitioner) may present a petition for it to be wound up by the court but an order will only be made on the petition if the court is satisfied on the balance of probabilities that the voluntary winding up cannot be continued with due regard to the interest of contributories or creditors.[229] The issue is whether the creditors or contributories will be prejudiced by the continuation of the voluntary liquidation. It has been held that the fact that a liquidator in a voluntary winding up was the appointee of the company's sole controlling shareholder is enough to justify making an order on the official receiver's petition but allegations of fraud on customers are not sufficient in themselves. All the evidence has to be considered by the court in making its decision.[230] The fact that under the Insolvency Act 1986 all liquidators must now be qualified insolvency practitioners and will be subject to regulation by professional bodies or the Department of Trade and Industry should make the use of this power even less common than it was formerly.

THE PETITION: FORM, SERVICE AND ADVERTISEMENT

14.97 A petition[231] to wind up a company should follow form 4.2 set out in the Appendix to the Insolvency Rules 1986 with only the variations necessitated by the circumstances of each particular case.[232] It will be headed with a description of the court in which it is presented including, in the case of a High Court petition a reference to the Chancery Division Group A. The full name of the petitioner and of the company to be wound up will be included together with the address of the company's registered office; its nominal share capital and the amount of capital paid up; and the principal objects of the company as set out in its memorandum of association. The ground on which a winding up order is sought is then set out. This part of the document must allege a case for winding up within s 122 of the Insolvency Act 1986—failure to do so will result in the dismissal of the petition with costs unless the court gives leave for the amendment of

---

228 Financial Services Act 1986 (Delegation) Order 1987 (SI 1987 no 942).
229 Insolvency Act 1986 s 124(5) and *Re J Russell Electronics Ltd* [1968] 1 WLR 1252.
230 *Re Medical Battery Co* [1894] 1 Ch 444.
231 See generally Palmer's 'Company Law' 24th Ed Vol 1 at paras 88.20 to 88.24.
232 Insolvency Rules 1986 r 12.7.

the document.[233] This is so even if there is evidence establishing a ground for an order.[234] Where fraud is alleged then the facts constituting fraud must be clearly stated in order to give an opportunity for a reply.[235]

14.98 The petition is presented at the office or chambers of the registrar who appoints a time and place for it to be heard. He endorses that information on the petition and sealed copies of it.[236] The petition will only be filed in court if it is produced with a receipt for the deposit payable on presentation.[237] In addition, copies for service on the company and exhibition with the affidavit of service must be delivered unless the company is the petitioner. If the company is in voluntary liquidation, subject to an administration order, in administrative receivership, subject to a voluntary arrangement or is an authorised institution under the Banking Act 1987, then a copy must be supplied to be sent to the existing liquidator, administrator, administrative receiver, supervisor of the arrangement or the Bank of England if, in each case, that person or body is not the petitioner. The copy petitions must be despatched to those persons on the next business day after it was served on the company.[238] On payment of the appropriate fee every director, contributory or creditor of the company is entitled to be given a copy of the petition by the petitioner's solicitor within 2 days of requesting it.[239] A petition to wind the company up can be presented after an administration petition has been presented but its advertisement will be restrained and no further steps on it will be allowed until the hearing of the administration petition.[240]

14.99 The date of the presentation of the petition is the date on which a winding up by the court commences unless a voluntary winding up has already begun in which case the date of commencement is the date on which the winding up resolution was passed.[241] This makes it vital to be able to establish the date on which a petition was presented. In the absence of bad faith or collusion attaching to the presentation of the first petition petitions rank according to the date of presentation and not the date of advertisement. Such factors may cause the first one to lose priority.[242]

233   *Langham Skating Rink Co* (1877) 5 Ch D 669. Even a discrepancy between the name of the company in the petition and its name in a judgment on which the petition is based can be fatal, although a different creditor may be substituted—*Re Goldthorpe & Lacey Ltd* (1987) 3 BCC 595.
234   *Re Wear Engine Works Co* (1875) 10 Ch App 188.
235   *Re Rica Gold Washing Co* (1879) 11 Ch D 36.
236   Insolvency Rules 1986 r 4.7(5) and (6).
237   *Ibid* r 4.7(2).
238   *Ibid* r 4.7(3), (4) and 4.10.
239   *Ibid* r 4.13.
240   *Re a Company (001992 of 1988)* [1989] BCLC 9.
241   Insolvency Act 1986 s 129.
242   *Re Building Societies Trust* (1890) 44 Ch D 140.

14.100   The petition must be verified by an affidavit to the effect that the statements in it are true or are true to the best of the deponent's knowledge, information and belief. If the petition is in respect of debts due to different creditors, the debts to each creditor must be separately verified. The affidavit must be sworn by the petitioner or by an officer of a corporate petitioner, a solicitor who has been concerned in the matter, or some responsible person who has been duly authorised to make the affidavit and has the requisite knowledge of those matters.[243] The petition must be exhibited to the affidavit verifying it and will be *prima facie* evidence of the statements in the petition; even if it amounts to hearsay evidence.[244]

14.101   Every petition must be advertised once in the *London Gazette* not less than 7 business days before the day fixed for a hearing and, if the petitioner is someone other than the company, not less than 7 business days after service and not less than 7 such days before the day fixed for the hearing.[245] The court has power to direct otherwise[246] and a trifling defect in an advertisement which has misled no-one will not invalidate the petition. A slight misspelling of the company's name which is unlikely to mislead or cause confusion, or an error about the last date for service of a notice to appear which do not mislead will be waived by he court under Rule 7.55 of the Rules.[247] A failure to advertise the petition in accordance with the rules may result in its dismissal.[248] The court has power to extend the time laid down by the Act or the Rules for advertising or for doing any other act or taking any proceedings either before or after the time has expired and on such terms, if any, as it thinks fit.[249] The court may restrain the petitioner from advertising his petition if it holds that the petition is an abuse of the process of the court but not on the basis of the possibility of an administration order, unless the company undertakes to present such a petition.[250]

14.102   Any petition not being presented by the company itself must be served on the company at its registered office or, if there is none, or it is not practicable to serve it there, at its last known principal place of business. It is served by being handed to a person who there and then acknowledges

---

243 Insolvency Rules 1986 r 4.12.
244 *Ibid* r 4.12(3) and (6) and *Re Koscot Interplanetary (UK) Ltd* [1972] 3 All ER 829; and see paras 160 *et seq*, *infra* on the hearing of the petition.
245 r 4.11(2).
246 This may include advertisement in a newspaper other than the *London Gazette* – r 4.11(1) and 4.11(3).
247 *Re J & P Sussman* [1958] 1 WLR 519; *Re Broad's Patent Night Light Co* [1892] WN 5; and *Re Videofusion* [1974] 1 WLR 1548.
248 Insolvency Rules 1986 r 4.11(5).
249 *Ibid* r 4.3.
250 *Charles Forte Investments Ltd v Amanda* [1964] Ch 240 and *Re Manlon Trading Ltd* (1988) 4 BCC 455.

himself to be, or who the server believes to be, a director or other officer or employee of the company, or a person who acknowledges himself to be authorised to accept service. In the absence of such a person the petition can be left at the registered office or place of business in such a way that it is likely to come to the attention of a person attending there. Otherwise the directions of the court may be sought to permit service in some other way.[251] Service is proved by an affidavit exhibiting a sealed copy of the petition and any order for substituted service. The affidavit must be filed in court immediately after service.[252] At least 5 days before the hearing of the petition, the petitioner or his solicitor must file in court a certificate of compliance with the rules for service and advertisement in Form 4.7. Failure to do so may result in the dismissal of the petition.[253]

14.103   Only one petition will normally succeed in respect of each of a number of companies to be wound up even if they have common shareholders, unless they form part of a group of companies.[254] This rule is designed to save costs. If more than one petition is presented in respect of the same company, a creditor may be substituted for a member but readvertisement will usually be ordered, as a contributory's petition has now become a creditor's petition.[255]

14.104   No duty of care is owed by one litigant to another in respect of the way litigation is conducted in relation to the service of process or other procedural steps. Consequently service of a winding up petition at the wrong address, resulting in the making of a winding up order when the company does not appear, does not form the basis for a damages claim by the company against the petitioner.[256] There is no right to withdraw a petition once it has been presented and a withdrawal obtained by lying to the court will not be allowed to stand.[257]

14.105   The premature advertisement of a petition will not automatically lead to it being struck out. However, advertisement before presentation may well result in such an order unless a supporting creditor is substituted for the original petitioner although if the company is already in voluntary liquidation no harm will be done and the general rule will not be applied.[258] Where service on an incorrect address, caused by an error at the Companies

251   Insolvency Rules 1986 r 4.8.
252   *Ibid* r 4.9.
253   *Ibid* r 4.14.
254   *Re a Company* [1984] BCLC 307.
255   *Re Creative Handbook Ltd* [1985] BCLC 1.
256   *Business Computers International v Registrar of Companies* [1987] BCLC 621.
257   *Re Wavern Engineering Co Ltd* (1987) 3 BCC 3.
258   *Re Signland Ltd* [1982] 2 All ER 609; *Re Roselmar Properties* (1986) 2 BCC 156.

Registry, is corrected after the advertisement of the petition and the company suffers no prejudice because the advertisement brings in supporting creditors there will be a hearing on the merits and the petition will not be struck out.[259]

THE GROUNDS FOR A WINDING UP BY THE COURTS

14.106 A winding up petition can succeed only if the petitioner establishes a ground. Seven such grounds are contained in the Insolvency Act 1986 and any one of them will suffice for this purpose. They will be dealt with in turn—the most commonly used grounds, of the company's inability to pay its debts and the opinion of the court that a winding up would be just and equitable, being considered last. The ground applicable only to petitions by the Secretary of State under s 440 of the Companies Act 1985 has already been dealt with[260] and the grounds available in respect of banks, insurance companies and deposit taking companies will be considered after the grounds generally applicable to all companies.[261] The grounds for a winding up order are set out in s 122(1) of the Insolvency Act 1986.

Special resolution; s 122(1)(a)

14.107 If the company has resolved by special resolution that it be wound up by the court, that is a ground for an order under s 122(1)(a). This ground is almost entirely otiose as a special resolution may be used to begin a voluntary liquidation of the company without the need for any other ground. Since, even after the reforms to the procedure of winding up by the court to be found in the Insolvency Act 1986, a voluntary liquidation will be speedier and cheaper it is hard to envisage any circumstances in which this ground would be attractive as a means of winding up a company.

Public companies not complying with share capital requirements; s 122(1)(b)

14.108 It is a ground for a winding up order that, being a public company which was registered as such on its original incorporation, the company has not been issued with a certificate under s 117 of the Companies Act 1985 confirming its compliance with the Act's requirements for the minimum permitted nominal value of its allotted share capital. More than a year must

---

259 *Re Corbenstoke Ltd* (1989) 5 BCC 197; and see *Re Garton (Western) Ltd* (1989) 5 BCC 198.
260 See paras 14.90–95 *supra.*
261 See paras 14.153–158 *infra.*

have elapsed since the company's first registration. This ground, which may support a petition by the Secretary of State for Trade and Industry or by any other petitioner,[262] is a means of policing the adherence of public companies to the rules for the minimum nominal value of the allotted share capital of public companies—the current figure of £50,000 is laid down by s 118(1) of the Act but may be varied by order.

14.109   A company which is unable to comply with s 117 and 118 of the Companies Act 1985 may re-register as a private company by following the procedure laid down in ss 53 to 55 of the Act. This requires a special resolution to re-register and to make necessary alterations to the company's memorandum and articles of association and an application in the prescribed form to the Registrar of Companies.[263] The application to re-register is then subject to a right of the holders of an aggregate of 5% in the nominal value of the company's issued share capital or any class of it or of 50 of the company's members within 28 days of the passing of the resolution to apply to the court.[264] This may result in the cancellation or confirmation of the resolution by court order on such terms and conditions and with such directions as the court thinks fit.[265] In the absence of any application to the court within the 28 day period allowed, or after the making of a court order confirming the resolution as a result of such an application, the registrar should issue a certificate of incorporation suitable to a private company and from the date of the issue of that certificate the company becomes a private company and the alterations to the memorandum and articles specified in the special resolution take effect.[266]

Old public companies; s 122(1)(c)

14.110   Section 122(1)(c) lays down the ground that the company is an 'old public company' registered as such immediately before 22nd December 1980. This ground applies to those companies which were registered as public companies before the relevant provisions of the Companies Act 1980 came into force and which have failed to re-register as either public companies or private companies.[267] A petition on this ground may be brought by the Secretary of State for Trade and Industry or by others entitled to petition.[268] Such petitions are likely to be increasingly rare as time passes after the relevant date.

---

262 Insolvency Act 1986 s 124(4).
263 Companies Act 1985 s 53(1) and (2).
264 *Ibid* s 54(1), (2) and (3). If the company has no share capital, 5% of the members or 50 members (whichever is fewer) will suffice.
265 *Ibid* s 54(1) and (5) to (9).
266 *Ibid* s 55.
267 Companies Consolidation (Consequential Provisions) Act 1985 s 1.
268 Insolvency Act 1986 s 124(4).

Suspension of business; s 122(1)(d)

14.111 A petition can succeed on the ground that the company has suspended its business for a whole year or did not commence its business within a year from the date of its incorporation. Despite the wording of the statutory provision the courts have held that this ground requires that the company should have an intention to abandon its business if it is to be wound up for the suspension of its business for a year. Where a company was formed to build, use and let assembly rooms, suspended all operations as a result of a trade depression after rooms had been built, an order was refused owing to the absence of an intention to abandon business. The court has a discretion and will have regard to the wishes of the majority of members in exercising it.[269] The opinion of such shareholders whether the business has been abandoned will also be considered.[270] Where only one of several main objects of the company is abandoned, this will not be enough to establish the failure to commence or the suspension of its business.[271]

14.112 A company is not regarded as carrying on its business by merely holding board meetings if no attempt is being made to carry out its objects but it has not suspended its business if it becomes a holding company with shares in subsidiaries which pursue its own objects.[272] Where there is a prospect of business being commenced in a reasonable time a winding up order will not be made because more than a year has elapsed since the company's incorporation if there is some explanation to account for the delay and in such circumstances a petition will be dismissed. An adjournment is inappropriate because of the relation back of the commencement of any later winding up order to the date of presentation of the petition. This relation back will imperil or invalidate acts done before the order is made.[273]

14.113 It is improbable that a petition on this ground will succeed where some business which falls within the company's main objects has been carried out[274] or where this is likely to occur in the future.[275] This attitude and the regard had to the wishes of a majority of members by value reflects the unwillingness of the courts to gainsay the commercial decisions of those in control of a company on the timing of its business activities on the

---

269 *Re Middlesburgh Assembly Rooms Co* (1880) 14 Ch D 104.
270 *Re Tomlin Patent Horse Shoe Co Ltd* (1886) 55 LT 314.
271 See *Re Langham Skating Rink Co* (1877) 5 Ch D 669 and *Re Norwegian Titanic Iron Co* (1866) 35 Beav 223 respectively.
272 *Re Langham Skating Rink Co* (note 271 above) and *Re Eastern Telegraph Co* [1947] 2 All ER 104.
273 *Re Metropolitan Railway Co Ltd* (1867) 36 LJ Ch 827.
274 *Re Capital Fire Assurance Association* (1882) 21 Ch D 209.
275 *Re Metropolitan Railway* (note 273 *supra*).

application of a minority.[276] A minority with a substantial grievance will be better advised to apply for relief on the 'just and equitable' ground[277] or, in the alternative, under s 459 of the Companies Act 1985. A defunct company may be removed from the register under s 652 of the Companies Act 1985.

Number of members below minimum s 122(1)(e)

14.114 A company may be wound up if the number of its members is reduced below two. This enables a member who is unable to transfer one or more of his shares to a nominee to escape the personal liability for the debts of the company which, after a period of 6 months, will be imposed on him under s 24 of the Companies Act 1985. A member need not have held his shares for 6 months or have obtained them on the death of a former member to petition on this ground.[278] Former members who are contributories within the meaning of the Act do not count as members for the purpose of the statutory minimum of two. A personal representative of a deceased member or the trustee of a bankrupt member may be registered as the holders of shares which devolve upon them and will be regarded as members once such registration has occurred.[279] It is unlikely that a creditor would wish to use this ground and his ability to do so is doubtful as he would gain nothing from the winding up except the payment of his debt. Difficulty on this score indicates the company's inability to pay its debts and it is on that ground that the creditor should proceed.

Inability to pay debts

14.115 This is the ground on which the great majority of petitions are presented and amounts to a contention that the company is insolvent. It will almost invariably be used by creditors. It is unlikely that a holder of fully paid up shares could succeed on it as he would not benefit from the making of a winding up order. However, a member of an unlimited company; a holder of partly paid shares; or a member of company limited by guarantee might succeed in obtaining a winding up order on this ground if he established that his potential contribution would thereby be reduced and if the amount of his contribution was significant. The ground to be made out is simply an inability to pay debts and once this has been established the court may make a winding up order. However, s 123 of the

---

276   *Re Middlesburgh Assembly Rooms Co* (1880) 14 Ch D 104 at 109.
277   See para 14.131 *infra.*
278   Insolvency Act 1986 s 124(2).
279   *Re Bowling and Welby's Contract* [1895] 1 Ch 663; and see s 22(2) of the Companies Act 1985.

Insolvency Act 1986 provides two specific factual circumstances in relation to the failure to meet particular debts in which a company is deemed to be unable to meet its debts. It also provides two definitions (based on a company's overall financial position) of the phrase 'inability to pay its debts'.

Overall financial position

14.116 The Act's definitions of those financial circumstances which will result in a company being deemed to be unable to pay its debts indicate that insolvency can take two forms. It may be that the company is unable to find the cash to pay debts when they are due for payment. In the past this was the sole criterion for the purpose of a winding up petition and contingent and prospective liabilities were ignored in deciding whether a company was unable to pay its debts although this might be taken into account if a petition were presented for winding up on the ground that this was just and equitable.[280] This definition also ignores the existence of assets which are difficult to realise and ignores the possibility of payment in full in the future. A company whose assets exceed its liabilities may still be unable to pay its debts. This represents a cash flow crisis but will amount to insolvency and permit a winding up order to be made. Since creditors are entitled to demand payment on time it is reasonable that this should be so.

14.117 Section 123(1)(e) makes it clear that proof to the satisfaction of the court that a company is unable to pay its debts as they fall due will result in the company being deemed to be unable to pay its debts. This focuses on debts presently due, but it is submitted that it also enables the court to look at the future cash flow of the enterprise to see whether future debts—enforceable when a particular date arrives—will be paid when they fall due. It will exclude a consideration of contingent and prospective liabilities as what has to be proved is that the company is unable to pay its debts as they fall due. This contemplates the present ability to pay and although regard must be had to debts as they fall due in the future those that are contingent or prospective will not be taken into account.[281]

14.118 If the company can pay all creditors who have demanded payment of debts already due out of its liquid assets it is able to pay its debts as they fall due. If it would be possible to meet all such debts from the immediate (albeit improvident) realisation of its assets then, again, this 'cash flow' test of insolvency will be passed and a winding up order will be refused if the petition is brought purely on the evidence of the company's financial position without the use of the specific factual grounds for this form of

280 Companies Act 1862 s 80(4) and *Re European Assurance Society* (1869) 9 LR Eq 122.
281 See s 123(2), where contingent and prospective liabilities are taken into account.

insolvency provided in s 123(1)(a) to (d).[282] However, even if a company can pass the 'cash flow' test of solvency a petition on the ground that it is unable to pay its debts will still succeed if it is proved to the satisfaction of the court that the value of the company's assets is less than the amount of its liabilities, taking into account its contingent and prospective liabilities.[283] This test involves a valuation of assets and of liabilities as at the date of the petition, taking full account of contingent and prospective liabilities. A deficit will give grounds for a winding up order even if the company is at present paying its debts as they fall due. Where this is done by applying present income to discharge past liabilities then a winding up order may be made if the value of all assets is less than the total of current, contingent and prospective liabilities.

14.119   Where this test is applied the value of assets should be determined without assuming an early forced sale. The availability of uncalled capital will be taken into account and a gradual process of realisation of assets will be assumed as a means of paying accrued and prospective liabilities. Profits from continued business and the costs incurred in carrying it out will be ignored[284] but the costs of realising the assets will presumably be taken into account. The fact that a creditor's claim is based on the allegation that money is held by the company as a constructive trustee of money had and received does not make his debt contingent or one the value of which is unascertained.[285]

14.120   The fact that debts could be paid only with borrowed money does not of itself establish the company's inability to pay debts as they fall due and in assessing the company's balance sheet position under the pre-1986 provision it was not sufficient to add together all liabilities including the prospective and contingent ones and to set them against the assets. The time at which prospective and contingent liabilities would become present liabilities had to be taken into account and evidence of long term loan agreements could indicate that such a change was not imminent.[286] It would seem that the same principle should apply to s 123(2) as, like the reference to contingent and prospective liabilities in the previous provision, it states that they are to be 'taken into account' and does not indicate that they are to be treated in the same way as present liabilities. The court exercises a discretion whether to make an order even if it is satisfied that a

---

282   See *In Re Capital Annuities Ltd* [1979] 1 WLR 170 at 183 to 188 which deals with the predecessor provision to s 123(1)(e).
283   Insolvency Act 1986 s 123(2).
284   *Re European Assurance Society* (note 280 above); and see Pennington, 'Company Law' 5th ed p 859.
285   *Re Prime Metals Trading Ltd* [1984] BCLC 543.
286   *Re a Company* [1986] BCLC 261.

ground under the Insolvency Act 1986 is made out. However, the mere hope or expectation of assets to which the company has no right will not defeat a petition if, without them, the company is unable to pay its debts.[287]

14.121 Since the emphasis in the great majority of petitions is on the company's inability to pay debts as they fall due—the demand procedure under s 123(1)(a) is the usual basis for a petition—the court is likely to display some caution in exercising its discretion to make a winding up order on the basis of insolvency as the result of an overall deficit. The method employed to value assets and to assess the level of contingent and prospective liabilities will require careful scrutiny although calculations made in accordance with the rules laid down in the Companies Act 1985 for drafting accounts in accordance with the conventions and guidelines used by the accountancy profession, will doubtless be accepted as giving a true and fair view of the existence and size of any deficit.

14.122 Where the possibility exists of the survival of all or part of the company's undertaking as a going concern an administration order may be appropriate. It will be necessary to establish that the company's undertaking or part of it may survive, or that there is a chance of a more advantageous realisation of assets in the future, or that a composition or arrangement with creditors may be possible before an order can be made. Such an order can be sought in a petition brought by the company, its directors or a creditor. It will not be available on a contributory's petition. Such an alternative may be appropriate where creditors—particularly those holding a floating charge—believe that a cash flow crisis can be overcome or where it seems that there is some prospect of an increase in asset values or speedy reductions in levels of liability. A full discussion of the administration procedure, and the moratorium which it provides against claims on the company's assets, will be found in chapter 13. In practice the difficulties involved in establishing this ground on the basis of the company's 'cash flow', or of a deficit on its balance sheet, are usually avoided by the use of the specific factual procedures based on neglect to pay debts after due notice or failure to satisfy a levy of execution.

14.123 In addition to the circumstances in which a company is deemed by the statute to be unable to pay its debts, facts such as a continuing failure by a company to honour its bills of exchange or cheques, or its statement that it has insufficient assets to make it worthwhile for a creditor to levy execution, can be sufficient evidence of the company's inability to pay its debts.[288]

---

287 *Byblos Bank SAL v A L Khudairy* [1987] BCLC 232 (a case on the interpretation of a debenture).
288 *Re Globe New Patent Iron and Steel Co* (1875) LR 20 Eq 337; and *Flagstaff Silver Mining Co of Utah* (1875) LR 20 Eq 268.

Statutory demand

14.124   Section 123(1)(a) of the Insolvency Act 1986 provides that a company will be deemed to be unable to pay its debts if it neglects to pay, or secure or compound for, a sum due to the reasonable satisfaction of a creditor for 21 days after service of a written demand in the prescribed form requiring payment of the debt. The procedure applies only to debts of £750[289] or more and the demand must be served on the company at its registered office by being left there.[290] The 21 day period must consist of whole days and must not include the day on which the demand was served.[291] The petition must not be presented until the whole of the 21 day period has expired. If this rule is not observed no order is possible even if there has been no payment by the date of the hearing.[292]

14.125   The statutory demand must be in writing, dated and signed either by the creditor or by someone authorised to make the demand on his behalf.[293] It should follow Form 4.1 in the appendix to the Insolvency Rules 1986 as closely as possible. In particular, the amount claimed must be stated and the consideration for it or the way in which it arises must be set out.[294] The demand must be limited to the amount of interest or other accruing charges accrued at the date of the demand and the amount, or rate, of the interest or charge set out, as well as the ground on which it is claimed.[295] The demand must explain to the company the fact that non-compliance may lead to proceedings for winding up, the time within which compliance is required to avoid that result and the methods of compliance open to the company.[296] The company must be informed how its officer or representative can communicate with named individuals to secure, or compound for, the amount demanded and the address and telephone number of such individuals must be supplied.[297]

14.126   It seems that if the essential information is included in the demand it will be a valid statutory demand and will be effective. The Court of Appeal has ruled that this is the case in bankruptcy in a case in which the wrong form was used on the basis that the Act and the Rules amount to a new code which is to be construed by the canons of construction and not fettered by technical rules developed under the old law. However, that decision was made in the context of bankruptcy and Rule 6.5(4) gives the court a

---

289   This figure may be changed by regulations.
290   s 123(1)(a).
291   *Re Lympne Investments Ltd* [1972] 1 WLR 523.
292   *Re Catholic Publishing & Bookselling Co Ltd* (1864) 2 De G J & S 116.
293   Insolvency Rules 1986 r 4.4(2) and (3).
294   r 4.5(1).
295   r 4.5(2).
296   r 4.6(1).
297   r 4.6(2).

discretion to set aside a demand.[298] As there is no such provision in the Rules, in cases of corporate insolvency, a failure to include the information required by the Rules may be fatal since a defective demand that is nonetheless a demand cannot be set aside. However, by analogy, minor inaccuracies that do not mislead or prejudice the company should not make the demand invalid.

14.127   This procedure can only be used in respect of a debt that is due and presently payable. A statutory demand cannot be made for a contingent or prospective debt.[299] The demand must relate to a liquidated sum and a demand for a fixed price, less an unliquidated amount claimed by the company from the creditor for breaches of the contract in question, will not satisfy the statutory provision.[300] A refusal by the company to pay part or all of the amount claimed on the grounds that it has a reasonable and substantial defence to the claim will result in a refusal of a winding up order.[301] Where only part of the sum demanded is disputed the company need not have paid the balance as it could not know the sum due. Its willingness to pay a lesser amount, together with a *bona fide* dispute on substantial grounds on the balance, will be sufficient to prevent an order being made on the creditor's petition.[302] On the other hand, overstatement *per se* will not affect the validity of the demand if the undisputed amount exceeds the statutory minimum.[303] A creditor who uses the statutory demand procedure when unaware that the company will raise a defence will be ordered to pay the costs of a hearing of the company's application to restrain the petition because he is at risk by using this procedure rather than the service of a writ for the debt.[304] A failure to comply with the requirements of the Rules[305] on the form of the demand will be fatal to the creditor's petition. A failure to deliver the demand to the company's registered office (as in the case of a telex[306]) will likewise prevent an order unless the company has no registered office in which case delivery to an 'unregistered' office of the company will suffice.[307]

14.128   Although s 123(1)(a) provides that a creditor, 'by assignment',

298   *Re A Debtor (No 1 of 1989)* [1988] 1 WLR 419.
299   *New Travellers Chambers Ltd v Cheese & Green* (1894) 70 LT 271; and *Re Bryant Investment Co Ltd* [1974] 1 WLR 826.
300   *Re Humberstone Jersey Ltd* [1977] 74 LS Gaz 711.
301   *Re Brighton Club and Norfolk Hotel Co Ltd* (1865) 35 Beav 204 and *Re Lympne Investments Ltd* [1972] 1 WLR 523.
302   *Re a Company* [1984] 1 WLR 1090; and see para 14.67 above on disputed debts.
303   *Re Tweeds Garages Ltd* [1962] 2 WLR 38.
304   *Cannon Street Entertainment Ltd v Handmade Films (Distributors) Ltd* (1989) 5 BCC 207.
305   rr 4.4 to 4.6.
306   *Re a Company* [1985] BCLC 37.
307   *Ibid* and *Re British and Foreign Generating Apparatus Co Ltd* (1865) 12 LT 368.

may use the statutory demand procedure, a demand by a creditor not capable of giving a valid discharge will not be sufficient basis for a petition. An equitable assignee falls within the category of creditors under s 124(1) for the purpose of presenting a petition, but the equitable assignee of part of a debt can only petition on the basis of a statutory demand if he is supported by the person entitled to the balance of the debt. Otherwise he must establish insolvency by means of the general state of the company's affairs.[308] Where a statutory demand has been served and is unsatisfied, any creditor or contributory may petition on the basis of it. Such action is not limited to the person who served the demand.[309]

14.129   Payment of the debt before the petition is presented will result in the dismissal of the petition with costs unless another creditor is substituted under Rule 4.19 of the Insolvency Rules 1986.[310] Payment after the order is made will not. Satisfaction of the statutory demand within the 21 day period will discharge that particular demand and other creditors must establish the company's inability to pay its debts by reference to their own statutory demands or to some other evidence.[311] Subject to the need to obtain a judgment against the company if there is likely to be a dispute over the debt, or over whether the sum due will reach the minimum amount for the use of the statutory demand procedure, the procedure of demanding payment is the most convenient method of seeking to wind up a company for non-payment of debt.

Execution unsatisfied
14.130   Where execution or other process issued on a judgment, decree or other order of any court in favour of a creditor of the company, is returned unsatisfied in whole or in part the company will be deemed to be unable to pay its debts.[312] This will usually mean that a *nulla bona* has been returned to a writ of *fieri facias* although a failure to satisfy a warrant of execution issued in the county court will equally fall within the provision. Where this method is used to establish the company's inability to pay its debts the court may exercise its discretion to make a winding up order even if the amount of the debt is less than the minimum required for the use of the statutory demand procedure.[313] Information from the company or its solicitor or other agent that the company has no assets on which execution

---

308   *Re Steel Wing Co* [1921] 1 Ch 349.
309   *Re Anglesea Island Coal and Coke Co Ltd ex p Owen* (1861) 4 LT 684.
310   *Re William Hockley Ltd* [1962] 1 WLR 555.
311   s 123(1)(a) refers to neglect 'to pay the sum or to secure or compound for it' during the three-week period as the basis for the assumption of inability to pay the debt.
312   s 123(1)(b), which applies to England and Wales. S 123(1)(c) and (d) apply to Scotland and Northern Ireland respectively.
313   *London & Birmingham Flint Glass & Alkali Co Ltd ex p Wright* (1859) 1 De G F & J 257.

may be levied is sufficient evidence on which to establish that a company is unable to pay its debts without it being necessary to levy execution. If the debt is in fact paid before an order is made the creditor will be awarded his costs.[314]

The just and equitable ground; s 122(1)(g)

14.131 A winding up order may be made if the court is of the opinion that it is just and equitable that the company should be wound up. The situations which fall within this ground cannot be categorically listed as the generality of the words 'just and equitable' are not to be reduced but confer a discretion on the court which is exercisable judically on the basis of the facts of each case. It is not to be construed *ejusdem generis* with the other six grounds on which an order may be made and is therefore capable of broad application on the basis of principles of fairness and equity.[315]

14.132 The ground will seldom, if ever, be used by creditors. Although contingent creditors have *locus standi* to petition on this ground the appropriate basis for such action is normally the company's failure to pay its debts. If an action is currently underway against the company its success will permit the creditor to use the non-payment of a judgment debt as a ground to petition and if it fails then the dismissal of the winding up petition does no wrong to the creditor. On this basis a petition by a creditor on the just and equitable ground can be struck out as serving no useful purpose.[316]

14.133 The ground has most commonly been used as a means of relieving a minority of members of a company from oppressive behaviour by the majority or from a risk to their investment arising from the company's actual or proposed business activities. The latter use applies where the *raison d'etre* of the company has disappeared or where fraud or other malpractice or illegality is established or suspected. Similarly, the need of members to break a deadlock which has paralysed the activities of the enterprise may give rise to a petition under s 122(1)(g). Use of the provision by the company itself is possible where there is not a majority sufficient to pass a special or extraordinary resolution to begin a winding up voluntarily or by a petition under s 122(1)(a). However, some facts must be established, to justify the petition, beyond the wish of a simple majority to liquidate the company. Those facts may relate to the improper use of voting power to deprive the company of a remedy in respect of a wrong done to it, or the impossibility of carrying on the company's business in the light of the

---

314 *Re Flagstaff Silver Mining Co of Utah* (1875) LR 20 Eq 268.
315 *Ebrahimi v Westbourne Galleries Ltd* [1973] AC 360.
316 *Re a Company* [1988] BCLC 282.

attitude of the majority and of the directors.[317] If the reason for a petition by a simple majority of shareholders or the directors involves inequitable behaviour by the group which refuses to support a decision to wind the company up, the court may make an order. It is unlikely that a petition by the directors of a solvent company would succeed against the wishes of a majority of members unless the liquidation represented the only means of dealing equitably with the minority.

14.134   The broad nature of this ground makes it particularly appropriate that petitions by the Secretary of State for Trade and Industry are presented on the basis of justice and equity after it appears to him that it is expedient in the public interest that the company should be wound up. This decision is taken as a result of an inspector's report made under s 437 of the Companies Act 1985 or of the information and documents obtained under ss 447 or 448.[318] The fact that there are circumstances giving rise to suspicion about the way the company's affairs have been carried out will justify a winding up order on the application of the Secretary of State even if the company is already being wound up voluntarily and a substantial body of creditors opposes the petition.[319] The dishonest commercial practices of a company and the public interest as stated in evidence by the Secretary of State can be taken into account by the court in deciding whether to make an order.[320]

14.135   A petition by a member on this ground may similarly be upheld if the company is already in voluntary liquidation if matters affecting members require investigation. Although doubts about the voluntary liquidator are less likely to justify an order since the introduction of the requirement that he must be a qualified insolvency practitioner, the need to investigate the fees charged by that person's accountancy firm for audit work performed for the company in the past may arise as it did in the past.[321]

14.136   Most petitions by the Secretary of State under s 124(4) are likely to involve circumstances where there is some suspicion of impropriety in the conduct of the company's affairs. This is also the most likely fact situation in which an insolvent company will be subject to a winding up order on the basis of s 122(1)(g). Despite the need to recognise the open ended nature of the court's discretion to make a winding up order on the 'just and equitable'

---

317 *Re Anglo-Continental Produce Co* [1939] 1 All ER 99.
318 Companies Act 1985 s 4410 and Insolvency Act 1986 s 124(4); and see para 14.90 above.
319 *Re Lubin Rosen & Associates Ltd* [1975] 1 WLR 122, where it was held that the predecessor to s 124(5) did not apply to a petition by the Secretary of State.
320 *Re Walter L Jacob & Co Ltd* (1989) 5 BCC 244.
321 *Re Zinotty Properties Ltd* [1984] BCLC 375.

ground, it is convenient for the purposes of exposition attempt to classify the cases in which petitions based on that ground have succeeded.

Fraud, illegality and the need for investigation

14.137 The court will order a company to be wound up if the objects for which it was founded are illegal.[322] However, if it is obvious from the face of the objects clause in the company's memorandum of association that its objects are illegal, the registrar may refuse registration or the Attorney General may apply for an order to this effect.[323] Where a company is a fraudulent enterprise in its inception then an order may be made where this is the only means of obtaining the shareholders' money from the fraudulent promoters who hold it. For example, the sale of a firm to the company for an exorbitant price on the basis of a deception induced by the similarity of its name to that of a well known firm was sufficient to justify a winding up order on this ground.[324] Similarly where a secret agreement ensured that the promoter/directors did not pay for their own shares, the fraud justified a winding up order as the company could be regarded as a 'bubble'.[325]

14.138 If the majority of the shareholders wishes the company to continue despite the possibility of fraud by the vendor of its main or sole asset and doubt about the existence of the asset this may induce the court to refuse an order. Fraud in itself or the issue of shares at a discount do not guarantee a winding up order as the court has a discretion in deciding whether to make such an order.[326] However, where an investigation is necessary the court can make an order to ensure that an independent liquidator is appointed or because of the dominant position of a particular member and creditor. This is possible even if a voluntary liquidation is under way and regardless of whether any assets will remain at the end of the day for distribution to unsecured creditors or shareholders.[327]

Disappearance of the company's substratum

14.139 The courts have been willing to order the winding up of a company on the ground that its main object or objects have either been abandoned or have become impossible to achieve. For the purpose of deciding this question the courts will look to the 'main objects' of the company and will

---

322 *Princess Reuss v Bos* (1871) 5 LR HL 176.
323 *Attorney-General v Lindi St-Claire (Personal Services) Ltd*, Financial Times 18 December 1980 and Sealy's 'Cases and Materials on Company Law' 3rd ed at p 10.
324 *Re Thomas Edward Brinsmead & Sons Ltd* (1867) LR 3 Eq 355.
325 *Re London & County Coal Co Ltd* (1867) LR 3 Eq 355.
326 s 125(1); and see *Re Nylstroom Co Ltd* (1889) 60 LT 477 and *Pioneers of Mashonaland Syndicate* [1893] 1 Ch 731.
327 *Re West Surrey Tanning Co* (1866) LR 2 Eq 737; *Re Peruvian Amazon Co* (1913) 29 TLR 384; and *Re Llandown Colliery Co* [1915] 1 Ch 369; and see ss 124(5) and 124(1).

distinguish objects from powers in a way that is now unusual for the purposes of determining whether an act of the company is *ultra vires*. Even when (as is usual) a company's memorandum of association contains a *Cotman v Brougham* clause together with a long list of different business activities so that each object and power is said to be a main object, the court will decide the purposes for which the company is formed and which therefore constitutes its substratum.[328] This contrasts with the approach adopted in deciding whether or not a transaction is *ultra vires* when no object will be regarded as ancillary to any other if the objects clause specifies that this is so. The substratum of the company will be established primarily by reference to the company's memorandum but a prospectus or circular to shareholders issued by the company, and its name, can be considered and may at least resolve any ambiguity in the objects clause.[329] Once the main objects of the company have been ascertained, proof that the company is no longer able to pursue any of them will provide a ground for a winding up order. If it can pursue some of those objects the abandonment of others will not amount to a failure of the substratum[330] but the fact that a company continues to exercise ancillary powers will not assist it.[331]

14.140   While it is clear that a winding up petition may succeed on the basis of the loss of a company's substratum, this is more likely to occur where an object, unambiguously central to the company's memorandum, is also narrow and specific. The exploitation of a particular invention after obtaining a specific patent will be impossible if the patent is not obtained and the company will then fall within this category.[332] Similarly, the impossibility of carrying out a contract which is the specific purpose of the company amounts to a loss of substratum.[333] The absence of adequate capital and the failure of a company to make profits may lead to the conclusion that a company is incapable of achieving its main objects and that its substratum no longer exists, but the court will be very reluctant to find that unprofitable operations indicate the impossibility of achieving the company's main objects.[334]

14.141   Although the use of a wide-ranging objects clause does not, in

---

328   *Cotman v Brougham* [1918] AC 514 at 520–521 per Lord Parker of Waddington.
329   *Re Thomas Edward Brinsmead* (note 324 above), where the primacy of the memorandum was emphasized; and *Re Crown Bank Ltd* (1890) 44 Ch D 634, where other documents were taken into account.
330   *Re Norwegian Titanic Iron Co Ltd* (1865) 35 Beav 223; and *Re New Gas Co* (1877) 5 Ch D 703.
331   *Re German Date Coffee Co* (1882) 20 Ch D 169.
332   *Re Bleriot Manufacturing Aircraft Co* (1916) 32 TLR 253.
333   *Re Suburban Hotel Co* (1867) 2 Ch App 737, where the emphasis on profitability arose from the erroneous view that the 'just and equitable' ground should be construed *ejusdem generis* with those concerned with insolvency.
334   *Re Kitson & Co Ltd* [1946] 1 All ER 435 and *Re Taldica Rubber Co Ltd* [1946] 2 All ER 763.

principle, prevent the identification of a main object which amounts to a substratum it increases the likelihood that the court will find that the company is still pursuing one of its multiple main objects. A company formed to acquire and take over as a going concern a specified business, and also to carry on a general type of business, does not lose its substratum by selling the specific business providing it carries on the general activity mentioned in the memorandum.This is so even if at a particular time its board have decided to abandon that type of business altogether.[335]

14.142 Even where the sale or loss of most of the company's major assets is sufficient to amount to a loss of its substratum, the question of whether remaining matters, such as transfers of assets or claims for compensation, are best handled by a liquidator or by the company's directors, and the effect of any liquidation on concessions or other assets of the company will be taken into account in deciding whether to make an order.[336] There is no absolute right of the minority or of a bare majority of shareholders to insist on the dissolution of the company and the distribution of a surplus. Although the principle behind this category of winding up cases is that the shareholders' money should not be used in pursuit of an object which did not originally form one of the company's purposes, the justice of the case as it appears at the time of the hearing is relevant to the exercise of the court's discretion. The use of assets for new projects not contemplated when the company was set up may well lead to an order if it is combined with a failure of controlling members to comply with the party's reasonable expectations of an appointment to the board where there is a 'quasi-partnership' situation. This will be particularly so if the company's assets have been abused and if there has been a failure to administer the company properly.[337]

Paralysis of the decision-making process
14.143 Where two opposing groups or individuals have evenly balanced voting rights and have reached a stage of disagreement such that no decisions can be made, the company will be wound up on the just and equitable ground. If the sole two directors, who are also the only shareholders and who have equal voting rights, have such a poor relationship that no business can be carried on the court will dissolve the company even if there is an arbitration clause in the articles since every decision needed in the day to day life of the company cannot be referred to an arbitrator.[338] The fact that one of the directors has a casting vote at

335 *Re Kitson & Co Ltd* (note 334 *supra*).
336 See *Baku Consolidated Oilfields Ltd* [1944] 1 All ER 24 and *Eastern Telegraph Co Ltd* [1847] 2 All ER 104.
337 *Re Zinotty Properties* [1984] 1 WLR 1249.
338 *Re Yenidje Tobacco Co Ltd* [1935] Ch 693.

board meetings will not prevent the court from making a winding up order.[339] The court will, however, refuse a petition if the petitioner fails to put in evidence the relevant provisions of the company's articles in case they contain a means of resolving the deadlock.[340]

14.144 Where a decision is possible because shareholders are not in possession of equal voting power then a situation of deadlock will not normally be accepted as a reason for granting an order.[341] However, even where shareholdings are unequal, behaviour by a director and shareholder in failing to use his voting power to resolve the problem will justify a petition if this effectively stops the company's decision-making machinery from ever being set in motion and so prevents either the conduct of its business or the use of a provision in the articles which deals with the deadlock situation.[342]

The partnership analogy
14.145 In the leading case of *Ebrahimi v Westbourne Galleries Ltd*[343] Lord Wilberforce indicated the circumstances in which one of the parties involved in a company can be subjected to a winding up order on this ground because he takes advantage of his formal legal rights under the memorandum or articles of association of the company, or under the Companies Act 1985. In *Ebrahimi* this took the form of a resolution to remove the petitioner as a director. In such cases the court will exercise a broad equitable jurisdiction on the basis that behind the formal company structure 'there are individuals with rights, expectations and obligations *inter se* which are not necessarily submerged in the company structure'.[344] Equity will recognise those rights and enable the court to protect them by allowing a petition to succeed on this ground in cases where the relationship between the parties indicates that such rights, expectations or obligations exist. This will not be the case in all small or private companies as many of these are based on a purely commercial relationship, the basis of which is adequately and exhaustively provided for in the articles. As Lord Wilberforce pointed out:[345]

"The super-imposition of equitable considerations requires something more, which typically may include one, or probably more, of the following elements:
(i) An association formed or continued on the basis of a personal relationship,

339   *Re Davis & Collett Ltd* [1935] Ch 693.
340   *Re Davis Investments (East Ham) Ltd* [1961] 1 WLR 1396.
341   *Charles Forte Investments Ltd v Amanda* [1963] 3 WLR 662 at 676.
342   *Re American Pioneer Leather Co* [1918] 1 Ch 556.
343   [1972] 2 WLR 1289 at 1297–1298.
344   *Ibid* at 1297.
345   *Ibid* at 1298.

involving mutual confidence—this element will often be found where a pre-existing partnership has been converted into a limited company;
(ii) An agreement that all or some (for there may be *sleeping* members), of the shareholders shall participate in the conduct of the business;
(iii) restrictions on the transfer of the members' interest in the company—so that if confidence is lost, or one member is removed from management, he cannot take out his stake and go elsewhere.

It is these and analagous factors which may bring into play the just and equitable clause and they do so directly through the force of the words themselves. To refer, as so many of the cases do, to 'quasi partnerships' or 'in substance partnerships' may be convenient but may also be confusing."

14.146 The court may grant a winding up order in such cases after considering the nature of the relationship among those involved and any agreement or course of conduct between them. There is no need for a contract.[346] Where the founders of the company had an understanding that it should be used to carry out one particular project which has been completed the court will grant an order on the petition of a member who objects to the intention of the directors and majority shareholders of investing the resulting capital and profits in a similar further venture.[347] However, where there is no question of a limited purpose having been envisaged for the company, the court will take account of the fact that a director who has resigned remains a shareholder and may refuse a petition aimed at realising his investment on that ground if his participation in management was not part of the original understanding of the parties.[348]

14.147 Where the conduct of the majority indicates that they may use their powers as directors to determine the amount of dividend to be distributed and to continue a practice of allocating any surplus in the form of directors' salaries, the petitioners' continued status as a shareholder will not prevent an order.[349] There is no need to prove any improper or devious conduct on the part of the majority or of the other directors to justify an order but inability to prove at least some course of conduct or breach of a tacit understanding to justify the claim of the petitioner that he has been treated inequitably will prevent an order.[350] The fact that proper constitutional procedures were followed in the removal of directors or in making other decisions will not protect the majority but in a case where the petitioner has not, as a matter of practice, participated in day-to-day management in the past he cannot claim an order because he is prevented

---

346 *Re Fildes Bros Ltd* [1970] 1 WLR 592.
347 *Re Zinotty Properties Ltd* [1984] 1 WLR 1249, where the majority also proposed interest-free loans to companies in which they but not the petitioner had an interest. They had also failed to appoint the petitioner as a director as he legitimately expected.
348 *Re K/9 Meat Supplies (Guildford) Ltd* [1966] 1 WLR 1112.
349 *Ebrahimi v Westbourne Galleries* (note 343 *supra*).
350 *R A Noble & Sons (Clothing) Ltd* [1983] BCLC 273.

from beginning to do so providing he is given full rights as a director to attend and participate in board meetings.[351]

14.148   In some cases of this kind, and in most of those involving oppression or misconduct by the majority, the petition will seek an order under s 459 of the Companies Act 1985 in the alternative. This alternative remedy may prove a more satisfactory solution to the problems of such companies if it can be established that the company's affairs are being or have been conducted in a manner which is unfairly prejudicial to some part of the members including the practitioner. Under s 461 the court can exercise a wide discretion as to the order to be made and can, for example, require the majority to purchase the minority's shares at a fair price if the conduct required by s 459 is established. This contrasts with the remedy of winding up; a draconian solution which may hold limited benefits for each side.

14.149   If the majority has agreed to purchase the petitioner's shares at his request and has offered a fair price (or to agree to a mechanism to establish one) no winding up order on the just and equitable ground will be made despite the earlier exclusion of the petitioner director from the management of the company. This reflects the right of the court to reject a petition on the just and equitable ground if the contributory petitioners have acted unreasonably in seeking to have the company wound up rather than pursuing some other available remedy.[352]

Oppression and misconduct
14.150   It is possible to distinguish cases where the company's controllers (whether directors or shareholders, and regardless of the capacity in which they act) behave in a manner oppressive to the minority or are guilty of misconduct from those circumstances in which the partnership analogy applies. In cases of oppression or misconduct there is no need to establish the details of the relationship of the parties as a foundation for the court's intervention to protect the petitioner from the exercise, by other partner members, of their legal rights. This is not the basis of the application. Even a public limited company with shares quoted on the Stock Exchange could conceivably be subject to a winding up order on the just and equitable ground if, for example, the company's shares had their Stock Exchange quotation withdrawn as a sanction against the behaviour of the company's controllers in acting in breach of the City Code on Takeovers and Mergers

---

351   *Ebrahimi* (note 349 *supra*) and *Re Fildes Brothers Ltd* (note 346 *supra*); and see *AB & C Chewing Gum* [1975] 1 WLR 579 where breach of an established management participation agreement was held to justify an order.
352   *Re a Company* [1983] 1 WLR 927; and see s 125(2) of the Insolvency Act 1986.

or other self regulatory provisions and this resulted in loss or injury to the shareholders.[353]

14.151 However, serious or persistent acts of misconduct must generally be established and occasional acts or omissions will not be sufficient, particularly if such acts on the part of directors might be ratified by the majority in a general meeting, or if any frauds involved in the formation of the company might be so waived and transactions so confirmed.[354] This limitation only applies where a remedy is sought by the minority in circumstances to which the *Ebrahimi* case cannot apply and in cases of misconduct with sufficiently serious effects on the petitioner the courts will not hesitate to make an order on the basis that it is just and equitable to do so.

14.152 In cases where the controllers of the company misappropriate its funds; where directors use their powers in breach of their obligations to the company and in pursuit of their own ends; or where an understanding about the way in which the company is to be run is breached, an order can be made.[355] Where the company's affairs are managed in such a way that no annual general meetings are held, no accounts are produced or audited and no information is given to the minority, a petition can succeed if this is part of a pattern of oppression whereby it is intended to coerce the minority.[356] However, behaviour which amounts to a breach of a personal duty owed to the petitioner will not form the basis for an order where no conduct amounting to oppression occurs unless the circumstances are such that the partnership analogy elaborated in the *Ebrahimi* case can apply.[357] An unreasonable refusal to use an alternative remedy will result in a refusal to grant an order and indeed, the very existence of a more appropriate remedy may be a reason for refusing to grant an order in a case involving the breach of a duty owed to the petitioner personally.[358] In considering whether a petition on the just and equitable ground is likely to succeed it is essential to look to the breadth of those words and there is no need to fit a case into one of the categories developed by writers for the ease of exposition as the courts are free to apply the principle embodied in the ground to novel situations.[359]

353 *Re St Piran Ltd* [1981] 1 WLR 1300 at 1307.
354 *Re Irrigation Company of France ex p Fox* (1871) 6 Ch App 176.
355 See *Re Bleriot Manufacturing Aircraft Co* (1916) 32 TLR 253; *Re Lundie Brothers Ltd* [1965] 1 WLR 1051; and *Re AB & C Chewing Gum Ltd* [1975] 1 WLR 579 respectively.
356 *Loch v John Blackwood Ltd* [1924] AC 783.
357 *Re Gold Co* (1879) 11 Ch D 701.
358 Insolvency Act 1986 s 125(2); and see *Charles Forte (Investments) Ltd v Amanda* [1964] Ch 240 (refusal to register a share transfer).
359 *Ebrahimi v Westbourne Galleries Ltd* [1972] 2 WLR 1289.

Specialist grounds

14.153 In addition to the general grounds applicable to all companies, regulatory legislation which applies to particular business activities often provides for a company to be wound up if certain conditions are satisfied.

Insurance companies

14.154 Under the Insurance Copmpanies Act 1982 a number of additional grounds are laid down for the winding up of insurance companies on a petition presented by the Secretary of State for Trade and Industry. In addition, under s 53 of that Act it is possible for 10 or more policy holders with policies of an aggregate value of at least £10,000 to petition for a winding up order although they are limited to the grounds laid down in the Insolvency Act 1986. They require the leave of the court to present the petition and must both establish a *prima facie* case and provide security for costs before leave will be granted. A petition by the Secretary of State under s 54(1) and (4) of the Insurance Companies Act 1982 can be based on one of four grounds:

(a) that the company is unable to pay its debts under ss 123 or 222–224 of the Insolvency Act 1986 as the case may be;

(b) that the company has failed to satisfy an obligation to which it is subject under the Insurance Companies Act 1982 or the previous regulatory legislation;

(c) that the company has failed to keep or to produce accounting records in satisfaction of its obligations under ss 221 and 222 of the Companies Act 1985 and that the Secretary of State is unable to ascertain its financial position;

(d) that it appears to the Secretary of State expedient in the public interest that the company be wound up and, on presenting a petition, he succeeds in establishing to the satisfaction of the court that it is just and equitable that the company should be wound up.

14.155 Under s 57 a subsidiary of a company being wound up by the court under the Act may be wound up in conjunction with the liquidation of the principal company if the subsidiary or its creditors have claims against the principal company and the principal company took a transfer of the whole or part of the insurance business of the subsidiary. The same liquidator may be appointed and both liquidations are treated as commencing at the time of the presentation of the petition in respect of the principal company. The court must consider whether such an order is just and equitable and must be satisfied that one company is a subsidiary of the other. A whole group of companies may be dealt with together in this way.

An application for such an order may be made by any creditor of, or person interested in, any of the group companies.

Banks

14.156   Under s 92 of the Banking Act 1987, the Bank of England can petition for the winding up of an authorised institution or a former authorised institution. The petition is presented in the court with jurisdiction to wind up the company. An 'authorised institution' is a company which is authorised by the Bank of England under the Banking Act 1987 to accept deposits in the course of a deposit taking business. A 'former authorised institution' is a company which was an authorised institution, recognised bank or licensed institution under the Banking Act 1979 and continues to have a liability in respect of any deposit for which it had liability at the time when it had that status.[360] The power of the Bank of England to petition under s 92 also extends to a company which has accepted a deposit in the course of a deposit taking business in breach of s 3 of the Banking Act 1987 because neither the unauthorised institution nor the transaction in question were exempted from the need to be authorised under the Act.[361] A s 92 petition can be based on either the inability of the authorised or formerly authorised institution to pay its debts within the meaning of s 123 of the Insolvency Act 1986 or the court's opinion that it is just and equitable that the institution be wound up. If the institution has defaulted in an obligation to pay a sum due and payable in respect of a deposit it is deemed to be unable to pay its debts.[362]

Companies carrying on investment business

14.157   Under s 72 of the Financial Services Act 1986 and the order delegating powers to the Securities and Investment Board (SIB),[363] the Secretary of State for Trade and Industry and the SIB have concurrent power to petition for the winding up of companies carrying on an investment business. In order to facilitate the operation of the system of self-regulating organisations (SROs) set up by the Act, a person authorised by membership of such a body or certified by a recognised professional body under the Act can only be subjected to a petition under s 72 by the SIB or the Secretary of State with the permission of the SRO or the professional body in question.

14.158   The company[364] whose liquidation is sought must be an

---

360   Banking Act 1987 s 106(1).
361   *Ibid* s 92(6).
362   *Ibid* s 92(1).
363   Financial Services Act 1986 (Delegation) Order 1987 (SI 1987 no 942).
364   The power applies to unregistered companies, partnerships and overseas companies as well as registered companies—Financial Services Act 1986 s 72(2).

authorised person or appointed representative. An authorised person is one who has been authorised to carry on an investment business under Chapter III of Part I of the Financial Services Act 1986 and an appointed representative is a person exempted from the need to be authorised because of being an employee of an authorised person.[365] Section 72 also applies to a person whose authorisation has been suspended or terminated under the Act.[366]

14.159   A winding up order under s 72 can be granted on the ground that the company is unable to pay its debts within the meaning of s 123 of the Insolvency Act 1986 (or s 221 if it is an unregistered company). This is deemed to be the case if it has defaulted in an obligation to pay a sum due and payable under an investment agreement. Alternatively the petition can succeed on the just and equitable ground.[367]

THE HEARING

14.160   The procedural requirements as regards the contents, presentation and service of a petition have already been noted.[368] The affidavit sworn in support of the petition is regarded as adequate *prima facie* evidence of statements in the petition to which it relates by virtue of Rule 4.12(6) of the Insolvency Rules 1986. This is so even if it amounts to hearsay evidence but this rule and, where it is applicable, the rule giving special credibility to an inspector's report, do not amount to a general permission for hearsay evidence to be used in winding up proceedings.[369] They are perhaps best explained by the specific statutory provisions which apply to those documents.[370] Where fraud, misconduct or other unusual circumstances apply to a case, or where the partnership analogy lies behind a petition on the 'just and equitable' ground, further affidavits are required in addition to the statutory one and they should set out the facts and evidence on which the petitioner relies.[371] Any affidavit in opposition to a petition must be filed within not less than 7 days before the date fixed for the hearing[372] and a copy of it must be sent to the petitioner.[373] Any deponent may be cross examined at the court's discretion.[374]

365   *Ibid* ss 207(1) and 44
366   *Ibid* s 72(2).
367   *Ibid* s 72(1) and (3).
368   See paras 14.97 *et seq, supra.*
369   *Re Koscot Interplanetary (UK) Ltd* [1972] 3 All ER 829; but see *Re St Piran* [1981] 1 WLR 1300.
370   Companies Act 1985 s 441 and Insolvency Rules 1986 r 4.12.
371   *Re ABC Couple and Engineering Co Ltd (No 2)* [1962] 1 WLR 1236 and *Re Davis Investments (East Ham) Ltd* [1961] 1 WLR 1396.
372   Insolvency Rules 1986 r 4.18(1).
373   *Ibid* r 4.18(2).
374   *Re London Fish Market Co* (1883) 27 SJ 600.

14.161 Any party (other than the petitioner and the company) who wishes to appear at the hearing of the petition must give notice of his intention to the petitioner in the prescribed form no later than 4 pm on the day before the hearing (or the previous Friday if the hearing is on a Monday). The notice must give the name address and telephone number of the person who serves it. It must also state whether the intervener will support or oppose the petition. The special leave of the court is required for the appearance of a person who fails to give notice.[375] The petitioner must prepare a list of the names and addresses of all those who have given notice of their intention to appear at the hearing and hand it (or a statement that no notices have been received) to the court before the hearing begins.[376]

14.162 Where the petitioner fails to advertise his petition in time; agrees to its withdrawal, adjournment or dismissal; fails to appear; or does not apply for an order in the terms contained in the prayer of his petition, the court may substitute any contributory or creditor as petitioner. It must be satisfied that the person substituted could himself have petitioned and that he wishes to prosecute the petition. Such an order can be made at any time if there is failure to advertise the petition within the prescribed time limits or if the petition is withdrawn.[377] A creditor can be substituted for a contributory even where the original petition was on the just and equitable ground and will have to be amended. Readvertisement will be ordered in such a case.[378] Premature advertisement of a petition can result in the substitution of a different petitioner.[379] If the petitioner's debt has been paid between petition and hearing a secured creditor who appeared on the petition may be substituted and the question of the validation of the payment under s 127 of the Insolvency Act 1986 considered. Even a creditor who did not appear can be substituted on the grounds that he will petition at a later date in any event.[380] The same person can be substituted without readvertisement if he petitioned as a contributory but also has the status of contingent creditor as guarantor of the company's debt.[381]

THE DECISION AND THE ORDER

14.163 On hearing the petition the court has a discretion to dismiss it, adjourn the hearing conditionally or unconditionally, or to make any other

---

375 Insolvency Rules 1986 r 4.16 and Form 4.9; and *Re Green McAllan & Fielden Ltd* [1891] WN 127.
376 *Ibid* r 4.17.
377 r 4.19.
378 *Re Creative Handbook Ltd* [1985] BCLC 1.
379 *Re Signland* [1982] 2 All ER 609.
380 *Re McCarthy & Co (Builders) Ltd* [1976] 2 All ER 338 and *Re Western Welsh International System Buildings Ltd* (1985) 1 BCC 99290.
381 *Re Commercial and Industrial Insulators Ltd* [1986] BCLC 191.

order that it thinks fit (including an interim order). However, an order must not be refused only on the ground that the company's assets have been mortgaged for an amount equal to or greater than their value or that the company has no assets.[382] If a petition has been brought by contributories on the just and equitable ground and the court takes the view that relief is available by winding up the company or by some other means (for example an order under s 461 of the Companies Act 1985) but that in the absence of the other remedy winding up would be just and equitable then the order must be made unless the court considers that the petitioner acted unreasonably in refusing to pursue the other available remedy.[383]

14.164 Adjournment of a petition will rarely be allowed unconditionally because a lengthy period of paralysis and the possibility that transactions will be invalidated by the relation back of a winding up order made later to the date of the presentation of the petition, are highly disadvantageous to the company.[384] Rather than adjourn the petition the court will make a winding up order by substituting a different creditor as petitioner if that is possible.[385] However, if a brief adjournment is needed for evidence to be gathered, or for a compromise or scheme of reconstruction to be negotiated this will be allowed. In the latter case a prompt application for an administration order may be a more appropriate step. Even an adjournment to set up a voluntary arrangement will be refused if it is clear that on the balance of probabilities the majority of creditors required by Part I of the Insolvency Act 1986 will not support the proposal.[386]

14.165 In exercising its discretion whether or not to make an order, the court may have regard to the wishes of the creditors and the contributories (as it may in relation to all matters involved in a winding up) providing those views are proved to it by sufficient evidence. It may direct meetings to be held in order to ascertain those views.[387] If a creditor has an ulterior motive and is petitioning to gain a benefit not shared by other creditors (for example, to gain a lease that will be forfeited if the company is wound up) this may result in the dismissal of the petition as an abuse of the process of the court. However, ill motive is not in itself an obstacle to the success of a petition which will genuinely benefit the petitioners as a class.[388]

14.166 In the case of an insolvent company the views of creditors will

---

382   Insolvency Act 1986 s 125(1).
383   *Ibid* s 125(2).
384   *Re Boston Timber Fabrications Ltd* [1984] BCLC 328.
385   *Re Goldthorpe & Lacey Ltd* (1987) 3 BCC 595.
386   *Ibid*.
387   Insolvency Act 1986 s 195(1).
388   *Re a Company* [1983] BCLC 492.

carry preponderant weight and will usually be determined by reference to the value of debts although the court may take particular note of the views of a class of creditors more seriously affected by its decision and an order will not be refused where that would amount to forcing a creditor to grant an interest free loan.[389] Where a company is solvent and only shareholders' interests are in issue their views will be given preference; the majority, by reference to the voting rights conferred by the articles, will usually prevail.[390] However, neither in the case of creditors nor of contributories is the court bound to follow the views expressed or to prefer the view of a majority to that of a minority.[391] The public interest to be served by making an order may be taken into account when matters of commercial probity are in issue. This will always be the case where the Secretary of State for Trade and Industry presents a petition but it may apply in the case of a petition by a creditor or a contributory.[392] A creditor's right as against the company to an order does not prevent the court from considering the views of other creditors[393] but it has been held not to be appropriate for the court to take account of matters of public interest such as the effects of an order on employment.[394] This contrasts with the approach to be adopted when an application for an administration order is being considered.[395]

14.167 The court will sometimes be confronted with a petition after a voluntary liquidation has already begun. Certain guidelines have been developed for such cases. Section 124(5) permits a petition to be presented in those circumstances but provides that the court is not to make a winding up order unless it is satisfied that the voluntary liquidation cannot be continued with due regard to the interests of the creditors or contributories. A number of recent cases illustrate how the court reaches a decision on that question.

14.168 The appearance of the liquidator in charge of the voluntary winding up to oppose a petition lends support to the case for an order as it casts doubt on his impartiality.[396] On the other hand, his appearance to assist but not to press a view has no such effect. The greater expense and

---

389   *Ibid* s 195(2) and see *Re Lamburn Petroleum Products* [1979] 3 All ER 297; *Re Floors of Bristol (Builders) Ltd* [1982] Com. LR 55.
390   *Re Langham Skating Rink Co* (1877) 5 Ch D 669; Insolvency Act 1986 s 195(3).
391   See, for example, *re Clandown Colliery Co* [1915] 1 Ch 369 (where the dominant creditor was the chairman of the company who was running it for his own benefit) and *Re Southard & Co Ltd* [1979] 1 WLR 1198.
392   See *Re Krasnapolski Restaurant Co* [1892] 3 Ch 174 and *Re Lubin Rosen & Associates* [1975] 1 WLR 122.
393   *Re Chapel House Colliery Co* (1883) 24 Ch D 259 and *Re Western Canada Oil Lands and Works Co* (1873) LR 17 Eq 1.
394   *Re Craven Insurance Co Ltd* [1968] 1 WLR 675.
395   See ch 13 *supra*.
396   *Re Roselmar Properties (No 2)* (1986) 2 BCC 99157.

slower process involved in a compulsory liquidation will weigh against an order if the company is already in liquidation. The views of creditors who are also members are not to be ignored although they will be given less weight than those of outside creditors.[397] In the case of a members' voluntary liquidation in which the winding up has been unduly protracted and the payment of debts referred to in the declaration of solvency has been delayed an order will be made.[398] The need to investigate the reasons for the swearing of the declaration of solvency and for the continuation of the business by the liquidator at a loss are reasons for rational creditors to seek an investigation and can outweigh the possible extra cost and waste of time if an order is made.[399]

14.169 If a creditors' voluntary liquidation is already in progress, the court must have a good reason for overriding the wishes of the majority by value of the creditors who support that procedure. However, if independent creditors will be left with a strong and legitimate sense of grievance on grounds of commercial morality, an order can be justified; especially if some of the creditors supporting the voluntary liquidation are also members. An order can be made in such circumstances without impugning the integrity of the voluntary liquidator.[400] The fact that a thorough investigation of the affairs of the company provides the only chance of a dividend for unsecured creditors and that the overwhelming majority of ordinary trade creditors support an order, justify that course of action. Section 124(5) does not raise a presumption in favour of allowing the voluntary liquidation to continue.[401]

14.170 If no voluntary liquidation has begun reasons must be given for the opposition of a majority of creditors to a winding up order. The danger that, if no order is made, the creditors who wish to begin a voluntary liquidation will be outvoted with the result that the company will not be wound up at all, presents a strong argument in favour of a winding up order. It is strong enough to justify the making or an order on the petition of an administrative receiver who has realised sufficient assets to pay off the debenture holder despite the opposition of the trade creditors who wish to have a voluntary liquidation.[402] The rule that a petitioner pursuing a personal gain not shared by the class of creditors as a whole may have his

---

397　*Re Medisco Equipment Ltd* [1983] BCLC 305.
398　*Re Surplus Properties (Huddersfield) Ltd* [1984] BCLC 89.
399　*Re William Thorpe & Son Ltd* (1989) 5 BCC 156.
400　*Re Palmer Marine Surveys Ltd* [1986] BCLC 106; and *Re Lowestoft Traffic Services Ltd* [1986] BCLC 81.
401　*Re MCH Services Ltd* [1987] BCLC 535; and *Re Falcon (R J) Developments Ltd* [1987] BCLC 437.
402　*Re Television Parlour plc* (1988) 4 BCC 95.

petition dismissed applies when a voluntary liquidation has already begun. A landlord who will gain by retaining a premium and forfeiting a lease if an order is made has had his petition dismissed despite evidence of an unsatisfactory creditors' meeting and some doubts about the liquidator's behaviour in the existing voluntary liquidation.[403]

14.171 The costs of a successful petition and those of the company will usually be met from the assets of the company. One supporting creditor and one supporting contributory are also likely to be awarded their costs.[404] This will apply if the company appears only to consent to the petition—the costs of its unsuccessful opposition will not generally be allowed, so that a solicitor instructed on behalf of an insolvent company to oppose a petition will be well advised to seek indemnity from the directors.[405] There is no power to order directors to pay costs personally as they are not parties to the proceedings.[406] The general rule that an unsuccessful petitioner will have costs awarded against him will not apply where a creditor whose debt is undisputed acted reasonably in petitioning or where a creditor was misled by the company into presenting a hopeless petition against it.[407] Where costs are to be met from the company's assets the court may order that they should be deferred to the claims of the unsecured creditors if the petitioner knew that the company was insolvent and was already in receivership.[408] An appeal by the company against an order may be subject to an order for security for costs. This may be made against the directors or shareholders, if the order was granted against a solvent company on the petition of a contributory using the just and equitable ground, providing the petitioner's share of the assets of the company would otherwise be reduced by the order.[409]

14.172 The costs of a provisional liquidator should *prima facie*, be borne by the company if the petition is dismissed. This is laid down by Rule 4.30(3) and the discretion conferred by that rule will only be exercised in exceptional circumstances. It will not normally be used where a special manager behaved properly and carefully. The requirement that an applicant furnish costs for the appointment of the official receiver as provisional liquidator is not mandatory and the court may waive it in a

---

403   *Re Rhine Film Corporation (UK) Ltd* (1986) 2 BCC 98949.
404   *Re Humber Iron Works Co* (1866) LR 2 Eq 15.
405   *Re Bathampton Properties Ltd* [1976] 1 WLR 168.
406   *Re Reprographic (Euromat) Ltd* (1978) 122 Sol Jo 400.
407   *Re McCarthy & Co (Builders) (No 2)* [1976] 2 All ER 339; *Re Lanaghan Brothers* [1977] 1 All ER 265; *Re Arrow (Leeds) Ltd* [1986] BCLC 538; but see *Re Shusella Ltd* [1983] BCLC 505.
408   *Re Reprographic Exports* (note 406 above).
409   *Re E K Wilson & Sons Ltd* [1972] 1 WLR 791.

public interest case where the applicant is the Secretary of State for Trade and Industry.[410]

14.173   The winding up order made by the court will be drawn up by the registrar (with whom all necessary documents are left by the petitioner and every other person who has appeared on the hearing of the petition) no later than one day after the order was made.[411] The registrar need not appoint a venue for any person to attend to settle the order unless special circumstances make an appointment necessary.[412] The order is sent in triplicate to the official receiver who gazettes the order, advertises it in a local newspaper and serves a copy on the company.[413] At the time when the order is made notice is given to the official receiver of that fact.[414] A copy of the order must be forwarded forthwith to the Registrar of Companies by the company.[415]

14.174   An appeal from the decision of the Registrar of the Companies Court to make a winding up order is to a judge of the Companies Court— not the Court of Appeal.[416] It is a true appeal and there is not a hearing *de novo*. The circumstances are considered as at the date of the making of the winding up order so that even if the debt on which the petition was based has been paid between the two hearings the order will be upheld.[417] This rule is appropriate since once the order is made the commencement of the winding up relates back to the date of presentation of the petition and parties other than the company and the creditor may have been affected. Once the winding up of the company has begun every invoice, order for goods or business letter issued by or on behalf of the company, its liquidator, or the receiver and manager of its property must contain a statement that the company is being wound up if the company's name appears on the document. Default is punishable by a fine on the company and on any officer, liquidator or receiver or manager who wilfully and knowingly authorises or permits the default.[418] The date of the commencement of the winding up by the court will be the date of the presentation of the petition unless a winding up resolution had been passed earlier in which case the date of the resolution marks the commencement of the process.[419] All   proceedings   taken   in   the   voluntary   liquidation   are

410   *Re a Company (No 001951 od 1987)* [1988] BCLC 182.
411   Insolvency Rules 1986 r 4.20(2).
412   *Ibid* r 4.20(3).
413   *Ibid* r 4.21(1), (2) and (3).
414   *Ibid* r 4.20(1).
415   *Ibid* r 4.21(3) and Insolvency Act 1986 s 130(1).
416   *Re Calahurst Ltd* (1989) 5 BCC 318.
417   *Re Industrial and Commercial Securities plc* (1989) 5 BCC 320.
418   *Ibid* s 188(1).
419   *Ibid* s 129.

deemed to have been validly taken unless the court orders otherwise on proof of fraud or mistake.

THE EFFECTS OF A WINDING UP ORDER

14.175 At the commencement of the winding up or on the order being made a number of vital changes will take place in the legal position of the company and of those dealing with it. Those matters are dealt with here although the process of liquidation and all matters relating to the appointment and functions of provisional and other liquidators are the subject of chapters 15 to 19.

Rescinding or staying the winding up order

14.176 A winding up order is perfected by being drawn up, and up to that time it may be rectified or rescinded by the use of the court's inherent power.[420] The power will be exercised only with great caution because of the effects that the making of the order has on the creditors and others. The application for rescission must be made by a creditor or a contributory or the company jointly with such a person. It should normally be made within 3 or 4 days of the order and must be supported by an affidavit of assets and liabilities. A later application can only be justified by exceptional circumstances.[421] After the order has been drawn up rescission can only be justified if the order fails to reflect the intention of the court.[422] Only an appeal or an application under s 147 for the proceedings to be stayed can be used if the order is to be challenged on other grounds.

14.177 Once a perfected winding up order exists, the court will normally order a stay of the proceedings either altogether or for a limited time on an application under s 147 of the Insolvency Act 1986 rather than using its power to rescind.[423] However, because the existence of a winding up order on the record, even after it has been stayed, will affect the company's ability to obtain credit, a successful application to rescind (under Rule 7.47 of the Insolvency Rules 1986) can be made despite the fact that the order has been drawn up and stayed. This is so if the order is a nullity as is the case if it was made against the wrong company in error. In such a case the Registrar of

---

420 *Re Miller's Case* (1876) 3 Ch D 661.
421 Practice Directions [1971] 1 WLR 4 and 757.
422 *Tucker v New Brunswick Trading Co* (1890) 44 Ch D 249; *Re Orthomere Ltd* (1981) 125 Sol Jo 495.
423 *Re Intermain Properties Ltd* [1986] BCLC 265.

Companies is not under a duty under s 130(1) of the Insolvency Act 1986 to retain the order on his records and the court can order him to remove it from his files.[424]

14.178   An application to stay the proceedings under s 147 can be made by the liquidator, the official receiver or any creditor or contributory of the company. The court will exercise its discretion whether to stay the proceedings to take account of considerations of commercial morality and may refuse an order sought by the majority of the creditors if further investigation is necessary of the promotion, formation or failure of the company because, for example, the directors have been in breach of their statutory duty to furnish the liquidator with full information.[425] It is for those seeking a stay of the proceedings to prove their case.[426] No damages are available in negligence merely because a winding up order is made as a result of the failure of the petitioner to serve the petition correctly since no duty of care is owed by one litigant to another as regards the conduct of the litigation.[427]

Effect of winding up on proceedings against the company

14.179   Any action or proceedings brought by others against the company are affected at two stages. From the presentation of a winding up petition the company or any creditor or contributory can apply to the court for an order to stay the proceedings. The application is to the Companies Court unless the action to be stayed or restrained is in the High Court or the Court of Appeal in which case application is to that court. The court then has a discretion to stay or restrain the proceedings on any terms it thinks fit.[428] Such an application is made by summons in chambers.[429] This power also applies to a company in voluntary liquidation and is the only means whereby proceedings can be stayed in such a case as there is no automatic stay of proceedings.[430] An application under this provision can relate to distress as well as proceedings in the sense of litigation or process of execution.[431] The purpose of the provision is to ensure an equal distribution of assets among creditors who belong to the same class but a landlord has been allowed to continue with distress begun before the

---

424   *Re Calmex Ltd* (1988) 4 BCC 761.
425   *Re Telescriptor Syndicate Ltd* [1903] 2 Ch 174.
426   *Re Calgary and Edmonton Land Co Ltd* [1975] 1 WLR 355.
427   *Business Computers International Ltd v Registrar of Companies and Alex Lawrie Factors* [1987] BCLC 621; [1987] 3 WLR 1134.
428   Insolvency Act 1986 s 126(1).
429   See Insolvency Rules 1986 Part VII.
430   Insolvency Act 1986 s 112(1) and (2).
431   *Venners Electrical Cooking and Heating Appliances Ltd v Thorpe* [1915] 2 Ch 404.

commencement of the winding up owing to the absence of special circumstances to justify interference.[432]

14.180 When a winding up order is made or a provisional liquidator is appointed all actions and proceedings against the company are automatically stayed and no new actions or proceedings may be begun unless the court gives leave. Such leave may be subject to such terms as the court thinks fit.[433] This provision affects distress—even if the process was begun before the presentation of the petition—and interpleader proceedings.[434] The object of the provision is that all creditors should be treated *pari passu* in the winding up process and that there should not be a scramble for priority.

Avoidance of dispositions and share transfers

14.181 Section 127 of the Insolvency Act 1986 lays down that in a winding up by the court any disposition of a company's property or transfer of its shares made after the commencement of the winding up is void unless the court orders otherwise. The rule extends to alterations in the status of members by means other than share transfers and operates from the presentation of the petition. It applies to transactions which take place between the presentation of the petition and the making of the winding up order or the appointment of a provisional liquidator as well as later transactions. In such cases the court may be asked to validate transactions retrospectively.

14.182 There is some indication, from the case law, of the transactions which can be regarded as falling within the section. If the company entered into an unconditional contract for the sale of land before the commencement of the winding up and an order of specific performance would be available to enforce the contract, the completion of the sale after the commencement of the winding up by the transfer of the company's legal interest to the purchaser is not a disposition of property within s 127. The fact that the purchaser is the equitable owner of the property prevents the conveyance of the legal estate from amounting to a 'disposition' and the contract conferring equitable ownership was made outside the period covered by s 127. However, if the contract were either conditional or voidable a waiver of the condition or an affirmation of the voidable contract would amount to a disposition of the property.[435]

---

432 *D Wilson (Birmingham) Ltd v Metropolitan Property Developments Ltd* [1975] 2 All ER 814; *Re Bellaglade Ltd* [1977] 1 All ER 319.
433 Insolvency Act 1986 s 130(2).
434 *Eastern Holdings Establishment of Vaduz v Singer & Friedlander Ltd* [1967] 2 All ER 1192 and *Re Memco Engineering Ltd* [1986] Ch 86.
435 *Re French's (Wine Bar) Ltd* [1987] BCLC 499.

14.183 There is some uncertainty whether this principle applies to a contract to transfer shares since it has been held that specific performance of such a contract may be refused after the commencement of the winding up and that the court will not complete a transfer by putting the purchaser on the register of shareholders.[436] This may reflect the different effects of a transfer of shares as well as the fact that it is a transfer of shares and not a disposition of them that is avoided by the section. However, a notice given under the articles before the commencement of the winding up to convert preference shares into ordinary shares has been allowed to take effect afterwards.[437] A contributory retains *locus standi* to seek or oppose an order s 127 after the commencement of the winding up whether the order relates to a transfer of shares or some other transaction.[438]

14.184 All payments into and out of a bank account are regarded as dispositions of company property—not only the excess of payments out over payments in[439]—and the section can apply to dispositions of company property made indirectly by third parties as well as those made by the company. Where a director draws cash from the company's bank account by cheque and uses the cash to buy money orders which are in turn used to pay a creditor that is a disposition of company property as the bank notes and the money orders into which they are converted belong to the company and its property passes to the creditor.[440] An order to validate payments out of the company's bank account and to facilitate the continuation of its business will normally be granted on the application of the company through its directors before the hearing of a contributory petition on the just and equitable ground unless doubts about the company's solvency make it desirable to stop the depletion of its assets by continued trading.[441] This reflects the principle that the objections of a contributory will carry little weight against the view of the directors of a solvent company that a disposition is necessary or expedient in the interests of the company unless no intelligent and honest person could reasonably hold such a view.[442] Such an order may be limited to prevent the use of monies for the costs and expenses of individuals in the proceedings but the company will be allowed to meet its own costs of the winding up proceedings—although not of proceedings under s 459 of the Companies Act 1985.[443]

---

436   *Sullivan v Henderson* (1972) 116 Sol Jo 969 and *Emmerson's Case* (1866) 1 Ch App 433.
437   *Re Blaina Colliery* [1926] WN 30.
438   *Re Argentum Reductions (UK) Ltd* [1975] 1 All ER 608.
439   *Re Grays Inn Construction Co Ltd* [1980] 1 WLR 711.
440   *Re J Leslie Engineers Co Ltd* [1976] 1 WLR 292.
441   *Re a Company (07523 of 1986)* [1987] BCLC 200.
442   *Re Burton & Deakin* [1977] 1 WLR 390.
443   *Re Crossmere Electrical and Civil Engineering Ltd* (1989) 5 BCC 37; but see *Re a Company (005686 of 1988)* (1989) 5 BCC 79.

14.185   In the case of an insolvent company different considerations apply and the court will be anxious to uphold the principle of *pari passu* treatment for creditors. This principle applies to both prospective and retrospective validation. So long as the transaction would have been approved had application been made in advance then retrospective validation will be granted. An order can be made so long as there is no reduction in the assets available in the winding up so long as approval would have been given in advance of the transaction even if the refusal of retrospective validation would in fact increase the value of those assets.[444]

14.186   The principle of ensuring that assets are not depleted will not be broken by the authorisation of a sale of assets to pay off charges with the proceeds and the court will approve such a transaction providing it is satisfied that the charges in question are not vulnerable to an order setting them aside under the Insolvency Act 1986 or because of a failure to register them properly.[445] However, the argument that the company will not be damaged by a payment will not justify its retrospective validation if it was not made properly and responsibly under the threat of the winding up petition and with a view to assisting the company. A repayment of a director's advance to the company once he decides that it is irrecoverable will not be validated on the basis of such an argument.[446]

14.187   When a bank seeks the retrospective validation of payments to it by the company, it will not succeed if it is unable to show that it took precautions to check whether the company's account was being conducted properly and whether a petition had been issued. If many cheques are being returned unpaid and substantial cash withdrawals are being made this should put the bank on inquiry. The application by the court of the *pari passu* principle puts an onus on the applicant to show why transactions should be validated. That onus will not be discharged if the continuation of trading was of no benefit to the creditors of a hopelessly insolvent company and if there is no evidence that payments were being made out of the company's account in the normal course of business or to pay post petition debts.[447] The court's discretion under the section will be exercised with a view to the achievement of a *pari passu* distribution of assets to creditors. This principle is underlined by the fact that even a payment to the petitioner after the presentation of the petition in satisfaction of the statutory demand will not be validated if another creditor is substituted on the petition. The *pari passu* principle applies from the presentation of the petition.[448] The

444   *Re Tramway Building and Construction Co Ltd* [1987] BCLC 632.
445   *Re Sugar Properties (Derisley Wood) Ltd* [1988] BCLC 146.
446   *Re Webb Electrical Ltd* (1988) 4 BCC 230.
447   *Re McGuinness Brothers (UK) Ltd* (1987) 3 BCC 571.
448   *Re Western Welsh International System Buildings Ltd* (1985) 1 BCC 99296.

issue on a winding up petition is not solely between the petitioner and the company—the interests of other creditors will also be considered by the court when it exercises its discretion under s 127.

14.188 The court will seek to apply principles of fairness and equity in exercising its discretion.[449] Those principles were discussed by the Court of Appeal in *Re Gray's Inn Construction Co Ltd*.[450] In that case a bank failed in its attempt to have payments into the company's bank account between petition and order validated. The court took the view that validation should not be permitted if it would result in some pre-liquidation creditors being paid in full at the expense of others. Transactions taking place wholly after the commencement of the winding up might be validated as might those which increased or maintained the value of the company's assets in the interests of all the unsecured creditors. However, the mere fact that a bank's decision to continue a company's account was made on reasonable grounds and was based on adequate information at the time does not justify validation of payments into the account if this will cause some pre-liquidation creditors to gain at the expense of others. The bank was required to restore the amount lost to the fund available for distribution by the liquidator as all payments into and out of the account were held to be dispositions for the purpose of s 127; not merely the excess of payments out over payments in.

The effect on execution against the company

14.189 Section 128 avoids any attachment, sequestration, distress or execution which is put in force against the estate or effects of the company after the commencement of a winding up by the court. The other effects of liquidation on such steps against the company's assets are dealt with in paras 18.30–18.46.

The effect of winding up order on employees and agents of the company

14.190 The making of the winding up order operates to discharge the company's employees.[451] It is the making of the order which has this effect and there is no relation back to the date of the presentation of the petition. The order operates as a notice of discharge and terminates the contract of employment unless there is clear evidence of a waiver of that effect of the order by the liquidator to continue the employment of a person by the

449   *Re Clifton Place Garage Ltd* [1970] Ch 477.
450   [1980] 1 All ER 814.
451   *Re General Rolling Stock Co (Chapman's Case)* (1866) LR 1 Eq Cas 346.

company while its business is continued or to enter a new employment contract. The discharge amounts to a breach of the contract of service and enables employees to prove for damages.[452] If the business of the company is continued after the order is made and the employees continue to work the liquidator may be taken to have waived the effect of the winding up order as notice of discharge or, on behalf of the company, to have entered a new contract with the employee on the same terms as the old one.[453] To avoid these uncertainties it is usual for a liquidator to explicitly dismiss company employees whom he does not wish to employ for the purposes of the liquidation. Employees who are employed by the liquidator will be paid in full for work done after the winding up order is made as such salaries will form part of the expenses of the liquidation. The termination of the contract of employment as a result of the winding up order prevents the company from obtaining an injunction to restrain the former employee from acting in breach of a restrictive covenant not to compete with the company. As the company cannot perform its obligations under the contract it would be inequitable to grant it specific performance of the restrictive covenant.[454]

14.191 The status of employees as preferential creditors is dealt with in paras 19.32–19.37. They can prove for arrears of pay, commission and holiday pay and for any damages due as a result of their wrongful dismissal by virtue of the winding up order. Such damages are calculated on the basis of the remaining term of the employment contract with a deduction to allow for the possibility of new employment.[455] At common law the agency contracts of the company are similarly discharged by the making of the winding up order. In particular, the agency status of any receiver of the company's property will come to an end. However, this does not, in itself, make him an agent of the person who appointed him.[456] The termination of the agency created by a debenture under which a receiver was appointed does not affect his powers as receiver.

14.192 In the case of an administrative receiver, the powers conferred by s 42 and sch 1 of the Insolvency Act 1986 may survive the termination, under s 44(1)(a), of his status as agent on the company going into liquidation.[457] This is not free from doubt as s 42 lays down that the powers conferred on the administrative receiver by the debenture by virtue of which he was appointed are deemed to include the sch 1 powers except insofar as they are

452 *Re Oriental Banking Corporation (McDowall's Case)* (1886) 32 Ch D 366.
453 *Ibid* at 372; and see *English Joint Stock Bank Corporation ex p Harding* (1866) LR 3 Eq 341.
454 *Measures Brothers Ltd v Measures* [1910] 2 Ch D 248.
455 *Re English Joint Stock Bank (Yelland's Case)* (1867) LR 4 Eq 350.
456 *Gosling v Gaskell* [1897] AC 575.
457 That phrase means the time of the making of the winding up order in a winding up by the court not preceded by a voluntary liquidation—Insolvency Act 1986 s 247(2).

inconsistent with the provisions of the debentures. If the powers conferred by the debenture are said to be conferred as part of the administrative receiver's agency status then the fact that they are deemed to include the powers in sch 1 does not alter the basis on which all the powers—contractual and statutory—are conferred. If that basis disappears the powers may also cease to exist. For this reason it may be wise to continue the practice of conferring powers of attorney on administrative receivers to facilitate the sale of property after the agency powers have terminated.[458]

The effect on directors' status and powers

14.193   The making of a winding up order dismisses the directors of the company.[459] It also terminates their power to manage the company, as does any earlier appointment of a provisional liquidator.[460] Even the power of the directors to make calls on shareholders is terminated and replaced by the similar power of the liquidator.[461] The status of the directors as officers of the company does, however, remain so that they can be required to answer interrogatories.[462] The board also retains certain residual powers which have not been assumed by the liquidator or provisional liquidator. They include the power to instruct solicitors and counsel on the hearing of the winding up petition after a provisional liquidator has been appointed, and to appeal against a winding up order.[463]

PART 4: MEETINGS OF CREDITORS AND CONTRIBUTORIES

14.194   The Insolvency Rules 1986 lay down the procedures to be followed in connection with meetings of creditors and contributories. In this section those rules are described as they apply to any type of winding up. Where the rules vary according to whether a liquidation is compulsory or voluntary or, in the latter case, a members' or creditors' voluntary liquidation the text will deal with the different provisions. Unless that is done the rules dealt with can be taken to apply in all cases.

458   See *v David Samuel Trust Ltd* [1978] 1 All ER 616; *Barrows v Chief Land Registrar, The Times* 20 October 1977; Palmer's 'Company Law' 24th ed para 86.04 and Gore Brown on *Companies* 44th ed para 32–16.
459   *Measures Brothers v Measures* (note 454 above).
460   *Re Farrows Bank Ltd* [1921] 2 Ch 164 at 173–174; and *Re Mawcon Ltd* [1969] 1 WLR 78, in which a court order appearing to continue the powers of the directors after the appointment of a provisional liquidator was construed as an appointment of the directors as special managers.
461   *Fowler v Broad's Patent Night Light Company* [1893] 1 Ch 724.
462   *Madrid Bank v Bayley* (1886) LR 2 QB 37.
463   *Re Union Accident Insurance Co* [1972] 1 WLR 640; and *Re Diamond Fuel Co* (1879) 13 Ch D 400.

WHEN AND BY WHOM MEETINGS ARE CALLED

14.195   The Act lays down a number of provisions for calling meetings of creditors or contributories. The particular sections deal with different forms of winding up.

Calling meetings in a winding up by the court

14.196   In a compulsory liquidation the official receiver, while acting as liquidator, has power to summon meetings of the company's creditors and contributories to appoint a liquidator to replace him.[464] He has a duty to decide whether to do so within 12 weeks of a winding up order being made and to call the meeting if required to do so by one quarter in value of the company's creditors.[465] Section 139 provides for the nomination of a liquidator at the separate meetings of the contributories and the creditors called after the winding up order is made. The section also gives effect to the choice of the creditors, if they have nominated anyone, unless the court makes an order appointing the contributories' nominee to act jointly with, or in place of, the nominee of the creditors, or for the appointment of some other person.[466] Section 141 provides that the meeting called to choose a liquidator in a compulsory liquidation may appoint a liquidation committee or that a separate meeting may be called for that purpose. A liquidator other than the official receiver must call a meeting to appoint a liquidation committee if he is requested to do so by one third in value of the company's creditors.[467]

14.197   After those initial meetings, the liquidator in a winding up by the court may at any time summon general meetings of the contributories or the creditors for the purpose of ascertaining their wishes and he is obliged to do so at the request in writing of one tenth in value of the creditors, or the contributories as the case may be, or if directed to do so by a resolution of a meeting of the group in question.[468] Section 195 gives such a power to the court and s 160(1)(a) permits the rules to delegate it to the liquidator. Rule 4.54(1) achieves that delegation.

14.198   At the stage at which it appears to a liquidator, other than the official receiver, that the winding up of the company by the court is for practical purposes complete he is obliged to summon a final creditors'

---

464   Insolvency Act 1986 s 136(4).
465   s 136(5) and see para 14.222 below.
466   s 139(3) and (4).
467   s 141(2).
468   s 168(2).

meeting to receive his report and determine whether he is to have his release. He is required to ensure that sufficient sums are retained from the company's property to cover the expenses of summoning and holding that meeting.[469]

Calling meetings in a voluntary liquidation

14.199   In a members' voluntary liquidation, which does not require conversion into a creditors' voluntary liquidation because of the company's insolvency, only company general meetings will be called. The commencement of the liquidation and the appointment of the liquidator will be by resolution of the company at a meeting preceded by a declaration of solvency by the directors.[470] The company general meeting has power to fill vacancies in the office of liquidator, and, if the liquidation continues for more than a year, such meetings are required to be held annually to receive an account of the liquidator's conduct of the winding up.[471] In addition, s 165(4)(c) gives the liquidator power to call company general meetings during the winding up to obtain sanction or for any other purpose he thinks fit. A final company general meeting must be called to receive an account of the liquidation as soon as the company's affairs are fully wound up.[472] Section 95 requires a creditors' meeting to be called in a members' voluntary liquidation within 28 days of the liquidator forming the opinion that the company will be unable to pay its debts in full. As from the date of that meeting the winding up becomes a creditors' voluntary liquidation.[473]

14.200   In a creditors' voluntary liquidation the first meeting of creditors has to be called under s 98 within 14 days of the passing of the winding up resolution by the company general meeting. After those meetings, the liquidator may summon general meetings of the company for any purpose that he thinks fit under s 165(4)(c). A creditors' meeting may be called by any creditor (or by a continuing liquidator if there was more than one) under s 104 and Rule 4.101A to fill a vacancy in the office of liquidator. At the end of each year of the liquidation a company general meeting and a creditors' meeting must be called under s 105(1) to receive an account of the liquidator's conduct of the winding up. As soon as the company's affairs are fully wound up a final meeting of the creditors and of the company must be called for the receipt of final accounts before dissolution.[474] In any voluntary liquidation an application can be made to the court for it to

469   s 146(1) and (3).
470   ss 84, 89, 90 and 91(1).
471   ss 92(1) and (2).
472   s 94(1).
473   s 96 and see para 14.199 above.
474   s 106.

exercise its power to call meetings under s 195 to ascertain the wishes of the creditors and contributories.

NOTICE OF MEETINGS AND INFORMATION TO CREDITORS IN ANY WINDING UP

14.201   In a compulsory liquidation the venue of any meetings of creditors and contributories, called by the official receiver to nominate a liquidator to replace him, must be fixed by him not more than 4 months from the date of the winding up order.[475] Such meetings will only be held if the official receiver decides to call them under s 136(5)). Notice of the meetings must then be given to the court and to every creditor known to the official receiver or identified in the statement of affairs (in the case of the creditors' meeting) and to every contributory (in the case of a contributories' meeting).[476] Notice to the court must be given forthwith and notice to the creditors and contributories at least 21 days before the date fixed for the meeting.[477] Notice of the meetings must also be given by public advertisement.[478] The notices sent out to creditors must specify the time and date by which they must lodge proofs and (in the case of both creditors and contributories) any proxies permitted in order to be entitled to vote at the meeting.[479]

14.202   In those circumstances in which creditors can requisition a meeting under s 136(5)(c) or 168(2) they must conform to Rule 4.57 in requesting a meeting. It lays down that a list of the creditors concurring in the request and the amount of their claims, a statement of the purpose of the proposed meeting and written confirmation of the concurrence of each listed creditor should accompany the request unless one creditor qualifies to make the request without the assent of others, in which case only a statement of the purpose of the meeting is needed.[480] If the liquidator decides that the request has been properly made he must fix a venue for the meeting not more than 35 days after receiving the request and give 21 days' notice of both meeting and venue to the creditors.[481] Similar rules apply to requests by contributories for meetings of that group to be held.[482] In the case of a request to the official receiver under s 136(5)(c) for meetings of creditors and contributories to be summoned, which appears to him to be

---

475   Insolvency Rules 1986 r 4.50(1).
476   r 4.50(2).
477   r 4.50(3).
478   r 4.50(5).
479   r 4.50(4).
480   r 4.57(1).
481   r 4.57(2) and (3).
482   r 4.57(4).

properly made, he will fix a venue within 3 months of receiving the request, withdraw any notices he has issued under s 136(5)(b) which he has decided not to summon a meeting and issue notices in accordance with Rule 4.50.[483]

14.203 During the course of the winding up of a company by the court meetings may be summoned by the official receiver or the liquidator to ascertain the views of the creditors or the contributories.[484] In the case of such meetings at least 21 days' notice must be given to creditors and contributories specifying the purpose of the meeting and its venue.[485] The notice must also specify where and by what time and date (not more than 4 days before the meeting) creditors must lodge proofs and creditors and contributories should lodge proxies to be entitled to vote at the meeting.[486] Public advertisement in addition to individual notice of such meetings is optional unless the court orders that it should be done.[487] Notice of the final meeting called under s 146 of the Act at the end of the compulsory liquidation may be sent out with notice of any final distribution.[488]

14.204 Where a notice is required to be served by post it must be sent in an envelope addressed to the person on whom it is to be served and sent by first or second class post. It may be sent to the person's last known address and is presumed to be posted on the date of its post mark and to arrive on the second business day after posting if it is sent first class or the fourth day if sent second class.[489] A meeting is presumed to have been properly summoned and held even if all those to whom notice should have been sent have not received it.[490]

14.205 Where a statement of affairs has been submitted and filed in court in a compulsory liquidation the official receiver is to send a summary out to creditors and contributories with his comments unless he has already reported to them on the company's affairs.[491] The same obligation exists if the company has been released from its obligation to submit a statement of affairs.[492] The court may waive or limit these obligations on the basis of the cost of carrying them out, the assets available and the extent of the claims of the creditors or any class of them. The obligation ceases if the winding up is

483   r 4.50(6).
484   r 4.54(1).
485   r 4.54(2) and (3).
486   r 4.54(4).
487   r 4.54(6).
488   Insolvency Act 1986 s 146(2).
489   Insolvency Rules 1986 r 12.10.
490   r 12.16.
491   r 4.45.
492   r 4.46.

stayed by the court.[493] In a voluntary liquidation Rule 4.48 requires the liquidator to send to the creditors and the contributories, within 28 days of a meeting under s 95 or s 98, a copy or summary of the statement of affairs of the company and a report of the proceedings at the meeting. If no statement of affairs has been filed in the court in a compulsory liquidation or delivered to the registrar of companies in a creditors' voluntary winding up creditors are entitled to require the liquidator to supply a list of creditors and the amounts of their debts. It is an offence for a person to claim falsely the status of creditor or contributory with the intention of obtaining sight of documents which that person is not entitled under the Rules to inspect.[494]

14.206   The notice required for meetings under s 95 and 98 must be sent by post not less than 7 days before the date of the meeting and advertised once in the Gazette and at least once in a newspaper circulating in the locality in which the company's principal place of business was situated during the 'relevant period'.[495] The notice must specify the venue of the meeting and the time (not earlier than 12 noon on the business day before the date of the meeting) by which time and place creditors must lodge proofs and any proxies necessary to enable them to vote at the meeting.[496] For meetings called voluntarily by the liquidator during the course of the winding up to ascertain the views of the creditors or the contributories Rule 4.54 applies the same time limits and requirements as apply to a compulsory liquidation. In the case of any liquidation it is open to the court to order that notice of any meeting of contributories or creditors be given by public advertisement and not by individual notice. In deciding whether to make such an order the court will have regard to the cost of public advertisement, the assets available and the extent of the interest of contributories or creditors or any class of them.[497]

VENUE, CHAIR AND ADJOURNMENT IN ANY LIQUIDATION

14.207   All meetings in liquidations of all kinds must be held at a venue fixed with due regard to the convenience of the persons who are to attend other than the chairman. In particular they must always be summoned to begin between the hours of 10 am and 4 pm on a business day unless the court directs otherwise.[498] In a compulsory liquidation any meetings called

493   rr 4.47 and 4.48.
494   *Ibid* r 12.17 and 12.18.
495   Insolvency Act 1986 ss 95(2)(b) and (c) and 98(1)(b) and (c); and see para 14.20.
496   Insolvency Rules 1986 r 4.51(2).
497   *Ibid* r 4.59.
498   r 4.60(1) and (2).

by the official receiver will be chaired by him or by his nominee, who must be appointed in writing unless he is another official receiver or a deputy official receiver. In any other case the chairman will be the convener (normally the liquidator) or a person nominated by him in writing but in any event must be a qualified insolvency practitioner or an employee.[499] In a voluntary liquidation meetings other than those held under s 98 must be chaired by the liquidator or someone nominated by him in writing who satisfies the same requirements as a liquidator's nominee in a compulsory liquidation.[500] In the case of a creditors' meeting called at the beginning of a creditors' voluntary liquidation the chair will be taken by the director appointed by the board of the company under s 99(1) to preside over it. According to s 95(3)(c) and Rule 4.56(1) as amended by SI 1987/1919, the liquidator himself must preside over a meeting called in a members' voluntary liquidation under s 95.

14.208   The rules on the adjournment of meetings apply to all meetings of contributories and of creditors in any liquidation. The chairman may once only at his discretion suspend the meeting for up to 1 hour without adjourning it.[501] He may in his discretion adjourn the meeting to such time and place as seems appropriate and is obliged to do so if the meeting so resolves. This is subject to the exception that a meeting called to remove the liquidator which is chaired by him may only be adjourned with the consent of at least half by value of the creditors present in person or by proxy and entitled to vote.[502] It would seem that this provision of the Insolvency Rules ousts the common law power of a chairman to adjourn a meeting although the obligation to use it with a view to achieving the purpose of allowing the views of the majority to be validly ascertained will presumably apply.[503]

14.209   If a quorum is not present within 30 minutes of the time appointed for the meeting to commence then the chairman may adjourn it in his discretion.[504] Adjournment can only be for up to 21 days and if a meeting is adjourned for want of a quorum and no-one is present to act as chairman agreement by those present and entitled to vote will fix the date of the reconvened meeting. If no agreement is reached the adjournment is to the same time and place the following week or, if that is not a business day the first business day thereafter.[505] Where any meeting is adjourned proofs and

499   r 4.55.
500   r 4.56.
501   r 4.65(2).
502   rr 4.65(3), 4.113(3) and 4.114(3).
503   See *Byng v London Life Association Ltd* (1989) 5 BCC 227.
504   r 4.65(4).
505   r 4.65(5) and (6).

proxies may be used if lodged at any time up to midday on the business day immediately before the adjourned meeting.[506]

ATTENDANCE, VOTING AND PROXIES AT MEETINGS IN ANY WINDING UP

14.210   In any winding up the Rules provide for the convener of any meetings of creditors or contributories to give at least 21 days' notice of the meeting and of any adjournment of the meeting to such of the company's personnel as he thinks fit.[507] The company's personnel means present and past officers of the company or of another company that was its officer, and former employees of such companies who were employed or engaged under a contract for services within a year before the date of the appointment of the provisional liquidator or the company going into liquidation. It also includes former liquidators, administrators or administrative receivers of the company and those who took part in its formation within the one year period.[508]

14.211   The convener is also entitled to require such personnel to attend a meeting by giving them notice to that effect and they in turn may give reasonable notice of their wish to be present although the chairman of the meeting has the power to decide whether to admit them and to determine what intervention if any they may make in the meeting and the questions that may be put to them.[509] The chairman may adjourn the meeting to obtain the attendance of any of the company's personnel if it is desired to question him.[510] In a creditors' voluntary liquidation s 99(1) lays down that the directors of the company are under an obligation to appoint one of their number to preside at the meeting called under s 98 and that that person is under a duty to do so.

14.212   The 1986 reforms have changed the rules on voting at creditors' meetings to make it easier for decisions to be made. A majority in value of those present and voting in person or by proxy is now sufficient to pass a resolution under Rule 4.63(1). Under Rule 134 of the Winding Up Rules 1949 a majority in number was also required before a decision could be made. Most of the rules on voting apply to all meetings in a winding up of any kind. As a general rule a creditor is entitled to vote only if a proof of

---

506   r 4.65(7).
507   r 4.58(2) and (3).
508   Insolvency Act 1986 s 235.
509   Insolvency Rules 1986 r 2.58(4), (5) and (7).
510   r 2.58(6).

debt has been lodged and admitted and any necessary proxy has been duly lodged. However, the court can order (in any liquidation) that an individual or a whole class of creditors should be allowed to vote without having proved a debt and, in a creditors' voluntary liquidation, the chariman may allow a creditor to vote on being satisfied that the failure to prove the debt was the result of circumstances beyond his control.[511] A person can only vote in respect of an unliquidated debt or a debt whose value has not been ascertained if the chairman of the meeting agrees to put an estimated value on the debt and to admit a proof for that purpose.[512] A secured creditor must value his security, deduct that amount from the sum he is owed and vote only in respect of the balance.[513] For this purpose the fact that a creditor claims that the company holds an amount as money had and received or on a constructive trust is a proprietory claim but does not make the creditor a secured creditor or a person claiming a debt whose value has not been ascertained. Consequently his voting rights are unaffected.[514]

14.213 If a debt is secured by a current bill of exchange or promissory note a creditor can only vote if he is willing to treat the liability of all those liable on it before the company as security, value it and deduct it from his proof. This does not apply to the antecedent liability of a bankrupt individual or a company in liquidation.[515] The admission or rejection of proofs for the purpose of entitlement to vote is in the discretion of the chairman of the meeting as regards the whole or part of a proof but his decision is subject to appeal to the court by any creditor or contributory.[516] If the chairman is in doubt whether to admit a proof he is to mark it as objected to and allow the creditor to vote subject to the vote being declared invalid if the objection is later sustained. If on an appeal against the decision of the chairman his decision is reversed or varied the court may order that another meeting be called or make such other order as it thinks fit.[517] The official receiver or his nominee can never be held liable for the costs of an appeal and any other person who chairs a meeting can only be made liable for them if the court so orders.[518] The voting rights of contributories at their meetings will be those to which they are entitled at company general meetings subject to any provision of the company's articles affecting that right either generally or when the company is in liquidation.[519]

---

511   rr 4.67(1) and (2) and 4.68.
512   r 4.67(3).
513   r 4.67(4).
514   *Re Prime Metal Trading Ltd* [1984] BCLC 543.
515   Insolvency Rules 1986 r 4.67(5).
516   r 4.70(1) and (2).
517   r 4.70(3) and (4).
518   r 4.70(5) and (6).
519   r 4.69.

14.214   Frequently proxies will be held by the chairman of the meeting and in such a case if he is instructed to vote in favour of a resolution and no-one else proposes it he must propose it himself or notify his principal forthwith after the meeting of the good reason which he considered that he had for not doing so.[520] The Insolvency Rules 1986, as amended by SI 1987/1919, lay down the scope for the use of proxies and the procedures to be followed. Forms 8.1 to 8.5 are to be used. Proxies are for use at meetings of contributories or creditors called or summoned under the Act or the Rules and a proxy is defined as an authority given by the principal to the proxy-holder to attend and speak and vote at such a meeting as his representative.[521] It requires the proxy-holder to give the principal's vote on matters arising for determination at the meeting or to abstain or to propose a resolution to be voted on at the meeting. It can be either a 'one way' or a 'two way' proxy as the rules provide that it can require the proxy-holder to act either as directed or in accordance with his own discretion.[522]

14.215   Only one proxy may be given for any one meeting and it must be given to only one proxy-holder who must be an individual of at least 18 years of age. However, the proxy may specify one or more individuals to be proxy holder in the alternative in the order in which they are named in the proxy.[523] The chairman of the meeting may be appointed as proxy-holder and, in a compulsory liquidation, the official receiver may be appointed. The chairman and the official receiver are obliged to accept appointment. If no-one else does so, the chairman is required to propose a resolution in favour of which a proxy instructed him to vote unless he has a good reason for failing to do so. In the latter situation he must notify his principal of the reason forthwith after the meeting ends.[524]

14.216   Proxy forms must be sent out with every notice summoning a meeting of creditors or contributories[525] and they must not be sent out with the name or description of any person already inserted in them.[526] It is not permissible for the forms sent out by the convener of the meeting to provide for the appointment of the chairman or the liquidator as the proxy-holder. The form must be signed by the principal or some person authorised by him in which case the form must itself state the nature of the authority. Only a form sent out with the notice of the meeting at which it is to be used or one that is substantially similar to it is acceptable.[527]

520   r 4.64.
521   r 8.1(1) and (2).
522   r 8.1(6).
523   r 8.1(3).
524   rr 8.1(4) and (5) and 4.64.
525   r 4.60(3).
526   r 8.2(1).
527   r 8.2(2) and (3).

14.217 A proxy given for a particular meeting may be used at an adjournment of that meeting and if the official receiver is proxy-holder his deputy, any other official receiver or any DTI official authorised by him in writing may use it. Similarly a substitute chairman of a meeting may use those proxies held by the responsible insolvency practitioner in that capacity.[528]

14.218 If the proxy directs the holder to vote for or against a particular person's appointment as liquidator, that does not bind him if that person is nominated to act jointly with someone else. In such a case the holder can vote at his own discretion unless the proxy prevents such a course of action.[529] Similarly, unless the proxy states otherwise, the holder is free to cast the votes at his own discretion on any resolutions which are considered by the meeting but which are not dealt with in the proxy.[530] The proxy-holder may propose any resolution in favour of which the proxy would entitle him to vote.[531]

14.219 The proxies used for voting at a meeting are to be retained by the chairman and passed to the liquidator if that is someone other than he.[532] While they are held by the liquidator they must be available for inspection at all reasonable times on any business day by any creditor (if they were used in a creditors' meeting), any contributory (if they were used in a company or contributories' meeting) and by the directors of the company. In addition anyone attending a meeting is entitled immediately before or in the course of the meeting to inspect proxies and proofs submitted for the purpose of that meeting.[533]

14.220 A proxy is not permitted to vote in favour of any resolution which would directly or indirectly place him or his associate in a position to receive remuneration from the company's assets. This rule does not apply if the proxy specifically directs him to vote in that way but if the proxy is signed by the proxy-holder as a person authorised to do so he must produce to the chairman of the meeting a written authorisation establishing his right to sign it before using it to vote for a resolution in which he has a financial interest. A person other than the proxy-holder acting as chairman of the meeting is subject to the same rule if he uses proxies in that capacity and the proxy holder is deemed to be his associate for this purpose.[534]

528   r 8.3(1). (2) and (3).
529   r 8.3(4).
530   r 8.3(6).
531   r 8.3(5).
532   r 8.4.
533   r 8.5.
534   r 8.6.

14.221   A person representing a corporate body at a meeting on the basis of s 375 of the Companies Act 1985 must produce a sealed copy of the board resolution (or one certified by the body's secretary or a director of it) from which he derives authority to the chairman of the meeting. The authority of a person to sign a proxy form on behalf of a corporate principal is not required to be in the form of a resolution.[535]

RESOLUTIONS AND MINUTES AT MEETINGS IN ANY LIQUIDATION

14.222   A resolution is passed in a meeting by the majority in value of those present and voting in person or by proxy. The 'value' of contributories in this context is determined by the number of votes conferred on each one by the company's articles. If the resolution is for the appointment of a liquidator and there are two nominees the one who obtains most support is appointed but in a compulsory liquidation he must have the support of a majority in value of those present in person or by proxy and entitled to vote.[536] If there are more than two nominees election is by eliminating ballot unless one obtains a clear majority over both or all the others.[537] The chairman always has the power to put to the meeting a resolution for the appointment of two or more joint liquidators.[538] On a resolution for the appointment of a liquidator or any other resolution affecting the remuneration or conduct of a proposed or former liquidator the vote of the liquidator and of any partner or employee of his as creditor, contributory or proxy-holder must not be counted in the majority for passing the resolution.[539]

14.223   The chairman is required to ensure that minutes which record the resolutions passed are kept, signed by him and retained as part of the records of the liquidation. He must also ensure that a list of creditors or contributories attending the meeting is made and kept.[540] He must also ensure in a winding up by the court that certified particulars of all such resolutions are filed in court within 21 days of the meeting.[541] The minutes are admissible as evidence in insolvency proceedings without further proof if they are signed by a person appearing to be the chairman of the meeting or so describing himself. They are *prima facie* evidence that the meeting was

---

535   r 8.7.
536   r 4.63(1), (2)(a) and 4.63(2A).
537   r 4.63(2)(b) and (c).
538   r 4.63(3).
539   r 4.63(4).
540   r 4.71(1) to (3).
541   r 4.71(4).

duly convened and held, that all the resolutions passed at the meeting were duly passed and that all proceedings at the meeting duly took place.[542]

EXPENSES OF MEETINGS

14.224 The expenses of meetings called by the liquidator or the official receiver will be part of the expenses of the winding up and will be paid out of the assets. The same rule applies to the expenses of a meeting called under s 98 in a creditors' voluntary liquidation except that any payment to the liquidator or his associate must be approved by the liquidation committee, the creditors or the court and 7 days' notice of his intention to pay others must be given to the liquidation committee.[543] If meetings are held at the instance of anyone other than the liquidator or the official receiver, the expenses must be met by that person who must make a deposit of an amount specified by the liquidator or the official receiver as security for that payment.[544] However it is possible for the creditors' meeting to resolve that the expenses of that meeting and any meeting of contributories requisitioned at the same time should be met out of the assets of the company as an expense of the liquidation. A contributories' meeting may resolve that the expenses of calling it should be met out of the assets after all the company's debts have been paid in full.[545]

542   r 12.5.
543   r 4.62(3) and (4).
544   r 4.61(1) and (2).
545   r 4.61(3) and (4).

CHAPTER 15

The Liquidator

15.01 The role of the liquidator is central to the winding up process. Unlike a trustee in bankruptcy he does not take ownership rights in relation to company property although the company is not the beneficial owner ot its property after liquidation has commenced.[1] The existence of the company continues after winding up begins. The liquidator takes over the functions of management and control of the company and for this reason he cannot be regarded as a trustee. However, he owes fiduciary duties in respect of the way he conducts the process of liquidation.[2]

PART 1: APPOINTMENT OF THE LIQUIDATOR

GENERAL REQUIREMENTS FOR APPOINTMENT

15.02 Apart from the official receiver no person may act as a liquidator or provisional liquidator unless he is qualified to act as an insolvency practitioner in relation to that company.[3] The person appointed to act as liquidator must not have been subject to a disqualification order made by a court under the provisions of the Company Directors Disqualification Act 1986 which disqualifies him from acting as a director or a liquidator. However, a person subject to such a disqualification may be given leave to act by the court with jurisdiction to wind up the company.[4] If a person who is in office as liquidator ceases to be qualified to act as an insolvency practitioner, he must vacate office immediately unless he is the official receiver.[5] Similarly a person against whom a disqualification order is made must cease to act in order to avoid liability to a criminal penalty and personal liability for the debts of the company incurred at a time when he was involved, as liquidator, in its management.[6] A liquidator who acts or is willing to act on the instructions of a person who is subject to a

1 *Ayerst v C&K (Construction) Ltd* [1976] AC 167 HL.
2 See below para 15.58–15.75.
3 Insolvency Act 1986 ss 230(3) and (5), 388(1)(a) and s 89; and see ch 21 above.
4 Insolvency Act 1986 s 390(4)(b) and Company Directors Disqualification Act 1986 ss 1(1)(b) and 17(1)(b); and see ch 21 on the circumstances in which disqualification orders may be made.
5 Insolvency Act 1986 ss 171(4) and 172(5).
6 CDDA 1986 ss 13 and 15.

disqualification order at the time when he acts, or is willing to act, will also be personally liable for the debts of the company unless he has obtained the leave of the court.[7]

15.03 A liquidator must be an individual. It is not possible for a corporation to be appointed to fill this role as only individuals are qualified to act as insolvency practitioners.[8] Similarly, neither a bankrupt nor a patient within the meaning of the Mental Health Act 1983 can act.[9] Section 231 of the Insolvency Act 1986 lays down that if more than one person is appointed or is to act as liquidator, provisional or otherwise, the appointment or nomination giving rise to this situation must specify whether acts required or authorised to be done by a liquidator or provisional liquidator are to be done by all or any one or more of the persons holding office.

APPOINTMENT IN A COMPULSORY WINDING UP

Provisional liquidator

15.04 Section 135 of the Insolvency Act 1986 empowers the court to appoint a provisional liquidator at any time after the presentation of a winding up petition and before the making of the winding up order.[10] The court order will specify the functions which are to be carried out by the person appointed and may limit his powers.[11] It is common for the official receiver to be appointed as provisional liquidator. By virtue of s 230(4), any other person appointed must be a qualified insolvency practitioner. The application for the appointment of a provisional liquidator may be made by the petitioner, a creditor, a contributory, the company, the Secretary of State or any person who would be entitled to petition for a winding up order.[12]

15.05 An affidavit must support the application for the appointment of a provisional liquidator. It must set out:

(a) the grounds for the application;

(b) the consent of, and the adequacy of the qualifications of, any proposed appointee other than the official receiver;

---

7   *Ibid* ss 15(1)(b) and 3(b), and see ch 10.
8   Insolvency Act 1986 s 390(1).
9   s 390(4)(a) and (c).
10   s 135(1) and (2).
11   s 135(4) and (5).
12   *Re a Company* [1974] 1 All ER 256 and Insolvency Rules 1986 r 4.25(1).

(c) whether or not the official receiver has been informed of the application or furnished with a copy of it;

(d) whether the applicant is aware of actual or proposed voluntary arrangements under Part 1 of the Insolvency Act 1986;

(e) whether an administrative receiver or administrator is acting, or a liquidator in a voluntary winding up has been appointed;

(f) and the applicant's estimate of the value of the assets in respect of which the appointment is proposed.[13]

15.06 The official receiver is entitled to copies of the application or, if this is impracticable, to sufficient notice of the application to enable him to attend. He is also entitled to a copy of the affidavit. He may attend the hearing and make representation.[14] The court will make the appointment on such terms as it thinks fit if it is satisfied that sufficient grounds have been shown to justify such an order.[15] The order of appointment will specify the functions to be carried out by the provisional liquidator in relation to the company's affairs.[16] Sealed copies of the order are supplied to the appointee, the official receiver and any administrative receiver acting in relation to the company. The appointee is responsible for the transmission of such a copy to the company or its existing liquidator appointed in a voluntarily winding up.[17]

15.07 It is possible for the hearing on whether to appoint a provisional liquidator to be held *in camera* if damage to the company is possible and it cannot be ascertained whether the grounds in the petition are good. This is, however, an exceptional step and proceedings should be held in public at the earliest opportunity.[18] The notice required for the hearing can be waived under Rule 7.4(6) if the appointment is required as a matter of urgency, for example, to run down the company's business speedily.[19] The court will exercise its powers to appoint a provisional liquidator where the company does not contest the application, applies itself or consents if the official receiver is to be appointed.[20] However, it is clear from the wording of s 135 and from the more recent case law that the court has an unfettered power to appoint a provisional liquidator and that there is no need for special circumstances to be proved even if the company objects to the appointment.

13   r 4.25(2).
14   r 4.25(3).
15   r 4.25(4).
16   r 4.26(1).
17   r 4.26(2) and (3).
18   *Re London & Norwich Investment Services Ltd* [1988] BCLC 226.
19   *Re W F Fearman Ltd* (1988) 4 BCC 139.
20   *Re Cilfoden Benefit Building Society* (1868) 3 Ch App 462.

15.08   In *Re Union Accident Insurance Co Ltd*[21] Plowman J accepted that the question of whether to appoint a provisional liquidator would be resolved by deciding; firstly, whether the petitioner had made out a good *prima facie* case for a winding up order and (if that were established); secondly, whether it is right in the circumstances of the case that a provisional liquidator be appointed.[22] In that case, which involved a petition by the Department of Trade and Industry for the winding up of an insurance company, the public interest requirement that the solvency of the company should be maintained or that it should be wound up before its liabilities exceeded its assets, together with the greater ease with which certain sums due to the company could be recovered by a provisional liquidator, justified the appointment.

15.09   The existence of danger to the assets, obvious insolvency, or the company's admission that it has no defence to the petition cannot be regarded as an exhaustive list of the circumstances in which an appointment can be made.[23] There are cases where an appointment will be appropriate for the protection of the company's assets. The use of the test of a *prima facie* case for granting an application for a provisional liquidator goes further than is necessary to prevent frivolous or vexatious applications to eliminate any element of prejudice of the final issue of whether the petition will succeed. In most cases the petition will be on grounds of insolvency and even at an interlocutory stage that issue will be easy to decide. When this situation is combined with a need to protect the assets of the company, the success of an application can hardly be in doubt.[24] The protection of assets can take the form of steps to reduce liabilities by the closure of uneconomic parts of the company's operations, and a provisional liquidator, (with powers limited to taking possession, collecting and protecting assets but not distributing or parting with them), may close an office and dismiss staff.[25]

15.10   Despite early case law to the contrary,[26] it is clear that *ex parte* applications for the appointment of a provisional liquidator will be granted should circumstances of urgency and necessity be established.[27] In such cases an undertaking as regards damages will be required unless the Secretary of State for Trade and Industry applies in the public interest.[28]

21   [1972] 1 All ER 1105.
22   *Ibid* at 1110.
23   *Ibid* at 1109.
24   *Re Hammersmith Town Hall Co* (1877) 6 Ch D 112.
25   *Re Union Accident Insurance Co Ltd* [1972] 1 WLR 640.
26   *Re London & Manchester Industrial Association* (1875) 1 Ch D 466.
27   *Re Union Accident Insurance* (note 25 above).
28   *Ibid.*

On an application by the Secretary of State for Trade and Industry under s 440 of the Companies Act 1985, the public interest may justify the appointment of a provisional liquidator if the company's activities have been disreputable and an imposition on the public. There is no need to establish insolvency or that the assets are in jeopardy if there is *prima facie* evidence that the winding up petition will result in an order.[29]

15.11 Where two companies have a relationship such that the liquidator of each of them will represent conflicting interests it is right for the court to appoint a provisional liquidator of one of them to prevent the same person acting as voluntary liquidator of both companies.[30] The powers of a provisional liquidator are subject to some dispute. The purpose of an appointment of a provisional liquidator is to 'keep things *in status quo* and to prevent anybody from getting priority'[31] or to protect the property with a view to the winding up of the company.[32] If no winding up order is made his appointment should not interfere with the rights of third parties. In such circumstances there is no relation back of the commencement of the winding up to the date of the presentation of the petition and the right of priority obtained in the period during which the provisional liquidator was in office can be given full force.[33] In the *Dry Docks Corporation* case the priority obtained by a levy of distress for rates was not affected by the fact that it was levied and the rates were due at a time when the provisional liquidator was in office. Had the rating authority been aware of the appointment of the provisional liquidator then they would have been in contempt in failing to seek leave from the court to levy distress against property held by the provisional liquidator under the terms of a court order. In practice, the powers conferred on a provisional liquidator by the order appointing him are usually restricted. Thus he will usually be comissioned to preserve the assets of the company and perhaps to run its business. The order will usually expressly prohibit any disposal of assets or distribution by the provisional liquidator although the protection of assets can include a reduction in the level of the company's liabilities.[34]

15.12 Since at the time of the appointment of the provisional liquidator no winding up order has been made, it would clearly be wrong if the process of winding up could be effectively achieved by that officer. However, it is submitted that the power to preserve assets is to be interpreted in a dynamic manner which gives full legal authority to the provisional liquidator to do

29 *Re Highfield Commodities Ltd* [1985] 1 WLR 640.
30 *Re P Turner (Wilsden) Ltd* [1987] BCLC 149.
31 *Re Dry Docks Corporation of London* (1888) 39 Ch D 306 per Kay J at 309.
32 *Ibid* per Cotton LJ at 312.
33 *Ibid* per Fry LJ at 314.
34 *Re Union Accident Insurance* (note 25 above).

all acts that are necessary to preserve the position. This may include running the company's business and carrying out or entering contracts in pursuit of that end[35] as well as sealing documents necessary to prevent the forfeiture of valuable property.[36] In *Re ABC Coupler and Engineering Co (No 3)*[37] Plowman J expressed the view *obiter* that 'the word "provisional" in this context seems to imply a qualification not of the liquidator's powers but of the tenure of his office; he is a liquidator but his appointment is temporary'. This statement has been questioned in Palmer's *Company Law*[38] on the grounds that the *Dry Docks* case was not cited in *ABC Engineering*. The observations in the former case in the Court of Appeal and at first instance as to the purpose of the appointment of the provisional liquidator imply that the completion of the winding up process would be beyond a provisional liquidator's powers and this accords with good sense since he is acting before a winding up order has been made. One might add that s 144(1) of the Insolvency Act 1986 which derives from the Companies Act 1948 s 243(1) empowers a provisional liquidator, like a liquidator, to 'take into custody or under his control all the property and things in action to which the company appears to be entitled', while s 143, which deals with the liquidator's general functions, and s 167 together with sch 4, which confer specific powers, refer only to the 'liquidator'.

15.13   Rule 4.26(1) of the Insolvency Rules 1986 requires that the order of appointment should specify the functions to be carried out by the provisional liquidator in relation to the company's affairs. This implies that his powers and authority have their origins in the order of appointment. Section 135(4) states that the provisional liquidator shall carry out such functions as the court may confer on him but s 135(5) enables the court to limit his powers. Perhaps these two provisions can best be reconciled by suggesting that the powers to be conferred will be consistent with the functions given to the provisional liquidator by the court. An order conferring a function is likely to be interpreted widely so as to enable the provisional liquidator to terminate contracts and to reduce liabilities in order to preserve the company's assets.[39] Presumably the courts will accept that the provisional liquidator has the powers necessary to carry out any function which has been conferred upon him. If the company continues in business this may include the power to enter into contracts on behalf of the company. It is unlikely that a court would ever make an order conferring the function of conducting the entire liquidation on the provisional

---

35   See *Re Dry Docks Corporation* (note 31 above), where this was expressly authorised, and *Re Union Accident Insurance* (note 25 above), where it was accepted.
36   *Carden v Albert Palace Association* (1886) 56 LJ Ch 166.
37   [1972] 1 WLR 702.
38   23rd ed, p 1144.
39   *Re Union Accident Insurance Co Ltd* [1972] 1 WLR 640.

liquidator. Where a court wished to curtail powers which might otherwise be considered to flow from the functions described in the order it could do so under s 135(5).

15.14 On the appointment of a provisional liquidator the powers of the company's directors to act as such are determined and cannot be revived for so long as the provisional liquidator remains in office.[40] However, this does not prevent the exercise of certain residuary powers which remain in the hands of the directors. They are entitled to instruct solicitors and counsel to oppose the winding up petition or to appeal against a winding up order. They may also make interlocutary applications in the winding up proceedings, for example, to challenge the appointment of the provisional liquidator.[41] Sections 232 (supplies by public utilities) and 234 (the collection of the company's property) apply after the appointment of the provisional liquidator.

15.15 The applicant for the appointment of the official receiver as provisional liquidator must deposit with the official receiver, or secure to his satisfaction, a sum to cover his remuneration and expenses. The court determines the exact amount. Orders for additional sums to be deposited or secured may be made on the application of the official receiver after appointment if the original sum proves to be insufficient. The deposit is returned when a winding up order is made if expenses and remuneration can be met from the assets available as an expense of the liquidation.[42]

15.16 Where an insolvency practitioner is appointed as provisional liquidator security must be provided by the appointee.[43] The cost of providing the security falls on the provisional liquidator in the first instance but reimbursement will be proved out of the company's assets if no winding up order is made, and in the winding up if an order is made.[44] Failure to provide or keep up security empowers the court to remove the provisional liquidator or discharge the order appointing him and to give directions as to the appointment of a replacement. Costs may be awarded against the original appointee.[45]

15.17 The remuneration of an insolvency practitioner will be fixed by the courts. In arriving at a figure the court will take account of:

40 *Re Mawcon Ltd* [1969] 1 WLR 78 at 82.
41 *Re Union Accident Insurance Co Ltd* [1972] 1 WLR 640.
42 r 4.27; on priority see r 4.218(1)(c)(ii).
43 Insolvency Act 1986 s 390(3) and Insolvency Rules 1986 r 12.8.
44 r 4.28.
45 r 4.29.

(a) the time properly given by the provisional liquidator and his staff in attending to the company's affairs;
(b) the degree of complexity of the case;
(c) any respects in which exceptional responsibilities have fallen on him;
(d) the effectiveness with which his duties have been or are being carried out;
(e) the value and nature of the property dealt with.[46]

The remuneration and expenses of the provisional liquidator are to be paid from the assets of the company if no winding up order is made or as a cost of winding up if one is made. Where the official receiver was appointed they will be paid from the deposit held under Rule 4.27 if the assets are insufficient.

Termination of the appointment of a provisional liquidator

15.18 A provisional liquidator can be removed from office only by court order.[47] The order may be made on his own application or on that of any of the persons who could have applied for his appointment. That is, the petitioner, any creditor of the company, any contributory, the company, the Secretary of State or any other person entitled to present a winding up petition.[48] A common reason for removal will be the dismissal of the winding up petition. However, whether the appointment is terminated for that reason or any other, the court may give directions as to the accounts of the provisional liquidator's administration of the company's affairs and as to the payment of his expenses and remuneration from the property of the company which he may be authorised to retain for that purpose.[49]

Special managers

15.19 Section 177 of the Insolvency Act 1986 enables any liquidator or provisional liquidator to apply for the appointment of a special manager of the business or property of the company. The application can be made 'where the company has gone into liquidation or a provisional liquidator has been appointed'. A company 'goes into liquidation' if it passes a resolution for voluntary winding-up or an order for its winding up is made by the court at a time when no such resolution has been passed. In the absence of an earlier resolution the date of the winding up order, and not the date of presentation of petition, represents the date on which the

---

46   r 4.30(1) and (2).
47   Insolvency Act 1986 s 172(2).
48   r 4.31(1).
49   r 4.31 and r 4.30(3) and (3A) as amended by SI 1987 no 1919.

company 'goes into liquidation'. This means that if a winding up resolution is passed between the presentation of a winding-up petition to the court and the making up of the winding up order the company goes into liquidation at the date of the resolution and not at the date of the presentation of the petition which is the date at which winding up commenced under s 129(2).[50] The appointment of a provisional liquidator before a winding up order is made enables applications to be made for a special manager. In the case of a voluntary winding up only the liquidator may apply for a special manager but where the company is wound up by the court the application can be made by the provisional liquidator or the liquidator before or after the order is made.

15.20 The application may be made by a provisional liquidator or a liquidator whether or not the official receiver is acting in that capacity. Under s 566 of the Companies Act 1985 only the official receiver could make such an application. This enables a person with suitable skill and experience to be appointed to run the company.

15.21 The application for the appointment of a special manager may be made where it appears to the applicant that the nature of the company's property or the interests of creditors or members generally require such a step.[51] This would be the case where the continued operation of the company's business was likely to increase the value of assets ultimately available for distribution in the winding up.

15.22 When an application is made under s 177 for the appointment of a special manager, it is to be supported by a report setting out the reasons for the application and the estimated value of the assets in respect of which the appointment will be made.[52] The order of appointment will specify the duration of the appointment by fixing a period of time, providing for termination of the recurrence of the specified event, or making it subject to further court orders.[53] In any event the appointment may be renewed by order and terminates on dismissal of a winding up petition, discharge of a provisional liquidator without a winding up order having been made, or on the application of the liquidator or provisional liquidator.[54] A liquidator or provisional liquidator is required to apply to the court for directions if he forms the opinion that the employment of the special manager is no longer necessary or profitable for the company or if a resolution of the creditors is

---

50 s 247(2).
51 s 177(2).
52 Insolvency Rules 1986 r 4.20(1).
53 r 4.206(3).
54 r 4.210(1) and (2).

passed requesting the termination of the special manager's appointment.[55] It will terminate in accordance with the original order if a period was fixed for its duration.

15.23   Defects in the appointment or qualifications of the special manager will not affect the validity of his acts.[56] Appointment is conditional on the provision of security of at least the value of the assets estimated in the report presented by the applicant. The provision of such security is evidenced by a certificate filed by the applicant for the special manager's appointments.[57] The cost of security is initially to be met by the special manager but he is to be reimbursed from the assets, whether or not a winding up order is made.[58] Where a liquidation occurs he has priority as to payment of a cost out of assets under Rule 4.218(1)(e).[59]

The powers of the special manager
15.24   The powers available to a special manager are those which the court entrusts to him under s 177(3) of the Insolvency Act 1986. Those powers will normally enable him to manage the company's business although in a case where the appointment relates to some specific property they may be limited to the management of that property. The court has powers to direct that if the special manager carries out any of the functions of the liquidator or the provisional liquidator any provisions of the Insolvency Act 1986 will have effect in relation to the special manager as they would have in relation to a liquidator or provisional liquidator.[60] The directors of the company may, in appropriate circumstances, be appointed as special managers with powers specified in the order of appointment.[61] The remuneration of the special manager is fixed by the court.[62]

15.25   During his period in office a failure to provide or keep the security necessary will result in a report to the court by the liquidator or the provisional liquidator and the possible removal of the special manager or the discharge of the order appointing him. This order will give directions as to his replacement.[63] Accounts containing details of the special manager's receipts and payments must be produced for the approval of the liquidator or the provisional liquidator in respect of 3 month periods and a shorter period if necessary ending with the termination of the appointment. After

55   *Ibid.*
56   r 4.206(6).
57   r 4.207.
58   r 4.207(5) and (6).
59   See ch 19.
60   s 177(4).
61   *Re Mawcon Ltd* [1969] 1 WLR 78.
62   r 4.206(5).
63   r 4.208.

approval the special manager's payments and receipts are added to those of the liquidator or the provisional liquidator.[64]

The appointment of a liquidator in a compulsory winding up

15.26 Where a company is wound up by the court, the official receiver becomes liquidator of the company on a winding up order being made until some other person becomes liquidator. The official receiver will be its liquidator during the period of any later vacancies.[65] However, if the winding up order is made immediately upon the discharge of an administration order, or at a time when a supervisor is in office under an approved form under Part I of the Insolvency Act 1986, the person who has acted as administrator or supervisor may be appointed by the court as liquidator and the official receiver would not take office. He will then be under none of the duties which would follow his taking office as liquidator.[66] These provisions ensure that from the moment a winding up order is made a liquidator is in office. If the official receiver has previously been in office as provisional liquidator (as will usually be the case where such an officer is appointed) his role will undergo a transformation at the date of the winding up order. The sequence of events which follow is likely to depend on the value of the assets available to the company. Where the costs of liquidation are likely to be met by those assets and a surplus will exist the creditors may wish to appoint their own liquidator. If this is not the case then the official receiver will remain in office.

15.27 Under s 136(4) the official receiver has power, at any time when he is liquidator of the company (whether immediately after the winding up order or during a later vacancy) to call separate meetings of the company's creditors and contributories to choose a person to replace him as liquidator. He has a duty to decide as soon as practicable, within the 12 weeks beginning with the date of the winding up order, whether to exercise that power. If he decides not to call meetings he must give notice of his decision to the company's creditors and contributories within the 12 week period and the notice must contain an explanation of the right of one quarter by value of the company's creditors under s 136(5)(c) to insist on a meeting being convened.[67]

15.28 Where creditors representing one quarter by value of the company's debts require the official receiver to summon a meeting under

---

64 r 4.209.
65 s 136(1) to (3).
66 s 140.
67 s 136(5)(a)(b).

s 136(5)(c) the official receiver is discharged from his duty to decide whether or not to do so and to give notice of a decision to call no meeting. In making his decision as to whether to call meetings for the appointment of a liquidator the official receiver will have regard to the likely dividend which will be available to creditors after the costs of the winding up have been met. If the assets are insufficient to meet those costs then the official receiver will decide to remain in office.

15.29   At any time when the official receiver is in office as liquidator of a company he may apply to the Secretary of State for Trade and Industry for the appointment of some other person as liquidator in his place.[68] Where meetings of creditors and contributories called for the purpose of appointing a liquidator fail to do so the official receiver is required by s 137(2) to decide whether to refer the need of an appointment to the Secretary of State. The Secretary of State may choose whether or not to appoint a liquidator but if a person is appointed they must give notice of their appointment to all the company's creditors or, with the leave of the court, advertise the appointment in accordance with the court's directions.[69] The notice or advertisement must state whether the new liquidator proposes to call a creditors' meeting under s 141 to decide whether to appoint a liquidation committee and, if he does not intend to do so, set out the right of one tenth in value of the company's creditors to demand this be done.[70]

15.30   Where the official receiver decides under s 136(4) to summon meetings to appoint a liquidator or where one quarter by value of the company's creditors insist that such meetings be convened each meeting may nominate a person to be liquidator.[71] The nomination of the members' meeting will prevail only if the creditors fail to make a nomination. Where two different persons are nominated the creditors' nominee will be appointed unless, on an application by any contributory or creditor under s 139(4) within 7 days of the creditors nomination, the court appoints the members' nominee or some other person than the nominee of the creditors.[72]

15.31   Where two or more persons are appointed or nominated as liquidators the appointment or nomination must declare whether acts are to be done by them or to be done by all or any one or more of them.[73] This

68   s 137(1).
69   s 137(4).
70   s 137(5).
71   s 139(2).
72   s 139(3) and (4).
73   s 231.

procedure ensures that from the time the winding up order is made the liquidator will be in office. This is achieved without the necessity of an appointment by the court. In cases where the creditors and contributories make the appointment and have their separate meetings, the procedure is similar to that which applies in a voluntary windung up. This avoids the process of application to the court for an appointment which was formerly required. In other cases the official receiver will remain in office and may make use of the early dissolution procedure under s 202 of the Insolvency Act 1986 to avoid unnecessary costs where the company's assets are of little or of no value and there is no reason to investigate the company's affairs. The court attaches great importance to the right of the creditors' meeting to appoint a liquidator. An independent provisional liquidator will not be appointed as liquidator by the court as this would prevent the creditors having their vote at the first meeting although the provisional liquidator may be given permission to use that individual as a special manager.[74]

15.32   The time of appointment of the official receiver as liquidator will be the moment at which the winding up order is made.[75] Where a person is appointed liquidator by a meeting of creditors or by a meeting of contributories his appointment takes effect from the date on which it is certified by the chairman of the meeting. That date is endorsed on the copy certificate. The endorsed certificate is then sent by the official receiver to the liquidator. The certificate of appointment will only be issued by the chairman of the meeting after the person appointed has provided the chairman with a written statement to the effect that he is an insolvency practitioner duly qualified under the Act to operate as liquidator and that he consents to act.[76] Where a liquidator is appointed by the court under either s 139(4) because different persons were nominated by creditors' and contributories' meetings or under s 140 following an administration or voluntary arrangement the date of the appointment is the date of the order making it.[77] The order does not issue unless and until the person appointed has filed in court a statement to the effect that he is an insolvency practitioner and that he consents to act as liquidator in the case.[78]

15.33   The court sends two copies of the order to the official receiver and one is forwarded to the liquidator. The liquidator must then, within 28 days

---

74   *Re W F Fearman Ltd (No 2)* (1988) 4 BCC 141.
75   s 136(1) and (2).
76   r 4.100 as amended by SI 1987 no 1919.
77   r 4.102(4).
78   r 4.102(2).

of his appointment, give notice of the appointment to all creditors and contributories of the company of whom he is aware. Alternatively, if the court allows, he may advertise his appointment as directed by the courts.[79] The notice of advertisement must state whether the liquidator proposes to summon meetings of creditors and contributories for the purpose of establishing a liquidation committee or only to summon a meeting of creditors for that purpose and if he has no proposal to summon any such meeting it must set out the powers of the creditors under the act to force him to summon one.[80]

15.34 Where a liquidator is appointed by the Secretary of State the appointment is effective from the date specified in the certificate of appointment issued by the Secretary of State to the official receiver. Of the two copies issued to the official receiver one is forwarded to the liquidator and the other filed in court.[81] Where a liquidator is appointed by a creditors' or contributories' meeting or by a meeting of the company he must, on receiving his certificate of appointment, give notice of his appointment in a newspaper which he considers appropriate for ensuring that his appointment comes to the notice of the company's creditors and contributories. The expense of this notice is to be borne at the first instance by the liquidator but he will be reimbursed from the assets as an expense of liquidation. The liquidator must also forthwith notify his appointment to the Registrar of Companies.[82]

15.35 It will be noted that where different persons are appointed by a meeting of contributories and a meeting of creditors the official receiver has power to ensure that it is the appointment by the meeting of creditors which takes effect since it is for him to file the certificate and thus give effect to the appointments.

15.36 Where a liquidator is in succession to the official receiver the official receiver is required to put him into possession of the assets but the liquidator must discharge any bonds due to the official receiver on account of his expenses or advances made by him in respect to assets. It is possible for the liquidator to give the official receiver a written undertaking to discharge any balances with the first realisation of assets rather than to hand over monies on taking possession of the assets. The official receiver

---

79   r 4.102(3) and (5).
80   r 4.102(6).
81   r 4.104.
82   r 4.106.

has a charge on the assets in respect of any sums due to him but where the liquidator has realised the assets with a view to making those payments the charge does extend in respect of the sums deductible by the liquidator as expenses probably incurred in the realisation.[83]

15.37 The official receiver must hand over to the liquidator all such information relating to the affairs of the company in the course of the winding up as the official receiver considers to be reasonably required for the effective discharge of the liquidator's duties. He must also furnish a copy of any report made by the official receiver under the insolvency rules to creditors and contributories.[84] The liquidator is required from time to time, out of the proceeds of the realisation of assets, to discharge all guarantees which were properly given by the official receiver for the benefit of the estate and to pay all the official receiver's expenses.[85]

15.38 It is an offence for a person to give, agree to give or offer to give any valuable consideration to a member or creditor of a company with a view to securing the nomination or appointment of himself or any other person as the company's liquidator or to preventing the appointment or nomination of another person.[86] This offence only applies to corrupt inducements given to members or creditors of the company itself. It appears that such inducements given to members or creditors of some other company which is itself a creditor or member of the company which is to be wound up do not fall within the provision unless there can be said to be given to the other company.

15.39 Rule 4.150(1) provides that the court may order that no remuneration should be allowed out of the company's assets to any person by whom, or on whose behalf, improper solicitation has been used in obtaining proxies or procuring his appointment as liquidator. Where such an order is made Rule 4.150(2) provides that it overrides any resolution of the liquidation committee or the creditors and any other provision of the insolvency rules as to remuneration. Thus not only is an offence committed by a liquidator who offers corrupt inducements to obtain appointment but his remuneration is also placed at risk.

The effect of the appointment on the powers of the directors

15.40 The Act does not expressly state that the powers of the directors cease on the appointment of a liquidator in a compulsory liquidation as it

---

83 r 4.107(1) to (5).
84 r 4.107(7) and (8).
85 r 4.107(6).
86 *Re Farrow's Bank Ltd* [1921] 2 Ch 164.

does in s 91(2) and 103 in respect of a voluntary winding up. However it is clear from the case law that the function of the liquidator in acting on behalf of the company after his appointment means that there is no function left for the directors.[87] The only role left to them is to appeal against the winding up order which has deprived them of their powers.[88] They may still enjoy apparent authority to bind the company and that cannot be denied unless the making of the winding up order has been gazetted under s 42 of the Companies Act 1985. It is unclear whether they still hold office formally after the onset of compulsory liquidation.[89]

APPOINTMENT IN A VOLUNTARY WINDING UP

15.41   In the case of a members' voluntary winding up the company in general meeting is empowered to fill a vacancy and appoint one or more liquidators.[90] This confirms that the control of such liquidations remains in the hands of the members. Since the company is assumed to be solvent as a declaration of solvency will have been made in advance, the company in general meeting or the liquidator may sanction the continuance of some or all of the powers of the directors. In the absence of such sanction, the directors' powers cease.[91] When the liquidator is appointed at the meeting held to pass the winding up resolution, the notice of the meeting and resolution need not include the proposal to appoint liquidators.[92]

15.42   Any vacancy in the office of liquidator in such a liquidation may be filled by the company in general meeting unless an arrangement to the contrary has been made with the company's creditors.[93] That meeting may be convened by a single contributory or by any remaining liquidator but will otherwise be held in the manner provided by the Insolvency Act 1986 or the company's articles or, if the application is made by any contributory or by a continuing liquidator, in the manner laid down by the court.[94]

15.43   In all voluntary liquidations the court retains an overriding power to appoint a liquidator if none is acting and to remove one liquidator or appoint another.[95] Similarly in any voluntary liquidation where no liquidator is appointed after the winding up commences the powers of the

---

87   *Re Farrow's Bank* (note 86 above).
88   *Re Diamond Fuel Co* (1879) 13 Ch D 400.
89   *Measures Brothers Ltd v Measures* [1910] 2 Ch D 248.
90   Insolvency Act 1986 s 92(1) and see r 4.101A.
91   s 91(2).
92   *Re Trench Tubeless Tyre Co* [1900] 1 Ch 408 CA.
93   s 92(1) and see r 4.101A.
94   s 92(2) and (3).
95   s 108.

directors cease, except in so far as they may be used to dispose of perishable or other goods which are likely to diminish in value if they are not immediately disposed of or to do anything else necessary to protect the company's assets. In a creditors' voluntary winding up their power may also be used without sanction to do anything necessary to secure compliance with ss 98 and 99 which deal with creditors' meetings and statements of affairs respectively.[96] Any other exercise of the directors' powers is an offence. The registrar of companies may strike the company off the register and disolve it if he has reasonable cause to believe that no liquidator is acting.[97]

15.44 In a creditors' voluntary winding up the ultimate choice of liquidator is made by the creditors' meeting. At the separate meetings of the company and creditors called under s 98, each meeting may nominate a liquidator. Where creditors nominate a liquidator he takes office and the nomination of the company's meeting will only prevail if no liquidator is appointed by the creditors' meeting.[98] Since the company meeting is necessarily held first their nominee may take office before a creditors' meeting is called within the 14 days required by s 98(1)(a). That appointment is valid and effective but the liquidator appointed has limited powers during the period before the creditors' meeting is called.[99] Section 166(5) requires the liquidator in these circumstances to apply to the court for directions within 7 days of becoming aware of the default by the directors or the company under ss 98 or 99 in laying a statement of affairs before the creditors or in calling a meeting of creditors. The procedure and voting rights at the creditors' meeting are dealt with in chapter 14, part 4. However, it should be noted that under the Insolvency Rules 1986 the majority by value alone make the nominations.[100] It is not necessary for there also to be a majority in numbers of creditors.

15.45 If there are two nominees for appointment as liquidator the person with most support is appointed. At a contributories' meeting the support is measured by the votes conferred by the company's articles. At a creditors' meeting support is counted by reference to the value of debts due.[101] Where more than two nominees are put forward election is by process of elimination of the person with least support until one nominee has a clear majority over all the others. Only at that stage is he elected.[102]

96 s 114.
97 Companies Act 1985 s 652(4).
98 Insolvency Act 1986 s 100(1) and (2).
99 s 166(1), (2) and (3).
100 r 4.63(1).
101 r 4.63(1) and (2)(a).
102 r 4.63(2)(b) and (c).

15.46   Where different persons are nominated by the creditors' and members' meetings any director, creditor or member of the company may apply to the court within 7 days of the date of the creditors' nomination for an order a person nominated by the company be appointed instead of or jointly with the creditors' nominee or that some other person be appointed in place of the creditor's nominee.[103] Any vacancy in the office of liquidator may be filled by the creditors' meeting unless the liquidator was appointed by the court.[104] In that case an application to the court would be necessary under s 108(1). The offence of offering, giving or agreeing to give corrupt inducements to secure or prevent the appointment of a person as liquidator applies to voluntary winding ups as well as compulsory liquidations.[105]

15.47   Where the person appointed as liquidator by a creditors' meeting is not perceived by creditors of substantial value as being independent and they wish the affairs of the company to be investigated by the official receiver, the court may make a winding up order on that petition. Even if the majority by value favour a voluntary winding up their motives will be taken into account when the court exercises its discretion of hearing the winding up petition. Principles of fairness and commercial morality require that substantial independent creditors should not be left with a strong and legitimate sense of grievance.[106] This may override the general rule that the wishes of the majority by value and the additional expense of a compulsory winding up will carry great weight in the exercise of the court's discretion as to whether to make a winding up order when a voluntary one has already begun.[107]

15.48   Section 652(4) applies to enable the registrar to strike off a company from the register if he has reasonable cause to believe that no liquidator is acting. A liquidator appointed in a creditors' or members' voluntary winding up must publish notices of his appointment in the prescribed form in the *Gazette* and deliver the notice to the registrar of companies. Failure to do so is an offence.[108] The liquidator must give notice of his appointment in the newspaper that he thinks is most appropriate for ensuring that it comes to the notice of creditors and contributories. This obligation arises on receipt by the liquidator of his certificate of his appointment.[109] The duty is not imposed on a liquidator appointed by company meeting and

---

103   s 100(3).
104   s 104.
105   s 164.
106   *Re Palmer Marine Surveys Ltd* [1986] 1 WLR 513.
107   *Re J D Swain Ltd* [1965] 1 WLR 909; *Re Medisco Equipment Ltd* [1983] BCLC 305; and ch 14.
108   s 109.
109   r 4.106(1).

replaced by another appointed on the same day by a creditors' meeting.[110] The expense of this advertisement is borne by the liquidator but is reimbursed as an expense of the liquidation.[111]

PART 2: POWERS, DUTIES AND ROLE OF THE LIQUIDATOR

LEGAL STATUS OF THE LIQUIDATOR

15.49   The legal status of the liquidator cannot be precicely defined. In this section the general legal role of the liquidator is examined before the specific statutory powers conferred on him are considered. In addition to his specific statutory powers the liquidator has power as agent of the company. Similarly, whilst statutory duties are specifically imposed on the liquidator, his role as a fiduciary imposes additional duties and the common law tort of negligence imposes yet more. Like the company director whom he replaces, the liquidator has a role which blends the principles of agency and of trust. In some respects the precise role of the liquidator will vary as between a liquidator acting in a compulsory winding up who is regarded as an officer of the court and a liquidator in a voluntary winding up who does not fulfil that role. It has long been the reality that even in a compulsory winding up the liquidator acts under the supervision of the court rather than on its instructions. This is because, unlike a receiver appointed by the court or, possibly, a provisional liquidator, his powers were not exhaustively defined by the court order apointing him. They were based on statute and subject to court supervision. Under the Insolvency Act 1986 the distinction between a liquidator in a compulsory winding up and one acting in a voluntary winding up is even less significant since each is appointed by a similar process of members' and creditors' meetings and, in the usual course of events, neither is appointed by the court. However, the fact that the court is seised of the matter in a compulsory winding up inevitably extends the degree of control that the court can exercise and makes the liquidator an officer of the court. The agency and fiduciary elements in the liquidator's role are common to both types of liquidation.

The liquidator as agent

15.50   The liquidator's role as agent of the company is well established. The company is bound by any contracts which he makes on its behalf and the liquidator is not personally liable for such contracts or for costs in

---

110   r 4.106(2).
111   r 4.106(3).

actions brought on behalf of the company. Consequently, there being no agency on behalf of the creditors or members by virtue only of the liquidator's office, there can be no liability on his part to individual members or creditors for his conduct of the liquidation in the absence of fraud, dishonesty or a deliberate act.[112]

15.51 Where a solicitor is instructed by the liquidator to act on behalf of the company his costs are payable by the company's unless the liquidator has contracted to be personally liable. This rule is based on the nature of the liquidator's role as agent.[113] Such a contract requires strong evidence showing the liquidator's intention to bind himself personally in the absence of any interest on his part.[114]

15.52 The nature of the liquidator's role as agent of the company does not stem from the body which appoints him. In the members' voluntary winding up he is appointed by the company's general meeting but in a creditors' voluntary winding up he is usually appointed by a meeting of creditors. Similarly in a compulsory winding up an appointment will now usually be by a meeting of creditors, although formerly it was by the court. It is, however, clear that in all cases the liquidator is agent of the company.[115] This seems to relate to his function rather than the source of his appointment.

15.53 In *Re Trueman's Estate*[116] the agency powers were said to derive from the fact that the liquidator in a voluntary winding up replaces the directors and takes on their role in this respect. In *Re Anglo-Moravian Hungarian Junction Railway Company* a liquidator in a compulsory winding up was held to have the role of an agent on the grounds that 'he is appointed by the court to act for the company'.[117] This can be contrasted with the nineteenth century approach to receivers appointed by the court whose role was to act for the debenture holders and who acted under close control by the court.[118] However, in modern times such receivers have invariably been made agents of the company by the deeds which appointed them and s 44 of the Insolvency Act 1986 provides that an administrative receiver is 'deemed' to be the company's agent up to the time when it goes into liquidation.

15.54 As a consequence of the agency role of the liquidator he has actual

112 *Scott v Knowles* [1891] 1 Ch 717.
113 *Re Trueman's Estate* (1872) LR 14 Eq 278.
114 *Re Anglo-Moravian Hungarian Junction Railway Company* (1875) 1 Ch D 130.
115 *Ibid.*
116 (1872) LR 14 Eq 278 at 281.
117 (1875) 1 Ch D 130 at 133 per James LJ.
118 *Stead Hazel & Co v Cooper* [1933] 1 KB 840.

authority to bind the company to contracts. The rules as to such authority apply by reference to the liquidator's statutory powers. It is hard to see how any ostensible or apparent authority could be attributed to a liquidator as he is the controller of the principal and cannot obtain authority as a result of a representation made to a third party by any person with actual authority to bind the company as is required by the decision in *Freeman and Lockyer v Buckhurst Park Properties (Mangal)* Ltd.[119] Third parties will always be able to ascertain whether a particular act is within the list of statutory powers of the liquidator. However, in the case of those powers exercisable only with the approval of the court or the liquidation committee, it is submitted that if there is no publicly available information as to whether approval has been given third parties should be entitled to assume that such approval exists. This is based on the analogy of the rule in *Turquand's Case.*[120]

15.55 It is unclear whether s 35 of the Companies Act 1985 will be available to a third party if the liquidator exceeds his authority. The section refers only to 'any transactions decided on by the directors and any limitations under the memorandum or articles or the powers of the directors to bind the company. This wording excludes the acts of a liquidator since his dealings are not decided on by the directors and his powers are not likely to be limited under the memorandum or articles of association of the company except in those cases where a reconstruction is undertaken in accordance with the articles. However, it might be argued that the liquidator's role as 'governing body' of the company[121] brings him within the words used by the EEC Directive 68/151/EEC as an organ of the company and thus within the section. However, even if such an argument were to succeed, the limited effect of s 35 in dealing only with restrictions in the memorandum and articles will mean that it is rarely applicable to a liquidator. The liquidator has power to ratify acts of the company that were done before his appointment so long as such acts were within the capacity of the company when they were carried out.[122]

15.56 Although the liquidator is protected from personal contractual liability by his role as agent of the company, he may be liable for negligence in carrying out his task: 'being an agent employed to do business for a remuneration he is bound to bring reasonable skill to its performance'.[123] As all liquidators are qualified insolvency practitioners the level of skill

---

119   [1964] 2 WLR 618.
120   (1856) 25 LJ QB 317.
121   *Hillman v Crystal Bowl Amusements Ltd* [1973] 1 WLR 162, see also Companies Act 1989 discussed in ch 1.
122   *Alexander Ward Co v Samyung Navigation Co* [1975] 1 WLR 673.
123   *Re Silver Valley Mines Ltd* (1882) 21 Ch D 381 at 392.

required of them will reflect that status. Negligence in bringing an application to the court in error may result in the award of costs against the liquidator personally unless he has acted on proper professional advice in bringing the application. In any event, the refusal of a sanction requested from the court will not, in itself, lead to an award of costs against him personally.[124]

15.57 Proceedings for negligence cannot be brought against the liquidator by an individual creditor or member before the company has been dissolved. As agent of the company his duty is to the company and before dissolution a misfeasance summons is open to a dissatisfied creditor or member as a means of challenging a distribution alleged to be wrongfully made or a failure to deal properly with the company's assets. For these reasons an individual creditor or member has a remedy for negligence against the liquidator after the dissolution of the company has removed the possibility of action by way of misfeasance summons under s 212 of the Insolvency Act 1986.[125] As a general rule a misfeasance summons cannot be used to obtain damages for negligence at common law unless there has been some breach of fiduciary duty.[126] However a breach of the liquidator's statutory duty may be the subject of such proceedings.[127] A liquidator is not to be held liable for the acts of employees who are operating within the framework of a proper management structure providing the selection of the employee and the decision to delegate matters to him was not negligent in the light of the facts known to the liquidator.[128] This places him in an analogous position to that of a company director.[129]

The liquidator as fiduciary

15.58 The fiduciary role of the liquidator has been developed by the courts but also finds recognition in the Insolvency Act 1986 and the Insolvency Rules 1986. It is clear that the property of the company is no longer beneficially owned by it after the beginning of the winding up. The custody, control, and realisation of its property and the distribution of its proceeds are taken out of the hands of the company which remains the legal owner of it and vested in the liquidator over whom the company has no control.[130] This does not mean that the liquidator is a trustee for individual creditors and members of the company who are entitled to a share on

---

124   *Ibid.*
125   *Pulsford v Devenish* [1903] 2 Ch 625.
126   *Re B Johnson & Co (Builders) Ltd* [1955] Ch 634 at 648.
127   See para 15.58 below.
128   *Jobson v Palmer* [1893] 1 Ch 71 (a case involving the trustee of a scheme of composition).
129   *Re City Equitable Fire Insurance Co Ltd* [1925] Ch 407.
130   *Ayerst v C&K (Construction) Ltd* [1976] AC 167 at 180.

realisation.[131] It simply means the property is not at the disposal of its legal owner for its own benefit but must be used for the benefit of other persons. The distinction between the role of the trustee in bankruptcy who becomes the owner of the bankrupt's property and the liquidator who simply has control of the company and its property is of little importance.[132] Although he is not the legal owner of the company's property the liquidator is its 'governing body'.[133] The position of the liquidator is analogous to that of a company director, in that he owes duties to the company rather than to individual creditors or members of the company. The liquidator has been held not to be a trustee for the purpose of protection under the Trustee Act 1925 although this may be open to some doubt.[134] The liquidator owes fiduciary duties to the company. This can be said to be based on his role as trustee or as agent; both roles will give rise to similar duties. However, it might be argued that while the agency role reflects his function as it involves relations with the outside world, he is also under a fiduciary duty to the creditors and contributories to carry out the statutory function of gathering, realising and distributing the company's assets.

15.59 During the course of the winding up there are statutory mechanisms that can be used by individual creditors or contributories to ensure that the liquidation operates within the scope of the statutory scheme. In a voluntary winding up an application may be made to the court under s 112 for the determination of a question and for such order as the court thinks fit. In a compulsory winding up the exercise by the liquidator of his powers can be controlled by the court on an application under s 167(3) before the event or under s 168(5) after it is exercised. Misfeasance proceedings are also available at the suit of a creditor or contributory against the liquidator if, *inter alia*, he has been guilty of a breach of fiduciary duty to the company.[135] The existence of these mechanisms to ensure a proper use of a liquidator's powers makes the issue of whether he owes fiduciary duties to individual creditors or contributories less pressing than in the case of a company director. The availability of court intervention on the application of any creditor or contributory prevents the difficulties imposed on minority shareholders in a company not in liquidation by the rule in *Foss v Harbottle*.[136]

15.60 The specific fiduciary obligations of a liquidator like those of a

131   *Knowles v Scott* [1891] 1 Ch 717.
132   *In Re Oriental Inland Steam Co* (1874) 9 Ch App 557 at 560.
133   *Hillman v Crystal Bowl Ltd* [1973] 1 WLR 162.
134   See *Re Windsor Steam Company* [1928] Ch 609 and [1929] 1 Ch 151.
135   Insolvency Act 1986 s 212.
136   (1843) 2 Hare 461.

company director are to act honestly and to use his powers in good faith and not for any collateral purpose. In particular he must not allow his duty to come into conflict with his private interests. Additionally, there is an obligation on a liquidator to act impartially between different groups with interests in the winding up process. This last duty arises from his function in carrying out the statutory scheme and can be seen as the equivalent in this context of the director's duty to act in the interests of the company as a whole.[137]

15.61 The avoidance of any conflict between interest and duty is a fundamental consequence of the fiduciary relationship and a well established equitable principle.[138] It prohibits any secret profit or even the possibility of a conflict of interest between the interests of the fiduciary and those of the person whom he serves. Regulation 4 of the Insolvency Practitioners Regulations 1986[139] indicates the seriousness with which any breach of fiduciary duty will be regarded when the question of authorisation as an insolvency practitioner is considered.

15.62 The Insolvency Rules deal with the position of solicitor liquidators. Such a solicitor is prohibited from paying profit costs to his own firm if it or any partner in it is employed unless this is authorised by the liquidation committee, the creditors or the court.[140] It is clear that the duty not to make a profit from the fiduciary position will apply regardless of the contents of the rules:

> "There is between the joint liquidators on one side and the shareholders and creditors of the company on the other a fiduciary relationship which prevents the liquidators from making a profit out of their own trust."[141]

Although the *Gertzenstein* case dealt with the profit costs of a solicitor liquidator, it is clear that the principle is applicable to any profit taken by a liquidator from the winding up beyond his remuneration.

15.63 The use of information or business opportunities obtained by the liquidator in that capacity for personal advantage will also constitute a breach of fiduciary duty. In this respect the liquidators' position is the same as that of a company director and the duty is onerous.[142] Examples of breaches of this duty by liquidators are rare in the reported cases but any

---

137 See *Mills v Mills* (1938) 60 CLR 150.
138 See, eg, *Aberdeen Railway v Blaikie* (1854) 1 Macq 461.
139   SI 1986 no 1995.
140 Insolvency Rules 1986 r 4.128(3).
141 *Re Gertzenstein* [1937] Ch 115 at 116.
142 See *Regal (Hastings) Ltd v Gulliver* [1942] 1 All ER 443 and *Boardman v Phipps* [1967] 2 AC 46.

retention of secret profits made by a liquidator by use of his position or use of information obtained because of his role will result in accountability on his part. Thus in the Canadian case of *Christie v Edwards*[143] a liquidator was held liable to account for gains made by him under an arrangement whereby he would retain a large part of the company's assets in return for personally assuming the company's tax liabilities. His knowledge of the company's tax position had been gained in his position as liquidator and consequently he was regarded as making a secret profit. The requirement that the liquidator account for such profits can be imposed even after the company has been dissolved just as a director remains liable to account for his gains even after he has left office.[144] A breach of duty by making a secret profit can be discharged by full disclosure to the group affected, creditors or shareholders. It is submitted that disclosure to creditors will always be required but that disclosure to contributories may be unnecessary if there is no question of a contribution being required or of a surplus existing for distribution to shareholders. However, it would be safer to disclose to both groups. This again follows the position of the company director and contrasts with the position of where property is wrongfully appropriated by a liquidator acting in bad faith.[145]

15.64 The principle that the liquidator must not place himself in a position where his duty and his interest conflict is also expressed in the rules given in contracts with the company in which the liquidator has a personal interest. The Insolvency Rules 1986 deal with transactions between the liquidator and any associate of his entered into in the administration of the estate.[146]

15.65 The term 'associate' is defined in s 435 of the Insolvency Act 1986.[147] It includes spouses and relatives of the liquidator or his partners and partners and employees and employers of the liquidator as well as companies controlled by him. Where a transaction between a liquidator and his associate takes place the court has power to set it aside and to order the liquidator to compensate the company for any loss suffered in consequence of it.[148] The rule is without prejudice that the operation of any rule of law or equity which deals with the liquidator's fiduciary duties. The transaction in which the liquidator himself is interested will be liable to be

---

143   [1939] 1 DLR 158; [1940] 2 DLR 65.
144   *Christie v Edwards* [1939] 1 DLR 158; and see *Industrial Development Consultants v Cooley* [1972] 1 WLR 443.
145   See *Christie v Edwards* [1939] 1 DLR 158 at 165–6 and *Regal (Hastings) Ltd v Gulliver* [1942] 1 All ER 443 per Lord Russell at 389.
146   r 4.149(1).
147   See para 15.66. The Interpretation Act 1978 provides that this definition applies to the Rules as well as the statutes.
148   r 4.149(1).

set aside and will result in liability on the part of the liquidator to account for profits or to pay damages to the company. Others who receive property dealt with by the liquidator in breach of his fiduciary duties may be liable as constructive trustee.[149]

15.66 Transactions by the liquidator with his associates cannot be set aside under Rule 4.149 if they are entered into with the prior consent of the court or if it is shown that the transaction was for value and was entered into by the liquidator without knowing or having reason to suppose that the other party was an associate. The latter justification will only succeed if it is shown by the liquidator (on whom the onus of proof lies) that he did not know and had no reason to suppose that the relationship or 'associate' existed. This would seem to require proof that the liquidator was ignorant of the fact giving rise to the association. Thus his ignorance of the family relationship which causes a person to be his associate will be a defence. His ignorance that such a relationship comes within the definition of association will not. If a liquidator has information from which he should have deduced that a relationship exists between himself and the other party which amounts in law to an association his failure to realise that the relationship existed will deprive him of a defence as he had 'reasons to suppose' he was an associate.

15.67 Rule 4.149 extends the consequences of a breach of fiduciary duty to circumstances on which no such duty arises at law or equity. Dealings with particular relatives of the liquidator, his spouse or partner would probably have been outside the equitable rules but some situations will be governed by both sets of rules. Thus dealings with the company controlled by the liquidator will fall into both categories. Rule 4.149 will, however, apply whether or not the liquidator gains and, assuming he knows of the relationship or has reason to suppose it exists, the rule applies even if value is given to the company in return for its part in the transaction.

15.68 If a liquidator enters into a contract with the company or has an interest in such a contract he will be in breach of his fiduciary duty to the company. In *Silkstone Coal Co v Edey*[150] the court set aside the purchase of the undertaking of a company in a liquidation by a company acting merely as a trustee for the liquidator and as a front to ensure earlier court sanction for the sale. The profits made from the business since the sale and withdrawn by the liquidator had to be returned to the original company although no interest had to be paid on those profits. This transaction

149   *Selangor Rubber Estates Ltd v Cradock (No 3)* [1968] 1 WLR 1555; *Belmont Finance Corporation Ltd v Williams Furniture Ltd* [1979] Ch 250.
150   [1900] 1 Ch 167.

exemplified a conflict of interest and duty and a failure by the liquidator to use his powers in good faith. A misfeasance summons under s 212 of the Insolvency Act 1986 would be likely to succeed against the liquidator holding the profits of such a transaction.

15.69 Where there is a suspicion that the intimate connections between the liquidator and the company's former directors or others who might be subject to investigation by the liquidator will prevent or hamper independent action, the liquidator can be replaced on application to the court.[151] This reflects the requirement that there should be no hint of conflict between duty and interest of the liquidator and that he should be and should be seen to be independent 'and discharge his duties without favour to either side'.[152] A liquidator who has been a director of the company, who is the trustee in bankruptcy of its majority shareholder or who is a debtor of the company, lacks independence and can be removed.[152a]

15.70 The latter point represents the requirement of impartiality as well as independence. In this respect the liquidator's obligation is to act not only honestly but also in the interests in both contributories and creditors. Thus a liquidator wishing to bring proceedings in accordance with the wishes of contributories with nothing to lose at the expense of creditors without having regard to the expense and risk of failing to recover any assets can be replaced by someone who will take account of the interests of both groups.[153]

15.71 This indicates the need for a liquidator to act independently and impartially balancing the sometimes conflicting interests of the different groups involved in the winding up. He is clearly under this obligation in his dealings with assets, whether in the process of recovery or distribution. The obligation to achieve even handedness between creditors and contributories or different classes of each is a special responsibility of the liquidator which arises from his function under the statutes. In this respect an analogy may be drawn with the role of directors when dealing purely with matters of adjustment between the interests of different classes of shareholders.[154] In these circumstances the duty to act in the interests of the company becomes a duty to behave independently and impartially.

15.72 This duty applies to all conflicting individual interests and requires that in the event of a conflict being considered by the court the liquidator should supply the court with all the information it ought to have and should

151 *Re Charterland Goldfields Ltd* (1909) 26 TLR 130 and *Re Sir John Moore's Goldmining Co* (1879) 12 Ch D 325.
152 *Charterland Goldfields* (note 151 above) per Swinfen Eady J at 133.
152a *Re Corbenstoke (No 2)* (1989) 5 BCC 767.
153 *Re Rubber & Produce Investment Trust* [1915] 1 Ch 382.
154 *Mills v Mills* (1938) 60 CLR 150.

not take sides in such litigation at the cost of the company.[155] Where there is no such conflict of interests the liquidator has the right to use the powers conferred on him by statute to carry out the function given to him of collecting and distributing company assets. This includes the pursuit of actions against those thought to be liable to the company. However, a liquidator who acts in good faith and honestly fails to realise that a constructive trust attaches to company property with the result that he disposes of it will not be held personally liable despite having constructive knowledge of the trust.[156]

15.73 In making any decision involving the exercise of his powers a liquidator has an obligation to exercise an unfettered discretion personally and not to delegate the right to exercise discretion in matters requiring professional judgement. Section 165(3) and sch 4 para 12 of the Insolvency Act 1986 empower a liquidator to appoint an agent to do any business which the liquidator is unable to do himself. However, this does not authorise him to delegate any functions other than purely ministerial ones and any attempt to do so may result in the removal of the liquidator.[157] Matters which require a decision by the liquidator personally include drawing or accepting a bill of exchange,[158] and conveying company property.[159]

15.74 In the process of liquidation it is therefore vital that all major decisions and the execution of deeds or the formal creation of important contracts should remain in the hands of the liquidator personally. This is in contrast to the position of the company board of directors which is able, within the limits laid down by the company's articles of association, to delegate a large number of functions to subordinates, officers and employees. The powers conferred by the Act on a liquidator amount to a specific and personal grant of capacity to a person whose particular qualities and skills resulted in his appointment and are an important feature of the decision-making process. This nineteenth century concept of the role of the liquidator does not fit well with procedures which need to be adopted where large firms of accountants deal with the liquidation of large enterprises.

15.75 In the past joint liquidators had to act jointly and any attempt to delegate powers to one of their members failed.[160] This was always subject

---

155 *Re Tavistock Ironwork Co* (1871) 24 LT 605.
156 *Competitive Insurance Co v Davies Investments* [1975] 1 WLR 1240.
157 *Re Scotch Granite Co* (1868) 17 LT 533.
158 *Re London & Mediterranean Bank ex p Birmingham Banking Co* (1868) 3 Ch App 651; *ex p Agra & Masterman's Bank* (1871) 6 Ch App 206.
159 *Re Metropolitan Bank* (1876) 2 Ch D 366.
160 *Ibid.*

to the power of the court in a compulsory winding up to allow one or more only of joint liquidators who exercised specified powers.[161] Section 231 lays down a requirement that any appointment or nomination of joint liquidators or which will have the effect that more than one person will hold office simultaneously must declare whether any of their rights are to be done by all or any one or more officeholders. This provision will ensure that in future both the liquidators themselves and any persons dealing with them will be able to establish whether acts are required to be done jointly. The section does not, however, vary the underlying rule that, unless the nomination or appointment states that one or more acts may be done by any one or more of the joint officeholders, they must act jointly. Section 231 applies to all appointments or nominations of administrators, administrative receivers and provisional liquidators as well as liquidators. The fiduciary duty of the liquidator continues after the dissolution of the company and he can therefore still be sued by a creditor for handing assets to the contributories without paying a judgment debt.[162]

The liquidator as an officer of the court

15.76   The liquidator in a compulsory winding up has been held to be an officer of the court when carrying out certain functions. This does not apply to a liquidator in a voluntary winding up and even in a compulsory winding up it only applies when the liquidator is exercising those powers stated in the Act or the Rules, exercisable by him as an officer of the court.[163] The courts will not extend the principle to the liquidator in a voluntary winding up as this would extend the uncertainty inherent in the rule in *Re James* to the law in that area and such a liquidator is not appointed by or subject to the control of the court until application is made.[164]

15.77   Section 160(1) of the Insolvency Act 1986 provides for the rules to enable certain powers and duties of the court under that Act and the Companies Act 1985 to be exercised or performed by the liquidator as an officer of the court and subject to the court's control. Those powers and duties are:

(a) 'The holding and conducting of meetings to ascertain the wishes of creditors and contributories.' This function is conferred on the liquidator in a compulsory winding up by rules 4.54 to 4.71 which govern the calling of meetings and the procedure at them (see chapter 14, part 4). Section 168(2) of the Act specifically confers on the liquidator in a compulsory winding up

---

161   *Re Midland Land and Investment Corporation* (1887) 22 WN 58.
162   *Lames v Winram* (1987) 3 BCC 156.
163   *Commissioner of Customs & Excise v T H Knitwear Ltd* [1988] BCLC 195 and *Re Hills Waterfall Co* [1896] 1 Ch 947.
164   *Ibid.*

the power to summon meetings of creditors and contributories to ascertain their wishes. It also imposes on the liquidator the duty to do so when a meeting is requested in writing by one tenth in value of either group or directed to do so by a resolution of a meeting of one of the groups.

(b) 'The settling of lists of contributories and the rectifying of the register of members where required, and the collection and application of assets.' Rule 4.195 specifically delegates the duties of the court with regard to the settling of lists of contributories to the liquidator and Rules 4.196 to 4.201 lay down the procedure to be followed in carry out this task (see paras 17.11–17.17). Rule 4.196 specifically requires the liquidator to settle a list of contributories as soon as possible after his appointment and to rectify the register of shareholders with the court's approval. Section 359 of the Companies Act 1985 contains the original power for the court to rectify the register. Rule 4.179(1) specifies that the court's duties with regard to the collection of the company's assets on their application to discharge its liabilities are carried out by the liquidator as an officer of the court and subject to its control. Rule 4.179(2) confers the powers of a receiver appointed by the high court on the liquidator for the purpose of requiring and returning possession of the company's property. The major function of the liquidator as between company, creditors, and contributories is carried out as an officer of the court (see para 15.76).

(c) 'The payment, delivery, conveyance, surrender or transfer of money, property, books or papers to the liquidator'. Rule 4.185 makes the courts' powers under s 234 to these matters exercisable by the liquidator or the provisional liquidator if he had been appointed and imposes a duty on those of whom property is demanded to comply without avoidable delay.

(d) 'The making of calls.' Rule 4.202 confers this power on the liquidator as an officer of the court and subject to its control. However, the power is subject to the sanction of the liquidation committee or the court.

(e) 'The fixing of a time within which debts and claims must be proved.' Rule 4.54(4) stipulates that the notice issued by the liquidator calling a creditors' meeting shall specify a time and date not more than 4 days before the date of the meeting by which creditors must lodge proofs and proxies in order to vote at the meeting. It is noticeable that, wide as the powers are which the liquidator exercises an officer of the court, they omit circumstances in which he acts as an agent of the company to enter contracts with outsiders. The classic situation where this will occur will be activities related to the continuation to the company's business as opposed to those actions involving the gathering in and distribution of assets.[165] In that situation the liquidator (even in a compulsory winding up) is acting as an agent or representative of the company. In that capacity he avoids the

---

165 *Stead Hazel & Co v Cooper* [1933] 1 KB 840.

personal liability that could arise from actions taken as an officer of the court which cannot be liable as principal.

15.78 The major consequence of the status of the liquidator as an officer of the court is the application of the Bankruptcy Rule in *ex parte James*.[166] This rule demands that the liquidator as an officer of the court should act in a high minded and ethical manner. Money paid to him under a mistake of law will have to be returned even if no order for its return would be made between ordinary litigants.[167] This is an expression of the principle requiring the highest ethical standards from an officer of the court. He should not stand on his strict rights at law or in equity. In particular, assets should not be returned where the company has provided no consideration in return for the money or property.[168] The principle may be limited to cases where the company has been enriched at the expense of the person seeking to recoup an asset despite its broad origins as a general requirement of high minded and ethical behaviour.[169]

15.79 The courts have exhibited a reluctance to extend the scope of the rule even in respect of compulsory liquidations. Thus the principle has been said to have no application where the liquidator honestly tackles the difficult question of whether money is held on trust by the company or is available for the general body of creditors by arguing that the fund is not held on trust.[170] Similarly, the liquidator is not to be prevented by the rule from questioning the effect against him of a charge not registered under s 395 of the Companies Act 1985.[171] It is submitted that it is desirable to narrow the scope of this anomalous rule in the field of company liquidation. The fact that most liquidators in compulsory liquidations will be appointed by the creditors and subject to only the broadest court supervision makes distinctions between the behaviour demanded of them and that required of liquidators in a voluntary liquidation inappropriate. The divergence between the roles of the liquidators in different forms of insolvent liquidation is to be discouraged, particularly when the 'officer of the court' is not chosen by the court or closely directed by it.

THE DUTY OF CARE AND SKILL

15.80 The liquidator will invariably be a qualified insolvency practitioner and the court will therefore demand of him the level of care and skill which

---

166 (1874) 9 Ch App 609; and *Re Opera Ltd* [1891] 2 Ch 154.
167 *Re Temple Fire & Accident Assurance Co* (1910) 129 LT Jo 115.
168 *Re Regent Finance & Guarantee Corporation* [1930] WN 84.
169 *Government of India v Taylor* [1955] 1 All ER 292.
170 *Re Multi Guarantee Co Ltd* [1987] BCLC 257.
171 *Re John Bateson & Co Ltd* [1985] BCLC 259.

that qualification implies. It has long been acknowledged that as a paid functionary who is able to seek expert advice and, if necessary, the guidance of the court he is expected to show a high standard of care and diligence. That is not to say that he can be regarded as an insurer but merely that a high level of care and skill is required.[172] Thus a liquidator can be held accountable for paying amounts apparently due in respect of claims on an unenforceable marine insurance contract. In that case expert advice would have indicated that payment was unnecessary and the liquidator was consequently liable on a misfeasance summons. Most of the case law concerns the negligent admission and payment of claims or proofs or a failure to provide for foreseeable claims. They represent liability for a breach of a duty imposed on the liquidator by statute in failing to carry out his function with sufficient care and skill.

15.81   The application of assets to settle a disputed claim without seeking the approval of either the court or an extraordinary resolution at a company meeting has resulted in liability where the payment was not of an amount within a range which the court or the shareholders might have approved.[173] Liability in that case was held to exist in negligence if not in the liquidator's capacity as trustee. A failure to provide for claims can similarly give rise to liability. Thus when files in the liquidator's possession show that the company is liable for certain amounts there is an obligation to contact the claimant.[174] Failure to do so is a breach of statutory duty. Similarly, a liquidator aware that the company was a lessee and had assigned its interest under the lease should have made provision for the contingent liability that would arise if the assignees failed to pay rent or acted in breach of covenant. Failure to do so amounted to a negligent breach of his duty to find out from the books and papers of the company and the statement of its affairs who were its creditors and to communicate with those who had not submitted a claim.[175] A failure to advertise properly for creditors can similarly amount to a breach of the duty to seek out claims.[176]

15.82   The remedy available to a person damaged by negligence or a breach of statutory duty by the liquidator depends upon the stage reached by the winding up process. If the company has not yet been dissolved the appropriate remedy is a misfeasance summons under s 212 of the Insolvency Act 1986. A direct action for negligence by a creditor against a

---

172   *Re Home and Colonial Insurance Company* [1930] 1 Ch 102 at 125.
173   *Re Windsor Steam Coal Company* [1929] Ch 151.
174   *Re Armstrong Whitworth Securities Limited* [1947] 1 Ch 673.
175   *James Smith and Sons (Norwood) Ltd v Goodman* [1936] Ch 216; and see *Re Linda Marie* [1989] BCLC 46 for a recent example.
176   *Pulsford v Devenish* [1903] 2 Ch 625.

liquidator is not permitted at this stage.[177] The misfeasance summons will require the liquidator to remedy his breach of statutory duty in failing to accept a claim or in paying out assets unjustifiably. If the company has been dissolved at the end of the winding up process and the misfeasance summons procedure is no longer available a common law action against the liquidator will be permitted on the basis of negligence or breach of statutory duty.[178] This action is available despite the possibility of the restoration of the company to the Register under s 651 or s 653 of the Companies Act 1985.[179]

15.83 The care and skill required of the liquidator reflects his position as a paid and qualified professional. His behaviour will be judged on the basis of the practices of such a figure. He is subject to a higher level of duty than a company director because of the statutory duties imposed on him. The provisions of the Insolvency Act 1986 imposing minimum qualifications on insolvency practitioners and thereby on liquidators will lead to a consolidation of the high level of skill and care expected of the occupants of that office. This level of duty is applicable to decisions made by the liquidator in carrying out his specific statutory duties. However, in respect of decisions made in the ordinary course of carrying on the company's business the level of care and skill required should be that of the agent and not that of the statutory functionary gathering and distributing assets. Thus in that context it has been held that losses caused by the acts of employees will not be laid at the liquidator's door unless he is shown to have been negligent in his management of the business or in the selection of employees by the standards expected of a manager in the commercial world.[180] This view reflects the fact that in managing the continuing business of the company the liquidator is in the position of a commercial man running a company. He should therefore be judged by the level of his skill and experience in that field. In this situation his position is more closely analogous to that of a company director. In deciding whether to carry on the company's business in the interests of a beneficial winding up the liquidator is exercising his specialist statutory function and will therefore be held to the higher standard of skill that this implies.

THE STATUTORY POWERS OF THE LIQUIDATOR

15.84 As agent of the company, the liquidator has power to bind it to contracts without himself being personally liable on those contracts. Such

---

177 *Knowles v Scott* [1891] 1 Ch 717.
178 *Pulsford v Devenish* [1903] 2 Ch 625.
179 *Re Linda Marie* [1989] BCLC 46.
180 *Jobson v Palmer* [1893] 1 Ch 71 (a case involving the trustee of a debtor's composition).

powers stem from his replacement of the directors as the governing organ of the company. Thus, he is not liable to a solicitor whom he appoints to act on behalf of the company and he occupies premises as the company's agent and not in his own right.[181] A breach of a covenant not to assign in a lease is the liability of the company even if it was the liquidator who assigned the company's interest after it had gone into compulsory liquidation. This source of the power of the liquidator is, however, intimately linked with statutory provisions which spell out particular powers.

15.85   The statutory powers differ slightly as between compulsory and voluntary liquidation and as between creditors' and members' voluntary liquidation. However, in each case there are some powers which do not require any sanction before they are exercised by the liquidator and others which are either subject to some sanction or consent before they can be exercised or the exercise of which must be reported after their use. It is proposed to classify such powers in accordance with whether any consent or reporting requirement is imposed. It must be noted that ss 91(2) and 103 of the Insolvency Act 1986 lay down that the powers of the directors cease on the appointment of a liquidator in a members' or creditors' voluntary winding up respectively. The same rule applies in a compulsory winding up and this is laid down in the case of *Re Farrows Bank*,[182] although some residual powers are left to the directors.[183]

Unfettered powers

15.86   Most of the powers granted to a liquidator in any liquidation are exercisable by him by virtue of his office and without the need for any consent or sanction from any other body. This is subject to the general qualification that in the case of a winding up by the court s 167(3) of the Insolvency Act 1986 makes the liquidator's exercise of any of his powers subject to the control of the court. Any creditor or contributory may apply to the court with respect to any exercise or proposed exercise by the liquidator of one of his powers. It is for this reason that it is submitted that the liquidator in a compulsory winding up is an officer of the court and is therefore subject to the constraints mentioned above[184] as to dealing in an honourable manner. Apart from the court's role and the wider availability to any person 'aggrieved by an act or decision of the liquidator' of a right to apply to the court for the reversal or modification of his act,[185] the

---

181 *Re Wearmouth Crown Glass Co* (1882) 19 ch D 640; *Re Anglo Moravian Hungarian Junction Railway Co* (1875) 1 Ch D 130.
182 [1921] 2 Ch 164.
183 *Re Emmadart* [1979] Ch 540; *Re Diamond Fuel Co* (1879) 13 Ch D 400.
184 paras 15.76 *et seq.*
185 s 168(5) Insolvency Act 1986.

liquidator's powers are largely unfettered in both compulsory and voluntary liquidations. The liquidator in a compulsory liquidation is entitled to use his own discretion in managing the assets and distributing them among the creditors.[186]

15.87 In a voluntary liquidation the liquidator, a creditor or a contributory may apply to the court for the determination of any question arising in the winding up or the exercise of all or any of the powers the court would have in a compulsory liquidation.[187] In a voluntary winding up the court has to be satisfied that the determination of the question or the exercise of its power will be just and beneficial before it decides to make an order.[188] It will be somewhat more difficult to question his decision in a voluntary winding up but in each case the liquidator's use of his unfettered powers will usually be unchallenged.

15.88 In both types of winding up the unfettered use of his powers by the liquidator will not be susceptible of challenge in the courts in the absence of fraud or behaviour outside the scope of reasonableness. In *Leon v York-O-Matic*[189] Plowman J held that an application is a compulsory winding up under the predecessors of s 167(3) and s 168(5) could only succeed if the liquidator had acted fraudulently, with *mala fides*, or in a way in which no reasonable liquidator could have acted. He implied that were a substantial under-valuation of property established this might be evidence enabling the court to act on an application under one of those sections. He based his interpretation of the court's powers under these sections on the case law under a similar provision of the Bankruptcy Act 1914.[190] The specific provision that, subject to the provisions of the Act, the liquidator should use his own discretion clearly supports this view[191] and the non-interventionist approach of the courts. The 'control' granted to the court by s 167(3) is something of a long-stop.

15.89 Although, at first sight, it may appear that in a voluntary winding up the court would have less control over the way in which the liquidator exercises his power than it has in the case of a compulsory winding up, the courts take the same view of the circumstances in which they are willing to intervene. Thus in *Harold M Pitman v Top Business Systems (Nottingham)*

186 s 168(4).
187 s 112(1).
188 s 112(2).
189 [1966] 1 WLR 1450.
190 s 80.
191 s 168(4) Insolvency Act 1986.

Ltd[192] Nourse J applied the *Leon v York-O-Matic* test in the case of a voluntary winding up. He observed that:[193]

> "it would run very contrary to the view which the companies court has always taken of the desirability of a liquidator, whether in a winding up by the court or a voluntary winding up, being able to exercise his powers without undue fetters if I were to say that there were to be some lower standard to be established in order to enable the court to intervene".

Thus negligence on the part of the liquidator will not be sufficient to support an application under ss 112(1), 167(3) or 168(5). There must be behaviour which is fraudulent, done in bad faith or 'so utterly unreasonably and absurd that no reasonable man would do it'.

15.90 It is submitted that the test for court intervention in a voluntary winding up cannot be any less stringent than that applicable in a compulsory since in the latter the liquidator is to operate under the control of the court while no such provision is enacted in respect of a voluntary liquidation. However, s 112(2) suggests that an applicant under that provision must first satisfy the court as to the general test established in *Leon v York-O-Matic* and then establish that the exercise of the court's power will be 'just and beneficial'. This acknowledges that it will be more difficult to obtain a court order in the case of a voluntary winding up since the court is not 'in control'. The interests of third parties (for example the purchasers of assets sold by the liquidator) as well as those of creditors and contributories might be taken into account in deciding what is 'just'. What is 'beneficial' may be decided purely in the interests of the creditors or members since the winding up process is not intended to benefit others. The following powers may be exercised without any sanction or permission in all liquidations:

To settle a list of contributories and collect payment
15.91 The liquidator has power to settle a list of contributories which then becomes *prima facie* evidence of the liability of those named in it to be contributories. In a voluntary liquidation this power is conferred by s 165(4)(a) of the Insolvency Act 1986 which permits the liquidator to exercise this power of the court. In the case of a compulsory winding up this power is conferred by s 148(1) on the court. However, Rule 4.195 of the Insolvency Rules 1986 delegates this power to the liquidator as is permitted by s 160(1)(b) of the Insolvency Act 1986. This power may involve the rectification of the company's register of members and this may be done by the court if it is required. Where it will not be necessary to make calls for

---

192 [1984] BCLC 593.
193 *Ibid* at 597.

example because all shares are fully paid or to adjust the rights of the contributories *inter se* the liquidator may dispense with the need to draw up a list.[194] Rectification of the register by the liquidator requires special leave of the court and such leave or the sanction of the liquidation committee is required for a call to be made. This is laid down by Rule 4.196(1) and s 160(2). Details of the process of collecting the amounts due from contributories are dealt with in chapter 17. The power to make calls on contributories is exercisable without sanction by the liquidator in a voluntary liquidation[195] but is delegated to the liquidator subject to the sanction of the court or the liquidation committee in the case of a compulsory winding up.[196] The liquidator may prove in the insolvency of any contributory (corporate or individual) and receive a dividend in his or its bankruptcy, insolvency or sequestration as a separate debt due and rateably with the other creditors (sch 4 para 8). Similarly he is given specific power to take out letters of administration to any estate of a deceased contributory and do any other act necessary for obtaining the payment of money due from a contributory or his estate which cannot conveniently be done in the name of the company. For these purposes the money is deemed to be due to the liquidator himself (sch 4 para 11).

To summon meetings

15.92   The function of summoning meetings is a central feature of the liquidator's role. In a creditor's voluntary winding up the initial meetings of members and creditors will be called by the company.[197] However, a liquidator nominated by the company is under an obligation to apply to the court for directions if the company fails to call a creditor's meeting in accordance with s 98 of the Insolvency Act 1986.[198] He must make the application within 7 days of the date on which he was nominated by the company or the date on which he first became aware of the company's default, whichever is the later.[199] Failure to do so without reasonable excuse is an offence.[200] In such a winding up the liquidator is required to call a general meeting of the company and a meeting of creditors within 3 months of the end of the first year from the commencement of the winding up and of each succeeding year.[201] Final meetings of the company and the creditors must be called as soon as the company's affairs are fully wound up.[202] Details of the proceedings at these meetings are dealt with in

194   s 148(2); r 4.195.
195   s 165(4)(b).
196   rr 4.202 to 4.204.
197   ss 84(1) and 98(1).
198   s 166(5).
199   s 166(6).
200   s 166(7).
201   s 105(1).
202   s 106(1).

chapter 14, part 4 and paras 19.119–19.120. In a members voluntary winding up general meetings of the company must be called by the liquidator at the end of each year and at the end of the winding up process.[203] Where the liquidator forms the opinion that the company will be unable to pay its debts with interest at the official rate within the period stated in the director's declaration of solvency, he must call a creditors' meeting within 28 days of forming that opinion.[204] This converts the liquidation into a creditors voluntary winding up from the date of the creditors' meeting.[205] In any voluntary winding up the liquidator has an additional power to call general meetings of the company to obtain its sanction for any act which requires this or for any other purpose.[206] In a creditors voluntary winding up he will consult creditors through the liquidation committee set up under s 101 and full creditors' meetings will only be held when they are required by ss 105 or 106. While the liquidator holds the opinion that a company in members voluntary liquidation is solvent he need not hold any creditors' meetings and, indeed, has no power to do so. If his opinion as to the company's solvency changes he will call a s 95 meeting to convert the winding up into a creditors voluntary winding up. An application to the court under s 112 would be necessary to enable the creditors' meeting to be called in the course of a members' voluntary winding up to ascertain their wishes or to call a full creditors meeting in a creditors voluntary winding up outside ss 105, 106 or 166(5). Section 112 enables the court, on the application of the liquidator to use its power under s 195 in a voluntary liquidation. In a compulsory winding up s 168(2) empowers the liquidator to summon general meetings of the contributories (rather than the company) or the creditors for the purpose of ascertaining their wishes. He is obliged to call such a meeting if required to do so by a resolution of an earlier meeting of the creditors or contributories or at the written request of one tenth in value of the contributories or creditors. The power of the court to call s 195 meetings of creditors or contributories is also delegated to the liquidator by Rule 4.54 of the Company Insolvency Rules 1986. The only advantage in using the delegated power would appear to be the added right to determine the manner in which the meeting is to be conducted and to appoint its chairman as s 168(2) provides adequate power to actually call the meeting. Section 146(1) requires a liquidator other than the official receiver to call a final meeting of the creditors when it appears to him that the winding up is for practical purposes complete. The procedure applicable to meetings and their function in the winding up process are dealt with in chapter 14.

203 ss 93(1) and 94(1).
204 s 95(1) and (2)(a).
205 s 96.
206 s 165(4)(c).

The sale of the company's property, execution of documents and raising money on security

15.93 The power to sell any of the company's property by public auction or private contract, to transfer the whole of it to any person or to sell it in parcels is conferred by sch 4 para 6.[207] This power is wide in its scope and permits the sale of anything that can be described as the property of the company. There must be sale and the reference in the latter part of the provision to a transfer is to be read as a transfer after a sale. However, the consideration for a sale under the liquidator's power need not be cash.[208] A sale may be set aside if the liquidator is personally interested in it in breach of his fiduciary duty but this is a reflection of the nature of the liquidator's role and not a limitation on his power; the sale is only voidable and the title of a *bona fide* purchaser without notice of the liquidator's wrongdoing will be unimpeachable.[209] The nature of the property which may be subject to sale by a liquidator is subject only to the limitation that it must be property that is assignable.[210] Subject to this limitation any real or personal property may be sold as may things in action. Thus if the liquidator assigns, in general terms, all the property of a company this will include its right of action against directors who have been in breach of their duty to the company.[211] This will not prevent the use of the misfeasance procedure under s 212 of the Insolvency Act 1986 and that can result in a court order for an individual to contribute such sum by way of compensation in respect of a misfeasance or breach of fiduciary duty as the court thinks fit.[212] Such a statutory compensation order is separate from the right of action which the company has at common law for the breach of duty. An order under s 212(3)(a) that a person repay, restore or account for money or property may be akin to the common law action. However, even the right to this remedy, it is submitted, is not a chose in action in the hands of the company, as application must be by the liquidator, the official receiver, a creditor or a contributory.[213] If the liquidator sells goods the property in which has not passed to the company, he will be liable to perform the contract by paying the purchase price on the basis that he has elected to carry out the contract. This was decided in *Re Anchor Lines (Henderson Brothers) Ltd*[214] on the basis that the liquidator (in this case the official receiver as provisional liquidator) must be presumed to know about his lack of title in the goods

207 Applied by s 165(3) to voluntary liquidations and by s 167(1)(b) to compulsory liquidations.
208 *Re Agra and Masterman's Bank* (1896) LR 12 EQ 509n.
209 *Re Silkstone & Haigh Moor Coal Co* [1900] 1 Ch 167; and see eg *Pilcher v Rawlins* (1872) LR 7 Ch App 259 at 268–269.
210 *Nokes v Doncaster Amalgamated Collieries Ltd* [1940] AC 1014 at 1033.
211 *Re Park Gate Wagon Works Co Ltd* (1881) 17 Ch D 239.
212 s 212(3)(b).
213 See below Ch 16.
214 [1937] Ch 1.

and to intend to pass good title to the purchaser. This may be an application of the doctrine in the case of *Re James*[215] as to the role of an officer of the court. If this is so in such a presumption would only apply in the case of a compulsory liquidation. Apart from that consideration the rules as to title applicable to any particular form of property will operate in the same way in this context as they would in the case of any other buyer or seller. Thus, for example, in a case where the company was a buyer in possession with the permission of the seller, s 27 of the Sale of Goods Act 1979 would enable a buyer from the liquidator to obtain good title even if property had not passed to the company so long as the goods had been transferred or delivered to the buyer who was in good faith and unaware of the original seller's right in respect of the goods. In such a case the original seller would only have a right to prove in the liquidation for the price of the goods. Similarly, in a lease containing a covenant against assignment, the liquidator of a tenant company must obtain the landlord's consent to any assignment.[216] It is thus clear that the liquidator's power of sale does not confer any greater property rights than those already held by the company before winding up commenced. In *Re Farrow's Bank* it was established that since the company's leasehold interest does not vest in the liquidator he is not freed from the company's covenant with the landlord. The power of sale is therefore as extensive as that held by the company and no more extensive. The Act specifically confers the powers necessary to the transfer of property or the creation of agreements. The liquidator has power to do all acts and execute all deeds receipts and other documents in the name of and on behalf of the company.[217] It seems that this power must be exercised by the liquidator himself if it involves a major agreement or the conveyance or transfer of property of significant value.[218] However, the function of signing letters or other documents as part of the minor or day-to-day business of the liquidation can be delegated to agents of the liquidator as such matters are purely ministerial acts. It has even been suggested that the signing of a bill of exchange may be delegated to an agent,[219] although the acceptance of a bill may have to be achieved by the signature of the liquidator himself.[220] Similarly, the power to draw, accept, make and endorse bills of exchange or promissory notes with effect as if this had been done by or on behalf of the company in the course of business is specifically conferred on the liquidator by sch 4 para 9 of the Insolvency Act 1986. The use of the assets of the company as security to raise money required for the purpose of the winding up is specifically provided for by para 10 of sch 4 but

---

215 (1874) 9 Ch App 609.
216 *Re Farrow's Bank* [1921] 2 Ch 164.
217 Sch 4 para 7.
218 *Re Metropolitan Bank and Jones* (1876) 2 Ch D 366.
219 *Ex parte Agra & Masterman's Bank* (1871) 6 Ch App 206 at 211.
220 *Re London & Mediterranean Bank* (1868) 3 Ch App 651.

this power must not be used in a way which will prejudice the interests of existing debenture holders.[221] Such a power is most likely to be used in a situation where the liquidator is continuing the business of the company in the interests of the beneficial winding up. However the power is expressly limited to those circumstances.

Disclaimer of onerous property

15.94 This power can be exercised without sanction in any winding up subject to an application to the court by a person claiming an interest in the property or under any liability in respect of it for a court order under s 181. The use of this power is dealt with in paras 18.73–18.75 on the realisation of the company's assets.

Applications to the court

15.95 The liquidator has a range of powers of application to the court as part of the liquidation process. Such applications can be distinguished from proceedings brought or defended by the liquidator on behalf of the company and in its name. All of these powers can be exercised without prior sanction or permission. Applications will be made in accordance with Part 7 of the Insolvency Rules 1986. Section 168(3) provides the basic right of a liquidator in a compulsory winding up to apply to the court for direction in relation to any particular matter arising out of the winding up. In a voluntary winding up application may be made under s 112(1) by the liquidator (or any creditor or contributory) for the court's determination of any question arising in the winding up or exercise all or any of the powers available to the court in a compulsory winding up. In particular, the latter power may be used to obtain the stay of legal proceedings or execution against the company or its property. This will be granted in the case of a creditor's voluntary winding up where execution has not yet been levied but not in the case of a members' voluntary winding up in which the company is presumed to be solvent.[222] In a compulsory winding up the appointment of a provisional liquidator or the making of a winding up order have the effect of staying existing actions and proceedings against the company and preventing the commencement of new ones unless the leave of the court is obtained.[223] An application by the liquidator for relief against forfeiture can be brought by summons in the winding up proceedings.[224] A liquidator may apply for the appointment of a special manager under s 177 in any winding up and no prior sanction is required for such a step. The role of the special manager is dealt with in paras 15.19–15.25 above. Such an

---

221 *Re Regent's Canal Ironworks ex p Grissell* (1875) 3 Ch D 411.
222 *Westbury v Twigg* [1892] 1 QB 77; *Gerard v Worth of Paris Ltd* [1936] 2 All ER 905.
223 s 130(2) and see Ch 14.
224 *Re Brompton Securities Ltd (No 2)* (1988) 4 BCC 436.

application is most likely to be made in cases where the business of the company is to be carried on in the interest of a beneficial winding up.

Agents and residual powers

15.96   The liquidator in any winding up has a general power to appoint agents 'to do any business which the liquidator is unable to do himself'.[225] This encompasses the use of professional experts such as solicitors, valuers, and surveyors as well as the use of employees of the liquidator or his practice. It has already been noted that the liquidator must not delegate to agents those decisions or actions which demand the exercise of his personal discretion. Agents must be limited to purely ministerial actions. To complement his specifically enumerated powers the liquidator is entitled to 'do all such other things as may be necessary for winding up the company's affairs and distributing its assets'. This power is to be read *ejusdem generis* to the specifically listed powers in sch 4 Part III (ie those exercisable without sanction). Thus surplus assets cannot be distributed under this provision without a court order as s 154 of the Insolvency Act 1986 governs the distribution of any surplus among those entitled to it.[226] Likewise the residual provision is located among those powers which can be exercised without sanction and thus it cannot be used to justify acts which are specifically stated to be permissible only with the sanction of the court or the liquidation committee. The residual power underlines the liquidator's role as one of winding up the company and distributing assets but within that limited sphere it provides a useful adjunct to the listed statutory powers. It can be used to disclose documents to a creditor who is a potential litigant against the company or other companies in the same group.[226a]

Qualified powers in compulsory liquidations

15.97   There are four specific powers which require either sanctions from or notice to either the court or the liquidation committee in a compulsory winding up but not in a voluntary winding up. They are:

(a) the power to carry on the business of the company;
(b) litigation;
(c) making calls;
(d) disposal of property to a connected person.

Power to carry on the business of the company

15.98   The liquidator has power to carry on the business of the company so far as may be necessary for its beneficial winding up.[227] In a voluntary

---

225   Sch 4 para 12.
226a   *Re ACL Metals Ltd* (1989) 5 BCC 749.
226   *Re Phoenix Oil & Transport Ltd (No 2)* [1958] Ch 565.
227   Sch 4 para 5.

winding up this may be done without any sanction but in a compulsory winding up the court or the liquidation committee must authorise it.[228] The qualification that the power may only be used in so far as it is necessary for a beneficial winding up places an emphasis on the realisation and distribution of assets. Thus the court has refused to sanction the continuation of a business for a trial period in the mere hope that it will be sufficiently successful for more capital to be raised so that, after reconstruction, the company can be taken over as a going concern.[229] Such conduct does not fall within the scope of the realisation of assets which must be the liquidator's primary purpose. However, the intention to sell the company's business as a going concern or the gradual and profitable realisation of its assets may justify a continuation of the business over a substantial period. A *bona fide* and reasonable belief on the part of the liquidator as to the beneficial effects on the winding up of a continuation of the company business will be sufficient to justify that court action.[230] Since the introduction of the administration procedure, it will usually be appropriate to use that method of continuing the whole or part of the company's business in order to realise the company's assets more profitably or to sell all or part of its undertaking as a going concern. However, in cases where liquidation has already begun before that option has been properly considered or where, for some other reason, no administration order was possible a liquidator may still wish to continue the company's business. If he does so he will have the disadvantage of not benefiting from the moratorium available to the administrator. However, in a compulsory liquidation he will have the benefit of the stay of all proceedings and the requirement that new actions be commenced only with the leave of the court (s 130(2)). When a liquidator does choose to carry on the company's business, the onus of proof is firmly on the other party to a contract who wishes to escape liability to show that the business being carried out is not necessary for a beneficial winding up, if, indeed, it is possible for such a person to escape even then.[231]

Litigation

15.99 The power to bring or defend any action or other legal proceedings in the name of and on behalf of the company is available without sanction to the liquidator in a voluntary winding up but only with the agreement of the court or the liquidation committee in a compulsory winding up.[232] The need for consent extends only to litigation on behalf of the company against outsiders which does not constitute an application to the court in the

228 s 167(1)(a).
229 *Re Wreck Recovery & Salvage Co* (1880) 15 Ch D 353.
230 *Great Eastern Electric Co Ltd* [1941] 1 Ch 241.
231 *Hire Purchase Furnishing Co v Richens* (1887) 20 QBD 347.
232 s 167(1) and sch 4 para 4.

winding up. The latter is made by the liquidator personally.[233] If the company's assets have been vested in the liquidator personally by a court order under s 145(1) (as applied by s 112 in the case of a voluntary winding up) then he may bring or defend any action or proceedings relating to that property or which is necessary for the purpose of effectively winding up the company and recovering its property.[234] Where proceedings are brought by a liquidator without sanction in a compulsory winding up the other party is not permitted to object[235] and sanction may be given retrospectively although it should be sought before proceedings are begun.[236] It is possible for a liquidator to adopt proceedings started before the commencement of the winding up by a minority using the company's name without the right to do so.[237] However, the appointment of a liquidator terminates control by the wrongdoers for the purpose of the 'fraud on the minority' exception to the rule in *Foss v Harbottle*[238] because the company's right to litigate then vests in him. If the liquidator refuses to take action on the company's behalf a contributory or creditor may apply to the court for an order requiring him to do so. Sections 112 and 167(3) enable this course to be pursued in a voluntary liquidation and s 168(5) has the same effect if the winding up is compulsory. A reasonable demand by the liquidator for an indemnity before such an action was begun would be a good defence but the court could give the creditor or contributory the right to use the company's name at their own risk as to costs.[239] If the liquidator sues in the name of the company on grounds of breach of fiduciary duty by directors or on the basis of fraud or other wrongdoing by others, he may, as a preliminary, seek a Mareva injunction to prevent the removal of the assets of the defendants from the jurisdiction. He will not be required to give an unlimited cross-undertaking as to damages if he makes such an application.[240] The appointment of a solicitor by the liquidator to assist him with his functions does not require sanction or any other special step in a voluntary liquidation.[241] However, in a compulsory winding up the exercise of this power by a liquidator other than the official receiver must be the subject of notice to the liquidation committee (if there is one at the time of the appointment).[242]

233 *Re Silver Valley Mines Ltd* (1882) 21 Ch D 38.
234 s 145(2).
235 *Dublin City Distillery v Doherty* [1914] AC 823.
236 *Re London Metallurgical Co* [1897] 2 Ch 262.
237 *Danish Mercantile Co Ltd v Beaumont* [1951] Ch 680.
238 (1843) 2 Hare 461.
239 *Fargo v Godfroy* [1986] 3 All ER 279 and *Cape Breton Co v Fenn* (1881) 17 Ch D 198 at 208.
240 *Re DPR Futures Ltd* (1989) 5 BCC 603.
241 Insolvency Act 1986 sch 4 paras 12 and 13.
242 s 167(2)(b).

Making calls

15.100 In a compulsory winding up the liquidator may exercise the court's power to make a call and thus impose an obligation on contributories to pay the amount due on their shares.[243] Rule 4.202 makes this power exercisable by the liquidator as an officer of the court subject to the court's control and by virtue of s 160(2) the special leave of the court or the sanction of liquidation committee is required before any call is made. A meeting of the liquidation committee may be summoned with at least 7 days' notice to each of its members.[244] The notice must state the proposed amount of the call and the purpose for which it is to be made.[245] Where there is no liquidation committee, the sanction of the secretary of state may be obtained.[246] Where the official receiver is the liquidator the liquidation committee will not function and the sanction of the Secretary of State will always be required unless the Rules provide otherwise.[247] An application to the court for leave will be made *ex parte* and supported by an affidavit supporting the liquidator's application. The application must state the amount of the proposed call and the contributories on whom it is to be made. The court may require notice of the order to be given to the contributories concerned or other contributories or may direct that it be publicly advertised.[248] In a voluntary winding up the liquidator has power to make calls without the sanction of the court or the liquidation committee.[249]

Disposal of property to a connected person

15.101 Although no sanction is required by a liquidator in any type of winding up for a disposal of property to a person connected with the company, it is necessary for such a transaction to be notified to the liquidation committee.[250] A disposal could be by way of sale, gift, loan or other means. Such a use of the liquidator's power may not be in any sense colourable. However, this provision ensures that the liquidation committee is given information so as to be able to decide whether to challenge the transaction and seek to have it set aside. This is intended to complement the qualification requirements for liquidators in preventing the abusive sale of assets at artifically low prices to persons connected with the company. Where no liquidation committee exists it would seem that there is no obligation to notify the Secretary of State even in a compulsory winding up. Section 167(2) specifically lays down that the requirement to give notice

---

243 Insolvency Act 1986 s 160(1)(d) and r 4.202.
244 r 4.203(1) and (2).
245 r 4.203(3).
246 s 141(5).
247 s 141(4).
248 r 4.204.
249 s 165(4)(b).
250 ss 165(6) and 167(2)(a).

only applies if there is for the time being a liquidation committee. This function does not, therefore, exist if there is no committee and s 141(5) cannot therefore operate to require a liquidator in a compulsory winding up to notify the official receiver of the disposal under Rule 4.172(2) which permits him to exercise the Secretary of State's functions under s 141(5). The detailed definition of the circumstances in which a person is to be regarded as connected with a company are laid down in ss 249 and 435 of the Insolvency Act 1986. This is dealt with in chapter 20, paras 20.17–20.29 which deals with transactions between the company and such persons.

Powers exercisable only with sanction in all liquidations

15.102   Such powers may be grouped under three headings:

(a) Compromises of the claims of the company against debtors or contributories.
(b) Arrangements or compositions with the company's creditors or the payment of a class of creditors in full.
(c) Provisions for the benefit of employees.

In the case of each of these powers a liquidator in a members voluntary winding up will be required to obtain the sanction of an extraordinary resolution of the company. In a creditors' voluntary winding up he will require the sanction of either the court or the liquidation committee. If no liquidation committee exists the sanction of a meeting of the company's creditors is needed unless an application is to be made to the court. The liquidator in a compulsory winding up needs the sanction of the court or the liquidation committee. Should no committee exist then the sanction of the Secretary of State is required but this function has been developed upon the official receiver in cases where he does not himself act as liquidator. Where the official receiver acts as liquidator he must seek the sanction of either the court or the secretary of state. Rule 4.184(1) lays down that any permission given to a liquidator by the court or the liquidation committee must not be a general permission but must relate to a specific proposed exercise of the liquidator's power to which is relates. However, a person dealing in good faith and for value is not concerned to enquire whether any such permission has been given. For the purpose of enabling the liquidator to meet his expenses out of the assets, Rule 4.184(2) empowers the court or the committee to ratify acts which required permission but for which it was not given providing the liquidator acted in a case of urgency and sought ratification without undue delay.

Compromises with debtors or contributories and matters affecting assets
15.103   Sanction is needed for the exercise by the liquidator of his power

"to compromise, on such terms as may be agreed:
  (a) all calls and liabilities to calls, or debts and liabilities capable of resulting in debts, and all claims (present or future, certain or contingent, ascertained or sounding only in damages) subsisting or supposed to subsist between the company or alleged contributory or other debtor or person apprehending liability to the company, and
  (b) all question in any way relating to or affecting the assets or the winding up of the company,
and take any security for the discharge of any such call, debt, liability to claim and give a complete discharge in respect of its stock".[250a]

The power to compromise claims and rights will only exist where there is some dispute or question to be settled or where there is difficulty in enforcing the claim or rights. Cases on rights to compromise conferred by trust deeds securing debentures suggest that this is so.[251] However, a *bone fide* belief by the parties that there is a question to be settled will be sufficient to justify a compromise.[252] Such compromises and arrangements will require the sanction mentioned above, the nature of which depends on the type of winding up in question.

Arrangements or compositions with the company's creditors
15.104   Any payment of a class of creditors in full will require sanction. This is the case whether such action is taken as part of an arrangement or composition with creditors or as a unilateral act of the liquidator.[253] This is a reflection of the fundamental principle that in a winding up all creditors should rank *pari passu*. In chapter 19 the process of paying out the assets collected by the liquidator to creditors is dealt with at length. Similarly, it should be noted here that the power of the liquidator 'to make any compromise or arrangement with creditors' is subject to sanction. This includes a compromise or arrangement with any person claiming to be a creditor or having or alleging that they have any claim against the company or whereby the company may be rendered liable. Claims are included whether they are present or future, certain or contingent and ascertained or sounding in damages only.[254] This power will apply wherever there is a disputed claim which is to be compromised. It covers both individual settlements of claims and the wider negotiation of an arrangement covering a whole class of creditors or all creditors. However, in any case where

---

250a Sch 4 para 3.
251   See *Mercantile Investment & General Trust Co v International Company of Mexico* [1893] 1 Ch 484n and *Sneath v Valley Gold Ltd* [1893] 1 Ch 477 (cited in *Halsbury's Laws* vol 7 paras 11–27).
252   *Lucy's Case* (1853) 4 De G M & G 356 (cited in *ibid*).
253   Insolvency Act 1986 sch 4 para 1.
254   sch 4 para 2.

it is intended to distribute assets in a manner which does not conform to the existing rights of creditors, this power is not the appropriate one to use.[255] In such cases a scheme of arrangement under ss 1–7 of the Insolvency Act 1986, might be more appropriate than a liquidation and ss 110 and 111 of the Insolvency Act 1986 may be used in a voluntary winding up. Sections 425 to 427 of the Companies Act 1985 present a further possible means of making an arrangement which varies the rights of creditors. These possible solutions are discussed fully in chapter 22 on Voluntary Arrangements. The most likely use of the power conferred on liquidators by para 2 of sch 4 is to compromise individual claims or debts rather than to change the legal rights of creditors.

Provisions for the benefit of employees
15.105   Section 719 of the Companies Act 1986 empowers a company to make provision for present and former employees of the company or its subsidiaries in connection with the cessation or transfer of the whole or part of the company's business or undertaking. This section re-enacts s 74 of the Companies Act 1980 which reversed the decision in *Parke v The Daily News*[256] holding such payments to employees to be *ultra vires*. The power has to be exercised with the sanction of an ordinary resolution of the company general meeting or, if the articles or memorandum stipulate it, a resolution of the board or some other type of resolution of a general meeting requiring more than a simple majority of members' votes. All other requirements of the memorandum and articles must also be met. Section 187 of the Insolvency Act 1986 permits the liquidator to make a payment already decided on by the company under s 719 of the Companies Act 1985. If no such decision has been made, the liquidator may himself exercise the power after the company's liabilities have been met and the costs of winding up provided for so long as the company general meeting approves in accordance with s 719 and all other requirements of the memorandum and articles are satisfied. Thus a payment to employees or former employees of the company or its subsidiary is possible from the company's assets available to the members in any type of winding up. The sanction of an ordinary resolution of a company general meeting is required unless a resolution requiring more than a simple majority is needed by virtue of the company's memorandum and articles. Sanction by a board resolution will never be sufficient after a winding up has commenced.

---

255   *Re Trix Ltd; Re Ewart Holdings Ltd* [1970] 1 WLR 1421.
256   [1962] Ch 927.

PART 3: REMOVAL FROM AND VACATION OF OFFICE BY A LIQUIDATOR AND RELEASE

RESIGNATION

15.106 A liquidator is only permitted to resign in a limited range of circumstances. In the case of a winding up by the court this is done by giving notice to the court.[257] In a voluntary winding up notice is given to the registrar of companies.[258] In each case the resignation is effective from the date on which the notice is given as it takes place 'by' giving notice. Resignation is only permitted by calling a meeting of creditors in a winding up by the court or the creditor's voluntary liquidation or by calling a company meeting in a members' voluntary liquidation if a specified ground for resignation exists. The specified grounds are:

(a) ill health;
(b) an intention to cease practising as an insolvency practitioner;
(c) the existence of 'some conflict of interest or change of personal circumstances which precludes or makes impracticable the further discharge by him of the duties of liquidator'.[259]

The last ground is clearly intended to deal with the emergence of circumstances making the proper exercise of the liquidator's fiduciary role impossible such as obtaining a substantial interest in a company likely to purchase assets from the company being wound up. It presumably also deals with other factors such as the growth of other commitments on the part of the liquidator which cause no conflict but prevent him from spending an adequate amount of time on the liquidation. A change of firm by an insolvency practitioner or the illness of close relatives or other family difficulties could equally constitute the necessary change of circumstances. Providing the continued discharge of his duties can be shown to be precluded or made impracticable, resignation by this means will be possible.

15.107 Where two or more joint liquidators hold office any one of them may resign without prejudice to the continuation of the others in office if either he or the others take the view that it is expedient that there be a different number of liquidators in office. In the case of an insolvent liquidation the opinion as the expedience of a different number of joint

---

257 s 171(5).
258 s 172(6).
259 See r 4.108(4) on insolvent liquidations and r 4.142(3) on a members' voluntary liquidation.

liquidators must be shared by the person resigning and the other liquidators. In a members' voluntary winding up it can be his view or that of the others. This suggests that an individual taking this view may resign using this procedure even if his view is not shared by his colleagues in the members voluntary winding up but that there must be agreement in an insolvent liquidation.[260]

15.108   The procedure to be followed where a liquidator resigns in a creditors' voluntary winding up or a compulsory winding up begins with the calling of a meeting of creditors for the purpose of receiving the resignations. The notice of the meeting must stipulate this purpose and draw to the creditors' attention their right under Rules 4.121 or 4.122 to resolve against the release of the liquidator and the consequence of passing or failing to pass such a resolution.[261] The notice must be accompanied by an account of the liquidator's administration of the winding up including a summary of receipts and payments and a statement that his accounts have been reconciled with that held by the Secretary of State in relation to that liquidation.[262] A copy of the notice must be sent to the official receiver in a compulsory winding up.[263] If the meeting is inquorate the meeting is deemed to have been held, to have accepted the resignation and not to have resolved against the liquidator having his release.[264]

15.109   If the liquidator's resignation is accepted by the creditors' meeting in a creditors' voluntary liquidation, notice must be given forthwith to the registrar of companies by the liquidator.[265] If a new liquidator has been appointed in place of the one who has resigned the certificate of his appointment must be delivered forthwith to the new liquidator by the chairman of the meeting.[266] The new liquidator must advertise his predecessor's resignation and his release (if it has been given) when he gives notice of his own appointment.[267]

15.110   In a compulsory liquidation, where the creditors' meeting is not chaired by the official receiver, a copy of any resolution to accept the resignation, or to appoint a new liquidator or to refuse to release the resigning liquidator must be sent to the official receiver within 3 days. Where the resignation has been accepted or a new liquidator appointed a

260   See rr 4.108(5) and 4.142(4).
261   r 4.108(1).
262   r 4.108(3).
263   r 4.108(2).
264   r 4.108(6) inserted by SI 1987 no 1919.
265   r 4.110(2).
266   r 4.110(3).
267   r 4.112.

certificate to that effect must also be sent.[268] In addition, notice of the resignation must be sent by the resigning liquidator the court accompanied by a copy of the account circulated to creditors with the notice calling the meeting. A copy must also be supplied to the official receiver who will file it in court. The resignation is effective from the date on which that notice is filed.[269]

15.111 If, in any insolvent liquidation, a creditors' meeting summoned to accept the liquidator's resignation has resolved not to accept it the liquidator may apply to the court for an order giving him leave to resign.[270] Such an order will, if granted, specify the date from which any release is effective and it may include provisions as to matters arising in connection with the resignation.[271] In a compulsory winding up two sealed copies of the order will be supplied to the liquidator one of which must be sent by him to the official receiver.[272] In the case of a creditors' voluntary winding up one of the liquidator's two copies must be sent to the registrar of companies and none need be sent to the official receiver.[273]

15.112 The order of the court made under this rule will merely give the liquidator leave to resign. In the case of a compulsory winding up a copy of the notice of his actual resignation which is sent to the court must be sent to the official receiver who will act as liquidator in the absence of the appointment of a new liquidator.[274]

15.113 It would seem that an application to the court under Rule 4.111 will only be possible if the liquidator satisfies the grounds set out in Rule 4.108(4) or (5) as to when resignation to a creditors' meeting is permissible. If those grounds did not exist Rule 4.108 would not apply and any creditors' meeting would not have power even to resolve not to accept the resignation as is required before the court can give leave under Rule 4.111(1).

15.114 In a members' voluntary winding up a meeting of the company must be called to receive the liquidator's resignation. The notice must indicate that this is the purpose of the meeting and the same accounts and statement must be circulated to members as are required in the case of a creditors' voluntary winding up.[275] Notice of the liquidator's resignation

268 r 4.109(2) and (3).
269 r 4.109(4), (5) and (6).
270 r 4.111(1).
271 r 4.111(2).
272 r 4.111(3).
273 r 4.111(4).
274 r 4.111(5) and s 172(6) of the Insolvency Act 1986.
275 r 4.142(1) and (2).

must be given by him to the registrar of companies forthwith after the meeting and the fact that his predecessor resigned must be included in the notice of appointment issued by a new liquidator.[276] No procedure is laid down for a court to give leave for a liquidator to resign in a members' voluntary winding up if the company meeting resolves not to accept his resignation. In the absence of a quorum the meeting is deemed to have been held.[277]

CEASING TO BE A QUALIFIED INSOLVENCY PRACTITIONER

15.115 In a voluntary winding up a liquidator must vacate office if he ceases to be a qualified insolvency practitioner.[278] In a compulsory winding up the same rule applies to both a liquidator and a provisional liquidator unless he is the official receiver.[279] The concept of a 'qualified insolvency practitioner' is dealt with in chapter 10. However, it is important to note that to continue in office when no longer qualified to do so will amount to an offence under s 389(1). On vacating office for this reason a liquidator in a voluntary winding up must give notice of doing so to the registrar of companies and the Secretary of State for Trade and Industry forthwith.[280] In a compulsory winding up the notice must be given to the official receiver who will file a copy in court and give notice to the Secretary of State.[281]

VACATION OF OFFICE ON MAKING OF A WINDING UP ORDER

15.116 Where a winding up order is made in respect of a company already being wound up voluntarily the official receiver will automatically become the liquidator of the company until another person takes office.[282] Thus, although (in the absence of court order to the contrary) all proceedings taken in the voluntary winding up are deemed to have been validly taken,[283] the voluntary liquidator will vacate office when the winding up order is made. For the purposes of obtaining a release such a situation is equated by the rules to the removal of the voluntary liquidator by the

276   r 4.142(5) and (6).
277   r 4.142(4A) inserted by SI 1987 no 1919.
278   s 171(4).
279   s 172(5).
280   rr 4.135(2) and 4.146(2).
281   r 4.134(2).
282   s 136(2).
283   s 129(1).

court.[284] For the criteria to be applied in deciding whether to make a winding up order in these circumstances see paras 14.96 and 14.167–14.169.

REMOVAL OF A LIQUIDATOR

15.117 This process represents a sanction against unacceptable behaviour by a liquidator and a means for controlling the liquidation process. It is therefore open to the court, the creditors and the Secretary of State.

By the court

15.118 The court has power to remove a liquidator in both a voluntary and a compulsory winding up. Section 108 which, together with s 171(2) applies to the removal of a liquidator in a voluntary winding up, stipulates that the removal can take place 'on cause shown'. Section 172(2) which applies to a winding up by the court merely limits the procedures available for the removal of a liquidator to removal by court order or by a meeting of creditors (see below). However, Rule 4.119(2) makes it clear that cause must be shown for the removal of a compulsory liquidator. In the case of a provisional liquidator removal can only be by court order.

15.119 The criteria to be used by the court in deciding whether to grant an application to remove a liquidator do not seem to vary between a voluntary and a compulsory winding up. Some of the earlier cases dealt with the predecessor provision, s 141 of the Companies Act 1862, which required 'due' cause to be shown for removal. This may explain the suggestion of Jessel MR and Thesiger LJ in *Re Sir John Moore Gold Mining Company*[285] that the words mean something different from a power of the court to make an order when it thinks fit. The indication in that case that some unfitness must be shown on the part of the liquidator to justify removal flows from that view. This could include a conflict between the interest and duty of the liquidator.[286] The fundamental test is the interests of 'all those who are interested in the company being liquidated'. Thus a new appointment which will ensure a larger dividend to significant numbers of creditors may justify the removal of a liquidator who is not in any sense unfit.[287]

15.120 The interests to be considered will vary according to the

---

284 rr 4.126 and 4.147.
285 (1879) 12 Ch D 325.
286 *Ibid* at 331 and 332–3.
287 *Re Adam Eyton Ltd ex p Charlesworth* (1887) 36 Ch D 299.

circumstances of the case. If a company is solvent it will be those of the contributories. If there is no prospect of payment to anyone other than the secured creditors their interests will predominate. However, in cases where a liquidator is not seen to be independent even unsecured creditors with no prospects of being paid are entitled to demand a replacement of the liquidator by someone who will fulfil the role properly. The need to uphold commercial morality is in itself a factor to be considered.[288] While the applicant for removal must show some reason that need not involve unfitness or personal misconduct; a relaxed and complacent attitude on the part of the liquidator to misconduct by directors and a failure to investigate missing stock have been held to provide grounds.[289]

15.121 Now that the words 'due cause' have been replaced with a requirement merely to show cause (ss 108 and 172(2) of the Insolvency Act 1986 and the Insolvency Rules 1986, Rules 4.119 and 4.120) the width of the discretion has presumably expanded since the cases on the Companies Act 1862. The power conferred by the Insolvency Act 1986 on the creditors' meeting to remove a liquidator is further evidence of a legislative intention that the replacement of a liquidator should be possible not merely on the grounds that he is unfit but also in any circumstances where the interests of the creditors require it in an insolvent winding up. In a liquidation of a solvent company the interests of the contributories will prevail. In each case the court is likely to regard the creditors or contributories themselves as the best judges of their own interest. However, if there is a doubt as to the independence of a liquidator he may be replaced even against the wishes of the majority in value of the creditors to prevent substantial creditors from having a sense of grievance based on some reasonable cause.[290]

15.122 The procedure to be followed in applying for the removal of a liquidator allows for the dismissal of the application if the court takes the view that no sufficient cause is shown after the applicant has had the opportunity of an *ex parte* hearing with at least 7 days' notice.[291] An applicant may be required to provide a deposit or other security for costs and unless the court orders to the contrary the cost of the application will not be met from the company's assets.[292] The applicant must send to the liquidator notice of the venue as well as a copy of the application and of any evidence which he intends to adduce in support of it at least 14 days before

---

288 See *Rayland Financiers Association* (1878) 10 Ch D 269; and *Re Palmer Marine Surveys*
       [1986] 1 WLR 573, esp at 579–580—a case on the making of a winding up order where a
       voluntary liquidation was already in place., see also *Re Corbenstoke (No 2)* (1989)
       5 BCC 767.
289 *Keypack Homecare Ltd* [1987] BCLC 409.
290 *Re Palmer Marine Surveys* (note 288 above).
291 rr 4.119(2), 4.120(2) and 4.143(2).
292 rr 4.119(5), 4.120(5) and 4.143(4).

the hearing of an application which has not been dismissed after the *ex parte* hearing.[293] Copies of an order removing the liquidator are to be sent to the official receiver in the case of a compulsory winding up or the registrar of companies where the winding up is voluntary. The order may provide for matters arising from the removal and appoint a new liquidator in which case the requirements of Rules 4.102 or 4.103 as to an appointment must be complied with.[294]

By creditors' meeting or company meeting

15.123 The Insolvency Act 1986 provides for the removal of a liquidator by meetings of creditors or members. This reflects the tendency of the reforms introduced in the Insolvency Act 1985 to place the control of the liquidation process increasingly in the hands of the creditors or members, even where the liquidation is compulsory and might therefore be expected to be controlled by the court.

15.124 In a members' voluntary winding up the power to remove the liquidator is given to company general meetings by s 171(2)(a) of the Insolvency Act 1986. No special rules are laid down in the Act or the Insolvency Rules as to the procedure to be followed or the means of calling the meeting. Thus the rules laid down in the company's articles of association and in the Companies Act 1985 will have to be followed. However, if it is necessary that the general meeting of the company which decides to remove the liquidator should be 'summoned specially for that purpose'. This implies that the notice calling the meeting should clearly specifiy its purpose and that no other business should be dealt with at the meeting. A simple majority of votes will be sufficient to secure the liquidator's removal.

15.125 In a creditors' voluntary winding up the power to remove the liquidator is placed in the hands of a general meeting of creditors by s 171(2)(b). The meeting must be summoned specially for the purpose in accordance with the Insolvency Rules. The meeting must be summoned by the liquidator if 25% in value of the company's creditors request him to do so. In ascertaining whether 25% have made such a request all creditors connected with the company must be excluded from the list of those who have made the request.[295] This is intended to prevent the controllers of the company or those associated with them from disrupting the process of

---

293   rr 4.119(4), 4.120(4) and 4.143(4).
294   rr 4.119(6), 4.120(6) and 4.143(5).
295   r 4.114(1).

liquidation by calling such meetings. Paras 20.17–20.29 discuss the meaning of the phrase 'connected with' the company.

15.126 If the liquidator in a voluntary winding up was appointed by the court by the use of its power under s 108 of the Act the requirement as to summoning a meeting to consider his removal is more stringent. Section 171(3) lays down that the meeting should only be called if the liquidator himself thinks fit or the court orders unless those holding not less than half of the total voting rights of those entitled to vote at the meeting requests it. In the case of a members' voluntary winding up this means not less than half of the voting rights of members. In a creditors' voluntary winding up it means not less than one half in value of the company's creditors.[296]

15.127 The notice summoning the meeting must indicate that the removal of the liquidator is the purpose or one of the purposes of the meeting and must draw the attention of creditors to the rules as to the release of the liquidator in these circumstances.[297] While the liquidator or his nominee may chair the creditors' meeting, it is possible for some other person to be elected and if the liquidator or his nominee does chair the meeting and a resolution to remove the liquidator has been proposed then the consent of at least one half by value of the creditors present in person or by proxy and entitled to vote is needed for the adjournment of the meeting.[298] An ordinary majority by value of the creditors present and voting at the meeting will be sufficient to pass a resolution for the removal of the liquidator and this and all other rules as to the conduct of creditors meetings will apply in accordance with Chapter 8 of the Insolvency Rules 1986. However, where a meeting of creditors is to be held or is proposed to be summoned to remove the liquidator under Rules 4.113 or 4.114 the court has the power to give directions as the way in which it is to be summoned, the sending out and return of proxy forms, the conduct of the meeting, and any other matter which appears to the court to need regulation or control.[299] If the meeting resolves to remove the liquidator then the chairman of the meeting must send the certificate of the liquidator's removal to the registrar of companies unless the meeting also appointed a new liquidator in which case the certificate is passed to him for transmission to the registrar.[300] The removal of the previous liquidator must be advertised together with the appointment of the new one.[301]

---

296   s 171(3).
297   r 4.114(2).
298   r 4.114(3).
299   r 4.115.
300   r 4.117.
301   r 4.118.

15.128   In a compulsory liquidation removal of the liquidator by a company general meeting is never possible. However, the general meeting of creditors does have that power where the liquidator to be removed:

(a) was originally appointed by a creditors' meeting;

(b) or is the official receiver acting by virtue of s 136(3) in succession to a liquidator appointed as in (a);

(c) or the liquidator nominated by a meeting of contributories was appointed by the court in preference to the creditors' nominee;

(d) or the former administrator of the company was appointed liquidator by the court on making a winding up order immediately on the discharge of the administration order.

Where one of the above factors applies a general meeting of creditors may be called to remove the liquidator in accordance with the general rules applicable to the summoning of creditors' meetings in a compulsory liquidation. Thus the official receiver and the liquidator have a general power to call such meetings to ascertain the wishes of creditors in any matter relating to the winding up.[302] Alternatively the creditors may have specified by resolution at the meeting appointing the liquidator or some other creditors' meeting the times at which subsequent meetings are to be called. If this is the case the liquidator must call creditors' meetings at those times and such a meeting may resolve to remove the liquidator.[303] A request in writing by one tenth in value of the creditors of the company will impose an obligation on the liquidator to call a creditors' meeting if the request is accompanied by a list of the creditors concurring in the request and their respective claims in the winding up and written confirmation from each creditor of his concurrence. The latter requirement will not apply if the single creditor making the request has claims of a value sufficient to entitle him to requisition a meeting without the concurrence of others. A statement of the purpose of the proposed meeting is always required.[304] A venue for the meeting must then be fixed by the liquidator not more than 35 days from his recept of the request and 21 days' notice of the meeting and venue must be given to creditors.[305]

15.129   In the case of an attempt to remove a liquidator who:

(a) was appointed by the court (other than under ss 139(4)(a) or 140(1)); or

---

302   s 168(2) and r 4.54(1).
303   s 168(2).
304   *Ibid* and r 4.57(1).
305   r 4.57(2) and (3).

(b) was appointed by the Secretary of State; and
(c) if the official receiver is the liquidator (unless he became liquidator in succession under s 136(3) to a person appointed by a meeting of creditors)

a general meeting of creditors for the purpose of replacing the liquidator may only be called if the liquidator thinks fit or the court so directs or not less than one quarter by value of the company's creditors requisition the meeting.[306] The rules as to the details to be included with the requisition will be the same in such a case (see Rule 4.57).

15.130 In either case the notice issued to summon the meeting must indicate that the removal of the liquidator is the purpose or one of the purposes of the meeting and draw the attention of creditors to the rules as to the liquidator's release.[307] A copy of the notice must be sent to the official receiver at the same time as it is sent to the creditors.[308] As in the case of a voluntary winding up the liquidator or his nominee may be replaced as chairman of the meeting by a person elected by the meeting but if they do chair the meeting any adjournment must have the consent of at least one half of the creditors present in person or by proxy and entitled to vote.[309] If the official receiver does not chair the meeting copies of any resolution to remove the liquidator, appoint a new liquidator, or refuse to release the removed liquidator must be sent to the official receiver within 3 days by the chairman of the meeting. A certificate of the liquidator's removal and the appointment of a new liquidator must also be sent if such resolutions have been passed.[310] The official receiver must file a certificate of the liquidator's removal in court and the removal is effective from that date. Filing may occur after the Secretary of State has certified that the liquidator's account is reconciled with that held by the Secretary of State. Copies of the certificate of removal are sent by the official receiver to the outgoing liquidator and any newly appointed liquidator.[311] A simple majority by value of creditors may pass a resolution to remove the liquidator in accordance with the general rules as to the creditors' meeting but the vote of the liquidator or any partner or employee of his will not be counted.[312] A notice of appointment given by a new liquidator must state that his predecessor was removed and (if it be the case) given his release.[313] The court has the same general power to regulate and control any matter

---

306   s 172(3).
307   r 4.113(1).
308   r 4.113(2).
309   r 4.113(3).
310   r 4.113(4) and (5).
311   r 4.116.
312   r 4.63.
313   r 4.112.

relating to the calling or conduct of the meeting as it has in a voluntary winding up.[314]

Removal by the Secretary of State

15.131 This means of removal applies only to a liquidator in a compulsory winding up who is appointed by the Secretary of State.[315] Such an appointment may occur in the circumstances laid down in s 137(1) or (2). The official receiver may at any time when he is the liquidator request the Secretary of State to appoint a person in his place.[316] Alternatively, if meetings of creditors and contributories called by the official receiver under s 136(5)(a) fail to choose a liquidator the official receiver may decide to refer to the Secretary of State the need to appoint a liquidator.[317] In either case the Secretary of State has a discretion to decide whether to appoint a liquidator.[318] If he fails to do so the official receiver will remain in office as liquidator. A liquidator so appointed may be removed by the Secretary of State who must notify the official receiver and the liquidator of his decision to do so before it takes effect and specify a period within which the liquidator may make representations against the implementation of the decision to remove him.[319] At the end of that period the Secretary of State may implement his decision if the representations of the liquidator have not persuaded him to refrain from doing so. The Secretary of State must then file notice of his decision in court and send notice to the official receiver and the liquidator.[320] The liquidator must apply to the Secretary of State for his release in the same way as he would had he been removed by the court and the court has power to make any order in respect of him that it could have made had it removed him.[321]

THE DEATH OF A LIQUIDATOR

15.132 The death of a liquidator other than the official receiver terminates his period in office as the appointment is purely personal. It is the duty of the personal representatives of a deceased liquidator to give notice of the fact to the appropriate bodies. In a compulsory winding up the appropriate body is the official receiver who must give notice to the court for the

---

314　r 4.115.
315　s 172(4).
316　s 137(1).
317　s 137(2).
318　s 137(3).
319　r 4.123(1).
320　r 4.123(2).
321　r 4.123(3).

purpose of fixing the date of the liquidator's release. In a creditors' voluntary winding up it is the registrar of companies or the liquidation committee or one of its members. In a members' voluntary winding up the company's directors (or any one of them) and the registrar of companies bear this responsibility. In each case the notice must include the date of death.[322] Alternatively the personal representatives may be relieved of their duty if notice is give to the appropriate authority by a partner of the liquidator's firm who is a qualified insolvency practitioner or a member of the body recognised by the Secretary of State for the authorisation of insolvency practitioners or by any other person who produces a copy of the death certificate with the notice.[323]

COMPLETION OF THE WINDING UP

15.133 The liquidator who is in office at the completion of the winding up process will vacate office at that time. In a voluntary winding up the liquidator vacates office on giving notice to the registrar of companies of the holding of a final meeting, its date and the decisions of the meeting.[324] That notice which must be accompanied by a copy of the account presented to the final meeting must be given within one week after the meeting.[325] At this point the liquidator whose report was considered at the meeting vacates office. In a compulsory winding up the giving of notice to the court and the registrar of companies of the holding and decisions of the final meeting held under s 146 is the point at which the liquidator vacates office.

DUTIES OF THE LIQUIDATOR ON LEAVING OFFICE

15.134 Where a liquidator in any winding up ceases to be in office as a result of removal, resignation, or ceasing to be a qualified insolvency practitioner he must forthwith deliver up the assets to his successor as liquidator after deduction of expenses properly incurred and distributions made by the outgoing liquidator. He must also hand over to his successor the company's books, papers and other records and all papers and records of the liquidation including correspondence, proofs and other related papers appertaining to his administration of the winding up process.[326] In a compulsory winding up a liquidator who intends to vacate office by

---

322   See rr 4.132(1) and (4), 4.133(1) and 4.145(1).
323   rr 4.132(2) and (3), 4.133(2) and 4.145(2).
324   s 171(6).
325   ss 94(3) and 106(3).
326   rr 4.138(1) and 4.148.

resignation or otherwise at a time when unrealised assets remain, must give notice to the official receiver of his intention and inform him of the nature value and whereabouts of those assets.[327] Where a creditors' meeting is called to receive the liquidator's resignation or otherwise in respect of his vacation of office, the notice to the official receiver must be given at least 21 days before the meeting.[328] This will apply to a removal of the liquidator by the creditors' meeting as well as resignation by the liquidator. In a compulsory liquidation in which the winding up is for practical purposes complete the liquidator must file all proofs remaining with him in court.[329] The obligations of a liquidator to make returns and his other duties in relation to the winding up process are dealt with fully in chapters 16 and 19 on the process of winding up.

THE RELEASE OF A LIQUIDATOR

15.135 Before the reform of Insolvency Law in 1986, there was no statutory procedure for the release of a liquidator in a voluntary winding up. The release of the liquidator in a compulsory liquidation was a matter for the Secretary of State for Trade and Industry with an appeal to the court against his decision. The new rules stipulate the time at which the release is to be available and the effect of release. This reduces the number of cases in which the Secretary of State decides the question of whether to grant release. The effect of a liquidator being given his release is that from that time he is 'discharged from all liability both in respect of acts or omissions of his in the winding up and otherwise in relation to his conduct as liquidator'. However, this does not prevent the court from exercising its powers under s 212 of the Act if a misfeasance summons is issued against a person who has had his release.[330] The effects of release are therefore serious and it is important to consider the circumstances in which it is granted. The Insolvency Act 1986 provides for release in both voluntary and compulsory liquidations.

Release in a voluntary liquidation

15.136 Section 173(2) of the Insolvency Act 1986 provides for the release of a liquidator from a time which is laid down by reference to the manner in which the liquidator leaves office. A resigning liquidator in a voluntary winding up is released from the time of giving notice to the registrar of

---

327 r 4.137(1).
328 r 4.137(2).
329 r 4.138(2).
330 ss 173(4) and s 174(6).

companies of his resignation unless, in the case of a creditor's voluntary winding up, the creditors' meeting which accepted his resignation has resolved against his release.[331] If the meeting of creditors resolves to refuse him his release the former liquidator must apply to the Secretary of State for his release.[332] There is no provision in a members' voluntary winding up for a company meeting which accepts the liquidator's resignation to refuse him his release. A liquidator who is removed from office by a company general meeting or by a creditors' meeting which does not resolve against his release is released from the time at which notice is given to the registrar of companies under Rule 4.117 or 4.144(2) to the effect that he no longer holds office.[333] The fact of his release must be stated in the certificate of removal.[334] A liquidator who dies is released from the time at which notice is given to the registrar of companies that he has ceased to hold office.[335] If a liquidator in a members' voluntary winding up is removed by a company general meeting he is automatically released as there is no power for the company meeting to resolve against his release. He is therefore always released on notice of his removal being given to the registrar of companies. However, a liquidator in a creditors' voluntary winding up may be removed by a general meeting of creditors which resolves not to give him his release.[336] In such a case he must apply to the Secretary of State for his release, which will operate from the time the Secretary of State determines.[337] The same rule applies both in a members' and a creditors' voluntary liquidation to a person who vacates office because of ceasing to be qualified to act as an insolvency practitioner or who has been removed by the court.[338] In most cases a liquidator will leave office as a result of a company's affairs being fully wound up. In this case he has his release in a members' voluntary winding up from the time at which he vacates office. That is the time at which he gives notice to the registrar of companies that the final company general meeting called under s 94 has been held and of its decisions.[339] There is no right for that meeting to resolve against the release of the liquidator.

15.137 In a creditors' voluntary winding up the liquidator will be released on vacating office, that is at the time of sending notice to the registrar of companies that the final meetings required by s 106 have been held, providing the final creditors' meeting has not resolved against his

---

331 r 4.122(1) and (2) and r 4.144(3).
332 r 4.122(3).
333 s 173(2)(a).
334 r 4.122(2).
335 s 173(2)(a).
336 s 173(2)(b).
337 s 173(2)(b).
338 rr 4.146 and 4.144(3) and (4) respectively and s 173(2)(b).
339 ss 173(2)(d), 171(6)(a) and s 94(3).

release.[340] If it has so resolved he must apply to the Secretary of State for his release.[341] The release will then be effective from the date of the certificate sent by the Secretary of State to the registrar of companies and to the former liquidator.[342] This rule also applies to a liquidator in a creditors' voluntary winding up who resigns or is removed by the court or a creditors' meeting and who gains his release by applying to the Secretary of State.[343] A liquidator in a members' voluntary winding up who is removed by the court or who ceases to be an insolvency practitioner is also covered by these rules.[344] It is noteworthy that any liquidator who is removed from office by the court must apply to the Secretary of State for his release, whether the liquidation is a members' or a creditors' voluntary winding up, or, indeed, a compulsory liquidaton.[345] A liquidator who vacates office in a voluntary liquidation due to the making of a winding up order is to be treated as if he had been removed by the court and must apply to the Secretary of State for his release.[346]

Release in a compulsory liquidation

15.138 Where a company is being wound up by the court slightly different rules apply to the release of a liquidator and rules are also provided to deal with the release of a provisional liquidator. The time from which a former provisional liquidator has his release is determined by the court on application by him.[347] This will usually be the time of the making of the winding up order, but the court has an unfettered discretion. A distinction is drawn for the purpose of dealing with the release of liquidators in a compulsory winding up between the official receiver and other persons. Thus, when the official receiver is replaced as liquidator by some other person, he will have his release from the time at which he gives notice to the court of his replacement by a person nominated by a general meeting of creditors or contributories or appointed by the Secretry of State.[348] If he is replaced by a person appointed by the court, the court will determine the time from which he has his release.[349] The Secretary of State will decide the timing of the release if the official receiver gives him notice that the winding up is, for practical purposes, complete.[350] Before giving such notice to the Secretary of State, the official receiver must send to all the creditors who

340 ss 173(2)(e), 171(6)(b) and 106(3).
341 s 173(2)(e)(i).
342 rr 4.126(3) and 4.122.
343 r 4.122.
344 rr 4.144(5) and 4.146(3).
345 rr 4.121(3), 4.122(3)(b) and 4.144(3).
346 rr 4.136 and 4.147.
347 s 174(5).
348 s 174(2)(a).
349 s 174(2)(b).
350 s 174(3).

have proved their debts notice of his intention to do so and a summary of his receipts and payments as liquidator.[351] When the Secretary of State has decided the date from which the official receiver is to have his release he must give notice to the court of his decision and a copy of the summary of receipts and payments.[352]

15.139 Where a person other than the official receiver ceases to be liquidator, the rules as to the timing of his release are much the same as those that apply in a voluntary liquidation. Thus where he is removed by a general meeting of creditors which has not resolved against his release, has his resignation accepted by such a meeting, or dies, he has his release from the time at which notice is given to the court of the fact which terminates the liquidators period in office.[353] If a final meeting of the creditors called under s 146 does not resolve against the release of liquidator, he has his release from the time at which he gives notice to the court and the Registrar of Companies that the meeting has been held and of its decisions.[354] Where a liquidator (other than the official receiver) is removed by the court, the Secretary of State, or a meeting of creditors which resolves that he be not released he must apply to the Secretary of State for his release. The same rule applies to a liquidator whose release is withheld by a creditors' meeting which accepted his resignation or by a final meeting held under s 146 as well as a liquidator who ceases to be qualified to act as an insolvency practitioner.[355] Where application is made to the Secretary of State for the release of a liquidator the Department of Trade and Industry will seek all the information considered necessary to decide the matter. If the release has been refused by a creditors' meeting they will be concerned to establish the reasons for the refusal and to assess their validity. The procedures for the release of liquidators have been substantially rationalised by bringing into line the rules applicable in voluntary and in compulsory liquidations and by the presumption of release on vacation of office in cases of removal, resignation or the termination of a liquidation unless a resolution is passed to the contrary.

PART 4: REMUNERATION OF LIQUIDATORS

15.140 The method of fixing the remuneration of the liquidator in an insolvent liquidation is governed by the Insolvency Rules 1986. In a members' voluntary winding up it is a matter for agreement between the

---

351   r 4.124(1) and (2).
352   r 4.124(3).
353   s 174(4)(a) and (c) and rr 4.121(1) and (2) and 4.109(6).
354   s 174(d)(ii); s 172(8).
355   s 174(4)(b) and r 4.121(3).

company and the liquidator. Section 91 of the Insolvency Act 1986 does not re-enact the power conferred by s 580(1) of the Companies Act 1985 which allowed the general meeting which appointed a liquidator in such a winding up to fix his remuneration. The provisions of Rules 4.127 to 4.131 does not apply to a members' voluntary winding up[356] and Rules 4.139 to 4.150 do not deal with remuneration. However, s 115 of the Insolvency Act 1986 does allow the liquidator in a members' voluntary winding up to take his remuneration from the assets. It will be wise to seek general meeting approval for at least the basis for determining the liquidator's remuneration, although in many cases the board of directors will have power to fix it.[357]

15.141 The rules applicable to the liquidator in an insolvent liquidation (whether a creditors' voluntary winding up or a winding up by the court) provide that the liquidator is entitled to remuneration for the services he provides in that capacity.[358] The basis on which the remuneration of a liquidator other than the official receiver is fixed is decided by the liquidation committee (if one exists).[359] If there is no such committee or it fails to make the decision then the decision may be made by resolution of a meeting of creditors.[360] Failing a decision by either of these bodies the liquidator's remuneration will be in accordance with the scale laid down for the official receiver by the Insolvency Regulations 1986 SI 1986/1994 regs 19 to 22.[361] In any case in which the official receiver acts as liquidator, whether during the whole or part of the winding up, he will be remunerated in accordance with those Regulations as amended from time to time. The choice as to the remuneration of other liquidators is between a percentage of the value of the assets which are realised or distributed or of both in combination and payment by reference to the time properly given by the liquidator and his staff in attending to matters arising in the winding up.[362] Most liquidators will prefer the latter method.

15.142 In determining the basis on which the remuneration should be fixed or percentage to be used if that method is chosen the liquidation committee or the creditors' meeting must have regard to:

(a) the complexity of the case;
(b) any responsibility of an exceptional degree or kind falling on the liquidator as such in connection with the winding up;

356 r 4.1(1).
357 Table A art 70 (SI 1985 no 805).
358 r 4.127(1).
359 r 4.127(3).
360 r 4.127(5).
361 r 4.127(6).
362 r 4.127(2).

(c) the effectiveness with which the liquidator appears to have carried out or to be carrying out his duties as such;
(d) the value and nature of the assets with which the liquidator has to deal.[363]

15.143   Where joint liquidators are in office the apportionment of remuneration between them should be agreed by them but if this is not possible the dispute may be referred to the court for settlement by order or to the liquidation committee or a meeting of creditors for settlement by resolution.[364] The payment of profit costs for acting on behalf of the company to the firm or partner of a solicitor liquidator must be authorised in advance by the liquidation committee, a meeting of creditors or the court.[365] Once the remuneration of a liquidator has been fixed, the amount may be challenged by either the liquidator or creditors (respectively) on the grounds that it is too low or too high. A challenge by the liquidator may be made to a meeting of creditors if his remuneration has been fixed by the liquidation committee. The amount to be paid may then be increased by resolution.[366] Whichever body has fixed his remuneration the liquidator may apply to the court to order that the amount or rate be increased. This can be done after a decision by the liquidation committee or the creditors' meeting or if no remuneration was fixed by those bodies and he was paid the rate laid down in the regulations for the official receiver.[367] At least 14 days' notice must be given to the members of the liquidation committee of an application by the liquidator to the court. The committee may then nominate one or more of its members to appear or be represented and to be heard on the application.[368] If there is no liquidation committee, notice of the liquidator's application must be sent to such creditors as the court directs and those creditors may nominate one or more of their number to appear or be represented and be heard.[369] The cost of the application may be ordered to be borne out of the assets.[370] Where a liquidator is to be paid out of funds deposited with the Insolvency Services Account only money belonging to the company should be used although the court has a discretion to pay the official receiver's costs and charges out of property held by the company as trustee.

15.144   The remuneration of a liquidator or provisional liquidator can

---

363   r 4.127(4).
364   r 4.128(2).
365   r 4.128(3).
366   r 4.129.
367   r 4.130(1).
368   r 4.130(2).
369   r 4.130(3).
370   r 4.130(4) as amended by SI 1987 no 1919.

generally only be claimed out of the assets of the company and not from property which passes through his hands but is held by the company on trust for others.[371] However, the court can allow a claim by the liquidator for expenses and remuneration from a trust fund despite an absence of prior authority as a condition of the court giving effect to the equitable interest. This will be done where the company's assets are insufficient and the liquidator's work was necessary to realise the fund and in discharge of his fiduciary duty. Such remuneration is calculated by aggregating the company's assets with the trust fund to determine the total amount of remuneration as a percentage of the whole. The trust fund then bears the proportion of that total remuneration figure that its value bore to the aggregate value of the assets.[372]

371 *Re Exchange Securities and Commodities Ltd (No 2)* [1985] BCLC 392.
372 *Re Berkeley Applegate (Investment Consultants)Ltd (No 2)* (1988) 4 BCC 280 and *Re Eastern Capital Futures Co* (1989) 5 BCC 223.

The Winding Up Process: Investigation, Enforcement, Records and the Creditors' Committee

INSPECTION OF BOOKS AND PUBLIC AND PRIVATE EXAMINATIONS

16.01 In order to carry out his function of investigating the circumstances surrounding the company's insolvency the liquidator is given substantial statutory powers to obtain information. These powers are also useful in the process of gathering in the assets of the company but they are dealt with here as they do not only fit into that part of the winding up process. The duty of the liquidator to report certain matters to the official receiver or the Secretary of State for Trade and Industry may apply to the results of the processes dealt with here (see paras 16.36–16.46 below).

16.02 The Cork Report recommended that the procedure of a public examination of those connected with the company should be revived as no such examination had taken place since 1935.[1] The purpose of such proceedings would be to form the basis of reports, by the official receiver to the DTI, on the affairs of the company and possible offences by the company's officers; to obtain information for the purposes of the administration of the estate; and to give publicity to 'the salient facts and unusual features connected with the company's failure'.[2] In respect of private examinations the Committee took the view that a more liberal approach to the circumstances in which they were ordered should be encouraged and that the court should have power to order costs against a witness who witheld information. They deprecated any tendency only to allow private examination orally after the submission of answers to a written questionnaire in all cases. Any abuse by liquidators who failed to use other methods of obtaining information before applying for an examination would be remedied by allowing costs to be awarded against such officeholders. The power of the court under the Bankruptcy Act 1914 s 25 to order the payment of any debt due to the estate from the person examined should, according to Cork, be extended to company liquidations.[3] The Insolvency Act 1986 makes provision for both forms of examination. The liquidator may set in motion the private examination

---

1 paras 653 to 657.
2 *Ibid* para 655.
3 *Ibid* para 896–907.

procedure but, as was the case before the reform of the law, the official receiver must be involved before a public examination is possible, as that procedure forms part of the system of investigations with which he is concerned.

Inspection of the company's books

16.03 The liquidator has a general duty and power to take into his custody all the company's property except documents of title in the hands of mortgagees.[4] This includes all books, accounts and records. In addition to this underlying entitlement, s 234 gives specific powers to the court to make orders on the application of any officeholder which will assist the process of gathering assets and investigating the affairs of the company. These powers are applicable to a liquidator in a voluntary liquidation; a liquidator and a provisional liquidator in a compulsory liquidation and, indeed, to administrators and administrative receivers.[5] A court order may be obtained by an officeholder against any person who has in his possession or control any property, books, papers or records to which the company appears to be entitled. It will require that person to deliver, or otherwise effectively transfer, the property to the officeholder either forthwith or within such period as the court directs.[6] The power conferred on the court by s 234 is exercisable in a compulsory winding up by the liquidator and by any provisional liquidator who has been appointed.[7] In a voluntary winding up the liquidator would have to apply to the court to enforce the obligation to hand over property.

16.04 In addition to providing for a court order to be obtained under s 234(2), the section confers some protection on an officeholder who exercises 'self help' by seizing or disposing of property which is not the property of the company, if he believes on reasonable grounds that he has a right to deal with it in that way. In such circumstances the officeholder has a lien on the property, or the proceeds of its sale, for expenses incurred in the seizure or the disposal and he is not liable to anyone for any loss or damage resulting from his action unless they were caused by the negligence of the officeholder.[8]

16.05 Section 235 of the Act imposes an obligation on a wide range of persons linked with the company to assist the officeholder. They are

4 Insolvency Act 1986 s 144; and see *Engle v South Metropolitan Brewing and Bottling Company* [1892] 1 Ch 442.
5 s 234(1).
6 s 234(2).
7 Insolvency Rules 1986 r 4.185.
8 s 234(3) and (4).

required to attend the officeholder at such times as he may reasonably require and to give him any information concerning the company and its promotion, formation, business, dealings, affairs and property as he may reasonably require. Those subject to this obligation include former and present company officers, those who took part in its formation within a year before the company went into liquidation, current employees and those in its employment within that one year period and those who are, or have been within that one year period, officers or employees of another company that was an officer of the company within the same period. In the case of a company in compulsory liquidation anyone who has acted as administrator, administrative receiver or liquidator of the company is also included.[9]

16.06 Orders for the enforcement of this obligation may be made by the court on the application of the 'competent person' and such orders will be those that the court thinks necessary for the enforcement of the obligations imposed by the section.[10] For this purpose the 'competent person' is the official receiver, the liquidator, the provisional liquidator, the administrator or the adminstrative receiver as the case may be.[11] Such an order may award costs against the person against whom it is made.[12]

16.07 In a compulsory liquidation s 155 permits the court (at any time after the winding up order was made) to make an order that books and papers in the company's possession be open to inspection by creditors or contributories. The power contained in the section applies in a voluntary winding up by virtue of s 112. This power will be exercised by the court in the interests of the winding up to recover assets or to assist in the investigation of the behaviour of those in control of the company before it became insolvent. There is no automatic right for an order to be made at the request of creditors or contributories. No order will be made if its only purpose is to facilitate proceedings by an individual creditor for his own benefit against the directors of the company in circumstances which will not give rise to any accretion to the assets available in the winding up.[13] Section 191 lays down that where a company is being wound up, the books and papers of the company and of the liquidator are, as between the contributories and the company, *prima facie* evidence of the truth of all matters purporting to be recorded in them.

16.08 Any lien or other right to retain possession which a person is

9   s 235(3).
10   r 7.20(1)(c).
11   r 7.20(2)(d).
12   r 7.20(3).
13   *Re North Brazilian Sugar Factories Ltd* (1887) 37 Ch D 83.

entitled to in respect of the books, papers or other records of the company is unenforceable to the extent that its enforcement would deny possession of its subject matter to an officeholder. This applies in the case of the appointment of a provisional liquidator, a company going into liquidation, or the making of an administration order. It does not apply to a lien on documents which give title to property and which are held as such. It should be noted that the lien is simply made unenforceable to the extent necessary to allow possession of the papers books or other records to be taken by the officeholder.[14] This provision does however overcome the problem raised in the case of *Re Capital Fire Insurance Association*[15] in which it was held that a court order was necessary before the liquidator could obtain possession of documents subject to a lien. It is now the case that the general right to possession under s 144 applies to such documents so that s 234(2) need not be used merely because of the existence of a lien.

16.09 Documents which give title to property and are held as such and which are therefore still subject to an enforceable lien because of the exemption in s 246(3) can probably be the subject of an order under s 236(3) to allow inspection by the officeholder.[16] An order under s 234(2) would not be appropriate as the company is not entitled to the documents as against the person with a lien over them, and for the same reason the general right to possession under s 144(1) would not assist.

Private examination

16.10 Section 236 of the Insolvency Act 1986 provides for the court to summon to appear before it:

"(a) any officer of the company,
    (b) any person known or suspected to have in his possession any property of the company or supposed to be indebted to the company, or
    (c) any person whom the court thinks capable of giving information concerning the promoting, formation, business, dealings, affairs or property of the company".[17]

It is clear from the section that an order against a person connected with the company only after it ceased actively to carry on business, and possessing information only coming into existence then, is permissible if the information is of the kind referred to in s 236(2)(c). However, reports covered by legal professional privilege need not be produced.[18] Solicitors must specify that the privilege relates to clients other than the insolvent

---

14 s 246.
15 (1883) 24 Ch D 408.
16 *Re Aveling Barford* [1989] BCLC 122.
17 s 236(2). This can include, for example, an employee of the petitioning creditor—*Re Esal (Commodities) Ltd* [1989] BCLC 59.
18 *Re Highgrade Traders Ltd* [1984] BCLC 151.

company or group of companies and on what grounds the information is privileged.[19]

16.11 An order may be made on the application of the officeholder, liquidator, provisional liquidator, administrator, or administrative receiver. The official receiver may also apply in any case in which a winding up order has been made against the company whether or not he is the liquidator.[20] An injunction may be granted under s 37 of the Supreme Court Act 1981 to prevent the defendant from leaving the jurisdiction before the examination takes place.[21] The power conferred by this section can be used in a voluntary or a compulsory liquidation.[22] The section is essentially concerned with the power of the officeholder to obtain information. It does not deal with property rights. Consequently a lien (such as a solicitor's lien) over documents does not prevent an order for inspection as there is no need to remove the document from the lienee's possession.[23]

16.12 An application under the section must be in writing and be accompanied by a brief statement of the grounds on which it is made.[24] Those grounds need not be proved even *prima facie*; a fair suspicion may be sufficient to justify an investigation.[25] It is even possible to avoid full disclosure of the grounds alleged until the hearing if their revelation to the respondent is likely to lead to dissimulation or concealment although a liquidator in a voluntary winding up not being an officer of the court must support the ground with affidavit evidence. There is no requirement to submit written questions in advance.[26] The court has a discretion whether the examination is preceded by written questions and will balance the views of the liquidator against the need to avoid carrying out the examination in an oppressive or unfair manner. No order to produce documents will be made against a person who has not refused to do so.[27] The application will usually be *ex parte*.[28] It must identify the respondent[29] and state the purpose of the application. The stated purpose may be for the respondent:

"(a) to be ordered to appear before the court, or
 (b) to answer interrogatories (if so, particulars to be given of the matters in respect of which answers are required), or

19 *Re Aveling Barford* [1989] BCLC 122.
20 s 236(1).
21 *Re Oriental Credit* [1988] 2 WLR 172.
22 s 236(1) and s 234(1)(c) respectively.
23 *Re Aveling Barford* (note 19 above).
24 r 9.2(1).
25 *Re Gold Company* (1879) 12 Ch D 77 at 84.
26 *Re Rolls Razor Ltd (No 2)* [1970] 1 Ch 576.
27 *Re Norton Warburg Holdings Ltd* [1983] BCLC 235.
28 r 9.2(4).
29 r 9.2(2).

(c) to submit affidavits (if so, particulars to be given of the matters to which he is required to swear), or

(d) to produce books papers or other records (if so, the items in question to be specified)

or for any two or more of those purposes."[30]

16.13   The court will only order that an examination take place when it is required for the purpose of the liquidation. As in the case of an order under s 234, no examination will be ordered if its sole purpose is to assist the applicant in making a personal claim against the directors or the company and there will be no benefit to the winding up process.[31] Although the purpose of the provision is to facilitate the investigation of the company's affairs and the recovery of assets, there may be some cases where an examination will be refused because the procedure is being abused by a liquidator *qua* litigant to assist him in countering reverses that he has experienced in the litigation brought on behalf of the company.[32] However the mere prospect of litigation by the company against the respondent or others and the use of evidence obtained in the examination in it will not be sufficient to prevent an order for an examination. In this context it will be important to determine whether the liquidator has a genuinely open mind on the question of whether to litigate against a third party.[32a]

16.14   However, even a predisposition in favour of such action may not prevent an order from being made so long as the procedure is not being used to obtain an advantage as litigant or to surmount difficulties experienced in that role (see *Re Spiraflite Ltd*[33] and *Re Castle New Homes Ltd*).[34] No examination will be ordered where this would be oppressive, vexatious or unfair but those who have been involved in a company's affairs have a duty to assist the liquidator and a long delay in seeking an order will not be a bar to a successful application if earlier action would have been prevented by the existence of litigation which has now ended.[35] Where a contributory applies for an order he must show some benefit to himself as such and not rely solely on the public interest. His application carries less weight than that of an independent professional acting as liquidator and will not be allowed if it merely furthers some ulterior motive such as the harassment of a bank seeking to enforce a guarantee given by the applicant.[36]

16.15   The Court of Appeal has laid down that the purpose of s 561 of the

---

30   r 9.2(3).
31   *Re Imperial Continental Water Corporation* (1886) 33 Ch D 314.
32   See for example *Re Bletchley Boat Company Ltd* [1974] 1 WLR 630.
32a   *Re Cloverbay Ltd* (1989) 5 BCC 732.
33   [1979] 1 WLR 1096 per Megarry J at 1102.
34   [1979] 1 WLR 1075.
35   *Re J T Rhodes Ltd* [1982] BCLC 77.
36   *Re Embassy Act Products Ltd* [1988] BCLC 1.

Companies Act 1985 (the predecessor provision) is to assist the liquidator to carry out his functions more effectively, For that reason the court will normally seek to assist the liquidator. In the context of a group of companies it is proper for the liquidator of the parent company to make available to the directors or liquidators of subsidiaries information obtained under the section which will assist in the process of getting in the assets of the subsidiaries for the benefit of both companies, although the court's order to this effect may limit that requirement to named subsidiaries. This principle was applied by the court despite the fact that the information to be disclosed was likely to assist the subsidiaries in litigation against the petitioning creditor in both the United Kingdom and the United States and an earlier agreement by the liquidator in a compromise to refrain from such disclosure without the permission of the petitioning creditor's solicitor.[37]

16.16 Whenever a person is required to appear before the court they will also be required to submit an affidavit, answer interrogatories, or produce books or papers. The rule does leave open the possibility of a practice of requiring that interrogatories be answered before an appearance is required. The section can be used to require the attendance of any person whom the court thinks capable of providing the information referred to in s 236(1)(c). The respondent need not have been involved in the management of the company and he can be required to give information or provide documents that came into existence before the liquidation began.[38]

16.17 Whatever the purpose of the application is said to be the court always has the power to make any of the orders specified in the section.[39] The section contemplates orders summoning a person to appear, requiring him to submit an affidavit containing an account of his dealings with the company, or requiring the production of books, papers or other records in his possession or under his control relating to the company and its promotion, formation, property and activities.[40] The court's order must be served forthwith on the respondent.[41] If he is required to appear the venue must be specified and must be for a date at least 14 days after the date of the order.[42] If affidavits are required the order must state the time limit for their submission and the matters with which they are to deal while an order for the production of books or papers must stipulate the time and manner of the compliance required.[43]

---

37 *Re Esal (Commodities) Ltd* [1989] BCLC 59.
38 *Re Highgrade Traders Ltd* [1983] BCLC 137.
39 r 9.3(1).
40 s 236(2) and (3).
41 r 9.3(5).
42 r 9.3(2).
43 r 9(3) and (4).

16.18   The section lays down enforcement procedures to deal with a breach of the orders of the court. They apply to a person who fails without reasonable excuse to appear before the court when summoned to do so or where there are reasonable grounds for believing that a person has absconded or is about to abscond to avoid appearing before the court.[44] In these circumstances the court can issue a warrant for the arrest of the person in question and for the seizure of any books papers or other records or company property in his possession. The person may then be kept in custody and things seized under the warrant held until that person is brought before the court or a further order is made.[45]

16.19   A warrant is issued to the bailiff in the county court, or the tipstaff in the high court, or to a constable.[46] A person seized under the warrant will be brought before the court forthwith for examination but if that is not immediately possible he will be delivered into the custody of the governor of a prison designated in the warrant and produced when the court requires him. The arrest and any delivery into custody must be reported to the court. The court will fix the earliest possible date for the examination to take place and order delivery by the prison governor while giving notice of the venue of the examination to the person who applied for the warrant.[47] A warrant may be executed by any county court in its own district at the request of the court which issued it.[48]

16.20   Examination of a person under s 236 is on oath whether it is done orally or by interrogatories.[49] It may be attended by the officeholder who applied for it who may put questions to the person being examined either in person or by a solicitor or counsel.[50] Any other person who could have applied for an order may attend the examination and put questions with the leave of the court if the applicant does not object but the questions must be put through the applicant.[51] A creditor who supplied the information which led the applicant to apply for an examination may similarly put questions through the applicant if he does not object and if the court gives leave.[52] The respondent is entitled to be represented by solicitor or counsel who may put questions to enable him to explain or qualify his answers and make representations on his behalf but such representation is at his own expense.[53] If the respondent was required to answer interrogatories the

44   s 236(4).
45   s 236(5) and (6).
46   s 236(5) and r 7.21(2).
47   r 7.23.
48   r 7.24.
49   s 237(4).
50   r 9.4(1).
51   r 9.4(2).
52   r 9.4(4).
53   r 9.4(5).

court will direct him as to which questions he must answer and whether any answers need be in affidavit form.[54]

16.21 The court may order that a person who would be subject to examination if he were within the jurisdiction will be examined in any part of the United Kingdom or in a place outside it.[55] A written record of the examination will be kept and this will be read over to, or by, the respondent who will be required to sign it. That record may then be used as evidence of any statement made by the respondent in the examination in any proceedings.[56] The written record, replies to interrogatories, and affidavits of the respondent are not normally filed in court and are not open to the public. They are only open to inspection by the officeholder. Similar restrictions apply to the part of the court file showing the grounds for the application under s 236 and copies of proposed interrogatories. A court order may be made to permit others to have access to these documents.[57]

16.22 The cost of proceedings under s 236 may be ordered to be paid by the respondent if it appears to the court that the examination was made necessary by the unjustifiable refusal of the respondent to provide information at an earlier stage.[58] The official receiver cannot be ordered to pay the costs unless he applies as liquidator and the normal order will be that the costs be borne by the company. However, if an order is made under s 237 for the delivery up of property or the discharge of a debt, the costs of the application may be ordered to be paid by the respondent.[59]

16.23 In accordance with the recommendations of the Cork Report, the Insolvency Act 1986 allows for orders to be made requiring the person subject to the private examination to deliver up company property in his possession to the office holder or to pay to him the whole or part of any debt due from the respondent to the company. Such orders may be made if it appears to the court, on consideration of any evidence obtained under s 236, that the respondent has company property in his possession or is indebted to the company as the case may be.[60] The power of enforcement conferred by s 237 only arises if it is evidence obtained in the private examination which makes it appear to the court that a debt is owed by the respondent or that company property is held by him but it is not only against the respondent that an order under the section can be made. If

54 r 9.4(3).
55 s 237(3).
56 r 9.4(6).
57 r 9.5.
58 r 9.6(1).
59 r 9.6(2) and (3).
60 s 237(1) and (2).

evidence obtained in the private examination indicates the existence of a debt or that company property is possessed by someone other than the respondent, the order may be made against the debtor or the person in possession of the property. In each case an order can only be made on the application of the office holder.

Public examination

16.24 The official receiver has an important role in the investigation process in the case of companies in compulsory liquidation. Section 131 empowers him to require that a statement of affairs be provided where a winding up order has been made or a provisional liquidator appointed by the court. This obligation can be imposed by the official receiver on some or all of the persons referred to in s 131(3). The list is the familiar one:

(a) present and past company officers;

(b) such of the present employees and of those employed within one year before the date of the winding up order or the appointment of the provisional liquidator (with the concept of 'employment' including those employed under a contract for services[61]) as the official receiver believes to be capable of giving the required information;

(c) those who took part in the formation of the company during that same one year period; and

(d) those who have been employed by, or officers of, a corporate officer of the company within the one year in question.

16.25 The contents of the statement of affairs are set out in s 131(2) and Rules 4.32 and 4.33. It must contain all the information required by Form 4.17. This includes:

(a) particulars of the company's assets and liabilities;

(b) the names and addresses of the company's creditors;

(c) the securities held by them and the dates when they were given.

The statement must be verified by the affidavit of the persons required to submit it and others may be required to file affidavits of concurrence.[62] The statement must be provided within 21 days of the notice demanding it but this period can be extended by the official receiver who may also relieve a person of the obligations that he has imposed on them under the section.[63]

---

61 s 131(6).
62 r 4.33.
63 s 131(4) and (5).

If such dispensations are refused by the official receiver an appeal to the court is possible.

16.26   A failure to comply with an obligation imposed by the official receiver makes a person liable to a fine and, for continued contravention, a daily default fine.[64] A duty is placed on the official receiver, by s 132, to investigate the cause of any failure of the company and any matters related to the promotion, formation, business, dealings and affairs of the company in all cases in which a winding up order is made. He will then make such report to the court as he thinks fit. That report is *prima facie* evidence of the facts stated in it in any proceedings.[65]

16.27   Although the official receiver has the function of investigating the company and preparing a report, the process of public examination is not restricted by the statute to the period after the report has been compiled and submitted to the court. The official receiver may apply to the court for an order for a public examination at any time before the dissolution of a company being wound up by the court. The persons who may be subject to such an examination are any past or present officer of the company; any former liquidator, administrator or receiver (this is not limited to an administrative receiver); and any other person who is or has been concerned or has taken part, in the promotion formation or management of the company.[66] In the case of a person in the last category the application to the court must be accompanied by a report by the official receiver which indicates the grounds on which he claims that the person falls within that category. The court may rescind its order if it is satisfied that those grounds are not made out.[67]

16.28   In the absence of a court order to the contrary, the official receiver is required to apply for a public examination if he is requested to do so by either one half in value of the company's creditors or three-quarters in value of the company's contributories.[68] Such a request must be in writing and be accompanied by a list of the creditors or contributories concurring in it together with written confirmation of that concurrence unless the requisitioning creditor or contributory has a debt or shareholding sufficient for a requisition without the concurrence of others.[69] The request must name the proposed examinee and specify his relationship with the company

---

64   s 131(7).
65   s 132(2).
66   s 133(1).
67   r 4.211(2)(a) and (4).
68   s 133(2).
69   r 4.213(1).

and the reasons for the request for an examination.[70] Before the official receiver is obliged to apply in accordance with the requisition he may require the requisitionists to provide such sum as he thinks appropriate as security for the expenses of the public examination. If the examination is ordered to take place the court may order that the resulting expenses be paid a specified proportion out of that sum instead of out of the assets.[71] Subject to the provision of such security the official receiver is obliged either to apply to the court within 28 days of receiving the requisition or, if he is of the opinion that the request is unreasonable, apply to the court for an order relieving him of his duty to apply for a public examination.[72] If he is relieved of that duty on an *ex parte* application a copy of the order must be sent to the requisitionists and if the court dismisses his application for relief he must apply for the public examination forthwith.[73]

16.29   On an application for a public examination the court is required to direct that the person to whom the application relates shall attend on the day that it appoints and be publicly examined. The examination relates to the promotion formation or management of the company; the conduct of its business or affairs; or that person's conduct or dealings in relation to the company.[74] The order is served on the person to whom it relates forthwith.[75] Service will normally be by post but if, in the report that he submitted with the application, the offical receiver has indicated that there is no reasonable certainty that service by post will be effective, then service by some other means will be directed by the court.[76] In addition to the service of the order on the examinee, 14 days' notice of the hearing will be served by the official receiver on the liquidator (if that is not the official receiver); the special manager (if any); and all creditors and contributories of the company known to the official receiver or identified in the statement of affairs. If the official receiver thinks fit, he may cause an advertisement of the order to be given in one or more newspapers at least 14 days before the hearing but this should not be less than 7 days after the notice was served on the examinee unless the court orders to the contrary.[77]

16.30   At the public examination the official receiver; the liquidator; a special manager; any creditor who has tendered a proof; and any contributory may all take part and ask questions.[78] They may appear by

70   r 4.213(2).
71   rr 4.213(3) and 4.217(1).
72   r 4.213(4) and (5).
73   r 4.213(5) and (6).
74   s 133(3).
75   r 4.211(1).
76   r 4.211(3).
77   r 4.212.
78   s 133(4).

solicitor or counsel with the approval of the court and may, in any case, authorise someone else in writing to ask questions on their behalf.[79] The examinee has an unqualified right to be represented at the examination at his own expense and his solicitor or counsel may put to him such questions as the court allows to enable him to explain or qualify his answers and may make representations on his behalf.[80] The examinee is examined under oath and must answer all questions which the court allows to be put to him or puts to him itself.[81] A written record of the examination will usually be kept and the examinee shall sign and verify it by affidavit after reading it or having it read over to him.[82] It may then be used as evidence against the examinee of any statement made by him in the course of the examination.[83]

16.31 The court may adjourn the examination if criminal proceedings have been instituted against the examinee and the court is of the opinion that the continuation of the hearing will prejudice a fair trial.[84] There is also a general power for the court to adjourn the hearing to a fixed date or generally. If it is adjourned generally the court may on the application of the examinee or the official receiver fix a venue and give directions on the notice to be given of the resumed hearing.[85] If it is the examinee who applies for the resumption of a hearing adjourned generally he may be required to meet the cost of the notices and to deposit an amount for that purpose.[86] In no circumstances can the costs of the public examination fall on the official receiver personally.[87] They are normally met from the assets of the company.

16.32 After an order for a public examination has been made the court may punish non-attendance, for which there is no reasonable excuse, as a contempt of court.[88] It may also issue a warrant for the arrest of a person who fails to attend without reasonable excuse or someone whom there are reasonable grounds to believe has absconded or is about to abscond with a view to avoiding or delaying his examination. The warrant may also authorise the seizure of books, papers and other property in that person's possession and the court may authorise the detention of the person in custody and the retention of documents or property. These procedures operate in the same way as they do for a private examination.[89]

---

79 r 4.125(2).
80 r 4.215(3).
81 r 4.215(1).
82 r 4.215(4).
83 r 4.215(5).
84 r 4.215(6).
85 r 4.216(1) and (2).
86 r 4.216(3).
87 r 4.217(2).
88 s 134(1).
89 s 134(2) and (3).

16.33 If the examinee suffers from some mental disorder or physical affliction or disability making him unfit to undergo or attend the examination the court may stay the order or give directions for the place and manner in which it is to be carried out.[90] It may take place at a hospital bedside or at the home of the examinee. An application to this effect can be made by a person appointed by a court to represent the examinee; a relative or friend of the examinee; or the official receiver.[91] If it is made by someone other than the official receiver, at least 7 days' notice of the application shall be given to the official receiver and the liquidator; a deposit certified by the official receiver, sufficient to cover the additional costs of any examination that may be ordered on the application, must be given to him; and unless the examinee is a patient under the Mental Health Act 1983 the application must be supported by the affidavit of a doctor on the examinee's mental and physical condition. If the official receiver applies he may do so *ex parte* and produce evidence in the form of his own report.[92]

16.34 The present procedure for public examinations should make it easier for them to take place. It is no longer necessary for the official receiver to make a 'further report' alleging fraud before an order for a public examination can be made. In any case where such a proceeding is necessary to give publicity to the circumstances surrounding the demise of the company's business, or to collect assets, or form the basis for the official receiver's report on possible offences or malpractice, an order can be made. However, it is still unlikely that public examinations will be held in cases where the assets are inadequate to meet the cost of the proceeding.

16.35 In a voluntary liquidation it will still be possible for the court to order a public or a private examination as s 112(1) enables the court to make any order that it could have made in a compulsory liquidation.[93] That was the case under the previous law when a further report was required in a compulsory liquidation. The reasoning in the *Campbell Coverings* case is even more appropriate in the context of the present law.

DUTY OF THE LIQUIDATOR TO REPORT MATTERS TO THE AUTHORITIES

16.36 In order to assist in the enforcement of the obligations of company officers and others, the legislation imposes a duty on the liquidator to

90 r 4.214(1).
91 r 4.214(2).
92 r 4.21(3) and (4).
93 *Re Campbell Coverings Ltd (No 2)* [1954] 1 Ch 225.

report certain matters to those authorities capable of mounting a fuller investigation than it is possible for the liquidator to undertake. This acknowledges the limits on the ability of the liquidator to deal with matters in which a public interest requires prosecution or at least a full investigation. Even if the assets of the estate are sufficient to permit a full investigation it may not be in the interests of the creditors for them to be used in that way. In some cases, the public interest in upholding proper standards of commercial morality, and the interests of the creditors in maximising the assets available for distribution in the liquidation, will coincide. However, if there is no prospect of a contribution being made to the assets either by the setting aside of a challengeable transaction or by an order being made that a person should personally contribute to the assets because, for example, of their involvement in wrongful trading, the liquidator can hardly be expected to spend the assets of the estate in the pursuit of wrongdoers. This problem is resolved by the legislation by which a duty is imposed to report certain matters to public authorities and to co-operate with any investigation begun by them.

16.37   Certain reports are required from the liquidator as an integral part of the process of winding up the company. After the final creditors' meeting in a voluntary winding up the liquidator is required to send a copy of his account and a return of the fact that the meeting was held to the registrar of companies.[94] Similarly, notice of the final creditors' meeting must be given to the court and the registrar of companies in a compulsory liquidation.[95] During the course of any type of liquidation annual details of its progress must be sent to the registrar of companies.[96] Such reports to Companies House will be publicly available but are not in the hands of an authority that will use them for investigative purposes.

16.38   In a compulsory liquidation, there is an additional obligation on a liquidator other than the official receiver to co-operate with that officer by meeting his reasonable requirements for information, the chance to inspect books, papers and other records, and other assistance. The test for what must be supplied to the official receiver hinges on his reasonable requirements for the purpose of carrying out his function in relation to the winding up.[97] This obligation will clearly be useful in the investigation of the company's affairs but it does depend on the initiative coming from the official receiver. It is also restricted to cases of winding up by the court in which the official receiver does not act as liquidator.

94   ss 94(3) and 106(3).
95   s 172(8).
96   s 192, failure to do so can lead to a court order requiring compliance and imprisonment
     for contempt if it is disobeyed; *Re S & A Conversions Ltd* (1989) 4 BCC 384 CA.
97   s 143(2).

16.39 In all cases of compulsory liquidation the official receiver has the function of investigating the causes of the company's failure and the conduct of its affairs from its promotion onwards.[98] If he is not the liquidator the duty of the liquidator under s 143 ensures that the investigation can proceed. If he is liquidator the s 235 duty to co-operate with the officeholder and the devolution of the power of the court to enforce it to the liquidator will provide an important resource. In addition the power to institute, a private examination under s 236 as liquidator and a public examination under s 133 as official receiver, are likely to be important.

16.40 In addition to these safeguards, s 218(1) empowers the court, on the application of any person interested in the liquidation or on its own motion, to direct the liquidator to refer any matter to the Director of Public Prosecutions if it appears to the court that any past or present officer of the company, or any member of it, has been guilty of a criminal offence in relation to it. Presumably no more than reasonable grounds for suspicion need be established to obtain such an order. Although the section is not expressly limited to circumstances in which the official receiver is not the liquidator, it is most likely to be used on the court's own motion in such cases. It does however give creditors or contributories the chance to challenge a decision by the liquidator, whoever he is, not to refer matters to the Director of Public Prosecutions.

16.41 A duty is imposed by s 218(2), on a liquidator other than the official receiver in a compulsory liquidation, to inform the official receiver of any offence which it appears to him has been committed by a past or present officer or a member of the company in relation to the company. This ensures that the oficial receiver has the necessary information on which to base an investigation of the alleged offence or to decide to call in the Director of Public Prosecutions.

16.42 In a voluntary winding up it is always possible for the official receiver, the Secretary of State or a disgruntled creditor or member to petition for a winding up order if the liquidator is not regarded as having investigated the company's affairs with sufficient diligence.[99] Since the liquidator will be a qualified insolvency practitioner this should rarely occur for reasons other than the absence of assets but the conversion of the liquidation into a compulsory one will bring into play the powers and duties of the official receiver, as well as the expertise and resources which are available to him but perhaps not to a private sector liquidator.

---

98 s 132(1).
99 See ch 14.

16.43 However if the liquidation remains voluntary slightly different procedures can be used to investigate wrongdoing. Section 218(4) imposes an obligation on the liquidator in a voluntary liquidation to report apparent offences by past or present officers or by members to the Director of Public Prosecutions rather than the official receiver. The report must be made forthwith and the duty of the liquidator extends to furnishing the Director with any information and any facilities for the inspection and copying of documents that he requires. The only limitation on this duty is that the information or documents must be in the possession or under the control of the liquidator and must relate to the matter in question. This wide investigatory power exists without the need for anything other than a requirement on the part of the Director of Public Prosecutions. The court has power to direct the liquidator to make such a report if he has failed to do so and a report made after the direction gives rise to the same powers on the part of the Director of Public Prosecutions and the Secretary of State as a report made under s 218(4).[100]

16.44 A further weapon at the disposal of the Director is his power to refer a matter, on which he has received a report under s 218(4) or 218 (5), to the Secretary of State for Trade and Industry who is then obliged to investigate it.[101] As part of that investigation process the Secretary of State may use all the powers that an inspector appointed under the Companies Act 1985 would have.[102] This enables him to investigate the group of companies, of which the one in liquidation forms a part, to require the production of documents and the appearance of corporate officers and agents, to examine on oath, to call for details of directors' bank accounts in certain circumstances and to have any obstruction of his investigation dealt with as contempt of court.[103] Any answers given by a person to questions put in such an investigation may be used as evidence against him.[104]

16.45 In any case in which a report or reference is made under s 218 and a criminal prosecution by the Director of Public Prosecutions or the Secretary of State follows, a duty is imposed on the liquidator and all agents and officers of the company past and present to give all the assistance in connection with the prosecution that they reasonably can to the Director or the Secretary of State. This obligation is expressly extended to any solicitor, banker or auditor of the company even if they are not its officers. it does not, however, extend to the defendant in the criminal proceedings.[105]

100 s 218(5).
101 s 218(5)(a).
102 ss 218(5)(b) and 219(1).
103 See ss 433–436 Companies Act 1985.
104 s 219(2) Insolvency Act 1986.
105 s 219(3).

16.46 The court may direct that assistance be given on the application of the Secretary of State or the Director. A liquidator against whom such an application is made may be ordered to bear its costs personally unless his failure to comply was the result of the absence of sufficient company assets for him to do so.[106] In the case of a solicitor the issue of professional legal privilege should not arise in this context as assistance to the authorities in the prosecution of those guilty of offences against the company cannot be a breach of his obligations to the company. It is the company's solicitor who is required to assist, not the solicitor of its officers or members. The police will also have a role in the investigation of crimes committed against the company and they will operate in conjunction with the Director of Public Prosecutions and the Department of Trade and Industry.

ACCOUNTS AND THE HANDLING OF MONIES

16.47 In addition to the requirements as regards records and accounts imposed on all insolvency practitioners and dealt with in chapter 10, a liquidator has specific and detailed duties imposed upon him. Those duties involve the use of the Insolvency Services Account (particularly in a compulsory liquidation) and the maintenance of accounts and records of the liquidation process as well as any continuation by the liquidator of the company's business.

The Insolvency Services Account

16.48 Sections 403 to 409 of the Insolvency Act 1986 continue the system of an Insolvency Services Account at the Bank of England which existed before the reform of the law. The purpose of the system is to finance the running of the Insolvency Service by the interest that accrues on the monies deposited in the account. The effect of this is that creditors bear the cost of the system to the extent that it is financed in this way. It is arguable that the community at large should meet this cost through the Treasury or that those who use companies should meet it through an addition to the fee for company registrations. However, since the 1986 reform the old system has been continued without substantial revision. The main significance of this system for the process of liquidation is the obligation imposed on liquidators to use the Insolvency Services Account. The duties involved vary according to whether the winding up is compulsory or voluntary.

16.49 In a compulsory liquidation the liquidator is required to pay all

---

106 s 219(4).

money received by him as such in the course of carrying out his functions without any deductions into the Insolvency Services Account kept by the Secretary of State for Trade and Industry at the Bank of England.[107] Remittances are to be sent through the bank Giro system or direct to the Bank of England, with the appropriate form from the department of Trade and Industry, once every 14 days or forthwith if £5000 or more has been received.[108] The only exception to this rule in a compulsory winding up occurs if the liquidator chooses to exercise his power to carry on the business of the company. In that case he may be authorised by the Secretary of State to open a local bank account and to make payments into and out of the bank specified in the authorisation, instead of the Insolvency Services Account, up to a limit laid down by the DTI.[109] A local bank account must be a current account with a bank in England and Wales recognised as such under the Banking Act 1987 and must be held in the locality in which the business is carried on, or in the neighbourhood of the district in respect of which the court which made the winding up order has jurisdiction.[110] Before granting an authorisation the Secretary of State must be satisfied that an administrative advantage will be derived from the existence of such an account.[111]

16.50 A separate account must be opened for each insolvent company and money provided or a specific purpose must be clearly identifiable in a separate account. Monies received for the purpose for which the account was opened may be paid into the loal bank account of the company to which they relate instead of the Insolvency Service Account. Receipts connected with the business of the company may be put through the account authorised for that purpose but any other receipts in the course of the liquidation (eg the proceeds of the sale of assets not sold in the course of business) may not.[112] The liquidator must keep proper records of all money paid into or out of local bank account and this includes documentary evidence.[113] Any surplus over the authorised limit must be paid into the Insolvency Services Account forthwith as must the whole balance on the account if the authorisation is revoked, or the liquidator vacates office or ceases to carry on the business of the company.[114] A certificate of the balance standing to the credit of the company in the

---

107   reg 4(1) of the Insolvency Regulations 1986 (SI 1986 no 1994) as amended by SI 1987 no 1959. See ss 403 to 410 of the Insolvency Act 1986 on the administration of the Insolvency Services Account by the Secretary of State.
108   *Ibid* reg 4(2) to (4).
109   reg 6(1).
110   reg 2(1).
111   reg 6(1).
112   reg 6(2) and (3).
113   reg 6(4).
114   reg 6(5) and (6).

Insolvency Services Account can be obtained by the liquidator on written application to the Secretary of State.[115] A breach of the rules regarding the payment of money into the Insolvency Services Account which is not explained to the satisfaction of the Secretary of State results in an obligation on the liquidator to pay interest at the rate of 20% per annum on the amount which he failed to pay in and liability for any expenses occasioned as a result of his default.[116]

16.51   In a voluntary liquidation the rules impose a less onerous obligation on the liquidator in relation to the use of the Insolvency Services Account. He is required to pay into the Account the balance of funds in his hands or under his control relating to the company (including unclaimed or undistributed assets or dividend) which he does not consider that he needs to retain for the immediate purposes of the liquidation. This obligation arises at the expiration of each 6 month period after the date of his appointment and the payment must be made within 14 days of the end of the 6 months.[117] By judicious management of the funds he handles the liquidator in a voluntary winding up may avoid the need to make any payments into the Account at all.

16.52   Money held in the Account may be used for the payment of the expenses of insolvency proceedings or by way of distribution and on the written application of the liquidator the Secretary of State may either authorise payment to the liquidator or direct that cheques be issued for delivery by the liquidator to the person to whom the payments are to be made.[118] A balance can be certified at the request of the liquidator in the same way as monies held in the Account in a compulsory liquidation.[119]

Administrative and financial records and audits

16.53   Reg 8 of the Insolvency Regulations 1986 lays down the requirements applicable in all liquidations regarding administrative records.[120] The liquidator is required to prepare and keep such records in relation to each company for which he acts. They must contain:

(a) the minutes of the proceedings at any meeting of creditors and contributories including a record of every resolution passed at the meeting;

---

115   reg 11.
116   reg 7.
117   reg 24.
118   reg 25.
119   reg 29 and 11.
120   reg 26 applies it to voluntary liquidations.

(b) the minutes of the proceedings at any meeting of the liquidation committee;

(c) the record of every resolution passed at any meeting of the liquidation committee;

(d) a copy of every resolution passed by post and a note that the concurrence of the liquidation committee was obtained;[121]

(e) any other matters which may be necessary to give an accurate record of his administration.

16.54   In a compulsory liquidation the liquidator is required to prepare and keep separate financial records for each company in respect of which he acts and must enter all receipts and payments in them from day to day.[122] If he carries on the business of the company he must keep separate trading accounts (including details of local bank account transactions) and incorporate weekly totals of receipts and payments in the overall liquidation accounts kept under reg 9(1).[123] The overall financial records must be submitted to the liquidation committee as they require and if they are dissatisfied with the accounts they may seek an audit by complaining with reasons to the Secretary of State.[124] The records must be retained six years after the last liquidator leaves office. Previous liquidators must pass them to their successors.[124A] This system places control of the finances of the liquidation in the hands of the liquidation committee even in a compulsory liquidation. Copies of the accounts must be sent to any creditor or contributory and to any director of the company in liquidation at their request free of charge within 14 days of the later of the accounts being sent to the Secretary of State under reg 12 or of the liquidator's receipt of the request.[125]

16.55   Each year during the tenure of the liquidator in a compulsory winding up, he must send his accounts to the Secretary of State in Form 1 accompanied by bank statements relating to any local bank account being used.[126] The first accounts must be accompanied by a summary of the statement of affairs showing realised assets and the reasons for the non realisation of any assets not realised.[127] If no statement of affairs has been submitted he must send a summary of all known assets and the state their realisation has reached.[128] The Secretary of State may require that the

121   r 4.167 of the Insolvency Rules 1986 provides for this.
122   reg 9(1) Insolvency Regulations 1986.
123   reg 10.
124   reg 9(2).
124A   reg 10A.
125   reg 13.
126   reg 12(1) and (2).
127   reg 12(3).
128   reg 12(4).

accounts submitted be audited and whether or not he does so the liquidator must be able to produce any vouchers, information, accounts, books and other records on demand at his own premises if necessary.[129] The authorisation of the official receiver is required for the destruction or disposal of the company's books, papers and other records in a compulsory liquidation but providing this is obtained the destruction can take place at any time.[130] In a voluntary winding up the liquidator may destroy these documents at any time after the expiration of one year from the date of dissolution of the company.[131] The accounts must be sent within 30 days of the end of each 12 month period after the liquidator takes office.[132] When the liquidator leaves office the last accounts covering the period since previous accounts were sent must be sent within 14 days of the date on which he vacates office.[133]

16.56 In a creditors' voluntary winding up the liquidation committee can determine the financial records that the liquidator is required to keep. If there is no liquidation committee the creditors make this decision. The records he is required to keep must have all receipts and payments entered including any relating to the Insolvency Services Account. Those records must be submitted to the committee, or the creditors if there is no committee, when they require them for inspection.[134] If he is required to do so by the Secretary of State, the liquidator in a voluntary winding up must send him an account of all his receipts and payments as liquidator in relation to the company. Each such account must be certified by the liquidator and the Secretary of State may insist that it be audited. Whether or not an audit is required, the liquidator must produce on demand for the DTI any vouchers, information, books, accounts or other records of the company—at the liquidator's own premises if necessary.[135]

16.57 The regulations clearly require that comprehensive accounts be kept as all payments and receipts must be entered up but the format is left to the liquidation committee or the creditors' meeting. If the liquidator in a creditors' voluntary winding up carries on the company's business the rules in reg 10 apply as regards the maintenance of separate accounts for the business and the entry of totals in the main liquidation accounts.[136]

16.58 Creditors, contributories and directors of the company in volun-

129 reg 12(7).
130 reg 14.
131 reg 32.
132 reg 12(5).
133 reg 12(6).
134 reg 27.
135 reg 30.
136 reg 28.

tary liquidation are entitled on request to be sent, free of charge, a copy of the statement sent to the registrar of companies under s 192 of the Insolvency Act 1986.[137] The copy is to be sent within 14 days of his receipt of the request or of it being sent to the registrar, whichever is later.[138]

Unclaimed funds and payments of dividend

16.59 In all liquidations, whether compulsory or voluntary, all monies in the hands of the liquidator or former liquidator at the date of the dissolution of the company, or the earlier vacation of office by the liquidator, which represent unclaimed or undistributed company assets or dividends, or other sums due to members as such, must be paid forthwith into the Insolvency Services Account.[139] Any person seeking to claim such monies may apply to the Secretary of State who will make a payment on production of the evidence he requires. An appeal lies to the court against a refusal of the Secretary of State to make such a payment.[140]

16.60 In a voluntary liquidation the liquidator is required to give the Secretary of State particulars of any money in his hands or under his control representing unclaimed or undistributed assets, dividends or other sums due to members as such within 14 days of being requested to do so. The details required by the Secretary of State can be any needed to assist the him in ascertaining or getting in any money payable into the Insolvency Services Account. The liquidator may be required to certify the particulars that he furnishes. This duty applies to current and former liquidators whether or not the company has been dissolved.[141] The winding up is not concluded by the dissolution of the company until such amounts have been paid into the Account.[142] Money on deposit at interest or invested will be regarded as being under the control of the liquidator for this purpose.[143]

Investments

16.61 The monies held in the Insolvency Services Account which the liquidator does not need for the immediate purposes of the winding up can be invested in government securities credited to the account of that company if the liquidator requests the Secretary of State, in writing, to do so. The investments made may then be realised at the request of the

137 See reg 31(1).
138 reg 31(2).
139 reg 16 applied to voluntary liquidations by reg 33.
140 reg 17 applied to voluntary liquidations by reg 33.
141 reg 35.
142 Insolvency Rules 1986 r 4.223(2).
143 Insolvency Regulations 1986 reg 18(8).

liquidator when the money is required for the immediate purposes of the winding up. The written request of the liquidator is sufficient authority for the investment or sale by the Secretary of State.[144] A new request has to be made if additional sums paid into the Insolvency Services Account to the credit of the company are to be invested—and this applies to interest on or the proceeds of existing investments which must be paid into the account. Interest is paid on sums in respect of which notice is given at the rate of $3\frac{1}{2}$ per cent per annum on any amount in excess of £2000 standing to the credit of the company in the Account.[145] These provisions apply to all liquidations but in the case of a company being wound up voluntarily the regulations expressly require the liquidator to realise other investments that he holds if he reaches a point at which he is required to pay that money into the Insolvency Services Account because it is not necessary to retain that part of the funds for the immediate purposes of the liquidation after the end of a 6 month anniversary of his appointment. Any money invested or deposited at interest by him is deemed to be money under his control for the purpose of the regulations.[146] However any money invested in government securities may be transferred to the control of the Secretary of State instead of being realised if the Secretary of State agrees. The securities may then be realised by the Secretary of State and the proceeds paid into the Insolvency Services Account if the money they represent is required for the immediate purposes of the liquidation. They effectively form part of the assets in the Account.[147]

SUMMARY PROCEEDINGS

16.62 The liquidator in the process of winding up can take summary proceedings to enforce a number of liabilities against persons who owe obligations to the company. This can be distinguished from his power to commence proceedings in the name of the company.[148] This method of proceeding is faster and more straightforward than the use of the company name and can be done without the sanction required in a compulsory liquidation for an action on behalf of the company and in its name.[149] The liabilities that can be enforced summarily are:

(a) certain payments by contributories;

---

144   reg 18(1)(2) and (3).
145   reg 18(4) to (7).
146   reg 18(8).
147   reg 18(8) and (9).
148   See para 15.99 *supra*.
149   See ch 15 and Insolvency Act 1986 sch 4 para 4.

(b) delivery of books papers and other property;
(c) the liability of persons guilty of 'misfeasance'.

Payments by contributories etc

16.63   Rule 4.205(2) permits the liquidator to apply to the court for an order to enforce payment, by a contributory, of an amount due on a call after the call has been properly made and notice has been served on the contributories (see paras 17.20–17.29 for the procedure for making calls). Apart from this specific provision relating to the payment of unpaid capital which has been called, it is possible for the liquidator to enforce summarily the liability of a person on the list of contributories to pay any money due from him to the company other than money due on a call.[150] This power can be used against a personal representative listed as a contributory. In the case of an unlimited company or a contributory to a limited company who is a director or manager whose liability is unlimited, a set off is allowed of any amount due to the contributory as a member of the company other than as dividend or profit.[151] In the case of any company, money due on any account to a contributory can be set off if all the creditors have been paid in full together with interest at the official rate. These limits on the right of set off available to a contributory only apply when this procedure is used. The courts tend to restrict the use a liquidator can make of the summary remedy. It can be used to recover dividends paid to contributories out of capital.[152] Amounts paid to contributories by the liquidator in ignorance of liabilities of the company, which can only be met by the use of the money paid out to a contributory, may also be collected under this power if the contributory was aware of the company's unpaid debts.[153]

16.64   However, although the section does not expressly limit the sums which can be claimed under it to amounts due from the contributory as such, the fact that a contributory is not entitled to a right of set off in respect of unpaid capital or amounts claimed on the basis of an excessive distribution but can claim such a right in respect of other debts, would make it inequitable to allow him to be summarily dealt with under the section for the latter debts as the section clearly limits the right of set off when it is used.[154] Since the case of *Re Marlborough Club Company*[155] lays down that a member who has fully paid his shares may not be added to the list of contributories simply to enable the liquidator to use the summary

150   Insolvency Act 1986 s 149(1).
151   s 149(2).
152   *Re Mercantile Trading Co (Stringer's case)* (1869) 4 Ch App 475.
153   *Re Aidall Ltd* [1933] 1 Ch 323.
154   *Re Whitehouse & Co* (1878) 9 Ch D 595.
155   (1868) LR 5 Eq 365.

procedure to claim other debts from him, the courts are unlikely to allow the liquidator to use that method to recover a debt unconnected with his status as a contributory against someone who happens to be on the list because his shares are partly paid.[156]

Enforcing the delivery of books, papers etc

16.65   We have noted the provisions of s 234 regarding the power of the court to order a person to hand over or transfer property, books, papers or records to the office holder. This is an application that can be made summarily by the liquidator in a voluntary winding up. In a compulsory winding up the power to make such an order is conferred on the liquidator or provisional liquidator by Rule 4.185. In such a liquidation the court need not be requested to make an order to place the person under a specific obligation. The liquidator will do that and will only have recourse to the court for the enforcement of the order that he has made. The section applies to all officeholders—administrators, provisional liquidators and administative receivers as well as liquidators—and is wider than the previous provision which named certain persons as being subject to the obligation by reference to their relationship with the company.[157] The new provision applies to anyone who has property, to which the company appears to be entitled, in his possesion or control regardless of his relationship with the company and, as has been noted, applies to all officeholders.

Misfeasance summonses

16.66   Section 212 of the Insolvency Act 1986 provides a summary method of recovering money or property or obtaining compensation on behalf of a company in liquidation. The section is the successor to a provision which has long existed in company law and which was last found in s 631 of the Companies Act 1985. It applies only during the course of the winding up of a company.

The applicants

16.67   An application can be made under s 212 by the official receiver, the liquidator, or any creditor or contributory of the company.[158] Although a contributory can only apply with the leave of the court he may apply with such leave even if he will fail to benefit from any order that the court may make because, for example, even after the order the liabilities of the company will exceed its assets.[159] In this respect the section amends the

---

156   See Pennington, "Company Law", 5th ed p 910.
157   See s 551 of the Companies Act 1985.
158   s 212(3).
159   s 212(5).

pre-existing law which only permitted such an application if the contributory stood to gain from an order.[160] The section can be used by these applicants in either a voluntary or a compulsory liquidation. The section provides a means whereby the liabilities of certain people to the company can be enforced by the members and the creditors as well as the liquidator or the official receiver. The difficulties presented to the member by the rule in *Foss v Harbottle* can be avoided if the company is in liquidation. The use of this procedure by the liquidator or the official receiver is likely to be preceded by a public or private examination of the respondent which will assist in the process of gathering information for use as evidence in the misfeasance proceedings.[161]

The respondents

16.68 The section provides for the use of a misfeasance summons against a wide range of respondents. The procedure can be used against any person who:

"(a) is or has been an officer of the company;
(b) has acted as liquidator, administrator or administrative receiver of the company, or
(c) not being a person falling within (a) or (b), is or has been concerned, or has taken part, in the promotion, formation or management of the company".[162]

16.69 An 'officer' of a company is defined in s 744 of the Companies Act 1985 as including 'a director, manager or secretary'. The word 'director' includes 'any person occupying the position of director, by whatever name called'.[163] It seems that the expression 'manager' includes any person who exercises a supervisory control related to the general administration of the company or which reflects its general policy.[164] Such a person is an officer without being on the board. An auditor has been held to be an officer of the company for this purpose.[165] A receiver and manager does not fit into the category of either officer or manager as his work in managing the company is done on behalf of the debenture holders and not the company.[166] However, an administrative receiver will now fall within s 212(1)(b).

16.70 It has been held in the past that *de facto* directors who acted as directors without being properly appointed came within this category if their misfeasance resulted in loss to the company.[167] Similarly, the

---

160   *Cavendish Bentinck v Fenn* (1887) 12 App Cas 652.
161   See paras 16.10 to 16.35 *supra* re private and public examinations.
162   s 212(1).
163   Companies Act 1985 s 741(1).
164   *Re a Company* [1980] Ch 138 (reversed on other grounds by [1981] AC 374).
165   *Re London and General Bank* [1895] 2 Ch 166.
166   *Re B Johnson & Co (Builders) Ltd* [1955] 1 Ch 634.
167   *Coventry and Dixon's Case* (1880) 14 Ch D 660.

procedure can be used against a retired director who is a party to the misfeasance.[168] However, where a person who has taken part in the management of the company does not fall within the definition of a director or manager he will in any event be caught by s 212(1)(c). A solicitor paid by means of a fixed salary will fall within the definition of an officer[169] but not one who is used as advisor or agent in the usual way.[170] Other independent agents or consultants will not be officers.[171] The question of whether a business consultant or other independent agent takes part in the management of the company and may thus be made a respondent under s 212(1)(c) will be a question of fact. The courts would not allow a company to avoid the section by hiring independent contractors from firms of management consultants to perform the functions of managers or directors. The actual function performed by the individual will be crucial and the test is likely to hinge on the authority conferred on him in practice to make decisions or participate in policy making on managerial matters. The section cannot be used against an employee who did not have such a role even if, because of his relationship to the controlling director he has received substantial amounts of company money. Such a person has to be pursued on the basis of a constructive trust.[172]

16.71   An application may not be made against an administrator or a liquidator after he has obtained his release without the leave of the court.[173] Any promoter of the company will be a possible respondent under s 212(1)(c) as will others with a significant role in the formation of the company. Independent professionals acting as agent or adviser are not likely to be included but those who, for example, engage in the sale of property to the company while also assisting in its creation will be covered by the section. A promoter who makes secret profits may be the respondent in misfeasance proceedings.[174]

The rights enforceable
16.72   The misfeasance summons procedure can be used when in the course of the winding up of a company it appears that a person in one of the categories who may be made respondents:

> "has misapplied or retained, or become accountable for, any money or other property of the company, or been guilty of any misfeasance or breach of any fiduciary or other duty in relation to the company".[175]

---

168 *Curtis's Furnishing Stores Ltd v Freedman* [1966] 1 WLR 1219.
169 *Re Liberator Permanent Benefit Building Society* (1894) 71 LT 406.
170 *Re Great Western Forest of Dean Coal Consumers Co Ltd* (1886) 31 Ch 42.
171 *Openshaw v Fletcher* (1916) 32 TLR 372.
172 *Re Clasper Group Services Ltd* (1988) 4 BCC 673.
173 s 212(4).
174 See, for example, *Gluckstein v Barnes* [1900] AC 240.
175 s 212(1).

This contrasts with the wording of s 631 of the Companies Act 1985 which reflected the wording of the provision as it had existed over the years. It applied where a person in the class of potential respondents had:

> "misapplied or retained or become liable or accountable for any money or property of the company, or been guilty of any misfeasance or breach of trust in relation to the company".[176]

The one substantial change is the amendment of 'any misfeasance or breach of trust' to 'any misfeasance or breach of any fiduciary or other duty'. It will be submitted below that the change does affect the scope of the section, particularly in relation to negligence. However, subject to that significant change much of the case law that grew up around the provision in the past remains applicable to s 212.

16.73 It is clear from the wording of the section and from the case law that it is only the claims of the company which can be the subject of a misfeasance summons. Any misfeasance or breach of duty must be in relation to the company. Where the company does not suffer loss and the behaviour complained of would not be susceptible to action in the courts by writ the misfeasance summons procedure cannot be used either. This rule precludes an action for a wrong such as acting as a director without holding qualifying shares.[177] Similarly, if a breach of fiduciary duty or misfeasance is against a contributory personally the procedure cannot be used by the aggrieved person. The sale of shares in a company being reconstructed which belong in equity to a member does not give the member the right to use the misfeasance procedure against the liquidator responsible for the sale—that would amount to allowing the enforcement of a personal right, not one which belongs to the company.[178] This underlines the fact that while the section can be used by individual creditors or (with leave) contributories, they can only use it to enforce certain rights of the company.

16.74 Even in relation to claims which are those of the company, it is clear that the section is procedural and does not, in itself, create new rights or add to existing obligations. This is clear from its wording which deals with misapplication or retention of, and accountability for, company property. All of these concepts presuppose an underlying set of legal rules defining company property; the nature and extent of misapplication of it or accountability for it; and the circumstances in which its retention is unjustifiable. Similarly the references to 'misfeasance' and breach of duty presuppose existing definitions. The case law has always followed this view of the section:

---

176   s 631(1).
177   *Coventry and Dixon's Case* (1880) 14 Ch D 660.
178   *Re Hill's Waterfall Estate & Gold Mining Co* [1896] 1 Ch 947.

"it has been settled and I think rightly settled that [s 165 of the Companies Act 1862] creates no new offence, and that it gives no new rights, but only provides a summary and efficient remedy in respect of rights which apart from that section might have been vindicated either at law or in equity".[179]

"The acts which are covered by the section are acts which are wrongful, according to the established rules of law or equity."[180]

However, the description of the remedy provided by the section as summary does not mean that it is limited to simple or straightforward cases which do not give rise to complex issues of law or fact. This early view was discredited in *Re Mercantile Trading Co (Stringer's case)* since it would act as an incentive to respondents to raise spurious difficulties to ensure that some fuller proceedings were required.[181]

16.75 Similarly, although the section itself does not create new rights and liabilities, those new obligations and rights created by virtue of the winding up process itself can be the subject of misfeasance proceedings.[182] If the applicant can show, for example, a preference or a transaction at an undervalue an order can be made in the company's favour on the summons despite the fact that such rights can only exist as a result of the commencement of the winding up itself, or the previous existence of an administration order. This remains a right of the company although it could not exist apart from the insolvency proceedings to which it is subject.[183]

16.76 The concept of a misfeasance and, under the old provision, of a breach of trust has been elaborated by the case law. Under s 212 a breach of a fiduciary duty is likely to have a similar meaning to 'breach of trust'. It has been said that:

"there is no such distinct wrongful act known to the law as 'misfeasance' ".[184]

It was held in that case that common law negligence did not fall within the section as then drafted but it was said that a wrongful act involving the misapplication of property in the hands of the respondent would be covered, as would conduct falling between those two ends of a spectrum of behaviour. The section was said to be limited to situations where:

"there has been something in the nature of a breach of duty by an officer of the company as such which has caused pecuniary loss to the company. Breach of

---

179 *Cavendish Bentinck v Fenn* (1887) 12 App Cas 652 per Lord Macnaghten at 669.
180 *Re B Johnson & Co (Builders) Ltd* [1955] 1 Ch 634 per Evershed MR at 648.
181 (1869) LR 4 Ch App 475 per Sir C J Selwyn LJ at 486.
182 *Re National Funds Assurance Co* (1878) 10 Ch D 118 at 125.
183 See eg *Re Washington Diamond Mining Co* [1893] 3 Ch 95.
184 Per Evershed MR in *Re B Johnson & Co (Builders) Ltd* [1955] 1 Ch 634 at 648.

duty of course would include a misfeasance or a breach of trust in the stricter sense, and the section will apply to a true case where there has been retention of money or property which the officer was bound to have paid or returned to the company".[185]

Thus the section does not apply to every claim of the company against those in the list of potential respondents. There is a need to establish some conduct in the nature of a breach of trust or some other breach of duty involving the wrongful retention of the company's property. The payment of dividends out of capital, granting a fraudulent preference and such breaches of the fiduciary duties of directors and promoters as the making of secret profits have been held in the past to be within the section.[186] The last mentioned behaviour may either be regarded as a misfeasance by breach of trust or the retention of the profit which in equity is the property of the company. It is clear that agreement to acts that are unlawful in themselves, under the *ultra vires* rule, will also make a director liable under the section as such decisions are a breach of the duties of directors.

16.77   It is clear that s 212 applies to any breach of fiduciary duty by a director or some other person in the class of potential respondents. It has always been accepted that there is no need to prove fraud to establish the right to bring an action under the provision and it has been said that 'misfeasance' does not necessarily involve moral turpitude but applies to any misappropriation or wrongful retention of company property.[187] The fiduciary obligations of directors are owed to the company and involve acting *bona fide* in the interests of the company. There is now no doubt that in a case of clear insolvency the interests of the company include the interests of creditors and consequently a liquidator has the choice of using either s 212 or an action by the company to recover money that was misappropriated.[188]

16.78   It would seem that the wording of s 212 may open up the possibility of an action for negligence by the use of the section. This has been held not to be available on the basis of the absence of any separate legal concept of misfeasance and the need for a breach of fiduciary obligation or some other wrongful act involving the misapplication or wrongful retention of company property. However, the present section refers to a breach of a

---

185   Per Maugham J in *Re Etic Ltd* [1928] Ch 861 at 873, cited with approval by Evershed MR in *Re B Johnson & Co (Builders) Ltd* [1955] 1 Ch 634 at 649.
186   See *Re National Funds Assurance* (note 182 above); *Re Washington Diamond Mining Co* (note 183 above).
187   See *Re Sale Hotel and Botanical Gardens Ltd ex p Hesketh* (1898) 78 LT 368 at 370, and *Selangor United Rubber Estates Ltd v Craddock* [1967] 1 WLR 1168 at 1173–4.
188   *Winkworth v Edward Baron Development Co Ltd* [1987] BCLC 193 HL; and *Liquidator of West Mercia Safetywear Ltd v Dodd* [1988] BCLC 250.

fiduciary or other duty in relation to the company. It is hard to see how one can argue for the interpretation of the phrase 'other duty' in this context as being limited to duties of a fiduciary nature. A duty can only be 'other' than a fiduciary duty if it is different from it. On the construction of the new section an action for a breach of the duty of care in negligence may be possible by this means. Similarly an action for the breach of a statutory duty by a director, liquidator or other officeholder may now be possible by means of a misfeasance summons. Such actions will only succeed where the breach of duty has resulted in some loss to the company as the remedies available take the form of restoring or accounting for property or money or contributing a sum as compensation. There is no reason why such remedies should be regarded as inappropriate in a case of negligence or of breach of statutory duty where loss has accrued to the company. Indeed the case law on the old section allowed a claim against a liquidator for paying an invalid claim in breach of statutory duty by negligent behaviour.[189] Negligence by an auditor which led to a misapplication of assets has been held to be within the scope of the remedy.[190] While it is true that in each of these cases there was a misapplication of company assets associated with the negligence it is hard to see why that should remain a requirement under the new section (if ever it was one). The section offers the remedies of compensation on the one hand and the return of property or an account for money on the other. The former is appropriate to a negligence claim. It also gives alternative circumstances in which the section can apply:

(a) guilt of a misfeasance,
(b) breach of fiduciary duty,
(c) breach of some other duty and,
(d) behaviour involving retaining, misapplying or becoming account-able for money or property.

This strongly suggests that conduct falling into any one of those categories is within the scope of the section as it now stands. For these reasons it is submitted that the new section opens up the possibility of a claim for negligence or breach of statutory duty against one of the potential respondents providing that the breach of duty occurred in relation to the company.

16.79 The only substantial argument against this view is that in an application by way of misfeasance summons no right of set off is available to the respondent for any amount due to him from the company in respect of

189 See *Re Windsor Steam Coal Co (1901) Ltd* [1929] 1 Ch 151.
190 *Re Kingston Cotton Mill Co (No 2)* [1896] 2 Ch 279.

the amount that he is ordered to pay.[191] However, the court has a discretion in respect of the order that it makes under s 212(3)(b) as the section lays down that the respondent may be ordered to contribute such sum as the court thinks just to the assets of the company by way of compensation in respect of the breach of duty. The court could order the payment of an amount which took account of any right of set off on which the respondent could have relied had the action been brought by writ. This would avoid any discrimination on the grounds of the procedure used.

16.80 The remedy of a misfeasance summons is no longer available after the dissolution of the company.[192] The provisions of the Limitation Act 1980 applicable to the proceedings will depend on the underlying claim being made; whether it be for breach of trust or negligence or on some other basis. This rule reflects the fact that no new rights are created by the section and the provisions applicable are those which deal with the underlying cause of action.

Orders available
16.81 The court is restricted by the wording of s 212 in the range of orders that it can make. Section 212(3) provides for the court, on application being made under the section, to examine the conduct of the respondent and:

> "compel him
> (a) to repay, restore or account for money or other property or any part of it, with interest at such rate as the court thinks just, or
> (b) to contribute such sum to the company's assets by way of compensation in respect of the misfeasance or breach of fiduciary or other duty as the court thinks just."

This excludes other forms of relief. Injunctive relief will not be available other than for the purposes set out in s 212(3)(a). It is not possible for the court to order the rescission of a contract.[193] Similarly an order to pay a debt due to the company is not possible as it is neither an order for the restoration or repayment of money or property nor the award of compensation for breach of duty.[194]

16.82 However where the court is awarding a 'just sum' as compensation under s 212(3)(b), it has a discretion over the amount to be awarded and need not award the amount that would have been payable if proceedings had been brought by writ rather than by misfeasance summons. This is clear from the wording of the section and is confirmed by a number of

---

191   *Re Anglo-French Co-operative Society ex p Pelly* (1882) 21 Ch D 492.
192   *Pulsford v Devenish* [1903] 2 Ch 625.
193   *Re Centrifugal Butter Co Ltd* [1913] 1 Ch 188.
194   *Re Etic Ltd* [1928] 1 Ch 861.

decisions in which this discretion was used. In the case of *Re Home and Colonial Insurance Co Ltd*[195] the liquidator was required only to pay an amount sufficient to meet the debts of the company rather than the amount he had paid out on a legally invalid insurance policy which the company's members would have honoured had the company been solvent and which was regarded as a liability for the purpose of the winding up resolution passed by the members.[196] This rule gives rise to a choice of action where a breach of duty comes within s 212. The court could not exercise a discretion to reduce the amount of damages payable if the action were brought by writ. However, once the company is in liquidation it will be a matter for the liquidator whether an action is brought in the name of the company for a breach of duty. A contributory or creditor may apply under s 212. If they wish proceedings to be brought in the name of the company they would have to seek an order forcing the liquidator to do this.[197] The summons may be dismissed without costs or costs may be awarded against the respondent even if there is no pecuniary loss to the company and no order is made.[198]

Procedure

16.83 It is likely that in many cases the evidence on which proceedings by way of misfeasance summons are based will be obtained by the use of a private or public examination.[199] The verified notes of the public examination of persons who were subjected to that procedure can be used as evidence against them in the misfeasance proceedings of any statement they made in the course of the examination.[200] Similarly the written record of a private examination under s 236 may be used in this way.[201] In addition any report of the official receiver made under s 132, in a winding up by the court, is *prima facie* evidence of the facts contained in it.[202] If the private examination shows that a person is indebted to the company the court can make an order under s 237(2) that the debt be paid. However, where the evidence is of some breach of duty or the retention of money or property the appropriate procedure will usually be by way of a misfeasance summons.

16.84 The particular nature of the matters which can be dealt with by the

195 [1930] 1 Ch 102.
196 See also *Re Sunlight Incandescent Gas Lamp Co* (1900) 16 TLR 535 and *Re VGM Holdings* [1942] Ch 235.
197 *Fargo Ltd v Godfroy* [1986] 3 All ER 279.
198 *Re Republic of Bolivia Exploration Syndicate Ltd* [1914] 1 Ch 139; and see *Halsbury's Laws* vol 7 para 1197.
199 See paras 16.10–35 above.
200 r 4.215(5).
201 r 9.4(7).
202 s 132(2) and r 7.9(3).

use of this procedure means that it is not possible for a respondent to use the third party procedure to join a person as a respondent and obtain a contribution or indemnity from them.[203] Among the respondents to the proceedings as brought by the applicant it is possible for the court to allow an indemnity when it makes its order.[204] The rules on the procedure for misfeasance summons are those laid down in Part VII of the Insolvency Rules 1986.[205]

THE LIQUIDATION COMMITTEE

16.85 The control of the liquidation process by the creditors is an essential part of every insolvent winding up. It takes place by means of the creditors' meetings which are required, by the Insolvency Act 1986, to be held at various stages of the process. In addition the creditors may wish to have a supervisory role in the period between creditors' meetings by means of a smaller and more effective body than the meeting of all creditors. It is for this reason that the legislation provides for the creation of a liquidation committee. This is the name now given to the body formerly known as the Committee of Inspection.

Appointment of the committee

16.86 In a creditors' voluntary liquidation the first meeting of creditors (held under s 98 of the Insolvency Act 1986) or any later creditors' meeting may decide to appoint a liquidation committee. The committee must have no less than three and no more than five members and will perform the functions conferred on it by the Act.[206] The company may nominate not more than five persons to serve on the committee either at the meeting at which they pass the winding up resolution or at a later meeting. The creditors have power to resolve that some or all of those persons should not serve and if they do so resolve the company nominees will not be committee members. This will be so unless the court directs otherwise and if an application is made to the court for such a direction it may appoint persons other than those chosen by the company.[207] This rule gives ultimate control to the creditors in the same way as the procedure which applies to the appointment of the liquidator.[208]

203   *Re A Singer & Co (Hat Manufacturers) Ltd* [1943] Ch 121.
204   *Re Morcambe Bowling Ltd* [1969] 1 WLR 133.
205   SI 1986 no 1925.
206   s 101 and r 4.152(2).
207   s 101(2) and (3).
208   See ch 15.

16.87 In a compulsory liquidation s 141 gives the decision whether a liquidation committee should be set up to the meetings of creditors and contributories called to appoint a liquidator.[209] The liquidator may call meetings of both creditors and contributories for this purpose at a later stage and can be required to do so by one tenth in value of the company's creditors.[210] In each case the meetings may establish the committee if they decide that one should be set up. If the meetings of the two groups do not agree on the issue of whether there should be a committee then a committee will be established providing one meeting has decided to do so.[211]

16.88 The official receiver has no power to summon meetings for the purpose of deciding to set up a committee and cannot be required to do so. At any time when he is the liquidator of the company the committee has no power or obligation to carry out its functions. In these circumstances its functions are carried out by the Secretary of State for Trade and Industry who also has that responsibility if there is no committee in a liquidation in which the official receiver is not the liquidator.[212]

16.89 If all the creditors in the liquidation are paid in full with interest, the liquidator's certificate to that effect must be filed in court in a compulsory liquidation or sent to the registrar of companies in a voluntary winding up.[213] From that time the creditor members of the liquidation committee leave office but the committee stays in existence until it is abolished by a meeting of contributories or until 28 days after the issue of the liquidator's certificate at which time it ceases to exist if there are fewer than three contributory members. The contributories have 28 days to save and take over the committee if there are not already at least three contributory members who remain in office. The committee is, however, unable to act in the 28 day period if it has fewer than three contributory members—it remains in a state of suspension.[214] The committee may be returned to full strength by the co-option of contributories by the liquidator or their appointment by a meeting of contributories.[215] All the rules on liquidation committees apply to a committee of contributories with the necessary amendments to take account of the absence of creditor members.[216]

16.90 The membership of the liquidation committee in a compulsory liquidation must consist of not more than five or less than three creditors

---

209 s 141(1).
210 s 141(2).
211 s 141(3).
212 s 141(4) and (5).
213 r 4.171(1)–(3).
214 r 4.171(5) and (6).
215 r 4.171(7).
216 r 4.171(8).

elected by the creditors' meeting and may include up to three contributories in a solvent winding up.[217] A solvent winding up for this purpose is one in which the company is being wound up on grounds other than its inability to pay its debts.[218] In a case where the meeting of creditors does not resolve to set up a liquidation committee or resolves not to do so a meeting of the contributories may appoint one of their number to apply to the court which may direct the liquidator to call a meeting of creditors which is treated as a s 141 meeting and which can decide to set up a committee and do so. If that meeting does not decide to set up a liquidation committee the contributories may do so and the committee shall consist of at least three and not more than five contributories.[219] It is only by the use of this procedure that contributories can serve on the liquidation committee of a company being wound up by the court on the basis that it is unable to pay its debts. It is unlikely that the procedure will be used often.

16.91 A member of the committee representing creditors must himself be a creditor. Such a member is qualified to serve so long as his debt is not fully secured and he has lodged a proof of it which has been neither wholly disallowed for voting purposes nor wholly rejected for the purposes of distribution.[220] A person whose proof has been allowed only in part for both purposes may serve. Corporate members may serve by means of a duly authorised representative holding a letter of authority signed on behalf of the corporate member.[221] A member representing the interests of contributories must be a contributory (see paras 17.03–17.10 for the definition of a contributory) although a member may be represented at meetings by a duly authorised person of his choice.[222]

16.92 It would seem that under the new rule it is still open to a creditor who is unrepresented on the committee to apply to the court for an order that a new creditors' meeting be convened with a view to giving him representation. This is only likely to succeed in exceptional circumstances and if the creditor was unable to be represented through no fault of his own. The example from the case law is of a creditor whose debt exceeded the aggregate of all other debts of the company and who was unable to attend the original creditors' meeting which appointed the committee because he was foreign and was unaware of the liquidation and had not proved his debt at that time[223] and where the committee had reached its maximum membership and no member was willing to retire. Such an application will

217   r 4.152(1).
218   r 4.151(b).
219   r 4.154.
220   r 4.152(3).
221   r 4.159(1) and (2).
222   See r 4.159.
223   See *Re Radford & Bright Ltd (No 1)* [1901] 1 Ch 272.

not be necessary if it is possible for the new member to be added to the committee by the operation of the normal rules.

16.93 The liquidation committee only comes into being with authority to act when the liquidator issues a certificate that it is duly constituted.[224] The certificate is issued after the chairman of the meeting (if that is not the liquidator) notifies the liquidator of the resolution to establish the committee and after the necessary minimum number of members has agreed to act. No-one may act as a member until they have agreed to do so. In a compulsory liquidation the certificate and any later amendments to it are filed in court and in a voluntary liquidation it is sent to the registrar of companies. Any change in the committee's membership is similarly filed or reported.[225]

Proceedings of the liquidation committee

16.94 The time and place of meetings of the liquidation committee is left to the liquidator in the first instance. He is required to call a meeting within three months of his appointment or of the establishment of the committee whichever is later and after that first meeting on dates specified by resolution of the committee at a previous meeting or within 21 days of receiving a request to call a meeting from a creditor member or his representative.[226] Notice of the time and place of the meeting must be given to every member of the committee by the liquidator unless this requirement is waived at or before the meeting. Such notice may be given to a member's representative who is designated for that purpose.[227] Meetings are chaired by the liquidator or his nominee; who must either be a qualified insolvency practitioner or an employee of the liquidator or his firm with experience of insolvency matters.[228] The quorum for meetings is two (in the case of a winding up by the court they must be creditor members) after notice has been duly given.[229]

16.95 For the purposes of participation in any of the business of the committee a member may be represented by a duly authorised representative who holds a letter of authority which must be produced to the chairman at his request on pain of exclusion if the authority appears to be deficient.[230] A member may not be represented by a corporate body or an

---

224 r 4.153.
225 r 4.153(2)–(8).
226 r 4.156.
227 r 4.156(3).
228 r 4.157.
229 r 4.158—this rule appears to take no account of committees established under r 4.154 by contributories.
230 r 4.159(1)–(3).

undischarged bankrupt or person subject to a composition or arrangement with his creditors and no one person can act as representative of more than one member at a time or as a member and a representative at the same time.[231]

16.96 Voting rights on the committee vary as between a committee in a compulsory liquidation and one which operates in a voluntary winding up. In all cases each committee member has one vote which may be cast by a representative. However, in an insolvent compulsory liquidation a resolution is passed by a majority of the creditor members who are present or represented and voting and the votes of the contributory members do not count although they are recorded. If the liquidation is effectively a solvent one and the committee consists entirely of contributories because it was set up under Rule 4.154 or the creditor members have left under Rule 4.171 after all debts have been paid in full all the members are treated as if they were creditor members and may have their votes counted. The resolutions passed by the committee must be recorded, signed by the chairman and retained as part of the records of the liquidation.[232] In a voluntary winding up a simple majority of all committee members is required and resolutions are to be similarly signed recorded and retained.[233]

16.97 Resolutions may be agreed by post. This is done by the liquidator sending a copy of a statement incorporating the proposed resolution to all committee members of their representatives designated for the purpose. If more than one resolution is proposed it must be possible to express support for or dissent from each one.[234] In the absence of a request from a committee member for the liquidator to convene a committee meeting the resolution is deemed to have been passed when the majority notify the liquidator in writing of their assent to it. In the case of a compulsory liquidation only creditor members of the committee may request a meeting and it is a majority of such members who must assent to the resolution. In a creditors' voluntary liquidation all members have the right to demand a meeting and to assent to the resolution.[235] This reflects the voting rights of the committee itself. In each case a copy of all resolutions passed in this way and note of the committee's concurrence must be kept with the liquidation records.[236] Rule 4.172A[237] validates the acts of the committee regardless of

---

231 r 4.159(4) and (5).
232 r 4.165.
233 r 4.166.
234 r 4.167(1) and (2).
235 r 4.167(3)–(6).
236 r 4.167(7).
237 Inserted by SI 1987 no 1919.

any defect in the appointment, election or qualifications of any member or member's representative or in the formalities of establishing the committee.

Vacation of membership

16.98 A person's membership of the committee may end by resignation in writing delivered to the liquidator. Alternatively, he can be removed by a resolution of a meeting of creditors in the case of a creditor member, or a meeting of contributories in the case of a contributory member. Fourteen days' notice of the intention to move the resolution is required in either case.[238] Membership terminates automatically if a member becomes bankrupt or compounds or arranges with his creditors but in the case of bankruptcy the trustee replaces the member on the committee.[239] Absence from three consecutive committee meetings and a failure to be represented at them terminates membership unless the committee resolves at the third meeting not to apply the rule.[240] In the case of a creditor member membership terminates automatically if he ceases to be a creditor or is found never to have been one.[241]

16.99 Vacancies on the committee can be left unfilled if the liquidator and a majority of the remaining members representing the same interest (creditors for creditor members and contributories for contributory members) agree so long as the total number of members does not fall below the minimum of three.[242] Alternatively the vacancy may be filled by a creditor or contributory (as the case may be) chosen by the liquidator with the agreement of the majority of creditors or contributories and the consent of the individual nominated.[243] A third possible course of action is for a meeting of the whole body of creditors or contributories to be called with at least 14 days' notice of the purpose of the meeting to resolve who should fill the vacancy. The notice need not name the nominee.[244] In the case of the vacancy being filled by a contributory's meeting in a creditor's voluntary liquidation, the creditors' meeting may veto the nominee in which case a court direction will be required for that person or some other contributory to be able to serve.[245] In the case of any vacancy being filled at a meeting of creditors or contributories the chairman of the meeting must notify the liquidator of the appointment.[246]

---

238 rr 4.160 and 4.162.
239 r 4.161(1)(a) and (2).
240 r 4.161(1)(b).
241 r 4.161(3).
242 rr 4.163(2) and 4.164(2).
243 rr 4.163(3) and 4.164(3).
244 rr 4.163(4) and 4.164(4).
245 r 4.164(5).
246 rr 4.163(5) and 4.164(6).

16.100 The expenses of the members of the liquidation committee can be met out of the assets (see para 19.01 for their priority). The expenses covered are the reasonable travelling expenses of members directly incurred by them in respect of attendance at committee meetings or otherwise on the committee's business.[247]

Transactions by committee members and their associates

16.101 A range of people connected with the committee is bound by the rules to refrain from transactions of three kinds with the company without the consent of the court or the agreement of the committee after full disclosure of all relevant information about the circumstances of the transaction. This rule applies to committee members, their representatives, the associates of either of them and anyone who has been a committee member within the last 12 months.[248]

16.102 The inclusion of the associates of committee members and of their representatives makes this a broad provision.[249] Great care will have to be taken about the associated companies of corporate committee members. The difficulty of entering post liquidation transactions with the company may inhibit certain creditors from serving on the committee; especially if the company's business is to be carried on during the liquidation. Even if the business will not be continued a creditor interested in purchasing company assets may be unwilling to serve on the liquidation committee owing to the need for disclosure to the other committee members of the transaction for their prior approval if court proceedings are to be avoided. The same considerations apply to the representatives of committee members who may have associations with individuals or corporations; a corporation may not be a representative. The rule against transactions by associates does not apply to former committee members who have served within the last 12 months. It is only such former members themselves who are caught by the rule. The transactions in question are those whereby a person caught by the rule:

"(a) receives out of the company's assets any payment for services given or goods supplied in connection with the administration, or
(b) obtains any profit from the administration, or
(c) acquires any asset forming part of the estate."[250]

16.103 It will be noted that (a) deals with any situation in which payment

247 r 4.169.
248 r 4.170(1).
249 See para 20.18 for the definition of 'associates'.
250 r 4.170(2).

is received out of the estate for goods or services supplied. There is no need to show any imbalance in the value received and given in favour of the committee member. The provision would apply even if greater value were given to the estate than was received from it. It is the receipt of any payment from the company assets which is covered by that paragraph. Similarly if an asset is acquired from the estate there is no need to show that it was acquired at an undervalue before the provision applies and the profit made by a committee member need not be a secret profit for the rule to deal with it. For obvious reasons the rule only applies to dealings with the estate and does not affect transactions with the company before the liquidation began. The stringency of the rule is mitigated by the provision of a number of methods whereby behaviour otherwise in breach of the rule can be sanctioned in advance or approved retrospectively.

16.104   The circumstances in which retrospective leave can be obtained are very circumscribed. Only the court can grant this relief; it is not within the power of the committee. The leave must be sought 'without undue delay' and it can only be granted if the transaction was entered into either as a matter of urgency or by way of performance of a contract 'in force' before the date on which the company went into liquidation.[251] It is likely that the concept of 'a matter of urgency' will be strictly construed by the court. One would envisage urgent circumstances as those in which the member sold something to the company which was unavailable from any other source at anything other than a much higher price or where delay in delivery would cost the estate dear unless the committee member or his associate supplied the goods or services in question. It is certainly likely that the economic consequences for the estate of any possible alternative transaction will be an important criterion in this context. A prior contractual obligation to carry out the transaction must have arisen by virtue of a contract made before the date of the winding up resolution or order. It need not have been made before the petition was filed in a compulsory liquidation.

16.105   If these factors do not exist a person caught by the rule must obtain leave for the transaction from the court (which has an unfettered discretion whether to grant it) or the prior sanction of the liquidation committee which can only agree if all the circumstances are disclosed to it and it is satisfied that the member or associate will be giving full value in the transaction.[252] No member of the committee or representative of a member may vote on a resolution of the committee to give sanction for a transaction if he is to participate directly or indirectly in it.[253] This excludes both the

251   r 4.170(3)(b).
252   r 4.170(3)(a) and (c).
253   r 4.170(4).

member who is or whose associate is a party to the transaction and his representative as well as any other member or representative directly or indirectly participating in it.

16.106   If a transaction prohibited by the rule is entered into without leave or consent then the court has power on the application of any interested person to set it aside and make such other order as it thinks fit including an order against the person who entered into it, requiring an account of profits or compensation for loss to the estate.[254] These statutory powers reflect the remedies available in the case of directors who are in breach of their fiduciary duties to a company. The court may allow the payment of out of pocket expenses and the cost price of goods supplied if there has been no previous sanction for the transaction.[255]

16.107   If an application is made against an associate of either a committee member or a member's representative it is a defence to the proceedings for the associate to prove to the court's satisfaction that he entered the transaction without any reason to suppose that in doing so he acted in contravention of the rule.[256] This defence may save those with a remote connection with a committee member or representative from the consequences of the breadth of the definition of an 'associate'. However, it would seem that the defence places the onus of proof on the respondent and that only a misapprehension about the facts will satisfy the court and not an error of law. Ignorance of the existence of the relevant relationship will suffice but ignorance of the legal effects of a known relationship will not. The necessary state of mind must exist at the time of entering into the transaction. Unless the court orders to the contrary the costs of an application under the rule will not be met out of the assets of the company.[257]

Functions of the liquidation committee

16.108   The functions of the liquidation committee are set out in the Insolvency Act and the Rules. The committee has a role in receiving and gathering information from the liquidator about the progress of the winding up. The liquidator is required by Rule 4.168(2) to send a written report to each committee member every 6 months on the progress of the winding up and any matters arising in connection with it to which the liquidator considers that the committee's attention should be drawn. The

---

254   r 4.170(5).
255   *Re Spink ex p Slater* (1913) 108 LT 811.
256   r 4.170(6).
257   r 4.170(7).

committee is entitled to direct the liquidator to send such a report at any time but not more frequently than every 2 months.[258] In addition to this power the committee is generally entitled to a report from the liquidator on all matters that appear to him to be, or that the committee indicates to him are, of concern with respect to the winding up.[259] Any major development between the regular reports should be reported to committee members on the initiative of the liquidator. If the committee indicates specific matters which require a report the liquidator may refuse to provide the information sought if he takes the view that:

> "(a) the request is frivolous or unreasonable, or
> (b) the cost of complying would be excessive, having regard to the relative importance of the information, or
> (c) there are not sufficient assets to enable him to comply."[260]

16.109   The last reason will justify non compliance however important the information. The process of weighing the importance of the information against the cost of providing it should be carried out by the liquidator with a view to his basic function and fiduciary duties. Information which may result in the probable collection of further substantial assets—because for example it may lead to an order that a former director contribute to those assets—should be more readily provided than information which does not have that effect. The creditors, through the committee members, are entitled to details of the progress of the liquidation process and only greatly excessive cost should be used to justify a refusal to state the current or recent situation in that respect.

16.110   If the committee is set up more than 28 days after the liquidator takes office he must report on his actions so far in summary form and answer their questions on this. However new individual committee members do not have a right to more than a summary report of earlier matters on taking office.[261] These rights of the committee do not disentitle it or its members from inspecting the liquidator's records of the liquidation and seeking explanations from him on any matter within the committee's responsibility.[262]

16.111   Apart from its entitlement to information from the liquidator the committee has a role in controlling the exercise of certain of his powers. (See para 15.97–15.105 on the powers of the liquidator.) In both compulsory and creditors' voluntary liquidations the sanction of either the court or the liquidation committee is required before the liquidator exercises the powers

---

258   r 4.168(1).
259   r 4.155(1).
260   r 4.155(2).
261   r 4.155(3) and (4).
262   r 4.155(5).

set out in Part I of sch 4 of the Act.[263] These powers include the payment of a class of creditors in full, the power to make compromises and arrangements of claims against the company and the power to compromise calls and debts or liabilities due to the company or other questions affecting company assets. In a compulsory winding up the sanction of the court or the committee is also needed for the exercise of the powers set out in Part II of the schedule which can be exercised without sanction in a creditors' voluntary liquidation.[264] This list consists of the power to bring or defend legal proceedings in the name of the company and the power to carry on its business.[265] It is also necessary for a liquidator other than the official receiver to give notice to the committee of the exercise by him of his powers by the disposal of any property to a person connected with the company (see para 20 and s 249 for the meaning of that expression) or the employment of a solicitor to assist him in carrying out his functions.[266] In a voluntary liquidation the disposal of property to a connected person must be reported but the appointment of a solicitor need not be.[267]

16.112 It is not possible for the committee to give a general permission in a compulsory liquidation for the exercise of the powers conferred on the liquidator by sch 4 Parts I and II; it must deal with each separate proposed exercise of a power. However, a person dealing with the liquidator in good faith and for value is not concerned whether such permission was given.[268] The permission should normally be given in advance of the exercise of the power but it is possible for the committee to ratify an act done without permission to allow the liquidator to meet his expenses from the assets if it is satisfied that he acted in a case of urgency and has sought ratification without undue delay.[269] The ratification is not necessary to validate a transaction as against a third party who entered into it in good faith and for value but it will presumably suffice to validate the liquidator's exercise of his power in favour of a third party who does not satisfy those criteria so long as the committee has full knowledge of all the circumstances of the transaction. Rule 4.184 applies to the sanction of the court when that is required in the same way as it applies to the committee and when the committee's function is being performed by the Secretary of State or the official receiver it applies to them. It has been noted in paras 15.140–15.144 that the committee has a major role in the determination of the remuneration to be paid to the liquidator (see Rules 4.127–4.131).

263 ss 165(2) and 167(1).
264 s 167(1).
265 Sch 4 paras 4 and 5.
266 s 167(2).
267 s 165(6).
268 r 4.184(1).
269 r 4.184(2).

16.113   Where no liquidation committee exists in a compulsory liquidation its functions are vested in the Secretary of State but will in practice be
performed by the official receiver.[270] If the official receiver is the liquidator
in such a winding up the DTI will carry out the committee's functions.[271] In
either case the requirements of the Act and Rules as regards notices to be
given or reports made to the committee by the liquidator do not apply
except to enable the committee to require a report.[272] The obligation to
provide regular reports and to report matters believed to be likely to be of
interest to committee members abates but a report must be provided on
demand unless one of the justifications for noncompliance in Rule 4.155(2)
applies. Where a winding up order is made immediately on the discharge of
an administration order and the former administrator is appointed as
liquidator the rules are adapted to allow for the continuation of a creditors'
committee which existed during the administration in the role of
liquidation committee (see Rules 4.173–4.178).

REPORTS TO CREDITORS

16.114   In addition to the use of the liquidation committee as a source of
information to creditors, the legislation provides for the provision of
information to individual creditors directly. In a creditors' voluntary
liquidation the liquidator must send to the creditors and contributories of
the company that are known to him or, if a statement of affairs has been
prepared, are identified in it, a copy or summary of that statement and a
report of the proceedings of the first creditors' meeting held under s 95 or
98.[273] A liquidator who was formerly an administrator must give such
information to creditors of whom he was not aware as administrator.[274]

16.115   In a compulsory liquidation the official receiver has a duty to
report at least once to the creditors and contributories and if he has not
already done so must report after the statement of affairs is prepared.
Where there has been an earlier report the report on the statement of affairs
need only be given if there are additional matters which the official receiver
believes should be brought to the attention of contributories and
creditors.[275] A similar obligation applies if the official receiver has released
the company from the obligation to submit a statement of affairs.[276] These

---

270   s 141(5) and r 4.172(2).
271   s 141(4).
272   r 4.172(1).
273   r 4.49.
274   r 4.49A, inserted by SI 1987 no 1919.
275   rr 4.43 and 4.45.
276   r 4.46.

obligations of the official receiver may be abrogated by the court on his application on which the court will have regard to the cost of reporting, the interests of creditors and contributories or any class of them and the assets available in the liquidation.[277]

16.116   At each stage of the liquidation process the liquidator will have to produce an account of his activities to the whole body of creditors or (in a members' voluntary liquidation) contributories.[278] A failure by the liquidator to file, deliver or make any return or document can lead to the service of 14 days' notice requiring him to do so. Failure on his part to make good the default can result in a court order on the application of any creditor or contributory or the registrar of companies. The order will specify a time limit for compliance and the costs of the application can be awarded against the liquidator.[279] In addition, the liquidator may be liable to a criminal penalty for his initial failure whether or not he makes good his default after service of the notice or the making of a court order.[280] Chapter 14 deals with the rules on calling and holding creditors' meetings.

---

277   r 4.47.
278   ss 93(2), 94(1), 96(3), 166(4), 105(2) and 106(1) apply to the annual and final meetings in each case for a voluntary liquidation and s 146(1)(a) to the final meeting in a compulsory winding up.
279   s 170.
280   s 170(4), and ss 93(3), 94(4), 94(6), 95(8), 98(6), 105(3), 106(4), 106(6) and 166(7), which create criminal offences relating to the failure to call meetings or to provide information.

CHAPTER 17

Contributories

SIGNIFICANCE OF CONTRIBUTORIES

17.01 Apart from the assets owned by the company itself which have to be marshalled to achieve the purpose of the winding up and to fulfil the duty of the liquidator,[1] the liquidator also needs to ensure that the contributories pay what they are required by law to contribute. In most cases the shareholders in the company will have no liability on its liquidation as s 74(2)(d) of the Insolvency Act 1986 limits their liability to the amount, if any, unpaid on their shares. In most modern companies shares are issued fully paid so the liability of members as such will be non-existent. It is important to bear in mind this qualification to the usefulness of the procedure for gathering the contributions of members when dealing with the collection of resources for the insolvent company from this source.

17.02 In an unlimited company, a company limited by guarantee or a company with partly paid shares, the rules will result in some increase in the resources available to creditors. In all liquidations lists of contributories have to be compiled and it is important to know the identity of contributories because of their rights, for example, to petition for a compulsory liquidation, to receive information about the progress of the liquidation, and to participate in meetings or to invoke investigative procedures. This makes it important to emphasise the definition of a contributory although the procedures for calling on them to provide resources will also be considered.

DEFINITION OF A CONTRIBUTORY

17.03 Section 79(1) of the Insolvency Act 1986 defines the word 'contributory' as including every person liable to contribute to the assets of the company in the event of it being wound up but excludes persons so liable only because of a declaration of the court of a requirement that they contribute owing to their participation in fraudulent or wrongful trading.[2]

1 See ch 18.
2 s 79(2).

For the purpose of proceedings for determining who is deemed a contributory and all prior proceedings the expression includes anyone alleged to be a contributory.[3] This last provision does not pre-empt a decision on the issue. It only means that such a person should be placed on the list of contributories and treated as such before final determination is made. The persons effectively included in the definition by virtue of their liability to contribute to the company's assets are listed below.

Every past and present member of the company[4]

17.04   The expression 'member' of a company includes for this purpose a person who is not a member but to whom shares have been transferred or transmitted by operation of law such as the unregistered purchaser of shares or the personal representative of deceased member.[5] Past members are absolved of liability if they ceased to be members more than one year before the commencement of the winding up[6] and they are not liable for debts contracted after their membership ceased.[7] To the extent that such debts have been paid or released (before the call was made) or have had a dividend paid they are not liable for them even if the past member bought up the relevant debts and caused them to be released.[8] A compromise between an A list contributory (ie a present member) and the liquidator which relieves the contributory from his liability does not absolve the past member who held the same shares (a B list contributory) from his liability.[9] The B list contributory would have to seek indemnification from the A list contributory in those circumstances.[10]

17.05   The procedure followed is to apply the proceeds of the call on present members to all debts regardless of the date on which they were incurred and then, when those assets are exhausted, to discover the liability of past members by finding out which debts were incurred at dates before particular individuals ceased to be members.[11] However, once the liability of past members has been discovered in this way the amount that they pay on the call on them goes into the general fund of the company and is not used for the particular debts incurred while individual past members where members.[12] It is unclear whether B list contributories are liable to

---

3   s 79(1).
4   s 74(1).
5   s 250.
6   s 74(2)(a).
7   s 74(2)(b).
8   *Re Apex Film Distributors Ltd* [1960] Ch 378; and see *Re Blakeley Ordnance Co* (1873) 8 Ch App 800.
9   *Helbert v Banner, Re Barned's Bank* (1871) LR 5 HL 28.
10   *Roberts v Crowe* (1872) LR 7 CP 629.
11   *Re Blakeley Ordnance Co* and *Helbert v Banner, re Barned's Bank* (nn 8 and 9 above).
12   *Webb v Whiffin* (1872) LR 5 HL 711.

contribute towards all the expenses of the winding up or only to the proportion of the expenses attributable to the collection of their own contribution.[13] It is submitted that since the costs of the winding up include expenses incurred in ascertaining the existence and extent of the liability of B list contributories, their contribution to those costs should not be limited by a reference to the direct cost of collecting their contributions.

17.06 In addition, past members are only liable at all if the present members are unable to satisfy the contributions required of them.[14] In the case of a limited company, this does not mean that the past members are liable to contribute if there are insufficient assets to pay all the debts and liabilities after the present members have paid the full amount due on their shares. The system works on the basis that the past members are not to be liable at all if the present members as a class have paid the full amount due on the shares. The liability of past members represents a 'fall back' liability.

17.07 For both past and present members the contribution required is limited in the case of a company limited by shares to the amount (if any) unpaid on their shares and in the case of a company limited by guarantee to the amount undertaken to be paid in the memorandum of association together with any amount unpaid on any share capital held if the company was formed at a time when such companies could have share capital and chose to have some.[15] Fully paid shareholders do fall within the definition of contributories and should be included on the list as a matter of course if there is likely to be any distribution of surplus capital.[16] If there is no such likelihood, they may still be included on the list if they so desire since they are contributories. The status of such shareholders as contributories is important from the point of view of policing the winding up process. Such a person who suspects that a fuller investigation may make further assets available is in a better position to press for it to take place than a person who is neither a creditor nor a contributory. Even past members who have no liability are within the definition and may insist on exercising the rights of contributories.[17] Although the position regarding past and present members who have a nil liability to the company may seem odd in the light of the basic definition of a 'contributory' in s 79(1) (which refers to a person liable to contribute to the assets of the company in the event of its being wound up) it seems that s 74(1) defines a contributory as every present and

---

13 Compare *Webb v Whifin* (above) per Lord Chelmsford at 726 with *Re Blakeley Ordnance Co.* (1873) 8 Ch App 800 at 810.
14 s 74(2)(c).
15 s 74(2)(c).
16 s 74(2)(d) and (3).
17 *Re National Savings Association* (1866) LR 1 Ch App 547; and *Re Anglesea Colliery Co* (1866) 1 Ch App 555.

past member, while s 74(2) defines the circumstances in which liability may be enforced. The definition of a contributory is not limited by such matters as the fact that shares are fully paid up or that a member need not pay if he ceased to be a member a year or more before the winding up commenced.[18]

Private company purchasing own shares from capital

17.08   If a private company has used the procedure provided by ss 171 to 181 of the Companies Act 1985 to purchase or redeem its own shares from capital and its winding up commences within one year of the date on which that paymemt was made, the directors who signed the statutory declaration made under s 173(3) become contributories to the extent of the amount paid out of capital to redeem or purchase the shares or the amount needed to pay the company's debts and liabilities and the expenses of winding up (whichever is less). The person whose shares were purchased or redeemed is a contributory up to the amount he received in respect of his shares and the directors are jointly and severally liable with him for that amount.[19] The liability accrues regardless of whether there is any other basis of liability but the word 'contributory' when it appears in the articles of association of a company is not to be taken to include such contributories.[20]

17.09   The liability of the vendor or redeemer of the shares is limited to the amount paid in respect of his shares but the directors are jointly and severally liable with each such person for that amount and may thus potentially have to pay the full amount of payment made for all such shares if the shortfall in the company's assets is sufficiently large. Any person who pays an amount to the company's assets by virtue of the provision may apply to the court for an order that someone jointly and severally be made liable to pay an amount that the court considers just and equitable, to him.[21]

Directors and managers with unlimited liability

17.10   In the unusual situation where a limited company has been set up with a provision that the liability of its directors and managers be unlimited, such officers are contributories on the basis of unlimited liability in that capacity; as compared with the liability of members who are not such officers whose liability will be limited in the usual way.[22] Section

---

18   See *Re Consolidated Goldfields of New Zealand Ltd* and *Re Anglesea Colliery Ltd* (above).
19   s 76(3) Insolvency Act 1986.
20   ss 76(1),(2) and (5) and 79(3).
21   s 76(3)(4).
22   s 75.

306(1) of the Companies Act 1985 provides for the possibility of such a company if the memorandum of association sets up that arrangement. The practice is uncommon.

SETTLEMENT OF LIST OF CONTRIBUTORIES

17.11 In a compulsory liquidation the task of settling a list of contributories is carefully regulated by the Act and the Rules. In a voluntary liquidation it is a task which the liquidator has power to perform but no detailed rules are laid down as to the manner in which he is to proceed.[23]

17.12 In a winding up by the court, the power to settle a list of contributories is given to the court by s 148(1) although the court may dispense with the list if calls appear not to be necessary and the rights of the contributories *inter se* will not need adjustment.[24] The discretion arises if calls and the adjustment of rights appear not to be necessary but in exercising it the court will balance the likely dangers of failing to compile a list against the expense and difficulty of doing so.[25] In the case of the solvent liquidation of a large company whose shares are held in small batches the discretion to dispense with a list will not be exercised if there is a danger that some shareholders will be missed in the process of returning capital if the full procedure set out in the Rules is not followed.[26]

17.13 In fact the court's power to make the list is delegated to the liquidator although the power to rectify the company register also conferred on the court by s 148(1) can only be exercised by him with the special leave of the court.[27] The official receiver, acting as provisional or full liquidator, has the same powers as any other liquidator in this respect.[28]

17.14 The Rules lay down the procedure to be followed in settling the list. If the company's shares are fully paid it is common practice to refrain from settling a list although the definition of a contributory in the statute and the obligation to compile a list make the legality of such a practice questionable. It is usual to settle an 'A' list and a 'B' list. The former consists of present members and the latter of past members whose membership ceased within 12 months before the commencement of liquidation. The

23   s 165(4).
24   s 148(2).
25   *Re Phoenix Oil Transport Co. Ltd* [1958] 1 Ch 560 at 565.
26   *Re Paragon Holdings Ltd* [1961] 1 Ch 346.
27   s 160(1)(b) and (2) and r 4.195.
28   *Re English Bank of the River Plate* [1892] 1 Ch 391.

liability of members on the B list only arises if those on the A list are unable to satisfy the contributions required of them and the past members can only be made liable for debts and liabilities incurred during their membership of the company.[29] For this reason the case law has developed the rule that a B list should only be settled after the court has given directions to that effect on being satisfied that the present members will probably be unable to pay the full amount required of them.[30] In the process of settling the list the Act requires that a distinction be made between those liable in their own right and those (such as personal representatives or trustees in bankruptcy) who are contributories only as representatives or as a result of their liability for the debts of others.[31]

17.15   The liquidator is required to settle the list and, if necessary, rectify the register of members with the court's approval as soon as possible after his appointment. Such duties are performed as an officer of the court.[32] The rules require the list to make the distinction between the different classes of contributory; with particular reference to the identification of those liable in their own right and those liable as representatives.[33] The list will also indicate those contributories who are liable as directors or managers with unlimited liability or as the recipients of payments for the purchase or redemption of the company's own shares in the few cases in which such contributories exist. The name, address and shareholding of each contributory will be recorded on the list with a record of the amount called and paid up in the case of shares not fully paid up.[34]

17.16   The 1986 Insolvency Rules simplify the procedure for settling the list by excluding the hearing before the liquidator which used to take place if a contributory challenged his inclusion in the list. The new procedure involves the liquidator giving, to every person included in the list, notice of the fact that he has settled it and of the extent of the interest of which that person has been included (the number of shares, the amount paid and called up in respect of them) and the fact that a call may be made in respect of any shares not fully paid up and his liability in that event as result to being included in the list.[35] The rules do not stipulate in detail the information to be given in the list in the event of the inclusion of a person on a basis other than membership of the company. The details of the extent and basis of such a liability should be set out in such a case.

29   ss 74(2)(a)(b) and (c).
30   See eg *Re Blakeley Ordnance Co* (1867) LR 4 Eq 135.
31   s 148(3).
32   r 4.196.
33   r 4.197(1).
34   r 4.197(2).
35   r 4.198(1) and (2).

17.17 The notice must inform its recipient of his right to object to any entry in, or omission from, the list within 21 days of the date of the notice.[36] Within 14 days of receiving such an objection the liquidator must respond by giving notice to the objector of specified amendment that he has made to the list or that he considers the objection not to be well founded and refuses to amend the list. In either case the notice must inform the objector of his right to apply to the court for the amendment of the list under Rule 4.199 within 21 days of receiving it.[37] The liquidator can only be liable for the costs of the application if the court makes an order. The official receiver can never be made personally liable for them.[38] The liquidator has a general power to vary or add to the list of contributories from time to time but must follow the same procedures as apply when it is first compiled in respect of notice and the right of those included to object each time its contents are changed.[39] In a compulsory liquidation the list is conclusive evidence of the liability of those appearing on it to pay the sums listed as due from them once the call procedure has been followed.[40] In a voluntary liquidation the list is only *prima facie* evidence of the liability of those included in it and consequently the procedure set out in the Rules for giving notice of the compilation of the list and dealing with objections does not apply.[41]

RECTIFYING THE REGISTER OF MEMBERS

17.18 This process is dealt with in the same way and on the basis of the same principle during the liquidation of the company as it is at any other time. The liquidator needs the special leave of the court to do this and if he includes a person in the list of contributories who does not appear on the register of members and that person objects to his inclusion on the list, the court must be satisfied that the applicant's name was improperly omitted from the register before the objection will be overruled.[42]

17.19 An order rectifying the register may be made on the grounds that a share issue was void; for example because the shares were unlawfully issued at a discount.[43] An allotment of shares may be avoided on the grounds that the company made a misrepresentation which induced the person registered to subscribe although in such a case the agreement must have been repudiated before the commencement of the liquidation and followed

---

36 r 4.198(3).
37 r 4.198(4).
38 r 4.201.
39 r 4200.
40 ss 150(1) and 152(1).
41 s 165(4)(a) and *Brighton Arcade Company v Dowling* (1868) LR 3 CP 175.
42 *Re Macdonald, Sons and Co* [1894] 1 Ch 89.
43 *Re Derham and Allen Ltd* [1946] Ch 31.

by efforts by the person on the register to have his name removed.[44] Under s 359(3) of the Companies Act 1985 the court, in dealing with the question of the rectification of the register, may deal with issues between two rival claimants to shares as well as matters between the company and the individual shareholder. In the case of a transfer of shares that has not been registered or the registration of an invalid transfer the court will not rectify the register on the liquidator's application if the error came about as a result of the default of the company as he stands in its shoes. This does not affect the right of the transferor or the transferee to obtain rectification.[45] Where a transfer has been completed before the commencement of the liquidation the liquidator cannot have it set aside on the grounds that it was made so that the transferor could avoid liability, nor can he take advantage of any right that the transferee may have to set it aside on the grounds of a misrepresentation made by the transferor. However, if the articles of the company give the directors the right to prevent the registration of the transfer they may do so.[46] The existence of a misrepresentation might lead the court to refuse to order the specific performance of a pre-liquidation agreement once the liquidation has begun. A rectification of the register made by the court after the commencement of a winding up can be retrospective to make the person whose name is substituted a contributory although such an order will include any provisions necessary to protect the rights of an innocent third party.[47]

CALLS AND THE LIABILITY OF CONTRIBUTORIES

17.20 Section 80 lays down that the liability of the contributory creates a debt in the nature of a speciality accruing from the time when the liability commenced but only payable at the times when calls are made for enforcing the liability. Since the debt is a specialty, the limitation period is 12 years.[48]

17.21 The death of a contributory before his name is placed on the list results in his personal representatives being liable in the course of administration of the deceased's estate to contribute and they are contributories whose names can be added to the list. Their liability is only as personal representatives but if they default, proceedings can be taken by the liquidator to administer the deceased's estate and to compel payment.[49]

---

44 *Re Overend Gurney and Co* (1867) LR 2 HL 325 at 353 and *Whiteley's Case* [1900] 1 Ch 365.
45 *Re Joint Stock Discount Co* (1867) 3 Ch App 119 and *In Re Hercules Insurance Company* (1870) LR 9 Eq 589.
46 *Re Discoverer's Finance Corporation Ltd* [1910] 1 Ch 312.
47 *Re Sussex Brick Co* [1940] 1 Ch 598.
48 Limitation of Actions Act 1980 s 8(1).
49 Insolvency Act 1986 s 81.

If the contributory dies after his name is added to the list of contributories, then s 80 ensures that his liability is a debt payable during the administration of his estate. Similarly, s 82 provides for the trustee of a bankrupt contributory to represent him for all purposes whether the bankruptcy occurred before or after the list of contributories was drafted. He may be called upon to admit proof of the bankrupt's liability and liability on future calls may be given an estimated value for this purpose.

17.22 At the commencement of a winding up the liability of the members is frozen. No transfer of the company's shares or alteration of the status of its members may occur without a court order in the case of a compulsory liquidation and in a voluntary liquidation the transfer of shares is only permitted to, or with, the sanction of the liquidator while a change in the status of members can only occur by a court order obtained under s 112.[50] The liabilities of past and present members, of those involved in the purchase or redemption by the company of its own shares and of directors and managers whose liability is unlimited as a result of the company's constitution have been outlined above.

17.23 It should be noted that, in the case of a company which is limited at the time of the commencement of the winding up but was unlimited at some earlier time, past members whose membership has ended since the company's re-registration are liable to contribute if the liquidation begins within 3 years of re-registration. This is in respect of debts and liabilities contracted before the company changed its status and liability is unlimited. If no-one who was a member of the company at the time of re-registration is an existing member at the commencement of the liquidation then anyone who was either a present or a past member of it at the time of re-registration is liable even if the A list contributories have paid in full. A person who ceased to be a member within one year before the date of the re-registration remains potentially liable as a past member if liquidation commences within 3 years after the date of re-registration.[51] However, such liability is limited to debts incurred before the date of re-registration.

17.24 In the converse situation s 78 protects a member of a former limited company which re-registered as unlimited before the commencement of the liquidation if his membership ceased before the company was re-registered. He is absolved from any liability in excess of that which he would have incurred had the company not re-registered unless he has been a member of the company since it became an unlimited company.

50 s 88 and 127.
51 s 77.

17.25 The power of the court to make calls on contributories in compulsory liquidation is delegated to the liquidator as an officer of the court.[52] In a voluntary winding up the power is conferred by on him s 165(4)(b). Section 150(1) allows for a call to be made either before or after the sufficiency of the company's assets have been ascertained and at any time after the making of the winding up order. The call may be based on the estimated amount of the company's liabilities without proofs from creditors having yet been received or admitted.[53] As has been noted no call can be made on contributories on the B list until those on the A list have defaulted. Thus a single call cannot simultaneously be made in respect of the two lists and a notice, warning that a call would be made if necessary, is not itself a call.[54] However, a separate call on the B list contributories can be justified on the basis of the probable inability of A list contributories to satisfy their obligations.[55] This rule has the same basis as the rule that no B list should be compiled until it is clear that the A list contributories will not be able to meet their obligations.

17.26 The call is made on any contributories on the list for any money considered necessary to satisfy the company's debts and liabilities and the expenses of the winding up or for the adjustment of the rights of the contributories *inter se*. The decision on the amount to be called and by whom it is to be contributed is made by the liquidator and his decision can be enforced by order of the court.[56] The probability of some contributories failing in whole or in part to pay the amount due from them can be taken into account by the liquidator in making the call.[57]

17.27 The court order may require the money due on a call, or as a debt ordered to paid under s 149(1), to be paid to the liquidator's account at the Bank of England rather than to the liquidator and such an order will be enforceable in the same way as an order that the liquidator be paid.[58] An order that a contributory pay money is conclusive evidence of the fact that the money it requires to be paid is due and of all other pertinent matters stated in it. This is despite the summary nature of the order. The right of appeal against the order is, however, preserved.[59]

17.28 The court may order the arrrest of a contributory at any time before

---

52   s 160(1)(d) and r 4.202.
53   *Re Contract Corporation* (1866) 2 Ch App 95.
54   *Re Apex Film Distributors Ltd* [1960] Ch 378.
55   *Helbert v Banner* (1871) LR 5 HL 28.
56   r 4.205(2) and 150(1).
57   s 150(2).
58   s 151(1).
59   s 152.

or after the making of the winding up order and whether or not a call has yet been made. The ground for an order for his arrest and the seizure of his books, papers records and personal moveable property is proof that there is probable cause for believing that he is about to quit the UK or otherwise abscond or remove or conceal his property for the purpose of evading the payment of calls.[60]

17.29 In a compulsory winding up the special leave of the court or the sanction of the liquidation committee is required before the liquidator may make a call.[61] The sanction of the committee will normally be sought if one exists as this procedure is much cheaper than an application to the court. A meeting of the committee can be convened for this purpose by 7 days' notice being given to each member by the liquidator. The notice must be state the amount of the proposed call and the purpose for which it is intended to be made.[62] If the leave of the court is sought for the call to be made the liquidator will apply *ex parte* and support his application with an affidavit and will state in it the amount of the proposed call and the identity of the contributories on whom it is made. The court may direct that notice of the application be served on the contributories individually or that it be advertised publicly.[63] In any event notice of the call must be given to the contributories after sanction or leave has been obtained for it and must specify the amount due from the person on whom it is served in respect of the call and whether the leave of the court or the sanction of the call and whether the leave of the court or the sanction of the liquidation commitee has been obtained. Payment of that amount may be enforced by the court.[64] In a voluntary liquidation the liquidator does not need leave or sanction to make a call but s 112 enables him to use the same summary procedure for the enforcement of the calls which he does make by seeking a court order under s 150(1).

SET OFF BY CONTRIBUTORIES

17.30 The rules on set off between an insolvent company and its creditors are dealt with in chapter 18. In the case of a call on a contributory by a limited company of which he is also a creditor, no set off is permitted. This rule applies to the debt itself and to any dividend declared in the winding up. After all calls due have been paid the contributory is treated in the same way as any other creditor and is entitled to the dividend due on his debt in

---

60   s 158.
61   s 160(2).
62   r 4.203.
63   r 4.204.
64   r 4.205.

accordance with the principle of *pari passu* distribution.[65] The whole basis for this rule is the prevention of a full payment of members' debts by set off when other creditors obtain a limited dividend. The contributory is not in the same position as other creditors whose debts arose before the commencement of the liquidation and not by virtue of the special obligations imposed on members of the company. This rule applies to the estate of a deceased contributory as it does to a claim against the contributory himself.[66]

17.31 The absence of a right of set off applies both to a call by the liquidator and to unpaid calls by the directors made on partly paid shares before the company went into liquidation.[67] The same principle would apply to an instalment due on a share issue. This rule does not apply in the case of an unlimited company or to a director or manager who is a contributory to the extent that his status as such depends on a provision of the articles imposing unlimited liability on such persons. In such cases the call may allow a set off:

> "any money due to him or the estate which he represents from the company on any independent dealing or contract with the company but not any money due to him as a member of the company in respect of any dividend or profit".[68]

This statutory modification to the general rule is consistent with the principle of *pari passu* distribution as the liability of the contributory is unlimited until all the company's debts are paid.[69]

17.32 Whether or not the company is limited, a right of set off is permitted to the contributories after all the creditors have been paid in full with interest at the official rate. However, this right of set off only applies to calls made after the payment of those debts.[70]

17.33 If a contributory becomes bankrupt before or after his name is placed on the list of contributories his trustee in bankruptcy represents him for all purposes of the winding up and thus is a contributory in that capacity.[71] The liability of the bankrupt as a contributory can be the subject of proof in the bankruptcy and will be paid as a debt in the bankruptcy, the estimated value of future calls may also be proved.[72]

65 *Grissell's Case* (1866) 1 Ch App 528.
66 *Re Peruvian Railway Construction Co* [1915] 2 Ch 144.
67 *Re Whitehouse & Co* (1878) 9 Ch D 595.
68 s 149(2).
69 See *Re International Life Assurance Association* (1870) LR 10 Eq 312 and a dictum of Lord Chelmsford in *Grissell's Case* above at 536.
70 s 149(3).
71 s 82(1) and (2).
72 s 82(3) and (4).

17.34 Section 323 of the Insolvency Act 1986 re-enacts the provisions of s 31 of the Bankruptcy Act 1914 and thus preserves the rule that, if a contributory is bankrupt, set off is permitted between his estate and the company to reduce the amount payable on the call or to reduce the amount due from the company to the bankrupt's estate. The decisions in both of the cases on this point are based on the existence of two separate systems and two statutes for personal and corporate insolvency.[73] The Insolvency Act 1986 preserves two distinct systems and is likely to result in a similar ruling in the future despite the fact that one statute now governs both areas of law. Parliament can be presumed to have intended to retain the well established rule since it has not changed the wording of the provisions in question in any relevant way.

17.35 Oddly, the position of an insolvent corporate contributory is distinguished from that of the insolvent individual and set off is prohibited where the corporate contributory is in liquidation. This was justified on the basis that there is no separate system involved in these circumstances.[74] It is submitted that the law should be changed so that the general rule in *Grissell's* case which prevents a set off applies in all cases. It is hard to justify the different treatmemt of an insolvent company as there is no practical distinction between the position of a bankrupt and a company in liquidation.

17.36 Any adjustment of the rights of contributories *inter se* may be carried out by court under s 154 in a compulsory liquidation or by the liquidator under s 165(5) if the winding up is voluntary. This process is considered in chapter 19 on the distribution of assets.

---

73 *Re Duckworth* (1867) 2 Ch App 578 and *Re Universal Banking Corporation* (1870) 5 Ch App 492.
74 *Re Auriferous Properties Ltd* [1898] 1 Ch 691.

CHAPTER 18

The Winding Up Process: Gathering Assets

18.01 The process of gathering assets is part of the function of the liquidator in all forms of winding up. It is the first step after appointment and includes any urgent steps necessary to secure assets at risk. Section 143(1) spells out that in a compulsory winding up one of the functions of the liquidator is to 'secure that the assets of the company are got in'. In the case of a voluntary liquidation s 91(1) and 100(1) (dealing with members' and creditors' liquidation respectively) give the purpose of the liquidator as winding up the company's affairs; a process that includes gathering assets. Section 166(3)(a) permits this process to continue during the period before a creditors' meeting is held without the sanction of the court even where the liquidator in a creditors' voluntary liquidation was appointed by the company.

18.02 In general the assets available to the liquidator for the purposes of the winding up consist of all those owned by the company at the date of the commencement of the liquidation. This excludes any which have been validly disposed of since that date and the rights gained by the liquidator are no better than those of the company. Property held by the company on trust is held in the same way by the liquidator; property leased by the company which is in its possession but is not owned by it (for example because of the effect of a valid *Romalpa* clause) is not available to the liquidator (see chapter 9). The same principle ensures that any consensual security interests by way of fixed or floating charge or mortgage and any created by operation of law (such as liens) will, in principle, continue to affect the assets in the hands of the liquidator. This is subject to specific provisions of the legislation setting aside or otherwise limiting such interests (see chapter 20 on setting aside transactions). In gathering assets the liquidator will be bound by any estoppel which is binding on the company although that is not the case when he is engaged in distributing the proceeds of realisation to creditors and contributories.[1]

18.03 The liquidator may add to the assets available by using the powers discussed in chapter 20 to set aside transactions which took place before the

---

1 *Re Exchange Securities and Commodities Ltd (No 3)* (1987) BCC 48

commencement of the liquidation and which depleted the company's assets. Similarly, the right to pursue directors guilty of wrongful trading or any persons guilty of fraudulent trading may be a means of increasing the value of of the assets available to creditors (see chapter 21). Such measures are additional to any right the company itself may have to sue directors for breach of fiduciary duty or to pursue other wrongdoers to increase the level of its assets. The liquidator will be able to institute such proceedings in the name of the company. In any action brought by the liquidator in the process of gathering assets, the question of whether the plaintiff company should be required to provide security for costs under s 726 of the Companies Act 1985 will be decided by the court by weighing the oppressive results of making such an order against the risk to the defendent of the insolvent company being unable to pay his costs.[2]

18.04   The assets of the company do not vest in the liquidator in the way that those of an individual insolvent vest in the trustee in bankruptcy, although the court has a little-used power to order that this should happen.[3] However, after the commencement of the liquidation the company is no longer the beneficial owner of its property[4] as it is held for the benefit of creditors and contributories. Despite this there is no trust in the full sense as those groups have no equitable interests in the assets. In considering the assets available to the liquidator, his power to disclaim onerous property is dealt with first. Particular rules affecting different types of property are then considered.

PART 1: THE RIGHT TO DISCLAIM PROPERTY

THE PROPERTY WHICH MAY BE DISCLAIMED

18.05   In the case of both voluntary and compulsory liquidations the liquidator is given the right under s 178 and 179 to disclaim on behalf of the company, onerous property. The property in question is defined in s 178(2) as any unprofitable contract or any other property of the company which is unsaleable, not readily saleable or which is such that it may give rise to a liability to pay money or perform any other onerous act. Property can be disclaimed if it is unsaleable even if no onerous obligation attaches to it or if it may give rise to liability in the future, even if it is saleable, at the time of disclaimer. This contrasts with the position before 1986.[5]

---

2 *Aquila Design (GRP Products) Ltd v Cornhill Insurance plc* (1987) 3 BCC 364
3 Insolvency Act 1986 s 145
4 *Ayerst v C & K (Construction) Ltd* [1976] AC 167
5 See *Re Potters Oils Ltd* [1985] BCLC 203

18.06 Property may be disclaimed even if possession of the property has been taken by the liquidator, or he has tried to sell it or has otherwise exercised ownership rights in respect of it.[6] However, the power is intended to avoid loss falling on the company and not to increase the level of its profits from a particular transaction. A contract to sell an asset cannot be disclaimed merely because the asset can be sold more profitably elsewhere.[7] Although the rights under a contract of sale may be unassignable and thus unsaleable such a situation is governed by s 178(3)(a) which deals with contracts and the contract is not 'unprofitable' unless its execution would result in a loss to the company, that is to say, a net reduction in the assets of the company would result from both sides carrying out their contractual obligations. It is not possible to argue that the rights under such a contract are within the category of 'other property of the company which is unsaleable' referred to in s 178(3)(b).

Procedure

18.07 In order to exercise his power of disclaimer, the liquidator must serve the prescribed notice.[8] Rule 4.187 requires that the notice contain particulars of the property to be disclaimed so that it can be easily identified and that the notice be signed by the liquidator and filed in court. The court endorses it with the date of filing, seals it, and returns it to the liquidator by hand or first class post. The liquidator must then serve the notice in accordance with Rule 4.188 within 7 days after its return to him by the court. The parties entitled to service of the notice are:

(a) In the case of the disclaimer of a leasehold, every person who to the liquidator's knowledge claims as underlessee or mortgagee under the company (Rule 4.188(2));

(b) In every case, every person who to his knowledge claims an interest in the disclaimed property or is under a liability in respect of it which is not discharged by the disclaimer. This will include the landlord in the case of the disclaimer of a lease and the assignor of property to be disclaimed by the assignee company (Rule 4.188(3)).

(c) All known parties to an unprofitable contract which is to be disclaimed and all other persons known to be interested in it (Rule 4.188(4)).

A person who was known by the liquidator to have an interest in the disclaimed property entitling him to a notice must be given one as soon as

---

6   s 178(2)
7   *Re Bastable* [1901] 2 KB 518
8   s 178(2)

that interest comes to the liquidator's knowledge unless the court waives compliance with the requirement or that person has in fact been made aware of the disclaimer and its date (Rule 4.188(5)). Additional notices may be given by the liquidator under Rule 4.189 at any time to persons who ought in the opinion of the liquidator to be informed in the public interest or for other reasons. The court must be notified under Rule 4.190 of the names, addresses and interests of all persons to whom any notice has been sent.

18.08   Section 178(5) allows a person interested in the property of the company to require a decision from the liquidator whether he will exercise the right of disclaimer. By serving a notice to elect in Form 4.54 or substantially similar form either personally or by registered post on the liquidator (Rule 4.191), the applicant forces the liquidator either to serve a notice of disclaimer within 28 days (or a longer period allowed by the court) or to forego his right to disclaim the property. The procedure prevents the liquidator from inflicting uncertainty on the other party for an indefinite period.

18.09   Conversely, if the liquidator is uncertain whether a person is interested in property or not he can serve notice under Rule 4.192. This results in an obligation on the person on whom the notice was served to notify the liquidator of the extent and nature of any interest which he claims and whether he makes such a claim. This must be done within 14 days and failure to comply entitles the liquidator to assume that the person has no interest in the property which would prevent or impede its disclaimer. If the disclaimer is to be challenged the onus rests on the person seeking to show that it is invalid. They must establish that the liquidator was in breach of duty as regards giving notice or in some other respect (Rule 4.193).

Effect of disclaimer

18.10   A disclaimer determines, from its date, the rights, interests and liabilities of the company in, or in respect of, the property disclaimed. However it does not affect the rights and liabilities of any other person except so far as is necessary for the purpose of releasing the company from liability.[9]

18.11   Disclaimed property vests in the Crown as *bona vacantia* unless the property in question is a fee simple interest in land in which case it probably escheats to the Crown[10] or is an interest in lease in which case it

---

9   s 178(4)
10   Per Jessel MR in *Re Mercer & Moore* (1880) 14 Ch D 287 at 295

has been held that the lease terminates on disclaimer.[11] In the case of land subject to a rentcharge which is disclaimed and vests by operation of law in the Crown or any other person the liability for sums due does not attach personally to the new owner unless he takes possession or control of the land or occupies it.[12] It is unclear when liability attaches to the Crown if other types of property are involved but it can be argued that such liability is incurred immediately as s 180 would otherwise be unneccessary.

18.12   In addition to the provision of s 178(4)(b) which prevents any unnecessary effect on the rights or liabilities of others as a result of disclaimer, s 178(6) gives persons who sustain loss or damage as a result of a disclaimer the right to prove in the liquidation for such loss or damage. They are deemed to be creditors of the company for that purpose.

18.13   The effect of a disclaimer on a surety or on the original lessee where the liquidator disclaims the lease of which the company was an assignee is uncertain. Section 178(4) lays down that the disclaimer operates to terminate the liability of the company but only affects the liabilities of others to the extent necessary to achieve this. Is the release of the original lessee or of a surety of the company's liability necessary for the purpose of releasing the company? In *Stacey v Hill*,[13] a bankruptcy case, the fact that the surety was entitled to an indemnity from the bankrupt was held to mean that the liability of the surety was determined by the disclaimer to avoid continuing the liability of the bankrupt. However the logic of applying the section to affect the liability of parties other than the company to the minimum extent necessary to release the company, is to retain the liability of the surety but to deny him his indemnity against the company. This approach has been followed in the analogous situation of a lessee who had assigned the lease to the company whose liquidator disclaimed it.[14] Such an approach may do an injustice to the surety or original lessee but it does seem to follow the intent expressed in the wording of s 178(4). It can also be based on the fact that in *Stacey v Hill* the obligation of the surety can be argued to have terminated because of the termination of the lease on the disclaimer.

Vesting orders

18.14   Section 181(3) empowers the court to make an order vesting property disclaimed under s 178 in any person who claims an interest in it

11   Per Maugham J in *Re Katherine et Cie* [1932] 1 Ch 70 at 73
12   s 180
13   [1901] 1 KB 660
14   *Warnford Investments Ltd v Duckworth* [1979] Ch 127

or who is under a liability in respect of it which was not extinguished by the disclaimer. The order may require the property to be vested in or delivered to the person in question or a trustee for that person. An order in favour of a person who is under a liability in respect of the property can only be made if it appears to the court just to do so for the purpose of compensating that person. This probably means that no windfall benefit should accrue as a result of the order and s 181(5) provides for the effect of any vesting order to be taken into account in assessing any damages or compensation claimed by the person under s 178(6). If the value of the property vested in the person is less that the amount of their loss they can only claim the balance under s 178(6). It is open to the court to make a vesting order on any terms that it thinks fit. If the value of the property exceeds the loss of the person in whom it is to be vested the court might order that person to pay an amount to the liquidator to ensure that only the amount necessary to compensate for the disclaimer is gained.

18.15   The effect of the vesting order is to remove ownership or, in the case of delivery, possession from the Crown and to vest it in the person in whose favour the order is made without the need for any conveyance assigniment or transfer.[15] An application for a vesting order may be made under s 181(2) by a person claiming an interest in the property or by a person under a liability not discharged by the disclaimer. The application to the court must by made under Rule 4.1294(1) within 3 months of the applicant becoming aware of the disclaimer or of his receiving the liquidator's notice of disclaimer (whichever is earlier). The application must be filed together with an affidavit stating whether the claim is based on an interest in property or an undischarged liability; the grounds for the application and the date on which the applicant received notice of the disclaimer or otherwise became aware of it.[16] A venue is then fixed by the court and the applicant must give notice of that and a copy of the application and the affidavit to the liquidator within 7 days.[17] At the hearing the court may order that notice of the application be sent to other persons.[18] The liquidator and the applicant are sent sealed copies of the order of the court.[19]

Disclaimer of leaseholds

18.16   The rules on the disclaimer of leaseholds and vesting orders in relation to such property take account of the interests of underlessees and

15   s 181(6)
16   r 4.194(3)
17   r 4.194(4)
18   r 4.194(5)
19   r 4.194(6)

mortgagees who claim under the lessee company and of those under liability to carry out the obligations of the company. By virtue of s 179(1), a disclaimer under s 178 of 'any property of a leasehold nature' does not take effect unless a copy of the disclaimer has been served on every person claiming as an underlessee or a mortgagee under the company. This is an additional requirement over and above the need to serve the appropriate notice under s 178. The underlessee or mortgagee has a period of 14 days from the date on which the last notice was served under s 179 to apply under s 181 for a vesting order to be made. The disclaimer only takes effect if no such application is made or if the court directs that it should take effect despite the fact that the application has been made. In the latter case— whether the order is in place of or in combination with a vesting order—the court has power under s 179(2) to make such orders as it thinks fit with respect to fixtures, tenant's improvements and any other matters arising out of the lease. Where a vesting order is made under s 181 but the effect of the disclaimer has been suspended under s 179, the order under s 181 will include a direction giving effect to the disclaimer unless other applications under s 181 are pending at the date of the order.[20]

18.17   An underlessee or mortgagee has to choose whether to seek a vesting order which gives him the interests of the company subject to certain liabilities and obligations or to be excluded from all interest in the property. This is because s 182(1) lays down that that the court may only vest property of a leasehold nature in such a person on terms making that person subject to either the same liabilities and obligations as applied to the company under the lease at the commencement of the winding up or the liabilities and obligations of an assignee of the lease from the company at that date. The fact that the obligations and liabilities are defined by reference to the commencement of the winding up means that the effect of the liquidation on the lease can be disregarded. However the choice of the basis on which liabilities will be imposed is a matter for the court.

18.18   The distinction between them relates to the treatment of breaches of the covenants in the leases of which the company has been guilty. If the lease is vested on the basis of the company's liabilities at the commencement of the liquidation, the underlessee or mortgagee will be personally liable for the company's previous breaches of covenant and will have privity of estate with the landlord if the company was the original lessee. If, on the other hand, the vesting order takes effect as if there had been an assignment of the company's interest, liability for rent and for breaches of covenant only operate from the date of the commencement of the winding up and there is

20   r 4.194(7)

no privity of estate between underlessee or mortgagee and landlord with the liability throughout the duration of the lease that would imply. If the underlessee does not seek a vesting order and the property is vested in another the underlessee's interest in the property is destroyed and he has no right of occupation and is not liable to pay rent or any of the other covenants of the lease.[21]

18.19   The decision is made at the discretion of the court but in any case where assignment by the company was permitted only with the landlord's consent or in which the company held as assignee, the vesting order will carry with it the full liability of the company as at the commencement of the winding up. This is because the test for exercising the discretion in favour of the underlessee or mortgagee by imposing liabilities on the basis of assignment is that this will place him in no better position and the landlord in no worse position than if there had been no disclaimer.[22] Since most leases are likely to require the landlord's consent for assignment, vesting on the basis of the liability of an assignee will be uncommon.

18.20   Section 182(2) provides that where only part of the property comprised in the lease is vested in the underlessee or mortgagee the obligations and liabilities imposed on the person in whom it is vested only relate to that part of the property. If the underlessee or mortgagee refuses to accept a vesting order on those terms not only is he excluded from all interest in the property by virtue of s 182(4); he is also likely to see the interest of the company vested in a person who is liable to perform the lessee's covenants under the lease freed and discharged from any estates incumbrances or interests created by the company; including his own. Section 182(3), which empowers the court to make such an order, applies for the benefit of a person who is liable jointly or alone; personally or in a representative capacity. For example a lessee from whom the company took an assignment of the lease of or a surety of the company's liabilities under it could benefit from this provision.

18.21   The system set up by the Act is to give the first right to a vesting order to an underlessee or mortgagee claiming under the company. If they refuse to accept the liabilities which go with such an order they will lose their interest in favour of a person who is liable to fulfil the company's obligation under the lease. If the landlord has assigned his interest there is no transfer to the assignee of the benefit of a guarantee of the tenant's obligations. Consequently the assignee cannot object to the liquidator's

---

21   *Re A E Realisations (1985) Ltd* [1987] BCLC 486
22   See *Carter & Ellis ex p Savill Bros* [1905] 1 K B 735—a bankruptcy case—per Vaughan Williams J at 746—747

disclaimer of the lease on the ground that this ends the guarantee and this causes loss to the assignee. The fact that the dissolution of the tenant company will end the guarantee if its terms limit it to the period when the leasehold interest is vested in the company deprives the assignee of a right to object to disclaimer even if the benefit of the guarantee has passed to him.[23]

PART 2: GATHERING PARTICULAR ASSETS

18.22   Certain considerations apply to the availability to the liquidator of assets which take the form of particular types of property.

LAND

18.23   The question of the company's title to land is resolved in the same way after liquidation as it is before. This will be by reference to the title deeds in the case of unregistered land and the entry on the register if the land is registered. The validity of the title of the company will not be impugned by the commencement of the liquidation. It is more likely that there will be special considerations if the company is the lessee of land. Most leases will have a provision for the forfeiture of the lease in the event of the company going into liquidation and the effect of such a clause must be considered by the liquidator as it clearly affects the asset which comes into his hands. Such a provision prevents the division of the interest of the company among the creditors. However, the clause only operates against a lessee company still in possession. If the company has assigned its interest before the commencement of the winding up its liquidation will not determine the lease as the covenant runs with the land.[24]

18.24   If the landlord seeks to forfeit the lease the liquidator can apply for relief against this. Section 146 of the Law of Property Act 1925 requires the landlord to serve notice on the company of his intention to forfeit the lease because of the liquidation of the company. The notice must give details of the breach of covenant involved and require compensation for it.

18.25   There are two sets of circumstances where this limitation on the landlord's right to seek forfeiture on this ground does not apply. First, if the lease is of agricultural or pastoral land, mines or minerals, a public house, a furnished dwellinghouse or any property for which the personal qualifica-

23   *Re Distributors and Warehousing Ltd* [1986] BCLC 129
24   *Horsey Estate Ltd v Steiger* [1899] 2 QB 79

tions of the lessee are important for the preservation of the value or character of the property or because it is near to the property of the lessor or someone holding under him. In these circumstances, s 146(9) of the Law of Property Act 1925 lays down that the section does not apply to a condition for the forfeiture of the lease on the liquidation of the company or because execution is levied against it. In such a case no notice is required under the section and there is no right for the liquidator to apply for relief against forfeiture. Secondly, the right of the liquidator to apply for relief against forfeiture only lasts for one year from the commencement of the winding up. Forfeiture after that time is possible without the need for the notice or the right of the liquidator to apply for relief. If the company's interest is sold within the one year period, the rights conferred by the section apply forever in relation to forfeiture on the basis of the liquidation or any execution levied before the sale of the company's interest.[25] A sale for the purpose must be completed by conveyance or have been agreed by an unconditional contract.[26] If there is no sale within the year the landlord's right to forfeit the lease is unfettered after the end of that period and the court has no inherent power outside the statute to grant relief in cases involving insolvency.[27] An application for relief against forfeiture made within the one year period can result in relief even if it is not heard until after the one year period is up.[28] It is a matter of some importance that the liquidator seek to negotiate a sale of the lease to be effective within the one year period unless he is to decide to disclaim the lease.

18.26   If arrears of rent have accrued before the commencement of the winding up, the lease may well provide the landlord with a right of re-entry. The landlord will normally be granted possession on this basis if the rent is not paid. The liquidator, if he wishes to make use of the company's existing premises, will have to pay off the arrears of rent to avoid possession. In *General Share and Trust Co v Wetley Brick and Pottery Co*[29] the Court of Appeal made it clear that the operation of a proviso for re-entry for non-payment of rent was not affected by a liquidation as possession could only be denied to the landlord by an unlawful act of the tenant.[30] The application is dealt with by the court granting liberty to re-enter. Such an order is necessary under s 130(2) of the Insolvency Act 1986 which suspends actions against the company and prohibits the commencement of new ones without the leave of the court in a compulsory winding up from the date of the order or of the appointment of a provisional liquidator. In the case of a

---

25   s 146(10)
26   *Re Henry Castle & Sons Ltd*(1906) 94 LT 396
27   *Official Custodian of Charities v Parway Estates Ltd* [1984] BCLC 309
28   *Pearson v Gee & Braceborough Spa Ltd* [1934] AC 272
29   (1882) 20 Ch D 260
30   See remarks of Jessel MR at 267

voluntary winding up no such order is necessary unless the court has made an order under s 112 preventing proceeding against the company. On an application under s 112 the court will apply similar principles to those used under s 130.[31]

18.27	An order giving leave to re-enter in the winding up proceedings will be made even if there are subtenants of the company who cannot be heard in that action as they will receive notice before a writ of possession is used by the landlord to enforce possession and they can then apply for relief against forfeiture.[32] This is so even if someone other than the liquidator is the sole occupant. Possession will be granted against the liquidator and the occupant can seek relief at a later stage.[33] The right of the company to apply for relief from forfeiture or from the landlord's exercise of his right of re-entry under s 146(2) of the Law of Property Act 1925 exists in this case but is unlikely to be successful unless the arrears of rent are to be paid in full. The judgment on whether to make such payments will be made by the liquidator on the basis of the value of the lease. If the arrears are paid off in full, relief will be granted despite the fact that the company is insolvent. The landlord's argument that this may lead to problems with the payment of future rent will carry no weight because such problems can be dealt with when they arise. The risk to the landlord in this situation is no worse than in the case of other impecunious tenants.[34]

18.28	Any protection enjoyed by the company under the Landlord and Tenant Act 1954 will not be affected by the liquidation as such but the cessation of trade or business may mean that the premises are no longer occupied by the tenant for the purpose of a business that it carries on.[35] If the Act applies there will be the possibility of continuing or renewing the tenancy beyond its contractual term and this will affect its value. It is always possible for the liquidator to negotiate a surrender of a lease with the landlord if he needs to dispose of the property and the lease has no market value.

CHATTELS

18.29	The major issue likely to affect the control of the liquidator over chattels after the commencement of a winding up is the fact that they are

31	*Westbury v Twigg & Co* [1892] 1 QB 77
32	See *Re Blue Jeans Sales Ltd* [1979] 1 All ER 641
33	*Re Brompton Securities Ltd* (1988) 4 BCC 189
34	*Re Brompton Securities Ltd (No 2)* (1988) 4 BCC 436
35	Landlord and Tenant Act 1954 s 23(1)

subject to distress or execution. Execution may also be a factor affecting land or debts owned by the company. Chapter 6 deals with the process involved in each of these matters and the circumstances in which distress may be levied or execution granted against assets. However the existence of the liquidation itself has certain consequences as a range of statutory provisions seek to preserve the *pari passu* treatment of creditors in the winding up process by limiting as far as possible the rights of those who have levied execution or distress or otherwise begun proceedings against the company.

Effect of liquidation on distress or execution

18.30   First, s 128(1) avoids 'any attachment, sequestration, distress or execution put in force against the estate or effects of the company after the commencement' of a winding up by the court. This protects the assets from that stage onwards in such a liquidation. The section applies to distress for rent, rates and taxes and to all forms of execution, equitable as well as legal. The case law lays down that the provision is subject to a power of the court to give leave for execution to be levied despite the absence of any qualification to the wording of the section.[36] This view was upheld by the Court of Appeal in *Re Lancashire Cotton Spinning Company*[37] and followed in later cases despite the enactment of what is now s 183 with just such an express qualification in s 183(2)(c).[38] It is clear that the power of the court to give leave for distress or execution to continue applies and modifies the word 'void' which is used in s 128 as regards the effect of winding up on such processes.

18.31   Leave to continue with distress or execution begun before the commencement of the winding up or for such steps to be initiated after that time is seldom given because the principle of *pari passu* treatment of creditors in the liquidation would be violated. The circumstances in which the court will give leave are limited to those in which force has been used to prevent the levy of execution immediately before the commencement of the winding up (as in the case of *Re London Cotton Co*[39] where the door was shut in the face of the sheriff when he came to levy execution) or where fraud and trickery are used to postpone the execution or the creditor levying execution changes his position on the basis of the act of the company, this was the case in *Rudow v Great Britain Mutual Life Assurance Society Ltd*[40]

---

36   See *Re Exhall Coal Mining Co Ltd* (1864) 4 De GJ & Sm 377
37   (1887) 35 Ch D 656
38   See *The Constellation* [1965] 1 WLR 272
39   (1886) LR 2 Eq 53
40   (1881) 17 Ch D 600

where the creditor incurred liability for costs on the basis of the company's liability to indemnify her and the company did not inform her of imminent winding up proceedings. The latter case is an indication of how the court might exercise its discretion under s 128 although it dealt with the predecessor of s 126 giving the court power to restrain proceedings against the company between the petition and the winding up order.

18.32 The power of the court under s 126(1) after the presentation of a winding up petition and before an order is made to restrain further proceedings in an action or proceeding begun before the petition was presented applies to execution and to distraint. However, this discretion will normally be exercised to allow the continuation of the distress or excution unless there are circumstances (such as unfair dealing) making it inequitable to allow the creditor to continue the proceedings. The benefit, to the other creditors in the winding up, of restraining the proceedings does not of itself amount to such a special reason.[41] In the case of a landlord levying distress, the proceeds of a sale will be available to the preferential creditors under s 176 if the sale takes place within 3 months before a winding up order was made. However, s 183 on the effect of the commencement of winding up on executions or attachments does not apply to distress for rent.[42] The enforcement of a charge or a lien over the company's property will be allowed to continue as it is closer to the enforcement of an existing security over property than to proceedings against the company.[43] A similar approach applies to a payment into court by the company under RSC Order 22 as the other party in the action is regarded as a secured creditor and removal of the money by the liquidator will not normally be allowed by an exercise of the court's discretion because the liquidation of the defendant company is not in itself sufficient to justify such a decision.[44]

18.33 The restriction in s 128 extends to distraint by a landlord insofar as he is using the remedy after the commencement of the winding up and as a creditor of the company. He may distrain for rent due for the period after the commencement of the winding up if the property has been retained by the liquidator for continued use or an advantageous disposal. However some definite decision must have been made by the liquidator to retain the property for such a purpose. It is not enough that he has failed to dispose of it. Any evidence of a new lease in the name of the liquidator or of occupation by him jointly with the company may result in the landlord not having the

41 *Re Bellaglade Ltd* [1977] 1 All ER 319
42 *Ibid*
43 *Blackeley v Dent* (1876) 15 WR 663
44 *Sherrat (WA) Ltd v John Bromley (Church Stretton) Ltd* [1985] QB 1038

right to distrain against company goods for post-liquidation rent. That debt will be due from the liquidator if there is a new agreement with him or will be apportioned if the occupation was joint.[45] The landlord may also use his right of re-entry for non-payment of rent to obtain rent due for the period before the commencement of the winding up.

18.34   Distress against goods which are on the company's premises but which do not belong to it in respect of rent due from the owner of those goods is permissible as the prohibition in s 128 applies only to 'the estate or effects of the company'. This exception could give rise to interesting possibilities in the case of groups of companies in which one goes into liquidation at a different time from other members of the group but has property on its premises belonging to a company which owes rent.

Effect of liquidation on actions or proceedings

18.35   Section 130(2) prevents any 'action or proceeding' being proceeded with or commenced against the company or its property without the leave of the court after a winding up order has been made or a provisional liquidator appointed. In *Re Memco Engineering*[46] it was held that distress levied by the Customs and Excise authorities under the VAT legislation was an action or proceeding but that leave to continue it by sale of the goods distrained would be granted in the absence of any special reasons such as unconscionable conduct or undue delay on the part of the distrainor making it inequitable to decide in this way. This was an application of *Herbert Berry Associates Ltd v Inland Revenue*[47] in which the House of Lords refused to restrain a levy of distress begun before the commencement of a voluntary liquidation under what is now s 112 on the basis that there was nothing making it inequitable to allow the distrainor to retain the property. It seems a somewhat strained interpretation of the section to hold that distress is an 'action or proceeding' but that does appear to be the case. In general an application under s 112 to restrain a levy of distress in a voluntary liquidation will be dealt with on the same principles as apply to a compulsory liquidation.[48]

18.36   A counterclaim by a defendant against the company is regarded as a proceeding and so should only be made after the winding up order has been made with the leave of the Companies Court to ensure an orderly process of winding up.[49] The commencement of an action will not normally be

---

45   See *Re ABC Coupler & Engineering Co Ltd* [1970] 1 All ER 650 and the cases cited there
46   [1985] 3 All ER 267
47   [1978] 1 All ER 161
48   *Re South Rhondda Colliery Co* [1928] WN 126
49   *Langley Construction (Brixham) Ltd v Wells* [1969] 1 WLR 503

permitted if proof of the debt in the liquidation is the appropriate way of dealing with the case. The use of the liquidation process to deal with the claims is cheaper and faster and even in cases where the plaintiffs claim to be the beneficial owners of property in the hands of the company the liquidator's role ensures that the claims of all classes are fairly dealt with.[50] The approach of the court under s 130(2), like its approach under s 183(2)(c) (see paras 18.38—18.46), is to do what is right and fair according to the facts of each case. A creditor who had effectively encumbered a vessel with his claim by issuing a writ and entering a caveat in the Admiralty register was allowed to proceed with the action even if he was not, strictly, a secured creditor.[51] The general principle will be that claims are best dealt with in the winding up and leave to bring or continue proceedings should be refused unless it is unfair to insist on this because, for example, the right to be enforced is analogous to that of a secured creditor.

18.37 The use of the court's discretion to protect property rights is confirmed by the approach to actions for specific performance. It is well established that actions for the specific performance of agreements for the sale of the company's real property will normally be allowed where the claim to that remedy is unimpugnable. This reflects the fact that the plaintiff had equitable ownership rights to the land and would be deprived of them and left to prove in the winding up for damages if he were not permitted to proceed with his claim for an order of specific performance. Any issue about the adequacy of the consideration for the property can be dealt with in the action for specific performance.[52]

Incomplete execution or attachment

18.38 Where an execution or attachment is incomplete at the commencement of a winding up s 183 and 184 govern the situation. They prevent the retention of the benefit of the process by the creditor as against the liquidator. These sections apply to both voluntary and compulsory liquidations. Section 183 lays down that if the creditor levying execution had notice of a meeting having been called at which a resolution for voluntary liquidation was to be proposed, the process of execution must be complete before that date if the benefit of it is to be retained against the liquidator. If the winding up is compulsory the date of the presentation of the petition will apply. The rule applies to the execution levied against the land or goods of the company and the attachment of its debts. For the purpose of the Act, the definition of the completion of such processes is:

50   *Re Exchange Securities and Commodities Ltd* [1983] BCLC 186
51   *Re Aro Co Ltd* [1980] 1 Ch 196
52   See *Re Coregrange* [1984] BCLC 453

(a) execution by the seizure and sale of goods or the making of a charging order against them under s 1 of the Charging Orders Act 1979;

(b) execution by the seizure of land, the appointment of a receiver or the making of a charging order under s 1 of the 1979 Act;

(c) attachment of a debt by receipt of it.[53]

18.39   A charging order is only complete when an order absolute is made; an order *nisi* is not sufficient.[54] The expression 'goods' in the section includes all chattels personal and 'the sheriff' includes any officer charged with the the execution of a writ or other process.[55] The 'benefit' of the execution or attachment means the charge conferred by it and the right to take the steps necessary to complete it.[56] It includes the right to obtain a garnishee order. One consequence of this definition is that money paid under the execution before the creditor had notice of the meeting at which a winding up resolution was to be passed or before the presentation of a petition can be retained if it is not obtained by making use of the charge which represents the 'benefit' of the execution.[57] It also follows that money paid to the sheriff to avoid sale is not part of the benefit of the execution.[58] Distress is not regarded as execution for the purpose of this provision.[59]

18.40   The rule in s 183(1) is modified by s 183(2) in two respects. First, a person who purchases in good faith, under a sale by the sheriff, goods on which execution has been levied obtains a good title against the liquidator.[60] Consequently there can be no claim against the goods in such a case. Secondly, the rights conferred on the liquidator by s 183(1) to take the benefit of an incomplete execution can be set aside by the court in favour of a creditor 'to such extent and subject to such terms as the court thinks fit'.[61] The court will exercise this discretion on the basis of seeking to achieve fairness.[62] The general principle that all creditors rank equally in the winding up is important and the court will not accept an argument that certain class of creditor (such as those who claim a beneficial interest in property held by the company) cannot rely on the liquidation process to deal with their claim.[63] Factors such as fraud or dishonesty on the part of

53   s 183(3)
54   *Roberts Petroleum v Bernard Kenny Ltd* [1983] BCLC 28
55   s 183(4)
56   See *Re Andrew* [1937] Ch 122 and *Carribean Products v Swains Packaging Ltd* [1966] 1 Ch 331
57   *Ibid*
58   *Re Walkden Sheet Metal Co* [1960] Ch 170
59   *Re Bellaglade* [1977] 1 All ER 319
60   s 183(2)(b)
61   s 183(2)(c)
62   *Re Grosvenor Metal Co* [1950] Ch 63
63   *Carribean Products v Swains* (note 56 above)

the company in preventing the completion of the execution will make an order in favour of the creditor more likely and requests or pressure by the company officers on the creditor which fall short of trickery but delay the completion of the execution can have the same effect.[64]

18.41 However not all delays by the company which prejudice the creditor will have this effect. The court will assess the position on the information before it and will have regard to the importance of *pari passu* treatment for creditors in the liquidation. In a case where the creditor in question is one member of a class (eg trade creditors) it is difficult to determine at what point the execution would have been completed if there had been no winding up. Would other creditors likewise have levied execution but for the company stalling? It may be that steps to complete the execution earlier would have led to an earlier commencement of the winding up and the court will be reluctant to enage in such speculation.[65] For these reasons it will be difficult to persuade the court to exercise its discretion unless the creditor seeking a dispensation is in a unique position.

18.42 Under s 184 even the proceeds of an completed execution levied against goods can be taken by the liquidator in either a compulsory or a voluntary winding up providing notice of the appointment of a provisional liquidator, the making of a winding up order or the passing of a resolution for the voluntary liquidation of the company has been served on the sheriff. If the notice is served on the sheriff before the sale of the goods or the completion of the execution by the receipt or recovery of the full amount of the levy, goods and any money seized or received in part satisfaction of the execution must be delivered to the liquidator when he requires the sheriff to do so subject to a charge on the goods or money for the costs of the execution. The liquidator may sell all or part of the goods to satisfy the charge.[66]

18.43 If goods are sold or money is paid to avoid sale under an execution for a judgment for more than £500 the sheriff must retain for 14 days the balance of the proceeds of sale or money paid to avoid sale after deducting the costs of the execution. If he is served with notice within that time of a meeting being called to consider a winding up resolution or the presentation of a winding up petition he must pay the balance to the liquidator if the resolution is passed or a winding up order is made. The liquidator may retain that balance as against the execution creditor.[67]

---

64   *Re Grosvenor Metal Co* [1950] Ch 63 and *Re Sudair International Airways* [1951] Ch 165
65   See *Re Redman Builders* [1964] 1 WLR 541, following *Re Vron Colliery Co* (1882) 20 Ch D 442
66   s 184(1) & (2)
67   s 184(4)

While the right to defeat the execution creditor's title under s 184(4) applies to money paid to avoid a sale, the requirement to deliver up money under s 184(2) only applies to money seized or paid in satisfaction of the execution and does not apply to money paid to avoid a sale.[68] The court has a discretion to set aside the rights of the liquidator under s 184(5) to such extent and subject to such terms as it thinks fit. The criteria for the exercise of that discretion are the same as those which apply to the discretion conferred on the court under s 183(2)(b).

18.44 Section 42 of the Companies Act 1985 which is derived from s 9(4) of the European Communities Act 1972 lays down that a company is not allowed to rely, against other persons, on the making of a winding up order or the appointment of a liquidator in a voluntary winding up unless that event has been officially notified or is shown by the company to have been known to the person concerned at the material time. Official notification means the publication in the *London Gazette* by the Registrar of Companies of a copy of the winding up order or the appointment under s 711(1)(p) of the Companies Act 1985 or s 109 of the Insolvency Act 1986.[69] Gazetting does not constitute notice to the whole world. Actual notice is still required before a landlord loses his right to forfeit by accepting rent after the company is in liquidation.[70]

18.45 It is uncertain whether that provision affects the operation of s 183 and 184 by allowing a third party to argue that in the absence of official notification or the discharge by the company of the burden of proof that there was actual knowledge, the rights of the liquidator under the sections cannot operate. Such a result can only arise if the company is relying on the making of a winding up order or the appointment of a liquidator. Under s 183 reliance is placed on the presentation of the petition or the passing of a winding up resolution (as the test is whether the execution was completed before the commencement of the winding up) or on notice of a meeting to consider the passing of a resolution for voluntary liquidation. Reliance is not placed on the making of the winding up order. It could be argued that reliance is placed on the appointment of the liquidator in a voluntary winding up in the sense that he must hold office before the section can apply. However, the section bases his right against the judgement creditor on the resolution or notice of it and not on his appointment.

18.46 Section 184 which is directed at the sheriff poses greater problems in that it bites when notice that a winding up order has been made is served on

68 *Marley Tile Co v Burrows* [1978] QB 241
69 s 711(2)
70 *Official Custodian of Charities v Parway Estates Ltd* [1984] BCLC 309

the sheriff, a provisional liquidator appointed or a winding up resolution passed. This raises the prospect that, in a compulsory liquidation in which the making of the order is the trigger for the section to apply, s 42 might operate. However, this should cause no difficulty. Under s 184(1) it is against the sheriff that the company, through the liquidator, is relying on the making of the order—not the creditor. The section can only operate if notice has been served on the sheriff. . Even in the limited circumstances in which the company might be said to rely on the making of a winding up order actual notice to the sheriff satisfies the requirement of s 42.

Sale of goods contracts

18.47　The right of the company to take delivery of goods which it has agreed to buy will be dependent on the terms of the contract. The unpaid vendor's lien and right of stoppage *in transitu* may be exercisable because of the insolvency of the purchasing company and may entitle the seller to refuse delivery.[71] If the goods have been delivered there may be a question whether property in them has passed and the contract may seek to protect the vendor's position by the use of a retention of title clause.[72]

CHOSES IN ACTION

18.48　The right of the liquidator of the company to intangibles follows the same general principles that apply to other property. His title is that of the company and he takes subject to security rights created earlier[73] and the ownership rights of others to whom, for example, receivables have been sold.[74] Similarly funds held on trust for others are not available for use in the liquidation.[75]

Third Parties (Rights Against Insurers) Act 1930

18.49　In the case of insurance policies held by the company the liquidator can claim just as the company could by adhering to the conditions of the policy including, for example, the need to notify the insurer within a certain time of the event giving rise to the claim. Where an insurance policy covers the liability of the company to a third party then the Third Parties (Rights

71　See ch 6
72　See ch 9
73　See ch 4
74　See ch 9
75　See ch 9

Against Insurers) Act 1930 applies. This provides for a statutory right of subrogation where the insured is a company and it goes into liquidation or receivership or is the subject of a voluntary arrangement approved under Part I of the Insolvency Act 1986. In such cases the rights of the company against the insurer under the insurance contract are transferred to and vest in the third party.[76] Liability on the part of the company must be established for the transfer to take place. A right which does not exist and which is incapable of coming into existence cannot be enforced. This will be the case where no proceedings were issued before or during the liquidation and it is impossible to revive the company after it has been dissolved.[77]

18.50 However, liability can have been incurred either before or after the insolvency proceeding which gives rise to the statutory subrogation. The liquidator is under an obligation to give, to a person claiming that the company is liable to him, any information he reasonably requires in order to find out whether rights have been transferred to him under the Act and for the purpose of enforcing such right.[78] Where the liability of the insurance company under the policy is subject to a condition precedent that they be notified of the accident giving rise to the claim and of any proceedings, they can defeat the victim's claim if they were not notified of the proceedings even if they have suffered only slight prejudice.[79] It is not possible for the insurance company to set off any unpaid premiums on the policy against the rights of the third party. It will have to prove for such sums in the winding up.[80]

Set off

18.51 The efforts of the liquidator to collect debts due to the company in gathering the assets in the winding up may be met by the claim that the debtor is also a creditor of the company. Were he merely to prove in the company's liquidation for its debt to him he would suffer loss if he is more solvent than the company. For this reason the rules applicable to a liquidation allow a right of set off which is more extensive than that which would be available in equity if there were no winding up or bankruptcy.

18.52 If the debtor is insolvent and will ultimately pay a lower dividend to its creditors than the creditor company the latter will gain from the right of set off. In all other cases the other creditors will lose as the right of

---

76 s 1(1) Third Parties (Rights Against Insurers) Act 1930
77 *Bradley v Eagle Star Insurance Co* (1989) The Times 3 March HL
78 *Ibid* s 2
79 *Pioneer Concrete (UK) v National Employer's Mutual Insurance Association* [1985] 2 All ER 395
80 *Murray v Legal and General Assurance Society Ltd* [1970] 2 QB 495

set off will result in the creditor being able to set off the debt due from him to the company and effectively receiving full payment. However, since the issue of set off arises in relation to debts due to the company from persons who are also its creditors it is dealt with in this section on the gathering in of assets rather than the section on the distribution of the amount realised after the assets have been collected in the liquidation process.

18.53 The rules of set off which apply when a company is in liquidation are those developed in the context of bankruptcy law. In addition to the set off available because of the rules of equity, which are of general application and therefore apply to receiverships, a wider range of transactions can be the subject of set off in a liquidation. Contractual arrangements for set off on a basis different from that applied by the Insolvency Rules are not permitted.[81]

18.54 Before the Insolvency Rules 1986[82] s 612 of the Companies Act 1985 applied the rules of bankruptcy on the debts provable and the valuation of liabilities in company liquidations. Since the repeal of that section by the Insolvency Act 1986 the rules on those matters are to be found in the Insolvency Rules 1986. Rule 4.90 provides for the set off of debts due from the company against those due to it and lays down the circumstances in which this can be done. The rule sets out principles virtually identical to those developed in bankruptcy law and wider than those governing set off in equity. The rule applies where, before the company goes into liquidation, there have been mutual credits, debts or other mutual dealings between the company and a creditor of the company proving or claiming to prove in the liquidation.[83] The purpose of the rule has been said to be to do substantial justice between the parties and not only to avoid cross actions as is the case with equitable set off.[84]

Scope of set off
18.55 A wide range of claims is covered by the rule. A preferential creditor can use it but must set off his debt rateably between the preferential and non-preferential elements of his claim. This was laid down in a case involving a set off between amounts owed to the Department of Health and Social Security and sums due to the company for VAT inputs; a common area for the application of set off.[85] The court laid down that the whole of the set off could not be applied to the non preferential debt as the nature of set off was an accounting exercise and the principle of 'equality is equity'

---

81   See below para 18.3.3.2.4
82   SI 1986 no 1925
83   r 4.90(1)
84   *Re D H Curtis (Builders) Ltd* [1978] Ch 162 at 173
85   See para 18.62–18.64 below on the position on debts to Goverment Departments

should apply as between different creditors. This was best achieved by a rateable set off of the credit.[86]

18.56   A debt which is secured can itself be the subject of set off.[87] If the security is realised before the commencement of liquidation any surplus held by the creditor can be set off against unsecured debts due to him from the company as mutual money claims exist before the commencement of the liquidation.[88] However, if the realisation only takes place after the commencement of the liquidation the surplus will not exist as a debt, credit or other mutual dealing between the creditor and the company before the company goes into liquidation and thus Rule 4.90(1) cannot apply and no set off will be permitted. The rules on set off by contributories are dealt with in paras 17.30—17.36 above.

18.57   There has been some uncertainty in the past whether contingent debts could be set off. It is submitted that it is now clear that this is the case. There is no doubt that a certain liability is within the rules if the amount due can be ascertained when the account is taken although that was not the case at the time of the commencement of the liquidation so long as the obligation existed then.[89] However, in *Carreras Rothmans Ltd v Freeman Mathews Treasure Ltd*[90] it was held that a contingent obligation to pay is not a debt due even if the contingency later occurs and a contract under which the the obligation arises was made before the commencement of the liquidation. This was distinguished from the situation in which the quantification of the amount due depended on a contingency which occurred after the winding up commenced.

18.58   This was not followed in *Re Charge Card Services Ltd*.[91] In that case the right to set off contingent debts was supported on the basis of the fact that such debts are provable and that the distinction between a debt, the amount of which, is dependent on a contingency and one, the existence of which depends on a contingency is one of degree and not of kind.[92] The view put forward in *Re Charge Services Ltd* was based on a thorough analysis of the legislative history of the provision of the Bankruptcy Act in issue, and of the relevant authorities. It is also supported by the fact that the wording of Rule 4.90(2) requires an account to be taken of what is 'due' from each party and that other rules clearly envisage proof of contingent

86   *Re Unit 2 Windows Ltd* [1985] 1 WLR 1383
87   *McKinnon v Armstrong* (1877) 2 App Ca 531
88   *Re H E Thorne & Son* [1914] 2 Ch 438
89   *Re Daintry* [1900] 1 QB 546
90   [1985] Ch 207
91   [1987] Ch 510
92   Per Millett J at 523

debts.[93] This reinforces the logic of the argument in *Re Charge Card Services Ltd* and confirms that the contingent debts can be set off. The right to set off amounts due extends to claims based on statute as well as those made on the basis of contracts.[94]

18.59   The right set off may be limited by the fact that double proof is not allowed in a liquidation.[95] A claim, based on the right of a surety who has not yet paid the debt, insisting that the principal pays the debt cannot be set off. If the surety is allowed to prove for the amount to which he will be entitled if he makes a payment as surety, it remains possible that the original creditor will also prove for the same debt. Since proof is not allowed set off is not permissable.[96] If the surety pays the company's debt after the commencement of its liquidation set off will be unavailable as the right to payment must exist at that time and the claim only arises on payment. The same difficulties will confront co-sureties claiming among themselves.[97] In the absence of payment by a surety in full before the commencement of the liquidation set off will not be available to him. This is particularly likely to arise in the case of cross guarantees by members of a group of companies.

18.60   The requirement that the mutual credits or debts existed before the company went into liquidation means that a claim must have been vested in the party seeking to set it off at that time. Thus a later assignment of the claim will prevent the assignee from claiming a set off.[98] Similarly, if a transaction giving rise to a credit or debt was with the liquidator there can be no set off as this must have occurred after the company went into liquidation. Rule 4.90(3) lays down that the account taken by way of set off must exclude sums due from the company to the other party if they became due at a time when that party had notice of a pending winding up petition or that a s 98 creditor's meeting had been summoned.

Mutuality
18.61   Rule 4.90(1) requires that debts, credits or dealings be mutual before set off can apply to them. This reflects the bankruptcy rules that preceded the Insolvency Rules and has been the subject of substantial case law. It is necessary to show an intention on the part of both parties to continue dealings with each other extending credit in respect of individual sums of money on each side until an account is made. In the context of

---

93   See especially r 4.86
94   *Re D H Curtis (Builders) Ltd* [1978] Ch 162
95   See paras 19.39 *et seq infra*
96   *Re Fenton* [1931] 1 Ch 85
97   Brown v Cork [1985] BCLC 363 at 368; and see r 4.90(1)
98   *Re Milan Tramways Co ex p Theys* [1884] 25 Ch D 587

banker and customer running a current account, or of any other continuing course of dealings between two parties, the courts are likely to find mutuality so long as there is an express or implied intention that the sums due on each side will be brought into account periodically. By contrast isolated dealings, or those which are part of a complex of mutual dealings but are singled out by the paries for separate settlement apart from the running account, will not be included.[99]

18.62   A transaction in which property is handed over for a special or specific purpose, of a kind which means that it would be a misappropriation to use the property for a purpose other than that for which it was paid, is excluded and cannot be the subject of set off. This will cover the situation in which property is held as bailee or trustee or in some other fiduciary capacity.[100] Lack of mutuality for this reason can be explained on the basis of the different nature of the dealings or of the fact that the debts were not between the parties in the same right if one of them holds as a fiduciary.[101] A similar lack of mutuality on the basis that different parties are effectively involved applies where one dealing is with an individual in his private capacity and the other is with him as a partner in a firm or where the acts are done personally and as executor.[102]

18.63   It is generally accepted that for this purpose the Crown is a single party and thus different government departments can set off each other's debts; as where the Inland Revenue sets off tax due against payments due to the company from HM Customs and Excise in respect of VAT. However, RSC Order 77 Rule 6 lays down that no person may plead a set off in proceedings by the Crown if the set off arises out of a claim to repayment of, or in respect of, any taxes, duties or penalties and that in any proceedings in which the Crown sues or is sued in the name of a government department, leave of the court is required for a set off to be raised if its subject matter relates to a different government department.

18.64   In *Re D H Curtis (Builders) Ltd* it was clearly established that the right of set off does apply to the Crown and is not limited to contractual claims. This was followed in *Re Cushla*.[103] However, the issue of whether leave was required for the Crown to claim set off between debts due to and from different government departments was not raised in either case but was dealt with by concession. Since the cases held unequivocally that the predecessor provision to Rule 4.90 applied to such debts it is possible that it

---

99   See *Rolls Razor Ltd v Cox* [1967] 1 QB 552 per Winn LJ at 575
100   *Re Mid-Kent Fruit Factory* [1896] 1 Ch 567
101   *Lee & Chapman's Case* (1885) 30 Ch D 216
102   *West v Pryce* (1825) 2 Bing 455
103   [1979] 3 All ER 415

follows that the RSC requirement of leave is overruled. Alternatively, it seems clear that the concern with justice between the parties which underlies the set off rules in bankruptcy and liquidation would justify a virtually automatic grant of leave if an application were required and were made. It is possible that a set off involving transactions of a different nature which were not comparable on each side and therefore not commensurate could fall outside the set off rules.[104] This might be the case if the Crown sought to set off a debt resulting from a commercial transaction against an amount due as tax. However it has been held that a debt due to a company from a Area Health Authority acting as agent for the DHSS for services provided on a commercial basis can be set off against amount due to the DHSS from the company because mutuality exists.[105] Attempts to amend the Insolvency Act 1985 to prevent the treatment of the Crown as a single entity were unsuccessful during its legislative passage.

18.65 Mutuality requires that the claims on each side should be in respect of pecuniary liabilities and consequently a claim for the return of goods cannot be set off against a money claim. This was first established in the case of *Eberle's Hotels and Restaurant Co. Ltd v Jonas*.[106] In that case a claim for the value of goods made in a detinue action was held not to be capable of being set off against debts. This rule does not, however, apply to goods in a party's hands for the purpose of conversion into money. In *Rolls Razor v Cox*[107] an agent who had been involved in mutual dealings with the company was held by the Court of Appeal to be entitled to set off both money, belonging to the company but held by him, and company goods held for the purpose of sale against commission due to him from the company, but he could not set off the value of goods held by him for the purpose of use rather than sale.

18.66 When a debt is assigned the assignee *prima facie* takes subject to the equities which exist between the assignor and the debtor at the time of assignment. That will include a right of set off in respect of claims arising before assignment. However, if set off is claimed in respect of later transactions or liabilities it will only be available if the claims arise out of the same contract which gave rise to the assigned debt and are closely intertwined the the debt.[108] It is also essential that the result of assignments should leave mutual debts or credits between the parties claiming set off. The holder of an insurance policy who has mortgaged it to the insurance

104 *Re D H Curtis (Builders) Ltd* [1978] Ch 776
105 *R A Cullen Ltd v Nottingham AHA* (1986) BCC 99367
106 (1887) 18 QBD 459
107 [1967] 1 QB 552
108 *Government of Newfoundland v Newfoundland Railway Commpany* (1883) 13 App Cas 199

company can set off the value of the policy against the amount due on the mortgage if the company goes into liquidation but if the company has effectively assigned the mortgage he will not be able to do so as a completed assignment (in law or equity) will mean that the amount due on the mortgage is no longer payable to the company.[109] Assignment of a chose in action by a company after it is in liquidation will be subject to set off. Only the balance due to the company after set off is available to the assignee.[110] By analogy to the rule which prevents the set off of the amount due from a contributory (see para 17.30—17.36), directors are not permitted to set off amounts which they are required to pay the company as a result of misfeasance against amounts due to them from the company.[111]

The account

18.67   Rule 4.90(2) lays down that an account is to be taken of what is due from one party to the other in respect of the mutual dealings which have taken place between them and that the sums due on each side should be set off against each other. Only any balance on the account is provable in the liquidation or (as the case may be) payable to the liquidator as part of the assets of the company.[112] As has been noted above, sums due from the company to the other party must not be included in the account if that party had notice, at the time they became due, that a meeting of creditors had been summoned under s 98, or that a petition for the winding up of the company was pending.[113]

Exclusion of set off

18.68   The courts have laid down that the set off rules cannot be excluded by the agreement of the parties and cannot be renounced or waived. This view is based on the use of the word 'shall' in the provision and the need for the administration of the estates of insolvents in a proper and orderly way.[114] It follows from this that any contractual right of set off that seeks to go further than the statutory provision will be struck down. Such a fate will befall any arrangement which tries to replace the *pari passu* payment of debts required by s 107 with some other system such as the clearance of a complex range of transactions, whether or not set off is involved.[115]

18.69   It is for this reason that the Companies Act 1989 seeks to prevent

---

109 *Re City Life Assurance Company Ltd* [1926] Ch 191
110 *Farley v Housing and Commercial Developments Ltd* [1984] BCLC 442
111 *Re Anglo-French Co-operative Society ex p Pelly* (1882) 21 Ch D 492
112 r 4.90(4)
113 r 4.90(3)
114 See r 4.90(2) & (3) and *National Westminster Bank v Halesowen Presswork* [1972] AC 785
115 *British Eagle International Airlines Ltd v Compagnie Nationale Air France* [1975] 1 WLR 758

the general law of insolvency from applying to arrangements made by recognised investment exchanges and recognised clearing houses for dealing with the default of members, or others dealt with by the rules of the Exchange. It was feared that without such legislation those arrangements would be regarded as an attempt to contract out of the general law of insolvency and would thus be unenforceable. The principle of set off is extended to what are, in effect, clearance schemes by the Act and the statutory instruments to be made under it. However the statutory provisions will apply only to the rules of the markets referred to and then only to the provisions concerned with the dealing contracts of defaulting members of those markets and certain charges given to secure their obligations in connection with such transactions.[116]

The statutory rescission of contracts

18.70 Apart from the possibility of the rules of set off applying to the debts due to the company, the Insolvency Act 1986 permits the other party to a contract with the company to apply to the court for rescission so that there are no longer any obligations to carry out the agreement. The aim of this provision is to allow a person who has entered a contract with the company to avoid the need to perform his part of an executory contract when he will be left with no more than the right to prove in the liquidation for a dividend in respect of the consideration due to him from the company. It has a similar basis to the set off rules which are meant to prevent the injustice of a creditor having to hand over the full amount due from him to the company and to receive only a dividend in respect of the amounts due to him. It is possible that the effect at common law of the company going into liquidation will be to terminate a contract automatically or to give the other party the right to rescind it if the liquidation or actions of the liquidator represents a sufficiently serious breach of the agreement.[117]

18.71 Section 186(1) gives the court a right to rescind a contract between the company and the applicant on such terms as to the payment of damages for non performance by, of to, either party or otherwise as the court thinks just. Application can be made by a person who is, as against the liquidator, entitled to the benefit or subject to the burden of a contract made with company. Any damages payable to a party other than the company are provable in the winding up.[118]

---

116 Companies Act 1989 Part VII. Because of the specialist nature and limited application of these rules, they are not dealt with in this book.
117 *Sale Continuations Ltd v Austin Taylor & Co Ltd* [1968] 2 QB 849.
118 s 186(2)

18.72 The section can apply whenever a contract has not been fully performed and is not, in terms, limited to wholly executory contracts. The court is not obliged to look at the whole range of dealings between the parties and is perfectly entitled to rescind only one or more of several contracts between them.[119] It will be difficult for the liquidator to resist an application for rescission unless he is able to assure the court that the contract will be performed in full.

THE REALISATION OF ASSETS

18.73 The liquidator will wish to realise the assets once he has gathered them in. It is possible to distribute assets *in specie* to those entitled in the liquidation. That is an unusual procedure and is only permissible if the liquidation committee consents and if the property to be divided between creditors cannot be readily or advantageously sold because of its peculiar nature or other special circumstances.[120] Similarly, it is possible for the liquidator to hive down the entire business of the company and to dispose of it as a going concern or to sell off particular assets separately. The judgment on which course to pursue will be based on the opinion of the liquidator on the method likely to result in sale for the best value and with the greatest security of payment. The powers and role of the liquidator have been dealt with in chapter 15. They permit sale by a variety of means. There is no need to sell for cash and the property which can be sold includes land, chattels and things in action; including the right to sue the company's directors for misfeasance.[121] In selling the assets of the company he must carry out his duties without negligence and in accordance with his position as a fiduciary. This involves ensuring that a reasonable price is obtained and that any advertiements are accurate.[122] He should obtain a valuation of assets from an independent competent valuer and may also seek advice from such a source on whether by private treaty or by auction is preferable and on the best means of advertising the sale. It is usual for the liquidator to prepare full schedules and lists of the property which is available for realisation.

18.74 A decision by the liquidator to sell an asset can only be challenged on the basis of fraud, a failure to excercise discretion in good faith or a proposal to do something that no reasonable man could do. Negligence is not sufficient to justify an order preventing a proposed sale and a statement

119   *Re Castle* [1917] 2 KB 725
120   r 4.183
121   *Re Park Gate Wagon Works Co* (1881) 17 Ch D 234
122   See *Cuckmere Brick Co Ltd v Mutaual Finance Ltd* [1971] 2 All ER 633

of claim which seeks to prevent sale and fails to allege facts supporting one of the grounds on which a sale may be challenged will be struck out.[123]

18.75 In addition to the fiduciary duties imposed by the courts, Rule 4.149 lays down that the court may set aside any transaction between the liquidator and an associate of his on the application of any interested person and order the liquidator to compensate the company for any loss that it has suffered in consequence of the transaction. An associate for that purpose has the same meaning as in the Insolvency Act 1986.[124] The rule does not apply if the transaction was entered into with the prior consent of the court or is shown to the court's satisfaction without knowledge or reason to suppose that the person concerned was an associate.[125] The rule is without prejudice to any remedies available in law and equity.[126] Once the assets have been gathered and realised the proceeds must then be distributed in accordance with the rules contained in the Act and the Insolvency Rules.

123   *Harold Pitman & Co v Top Business Systems (Nottingham) Ltd* [1984] BCLC 593
124   See para 20.18 below
125   r 4.149(2)
126   r 4.149(3)

CHAPTER 19

The Distribution of Assets on Winding Up and the Dissolution of the Company

GENERAL ORDER OF DISTRIBUTION OF ASSETS

19.01 Assets subject to security rights are outside the liquidation and consequently are used to meet the claims of secured creditors. Only any balance remaining will fall into the assets available to the liquidator for distribution in the winding up. Secured creditors will be able to prove in the liquidation for amounts due to them over and above what they have realised by the use of their security and, in the case of a floating charge, the preferential creditors will have priority over the holder of the charge. However, subject to those qualifications which are dealt with more fully at the appropriate points in this chapter, the order of distribution discussed here does not affect property that is subject to security rights or the debts secured on it.

19.02 After the claims of the secured creditors have been met out of the property which was subject to their security, the liquidator will apply the assets in the liquidation in accordance with the order laid down in the Insolvency Act 1986. Subject to the priority accorded to the expenses of the liquidation and to the preferential debts the principle of *pari passu* distribution applies.

19.03 The Act's provisions cannot be varied by any arrangement between the parties to a contract. In *British Eagle International Airlines v Compagnie Nationale Air France*[1] a clearing house arrangement made between airlines in respect of amounts due between them could not be enforced as it was held to amount to an attempt to contract out of what is now s 107 of the Insolvency Act 1986. Such an arrangement was held by the House of Lords to be contrary to public policy as a breach of the principle of *pari passu* distribution.

19.04 The following list summarises the order of distribution that may be deduced from the Act and the Insolvency Rules 1986 and refers to the section of this chapter which deals with each type of claim.

(a) Expenses of the liquidation (paras 19.06 *et seq*);

1 [1975] 1 WLR 758.

(b) Preferential creditors (paras 19.17 *et seq*);

(c) Ordinary debts (paras 19.39 *et seq*);

(d) Post-liquidation interest on debts (paras 19.73–76 and 19.99);

(e) Debts postponed under s 215(4) of the Insolvency Act 1986 and costs subject to a *Bathampton* order (para 19.100).

19.05   The following are amounts payable to contributories:

(a) Any liability of the company on agreements to buy or redeem shares under s 178(4) of the Companies Act 1985 (paras 19.101–2);

(b) Debts owed to past or present members in their character as members before the commencement of the liquidation rank here by virtue of s 74(2)(f) (paras 19.103–4);

(c) Expenses of summoning and holding a meeting of contributories at the requisition of contributories if the meeting resolves that they should be paid out of assets. Rule 4.61(4). This claim ranks here as all preceding payments are to creditors or interest on debts due to creditors and the rule subordinates these expenses to such claims. Even a claim under s 178 of the Companies Act 1985 is a debt (para 19.105);

(d) Return of capital to members up to the nominal value of shares as far as paid up (paras 19.106–112);

(e) Distribution of surplus to contributories in accordance with s 107 and 154 of the Insolvency Act 1986 (paras 19.113–17).

THE EXPENSES OF WINDING UP

Priority of expenses

19.06   It is clear from s 175(1) and (2)(a) that the expenses of winding up have priority over preferential debts which in turn have priority over other debts. That section applies to any winding up whether it is voluntary or compulsory. The rules as to the order of payment of the different expenses among themselves are also similar in both compulsory and voluntary liquidations.

19.07   Section 156 gives the court a discretion to determine the order of priority in which the expenses of winding up should be paid out of the assets of the company if those assets are insufficient to satisfy the liabilities. That section applies only to winding up by the court but an application under s 112 could be used to request an exercise of the same discretion in a voluntary liquidation. It is submitted that the court could exercise that discretion despite the provision of Rule 4.220(1) which only makes the priorities laid down in Rule 4.218(1) subject to a contrary court order in compulsory liquidations. The power given in s 112(1) of the Act would override the provision of the Rule which appears to limit the court's discretion in voluntary liquidations. Section 115 lays down that in a voluntary liquidation all expenses properly incurred (including the remuneration of the liquidator) are to be paid out of the company's assets in priority to all other claims.

19.08   It is this priority accorded to liabilities incurred by the liquidator after the commencement of the liquidation which enables him to carry out his function by entering contracts or otherwise incurring debts. Creditors are aware that they can claim with priority over all pre-liquidation debts; including those due to preferential creditors.[2] This facilitates the continuation of the business of the company to the extent that this is necessary for a beneficial winding up.

Usual order of priority of expenses *inter se*

19.09   If the court does not make any order on the priority to be accorded to the different expenses of the liquidation and the assets are insufficient to meet all of them, then Rule 4.218 will apply to determine the order of payment. The order laid down by the rule is as follows:

(a) Expenses properly chargeable or incurred by the official receiver or the liquidator in preserving, realising or getting in any of the assets of the company. This includes the costs of employing a shorthand writer, if appointed by court order at the instance of the official receiver in connection with an examination.[3] It also includes such costs, expenses and liquidator's remuneration as the court has allowed in relation to a voluntary winding up where a compulsory liquidation follows it.[4] If the company goes into voluntary liquidation between the presentation of the petition for compulsory liquidation and the making of the order the voluntary liquidator's expenses may also be included.[5] The costs of a petition for an administration order presented at the same time as the winding up petition can also be included.[6] However, in the absence of a threat by the landlord to forfeit a lease, liabilities incurred by the liquidator to the landlord to allow for the continuation of the business and the assignment of the company's interest in the lease are costs of the

---

2   *Re Great Eastern Electricity Co* [1941] 1 Ch 241.
3   Insolvency Rules 1986 r 4.218(2).
4   r 4.219.
5   *Re A V Sorge & Co Ltd* (1986) 2 BCC 99, 306.
6   *Re Goscott (Groundworks) Ltd* [1988] BCLC 0000.

advantageous realisation of an asset rather than expenses incurred in preserving it.[7]

(b) Any other expenses incurred or disbursements made by the official receiver or under his authority, including those incurred or made in carrying out the business of the company.

(c) (i) The fee payable under any order made under s 414 for the performance by the official receiver of his general duties as official receiver.

(ii) Any repayable deposit lodged by the petitioner under any such order as security for the fee mentioned in subparagraph (i). Fees under the section are laid down in the Insolvency Fees Order 1986 SI 1986 no 2030.

(d) Any other fees payable under any order made under s 414, including those payable to the official receiver and any remuneration payable to him under general regulations.

(e) The cost of any security provided by a provisional liquidator, liquidator or special manager in accordance with the Act or the Rules.

(f) The remuneration of the provisional liquidator (if any) in a compulsory liquidation. This does not include the remuneration of some other person appointed to collect assets before the commencement of a voluntary winding up. Such a person can only claim expenses incurred to enable the resolution to be passed.[8]

(g) Any deposit lodged on an application for the appointment of a provisional liquidator.

(h) The costs of the petitioner, and of any person appearing on the petition whose costs are allowed by the court. These costs include those of the original petitioner where the successful petitioner was substituted for that person but only to the extent that the activities of the original petitioner contributed to a winding up order being obtained. This includes the presentation fee and advertising costs but not the costs of preparing the petition and appearing at the hearing which had to be incurred a second time.[9]

(i) The remuneration of the special manager (if any).

(j) Any amount payable to a person employed or authorised under chapter 6 of Part 4 of the Rules to assist in the preparation of a statement of affairs or accounts. This refers to Rules 4.37 and 4.41.

(k) Any allowance made, by order of the court on an application for release from the obligation to submit a statement of affairs or for an extension of time in submitting such a statement.

(l) Any necessary disbursements by the liquidator in the course of his

7 *Re Linda Marie Ltd* [1989] BCLC 46.
8 *Re Sandwell Copiers Ltd* [1988] BCLC 209.
9 *Re Bostels* [1968] 1 Ch 346.

administration (including the expenses incurred by members of the liquidation committee or their representatives and allowed by the liquidator under Rule 4.169, but not including any payment of capital gains tax in circumstances referred to in Rule 4.218(1)(p)).

(m) The remuneration or emoluments of any person who has been employed by the liquidator to perform any services for the company as required or authorised by or under the Act or the Rules. This deals with a wide range of payments as the powers of the liquidator to employ agents are wide. Rule 7.34 allows the liquidator to either insist on the taxation of such expenses costs or charges or to agree them. The liquidation committee can insist on taxation. The rule provides for the payment of amounts on account if there is to be taxation in return for an undertaking to repay any amount found to have been overpaid.

(n) The remuneration of the liquidator, up to any amount not exceeding that which is payable to the official receiver under general regulations. That amount is to be found in the Insolvency Regulations 1986 SI 1986 No 1994.

(o) The amount of any capital gains tax on chargeable gains accruing on the realisation of any asset of the company (without regard to whether the realisation is effected by the liquidator, a secured creditor, or a receiver or manager appointed to deal with the security).

(p) The balance, after payment of any sums due under Rule 4.218(1)(o) (para 19.09(n) above) of any remuneration due to the liquidator. See para 15.140 on the rules governing the procedure for fixing the remuneration of the liquidator.

19.10   The power of the court to make an order for costs is unaffected by these rules.[10] If the court orders that the costs of proceedings are to be paid out of the assets of the company directly, or by the liquidator from those assets, they can be taken from the assets as soon as the order is made without regard to whether the assets are sufficient to meet the other expenses of the winding up unless the liquidator can establish the existence of other claims that rank ahead of, or *pari passu* with, the litigant's costs.[11] Only the liquidator's costs of realisation have priority.

19.11   A solicitor employed in the winding up is paid out of the assets and not by the liquidator personally but he has a lien over any fund recovered by the use of his services and can enforce it with a charging order; even if the order is sought after the company is in liquidation and the fund was recovered before the commencement of the winding up.[12] Both litigious

---

10   r 4.220(2).
11   *Re Staffordshire Gas Co* [1893] 3 Ch 523 and *Re London Metallurgical Co* [1895] 1 Ch 758.
12   *Re Trueman's Estate* (1872) LR 14 Eq 278 and *Re Born* [1900] 2 Ch 433; and see paras 6.15–24 *supra*.

and non litigious costs in a liquidation are normally taxed on a common fund basis but the court has a discretion to order taxation on, for example, a trustee basis if the liquidator sought an order to expedite the distribution of assets.[13] Property subject to a security interest is not available to meet the costs of the winding up unless the liquidator is claiming the costs of realising the property for those who are entitled to it.[14]

19.12 In *Re Barleycorn Enterprises Ltd*[15] it was held that the expenses of the winding up have priority over both the preferential debts and a floating charge which has not crystallised before the commencement of the liquidation. However, if the floating charge crystallised before the commencement of the liquidation, the assets over which the receiver was appointed, or of which possession was taken, ceased to be assets in the winding up and were not available for the expenses of that process.[16] Since those cases were decided two changes have occurred.

19.13 Section 251 of the Insolvency Act 1986 defines a floating charge for the purpose of the Act as a charge which as created was a floating charge. This, together with the provisions of s 40 of the Act, means that the preferential debts are given priority over the claims of the holder of a debenture secured by a floating charge in any case in which a receiver is appointed on behalf of the debenture holders; even if the floating charge had crystallised before the receiver was appointed. The preferential creditors are to be paid out of the assets coming into the hands of the receiver in priority to the claims of the debenture holders. That provision applies if the receiver is appointed at a time when the company is not in the course of being wound up but the amount paid to preferential creditors can be recouped from the assets available for unsecured creditors if they are of sufficient value.[17] Section 196 of the Companies Act 1985 gives the same priority if possession is taken of assets by or on behalf of debenture holders secured by a floating charge.[18]

19.14 If it is accepted that the basis for the priority accorded to the expenses of the winding up is that they are payable before the preferential debts, it may be that they will now have priority whenever such debts are paid in advance of debenture holders; even if crystallisation occurred before the commencement of the winding up.

---

13 *Re Nation Life Insurance Co* [1978] 1 WLR 45.
14 *Re Regents Canal Ironwork Co* (1876) 3 Ch D 411.
15 [1970] 1 Ch 465.
16 *Re Christonette International* [1982] 1 WLR 1245.
17 s 40(2) and (3).
18 Sch 13 Insolvency Act 1986.

19.15   The fact that the case of *Re Brightlife*[19] has upheld the validity of automatic crystallisation clauses in floating charges means that in most cases crystallisation will occur before or simultaneously with the commencement of liquidation; even if a receiver is appointed or possession taken of the assets after the winding up has commenced. This is the result of the standard provision in floating charge documents stipulating that the charge crystallises when the company goes into liquidation. The criterion for the priority of the expenses of the liquidation may therefore become the date of the appointment of a receiver or of possession being taken of the assets in relation to a liquidation rather than crystallisation as it is the former which determines the position of the preferential creditors.

19.16   A guarantor of a company's debt who pays off that debt takes the priority that the creditor would have had in the winding up so that if an expense of the liquidation is paid off the guarantor will have that level of priority.[20]

PREFERENTIAL DEBTS

19.17   Certain debts have long been given preference in winding up and bankruptcy by statutory provision. The 1986 reforms of insolvency law substantially reduced the range of debts with this status; partly as a result of a government defeat in the House of Lords during the passage of the Insolvency Act 1985. The preferential rights of the state to taxes were cut down to those taxes held by the insolvent after being collected from others under systems such as PAYE, Betting Tax or VAT collection. The state's right to arrears of corporation tax was removed. The debts which now have priority are specified in s 386 and sch 6 of the Insolvency Act 1986 read with sch 3 to the Social Security (Pensions) Act 1975.

The priority of preferential debts

19.18   The preferential debts are those debts which by virtue of the Act are given priority over the claims of unsecured creditors and the holders of floating charges. They have no priority over fixed charges and no claim to any surplus remaining after a fixed charge is paid off. Such an amount must be handed over to the person entitled to it; a later chargee, the company, or the liquidator if the company is being wound up.[21] For this reason banks

19   [1986] 3 All ER 673.
20   *Re Downer Enterprises Ltd* [1974] 1 WLR 1460.
21   See *Re Lewis Merthyr Consolidated Collieries Ltd* [1929] 1 Ch 498 and *Re G L Sanders Ltd* [1986] BCLC 40.

and other major lenders to companies will seek to gain fixed charges over the widest possible range of assets; including, for example, book debts.

19.19 Section 175 of the Insolvency Act 1986 lays down that the preferential debts specified in s 386 and sch 6 of the Act are to be paid in priority to all other debts in a winding up. The fact that the rule applies to the winding up indicates that those debts dealt with outside liquidation by security on assets are not covered by the provision of the section. However, s 40 of the 1986 Act and s 196 of the Companies Act 1985, as substituted by the 1986 Act, lay down that preferential debts are to have priority over the claim of debenture holders, secured by a floating charge out of the assets, coming into the hands of the receiver or taken into the possession of the debenture holders.[22] Those sections apply when the debenture is secured by a charge which, as created, was a floating charge, even if it has become a fixed charge by crystallising before possession was taken or the receiver was appointed. In each case the provision applies to companies which are not in the course of winding up. Section 175 will operate to the same effect if the company is being wound up when the receiver is appointed or possession is taken as the assets will be part of the liquidation at that point. All three provisions ensure that the burden of the preferential debts falls on the unsecured creditors and that they are only effectively met by the holders of floating charges to the extent that the funds available to pay unsecured creditors are exhausted before the preferential debts have been paid in full. If they are met from assets in the possession of debenture holders or in the hands of their receiver before the commencement of the winding up then the payments can be recouped as far as possible from the assets of the company available for the payment of the general creditors.[23] If they are paid in a liquidation the funds available to general creditors are exahusted before property subject to a floating charge is touched.[24]

19.20 In a compulsory liquidation, s 176 confers priority on the preferential debts over goods subject to distress and the proceeds of their sale if distress occurred in the three months before the date of the winding up order. This is done by subjecting such goods or money to a charge. The charge is for the amount of the company's preferential debts to the extent that the company's property is for the time being insufficient to meet them. The section ranks a person who surrenders goods or makes a payment by virtue of the charge as a preferential creditor against the other assets of the company in respect of the amount raised by the sale of the goods surrendered or the amount of the money paid to the company.[25]

---

22 ss 40(2) and 196(2).
23 See ss 175(2)(b) and 40(3).
24 Companies Act 1985 s 196(4).
25 Insolvency Act 1986 s 176(3).

19.21   The section applies where a person 'has distrained' in the three month period. This includes a landlord or other distrainor of the company's goods who levied distress before the beginning of the three month period but sold the goods within it. In *Re Memco Engineering*[26] Mervyn Davies J held that a person could only be regarded as 'having distrained' once goods seized had also been sold.[27] The section is expressed to be without prejudice to s 128.[28] Distress put in force against the company's estate or effects after the commencement of the winding up will be void. The commencement of the winding up is the date of the petition but the three month period under s 176 runs from the date of the winding up order.

19.22   Preferential debts rank equally among themselves after the expenses of the winding up and are to be paid in full unless there are insufficient assets to meet them in which case they abate in equal proportions.[29] If a receiver or a liquidator fails to meet the claims of the preferential creditors out of assets available for that purpose before distributing them he will be liable in damages to those with preferential claims.[30] Preferential creditors who also hold security are entitled to appropriate the sum raised by the realisation of that security to the non preferential element of their debt to enable them to claim as preferential creditors in respect of the balance.[31] This contrasts with the ruling that any set off to which a preferential creditor is entitled must be applied rateably to preferential and non preferential debts.

The 'relevant date'

19.23   In the case of many of the categories of debt listed, the amount on which priority is conferred will be calculated by reference to the 'relevant date'. The meaning given to this phrase depends on the situation in which the preferential debts are being considered. Section 387(2) lays down the definition for the purpose of the right of preferential creditors under s 4 to prevent a decision to reduce their priority or to pay different dividends to different preferential creditors in a voluntary arrangement under Part I of the Act. In such a case it is the date of any administration order which has been made or, if none exists, the date of the approval of the voluntary arrangement unless the company is in liquidation in which case the relevant date for a liquidation applies.

---

26   [1985] 3 WLR 875.
27   *Ibid* at 882.
28   s 176(10) and see para 14.00 *supra*.
29   s 175(2)(a).
30   *Westminster Corporation v Haste* [1950] 1 Ch 442.
31   *Re William Hill (Contractors) Ltd* [1967] 2 All ER 1150.

19.24 When a company is being wound up by the court the relevant date is the date of the winding up order unless:

(a) a provisional liquidator was appointed in which case it is the date of his appointment; or

(b) the winding up order was made immediately on the discharge of an administration order in which case it is the date of the administration order; or

(c) the company was in voluntary liquidation before the date on which the winding up order was made in which case it is the date of the passing of the winding up resolution.

If a company is in voluntary liquidation the relevant date is the date of the passing of the winding up resolution.[32] In the case of a company in receivership the 'relevant date' is the date of the appointment of the receiver.[33]

The categories of preferential debts

19.25 Schedule 6 to the Act sets out five categories of preferential debt.

Category 1; Debts due to the Inland Revenue

19.26 These debts are restricted to amounts due from the company in respect of the tax liability of others which the company was responsible for handing over to the Inland Revenue. Corporation Tax is not included but the preference extends to sums due at the relevant date from the company in respect of deductions of tax from payments of emoluments to employees or amounts handed over to subcontractors in the construction industry in the 12 months before the relevant date. In respect of employees the deductions are those required under s 204 of the Income and Corporation Taxes Act 1970 which deals with the PAYE system less the amount of any repayments of income tax liable to be made by the company during that period. Section 69 of the Finance (No 2) Act 1975 specifies the deductions to be made from amounts handed over to subcontractors in the construction industry.

Category 2: Debts due to the Customs and Excise

19.27 These debts are, once again, predominantly amounts collected by the company rather than duties levied directly on its own activities. Such debts include any Value Added Tax which is referrable to the period of six

---

32 s 387(3).
33 s 387(4).

months immediately before the relevant date. To determine the tax which is referrable to that period it is necessary to establish the prescribed accounting period to which tax is attributable. Such periods are prescribed by regulations made under the Value Added Taxes Act 1983. If the whole of the prescribed accounting period falls within the six month period the whole amount of the VAT attributable to that accounting period is referrable to those six months. If there is not a complete overlap the proportion of VAT referable to the six month period will be the proportion of the tax attributable to the accounting period which is equal to the proportion of that period which falls within the six month period. If the insolvent company is part of a group of companies which has elected for group treatment the preference extends to the whole amount of VAT due from every group company and referrable to the six month period.[34]

19.28   In addition to VAT the amount of any car tax, general betting duty, bingo duty, pool betting duty recoverable from an agent collecting stakes or gaming licence duty which is due from the company at the relevant date and became due within the 12 month period immediately before that date is given priority.

19.29   Where a VAT refund was paid to the company's suppliers under the VAT (Bad Debt Relief) Regulations 1978 on the basis that the company was apparently insolvent and they had proved for their debts exclusive of VAT, there is no obligation on the liquidator to pay the amount of the refund to the Customs and Excise if the company proves to be solvent and capable of distributing money to contributories.[35]

Category 3: Social security contributions
19.30   Preference is conferred on sums due from the company on the relevant date and which became due in the preceding 12 months on account of primary or secondary Class 1 contributions under the Social Security Act 1975 or the equivalent Northern Ireland legislation. Although Class 2 and Class 4 contributions in respect of that period are also listed in the schedule a company is not likely to be liable for such contributions.

Category 4: Contributions to occupational pension schemes
19.31   Any sum due from the company under sch 3 of the Social Security Pensions Act 1975 is given priority. This includes any amount due from the company as a contribution to a contracted out pension scheme payable in the 12 months immediately before the relevant date subject to a maximum

---

34   *Re Nadler Enterprises Ltd* [1981] 1 WLR 23.
35   *Re T H Knitwear (Wholesale) Ltd* [1988] BCLC 195.

limit. There is also liability for any earner's contribution to such a scheme which the company is liable to make in respect of earnings paid or payable to a member of the scheme during the four months immediately before the relevant date.

Catgory 5: Remuneration and other sums due to employees
19.32 A number of debts due to employees enjoy preferential status. They are:

(a) *Remuneration* An amount not exceeding the sum currently prescribed by the Secretary of State which is owed by the company to an employee or ex-employee and is payable by way of remuneration in respect of the whole or part of the period of four months before the relevant date. The meaning of remuneration for this purpose includes wages, salary, and all payments calculated by reference to time piecework or commission in respect of services rendered to the company in the period covered.[36] This is limited to the claims of employees and excludes independent contractors.[37]

Any remuneration payable in respect of a period of absence from work through sickness or other good cause or on holiday is deemed to be wages or salary for services rendered by the employee to the company during that period.[38]

In addition by virtue of sch 6 para 13(1)(b) and (2) the following payments are included in the definition of sums payable to a person by the company by way of remuneration:

(i) a guarantee payment under s 12(1) of the Employment Protection (Consolidation) Act 1978;

(ii) remuneration on suspension on medical grounds under s 19 of that Act;

(iii) any payment for time off for trade union activity under s 27(3), to look for work or arrange training under s 31(3), or to receive antenatal care under s 31A(4) of the 1978 Act;

(iv) remuneration under a protective award made by an industrial tribunal under s 101 of the Employment Protection Act 1978.

(b) *Holiday pay.* An amount owed, by way of accrued holiday pay in respect of any period before the relevant date, to a person whose employment has been terminated before, on, or after that date. If the employment has ended by reason of the employer going into liquidation or receivership, or because possession is taken of assets by debentureholders the calculation of the accrued holiday pay over the period before the

36 Sch 6 para 13(1)(a).
37 *Re General Radio Co Ltd* [1929] WN 172.
38 Sch 6 para 15(1).

employment ended is not to be affected by the termination of employment. Thus even if the contract or enactment which governs the holiday pay would prevent accrual for the whole period because the holiday will never be taken in full amount accruing up to the termination of employment will be payable.[39]

(c) *Loans to meet remuneration.* In addition to sums owed in respect of pay or holiday pay as defined in (a) and (b) above, loans used to make such payments can result in a similar priority for the lender. So much of any sum advanced for the purpose as has been used to pay a debt which if it had not been paid would have fallen within (a) or (b) is a preferential debt. This advantage will most frequently accrue to banks who will allow an account to be opened for the specific purpose of the payment of wages so as to gain full advantage from this preference. The rule in *Clayton's Case*[40] ensures that payments into a current account which is overdrawn are taken to pay off the earliest debts thus a carefully organised series of payments into the wages account will prevent some of the overdraft from representing advances for wages paid more than four months before the relevant date which would not have priority but will prevent the rule from operating to reduce the amount of debt that is attributable to wages.[41] If the bank has security for its loan it can appropriate the proceeds of its realisation to paying off its non-preferential debts so as to be able to claim as a preferential creditor for the maximum proportion of the unsecured debts.[42]

(d) *Reserve Forces Employment.* Up to a prescribed limit any amount ordered to be paid by the company under the Reserve Forces (Safeguard of Employment) Act 1985.

Amounts paid by the Department of Employment
19.33   Apart from the preference conferred on employees in the insolvency a further guarantee of certain amounts which do not wholly coincide with the preferences conferred by the Insolvency Act is available to employees under the Protection of Employment (Consolidation) Act 1978. The payments protected in this way are paid by the Department of Employment to the employees and recouped by the Department by means of a claim in the corporate insolvency.[43]

19.34   The right to claim from the Redundancy Fund under the

---

39 Sch 6 para 14.
40 (1816) 1 Mer 529.
41 *Re James R Rutherford & Sons Ltd* [1964] 1 WLR 1211.
42 *Re William Hall (Contractors) Ltd* [1967] 1 WLR 948.
43 Employment Protection (Consolidation) Act 1978 Part VII, extended by the Insolvency of Employer (Excluded Classes) Regulations 1983 (SI 1983 no 624) to cover employees in the police service and those who ordinarily work under their contract of employment within the territory of the members states of the EEC. The Act and the regulations together implement EEC Directive 80/987 (OJ L 283 28.10.80).

Employment Protection (Consolidation) Act 1978 applies to the whole or part of the following debts:

(a) Arrears of pay in respect of a period or periods not exceeding in aggregate 8 weeks. For this purpose 'pay' includes guarantee payments, remuneration on suspension on medical grounds, payment for time off to carry out trade union duties, to look for work or receive training or to receive antenatal care and remuneration under a protective award by an industrial tribunal.[44]

(b) Any amount that the employer is required to pay the employee for a period of notice or for failure to give notice under s 49 of the Employment Protection (Consolidation) Act 1978.[45]

(c) Holiday pay for a period or periods up to six weeks to which the employee became entitled during the 12 months ending with the relevant date.[46]

(d) Any basic award of compensation for unfair dismissal within the meaning of s 72 of the 1978 Act.[47]

(e) Any reasonable sum by way of reimbursement of the whole or part of a fee or premium paid by an apprentice or articled clerk.[48]

19.35 The relevant date for the purpose of these provisions is the date on which the employer became insolvent in relation to arrears of pay and holiday pay. In relation to a protective award or a basic award for unfair dismissal it is the latest of; the date on which the employer became insolvent, the date on which the employee's employment terminated and the date on which the award was made. For the purpose of any other amount it is the later of the date of termination of employment and the date on which the employer ecame insolvent.[49] A ceiling applies to any weekly payment to be made under s 122 by virtue of s 122(5) and the current Employment Protection (Variation of Limits) Order. An employee may complain to the industrial tribunal within three months of the date of a decision by the Secretary of State to refuse to make such a payment out of the Redundancy Fund.[50]

19.36 Where payments are made to employees under these provisions the rights and remedies of the employee are transferred to the Secretary of State for Employment (including the status of the employee as a preferential

---

44   Employment Protection (Consolidation) Act 1978 s 122(3)(a) and (4).
45   *Ibid* s 122(3)(b).
46   *Ibid* s 122(3)(c).
47   *Ibid* s 122(3)(d).
48   *Ibid* s 122(3)(e).
49   *Ibid* s 122(2), substituted by Insolvency Act 1975 s 218(3).
50   *Ibid* s 124.

creditor).[51] The right conferred on the Secretary of State is that he be paid in priority to any other unsatisfied claim of the employee, and in computing the maximum sums to be paid under the Insolvency Act 1986 as regards preferential claims the amounts paid to the Secretary of State are to be treated as if they had been paid to the employee.[52] If payments have been made to an occupational pension fund in respect of unpaid contributions under s 123 of the 1978 Act, the Secretary of State takes over the rights and remedies of those competent to act in respect of the scheme.[53] The Secretary of State thus has a 'super preference' over the employee himself in respect of those amounts in a liquidation. This does not apply in the case of an administrative receivership. In such a case the Secretary of State can only claim the dividend the employee would have received had the Secretary of State not paid the employee's claim.[54]

19.37 While the number of debts which retain preferential status may seem formidable their number was reduced substantially by the Insolvency Act 1985. Rates no longer have preference and with limited exceptions the taxes with preference are those (such as VAT and PAYE income tax) collected by the company and held for the revenue rather than those levied on the company.

Levies on coal and steel production
19.38 Debts due from a company in respect of any levies on the production of coal and steel referred to in Articles 49 and 50 of the European Coal and Steel Community Treaty and any surcharges for delay imposed under that Treaty are preferential debts. The Insolvency (ECSC Levy Debts) Regulations 1987 insert a new Paragraph 15A in sch 6 of the Insolvency Act 1986. The regulations have retrospective effect and apply to transactions entered into at any time.[55]

ORDINARY DEBTS

What is provable?

19.39 A central feature of the liquidation process is the procedure whereby creditors prove their debts in the liquidation and the liquidator decides whether to admit such proofs. There is a general rule that in any

---

51   *Ibid* s 125.
52   *Ibid* s 125(2).
53   *Ibid* s 125(3).
54   *Re Urethane Engineering Products Ltd* (1989) 5 BCC 614.
55   SI 1987 no 2093, which implements EC Commission Recommendation 86/198/ECSC (OJ L 144 29.5.86 p 40).

winding up—compulsory or voluntary—the liquidator must receive a claim either formal or informal and should not admit a debt merely because it appears in the company's books.[56]

19.40 The debts which are provable in a winding up are defined in Rule 12.3 of the Insolvency Rules 1986. This rule lays down that all claims by creditors are provable as debts against the company 'whether they are present or future, certain or contingent, ascertained or sounding in damages only'. The claims specifically stated not to be provable in a winding up include an obligation arising under a confiscation order made under s 1 of the Drug Trafficking Offences Act 1986.[57] Certain claims under s 6 of the Financial Services Act 1986 and s 49 of the Banking Act 1987 are not provable until all other claims of creditors have been paid in full with interest.[58] Similarly any claim, payment of which is to be postponed by virtue of the Insolvency Act 1986 or any other enactment in a bankruptcy or a winding up is not provable until other creditors have been paid in full with interest.[59] This prevents early proofs of a claim based, for example, on the company's liability on a contract to purchase its own shares.[60] The rule giving a right to prove, in all cases, is stated to be without prejudice to any enactment or rule of law under which a particular kind of debt is not provable on public policy grounds or otherwise.[61]

19.41 A 'debt' is defined as meaning any debt or liability to which the company is subject at the date on which it goes into liquidation or to which it may become subject after that date by reason of an obligation incurred before that date. It also includes interest payable on a debt in the period before the company went into liquidation and thus provable under Rule 4.93(1).[62] For the purpose of deciding whether a liability in tort is provable in a winding up the company is deemed to have become subject to that liability by reason of an obligation incurred at the time when the cause of action accrued.[63] A tort claim is provable if that date falls before the date on which the company goes into liquidation; the date of the passing of the resolution or of the making of the winding up order.

19.42 Since there must be a debt or liability before a proof can be entered,

---

56 *Re Compania de Electricidad de la Provincia de Buenos Aires Ltd* [1980] 1 Ch 146; and see paras 19.46 *et seq* on the need for a formal proof in a compulsory liquidation.
57 r 12.3(2).
58 r 12.3(2A)(a) and (b), substituted by SI 1987 no 1919.
59 r 12.3(2A)(c).
60 See paras 19.101–2 below.
61 r 12.3(3).
62 r 13.12(1).
63 r 13.12(2).

unenforceable obligations cannot be proved. This applies to claims based on transactions *ultra vires* the company in the sense of being outside its capacity.[64] However, in deciding whether a transaction is *ultra vires*, the provisions of s 35 of the Companies Act 1985 and the decision in *Rolled Steel Products (Holdings) Ltd v BSC*[65] should be borne in mind. After the enactment of the Companies Bill 1989 no claims will be prevented by the *ultra vires* doctrine for non-charitable companies. Statute barred claims should not be admitted to proof.[66]

19.43   In contrast to the law before December 1986, 'liability' for the purpose of the insolvency legislation means a liability to pay money or money's worth and includes liability in tort or bailment as well as statutory liability, liability for breach of trust or in contract, and liability arising out of an obligation to make restitution.[67] However, the debt or liability can be present or future, certain or contingent and its amount can be fixed or liquidated or capable of being ascertained by fixed rules or as a matter of opinion.[68]

19.44   The right to prove may arise because the person who proves is subrogated to the right of a creditor of the company having performed its obligation by paying the whole of a debt due from it in accordance with a surety or guarantee. However, the rule against double proof in a liquidation prevents more than one proof from being lodged in respect of a single debt or liability of the company. The rule against double proof originates in bankruptcy law but it is submitted that it is preserved by Rule 12.3(3) of the Insolvency Rules 1986. The rule applies whether the claims would be available to a single claimant or to more than one. It also applies where the debts ar created or secured by separate contracts so long as a single debt is involved.[69] A guarantor of a debt owed by the company can only prove if he has discharged the whole of the company's debt since if part only of the debt has been paid by the guarantor there may be a claim by the creditor in respect of it in addition to that of the guarantor.[70] However, if the debts paid by a guarantor have been fully discharged so that the creditor has nothing on which to base any proof and nothing to assign to any other

---

64   See, for example, *Re Jon Beaufort (London) Ltd* [1953] Ch 131; but contrast *Re New Finance and Mortgage Co Ltd* [1975] 2 WLR 443.
65   [1986] Ch 246.
66   *Re Art Reproduction Co Ltd* [1952] Ch 89; and see *Re Overmark Smith Warden* [1982] 1 WLR 1195 on the possible effect of an acknowledgement of debt in a statement of affairs prepared by an administrative receiver. See also *Re Joshua Shaw & Sons Ltd* (1989) 5 BCC 188, where the assets were distributed to contributories because the debts were statute-barred after a lengthy receivership.
67   r 13.12(4).
68   r 13.12(3).
69   *Re Oriental Commercial Bank* (1872) 7 Ch App 99.
70   *Re Fenton (No 2)* [1932] 1 Ch 178.

person then there will be no double proof and the claim of the guarantor can be admitted.[71]

19.45 By s 74(2)(f) a sum due to any member of the company in his character as such by way of dividends profits or otherwise is not deemed to be a debt of the company payable to that member in a case in which he is in competition with a creditor who is not a member. This rule extends to past as well as present members but does not prevent a proof for sums owed to a member in some other capacity if he has paid any calls in full. A shareholder of a bank which was in liquidation could prove for the balance due on his current account as that was not due to him in his character of member and he has paid all the calls made upon him by the company.[72]

Procedure for proving debts

19.46 A creditor who claims in the liquidation whether in writing or not is referred to as proving and any document by which he seeks to establish his claim is referred to as a proof.[73] In a compulsory liquidation a written claim is required unless the court has made an order to the contrary under Rule 4.67(2) but in a voluntary liquidation the liquidator may require a written claim but is not obliged to do so.[74] The proof must be in the prescribed form or a substantially similar form in a compulsory liquidation and has to be made out by, or under the directions of, the creditor or someone authorised by him in that behalf. This is so unless it is submitted by a Minister of the Crown or a government department in which case it must show all relevant particulars of the debt but need not be in the prescribed form.[75]

19.47 Subject to the power of the court to order otherwise, the rules require the liquidator in a compulsory liquidation to send out forms of proof to every creditor known to him or identified in the statement of affairs together with the first of:

(a) the notice to creditors under s 136(5)(b) of the official receiver's decision not to call a meeting of creditors; or
(b) the first notice calling such a meeting; or
(c) the notice of the liquidator's appointment by the court.

19.48 If the liquidator is appointed by the court in a winding up following

---

71 *Barclays Bank Ltd v TOSG Trust Fund Ltd* [1984] AC 626.
72 See *Re West of England Bank ex p Brown* (1879) 12 Ch D 823.
73 r 4.73(3).
74 r 4.73(1) and (2).
75 r 4.73(4) and (5).

an administration or a voluntary arrangement under ss 139(4) or 140 and is allowed to advertise his appointment in accordance with the court's directions he must send proof forms within four months of the date of the winding up order.[76] The proof must specify the amount of the claim at the date at which the company went into liquidation and whether it includes outstanding uncapitalised interest or value added tax. The creditor's name and address, details of any security held and of whether the debt is preferential as well as details of how and when the company incurred the debt must also be provided.[77] The proof must specify documents by reference to which the claim could be substantiated but they need only be produced if the liquidator or chairman of the creditor's meeting requires this for the purpose of substantiating all or part of the claim.[78]

19.49   The proof in a creditor's voluntary liquidation can be in any form.[79] However, the liquidator or the chairman of a creditors' meeting can call for details of any of the matters required to be contained in a proof in a compulsory liquidation or for documentary or other evidence if he considers such information necessary to clarify or substantiate the claim.[80]

19.50   If the liquidator requires it, the proof in any liquidation may have to be verified by an affidavit in the prescribed form. This requirement can be laid down even after a proof has been submitted and, in the case of a compulsory liquidation, the affidavit may be sworn by an official receiver or deputy official receiver or a duly authorised officer of the court or the DTI.[81]

19.51   Unless the court orders otherwise the cost of proving a debt is borne by the claimant but the cost of estimating its quantum under Rule 4.86 if it does not bear a certain value is payable out of the assets as an expense of the liquidation.[82]

19.52   So long as they are in the liquidator's hands, proofs may be inspected by contributories and by those creditors whose proofs have not been wholly rejected or by anyone acting on behalf of such persons at all reasonable times on any business day.[83] The rules provide for the transmission of proofs between liquidators or from the official receiver to

---

76   r 4.74.
77   r 4.75(1).
78   r 4.75(2) and (3).
79   r 4.73(6).
80   r 4.76.
81   r 4.73(7) and 4.78.
82   r 4.78.
83   r 4.79.

the liquidator when there is a change in the person administering the winding up.[84]

19.53 Once a proof has been submitted to the liquidator he has the task of admitting or rejecting it. He may do this in respect of the whole or part of the proof and if he rejects it in whole or in part he must prepare a statement of his reasons for doing so and send it to the creditor.[85] The creditor may then apply to the court within 21 days of receiving the statement for the liquidator's decision on the rejection of the proof or the preference accorded to it to be varied or reversed.[86]

19.54 A similar application may be made by any other creditor or by a contributory against the decision to admit or reject the whole or part of any proof within 21 days of the applicant becoming aware of the decision.[87] Such applications result in a venue being fixed, of which notice is sent to the liquidator and the creditor whose proof is in issue. On receipt of which the liquidator files the relevant proof and a copy of his statement (if appropriate) in court.[88] The costs of such an application cannot be awarded against the official receiver personally and are not borne by the liquidator personally unless the court so orders.[89] In the case of an application under this rule by a person ordinarily resident outside the jurisdiction the court may order that security of costs be provided by the applicant.[90]

19.55 Apart from the procedure laid down for the challenge of liquidator's decision on a proof, it is always possible for the amount claimed on proof to be varied or for the proof to be withdrawn by agreement between the liquidator and the person who submitted it.[91] In addition, the court has power to expunge a proof on the application of the liquidator where the latter thinks the proof has been improperly admitted or should be reduced or on the application of any creditor if the liquidator declines to interfere.[92]

Quantification of debts

19.56 Once the correct procedure has been followed for the admission of proofs the liquidator will be involved in quantifying the claims of those who

---

84 rr 4.80 and 4.81.
85 r 4.82.
86 r 4.83(1).
87 r 4.83(2).
88 r 4.83(3) and (4).
89 r 4.83(6).
90 *Re Pretoria Pietersburg Railway Co (No 2)* [1904] 2 Ch 359.
91 r 4.84.
92 r 4.85(1).

have proved in the liquidation. In doing so the liquidator is not bound by any estoppel raised by representations made by the company before the company went into liquidation. It is his duty to ascertain the true level of the debts due to the creditors and he is not bound by the statements of those who formerly controlled the company as to the amount due to individual creditors.[93] This rule applies to the distribution of the company's assets because of the liquidator's special statutory function. When he is collecting assets he can be bound by an estoppel since he obtains no better right than the company. Thus he cannot add a person, who lent to the company on the basis of a representation that its shares were fully paid, to the list of contributories who are due to pay on a call.[94]

19.57 The quantification of claims in a winding up will generally be on the basis of the value of the debt at the date of the commencement of the winding up.[95] Particular problems with the application of this principle are dealt with by the Rules.

Debts of uncertain value
19.58 Some debts which can be proved will not bear a certain value. This may be because they are subject to some contingency or for some other reason. In such cases the liquidator is required to estimate the value of the debt and is permitted to revise such estimates by reference to changes in the circumstances or in the information available to him. He must inform the creditor of his estimate and of any revision of it but the estimate for the time being represents the amount provable in the winding up in the case of that debt unless the court changes the amount.[96] Application to the court to challenge a disputed estimate of the value of the debt is possible under Rule 4.83 or under s 168 in a compulsory liquidation or s 112 in a voluntary winding up.

19.59 While all future and contingent debts are provable there is a difficulty in principle about the amount of dividend to be paid on debts of which payment is not due until after the date of the declaration of dividend.[97] In such a case Rule 11.13 lays down that the creditor's entitlement to dividend is to be calculated by reducing the amount of the proof by a percentage calculated by reference to the length of the period between the date on which a dividend is declared and the date on which payment of the debt would otherwise be due.[98] The balance of the amount

93 *Re Exchange Securities and Commodities Ltd (No 3)* (1987) 3 BCC 48.
94 *Bloomenthal v Ford* [1887] AC 156.
95 *Re Humber Ironworks and Shipbuilding Co Ltd* (1869) 4 Ch App 643.
96 r 4.86.
97 r 4.94.
98 See r 11.13(2).

of the debt is, however, payable to a creditor paid a reduced dividend in advance of the payment of post liquidation interest to other creditors under ss 189(2) or 328(4).[99]

19.60 Examples of future or contingent debts include the claim of a surety of one of the company's debts who has not yet paid the debt or any person seeking to claim on the basis of their entitlement to indemnity from the company for a future liability which has not yet arisen.[100] An applicant who is also seeking to show that the property is held by the company on trust for him can nonetheless prove for a fixed amount and will not be regarded as making a contingent or unliquidated claim.[101]

Negotiable instruments
19.61 A proof may be entered in respect of money owed on a negotiable instrument or security (such as a bearer bond) but the instrument or security itself or a certified copy of it must be produced if the liquidator so requires before the proof can be admitted.[102] If the party proving has received anything from other parties to a bill of exchange on which his claim is based he can only prove for the balance.[103]

Secured creditors
19.62 It is likely that many secured creditors will already have exercised a remedy in respect of their security before winding up begins. The property on which the debt due to them is secured will thus have been removed from the liquidation process. If the secured creditor has relied wholly on his security in this way he will not prove in the winding up at all. This course of action will be appropriate in cases in which the value of the security clearly exceeds the amount of the debt due to the creditor from the company. A plaintiff in an action against the company is regarded as a secured creditor to the extent of any payment into court by the company.[104] On the other hand, a beneficial owner of property held by the company as trustee cannot be classified as a secured creditor on the basis of his proprietary claim.[105] However, it is possible that the amount realised from the security will fall short of the full debt due to the secured creditor and in such a case he will prove in the liquidation for the balance.[106] If he has not realised his security the creditor may prove on the basis of having valued it in which case he

---

99   r 11.13(3).
100   *Re Paine* [1897] 1 QB 122.
101   *Re Prime Metal Trading Ltd* (1984) 1 BCC 99265.
102   r 4.87.
103   *Re Oriental Commercial Bank* (1868) LR 6 Eq 582.
104   *W A Sherratt v John Bromley (Church Stretton) Ltd* [1985] 1 All ER 216.
105   *Re Prime Metal Trading Ltd* (1984) 1 BCC 99265.
106   r 4.88(1).

must disclose in his proof its existence, the date on which it was given and its value.[107]

19.63   It is possible for a secured creditor to choose to surrender his security and prove for the whole of his debt in the liquidation as if it were unsecured but such a course will rarely be followed as the claim of the secured creditor will then rank *pari passu* with those of the other creditors.[108] If a secured creditor submits a proof of debt and omits to disclose his security he surrenders his security for the general benefit of creditors unless the court grants him relief on the ground that the omission was inadvertent or the result of honest mistake.[109] The concept of inadvertence has been said to point to forgetfulness or accident and not to apply in a case in which a definite valuation of a security was made and was understood to establish that it was worthless.[110] Although such an error would clearly amount to an honest mistake as to valuation it would hardly justify a failure to disclose the existence of the security at all. Ignorance that the proof failed to state that there is no security has also been held to be insufficient to amount to inadvertence where the creditor was aware of the existence of the security.[111]

19.64   The current rule allows the court, if it grants relief, to require the creditor's proof to be amended on such terms as may be just.[112] This gives a discretion which can be used to correct any injustice that might flow from the fact that the liquidator has changed his position on the strength of the proof and would seem to justify a flexible approach to the decision whether to grant relief. It may no longer be the case, that the fact that the liquidator has altered his position on the basis of the inaccurate proof, will automatically prevent the court from granting relief, as appears to have been the case in *Re Safety Explosives Ltd*.[113] The amount for which the creditor is permitted to prove might be varied to take account of this or his claim may, in part, be deferred to those of others to achieve fairness.

19.65   If a secured creditor has proved for his debt and wishes to alter the value which he has placed on his security in his proof of debt he may do so in any liquidation with the leave of the court or the agreement of the liquidator. However, if the creditor has, in a compulsory liquidation, either been the petitioner and placed a value on the security in the petition or has,

107   r 4.75(1)(g).
108   r 4.88(2).
109   r 4.96(1).
110   *In Re Piers* [1898] 1 QB 627 at 631.
111   *Re Safety Explosives Ltd* [1904] 1 Ch 226.
112   r 4.96(2).
113   n 111 *supra.*

whether he was petitioner or not, voted in respect of the unsecured balance of his debt, then the revaluation will require the leave of the court.[114]

19.66   The Rules lay down procedures for the realisation and redemption of the security and allow the liquidator to test its value. If the secured creditor has entered a proof the liquidator may at any time give notice to him that at the end of 28 days from the date of the notice the liquidator proposes to redeem the security at the value put on it in the proof.[115] The secured creditor then has 21 days or a longer period allowed by the liquidator to exercise his right to revalue the security (with the leave of the court if Rule 4.95(2) applies) and if the security is revalued the liquidator may only redeem it at the new value.[116] In any case in which redemption takes place the cost of transfer of the property must be met out of the assets.[117]

19.67   The secured creditor has the right, by a notice in writing, to put the liquidator to an election whether to exercise his right to redeem the security at the value then placed on it and, if notice is served, the liquidator has six months to exercise his power or to decide not to do so.[118]

19.68   If the liquidator is dissatisfied with the value which a secured creditor has placed on his security (either in his proof or on revaluation after notice of redemption has been served by the liquidator), the liquidator may require the property comprised in the security to be offered for sale. The terms of the sale will be those agreed between the liquidator and the creditor or those laid down by the court's directions. If the sale is by auction the liquidator on behalf of the company and the creditor on his own behalf may each appear at the sale and bid.[119] If the liquidator sells assets on behalf of a secured creditor he is entitled to take a sum for remuneration out of the proceeds of sale. The amount should be equivalent to the sum chargeable by the official receiver under general regulations in corresponding circumstances.[120]

19.69   In cases in which the creditor realises his security after he has valued it in his proof—whether or not the realisation was at the instance of the liquidator—the net amount realised is treated for all purposes as an amended valuation made by the creditor and is substituted for the

114   r 4.95(2).
115   r 4.97(1).
116   r 4.97(2).
117   r 4.97(3).
118   r 4.97(4).
119   r 4.98.
120   r 4.128(1).

valuation previously put on the security by him.[121] On realisation the creditor is entitled to principal, interest and costs out of the proceeds of sale unless the agreement creating the security provides otherwise.[122]

19.70 The definition of a secured creditor in s 248 of the Insolvency Act 1986 applies for the purpose of deciding to whom the Rules on proof apply. This defines such creditors as those who hold in respect of their debts security over the property of the company. 'Security' means any mortgage, charge, lien or other security.[123] In addition to those who hold a mortgage, charge or other consensual security, the expression applies to those with liens or other securities created by operation of law. The holder of a maritime lien or a lien available to a repairer, a solicitor or a banker will be included and it is those in this category who are most likely to fail to realise that they hold a security.[124] However, only security interests as such will bring those who hold them within the definition. The legal or beneficial owner of property does not have such an interest.[125]

Discounts
19.71 Rule 4.89 lays down that in quantifying the claims of creditors all trade and other discounts which would have been available to the company but for its liquidation are to be deducted except any allowed for immediate early or cash settlement of the debt.

Foreign currency debts
19.72 A debt incurred or payable in a currency other than sterling is to be converted into sterling for the purpose of proof. Conversion is at the official exchange rate at the date on which the company went into liquidation; that is the middle market rate at the Bank of England published for the date in question. In the absence of such a rate the court has to determine a rate to apply for this purpose.[126]

Post liquidation interest
19.73 The Insolvency Act 1986 lays down a new regime for the payment of interest in the liquidation of a company. It enables interest to be claimed on debts in respect of the period after the company goes into liquidation and thus changes the previous law in accordance with the recommendations of the Cork Report.[127]

121 r 4.99.
122 *Re Joint Stock Account Co (No 2)* (1870) LR 10 Eq 11.
123 S 248(d)(i).
124 See, for example, *Re Safety Explosives Ltd* (note 111 *supra*).
125 See ch 9.
126 r 4.91.
127 See *Amalgamated Investment and Property Co Ltd* (1984) 1 BCC 99104 and Cork Report (Cmnd 8558) para 1380 respectively.

19.74 Section 189 lays down a statutory rate of interest to be paid on the debt proved by a creditor in the winding up. Such interest is payable on any debt proved in the winding up including that part of any debt which represents interest on the remainder.[128] The statutory interest ranks after the payment of the debts proved in the winding up and before the application of the surplus to any other purpose; such as the repayment of capital.[129] Consequently, in a case in which a number of dividends are paid the dividends should first be attributed to repayment of the principal and any pre-liquidation interest (the latter is part of the debt proved according to s 189(1)) and only after those amounts have been paid in full should any payments be made for post-liquidation interest.

19.75 The interest is paid on debts proved in the winding up for the period during which they have been outstanding since the company went into liquidation.[130] All the interest under the section ranks equally regardless of whether that was the case for the debts on which it is payable.[131] The interest on the preferential debts ranks equally with that on the ordinary unsecured debts.

19.76 The rate of interest which is paid on debts under s 189 for the period after the company goes into liquidation is the higher of:

(a) the rate laid down under s 17 of the Judgments Act 1838 for the day on which the company went into liquidation[132] and
(b) the rate applicable to that debt apart form the winding up.[133]

Pre-liquidation interest
19.77 Interest for the period before the company went into liquidation is provable in the winding up as part of the debt, providing the debt bears interest.[134] The debt will be regarded as bearing interest if interest was 'reserved or agreed' before the company went into liquidation.[135] However the rule allows for a proof to include interest even if that was not the case providing one of two situations can be established.

19.78 The first is that the debt was due by virtue of a written instrument and payable at a certain time falling before the company went into

---

128   s 189(1).
129   s 189(2).
130   s 189(1) and (2).
131   s 189(3).
132   15% under SI 1985 no 437.
133   s 189(4).
134   r 4.93(1).
135   r 4.93(2).

liquidation. In such a case the creditor may prove for interest in respect of the period from the date on which the debt was due to the date on which the company went into liquidation. The rate will be that specified under s 17 of the Judgments Act 1838 for the latter date.[136]

19.79 If the debt does not fit within that category then it is only possible for the creditor to prove for interest for the pre-liquidation period if a written demand on the company was made by or on behalf of the creditor giving notice that interest would be payable from the date of the demand to the date of payment. The demand must have been served on the company before it went into liquidation and interest can only be claimed from the date of the demand to that date.[137] The rate of interest that can be claimed is the rate fixed under s 17 for the date on which the company went into liquidation or a lower rate specified in the demand.[138]

Periodic payments

19.80 If a creditor is proving for rent or some other payment of a periodic nature he may only prove for amounts due and unpaid up to the date when the company went into liquidation.[139] However, if a payment was accruing due at that date he may prove for the amount that would have been due then if the payment had been accruing from day to day rather than only for the last full instalment.[140]

19.81 If the agreement under which the payments were due terminates as a result of the liquidation or a breach of its terms on the part of the company, the other party will be able to prove for the loss he has suffered by way of damages for breach of contract but will not be able to prove for further instalments as future debts. It is a matter of construction of the agreement whether it terminates and whether this occurs automatically or only at the election of the other party to it. Most formally prepared leases or other agreements involving instalment payments will provide for termination on the company going into liquidation. In a lease of realty this will take the form of a forfeiture clause.

19.82 If the agreement has not terminated the creditor will have to prove for future payments under Rule 4.94.[141] However, as has been noted,[142] if the liquidator retains a lease of premises solely for the benefit of the

---

136 r 4.93(3) and (6).
137 r 4.93(4) and (5).
138 r 4.93(6).
139 r 4.92(1).
140 r 4.92(2).
141 *Re New Oriental Bank Corporation (No 2)* [1895] 1 Ch 753.
142 See paras 18.30 *et seq supra*.

liquidation the landlord will be entitled to rent for the post liquidation period as an expense of the winding up.[143] The same principle can presumably apply to a lease of chattels. The right of the liquidator to disclaim onerous property is dealt with in paras 18.05 *et seq*, above.

Set off

19.83   In quantifying the value of debts proved in the winding up the liquidator will take account of the rules as to set off which will affect the amount to be proved by creditors. That matter is dealt with in paras 18.51 *et seq*, above in the context of the collection of debts due to the company.

DIVIDEND AND FINAL DISTRIBUTION

Dividend

19.84   Once the process of gathering assets and quantifying debts is under way the possibility of some distribution among the creditors arises. The liquidator is required to make a distribution by way of dividend among the creditors in respect of debts that have been proved whenever he has sufficient funds in hand for the purpose.[144] This is subject to the retention of such sums as may be necessary for the expenses of winding up which have priority over all debts. The liquidator must give notice of his intention to declare and distribute a dividend.[145] Once it is declared, he must give notice of how it is to be distributed and details of the company's assets and affairs sufficient to enable creditors to understand the calculation of the amount of the dividend and the manner of its distributions.[146]

19.85   All distributions must be made on the basis that the debts of the company (other than preferential debts—for which see paras 19.18 *et seq*) rank *pari passu* and are to be paid in full unless the assets are insufficient in which case they abate equally.[147] This does not apply to secured debts in respect of which the creditor relies on his security because such claims are dealt with outside the process of liquidation.

19.86   The Insolvency Rules lay down how the liquidator is to calculate and distribute the dividend. He must make provision for any debts which

---

143 *Re ABC Coupler and Engineering Co Ltd (No 3)* [1970] 1 All ER 650.
144 r 4.180(1).
145 r 4.180(2) and 4.182A(1).
146 r 4.180(3).
147 r 4.181 applies this principle to a compulsory liquidation. s 107 of the Insolvency Act 1986 applies it in a voluntary winding up; and see *British Eagle International Airlines Ltd v Compagnie Nationale Air France* [1975] 1 WLR 758.

appear to be due to persons who may not have had sufficient time to tender and establish their proofs by reason of the distance of their place of residence. Similarly, he must provide for disputed proofs or claims and debts whose claims have not yet been determined.[148]

19.87 Creditors who have not proved their debts before the declaration of a dividend are not entitled to disturb the distribution of any dividend which was declared before proof of their debts. However, they are entitled to be paid the dividends which they failed to receive out of any money which is available for a further dividend distribution in priority to the payment of those further dividends.[149] The same rule applies if the amount claimed in the proof is increased after the payment of dividend.[150] If a proof is withdrawn or expunged after being admitted, the creditor is required to repay to the liquidator, for the credit of the company's estate, any overpayment of dividend.[151]

19.88 There is no action available as of right against the liquidator for any dividend but the court has power to order him to pay a dividend if he has refused to do so. In such a case the dividend will be paid out of the assets of the company but the liquidator may be ordered to pay out of his own money costs and interest at the statutory rate from the time when he withheld the dividend.[152]

19.89 While it is usual for the dividend in a winding up to be paid in cash as a result of the realisation of the company's assets, distribution *in specie* is possible. Rule 4.183 allows the liquidator, with the permission of the liquidation committee, to divide property amongst the company's creditors in its existing form and according to its estimated value. However, this procedure is only available if the property, from its peculiar nature or other special circumstances, cannot be readily or advantageously sold. This power is expressed to be without prejudice to the right of the liquidator to disclaim onerous property.

19.90 In the process of distribution the revaluation of the security of secured creditors may cause some difficulty.[153] If the revaluation results in a reduction in the unsecured claim of such a creditor any excess dividend which he received must be repaid to the liquidator for the credit of the

148 r 4.182(1).
149 r 4.182(2) and 4.182A(4).
150 r 11.8(1) and (2).
151 r 11.8(3).
152 r 4.182(3).
153 See generally paras 19.62 *et seq.*

company's estate.[154] If, on the other hand, the amount of the unsecured claim is increased and dividend has been underpaid, the creditor is entitled to receive the shortfall from any money available to pay further dividend in priority to such dividend, but he cannot disturb any dividend declared before the date of the revaluation; whether or not it has been distributed.[155] Any contravention by a creditor of a provision of the Act or the Rules as to the valuation of a security gives the court a discretion wholly or partly to disqualify the offending creditor from participation in dividend on the application of the liquidator.[156]

19.91 Rule 11.11 permits the assignment of a right to dividend and requires the liquidator to pay the assignee if given notice by the assignor of the assignment and the assignee's name and address. Even if there has been no assignment a creditor may give notice that he wishes his dividend to be paid to another person and the liquidator must comply if he is informed of that person's name and address.

The final distribution

19.92 When he has realised all the company's assets or—as many of them as, in his opinion, can be realised without needlessly protracting the winding up—the liquidator is required to give notice of a final dividend or of the fact that no dividend or no further dividend will be declared.[157] Part 11 of the Insolvency Rules lays down the content of the notice which must, *inter alia*, require claims against the company's assets to be established by a specified date.[158]

19.93 If application is made a liquidator may be required to postpone a distribution until late claims by potential creditors have been dealt with. The liquidator may raise this issue by applying for leave to distribute without awaiting such claims. The court will consider that matter by looking at the justice of the case and default or delay by the claimants is only one factor. In a case where the delay was not the fault of the claimants, who had a personal injury claim against the company, and the distribution that the liquidator sought to make was to contributories rather than creditors, leave to distribute without making provision for the claim was refused.[159]

19.94 Notice of the intention to declare a dividend must be given to all

154   r 11.9(2).
155   r 11.9(3).
156   r 11.10.
157   r 4.186(1).
158   r 4.186(2).
159   *Re R-R Realisations* [1980] 1 WLR 805.

creditors who have not proved their debts. The notice must specify 'the last date for proving' which must be the same for all creditors and not less than 21 days from the date of the notice. The notice must also state the intention of the liquidator to declare a final or interim dividend within the period of 4 months from the last day for proving.[160] The last date for proving represents a time limit for the final admission or rejection of proofs. Within 7 days after that date the liquidator is obliged to admit or reject in whole or in part or otherwise make provision for every proof that has been lodged, so far as it has not already been dealt with. He is not required to deal with any proofs lodged after that date but may do so if he thinks fit.[161] This procedure applies to contributories who wish to make claims as they are creditors for this purpose although their claims may be deferred under s 74(2)(f) because they are made in their character as members.[162]

19.95   The liquidator may postpone or cancel the dividend if an application is made to the court within the 4 month period to reverse or vary his decision on a proof, or for a proof to be expunged, or for the amount of a claim to be reduced and, without the leave of the court, he may not declare a dividend while such an application is pending. If the leave of the court is given the liquidator must make such provision for the proof as the court directs.[163] In the absence of grounds to postpone or cancel the dividend the liquidator is obliged to declare it.[164]

19.96   On the declaration of a dividend, the liquidator must give notice of dividend—which may be distributed at the same time as the dividend itself—to all creditors who have proved their debts.[165] The notice must include the following particulars of the insolvent estate:

(a) amounts raised by the sale of assets with detail so far as practicable of the amounts raised by the sale of particular assets;

(b) payments made by the liquidator in the administration of the estate of the company;

(c) any provisions made for unsettled claims or funds retained for particular purposes;

(d) the total amount to be distributed and the rate of dividend;

(e) whether and, if so, when any further dividend is likely to be declared.[166]

---

160   r 11.2.
161   r 11.3 and 4.182A(5).
162   *Re Compania de Electricidad de la Provincia de Buenos Aires Ltd* [1980] 1 Ch 186.
163   rr 11.4 and 11.5(2).
164   r 11.5(1).
165   r 11.6(1) and (3).
166   r 11.6(2).

19.97   The normal means of paying the dividend will be by post but by arrangement with the creditor it may be paid in another way or retained for him to collect.[167] If the dividend is paid on a negotiable instrument the amount of the dividend must be endorsed on the instrument or a certified copy.[168] If notice is given to the creditors, by the liquidator, that he will be unable to declare any or any further dividend it must state either that no funds have been realised in the liquidation or that the funds realised have been used or set aside to defray the expenses of the liquidation.[169]

19.98   The procedures laid down in Part 11 of the Insolvency Rules 1986 for the declaration and distribution of dividends apply to preferential creditors with appropriate adaptations to take account of the fact that they are a limited class.[170] After the last date for proving the liquidator will defray all the outstanding expenses of the winding up out of the assets and declare and distribute the final dividend without regard to the claim of any person in respect of a debt not already proved.[171] However, the court has power to postpone that date on the application of any person.[172]

POST LIQUIDATION INTEREST

19.99   As noted in paras 19.73–19.76 above, post liquidation interest on debts will be paid after all the debts have been paid in full. The final distribution will include payments of these amounts if a 100% dividend was paid on all debts which were proved in the liquidation.

SECTION 215(4) ORDERS AND BATHAMPTON ORDERS

19.100   If the court, on finding a person responsible for wrongful or fraudulent trading, has made an order under s 215(4) of the Act postponing the debts due to them from the company such persons will rank after the payment in full of all other debts and of post-liquidation interest on them. Similarly, if a court has made a *Bathampton* order in respect of costs unjustifiably incurred by the company in opposing the making of a winding up order, that amount will be recoverable after the payment of other debts and post-liquidation interest on them.[173] All claims which rank in this

---

167   r 11.6(4).
168   r 11.6(5).
169   r 11.7.
170   r 11.12.
171   r 4.186(3).
172   r 4.186(4).
173   See *Re Bathampton Properties* [1976] 1 WLR 168, where such an order was made in respect of the company's costs incurred after it could have consented to the winding up order.

position, behind debts and post-liquidation interest, are payable *pari passu.* Post liquidation interest on all categories of debt ranks equally.[174] All further claims are made by contributories and are dealt with under that heading.

DISTRIBUTIONS TO CONTRIBUTORIES

Liability arising from purchase or redemption of own shares

19.101 Section 178(4) of the Companies Act 1985 provides for the enforcement of any liability of the company that exists because the company agreed to buy its own shares or issued redeemable shares under Chapter VII of the Act after 15th June 1982 and has not bought or redeemed them before the commencement of the liquidation. The liability will not be enforceable if the terms of the purchase or redemption provided for shares to be redeemed or purchased at a date later than the commencement of the winding up.[175] There will also be no possibility of enforcement against the company if it could not have lawfully made a distribution of an amount equal to the price at which the shares were to have been redeemed or purchased at any time between the date on which purchase or redemption was to have taken place and the date of the winding up.[176]

19.102 If a payment can be enforced under s 178(4) it will rank after all other debts and liabilities of the company other than those due to the members in their character as such.[177] It also ranks behind the claims of other members based on their preferred rights as the holders of shares carrying rights as to capital or income which have priority over the rights as to capital of the shares to be bought or redeemed.[178] These amounts are paid to contributories either by way of redemption of their shares or as the price for the company's purchase of those shares. In either case the shares are treated as cancelled on redemption or purchase.[179]

Deferred debts to members

19.103 Section 74(2)(f) of the Insolvency Act 1986 lays down that any sum due to a member of the company in his character as such by way of

174 Insolvency Act 1986 s 189(3).
175 Companies Act 1985 s 178(5)(a).
176 *Ibid* s 178(5)(b).
177 *Ibid* s 178(6)(a).
178 *Ibid* s 178(6)(b).
179 *Ibid* s 178(4).

dividend profit or otherwise is not deemed to be a debt of the company payable to that member if he is in competition with any other creditor who is not a member of the company. Such amounts rank after all other liabilities of the company apart from the return of share capital and the division of any surplus among members.

19.104 Dividends which were declared or otherwise fell due before the commencement of the liquidation but which were not paid fall into this category.[180] In the absence of clear evidence of an express or implied agreement that unpaid dividend was left on loan with the company it will not be regarded as a debt due in some character other than that of member. This is despite the fact that unpaid dividend is regarded as a debt before the company goes into liquidation. Mere book entries will not amount to adequate evidence of a loan, particularly if the company had insufficient funds to pay the dividend and did not provide any other consideration to the member such as interest on the loan.[181] An amount due to a member in some other character, such as a normal trade debt or an amount specifically advanced by way of loan will not be affected by the rule in s 74(2)(f) and such a member will be able to prove that debt and will receive a dividend on it in the same way as other creditors with the corollary that the debt cannot be set off against a call.[182]

Expenses of contributories' meetings

19.105 Rule 4.61(4) provides for a meeting of contributories summoned on the requisition of contributories to decide that the expenses of summoning and holding the meeting should be payable out of the assets but such payment must rank after the payment of all creditors in full with interest.

Return of capital

19.106 After the payment of the expenses of the liquidation and of the debts the contributories will receive any remaining balance. The expression 'surplus assets' used in a company's articles or memorandum of association may either mean the amount remaining after debts and expenses have been paid, or the balance after those liabilities have been met and the shareholders have received a return of the capital paid up on their shares. The construction to be placed on the phrase will depend on the context in

---

180   *Re Consolidated Goldfields of New Zealand Ltd* [1953] Ch 689.
181   *Re L B Halliday & Co Ltd* [1986] BCLC 227.
182   *Grissell's Case* (1866) 1 Ch App 528; and see paras 17.20–29 on calls.

which it is used in a particular document.[183] If a contributory has died or become bankrupt his personal representative or trustee in bankruptcy is treated as a contributory by virtue of sections 81 or 82 of the Insolvency Act 1986.

19.107 In a compulsory liquidation s 154 lays down that the court is to adjust the rights of the contributories *inter se* and to distribute any surplus among the persons entitled to it. This means that the liquidator must apply to the court for an order whether the amount available is sufficient to repay capital in whole or in part or to distribute a surplus after capital has been repaid in full.[184] This rule has survived the 1985 reforms despite the tendency to reduce the degree of control by the court in compulsory liquidations and despite the repetition in s 143(1) of the provision giving the liquidator in such a winding up the function, *inter alia*, of distributing any surplus to those entitled to it.

19.108 Rule 4.221 lays down that an application to the court by the liquidator for an order authorising the return of capital should be accompanied by a list of the persons to whom the return is to be made and the amount to be paid to them. The list will include the same details of the persons involved as the settled list of contributories. The court is required to send a sealed copy of its order to the liquidator who will then inform each person of the rate of return per share and whether it is expected that any further return will be made.[185] Payments will normally be sent by cheque.[186]

19.109 In a voluntary winding up s 107 lays down that, subject to the application of assets to satisfaction of the company's liabilities, its assets are to be distributed among the members according to their rights and interests in the company unless the articles of the company provide otherwise. It seems that such a provision must lay down some other basis for distribution and a statement that no part of the assets is to be distributed to the members is not sufficient on its own to supplant the rule that distribution is to be among contributories.[187] Section 165(5) specifies that the liquidator is to adjust the rights of the contributories among themselves. It is, of course, possible for the liquidator to apply under s 112 for the guidance of the court

---

183 See, for example, *Re E W Savory Ltd* [1951] 2 TLR 1071 and *Re Ramel Syndicate Ltd* [1911] 1 Ch 749.
184 *Re Phoenix Oil and Transport Co Ltd (No 2)* [1956] 1 Ch 565.
185 r 4.222(1).
186 r 4.222(2).
187 See *Re Merchant Navy Supply Association* [1947] 1 All ER 894, where the provision in question was held to apply only to the company's profits as a going concern and not to a surplus on winding up.

in carrying out these functions but the Act makes it clear that he is entitled to make distributions among contributories without a court order.

19.110   The liquidator may use the procedure in Part 11 of the Insolvency Rules to fix a date by which shareholders or former shareholders must prove their debts and claims and to exclude those who fail to do so from the benefit of any distribution of assets as they are regarded as creditors for this purpose in respect of the amount due by way of dividends declared and not paid and the repayment of capital. After the exclusion of such members by the use of that procedure, monies are not regarded as being held on trust for them and the limitation period on proceedings to recover unpaid dividend is six years as it is not a speciality claim.[188]

19.111   The first step will be to use the surplus to repay capital. If the company has issued preference shares which are stated to have a preference as to capital as well as dividend then those shares must receive full repayment before any capital is repaid on other classes of share. In the absence of any further statement of the rights attached to such shares to participate in the surplus, their right to a full return of capital before the holders of other classes of share will be taken to exclude any right to participate in any remaining surplus after all capital has been repaid.[189] The rules laid down for the order of the repayment of capital in the company's memorandum and articles must be followed strictly.

19.112   If the company has only one class of share and the surplus is not large enough to repay capital in full then the contributories will be repaid rateably according to the number of shares they hold so that the loss falls on members in proportion to the nominal value of the shares that they hold.[190] If some shares have more paid up on them than others then the additional amount paid must be repaid with interest before the remaining surplus is distributed equally. This ensures an equal distribution without actually requiring those who have paid up less to pay money in and receive a different sum back.[191] Unless the company's articles provide that loss is to fall on the basis of the amount paid up on shares, the liquidator must make a call if that is necessary to ensure that those who paid more can be repaid.[192] Similarly, a contributory who has not paid a call due from him cannot receive any return of capital without making the payment required or (if he is due more than he owes) having an account taken.[193]

188   *Re Compania de Electricidad de la Provincia de Buenos Aires Ltd* [1980] 1 Ch 146.
189   *Scottish Insurance Corporation v Wilson & Clyde Coal Co* [1949] AC 462.
190   *Ex p Maude* (1870) 6 Ch App 51.
191   *Re Wakefield Rolling Stock Co* [1892] 3 Ch 165.
192   *Ex p Maude* (note 190 above) and *Re Kinatan (Borneo) Rubber* [1923] 1 Ch 124.
193   *Grissell's Case* (1866) 1 Ch App 528 and *Re West Coast Goldfields* [1906] 1 Ch 1.

Distribution of surplus after repayment of capital

19.113   The final application of assets remaining in the hands of the liquidator will involve their payment to contributories after all capital has been repaid on shares. In a company limited by guarantee all surplus will be distributed in this way if no share capital exists. This process will be governed by the rules laid down in the memorandum and articles of the company. It has already been noted that preference shareholders will be excluded from any share in such a surplus if they had a preference for the repayment of capital and are not expressly stated to be entitled to share the ultimate surplus.

19.114   The entitlement of preference shareholders to arrears of dividend from the surplus after capital has been repaid depends on the construction of the company's articles. If a dividend was declared before the commencement of the winding up, then the shareholder is a creditor entitled to claim after all other debts and expenses of winding up have been paid.[194] If this has not occurred then there will only be entitlement if the articles of the company or the terms of issue of the shares laid down that the profits of the company as a going concern should be applied in a particular way which includes the payment of dividend on preference shares. Such a provision ensures payment of the dividend out of the surplus if sufficient profits have been earned and replaces, to that extent, the general rule that the fact that part of the surplus represents profits does not mean that it is to be distributed as dividend rather than capital.[195]

19.115   If the articles or the terms of issue of preference shares lay down that preference share dividends are to be paid without specifying the date to which they are calculated they will only be paid for the period up to the commencement of the winding up and not up to the date of the repayment of capital to the preference shareholders.[196] Similarly, a limitation of the preference to dividend due at the commencement of the winding up will only give entitlement to sums for which the shareholder could have sued at that time; ie those which had been declared or which fell due automatically on a given level of profits being earned by the company.[197]

19.116   The construction of particular clauses which were commonly used in the past and are now avoided by draftsmen has been dealt with in a number of reported cases. It is sufficient for the purpose of this work to refer

194   See paras 19.103–4.
195   *Bishop v Smyrna and Cassaba Railway Co* [1895] 2 Ch 265 and *Re Crichton's Oil Co* [1902] 2 Ch 86.
196   *Griffith v Paget* (1877) 6 Ch D 511.
197   *Re Roberts and Cooper Ltd* [1929] 2 Ch 383.

the reader to the citation and discussion of those cases in the standard company law texts.[198]

19.117 The surplus remaining after capital has been repaid will be divisable among shareholders in proportion to the nominal value of their shares rather than the amount paid up unless the articles of the company or the terms of issue of the shares provide to the contrary.[199] However, this rule once again merely illustrates the importance of construing the articles of the company and acting in accordance with their stipulations.

DISTRIBUTIONS TO EMPLOYEES

19.118 Section 187 of the Insolvency Act 1986 makes provision for the distribution of assets to employees of the company if such a decision is made by the company before the commencement of the liquidation or by the use of the procedure laid down in s 187 itself. That process is dealt with in para 19.32 *supra*.

THE FINAL MEETINGS

19.119 The conclusion of the winding up process is marked by the meetings required by the Act at that stage to which the liquidator formally presents his final return and account. In a voluntary liquidation ss 94 and 106 deal with the meetings applicable to a members' or creditors' voluntary liquidation respectively. Under s 106 a general meeting of the company and a meeting of all its creditors is called so that the liquidator's account and his explanation of it can be laid before each meeting. The liquidator has an obligation to call the meeting as soon as the company's affairs are fully wound up. The account of the liquidator must show how the winding up has been conducted and indicate the disposition of the company's property. In the case of a members' voluntary liquidation s 94 only requires that the account be presented to a company meeting. In each case the meeting must be advertised in the *Gazette* at least one month before it is to take place to show the time, place and object of the meeting.[200] A return of the holding of the meeting to the effect that it was inquorate and a copy of the account must then be sent to the registrar of companies within one week after the date of the meeting.[201]

---

198   See for example Gore Browne on "Companies" para 14.4.1; Pennington's "Company Law" 5th ed pp 233–5 and Palmer's "Company Law" 24th ed paras 35–08 to 35–10.
199   *Birch v Cropper* (1889) 14 App Cas 525.
200   ss 94(2) and 106(2).
201   ss 94(3) and (5) and 106(3) and (5).

19.120 In a winding up by the court s 146(1) requires the liquidator to call a final general meeting of the company's creditors if it appears to him that the winding up is, for practical purposes, complete. The meeting receives his report and decides whether to grant the liquidator his release. Notice of the meeting may be served at the same time as notice of a final distribution.[202] After the meeting the liquidator must serve notice that it has been held and of its decisions on the Registrar of Companies.[203]

DISSOLUTION

19.121 The final stage in the liquidation process is the dissolution of the company. The procedure applicable to this varies between a voluntary and a compulsory liquidation.

Voluntary liquidation

19.122 In a voluntary liquidation the company is deemed to be dissolved three months after the Registrar of Companies registers the final account and return. The liquidator is required to file that document within one week after the final meeting in the case of a members' or creditors' voluntary liquidation by ss 94 and 106 respectively.[204] It is, however, possible for the liquidator or any other person who appears to the court to be interested to apply to the court for an order deferring the date of dissolution for such period as the court thinks fit.[205] If such an order is made the applicant must deliver an office copy of it to the registrar of companies for registration within seven days of the date of the order.[206] After the time limit for such applications is over it seems that only fraud on the part of the liquidator will justify setting aside the dissolution. So long as the liquidator believed that the company was fully wound up before his final account was made up, the precondition for holding the meeting and filing the return is satisfied. The consequent automatic dissolution of the company will not then be void even if it later appears that claims of which the liquidator was unaware did exist.[207] However, the power of the court under s 651 will be available.[208]

Compulsory liquidation

Early dissolution
19.123 In the case of a compulsory liquidation a procedure for early

---

202 s 146(2).
203 s 172(8).
204 See s 201(1) and (2) and paras 19.113 *et seq supra*.
205 s 201(3).
206 s 201(4).
207 *Re Cornish Manures Ltd* [1967] 2 All ER 875.
208 See para 19.137–19.140.

dissolution of the company is to be found in ss 202 and 203 of the Insolvency Act 1986. Those sections apply if the official receiver is the liquidator of the company and it appears to him that the realisable assets of the company are insufficient to cover the expenses of the winding up and that its affairs do not require any further investigation. In such a case he may apply at any time to the registrar of companies for the early dissolution of the company.[209] The company is then dissolved three months after the registration of the application unless the Secretary of State gives directions under s 203 on the application before the end of the three month period of the official receiver or any person who appears to be interested.[210]

19.124 This provision prevents the dissipation of public funds by the use of the full liquidation procedure by the Insolvency Service in cases in which there is neither any hope of meeting the expenses of that process from the company's assets nor any reason to suppose that further investigation of the history of the company is worthwhile. The reference to the company's realisable assets ensures that its ownership of worthless property such as debts which are impossible to collect or rights under contracts which are disadvantageous to it does not prevent the use of the procedure for an early dissolution.

19.125 Before applying to the registrar of companies the official receiver must give at least 28 days' notice to the company's creditors and contributories and to any administrative receiver of the company's assets of his intention to do so.[211] The date of that notice marks the point at which the official receiver as liquidator is no longer required to perform any duty to those parties or to the company under the Insolvency Act 1986 except the duty to apply to the registrar of companies for the early dissolution of the company.[212]

19.126 The notice to creditors and contributories also triggers the right of the official receiver or those on whom he has served it to apply to the Secretary of State for directions.[213] Such an application may be made on the grounds that the realisable assets of the company are sufficient to cover the expenses of winding up, or that the affairs of the company require further investigation or that for some other reason the early dissolution of the company is undesirable.[214] The Secretary of State's directions may provide for the winding up of the company to proceed as if no notice had

209   s 202(2).
210   s 202(5).
211   s 202(3).
212   s 202(4).
213   s 201(1).
214   s 203(2).

been served by the official receiver; thus reviving his duties as liquidator under the Act. They may also defer the date at which dissolution is to take place if they are given after the application to use the procedure has already been registered.[215]

19.127   The person on whose application the directions of the Secretary of State were given or the successful appellant against directions must register them with the registrar of companies within seven days.[216] The Secretary of State is required to send two copies of his directions to the applicant so that one of them can be sent to the registrar of companies.[217] An appeal to the court is available against the decision of the Secretary of State on an application for directions and the court is required to send two sealed copies of its order to the successful party so that one of them can be sent by that party to the registrar of companies.[218]

The usual procedure
19.128   If the procedure for early dissolution under ss 202 and 203 is not applicable because the realisable assets of the company are sufficient to pay the expenses of widning up or because an investigation of the company's affairs is regarded as desirable, s 205 lays down a procedure to be followed for dissolution which is similar to that laid down in s 201 for cases of voluntary liquidation. In such cases the dissolution takes place three months after receipt and registration, by the registrar of companies, of notice (from the liquidator under s 172(8)) of the holding of the final meeting and his vacation of office or of notice from the official receiver that the winding up of the company by the court is complete.[219] However, the Secretary of State has power to give a direction deferring the date of dissolution for such period as he thinks fit on the application of the official receiver or such other person as appears to him to be interested.[220] An appeal to the court is available against his decision and the applicant, or if there is an appeal, the person in whose favour it is decided, is obliged to file one of the two copies he is given of the court order or the Secretary of State's direction within seven days of it being made.[221]

19.129   The reforms of 1985 have ensured that a straightforward and automatic procedure exists for the dissolution of companies subject to winding up by the court so that reliance need no longer be placed on s 652

215   s 203(3).
216   s 203(5).
217   r 4.224.
218   s 203(4) and r 4.225.
219   s 205(1) and (2).
220   s 205(3).
221   s 205(4) and (6) and rr 4.224 and 4.225.

of the Companies Act 1985 for automatic removal from the register by the registrar of companies if a court order is to be avoided. However, that procedure may apply if there is no liquidator of a company being wound up or if its affairs appear to be fully wound up and the liquidator's returns have not been made for six months.[222]

Striking companies off the register

19.130 Section 652 lays down a procedure for a company to be struck off the register by the registrar of companies if he has reasonable cause to believe that it is not carrying on business or in operation. In such a case the registrar will send a letter by post inquiring whether the company is carrying on business or in operation.[223] If the letter is not answered within one month of being sent he must send a registered letter referring to the first letter and warning that if no reply is received within one month of the date of the second letter a notice will be published in the *Gazette* with a view to striking the name of the company off the register.[224]

19.131 If the company is in liquidation the registrar can omit those first two steps if he has reasonable cause to believe that no liquidator is acting or that the affairs of the company are fully wound up and he has received no return from the liquidator for a period of six months.[225] In such a case, or in a case where the letters required by ss 652(1) and (2) have elicited no reply or a reply to the effect that the company has ceased business or is no longer in operation, the registrar can publish in the *Gazette* and send to the company a notice that at the end of three months from its date the company will be struck off unless good cause is shown to the contrary.[226] At the end of the three month period the registrar can strike the company off the register if no cause to the contrary has been shown and on publication of notice in the *Gazette* that he has done this the company is dissolved.[227]

19.132 All notices to the liquidator of a company under this section can be addressed to him at his last known place of business. Notices and letters to the company can be sent to its registered office or to the care of one of its officers if it has no registered office. In the absence of any officer whose name and address is known it can be sent to the subscribers to the memorandum.[228]

222 s 652(4) Companies Act 1985 and see paras 19.130–133 below.
223 Companies Act 1985 s 652(1).
224 s 652(2).
225 s 652(4).
226 s 652(3).
227 s 652(5).
228 s 652(7).

19.133 After the dissolution of a company under the section the liability of all of its directors' managing officers and members can still be enforced as if it still existed and the court still has power to wind it up on a petition which requests its restoration to the register as a preliminary. The latter power exists even if a winding up order has already been made in ignorance of the fact that the company had been struck off as the restoration of the company will result in the property vesting in the liquidator.[229] No voluntary winding up of the company can commence after it has been struck off the register.

The effects of dissolution and striking off

19.134 After dissolution the court has no jurisdiction over the company as it does not exist and service of process is no longer possible. A party, such as an insurance company, entitled to a right of subrogation cannot sue in the company's name unless the cause of action was assigned by the company before it was dissolved.[230]

19.135 By s 654 of the Companies Act 1985, a company's property is deemed to be *bona vacantia* after its dissolution. This includes real property, leases and personalty (including choses in action such as its rights under contracts). It also includes property held by others on trust for the company but does not include property held by the company on trust for another person. *Bona vacantia* belong to the Crown or the Duchy of Lancaster or the Duke of Cornwall. The ownership rights vest in this way subject and without prejudice to orders under ss 651 or 653 for the revival of the company.[231] The possibility of orders under those sections does not affect the right of the person entitled to *bona vacantia* to dispose of the property or of any interest in it and the making of such an order does not affect a disposition although it may deal with other property previously vested in or held on trust for the company.[232] If property has been disposed of before an order under ss 651 or 653 is made the Crown (or other holder of *bona vacantia*) must pay the company the amount of the consideration received for the property or right or interest disposed of or the value of the consideration as at the date of the disposal or, if no consideration was received, the value of the property right or interest at that date.[233]

19.136 If the procedure in s 656 of the Companies Act 1985 is followed the

229 s 652(6) and *Re Thompson and Riches* [1981] 1 WLR 682.
230 *M L Smith (Plant Hire) Ltd v D Mainwaring* [1986] BCLC 342.
231 See para 19.137 *infra*.
232 Companies Act 1985 s 655(1) and (2)(a).
233 s 655(2)(b).

Crown can disclaim property to which it becomes entitled as *bona vacantia* on the dissolution of a company. The effect of this is that property to which a notice under that section relates is deemed never to have vested in the Crown under s 654.[234] Sections 178(4) and 179 to 182 of the Insolvency Act 1986 then apply as if the property had been disclaimed by a liquidator under ss 178 to 180 of that Act immediately before the dissolution of the company.[235]

Revival of dissolved companies

19.137 Section 651 of the Companies Act 1985 provides for the court to make an order declaring the dissolution of the company void. This may be used when a company has been dissolved under ss 201 to 205 of the Insolvency Act 1986 but not when the company has been struck off the register under s 652 of the Companies Act 1985. However, in the case of a company which is struck off, s 653 is available for its restoration but s 651 may be used as an alternative.[236]

Use of s 651

19.138 An application to the court under s 651 may be made within 12 years (2 years pending implementation of the Insolvency Act 1985) of the date of dissolution but an order may be made outside that period if application is made within it.[237] The application can be made by the liquidator of the company or by any other person appearing to the court to be interested. A 'liquidator' means someone who was liquidator at the date of dissolution; someone appointed afterwards can only apply as an interested person but fits that category because of a possible claim for a *quantum meruit* or a possible liability to the Crown for meddling in property which is *bona vacantia*.[238] However, a person who has no personal interest whatsoever—such as a solicitor acting for a plaintiff—is not within the definition as would be his client.[239]

19.139 The section does not lay down the criteria which the court is to use in deciding whether to make an order declaring the dissolution to have been void. The most obvious justification for an order is the existence of assets which may be used to meet the claims of creditors or members when they

234 s 657(1).
235 ss 657(2) and 658; and see paras 18.05 *et seq* for details of the provisions on disclaimer by a liquidator.
236 *Re Test Holdings (Clifton) Ltd* [1970] Ch 285.
237 s 651(1) as amended by Insolvency Act 1985 sch 6 para 45 from a day to be appointed; and see *Re Scad Ltd* [1941] Ch 386. The Companies Act 1989 s 141 extends the period to 20 years for personal injury claims by inserting a new s 651(4)–(7).
238 *Re Wood & Martin (Bricklaying) Contractors Ltd* [1971] 1 All ER 732.
239 *Re Roehampton Swimming Pool Ltd* [1968] 1 WLR 1693.

vest in the company on its revival. The existence of a claim against the company may also justify an order.[240] A right of action against officers of the company for wrongful or fraudulent trading or the possibility of setting aside transactions and thus making assets available for creditors will clearly be relevant.

19.140   The effect of an order under s 651 is that the dissolution becomes 'void'. However, in contrast to the position on revival under s 653, this does not validate acts of the company which took place between dissolution and revival. An arbitration award made in that period does not bind the company as it was made against a non-existent company[241] and even a misfeasance summons issued before the dissolution during the winding up of the company cannot be revived on the avoidance of the dissolution.[242] Once the order under s 651 is made it does revive the company with retrospective effect so that property revests in it without any further order unless the Crown has disposed of it in the meantime.[243]

Use of s 653

19.141   If a company's name has been struck off the register under s 652 of the Companies Act 1985 it may be restored by the court on the application of the company or any member or creditor of it who feels aggrieved by the striking off. The application must be made within 20 years from the publication in the *London Gazette* of the notice required under s 652.[244] It is difficult to see how the non-existent company can apply for its own restoration to the register. It seems that it has a purely provisional existence for the purpose of deciding who may apply for the restoration of its name to the register and it is not entitled to be heard on an application by a creditor by virtue of either s 653 or RSC O15 r6 which only applies if there is some matter in dispute and cannot assist a fully paid shareholder in this context.[245]

19.142   Application can be made by prospective or contingent creditors and by those with unliquidated claims against the company.[246] A personal representative of a deceased member can claim without being registered as a shareholder[247] but an assignee of a debt or transferee of a share who took his interest after the date of dissolution cannot. The applicant must have

240   *Ibid.*
241   *Morris v Harris* [1927] AC 252.
242   *Re Lewis and Smart* [1954] 1 WLR 755.
243   *Re C W Dixon Ltd* [1947] Ch 251 and s 655(2) (para 19.135 *supra*).
244   s 653(1) and (2).
245   See *Re Portra Frame Ltd* [1986] BCLC 533 and *Re H Clarkson (Overseas) Ltd* (1987) 3 BCC 606.
246   *Re Harvest Lane Motor Bodies Ltd* [1969] 1 Ch 457.
247   *Re Bayswater Trading Co Ltd* [1970] 1 WLR 608.

been a creditor at the date of the company's dissolution if he applies in that capacity; a surety who paid a debt of the company after that date cannot apply.[248]

19.143 Section 653 is only available if a company's name has been struck off the register but s 651 can also be used in that situation. Section 651 allows application by a wider range of people as all that is necessary is that an applicant appears to the court to be interested. However, the 20 year time limit for an application under s 653 is more generous than the 12 years prospectively allowed under s 651.

19.144 The criteria for the restoration of a company under s 653 are that the court is satisfied that the company was in operation or in business at the time of the striking off or that it is just that the company be restored to the register.[249] The latter requirement has been held to mean that there must be some really substantial benefit to members or creditors who petition for the restoration.[250]

19.145 Unless the company was already in liquidation when it was struck off the registrar of companies must be made a party to the proceedings to be able to make representations to in the public interest and on the grounds on which the company was struck off.[251] The Treasury Solicitor will also be involved, as the company's property will have devolved on the Crown as *bona vacantia*.

19.146 Once an office copy of the order restoring the company has been delivered to the registry of companies for registration, the company is deemed to have continued in existence as if its name had not been struck off the register.[252] The court may give such directions or make such provisions in the order as seem just to place the company and all other persons in, or as near as may be to, the position they would have been in if the company had not been struck off.

19.147 This means that, in contrast to the position under s 651, the company's acts and all matters affecting it are retrospectively validated by its restoration to the register. An application in the company's name in the county court for a new business tenancy is validated by its later restoration to the register. The court's power to give directions is merely intended to

---

248   *Re New Timbiqui Gold Mines Ltd* [1961] 1 All ER 865 and *Re Aga Estate Agencies Ltd* [1986] BCLC 346.
249   s 653(2).
250   *Re Lindsay Bowman* [1969] 1 WLR 1443.
251   *Re Test Holdings (Clifton) Ltd* [1970] Ch 285.
252   s 653(3).

complement the statutory rule that the company is deemed to have continued in existence during the *interregnum*.[253] Directions may protect the position of the company or others. They may deem a charge on the company's assets to have been duly delivered for registration under s 395 of the Companies Act 1985 on the date on which it was received by the registry despite the fact that the company did not exist at that time. Similarly, the running of time under the Limitation Act may be suspended by directions in the order if the petitioner or other creditors have been prejudiced and the company was not in liquidation at the date of dissolution.[254]

253 *Tymans Ltd v Craven* [1952] 2 QB 100.
254 *Re Boxco Ltd* [1970] Ch 442.

CHAPTER 20

Setting Aside Transactions

20.01 The right to set aside transactions in order to do justice to creditors and to prevent debtors from avoiding their obligations has a long history. The provisions now dealt with in s 423 to 425 of the Insolvency Act 1986 and which were previously contained in s 172 of the Law of Property Act 1925 have their origins in the Fraudulent Conveyances Act of 1571. Orders under this provision can be made even if the debtor has not been subject to insolvency proceedings and remain available to victims of such activities as well as to officeholders in an insolvency.[1] In addition to that provision the pre-1986 law permitted the avoidance of fraudulent preferences. This remedy was available once a person was formally adjudged insolvent and payments or property transfers could be set aside if they were shown to have been made with an intention to 'prefer' a particular creditor. The provision applied to insolvent companies and insolvent individuals. Insolvent individuals were also subject to the rule that settlements could be set aside under s 42 of the Bankruptcy Act 1914 while insolvent corporations could find that certain floating charges were voidable if insolvency ensued within 12 months and the company had not been solvent when the charge was granted.

20.02 The Insolvency Act 1985 enacted provisions which reflect a number of the recommendations of the Cork Committee. They have brought consistency to the rules applicable to both companies and individuals who become insolvent. The rules on preferences, transactions at an undervalue and the avoidance of floating charges reflect the concern of the Cork Committee to attack transactions not at arm's length by the operation of the time limits and the burden of proof. They also clarify the mischief with which the law is concerned by emphasising the loss of value to the company and thus the depletion of the assets available to its creditors as the key criterion. It is unfortunate that certain provisions—particularly s 240(1) which deals with the effect of a person's connection with the company on preferences and transactions at an undervalue—are difficult to interpret.

---

1 See paras 20.31 *et seq* below.

TRANSACTIONS AT AN UNDERVALUE

Application and nature of transaction

20.03   In common with the other remedies which facilitate the adjustment of prior transactions, the power to apply to the court for an order to set aside a transaction at an undervalue applies when a company is in administration or in liquidation.[2] This power is not available to an administrative receiver.

20.04   Section 238(2) allows an application to be made to the court if the company has at a relevant time[3] entered into a transaction at an undervalue with any person. A transaction at an undervalue is defined by s 238(4) in two alternative ways. A transaction whereby the company:

> "(a) makes a gift to that person or otherwise enters into a transaction with that person on terms that provide for the company to receive no consideration"

comes within the definition. In circumstances in which the company receives no economic benefit whatsoever the transaction will be regarded as being at an undervalue whether or not it can be classified as a gift. However, the definition also includes the situation in which:

> "(b) the company enters into a transaction with that person for a consideration the value of which, in money or money's worth, is significantly less than the value, in money or money's worth, of the consideration provided by the company".

20.05   It is important to note that the second part of the definition does not require that the consideration be in money or money's worth but only that it be valued in those terms. The process of valuation will be used to test the relative values given and gained by the company. The difference must be significant. It is thus clear that a *de minimus* rule applies but the word 'significant' suggests that more than that is intended. A test may be developed by the court which accepts a range of values within which the transaction will be unimpeachable. The difficulty of achieving an accurate valuation will vary with the nature of the property involved and the circumstances in which the transaction takes place; the presence or absence of a readily available market in the property in question being the most important factor.

20.06   The meaning of the word 'transaction' as it applies throughout the

2   See ss 238(1), 239(1), 244(1) and 245(1) Insolvency Act 1986; but contrast s 424, which permits an application by a 'victim'.
3   See paras 20.35–36 *infra*.

Insolvency Act 1986 is laid down in s 436. It is not limited to contractually binding agreements but includes any 'gift, agreement or arrangement'. The level of formality applying to the dealings of the company with a person makes no difference to their status as 'transactions'. The definition includes contracts of purchase or sale or for services, gifts, grants of security, guarantees or payments of debts, property transfers and less formal arrangements.

The statutory defence

20.07   Even if it is established that a transaction is at an undervalue and was entered into at a relevant time, a defence is provided by s 238(5). This prevents transactions which fall within the definition of undervalue because of the absence of consideration or its inadequate value from being impugned by an order of the court if two conditions are satisfied. First, the company must have entered the transaction both in good faith and for the purpose of carrying on its business. It must be shown that those acting on behalf of the company in connection with the transaction were acting *bona fide*. In this situation the state of mind of those regarded as the alter ego of the company will be attributed to it.[4] The motive for the transaction is also significant in that it must not only be *intra vires* the objects of the company but; 'for the purpose of carrying on its business'. It is submitted that that means a business which the company has in fact carried on in the past or which it has properly and in good faith decided to undertake in the future. It will not be sufficient to show that the transaction is one which could have been undertaken as part of a business authorised by the objects clause in the company's memorandum of association if the company has not in fact embarked on such a business. The second condition that must be satisfied is that there were reasonable grounds for believing at the time when the company entered into it that the transaction would benefit the company. This provides an objective test for the decision that the company would benefit from the transaction. It is likely that it will be harder to satisfy this test in cases where no consideration is provided to the company although even a gift may be made on the basis of its likely beneficial effects on the commercial activities of the company and a court may find that there were reasonable grounds for a belief in such benefits.

20.08   The structure of s 238 is such that the initital matters which require proof on an application by an administrator or a liquidator are the value

---

4   See *R v Andrews Weatherfoil Ltd* [1972] 1 WLR 118 and *Tesco Supermarkets Ltd v Nattrass* [1970] 2 QB 133. It would seem that the test established in those cases for the mental element required for a criminal charge will apply to the issue of a company's *bona fides*.

given on each side of the transaction and the time of the transaction. The defence that the transaction was entered into in good faith for the purpose of carrying on the company's business at a time when there were reasonable grounds for believing that it would benefit the company will require proof on the part of the party seeking to avoid an order setting the transaction aside. This should facilitate the task of the insolvency practitioner in seeking such an order in cases where negligence can be proved on the part of those responsible for deciding that the transaction was likely to benefit the company. It is possible for a transaction entered into in good faith for the purpose of the company's business to be set aside as a result of negligence in the assessment of the likelihood of benefit to the company.

20.09   It might be argued that this rule is unfair to the other party to a genuine but foolish commercial transaction entered into by the company in good faith. However, the requirement that the discrepancy in the value of the consideration be 'significant' provides some protection in cases where some consideration flowed to the company. In all cases it will be necessary for the administrator or the liquidator to show that the transaction took place at a 'relevant time'. For the purpose of the rules on transactions at an undervalue and preferences[5] the concept of the 'relevant time' is defined in s 240 of the Insolvency Act 1986.

The relevant time

20.10   The 'relevant time' applicable to both transactions at an undervalue and preferences is defined by s 240 of the Insolvency Act 1986. In determining the period that constitutes the 'relevant time' for the purpose of ss 238 and 239 a distinction is made between transactions with connected persons and other transactions. This method is used to achieve a balance between the need to protect legitimate commercial interests in the stability of transactions and the importance of protecting creditors of the company from abuses. In the case of all transactions s 240(1) calculates the period from the date of the 'onset of insolvency'; although transactions or preferences taking place in the period between the presentation of an administration petition and the making of an order are always included.[6] The 'onset of insolvency' is the date of the presentation of the petition on which the administration order was made in a case where the sections apply because of the making of such an order or the making of a liquidation order immediately on the discharge of an administration order. In any other case it is the date of the commencement of the winding up.[7] In the case of a

---

5   See paras 20.32–34 and 20.40–45 *infra*.
6   s 240(1)(c).
7   s 240(3).

compulsory winding up that is the date of the filing of the petition because of the doctrine of relation back unless an earlier resolution for voluntary winding up was passed, in which case it is the date of that resolution. In cases of voluntary liquidation the commencement of the winding up, and thus the date of the onset of insolvency, is the date of the passing of the resolution.[8]

20.11 Where the transaction or preference in question involves a party who is a person connected with the company the period is two years before the onset of the winding up.[9] The only exception to this is that a person who is connected with the company only by virtue of being an employee is not subject to the longer period for the calculation of the relevant time.

20.12 Section 240(1)(a) appears to lay down that either a transaction at an undervalue or a preference will have been entered into or given at a relevant time if it was given to, or entered into with, a connected person within two years before the onset of insolvency. However, the wording of the subsection could be construed as meaning that *all* transactions at an undervalue occur at a relevant time if they occur within two years before the onset of insolvency but that only preferences given to connected persons are challengeable within two years of such an onset. The latter view assumes that the words, 'which is given to a person who is connected with the company (otherwise than by reason only of being its employee)', qualify the word 'preference' and not the phrase 'transaction at an undervalue or of a preference'. The latter interpretation is supported by s 240(1)(b) which states:

> "in the case of a preference which is not such a transaction and is not so given, at a time in the period of six months ending with the onset of insolvency".

This indicates that para (b) of s 240(1) only applies to preferences which are not transactions at an undervalue and are not given to a person connected with the company.

20.13 The net effect of this interpretation is:

(a) transactions at an undervalue occur at a relevant time if they occur within two years of the onset of insolvency (subject to the provisions of subsection 240(2)) whether they are with persons connected with the company or not;

(b) preferences given to a person connected with the company can be challenged if they occur within two years before the onset of insolvency;

---

8 ss 86 and 129.
9 s 240(1)(a).

(c) preferences which are not also transactions at an undervalue and which are not given to connected persons can be challenged if given within a six month period before the onset of insolvency;

(d) both preferences and transactions at an undervalue are susceptible to challenge during the period between the presentation of a petition for an administration order and the making of the order.[10]

20.14 This interpretation is not consistent with the intention of the Cork Committee to create a different approach to 'connected persons' in respect of transactions at an undervalue. However, it is submitted that the literal interpretation of the statute results in the position that all transactions at an undervalue—including those which are also preferences—can be challenged if they occurred within two years before the onset of insolvency and that it is only in the context of preferences that a distinction exists between the relevant time as it applies where 'connected persons' are involved and the period applicable if transactions are with others.

20.15 In order for a transaction or preference to be treated as occurring at a relevant time, there is an additional requirement that the company was, at the time of the transaction, unable to pay its debts (in the same sense as applies for the purpose of a liquidation order—see para 14.115) or that it became unable to pay them in consequence of the transaction or preference. It is necessary that there be a causal link between the transaction and the company's insolvency unless the company was already insolvent at the date of the transaction or the preference. This conforms with the view of the Cork Committee that the mischief to be tackled by such a provision is the depletion of the resources which were, or might have been, available to the creditors in the insolvency proceedings. However, in order to avoid abuse by persons connected with the company there is a presumption in the case of transactions at an undervalue in which they are involved (but not in the case of preferences) that the company was already insolvent at the time of the transaction or became insolvent as a result of it.[11]

Connected persons

20.16 The definition of a person connected with a company is to be found in s 249 of the Insolvency Act 1986. It applies to all the parts of that Act concerned with corporate insolvency. It includes directors and shadow

---

10   This view is shared by Gregory *et al*, "A Guide to the Insolvency Act" 1985 pp 46–47; Milman, "Corporate Insolvency: Law and Practice" at pp 149–150 and I F Fletcher, the revision of Palmer's "Company Law" (24th ed)—see para 88.82A. For a contrary view see annotations to s 240(1)(a) in Current Law Statutes 1986.
11   s 240(2).

directors of the company. By s 741(1) of the Companies Act 1985 the expression 'director' includes; 'any person occupying the position of director, by whatever name called'. Section 741(2) defines a shadow director as; 'a person in accordance with whose directions or instructions the directors of the company are accustomed to act'. Persons who give advice in a professional capacity on which the directors act are excluded from this definition.

20.17 This basic definition of those who are connected to a company is expanded by reference to the concept of association which is defined in s 435 of the Insolvency Act 1986. The associates of directors and shadow directors and of the company itself are all included in the definition of connected persons by s 249 of that Act.

'Associates'

20.18 The definition of association works on mutual basis. If any person is an associate of another by virtue of the operation of the provisions of s 435 they are associates of each other for the purpose of the Act.[12]

Associates of individuals

20.19 A person is the associate of his or her husband or wife. The words 'husband and wife' include a former husband or wife and a reputed husband or wife.[13] After a divorce a former spouse remains an associate. It would seem that the parties to a void marriage would not be included in the concept of 'husband and wife' but by virtue of s 16 of the Matrimonial Causes Act 1973 the parties to a voidable marriage would be 'associates' as spouses. The concept of 'reputed' husband and wife would include those living together as husband and wife if the relationship was regarded by the world at large as analogous to marriage. It would be a question of fact for the court whether in the case of any given relationship there was reputed to be a marriage. It is unclear whether those among whom the parties are reputed to be spouses must believe in the permanence or the sexual nature of the relationship or in any other particular incidents of the married state. The use of the concept of reputed spouses may make the definition narrower than it would have been had the phrase 'living together as husband and wife' been used. The parties to a void marriage who cohabit will come within the definition of reputed spouses and even if they do not cohabit may be reputed to be spouses if they lead people to believe in the validity of their marriage.

---

12   s 435(1).
13   s 435(2) and (8).

20.20 Other relatives of an individual or of his or her spouse and the spouses of such relatives are 'associates' of that person. The relatives to whom this provision applies are: brothers and sisters; uncles and aunts; newphews and nieces; lineal ancestors; and lineal descendants. In the case of all of these relationships step children and adopted children are regarded as the children of the step parent or adoptive parent and relationships of the half blood are treated as relationships of the full blood. Illegitimate children are treated as the legitimate children of their mother and reputed father.[14]

20.21 All the other relationships between individuals which can amount to an 'association' under s 435 are of an economic nature. The relationship of employer and employee creates an association so that an individual is regarded as the associate of any person whom he employs or by whom he is employed.[15] Similarly a person is an associate of anyone with whom he is in partnership and with the spouse or other relative (within the categories outlined above) of a partner who is an individual rather than a company.[16] A trustee (whether individual or corporate) is an associate of a beneficiary of the trust; even if the trust is discretionary. He is also an associate of any person who is an associate of a beneficiary. A trustee of a pension scheme or an employee's share scheme within the definition in s 743 of the Companies Act 1985 and the trustee in bankruptcy of an individual are, however, excluded from this rule.[17]

Associates of corporate bodies
20.22 In s 435 the word 'company' includes any body corporate whether incorporated in Great Britain or elsewhere.[18] Any corporation aggregate is treated as a company for the purpose of this section and bodies such as industrial and provident societies and municipal corporations are included within the definition and so cannot be used to break the links which the definition forges to determine the question of association and (under s 249) of a connection between persons. By s 740 of the Companies Act 1985 the expression 'body corporate' does not include a corporation sole but does include a company incorporated outside Great Britain. A company is a person for the purposes of the section and consequently relationships of employer and employee, trustee and beneficiary, and of partnership which apply to individuals and create an association can equally create an association between a company and an individual or, in the case of a trust or a partnership, between a number of companies. In particular the

14   s 435(8).
15   s 435(4).
16   s 435(3).
17   s 435(5).
18   s 435(11).

directors and other officers of a company are treated as its employees.[19] Since only individuals can have relatives and spouses a company cannot be directly associated with a person only on that basis.[20] However, such relationships can create an association between an individual and a company with which his spouse or relative is associated in some other way.

20.23 In addition to the forms of association which can arise because of the fact of corporate personality, there are certain specific provisions in s 435 which define additional circumstances in which a company may be the associate of another company or of an individual. The association of a company with an individual or another company on a basis other than corporate personality involves the concepts of control and of association between controllers. A company is an associate of any person (individual or corporate) if that person has control of it. It is also associated with a person if he together with persons who are his associates have control of it.[21] The association of individuals with each other can be on the basis of relationships of blood or marriage. This would associate the company with all of the members of the controlling group. Equally, relationships between individual controllers might be economic; employer and employee; trustee and beneficiary or members of partnership. However, the relationships of partner or trustee and beneficiary might equally exist between companies.

20.24 In addition to the concepts of association applicable between individuals or to all persons whether corporate or individual, the section defines certain relationships of association which arise only between two or more companies. This arises in the following situations:

(a) where one person has control of both companies;
(b) where a person has control of one and persons who are his associates have control of the other;
(c) where a person has control of one and he and persons who are his associates have control of the other;
(d) where:
    (i) a group of two or more persons has control of each company and
    (ii) the groups consist of the same persons or would if one or more members of either group were treated as replaced by a person of whom he is an associate.

20.25 In all of these circumstances the companies affected by the relationship will be regarded as associates of each other. In each case the

---

19   s 435(3), (4), (5) and (9).
20   s 435(2).
21   s 435(7).

persons with control may be individuals or companies.[22] This gives rise to the question of what is meant by 'control' of a company in these circumstances. Section 435(10) defines this concept. It is possible for a company to be under the control of a number of persons who may be either individuals or corporate bodies. Control may be held for the purpose of the section in two different ways. It may be by direct or indirect control of votes or of the board of a company. Either will suffice to establish that control exists.

20.26 The scheme of the section is comparable with s 736(1) of the Companies Act 1985 which deals with the circumstances in which companies are regarded as holding and subsidiary companies. However, s 736 requires a company to hold more than half in nominal value of the equity in another company to create the subsidiary/holding company relationship on the basis of voting power, whereas s 435 requires control of only one third of the voting power. Similarly, control of the composition of the board is required as the other basis for control in s 736, whereas s 435 permits control to arise on the basis of only one director being accustomed to act on the directions or instructions of the controller.

20.27 The provisions of s 346 and part I of sch 13 of the Companies Act 1985 on when a person is to be regarded as connected with a director, for the purpose of the provisions on loans by the company to directors and to such persons, differ somewhat from the provisions of the Insolvency Act 1986 on 'connected persons'. Only the director's spouse and infant children or step children are regarded as connected to him for that purpose as compared to the wider group of blood relatives covered by s 435.[23] Association between a director and a company for that purpose requires only that the director and persons connected with him have an interest in or control over one fifth of the company's equity share capital or of the voting power at a general meeting, compared with the one third required for the purpose of the Insolvency Act provision.[24] It is only in determining the relationship between the ultimate controller of voting power and the company in which it is held that the figure of one third of the voting power of an intermediate company in actual control of the voting power is used.[25]

20.28 Voting control is defined as the entitlement to exercise or to control the exercise of one third or more of the voting power at a company general meeting or at the general meeting of a company which itself controls the

22   s 435(6).
23   s 346(2)(a) Companies Act 1985.
24   s 346(4).
25   s 346(4), (5) and (7) and sch 13 para 15.

company in question. Such control will be sufficient to make a person the controller of the company.[26]

20.29 Control may also be held by control of the board of the company or of that of a company which in turn controls the company in question. This is defined in terms of the fact that the directors or any of them are accustomed to act in accordance with the directions or instructions of the person with control. A person falling within the definition of a shadow director in s 741(2) of the Companies Act 1985 will be regarded as a controller of the company. Only one director need customarily act in accordance with a person's directions or instructions for that person to become a controller of the company of which the compliant individual is a director and of any companies controlled in turn by that company.[27] Where two or more persons together satisfy either of these tests then they are to be taken to have control of the company. This applies in addition to the specific provisions dealt with above on the joint control of a company by a number of persons.

The order

20.30 If a transaction at an undervalue is shown to have taken place at a relevant time, the court may make any order it thinks fit. The statute lays down that the purpose of the order is to restore the position of the company to what it would have been if the company had not entered into the transaction.[28] Provisions setting out examples of the uses which may be made of this broad power and imposing limits on the use which may be made of it for the protection of third parties are dealt with in paras 20.32–34 and 20.40–45 below as they apply to transactions at an undervalue and preferences respectively.[29]

TRANSACTIONS DEFRAUDING CREDITORS

20.31 S 423 to 425 of the Insolvency Act 1986 replace s 172 of the Law of Property Act 1925 and implement the recommendations of the Cork Report for the reform of that provision. They apply in cases of corporate and personal insolvency and permit an order to be made without any time limits. The grounds which must be established for an order to be made are based on the concept of a transaction at an undervalue but a particular

26   s 435(10)(b).
27   s 433(10)(a).
28   s 238(3) Insolvency Act 1986.
29   s 241.

intention must be established in this context which is not necessary under s 238 when a time limit is imposed for applications to the court.

Transaction at an undervalue

20.32 Section 423(1) defines a transaction at an undervalue in almost identical terms to those used in s 238(4). Only the addition for the purpose of applications relating to individuals of transactions in consideration of marriage distinguishes s 423(1). Gifts and transactions in which the company gives consideration of significantly greater value than it receives are within the definition.[30]

The purpose of the transaction

20.33 In addition to establishing the existence of a transaction at an undervalue, an applicant under s 423 must satisfy the court that the person entering the transaction did so for the purpose of:

> "(a) of putting assets beyond the reach of a person who is making, or may at some time make, a claim against him, or
> (b) of otherwise prejudicing the interests of such a person in relation to the claim which he is making or may make".[31]

20.34 It is clear that it is the company which is the person entering the transaction for the purpose of the section as the definition in s 423 of a transaction at an undervalue defines that person as the one receiving consideration of lower value than the consideration that it gives (or the one making the gift) and the section provides that the word 'debtor' is used to describe that party in s 424 and 425.[32] The purpose referred to in s 423(3) is that for which the transaction was entered into by the company. It is on the part of the company (as the 'person entering into such a transaction') that the necessary intention must be established.[33] The necessary prejudice need not be to the interests of a person with a current claim against the company. The statutory purpose can be established if the transaction affects (in the necessary way) a person who may make a claim. The purpose can either be to put assets beyond the reach of the actual or potential claimant or to prejudice his interests in some other way. Presumably any transaction designed to make the claim more difficult or more expensive to pursue will be within the definition. It is not necessary that the transaction should succeed in achieving the company's purpose for an application to succeed.

---

30   s 423(1)(c) Insolvency Act 1986.
31   s 423(3).
32   s 423(1)(a) and (b) and (5).
33   s 423(3).

Applicants

20.35 Section 424 lays down who may apply under s 423. If a bod͵ corporate is in liquidation or is subject to an administration order the application may be made by the official receiver, the liquidator or the administrator. In addition, a victim of the transaction may apply with the leave of the court in such a case.[34] If a victim of the transaction is bound by a voluntary arrangement approved under Part I of the Insolvency Act 1986, the supervisor of the arrangement can apply, but any victim of the transaction, whether bound by the arrangement or not, may also apply without requiring the leave of the court.[35] In any other case a victim of the transaction may apply.[36] This indicates that the remedy available under s 423 is not only available without any time limit but is available whether or not the company which entered into the transaction is insolvent or the subject of any insolvency proceedings. However, an administrative receiver has no standing as such in relation to transactions susceptible to challenge under s 423; although the creditor who appointed him may be a 'victim'. A victim of a transaction for the purpose of s 423 to 425 is a person who is, or is capable of being, prejudiced by it.[37]

20.36 Applications are made in the High Court or in a county court with jurisdiction to wind up the company.[38] In order to allow the court to make an order resolving all the difficulties created by a transaction and binding on all parties, each application is treated as made on behalf of every victim of the transaction in question.[39]

Court order

20.37 Section 423(2) gives the court a wide discretion to make any order it thinks fit if it is satisfied that the conditions defined in s 423 exits. The order will seek to restore the position to what it would have been if the transaction had not been entered into and to protect the interests of persons who are the victims of the transaction. S 425(1) lists examples of the uses which may be made of that discretion. They are *mutatis mutandis* the same as the examples furnished in s 241(1) which are discussed in para 20.51 *et seq.*

20.38 The only contrast worthy of note is the possibility, referred to in s 425(1)(a), of vesting property transferred as part of the transaction, in any

34 s 424(1)(a).
35 s 424(1)(b).
36 s 424(1)(c).
37 s 423(5).
38 s 423(4).
39 s 424(2).

person either absolutely or for the benefit of all the persons on whose behalf the application is treated as made. The applicant and the other victims of the transaction can share in the return of property transferred as part of the transaction. Section 241(1)(a) deals only with the vesting of property in the company.

20.39   The protection extended to third parties by s 425(2) is similar to that conferred by s 241(2) although the definition of 'relevant circumstances' in s 425(3) is limited to the circumstances by virtue of which an order under s 423 might be made. The court does have power to make orders affecting property held by third parties or imposing obligations on such persons subject to the protection by the Act of those taking a benefit from the transaction or an interest in property in good faith and for value without notice of relevant circumstances.[40]

PREFERENCES

20.40   Where a company is in liquidation or is subject to an administration order the liquidator or administrator may apply to the court if any preference has been given at a relevant time.[41] The purpose of the application will be to have the preference set aside. The act of preferring a creditor is a breach of the fiduciary duty of a director to the company as the interests of the company include the interests of creditors if the company is insolvent. In addition to the use of this provision action could be taken against the director under s 212. Proceedings at common law will also be available against the director. The person preferred will be liable as constructive trustee of the company's property if they were aware of the circumstances surrounding the payment.[42] A preference is defined in s 239(4) as anything done by the company or which it suffers to be done which has the effect, in the event of the company going into insolvent liquidation, of putting a creditor, surety or guarantor of a debt or liability of the company in a better position than he would have been in if that thing had not been done.

20.41   The most obvious example of a preference is the payment of a debt due to one creditor in advance of others who have equal or greater priority. However, the release of a guarantor or surety, the cancellation of a debt due to the company from a creditor which could not have been the subject of a set off in a liquidation or the part payment of a debt due from the company

---

40   s 425(2) and see para 20.51 *et seq.*
41   s 239(2).
42   *Liquidator of West Mercia Safetywear Ltd v Dodd* (1988) 4 BCC.

could all equally well amount to preferences. Any such transaction will have the effect of putting one creditor in a more favourable position than he would have been in had he been required to prove in the company's insolvent liquidation; the unsecured creditor who has been paid off before the onset of the insolvent liquidation might have received only a small dividend or no payment at all had he been required to prove in the winding up. The assets which were used to pay him in advance of the onset of the liquidation would have been available to other creditors had the payment not been made.

20.42   It is clear, however, that some limit must be placed on the scope permitted for the liquidator or administrator to challenge such preferences. This achieved by two of the provisions of s 239. First it is necessary that the preference was given at a 'relevant time'. This phrase is defined in s 240 which is dealt with in paragraph 20.35–20.36 above. Secondly, a certain intention is required on the part of the company before a preference is established.

20.43   The Act lays down that this mental element is required on the part of the company before a court order can be made on the basis that a preference was given. Section 239(5) prevents the court from making an order unless the company, in deciding to give the preference, was influenced by a desire to produce, in relation to the person to whom it was given, the effect of putting him in a better position than he would have been in if the preference had not been given. This does not require that the sole or even the major motive for the act which amounts to a preference was to improve the position of its recipient. It is only necessary to show that such a desire 'influenced' the company when it made its decision.

20.44   In the classic case in which the company argues that a debt was paid because of the threats and pressure brought to bear by the creditor it will be sufficient for the administrator or liquidator to show that the company was influenced to some degree by a desire to prefer that creditor. It will not be sufficient for the company to show that its predominant motive was something other than to confer a preference. It will have to show that it was not influenced at all by such a desire. However, it is clear that the onus of proof in this instance is on the office holder who is seeking a court order. The subsection prohibits the making of an order unless the company was influenced by the desire to give a preference. The existence of that influence is therefore a matter to be proved in the first place by those seeking the order.

20.45   This is a change to the pre-1985 law which required proof of preference as the predominant motive of the company in making the payment. It is now only necessary to show that a desire to prefer influenced the decision of the company. Even under the old law the fact that a payment was intended to be used by the preferred creditor to aid the insolvent business by channelling money into a new company to which the creditor lent it did not prevent the necessary mental element from being established.[43] *A fortiori* this will be the case under the 1986 Act.

20.46 The burden of proof on the issue of whether the company was influenced by a desire to give a preference is reversed by s 239(6) in cases where the preference was given to a person connected with the company at the time of the act amounting to a preference. There is then a presumption that the company was influenced by a desire to prefer unless the contrary is shown. In this situation a person is not regarded as connected to the company by reason only of being its employee. This provision, together with the extension of the 'relevant time' period to two years in the case of a preference given to a connected person, implements the recommendations of the Cork Report.[44] A bank which provides a report in the context of the company's inability to pay off an overdraft could bring itself within the definition of a shadow director and be held to be connected with the company if the company follows the advice contained in the bank's document.[45]

20.47 An act done in pursuance of a court order may still amount to a preference as the existence of the order alone does not prevent that outcome.[46] This prevents collusive proceedings by a creditor from justifying payment of his claim in advance of the claims of those with priority over him. The existence of a judgment or an order for execution may, however, be evidence of the absence of any desire to prefer as an influence on the decision made by the company. Likewise the fact that the payment made to a creditor was of an amount which greatly exceeded any claim he could make is not a ground for holding that it is not a preference.[47]

20.48 There is substantial scope for overlap between the concepts of a preference and a transaction at an undervalue as any case in which there is a loss of value to the company as a result of conferring a preference will fit both categories. It is clear that the legislation contemplates the application

---

43 *Re Clasper Group Services Ltd* (1988) 4 BCC 673.
44 See para 20.35–20.36 and Cork para 1287.
45 See Companies Act 1985 s 741 and *Re a Company (005009 of 1987) ex p Copp* [1989] BCLC 13.
46 s 239(7).
47 *Liquidator of West Mercia Safetywear* (note 42 *supra*).

of either concept to a single transaction.[48] If it is true that the period before the onset of insolvency which can be a relevant time is two years for a transaction at an undervalue whether the other party is connected with the company or not, it is important that a preference may be treated as such a transaction if it falls within both categories as otherwise it could only be challenged if it occurred within six months before the onset of insolvency unless it had been given to a connected person.

ORDERS OF THE COURT ON PROOF OF A PREFERENCE OR A TRANSACTION AT AN UNDERVALUE

Scope of court orders

20.49 When it is established that either a preference or a transaction at an undervalue has occurred the court has power to make such order as it thinks fit for restoring the position to what it would have been if the company had not given the preference in respect of which the order was made or entered the transaction which gave rise to the order.[49] Sections 423(2) and 425 make similar provision for orders in cases in which a transaction is held to fall within s 423. Para 20.38 deals with the minor variations necessarily applicable to such cases. Otherwise the observations in para 20.51 and 20.58 apply to such orders. The court has a wide discretion in relation to the order it makes with a view to achieving the statutory objective of restoring the company to the position it was in before the transaction or the preference took place. An order under s 238 or 239 may affect the property of a person who was neither the beneficiary of the preference nor the other party to the transaction at an undervalue. It may also impose an obligation on such a third party.[50] However, orders affecting third parties are limited by s 241(2) and (3). Such orders may not prejudice any interest in property acquired in good faith from a person other than the company for value and without notice of the relevant circumstances. Protection is thus afforded to persons who acquire an interest in property from the other party to the transaction or the preference or from a person deriving title from that party, providing they gave value and acted in good faith. The third party must also be without notice of the 'relevant circumstances'. The 'relevant circumstances' are those circumstances by virtue of which an order could be made should liquidation or administration follow within a particular period.[51] All of the

---

48   See s 240(1)(b).
49   ss 238(3) and 239(3).
50   s 241(2).
51   s 241(3)(a).

factors necessary to make it possible for the court to make an order are relevant. A third party who has no notice of any one such factor will not be amenable to a court order. Ignorance, for example, of the fact that the company was influenced by a desire to benefit the beneficiary of a preference would protect a third party taking the property for value and in good faith from the person preferred or his successor in title. Ignorance of any of the relevant circumstances will protect a person who dealt in good faith for value with a person other than the company even if he has knowledge of all the other relevant circumstances. If the period, within which the company must go into liquidation or administration after the preference or transaction took place, had already expired at the time at which the third party acquired his interest, it is also necessary that he have notice of the administration or the liquidation for him to be susceptible to a court order.[52]

Once property has passed to a person who gave value and took in good faith without notice no order can be made to prejudice an interest deriving from the interest of that person. Even if the current holder of an interest did have notice of the circumstances making an order possible no order could be made against him because his title derives from a person who satisfied all the requirements of s 241(2)(a). That paragraph stipulates that no order may 'prejudice any interest deriving from such an interest'.

In addition to the protection conferred by s 241(2)(a) against an order which will prejudice certain property interests of third parties, s 241(2)(b) protects certain persons against the possibility of an order requiring them to pay money to the administrator or the liquidator. That paragraph lays down that a person who received a benefit from a transaction or a preference in good faith for value and without notice of the relevant circumstances (defined as above) must not be required to pay a sum of money to the officeholder unless he was a party to the transaction at an undervalue or, in the case of a preference, he is to make the payment in respect of a preference given to him at a time when he was a creditor of the company. This means that only a party to a transaction at an undervalue or a person who later benefited from it but who lacked one of the elements of good faith, the provision of value, or the absence of notice of relevant circumstances can be ordered to make a payment to the administrator or liquidator. In the case of a preference only a creditor of the company can be made to pay despite receiving the preference in good faith, for value and without notice of the relevant circumstances.

20.50   The power of the court to make an order when the circumstances

---

[52]   s 241(3)(b).

laid down in s 238 and 239 exist is without prejudice to the availability of any other remedy. The right of the officeholder to litigate on the basis of the rules of common law or equity or of the provisions of the Companies Act 1985 is unaffected by the use of his powers under these provisions. This is expressly stated to apply to the situation where the transaction or the preference is beyond the powers of the company.[53] Action in the name of the company on the basis of the doctrine of *ultra vires*, or against officers or former officers on the basis of their breach of duty, or against others on the basis of the operation of the doctrine of the constructive trust all remain available. However, in granting a remedy to the company on the basis of such other causes of action a court would presumably take account of amounts recovered for the company under these sections of the Insolvency Act 1986.

Possible orders

20.51   Although the powers of the court to make orders is unfettered, subject to the protection conferred on third parties, the Act lists a number of examples of the orders which might be made in respect of transactions at an undervalue and preferences. This list indicates the range of the court's powers and the ways in which they may be used. It is without prejudice to the breadth of the discretion conferred by s 238(3) and 239(3) but is subject to the protection conferred on third parties by s 241(2). Section 241(1) illustrates the court's powers by listing possible orders to:

> **20.52**   "(a) require any property transferred as part of the transaction or in connection with the giving of the preference, to be vested in the company."

This amounts to a straightforward reinstatement of the company's previous position as regards property with which it parted. Para (g) below might be used to define the extent to which a party made to vest property in the company could claim in the insolvency. This power like all of the examples listed in s 241 may be used against the person to whom the preference was given or who was the other party to the transaction at an undervalue or against some other party who now holds the property in question. In the latter case its use would be subject to s 241(2).

> **20.53**   "(b) require any property to be so vested if it represents in any person's hands the application either of the proceeds of sale of property so transferred or of money so transferred,"

Such an order amounts to a form of statutory tracing. Money or other property which results from the disposal of the asset originally

---

53   s 241(4).

transferred as part of the transaction at an undervalue or preference can be subject to an order that it be vested in the company. In a case in which the property subject to the original transaction or preference has passed to a third party who acted in good faith, gave value and was ignorant of the 'relevant circumstances' the value given to the previous person in the chain of transfers of property will be susceptible to an order of this kind. Such an order might therefore be made against a party to the original transaction or preference or some other person in whose hands the money or other property subject to the order represents the results of the application of the original property.

20.54   "(c) release or discharge (in whole or in part) any security given by the company"

This paragraph does not specify to whom the security must have been given or its connection with the transaction at an undervalue or preference. However, the court's discretion will necessarily be used in accordance with the objective expressed in s 238(3) and 239(3) of restoring the position of the company to the *status quo ante* the transaction or preference. The test will be whether the security being set aside is one which was given in connection with the transaction or preference and whether it worsens the position of the company. A security which replaced an existing security in favour of the same party but which secured a larger amount as a result of the transaction or the preference would presumably only be discharged in part as that is all that would be necessary to restore the position of the company. The word 'security' in this context means 'any mortgage charge lien or other security'.[54] However, it is likely that only consensual securities will be the subject of an order.

20.55   "(d) require any person to pay, in respect of benefits received by him from the company, such sums to the officeholder as the court may direct"

This provision contemplates a situation where a person has gained a benefit from the company derived in some way from the transaction or the preference. The paragraph has to be read in the context of the primary purpose of any order made under these provisions which is the restoration of the position of the company to its pre-transaction or pre-preference position. The benefits in respect of which a sum is ordered to be paid must not only be obtained from the company but also have changed the company's previous position. It is unclear whether this paragraph covers interest earned on money obtained as a result of a transaction or a preference or profits made by the use of other property so obtained. However, even if such benefits cannot be regarded as being received from the company the court has power within its broad discretion to return the

---

54   s 248(b)(i).

company to the position it would have been in if the transaction had not taken place by ordering that interest or other benefits incidental to property be handed over to the company. This follows from the fact that had the transaction or preference not taken place such benefits would have flowed to the company.

20.56 "(e) provide for any surety or guarantor whose obligations to any person were released or discharged (in whole or in part) under the transaction, or by the giving of the preference, to be under such new or revived obligations to that person as the court thinks appropriate,"

This paragraph facilitates the restoration of the obligations of a surety of guarantor, not only for the benefit of the company as the creditor to whom the surety or guarantee is given, but also to any other person. Apart from the situation in which the preference or transaction at an undervalue involved the release of the obligations of a surety or guarantor of a debt or other liability due to the company, this paragraph enables the court to deal with circumstances in which the payment of a debt due from the company discharged the obligations of a person who had guaranteed it or stood as surety. In such a case the creditor might be ordered to repay the money handed over by the company by way of preference and the obligations of the guarantor of that debt would be revived or new obligations created for the benefit of the creditor who was preferred. The revival of an obligation may result in the obligation being regarded as having continued throughout the period from its original creation as if it had never ceased to exist but this is not a necessary interpretation of the distinction between new and revived obligations. The distinction may merely be that a revival of the former obligation would necessarily result in the content of the obligation being the same as it was formerly whereas a new obligation might be different, for example, in respect of the time for which it lasts or the amount guaranteed or in some other respect.

20.57 "(f) provide for security to be provided for the discharge of any obligation imposed by or arising under the order, for such an obligation to be charged on any property and for the security or charge to have the same priority as a security or charge released or discharged (in whole or in part) under the transaction or by the giving of the preference,"

This paragraph contemplates that an order may require that security be provided for the discharge of any obligation it imposes. It is possible that security might be imposed in a case where none existed before the preference or transaction took place. If a person is to be ordered to pay money to the company and will be able to do so only over a period of time then the obligation to do so might be ordered to be supported by security. In that case the priority of the security against that person's assets would date from the time of the court order. However, if the reason for ordering that a security or charge be provided is that the transaction at an undervalue or the preference involved the release or discharge of some existing security held by the company, the court may order that the new security is to have the same priority as the one which was released or discharged. In addition to requiring security for obligations imposed by the order, it is possible for the court to order a person to provide security for the discharge of an obligation arising under the order.

20.58 "(g) provide for the extent to which any person whose property is vested by the order in the company, or on whom obligations are imposed by the order, is to be able to prove in the winding up of the company for debts or other liabilities which arose from, or were released or discharged (in whole or in part) under or by, the transaction or the giving of the preference."

This example of the uses which the court might make of its powers provides for the reciprocal rights of a person whose property is vested in the company. This is likely to be no more than the right to prove in the company's liquidation as the company in respect of which the order is made is necessarily insolvent. In some cases this will amount to no more than the right of a creditor who has been ordered, for example, to repay a sum paid out by way of preference to prove in the company's winding up for the original debt. However, the paragraph also contemplates that an order may regulate a person's right to prove for a debt which arose from a transaction at an undervalue. This could occur if the transaction involved consideration of inadequate value being provided to the company in return for the transfer by it of an asset. In such a case the court might order a person to return the company asset and prove in the liquidation for the inadequate consideration which he provided at the time of the transaction. Similarly a person's right to prove in the liquidation for a debt originally due to him from the company which was released as part of the transaction at an undervalue might be regulated. The order may stipulate the value in respect of which a person proves in the winding up of the company. It is important to emphasise that the powers listed in s 241(1) are only examples of the court's discretion. In order to restore the position of the company the court may devise and use orders not referred to in that subsection.

EXTORTIONATE CREDIT TRANSACTIONS

20.59 Section 244 of the Insolvency Act 1986 permits the liquidator or administrator of a company to apply to the court for an order if the company is or has been a party to a transaction involving the provision of credit to the company.[55] Only such transactions entered into within three

---

55   s 244(1).

years before the date of the administration order or the date on which the company went into liquidation are susceptible to challenge[56] but subject to that time limit a contract to which the company 'has been' a party but which has terminated can be reopened. A company goes into liquidation at the date of a resolution for voluntary winding up or of a winding up order made in the case of a company not already in voluntary liquidation.[57] For this purpose the doctrine of relation back to the date of the presentation of a winding up petition does not apply as it would if the section referred to the commencement of the winding up.

20.60   A transaction will be for or will involve the provision of credit to the company (and thus fall within s 244(1)) in any situation in which payment by the company is deferred or, indeed, where an obligation of the company can be performed at a later date. It is not only a loan of money which will be covered but, for example, a sale of goods for which payment is deferred.

20.61   The court may make an order if it decides that the transaction is or was extortionate.[58] This is presumed in the case of any transaction which is the subject of an application unless the contrary is proved. A transaction is extortionate if, having regard to the risk accepted by the provider of the credit, its terms are or were such as to require grossly exorbitant payments to be made in respect of the provision of credit. It will be extortionate whether the grossly exorbitant payments are to be made unconditionally or in certain contingencies; such as may be laid down in a penalty clause. Even an agreement which does not require grossly exorbitant payments to be made will be extortionate if it 'otherwise grossly contravened ordinary principles of fair dealing'.[59] It is clear that the agreement need not be current when an application is made under the section; the definition of an extortionate transaction refers to its terms in both present and past tenses. Even if the company had fully paid all that was due by the time the application is made the transaction can still be reopened so long as it was entered into within the three year period.

20.62   The creditor will have to establish that the agreement is not extortionate by showing that the definition is not satisfied having regard to the risk that the creditor bore. The use of the word 'grossly', in relation to the exorbitant payments or the contravention of the ordinary principles of fair dealing must exist to make the transaction extortionate, will make the creditors task easier but the onus of proof is on him. All relevant factors will

---

56   s 244(2).
57   s 247(2).
58   s 244(2).
59   s 244(3).

presumably be taken into account in deciding whether a transaction is extortionate. They may include the relationship of the creditor to the company (although the Act does not distinguish between connected persons and others) and any financial pressure that the debtor company was under at the time when it agreed to the transaction.[60]

20.63   Unlike ss 238 and 239 which give a wide discretion to the court, this section only permits the court to make an order containing one or more of the provisions set out in s 244(4). It may set aside the whole or part of any obligation created by the transaction.[61] This can be an obligation imposed on either party so that as well as relieving the debtor of onerous obligations the court may reduce or cancel the obligations of the creditor if this is necessary to achieve a fair outcome in the light of the order made in favour of the debtor company.

20.64   The court may vary the terms of the transaction and the terms on which any security for the purpose of the transaction is held in other ways.[62] This might involve an alteration of the terms applicable to the termination of the agreement or to its duration. It may also order any person to pay to the officeholder sums paid to him by the company by virtue of the transaction. Such an order can however, only be made against someone who is or was a party to the transaction.[63] Any person, whether or not he is a party to the transaction, can be ordered to surrender to the liquidator or administrator any property that he holds as security for the purposes of the transaction.[64] There is a general power to order that accounts be taken between any persons in respect of the transaction.[65]

20.65   It is possible that a transaction falling under s 244 as an extortionate credit transaction will also be a transaction at an undervalue. If this is the case the powers conferred on the court by s 244 may be exercised concurrently with its powers under s 238.[66] If, for example, an exorbitant amount is to be paid in respect of the provision of credit it is likely that the company will be receiving consideration of significantly lower value than that which it is giving. If the transaction is treated as a transaction at an undervalue it will be necessary that it took place within two years before the onset of insolvency. Extortionate credit transactions can be challenged if they were entered into within three years before the

---

60   Compare s 138(2), (3) and (4) of the Consumer Credit Act 1974.
61   s 244(4)(a).
62   s 244(4)(b).
63   s 244(4)(c).
64   s 244(4)(d).
65   s 244(4)(e).
66   s 244(5).

making of the administration order or the company going into liquidation. On the other hand the powers of the court to make an order are wider in the case of a transaction at an undervalue. It is easier for an order to be made against a third party and the court has a wide discretion as to the orders that it makes. In dealing with an extortionate credit transaction it can only make the orders specified in s 244(4). The fact that the court's powers can be used concurrently in respect of the same transaction assists the officeholder in recovering assets on behalf of the creditors.

THE AVOIDANCE OF CERTAIN FLOATING CHARGES

20.66 Section 245 replaces s 617 of the Companies Act 1985 (formerly s 322 of the Companies Act 1948) and implements some of the recommendations of the Cork Report on the circumstances in which it should be possible to set aside floating charges granted shortly before insolvency proceedings begin.[67] The section applies to companies in liquidation or in respect of which an administration order has been made.[68] Floating charges can be attacked under the section only if they were created at a 'relevant time'.[69] For the purpose of this section a relevant time is the period between the presentation of a petition for an administration order and the making of the order[70] and certain periods ending with the 'onset of insolvency'; defined as the presentation of the administration petition or the commencement of the winding up.[71] The commencement of the winding up is the date of the passing of a resolution for voluntary liquidation or, if the company was not already in voluntary liquidation the date of the presentation of a winding up petition.[72]

20.67 The periods specified as defining the 'relevant time' vary according to whether or not the floating charge was granted to a person connected with the company. If the chargee is such a person the period is two years before the onset of insolvency.[73] In the case of any other chargee it is 12 months before that date.[74] In the case of a charge created in favour of a person not connected with the company within the period of 12 months before the onset of insolvency it is necessary to prove an additional factor before the charge is regarded as having been created at a relevant time. That factor is either that the company was unable to pay its debts within the

---

67 See Cork paras 1551 to 1566.
68 s 245(1).
69 s 245(2).
70 s 245(3)(c).
71 s 245(3).
72 ss 86 and 129.
73 s 245(3)(a).
74 s 245(3)(b).

meaning of s 123 at the time of the creation of the charge or that it became unable to pay them as a result of the transaction under which the charge was created.[75]

20.68 This provision prevents those closely connected with the company from obtaining security for themselves by taking a floating charge while the company is solvent and as part of a transaction which does not make it insolvent. If the company goes into liquidation or administration within two years its solvency at the time of the creation of the charge will not protect such persons as it would in the case of parties operating at arm's length. However, the invalidity would still be limited to the extent to which value was not given at the time of or after the creation of the charge.[76] It should be noted that the more stringent rules applicable to connected persons only apply if the charge is created in their favour; they do not apply if the present holder of the charge is a connected person to whom it has been assigned.

20.69 Once it is established that a floating charge on the company's undertaking or property was created at a relevant time invalidity follows except to the extent of value given at the time of the creation of the charge or earlier.[77] That exception to invalidity applies to the aggregate of a number of amounts. They are set out in s 245(2).

20.70 First, the charge is valid up to the value of so much of the consideration for its creation; 'as consists of money paid or goods or services supplied to the company at the same time as or after the creation of the charge'.[78] This provision puts a premium on ensuring that money goods and services are supplied as part of the consideration for the charge. The paragraph implements the Cork recommendation on the inclusion of services as well as goods.[79] It seems that money paid shortly before the charge is created will be regarded as paid 'at the same time as' the creation of the charge if it was paid in reliance on a promise to grant the charge.[80] The rule in _Clayton's case_ means that money, paid into the company's bank account after a charge securing further advances is issued, can be set against indebtedness of the company which existed before the charge was created.[81]

---

75 s 245(4).
76 s 245(2).
77 See s 251 and paras 5.11 _et seq supra_ for the definition of a floating charge.
78 s 245(2)(a).
79 Cork paras 1564–1565.
80 _Re Columbian Fireproofing Co_ [1910] 2 ch 120.
81 _Re Yeovil Glove Co_ [1965] ch 148. The recommendation of the Cork Committee that the rule established by this case be reversed was not implemented in the 1985 Act.

20.71 The value of goods or services for the purpose of s 2, defined as:

"the amount in money which at the time they were supplied could rea have been expected to be obtained for supplying goods or services in the ordinary course of business and on the same terms (apart from the consideration) as those on which they were supplied to the company".[82]

This allows the court to make its own assessment of the value actually provided to the company by reference to the market price at the time at which the goods or services were supplied. The consideration allocated by the parties to the transaction to the goods and services provided need not limit the court's power to determine their value.

20.72 In addition to the value of goods and services provided, the value of any discharge or reduction of any debt of the company which occurs at the same time as or after the creation of the charge is aggregated to ascertain the total amount not affected by the invalidity of the charge; providing the discharge or reduction amounts to part of the consideration for the charge.[83]

20.73 The amount of any interest payable on the amounts provided to the company under paras 245(2)(a) or (b) can be aggregated with the value of the benefits given to the company at the time of or after the creation of the charge and as part of the consideration for it. The charge, even if it was granted at a relevant time, will be valid to the extent of the aggregate of the value of the consideration actually provided at the time of or after the creation of the charge. For this purpose 'consideration' does not bear its strict contractual meaning.[84]

20.74 The effect of invalidity is to leave the debt secured by the charge as an unsecured debt which can be proved in a liquidation.[85] However, if a receiver appointed under the charge has already paid the debt before the presentation of an administration petition or the commencement of winding up, the payment by the receiver as agent of the company prevents any claim against the erstwhile debtor for the repayment of amounts received by him.[86]

---

82 s 245(6).
83 s 245(2)(b).
84 *Re Yeovil Glove Co* [1965] ch 148.
85 *Re Parkes Garage (Swadlincote) Ltd* [1929] 1 ch 139.
86 *Mace Builders (Glasgow) Ltd v Lunn* [1987] BCLC 55.

CHAPTER 21

Personal Liability of Directors and Others

21.01 This chapter focuses on those provisions applicable on the insolvency of a company which impose personal liability on its directors or others who are involved with it. It also deals with the circumstances in which a person may be disqualified from acting as a company director in the future as a result of events surrounding the insolvency of a company. However before examining those statutory provisions specifically applicable to insolvency, some general rules which govern personal liability are considered.

PART 1: PERSONAL LIABILITY

21.02 The corporate personality of a company prevents a director from incurring liability on the contracts of the company, or for its torts, unless he can be regarded as a party to the contract or as a tortfeasor. In the case of a contract the potential liability of the director will depend on the construction of the agreement and the circumstances surrounding it.[1]

Directors will often be required to provide personal guarantees of the debts of a company. If they do so they will incur personal liability. In addition, banks and similar financiers will often require a series of cross guarantees, by all the companies in a group for the liabilities of each member company, to the lender. In such a case a guarantee by the directors of one company in the group of that company's debts will, if it is properly drafted and supported by consideration, effectively make them liable for those obligations of the company whose debts they have guaranteed which result only from the guarantee by that company of the debts of other companies in the group. This will certainly be the case where the advance to the company in the group whose liability is guaranteed by another group member was made at the request of the guarantor company. Only evidence from the context of the agreement and the behaviour of the parties to it to a different effect will prevent the lender from relying on provisions in a guarantee document which achieve such a result. The consideration by the

---

1 See *Henry Brown & Sons v Smith* [1964] 2 Lloyd's Rep 476 and *The Swan* [1968] 1 Lloyd's Rep 5.

lender for the director's guarantee can be its accession to his request for a group facility and an advance to a company in the group.[2] It is possible for a director to incur effective personal liability for such debts of the whole group as are not paid out of the resources of its members if a creditor obtained a guarantee.

21.03 It is also possible that liability on a bill of exchange will exist if a director appears to have signed in a personal capacity and not as a representative of the company.[3] A failure accurately and legibly to mention the company's name in any bill of exchange, cheque, promissory note, or order for money or goods, will render any company officer or other person who signs it, or authorises it to be signed on behalf of the company personally liable if the company fails to pay the amount due.[4] The director or other person to be held liable must have been aware of the inaccuracy in the version of the company's name used and the misuse of the name must not be due to the error of the party seeking to hold the individual liable, because estoppel will apply in such circumstances.[5] There must be some signature on the document before a director can be held personally liable. Even if liability is to be on the basis of authorising a document to be signed there must be the signature of some other person. It seems that a printed name or one inserted by the use of a stamp will not be sufficient.[6]

21.04 The Court of Appeal has held that liability under s 349(4) cannot be avoided by obtaining an order for the rectification of the contract which was signed because that remedy is available only to give effect to the intentions of the parties not to enable a director to avoid personal liability.[7] There is no potential for a tort claim by creditors against a director for negligence resulting in the company's insolvency, because while the company is solvent the director owes no duty of care to its creditors.[8] However, equity recognises a duty on the part of the directors as the conscience of the company to preserve its assets for benefit of creditors and

> "to ensure that the affairs of the company are properly administered and that its property is not dissipated or exploited for the benefit of the directors themselves to the prejudice of the creditors".[9]

2 *Coglan v S H Lock (Australia) Ltd* (1987) 3 BCC 183 PC.
3 s 26 Bills of Exchange Act 1882; and see *Bondina v Rollaway Shower Blinds Ltd* [1986] 1 WLR 517.
4 s 349(2) Companies Act 1985.
5 See *John Wilkes (Footwear) Ltd v Lee International (Footwear) Ltd* [1985] BCLC 444 and *Durham Fancy Goods Ltd v Michael Jackson (Fancy Goods) Ltd* [1968] 2 QB 839.
6 *Oshkosh B'Gosh Inc v Dan Marbel Inc Ltd* (1988) 4 BCC 795.
7 *Blum v OCP Repartition SA* (1988) 4 BCC 771.
8 *Multinational Gas and Petroleum Co Ltd v Multinational Gas and Petroleum Services Ltd* [1983] 3 WLR 492.
9 Per Lord Templeman in *Winkworth v Edward Baron Development Co Ltd* [1986] 1 WLR 1512 at 1516.

WRONGFUL TRADING

21.05   The purpose of the provision now contained in s 214 of the Insolvency Act 1986 is to impose liability for negligent behaviour which involves the continuation of corporate trading so that debts are incurred which are unlikely to be repaid. It supplements the liability for fraudulent trading which continues to exist as a civil matter under s 213 and as a criminal offence under s 458 of the Companies Act 1985 (see para 21.3). The definition in s 214 of the behaviour that can result in an order against a director was subject to anxious scrutiny during Parliament's consideration of the Insolvency Act 1985 and in certain respects departs from the recommendations of the Cork Report.

Definition

21.06   Although the concept of 'wrongful trading' is referred to in the marginal note to the section, the conduct which forms the basis of a declaration by the court of liability relates to knowledge of, or negligence in relation to the company's prospects of avoiding insolvent liquidation. A defence is available to a person found to have had the necessary knowledge or to have been negligent if he took every step that he ought to have taken with a view to minimising the potential loss to the company's creditors. This contrasts with the recommendation of the Cork Report which involved a liability based on the company carrying on its business or incurring further debts or liabilities without a reasonable prospect of meeting them in full. The main application of the section is likely to be to cases involving trading or the conduct of the company's business. Its wider scope makes it potentially applicable to any failure to take the steps required to provide a defence in a case where the necessary knowledge or negligence in relation to the prospects of avoiding insolvent liquidation exists. The section only applies in cases in which a company is in liquidation. Contrary to the recommendations of the Cork Report it does not apply to companies in respect of which an administrative receiver has been appointed or which have been made the subject of an administration order. Section 214(1) permits an order to be made by the court only where it appears 'in the course of the winding up of a company' that the circumstances laid down in s 214(2) of the Act apply.

21.07   Section 214 does not apply to all the officers or managers of a company. It applies only to directors and shadow directors.[10] This means

---

10   s 214(1) and (7).

that only a person who is or has been a director of the company or in accordance with whose directions or instructions the directors of the company are or have been accustomed to act can be made personally liable under the section.[11] This excludes an auditor, company secretary or senior manager who has never been a director of the company unless the directors have customarily followed his directions or instructions. The fact that the directors act on advice given by a person in a professional capacity does not, in itself, make the adviser a shadow director. In the case of a subsidiary company it is possible that the holding company may be a shadow director if members of the subsidiary's board customarily follow its directions or instructions. Likewise an individual shareholder or a person otherwise unconnected with the company may come within the definition. It will be a question of fact in each case whether the directors of the company were accustomed to act in accordance with the directions or instructions of any particular person. The court is likely to have regard to the question of whether the relationship in any particular case was one which involved directions or instructions or only pressure or persuasion. Similarly, the frequency and regularity of communications which do fall within the definition and the response of the company's directors to them will determine the issue of whether those directors were 'accustomed to act' on them. It is possible for a bank which provides a report to a company in the context of a substantial overdraft, about which the bank is concerned, to become a shadow director of the company if the company follows the recommendations of the report.[12] A person who occupies the position of director will be subject to the section by whatever name his function is known.[13]

21.08 The Cork Committee took the view that liability for wrongful trading on the basis of negligence should extend to all officers of the company and that that term should be given a wide interpretation which would, for example, include auditors. However, the fact that it is the board which controls the company and which has the power to decide that the company should cease trading or be placed in liquidation or administration makes it reasonable that the potential liability should be limited to directors. It is they who, collectively, have access to all relevant information as well as having the power to act. To limit the scope of the section to this group and those who control them can therefore be justified, although the exclusion of auditors is not justified on this basis. Potential liability for fraudulent trading arises from dishonest behaviour by a wider range of individuals.

---

11   Companies Act 1985 s 741(2).
12   *Re a Company (005009 of 1987) ex p Copp* [1989] BCLC 13.
13   *Ibid* s 741(1).

Preconditions for an order

21.09   For the court to have the power to make an order under s 214 three further conditions have to be satisfied. They are contained in s 214(2).

Insolvent liquidation

21.10   First, the company must have gone into insolvent liquidation. Thus although s 214(1) applies in the course of any winding up, no order can in fact be made unless the company has gone into insolvent liquidation. This is essential to the whole scheme of the section as, if the company is not insolvent, there will have been no loss to creditors as a result of the behaviour of the director. However, the test of insolvency is applied at the time at which the company goes into liquidation. The fact that at the end of the liquidation process the debts of the company are all paid because, for example, transactions are set aside or contributions are made to its assets in accordance with an order under s 214 will not render s 214 inapplicable.

21.11   It should be noted that the definition of a company going into insolvent liquidation for this purpose in s 214(6) involves the insufficiency of its assets for the payment of its debts and other liabilities, together with the expenses of winding up at the time at which it goes into liquidation. That is the time at which a winding up resolution is passed or at which a winding up order is made if no earlier resolution has been passed.[14] It is clear that the fact that a company was still able to pay debts as they fell due at the time of liquidation will not prevent the section from applying if the assets are insufficient to meet the company's liabilities. A policy of 'robbing Peter to pay Paul' which ends in liquidation can leave the directors vulnerable to an order under the section. Conversely, a failure to pay a debt due to liquidity problems will not bring the section into operation if the assets are sufficient to meet all the liabilities of the company, and the expenses of the winding up, at the time when the company goes into liquidation but debts are unpaid due to problems with the realisation of the assets. This is in accordance with the policy of the section because in such a case no creditor suffers, and the circularity of taking account of accretions to the company's assets during, and as a result of, the winding up process is avoided.

Knowledge or negligence

21.12   The second requirement laid down in s 214(2) relates to the knowledge or negligence of the director against whom an order is sought. Section 214(2)(b) requires that:

"At some time before the commencement of the winding up of the company,

---

14   s 247(2).

that person knew or ought to have concluded that there was no reasonable prospect that the company would avoid going into insolvent liquidation."

The first point to note is that the relevant time at which the director's state of mind is considered is before the commencement of the winding up of the company. That is the date of the presentation of the winding up petition in a compulsory winding up, or of an earlier winding up resolution. This contrasts with the use of the concept of the company going into liquidation in para (a) of the same subsection which deals with the date at which the section applies. Thus an application is possible only after the date of the order in a compulsory liquidation and the state of mind of the director and the information available to him before the hearing of the petition, but after it has been presented cannot be taken into account. This is consistent with the policy of holding directors accountable for their action or inaction only at a time when they can be expected to take some step to protect creditors. Once a petition has been presented it is reasonable to permit the directors to await the hearing of the petition. The paragraph then requires that knowledge or negligence be established as to the prospects of the company avoiding insolvent liquidation.

21.13 A director will be within the scope of the section if he knew that there was no reasonable prospect that the company would avoid going into insolvent liquidation. The knowledge available to him is a matter of evidence and this element of the test is subjective. However, the matter of which he is required to have knowledge is that there is 'no reasonable prospect' of the company avoiding insolvent liquidation. This means that the information available to the director is a question of fact but that there is an objective element to be established as to the forecast made on the basis of the facts known to the director. It is clear that an excessively sanguine view of the company's prospects will not protect a director who has information which would indicate to a reasonably diligent person that there was no prospect of the company avoiding insolvent liquidation. Thus even where evidence as to the knowledge of the director forms the basis for liability, the conclusions to be drawn from that information are to be tested objectively. For this purpose the provisions of s 214(4) apply.

21.14 A major feature which distinguishes the provision on wrongful trading from the procedure available under s 213, which defines fraudulent trading, is the possibility of liability on the grounds of negligence. A director can come within the scope of s 214 if he 'ought to have concluded' that the company had no reasonable prospect of avoiding insolvent liquidation. For the purpose of determining the facts that a director ought to have known or ascertained and the conclusions he ought to have reached, s 214(4) lays down the test of the 'reasonably diligent person'. This hypothetical figure embodies the level of skill, knowledge and experience from which the knowledge, foresight and (for the purpose of the defence in s 214(3)) actions expected of a particular director are deduced. For the purpose of this provision, the standards of care and skill required of directors are considerably higher than those applied at common law, and classically expounded in the case of *Re City Equitable Fire Insurance Co Ltd.*[15]

21.15   At common law, the director is expected to exhibit in the performance of his duties only the degree of care and skill that can be expected of a person of his knowledge and experience. He is not bound to give continuous attention to the affairs of his company and he may delegate duties to an official, in accordance with the articles and as the exigencies of business dictate, without being held liable for the dishonesty of that official in the absence of grounds for suspicion.[16] This is the level of duty imposed on directors. In the case of an executive director, it is likely that a higher level of duty will be imposed under the contract of service applicable to him. That duty will reflect the functions which he is required to perform under that contract and his level of professional qualification and experience.

21.16   Section 214(4) lays down a criterion applicable to all directors for the purpose of wrongful trading. It cumulatively imposes both objective and subjective standards on a director against whom an application is made under the section. His knowledge, conclusions or actions are judged against those to be expected of a reasonably diligent person. That person is taken to have two levels of general knowledge, skill and experince. He has attributed to him the general knowledge, skill and experience reasonably to be expected of a person carrying out those functions which the director in question carries out or which have been entrusted to him, but not carried out by him (s 214(5)). In addition he is assumed to have the general knowledge, skill and experience which the director in question actually has. The standard is set by the reasonably diligent person. One would expect a reasonably diligent person to read papers provided to the Board and to attend most board meetings in the absence of a good reason for failing to do so. It is submitted that it would be open to the court to hold that a reasonably diligent person would play his full role in ensuring that the board sets up appropriate systems to monitor the performance of the company, and to provide accurate information rapidly to the management. It is likely that the nature of the activities undertaken will depend on the

---

15   [1925] Ch 407.
16   See *ibid* at 428–429.

level of knowledge, skill and experience to be assumed in a particular case, while the frequency and energy with which they are undertaken will be established by a fixed standard of diligence. The test as a whole is based on the specific knowledge and the conduct to be expected of a reasonably diligent person with the specified level of general knowledge, experience and skill and the conclusions likely to be reached by such a person. The inclusion of the concept of diligence ensures that an objective test applies to the level of activity expected of the director as well as the basic level of skill, general knowledge and experience to be attributed to him.

21.17 To apply the section to a director on the basis of actual knowledge requires proof that there was knowledge of no reasonable prospect of avoiding insolvent liquidation. To apply it on the basis of negligence involves proof of the conclusions that the person ought reasonably to have reached. The latter will involve an assessment of the person's actual knowledge of specific information. He will be taken to know that which he does know and also that which would be known to the reasonably diligent person with the level of general knowledge, skill and experience cumulatively laid down in the subsection. A director with actual knowledge of all relevant information is judged by the reasonably diligent person's standards in relation to the conclusions he ought to have reached from that information. A director not in possession of all relevant information may be taken to have the specific information that he would have had had he complied with the standard applicable to him under s 214(4). He will then also be taken to have drawn the conclusions which that standard requires of him. The standards of general knowledge, skill, and experience laid down in s 214(4) ensure that the director is judged against the higher of two levels. The first is the level that may reasonably be expected of a person carrying out the functions that the director concerned either carried out or was entrusted with. To ascertain the relevant functions it is necessary to look to two things. First, the functions actually carried out by this person. He may have officially have had a narrow range of responsibilities—for example, the supervision of only the company's marketing strategy. Since that function was entrusted to him he will be judged by the standards that it reasonably requires even if he failed to carry it out. In addition, if he carried out functions which had not been entrusted to him he will be measured by the standards demanded of one with his *de facto* role in the company. This system meets the objection that can be raised against a single standard applied to all directors without variation. The qualified engineer who is the production director, and the qualified accountant who is the finance director can hardly be expected to have the same level of competence as each other in respect of each of those functions. On the other hand, the functions which determine the standard against which a director is to be judged cannot be artificially limited by an official job description which is ignored in practice. The functions actually performed by the director and those entrusted to him, but not carried out, are both used to set the standard.[17] Thus in a case such as *Hely Hutchinson v Brayhead Ltd*[18] or *Freeman & Lockyer v Buckhurst Park Properties (Mangal) Ltd*[19] the *de facto* performance by an individual of the functions of a managing director would impose the standards to be reasonably expected of a managing director on him, despite the absence of any formal appointment to that office.

21.18   The size of the company's business undertaking and the field within which it operates will also be relevant in analysing the function involved. Thus in *Re Produce Marketing Consortium Ltd*[20] Knox J accepted that the general knowledge, skill and experience reasonably to be expected of a director of a small company, in a modest way of business and with simple accounting procedures and equipment, would be less extensive than for someone on the board of a large company with sophisticated procedures. However, he also accepted that certain minimum obligations would be assumed in all cases and that they included the requirements of the Companies Act 1985 as to accounts and records. While any specialised function either carried out by a director or entrusted to him without being carried out can determine the standard to be applied in his case, a director who has no specialist function beyond his role as a member of the board will be subject to a minimum standard applicable to a person in that position. It might be argued that in such a case the standard imposed by the section will coincide with that imposed by the common law. However, it is submitted that the section requires the application of some minimum objective standard not limited by the actual knowledge and experience of the individual in question. This is supported by the view expressed by Knox J in *Re Produce Marketing Consortium Ltd* on the minimum requirements laid down by the Companies Act 1985.

21.19   Paragraph (b) of s 214(4) of the Insolvency Act 1986 adds to the objective standard laid down in para (a) 'the general knowledge, skill and experience that that director has'. Since this is added to the objective standard laid down in the first paragraph, it cannot be true for the purposes of this section that 'a director need not exhibit . . . a greater degree of skill than may reasonably be expected from a person of his knowledge and experience'.[21] Paragraph (b) applies the standard of what is reasonably to

17   See s 214(5).
18   [1968] 1 QB 549.
19   [1964] 2 QB 480.
20   (1989) 5 BCC 569.
21   *Re City Equitable Fire Insurance Co* [1925] Ch 407 at 427.

be expected of a person with his knowledge, skill and experience cumulatively to the standard set by para (a). This suggests that the courts are expected to apply a standard which relates to the function of a director who is simply a board member. Perhaps this standard will be devised with reference to the monitoring and supervisory function that the business world expects a board of directors to perform in the case of a company of substantial size. Such a function is particularly appropriate to non-executive directors. In the case of directors of incorporated small businesses, the functions actually performed by those active in management are likely to cause a higher standard to apply. The minimum standard based on a monitoring function would apply to board members not active in management.

21.20   The minimum obligation imposed on all directors to ensure that proper records and accounts are kept in accordance with the Companies Act 1985 results in directors being taken to know, for the purpose of the section, not only the facts revealed by the records actually kept, but also those which would have been revealed had proper accounting records been maintained. The time at which they will be taken to have this additional information will be the time at which such records would have been available had the statutory requirements been observed.[22] In every case the specific knowledge, actions and ability to reach conclusions expected of a director will be those reasonably expected of a person with his actual general knowledge, skill and experience. If the functions the individual performed or was entrusted with would raise more demanding expectations, then it is against that higher standard that he will be judged. The courts will recognise the function of a director as itself laying down an objective standard below which no individual director may fall. However low the individual's level of knowledge and experience may be, the objective standard required by virtue of being entrusted with the function of being a Board member should provide a minimum standard. In the case of shadow directors, the function actually carried out is likely to be of greater significance as no function may have been entrusted to the individual. This approach contrasts with the tendency of the common law to use the individual's actual level of knowledge and experience to limit the level of skill he is expected to display.

Commencement
21.21   The person against whom an application is made under the section must have been a director or shadow director of the company at the time at which he knew, or ought to have concluded, that there was no reasonable

---

22   *Re Produce Marketing Consortium,* (1989) 5 BCC 569.

prospect of the company avoiding going into insolvent liquidation. That time must also have been not earlier than the commencement date—28 April 1986.[23] It is therefore important that the knowledge or negligence of the director be established in relation to some event or omission so that it can be proved that he held office at the time and that the knowledge or negligence existed before the commencement date.

The statutory defence

21.22   Section 214(3) provides that the court will have no power to make an order under the section if it is satisfied that the director against whom an application has been made took every step that he ought to have taken to minimise the potential loss to the company's creditors. The question of the steps that a person 'ought to have taken' for this purpose is determined on the assumption that he knew that there was no reasonable prospect of the company avoiding insolvent liquidation. This prevents the use of the argument that in this subsection the limited actual knowledge of the individual can justify inaction in a case where the limited knowledge is a result of his negligence. In order to ascertain the steps that an individual ought to have taken, the standards laid down in s 214(4) are used. The 'reasonably diligent person' test is applied on the basis of the higher of the two standards laid down in that subsection. It is hard to envisage how a person who is held to have been negligent in failing to know that the company had no reasonable prospect of avoiding insolvent liquidation could successfully establish this defence. If there was no actual knowledge, it is unlikely that the steps required by the standard laid down in subsection (4) will have been taken. A director should succeed in this defence if he shows that he argued in favour of an application for an administration order or for voluntary liquidation. It may be sufficient that he argued in favour of the company instructing a solicitor, accountant or qualified insolvency practitioner to investigate its affairs and advise the board. The steps taken by the individual need not result in action if he is outvoted on the board. However, it is arguable that a director who is also a shareholder must use any power that this gives him in addition to those steps open to him as a director. In a small company the availability of a contributory's winding up petition or an application under s 459 of the Companies Act 1985 may be relevant. The courts will have to determine the degree of persistence required of a director who wishes to rely on this defence. The defence is vital for company doctors who are appointed to the board at a time when the company is already in financial difficulties and who proceed with a rescue attempt.

---

23   s 214(2)(c) and proviso.

21.23 The time at which the steps required by s 214(3) must be taken is 'after the condition specified in subsection (2)(b) was first satisfied in relation 'to the person using the defence'. It is easy to see that the steps should be taken soon after actual knowledge is obtained when the application is based on such actual knowledge. However, in a case of negligence it may be harder to establish the point at which the condition in s 214(2)(b) was satisfied. In a case where a negligent failure to obtain information or to draw the appropriate conclusions from available information is followed by actual knowledge, it is clear that the steps needed for a successful defence must be taken soon after the paragraph's condition is first satisfied. Such steps taken after the later acquisition of actual knowledge would not satisfy the precondition of the defence. They would presumably be taken into account by the court when the level of the director's contribution was fixed. In respect of a summons brought for an order under s 214, the court's power to grant relief under s 727 of the Companies Act 1985 does not arise. This was held to be the case at first instance on an application to strike out a paragraph of a director's defence in the earliest s 214 application to reach the courts.[24] In that case it was accepted that Parliament could not have intended s 727 to be available on the basis of honest and reasonable behaviour when an objective test is specifically laid down in s 214 itself. However, it seems likely that s 214 does implicitly impose a duty on directors by imposing a sanction on them for not behaving in the way that the law requires as the argument that the relief in s 727 of the 1985 Act on the ground that no duty existed was rejected.

The application

21.24 Section 214(1) permits only the liquidator to apply to the court for an order in respect of wrongful trading. This is in contrast to the recommendation of the Cork Report that once the company was in liquidation or receivership or had been made subject to an administration order, an application for an order could be made by any creditor or contributory as well as the liquidator, receiver, administrator or the official receiver.[25] The fact that the remedy is only available when a company goes into insolvent liquidation explains the exclusion of applications by a receiver or an administrator. The fact that all liquidators must be qualified insolvency practitioners is assumed to mean that applications will be made in all appropriate cases without a right of application being granted to creditors and contributories or the official receiver. The liquidator can give evidence or call witnesses on the hearing of an application under this section or s 213. An application for an order in respect of wrongful trading

---

24   *Re Produce Marketing Consortium Ltd* (1989) 5 BCC 399.
25   Cmnd 8598 para 1806.

will be made under rule 7 of the Insolvency Rules 1986 which governs the form and contents of the application, the rules as to its filing and service and the hearing. Section 214(8) makes it clear that the section is without prejudice to s 213 which is concerned with fraudulent trading. Thus it is possible for a person to be subjected to an order under both sections.

FRAUDULENT TRADING

21.25   The concept of fraudulent trading has survived the changes of the 1980's and remains as the basis for a criminal offence under s 458 of the Companies Act 1985 and of civil liability under s 213 of the Insolvency Act 1986. The criminal offence applies whether or not the company has been, or is in the course of winding up. This change was introduced by s 96 of the Companies Act 1981 and is consolidated in the provision of the 1985 Act. By contrast, the power of the court to make an order under s 213 of the Insolvency Act 1986 is only available if, in the course of a winding up, the conditions specified in the section appear to the court to exist in relation to the conduct of the business of that company. Section 213(2) permits the court to order persons to make such contributions as it thinks proper to the assets of the company on the application of the liquidator. The power of the court exists if it appears that any business of the company has been carried on either with the intent to defraud creditors (of the company or of any other person) or for any fraudulent purpose. The order may be made against persons who were knowingly parties to the carrying on of the business in that manner. The offence in s 458 of the Companies Act 1985 is defined in similar terms in respect of both the conduct required and the parties liable to conviction. It is necessary to consider in turn the meaning of the concept of fraudulent trading and the nature of the parties against whom an order can be made.

The meaning of fraudulent trading

21.26   The provisions in s 213 and s 458 both consist in two separate forms of behaviour.[26] They deal with carrying on any business of the company with intent to defraud creditors. The creditors in question can be those of the company or those of any other person. In addition, they deal with a second form of fraudulent trading which involves carrying on any business of the company for any fraudulent purpose. It is not only behaviour intended to defraud creditors that comes within the scope of the sections, although that is by far the most common situation to which they apply. A

---

26   See *R v Inman* [1967] 1 QB 140.

fraudulent purpose could involve a scheme to defraud customers or shareholders who were not creditors.[27] In the case of an application by the liquidator under s 213, the contribution to the assets of the company will go to assist in paying creditors and the attitude of the court to the amount to be paid may be influenced by the identity of the victims of the fraud. Litigation against the company by defrauded customers or other victims may result in them becoming creditors at that stage, although the fraud that was originally perpetrated could not be described as the conduct of a business with intent to defraud creditors. Unlike s 214 which deals with wrongful trading, s 213 is not limited to cases of insolvent liquidation. It is therefore possible that an order under the section could result in a return of capital or the distribution of a surplus to contributories.

21.27 Since it can be any business of the company that is carried on in a way which amounts to fraudulent trading, there is no need to establish that the business that was carried on in that way was its only business or even its main business. The concept of carrying on a business had not been taken by the courts in this context to be limited to the normal trading activities of a company. Thus in *Re Sarflax Ltd*[28] the collection of assets acquired in the course of business, and their distribution in the discharge of obligations incurred in that process was held to be capable of constituting the carrying on of a business. Seeking an order or accepting an advance payment in respect of one customer only can amount to carrying on a business and the requirement of an intent to defraud creditors can be satisfied when only one creditor is involved.[29] A single dishonest transaction carried out in the course of business can be sufficient.[30]

21.28 Whether intent to defraud or some other fraudulent purpose is alleged the central requirement for successful action against those involved is that there must be fraud. It is the meaning of this concept which has presented the major difficulties with this provision. In *Re Patrick and Lyon Ltd*[31] Maugham J gave the well known indication that:

> "The words 'defraud' and 'fraudulent purpose', where they appear in the section in question are words which connote actual dishonesty involving, according to current notions of fair trading among commercial men, real moral blame."

He went on to state that this distinguishes the use of the word in this section from its wider meaning in the parts of the Act dealing with fraudulent

---

27   *R v Kemp* [1986] BCLC 217.
28   [1979] 1 Ch 262.
29   *Re Cooper Chemicals Ltd* [1978] 1 Ch 262.
30   *R v Lockwood* (1986) 2 BCC 99, 333.
31   [1933] 1 Ch 786.

preferences, although he acknowledged that he was not providing a comprehensive definition of the term. On the facts of that case, he was not convinced that the necessary deliberate behaviour had been established to justify an order. This view is often contrasted with the statement of the same judge in the case of in *Re William C. Leitch Brothers Ltd*[32] where he stated that it is proper to infer that the company is carrying on its business with intent to defraud its creditors if it continues to carry on its business and to incur debts when the directors know that there is no reasonable prospect of the creditors ever receiving payment of those debts. It will be noted that this was described as a proper inference and not as an inevitable conclusion. The passage clearly confirms the need for knowledge on the part of the directors that the debts are not likely to be paid. Subsequent case law establishes that it is not necessary to show knowledge that there is no reasonable prospect that the debts will ever be paid. It is enough that there was a realisation at the time when the debts were incurred that there was no reason to think that funds would become available to pay the debt when it became due or shortly thereafter.[33] It has been said that the section:

"Is one which requires a successful applicant to allege and prove the respondent's knowing participation in dishonesty."[34]

21.29   Knowingly to run up debts is dishonesty when it is done with knowledge that they cannot be paid, but the burden lies on the applicant under s 213 or the prosecution under s 458 to allege and prove the facts from which knowing participation in the dishonesty can be inferred. The mere fact that a warranty was given or a representation made on behalf of the company to induce a person to enter a contract with it is not sufficient basis in itself for an inference of dishonesty, on the part of the respondent who gave the warranty or made the representation, even if he knows that a substantial claim on the warranty cannot be met by the company. It is necessary to prove recklessness or intention as to the likelihood that the company will be called upon to honour its commitment in addition to knowledge of its inability to do so. The creation of a potential liability against a background of financial difficulty is not sufficient in itself to give rise to liability for fraudulent trading.[35] The need for an element of dishonesty is further supported by the fact that an allegation that one creditor was preferred over another is not sufficient to support a claim under s 213. The liquidator's application can be struck out if that is the only allegation that it makes.[36] Dishonesty must be proved as part of the

---

32   [1932] 2 Ch 71.
33   *R v Grantham* [1984] 1 QB 675 per Lord Lane CJ at 682.
34   *Norcross Ltd v Amos* (1980) unreported Transcript 0079 of 1980 Lexis and (1981) 131 NLJ 1213 per Oliver LJ.
35   *Ibid.*
36   *Re Sarflax Ltd* [1979] 1 ch 592.

allegation of either intent to defraud or of fraudulent purpose in both civil and criminal proceedings.[37]

21.30 The mere fact of a person providing a 'comfort letter' and providing assurances of continued support for the company on which creditors rely, is not in itself sufficient to establish a fraudulent intent or to permit the inference of such an intention. The fact that in changed circumstances the statement is not honoured does not establish and does not permit the inference that the statement was anything other than an honest statement of intent at the time at which it was made.[38] This was said *obiter* in a case involving a holding company which had provided this form of support for its subsidiary but had later decided to allow the latter company to fail. It is consistent with the emphasis in all the decided cases on the need to prove fraud and dishonesty to establish fraudulent trading. With the creation of the concept of wrongful trading, the use of s 213 is likely to be limited to cases where the person against whom an order is sought was neither a director nor a shadow director at the time of the events which form the basis of the application. Section 214 is likely to be used in any case in which it is available, as the same orders can be obtained on the basis of negligence or knowledge without the need to prove fraud or dishonesty. Apart from the use of s 213 against parties who are not subject to s 214, prosecution under s 458 of the Companies Act 1985 will remain available.

The parties to fraudulent trading

21.31 Section 213(2) permits the court to impose liability on:

> "any persons who were knowingly parties to the carrying on of the business in the manner above mentioned".

Criminal liability under s 458 of the Companies Act 1985 applies on the same basis. It is clear from the wording of the two provisions and from the case law that this means that there must be knowing participation in dishonesty.[39]

21.32 On the basis of this test, a creditor can be a party to the fraudulent trading if he accepts money which he knows has been procured by carrying on the business with intent to defraud creditors for the very purpose of making the payment. In such a case 'a man who warms himself with the fire of fraud cannot complain if he is singed'.[40] However, a creditor who merely presses for payment when he knows that no money will be available to him if the debtor remains honest will not be liable, as the honest debtor may

---

37   *R v Cox & Hodges* [1983] BCLC 169 per Watkins LJ at 175.
38   *Re Augustus Barnett & Son Ltd* [1986] BCLC 170.
39   *Norcross v Amos* (footnote 34 above).
40   *Re Cooper Chemicals* [1978] 1 Ch 262 per Templeman LJ at 268.

begin insolvency proceedings.[41] It has been held that the process of determining whether a person falls within this provision requires that there be a finding 'that someone has done an act which can be described as carrying on some business of the company and that in doing so he had an intent to defraud'.[42] A person who has an intent to defraud or pursues some other fraudulent purpose cannot be subject to an order or a conviction if that person was not carrying on the business of the company, and those who were did not have the necessary intention or purpose. Once it is established that there was at least one person who was carrying on a business of the company with the necessary mental state, then is it possible to obtain an order or a conviction against others who are knowingly party to that activity, but are not carrying on the business themselves.[43] Providing these conditions are satisfied, a shareholder or a creditor or a person with no such relationship with the company can be made liable for fraudulent trading. In *Re Gerald Cooper Chemicals Ltd*[44] it was held to be possible for a creditor to be liable. In principle, it would be possible for a management consultant or professional adviser who had the necessary intention to be held liable as a party to fraudulent trading being carried on by others, or as an actor in fraudulent trading themselves if they were sufficiently closely involved in controlling the company's activities.

21.33   In order for a person to be found to be a party to fraudulent trading, it must be found that he 'participates in', 'concurs in', or 'takes part in' the carrying on of the business. This involves some positive steps on his part. A failure on the part of a company secretary to give advice as to the company's financial position, which might amount to negligence or a breach of his contract with the company, does not in itself make him a party to fraudulent trading.[45] The court has to consider the nature and degree of the participation of the person in question in each case to determine whether their role was sufficiently active to bring them within the scope of the section. It would seem from the *Maidstone Buildings* case that an omission is insufficient to make a person a party to the conduct of the business in the prohibited manner and that a positive act is required.

THE COURT ORDER UNDER SS 213 AND 214

21.34   The court is empowered in the case of each section to declare that a person within the scope of the section in question is:

41   *Ibid.*
42   *Re Augustus Barnett & Son Ltd* [1986] BCLC 170.
43   *Ibid.*
44   [1978] 1 Ch 262.
45   *Re Maidstone Building Provisions Ltd* [1971] 1 WLR 1085 per Pennycuick VC at 1092–1093.

"to be liable to make such contribution (if any) to the company's assets as the court thinks proper".[46]

No further guidance is given to the court as to the criteria to be employed in assessing the amount which is to be contributed by the person against whom the order is made. In *Re a Company*[47] Peter Gibson J said *obiter*:

> "Whilst the Act does not state how much can be recovered under these sections, the additional costs and debts incurred at a time when the company should have ceased trading .... provide a likely measure of those contributions."

This would seem to be an obvious starting point in any attempt to assess the liability to be imposed under the sections. It represents the maximum amount that can fairly be imposed as it represents the full amount of the loss suffered by the company's creditors as result of the activity to which the section applies. In the case of each individual, the amount may vary as justice would demand that a person be held liable only for those losses incurred after he first became a party to the fraudulent trading, or the time at which he first had the knowledge or would have had it but for the negligence which forms the basis of his liability for wrongful trading. In cases in which the company should have ceased trading at a date earlier than the first act or omission which makes an individual liable under the sections, only the later date at which the individual's involvement began should represent the starting point for the calculation of his maximum liability.

21.35   In a case in which several persons are all liable under one or both of the sections, the court will wish to have regard to the means of each person with a view to ensuring the recovery of the maximum amount for the creditors in the liquidation. However, the maximum liability of each individual should not exceed the amount suggested in the last paragraph. It is submitted that it would not be appropriate for the court to have regard to the culpability of a person to whom one of the sections applies in determining the mount of the contribution that he will be ordered to make. The question of whether liability is based on dishonest conduct under s 213, actual knowledge under s 214 or negligence under that section, should not affect the court's decision. The Act imposes liability on the basis of behaviour which is defined as falling below the standard demanded of those involved in the management of companies. To allow those who fall within its scope because of negligence to escape with a lower level of liability would frustrate its intention to allow for the compensation of creditors. This

---

46   ss 213(1) and 214(1).
47   [1987] 3 WLR 339 at 354.

would suggest that it is only where there would be a surplus after the payment of all creditors, if the maximum contribution were required, from all those against whom orders are to be made that the question of the extent of their moral culpability should affect the decision as to the level of their contribution. In *Re Produce Marketing Consortium Ltd*[48] Knox J accepted that s 214 gave rise to a primarily compensatory jurisdiction rather than a penal one. Consequently, the amount of the contribution should be assessed by reference to the depletion in the company's assets that resulted from the conduct that gave rise to the court's discretion. However, he was unwilling to spell out limits on the very wide discretion conferred on the courts by Parliament and refused to ignore the absence of fraudulent intent in fixing the amount of the contribution to be ordered. While accepting that that factor should not result in the award of a low or nominal amount, he took it into account in awarding £75,000 rather than the £107,000 claimed. It is submitted that such a mitigation of the principle that the provision is compensatory is undesirable.

21.36   Both sections are concerned with supplementing the assets available in the liquidation. It has already been noted that only the liquidator may apply under each of these sections. Individual creditors cannot do so, and both sections make it clear that it is not now possible for the court to make an order that payment be made to a particular creditor. Even if dishonest conduct under s 213 is involved, the criminal sanctions available under s 458 of the Companies Act 1985 should be used for the purpose of punishment rather than an exemplary award under s 213 of a higher amount than was lost to creditors, as a result of the behaviour of the person concerned. In *Re Cyona Distributors Ltd*[49] Lord Denning suggested that an exemplary order may be made and that under the pre 1986 law an order could be made for payment direct to an individual creditor. The latter observation was supported by Templeman J in *Re Gerald Cooper Chemicals.*[50] In the *Cyona* case it was found that the fact that a creditor was paid as a result of threatening proceedings against individuals for fraudulent trading does not impress the amount paid with a trust in favour of the general body of creditors.

21.37   The court has a discretion by virtue of s 215(2) when making a declaration under either of the sections, to give such further directions as it thinks proper for giving effect to the declaration. In particular, it may make the liability it imposes a charge on any debt or obligation due from the company to the person against whom the declaration is made, or on any

---

48   (1989) 5 BCC 569.
49   [1967] 1 Ch 889 at 902.
50   [1978] 1 Ch 262.

mortgage or charge he has on the assets of the company or any interest he has in such a mortgage or charge. This power extends to the imposition of a charge on a debt, obligation or mortgage; or a charge held by or vested in an assignee from or through the person, subject to the declaration or any person acting on his behalf as well as such assets or securities held by the person to whom s 213 or 214 applies or a person acting on his behalf. For this purpose an assignee is defined in s 215(3) as including a person to whom the debt, obligation, mortgage or charge was issued or transferred or in whose favour it (or an interest in it) was created, providing these things were done by the directions of the person made liable by the declaration. These transactions need not be carried out by that person if they were done at his direction. Protection is given to assignees who give valuable consideration (other than by way of marriage) in good faith and without notice of the ground on which the declaration is made. Such persons are excluded from the definition of an assignee by s 215(3)(b) and ignorance of the facts which form the basis of the declaration protect such third parties.

21.38   Where a debt, obligation or security is charged by the court under s 215(2), orders may be made from time to time as they are necessary to enforce that charge.[51] In addition, if the person against whom the s 213 or 214 declaration is made is a creditor of the company, the court may direct that the whole or any part of any debt due to that person from the company and any interest on it shall be subordinated to all the company's other debts and the interest on them. This order will effectively allow the other creditors to have access to the company's assets ahead of the person guilty of fraudulent or wrongful trading. The power to subordinate debts can be used in conjunction with an order that payment be made by the person subjected to the declaration and the power to charge debts, obligations or securities could be used to assist in the enforcement of the payment order. Any debts subordinated to those of other creditors will not be charged with the amount of the payment required.

PHOENIX COMPANIES

21.39   Section 216 and 217 of the Insolvency Act 1986 deal with the problem of the Phoenix company. This is the abuse whereby the controllers of an insolvent company would place it in liquidation or receivership (if they were holders of a floating charge over its assets) and by the use of a sympathetic liquidator or receiver ensure that the business of the company was sold for substantially less than its market value to another company

---

51   s 215(2)(b).

controlled by the same individuals. The new company would have a registered name or a business name used for trading purposes which was identical with, or similar to that of, the old company. By these means the creditors of the original company recovered little or nothing from the debts due to them and had insult added to injury by the continuation of the business under an identical or similar name by the same individuals using a new company. Sections 216 and 217 deal with this problem by imposing civil and criminal liability on persons involved in such activities. The provisions of the Company Directors Disqualification Act 1986 are also relevant in this situation but are dealt with in paras 21.46 *et seq* below.

21.40   For s 216 to apply, a company must have gone into insolvent liquidation on or after 29th December 1986.[52] This means that a winding up order was made or a winding up resolution was passed on or after that date, and at a time when the company's assets were insufficient for the payment of its debts and other liabilities and the expenses of winding up.[53] If the section applies to a company, certain prohibitions are imposed on a person who was a director or a shadow director of that company at any time in the period of 12 months ending with the day before it went into liquidation.[54] Such a person may not, at any time in the 5 years beginning with the day on which that company went into liquidation, do any of the following:

(a) be a director of any other company known by a prohibited name,
(b) be concerned or take part in any way, directly or indirectly
   (i) in the promotion, formation or management of any such company, or
   (ii) in the carrying on of a business (other than by a company) under a prohibited name.[55]

For the purpose of the section a name is prohibited if it is either a name by which the original company was known at any time in the 12 month period before it went into liquidation, or a name which is so similar to such a name as to suggest an association with that company.[56] The use of the concept of a name by which a company is or was known is expressly stated to include any name under which it carried on business at the time in question as well as its own name.[57] This applies to names used by the original company during the 12 months before it went into liquidation and to names used by

52   s 216(1).
53   ss 216(7) and 247(2).
54   s 216(1).
55   s 216(3).
56   s 216(2).
57   s 216(6).

any other company with which its former director or shadow director is later connected. It should be noted that if a name was used by the original company within the 12 month period, the prohibition applies to the use of it by a former director or shadow director even if that person did not hold that position at the time at which that name was used.

21.41 The restrictions imposed by the section are very broadly defined and are analogous to those imposed on a person subjected to a disqualification order under the CDDA 1986. A person affected by s 216 is excluded from holding a directorship in a company with a prohibited name and from any direct or indirect concern or participation in either the promotion, formation or management of a company or the carrying on of an unincorporated business which uses the prohibited name. This covers a wide range of activities including the role of shadow director. In *R v Campbell*[58] the comprehensive nature of this formulation was noted and was held to prevent the person to whom it applied from being part of the management and central direction of the affairs of the company. Under s 216, this would also apply to carrying on an unincorporated business. A person who acts as a management consultant or 'company doctor' and advises directors or other controllers on the financial and management structure of a business is likely to be directly or indirectly concerned in its management. This will be a breach of this section if a prohibited name is being used as will any participation in the promotion or formation of a company. It is not a breach of the section to be involved in the inception of an unincorporated business without participating in carrying it on.

21.42 Section 216(4) lays down that it is a criminal offence to act in breach of the section. Punishment is by the statutory maximum fine or 6 months imprisonment for a summary conviction, and 2 years imprisonment and an unlimited fine for a conviction on indictment.[59] In addition, s 217 provides for civil liability in respect of breaches of s 216. Such liability exists by virtue of the section if its requirements are satisfied. Unlike ss 213 and 214, it is not for the court in its discretion to decide on the level of the contribution that will be imposed. The liability is for all the 'relevant debts' of the company and this concept is defined by reference to the time at which the debts are incurred. The liability is imposed on two categories of person:

(a) a person who, in contravention of s 216, is involved in the management of a company,[60] and

(b) a person who:

---

58 [1984] BCLC 83.
59 sch 10.
60 s 217(1)(a).

(i) is involved in the management of a company, and
(ii) acts or is willing to act on instructions given (without the leave of the court) by a person whom he knows at that time to be in contravention of s 216 in relation to that company.[61]

For the purpose of both bases of liability and, indeed, of the whole of s 217 involvement in the management of a company is defined as meaning either being a director of the company or being directly or indirectly concerned in or taking part in the management of the company.[62] Any director will automatically be regarded as being involved in the management of the company whether he participates in its activities or not. Others can come within the definition on the basis of their actual role in management.

21.43 Once it is established that a person involved in the management of a company acted on the instructions of someone whom he knew at that time to be contravening s 216, a presumption of continued willingness to act on that person's instructions applies unless the contrary is proved.[63] This will increase the number of debts for which such a person is liable to include those incurred by the company in the period of presumed willingness to act on the instructions of the wrongdoer as well as those incurred during the period when the instructions were being acted upon.

21.44 Personal liability under s 217 for the 'relevant debts' of the company is joint and several with any other person so liable.[64] The debts for which personal liability is imposed by s 217 are those incurred by the company at the time when the person made liable was acting in breach of the section. For someone made responsible for the debts by their involvement in the management of the company, the debts in question are those incurred by the company at a time when that person was either a director or directly or indirectly participated in the management of the company contrary to s 216. A person who acts or is willing to act on the instructions of someone then known by them to be in contravention of the section the debts for which they are responsible are those incurred by the company at a time when they acted or were willing to act in that way. In each case the responsibility imposed by the section extends to other liabilities incurred by the company at the time in question as well as debts.[65]

21.45 Section 217 is concerned only with companies because a person

61 s 217(1)(b).
62 s 217(4).
63 s 217(5).
64 s 217(2).
65 s 217(3).

who carries on an unincorporated business in breach of s 216 will necessarily be personally liable for its debts as a sole trader or a partner. Sections 216 and 217 extend to companies which can be wound up under Part V of the Insolvency Act 1986 as well as registered companies. Unregistered companies are subject to the 'Phoenix' rules.[66]

EXCLUSIONS FROM THE 'PHOENIX' RULES

21.46   The width of the prohibition imposed on the use of company names by s 216 is mitigated by the possibility of excluding the operation of the section. Section 216(3) provides that the prohibition in that subsection on holding a directorship, participating in the promotion, formation or management of a company or carrying on an unincorporated business using a prohibited name does not apply if the leave of the court is obtained or if prescribed circumstances apply.

Leave of the court

21.47   An application should be made to the court in advance of the act which would be a breach of s 216(3). The application will be dealt with under Part 7 of the Insolvency Rules. If no leave is obtained from the court in advance of the act in question Rule 4.229 of the Insolvency Rules[67] may assist if an application is made by the director or shadow director of a company which goes into liquidation within 7 days of the date on which it went into liquidation. The leave of the court must be granted not later than 6 weeks from the date of the liquidation but providing the court hears the application within that period the acts of the applicant from the date on which the company went into liquidation to the date on which the court disposes of the case will not breach s 216(3) whether or not the court grants leave. This provision is only likely to be of assistance if the company or business with which the applicant is connected and which is using a prohibited name already exists when the original company goes into liquidation or is set up very soon afterwards. This is a form of *interim* relief which could be particularly useful in the case of a group of companies with similar names and interlocking directorships if only one group member goes into liquidation. In any application for leave under s 216(3) the court may call on the liquidator or any former liquidator of the liquidating company to report on the circumstances in which it became insolvent and the extent of the responsibility of the applicants for that event.[68]

---

66   See para 14.03–14.06 as to the companies that can be wound up under the Act.
67   As amended by SI 1987 no 1919.
68   r 4.227.

Cases where leave is not required

21.48   There are two 'excepted cases' in which the prohibition in s 216(3) will not apply to a person despite the absence of leave from the court for his activities. The first deals with the use of a successor company, a practice which is likely to be involved where the original business or part of it is hived off. The second is concerned with the use of a prohibited name by an existing company.

21.49   Rule 4.228 applies if a successor company acquires the whole or substantially the whole of the business of an insolvent company under arrangements made with a qualified insolvency practitioner. The practitioner who makes those arrangements must be acting as the liquidator, administrator, administrative receiver or supervisor of a voluntary arrangement under the Act in respect of the insolvent company. To protect a person who would otherwise infringe s 216(3) notice naming him must be given to the creditors of the insolvent company.[69] The notice must be given within 28 days from the 'completion of the arrangements'. This will usually mean the transfer of the business from the insolvent company to the successor company and it may be that the word 'completion' is used in the sense of the performance of a contractual obligation to transfer. However, if other acts can be described as part of the arrangements under which the business was transferred then the completion referred to may take place later than the transfer of the business. The appointment of the person in question to the board of the successor company might be such an act if it represents the completion of the arrangements. The notice must specify the name and registered number of the insolvent company and describe the circumstances of the acquisition of its business by the successor company. Details of any change of name by the successor company and of the prohibited name it has assumed or proposes to assume must also be set out.[70] In addition the name of the person who is to be protected from the application of s 216 by the notice must be given together with particulars of the nature and duration of his directorship or shadow directorship of the insolvent company. This information is given with a view to the named person being associated with the management of the successor company or being a director of it.[71] If effective notice is given the person named in it is free to act in the ways mentioned in s 216 in relation to the successor company without the leave of the court.[72]

21.50   The second case in which the section's effects can be excluded

---

69   r 4.228(1).
70   r 4.228(2).
71   r 4.228(3).
72   r 4.228(4).

without recourse to the court is where the company known by a prohibited name has been so known throughout the whole of the 12 months ending with the day before the liquidating company went into liquidation. Providing the company with the prohibited name has not been dormant at any time during that 12 month period, the leave of the court is not required for any person to be a director of that company or to engage in activities in relation to it that would otherwise be forbidden by s 216.[73] The existence of these exceptions mitigates the severity of the broad prohibition on the use of a prohibited name imposed by the section.

PART 2: DISQUALIFICATION OF DIRECTORS

The Company Directors Disqualification Act 1986 consolidates the rules on this topic. In this section it is proposed to consider in outline the general provisions of the Act for disqualification and to look in greater depth at the rules on disqualification in cases involving insolvency.

THE NATURE OF A DISQUALIFICATION ORDER

21.51   The Act gives the court power, or in some circumstances, a duty to make a disqualification order against a person. If such an order is made the person is prohibited from a range of activities. Section 1 lays down that the order will forbid the person against whom it is made from being, during the period for which the order lasts, a director, liquidator, administrator or receiver or manager of a company. In addition such a person may not:

"in any way, whether directly or indirectly, be concerned or take part in the promotion, formation or management of a company".

In each case the leave of the court may be obtained to authorise the behaviour in question.

21.52   It is clear that the prohibition on participation in the promotion, formation or management of a company is very wide. In *R v Campbell*[74] it was held that a company doctor who advised directors on financial and management structures might well be concerned directly or indirectly in the management of the company and that the section had the effect of preventing disqualified persons from being part of the management and central direction of the company's affairs at all. It will be noticed that the prohibition in this section does not extend to participation in an

73   r 4.230.
74   [1984] BCLC 83.

unincorporated business. Otherwise it is similar to the provision of s 216 on Phoenix companies.[75]

21.53 Although no specific reference is made to the role of shadow director carried on by a person subjected to a disqualification order, s 1(1)(d) of the Act will encompass anyone who provides directions or instructions on which the directors of a company are accustomed to act since such a person would be sufficiently involved with the central management and control of the company to fall within that paragraph.

21.54 The disqualification order made by the court will specify the period for which the disqualification is to last. The maximum period of disqualification varies according to the ground on which the order is made and in the case of s 6 a minimum period is specified. If an order is made against a person who is already subject to an order the periods provided for in the two orders will run concurrently so that, in effect, the disqualification will last for the longer of the two periods.[76]

Section 1(4) makes in clear that a disqualification order can be made on grounds consisting of or including matters other than criminal convictions despite the potential criminal liability of the respondent in respect of those matters.

21.55 A person applying for leave to engage in an activity prohibited by a disqualification order to which they are subject must apply to the court with jurisdiction to wind up companies generally if the leave is to promote or form a company. In all other cases the application must be made to the court with jurisdiction to wind up that particular company; this will vary according to the value of its paid up share capital.[77] When the application for leave is heard and the disqualification order made on the application of the Secretary of State, the official receiver or the liquidator of a company then that person is obliged to appear at the hearing and to draw the attention of the court to any matters that he considers to be relevant. He may also give evidence or call witnesses.[78]

21.56 Once a disqualification order is made details of the order and of any variation of it or leave granted by the court for a person to do things which would otherwise be prohibited, will be sent by an officer of the court to the Department of Trade and Industry which runs a register of disqualification orders that is open to inspection by the public.[79]

---

75 See paras 21.46 *et seq* above.
76 Company Directors Disqualification Act 1986 s 1(2) and (3).
77 s 17(1).
78 s 17(2).
79 s 18 and Companies (Disqualification Orders) Regulations 1986 (SI 1986 no 2067).

CONSEQUENCES OF BREACH OF AN ORDER

21.57 Acting in contravention of an order is a criminal offence. On indictment a conviction leads to up to 2 years' imprisonment and/or a fine. A summary conviction results in up to 6 months' imprisonment and/or a fine.[80] If the offence is committed by a corporate body it is possible for any director, manager, secretary or other similar officer of that body or anyone purporting to act in such a capacity to be guilty of the offence providing the offence occurred with his consent or connivance or was attributable to his neglect.[81] The members of a corporate body are treated as if they were directors of it for this purpose if its affairs are managed by them.[82] A corporate body might be liable for the breach of an order either because one has been made against it as a director of a company or because it is a party to the offence of an individual against whom an order existed.

21.58 In addition to the criminal sanction against those guilty of breach of a disqualification order, personal liability is imposed for the company's debts on the basis of such behaviour. Section 15 provides for this in a manner similar to s 217 of the Insolvency Act 1986 which applies to the debts of a Phoenix company. Such responsibility arises when a person is involved in the management of a company either in breach of a disqualification order or while he is an undischarged bankrupt. Involvement in the management of a company includes being a director of it and being concerned (whether directly or indirectly) or taking part in its management.[83] The latter element is wide enough to include acting as a liquidator, receiver or administrator of a company.

21.59 Liability is also imposed on anyone who is involved in the management of a company and who acts or is willing to act on the instructions of a person whom he knows at that time to be subject to a disqualification order or to be an undischarged bankrupt; providing those instructions are given without the leave of the court. A person who is once proved to have acted on such instructions is presumed, unless the contrary is shown to have been willing to act on that person's instructions at any time from then onwards.[84]

21.60 Responsibility for debts under the section is joint and several with others liable for them whether under the section or otherwise.[85] The debts

---

80   Company Directors Disqualification Act 1986 s 13.
81   s 14(1).
82   s 14(2).
83   s 15(1)(a) and (4).
84   s 15(1)(b) and (5).
85   s 15(2).

for which liability is imposed are those incurred at any time when the person who is to be responsible for them was involved in the management of the company or was acting or willing to act on the instructions of the undischarged bankrupt or person subject to an order; depending on the basis on which liability is imposed.[86]

APPLICATIONS FOR DISQUALIFICATION ORDERS

21.61 Application for an order under ss 6 or 8 of the Act can be made only by the Secretary of State for Trade and Industry. However, officeholders are required to report to the Secretary of State if they believe that the conditions in s 6 are satisfied and he may direct that the official receiver bring the proceedings.[87] In the case of an application to disqualify a person under ss 2 to 5 of the Act, an application may be made by the liquidator, or any past or present member or creditor of a company in respect of which that person is alleged to have committed an offence or a default as well as by the Secretary of State or the official receiver.[88] If the application is in fact made by the official receiver, the Secretary of State or the liquidator, the applicant is required to appear at the hearing and to draw the attention of the court to anything that he considers to be relevant. He has power to give evidence and to call witnesses.[89] Whoever makes the application, 10 days' notice must be given, to the person against whom the order is to be sought, of the intention to apply. The respondent may appear and give evidence or call witnesses.[90]

21.62 The procedure on an application under ss 6 or 8 of the Act is laid down in the Insolvent Companies (Disqualification of Unfit Directors) Proceedings Rules 1986.[91] The application is by originating summons in the High Court or originating application in the county court.[92] The summons together with copies of the affidavit evidence in support of the application which must be filed at the time of the issue of the summons must be served on the respondent. The report of the official receiver will be treated as verified by his affidavit if the application is made by him. The affidavit (or the official receiver's report) must contain a statement of the matters by reference to which the respondent is alleged to be unfit to take part in the management of the company.[93]

---

86 s 15(3).
87 See paras 21.88 *et seq* below.
88 s 16(2).
89 s 16(3).
90 s 16(1).
91 SI 1986 no 612.
92 r 2.
93 r 3.

21.63 The summons must be endorsed with information about the maximum and minimum periods of disqualification available to the court on the application and the period that can be imposed summarily.[94] Service is by first class post to the respondent's last known address and is accompanied by a form on which the respondent can acknowledge service.[95] Evidence in affidavit form may be filed by the respondent within 28 days of the date of service and a copy of it must be served on the applicant forthwith.[96] The applicant may then file and serve further evidence in reply within 14 days from receiving a copy of the evidence of the respondent.[97] The hearing of the application is before the Registrar in the first instance and takes place not less than 8 weeks after the date of issue of the summons. The hearing may either result in a summary determination or in an adjournment because of the registrar's opinion that disqualification for a longer period than the 5 years which can be imposed summarily is appropriate or that questions of law or fact not suitable for summary disposal arise in the case. If the hearing is adjourned it may either be resumed before the Registrar or transferred to be heard by a judge.[98] A disqualification order may be made in the absence of the respondent but such an order can be set aside or varied by the court on whatever terms it thinks just.[99]

21.64 Proceedings for an order are civil and there is no need for detailed charges to be set out or for the official receiver to be restricted to the affidavit evidence filed initially. If new affidavit evidence is filed an adjournment can be granted to enable the director to prepare an answer to the new allegations.[100]

Any disqualification order made will take effect at the beginning of the 21st day after the day on which it is made unless the court directs otherwise.[101]

DISQUALIFICATION ORDERS ON GROUNDS NOT NECESSARILY INVOLVING INSOLVENCY

Conviction for an indictable offence

21.65 Section 2(1) of the Act provides for the disqualification of a person who has been convicted of an indictable offence in connection with the

---

94 r 4.
95 r 5.
96 r 6(1).
97 r 6(2).
98 r 7.
99 r 9.
100 *Re Churchill Hotel (Plymouth) Ltd* (1988) 4 BCC 112.
101 r 8.

promotion, formation, management or liquidation of a company or with the receivership or management of its property. The meaning of the phrase 'indictable offence' is given in s 5 and sch 1 of the Interpretation Act 1978. It means any offence which if committed by an adult is triable on indictment whether it is exclusively triable in that way or triable either on indictment or summarily. The disqualification order can be made by a court which has jurisdiction to wind up the company in relation to which the offence was committed or by the court by or before which the person was convicted of the offence. In the case of a court of summary jurisdiction, any magistrates' court acting for the same petty sessions area has this power.[102]

21.66   The maximum period of disqualification under s 2 is 15 years unless the order is made by a court of summary jurisdiction in which case it is 5 years.[103]

For the purpose of s 2 it is necessary that the person against whom the order is to be made has been convicted of an offence. However, the section is sufficiently widely drafted to cover offences under the Theft Act 1968 or other offences of dishonesty in addition to offences under the Companies Act 1985 or the Insolvency Act 1986. The offences may be committed against outsiders as opposed to the company itself or its members providing they fall within the scope of the matters described by this section and involve the promotion, setting up or management of a company or its liquidation or receivership.[104]

21.67   The concept of an offence committed in connection with the management of a company covers the conduct of both its internal and its external affairs. Carrying on an insurance business through a limited company is a function of management and if that function is carried out unlawfully in a way which results in a conviction for an indictable offence then a disqualification order may be made by the court under the section.[105]

Persistent default in complying with companies legislation

21.68   Section 3(1) of the Act permits a court to make a disqualification order against any person whom it considers to have been persistently in default in relation to the requirements of the companies legislation for any return, account or other document to be delivered or sent to or filed with the registrar of companies. This section provides for a maximum

---

102   s 2(2).
103   s 2(3).
104   See *R v Austen* (1985) 1 BCC 99, 528.
105   *R v Georgiou* (1988) 4 BCC 322.

disqualification period of 5 years.[106] The order may be made by any court with jurisdiction to wind up any of the companies in respect of which a default is alleged to have occurred.[107]

21.69 Persistent default for the purpose of s 3 may be proved in any manner but a person adjudged guilty of three or more defaults in the 5 years ending with the date of the application unders s 3 is conclusively taken to have been persistently in default.[108] The concept of being adjudged guilty of a default is defined in s 3(3) as including a conviction for an offence consisting of a person's failure to comply with or contravention of such a provision either on his own part or on the part of any company. In addition, the making of a default order against him by a court enforcing the delivery of accounts or returns by the company or its receiver, manager, or liquidator amounts to being adjudged guilty of a default whether it is the result of non-compliance on his own part or on the part of a company.[109]

21.70 Section 3 permits an order to be made as a result of the accumulation of a number of defaults on the part of a person. Since the defaults have to be persistent a single conviction or default order will not be sufficient unless other defaults are proved by evidence other than convictions or default orders. However, a number of such orders all made on the same occasion can cumulatively give rise to liability under the section. An order under the section must therefore be made by the court in which a company involved could be wound up.

21.71 Section 5 permits a court of summary jurisdiction to make a disqualification order against a person on his conviction for a summary offence of the kind dealt with in s 3 if the defendant has, during the 5 years ending with the date of conviction, a total of three default orders and offences against him. The offences of which he is convicted on the occasion on which the order is made can be included in the calculation for this purpose. Earlier offences can be either indictable or summary but the conviction which gives rise to the power the make the order must be of a summary offence. For this purpose a summary offence is one defined in sch 1 of the Interpretation Act 1978 as an offence which if committed by an adult is triable only summarily. The default orders which are to be taken into account for the purpose of s 5 are those listed in s 3(2)(b).

Section 5 permits disqualification for a total of five years.[110]

21.72 There is no need to show blameworthiness on the part of a person to

106   s 3(5).
107   s 3(4).
108   s 3(2).
109   s 3(2)(b).
110   s 5(5).

justify an order under these provisions. The concept of persistent default refers only to the number of occasions on which default has occurred and not necessarily to convictions for such behaviour. The fact that a person was subject to substantial pressures which caused the default and was guilty of no fraudulent intent does not prevent the court from making an order.[111]

Disqualification after the investigation of a company

21.73   The Secretary of State for Trade and Industry can apply to the court for an order to be made against a person who was a shadow director or a director of a company which has been subject to an investigation or inspection under certain provisions of the Companies Act 1985 or the Financial Services Act 1986. The Secretary of State can apply if he has reached the conclusion that it is expedient in the public interest that a disqualification order be made. This conclusion can be reached as a result of an inspector's report made under s 437 of the Companies Act 1985 or ss 94 or 177 of the Financial Services Act 1986. Alternatively it can be based on information or documents obtained under ss 447 or 448 of the Companies Act 1985 or s 105 of the Financial Services Act 1986.

21.74   Application is made to the High Court which may make a disqualification order for a period of up to 15 years if it is satisfied that the director or shadow director's conduct in relation to his company makes him unfit to be concerned in the management of a company.[112] The criteria used to determine the question of the unfitness of such a person are the same as those applied under s 6.[113]

GROUNDS SPECIFICALLY RELATING TO CORPORATE INSOLVENCY

21.75   Sections 2, 3, 5 or 8 could apply as a result of events that take place or come to light at the stage of a company's life when it is insolvent. However, it is not a precondition of the application of those sections to a person that the company involved should be insolvent or subject to insolvency procedures. This is the case with ss 4, 6 and 7.

Fraud becoming apparent in the course of winding up

21.76   Section 4(1) permits a court with jurisdiction to wind up a company[114] to make an order disqualifying a person if it appears to the

---

111 See *Re Arctic Engineering Ltd (No 2)* [1986] BCLC 253.
112 ss 8(2)–(4).
113 See para 21.88 *et seq* below.
114 s 4(2).

court in the course of the winding up of a company that he has been guilty of certain behaviour. The behaviour in question can be fraudulent trading under s 458 of the Companies Act 1985 in which case there is no need for the person to have been convicted of the offence or to be an officer of or officeholder in relation to the company.[115] Alternatively, an order can be made on the basis of the fact that the defendant has been guilty while an officer or liquidator of the company or receiver or manager of its property of any fraud in relation to the company or of any breach of duty in the capacity in which he acted.[116] This permits an order to be made for any breach of duty by a director, shadow director,[117] receiver or liquidator of a company. Such a breach may be fraudulent but this is not necessary for the section to apply.

Wrongful trading

21.77   In addition to the possible disqualification under s 4, of a person liable for the criminal offence of fraudulent trading, a court which makes an order under s 213 or 214 of the Insolvency Act 1986 requiring a person to make a contribution to the assets available to the company's creditors, may disqualify that person for up to 15 years. This power may be exercised by the court on its own initiative whether or not anyone has applied for a disqualification order and is not dependent on the existence of liability for any criminal offence.[118]

Unfitness in the context of insolvency

Investigation and report
21.78   Only the Secretary of State for Trade and Industry or (in the case of a compulsory liquidation) the official receiver can apply to the court for a disqualification order against a director or shadow director under s 6 of the Act on the basis of his unfitness to hold office.[119] However, s 7(3) of the Act requires the officeholder responsible under that subsection to report to the Secretary of State if it appears to him that the conditions laid down in s 6 are satisfied in respect of a person who is or has been a director or shadow director of the company. The officeholders responsible for this function are the administrator or administrative receiver if the company is subject to an administration order or is in receivership. If the company is being wound up by the court it is the official receiver and, if it is being wound up voluntarily, the liquidator.

---

115   s 4(1)(a).
116   s 4(1)(b).
117   s 4(2).
118   s 10 and see para 21.65 *supra*.
119   See *Re Probe-Data Systems Ltd* (1989) 5 BCC 384.

21.79 The Insolvent Companies (Reports on Conduct of Directors) No 2 Rules 1986[120] impose an obligation on officeholders to report to the Secretary of State on the forms prescribed in those rules.[121] They further ensure that the officeholder to whom it appears that the company has at any time become insolvent must furnish a return within 6 months of the 'relevant date' on every person who was on that date a director or shadow director of the company or had been a shadow director or director at any time in the 3 years immediately preceding that date.[122]

21.80 The return must either state that the officeholder has not submitted a report on those persons because he does not have sufficient information to hand or because as at the date of the return he has not become aware of any matters which would require him to make a report under s 7(3) of the Act. If he states that insufficient information is to hand he must state when he expects to submit a report. If no report is made under s 7(3) of the Act the officeholder will have to explain that this is because he does not believe at the date of the return that a report is necessary or that he has insufficient information.[123]

21.81 Failure to submit either a report under s 7(3) or a return explaining why none has been submitted results in a fine being imposed on the officeholder unless he has reasonable cause for his failure to comply with the Rules.[124] It should be noted that either a report or a return must be submitted in respect of every person who falls within Rule 4(2) because they are or (within 3 years before the relevant date) have been a director or shadow director of the company.

21.82 For the purpose of the Rules the relevant date is the date of the appointment of an administrator in the case of an administration order or of an administrative receiver who is not the successor to one who died or vacated office under s 45 of the Insolvency Act 1986 in the case of a receivership. In the case of a creditors' voluntary winding up it is the date on which the winding up resolution was passed. If the liquidation began as a members' voluntary winding up it is the date on which the liquidator formed the opinion that at the date on which the company went into liquidation the company was insolvent.[125] The Rules do not apply to winding up by the court as the official receiver is the responsible officeholder under s 7 in such a liquidation. The responsible officeholder for

---

120 SI 1986 no 2134.
121 r 3.
122 r 4(1), (2) and (5).
123 r 4(5).
124 r 4(7).
125 r 4(4).

the purpose of the duty to furnish a return in compliance with Rules 3 and 4 is the person in office at the date on which a return is required or the one who vacated office nearest to that date.[126]

21.83   In addition to the general obligation of the officeholder to furnish a return to the Department of Trade and Industry, s 7(4) of the Act gives power to the Secretary of State or the official receiver to require a present or former liquidator, administrator or administrative receiver of a company to furnish him with such information as he may reasonably require for the purpose of exercising or deciding whether to exercise any function under s 7 of the Act. The information will be with respect to any person's conduct as a director or shadow director of the company.[127] The requirement can extend to the production and inspection of books, papers and other records relevant to that person's conduct in that capacity.[128]

Compliance with a requirement laid down under s 7(4) can be enforced by a court order made on the application of the Secretary of State or the official receiver.[129]

The order on the basis of unfitness
21.84   As has already been noted, an application under s 6 must be made by the Secretary of State or, if he so directs in the case of a company being wound up by the court, the official receiver.[130] An application is made to the court in which a company in compulsory liquidation is being wound up, the court which made any administration order in force in relation to the company, the court with jurisdiction to wind up a company in voluntary liquidation, or, in any other case, the high court.[131]

21.85   The court is under a duty to make an order for a minimum period of 2 years (with a maximum of 15 years) if it is satisfied that the person against whom the order is to be made is or has been a director or shadow director of a company which has at any time become insolvent and that his conduct as a director of that company makes him unfit to be concerned in the management of a company.[132]

21.86   There is no need to establish that the company became insolvent while he was a director; it is enough if that happened after he ceased to be a director or shadow director.[133] A company is regarded as becoming

126   r 4(5).
127   s 7(4)(a).
128   s 7(4)(b).
129   r 5.
130   s 7(1).
131   s 6(3).
132   s 6(1) and (4).
133   s 6(1)(a).

insolvent for the purpose of the section if an administration order is made in relation to it or an administrative receiver of it is appointed.[134] Alternatively it becomes insolvent if it goes into liquidation at a time when its assets are not sufficient for the payment of its debts and other liabilities (including the expenses of winding up).[135] It goes into liquidation at the time when a winding up order is made or an earlier winding up resolution is passed and it is at this point that its solvency will be judged.[136]

21.87   The conduct of a person which is taken into account in deciding whether he is unfit can either be limited to his conduct as a director of the company in question or can be such conduct taken together with his conduct as a director of another company or companies.[137] While his conduct in relation to the insolvent company must form part of the evidence leading to the conclusion that he is unfit, his behaviour in relation to other companies—which need never have been insolvent—can also be taken into account. Conduct as a shadow director is also relevant.[138] The respondent's conduct in relation to any matter connected with or arising out of the insolvency of a company is expressly included as regards both the insolvent company which has triggered the application and any other company in relation to which the conduct of the respondent is being considered.[139] The matters to be considered in determining whether the respondent's conduct makes him unfit to be concerned in the management of a company are dealt with in s 9 and sch 1 of the Act.[140] Any application brought under s 6 for a disqualification order must be made with the leave of the court if it is made more than 2 years after the company became insolvent.[141]

The criteria for unfitness
21.88   Section 9 provides that for the purpose of determining whether a person's conduct as a director or shadow director of a company makes him unfit to be concerned in the management of a company, the court shall have regard to sch 1 of the Act. That schedule can be amended by statutory instrument.[142] Part I of the schedule applies in all cases. Part II also applies in those cases in which the company in respect of which the person's behaviour is being considered has, at some stage, become insolvent.[143] Both parts will always apply to the company whose insolvency triggered

134   s 6(2)(b) and (c).
135   s 6(2)(a).
136   s 22(3) and Insolvency Act 1986 s 247(2).
137   s 6(1)(b).
138   s 6(3).
139   s 6(2).
140   See paras 21.88 *et seq* below.
141   s 7(2), *Re Tasbian Ltd* (1989) 5 BCC 729.
142   s 9(4) and (5).
143   s 9(1).

the application. It is possible that only Part I will apply to other companies with which the respondent has been involved.

21.89   The matters to be taken into account in all cases include misfeasance and breach of duty by the director in relation to the company, his misapplication or retention of the company's property or money and any conduct by the director giving rise to an obligation to account for property or money.[144] The reference to breach of duty presumably refers to duties already owed and so does not impose additional duties on shadow directors (to whom the schedule applies). Such a person could however be accountable as a constructive trustee or guilty of the misapplication or retention of company property. In addition, the extent of any liability of the respondent for the company entering into a transaction liable to be set aside under ss 423 to 425 of the Insolvency Act 1986 as transactions at an undervalue and for any failure of the company to comply with the Companies Act requirements for maintaining and preserving accounting records, registers of directors, members and charges or making annual returns or of the directors to prepare annual accounts or to sign the balance sheet and annexed documents.[145]

21.90   Where the company has become insolvent the court will also consider the extent of the director's responsibility for the causes of the company becoming insolvent and for its failure to supply any goods or services which have been paid for in whole or in part.[146] If the company has entered into any transaction or given any preference liable to be set aside under ss 127 or 238 to 240 of the Insolvency Act 1986, the extent of the respondent's responsibility for the company's action will be taken into account as will his own failure to comply with any obligation imposed by specified provisions of the Insolvency Act 1986 to provide a statement of affairs, to attend a creditor's meeting or to deliver up company property or co-operate with a liquidator.[147] If the directors have failed to comply with s 98 of that Act by not calling a creditor's meeting in time when the company goes into creditor's voluntary liquidation then the extent of the respondent's responsibility for that failure will be taken into account.[148] These matters apply to any company of which the respondent has been a director or shadow director which has in fact become insolvent; not only the company whose insolvency triggered the application for a disqualification order.[149]

144   sch 1 paras 1 and 2.
145   paras 3, 4 and 5; and see eg *Re Western Welsh International Systems Building Ltd* (1988) 4 BCC 449.
146   paras 6 and 7.
147   paras 8 and 10.
148   para 9.
149   s 9(1).

21.91   All references in the schedule to provisions of the Companies Act or the Insolvency Act include the corresponding provision in force before that provision came into force.[150] The breadth of the matters dealt with in the schedule indicates that s 6 can readily be used to obtain disqualification orders. The court is obliged to make an order disqualifying the respondent for at least 2 years if it is satisfied that there has been conduct making that person unfit.

21.92   It seems that conduct as a *de facto* director can be taken into account even if there was no valid appointment to the office of director.[151] A director who shirks his duties and fails to supervise effectively those to whom tasks are delegated can be guilty of misconduct although all positive acts were done by subordinates but the delegation of responsibility for records to a chartered secretary is mitigation which can reduce the length of the disqualification.[152]

21.93   The courts decide the issue of unfitness by exercising a discretion after considering all the circumstances surrounding the director's conduct in relation to the companies with which he has been involved. Conduct in relation to the insolvent company may be considered first and then conduct as a director of other companies. The whole of the director's conduct is considered and not merely that which violates a particular provision of the Companies Act or the Insolvency Act but there must be a finding of a serious failure, whether deliberate or through incompetence, to perform the duties of a director before an order can be made.[153]

21.94   Misconduct short of wrongful trading will suffice. Imprudent or improper behaviour such as failing to hand over PAYE deductions or other Crown debts; failing to keep proper accounts as between related companies; failing to file Companies Act returns on time and running an undercapitalised business at a loss are all examples of relevant misconduct.[154] However, the court considers the whole of the director's conduct and in *Re Bath Glass Ltd* some such vices were outweighed by the preparation during the company's trading life of proper budgets, the provision of security from personal assets for corporate debts, the use of professional advisers and a belief (which the court did not consider wholly

---

150   s 9(3).
151   *Re Lo Line Electric Motors* [1988] BCLC 698 (a case on s 300 of the Companies Act 1985).
152   *Re Majestic Recording Studios* [1989] BCLC 1 and *Re Rolus Properties* (1988) 4 BCC 446.
153   *Re Bath Glass Ltd* (1988) 4 BCC 130.
154   See *Re Stanford Services* [1987] BCLC 607; *Re Churchill Hotel (Plymouth) Ltd* (1988) 4 BCC 112; and *Re Bath Glass Ltd* (n 153 *supra*).

irrational) on the part of the directors that the company could trade its way out of difficulties. On weighing the factors in that particular case the court concluded that a disqualification order was not appropriate. However, earlier acts in accordance with professional advice will not mitigate later behaviour in trading with an evidently insolvent company.[155]

21.95 Another basis on which a court may decide to refrain from disqualifying a director appears to be the effects of the order on others. In *Re Churchill Hotel (Plymouth) Ltd* disqualification was avoided because the directors ran other successful companies which employed a substantial number of people and had been guilty of no misconduct in respect of those companies. This later behaviour could be taken into account and apparently outweighed their behaviour in financing an undercapitalised and loss making company by improperly retaining monies due to the Crown and failing to file Companies Act returns on time. However, in *Re Majestic Recording Studios* the efficiency exhibited in running later companies was not sufficient to outweigh irresponsible behaviour in relation to earlier ventures.

21.96 In the absence of gross incompetence, the continuation of a business while assured by an independent person that he will assist in keeping the company afloat for an orderly wind down of its activities, will not become a basis of disqualification simply because Crown monies were retained. In such a case the court is unlikely to find a lack of commercial probity sufficient to warrant disqualification; especially if directors invested large amounts of their own money in the company in an attempt to save it.[156]

It is also possible for a limitation to be placed on a disqualification order to allow the disqualified person to act as director of a particular company and that permission may be made conditional the court's approval of fellow directors who may, for example, be required to be chartered accountants.[157]

21.97 The question of how extensive the use of the section will be depends on the readiness of the DTI to use it, the quality of the information passed to them by officeholders and the willingness of the courts to accept that behaviour that is not morally blameworthy should result in disqualification under the section. It is submitted that the courts are unlikely to interpret the judgment in *Re Dawson Print Group Ltd*[158] as limiting their discretion by

155 *Re McNulty's Interchange Ltd* (1988) 4 BCC 533.
156 *Re C U Fittings Ltd* (1989) 5 BCC and *Re Douglas Construction Services* [1988] BCLC 397.
157 *Re Majestic Recording Studios* (note 152 above).
158 [1987] BCLC 601.

requiring proof of serious breaches of commercial morality or gross incompetence. Such limitations are not consistent with the broad discretion conferred by the Act. It is, however, clear that disqualification will be less frequent than it would have been under the original government proposal in the Insolvency Bill 1985.

CHAPTER 22

Voluntary Arrangements

THE LIQUIDATOR'S POWERS

22.01 The liquidator in any liquidation has power to make any compromise or arrangement with creditors or compromise with contributories and other debtors of the company, but in each case the sanction of the court or the liquidation committee is required.[1] In addition, para 13 of sch 4 of the Act gives liquidators general power to do all things that may be necessary for winding up the affairs of the company and distributing its assets. In a voluntary winding up ss 110 to 111 of the Act may also be used to carry out a reconstruction of the company by the sale of its undertaking in return for shares. In a compulsory liquidation the court may sanction a similar transaction.[2] The fact that the power in relation to contributories is limited to a compromise and does not extend to an arrangement probably means that s 425 of the Companies Act 1985 or ss 1–7 of the Insolvency Act 1986 should be used for the reconstruction of a company rather than making use of the general powers of the liquidator by making *ad hoc* requests for sanction under sch 4. Since the legislature has provided those procedures the courts should not encourage the use of other methods.

SECTIONS 110–111 OF THE INSOLVENCY ACT 1986

22.02 It is possible for a company in voluntary liquidation to engage in a reconstruction under ss 110 and 111 of the Insolvency Act 1986. The sections apply in cases where the liquidator proposes to transfer or sell the whole or part of the company's business or property to another company and to receive in return (for distribution among its members) shares, policies or other like interests, or to arrange for the members to receive directly a right to participate in profits or some other benefit from the transferee company.[3]

22.03 In the case of an insolvent company, this can only be done by means of a creditors' voluntary winding up and in such a case the liquidator must have the sanction of the court or the liquidation committee to receive such

---

1 ss 165(1) and 167(1) and sch 4 Part 1, Insolvency Act 1986.
2 *Re Agra and Masterman's Bank* (1866) at (1871) LR 12 Eq 509n.
3 s 110(1), (2) and (4).

assets in compensation for the sale of the company's property or business.[4] Under ss 582(2) and 593 of the Companies Act 1985 the sanction, of both a special resolution of the company and either the creditors' committee or the court, was required. The wording of s 110(3) suggests that only the sanction of the committee or the court may be required in a creditors' voluntary liquidation. The first paragraph of the subsection lays down that in 'the case of a members' voluntary winding up' the sanction of a special resolution is required. The second paragraph is preceded by the word 'and' but states that in a creditors' voluntary winding up the necessary sanction is that of the court or the liquidation committee. The grammatical meaning of the subsection would seem to be that the in a creditors' voluntary winding up only para (b) applies while para (a) applies only to a members' voluntary liquidation.

22.04   Section 165 and sch 4, paras 6, 7 and 13 of the Insolvency Act 1986 indicate that the transfer of company assets in return for consideration of the kind envisaged in s 110 and the distribution of that consideration to the members is within the liquidator's powers without the need for a special resolution of the company. This is true of a liquidator in either a members' or a creditors' voluntary winding up. From *Re Agra & Masterman's Bank*[5] it is clear that such a transaction can be carried out in a compulsory liquidation. The requirement of a special resolution in the case of a voluntary liquidation must be intended to achieve more than the authorisation of the transaction. The point of the sections is to force all the members (subject to their rights under s 111) to accept the compensation available to them under the scheme if a 75% majority has decided to do so.[6] To interpret the Act as not requiring a special resolution would prevent s 111 from applying to creditors' voluntary liquidations and would thus deprive the members of the protection it confers.

22.05   In cases where the company is in fact insolvent there will be no return to the members as all assets will be used up in paying the expenses of liquidation or the creditors. However, the provisions of ss 110 and 111 might be used in a creditors' winding up where no members' voluntary winding up was possible because uncertainty about the quantum of assets or debts prevented the directors from making the declaration of solvency necessary for a members' voluntary liquidation. If, at the end of the day, assets were distributed to the members in such a case it would be anomalous for the members to be deprived of the protection of s 111. For these reasons any liquidator contemplating the use of ss 110 and 111 in a creditors'

4 s 110(3)(b).
5 (1866) at (1871) LR 12 Eq 509n.
6 s 110(5).

voluntary liquidation should ensure that a special resolution of the company is passed until it becomes clear how the courts are going to interpret s 110(3). The special resolution is invalid if a winding up order is made within 1 year of the passing of the resolution unless it is sanctioned by the court.[7] That sanction can only be given in compulsory liquidation proceedings.[8]

22.06   Section 111(2) gives members the right to insist that the liquidator choose between buying them out at a price fixed by agreement, or arbitration, or not carrying out the special resolution. This procedure can be used by members who did not vote for the resolution and who served notice on the liquidator within 7 days of the passing of the resolution. It is only available where a resolution has been passed under s 110.[9] The money to buy out the minority must be paid before the company is dissolved and will be raised in the way laid down in the resolution.[10] This right of shareholders to dissent is normally taken to preclude an application on their part for the company to be wound up compulsorily but such a petition may succeed if the arrangement is impeachable for unfairness.[11] In a case falling outside the sections because it involves a compulsory liquidation, a court authorising a similar arrangement will permit dissenting contributories to be bought out for cash.[12]

22.07   Since the procedure under ss 110 and 111 takes the form of a voluntary liquidation of the company the order of application of the assets which come to the company will ensure that creditors are paid before any assets are handed over to members. The proceeds of the sale or transfer must be applied to pay the expenses of the liquidation, the debts of the company and to buy out dissenting shareholders. If necessary, non-cash assets received as part of the price in the sale must themselves be sold or used as security to raise money for these purposes. Only after this process is complete will the assets received by the liquidator be distributed to the members of the company. The liquidator will be personally liable if he fails to distribute assets in the appropriate order.[13]

22.08   If, in the case of a members' voluntary liquidation, the very existence of the sale or transfer to which s 110 applies is regarded as prejudicial to the interests of the creditors they can petition for the company to be wound up and thus require the court's sanction for the s 110

7   s 110(6).
8   *Re Callao Bis Co* (1889) 42 Ch D 169.
9   s 111(1).
10   s 111(3).
11   *Re Consolidated South Rand Mines* [1909] 1 Ch 491.
12   *Re General Motor Cab Co* [1913] 1 Ch 377 at 384.
13   *Pulsford v Devenish* [1903] 2 Ch 625.

resolution but they cannot use s 112 during the course of the voluntary liquidation.[14] Where the company is subject to a creditors' voluntary liquidation, they will be able to make their views known when the sanction of the court or of the liquidation committee is sought.

VOLUNTARY ARRANGEMENTS UNDER PART I OF THE INSOLVENCY ACT 1986

22.09   The provisions of the Insolvency Act 1986 on voluntary arrangements are intended to facilitate the process of making a legally binding agreement between a company and its creditors and members. An agreement at common law requires the unanimous agreement of those who are to be bound by it and if that procedure is used a minority who disapprove of the arrangement can prevent its realisation. The difficulties associated with the use of ss 425–427 of the Companies Act 1985 are noted below.[15] Sections 1–7 of the Insolvency Act 1986 provide a method of achieving a binding voluntary arrangement by a two thirds majority by value of the company's creditors without the need for a court order either to call the meetings or to approve the proposal but with the possibility of a challenge in court on limited grounds after the arrangement is approved. The difficulty of retaining confidentiality while negotiating such an arrangement may mean that in practice companies in administration are the group most likely to use the section because once an administration order is made the protection of the statutory moratorium is in place while discussions about an arrangement proceed. However, a voluntary arrangement is available in principle as an alternative solution to winding up or to an administration order. Indeed the provisions can be used whether or not the company is insolvent and may thus be available in cases where liquidation or an administration order cannot be used. The capital structure of the company can be altered by the use of this procedure. For example, debt may be converted into equity to change corporate gearing, or the amount and status of the company's debt may be revised. The agreement of secured or preferential creditors is, however, required if the right to enforce security or the priority attached to the preferential debt is to be affected by the arrangement.[16]

The proposal and the nominee

22.10   A proposal for a voluntary arrangement under the Act may be made to the company and to its creditors. The proposal must be for a

---

14   *Re Callao Bis Co* (1889) 42 Ch D 169.
15   See paras 22.56 *et seq.*
16   s 4(3) and (4).

composition in satisfaction of the company's debts or a scheme of arrangement of its affairs.[17] A scheme of arrangement can include any reorganisation of the company's capital. In the context of s 425 of the Companies Act 1985 it has been held not to be limited to arrangements in the nature of a compromise although something which confiscates rights and gives nothing in return has been said to fall outside the meaning of the expression.[18] In contrast to s 425, the word 'compromise' does not appear in s 1 of the Insolvency Act 1986. A composition in satisfaction of the company's debts is an agreement between the company and some or all of its creditors by which they agree to accept less than the sums due to them in full satisfaction of their debts.[19] The proposal made under s 1 may have features of both an arrangement and a composition since creditors may relinquish some of their rights as part of a scheme whereby the capital structure of the company is revised.

22.11   The directors have power to make such a proposal providing the company is not being wound up and does not have an administration order in force in respect of it. If the company is in liquidation or the subject of an administration order a proposal may be made by the liquidator or the administrator respectively but not by the directors.[20] No other body has the power to make a proposal so such a step cannot be taken by an administrative receiver or by the company in general meeting, although either of those parties could seek to persuade the person with a right to do so to make a proposal.

22.12   A proposal under s 1 of the Act must provide for the appointment of a person known as 'the nominee' to act as trustee of the arrangement or otherwise for the purpose of supervising its implementation. This person must be qualified to act as an insolvency practitioner in relation to the company.[21] The procedure for the preparation of the proposal varies according to whether the proposal is made by the directors or by an administrator or liquidator and in the latter case whether the liquidator or administrator will himself be the nominee or will appoint another insolvency practitioner.

Proposal by directors

22.13   The directors prepare a proposal so that the qualified insolvency practitioner who is to act as nominee can make his report on it to the

---

17   s 1(1).
18   See *Re Guardian Assurance Co Ltd* [1917] 1 Ch 431 and *Re NFU Development Trust Ltd* [1973] 1 All ER 135.
19   See, for example, *Re Hatton* (1872) 7 Ch App 723 at 726.
20   s 1(3).
21   s 1(2).

court.[22] The Rules lay down the contents of the proposal. It must provide a short explanation of why the directors take the view that a voluntary proposal under the Act is desirable and why creditors are likely to concur in it.[23] This will be easier to achieve if the directors have had preliminary discussions with at least the largest creditors of the company and in practice it is likely that the insolvency practitioner who is the nominee under the proposal and who will become the supervisor will have had a major role in preparing the proposal and in the discussions with the creditors of the company.

22.14 This process of discussion and preparation which is necessary before the statutory provisions are used gives rise to the problem that the rumours at that preliminary stage may cause individual creditors to jump the gun and enforce their security or seek to put the company into liquidation before a proposal is drafted. This is one of the reasons for assuming that the statutory procedure is most likely to be used by the administrator of a company who has the benefit of the statutory moratorium which flows from the administration order. One of the grounds for an administration order is the possibility of making a voluntary arrangement under these provisions.

22.15 Rule 1.3(2) lays down the detailed matters which have to be stated in the proposal. They are:

(a) The company's assets, their estimated value, the extent to which they are charged in favour of creditors and the extent to which particular assets are to be excluded from the voluntary arrangement. These matters are to be included insofar as they are within the immediate knowledge of the directors. This suggests that an exhaustive investigation is not required for the purpose of compiling the proposal.

(b) Particulars of any property to be included in the arrangement (other than the company's own assets) and of the source of such property and the terms on which it is to be made available.

(c) Details of the nature and amount of the company's liabilities so far as they are within the immediate knowledge of the directors and of how they are to be dealt with by the arrangement, for example by being met, postponed or modified must be included. More specifically the proposal must explain how preferential and secured creditors and creditors who are persons connected to the company within the definition in s 249 of the Insolvency Act 1986 are to be treated. If the directors know of

22   r 1.2.
23   r 1.3(1).

circumstances making it possible that claims would be made to set aside certain transactions if the company went into liquidation then that information must be disclosed.[24] In addition, the proposal must reveal whether and, if so, how, the company is to be indemnified wholly or partly in respect of such claims under the voluntary arrangement.

(d) Details of any existing guarantees given by others of the company's debts stating which of the guarantors, if any, are persons connected with the company and whether any guarantees are to be given for the purpose of the arrangement and, if so, whether any security is to be given or sought.

(e) The proposed duration of the voluntary arrangement and dates of distributions to creditors with estimates of their amounts.

(f) The amount to be paid to the nominee for expenses and remuneration and the manner in which it is proposed to pay those of the supervisor when the arrangement is in place. Rule 1.28 defines the fees, costs, charges and expenses which can be incurred for any of the purposes of the voluntary arrangement. They include any disbursements of the nominee prior to the approval of the scheme and any remuneration for his services as nominee agreed with the company or the liquidator or administrator. In addition any fees, costs, charges or expenses sanctioned by the terms of the arrangement or correspondent to those payable in an administration or a winding up, are included.

(g) The way in which funds held for the purpose of the arrangement are to be banked, invested and dealt with pending distribution to creditors and how funds held for the payment of creditors but not used for that purpose at the end of the arrangement are to be dealt with.

(h) The manner in which the business of the company is proposed to be conducted during the course of the arrangement with details of any further credit facilities which it is intended to arrange for the company and how the debts so arising are to be paid.

(i) The name, address and qualification of the person it is intended to appoint as supervisor of the voluntary arrangement, details of his functions and confirmation that so far as the directors are aware he is a qualified insolvency practitioner.

22.16   In addition to the matters which the Rules require the proposal to deal with, it must lay down the powers to be conferred on the supervisor as he is not given powers by the Act in the way that the administrative receiver, administrator and liquidator are. If he is to have agency powers this must be spelt out. His right of indemnity should also be made clear. These matters will be particularly important in cases where he will be involved in

---

24   The transactions in question are those that may be attacked under s 238 (transactions at an undervalue); 239 (preferences); 244 (extortionate credit transactions) or 245 (invalid floating charges).

continuing the business of the company while the voluntary arrangement is carried out.

22.17 A comprehensive plan for the execution of the arrangement must be included in the proposal as the whole implementation of the scheme will be carried out in accordance with that document as approved by the meetings of creditors and members. This once again underlines the need for full discussion and negotiation with all interested parties in advance of the commencement of the formal procedures laid down in the Act and the Rules. Up to the time at which the nominee's report is delivered to the court under s 2(2) of the Act, the directors' proposal may be amended with the written agreement of the nominee.[25] Once the directors' proposal has been drafted the directors deliver to the intended nominee, or a person authorised to receive documents on his behalf, written notice of their proposal together with a copy of it. If the nominee agrees to act he endorses a copy of the notice to that effect and returns an endorsed copy to the directors at the address specified by them in the notice for that purpose.[26]

22.18 Within 28 days from the date of the endorsement of the notice (or such longer period as the court may allow) the nominee must submit a report to the court under s 2(2) of the Act stating whether in his opinion meetings of the company and of its creditors should be called to consider the proposal and, if he believes that they should be called, suggesting times, dates and places for such meetings. An annex to the report must contain his opinion of the proposal if he recommends that meetings be called or, if he does not take that view, the reasons for his opinion that they should not be called.[27] A copy of the proposal and a copy or summary of the statement of affairs must be sent to the court with the nominee's report.[28] A copy of the report and of the nominee's comments must be sent to the company and any director, member or creditor is entitled to inspect the court file after the nominee's report has been filed in the court.[29] Section 2(3) lays down that to enable the nominee to prepare his report he must be provided with a statement of affairs in addition to a copy of the proposal. The statement of affairs must be certified as correct to the best of their knowledge and belief by two or more directors of the company or the company secretary and one director.[30]

22.19 Rule 1.5(1) requires the directors to deliver the statement of affairs

25   r 1.3(3).
26   r 1.4.
27   r 1.7(2).
28   r 1.7(1).
29   r 1.7(3) and (4).
30   r 1.5(4).

within 7 days of delivering their proposal to him unless he allows a longer period. The statement of affairs must supplement, amplify and clarify the information already given in the proposal and, in particular, should:

(a) list company assets in a set of categories which facilitate easy identification, with estimated values given for each category;

(b) give details of property on which claims against the company are secured;

(c) give names and addresses of all creditors, divided into those that are preferential, those which are secured and those which are unsecured with details of the amount of their claims;

(d) give particulars of any debts due to or by the company to or by persons connected with it;

(e) names and addresses of company shareholders and details of their shareholdings.

In addition the statement of affairs must give such other particulars as the nominee may require in writing for the purpose of making his report to the court.[31]

22.20   The statement must be made up to a date not earlier than 2 weeks before the date of the notice served on the nominee by the directors unless the nominee allows an extension but this may not be to a date more than 2 months before the date of the notice delivered by the directors. If an extension is granted the nominee must give reasons in support of that decision in his report to the court.[32]

22.21   In addition to the information provided to the nominee in the proposal itself and the statement of affairs, the nominee can insist on certain details and explanations if it appears to him that he cannot properly prepare his report to the court without them. This includes details of previous proposals for voluntary arrangements under the Act and further and better particulars of the circumstances in which, and the reasons why, the company is insolvent or is threatened with insolvency, but extends to any information with respect to the company's affairs that the nominee thinks is necessary for the preparation of his report.[33] The nominee may also insist that the directors inform him whether and in what circumstances any present directors (or persons who have been directors during the period of 2 years before the date on which the report was delivered to the nominee) have, at any time, been concerned in the affairs of another company which

---

31   r 1.5(2).
32   r 1.5(3).
33   r 1.6(1).

has become insolvent, or have themselves been adjudged bankrupt or entered into an arrangement with their creditors.[34] The nominee must be given access to the company's accounts and records for the purpose of preparing his report and considering the directors' proposal.[35]

22.22 On an application made by the person intending to make a proposal for a voluntary arrangement the court may order that the nominee be replaced by another qualified insolvency practitioner if he has failed to submit his report to the court.[36] At least 7 days' notice of the application must be given.[37]

A proposal by a liquidator or administrator

22.23 The requirements as to the proposal and the statement of affairs apply to cases in which an administrator or a liquidator makes the proposal with slight necessary amendments. If the administrator or the liquidator is to appoint some other insolvency practitioner to be the nominee he must prepare his proposal and give notice to the intended nominee in the same way as the directors do if they are making the proposal.[38] He must also serve a copy of the proposal and the name and address of the insolvency practitioner who has agreed to act as nominee on the official receiver if the company is being wound up by the court.[39] If he is himself acting as the nominee, the administrator or liquidator must include in his proposal all matters that the directors are required to include in theirs and such other matters as he considers appropriate to enable members and creditors to reach an informed decision on the proposal.[40] If the company is being wound up by the court a copy of the proposal must be served on the official receiver.[41] However, he does not need to prepare a report on the proposal or file the documents with the court.

Summoning meetings

Nominee not liquidator or administrator
22.24 In any case in which the nominee is not the liquidator or the administrator of the company—whether the proposal has been put forward by the directors or an administrator or liquidator—the person making the

---

34   r 1.6(2).
35   r 1.6(3).
36   s 2(4).
37   r 1.8.
38   r 1.12(1) to (5) and (7).
39   r 1.12(6).
40   r 1.10(1).
41   r 1.10(2).

report to the court has to summon the meetings of the company and of its creditors for the time, date and place set out in the report unless the court directs otherwise.[42] If the nominee, in his report to the court, recommends that the meetings be called, the meetings must be held not less than 14 days nor more than 28 days from the date on which the report was filed in court.[43] At least 14 days' notice of the meetings must be given. In the case of the creditors' meeting the notice must be sent to all creditors of whose claim and address the nominee is aware; both those whose names appear in the statement of affairs and all other creditors. For the members' meeting the notice must be sent to everyone who, to the best of the nominee's belief, is a member of the company.[44]

22.25 Each notice must specify the court to which the nominee's report under s 2 of the Act has been delivered and must list the majorities required at the meeting for the proposal to be approved. The notice must also be accompanied by a copy of the proposal, a copy or (if the nominee so decides) a summary of the statement of affairs and the nominee's comments on the proposal. If a summary of the statement of affairs is sent it must include at least a list of creditors and the amount of their debts.[45]

22.26 In any case in which someone other than the liquidator or the administrator is to be the nominee under the proposal, creditors or members may apply to the court for a direction that the meetings be not held on the dates and at the times proposed or at all. The court is likely to be guided by the view of the nominee in determining this question but has power to decide not to hold the meetings at all even where the nominee has recommended that a voluntary arrangement is appropriate. In the case of a proposal by the liquidator or the administrator with a different person acting as nominee it is perhaps more likely that a proposal would be approved against the wishes of the nominee. However cases of disputes between nominees and the proposers of the scheme are likely to be rare since the nomination is made by the proposers and the proposal is likely to have been discussed extensively with the nominee before it is formally submitted to him.

Liquidator or administrator himself the nominee
22.27 In cases where the liquidator or the administrator is the nominee s 3(2) lays down that he should simply summon meetings of creditors and members without first filing the proposal with the court. The notice he must

---

42 s 3(1).
43 r 1.9(1).
44 s 3(3); r 1.9(2) and r 1.12(7).
45 rr 1.9(2) and (3) and 1.12(7).

give is the same as that required in other cases apart from the fact that he need not send his comments on his own proposal.[46] The effect of the rules is that creditors and members do not have the possibility of challenging the decision to seek a voluntary arrangement in the court at this early stage if the nominee is to be the administrator or liquidator of the company. This is based on the fact that a qualified insolvency practitioner is already in control and will supervise the voluntary arrangement if it is approved. However, the right of challenge under s 6 which exists after the meetings have approved the proposal does apply in these cases.

All meetings

22.28 In all cases regard must be had to the convenience of the creditors in fixing the venue of both the members' meeting and the company meeting. The creditors' meeting must take place first but the two meetings are to be on the same day and must both commence between the hours of 10 am and 4 pm. Proxy forms must be sent out with the notice each of the meetings.[47]

The decision on a proposal and its effects

22.29 The decision whether the proposal is to be accepted and the voluntary arrangement implemented is taken by the meetings of the members of the company and of its creditors.[48] The proposal may be approved with or without modifications which can confer functions, intended for the nominee according to the proposal, on some other qualified insolvency practitioner. However, the Act limits the modifications which can be adopted by excluding those which would cause the proposal to cease to be a composition in satisfaction of the company's debts or a scheme of arrangement of its affairs.[49] Likewise, the meeting cannot approve a proposal or modification which affects the right of a secured creditor of the company to enforce his security without his concurrence.[50] Nor can it agree to reduce the priority accorded to preferential debts or to provide for the payment of lower proportions of some preferential debts than of others without the concurrence of the creditor in question.[51]

22.30 The Rules lay down the procedures to be followed at the meeting, the voting rights of members and creditors and the majorities needed to approve the proposal.[52] The members' meetings, those of the creditors and

46   r 1.11.
47   r 1.13.
48   s 4(1).
49   s 4(2).
50   s 4(3).
51   s 4(4).
52   s 4(5).

any combined meetings are to be chaired by the convener if he is present.[53] If he is unable to attend he may nominate another qualified insolvency practitioner or an employee of the convener or his firm who is experienced in insolvency matters to act as chairman.[54] The chairman is not permitted to use any proxy held by him to vote to change the level of remuneration or expenses proposed for the nominee or the supervisor unless he is following the specific directions of the proxy.[55]

22.31   In addition to the notices sent out to convene the meetings, 14 days' notice to attend must also be given to the directors of the company and anyone whose presence the convener requires and who has been an officer or a director of the company in the 2 years immediately preceding the notice.[56] However, such people may be excluded from attendance at the whole or any part of a meeting if the chairman thinks fit; whether or not a notice has been sent to the person excluded.[57] The meetings will be presumed to have been duly summoned and held despite the fact that some of those to whom notice was to be given have not received it providing it was sent out.[58] However, only those who 'had notice' of the meeting and were entitled to vote at it will be bound by the arrangement after it is approved.[59]

22.32   At the meeting of creditors the right to vote is conferred on those to whom notice of the meeting was sent and the votes are calculated on the basis of the value of the creditor's debt at the date of the meeting or, if the company is being wound up or is the subject of an administration order, the date of its going into liquidation or of the administration order.[60] No vote is allowed in respect of an unliquidated debt or one whose value is not ascertained unless the chairman agrees to give it an estimated minimum value for the purpose of the right to vote.[61] Those not entitled to vote will not be bound by the arrangement and may therefore have to be paid off in full to prevent them from making claims.[62] This includes those whose debts arose after the company went into liquidation or after an administration order was made as well as those whose unliquidated debts or debts of unascertained value are not given an estimated value for voting purposes. This rule will encourage the chairman to estimate the value of such debts.

---

53   r 1.14(1).
54   r 1.14(2).
55   r 1.15.
56   r 1.16(1).
57   r 1.16(2).
58   r 12.16.
59   s 5(2)(b).
60   r 1.17(1) and (2).
61   r 1.17(3).
62   s 5(2)(b).

Those, such as secured creditors, who are entitled to vote but whose votes do not count will be bound by the arrangement.

22.33 The chairman's decision in respect of these matters can be appealed to the court by any member or creditor.[63] If he is in doubt about whether to admit a claim for the purpose of voting he should mark it as objected and allow the creditor to vote subject to the vote being declared invalid later if an objection to the claim is upheld.[64] If the court reverses or varies the chairman's decision or declares a creditor's vote invalid, it has power to order that a further meeting be summoned or to make any other order it thinks just. However, these powers can only be exercised if the court considers that unfair prejudice or material irregularity arise from the matter.[65] An appeal to the court against the chairman's decision must be made within 28 days of the first report of the result of the meeting being filed in court under s 4(6) of the Act.[66] The chairman of the meeting is not personally liable for any costs incurred in such an appeal.[67]

22.34 The majority required at a creditors' meeting for a resolution to approve a proposal or modification is in excess of three quarters in value of creditors present in person or by proxy and voting on the resolution.[68] For any other resolution it is one half in value of that group.[69] A creditor's vote in respect of a claim or part of a claim will not be counted if no written notice of the claim has been given at or before the meeting to the chairman or the convener or if the claim or part of it is secured. If the claim relates to a debt wholly or partly on or secured by a current bill of exchange or promissory note, the vote will only count if the creditor is willing to treat the liability of all those whose liability to him is antecedent to that of the company and who are not bankrupt or (in the case of companies) in liquidation as security in his hands and to estimate the value of that security and deduct it from the claim for voting purposes.[70] Even if it has received the necessary majority of those voting in person or by proxy, a resolution is invalid if those voting against it include more than half in value of the creditors to whom notices of the meeting were sent and who are neither connected to the company nor unable to have votes counted because they gave no notice of claim or have security.

22.35 It is for the chairman to decide who falls into these categories and in

63 r 1.17(5).
64 r 1.17(6).
65 r 1.17(7).
66 r 1.17(8).
67 r 1.17(9).
68 r 1.19(1).
69 r 1.19(2).
70 r 1.19(3).

deciding whether someone is connected with the company he may use information provided under the rules in the statement of claim, by company officers, in the proposal or in the nominee's report to the court. Any proxies used by the chairman on a resolution to alter the level of remuneration or expenses payable to the nominee or the supervisor without following a specific direction in the proxy do not count. The rules on appeals to the court against the decision of the chairman apply to these matters as they do to the qualification of creditors to vote.[71]

22.36   At the members' meetings called to consider the proposal the voting rights of members depend on the provisions of the articles. The shares or other interest that a person has as a member of a company (for example, the guarantee in the case of a company limited in that way) will confer the number of votes laid down in the company's articles for his particular interest.[72] This means that in companies which have different classes of share with different voting rights those rights can be exercised at the members' meeting which considers the proposal. The rules lay down one exception to that rule. If a member would have no vote under the company's articles he is nonetheless entitled to cast one vote for or against the proposal or any modification of it.[73] However, a vote cast under that rule is to be left out of account in determining whether the necessary majority has been achieved at the meeting for a resolution to pass.[74] Similarly a use of a proxy vote by the chairman to alter the level of remuneration or expenses payable to the nominee or supervisor except when specifically directed by the proxy will not be counted in determining the majority.[75]

22.37   Under the rules the majority required at a members' meeting is more than one half in value of the members present in person or by proxy and voting on the resolution. Value is determined by the number of votes conferred on each member by the company's articles.[76] Most commonly this will be one vote per share. The company's articles can expressly provide for a different majority and that provision will prevail over the general rule.[77] Such a provision might stipulate that a majority of two thirds or three quarters is required, or it might require a simple majority of all members and not only those present in person or by proxy and voting on the resolution. It is not in the interests of companies to make the agreement

71   r 1.19(4)–(7).
72   r 1.18(1) and (3).
73   r 1.18(2).
74   r 1.20(2).
75   r 1.20(3).
76   r 1.20(1) as amended by SI 1987 no 1919.
77   r 1.20(1).

of voluntary arrangements more difficult and special provisions in the articles should only be used to protect the special interests of particular groups of members.

22.38 On the day on which they are held the meetings of the creditors and of the members may be adjourned from time to time and, if the chairman thinks fit, they may be held together for the purpose of getting their simultaneous agreement to the proposal with the same modifications (if any have been suggested).[78] If the necessary majority is not obtained at each meeting on that day the chairman may adjourn the meetings for not more than 14 days. If it is so resolved he must adjourn them for such a period.[79] On every occasion when there is an adjournment of one of the meetings, the other one must be held on the same business day and no adjourned meeting can be held more than 14 days after the date of the original meetings.[80] If the adjourned meetings are dealing with a proposal from the directors of the company the nominee must notify the court of each adjournment.[81] If the proposal with the same modification (if any) is not approved by both meetings after their final adjournment then it is deemed to have been rejected.[82] These rules ensure that there is certainty as to the time within which a decision will be reached on the proposal.

22.39 If the voluntary arrangement is approved by the meeting of creditors and two or more insolvency practitioners are appointed to act as supervisor of the arrangement then the meeting may pass a resolution laying down whether they can only act jointly or each have power to act. This can either be done when the members' meeting has also approved the arrangement or in anticipation of that approval.[83] If a resolution is moved at either meeting to appoint a person other than the nominee as supervisor of the arrangement that person's written consent to act and his written confirmation that he is qualified to act as an insolvency practitioner in relation to the company must be produced to the chairman at or before the meeting.[84]

22.40 The chairman of each meeting is required to report the result of the meeting to the court after their conclusion.[85] The report must state whether the arrangement was approved and if so with what modifications (if any) as

78 r 1.21(1).
79 r 1.21(2).
80 r 1.21(3) and (4).
81 r 1.21(5).
82 r 1.21(6).
83 r 1.22(1) and (2).
84 r 1.22(3).
85 s 4(6).

well as the text of the resolutions taken and the decision on each one. It must list the creditors and members present or represented at the meetings and how they voted on each resolution and any other information that the chairman thinks it appropriate to include.[86] The report must be filed with the court within 4 days after the meetings and notice of the result of the meetings must then immediately be sent to each person who was sent notice of the meeting.[87] If the proposal was approved with or without modifications then a copy of the chairman's report must also be sent to the registrar of companies.[88]

22.41 After the approval of the voluntary arrangement by each of the meetings either without any modifications or with the same modifications the arrangement takes effect as if made by the company at the creditors' meeting and binds every person who had notice of and was entitled to vote at that meeting as if he was a party to the voluntary arrangement whether he was present or represented at the meeting or not.[89] From that time the arrangement binds all creditors who had votes; including secured creditors whose votes do not count towards the majority and whose interests may not be affected by the arrangement. It also binds the company as it is taken to have made the arrangement at the meeting of creditors.

22.42 If the company is being wound up or an administration order is in force the court may make an order to stay all proceedings in the winding up or to discharge the administration order or give such directions with respect to the conduct of the winding up or the administration as it thinks appropriate to facilitate the implementation of the arrangement.[90] However that power cannot be exercised earlier than 28 days after the day on which a report of the meetings has been made to the court under s 4(6) or at a time when an application to challenge the arrangement or an appeal in respect of such an application is pending or within the period allowed for such an appeal.[91]

Challenges to the arrangement

22.43 Section 6 allows a challenge to to be mounted in the court to the arrangement on one or both of the grounds that:

(a) the arrangement unfairly prejudices the interests of a creditor member or contributory of the company; or

---

86   r 1.24(1).
87   r 1.24(4).
88   r 1.24(5).
89   s 5(1) and (2).
90   s 5(3).
91   s 5(4).

(b) there has been some material irregularity at or in relation to either of the meetings.[92]

Such an application can be made to the court by any person who was entitled to vote at either meeting according to the rules, the nominee or a person who replaced him, or the liquidator or administrator if the company is in liquidation or subject to an administration order.[93] The application must be made within 28 days after the first day on which a report of the result of the meetings has been filed with the court.[94]

22.44　It is clear that the meaning of 'unfairly prejudicial' in this context will be similar to that applied to the phrase under s 459 of the Companies Act 1985. It may import wider equitable considerations in addition to strict rights.[95] It has been said that the words connote:

> "that there must be harm or prejudice and that such harm must be unfair harm. It plainly implies that there may be harm that is not unfair, and harm, to be within the section, must be alleged to be unfair . . .".[96]

The fact that the prejudice must be unfair makes it clear that the mere fact that a creditor is worse off than he would have been had no arrangement been approved will not be sufficient to support a challenge. Equally, it is unlikely that the effects of the arrangement on a creditor will be regarded as unfair if he supported the arrangement in its final form at the meeting. However, in this context it is not necessary that the applicant be the person unfairly prejudiced by the arrangement (there is no requirement to this effect and the liquidator or administrator is unlikely to be personally affected) or that only part of the body of creditors or members or contributories be unfairly prejudiced as is the case under s 459.

22.45　The existence of an irregularity can form the basis of a successful challenge if it occurred at or in relation to either meeting. It could apply to the conduct of the meeting or matters such as notice or adjournments. However, the irregularity must be material. This means that a merely formal irregularity which had no effect on the outcome of the meeting will not suffice. Unless a successful application is made under s 6 an approval of an arrangement given at a meeting summoned under s 3 of the Act is not invalidated by any irregularity.[97]

92　s 6(1).
93　s 6(2).
94　s 6(3).
95　*Re a Company (No 00477 of 1986)* [1986] PCC 372.
96　Per Harman J in *Re a Company (No 001761 of 1986)* [1987] BCLC 141.
97　s 6(7).

22.46   If the court is satisfied that one of the grounds is made out it may make an order under s 6(4). Such an order may revoke or suspend the approvals given by the meetings and/or give a direction to a person for the summoning of further meetings to consider any revised proposal that may be made by the person who made the original proposal. These powers may be used whichever ground resulted in a successful challenge to the arrangement but are likely to be most appropriate when the challenge was based on the contents and effects of the arrangement rather than a procedural irregularity. If the order is based on a procedural irregularity it may revoke or suspend the approval given by a meeting affected by that problem and/or order that a further meeting be convened to reconsider the original proposal.[98] If the court directs that further meetings be called to consider a revised proposal and is later satisfied that the person who submitted the original proposal does not intend to submit such a proposal it must revoke its direction and revoke or suspend any approval given at the previous meetings.[99]

22.47   The court has power to give such supplemental directions as it thinks fit if it makes an order on an application under s 6. In particular, it may give directions in respect of things done after the approval of the voluntary arrangement by a meeting.[100] This enables the court to undo any steps which may have been taken before its order is made and takes account of the fact that the effects of the arrangement and its binding nature arise as soon as the meetings have approved the arrangement.

22.48   If the court makes an order under s 6 to revoke or suspend the approval given at a meeting, the person who applied for the order must serve a copy of it on the supervisor and on the person who proposed the voluntary arrangement. If the proposal emanated from the directors, service of one copy at the company's registered office will suffice.[101] If the order includes a direction that a person summon a new meeting then a copy must also be served on that person by the person on whose application the order was made.[102] On receiving a copy of the order, the proposer of the arrangement must forthwith give notice of it to all those who were sent notice of one of the meetings and anyone else who appears to be affected by it. The proposers must also give notice to the court within 7 days of receiving their copy of the order of whether they intend to make a revised proposal or invite reconsideration of the original one.[103] A copy of the

---

98   s 6(4).
99   s 6(5).
100   s 6(6).
101   r 1.25(2).
102   r 1.25(3).
103   r 1.25(4).

court's order must be delivered to the registrar of companies by the person on whose application it was made within 7 days of it being made.[104]

Implementing the arrangement

22.49 After the approval of the arrangement the nominee becomes known as the supervisor of the arrangement.[105] The directors, liquidator or administrator of the company must then do all that is necessary to put the supervisor in possession of all the assets of the company included in the arrangement. This, of course, is not necessary where the liquidator or administrator himself becomes the supervisor.[106] If the company is in liquidation or subject to an administration order the supervisor must discharge (or give a written undertaking to discharge out of the first realisation of assets) any balance due to the administrator, official receiver or liquidator by way of remuneration, fees, costs or expenses properly incurred and payable under the Act or the Rules and any advances made in respect of the company before it went into liquidation or was made subject to an administration order.[107] The liquidator, official receiver or administrator have a charge on the assets included in the arrangement for the outstanding balance of such amounts which is subject only to the proper costs and expenses of the supervisor's realisation of such assets.[108] In addition, the supervisor is from time to time to use the proceeds of the realisation of assets to discharge any guarantees properly given by the liquidator, administrator or official receiver and to pay his expenses.[109] It is when a company is being wound up by the court that the official receiver is included in the category of insolvency practitioners who benefit from these rules and in such cases he benefits whether he acted in the capacity of liquidator or not and has priority over the liquidator in respect of sums due to him.[110]

22.50 During the course of the implementation of the voluntary arrangement any of the company's creditors or anyone else dissatisfied with any act, omission or decision of the supervisor may apply to the court. The court may make such order as it thinks fit on such an application including confirming, reversing or modifying any act of the supervisor or giving him directions.[111] In addition the supervisor (like a liquidator in a winding up)

104 r 1.25(5).
105 s 7(2).
106 r 1.23(1).
107 r 1.23(2) and (3).
108 r 1.23(4).
109 r 1.23(5).
110 r 1.23(6).
111 s 7(3).

may apply to the court for directions in relation to any matter arising under the voluntary arrangement. He is also included in the list of persons who may apply to the court for a winding up or administration order in relation to the company.[112]

22.51 The court has a power to appoint supervisors in addition to or in replacement of one or more existing officeholders if it is expedient to do so and difficult, inexpedient or impracticable for it to be done without a court order.[113] In many cases it will be possible for this to be done without application to the court by a procedure laid down as a term of the scheme of arrangement itself.

Accounts, reports and records

22.52 During the course of implementing the voluntary arrangement the supervisor is required to keep accounts and records of his dealings and, in particular of all receipts and payments of money. This obligation is imposed if the arrangement authorises or requires him to carry on the company's business or trade on its behalf or in its name, to realise its assets or otherwise to administer or dispose of any of its funds.[114]

22.53 Every 12 months, beginning with the date of his appointment, the supervisor must prepare an abstract of receipts and payments and send copies of it with his comments on the progress of the arrangement to the court, the registrar of companies, the company, all the creditors who are bound by the arrangement and the company's auditors if it is not in liquidation. The company's members who are bound by the arrangement should also be sent this information unless the court has dispensed with that requirement or ruled that it may be carried out by advertising the availability of the abstract.[115] The abstract must cover the period from the date of appointment or from the date of the last abstract and must be sent within 2 months of the end of the period it covers.[116] If the supervisor is not authorised or required to carry on the business, realise assets or administer or dispose of funds, or if there are no receipts or payments in a given period he must still send a progress report to those mentioned above at the specified times.[117] The dates on which reports or abstracts are to be sent out can be varied by the court on the application of the supervisor.[118]

---

112   s 7(4).
113   s 7(5) and (6).
114   r 1.26(1).
115   r 1.26(2) and (5)(a).
116   r 1.26(3).
117   r 1.26(2) and (4).
118   r 1.26(5)(b).

22.54 At any time before or after the completion of the voluntary arrangement the Secretary of State for Trade and Industry may require the supervisor to produce for inspection all his records and accounts in respect of the arrangement and copies of the abstracts and reports that he has provided either at his premises or elsewhere.[119] The supervisor has a statutory duty to comply with any requirements imposed under Rule 1.27. The Secretary of State may have the accounts and records audited and must be given such further information and assistance as he needs for that purpose.[120]

Completion of the arrangement

22.55 Rule 1.29 lays down that notice of the full implementation of the arrangement must be sent to all the creditors and members of the company who are bound by it not more than 28 days after its final completion unless the court extends the period on the application of the supervisor. A report summarising all receipts and payments made by the supervisor and explaining any difference between the actual implementation of the arrangement and the contents of the proposal as approved by the meetings must accompany the notice. Both documents must also be sent to the court and to the registrar of companies.

ARRANGEMENTS AND RECONSTRUCTIONS UNDER SS 425 TO 427

Scope of s 425

22.56 The provisions of ss 425 to 427 of the Companies Act 1985 are available where any 'compromise or arrangement' is proposed between the company and its creditors or any class of them or the company and its members or any class of them.[121] The word 'arrangement' is stated in s 425(6)(b) to include a reorganisation of share capital by either consolidating shares of different classes or dividing shares into different classes or both. It seems that the terms are very wide. A 'compromise' will exist only where there is some controversy over the rights of the parties to it or some difficulty in the enforcement of rights. Classically, it will involve the part payment of a claim.[122] Indeed, where creditors are not to be paid in strict accordance with their rights in a winding up, s 425 or ss 1–7 of the

---

119   r 1.27(1) and (2).
120   r 1.27(3).
121   s 425(1).
122   See *Mercantile Investment & General Trust v International Co of Mexico* [1893] 1 Ch 484 at 489n.

Insolvency Act 1986 are the appropriate methods to use. The sanction of the court under s 167 should not be used as a substitute for such procedures as this deprives the dissenting creditors of their right to express their views to the court and to enjoy its protection.[123]

22.57 An 'arrangement' need not involve such an element and is not qualified in meaning by being adjacent to the word 'compromise'. There need be no dispute or difficulty to be resolved for an arrangement within the meaning of the section to exist.[124] However, it has been held that in each case there must be some element of give and take and not merely the abandonment of rights without any advantage accruing in return.[125] There must be some contractual element for an arrangement to exist and the company must be a party to it for s 425 to apply.[126]

22.58 A scheme proposed under s 425 must not be *ultra vires* the company or illegal.[127] If it involves a reduction of the capital of the company it will be necessary for the procedures laid down by the Act for such a step to be used in addition to s 425. Sections 135 to 141 will apply to the reduction of share capital but reductions carried out in accordance with those sections will not need to use the procedures in ss 159–181 for the purchase or redemption by the company of its own shares.[128] If the company is to provide financial assistance for the purchase of its shares under the proposal, s 151 of the Act will not apply so long as the s 425 scheme is approved by the court.

22.59 Unlike ss 110–111 of the Insolvency Act 1986, the s 425 procedure can be used if the company is not to be wound up. It can also provide a means of agreeing that debenture holders will take shares in place of their security against the wishes of a minority.[129] Sections 1 to 7 of the Insolvency Act 1986 cannot be used in this way, as the right of secured creditors to enforce their security can only be affected with their concurrence under those provisions.

The procedure under ss 425 to 427

Convening class meetings
22.60 Section 425(1) requires an application to be made to the court for meetings to be summoned of the members or class of members or creditors

---

123 See *Re Trix Ltd* [1970] 1 WLR 1421.
124 See *Re Guardian Assurance Co* [1917] 1 Ch 431.
125 *Re NFU Development Trust Ltd* [1972] 1 WLR 1548.
126 See *Re Savoy Hotel Ltd* [1981] 3 All ER 646.
127 *Re Oceanic Steam Navigation Co* [1939] Ch 41.
128 s 143(3)(b) Companies Act 1985.
129 *Re Empire Mining Co* (1890) 44 Ch D 402.

or class of creditors with whom the company proposes to make the compromise or arrangement. The meeting will then be summoned in the manner the court directs. The application to the court is made by a summons for directions which can be taken out by the company, its liquidator or administrator or any creditor or member of the company. Since the company must be a party to the scheme under s 425(1), the company should approve it by the decision of the board or of its general meeting and if there is no prospect of such approval the court will exercise its discretion by deciding not to call the meetings as they would not serve any useful purpose.[130] No approval for the scheme is required of any class unaffected by the proposed scheme or merely gaining a concession or gift from it.[131]

22.61 It will sometimes be difficult to determine what constitutes a class for the purpose of deciding whether separate meetings are necessary of different groups of members or creditors. The criterion to be applied was laid down by Bowen LJ in *Sovereign Life Assurance Co v Dunn*:[132]

> "We must give such a meaning to the term 'class' as will prevent the section being so worked as to result in confiscation and injustice, and . . . it must be confined to those persons whose rights are not so dissimilar as to make it impossible for them to consult together with a view to their common interest."

In that case the interests (as creditors) of policy holders in an insurance company whose policies had matured were sufficiently different from those of policy holders whose policies had not matured to make separate meetings necessary. It is clear that separate class meetings of preferential, secured and unsecured creditors must be held.

22.62 If shares are divided into different classes a meeting must be summoned of those holding each class. Separate meetings must be held of those with fully paid and partly paid shares.[133] In a scheme which was intended to result in the takeover of the company by a different company, a member holding over 50% of the share capital of the former company which was itself a wholly owned subsidiary of the latter company was held to be a member of a separate class from all the other members—despite the fact that they all held ordinary shares.[134] One of the reasons for the expense and difficulty involved in using these provisions is the fact that if the applicant does not call the necessary meetings of all separate classes that

---

130 *Re Savoy Hotel Ltd* [1981] 3 All ER 646.
131 *Re Tea Corporation* [1904] 1 Ch 12.
132 [1892] 2 QB 573 at 583.
133 *Re United Provident Assurance Co* [1910] 2 Ch 477.
134 *Re Hellenic & General Trust Ltd* [1976] 1 WLR 123.

objection will only be raised on the petition for the court's sanction after the meetings have been held and not on the hearing of the originating summons requesting the court to summon the meetings.[135]

22.63 Section 426(2) and (4) lay down that with every notice sent out to a creditor or member to summon a class meeting there must also be a statement explaining the effect of the proposed scheme, any material interests of directors of the company or trustees of its debentures (as such or as members or creditors) and any differences between the way those interests will be affected by the scheme and the way it will affect the like interests of others. If the meetings are advertised the availability of the statement free of charge to all members and creditors must be contained in the advertisement.[136] Section 426(7) imposes a duty on the directors of the company and the trustees of its debentures to give the company notice of matters relating to themselves that may be necessary to enable it to carry out the requirements of the section. Failure by the company to provide the information required amounts to an offence by the company and any of its officers (including the liquidator and the trustee of a deed securing debentures) who cannot show that his default was the result of the failure of another person who was a director or a trustee of debentures to supply the necessary particulars of his interests.[137]

22.64 The court will ensure that the explanatory circular is fair and as that, as far as possible, it gives all the information necessary to enable those who receive it to decide how to vote.[138] The requirement for the disclosure of the interests of the directors is so strict that failure to do so can only be justified on the basis that the omission is *de minimis* and could not influence the mind of a reasonable shareholder. In particular, any change in the interests of a director between the date of sending the circular and the date of the meeting must result in a new circular being sent out unless it can be shown that no reasonable person would change his view of the scheme if he were aware of the change in question.[139] This requirement does not appear in s 426 but failure to circulate information about a change in interests will affect the court's willingness to confirm the scheme after the meetings.[139a]

The meetings
22.65 The court's directions will govern the conduct of the meetings. A majority of three quarters in value of those present and voting in person or by proxy is required in each meeting before the compromise or

135   Practice Note [1934] WN 142.
136   s 426(3) and (5).
137   s 426(6).
138   *Re Dorman Long & Co Ltd* [1934] Ch 635.
139   See *Re Jessel Trust* [1985] BCLC 119 and *Re Minster Assets plc* [1985] BCLC 200.
139a See *Re MB Group Ltd* (1989) 5 BCC 684.

arrangement can be sanctioned by the court.[140] In the case of a company limited by shares the value attributable to the interest of a member will be easy to determine. However, even in the case of a company limited by guarantee without a share capital the expression is to be taken to the value of the stake that each member has in the company—in that case the amount to which he is entitled on a distribution.[141] In estimating the voting rights of any class of creditors a liquidator is not bound by any estoppel based on a representation made by the company before liquidation began even if the estoppel would affect the value of the debts of those creditors.[142]

Court sanction and orders

22.66 After the approval of the scheme by the meetings of creditors or members, the court must give its sanction to make the compromise or arrangement binding. The court exercises a discretion in deciding whether to grant its sanction to the scheme. It will first of all consider whether the scheme has been approved in accordance with the provisions of the Act. This will involve considering any objections to the groups regarded as constituting classes for the purpose of holding the meetings, the question of whether the scheme is a compromise or an arrangement which can be dealt with under s 425 and whether the notice and statements issued for the meeting conformed with the Act.

22.67 In addition it will look to the question of whether the scheme was made in good faith and is fair and reasonable. The test of fairness and reasonableness is whether an intelligent and honest man acting in respect of his interest might approve the proposal.[143] In general it will be assumed that shareholders acting honestly are better judges than the court of what is to their commercial advantage. However, the scheme may be refused court sanction despite votes in its favour if it is shown that the majority in a class voted in the way that they did because of their interests as shareholders of another class.[144] The scheme must not be a fraud on the minority. It must be one that can reasonably be considered by sensible business people to be for the benefit of the class as such and not a mere confiscation. The object of the section is not that 'one person should be a victim and that the rest of the body should feast upon his rights'.[145] The scheme, after it is sanctioned by the court, will not take effect until an office copy of the court order giving sanction is registered with the registrar of companies.[146] It is then binding

---

140 s 425(2).
141 *Re NFU Development Trust Ltd* [1972] 1 WLR 1548.
142 *Re Exchange and Commodities (No 3)* (1987) 3 BCC 48.
143 *Re English, Scottish and Australian Chartered Bank* [1893] 3 Ch 385 at 399.
144 *Carruth v ICI* [1937] AC 707 at 769.
145 *Re Alabama, New Oreleans, Texas & Pacific Junction Railway Co* [1891] 1 Ch 213.
146 s 425(3).

on all creditors, all members of the company or all members of the class with whom it was made and on the company or its liquidator. Even the minority who voted against it are bound.

22.68 Section 427 permits the court to make a number of orders to assist in carrying out a scheme once it has been approved. These powers can be used on granting the sanction of the court or at a later date. They are applicable in cases where the compromise or arrangement was proposed for the purpose of or in connection with the reconstruction of the company or the amalgamation of two or more companies and the whole or any part of the undertaking or property of a company is to be transferred to another company under the scheme.[147] In such cases s 427(3) enables the court to provide for:

(a) the transfer of the whole or part of the undertaking, property or liabilities of a transferor company to a transferee company;

(b) the allotment or appropriation in accordance with the scheme of any shares, debentures, policies or like interests in a transferee company;

(c) the continuation of or by the transferee company of legal proceedings pending by or against the transferor company;

(d) the dissolution without winding up of a transferor company;

(e) provisions (of a kind and at a time that the court directs) to be made for those dissenting from the compromise or arrangement;

(f) incidental, consequential and supplemental matters necessary fully and effectively to carry out the reconstruction or amalgamation.

Such orders have the effect of vesting any property and imposing any liabilities that they transfer in the transferee company. If the order so directs the property can be freed from any charge which was to cease to have effect by virtue of the scheme.[148] An order under the section must be registered with the registrar of companies within 7 days of being made.[149]

Mergers and divisions of public companies

22.69 A new s 427A and sch 15A were inserted in the Companies Act 1985 by statutory instrument to implement the requirements of the Third Company Law Directive of the EC with effect from 1 January 1988.[150] Sections 425 to 427 have effect subject to the new section and the schedule as regards those schemes to which they apply and in which no application

147 s 247(2).
148 s 427(4).
149 s 427(5).
150 Companies (Mergers and Divisions) Regulations 1987 (SI 1987 no 1991); and see Directive 78/855/EEC OJ L295/36 of 20 October 1978.

was made to the court before under s 425(1) before 1st January 1988.[151] The new section does not apply to compromises or arrangements if the company in respect of which they are made is being wound up.[152] However, in the case of a company subject to an administration order or administrative receivership they can apply. They apply to any proposed compromise or arrangement of the kind specified in s 425(1) involving a public company in either a scheme of reconstruction or an amalgamation of two or more companies if the consideration for the transfer or each of the transfers involved is to be shares in the transferee company or companies receivable by members of the transferor company or companies.[153] It must be emphasised that these provisions do not apply to takeovers by the acquisition of shares in a company whether by cash offer or an exchange of shares but only to schemes of arrangement and reconstructions.

22.70   It is a further precondition for the application of the provisions that the compromise or arrangement falls into one of the cases set out in s 427A(2).[154] Those cases are that under the scheme:

(1) The undertaking, property and liabilities of the company in respect of which the scheme is proposed are to be transferred to another public company other than one formed for the purpose of or in connection with the scheme.

(2) The undertaking, property and liabilities of each of two or more companies (including the one in respect of which the scheme is proposed) are to be transferred to a company set up for the purpose of or in connection with the scheme. The latter company need not be a public company.

(3) The undertaking, property and liabilities of the company in respect of which the scheme is proposed are to be divided among or transferred to two or more companies each of which is either a public company or a company formed for the purpose of or in connection with the scheme.[155]

22.71   If a scheme affected by s 427A is proposed under s 425, the pre-existing transferee company, its administrator if it is subject to an administration order, or any of its members or creditors can apply to the court for an order that meetings of the shareholders or creditors of that company or of classes of them be summoned. Schedule 15A lays down rules for the procedures to be followed and the information to be provided in cases to which s 427A applies. It is not proposed to deal with those rules in

151   s 427A(1) and (5).
152   s 427A(4).
153   s 427A(1)(a) and (c); and see s 427A(8) for definitions.
154   s 427A(1)(b).
155   s 427A(2).

detail here. They essentially import requirements laid down in the directive for the procedure to be followed. Those rules are intended to protect the interests of shareholders in each pre-existing company involved by ensuring that full information about the proposed scheme is available to them and that a draft scheme has been approved by the directors of all pre-existing companies involved.[156] In particular, the schedule specifies the documents and information to be made available and they include a director's report on the scheme and a separate independent expert's report.[157]

22.72 The rights of holders of securities to which special rights attach but which are not held in the capacity of shareholder or creditor are protected.[158] The rights of shareholders of pre-existing transferee companies are protected by the requirement that meetings be held and that a 75% majority approves the scheme. This is in addition to the requirement under s 425(2) for a similar majority in the case of creditors and members (and classes of them) of the company subject to the arrangement or reconstruction.[159]

22.73 The court will stipulate in its order the date on which the transfer of the assets or undertaking under the scheme and any dissolution of a company will take effect and, if necessary, a date not more than 6 months later by which any further steps to achieve a transfer must have been taken.[160]

AGREEMENTS WITH CREDITORS AT COMMON LAW

22.74 It is possible to create a contract between a company and any particular creditor or creditors to change the rights of the creditor.[161] So long as consideration is provided it is possible to agree a composition with creditors outside the provisions of the Insolvency Act 1986 and the Companies Act 1985. In a composition agreement the consideration which ensures that part payment of a debt operates as a discharge of the whole debt can be the agreement among creditors that each will forgo part of their claim. Alternatively it could be the provision of shares in the company or consideration in some other non-cash form in return for the release of its obligation. This may be any agreement to accept payment of less than the amount due in full satisfaction of a claim or a permanent or temporary

156 sch 15A paras 2, 3, 6 and 10.
157 *Ibid* paras 4 and 5.
158 *Ibid* para 8.
159 *Ibid* para 1.
160 *Ibid* para 9(2) and (3).
161 See *Hirachand Punamchand v Temple* [1911] 2 KB 330.

agreement that claims will not be enforced. It would even be possible to convert debt to equity or arrange a reconstruction of the company by these means.The difficulty with such arrangements is the fact that every creditor must enter the agreement if all are to be bound. Any one creditor can demand payment in full and threaten to petition for the company to be wound up or otherwise to enforce his debt. For these reasons, it is unlikely that an agreement at common law will be used to reach a settlement in any but the simplest cases. Sections 1 to 7 of the Insolvency Act 1986 provide a means of achieving an arangement by majority vote and may be used in combination with an administration order. Sections 110 to 111 of that Act and 425 to 427 of the Companies Act 1985 provide other possible solutions to this problem based on majority decisions.

22.75   In the past it has been possible to persuade a court to dismiss a winding up petition on the ground that a majority of the creditors have for good commercial reasons voted at an informal creditors' meeting for an informal winding up procedure.[162] It is likely that the court will now expect such a case to be dealt with under Part I of the Insolvency Act 1986. The similar tendency for the courts to refuse to complete garnishee proceedings or a charging order if this will prevent an informal arrangement can also be expected to be superseded by a requirement that Part I be used as a condition of success by the company in such proceedings.[163] A court may be willing to give a short adjournment to allow a Part I scheme already in preparation to be completed.

---

162   *Re Brendacot Ltd* (1986) 2 BCC 99164.
163   *D Wilson (Birmingham) Ltd v Metropolitan Property Developments Ltd* [1975] 2 All ER 814 and *Rainbow v Moorgate Properties Ltd* [1975] 1 WLR 788.

Index

Note: All references are to paragraph numbers.

Accountants—
 liens, 6.12
Accounts—
 default in complying with legislation, 21.68–21.72
 financial records—
  compulsory winding up, 16.54–16.55
  voluntary winding up, 16.56–16.59
 generally, 16.47
 Insolvency Services Account—
  compulsory winding up, 16.49–16.50
  generally, 16.48
  investments, 16.61
  unclaimed funds, 16.59–16.60
  use of money in, 15.143, 16.52
  voluntary winding up, 16.51
 payments of dividends, 16.59–16.60
 special managers, 15.25
 unclaimed funds, 16.59–16.60
 voluntary arrangements, 22.52–22.54
Administration orders—
 administrative receiver already appointed, 13.23
 administrators, *see* Administrators
 application—
  affidavit, 13.09, 13.11
  applicant, 13.05, 13.08
  directors' position, 13.08
  hearing, 13.12, 13.23
  notice, 13.12
  petition, 13.09, 13.12
  report recommending, 13.10, 13.11
  service, 13.12
 banks, 13.22
 conditions, 13.13–13.16
 Cork Report, 13.01–13.02
 creditor protection, 13.118, *and see* Creditors' committee *and* Creditors' meetings
  (administration orders)
 discharge, 13.54, 13.114, 22.42
 discretion to make, 13.17
 duration, 13.33
 effects, 13.27–13.28, 13.43–13.44
 exclusiveness, 13.32
 generally, 13.03
 insurance companies, 13.22
 interim, 13.24, 13.56
 invoices, 13.46

Administration orders—*cont*
  meetings—
    creditors', *see* Creditors' meetings (administration orders)
    members', 13.105
  moratorium, 13.25–13.26, 13.28, 13.34–13.40
  notice, 13.47
  prohibition on enforcement of securities, 13.37
  refusal, 13.18, 13.21
  remedies, 13.45
  repossession of goods during, 13.36, 13.38–13.40
  retention of title agreements, 13.39–13.40
  secured creditor's enforcement during, 13.35
  statement of affairs—
    affidavits, 13.51
    application to court, 13.52
    content, 13.51
    costs, 13.52
    disclosure, exclusion, 13.53
    notice requiring, 13.48
    persons liable, 13.49–13.50, 13.52
    time to submit, 13.50, 13.52
  statutory purposes, 13.14–13.16, 13.19–13.20
    variation, 13.54
  unfair prejudice, 13.102, 13.129–13.131
  use, 13.06–13.07
  utilities' supplies, 13.41–13.42
  variation, 13.54
  veto of holder of floating charge, 13.03–13.04, 13.23, 13.69
  voluntary arrangements, *see* Voluntary arrangements
Administrative receivers—
  accounts—
    ceasing to act, 12.26
    enforcement, 12.27
    first, 12.26
    form, 12.26
    submission, 12.25
  acting severally, 11.36
  administration order, position on, 13.26, 13.28–13.29, 13.31–13.32
  agency—
    background, 12.01
    responsibility of debenture holder, 12.04
    special position, 12.02–12.03
    termination, 12.05
  appointment—
    acceptance—
      mode, 11.42
      time in which to make, 11.40
    defect in, 11.31
    exercise of power, 11.23
    grounds for, 11.19–11.22
    invalid—
      indemnity, 11.26, 11.29–11.30
      protection of third persons, 11.32
    joint receivers, 11.35–11.38
    liquidation, company in, 11.39
    method, 11.33–11.34

Administrative receivers—*cont*
  notification—
    advertisement, 11.45, 11.50
    business communications, 11.43
    company, 11.46
    contents of notices, 11.47
    creditors, 11.46
    proof, 11.49
    register of charges, 11.44
    unnecessary, 11.51
    writing, 11.49
   time, 11.41
  validity—
    debenture's validity, 11.26–11.28
    generally, 11.24
    satisfaction of debenture's conditions, 11.25
  compulsory winding up, effect, 14.192
  Cork Report, 11.03–11.04, 11.09
  definition, 11.05–11.08
  disqualifications—
    corporate bodies, 11.16
    generally, 11.15
    insolvency practitioner disqualifications, 11.18
    undischarged bankrupts, 11.17
  documents—
    categories, 12.30
    confidentiality, 12.96–12.97
    ownership, 12.29–12.30
  duties—
    care, 12.64–12.66
    certificate of insolvency, issue, 12.61–12.62
    conflict of interests, 12.68
    contractual, 12.67
    creditors—
      committee, *see* Creditors' committee (administrative receivership)
      meeting, 12.40
      secured, 12.88–12.92
    enforcement, making returns, 12.27
    fiduciary, 12.68
    generally, 12.63
    officeholder, as, 12.94–12.95
    position of—
      debenture holder, 12.66
      guarantor, 12.65
      third parties, 12.95
    publicise appointment, 12.31
    report—
      content, 12.37–12.39
      limited disclosure of content, 12.36, 12.39
      liquidation, 12.35
      meeting of unsecured creditors, 12.33–12.34
      recipients, 12.32–12.34
      registrar of companies, 12.36
      time for preparation, 12.32
    supply of information, 12.28–12.30
  employment contracts, 12.09, 12.86–12.87
    remuneration as preferential debt, 12.128

Administrative receivers—*cont*
  ending receivership—
    death, 12.138
    distribution, 12.120–12.125
    notice, 12.120
    order of payment, 12.120–12.122, 12.125–12.126
    preferential creditors, 12.127–12.131
      categories, 12.128
    protection for administrative receiver, 12.131
    removal, 12.135–12.136
    resignation, 12.137
    vacation of office, 12.132–12.134
  examination of people by court—
    abroad, 12.105
    costs, 12.111
    enforcement by court, 12.109–12.110
    generally, 12.102–12.108
  independence, 12.135
  liquidation—
    accounting to liquidator, 12.116
    appointment after, 12.115
    effect, 12.112–12.119
    position after, 12.05–12.06, 12.112
    public examination, 12.119
    remuneration on, 12.117–12.118
    status on, 12.06, 12.113
  origins, 11.02–11.04
  personal liability for contracts—
    Cork Report, 12.07
    employment contracts, 12.09
    exclusion by administrative receiver, 12.12
    general position, 12.07
    indemnity, 12.11
    prior to appointment, 12.08
    set off, 12.10
  powers—
    borrowing, 12.83
    codification of, 5.04, 7.11
    cooperation with, requiring, 12.101–12.102
    court's guidance, 12.71, 12.120
    debenture prevailing over statute, 12.69, 12.72
    delivery up of company property to, 12.100
    disputes about exercise, 12.73
    general, 12.72
    generally, 12.69–12.70
    hive-down, 12.84–12.87
    information, requiring, 12.101
    officeholder, as, 12.94–12.95
    property—
      charged, 12.88–12.92
      expenses, 12.75
      getting in, 12.75–12.77
      leasing, 12.78–12.79
      meaning, 12.70
      selling, 12.78–12.80
        charged property, 12.88–12.92
      undervalue transactions, 12.77

Administrative receivers—*cont*
    protection of third persons, 12.74
    sale of company as going concern, 12.81–12.83
    summoning people before court, 12.102–12.111
      examination abroad, 12.105
    trading, continuance, 12.81–12.83
  professional code, 11.10
  protection of third persons, 11.32, 12.74
  qualifications, 11.09–11.14
  statement of affairs—
    concurrence in, 12.19
    content, 12.15
    deponents—
      application to court by, 12.22–12.24
      expenses, 12.17
      notice to, 12.14
      release from obligations, 12.21–12.22
    discretions of administrative receiver, 12.21–12.22
    duty to obtain information, 12.13
    form, 12.16
    limited disclosure, 12.18
    time for submission, 12.20–12.21
      extension, 12.21–12.22
    verification, 12.16
  utilities' supplies, 12.98–12.99
  value added tax, certificate of insolvency, 12.61–12.62
  see also Insolvency practitioners
Administrators—
  appointment, 13.27, 133.55–13.56
  court's directions, 13.62
  discharge, 13.65
  duties—
    accounts, submission, 13.88
    agent, as, 13.83, 13.84
    breach, sale at loss, 13.81
    comparison with—
      director, 13.83
      liquidator, 13.83, 13.84
    conflict of interests, 13.83
    fiduciary, 13.83
    getting in company's property, 13.85
    management, 13.86
    meetings of creditors, 13.87
    owed to company, 13.83
    proposals, acting in accordance with, 13.86
    reports, 13.114, 13.118
  interim, 13.56
  notice, 13.55
  powers—
    agent of company, as, 13.66
    charged property—
      crystallisation, 13.73
      disposal, 13.73
      floating charges, 13.69–13.73, 13.81, 13.91
      generally, 13.68–13.69
      goods, third party's, 13.73
      liens, 13.73

Administrators—*cont*
 loss on sale, 13.81
  order for disposal, 13.73–13.80, 13.82
  priority retention, 13.69–13.72
  unfair prejudice, 13.82
  value decline, 13.81
 consent necessary, 13.59–13.60
 control of company, 13.59–13.60, 13.63–13.65
 employees—
  adoption of existing contracts, 13.91, 13.92
  appointment, 13.67
  termination of contracts, 13.92
 general, 13.58–13.62
 generally, 13.57
 hive-down, 13.64
 limitation, 13.62
 meetings, calling, 13.63
 property—
  gathering in, 13.61
  schemes, 12.93
 realising company's property, 13.61
 retention of title cases, 13.72
 third parties, 13.66–13.68
  protection, 13.66, 13.77
 winding up petition, 13.65
 within company, 13.59–13.60, 13.63–13.65
 proposals—
  acting in accordance with, 13.86
  annexed statement, 13.103
  approval, 13.114
  consideration, 13.106–13.117
  continuation of business, 13.100
  creditors, function, 13.101
  guidelines on procedures, statutory, 13.101
  meetings—
   creditors, *see* Creditors' meetings (administration orders)
   members, 13.105
  presenting, 13.104–13.105
  producing, 13.99, 13.103
  rejection, 13.114
  reports, 13.114
  revision, 13.115–13.117
 provisional liquidator, as, 13.65
 qualification, 13.55
 release, 13.93
 remuneration—
  basis, 13.94
  fixing, 13.94–13.95
  increasing, 13.95, 13.97
  joint administrators, 13.95
  reduction, 13.98
  solicitor administrator, 13.96
  vacation of office, 13.90, 13.91
 resignation, 13.89
 vacation of office—
  death, 13.89, 13.93
  generally, 13.89

Administrators—*cont*
    liabilities incurred during administration, 13.91
    notice, 13.89
    order to—
        fill vacancy, 13.55, 13.89
        remove administrator, 13.89
    remuneration and expenses, 13.90, 13.91
    see also Insolvency practitioners
Aircraft as security—
    generally, 3.28
    liens, 8.135
    possession, 7.09
    registration of charges, 8.40, 8.135
    priority, 8.135

Book debts as security—
    assignment to factor, 4.47–4.48
    creation, 4.35
    equitable charge, 4.35–4.36
    fixed charge, 4.39–4.45
    floating charge, 4.42–4.46
    future debts, 4.35–4.37
    legal mortgage, 4.37
    meaning of book debt, 4.38
    priorities, 4.39
    registration, 4.38, 8.35–8.37
Borrowing—
    agency—
      powers—
        authority—
          apparent, 1.18
          before Companies Bill 1989, 1.20–1.21
          Companies Bill 1989, 1.22–1.27
          express, 1.15
          implied, 1.16
          none, 1.19
          rule in *Turquand's* case, 1.17
        generally, 1.13
        limitation, 1.14
        management, 1.14
    capacity of company—
      before Companies Bill 1989, 1.02–1.09
      Companies Bill 1989, 1.10–1.12, 1.22–1.27
      'decided on by directors', 1.07–1.08
      implication of power, 1.04
      objects clause, 1.02–1.03
      trading company, 1.02, 1.04
      ultra vires—
        doctrine, 1.02–1.09
        effect of—
          application, 1.05
          good faith, 1.06, 1.08
        extension of term, 1.03
        tracing money, 1.09
    generally, 1.01
    security interests—
      common law, 1.29—1.31

Borrowing—*cont*
   Diamond Report, 1.36
   equitable—
      charge, 1.32, 1.34
      mortgage, 1.33–1.34, 5.02
     fixed charge, 5.01–5.02
     floating charge, 1.35
     future property, 1.29–1.30, 1.32
     generally, 1.28
     mortgage, 1.29
     pledge, 1.31

Charges of land—
   advantages, 2.05
   equitable, 1.32, 1.34, 2.14–2.15
     registered land, 2.15
   floating, *see* Floating charges
   see also Mortgages of land *and* Registration of company charges
Charging orders—
   absolute—
      effect, 6.82
      making, 6.78–6.79
      refusal, 6.78–6.79, 6.82
   application for, 6.76
   availability, 6.76
   beneficial interests, 6.75
   enforcement, 6.80–6.82
   incomplete at liquidation, 18.39
   injunction with, 6.81
   nature, 6.80
   nisi, 6.76, 6.82
   notice, 6.77
   priority, 8.140
     floating charges, 8.93
   procedure, 6.76
   registration, 6.80–6.81
   use, 6.74
Charitable company—
   Companies Bill 1989, 1.11–1.12
Chattels as security—
   generally, 3.01
   imported goods exemption, 3.09
   mortgage—
     equitable—
       creation, 3.05
       future property, 3.05–3.06, 3.09
       hypothecation letter, 3.08–3.09
       registration by company, 3.07, 8.128
     generally, 3.02
     legal—
       creation, 3.03
       fraud, 3.04
     priority, 8.128
     registration, 8.128
   pledge, *see* Pledge of chattels
Choses in action as security—
   equitable assignment—
     creation, 4.10–4.12

Choses in action as security—*cont*
  legal choses in action, 4.14
  notice, 4.13
  generally, 4.02–4.04
  meaning of choses in action, 4.01
  personal chattels distinguished, 4.02
  priority—
    generally, 8.112
    rule in *Dearle* v *Hall*—
      knowledge of assignee, 8.115
      nature of notice, 8.116–8.117
      property covered, 8.113–8.114
      stop notices, 8.118
  registration, 4.04
  statutory assignment—
    creation, 4.05–4.07
    equitable choses in action, 4.06
    notice, 4.08
    prior equities, 4.09
Committee of inspection, *see* Liquidation committee
Compulsory winding up—
  affidavits, 14.100, 14.160
  banks, 14.156
  commencement, 14.99, 14.174
  discretion of court, 14.88, 14.163
    exercise, 14.165–14.166
  effects—
    administrative receiver, on, 14.192
    agents of company, 14.191
    avoidance of—
      dispositions, 14.181–14.182, 14.184–14.186
      share transfers, 14.181–14.183
    directors, 14.193
    employment contracts, 14.190–14.191
    execution against company, 14.189
    generally, 14.175
    proceedings against company, 14.179–14.180
    validation of dispositions, 14.185–14.187
      court's discretion, 14.188
  employment contracts, 14.190–14.191
  grounds—
    generally, 14.106
    inability to pay debts—
      administration order for part undertaking, 14.122
      amount, 14.130
      cash flow, 14.117–14.118, 14.122
      evidence, 14.123
      execution unsatisfied, 14.130
      generally, 14.115
      overall financial position, 14.116–14.123
      statutory demand, 14.124–14.129
      value of assets less than liabilities, 14.118–14.119
    just and equitable—
      construction, 14.131
      deadlock, 14.143–14.144
      disappearance of company's substratum, 14.139–14.142
      fraud, 14.137–14.138
      illegality, 14.137

Compulsory winding up—*cont*
    investigation, need, 14.138
    misconduct, 14.150–14.152
    oppression, 14.150–14.152
    partnership analogy, 14.145–14.149
    unfair prejudice, 14.148
    unreasonable behaviour of contributory petitioners, 14.149
    use—
        by creditors, 14.132
        generally, 14.133, 14.135
    number of members below minimum, 14.114
    public companies—
        non-compliance with share capital requirements, 14.108–14.109
        old, 14.110
    special resolution, 14.107
    specialist, 14.153–14.159
    suspension of business, 14.111–14.113
hearing, 14.160–14.162
insurance companies, 14.95, 14.154–14.155
investment companies, 14.95, 14.157–14.159
jurisdiction—
    case stated for High Court, 14.57
    county court, 14.51–14.53, 14.56
    High Court, 14.51, 14.53–14.54
    petitions in both High Court and county court, 14.55
liquidation committee, *see* Liquidation committee
liquidator, *see* Liquidators
meetings—
    calling, 14.196–14.198
    final creditors' meeting, 14.198
    notice, 14.201, 14.203
    official receiver's position, 14.196, 14.201, 14.203, 14.207
    see also Meetings
order—
    appeal against, 14.171, 14,174
    costs, 14.171
    drawing up, 14.173
    just and equitable ground, 14.163
    notice, 14.173, 14.174
    nullity, 14.177
    public interest, 14.166
    rectification, 14.176
    rescission, 14.176, 14.177
    service, 14.173
    stay, 14.176–14.178
petition—
    adjournment, 14.164
    advertisement—
        failure to make, 14.162
        generally, 14.101
        premature, 14.105, 14.162
        readvertisement, 14.162
    costs, 14.171
    form, 14.97
    group of companies, 14.59, 14.103
    injunctive relief, 14.72–14.73, 14.89
    multiple, 14.59

Compulsory winding up—*cont*
    opposition of majority of creditors, 14.170
    presentation, 14.98–14.99
    restraint of prosecution, 14.72–14.74
    service, 14.98, 14.102, 14.104
    several, 14.103
    verification, 14.100, 14.160
    voluntary liquidation already begun, 14.167–14.170
    withdrawal, 14.162
    petitioners—
    administrator, 14.64
    Bank of England, 14.156
    company, 14.61–14.62
    contributory—
      deceased, 14.80
      gain from winding up, 14.84–14.85
      generally, 14.77–14.78
      interest in winding up, 14.86–14.87
      majority rule, principle, 14.88, 14.89
      meaning, 14.77
      restrictions, 14.81–14.83, 14.89
      trustee in bankruptcy of, 14.79
    creditor—
      contingent creditor, 14.70
      debt's existence, 14.69
      dispute about debt, 14.71
      executor of deceased creditor, 14.66
      garnishor, 14.68
      generally, 14.65–14.66
      judgment creditor, 14.75
      majority's views, 14.88
      malicious, 14.74
      opposition, 14.76
      unliquidated claims, 14.67
    directors, 14.62–14.63
    ill motive, 14.165
    joint, 14.59, 14.76
    possible, 14.58, 14.60
    receiver, 14.64
    Secretary of State—
      generally, 14.90
      investigation, 14.91–14.92
      just and equitable, 14.91, 14.134, 14.136
      non-compliance with statutory requirements, 14.95
      public—
        companies, 14.95, 14.108, 14.110
        interest, 14.91, 14.93
      specialist powers, 14.95, 14.154, 14.157
      trading practices of company, 14.94
    Securities and Investment Board, 14.157
    substitution by court, 14.162, 14.164
  refusal, 14.76, 14.88
  relation back doctrine, 14.40, 14.53, 14.112
  reports, 16.115, 16.116
  resolutions, possible, 14.30
  statement of affairs, 14.205
  stay of other proceedings, 14.179–14.180

Compulsory winding up—*cont*
  see also Winding up
Conditional sale agreements—
  generally, 9.60
  insolvency, 9.64
  statutory moratorium, 9.59
Contributories—
  arrest, 17.28
  calls—
    evasion, 17.28
    leave for, 17.29
    making by—
      court, 17.25, 17.27
      liquidator, 17.25–17.26, 17.28
    sanction of liquidation committee, 17.29
  definition—
    Act, 17.03
    deemed contributory, 17.03
    past members, 17.04–17.07
    present members, 17.04–17.07
  directors, 17.08–17.10
  liability—
    bankruptcy, 17.21, 17.33–17.34
    death, 17.21
    nature, 17.20
    personal representatives, 17.21
    winding up commencement, effect, 17.22–17.24
  managers, 17.10
  own shares purchased by private company, 17.08–17.09
  rectifying register of members, 17.18–17.19
  set off, 17.30–17.36
    insolvent corporate contributory, 17.35
  settling list—
    amendments, 17.17
    classes, 17.14–17.15
    court's power, 17.12–17.13
    dispensing with list, 17.12
    evidence of liability, 17.17
    liquidator's power, 15.91, 17.02, 17.11, 17.15–17.17
    notice of inclusion, 17.16–17.17
    official receiver, 17.13
    procedure, 17.14–17.17
  significance, 17.01–17.02
Creditors' committee (administration orders)—
  administrator's attendance, 13.124
  certificate of due constitution, 13.122
  constitution, 13.122
  discharge of order, committee as liquidation committee, 16.113
  function, 13.121
  meetings, 13.123–13.124
  membership—
    dealings by, 13.128
    expenses, 13.127
    termination, 13.125
    vacancy, 13.126
  setting up, 13.121

Creditors' committee (administrative receivership)—
    actions, 12.48–12.50
    administrative receiver attending before, 12.42–12.44
    certificate of due constitution, 12.48
    confidentiality of insolvency records, 12.96
    expenses, 12.56
    functions, 12.41—12.42
    meetings—
        chairman, 12.52
        holding, 12.51—12.52
        procedure, 12.53
        resolutions—
            passing, 12.53
            postal, 12.54–12.55
    membership—
        automatic termination, 12.58
        generally, 12.45–12.47
        removal, 12.59
        resignation, 12.57
        vacancies, 12.60
    setting up, 12.40
Creditors' meetings (administration orders)—
    administrator's—
        actions, unfair prejudice, 13.102, 13.129–13.131
        duty, 13.87
    calling, 13.107–13.108
    conduct, 13.106
    purpose, 13.106, 13.113
    reports, 13.114
    requisitioning, 13.119–13.120
    resolutions, 13.112
    role regarding proposals, 13.101–13.102
    voting, 13.109–13.111

Debentures—
    registration, 8.26–8.27
    see also Administrative receivers *and* Floating charges
Disclaimer of property, *see* Gathering assets, disclaimer
Disqualification of directors—
    applicants, 21.61, 21.78
    application for order, 21.61–21.63, 21.84
    civil liability, 21.58–21.60
    criminal liability, 21.57, 21.59–21.60
    evidence, affidavit, 21.62–21.64
    grounds—
        insolvency not necessarily involved—
            conviction for indictable offence, 21.65–21.67
            default in complying with legislation, 21.68–21.72
                blameworthiness, 21.72
            inspection, company subject of, 21.73–21.74
            investigation, company subject of, 21.73–21.74
        potential criminal liability, 21.54
        relating to corporate insolvency—
            fraud in winding up, 21.76; *see also* Personal liability, fraudulent trading
            generally, 21.75

Disqualification of directors—*cont*
    unfitness—
        court's decision, 21.93–21.97
        criteria, 21.87–21.97
        investigation, 21.83
        report, 21.61, 21.78–21.82
        wrongful trading, 21.77; *see also* Personal liability, wrongful trading
    hearing, 21.63
    adjournment, 21.63, 21.64
    joint liability, 21.60
    notice of intention to apply, 21.61
    order—
      breach, consequences, 21.57–21.60
      effect, 21.51–21.52
        date of, 21.64
      leave to act, 21.51, 21.55
      making, 21.63
      nature, 21.51–21.56
      period, 21.54
      register, 21.56
      shadow directors, 21.53
      unfitness, 21.85–21.87
        limitation on order, 21.96
    procedure, 21.62–21.64
    report to Secretary of State, 21.61, 21.78–21.82
    returns on directors, 21.79–21.82
    several persons, 21.60
    see also Personal liability
Dissolution of company—
    compulsory winding up—
      early dissolution, 19.123–19.127
      usual procedure, 19.128–19.129
    defunct companies, 14.113, 19.130–19.133
    effects, 19.134–19.136
    generally, 19.121
    property as *bona vacantia*, 19.135
    disclaimer by Crown, 19.136
    revival of company—
      generally, 19.137
      use of—
        s 651, 19.138–19.140
        s 652, 19.141–19.147
    striking off register, 14.113, 19.130–19.133, 19.137
    effects, 19.133–19.136
    subrogation rights, 19.134
    voluntary winding up, 19.122
    deferring, 19.122
Distress—
    common law, 6.92
    generally, 6.92
    liquidation's effect on, 18.30–18.35
    Magistrates' Courts Act 1980, 6.122–6.124
    priority, 8.142
    rates, 6.115–6.121
    rent—
      exceptions to seizable goods, 6.97–6.99
      floating charges, 8.95–8.96

Distress—*cont*
    fraudulent removal of goods, 6.97
    generally, 6.93–6.96
    liquidation, 18.33–18.34
    procedure, 6.101–6.105
        third parties' intervention, 6.106–6.108
    rent charge, 6.95
    subject matter, 6.97
    third party's goods, 6.98–6.100
    taxes, 6.109–6.114
Distribution of assets on winding up—
    costs, Bathampton orders, 19.100
    Department of Employment payments, 19.33–19.36
    dividend—
        assignee, 19.91
        basis of distribution, 19.85
        calculation, 19.86
        distribution, 19.84, 19.86–19.87
        in specie, 18.73, 19.89
        final, 19.92–19.98
        further, 19.87, 19.90
        order to pay, 19.88
        overpayment, 19.87, 19.90
    expenses of winding up—
        court's—
            discretion, 19.07
            power to make costs order, 19.10
        floating charges, position, 19.12–19.15
        guarantor of company's debt, 19.16
        order *inter se*, 19.09–19.16
        priority, 19.06–19.08
        solicitor's fees, 19.11
    final—
        distribution, 19.92–19.98
        meetings, 19.119–19.120
    general order of distribution, 19.01–19.05
        variation, 19.03
    ordinary debts—
        definition of—
            debt, 19.41
            liability, 19.43
        provable—
            double proof, rule against, 19.44
            generally, 19.40
            members, to, 19.45
            not, 19.40
            proof, 19.39
            tort claim, 19.41
            ultra vires, 19.42
            unenforceable obligations, 19.42
        proving, procedure—
            admission, 19.53–19.54
            affidavit, 19.50
            cost, 19.51
            expunging proof by court, 19.55
            inspection of proofs, 19.52
            liquidator's duty, 19.47–19.48, 19.53

Distribution of assets on winding up—*cont*
    proof, 19.46, 19.48–19.49
    rejection, 19.53–19.54
    variation of amount claimed, 19.55
    withdrawal of proof, 19.55
  quantification—
    contingent debts, 19.58–19.60
    costs, 19.51
    definition of secured creditor, 19.70
    discounts, 19.71
    estoppel, 19.56
    foreign currency debts, 19.72
    future debts, 19.59–19.60
    generally, 19.56–19.57
    interest—
      post liquidation, 19.73–19.76, 19.99, 19.100
      pre-liquidation, 19.77–19.79
      rate, 19.76
    negotiable instruments, 19.61
    periodic payments, 19.80–19.82
    sale of secured property, 19.68–19.70
    secured creditors, 19.62–19.70
      redemption of security, 19.66–19.67
    set off, 19.83; *and see* Gathering assets, set off
    uncertain value, 19.58–19.60
  subrogation, 19.44
postponed debts, 19.100, 21.38
preferential debts—
  abatement, 19.22
  categories, 19.25–19.32
  changes in law, 19.37
  compulsory winding up, 19.20–19.21
  Customs and Excise, 19.27–19.29, 19.37
  employees'—
    holiday pay, 19.32, 19.118
    loans to meet remuneration, 19.32, 19.118
    remuneration, 19.32, 19.118
    reserve forces, 19.32
  generally, 19.17
  Inland Revenue, 19.17, 19.26, 19.37
  levies on coal and steel production, 19.38
  occupational pension scheme contributions, 19.31
  priority, 19.18–19.22
  ranking among selves, 19.22
  relevant date, 19.23–19.24
  social security contributions, 19.30
  value added tax, 19.27–19.29, 19.37
secured creditors, 19.01
to contributories—
  bankrupt contributory, 19.106
  capital return, 19.106–19.112
  classes of shareholder, 19.111–19.112
  compulsory winding up, 19.107–19.108
  deceased contributory, 19.106
  deferred debts, 19.103–19.104
  expenses of meetings, 19.105
  own shares purchase or redemption by company, 19.101–19.102

Distribution of assets on winding up—*cont*
    surplus after capital repayment, 19.113–19.117
    voluntary winding up, 19.109
  to employees, 19.118

Enforcement of security interest—
  availability of remedies, 7.02
  equitable—
    charges, 7.04
    mortgages, 7.04
  foreclosure—
    availability, 7.02, 7.31–7.32
    effect, 7.31
    obtaining, 7.32–7.33
    use, 7.04
  generally, 7.01
  judicial sale, 7.32, 7.33
  possession—
    aircraft, 7.09
    chattels, 7.08
    choses in action, 7.10
    equitable mortgages of land, 7.07
    order, 7.07
    pledge of chattels, 7.06
    ships, 7.09
    use, 7.05
    writ, 6.60–6.61
  preservation of security, 7.03
  receivership—
    appointment of receiver, 7.12–7.13
    equitable mortgages, 7.15
    generally, 7.11
    powers—
      of receiver, 7.14
      to appoint—
        arising, 7.13
        exercisable, 7.13
    use, 7.16
  rights of mortgagees, 7.03
  sale by mortgagee—
    application of proceeds, 7.28–7.29
    duty of mortgagee, 7.22–7.25
      breaches, 7.23–7.24, 7.26
    equitable—
      charge, 7.18
      mortgage, 7.20
    possession sought first, 7.30
    prior incumbrances, 7.28–7.29
    purchaser's protection, 7.21, 7.26
    right, 7.17
    self, to, 7.27
    statutory power, 7.20
Examination, *see* Investigation
Execution—
  carrying out, 6.52
  charging orders, *see* Charging orders
  conditions for, 6.51

Execution—*cont*
  delivery, 6.62–6.63
  fieri facias, 6.55–6.59
  garnishee proceedings, *see* Garnishee proceedings
  liquidation's effect on, 18.30–18.32
    incomplete execution, 18.38–18.46
  liquidator's position, 6.53
  Mareva injunctions, 6.90, 6.91
  payment into court, 6.91
  possession, 6.60–6.61
  priority—
    charging orders, 8.140
    distress, 8.142
    fieri facias, 8.138
    garnishee orders, 8.139
    generally, 6.54, 8.137
    receiver, execution, 8.141
  receiver, appointment, 6.85–6.89
  sequestration, 6.64–6.65
  stop—
    notices, 6.84, 8.118
    orders, 6.83–6.84
  use, 6.50
  walking possession of goods, 6.59

Factoring—
  generally, 9.65
  liens, 6.29–6.30
  notice, 9.67
  priorities, 9.67–9.68
  relationship with—
    administration, 9.68
    floating charge, 9.65–9.66
    liquidation, position on, 9.68
    receivership, 9.68
Floating charges—
  creation, 5.16
  crystallisation—
    automatic, 5.31, 5.34, 5.36–5.41, 5.43
    cessation of business, 5.29–5.31
    chargee's actions—
      enforcing, 5.28
      receiver appointed, 5.27
    creditors' acts, 5.32–5.35
    deemed continuance as floating, 5.25
    effects, 5.46
    later floating charges' effect, 5.32–5.33
    liquidation, 5.26
    notice effecting, 5.37–5.39
    partial, 5.42–5.44
    preferential creditors' rights, 5.34–5.35
    reconstruction of company, 5.26
    reflotation of charge, 5.45
    third parties' position, 5.36, 5.39
    time, 5.24
    winding up, commencement, 5.26
  debentures, 5.09–5.10

Floating charges—*cont*
  development—
    background, 5.03–5.05
    Cork Report, 5.05–5.06
    effect of Insolvency Act 1985, 5.06–5.07
    justification, 5.08
    uses, 5.09
  distress for rent, 8.95–8.96
  enforcement, receivership and sale, 7.30
  extent, 5.17–5.18
  invalidity, 20.66–20.74
  legal nature—
    description, 5.13–5.15
    generally, 5.11
    origin, 5.12
  negative pledge clause, 5.23
  ordinary course of business—
    continuance of charge, 5.19
    disposal, large part of undertaking, 5.21–5.22
    evidence of past activities, 5.22
    outside such course, 5.19
    purchase of business's products, 5.20
    ultra vires transaction, 5.22
  origin, 1.35
  overdraft, 5.09
  priorities—
    against fixed charges, 8.79–8.87
    between floating charges, 8.78
    charging order, 8.93
    crystallisation, after, 8.84
    execution, 8.89–8.94
    fieri facias, 8.89–8.91
    garnishee order, 8.92
    generally, 8.77
    liens, 8.88
    Mareva injunction, 8.94
    sequestration, 8.94
  registration, 8.38
  rents due from subtenants, 8.96
  veto of holder to administration order, 13.03–13.04, 13.23, 13.69
  winding up, position on distribution of assets, 19.12–19.15
  see also Administrative receivers

Garnishee proceedings—
  application of proceedings, 6.66, 6.68–6.70
  bank accounts, 6.69
  garnishee's—
    position, 6.67. 6.73
    rights, 6.71
  incomplete at liquidation, 18.39
  order—
    absolute, 6.72–6.73
    enforcement, 6.72
    nisi, 6.72
    refusal, 6.73
  priorities, 6.70, 8.139
    floating charges, 8.92

Garnishee proceedings—*cont*
  procedure, 6.72
  use, 6.67
Gathering assets—
  adding to, 18.03
  chattels—
    effect of liquidation—
      actions, 18.35–18.36
      counterclaims, 18.36
      distress, 18.30–18.35
      execution, 18.30–18.32
      incomplete execution, 18.38–18.46
      proceedings, 18.35–18.36
    generally, 18.29
    sale of goods contracts, 18.47
  choses in action—
    generally, 18.48
    insurance policies, 18. 49–18.50
    third parties' rights against insurers, 18.49–18.50
  contracts, rescission by court, 18.70–18.72
  disclaimer—
    decision by liquidator, election, 18.08
    effect, 18.10–18.13
    leaseholds—
      fixtures, 18.16
      guarantee, 18.21
      liabilities' imposition, court's power, 18.18–18.19
      mortgagees, 18.16–18.20
      original lessee, effect on, 18.13
      part, 18.20
      termination, 18.11
      underlessees, 18.16–18.20
      vesting order, 18.21
    loss resulting, 18.12
    notices, 18.07–18.09
    procedure, 18.07–18.09
    property, 15.94, 18.05–18.06
    restriction on, 18.06
    surety's position, 18.13
    vesting—
      in Crown, 18.11, 18.15
      orders, 18.14–18.15, 18.21
  estoppel, 19.56
  generally, 18.01–18.02
  incomplete execution, 18.38–18.46
  land—
    effect of liquidation, specific performance, 18.37
    incomplete execution, 18.38
    leaseholds—
      business tenancies, 18.28
      forfeiture by landlord, 18.24–18.25, 18.27, 18.44
      re-entry by landlord, 18.26–18.27
      rent in arrears, 18.26–18.27
      sale, 18.25
      title, 18.23
      see also disclaimer, leaseholds
    title, 18.23

Gathering assets—*cont*
  realisation of assets, 18.73–18.75
  set off—
    account, 18.67
    Companies Bill 1989, 18.69
    Crown, 18.63–18.64
    exclusion, 18.68–18.69
    generally, 18.51–18.54
    mutuality, 18.61–18.66
    scope, 18.55–18.60
    waiver, 18.68
  vesting of property, 18.04

Hire purchase—
  generally, 9.60
  insolvency, 9.64
  statutory moratorium, 9.59

Insolvency practitioners—
  acting as, 10.04–10.05
  authorisation by competent body—
    application, 10.10
    competent bodies, 10.09
    criteria, 10.11–10.19
    educational qualifications, 10.16
    experience, 10.17–10.19
    generally, 10.09
    grant, 10.11
    notice to applicant, 10.20
    period, 10.11
    procedure, 10.20–10.24, 10.27
    refusal, notice, 10.20, 10.23
    withdrawal, 10.12–10.15
      notice, 10.20, 10.23
  bond, 10.34
  certificate of specific penalty, 10.34–10.35
  Cork Report, 10.02
  corporate bodies, 10.32
  disqualifications, 10.31–10.33
  generally, 10.01
  origins of qualification system, 10.02–10.03
  receivers appointed by—
    court, 10.04
    fixed chargees, 10.04
  recognized professional bodies, 10.06–10.08
  records, 10.36–10.38
  surety, 10.34–10.35
  tribunal—
    composition, 10.24, 10.25
    procedure, 10.24, 10.26–10.30
    reference to, 10.20–10.22
  unqualified person acting as, 10.04
Insurance policies as security—
  creation of security, 4.17
  generally, 4.15
  life policies, 4.15
  mortgages, 8.127
    priority, 8.127

Insurance policies as security—*cont*
  premiums, 4.18
  registration, 4.16
Intellectual property as security—
  copyright—
    design right, 4.64
    equitable mortgages, creation, 4.63
    future, 4.63
    legal mortgages, form, 4.62
    registration, 4.63
  generally, 4.58
  patents—
    assignments, 4.59–4.60
    licences distinguished from assignments, 4.60
    mortgages, 4.59
    priority, 8.119–8.122
    register, 8.119–8.122
    registration of mortgages, 4.61
  registered designs, 4.65–4.66, 8.124
    priority, 8.124
  registration of charges, 8.41
  trade marks—
    priority, 8.123
    register, 8.123
    registered—
      assignment, power, 4.67–4.68
      creation of mortgages, 4.69
    restrictions on assignment, 4.68
    unregistered, 4.67
Investigation—
  accounts, *see* Accounts
  administrative records, 16.53
  Cork Report, 16.02
  court orders, 16.03, 16.06–16.07, 16.09
  examination, 16.35; *see also* private examination before court *and* public examination
  inspection of company's books—
    compulsory winding up, 16.07
    generally, 16.03
    lien of other party, 16.08
    voluntary winding up, 16.07
  liquidator's—
    lien, 16.04
    powers, 16.01
    reports to authorities—
      criminal offences, 16.40–16.41, 16.43, 16.46
      generally, 16.36–16.39
      reference to—
        Director of Public Prosecutions, 16.40–16.41, 16.46
        Secretary of State, 16.44–16.46
      solicitor's position, 16.45–16.46
    right to have cooperation, 16.05
  private examination before court—
    appearance, 16.16
    applicant, 16.11, 16.14
    application for, 16.12
    costs, 16.22

Investigation—*cont*
    group of companies, 16.15
    hearing, 16.20
    injunction, use, 16.11
    legal professional privilege, 16.10
    order—
        delivery up of company property, 16.23
        enforcement, 16.18–16.19
        generally, 16.13–16.14, 16.17
        payment of debt, 16.23
        refusal, 16.13–16.14
    outside jurisdiction, 16.21
    provision for, 16.10
    purpose, 16.12, 16.15
    public examination—
        application, 16.27–16.28
        costs, 16.31
        examinees, 16.27–16.29
            disabled, 16.33
        generally, 16.34
        hearing, 16.30
            adjournment, 16.31
        non-attendance, 16.32
        official receiver's role, 16.24, 16.26–16.28
        order—
            notice, 16.29
            service, 16.29
        retention of documents, 16.32
        statement of affairs—
            contents, 16.25
            provision, 16.24–16.25
        unreasonable request for, 16.28
    title deeds, 16.03, 16.08–16.09

Land as security, *see* Charges of land *and* Mortgages of land
Leasing—
    financial lease, 9.62–9.63
    generally, 9.59–9.60
    insolvency, 9.64
    operating lease, 9.61
Liens—
    accountants, 6.12
    agents, 6.10–6.11
    bankers, 6.24–6.26
    books of company, 6.02
    common—
        carriers, 6.08
        law, 6.06–6.07
    contractual, 6.03–6.04
    custodians of goods, 6.10
    equitable, 6.38, 6.45
    factors, 6.29–6.30
    forms, 6.03–6.05
    general, 6.07–6.13
    improvement of another's property, 6.45
    innkeepers, 6.09
    insurance brokers, 6.28

Liens—*cont*
  maritime—
    cargo, 6.48
    crew, 6.48, 8.133–8.134
    damage by navigation, 6.48, 8.133–8.134
    lienees, 6.48
    priority—
      between liens, 8.133–8.134
      over mortgages, 8.132
    salvage, 6.48, 8.133–8.134
    ship repairers, 6.11, 6.46, 8.134
    statutory, 6.49
    types, 6.46–6.47
  misrepresentation, 6.06
  particular, 6.07, 6.08–6.12
  partnership property, 6.45
  possession, 8.136
  priority, floating charges, 8.88
  purchasers, 6.44
  repairing goods, 6.11
  sale of goods—
    buyer's disposition, 6.34
    insolvency, 6.37
    possession with seller, 6.32
    resale, right, 6.35–6.36
    stoppage in transit, 6.33–6.35
    unpaid seller's rights, 6.31, 6.34–6.35
    withholding delivery, 6.33
  ships, *see* maritime
  solicitors—
    charging order, 6.23
    client account funds, 6.21
    discharge of lien, 6.20
    extent of lien, 6.14
    inspection of documents, 6.17
    joint account funds, 6.22
    loss, 6.18
    non-availability of lien, 6.15–6.16
    particular lien, 6.21
    priority, 6.18
    production of documents, order, 6.17
    withdrawal from case, 6.19
  stockbrokers, 6.27
  trust property, 6.45
  vendors—
    application, 6.39–6.40
    assignment, 6.44
    enforcement, 6.43
    replacement by security interest, 6.41–6.42
    subrogation, 6.39
    successors of purchaser, 6.43
Liquidation, *see* Winding up
Liquidation committee—
  abolition, 16.89
  appointment—
    compulsory, winding up, 14.196, 16.87
    creditors' voluntary winding up, 14.28, 16.86

Liquidation committee—*cont*
    official receiver's position, 16.88
    Secretary of State's responsibility, 16.88
  calls, sanction by, 17.29
  certificate of due constitution, 16.93
  expenses, 16.100
  functions, 16.108–16.113
  generally, 16.85
  liquidator, relationship with, 16.108–16.112
  meetings, 16.94
  membership, 16.90–16.93
    vacation, 16.98–16.99
  none, compulsory winding up, 16.113
  proceedings, 16.94–16.97
  representation, 16.95
  resolutions, 16.97
  suspension, 16.89
  transactions—
    by—
      associates, 16.101–16.107
      members, 16.101–16.106
      representatives, 16.101–16.106
    retrospective leave, 16.104
  voting, 16.96
Liquidators—
  appointment—
    compulsory winding up—
      court's approach, 15.31
      date of appointment, 15.32
      effect on directors' powers, 15.40
      following administration order, 15.26
      inducements to secure nomination, 15.38–15.39
      notice, 14.201, 15.33–15.34
      official receiver—
        position, 15.26–15.27
        powers, 14.196
        replacement for, 15.27–15.29
        Secretary of State to make replacement, 15.29, 15.34
        succeeding to, 15.36–15.37
      provisional liquidator, *see* provisional
      several nominees, 15.30–15.31, 15.35
      supervisor, 15.26
    corporation, 15.03
    general requirements, 15.02–15.03
    resolutions, 14.222
    several, 15.03
    voluntary winding up—
      court's powers, 15.43, 15.47
      creditors', 14.28, 15.44
        effect on directors' powers, 14.15, 14.18, 14.44, 15.43
      inducements to secure appointment, 15.46
      members', 14.37, 14.39–14.40, 14.199, 15.41–15.42
        effect on directors' powers, 14.15, 14.44, 15.41, 15.43
      no liquidator acting, 15.43, 15.48
      notice, 15.48
      several nominees, 15.45–15.46
  certificate of creditors' full payment, 16.89

Liquidators—*cont*
cessation, qualified insolvency practitioner, 15.115
contracts, binding company, 15.50, 15.54, 15.84
  self and company, 15.68
court—
  applications to, 15.95
  intervention, 15.59, 18.75
death, 15.132, 15.136
disqualification, 15.02–15.03
duties—
  care, 15.80–15.83
  conflict of interests, avoidance, 15.60–15.61, 15.64–15.66, 15.68–15.72
  delegation, 15.73–15.75, 15.96
  fiduciary, 15.60–15.63
  impartiality, 15.70–15.72
  investigation, *see* Investigation
  leaving office, 15.134
  skill, 15.80–15.83
final account and return, 19.122
gathering assets, *see* Gathering assets
generally, 15.01
insufficiently diligent, 16.42
joint, 15.75, 15.143
  resignation, 15.107
legal status—
  agent, 15.49–15.57
  fiduciary, 15.49, 15.58–15.75
  generally, 15.49
  officer of court, 15.49, 15.76–15.79
liability—
  employees' acts, 15.57
  exceeding authority, 15.55
  generally, 15.50
  negligence, 15.56–15.57, 15.80–15.82
liquidation committee, relationship with, 16.108–16.112
meetings—
  final, 19.119–19.120
  notice, 14.206
misfeasance summons, 15.57, 15.82; *and see* Summary proceedings by liquidator,
  misfeasance summonses
powers—
  applications to court, 15.95
  appointment of agents, 15.96
  arrangements with creditors, 15.104
  benefiting employees, 15.105
  borrowing, 15.93
  carrying on company's business, 15.98
  collecting contributories' payments, 15.91, 15.100, 17.01
  compositions with creditors, 15.104
  compromises of company's claims, 15.103
  control by liquidation committee, 16.111
  dislaimer, onerous property, 15.94, 18.05–18.06
  disposal of property to connected person, 15.101
  execution of documents, 15.93
  exercise—
    compulsory winding up, 15.88, 15.90
    question arising, 15.87–15.89
    voluntary winding up, 15.87–15.90

Liquidators—*cont*
  investigation, *see* Investigation
  litigation, 15.99
  making calls, 15.100
  payment of creditors in full, 15.104
  realisation of assets, 18.73–18.75
  reconstruction of company, 22.04
  residual, 15.96
  sale of company's property, 15.93
  settling contributories' list, 15.91, 17.02, 17.11, 17.15–17.17
  statutory—
    generally, 15.84–15.85
    qualified, compulsory winding up, 15.97–15.101
    sanction necessary, 15.102–15.105
      ratification later, 15.102
    unfettered, 15.86–15.96
  summoning meetings, 15.92
  voluntary arrangements, 22.01, 22.11
  provisional—
    affidavit, 15.05
    application for, 15.04–15.06
    appointment by court, 15.04, 15.06–15.10
      in camera, 15.07
    directors—
      effect on powers, 15.14
      relationship with, 15.14
    expenses, 14.172, 15.15, 15.17
    functions, 15.13
    official receiver—
      as, 15.04
      notification, 15.06
      remuneration, 15.15, 15.141
      winding up order, 15.26
    powers, 15.11–15.13
    priorities, 15.11
    protection of assets, 15.09, 15.12
    relationship between companies, 15.11
    release, 15.138
    removal, 15.18
    remuneration, 15.17
    Secretary of State's application, 15.10
    security, 15.16
    special managers, 15.19–15.25
    urgent cases, 15.07, 15.10
    winding up, relationship with, 15.12, 15.13
  release—
    compulsory winding up, 15.138–15.139
    effect, 15.135
    generally, 15.135
    official receiver, 15.138
    provisional liquidator, 15.138
    voluntary winding up, 15.136–15.137
  removal—
    court, 15.118–15.122
      appointee, 15.129–15.130
    creditors' meeting, 15.123, 15.125–15.128

Liquidators—*cont*
   generally, 15.117
   members' meeting, 15.123–15.124, 15.126
   official receiver, 15.129–15.131
   Secretary of State, 15.131
     appointee's removal, 15.129–15.130
   remuneration—
     challenge to amount, 15.143
     claim, 15.144
     fixing, 15.140–15.142
     Insolvency Services Account, use, 15.143
     joint liquidators, 15.143
     none, court order, 15.39
     official receiver, 15.141
   reports by, 16.114, 16.116, 21.78–21.79
   resignation, 15.106–15.114
   solicitor—
     as liquidator, 15.62
     instructed by liquidator, 15.51
   special managers—
     accounts, 15.25
     application, 15.20–15.22
     appointment, 15.19, 15.22–15.23
     powers, 15.24
     remuneration, 15.24
     security, 15.23, 15.25
     termination, 15.22, 15.25
   summary proceedings, *see* Summary proceedings by liquidator
   transactions, setting aside by court, 18.75
   vacation of office—
     completion of winding up, 15.133
     generally, 15.02
     voluntary winding up, 15.46, 15.116
   vesting of property, 18.04
   see also Insolvency practitioners

Mareva injunctions, 6.90, 6.91, 8.94
Meetings—
   adjournment, 14.208–14.209
   attendance, 14.211
   court's power to call, 14.200
   creditors', *see* Creditors' meetings (administration orders)
   expenses, 14.224
   final, 19.119–19.120
   generally, 14.194–14.195
   liquidator's power to summon, 15.92
   minutes, 14.223
   notice—
     giving, 14.206
     personnel of company, 14.210–14.211
     service, 14.204
   proxies, 14.214–14.221
   request by—
     creditors, 14.202
     official receiver, 14.202
   resolutions, 14.222
   venue, 14.207

Meetings—*cont*
  voting, 14.212–14.213
Mortgages of land—
  equitable—
    deposit of title deeds, 2.08–2.13
    equitable interest, 2.16
    generally, 1.33–1.34, 2.07
    part performance, doctrine, 2.08, 2.10
    possession, 7.07
    registration, 2.11
  foreclosure, 7.31–7.33
  generally, 1.29, 2.01
  legal—
    agreement to create, 2.14–2.15
    disadvantage, 2.05
    form, 2.03
    grant, 2.02
    leasehold, 2.04
  priority—
    competition between—
      mortgages protected by deposit, 8.101–8.104
      protection by deposit and registration, 8.105
      registrable mortgages, 8.106–8.107
    deposit of deeds with mortgagee, 8.98, 8.100
    equitable interests, 8.98–8.99
    generally, 8.04, 8.11–8.12, 8.97
    legal estate, 8.98
    registered land—
      caution, 8.109–8.110
      notice, 8.109–8.110
      registered charge, 8.108, 8.110
      unregistered mortgages, 8.109–8.111
  receiver, appointment, 7.12–7.15
  registered land, 2.06
  rights of mortgagees, 7.03
  sale by mortgagee, 7.20–7.30
  see also Registration of company charges

Negotiable instruments as security—
  bills of exchange, negotiation, 4.50
  deposit, 4.54
  face value differing from debt, 4.52
  fraud, 4.54
  generally, 4.55
  meaning of negotiable instruments, 4.49
  mortgages, 4.51, 4.53
  negotiation, 4.49–4.50
  pledges, 4.53

Operation of law giving security—
  basis of non-consensual security, 6.01–6.02
  forms of security, 6.01
Ownership rights as security—
  insolvency of company, position, 9.03, 9.05
  methods—
    Diamond Report, 9.02
    generally, 9.01

Ownership rights as security—*cont*
  misleading effects, 9.04

Payment into court, 6.91
Personal liability—
  directors—
    bills of exchange, 21.03
    contract, 21.02, 21.04
    estoppel, 21.03
    guaranteeing company's debts, 21.02
    signature, 21.03
    tort, 21.02, 21.04
  fraudulent trading—
    any fraudulent purpose, 21.26
    applicant, 21.36
    business of company, 21.27
    charge by court, 21.37–21.38
    civil liability, 21.25
    comfort letters, 21.30
    contribution to company's assets, 21.34–21.35
    criminal liability, 21.25, 21.31–21.32, 21.36
    defrauding creditors, 21.26
    knowledge, directors', 21.28–21.29
    meaning, 21.26–21.30
    onus of proof, 21.29
    order, 21.34–21.38
    parties, 21.31–21.33
    postponement of debts by court, 19.100, 21.38
    relationship with wrongful trading, 21.24
    secretary, company, 21.33
    use of provision, 21.30
  Phoenix companies—
    application of provision, 21.40–21.41, 21.45
    civil liability, 21.39, 21.42
    contribution imposed, 21.42–21.43
    criminal liability, 21.39, 21.42
    exclusions from rules—
      generally, 21.46
      leave of court, 21.47
      prescribed circumstances, 21.48–21.50
      protection of person, 21.49
      successor company, 21.48–21.49
    interim relief, 21.47
    joint liability, 21.44
    problem, 21.39
    prohibited name, 21.40–21.41, 21.46, 21.50
    restrictions, 21.40–21.41
    several persons, 21.44
  wrongful trading—
    applicant, 21.24, 21.36
    application, 21.24
    charge by court, 21.37–21.38
    contribution to company's assets, 21.34–21.35
    defence, statutory, 21.06, 21.22–21.23
    defendants, possible, 21.07–21.08
    definition, 21.06
    hearing, 21.24

Personal liability—*cont*
    minimising potential loss, 21.22
    order, 21.34–21.38
    postponement of debts by court, 19.100, 21.38
    preconditions for order—
        commencement date, 21.21
        functions of director, 21.17–21.20
        insolvent winding up, 21.10–21.11
        knowledge, 21.12–21.13, 21.15–21.20
        negligence, 21.12, 21.14–21.20, 21.22–21.23
    purpose of provision, 21.05
    relationship with fraudulent trading, 21.24
Pledge of chattels—
    bill of lading as, 3.12–3.15
    completion, 3.11
    creation, 3.10
    form, 3.02
    generally, 1.31, 3.16
    possession—
        attornment, 3.12
        constructive delivery, 3.11
        enforcement position, 7.06
        generally, 8.136
        third party's, 3.12
        trust receipt, 3.15
    trading companies, 3.12–3.13
Priority of security interests—
    Bills of Sale Acts, 8.129
    further advances—
        absence of notice, 8.21–8.22
        agreement between mortgagees, 8.20
        bank lenders, 8.22
        obligation to make, 8.23
        registered land, 8.24
        tacking, 8.19
    generally, 8.01–8.03
    loss—
        conduct of holder, 8.05
        constructive notice, 8.05
        fraud, 8.06, 8.08
        notice, 8.05
        release of deeds during mortgage, 8.07–8.09
    mortgages, *see* Mortgages of land, priority
    nemo dat rule, 8.10
    notice outside registration systems—
        actual notice, 8.13
        constructive notice, 8.14–8.17
        generally, 8.11–8.12
        imputed notice, 8.18
        knowledge, 8.13

Receivers—
    administration order, position on, 13.28–13.32
    appointment—
        for judgment creditors, 6.85–6.89
        method, 11.34
        official receiver, 12.119

Receivers—*cont*
  enforcement of security interest, 7.11–7.16
  expenses, 6.89
  extension of authority, 6.86
  origins, 11.02
  powers, 5.04
  priority in execution, 8.141
  remuneration, 6.89
  role, 11.01
  see also Administrative receivers
Reconstruction of company—
  assets, order of application, 22.07
  buying out minority members, 22.06
  creditors' interests, 22.08
  generally, 22.01–22.02
  insolvent company, 22.03–22.05
  liquidator's powers, 22.04
  special resolution, creditors' winding up, 22.03–22.06
  under Companies Act 1985—
    orders, 22.68
    public company, 22.69–22.73
Registration of company charges—
  Companies Bill 1989—
    avoidance of charge, 8.71, 8.73
      court order preventing, 8.74
    effects of registration, 8.75
    extension of registration time, 8.70–8.72
    failure to register, 8.69
    generally, 8.61
    inaccurate particulars, 8.70, 8.73
    notification of crystallisation, 8.68
    overseas companies, 8.76
    priorities, 8.72
    registrable charges, 8.62–8.67
  effect of registration—
    constructive notice, 8.57–8.59
    inaccuracy of information, 8.60
    judicial review, 8.56
    validity of registration, 8.55
  extension of registration time, 8.51–8.54
  failure to register—
    correction, 8.51–8.54
    effect, 8.42, 8.44–8.46
    invalidity of security, 8.42, 8.44–8.46
    priority of later charge, 8.47–8.50
  rectification, 8.51–8.52
  registrable charges—
    aircraft, 8.40
    bills of sale, 8.29–8.32
    book debts, 8.35–8.37
    calls made, 8.39
    debentures, 8.26–8.27
    floating charges, 8.38
    generally, 8.25
    goodwill, 8.41
    hire purchase, 8.32
    imported goods, 8.31

Registration of company charges—*cont*
    intellectual property, 8.41
    land, 8.33–8.34
        further registration, 8.33–8.34
    register, 8.25
    ships, 8.40
    uncalled share capital, 8.28
    responsibility for registering, 8.43
Reports—
    failure to make, 16.116
    to—
        contributories, 16.114–16.116
        creditors—
            compulsory winding up, 16.115, 16.116
            voluntary winding up, 16.114, 16.116
    see also Investigation, liquidator's reports to authorities
Retention of title—
    annexation of goods to real property, 9.21
    charges, 9.14–9.16, 9.19, 9.21, 9.46–9.47
    conditional sale of goods, 9.07
    contractual terms, 9.08
    co-ownership provision, 9.17–9.19
    Cork Report, 9.48
    detachable goods, 9.13
    entry and repossession of goods, 9.08
    equitable title, 9.09
    mixed goods, 9.11–9.21
    proceeds of sale—
        case law, 9.31–9.41, 9.44
        charge, 9.43–9.44
        fiduciary relationship, 9.27–9.30, 9.41–9.43, 9.45
        generally, 9.26
        separate account, 9.41, 9.44
        surplus monies, 9.45
    securing whole account, 9.45–9.48
    seller's title, extinction, 9.24–9.25
    separate storage of goods, 9.20
    sub-purchaser's title, 9.23–9.24
    subsale of goods, 9.22–9.25
    tracing, 9.12, 9.14, 9.30, 9.41
    unmixed goods before subsale, 9.07–9.10
    use, 9.06
Romalpa clause, *see* Retention of title

Setting aside transactions—
    background, 20.01–20.02
    Cork Report, 20.02
    defrauding of creditors—
        applicants, 20.35
        application, 20.36
        generally, 20.31
        order, 20.37–20.39
        protection of third parties, 20.39
        purpose of transaction, 20.33–20.34
        undervalue, transaction, 20.32
        vesting of property, 20.38
    extortionate credit transactions, 20.59–20.65

Setting aside transactions—*cont*
  floating charges, invalidity, 20.66–20.74
  orders—
    discretion of court, 20.49
    guarantor, 20.56
    payment, 20.55
    possible, 20.51–20.58
    proving in winding up, right, 20.58
    reinstatement of position, 20.51–20.52, 20.54
    scope, 20.49–20.50
    security, provision, 20.57
    tracing, 20.53
  preferences—
    application, 20.40
    challenge to, 20.13, 20.15
      limitation, 20.42
    definition of preference, 20.40
    examples, 20.41
    intention of company, 20.43–20.46
    liability of person preferred, 20.40
    onus of proof, 20.44–20.46
    orders, 20.49–20.58
      action pursuant to, 20.47
    protection of third parties, 20.49
    relationship with transaction at undervalue, 20.48
  undervalue—
    application, 20.03–20.04
    associates—
      generally, 20.18
      of—
        corporate bodies, 20.22–20.29
          control, 20.23–20.29
        directors, 20.27
        employers, 20.21
        individuals, 20.19–20.21
    availability of power, 20.03
    business's purpose, 20.07
    connected persons, 20.16–20.17
      employees, 20.11
    defence, statutory, 20.07–20.09
    definitions—
      associates, 20.18
      connected persons, 20.16
      relevant time, 20.10
      transaction, 20.06
      undervalue, 20.04
    extortionate credit transaction as, 20.65
    gift, 20.04
    good faith, 20.07
    inability of company to pay debts, 20.15
    negligence, 20.08
    onset of insolvency, 20.10
    orders, 20.30, 20.49–20.58
    proof, onus, 20.08
    protection of third parties, 20.09, 20.49
    reasonable grounds, 20.07
    relationship with preferences, 20.48

Setting aside transactions—*cont*
    time, relevant, 20.10–20.15
    valuation, 20.05
Shares—
    cancellation, 4.19–4.20
    issue void, 17.19
    mortgages—
        creation, rules, 4.22
        equitable, 4.30–4.32
        generally, 4.19
        legal—
            creation, 4.25
            effect, 4.23, 4.26
            partly paid shares, 4.27
            refusal to register transfer, 4.28
            restricted shares, 4.28–4.29
            voting rights, 4.26
        own shares of company, 4.19–4.21
        priorities, 4.22, 8.125–8.126
        registration. 4.24
        stop notice, 4.22, 8.126
    partnership—
        changing, 4.34
        company as partner, 4.33
    transfers, effect of winding up resolution, 14.43
Ships—
    bottomry bonds, 3.26–3.27, 8.132–8.134
    cargo as security, 3.25
    equitable mortgages, 3.22–3.23, 8.130
    fieri facias, 6.58
    generally, 3.17
    legal mortgages—
        effect, 3.19
        fishing vessels, 3.20–3.21
        form, 3.18
        registration, 3.18, 3.23, 8.130
    liens, 6.11, 6.46–6.49, 8.132–8.134
    possession, 7.09
    priority of security interests—
        further advances, 8.131
        liens, 8.132–8.134
        operation of law, 8.132–8.134
        register of shipping, 3.18, 8.130–8.131
    registration of charges, 8.40
    respondentia bonds, 3.26–3.27
    rights of mortgagee, 3.23–3.25
    sale by mortgagee, 7.19
Solicitors—
    liens, 6.14–6.23, 19.11
    payment of fees on winding up, 19.11
Special managers, *see* Liquidators, special managers
Summary proceedings by liquidator—
    enforcement of delivery—
        books, 16.65
        property, 16.65
        records, 16.65
    generally, 16.62

Summary proceedings by liquidator—*cont*
  misfeasance summonses—
    applicants, 16.67
    availability, 15.57, 16.80
    breach of—
      duty, 16.76, 16.78–16.79
      trust, 16.76–16.77, 16.80
    company claims, 16.73–16.75
    compensation, 16.79, 16.81–16.82
    concept of misfeasance, 16.76
    employees, 16.70
    generally, 16.66
    negligence, 16.76, 16.78, 16.80
    orders available, 16.81–16.82
    payments by contributories, 16.63–16.64
    procedure, 16.83–16.84
    respondents, 16.68–16.71
    restoration of property, 16.81
    rights enforceable, 16.72–16.80
    set off, 16.79
    third parties, 16.84
    winding up process, 16.75
Supervisors, *see* Insolvency practitioners *and* Voluntary arrangements, supervisor

Trust fund interest as security—
  generally, 4.56–4.57
  possession, 7.10
Trust property—
  accounting system, 9.53, 9.57
  advance payments as, 9.58
  bank deposits, 9.54
  certainty, 9.52
  constructive trust, 9.50
  express trust, 9.50
  indentification of property, 9.50
  implied trust, 9.50
  intention of parties, 9.52
  records, importance, 9.53
  resulting trust, 9.51
  tracing, 9.55–9.57
  unavailability on liquidation, 9.49–9.50
  see also Trust fund interest as security

Unregistered company—
  winding up, 14.03–14.04

Voluntary arrangements—
  accounts, 22.52–22.54
  availability, 22.09
  challenges, 22.43–22.48
  common law agreements with creditors, 22.74
  completion, 22.55
  composition, 22.10, 22.74
  court's order to facilitate, 22.42
  generally, 22.09, 22.75
  implementation, 22.49–22.50
  irregularity, 22.43, 22.45

Voluntary arrangements—*cont*
liquidator's powers, 22.01, 22.11
meetings—
adjournment, 22.38
decision on proposal, 22.29
none, 22.26
procedure, 22.30–22.31
result, report to court, 22.40
summoning—
adminstrator as nominee, 22.27
generally, 22.28
liquidator as nominee, 22.27
nominee not liquidator or administrator, 22.24–22.26
voting, 22.32–22.37
nominee—
agreement to act, 22.17
liquidator's proposal, 22.23
qualification, 22.12
replacement, 22.22
report of, 22.18, 22.21–22.22
supervisor, becoming, 22.49
proposal—
acceptance, 22.29, 22.40
administrator's, 22.11, 22.23
amending, 22.17, 22.29
contents, 22.15–22.17
court winding up, 22.23
directors', 22.11, 22.13–22.22
discussions, need, 22.14, 22.17
effect, 22.41
generally, 22.10, 22.12
liquidator's, 22.11, 22.23
Secretary of State's inspection, 22.54
statement of affairs, 22.18–22.20, 22.23
supervisor—
court's guidance, 22.50
implementation of arrangement, 22.49–22.50
joint, 22.39
non-nominee, 22.39
powers, 22.16
records, 22.52–22.54
replacement, 22.51
under Companies Act 1985—
EC Third Company Law Directive, 22.69–22.73
orders, 22.68
procedure—
court's sanction, 22.66–22.67
explanatory circular, 22.63–22.64
meetings—
application to court, 22.60
conduct, 22.65
convening, 22.60–22.63
notice, 22.63
scope, 22.56–22.59
unfair prejudice, 22.43–22.44
Voluntary winding up, creditors'—
general meetings of company, 14.200

Voluntary winding up, creditors'—*cont*
  generally, 14.07
  liquidation committee, *see* Liquidation committee
  liquidator, *see* Liquidators
  meetings of creditors—
    annual, 14.200
    chairman, 14.207
    conduct, 14.31
    control by, 14.28
    final, 14.200
    first, 14.200
    information, advance, 14.22–14.23
    need for, 14.19, 14.21
    notice, 14.19–14.20, 14.22–14.23
    president, 14.24
    statement of affairs—
      preparation, 14.24–14.26
      receiving, 14.28
      timing, 14.27
    see also Meetings
  protection of creditors, 14.17
  reports, 16.114, 16.116
  resolution—
    action following, 14.19
    appointing liquidator also, 14.15
    challenge to validity, 14.13
    effect on directors' powers, 14.15–14.16, 14.18
    first creditors' meeting, 14.29
    irregularly called meeting, 14.12–14.13
    notice of, 14.14–14.15
      meeting, 14.10
    procedure for passing, 14.10–14.30
    type, 14.08–14.09
    without meeting, 14.11
    written agreement, 14.11
  statement of affairs, 14.205
  see also Winding up
Voluntary winding up, members'—
  commencement, 14.32
  conversion into creditors' liquidation, 14.27, 14.36, 14.37, 14.40
  creditors' meetings during, 14.37–14.39
  directors' statutory declaration, 14.33–14.36
  liquidator, *see* Liquidators
  meetings—
    chariman, 14.207
    creditors', 14.199
    general meetings, 14.199
      final, 14.199
    see also Meetings
  statement of affairs, 14.205
  see also Winding up

Winding up—
  compulsory, *see* Compulsory winding up
  conversion from voluntary to compulsory, 16.42
  decision, 14.02
  definition of company for purposes of, 14.05

Winding up—*cont*
distribution of assets, *see* Distribution of assets on winding up
effects of resolution—
    business of company, 14.41–14.42
    directors' powers, 14.44
    employment contracts, 14.45–14.46
    proceedings against company, restraining, 14.47–14.50
    share transfers, 14.43
    status of company, 14.42
gathering assets, *see* Gathering assets
international organisation, 14.03
investigation, *see* Investigation
meetings, *see* Meetings
methods, 14.06
nature, 14.01
official receiver's power to petition, 14.96
procedure, 14.03
relationship with administration order, 13.26, 13.28, 13.32, 13.65
stay—
    other proceedings, 14.179–14.180
    voluntary arrangement approved, 22.42
unregistered company, 14.03–14.04
voluntary, *see* Voluntary winding up
Writs—
    delivery, 6.62–6.63
    execution, 6.54; *and see* Execution
    fieri facias, 6.55–6.59, 8.89–8.91
    possession, 6.60–6.61
    sequestration, 6.64–6.65, 8.94